THE COLLECTED WORKS OF
SAMUEL TAYLOR COLERIDGE 12

MARGINALIA

General Editor: KATHLEEN COBURN

THE COLLECTED WORKS

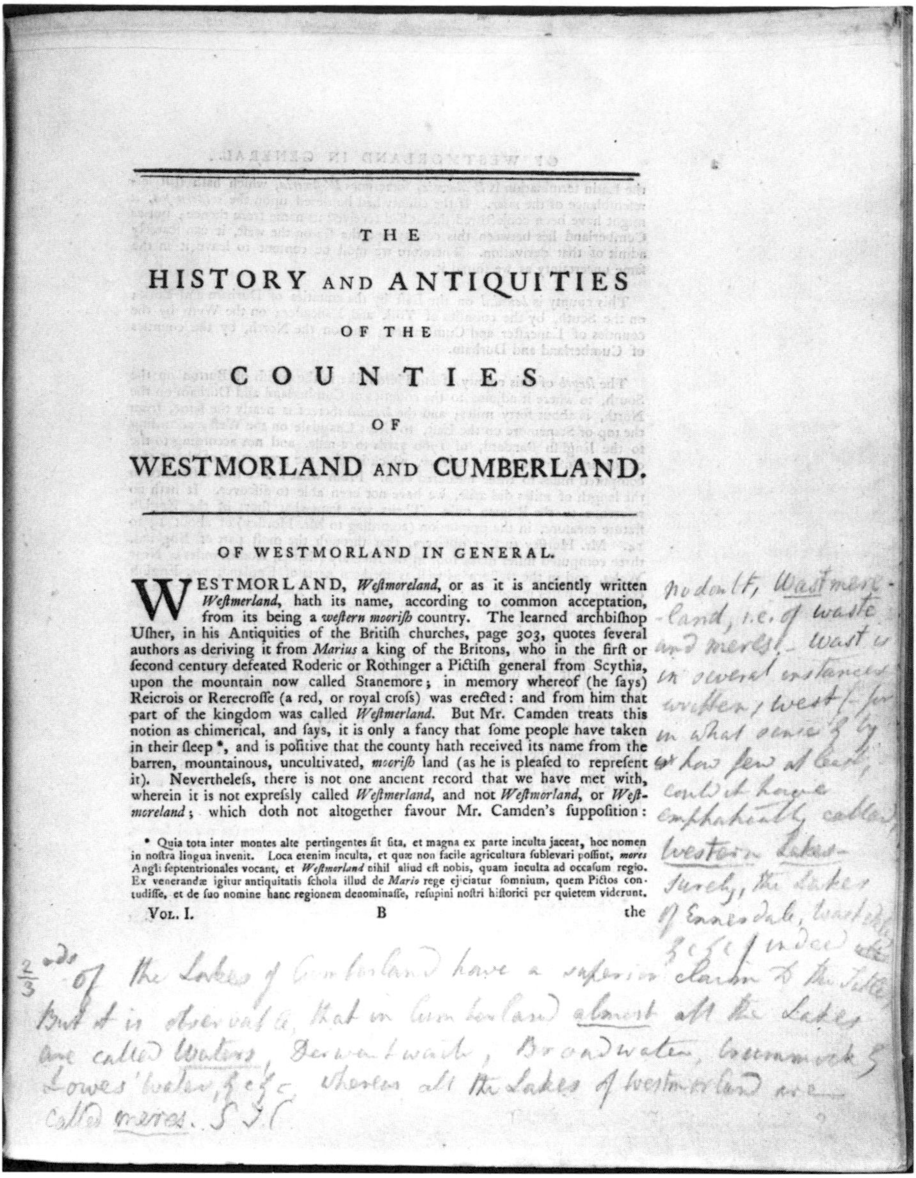

THE

HISTORY AND ANTIQUITIES

OF THE

COUNTIES

OF

WESTMORLAND AND CUMBERLAND.

OF WESTMORLAND IN GENERAL.

WESTMORLAND, *Weſtmoreland*, or as it is anciently written *Weſtmerland*, hath its name, according to common acceptation, from its being a *weſtern mooriſh* country. The learned archbiſhop Uſher, in his Antiquities of the Britiſh churches, page 303, quotes ſeveral authors as deriving it from *Marius* a king of the Britons, who in the firſt or ſecond century defeated Roderic or Rothinger a Piƈtiſh general from Scythia, upon the mountain now called Stanemore; in memory whereof (he ſays) Reicrois or Rerecroſſe (a red, or royal croſs) was erected: and from him that part of the kingdom was called *Weſtmerland*. But Mr. Camden treats this notion as chimerical, and ſays, it is only a fancy that ſome people have taken in their ſleep *, and is poſitive that the county hath received its name from the barren, mountainous, uncultivated, *mooriſh* land (as he is pleaſed to repreſent it). Nevertheleſs, there is not one ancient record that we have met with, wherein it is not expreſsly called *Weſtmorland*, and not *Weſtmorland*, or *Weſt-moreland*; which doth not altogether favour Mr. Camden's ſuppoſition:

* Quia tota inter montes alte pertingentes ſit ſita, et magna ex parte inculta jacet, hoc nomen in noſtra lingua invenit. Loca etenim inculta, et quæ non facile agricultura ſublevari poſſint, *mores* Angli ſeptentrionales vocant, et *Weſtmorland* nihil aliud eſt nobis, quam inculta ad occaſum regio. Ex venerandæ igitur antiquitatis ſchola illud de *Mario* rege ejiciatur ſomnium, quem Piƈtos con-tudiſſe, et de ſuo nomine hanc regionem denominaſſe, reſupini noſtri hiſtorici per quietem viderunt.

VOL. I.   B   the

[Handwritten annotations in margin and bottom, partially legible:]

no doubt, Waſtmere-land, i.e. of waſte and meres. waſt is in several instances written, weſt for ... in what sense & by how few at ... could it have emphatically called weſtern Lakes. Surely, the lakes of Enneſdale, Waſt &c &c indeed ...

⅔ of the Lakes of Cumberland have a superior claim to the Title. But it is obſervable, that in Cumberland almost all the Lakes are called Waters, Derwentwater, Broadwater, Crummock & Lowes' water, &c. wheras all the Lakes of Weſtmorland are called meres. S.T.C.

THE COLLECTED WORKS OF

Samuel Taylor Coleridge

Marginalia

III

Irving to Oxlee

EDITED BY

H. J. Jackson and
George Whalley

ROUTLEDGE

✠ BOLLINGEN SERIES LXXV
PRINCETON UNIVERSITY PRESS

This edition of the text by Samuel Taylor Coleridge is
copyright © 1992 by Princeton University Press

The Collected Works, sponsored by Bollingen Foundation,
is published in Great Britain by Routledge
11 New Fetter Lane, London EC4P 4EE
ISBN 0-415-07648-X
and in the United States of America
by Princeton University Press, Princeton, New Jersey
ISBN 0-691-09954-5
LCC 87-104402

Library of Congress Cataloging-in-Publication Data
(Revised for vol. 3)
Coleridge, Samuel Taylor, 1772–1834.
Marginalia.

(Bollingen series; 75) (The collected works
of Samuel Taylor Coleridge; 12)
Includes bibliographical references.
Contents: 1. Abbt to Byfield—2. Camden to
Hutton—3. Irving to Oxlee.
I. Whalley, George, 1915–1983. II. Title.
III. Series. IV. Series: Coleridge, Samuel
Taylor, 1772–1834. Works. 1969; 12.
PR4470.F69 vol. 12 [PR4480]   87-104402
ISBN 0-691-09879-4 (Princeton University Press: v. 1)
ISBN 0-691-09889-1 (Princeton University Press: v. 2)
ISBN 0-691-09954-5 (Princeton University Press: v. 3)

The Collected Works constitutes
the seventy-fifth publication in Bollingen Series

The present work, number 12 of the Collected Works,
is in 5 volumes, this being 12: III

Designed by Richard Garnett

Printed in the United States of America
by Princeton University Press

CONTENTS

━━━━━━━━━━━ III ━━━━━━

Marginalia

[† designates a "Lost Book"—a book reported to contain marginal notes in C's hand but which the editor has not been able to find and for which no transcript of marginalia is known to exist.]

Contents

LIST OF ILLUSTRATIONS

FOREWORD

A T THE TIME of his death in 1983, George Whalley's work on the *Marginalia* was already well advanced. He had solved the basic conceptual and practical problems of the edition in Volume I, which fixed the general format of the volumes yet to come; he had made corrections to the proofs of Volume II; he had assembled transcriptions of virtually all the remaining entries, and written notes for most of the authors whose names begin with I or J, as well as those of the later authors—Lacunza, Leighton, Taylor, and all the Germans—for whom he had the reinforcement of a coeditor. With funds from the Social Sciences and Humanities Research Council of Canada, he had also begun the process that has continued at Toronto in the efficient hands of Freda Gough and Rea Wilmshurst and that is now almost complete, the transferring of all the text of the marginalia onto a word-processor. With the active and thoughtful co-operation of Elizabeth Whalley, his machinery and records and working papers were transferred to Toronto to save his successor years of labour. I have carried on where he left off, checking every text in Volume III against the original, completing or revising the notes that I inherited, and supplying annotation for the titles that remained. In this volume, though all editorial decisions were ultimately mine, I have been constantly aware of standards that had been established long before I came upon the scene, and that often took the decisions out of my hands; these standards are a small part of George Whalley's rich intellectual legacy.

The acknowledgments of obligation that follow are all my own; the prefatory remarks in the earlier volumes recognise some of the assistance that George Whalley had had for later titles, and any that I am not aware of will, I hope, be brought to my attention before the final volume is published. An enterprise on this scale needs all the help it can get, and we have been wonderfully fortunate in both institutional and individual support. Funds from the Social Sciences and Humanities Research Council of Canada provided both the computer equipment that I have mentioned and released time for me when I was getting started; a General Research Grant from the Social Sciences and Humanities Committee of the University of Toronto paid for some essential supplies; the

Princeton University Press has kept the Coleridge Office running and has generously covered travel expenses, besides giving the edition steady encouragement through the benevolent administration of Elizabeth Powers.

I have in the last few years travelled to libraries diverse in practically everything but their kindness to the new reader trying to find her way about. In England, thanks due are most gratefully rendered: to Gaye Blake Roberts and the staff of the Wedgwood Museum in Barlaston, Stoke-on-Trent, and particularly to the Archivist, Dr Ian Fraser, who discovered the document printed as an annex to LESLIE; to Christine Fyfe, at the Library of the University of Keele; to the staff of the Wisbech and Fenland Museum in Wisbech, Cambridgeshire; to Joanna Parker, at the library of Manchester College, Oxford; and to Jeff Cowton and his associates in the Wordsworth Library at Grasmere, who even rustled up a rainbow at the end of my first visit there. I am also indebted for assistance to several collections in London: to the handsome surroundings and unruffled help of the library of the Victoria and Albert Museum; to Dr Williams's Library; to Sion College Library; to the Wellcome Institute of the History of Medicine; and to the library of University College. My greatest debt, however, is to the incomparable British Library, the best place in the world to work on Coleridge, where I have spent many happy summers and have come to enjoy even the inevitable noise of pneumatic drills outside the windows of the North Library.

The major North American Coleridge Collection is at Victoria College in the University of Toronto; here I am among friends and have been able to take for granted—which is not to say it is not appreciated—the tireless co-operation of the Librarian, Robert Brandeis, and the library staff, especially Lila Laakso, Ann Black, and Irene Dutton. Other substantial collections that have put up with more trouble than they can have bargained for from this quarter are the Huntington Library in San Marino (and particularly Thomas V. Lange), the Houghton Library at Harvard, the Berg Collection at the New York Public Library, the Beinecke Library at Yale, and the Humanities Research Center in the University of Texas at Austin, where Cathy Henderson presides over an exceptionally fleet-footed staff. Smaller collections (as far, at least, as Coleridge is concerned) have also treated my sometimes whirlwind visits with great courtesy and made them memorable: the Folger Shakespeare Library and the Library of Congress in Washington; the Pierpont Morgan Library and Columbia University Library in New York; the Clark Library at UCLA; the Rare Books Department of Firestone Library at Princeton University; the University of Chicago Library and the

Newberry Library, also in Chicago; the Rare Books Division of Johns Hopkins University in Baltimore; Brandeis University Library in Waltham, Massachusetts; the Lilly Library at Indiana University in Bloomington; the Rosenbach Museum and Library, the Academy of Fine Arts, and the library of the College of Physicians, all in Philadelphia; and the Department of Rare Books in the Perkins Library at Duke University in Durham, North Carolina, where J. Samuel Hammond genially bent a rule or two on Coleridge's behalf.

It is not because Coleridge was a genius or a polymath that anyone attempting to "explain his explanation" must take lessons in humility. He was not, in his time, alone in being able to read several languages or in being a generalist with an interest in many fields that we have fenced off from one another since then. Many—perhaps most—of his similarly educated contemporaries would present comparable challenges to the editor had their papers been preserved and approached with the same degree of attention to detail as Coleridge's. It would, however, require a genius or polymath to reproduce his kind of knowledge today, and it has been clear from the start that this edition could not be achieved single-handed. The sunny side of this potentially depressing fact is that one learns in the most agreeable way that academic research does not have to be an isolated activity. In the preparation of this volume I have called on the learning and good will of colleagues near and far, and have never had occasion to regret the appeal. At the University of Toronto, I have exploited old friends and made new ones. In my own department, English, Hugo de Quehen was able to identify a passage in Swift that had eluded me; Roberta Frank made light of linguistic inquiries touching on Old German, Old English, Icelandic, and what I think of as Old Esperanto; Dorothy Parker and Brian Parker carried my problems as far away as Australia, and brought them back solved; Allan Pritchard offered fruitful advice on the Great Wallop; and as a graduate student, Lisa Darrach helped with Luther. From the History Department, I drew on John Beattie's unmatchable knowledge of eighteenth-century law and legal systems, Jim Estes' expertise in the history of the Reformation, and Walter Goffart's deep sympathy with the mind of the computer. Trevor Levere, in the Institute for the History and Philosophy of Science and Technology, has been an unfailing resource in all sorts of scientific inquiries, combining with his grasp of Romantic science an understanding of Coleridge's idiosyncratic ways of thinking. John Warden of Scarborough College's Division of Humanities has coped cheerfully with some mind-boggling classical problems, and E. J. Revell of Near Eastern Studies most courteously supplied the knowledge of Hebrew and of bib-

lical criticism necessary to gloss a line in Leighton that Coleridge him-
self did not understand. Outside Toronto, my constant recourse is to
other Coleridge editors, particularly J. C. C. Mays of University Col-
lege Dublin, whose edition of Coleridge's *Poetical Works* overlaps to
some extent with the marginalia, and Anthony Harding of the University
of Saskatchewan, whose work on the fifth volume of the *Notebooks* re-
quires the same miscellany of skills as the marginalia, and whose learn-
ing especially in German and theological matters is far ahead of mine.
Others without the same responsibility for Coleridge have extended
kindness to him: Barbara Rosenbaum of the *Index of English Literary
Manuscripts*, in London; Eric Stanley at Oxford; Michael Petry at the
Erasmus University in Rotterdam; Marion Faber of Swarthmore Col-
lege; Mark U. Edwards, Jr, of Purdue University; and Howard Weinbrot
from the University of Wisconsin at Madison, who allowed himself to
be caught up in Ulysses' Knot in the British Library. At the copy-editing
stage, Eric Van Tassel and Jane Van Tassel worked through the text with
meticulous care and contributed to it substantively when they asked in-
telligent questions and at the same time tactfully slipped me the answers.

The scholars named as coeditors for individual titles were in general
consulted for specialised information by George Whalley at an early
stage of the project, and were identified by him in the Introduction to
Volume I. Whatever he received from them he absorbed into his own
notes. There are, however, two exceptions to this rule. John Beer, the
editor of *Aids to Reflection* in this series, has from start to finish been
closely involved with the Leighton marginalia (and incidentally with
other titles as well) and is a true collaborator. Raimonda Modiano's role
as coeditor of most of the German titles—assisted by a Grant-in-Aid
from the American Council of Learned Societies and a grant from the
American Philosophical Society—has also entailed an extraordinary
share of the editorial labours, including the selection and translation of
passages commented on, the checking of texts, and the writing of notes,
especially but not exclusively those concerned with the philosophical
contexts of Coleridge's remarks. Her help has been absolutely indis-
pensable, and I look forward with tolerable equanimity to Schelling,
Steffens, and Tennemann, knowing that she will have been there before
me.

Four others have been consulted not just now and then but regularly
throughout the past five years. Bart Winer, the associate editor for the
edition until his death in February 1989, had steered many other vol-
umes through the press and was a committee of editors in himself, with
a way of making problems disappear almost as soon as they were raised:

although he did not study it in its final form, he was a dependable guide to this volume from its inception. Lorna Arnold acted as classical consultant for this as for all the other titles in the series, and saved me from numberless blunders as well as from probably months of inefficient hunting in largely unfamiliar territory. Rea Wilmshurst has given Coleridge the benefit of her eagle eyes and hummingbird fingers day after day, taking upon herself a large part of the labour of this labour-intensive project. And my husband, J. R. de J. Jackson, is the first to whom I turn when I'm stuck, and nine times out of ten the last as well.

Toronto, Ontario, December 1989   H. J. JACKSON

EDITORIAL PRACTICE, CONVENTIONS, AND ABBREVIATIONS

F OR the definition of "marginalia", "textus", and "submarginalia" see *CM* I xxiii–xxvi. For special terms such as "fly-pages", "annex", "ms transcript", "quasi-marginalia", "lost book", and "marked book" see I xxx–xxxii.

All marginalia are transcribed literatim from the original mss, whenever these were available to the editor: cancelled words and phrases are restored; idiosyncratic spellings and obvious misspellings are reproduced without comment; slips of the pen and accidental repetitions are also reproduced, normally with explanation in a textual note. See I xxiii. A second parenthesis or quotation mark omitted by oversight is supplied by the editor without comment unless the placing of the mark is in doubt. Illegible deletions are omitted.

The annotated books are entered in alphabetical order of the authors, and within an author-entry in alphabetical order of title. Reference to annotated books within this edition is made by short title (identifiable from the running headlines) to which the serial number of a particular annotation can be attached: e.g. DONNE *Sermons* COPY B **57**. (Bold figures are used only for serial numbers of marginalia.) Editorial footnotes are identified by attaching the number of the footnote indicator to the abbreviated title of the book: e.g. DONNE *Sermons* COPY B **57** n 2. See also I xxix–xxx.

CONVENTIONS USED IN TRANSCRIPTION

[wild]	A reading supplied by the editor when the word has been lost from the ms by cropping or physical damage
[not]^a	A word inserted by the editor to supply an unintentional omission on Coleridge's part, or to clarify the sense of an elliptical or ambiguous phrase. The accompanying textual note *a* accounts for the insertion
[? wild]	An uncertain reading
[? wild/world]	Possible alternative readings
[. . .]	An illegible word or phrase

[. . . . .]	A passage of undetermined extent illegible through rubbing or off-setting, or lost by cropping or other physical damage
⟨ ⟩	A word or passage inserted between the lines, or marked for insertion from another part of the page (in which case a textual note is provided). An inserted word or passage is not so marked when it follows immediately upon a cancellation in the ms

ABBREVIATIONS

Place of publication is London, unless otherwise noted. Special abbreviations that apply only to certain author-entries or book-entries are given in the appropriate headnote.

Allsop	[Thomas Allsop] *Letters, Conversations and Recollections of S. T. Coleridge* (2 vols 1836)
AM	S. T. Coleridge *The Rime of the Ancient Mariner*
AR (1825)	S. T. Coleridge *Aids to Reflection* (1825)
AR (*CC*)	S. T. Coleridge *Aids to Reflection* ed John Beer (London & Princeton in preparation = *CC* IX
AV	The "Authorised Version"—or "King James Version"—of the Bible, in modern orthography
BCP	*The Book of Common Prayer and Administration of the Sacraments and Other Rites and Ceremonies of the Church According to the Use of the Church of England*
BL (1817)	S. T. Coleridge *Biographia Literaria; or Biographical Sketches of My Literary Life and Opinions* (2 vols 1817)
BL (1847)	S. T. Coleridge *Biographia Literaria* ed H. N. and Sara Coleridge (2 vols 1847)
BL (*CC*)	S. T. Coleridge *Biographia Literaria* ed James Engell and W. Jackson Bate (2 vols London & Princeton 1983) = *CC* VII
BM	British Library, Reference Division, formerly "British Museum Library"
BMC	*The British Museum Catalogue of Printed Books*
B Poets	*The Works of the British Poets* ed Robert Anderson (13 vols Edinburgh & London 1792–5; vol 14 1807). The annotated copies are referred to as "ANDERSON"
Bristol LB	George Whalley "The Bristol Library Borrowings of Southey and Coleridge" *Library* IV (Sept 1949) 114–31
C	Samuel Taylor Coleridge
C&S	S. T. Coleridge *On the Constitution of the Church and State, According to the Idea of Each* (2nd ed 1830)

C&S (*CC*)	S. T. Coleridge *On the Constitution of the Church and State* ed John Colmer (London & Princeton 1976) = *CC* x
CC	*The Collected Works of Samuel Taylor Coleridge* general ed Kathleen Coburn (London & Princeton 1969–)
CCD	J. Robert Barth, S.J. *Coleridge and Christian Doctrine* (Cambridge MA 1969)
CIS	S. T. Coleridge *Confessions of an Inquiring Spirit and Some Miscellaneous Pieces* ed H. N. Coleridge (1849)
CL	*Collected Letters of Samuel Taylor Coleridge* ed Earl Leslie Griggs (6 vols Oxford & New York 1956–71)
C Life (*G*)	James Gillman *The Life of Samuel Taylor Coleridge* (1838)
CM (*CC*)	S. T. Coleridge *Marginalia* ed George Whalley and H. J. Jackson (London & Princeton 1980–) = *CC* xii
CN	*The Notebooks of Samuel Taylor Coleridge* ed Kathleen Coburn (New York, Princeton & London 1957–)
C Pantheist	Thomas McFarland *Coleridge and the Pantheist Tradition* (Oxford 1969)
CRB	*Henry Crabb Robinson on Books and Their Writers* ed Edith J. Morley (3 vols 1938)
C 17th C	*Coleridge on the Seventeenth Century* ed R. F. Brinkley (Durham NC 1955)
C Talker	R. W. Armour and R. F. Howes *Coleridge the Talker* (1949)
DC	Derwent Coleridge
DCL	Dove Cottage Library, Grasmere
De Q	Thomas De Quincey
De Q Works	*The Collected Writings of Thomas De Quincey* ed David Masson (14 vols Edinburgh 1889–90)
DNB	*Dictionary of National Biography* (1885–)
DW	Dorothy Wordsworth
DWJ	*Journals of Dorothy Wordsworth* ed Ernest de Selincourt (2 vols 1941)
DWJ (M)	*Journals of Dorothy Wordsworth. The Alfoxden Journal 1798* [and] *The Grasmere Journals 1800–1803* ed Mary Moorman (Oxford 1971)
EC	*The English Catalogue of Books (Including the Original "London" Catalogue [of 1786 for 1700–86]) . . . Issued in the United Kingdom . . . 1801–1836* ed R. A. Peddie and Q. Waddington (1914)

Ed Rev	*The Edinburgh Review* (Edinburgh & London 1802–1929)
EHC	Ernest Hartley Coleridge
EOT (CC)	S. T. Coleridge *Essays on His Times in "The Morning Post" and "The Courier"* ed David V. Erdman (3 vols London & Princeton 1978) = *CC* III
Friend (CC)	S. T. Coleridge *The Friend* ed Barbara E. Rooke (2 vols London & Princeton 1969) = *CC* IV
Gillman SC (1843)	*Catalogue of a Valuable Collection of Books, Including the Library of James Gillman, Esq* (Henry Southgate 1843). Marked copies: BM SC Sg 64 (2) and Sg a 53
G Mag	*The Gentleman's Magazine* (1731–1907)
Göttingen LB	A. D. Snyder "Books Borrowed by Coleridge from the Library of the University of Göttingen, 1799" *Modern Philology* xxv (1928) 377–80
Green List	VCL MS 18, a handlist of C's books prepared by Mrs J. H. Green c 1863
Green SC (1880)	*Catalogue of the Library of Joseph Henry Green . . . Sold by Auction* (Sotheby Jul 1880). Marked copy: BM SC S 805 (1)
Green SC (1884)	*Catalogue of Scarce and Valuable Books, Including a Remarkable Collection of Coleridgeiana* (Scribner & Welford, New York 1884)
HC	Hartley Coleridge
HCL	*Letters of Hartley Coleridge* ed Grace Evelyn and Earl Leslie Griggs (Oxford 1936)
HC Essays	*Essays and Marginalia by Hartley Coleridge* ed Derwent Coleridge (2 vols 1851)
HC Poems	*Poems by Hartley Coleridge, with a Memoir of His Life by His Brother* [Derwent Coleridge] (2 vols 1851)
HCR	Henry Crabb Robinson
Healey	George Harris Healey *The Cornell Wordsworth Collection* (Ithaca NY 1957)
HEHL	The Henry E. Huntington Library and Art Gallery, San Marino, CA
HNC	Henry Nelson Coleridge
H Works	*The Complete Works of William Hazlitt* ed P. P. Howe (12 vols 1930–4)
Kant *C d r V*	Immanuel Kant *Critik der reinen Vernunft*

Kant *VS*	Immanuel Kant *Vermischte Schriften* (4 vols Halle & Königsberg 1799–1807)
Kemp Smith	Norman Kemp Smith tr *Immanuel Kant's Critique of Pure Reason* (rev ed 1933)
L & L	*Coleridge on Logic and Learning* ed Alice D. Snyder (New Haven & London 1929)
LCL	Loeb Classical Library
Lects 1795 (CC)	S. T. Coleridge *Lectures 1795: On Politics and Religion* ed Lewis Patton and Peter Mann (London & Princeton 1971) = *CC* I
Lects 1808–1819 (CC)	S. T. Coleridge *Lectures 1808–1819: On Literature* ed Reginald A. Foakes (2 vols London & Princeton 1984) = *CC* VI
Levere	Trevor H. Levere *Poetry Realized in Nature: Samuel Taylor Coleridge and Early Nineteenth-Century Science* (Cambridge 1981)
LL	*The Letters of Charles Lamb to Which Are Added Those of His Sister Mary Lamb* ed E. V. Lucas (3 vols 1935)
LL (M)	*The Letters of Charles and Mary Anne Lamb* ed Edwin W. Marrs, Jr (3 vols Ithaca NY 1975–8)
L Life	E. V. Lucas *The Life of Charles Lamb* (1921)
L Works (1903)	*The Works of Charles and Mary Lamb* ed E. V. Lucas (5 vols 1903)
Logic (CC)	S. T. Coleridge *Logic* ed J. R. de J. Jackson (London & Princeton 1980) = *CC* XIII
Lost List	A handlist prepared by George Whalley of books known to have been annotated by C but not located at the time this edition went to press. An incomplete version was published in *Book Collector* XVII (1968) 428–42 and XVIII (1969) 223
LR	*The Literary Remains of Samuel Taylor Coleridge* ed H. N. Coleridge (4 vols 1836–9)
LS (CC)	S. T. Coleridge *Lay Sermons* [being *The Statesman's Manual* and *A Lay Sermon*] ed R. J. White (London & Princeton 1972) = *CC* V
Method	*S. T. Coleridge's Treatise on Method as Published in the Encyclopaedia Metropolitana* ed Alice D. Snyder (1934)
Migne *PL*	*Patriologiae Cursus Completus . . . Series Latina* ed J. P. Migne (221 vols Paris 1844–64)

Misc C	*Coleridge's Miscellaneous Criticism* ed T. M. Raysor (1936)
M Mag	*The Monthly Magazine* (1796–1843)
Mrs C	Sara Coleridge née Fricker (wife of C)
MW	Mary Wordsworth née Hutchinson (wife of WW)
N	Notebook of Samuel Taylor Coleridge (numbered or lettered) in ms. References are given by folio
NED	S. T. Coleridge *Notes on English Divines* ed Derwent Coleridge (2 vols 1853)
NLS	S. T. Coleridge *Notes and Lectures upon Shakespeare and Some Other Old Poets and Dramatists with Other Literary Remains* ed Sara Coleridge (2 vols 1849)
NTP	*Notes, Theological, Political and Miscellaneous* ed Derwent Coleridge (1853)
NYPL	New York Public Library
ODCC	*The Oxford Dictionary of the Christian Church* ed F. L. Cross (1971)
OED	*The Oxford English Dictionary* (12 vols Oxford 1970)
p-d	paste-down. See "Editorial Practice" *CM* I xxx
Phil Trans RS	*The Philosophical Transactions of the Royal Society* (1665–1821)
P Lects (1949)	*The Philosophical Lectures of Samuel Taylor Coleridge* ed Kathleen Coburn (London & New York 1949)
PML	The Pierpont Morgan Library, New York
PW (EHC)	*The Complete Poetical Works of Samuel Taylor Coleridge* ed E. H. Coleridge (2 vols Oxford 1912)
QR	*The Quarterly Review* (1809–1952)
RS	Robert Southey
RX	John Livingston Lowes *The Road to Xanadu* (rev ed Boston 1930)
SC	Sara Coleridge (daughter of C, and wife of HNC)
SC Life	Earl Leslie Griggs *Coleridge Fille. A Biography of Sara Coleridge* (Oxford 1940)
SC Memoir	*Memoir and Letters of Sara Coleridge* [ed Edith Coleridge] (2 vols 1873)
SH	Sara Hutchinson
Sh C	*Coleridge's Shakespearean Criticism* ed T. M. Raysor (2nd ed 2 vols 1960)

S Letters (Curry)	*New Letters of Robert Southey* ed Kenneth Curry (2 vols New York & London 1965)
SM (*CC*)	S. T. Coleridge *The Statesman's Manual* in *Lay Sermons* ed R. J. White (London & Princeton 1972) = *CC* v
Southey SC (1844)	*Catalogue of the Valuable Library of the Late Robert Southey* (Sotheby, May 1844). Marked copy: BM S–C S 252 (1)
SW & F (*CC*)	S. T. Coleridge *Shorter Works and Fragments* ed H. J. Jackson and J. R. de J. Jackson (2 vols London & Princeton in preparation) = *CC* xi
TL	S. T. Coleridge *Hints towards the Formation of a More Comprehensive Theory of Life* ed Seth B. Watson (1848)
TT	*Table Talk of Samuel Taylor Coleridge* ed H. N. Coleridge (rev ed 1836). Cited by date
VCL	Victoria College Library, University of Toronto
Watchman (*CC*)	S. T. Coleridge *The Watchman* ed Lewis Patton (London & Princeton 1970) = *CC* ii
WL (*E* 2)	*Letters of William and Dorothy Wordsworth; the Early Years* ed Ernest de Selincourt, rev Chester L. Shaver (Oxford 1967)
WL (*L* 2)	*Letters of William and Dorothy Wordsworth; the Later Years* ed Alan G. Hill (Oxford 1980–)
WL (*M* 2)	*Letters of William and Dorothy Wordsworth; the Middle Years* ed Ernest de Selincourt, rev Mary Moorman (2 vols Oxford 1969–70)
W Library	Chester L. Shaver and Alice C. Shaver *Wordsworth's Library. A Catalogue Including a List of Books Housed by Wordsworth for Coleridge from c. 1810 to c. 1830* (New York & London 1979)
W Life	Mary Moorman *William Wordsworth: a Biography* (2 vols Oxford 1957–65)
W Prose	*The Prose Works of William Wordsworth* ed W. J. B. Owen and J. W. Smyser (3 vols Oxford 1974)
WPW	*The Poetical Works of William Wordsworth* ed Ernest de Selincourt and Helen Darbishire (5 vols Oxford 1940–9)
WW	William Wordsworth

MARGINALIA

EDWARD IRVING
1792–1834

For Missionaries after the Apostolical School, a series of orations. In four parts. I. The Doctrine. II. The Experiment. III. The Argument. IV. The Duty. London 1825. 8°.

British Library C 61 c 8

Preface dated *"January*, 1825." Three-page dedication "To Samuel Taylor Coleridge, Esq." Inscribed on p⁻2 "From the Author To his dear friend & kind Instructor Samuel Taylor Coleridge". Two notes in pencil in an unidentified hand, referring to Irving's text and not to C's notes, appear on pp 51, 82; it was probably the same hand that underlined in pencil a double negative on p 63.

In *AR* (1825) 372n–3n C acknowledged his friendship with Irving and praised his Luther-like spirit. Four years later, however, he found it necessary to make "a frank declaration" about Irving in *C&S (CC)* 142*, since—partly because of the dedication of this work—his name had come to be associated with Irving's very dubious doctrines. Other works of Irving's annotated by C are *Sermons* and Lacunza.

DATE. Between 1825 (after May, when *AR* was published) and 1827.

COEDITOR. James Boulger.

1 half-title verso

The 12 last verses of Mark's Gospel b̶y̶ on internal & external evidence are by all the later School of Biblical Criticism asterisked as spurious.[1] Manifest echoes of misunderstood passages in the Acts of the Apostles[2]—while the texts in the two other Gospels κατα σαρκα[3] must, I think,[a]

---

a The note is incomplete

[1] For Mark 16.9–20 as a later addition to the gospel see BIBLE COPY B **101** and n 1, HOOKER **39** at n 3. By "the later School of Biblical Criticism" C would normally mean the "Neologists" Eichhorn, Schleiermacher, Rosenmüller, Herder, Lessing— "those *critical* dreadnoughts" in LACUNZA **6**. Eichhorn *Neue Testament* I 576–9, however, defends the authenticity of these verses, setting forth in detail the evidence of the codices and scholia, drawing per-

haps on Rosenmüller's *Scholia in Novum Testamentum* (5 vols Nürnberg 1803–15); in N 26[.27] ff 55–55ᵛ and 26[.29] f 58 (27 Jul 1827) C expresses surprise at Eichhorn's conclusion. It does not appear that Schleiermacher, Herder, or Lessing discusses the authenticity or "spuriousness" of Mark 16.9–20. See also *CN* IV 5169 and 5371 ff 7ᵛ–8.

[2] These verses (Mark 16.9–20) seem to have been compiled from the other gospels

2   p xiii | Preface

To give it this more convincing and more living form, was the occupation of my little leisure from pastoral and ministerial duties, rendered still less, during the summer months, by the indifferen¢¢t state of my bodily health. And it was /\ not until the few weeks of rest and recreation which I enjoyed in the autumn, that I was able to perceive the true form and full extent of the argument which is necessary to make good my position.

better thus /\ in the few weeks— —autumn, that I first obtained an insight into the true form and full extent of the Argument, by which my position was to be maintained and by which alone it could be made good.

3   p xiii

The doctrine, of which I have convinced myself out of the Scriptures, and which I propose by the grace of God to demonstrate and <u>commend</u> . . .

apply*a
* "Commend" is never used in modern English, except as = to express approbation of.[1]

4   p xvi

Now, if I read the eleventh chapter of St. Paul's Epistle to the Hebrews, I find that . . . it was by *faith* that the cloud of witnesses . . . so mightily prevailed . . . whereas *prudence* or *expediency* is the substance of things present, the evidence of things seen. So that faith and prudence are opposite poles in the soul, the one attracting to it all things spiritual and divine, the other all things sensual and earthy. This expediency hath banished the soul of patriotic eloquence from our senate, the spirit of high equity from our legislation, self-denying wisdom from our philosophy, and of our poetry it hath clipt the angel wing and forced it to creep

---

a Having underlined "commend" in the text, C proposes an alternative word, "apply", in the margin

---

and from Acts—perhaps by Aristion, according to one interpretation of a tenth-century ms.

    1[3] The gospels "according to the flesh"—i.e. from a human point of view, as human history: the "synoptic" gospels Matt, Mark, and Luke as opposed to the gospel "according to the spirit", John. BLANCO WHITE *Practical Evidence* **1** n 2.

See also **11** n 2 below; and cf e.g. DONNE *Sermons* COPY B **16** and n 5, HERDER *Von der Auferstehung* **16** and n 5.

    3[1] *OED*, however, does not exclude for this period the meanings "recommend" or "present as worthy of notice or regard", subtly different from C's definition, and closer to Irving's intention than "apply".

along the earth. And if we look not to i̲t̲, it will strangle faith and make void the reality of the things which are not seen, & which are the only things that are real and cannot be removed.

it, according to the grammatical position, would have its antecedent in "Prudence". Better therefore, And unless we halt in time and stand on our guard, this Prudence, this all-mastering Expediency will strangle &c

5 p xvi | Continuing **4** textus

Money, money, money, is the universal cry.

1. 6 /\. the End and the Means! at once the Butt, the Shaft and the Bow! Money, the A and Ω[1] of the World's Idolatry!

6 p xvi | Continuing **5** textus

Mammon hath gotten the victory, and may say triumphantly (nay, he may keep silence and the /\ servants of Christ will say it for him), "Without me ye can do nothing."

/\ profest
Qᵞ professors?[1]

7 p xvii

And truth will not retaliate upon prudence the evil aim which she hath bent against her and all her daughters: but, upon the other hand, will bestow even upon prudence a heavenly form.

See "Aids to Reflection" from p. 13 to p. 28.[1]

8 p xx

The Jews required a sign (that is, *miracles), and the Greeks sought after wisdom, but it pleased God by the foolishness of preaching to save them that believe.

* a mistaken interpretation. Our Lord had just performed the most stu-

5[1] A traditional lament; cf 1 Tim 6.10: "the love of money is the root of all evil". Alpha and omega, the first and last letters of the Greek alphabet, allude to Rev 1.8, "I am Alpha and Omega, the beginning and the ending, saith the Lord."

6[1] The implication is that "professors" (in the Church or in the academy?) may not be practitioners of the doctrines they profess.

7[1] *AR* (1825) 13–28 consists of Aphorisms 20–32 at the end of the group of Introductory Aphorisms. Aphorism 20 states that the "high intent" to "form the human mind anew after the DIVINE IMAGE" is "comprised under three heads": "the prudential, the moral, and the spiritual"—the heads under which the aphorisms in *AR* are grouped. Introductory Aphorisms 21–2 and 29 are on the subject of prudence.

pendous of his miracles before their eyes, when (and N.B. *prompted* by this miracle & in *consequence* of it) they required THE SIGN—i.e. the open assumption of the Regal Power—i.e. that he would issue a Proclamation.[1]

9 p xxi

Those five offices mentioned by the Apostle in the Epistle to the Ephesians, "apostles, prophets, evangelists, pastors, and teachers," are not offices for a time but for all times, denoting the five great divisions of duty necessary for the prosperity of the Church . . .

PENTAD 1. Prothesis. 2. Thesis. 3. Antithesis. 4. Indifference or Amphotéric 5. Synthesis.[1]

1 Apostles
2. Prophets   4. Pastors.   3. Evangelists
5. Doctors.[2]

10 p 43 (misprinted 34), pencil | Oration 1 "Messiah's Constitution for the Missionary Estate"

I cannot help thinking that the men [the twelve Apostles] were well endowed for their work, and that their work was worthy of the endowment, and that they would find in the worst of climes (as verily they did, for these same twelve planted the Gospel far and near, from India to the British Isles,) a class of men, and that the highest, to give them welcome.

? a Legend: and irreconcilable with St Paul's Assertion, that to him exclusively the Gentile Missions were entrusted—while the 12 sought the lost sheep of Israel, first, in the towns and villages of Palestine; afterwards, in Babylon, Ephesus, Alexandria; in short, wherever there was Jewish Settlement & Synagogue.[1] If there be (which I grievously doubt)

8[1] Irving is paraphrasing 1 Cor 1.22–5, which echoes Matt 12.38: "Master, we would see a sign from thee"—the Pharisees' attempt to trap Jesus into a confession of blasphemy after he had healed the man "possessed with a devil, blind and dumb". In John (e.g. 2.18, 6.30) a "sign" can mean a miracle, but not in the synoptic gospels. C correctly says that the sign the Pharisees sought was a declaration that Jesus was the Messiah come as King of the Jews to hold "Regal Power" (not a biblical phrase). Cf Pilate in John 19.14–22.

9[1] For the terms of the Logical Pentad see IRVING *Sermons* 2 at n 1. The middle term—here numbered "4"—is sometimes called "Mesothesis", for which "Amphoteric"—"[partaking] of both [Thesis and Antithesis, and of Prothesis and Synthesis]"—is an unusual alternative or a gloss. Cf *C&S* (*CC*) 233.

9[2] Five orders of ministry are suggested by Eph 4.11, three orders by 1 Cor 12.28.

10[1] For "Paul's Assertion" see esp Acts 13.43–8 (including "lo, we turn [from the Jews] to the Gentiles"), and cf

any truth in the tradition of Peter's episcopacy & martyrdom at Rome, in this way only must it be explained—viz. that he confined himself to the Jewish Transteverine Settlers.[2]

11 pp 50–1 | Oration 2 "The Perpetuity of this Missionary Constitution, Proved"

[Irving argues that the instructions contained in Matt 10.5–42, which he reprints on pp [1–2] as "the missionary charter", "are of continual obligation, present the everlasting type of the missionary character, and are not by any human authority to be altered or abridged." (46)] Therefore, let what hath been said suffice for showing the evidence, which the document yields to its own durability, and the express denial which it gives to every daring temporizer . . .

Unanswerable by such Antagonists as M[r] I. had in his mind's eye or was likely to meet with. But I cannot exclude the thought from my mind, that this whole Speech, like the Sermon on the Mount,[1] are instances & proofs of the plan, on which the first Gospel was written—in other words, of the principle, on which the κηρύγματα which were the materials common to all the three Gospels τὰ κάτα σάρκα;[2] were [? first/put] idea. It is eh the distinctive Character of Matthew (I use the name merely to signify the compositor of the our first Gospel) to bring together all the sayings that Christ had uttered at different times and occasions on some one time, place or occasion/ seemingly regardless of slight inconsistencies consequent thereon.[3] This strengthens M[r] Irving's Argument.

"a teacher of the Gentiles" in Rom 15.15–16, Eph 3.7–9, 1 Tim 2.7, 2 Tim 1.11. For the apostles "preaching the word to none but unto the Jews only" see Acts 11.19, but cf Acts 11.20–5, 14.1–5. Neither Acts nor the Pauline epistles suggest such clearcut constituencies for the apostles' missions as C implies.

10[2] The tradition of Paul's episcopacy and martyrdom at Rome comes primarily from the apocryphal *Acts of St Paul*, largely compiled in the late second century from Acts and the Pauline epistles. According to Acts, Paul was first brought to Rome as a captive and kept there under house arrest for two years. He was then apparently allowed to travel to Spain, arrested again at Troas (2 Tim 4.13), brought to Rome, and killed there—beheaded, according to Tertullian—in the Neronian persecution of A.D. 67 (Eusebius). According to the *Acts of St Paul*, he was killed on the banks of the Tiber three miles from Rome, but that does not necessarily imply a mission to the Jews who lived across the Tiber ("Transteverine" being C's rendering of Italian *trastiburino*, "across the Tiber"). There is no reason to doubt the tradition of Paul's martyrdom; probably Eph, Phil, Col, Philem were written during his second period in Rome.

11[1] Matt 5–7; cf Luke 6.20–49.

11[2] The "proclamations" common to the three gospels "according to the flesh", the three synoptic gospels (1 n 3 above). Κήρυγμα is regularly translated "preaching" in AV (e.g. Matt 12.41, Luke 11.32, Rom 16.25), the word "sermon" not occurring in AV. It is a key term for the German Neologists and for C, often distinguished from δόγματα, dogma: see *CN* IV 5336, HERDER *Von der Auferstehung* **16**.

11[3] See HERDER *Von der Auferstehung* **11** n 1.

12 p 79

For if these [instructions] be cast aside, I, for one, see not upon what scriptural basis a Missionary Society resteth. . . . . But these instructions remaining, I perceive the use of a Missionary College, to see them carried into effect; and I see the calling of a Missionary to be the highest upon earth, and the nearest unto God; I see that he is a messenger not of time but of eternity . . .

This is the weakest part—*how* can and on what plan should, a College claim or exercise superintendence of *such* Missionaries?   *S. T. C.*

13 pp 131 (at the end of the text) and +1 | "Conclusion—From the Missionary Doctrine"

Whether, in fine, we are to open in the hearts of our Missionaries inlets to every spirit of hypocrisy, avarice, and ambition, and close as many inlets to the SPIRIT OF TRUTH, quenching by our prudences and policies the one everlasting Spirit of God, and giving vent to as many spirits, crusading, jesuitical, commercial, or political, as there are diverse ages in the Church, which are not, like the ages of the world, fourfold,—of gold, of silver, of brass, of iron,—but manifold, according to the degree of impurity and incompleteness in the doctrine which is preached, and the degree of laxness or lordliness in the discipline which is administered in the Churches.

A noble Specimen of manly principle and manly eloquence. If Mr I. have published a second part, I have not seen ⟨it⟩[1]—Even if he has, it is still to be regretted that he had not in the very outset of his argument met the main objection of his Antagonists, the *miraculous* Gifts of the Apostolic Missionaries.[2] This for the majority of his Hearers and Readers hangs, like a dead weight, around the neck of his Reasoning—They say to themselves—To whom Christ commanded a super-natural independence of human Means and Aids, to them in the same commission he delegated super-human powers—in applying the statute therefore we must qualify the duties imposed by the difference of the powers conferred for their performance.—This Argument Mr Irving should have met at the outset: for the Removal of this obstacle is as the foundation of all, he would build up: inasmuch as not being removed it prevents the foundation from being laid.   S. T. C.

13[1] Here C's writing reaches the printed formula "END OF THE FIRST PART." No continuation by Irving is provided here or elsewhere.

13[2] In Matt 10.5–42, esp 10.8.

Ah! how easy and how difficult would it be to reduce this objection to a mere fraction of its assumed weight!—I question whether Mr Irving himself would not anathematize his volunteer Ally, and disclaim with vehemence this auxiliary ~~Force~~ Contingent! The time is not yet come, for men to believe what they ⟨would⟩ actually find in Luke's Acts of the Apostles if they looked at the contents with the naked Eye—instead of Katterfelto's Glass, that shewed 500 non-descript Animals, each as lar[g]e^a as his Black Cat, in a drop of water.—³

14   pp ⁺2, ⁺1

The two most uncommon things in the World are the Love of the Good, *as* good, and the Love of the True *as* Truth—each *absolutely* and only for itself. And of these two uncommon things the latter is the more uncommon. I do not mean Veracity, or the man's abhorrence of ~~saying~~ Falsehood or of saying what he does not think—that he does so *think*, must be grounded in no other interest but the desire of thinking the Truth.¹ Again: I do not mean partially, or generally, but as a principle, operating without exception. The former rare excellence I could confidently attribute to my Friend, Edward Irving; but not with equal confidence, or so unexceptionally, the latter. For instance: I cannot help, believing, that his imagination that the XXth Chapter of the Revelations² favors the doctrine of a future Millennium prevents him from seeing, that it is a mere imagination; & that the passage was actually intended to evacuate theise favorite fancy of the Jews and Jewish Converts by substituting under the same name the anticipation of the Establishment of Christianity as the Religion of the Empire.³*   S. T. C.

* I say this with less suspicion of any counterwarp in my own mind, that (only cutting all connection with Daniel and the Apocalypse) I am inclined to think in the main with him & Lacunza respecting the Second Coming of our Lord.

---

^a Possibly "huge": the word is squeezed in above the footnote to **14**, which must have been written before this postscript to **13**

13³ Gustavus Katterfelto (d 1799), Prussian conjuror and quack: see BLANCO WHITE *Practical Evidence* **10** n 1.

14¹ For the distinction between truth and veracity see BAXTER *Reliquiae* COPY B **46**.

14² The vision of the Millennium and the Resurrection, and the defeat of the Devil. For C on "the fiction of the Millennium" see FLEURY **31** and nn 1, 2.

14³ See LACUNZA **2** and **47**, and *C&S* (*CC*) 139–40 n *. Cf. also EICHHORN *Neue Testament* COPY A **33** n 4.

Sermons, Lectures, and Occasional Discourses. 3 vols. London 1828. 8°.

The title-page of each volume gives a general title to the contents of that volume, recorded in CONTENTS below. Vol I is dedicated to Irving's congregation, II to Mr and Mrs Basil Montagu, III to Henry Drummond. The work appeared in Nov 1828, but internal dates establish the order in which the volumes were prepared for the press, Vol II Preface being dated 28 Sept 1827, Vol III Dedication 10 Jan 1828, Vol I Epistle Dedicatory 10 Nov 1828. The three volumes are continuously paginated; after Vol I had been set and printed, however, two sermons were added with a clumsy pagination of their own, the final page number of the original setting being given in parentheses with new roman numerals following: Sermon 3 is paginated (140)i–(140)cxcv. An additional complication is that on verso pages the roman numerals appear first, e.g. cx(140).

British Library C 126 i 8

Inscribed on the title-page of Vol I: "To my Sage Counseller & most honoured Friend Samuel Taylor Coleridge Esq   E. Irving". Monogram of John Duke Coleridge on Vol I title-page; "S. T. C." label on title-page of each volume. A note by EHC inserted at I 24/5. C has written most of his annotations in Vol I, into which he bound a few extra leaves (**17**) to carry his notes.

CONTENTS. Each volume has a general title given on the title-page. Prefaces and dedications are omitted from this table. Vol I The Doctrine of the Incarnation Opened in Six Sermons: "That the Beginning and Origin of the Mystery that the Eternal Word should take unto himself a body, is the holy will and good pleasure of God" (1–66); "The End of the Mystery is the Glory of God" (67–139); "The Method of accomplishing the Mystery, is by taking up the Fallen Humanity into the Personality of the eternal Son of God" (140–(140)cxcv); "The Preparation for and the very Act of the Incarnation" (cxcvi(140)–211); "The Fruits of the Incarnation" (212–328); "Conclusions concerning the subsistence of God and the subsistence of the Creature, derived from reflecting on the Incarnation" ((328)i–(328)lxvii). Vol II Lectures on the Parable of the Sower: "Introductory" (343–83); "Seed on the Way-side" (384–454); "Seed on the Rock" (455–514); "Seed among Thorns" (515–603); "Seed in a good and honest Heart" (604–86); "Supplementary Lecture" (687–772). Vol III On Subjects National and Prophetical, Seven Discourses: "On Education" (781–846); "The three unclean Spirits" (847–92); "God's Controversy with the Land" (893–963); "Drying-up of the Euphrates" (964–1024); "The Curse (Gen. iii.) as to Bodily Labour" (1025–93); "The Kings of the East or the Ten Tribes" (1094–1198); "Curse and Remedy of Ireland's Evil Condition" (1199–1253).

DATE. Nov–Dec 1828 (shortly after publication in Nov) to c Feb 1829 (cf *CL* VI 785). Dated in ms 25 Dec 1828 (**24**), 1 Jan 1829 (**29**), "1828" (**29** PS).

COEDITOR. James Boulger.

1   1 ⁻9⁻⁻4ᵃ

⟨Observe.—The "*pre-*" in the following Remarks must not be referred to priority in time, every imagination of which must be vigilantly excluded in our contemplation of Eternal Verities;—but ⟨to⟩ the order of thought or ideal Genesis.[1] In the Acorn the Root and the Trunk co-exist; but still in the order of necessary thought the Root is first or deepest.—⟩

Would to heaven, I could induce the high heart and vehement intellect of my friend, Edward Irving, to devote one quiet genial day of Spring or Autumn to the Contemplation of God under the form of Absolute Identity, [? ~~or that he~~] preparing for it by meditation on the Evangelist's Θέον οὐδεις ἑώρακεν ουδε ποτε;[2] so namely as to fix and master the difference of the Θεος in this, the 18ᵗʰ verse, and the Θεος likewise without an article before it, in the first verse of the same Chapter: in which latter it partakes of the character of a Predicate, referred to a Subject by the intervening Verb Substantive—και ὁ λογος ἦν Θεος.[3] The former (*in v. 18ᵗʰ*) on the contrary, admits not of a Verb Substantive preceding it, either with or without a Noun Substantive as the proper or prior Nominative Case. The Father *is* seen in the only-begotten Son, as the objective visibility, the **Person*, of the Father: and of the Father we must say, Ο πατηρ εστι 'Ο̲ θεος.—Περι Θεου ου τλημι λεγειν, οτι εστι· ἀλλ᾽

* This alone, did no other objections exist, should have forbidden the use of the term, person, instead of υποστασις, or subsistency—applicable alike to F., S, and H. G., while the son only is the Person of the Father[4]

ᵃ In the present state of the volume (rebound in 1951) pp ⁻4/⁻3 constitute the stub of a sheet (pp ⁻6–⁻3) guarded in. This was evidently the state of the flyleaves when C used the book, because he has written three lines of ms on the recto of the stub (p ⁻4), and has numbered three of the front flypages (i.e. pp ⁻7, ⁻6, ⁻5) as 3, 4, and 5. See also **17** n 4 below.

1[1] For C's use of the prefix *pre* or *prae* see BÖHME **6** n 8.

1[2] John 1.18 (var), evidently quoted from memory: "No man hath seen God at any time."

1[3] John 1.1, "and the Word was God", which is literally what C—translating AV English—has written in Greek. (The actual Greek NT text is και Θεὸς ἦν ὁ λόγος, lit "and God was the word".) For C's view on the significance of the "Verb Substantive"—i.e. "to be"—see e.g. *Logic (CC)* 16–19, and cf **2** at n 3 below. The other issue here, the presence or absence of the definite article, reflects a contemporary theological controversy initiated by the

publication of Granville Sharp's *Remarks on the Use of the Definitive Article in the Greek Text of the New Testament* in 1798. Sharp was supported by Christopher Wordsworth and by C's college friend T. F. Middleton. Cf BIBLE COPY B **102** n 1, and **2** at n 13 below.

1[4] For C's objection to the Trinitarian use of "Person" as equivalent to ὑπόστασις (substance, "ground" in **7** below) see CHANNING **1** and n 2, FLEURY **56** and n 3, and **40** below. "Subsistency" is an abstract noun derived from *hypostatis*—*substantia*—'standing-under"; cf **2** n 14 below.

οτι παντα εστι απ' αυτου.[5]— For I speak of that Absolute Subjectivity which cannot be an Object, nor have any Object as its proper Correlative or Antithesis: as with less declination from the truth, with less disturbance & contravention of the unique Idea, the Father may be affirmed to have in the Son.

Of this Absolute Subject ~~we~~ it cannot be said, that he is All or the whole: nor dare we speak of his Unity, but ⟨we must think of the Abs. Subj.,⟩ as the immanifestable Ground (= βύσσος ἄβυσσος)[6] and Giver of Unity; ~~the Antecedent and~~ even as in all Distinction he is ~~pre-~~ likewise supposed, ⟨as the Ground and Precondition thereof.⟩ The Father is known as distinct from the Son, and the Son from the Spirit; and the Father, the Son, and the Spirit are in inseparable Unity, in that the ⟨Absolute Subject⟩ is supposed the imperturbable indistinguishable ONE in all; and ~~in~~ only by being ⟨thus⟩ supposed ~~as such it in for~~ is itself ~~is~~ rendered distinguishable by and for the finite discursive intellect. ~~become distinct.~~

But where shall Man find the Mirror, in whose ~~own~~ image he may make this Mystery of Mysteries not indeed comprehensible but dimly intelligible? I answer—In his Will, as the source, ground and condition of his responsib⟨i⟩lity: in the IDEA of the Will, left after the exclusion of its Imperfections, as finite, of its corruptions, as fleshly; and lastly, in the Idea of THE GOOD.—[7]

After this Ascent hath been attained, it will no longer be Sound without Meaning for my Friend, when he hears it said—That the Absolute Subject in the eternal Act of Self-affirmation begetting the Son, ⟨or (which means the same)⟩ uttering the only-begotten WORD[8] is at once the I AM, and the Father.[9] ~~It is~~ The ⟨Air of the intellectual World cleansed from the⟩ glittering Dust-atoms and Moats of the fancy; the busy disursion[a] of the Understanding ⟨suspended,⟩ and the stubborn in-

---

[a] A slip for "discursion"

1[5] "The father is *the* god.—About 'god' I do not dare to say that he is; but that all things are from him." With the last clause cf John 1.3: πάντα δι'αυτοῦ ἐγένετο. Τλημμ is intended, on a classical analogy, for τολμάω: see e.g. Rom 5.7, 1 Cor 6.1.

1[6] "Depthless depth". See BÖHME **72** n 1.

1[7] Of many comparable statements indicating the special status of the will in C's thought at this time, cf esp *CL* VI 641, *C&S* (*CC*) 123 and n, *AR* (1825) 328.

1[8] This phrase seals the relation in C's mind between his pun on "outerance" and "utterance" (BÖHME **100** n 2) and the creative activity of the Word as in John 1.3: "All things were made by him . . .".

1[9] For God the Father as "I AM"—a traditional identification based on Exod 3.14, but embracing also C's views on the verb substantive and fundamental tenets of post-Kantian philosophy—see also **15** at n 5, **54** at n 10 below; *BL* (*CC*) I 272–5; DONNE *Sermons* COPY B **110**.

trusions of Time and Space, repelled—let him but once have raised his Spirit to the contemplation of Deity under the form of Identity, as the Absolute Will essentially Causative of *all* Reality and therefore of his own (Causa Sui)[10] he will welcome the appropriateness not shrink from the scholastic strangeness, of the ~~Tri-une~~ terms Ipseity, Alterity and Community,[11] as Exponents of the eternal Distinctities, in which God is the Father, the Son, and the Spirit—the Subjective, = the I Am, the Objective = the Jehova;[12] the subjectively Objective = the Holy Ghost, or eternal Procession of Life and Love, Communicant and Communicated.

One practical Conclusion He will not fail to deduce from the above, namely, never in any act to introduce any one of the Divine Tri-unity without a clear intuition of the Co-presence of all—Will, Light, Life! Good, Truth, Wisdom. For lest it never be absent from the mind, that if the Distinctityies of the Deity be incomparably more real, essential and incomprendible, than the corresponding Names, viz. the I, the Reason, and the Personal Life or Spirit in a regenerate Man, the Unity likewise is in the same transcendency more perfect—in as much as it alone is perfect, in short absolute. As therefore in every ~~Act~~ manifestation it is *the Man* that acts, and not ~~either the~~ *ᵃ* ~~power some~~ any one ~~of~~ Power singly, tho' it may very well happieren, that this Power may give the distinct form, name and character to the Act: so is it God, the one incomprehensible God, that is manifested in every work of God: and still less, than in the case of a human Individual, dare we think ~~o~~ that the Son is acting without the Holy Ghost, while the Father looks on as from a distance; or that the Father can act without ~~his~~ the Son, and the Holy Ghost, who are *his* Word and *his* Breath.—

I trust, that no spell of Vanity is upon me when I ~~say t~~ declare my belief, that a stedfast and calm consideration of the points urged in these four pages would have induced my reverend Friend to greatly modify the language at least, if not the doctrines themselves, in sundry paragraphs of this Volume. Nor is it only ⟨in⟩ the matter of the Trinity that I have wished for a revisal⟨.⟩ ~~of~~ Two other questions have ~~started~~ been called up in my mind by portions of the ⟨four⟩ first Discourses[13]—the

ᵃ Blank space left in ms

1[10] "Self-Cause", "Cause of Himself".

1[11] C's notes 2 and 3 below expand upon the significance of these terms. Cf the tetractys in GREW 1.

1[12] For the identification of Christ as the "Jehova-Word", see also BIBLE COPY B

11, 55; EICHHORN *Neue Testament* COPY B 10.

1[13] Vol I consists of six sermons on the Incarnation (see headnote); C's annotations in this volume end with Sermon 4 (**49** below).

first, respecting an apparent confusion of the Flesh, which our Lord *became* (και εγενετο σαρξ)[14] He came doubtless, with the *Seed* which he took on him (Hebrews ⟨c.⟩ II. ⟨v⟩ 16.). i.e. if the textual version is preferred to the marginal[15]—⟨the confusion of ⟨this⟩ material⟩ with the [? ~~core/corp~~] Organismus which in Jesus as in other men existed ~~in~~ only in transitu,[16] never the same in any two successive moments, and which I can conceive only as the Product, and as such the representative Sign of that Body which cleansed from Sin by him who ⟨therein⟩ had conquered Death & Sin, ~~in the Body~~ was capable of glory and actually glorified so as to enter into the Person of the Son of God.[17] There is another sense of the word, flesh, I ~~know;~~[a] am aware; but I ~~know~~ am likewise aware, who it was who refused to know Christ himself according to it.[18]
—Now my first Question is—Can we suppose that any momentous & essential Constituent of the Redemption by the Word incarnate was passed over by the Evangelist John, without even an allusion to it? If not, ~~it does~~ is not the language in more than one passage of these Discourses concerning the Material Organism such as it would be almost equally difficult to reconcile with Reason and the declarations of St John?—My next question refers to the fall of the Angels? If the Paradise Lost were part of the Canon, *then* I should have found no objection.—

But to ground a System on a possible interpretation of two or three obscure Texts, to which the best recent Interpreters attach a very different meaning, namely, the apostate Hierarchy before the Flood—this I think *rash*.[19]

2 1 $^-$2-$^-$ 1, title-page verso ([ii]), [iii]–vii

It may assist the Pupil's Efforts and help to put his mind in a fitter state

---

[a] Semicolon not deleted in ms

1[14] John 1.14 (actually σάρξ ἐγένετο): "And the Word was made flesh". For C's preference for the translation "became" see LEIGHTON COPY C **44** n 1, FLEURY **98** and n 4, and *AR* (1825) 16n. It was the question of Irving's treatment of "the flesh" of Christ that led eventually to his excommunication, formal charges arising from his *Christ's Holiness in the Flesh* (1831).

1[15] For the detail of Heb 2.16, including "he took on *him* the seed of Abraham", see 5 at n 1 below.

1[16] "In passing".

1[17] Cf John 13.31–2, 17.1–5. These two meanings of the term "flesh" are clarified in **12** and **29** below.

1[18] That C refers to Paul is confirmed by a similar statement in DONNE *Sermons* COPY B **16**, where the question of the relationship of Christ to Mary and Joseph is raised: "It is a point of religion for me to have no belief one way or the other—I am in this way like St Paul more than content not to know Christ himself ως κατα σαρκα." In the third sense, then, "according to the flesh" means "in human terms".

1[19] The fall of the rebel angels is mentioned in Rev 12.7–9, Jude 1.6, 2 Pet 2.4. The commentators interpreting those texts as references to an "apostate Hierarchy" have not been traced.

for comprehending the highest form of thinking by beginning with the lower, & after he has been familiarized with this, then to direct his attention on those Terms which arise out of the consideration of the Finite and cannot be applied to the Absolute.—[a]

With this view we may commence with the Logical Pentad

Prothesis

Thesis   Mesothesis   Antithesis
Synthesis.[1]

Now it will first be necessary to make the Student see, that the Mesothesis, or Indifference of the Thesis and Antithesis; that which may be either according as the relation is, or both at once but in different relations—(Thus the infinitive in Grammar expresses the indifference of Being and Act, or Noun and Verb. It is neither exclusively but may be either, to a Verb it may be the Noun, as the Object = in the Accusative Case, or the Subject = in the Nominative—or both, the Noun to a Verb, and the Verb to a Noun. Example.

For not *to-dip* the hero in the Lake
Could save the Son of Thetis from to die.
ου γαρ βαπτιζειν τον ηρωα εν στυγι
εδυνατο σωζειν τον πηλειδην απο του θνησκειν.—[2]

Here the infinite[b] βαπτιζειν, or to dip, is a Noun and the Nominative Case to the Verb, εδυνατο, could save, and at the same time it is a Verb to the Noun, τον ηρωα, the hero, and *governs* it as its Accusative.)

Now first, I say, the Student must be made see[c] that this must be omitted ~~when names for~~ in the exposition of the Forms, under which the Absolute is contemplable. Thus by way of illustration, not as instance (for the Mesothesis must be of the same class with the Thesis & ~~Mes~~

---

[a] Here C has written "Turn over leaf.—" and has resumed the note on p ⁻1 with "From over leaf, 1. 7.—"

[b] A slip for "infinitive"

[c] "see" is the first word p [ii], title-page verso; C had also written "see" as a catchword at the foot of p ⁻1

2[1] For the terms of the Logical Pentad (repeated in the schema below) see also IRVING *For Missionaries* 9 and n 1, *CN* III 4427 and n, *CL* VI 818; also BÖHME **6** n 10 and **107** n 2. For the tetractys as the same as the pentad but without the Mesothesis (or *punctum indifferens* of e.g. *AR*—1825–330) see FLEURY **92** and n 2, *CN* III 4432, 4436.

2[2] The Greek appears to be C's own translation, but the English lines appear in several of C's statements about the infinitive, or "Verb-Substantive". C adopted the verses—from Spenser *The Ruins of Time* lines 428–9 (var)—from James Harris's *Hermes* (1751): *Logic* (*CC*) 17 n 3.

Antithesis) ~~let~~ Derwent may be conceived as the Indifference or Meso-
thesis of Father and Son—Son in relation to me, Father in relation to my
Grandson.[3] But when we speak of the Divine Paternity, unique, absolute
and comprehending all paternity in one eternal Act, and of the Divine
Filiety,[4] ~~contained~~ receiving and containing all in its own Plèroma[5] (=
the WORD that expresseth every Word that cometh from the Mouth of
God!)[6] it is self-evident, or rather an identical proposition that no third
can be either. ~~Most~~ It is, therefore as true in philosophy as it is orthodox
in faith, to profess that the filial Word is μονογηενς,[7] the only-begotten
of the Father. The Father *begetteth* the Son, while he *proceedeth* in and
with the Spirit, even as the Spirit proceedeth from and with the Father
thro' the Son.[8]

~~For the same reason, it~~ Again—if there can be no mesothesis, still
less, if less could be, can there be any proper Synthesis, or Compound
of both—only that here a higher form is substituted: and to express this,
~~I instead of~~ omitted I say that the Synthes[a] is *exchanged* for that absolute
Form, of which it is a dim and imperfect analogon.—further, to distin-
guish the intelligential Light by which ~~we~~ the Absolute is made known
to us from the Faculty by which we seek to understand and distinguish
the finite, I have named the Science which has the former for its subject
Noetic, from Noûs,[9] and the latter Logical, and call the Absolute Forms
the noetic Tetractys, the Forms of the Finite or Conditional the logical
Pentad.

---

[a] A slip for "Synthesis", caused perhaps by the following verb "is"

2[3] DC was married on 6 Dec 1827; his son Derwent Moultrie was born 17 Oct 1828.

2[4] "Sonship": C does not use this word elsewhere, and the *OED* records no exam-
ple of its use before J. S. Mill's *Logic* (1851).

2[5] "Fulness", "plenitude", a Gnostic term that C uses fairly frequently in theo-
logical writings, e.g. *CN* iv 5233 and n, BIBLE COPY B **131** n 5.

2[6] An allusion to Matt 4.4, "Man shall not live by bread alone, but by every word
that proceedeth out of the mouth of God."

2[7] "Only-begotten", as C invariably translates the Greek word, following John
1.14, 18.

2[8] The doctrine of procession, based on such texts as John 8.42 (". . . I proceeded

forth and came from God; neither came I of myself, but he sent me") and 15.26 ("The
Spirit of truth, which proceedeth from the Father") and enshrined in the formula of
the Nicene Creed ("I believe in the Holy Ghost . . . Who proceedeth from the Fa-
ther and the Son"), normally discriminates between the Holy Ghost and the other per-
sons of the Trinity; C, however, insists on their integrity and equality.

2[9] Cf FLEURY 32: "Nous = the pure Reason: Logos = the intelligential Imagi-
nation, or Reason manifesting itself in *forms*; Phronesis = the Understanding".
With "noetic" cf *Logic* (*CC*) 293 and LU-
THER *Colloquia* **40** ("my Noetic or Doc-
trine & Discipline of Ideas")—but the ad-
jectival form is not C's coinage.

The noetic Tetractys,		The logical Pentad	
Identity		Prothesis	
Ipsëity Alterity	Thesis:	Mesothesis: Antithesis
Community		Synthesis.	

Now the contemplation of *Deity* under the first form of the Tetractys, i.e. Identity—the unarticled Θεον of John I. v. 18.[10]—this is the Height above all Height, the Deeper yet of all Depths.[11] Well for him, to whom the ~~Truth and~~ Certainty therefof ~~are~~ is made known, tho' but negatively, by seeing the impossibility of the Contrary! But blessed is He, ~~to~~ on whom tho' but once, in but one Sabbath moment, the Truth itself is presented—tho' as the Sun in the Rent of a dark Cloud which instantly closes again. ~~In the succeeding holy Gloom~~ It is the Soul of Faith: and what if a Darkness follows? The Soul feels the pressure of the Sealing tho' unable to discern the character and image.[12]—I trust, the time will come, when Mr Irving will have contemplated the Trinity in the light of the Absolute ONE, for so only can the mind be secure against the risk of Tritheism[13] by the too exclusive attention to the Distinctities under the unhappy translation of hypostasis by Person, and of thus introducing diversity of Attributes where only the eternal Proprieties of Form, ⟨Subsistency,⟩[14] and essential Relations dare be affirmed. That the Word became Flesk,^a I believe: for I find it declared in the Gospel of John[15] ~~but~~ and of the conception of Jesus in the womb of a Virgin impregnated by a Spirit I find two different relations prefixed, one to the first, the other to the third, Gospel. But I must see more reason, than ~~I~~ hitherto I have been able to discover, for considering these "evangelia infantiæ" of apostolic age and authority, before I think myself bound to have any opinion on the subject.^b16

---

^a A slip for "Flesh"

^b Here, at the top of I vii, the note ends with a line drawn across the page to separate the last two lines of ms of **2** from the beginning of **4**, which had already been written on I vii–viii

2[10] See **1** at n 2 above.

2[11] See **1** at n 5 above.

2[12] A Pauline image: cf 2 Cor 1.22, Eph 1.13, 4.30.

2[13] C repeats this charge, **29** at n 9 below.

2[14] For the proper translation of *hypostasis* as "subsistency" see **1** at n 4 above.

2[15] John 1.14, as **1** n 14 above.

2[16] Matt 1.18–25, Luke 1.26–38, parts of the "gospels of the infancy" that C, with certain German textual scholars, believed to be late additions to the first and third gospels: cf CHILLINGWORTH COPY B 2 n 2, F. E. D. Schleiermacher *A Critical Essay on the Gospel of St. Luke* tr Connop Thirlwall (1825) lxxxix. The term "evangelium infantiae" does not itself appear to have been used by the German scholars; C has adopted the title of one of the texts of the NT Apocrypha (of which he annotated a copy in 1826: BIBLE *NT Apocrypha*).

3   I ⁻2

Identity
Absolute Will, the alone Good.

Ipseity[1]
The ~~Father,~~ I AM, who in affirming himself begetteth
the Son & is thus the Father—

Alterity
The Son—Mind, I Subsistent Idea /[2]

Community
Spirit, Life, Love.

answering to the four forms of Logic,

Identity
Thesis   Antithesis
Synthesis.

4   I vii–viii | Preface

This is the redemption, this is the at-one-ment, which was wrought in Christ, to redeem the will of a creature from the oppression of sin, and bring it to be at one with the will of the Creator. . . . What a calumny it is then, ~~What a hideous lie,~~ to represent us as making Christ unholy and sinful, because we maintain that he took his humanity completely and wholly from the substance, from the sinful substance, of the fallen creatures which he came to redeem!

Mr Irving's Assailants have, it is probable, mistaken Appetence for Will, or confounded the two terms, supposing them synonomous, like swerve and deviate.[1] In like manner they ~~seemed~~ to have overlooked the important distinction between the Sin *of* a Man, i.e. proper & personal Guilt, and Sin *in* a Man, rightly called Sin inasmuch as it is the Offspring, ~~and~~ effect and consequence of an evil Will, tho' it may be opposed to and overcome by, the Will of the Person.[2]

3[1] "Himselfness", "selfhood" (not C's coinage), used of the Father also in e.g. Böhme **111** n 1, Fleury **70** n 2. Cf **1** at n 11 above.

3[2] For "subsistence" see **1** n 4 above; "alterity" or "otherness" is the traditional counterpart to "ipseity".

4[1] Characteristically desynonymising,

C distinguishes "appetence" as natural or carnal desire from "will", which is essentially spiritual. J. A. Heraud recorded a conversation between C and Irving in which the same distinction is invoked: *C Talker* 259–60; cf *AR* (1825) 278–9.

4[2] C's views on original sin are most fully expounded in *AR* (1825) 251–87.

5 I 2–3, completed on I $^+$1–$^+$4 | Sermon 1

This fall of man was also the formal cause of the Incarnation; that is to say, what gave to the purpose of God its outward form and character, requiring his Son to take upon him the nature of man, and not of angels, to be under the law, and to bear the curse of death, as it is written (Heb. ii. 14, 15), * "Forasmuch then as the children are partakers of flesh and blood, he also himself likewise took part of the same; that through death he might destroy him that had the power of death, that is, the devil; and deliver them who through fear of death were all their lifetime subject to bondage."

* The verse cited is the 16th of the 2nd chapter of Hebrews, a most perplexing verse from the extreme difficulty of deciding whether the textual or the marginal Translation express the right meaning of the original Greek; which may be construed both ways.[1] This is not the only instance of the ambiguity to which the too various offices of the Genitive Case ~~makes~~ exposes the Greek Language. Doubtless, the addition of an Ablative Case by the Latins was a needful improvement of the Declension of Nouns.[2] The marginal Version seems the more obvious rendering of the text, but the other which the translators adopted agrees better with the Context.   S. T. C.^{a}

There is perhaps no book in the whole new testament which in so great a degree as the †Epist. to the Hebrews demands on the part of the

† On very insufficient grounds and in the face of unanswered objections attributed to St Paul—to the Apostle who had anxiously warned the church against the innutritious flatulent qualities of the GNOSIS (most absurdly and injuriously rendered KNOWLEGE in our Established Version)/[3] have we attributed a Work written in the Alexandrian Dialect which carries the Gnosis, or typical and allegorical accommodation of the plain Letter & obvious meaning of the Old Testament to the utmost

^{a} Here C has written "*See Blank Leaf ad finem hujus Tomi*: A." and has resumed the note on I $^+$2 with "A. p. 3."

5[1] Heb 2.16, AV: "For verily he took not on *him the nature of* angels; but he took on *him* the seed of Abraham." Marginal gloss: "he taketh not hold of angels, but of the seed of Abraham he taketh hold". Cf the citation of this text above (in a note presumably written later than this one), **1** at n 15.

5[2] In a note to MATTHIAE (**10**), however, C refers to the Latin ablative as "a mere refinement".

5[3] 1 Cor 8.1: "Knowledge puffeth up, but charity edifieth." As C points out, "Knowledge" translates the Greek γνῶσις, which C consistently prefers to consider as referring more narrowly to "the science of detecting the mysteries of faith in the simplest texts of Old Testament History, to the contempt or neglect of the literal & contextual sense": DONNE *Sermons* COPY B **39**; cf EICHHORN *Neue Testament* COPY B **5**.

Commentator and Interpreter the union of Sound Learning, sober Judgement, and that rare Gift of imagination which enables the possessor to think, feel, and reason in the form and character of a distant Age under circumstances the most diverse from his own. As an Artist, making a portrait of himself, recurs at brief intervals to the Reflection in the Looking-Glass in order to keep alive in his mind the total impression of the Countenance while he is employed on some one single Feature; and will occasionally alter the position of his Head in order to contemplate the same features under a different mood or direction: so must the Student of this Epistle ever and anon refresh his mind by contemplating the Synopsis of the whole faith in Christ in the Mirror of the Idea.—For instance—I select a passage from this Epistle, and I consider ~~three~~ 3 points—first, what is the particular truth, of which the Writer endeavors to convince his intended Reader? secondly, ⟨to⟩ what sort of Readers the Writing was specially addressed? thirdly, how, by what illustrations, by what manner of inferences and deductions, the legitimacy of which was previously ⟨an⟩ allowed & familiar principle in the Reader's mind, was he most easily to be convinced?—Then I would take the same truth, and ~~suppose~~ instead of Apollos reasoning with a Jew whose Learning con-

---

height compatible with the claim ~~to~~ of having been composed under *Apostolic* Inspiration, ~~or~~ i.e. ⟨that⟩ which ~~is~~ retains its edifying power and binding Authority in *all* ages & in all churches—to such a height indeed, that the Catholic Church hesitated for nearly three Centuries before ~~they~~ she put the seal on its Canonicity. That the Church decided wisely and rightly in its final admission, I do not entertain the least doubt. It is a precious Relic of the Apostolic Age, and, I will add, of the Apostolic Spirit—and its Value for *us* is increased by the very circumstance, that it was written by a learned and eloquent Convert from the great ⟨Synagogue, which stood almost in⟩ *rival⟨ry⟩* ~~of~~ with the ancient Church in Palestine, notwithstanding ~~the~~ her high Prerogative of the Temple and its splendors. Thus we have a double Testimony of the Apostolic Faith before the destruction of the Temple—Paul, and (according to Luther's happy conjecture) Apollos.[4]

[5][4] Eichhorn may have been C's source for the information about Luther's theory that Apollos was the author of the Epistle to the Hebrews (BIBLE COPY B **134** n 1)— speculation that C refers to approvingly more than once, e.g. KANT *Religion* **3**, *TT* 6 Jan 1823, 1 May 1823. The debate about the canonicity of Heb is summarized by e.g. J. D. Michaelis *Introduction to the New Testament* ed Herbert Marsh (4 vols Cambridge 1801) IV 266: ". . . some Latin writers in the fourth century received it, among whom was Jerom himself: yet even in the time of Jerom the Latin church had not placed it among the canonical writings".

sisted almost exclusively ~~of the Laws~~ in his acquaintance with the Laws and Institutes of Moses, the history of his own Nation, the ~~revered~~ Hymns, Oracles, and Aphorisms of its inspired Teachers, together with the comments of the Lawyers & the Traditions of the Doctors, ~~at~~ in highest repute at the given Period—I would suppose Sᵗ Paul in Arabia laboring to make the same truth intelligible and convincing to a Sheik or Nomad Chief in his Tent with his Camels, ~~and~~ Flocks, and Sheep-dogs—~~around~~ basking on the Sands before him⸝—who had never seen a Temple, or led a Victim to the Altar—Again, I would suppose the Apostle Thomas essaying to impress the same truth on the mind of a Brahmin who held the shedding of Blood in abhorrence, and placed the seat of Life exclusively in the Nervous System.[5] In this manner I should enable myself to distinguish that which appertained to the substance from that which belonged to the Drapery. But on the other hand neither would I forget, that some Drapery the Truth, which is the Substance, must have in all cases, and that to the Truths of an instituted Religion, which has an historic pole as well as an *ideal* or spiritual, and in which the Historic is as essential a *constituent* as the other, tho' it may be of subordinate dignity as being for the sake of the other, there must be an adherent Drapery, indetachable from the Substance: and that in the institution of the Christian Faith and of the Church in Christ, the Hebrew History and the prior Dispensations to the Hebrew People supplied the adherent Drapery. The Christian *Corpus Veritatum*[6] is not to be compared to an Artist's *Layman*, on which now this, now another Costume may be tried but to a finished Statue of a great Sculptor, ~~in~~ where the ~~Senator and the investing Toga~~ same Marble under the same plastic Master hand rises into the Senator and the investing Toga.

Now the main characteristic error of the far and wide-extended Gnostic Heresy was, that in their multifarious Schemes of Christianity the Christ, whom they were willing to acknowlege, αγγελων, ου σπερματος Αβραμ επιλαμβανεται[7]—of IDEAS, or imaginary Beings impersonating ideas, rejecting the[a]

---

[a] The note remains incomplete

[5] The apocryphal *Acts of St Thomas* is the source of the tradition that Thomas, the "doubting apostle", took the gospel to India and was martyred there. No source has been discovered for C's statement about the Brahmins' view of the nervous system; their prohibition of bloodshed, however, was common knowledge: cf Bernard Picart *Ceremonies and Religious Customs of the Various Nations of the Known World* (7 vols 1733–7) III 273, 366.

[6] "Body of Truths".

[7] "He [Christ] took on him [the nature] of angels, not of the seed of Abraham"—Heb 2.16, var and inverted. Cf 5 n 1 above.

6 I 6–7

Which aspect . . . of the Divine character [i.e. God's will to make known "the grace and mercy, the forgiveness and love which he beareth towards those who love the honour of his Son"], could never be beheld by a creature unfallen; forasmuch as grace, and mercy, and forgiveness, do necessarily presuppose and require guilt, and offence, and hatefulness, for the objects upon which to put themselves forth, as necessarily as the power, and wisdom, and order, and harmony of creation require a chaos, and confusion, and darkness which they may adorn, and order, and bless.

Yet it might seem a manoeuvère not to be worthily conceived of the Divine Wisdom and Goodness, to fore-ordain "guilt and offence and hatefulness" in order to make a shew of "Mercy, and Forgiveness"— or even to create Confusion, and Disorder for the sake of converting the Chaos into Order, Light and Beauty—tho' in the latter case, on the vulgar notion of a Chaos as insensate formless Matter,[1] it may be deemed indifferent, inasmuch as no suffering is inflicted. I notice this for the purpose of preparing the mind of a theological Inquirer for the absolute necessity of going farther back—even to that Fall, of which Time, and τὰ μὴ θέος[2] were themselves the necessary Result—of recurring, I say, to that View, in which the Creation of the material universe appears as the first Act of the Redemption by the Spirit & the Word.[3]

7 I 8–18

[Eph 3.8–11:] "Unto me . . . is this grace given, that I should preach among the Gentiles the unsearchable riches of Christ . . . to the intent that now unto the principalities and powers in heavenly places might be known, by the church, the manifold wisdom of God, according to the eternal purpose which he purposed in Christ Jesus our Lord." * Upon which word "now," I remark, that we, that the principalities and powers in heavenly places, that all created beings, shall have no other revelation than we now possess in the church concerning the manifold wisdom of God . . .

* This just and pregnant Remark is capable of a Proof little below Self-

---

6[1] For C's view that Chaos was not confusion but "the mere state of potentiality" see his note in John WEBSTER p 186, and cf BÖHME **53**, **146** n 1.

6[2] "The things [that are/were] not God".

6[3] C repeats this phrase in **54** below, as

one of the essential points of his disagreement with Irving. Cf his assertions about "the great redemptive process which began in the separation of light from Chaos . . . and has its end in the union of life with God" in *C&S* (*CC*) 113.

evidence. Christ has been revealed in his identity with the Logos, ⟨i.e. as the⟩ Substantial personal Reason in whom Life is—the universal communicative Reason "who lighteth *every* Man",[1] & therein constitutes the proper Humanity. Christ, ὁ ἀληθης, the True, *is* ἡ ἀληθεῖα, the Truth.[2] If then Christ be Truth, self-subsistent tho' (and herein, *Nota bene*, consists the fundamental difference of the Gospel faith from Spinosism) *not* self-originant;[3] *living, καὶ ὄντως οὖσα,*[4] (i.e. no accident, property or faculty having its *ground, τὴν αυτῆς ὑπόστασιν,*[5] in another) and yet universal—then whatever is Truth, [(]as distinguished from the mere facts or phænomena in which it manifests itself) must be Christ. What Post-script or Supplement can be imagined to this Revelation? What other can Men or Angels receive? It is a continuous, ever unfolding Revelation, which having once had its reality established as history & historic Fact, must for all future ⟨time⟩ have its manifestation and individual Growths inwardly by communion of the H. Spirit, or outwardly by the Light of Providence whether in the Natural World, symbolically, or in the moral world, by the evidence of Fulfilment.

S. T. C.—

Briefly, if Christ be Truth, whatever is known as true, must be of Christ.*

* Observe. I speak of knowlege by *insight*, and of Insight (i.e. intuitûs intellectualis)[6] of the Truth, in distinction from the Sight or perception of a Fact or Appearance. In propriety of Speech, the alone truth of a Thing is the Law that constitutes that Thing, and is at once its antecedent Ground and its abiding Reality; and every such Truth, having a Law for its Object, is an *Idea*. But again every Thing exists in a communion of Action and reaction with other things & mediately with every other thing; and the knowlege of a Thing is imperfect without a knowlege of its Relations. But this is possible only by means of some higher Idea, which comprehends A.B.C. as *one*: and this again is rendered intelligible by some yet higher Idea, till we arrive at the Universal

---

7[1] John 1.9.

7[2] C has translated both Greek words. Although this statement is based upon NT texts (e.g. John 14.6, "I am the way, the truth and the life"), the term ἀλήθεια, "truth", has special significance for C in this note in being connected, by an ingenious play on words for which there is no authority in Greek, with the terms "breath" and "Logos" or "Word", i.e. Christ. C divides ἀλήθεια into ἄλη θεῖα,

which he translates as "divinus halitus", "divine breath": cf *CN* III 4319 f 125 and n, 4483; N21½.116.

7[3] C's invariable objection to "Pantheism; or the Scheme of Spinosa": cf HILLHOUSE 1 at n 5.

7[4] "And really being".

7[5] "Its own ground", C identifying "ground" and ὑπόστασις (*hypostasis*), the "subsistency" of 1 n 4 above.

7[6] "Of *intellectual* insight".

IDEA, involving ~~all~~ and *eminenter* seu in formâ absolute~~ly~~a[7] including all true distinctions of all true Being, itself truly *Being*, and the Identity of Truth and Being—the Form of all Forms, the Being of all Beings, o μονογενης,[8] the eternal self-manifestation of the Holy One, sui ipsius per suum *Alterum* (alterum *in* Deo, non alium *a* Deo).[9] This is the Doctrine, profound beyond comparison, yet so clearly and expressly set forth by the Evangelist John, in whose divine Oracle it appears as a Light in the Depths irradiating the Depths! This is that Mystery, of which the other great Apostle tells us, that in it all treasures of knowlege are involved.[10]—Briefly, this is the unique exclusive Character of God, the Absolute, that his BREATH, or Spirit, and his WORD, are not as in finite Beings, the accidents or attributes of some one, but truly *subsist*, & have their *hypostasis in* themselves, tho' of and from the Father— Hence the force of the term, Logos πρoς τον θεoν,[11] the preposition, inadequately nay defectively rendered "with", expressing the distinctè indivisum, inseparable yet distinct, which is further explained by the Word's having life in him self.[12]—The Word is uttered, but likewise it speaks; the Spirit is shed forth, but likewise it proceedeth. It is aweful to reflect in how admirable a manner Man contains in himself the image & outshadowing ϕ of this Mystery. His Will giveth birth to the Articulative Energy, but the Word goeth not forth without the Breath—which proceedeth from the Will thro' the medium of the Articulation. In the order of the genesis the *form* is first; but in the order of manifestation to the Creature the Breath, = the Vowel, sometimes begins, sometimes follows: El: Jah.[13]

8 I ⁻2[a], referring to I 17

. . . the holiness of God was, in a most marvellous way, illustrated in

---

[a] This annotation was written before **2**, the beginning of which is cramped into the space left at the head of I ⁻2

7[7] "Eminently or in absolute form".

7[8] "The only-begotten" (as in John 1.14, 18).

7[9] I.e. "of him himself through his *Other*" (other *in* God, not different *from* God)".

7[10] I.e. Paul, in Col 2.2–3, "the mystery of God, and of the Father, and of Christ; In whom are hid all the treasures of wisdom and knowledge".

7[11] "The Word *with* God": John 1.1.

7[12] John 1.4, "In him was life; and the life was the light of men." C's objection to the AV translation "*with* God" is recorded

also in *TT* 6 Jan 1823, where he proposes instead that πρòς signifies "the utmost possible *proximity*, without *confusion*".

7[13] C's illustration is not strictly correct: all the Hebrew letters are consonants, the vowels being provided in diacritical pointing. *El* (the first syllable of e.g. *Elohim*, and the last syllable of many names, e.g. Daniel, Emmanuel) begins with a consonant in Hebrew no less than *Yah* (the first syllable of the primitive name of God in Gen, corrupted in English into *Jehovah*). C might have encountered this idea in his philological reading, e.g. in J. C. Adelung

the midst of his love; yea, and over his love. Yes, I will say *over* his love; for holiness is the column of the Divine majesty and power, the root and trunk of that tree, of which goodness and wisdom, mercy and love, are the various branches, flowers, and fruits.

P. 17. ἐστῆσμος + ατραχισμῳ.[1] But how will Mr I. answer the Objection of an Athanasian—from the equal possession of all the divine perfections, self-origination alone excepted, by the Father and the Son. If from the paternal holiness there result an impossibility of forgiveness = 0, then from the filial Holiness, there must result 0: and $0 + 0 = 0$.

9 I 18–19

Their case [that of the fallen angels] was passed by, while ours was chosen for the manifestation of grace and truth:* which is, therefore, devoutly to be contemplated as an act of sovereignty in the midst of mercy; for there must be sovereignty in all God's acts, else he were no longer gracious. . . . It needed to be shewn that God could punish sin unchangeably; or, in other words, that the proper nature of sin is to propagate and increase itself for ever. There must be a monument of all the Divine attributes, and this of the fallen angels is the monument of his unextinguishable hatred of sin.

* Were I assured that not only the inherent necessity of a delapsûs ad infinitum[1] of an imperishable impenitent Soul was here held forth; but that our Saviour meant likewise to inform us, that such a state was not only ideally possible, all the conditions supposed actually existing but *really* ~~was~~ the predestined State of many; and further, were I assured that the ⟨continuance of the⟩ personal high perfections of Reason and Conscience, with Self-consciousness, the Offspring of these (for Conscience is the ground and indispensable Condition of Self-Consciousness) ~~wereas~~ meant to be included in the eternal Death; and further yet, were I persuaded that Eternal Death was synonimous with Everlasting Torment;—neither of which three positions I am at all assured, still I should as little venture to assert, that "God *punished* Sin unchange-

---

Mithridates I (1806) vi–vii, where the priority of vowels is discussed.

8[1] "*Estēsmos + atrichismos*"—i.e. a Coleridgeism with a Calvinism, the "Coleridgeism" referring probably to the figure of the tree, which C uses e.g. *CL* VI 628, *AR* (1825) 2–3. Ἄτριχος, "hairless", appears to be given—like θάλαρχος ("bald")

in **50** below—as a synonym for *calvus*, "bald", a fanciful root for "Calvin".

9[1] "A fall to infinity". Irving quotes Isa 66.24 (var): "They shall go forth, and look upon the carcases of the men who have transgressed against me; for their worm dieth not, neither shall their fire be quenched."

ably'', or dare attribute to essential Love ''an inextinguishable hatred,'' as, supposing a man to have wilfully pulled his eyes out, I would say, that the Sun inflicted incurable Blindness on him. O that Mʳ I. would but compare the texts on which he grounds th*d*is dogma with those of a contrary import in ⟨respect of⟩ number, and certainly of interpretation!

10   I ⁻2, referring to I 18 | **9** textus

p. 18. * Sovereignty in this Sense an absolute contradiction to Holiness—& this attempt to cut a knot which he could it can not untie, the knot too of his its own making, I regard as the radical error of Calvinism.

11   I 19–25

I cannot help—notwithstanding the unfeigned and earnest respect, in which I hold Mʳ Irving, I yet cannot help at times comparing him in my fancy to a Hornet or Dragon-fly who having been caught and bound in the strongly-woven Spider-web of Calvinism had at length by vigorous efforts liberated himself, shattered left the Web, ruined rent and ruined but alas! carried off with him a portion of the Threads & viscous bonds that impede the free action of his Wings, and render his flight unsteady and bewildered—now soaring by his native vigor, now sinking by the weight of his still adhering bondage.—He writes like a fugitive from modern Calvinism, who has freed the chain from the Staple-ring, but not his ancles from the Chain.¹ Mʳ Irving feels the grandeur and the moral necessity of that view of the redemptive Act which places it in the WILL and its holy causative yea creative and re-generative energies; but he cannot, rather he will not, leave hold of the old prison-mumpsimus² of the Debtor and Creditor Account, so much pain & suffering for so much Sin, and of the accompanying contrariety of goodness and compassion in the self-substituted Debtor, or Debtors Proxy, the Son, to the enraged and (in strange contradiction to his asserted reasonless Sovereignty!) incapable-of-forgiving-Justice of the Father.³ And in order to palliate the off reconcile this conception if not to his reason yet to his fancy and feelings he gives an exaggerated picture of our Lord's physical and mental *Sufferings* ⟨of Jesus⟩ out of all warrant of the Gospel

---

11¹ The image of the staple that holds a chain fast is fairly common in C's writings: cf *BL* (*CC*) I 266, *Friend* (*CC*) I 455. C's habitual distinction between Calvinism and ''modern Calvinism'' appears in e.g. A. FULLER **4**, *AR* (1825) 153–5.

11² ''Mumpsimus'', a traditional notion obstinately adhered to (as in BAXTER *Reli-*

quiae COPY A **44[b]**), is here represented as a confining ''prison''.

11³ C had expounded the inadequacy of the ''Debtor and Creditor'' concept of redemption in *AR* (1825) 319–26, and he refers to Irving's acceptance of his views in **32** below.

Record, which speaks of Temptations indeed, related doubtless by our Lord for the instruction of his Apostles (for they all refer to the great principles of their Conduct as Preachers of the Word endued with supernatural Powers)—but of Temptations calmly and triumphantly overcome—and in all else relates nothing that in intensity or continuity of *Suffering* exceeds what we read of as endured by the Martyrs and Missionaries of the first or even the latter ages. It is most observable, and most worthy of Observation, that in the statement of his higher views, the mysterious death-conquering energy of the sinless Will, and the *possibility* of re-union with Deity atchieved for the human race by the actual Union of Deity with that divine Humanity which is the *Ground* of the humanity or spiritual Personëity in every Person; he regularly repeats his sentiments in equivalent words cited fom the Scriptures; while in the exhibition of his Calvinistic remnant he either ~~gives~~ refers to no scripture warrant, or presents it thro' the Katterfelto Glass of an extravagant Paraphrase.[4]

12   I 24, 26–8

This was a great, a very great apparent stigma, which the perfect obedience of Christ in human flesh removed, proving unequivocally that it was made for flesh, and would have blessed humanity, had its gracious intention and adaptation not been crossed and prevented by the fall of our first parents, and the consequent apostacy of the will of man . . .

Startling Assertions in palpable contradiction to other Assertions of the same Writer no less startling—namely, that only by the constant Action of Omnipotence exerted by the H. Ghost was Christ himself able to fulfil the Law in the Flesh![a][1]

I am persuaded, that the term "Flesh" in the few places in which it is not spoken of as the product and reproducent of Sin, as the Prison-house from which we are to be finally redeemed by Christ, is used negatively, for the purpose of unsensualizing the still gross apprehensions of the Disciples, of withdrawing, namely, their thoughts & fancies from the

---

[a] Here C has written "See *MSS*. p. 26." So far the note had been written in the outer margin of I 24 opposite the textus. Since the head- and foot-margins of I 24–5 were already filled with the last part of **11**, I 26 was the nearest unused space in which to continue **12**

11[4] For the magician Katterfelto, see IR-VING *For Missionaries* **13** n 3 above.

12[1] The latter notion occurs especially in Sermon 3, e.g. p 140(xvii): ". . . I believe it to be necessary unto salvation that a man should believe that Christ's soul was so held in possession by the Holy Ghost, and so supported by the Divine nature, as that it never assented unto an evil suggestion, and never originated an evil suggestion . . .". C repeats his objection in **25** below.

visible Organs of our Lord to his true spiritual Body. *Not* this outward Shell, this σκηνὴ, which you see,[2] is *my* flesh, or *my* Blood.[3] No! that ⟨by⟩ which and *to* which you must ⟨be⟩ assimilated or you cannot have abiding Life, that is *my* flesh (i.e. seat of Power, the flesh being the Muscular Substance) and *my* Blood—i.e. seat and material of Vitality. But I am wasting words, I fear.—for even if I could succeed in demonstrating the erroneousness of these views, I should still be unable to substitute the truth, not having previously laid the foundation by opening out the proper essence & character of Hades, or the Evil Spirit,[4] whereof we are to predicate the most perfect contrariety to the Divine Idea, that is compatible with being the Subject of any Predicate. And as little, in my belief, is it possible to understand the full and true import of the Incarnation without contemplated[a] the same as grounded on the Antecedent Incorporation—as the informing WORD, the Lux lucifica—.[5]

13   I 38–9

And here let us begin with a text which containeth the truth in questions stated in the bluntest, baldest way possible. 1. Pet. iii. 18: "For Christ also hath suffered for our sins, the Just for the unjust." . . . Which act of suffering for our sins is oft concentred in its great closing scene, the cross . . . [Irving then quotes other texts on vicarious suffering.]

I will not, ~~I~~ the sense of truth will not permit me to, deny, that a Jew of the Apostolic Age ~~w~~could hardly fail to understand the sentences here ~~quo~~ cited, as asserting the doctrine of vicarious Suffering and Sin by proxy: and this being the case, ~~then~~ the presumption is that the Writer of this Epistle, likewise ~~of~~ by birth and education a Jew, intended to be so understood; and unless some direct proof to the contrary can be adduced (and I know of none such) this must be admitted to be the true sense of the passage. For Mʳ Irving then the question is put at rest. Scripsit Petrus: ergo, demonstratum est[1]

---

[a] A slip for "contemplating"

12[2] "Tent", in OT the temporary abode of Yahweh before the tabernacle was built, in Heb 8–9 the body of Christ himself, the "more perfect tabernacle, not made with hands" (9–11).

12[3] Cf "This is my body. . . . this is my blood" in the BCP Communion service, from 1 Cor 11.24 on the authority of Matt 26.26–8, Mark 14.22–4, Luke 22.19–21. The true nature of "body" is further considered below, **29** at n 14 and following.

12[4] For Hades (commonly mistranslated as "Hell", according to C in **42** below) as "the hidden and dark Ground of the Glorified New Earth" see **51** below at n 20; and cf DONNE *Sermons* COPY B **123**.

12[5] "Light-making light" (from Augustine): cf BÖHME **80** n 1.

13[1] "Peter wrote it; therefore, it is proved (i.e. beyond question)."

14 ɪ 65–6

Secondly, as Christ did not his own will to glorify himself, but forewent the sovereignty, the Divine and uncreated liberty thereof, and learned obedience as a servant, boring his ears,* as a willing slave, and delighting to be under the law ̄ . . . so we must in like manner yield ourselves to the holy will of God . . .

* Sundry Persons who call themselves Christ's Ministers, are more willing to bore the ears of others. I ~~make~~ knowingly offend my own feeling by this Levity, that I may draw attention to the danger of using these too bold metaphors, not applied by the Sacred Writers to our Lord, especially where, as in this instance, the custom ~~is~~ does not obtain in this ~~custom~~ountry, and therefore the allusion ⟨is⟩ unintelligible to the People in general.

15 ɪ 66–70[a] | Sermon 2

In the Solar radiance three sorts of Rays are emitted, the chemical or formative, the calorific and the lucific, i.e. power, warmth and light. In the divine Glory (a metaphor taken from the Sun) Will, Mind and Spiritual Life are eradiated.[1] It is therefore perfectly indifferent, whether I say, that the End of the Utterance and Incarnation of the WORD, i.e. Creation and Redemption, was the Glory or Glorification of God, or that the End was ⟨the communication of⟩ the greatest possible Holiness and Beatitude: for both mean the same—in the first, it is conveyed ~~by~~ in a metaphor, in the second, without any.[b] The Holiness and Beatitude communicated *are* the Glory, the eradiations of his transcendent goodness wherewith he glorifieth himself. To say therefore that they are for his Glory is the same as saying, God's glory is for the[c] Glory of God. And even this, strange as it sounds *may* be said. For in the Absolute transcendent Acts of the Eternal ONE there is neither End nor Means, but the Identity of both: i.e. that which in a higher form (*eminenter*, as the

[a] C actually began his note p 67, then went back to p 66, and from there to pp 68–70

[b] In the foot-margin of ɪ 66 (the head having been filled with the last three lines of **14**) C has written "*continued from the last line of the page opposite.*"

[c] Here C has written "*turn to p. 68*"

15[1] This note may have been provoked by the phrase "the Glory of God" in the title of Sermon 2. For the sun as "the earliest Symbol of the Tri-une God" see BÖHME **169** and n 1; C's most fully developed explanation of the metaphor of "glory" appears in LEIGHTON COPY C **50** below. C's science is up to date: William Herschel's discovery of the infrared spectrum in 1800 was presented as a discovery of invisible "rays of heat" in light, and some investigators proposed that the chemical effects of light might be produced by analogous invisible *chemical* rays. See e.g. Rees's *Cyclopaedia* "RAYS of Heat".

Schoolmen say)[2] contains both as one. When the profoundest Divines assign to the Absolute Good, the incommunicable name, Causa Sui, αυτοπατωρ,[3] they imply that the Most High ~~is~~ God is his own End—and the literal Rendering of the Hebrew words, in which God declared his ⟨own⟩ Being, is, I shall be that I will to be![4] O height above all height! We owe ⟨adoration of⟩ thanksgiving to God even for his ⟨own⟩ essential Perfections! For even these are the eternal Births of the Absolute Freedom, the uncomprehended all-comprehending Causality of the Holy Will, the Abysmal GOOD.[5]

16 ɪ 70–1, concluded in pencil

* And that great gathering of the heavenly host to look upon the scene, their earnest zeal to celebrate the act with ascriptions of praise, doth manifest that they were interested in no ordinary degree in that which then began to be accomplished upon the earth. . . . and above all, because it is one constituent part of the mystery of godliness, that "God was seen of angels," we conclude that the relation of all the heavenly intelligences towards the Godhead is in some way dependent upon . . . the incarnation of the Son of God . . .

* Unable to satisfy myself that the document here relied on is of Apostolic date or authority; and ~~even were it the work~~ whatever its date may be, yet holding it for symbolic poesy, I am reduced to the necessity of acknowleging[a], that I do not know what the Author of the Epistle intended by "seen of Angels"—or to what part of our Lord's History he alludes.[1] Possibly to the Transfiguration, possibly to the close of the Temptation, not improbably to both, both narratives forming a part of all the Gospels, & therefore doubtless of the Original Gospel⸘ but assuredly not to the Shepherds' Vision.[2]

[a] From here, beginning with the comma, the note is written in pencil

15[2] "Eminently"—for the scholastic sense of which see BÖHME **12** n 1.

15[3] "Cause of himself, God self-father".

15[4] Exod 3.14: "I AM THAT I AM" and "I AM", a crucial text for C: cf **1** n 9 above.

15[5] The apparently oxymoronic phrase "Abysmal GOOD" is related to the *byssos abyssos* of **1** n 5 above, and to the "Height above all Height, the Deeper yet of all Depths" of **2** at n 11, height and depth becoming interchangeable dimensions of the unimaginable and incomprehensible.

16[1] 1 Tim 3.16: C agrees "with Eichhorn and Schleiermacher" in rejecting this epistle as Pauline, in ETERNAL PUNISHMENT **16**.

16[2] C disagrees with Irving, who supposes the phrase to refer to the "Shepherds' Vision" at the Nativity.

17 ɪ 72–5

This [text "Rejoice, ye heavens, and they that dwell in them; for the accuser of the brethren is cast down, which accused them before our God day and night" (Rev 12.10)] suggesteth to us a still higher sense of the words of Paul, in the Epistle to the Colossians, commented upon in the preceding sermon, where it is written of the person and office of Christ, *"It pleased the Father that in him should all fulness dwell; and having made peace through the blood of his cross, by him to reconcile all things unto himself; whether they be things in earth or things in heaven."

* It is in this and in other texts of the same or similar import, that I seem to myself to find the true ~~and~~ sense of the doctrine of Imputed Righteousness,[1] and of the tenet, often but most untruly made characteristic of the Calvinistic Scheme, and attributed exclusively to Calvin & his followers, that Man is Justified by the Righteousness of the Son of Man alone; whereas if I dared ~~assign~~ connect this doctrine with any one name in particular, not as alone holding and teaching the same but as giving an especial prominence, and life-and-death importance thereto, as the ~~especial~~*a* very sign and condition stantis vel cadentis ecclesiæ,[2] it would be LUTHER.[3] But in fact, this Tenet was common to all the Churches of the Reformation at their first foundation. By the *true* sense I mean, first *a* sense, a meaning that can be conceived or contemplated as real, & which therefore must be actually possible—In other words, that the doctrine is intelligible as an idea. Secondly, that ⟨it⟩*b* is compatible with the principles and postulates of Morality.—The steps, by which from the *pleroma* of the Son I pass to the Article in question, will be found in paper & gummed on among the additional blank leaves to this Volume*c*[4]—/ where, I trust, will be found a fresh example in proof of a long-cherished Conviction of mine, that the so called *Mysteries* of our Faith are indispensable to the right understanding of the moral precepts, nay, to their reception as moral

a Cancelled in pencil, the substituted word "very" also in pencil. The change was perhaps made at the same time that **18** was written above **17**, also in pencil, on the same page

b Added in pencil

c See **20** below

17[1] Cf C's note in BIBLE COPY B **137**: "It is not, we must dare think it, *our* righteousness, but the righteousness of Christ imputed to us. But yet it must be the Righteousness of Christ *in* us . . .".

17[2] "Of the standing or falling of the church".

17[3] For C's welcoming the doctrine of justification by faith articulated by Luther and adopted by the Calvinists see e.g. LUTHER *Colloquia* **49, 52**.

17[4] I.e. the long note **1**. *Pleroma*, "fullness", is used and defined in **2** at n 5 above.

18   I 73, pencil

. . . in the holy Scriptures he is revealed to possess one place by peculiar property, and to fill it with most glorious effulgency. "Thus saith the High and Lofty One that inhabiteth eternity, whose name is Holy, I dwell in the high and holy place;" where the word in the Hebrew is the same which is usually rendered in the Greek by the word which we translate "highest."

N.b. By the Rule of Parallelism in Hebrew Poesy, the 2ⁿᵈ Clause must ~~express~~ repeat the sense of the first Clause in a different form of words. "The high & holy place", therefore, must mean Eternity, and not a *somewhere* Saloon, as Mʳ Irving fancies.[1]

19   I 74, pencil, the text of the whole of I 74 marked in the margin with a pencil line

It is not likely that the heavenly host would have ascribed such a marvellous property to the birth of Messiah, as that it should glorify God in the highest, and still less likely is it that his disciples should do so, unless the same had been revealed and written of Messiah in the holy Prophets, to which therefore I would go back and search for the light which they afford us upon this great subject. And I begin with a passage in the xlixth chapter of Isaiah, where it is thus written: "The Lord hath called me from the womb; from the bowels of my mother hath he made mention of my name. And he hath made my mouth like a sharp sword; in the shadow of his hand hath he hid me, and made me a polished shaft: in his quiver hath he hid me; and said unto me, Thou art my servant, O Israel, in whom I will be glorified." That he speaketh here, of Messiah, the true *Israel*, or *Prince of God*, and not of the literal Israel, or Jacob, is manifest not only from the grandeur of the expressions, but also from the words which follow, wherein Messiah complaineth of his ineffectual mission to his brethren. "Then I said, I have laboured in vain, I have spent my strength for nought, and in vain: yet surely my judgment is with the Lord, and my work with my God."

All this is very well made out, on the plan adopted↓. *In suo genere*,[1] it is sound and scholarly; soberly grounded & happily built up.ᵃ S. T. C.

ᵃ The words "built up" are overtraced in ink in C's hand; and the afterthought, written after "S. T. C.", is in the same ink

18[1] Irving, quoting Isa 57.15, correctly observes that the Hebrew word *marom* ("the high and holy *place*" in AV, though elsewhere in AV translated as "the high and lofty") is taken as equivalent to the Greek ὕψιστος, "highest", in the Septua-gint. C invokes the "Rule of Parallelism" established by Robert Lowth in *De sacra poesi Hebraeorum* lect 19 (Oxford 1753) 177–96, in order to challenge Irving's interpretation.

19[1] *"In its own kind"*.

But yet see * ad finem.[2]

20   I 74/5, two single leaves (4 pp) guarded in, referring to I 74

* Note to p. 74[1]

On the Principle of interpretation hitherto applied to the Hebrew Oracles and sanctioned by the authority of a long Succession of learned and orthodox Divines, both the selection and the exposition of the Texts here cited do, as I have acknowleged, evince the hand of a Master: and the whole passage is in my friend's happiest manner. But on a subject of such high concernment I dare practice neither equivocation nor concealment: and must therefore ~~ask If~~ inquire into the truth of the Principle itself ~~Mr. I. and to this~~ before I dare adopt the inferences which M[r] Irving has drawn from the Texts on the presumption of its Truth. Now to this I can only express a very qualified Assent by subjoining what will, I fear, amount pretty nearly to a declaration of its falsity. ~~There~~ It is Truth; ~~therein;~~ but not the whole truth.—[? ~~far~~] ~~better~~ The consequence is inevitable. What is not the whole truth, is not *the* Truth—is not the true Principle. I prefer therefore to say at once, that it seeks a ground on a part of the truth—[? ~~then almost~~] ~~that~~ At all events, then, (you will say,) it is partially true.—Nay!—for a Half-truth substituted for, and assumed to be, the whole truth, is total Error, ~~and an error too griev of the most dangerous kind: more dangerous than that because more plausible~~ and of a kind especially to be eschewed, as more dangerous because more plausible, and of less easy detection. Now the Principle here in question rests on the Assumption, that in the prophecies unfolding the great scheme of Redemption only one Spiritual Agent or Functionary ⟨in addition to God the Father⟩ is spoken of, ~~namely, besides Christ the Saviour besides~~ namely, the Saviour Christ—Or perhaps my meaning would be clearer if I say, that this Principle goes on the supposition, that the only Spiritual Persons or Personages introduced are the Father ⟨~~and Christ: to the former⟩ ⟨to whom the Commentators apply the names Jehovah, God, the Lord, the Lord God &c⟩ and Christ,~~ and Christ, the names Jehovah, God, the Lord, the Lord God, being understood of the former exclusively: while ~~in~~ the grand idea of the Latter, ~~the Delight of ⟨the⟩ Law~~ found in Moses and the Prophets, as the Redeemer, the Reconciler, and the Desiderium Gentium, the Yearned for of the Nations,[2] is ~~by the~~ almost ~~without exception~~ all[a] our Expositors,

[a] C presumably meant "by almost all", forgetting that "by" had been deleted

19[2] From the asterisk "to the end"— i.e. **20** following.
   20[1] I.e. textus of **19** above.

20[2] Actually "desideratus cunctis gentibus", "the Desire of all nations", in the Vulgate and AV, Hag 2.7. C's fondness for

and in a marked degree by Mr Irving, mixed up and debased with the Dross of the Dream-book compiled under the name of Daniel and the ruinous & fleshly fancies entertained by the Jews from the time of Alexander the Great of a ⟨Messiah King, a⟩ Warrior Monarch & Conqueror, a magnified David, who was to bring the Gentile Nations in subject and subordination to the united kingdom of Judaea and Israel as the Premier Nation of the World.[3] Alas! that a carnal Superstition, which has been the main cause and instrument of the calamities and degradation of the Jews, which was and continues to be the unsightly Ulcer of the Synagogue, should have infected the Church of Christ, should ha still be allowed to taint the faith of the professed Followers of the meek and holy Jesus.

21   I   75, pencil, a few words overtraced in ink, the whole page marked with a pencil line in the margin

Jacob, being left alone of all his kindred, wrestled with the Lord until the breaking of the day, and was not prevailed against, wherefore he was called no more Jacob but Israel. . . . Even so Jesus, being left alone, wrestled, I may say, with God, from the time that he said upon the cross, *"My God, my God, why hast thou forsaken me?" during all the night of the hour and power of darkness, until the breaking of the morning of his resurrection . . .

* [a]By *giving out* aloud[b] the first[c] verse of the [d]22nd Psalm,[e] Christ here reminds John and his Mother that what they were weeping at, was the fulfilment of the first half of the prophecy—proof that the 2nd, his Triumph, would no less be fulfilled.[1]

22   I   75, pencil[f] | **21** textus

* I am always grieved when this most affecting Instance of Christ's

[a-b] Overtraced in ink by C
[c] Word overtraced in ink by C
[d-e] Overtraced in ink by C
[f] This note is written in the gutter and crowded into the space left in the foot-margin by the conclusion of **17**. **22** and **23** seem to have been written at the same time

---

the term "desiderium" (long since taken over into English from Latin) may be seen in e.g. BÖHME **52** n 2, *CL* IV 697, 966.

20[3] In the controversy over the authorship and status of the Book of Daniel, C came at last to adopt the now commonly held view that it was "a Forgery of the age of Antiochus Epiphanes" (PAULUS **43**): cf EICHHORN *Alte Testament* **48**, *CN* IV 4615 and n. *TT* 13 Apr 1830 clarifies his objec-

tions: "With the exception of the book of Daniel, which the Jews themselves never classed among the prophecies, and an obscure text of Jeremiah, there is not a passage in all the Old Testament which favours the notion of a temporal Messiah."

21[1] C's consistent interpretation of the words recorded in Matt 27.46 and Mark 15.34: cf **42** below, BIBLE COPY B **32**, LEIGHTON COPY C **46**.

Love & tender Thoughtfulness for others in the midst of his own Sufferings, is turned into an unintelligible Cloud, to which the Writers themselves can assign no distinct shape of meaning.

23 I 77

In the narrative of the raising of Lazarus, recorded in the xith chapter of Luke, we find our Lord thus answering the message of his sickness: "This sickness is not unto death, but for the glory of God, that the Son of God might be glorified thereby." And being come to the place of the sepulchre, he further saith, "Said I not unto thee, that if thou wouldest believe, thou shouldest see the glory of God?" This glory of God, therefore, for which Lazarus's sickness and death was ordained, consisteth in something which Martha should see if she believed; that is, it consisted in the mighty work of raising Lazarus from the dead. And that other miracles were manifestations of the same glory is further evident from that which the Lord answered of the blind man: "Neither hath this man sinned, nor his parents; but that the works of God should be made manifest in him." So also he is said "to have manifested forth his glory" in the marriage supper of Cana, when he changed the water into wine. We may conclude, therefore, in general, that the glory of God was shewn forth in the mighty acts of Christ, which he did during the days of his flesh; because, as I have oft explained to you, they were but the fore-shewings and forerunners and first-fruits of that glorious power which he is to exercise over the whole world, in the time of his kingdom.

Had Mr Irving steadied his mind by fixing in it the primary sensuous meaning of Glory, he would have found in all these Texts so many examples of the interpretation given by me p. 66, 67.[1]

24 I 80–1

. . . one thing is manifest from these three several instances, that the glory which Christ brought to his Father consisteth in the manifestation of things, in the doing of works, in mighty achievements of power, and manifestations of goodness; and not in mere abstract revelations to the mind,—that is, not in doctrines or ideas merely, but in acts and deeds, whereof ideas are the laws, and doctrines the prophetic declarations. This I count a very important remark, which will help us greatly in the sequel.

The *Remark!*—The Principle here introduced would, I am persuaded,

---

23[1] **15** above.

have been more generally understood, if my Friend had enunciated the same in my own words—viz. Religion is distinguished from Philosophy on the one hand, and from History on the other, by being both in one— All its Facts are intelligential Truths, all its Truths are Historical Facts.—The two equally indispensable Factors of a Religion are Ideas and Facts manifesting ideas. Corollary. A Religion not revealed, or a Natural Religion, is a contradiction in terms.[1]   S. T. Coleridge

Christmas Day, 1828.

25 1 139 (blank half-page at end of Sermon 2, 140, (140)i[a] | Sermon 3 pt 1 "The Composition of Christ's Person"

My active and positive Belief commencing where, I am persuaded, the Gospels in their first forms of commenced, from the Baptism of John; and assured, that Paul, John and Peter, whose Amanuensis & Interpreter Mark was, either were ignorant of the traditions prefixed to Luke's Gospel and concorporated with the Greek Edition of the Gospel of the Hebrew Church attributed to Matthew;[1] or did not regard them as necessary parts of a Christian Faith; yet with a respectful acquiescence in & a filial non-resistence (of mind no less than of tongue and hand) to so the old and constant a doctrine of the Catholic Church, that Jesus was conceived of the Holy Ghost & born of Mary a Virgin;—I cannot be supposed to feel much these interest in these somewhat startling Speculations of my friend according ⟨to which⟩ the Holy Ghost by a distinct and peculiar agency performed the office of an additional placenta in secreting and forming out of Mary's flesh & blood a fit body for the Son of God, which yet however remained *sinful* flesh, requiring his (the Holy Ghost's) continued energy and presence to keep in check, &c &c.[2] But surely I cannot be wrong in wishing that he would either enunciate his doctrines in the words of Scripture, or attach a less terrific importance & in a less angry and imperious tone, to statements & assertions in words of his own finding, that are no where directly asserted or declared in Scripture, and which so many pious both learned and pious Divines have not considered deducible therefrom. But alas! there are too many of these heat-

---

[a] See bibliographical note to title for the anomalous pagination

24[1] C repeats an assertion made in *AR* (1825) 176.

25[1] For C's views on the "evangelia infantiae" see **2** above at n 16, and cf **36** below.

25[2] C objects not to a particular passage, but to the general line of argument in Sermon 3. Given the problem of the combination of divine and human nature in the Incarnation, Irving suggests that the Holy Ghost was God's agent, forming "the body [of Christ] in the womb of the virgin", xiv(140), but that because the time for his glorification had not come, "he appeared not in the glorious raiment of a conqueror . . . as he shall appear when he cometh the second time", xiv(140).

pimples and fever-spots on the fair and manly face of my Friend's Elocution.   S. T. C.

26   ı viii(140)

Now, concerning the time and manner of our Lord's receiving this reasonable soul, *I believe it to have been at the same time, and after the same manner, in which the rest of the children receive it; in opposition to those who hold the pre-existence of Christ's human soul, or that it was made before the creatures, for the Son of God to possess and unite himself to, and with it and by it to create all things visible and invisible, and afterwards to come in it and join himself to the substance of the Virgin Mary.

* That is, I know nothing about it. How much better would it have been to have made the same frank avowal on the greater number of the questions preceding!

27   ı x(140)–(140)xvii

God at first, when he had created man, breathed into his nostrils the breath of life, and he became a living soul. Such a living soul is, therefore, the definition of man: "the first Adam was made a living soul." Again; it is said, "the body returneth unto the dust, and the soul to him that gave it." Man, therefore, is a body of dust and a soul given by God, in a state of living union. Man is not a body of flesh, nor is man a disembodied soul; but these two in living union constitute a man. From the time that Christ was conceived by the Holy Ghost in the womb of the Virgin was he both body and soul of man. He was not soul of man before he was body of man; but he was soul and body of man from the same moment of his conception.

I remember but one place in Scripture, in which the word, Soul, is used in its present popular Sense as the Antithesis to Body, or as a Jewel to its containing Casket: but this one place is of highest authority, it being that in which Christ exhorts his Disciple[a] not to fear Man who can only hurt their Bodies but God who can destroy both Body and Soul in ~~Hades~~ Gehenna. It would be desirable, had it been possible, to ascertain the Syro-chaldaic Word used by our Lord.[1]—It would, however, be refining too much to treat a ~~moral~~ rule or sentiment of practical Morality ad-

---

[a] A slip for "Disciples"

27[1] Matt 10.28: "And fear not them which kill the body, but are not able to kill the soul: but rather fear him which is able to destroy both soul and body in hell." The critical word is apparently the original of AV "kill": see n 2 below.

dressed to simple and unlearned Jews as a scientifically stated meta-physical Proposition. The former must be interpreted by the ⟨then⟩ known intention ⟨of the Speaker, ~~and~~⟩ and ~~particular~~ declared Object of the whole Speech. In the latter only dare we impose as ⟨binding⟩ truths whatever can be logically deduced from the particular words and their relative position. It would, I say, be over-refining to infer that ἀποκτεῖναι is here contra-distinguished from ἀπολέσαι, *kill* or *kill off* from destroy,[2] because after the *killing* by a Mortal in this world the body is still existing to be destroyed εν γεεννῃ, in Gehenna. The very word, Gehenna, i.e. Tophet or the vale of Hinnom, a spot of ill repute near Jerusalem, should teach us better.[3] The ~~thought~~ truth meant and alone meant to be understood, was—Fear not them who can only touch the surface and *shew* of your Being, who can shatter your Spectacle-glasses, not reach your eyes, but fear him whose power extends over your whole Being, and can penetrate, like a consuming fire into the ground and sub-stance of your Individuality, as well as destroy the organ and medium by which it is manifested. Yet it need only that a man should be in love with a theory, to make him find in this text a proof [of][a] a twofold Body, a phænomenal or material = σωμα ὑλήειδες, and a substantial or psy-chical Body = σῶμα ψυχόειδες.[4] Indeed, if my ~~mem~~ fancy does not counterfeit memory, Emanuel Swedenborg cites th*d*is text in support of some such notion,[5] which has had its adherents among philosophers and physiologists of no mean name—Ex. gr. Dʳ H. More, Platner, Ab. Tucker or E. Search.[6] On the other hand, I regard Sᵗ Paul's distinctions

---

[a] Word supplied by the editor, C perhaps having been misled by his having written the letters "of" in the word "proof"

27[2] AV translates ἀποκτεῖναι as "to kill" and ἀπολέσαι "to destroy" consis-tently, preserving for NT Greek the same distinction that clearly exists in both clas-sical Greek and English.

27[3] C draws attention to the history of the term translated "hell" in NT, the He-brew *Ge-Hinnom*, the Vale of Hinnom, re-ferring to a site once used for human sacri-fices: cf *Lects 1795* (*CC*) 342 and n 1, ETERNAL PUNISHMENT 1 n 4.

27[4] "A matter-like body" and "a soul-like body". In a note of 1809, C himself asserted the existence of a twofold body, a "body terrestrial" and a "body celestial" as in 1 Cor 15.40: *CN* III 3558 f 28. Cf BROOKE 24, PEARSON 1, and esp LEIGH-TON COPY B 5.

27[5] Swedenborg cites the verse several times, but the passage that lends itself best to C's interpretation appears to be *The Apocalypse Explained* § 750 d, which is concerned with the use of the word "soul" as referring to spiritual life (though it may also refer to the life of the body, as in § 750 c).

27[6] C annotated at least four works by the Cambridge Platonist Henry More (1614–87) as well as the *Philosophische Aphorismen* (2 vols Leipzig 1793, 1800) of Ernst Platner (1744–1818): see MORE and PLATNER in *CM* (*CC*) IV. His copy of *The Light of Nature Pursued* (2 vols 1768) by Abraham Tucker (1705–74), published un-der the pseudonym "Edward Search", is at VCL. The doctrine of the twofold body does not seem to appear explicitly as a topic in Platner or Tucker, nor do C's notes

of Body, Soul and Spirit as no less true philosophically tha~~t~~n important in the religious Consequences,[7] the nature of the Body being in every [? de] State determined by the System, with which the ~~St~~ Soul stand in intercommunion, and from which the *material informanda*[8] is assimilated.—In the Earth earthy[9] and subsisting only under the condition of a continual flux, and by its apparent identity under actual change affording a strong presumption of the abidingness of the Soul. In the heavens, the Realm of Incorruption, a celestial incorruptible Body.[10] But of disembodied or bodiless finite BEINGS having individuality, the great Apostle knows nothing, blessed or accurst, above or below. Spirits indeed taking possession both of Souls and Bodies are often spoken of;[11] but were it certain, that all Souls are Spirits, it does not follow that all Spirits are Souls.

28 I (140)xxix–xxxiv(140)

And I may observe, by the way, that the universality, the stability, the unchangeableness of this, the law of all body of Adam descended, doth raise into a very high and vast importance those exceptions of Enoch and Elias,!!* the only ones which have ever been permitted—and undoubtedly not without the gravest causes and greatest ends permitted. . . . And yet, to the end that in this also he might have the pre-eminence, the transfiguration upon the Mount was given, and Elias made to attend upon the changed Lord; in order to signify and shew, that not only did the resurrection stand in Christ, but likewise the changing of the living, the rapture of the saints, which was foreshadowed in the rapture of Elias.

* As to the first, viz. Enoch, I have no doubt that the true and only meaning of the verse in Genesis is that Enoch died in his Youth[1]—the first instance, perhaps, of a premature Death without violence—and of the second, viz. Elias, I have little doubt, that the passage in Kings is a poetic Paraphrase of the Fact, that Elijah departed (gave up his Spirit) in

on PLATNER raise the issue, but he may have found it implied in those works. Henry More, however, does invoke the distinction between the terrestrial and the celestial body in *An Explanation of the Grand Mystery of Godliness: Theological Works* (1707) 98.

27[7] C refers to 1 Cor 15, and especially to the verse quoted by Irving, in which the distinction between soul (ψυχή) and spirit (πνεῦμα) is unusually clear: "The first man Adam was a living soul; the last Adam *was*

made a quickening spirit" (1 Cor 15.45).

27[8] "Material to be given form".

27[9] 1 Cor 15.47.

27[10] 1 Cor 15.40.

27[11] The word for such a "spirit" is always *pneuma*, e.g. Matt 12.43, Luke 11.24, Acts 19.12–16.

28[1] Gen 5.21–4, esp 22: "And Enoch walked with God after he begat Methuselah three hundred years, and begat sons and daughters".

the act of prophesying and under the full influence of prophetic Inspiration—His Spirit ascended ~~oin~~ in a fiery chariot to the God who gave it.[2]

S. T. C.[a]

PS. Again—the Transfiguration. Where does Mr Irving find it either declared or intimated by necessary Inference that Moses & Elias were present?[3] I think it very far from certain, that from the words of the Gospel Narrative of this incident we are under the necessity of holding that any living substantial Figures were communing with our Lord in the glory—and the opinion is not without its difficulties for a man who has attained to a view of the Christian Faith freed from the ~~laws~~ Costume of ⟨popular⟩ Judaism, as it existed in its motley Egypto-Græco-Persian Togs, and Embroideries at the Christian Era. But granting, that that[b] the luminous Appearances were Personal Beings, still I ask of Mr Irving, whence he learnt, on what testimony he grounds his right of thus positively determining that the glorious Apparitions were Moses and Elias?—(One of the oldest Pseud-evangelia makes them to have been Enoch and Elijah[4]—doubtless in order to ~~bring the im~~ evade the weighty objection of contradicting the positive declaration of Scripture, the important article of faith, that Jesus was the first-born of the Resurrection.)[5]—I know indeed as well as my friend, that Peter talking between Sleep & Awake expresses his Opinion, his "I dare say, it was" Moses and Elias![6] But I know likewise, and my friend would do well to remember, that this conjecture of the honest-hearted but somewhat hasty Apostle received neither countenance nor ⟨any⟩ word of confirmation, from our Lord. On similar evidence, that is, on the unconfirmed ~~and~~ conjectural interpretation of our Lord's words by the yet unenlightened Disci-

---

[a] C ends this note at the top of p xxx(140) with a caret, and uses the same symbol to take it up again at the foot of the page

[b] Word repeated, appearing at end of one line and beginning of next

28[2] Actually in a whirlwind, 2 Kings 2.11: ". . . there appeared a chariot of fire, and horses of fire, and parted them both asunder; and Elijah went up by a whirlwind into heaven".

28[3] Matt 17.1–13, Mark 9.2–13, Luke 9.28–36. Moses and Elias (Elijah) are named in all three accounts; the issue is whether they were in some sense *physically* present.

28[4] NT accounts of the Transfiguration of Christ (n 3 above) record the presence of two heavenly visitors, Moses and Elijah. No trace of Enoch as a substitute for Moses has been found in the NT Apocrypha, C's "Pseud-evangelia".

28[5] Col 1.18 (cf 1 Cor 15.20) declares Christ to be "the beginning, the firstborn from the dead; that in all *things* he might have the preeminence". If Moses appeared at the Transfiguration, it would be as one raised from the dead and Christ would not be the *first* so raised. Elijah and Enoch, however, had been carried directly to heaven.

28[6] Luke 9.32–3 describes Peter, a witness of the Transfiguration, as "heavy with sleep" and as addressing Christ "not knowing what he said".

ples, it has been taken for granted (against all hope of reconciling it with the words of Maachi*a*) that John the Baptist was Elias—[7]

29 I xxxiv(140)–lviii(140)[1]

For what else is corruption, but the consequence of sin? In Adam, in the Paradise of Eden, *in the world unfallen, there was perpetual health, and no vestige of decay; no autumn with its yellow leaf, no winter with its naked desolation, but one continued fulness of life, without any indications of change . . .

* Ecce, iterum![2] M*r* Irving surprizes me with the extent of his information! In what precious Relic of ante-diluvian, nay ante-lapsarian Chorography, has he discovered this anecdoton[3] respecting the unique properties and privileges of the Garden, which God set Adam to till?—Was it in the 2nd ~~and~~ or 3rd Book of Ezra? Or in the Book of Enos?[4]—I cannot persuade myself, that these Cabalistic Fancies can be for edification! Still less favorably am I inclined to appreciate these refinements & finedrawn inferences respecting the tangible Flesh, in which our Lord εσκηνωσεν, tented or tabernacled.[5] First, because my friend appears to me, in his recoil from the Volatilizers and frigorific Evaporators who confine the ~~vim et~~ vimque modumque operandi,[6] the operative force of Christ & the Christian Faith to Opinions, Arguments, Examples, and Facts that are to constitute an experience, these Facts being themselves contrary to all preceding and to all following experience, in proof of the certainty of a class of Facts that are to take place at the end of the World, placed beyond the possibility of any Experience—my friend, I say, recoiling

---

a I.e. Malachi: the tail of the "g" in "against" in the line above occupies the place where the "l" should be

28[7] After the Transfiguration, when the disciples questioned Christ about the prophecy regarding Elijah, that he would come before the day of the Lord (Mal 4.5), Christ answered, "Elias is come already. . . . Then the disciples understood that he spake unto them of John the Baptist" (Matt 17.10–13). John the Baptist emphatically denied that he was Elias (John 1.21).

29[1] As the page numbers suggest, this note refers not only to the brief textus given, but to the first section, 30 pages long, of Sermon 3. Internal evidence indicates that it was written certainly before **31**, **32**, and **34**, and probably before **30**, **33**, and **35**, and therefore that some of C's detailed notes were made during a second

(or later) reading of the work.

29[2] "Here we go again!"—a tag from Juvenal 4.1.

29[3] Transliterating the Greek ἀνέκδοτον, "unedited" or "unpublished": see Davison **10** n 4.

29[4] That is, the apocryphal books 1 and 2 Esdras (cf Eichhorn *Apokryphischen Schriften* **1** n 1) and the pseudepigraphical book of Enoch—non-scriptural and inappropriate sources, in C's view.

29[5] C gives the literal significance of the verb translated as "dwelt" in John 1.14: cf **12** n 2 above and Eichhorn *Neue Testament* COPY B **10** n 2.

29[6] "Force and manner of working".

from this extreme has plunged into the saddest error of the Romish Church, even the opposite extreme of condensing the great *Ideas*, the living Spiritual Verities, of the Gospel into *Idols*— = Things, i.e. ~~sens~~ phænomena or appearances defined either for sight or for the fancy by outlines.[7] Truly & sincerely, I had not deemed it *possible* that I could have read the assertions and positions contained in this discourse from p. xxix to p. xliv in a work of Mr Irvings![8] The glaring Tritheism—what do I say?—the palpable Tri-angelism,[9] the Holy Ghost being clearly the superior Person, the least confined and crippled of the three, and to all intents and purposes the true and only effective Agent in our Redemption—the strange enunciations of fancies the most startling without a single expression of the Sacred Writers to warrant, or that could even be supposed to have suggested them—and above all the continued attribution to the transitory material Body of Jesus, from which he in so many ways endeavored to wean & withdraw the still sensual minds of the disciples, all the powers, attributes, and functions of the mystical and spiritual Flesh and Blood of the Word that had become Man, constituting the proper *Humanity* (not combining with it as with an element already existing previously to the combination) the Flesh and Blood that nourish to life everlasting, the supersensual Body which *is* Life, and whereto we must be assimilated, assimilated to the divine food as the food inferior to ourselves is assimilated to our Bodies, or we *cannot* live! Nay, to so wild a frenzy is this *Superstition* carried (See Aids to Reflection—Superstitio = superstantibus attributio proprietatum quæ non nisi de Substantiis predicare licet)[10] that even to the identical ponderable, visible and evaporable drops of Blood, which without any authority of the Evangelists Mr Irving describes as absorbed by the Earth—i.e. the Soil on which the Cross stood, & uses such language as would be extravagant, had he been speaking of the Stream from a Scaffold on which fifty Men had been guillotined in the same Second, is invested with attributes not only exclusively [? ~~attrib~~] applicable to Spirits, but such as it would be Madness to assert of any other Spirit, but the Almighty Omnipresent

---

29[7] Ideas address the reason, idols the fancy. This is a variant of a distinction frequently made by C; an example that reveals a Baconian source is *Friend* (*CC*) I 491–3.

29[8] I.e. the page numbers of the first section of Sermon 3, beginning at **28** textus and continuing to **31**.

29[9] Cf the charge of tritheism, "three-god-ism", in **2** above (at n 13); "Tri-angelism" is a still greater reduction of the

Trinity.

29[10] *AR* (1825) 184 and n, which C quotes here from memory: "Superstition = assigning to appearances properties that ought to be predicated of substances alone." The point depends on the distinction between the prepositional prefixes *super* (over, above) and *sub* (under), "substance" lit "standing under".

God![11]—Alas! how large a portion of these lamentable Bewilderments might have been prevented, ~~by~~ had M[r] Irving merely begun with a cool and tranquil mind with an analysis of the term, Body—not in its universal sense as matter filling space; but as the visible Organismus of living Creatures.[12] In this sense, a Body is, I grant, neither an Ens logicum, nor an Ens imaginarium, but a true Ens reale,[13] objectively existing. Now of ~~Entia Realia~~ Realities, vel των objectivè existentium,[14] there are two sorts, that dare not be confounded—the one, unconditional, where the Object exists independent of the forms or combinations, in which at any given time it may be found existing—~~so~~ such, for instance, as Gold, Iron, Hydrogen &c. The other, conditional, and deriving their existence & in all strict use of words, their appropriate ~~name term~~ Name; from the Copula or unity of the Constituent elements, or of its Positive and Negative Fact ⟨~~only~~⟩.—Such, for instance, are—a Tune, or the geometrical Figures of Sand made by magnetic efflux, or the vibrations of Musical Glasses.[15]—The real Object in eas instances of this class, is neither A nor B, nor both of them together; but it exists as *a* unity—*not*, observe, *in* the *union* of the two constituents, as Atmospheric Air docs in the union of Oxygen & Nitrogen Gasses; but as a specific Unity, constituting the two Components that which they are become, i.e. *itself*. With the dissolution of the Unity, the Object ceases to exist.—Now to this class or sort of Realities our Bodies belong. The moment the Copula or

29[11] An example from p xlii(140), on which this part of C's note appears. Irving says, "And be it further observed, that the blood of a blameless life which fell from his cross upon the ground, and which the earth greedily drank up, is to her [the earth] the assurance of hope, and speaketh out from the ground better things than the blood of Abel, crying, not for vengeance, but for redemption. It is her baptism of blood; one of the witnesses which witnesseth of glory yet to come: for what the Holy Spirit is to man, the blood of a holy-man is unto the ground; because man is the life of the earth, as the Holy Spirit is the life of man."

29[12] C repeatedly insisted on the need for a scrupulous definition of the term "body", crucial in debates about the Incarnation, the Eucharist, and the Resurrection. On the one hand, the term had to be distinguished from such related words as "matter", though both Descartes and Kant had failed in this respect: *AR* (1825) 392n; Kant *Metaphysische Anfangsgründe* 8; cf Leighton copy c 7, *SM* (*CC*) 81 and n. On the other hand, different meanings of the word had to be distinguished from one another, as in C's discussion of the twofold body in 27 n 4 above. Cf Brooke annex, Hacket *Sermons* 22 n 2, Luther *Colloquia* 40, 91.

29[13] Neither a "logical thing" nor an "imaginary thing", but a "real thing".

29[14] "Or of the things existing objectively"—the Greek definite article being introduced in the Latin phrase to clarify the reference to existing *things* rather than to existence in the abstract.

29[15] Either the fashionable instrument invented about 1740—basically glasses partially filled with water, and struck with wooden rods—or Benjamin Franklin's refinement of it, the "glass harmonica" of 1762, which was operated by a player with wet fingers.

unitive Act and Presence of the Principium Vitale[16] (the Psyche or Animal *Soul* of St Paul, whence psychical is used by him as equivalent to carnal)[a][17] the *Body* ceases to be: tho' not from the vis inertiæ of the negative Factor, the *Stuff*, the *Shape* (= forma *apparens*) may for a longer or shorter time remain after the extinction or withdrawing of the operative *Form* (= *forma informans*, vel *forma substans*)[18]—still it is not a Body but a Carcase. And in strict propriety of language we cannot even say—the Body is now a Carcase, but must say—there is a Carcase instead of a Body—And when after a while the vis inertiæ of the Corse is overcome by the chemical Energies, there remain Lime, Carbon, Hydrogen, Nitrogen, Oxygen, Phosphorus, Sulphur, Iron, ⟨Ammonium⟩ singly or in other combinations. We may say, the *Carcase* is fallen abroad into these as it[b] component parts, but not that the *Body* is so, for the Lime, Carbon, &c never were *parts* of the Body, even because *the Body* is not a mere aggregate or Compositum, but the Copula or indivisible Unity.—To talk therefore of the Holy Ghost preserving the dead *Flesh* of Christ, nay, even the Blood that had separated from the Blood-vessels, from Corruption— ~~is in truth~~ what is it but calling in the Holy Ghost to do what a small quantity of Salt or Sugar, or a deep Frost, could have done as well! and which, in fact, the stimulating Gums &c in which the Corse had been laid, were perfectly competent to effect for the short interval between Friday Evening and Sunday Dawning.[19] If M[r] Irving could have had a Bird's Eye View of my mind during my perusal of these pages, and have seen how in consequence of the ⟨consecutive⟩ figures and images conveyed by him and which he insists on our taking in the literal sense, my imagination without and against my Will was *flashed across* and traversed by the most ludicrous recollections of Cookery and the various processes of Salting, Corning, Potting, Pick-

---

[a] A verb has been omitted here, perhaps "dissolves" or "ends"   [b] A slip for "its"

29[16] "Vital principle".

29[17] C refers apparently to Paul's use of the adjective (*psychikos*) in 1 Cor 15 esp 44: "There is a *natural* body, and there is a spiritual body" (AV).

29[18] The Latin phrases, beginning with *vis inertiae* (a Newtonian term appearing as early as 1794 in *CL* I 74), may be translated "inertial force", "apparent form", "informing [i.e. form-inducing] form, or substantial [i.e. under-standing] form". For "*sub*stans" see e.g. BLANCO WHITE 13 n 8, BIBLE COPY B 136 n 2.

29[19] C objects particularly to Irving's contention pp 1(140)–(140)li: ". . . like withering leaves, we shall drop off from him; like fruitless branches, be pruned away; like his own body of sin, drop into death and the grave; unless we shall have partaken of that regenerating power of the Holy Ghost which he partook in the tomb; which saved him from corruption, which shall deliver the regenerate out of corruption; which united his body, that was mortal and corruptible, unto his immortal part, consisting of soul and Second Person of the Godhead, and fixed it there in immortal union for ever and ever''.

ling, Preserving, Basting, he would have recoiled from the thought of having furnished the occasion and subject-matter of this involuntary Profaneness.—N.B. I do not deny, that for Amateurs of "Curious Questions", who read the Gospel Narrative in the spirit, and for the satisfaction, of their *Curiosity*, the circumstances of our Saviour's Visibility, ~~during~~ and his several Appearances during the interval between his Resurrection and his Ascension, will not be without sundry difficulties, and furnish abundant hints for questions, which I am better satisfied with the disposition to quash than I should be with the power of answering. If Mr Irving, however, feels an interest in speculations of this sort, I can refer to the Posthumous Sermons of Bishop Horsley on the nature of our Lord's Body after the Resurrection,[20] in which this Archaspistes Orthodoxiæ Angelicanæ[21] supports opinion which in former time would have gone near to rank him among the Docetæ.—[22]

P.S. As every new Instance in illustration of a Point increases the chance of rendering it intelligible to some one or more Readers, I will elucidate the *sort* of Realit~~y~~ies, among which ~~an~~ Organic Bodies stand, by taking flexile Wires and bending them into the cyphers 1828/ then unbending them and converting the same wires into S. T. C, the first ~~answering the~~ expressing pro tempore[23] an æra, the other being a personal Signature./ Which would you say, supposing you wished to speak accurately—that 1829[a] changed into S. T. C: or that the Wires, which a formative Power had employed to make the *conception* of the number of years since the Birth of Christ ~~an~~ perception, ~~or to render the intelligible sensible,~~ make a *form* of the *Intellect* a significant *Shape* for the Senses, were afterwards used by him to convey thro' the Senses the recollection of a Person—& then, perhaps, the same Wires might have gone to restrain the Cork of a bottle of Spruce Beer. Now what the Date of the Year, and the Personal Signature are to the Wire, that a Man's Body is to the Lime, Phosphorus, Ammonium, Nitrogen, Carbon, Oxygen, Hydrogen, and Iron which constitute its visibility, and tangible[b] in perfect indifference to the particular *Form* which they render visible and tangible.

---

[a] A slip for "1828"—the annotation written on 1 Jan 1829   [b] For "make it tangible"?

29[20] Samuel Horsley *Nine Sermons* (1815), Sermon 4 on the Resurrection, cited by C in C. BUTLER *Vindication* **1**, and q extensively in n 9.

29[21] "Principal champion of Anglican orthodoxy". C uses "archaspistes"—literally "chief shield-bearer"—as early as 1803 (*CN* I 1565); cf CHILLINGWORTH COPY A **1**.

29[22] Those who believe that Christ's physical form and suffering were mere *appearances*.

29[23] "For the time being".

It is possible, doubtless, that "bodies celestial"[24] may be, like Calorique (or Warmth-stuff as the Germans name it)[25] only in some higher and potenziated essence, simple, indecomponible, and unchangeably susceptible of the informing Life or Spirit, and consequently permanent. But it seems to me more probable, that a certain Circulation or Interchange takes place, only the reverse of that which obtains in our present state in which all things are significant of a *Fall*, and where the matter that gives place to newly assimilated Substance sinks from a higher to a meaner form of Being, or both may be in a certain sense combined, if we suppose what is at least supposable, a successive and progressive potenziation of the indecomponible Substance by the acts & influences of the informing Agent, by the presence and blest *Contagion* of the Spiritual Life which constitutes the imperishable *stuff* an angelic Body— Even in this world all Substances are not corpuscular or atomic. But M[r] I. has not yet had the momentous Doctrine of the double "I", the double Will, and the double Life revealed to him: or the true relations of Nature to God.[26]

1 Jan[y] 1829.　　　　　　　　　　　　　　　　　S. T. C.

30　ɪ xliv(140) | Pt 2

Besides these good effects, necessarily resulting from Christ's taking our fallen humanity, and of which not one would have resulted had he taken humanity in an unfallen state, there is another, to which divines of this age will be more alive; which is, that there could otherwise have been neither reconciliation nor atonement between God and man.

The word is the low German & Saxon attönen, in High German Versöhnen, to reconcile, expiate, appease.[1]

29[24] 1 Cor 15.40, "celestial bodies, and bodies terrestrial"; cf **27** nn 4, 10 above.

29[25] "Caloric" (Eng.), "calorique" (Fr.), "Wärmestoff" (Ger.), a term introduced by the reformers of chemical nomenclature in France in 1787 to refer to a material substance (commonly thought of as an elastic fluid) supposed to be present in all bodies, to which the phenomena of heat were attributed. Cf *CN* ɪv 5144 and n.

29[26] C complains later (**35**) of Irving's misapprehension of Coleridgean doctrines on such subjects as these. Cf a notebook entry of 19 Aug 1830: "O how pregnant & multiplicative is every truth—Long ago it was given me to see, that Faith implied an entireness of the Will. ~~Some~~ Soon after I saw, as a consequence of this, the necessity of asserting a double Will . . . [t]he divine & the natural—the Will of God, transcendently One, and the Will of Hades . . ." (N44.53).

30[1] C is correct about *versöhnen*, but no such verb as *attönen* existed even in Low German dialects. It appears that either C or some misleading source invented it as a hypothetical Germanic analogue to the Latin *adunare*, "to make one" or "unite". See **31** below.

31   ɪ xliv(140) | Continuing **30** textus

Those, indeed, who consider atonement as a bargain . . . will see little or nothing in the line of argument which I am now about to pursue. But those who . . . *understand atonement in its only scriptural sense, of at-one-ment, or reconciliation between the Holy Creator and the unholy creature; that which I am about to argue will appear of the greatest moment, and unanswerable.

* It is strange, that I, the originator of this sense of atonement, should have publickly, i.e. in a printed work, recanted it as a grave Pun:[1] and that Mr I. should have wedded himself to this cast-off Dalila! S. T. C.

32   ɪ liv(140)

Whence it follows, that, whatever he suffered, and, which is far more, whatever he forewent of infinite glory and blessedness in order to suffer, is all to be placed to the account of mankind, and not to his own account.

And yet this is the Man who in the ἐστῆσῇ fit[1] talks with contempt of "the Debtor and Creditor Scheme" of Redemption!![2] Mr I. *alarms* me with his shouldering mob of Inconsistencies! Here Calvinism & Popery stand like Mule & Ass with their heads in contrary directions: and here Mr I. ties them together by the Tails & then sets them a kicking!—

33   ɪ (140)lv

So that, as the whole earth stood in Adam's body represented, with the fate of Adam's body implicated, in it to stand and fall and be redeemed; so likewise the whole substance of organized flesh and blood, living, and dead, and to live, stood represented in the body of Christ which the Holy Spirit had formed from the virgin's substance, to stand or to fall according as this man newly constituted, this new thing created of God, should stand or fall.

Surely, Mr I. must have been dreaming, must have written in under Somnambulism! I can call to mind no book from which he could have taken it—unless he has met with some old volume written by some obscure Follower of Jacob Behmen.

31[1] A puzzling statement, for no *printed* recantation is known to have appeared in C's lifetime. The etymological analysis of "atonement" as "at-one-ment" (*not* original with C) appears in *SM* (*CC*) 55, where the note indicates later reservations recorded by C in James Gillman's copy of the work. C perhaps confused the printed and ms texts.

32[1] The "S. T. C. fit".

32[2] See **11** n 3 above.

34 I (140)lv

I cannot tell how this is, and I do neither say nor gainsay it, being minded only to speak what the Lord hath made me clearly to know.!!!!! I do indeed perceive this much, that no creature could pay the price of sin but by eternal separation from God, because I see it to have been so in the fallen angels . . .

Where did Mr I. *see* any Syllable about *fallen Angels*, except in the sense of Ministers, Bishops, in short, *Men*—[1]

35 I lvi(140) | Continuing **34** textus

. . . and if so, then the recovery of man must be accomplished by an act of power of an infinite measure; which act Christ's was, by that two-fold will or operation which was in him—one conversant with the Godhead, and enlarged to its infinite bounds; another conversant with the manhood, and restricted to its humble and suffering conditions—these two wills, or operations as the orthodox Fathers termed it, being necessary to compose any act of the person Jesus Christ. The I in him, embraced the infinite and the finite also; which gave to every action and feeling of his a character of infinity.

Whoo! a Will enlarged to a Bound! and to an *infinite* Bound! This a fragment of an Echo from ἐς τὴ σὴ[1] Alas! alas!

36 I lx(140)–(140)lxiii

How is the world to be reconciled unto God? . . . As in an individual, even Adam, the enmity came; so in an individual, even Christ, the reconciliation came. And as from the first individual, the enmity was propagated to many, yea to all; so from the latter individual is the reconciliation propagated unto many: as is the fall, so is the remedy. And how, then, was the reconciliation accomplished in the man Jesus Christ; and afterwards is it propagated from him unto other men?

⊦On the difficult question agitated in this & the following pages I do not, as the lawless contents of the preceding have forced me to do, *blame* Mr Irving. I have no right to do so: for he has the whole Choir of Divines— & the Authority of the Church, on his side: and I stand almost alone. But I regret that by his *willing* to exclude from his Understanding the

---

34[1] C repeatedly asserted that neither angels themselves nor any fall of angels forms part of the revealed Christian religion that teaches the fall of man. Cf HACKET *Sermons* **16**; also **1** at n 19 and **9** above.

35[1] "S. T. C."—cf **8**, **11**, **32** above.

many and solid reasons for *doubting*, if not for denying the Apostolicity of ⟨the⟩ two Evan. Inf.[1] (so far doubting, at least, as not to build any article of faith singly or mainly on these Scriptures) he has involved the question of the peccability in unnecessary and (I suspect) irremovable Difficulties—With *my* views, I subscribe to M[r] Irving's Position on the whole; but yet I must acknowledge that I assent ~~with~~ more promptly & fearlessly to the peccability of Jesus than to the peccability of the Christ. M[r] Irving himself would, perhaps, allow that it must have been a constantly diminishing Liability: and I, ~~who commencing~~ for whom the Gospel commences with and from the Baptism of John,[2] and who therefore see no reason why I should not receive in the literal sense the words—Today I have begotten thee![3] can readily suppose that the Object of the Temptation immediately sub~~stitut~~sequent, as far as our Lord himself was in view & not the future instruction of the Apostles, might have[a] the acquainting with the Power over the Tempter & the Temptations, which had accrued to him as the begotten Christ. And herein, that the eternally begotten Word was begotten again in Jesus *when time was*,[4] lies, if I mistake not, a Mystery of deep practical Concernment.

37   I (140)ci–(140)cv

As Reconciler, He took off the curse of the Law, which, though not openly imposed from the beginning, had been laid on in all its iron terrors by the covenant of Sinai, which I take to be the true covenant of works, according to that saying of the Apostle Paul, "The Law speaketh on this wise: He that doeth these things shall live in them." This Law, having kept, he had no right to die, but his right was to live in them.

This page, I confess, leaves no impression on my mind but that of a vain attempt to transmute Spiritual *Ideas*, the Intuitions of the pure Reason, into *Conceptions* of the Understanding; and eternal *Truths* into historical (I might say, biographical) *Facts*.[1] What does M[r] Irving mean by the *Law*? Not surely the ceremonial Law, which was at no time binding except on the Jewish People; & on these only, as long as they remained

---

[a] For "have been"?

36[1] Cf 2 at n 16 and 25 above. In PAU-LUS **2**, C says "that the only Parties whom had any interest in maintaining the genuineness of the Christopædia were Deists and Unitarians".

36[2] As suggested above at n 1, C discounts the texts concerned with the conception, birth, and childhood of Jesus, and considers the historically reliable texts as

beginning with the baptism of John in Luke 3.

36[3] Acts 13.33, q from Ps 2.7 by Paul in his sermon at Antioch.

36[4] Not a biblical phrase, unless C alludes to the more commonplace "when *the* time was" of e.g. 1 Sam 1.4, 20.

37[1] Vital distinctions for C, as in LU-THER *Colloquia* **41**, *C&S* (*CC*) 12–13.

a *State*. The moral Law then—as comprized *negatively* (for such is the *Legal* form of morality) in the X Commandments.[2] But how can the strict and adequate obedience to this Law by one Agent absolve all after him from the duty of following his example? But if Mʳ I. meant more and other than this by "Law", he should have premised his meaning.— It is from the *condemnation* of the Law by the conversion of Law into Grace, and by the implanting a living seed of Righteousness not our own, but which working as an organic Life in us shall transubstantiate the ground of our essential Being (i.e. the Will) to itself, that we are *absolved*.—not from the Law itself, not which but *our relation* to which, is changed. Now this working of Christ in the Elect, as a spiritual Germ, is the Holy Spirit given by and thro' Christ—& by Christ, as God, as the manifested only-begotten Son—& therefore in the order of the divine economy following, and consequent on, his ascension from his Individuality, as *a* man—~~his~~ the first act of his Glorification, when he *resumed* the Glory which he had with the Father before the World began[3]—For he *is* the *Glory* of the Father, relatively to the Godhead; and relatively to us the King of Glory: or God as the Glory of God.[4]

S. T. C.

38   ɪ (140)cix

Now the church, being on all hands the guardians of discipline, it follows that the church is her own head upon earth; or rather, to speak more correctly, the church hath no head upon earth, but is a body without a head; and you might as well give unto the king or civil magistrate, the keeping and administering of the sacraments as you give unto him the title of head of the church. It is a misnomer, to say the best of it, in our sister church; or, if it be not a misnomer,* then it is something infinitely worse.

* The Misnomer (for I admit, there *is* one) consists in the unhappy double meaning given to the word, Church. If instead of the Church, we had simply affirmed that the King is the Head of the National Clerisy, as well as of the Laity—the Head of the *whole* Estate, in both its Species, viz. the hereditable, and the elective—the Portion of the People, and those reserved in behoof of the Nation—that he is the Head, or Point

37[2] "The rules of prudence in general, like the laws of the stone tables, are for the most part prohibitive. *Thou shalt not* is their characteristic formula . . ." (*AR*—1825—14). C takes up Irving's conception of moral law again in **41** below.

37[3] "And now, O Father, glorify thou me with thine own self with the glory which I had with thee before the world was": John 17.5.
37[4] Cf **15** above.

of Union, of the *Proprietage* and of the *Nationalty*—I can conceive no rational, no loyal,[a] Objection to the Name.—[1]   S. T. C.

39   I   cx(140)

Seeing then that Christ's baptism with the Holy Ghost is really and truly, and to the fullest extent, the effecting of the Father's purpose of election, the bringing of his elect ones out of the unregenerate world, the implanting in them of a Divine person, who abideth for ever there where he hath once come, and shall not, cannot, be dislodged again for ever, it is most manifest that to believe in the Father's election, and to believe in Christ's active headship of the church, and to believe in the work of the Holy Ghost, is truly to believe in one and the same thing.—The election of the Father, the office of Christ to baptize with the Holy Ghost, and the actual sanctification of the Holy Ghost, are the three functions of the persons in the Godhead towards the accomplishing of the one work of our regeneration. Election, therefore, Christ's headship of the church, and regeneration of the Holy Ghost, must stand or fall together. Where election is not believed in, there Christ's high resurrection office to baptize with the Holy Ghost will be forgotten; and men will get no higher than his cross, burial, and forthcoming from the tomb, never attaining unto the discourse of his post-resurrection work, but losing him in the white cloud, and fancying him a dissolved wide-spread substance, instead of a personal presence, and an almighty power. They will dwell by the Jordan in their discourse, and in the towns of Galilee, and in the temple of Jerusalem, and at the foot of the cross on Calvary, and so forth, deciphering the justice, the charity, the nobility of all his works, but no higher ascending; preaching the imitation of his obedience, and using the Holy Spirit to help us to keep the law, which is to bring us back unto the law, from which Christ hath for ever delivered us. Where election is not believed, the humanity of Christ alone will be apprehended; not the mystery of his humanity, but the example of his humanity. Yea, they may attain unto the bodily measure of the Godhead, that was within such narrow conditions and under such dark veils concealed; but into that dignity, and majesty, and might Divine, which he hath since acquired, and doth now occupy in the heavens, bringing to pass every secret purpose of the invisible Father, making the Godhead's full purpose to be accomplished, and the hidden things to be made known;— into the mystery of the invisible Godhead, which he invisibly exerciseth

[a] Probably a slip for "logical"

38[1] The themes and terminology of this note, and particularly C's coinages "cler-   isy", "nationalty", and "proprietage", belong to *C&S* (1829).

in all chambers of creation, gathering out from thence the Father's hidden ones, and preserving them separate in the midst of all powers and preventions of darkness, and of sin;—into these noble offices of Christ, which pertain to him as the Baptizer with the Holy Ghost, they cannot enter who believe not in the election of the Father. For if they believe not that there is such a thing as an election of the Father, which Christ by baptism of the Holy Ghost is separating, and by headship of the church is governing, how can they believe or understand the doing or fulfiling of the same? They shear him of the beams of his glory; they take away from him the locks of his strength; they understand not his present Nazarite function, who said before his death, "I sanctify myself, (or I make a Nazarite of myself,) for their sakes, that they also might be sanctified by the truth;" who said also, "Henceforth, I will not drink of the juice of the vine, until I drink it new with you in my Father's kingdom." I say, the seven locks in which lie the mighty Nazarite's power, which are the seven Spirits of God, they shear him of, and bring him down to the dimensions of a common man, keeping him under the law, bringing his church under the law, and innumerable other grievances inflicting.

The whole of this Paragraph is excellent, and worthy of my friend, Irving. The Distinctities (= the divine *Persons* of the Pseudo-athanasian Creed)[1] do not, as elsewhere in my friend's Discourse,[a] predominate over the Unity.

40   I (140)cxi

. . . the Spirit's work; which being dissevered from the Father's election . . . doth fall away into . . . at best, some gracious communication of an undefined and undefinable power, blowing, like the wind, wheither it listeth. But to enter into the Spirit's personality, to believe in him not as the incomprehensible infinite, but as the Spirit of Christ, the same mind which was in Jesus Christ, <u>the child of Christ</u>, in form and feature, not of the Christ in flesh . . . but of the Christ in glory . . . must needs depart from the knowledge of those who will not know the election of the Father, and from the experience of those who will deny the election of the Father.

---

[a] C has accidentally inserted a closing parenthesis here

39[1] C's defence of his coinage "distinctity" is recorded in *C&S* (*CC*) 118 n 2. The plural here, however, has a specific theological significance, referring to the separate "persons" of the Trinity; C adopts the same usage in his "Formula fidei de sanctissima Trinitate": *LR* III 2. C refers to the Athanasian Creed consistently as false, a pseudo-creed: cf BÖHME **33** n 1.

This is too bold; but arises naturally out of the unhappy Term, *Person*, applied in the same sense to the Father, the Son, and the Spirit. In the right & strict use of the Word, the Son, υιος ο μονογενης, is alone the *Person* of the Father. See John's Gospel I v 18.—[1]

41 1 cxx(140)–cxxxiv(140), completed in pencil

And then, for greater manifestation, and for further punishment of sin, *he imposed the Law, which came by Moses, and was removed by Christ. The Law, therefore, is the great sign and standing monument of God's unreconciled mind towards men. . . . [cxxiv(140):] The Law is by the Apostle absolutely called sin, even as Christ, when under the Law, is likewise called sin. And that the Law hath sin, and not righteousness, for its object, is well declared in that passage, Rom. v.13: "Until the Law, sin was in the world; but sin is not imputed where there is no law."

* Here re-commences my perplexity: and again I ask, what Mr Irving means by the Law. In the two last words of the preceding ¶ph. he seems to mean the *Moral* Law.[1] But surely he could not mean to assert, that the Moral Obligations did not exist before the⟨ir⟩ fir promulgation in the Decalogue from Mount Sinai?—The ceremonial Law instead, that is, the Customs and Ordinances National which having been imposed by a lawful Authority bee acquired the force of Moral Obligation for every Member of that Nation, as long as a as Citizens of a particular State & during the its^a continuance as a State—*this* Law undoubtedly came by Moses; but was not abolished by Jesus Christ, in his *legislative* Character, but ceased of itself by the cessation of the State, when the Heaven & the Earth, i.e. the Hierarchy and the Nation, the Government and the Body politic collectively governed, had passed away.[2] We may say indeed, that it was abolished in consequence of Christ's Coming, because Christ Incarnate was the Fulfilment of the ceremonial, and abolished under the controlling power of Christ, as now the Providence of the World; but the fact that it was made binding on every native Jew during the whole interval from our Lord's Preaching to the destruction of the City & Temple proves that it was not abolished *by* Jesus. Not therefore

^a C cancelled "its" instead of "the"

40[1] The Greek phrase "only-begotten son" (as in **2** n 7 above) appears in this text. For C's objection to the theological use of the term "person" see **1** n 4 above.

41[1] On p cxx(140): ". . . the Holy Ghost's active service in delivering the soul from the law of the flesh, and from the curse of the Moral Law". C takes up again a problem aired in **37** above.

41[2] Christ said, "Heaven and earth shall pass away: but my words shall not pass away": Mark 13.31, Luke 21.33.

the Law, as peculiar to the Jewish State but the Law as equally obliga-
tory on Jew and Gentile because equally inscribed on the Tablets of the
Heart, can have be*ᵃ* intended: and therefore it cannot be the *Matter* of
the Law, but the Form, and the nature and direction of the Obliging
Motives, constituting the *matter* Law, which under Christ became Grace
& Truth. *ᵇ*Mʳ Irving has, (ὡς ἐμοίγε δοκεῖ)³ been misled thro' inadver-
tence to the fact, that ⟨tho'⟩ we may rest with unqualified confidence in
the truth of Sᵗ Paul's CONCLUSION, this is by no means universally the
case with his *Premises*: these being sometimes CONCESSIONS *argumenti
causâ*⁴ to his Antagonists—ex. gr. to the Rabbinical Doctors of his Age.
"Well! I will take for granted what you lay down as a Truth: yet even
from this no such *conclusion* would follow. Even from this Assumption
the more legitimate Conclusion would be,—&c &c./'' Now this is par-
ticularly applicable to Sᵗ Paul's Reasoning on THE LAW, which I first
understand when instead of the perplexity which must be the result of
comparing them with the Pentateuch, I collate them with the established
Dicta and maxim*ᶜ* of the Doctors of the Law, the Apostle's Predecessors
& Contemporaries. But, in this via ad veritatem per admissionem Falsi,⁵
let it ever be remembered, that in the Apostle's mind there is some
deeper, more universal, or (so to say) some ethical and metaphysical
Truth, of which the Mosaic Law is the Symbol, and representative
Term. Ex. gratiâ—x y z excited *ab extra*⁶ by Threat & Promise is THE
LAW: the same x y z evolved and growing *ab intra*⁷ from the Conformed
Will is Grace & Truth. Therefore the LAW itself, *as* Law, and indepen-
dent of the contingent Obedience or Disobedience, implies *Condemna-
tion*, i.e. the graceless & immoral state of the Subject so acted on, tho'
a perfect Obedience would suspend indefinitely the penalty or actual
infliction of the condemnatory Verdict—even as by regular Breathing
we at once attest and suspend the sentence of Death. But, says the Apos-
tle, a *perfect* Obedience is impossible thro' the very corruption, which
occasioned and required THE LAW⁸—i.e. that the Dictates of the Moral
Reason should be promulged in the form & with the penalties of, Law:
Therefore the Law commanding what *we* can not practice, is for us a
sentence of Condemnation—if taken as complete in itself and not as

---

ᵃ A slip for "been"   *ᵇ* The note continues in pencil without a paragraph break
ᶜ For "maxims" or "maximæ"?

41³ "(In my opinion, at least)".
41⁴ "For the sake of argument".
41⁵ This "way to truth by letting in
falsehood".

41⁶ "From outside".
41⁷ "From inside".
41⁸ C disagrees with Irving's interpre-
tation of Rom 5, esp 12–21.

preparative to, and therefore Spiritually inclusive of, the Redemption by Grace which by *translocation*[9] of the Law, by reversing its Starting-point & direction, makes it to become no longer Law, but the Power of Truth thro' a Life of Grace.   S. T. Coleridge—

42 I 200–4 | Sermon 3 [i.e. 4][a] ii

What, then, must the Son of Man's condition during three days and nights' abode in the heart of the earth have been! how abject, how dishonourable, how sorrowful! in order to stand between Jonah's misery and the misery of the Jewish people, the antitype of the former, and the prototype of the latter. It must indeed have been such as passeth all comprehension and belief: into the gulf whereof when he was passing downward, like Jonah into the open throat of that loathsome living sepulchre which widely opened its armed jaws upon the Prophet, he cried aloud, "My God, my God, why hast thou forsaken me! Father, into thy hands I commend my spirit."*

* I have more than once in Mr Irving's presence given the true interpretation of this most wildly perverted Text—have opened out the divine Wisdom & Goodness which our Lord here displayed: while at once to console the anguish and confirm the faith of Mary & John who were standing at some distance, he ~~gave out~~ recited, with a loud voice a verse which must have instantly reminded them of the 22nd Psalm—or as *we* should say, he *gave out* the 22nd Psalm, which the Jews did not by mentioning the Book ~~and~~ or Number of the Chapter or Psalm but by citing the first Verse.[1] He thus flashed upon their recollection, that the very Scene at that moment before their eyes with all its minute peculiarities were ever painted in this first Half of this prophetic Hymn—But if in this—/the Prophecy had been accomplished to the uttermost point, how was it possible for them to doubt the equal fulfilment of the latter half, announcing the triumph of the Saviour and the glorious establishment of his Kingdom, and the blessedness of all that had received him. The Overcoming of his own Agonies, even in the death-pangs occupied with lively compassion for others—the admirable appropriateness & the God-like majesty of the consolation—Yes! this was indeed a final Act worthy of him who in all things was to be our Exemplar!—But what shall I say of the portentous and unhallowed Fancies, which Mr I. has conjured up

---

[a] The sermon beginning on I 141 had already been numbered "III" before the new Sermon 3 was inserted at I 140/141

41[9] For C's compounds with *trans-* see GREW **3** n 1; "translocation", not a coin-   age, occurs also in FIELD **33** at n 3.
42[1] See **21** and n 1 above.

~~not from Paul~~ without a single sentence of either Gospel or Epistle ~~to~~ for his Sanction or even for his pretext, ~~but an~~ out of an interpolation of the Apostles' Creed ~~wh~~ of the Sixth Century, & which even then meant nothing more than verè mortuus est![2] If such lawless Fictions as M^r I has here fabricated of our Lord's Torments in *Hell* (o sad to meet in a discourse of the present day this vulgar mistranslation of *Hades*)[3] deserved a confutation, it would be enough to quote our Lord's own words, It is finished![4]—No! (says Mr Irving) it had but just begun! The worst was yet to come!! Alas! if Mr I. could see into my heart, he would do justice to the pain & regret with which I have written these animadversions!—

43 ɪ 202

And in token of his victory, he brought from the state of separate spirits as many of the saints as it seemed to him good; who also took their bodies from the grave, and went with him into glory.*

* (It would be a severe but not unmerited Chastisement to collect the numerous fictions of this sort under the name of the Gospel according to Irving.)

44 ɪ 205

Who [the apostates] are of two classes, the Pharisees and the Sadducees; the former adhering to their forms of ritual service, and their outward works of piety and charity; the latter adhering to their intellectual self-sufficiency and enlightened scepticism.*

* To which of the two classes do Scorn and the use of bitter Irony belong? As sure as the morning Twilight precedes the Sunrise, so surely must "enlightened Scepticism" go before enlightening Faith!

45 ɪ 206

While from the enlightened and philosophical (falsely so called) Sadducees—that is, our liberal and benevolent disbelievers in all the mysteries of our holy religion—you must expect the uttermost scorn and derision, as men of disordered minds and dangerous opinions. . . . But

---

42[2] "He really died": cf DONNE *Sermons* COPY B **125** and n 3, and LUTHER *Colloquia* **23** for the same objection to the words "He descended into Hell" in the Apostles' Creed.

42[3] In ɪ 200–2, Irving describes the period between Christ's death and his resurrection as the period of "his abode in the separate state" or Hell; he asserts that Christ conquered death and Hell by descending into death and Hell, and that on his departure from Hell he left hope to those imprisoned there. See also **43** textus.

42[4] John 19.30.

we must first drink of his cup, and be baptized with his baptism, in order to enter into his kingdom.

I grieve to say it, but for every single contemptuous Sentence published against Mʳ Irving, I would undertake to produce ten out of his own publications applied to others. And how can it be, that wise men should not be disgusted, to hear him boasting of his persecutions, & his cup of martyrdom, while he lives in the riot of popularity in his own World!

46   ɪ 207

"Now that he ascended, is it not also that he first descended into the lower parts of the earth?"*

* I cannot persuade myself, that this is the true rendering of the text, or that it gives Sᵗ Pauls meaning—It seems to me incomparably more probable, that εις τα νεϱτεϱα της γης¹—signify no more than—to this our sublunary world/—literally, to the lower parts of [? Wͦͬ] Earth/ the Genitive being used *appositively*; as = to the lower of the earth, or this lower earth. The context too requires that it should be an argument for Christ's pre-existence in the Bosom of the Father.²

47   ɪ 207

Aye, and more: I believe a state of activity, of active driving back and discomfiting of Satan's evil power in those regions: of wounding, and bruising, and vexing, and plaguing him,* and conquering and triumphing over him, and perpetuating the work which in those mansions the Lord did set on foot.

* What an amiable occupation Mʳ I. anticipates for himself & his friends! As Domitian killed flies ⟨in the Chambers of the Palace⟩ to prevent *Ennui*,¹ Mʳ Irving ⟨for the same purpose⟩ would be bruising, vexing and plaguing the *God of Flies*, i.e. Belzebub,² during his Vacation in the Chambers of Hades.

46¹ "To the lower [parts] of the earth". C is writing from memory, using—perhaps from Aeschylus *Agamemnon* 1617—τὰ νέϱτεϱα for "the lower places". The NT text, Eph 4.9, quoted var in textus, reads τὰ κατώτεϱα μέϱη, "the lower parts".

46² The phrase comes from John 1.18, q in Greek in **55** at n 10 below.

47¹ Titus Flavius Domitianus (ᴀ.ᴅ. 51–96), emperor, son of Vespasian, last of the Caesars. Suetonius tells how Domitian passed the time in catching flies and killing them with a bodkin.

47² Beelzebub, "the prince of the devils" in NT, e.g. Matt 12.24, is traditionally associated with the OT "Baalzebub" ("fly-lord"), mentioned in 2 Kings 1.2 as a "god of Ekron".

48 I 209

And to success in this, nothing will avail but earnestly and constantly to look unto Jesus, the author and finisher of our faith; who endured the cross, despising the shame, and is now set down at the right hand of God.

O si sic omnia![1]

49 I 211

Therefore, beloved brethren, this discourse, descriptive of Christ's sufferings, is a discourse exhortative and instructive to you to undertake the fellowship of the same: this discourse, descriptive of Christ's triumph over all his and your enemies, is a discourse full of assurance to every one who believeth in Christ. It is by spreading our souls in wide contemplation of the mighty work of God in the humiliation and exaltation of the Son of Man; it is by collecting our souls in intenser meditation upon the personal experiences of the Son of Man; that we shall grow into his image; and be led of the Holy Spirit into these the deep things of God, into which I have sought a little to introduce you this day. Therefore I do entreat you to "consider Him who endured such contradiction of sinners against himself, lest you also be weary and faint in your minds." He hath set us an example, that we should follow his steps.—"Now, the God of peace, who brought again from the dead our Lord Jesus, that Great Shepherd of the sheep, through the blood of the everlasting covenant, make you perfect in every good work, to do his will; working in you that which is well-pleasing in his sight, through Jesus Christ; to whom be glory for ever and ever. Amen."[a]

This concluding Paragraph—o what affectionate regrets does it awake in my heart, while it reminds me of my friend's saner days, when he was well content to know no more of Christ's History than the Gospels had preserved for him! and to unfold the plain meaning of the Evangelists Chapter-wise, instead of deducing meanings, say rather fancies, of his own from simple words or sentences, these too often mistranslated, and in more than one instance of suspicious Authenticity.[1]

S. T. Coleridge

50 II ¯2

The three predominant Ingredients of these Discourses are distinguished

---

[a] End of Sermon 4

48[1] "O, if only [it were] all like this!"   **49**[1] As in **42** above.

occasionally in the Marginal MSS by the Marks *Est.* for Εστησισμος;[1] *Phal.* for Φαλακρινισμος, (a Φαλακρος, Calvus)[2] or *Paraphal* for παρα-φαλακρινισμος, i.e. perverted Calvinism;[3] & lastly, by IR. for ΙϱϜινισμος.—[4]

51 II 333–49 | Dedication "To my dear and honoured friends, Basil Montagu Esq., and his wife, Mrs. Basil Montagu"

When the Lord . . . advanced me from the knowledge of my own flock and the private walks of pastoral duty, to become a preacher of righteousness to this great City . . . I became also an object of attack to the malice and artifice of Satan . . . at such a perilous moment the Lord in you found for me a Mentor, both to soothe my heart, vexed with cold and uncharitable suspicions; and to preserve my feet from the snares which were around my path; until, by the blessing of God upon you, and such as you, to whom I was a stranger, I have been brought to the conception and clear conviction of the great lameness and blindness of those who call themselves religious, whom heretofore I idolized, but whom now I take upon me when need is both to reprove and to instruct; and to the discovery of that truth, of which a son of the Calvinistic Church of Scotland should never have been ignorant, viz. the total perdition* of the world and its predestinate destruction . . .

* According to the Brahmin Theology, the Godhead is manifested in Nature in the trinity of ~~erea~~ Production, Destruction and Reproduction:[1] and there is in this a Hint, of which both a philosophic and a christian use may be made. Observe, its place corresponds to that of the Logos μονογένης[2] in the Christian Triad.—Now the proprieties of the Word are expressed in the terms, distinctive, evocative, separative, elective by selection.[3] It is Light, and the preceding are all properties of Light.

50[1] "Estēsismos", an S-T-C-ism, as in **8** at n 1 above, **56** n 1 below.

50[2] "Phalakrinismos (from [Greek] *phalakros* [bald], [Latin] *Calvus* [bald])"—hence a "Calvinism". Cf **8** n 1.

50[3] "Paraphalakrinismos", a going "beyond" Calvinism. C remarks upon Irving's Calvinistic tendencies in e.g. **10**, **11**, **32**, and esp **58**.

50[4] "Irvin[g]ismos", Irvingism, of which C complains in e.g. **42** at n 3 and **43** above. C did not in fact mark any passages with the abbreviations established here.

51[1] Common knowledge, but included in a work annotated by C that has a connection with this note (at n 17), DUBOIS p 367:

"The Hindus understand by the word *Trimurti*, the three principal divinities whom they acknowledge; namely, Brahma, Vishnu, and Siva. It signifies *three powers*, because the three essential energies of *Creation*, *Preservation*, and *Destruction*, severally pertain to these three gods."

51[2] "Only-begotten", as in **2** n 7 above.

51[3] These terms appear to be C's own, though influenced by the language of science, especially the "elective affinities" of chemistry. Cf James Hutton *A Dissertation upon . . . Light, Heat, and Fire* (1794) 50, where Hutton writes of "the elective affection of light".

But then it is Light *in actu*,[4] only where there is Life as the Correlative. The Word (or Logos) indeed hath life *in* itself, but still from the Father.[5] Now in the idea of Life as in all other realities there are two Factors or Constituents, viz. the Ground, and the Form manifesting the *Ground*.[6] Life is the *one*, or Vis unifica,[7] manifested in the Many. (Corollary— Affinity of Life and Beauty. Both are definable, *Più nel Uno*.)[8] The ⟨One (or the⟩ Unificence)[9] is the *Ground*, the Many (i.e. vis distinctio̶n̶guens, expandens, seu exponens, exhibens)[10] is the Form. O̶In whatever Subject, therefore, the *Ground* of Life is not, or no longer is, for that Subject Light ceases to be L̶i̶g̶h̶t̶, constructive, and becomes Destruction. Tha̶te Light, which is the beatitude (visio beatifica)[11] of Spirits—whose Will is the Will of the Father, is a consuming Fire to all Iniquity. The distinctive becomes *separative*, and works in both forms of Indistinction, the liquefying as in *sanies*, and the pulverizing.[12] It is the great Agent in the processes of Sloughing, ejecting, excommunicating: and for each of these we find express declarations in Scripture, and facts equally express and declarative in Nature. But further: every great Epoch of Reproduction, (Re-creation, Re-generation, New Birth) is preceded by a L̶ Destruction. The World (ævum, æon)[13] is brought to an end—a day of Judgement takes place—t̶h̶e̶ a new Ledger or Book of Life is opened, and only the Balance, the Net Profits are carried over. It is rendered highly probable by the recent investigations of Geologists that so it has been in each of the five great Epochs ⟨enumerated by Moses, as⟩ preceding the creation of Man.[14] But most observable, and of most profitable

---

51[4] "Actual, in action".

51[5] John 1.1–4 esp 4, "In him was life; and the life was the light of men."

51[6] As in **29** at n 18 above.

51[7] The "unity-making power".

51[8] "The Many in One", a definition C associated with St Francis of Sales, e.g. in *CL* VI 799, N50 f 31, though no precise source of the phrase has been discovered.

51[9] "One-making".

51[10] A "power differentiating, spreading out or setting forth, showing forth".

51[11] "Vision beatific", as in Milton *Paradise Lost* I 684.

51[12] C is presumably using "sanies" in its medical sense as referring to the serum or watery part of the blood, or to pus. With the "liquefying" and "pulverising" forces cf the account of the process of creation in C's important note of Aug 1818, *CN* III 4418 f 15ᵛ.

51[13] Both *aevum* and αἰων (here transliterated as "aeon"), Latin and Greek equivalents, mean primarily "eternity", thence an age, epoch, eon. The end of an era is associated with the Apocalypse.

51[14] I.e. the five first "Days or Periods" (*CN* III 4418 f 16) recorded in Gen 1. Among the "recent investigations of Geologists", C is probably thinking particularly of A. G. Werner's "Neptunian" system, which describes five distinct periods or epochs in the history of the earth, punctuated by repeated deluges. C would have read about Werner's system and about the disputes between his followers and those of James Hutton with their "Plutonian" theory about the igneous origins of rocks in both scientific and popular periodicals, *Phil Trans RS* and *Ed Rev*. Werner is mentioned in *TL* (1848) 67 as one of those who teach "the original fluidity of the planet".

Observation, is the Fact, that the ~~destructive~~ two great Revolutions, the dread destructive Moments of the existing Epoch, the one recorded, the other predictively denounced, in Holy Writings,[15] present the two ~~modes~~ forms of Death, above-mentioned, the two modes of destructive disorganization; the first, namely, the liquifactive or fluidific, a form of Death which is however the matrix of future Life, & the second, the pulverizing or incinerative Power which is, however, at the same time the purifying, which reduces the substance to a harmony with Light (which *and not the absurd theory* of strait Pores or infinitesimal thoroughfares, is the true ground & right solution of Transparency).[16]—Language bears its testimony/—purus from πῦρ, Fire; while the Greek αγνος, i.e. purus is found in the Latin *Ignis*. The Lamb, Agnus, the spotless, αγνος, ~~and~~ the consuming Fire, and ~~one~~ the purifying Water are one and the same with the Light of Life, the Living Light, whose indwelling Life is the alone true Light of Man.[17] But in the likeness and the difference of Water and Fire a yet deeper Mystery is involved = the suspension, the withholding of Mercy : to the bursting forth of Wrath. In the diluvial Devastation, the Figure of the Son, the Articulation of the Word, is withdrawn; in the *final* conflagration the Will of the Ground is stirred up—the Distinctive Power no longer neutralizes its negative ($-$ Elect? = Oxygen) and positive force ($+$ El? = Hydrogen) but receiving into itself the bitter will of the Ground shall oppose them in the fury of Conflict, the dilative shall be the fuel of the Contractive,[18] and all shall be bound up in the utter darkness, sealed up in Death, & have no *place* more.[19] Yet I doubt not, that God will be glorified therein. The

---

Theological controversies aroused by other geologists are mentioned in *TT* 2 Jun 1824.

51[15] The first was the Flood; the second, destruction in the "lake of fire" (the "second death") foretold in Rev 20.14–15.

51[16] The "absurd theory" that transparency in bodies arises from there being wide gaps between the particles of which they are composed is Newtonian; C had discussed and rejected it in a note written for *Joan of Arc*: *PW* (EHC) II 1112–13.

51[17] C suggests that etymology will support the connections he wishes to establish between purifying fire and water and Christ, the Lamb of God: the Greek *pur*, "fire", is linked to the Latin *purus*, "pure", and the Greek *agnos* (properly ἅγνος, *hagnos*), "unsullied", is associated with the Latin *agnus*, "lamb", as well as

with *ignis*, "fire". C may have been started on this line of speculation by DuBois. It appears in an extended form (with καίω, *kaio*, "burn", and *castus*, "chaste") in *CN* III 4418 f 15ᵛ. On "the Light of Life" see John 1.4, 9.

51[18] C's language here must be interpreted in the light of his expositions of Genesis in terms of *Naturphilosophie* and the Compass of Nature, e.g. BÖHME **95**, **97**; *CN* III 4420, IV 4555. The details of the scheme here coincide not with the earliest versions of the scheme but with the general pattern of the 1820s, in which the eastern pole represents dilation, oxygen, and negative electricity, and the western one contraction, hydrogen, and positive electricity.

51[19] Rev 20.11, "and there was found no place for them".

flameless Fire burns inward: the Contraction is absolute: and for this very cause ɳ there can be no contagion, no pollution. The evil is incommunicable, hath no *objective* Being & by its ~~perfect~~ absolute heterogeneity separated from the Good and immiscible, may be ~~the~~ nevertheless the Hades,[20] the hidden and dark Ground of the Glorified New Earth—the enemy placed for ever under the feet of the Blessed, the elastic Spring of their mystic Dance, the Rebound of their ever fresh Triumph—the Refection[a] of the Light of the Lamb which ~~filleth the Heavens with glory,~~ maketh the City of God resplendent, and filleth it with the reflexes of his Glory.—So it may be—& such are the forms which I seem to see dimly in the Mirror of Symbols, the laws & processes of ~~the~~ corporeal World organic and inorganic, as interpreted by the Revealed Word.—And I speak only as I see—: seeing dimly I speak uncertainly. But most assured am I, that ~~I can~~ Hell cannot be *manifested*, as my friend, Mr Irving, too narrowly interpret~~ed~~ing the last verse of Isaiah, supposes.[21] Can Hades (i.e. αειδης, or invisible)[22] be an Object of Vision? Light in utter darkness.—In this Belief I hesitate not to deem him in *error*; and on the Subject of the *Elect*, a truth in close connection with the Ideas of the Children of Perdition (Election and Damnation are as Construction and Destruction, as above shewn,) ~~I~~ Mr Irving will pardon me that I ~~S~~ hold him in the dark.—But of this momentous Article I will essay to speak what is given to me, on some future occasion; perhaps, as a comment on the Text, All Israel shall be saved.[23]

S. T. Coleridge

P.S. It will be against my will, and foreign to the intention of the concluding Sentences of this Note, if the Ideas there advanced should be ~~exprest with a dogmatic~~ understood as conveying my belief or judgement respecting the State of the Wicked after the dissolution of the material Body. I am content to know, that the result of our mortal probation is that we shall either rise above time, or sink below it; that the former is the ~~th~~ greatest Good that can be proffered~~mised~~ to a rational Creature, ~~as the Object to be desired,~~ the latter the ɱ greatest Evil that can be threatened. More than this it is my knowlege not to know; more than this it is my faith to withhold my thoughts from believing, and to walk humbly with the Lord my God.[24] All the Analogies of this Life make it sufficiently clear, that there is a *Dying* as well as a *Death*, and that from

---

[a] A slip for "Reflection"

51[20] Cf **12** n 4, **42** above; "Hades" is rendered "invisible" at n 22 below.

51[21] Isa 66.24, q by Irving ɪ 18–19 (**9** n 1 above).

51[22] Cf **42** and n 3 above: C reduces

the term etymologically to a negative prefix (ἀ-) before the verb "to see" (εἴδω).

51[23] Rom 11.26.

51[24] Mic 6.8 (var).

such, as have been recovered from Drowning or Strangling we learn, that in the lapses of a few Seconds the Soul may experience what it would take hours to narrate, enough of itself to alarm the indifferent and to scare the Guilty. That Guilt is a Perishing of the Soul on the one hand, and that the Soul is essentially imperishable on the other, ~~and that are~~ both are truths: that therefore, in which alone they can be reconciled, must likewise be a Truth—and this is, that it is an endless Perishing: even as a Body, all attraction having been withdrawn and no retarding medium in existence, must be infinitely falling. Now a truth of Science is equivalent to an historic Fact, only where all the requisite conditions are ascertained and ascertainable, for ~~all~~ the truths of all pure Science are conditional ~~or~~ relatively to their realization: and those of moral Science eminently so. But here the conditions can not be foreknown absolutely. ~~B~~ For all moral purposes, however, it is surely more than sufficient for any mind, capable of being ⟨at all⟩ acted on by motives, to be assured, that endless Perishing must be its fate, if God ~~does~~ should not resume his attracting force: and God has made no such promise—while to regard this truth as not ~~a f~~ equivalent to a future fact,—is the most ~~effectual~~ certain way to render ⟨it⟩ such—and ~~i~~of all preventives of God's mercy ~~the~~ we can conceive none so effectual as the presuming on that mercy as a motive for persevering in wickedness.—But if a man be beyond the reach of motives, all doctrines must be alike inefficacious. But ~~never~~ there are two considerations, which the Moralist and above all a Pulpit Moralist should never lose sight of—first, that motives influence the minds of men not according to their magnitude, but by their clearness, proportionateness to the imagination, ~~a~~ understanding and moral sense of the Individual—and the ~~weight~~ impulsive force increases with the proximity, & the speciality. A threat of giving up a whole City to military execution 30 years hence, if such or such a demand be not granted, will probably not influence any one citizen, as powerfully as the threat of a sound horsewhipping to be administered to *his* particular back & shoulders on the next morning. Secondly, that a far, very far greater share in the determination of mens Actions is attributed to Motives, than either Experience or the principles of Psychology will warrant.[25] The mass of the population are below the influence of motives, and are governed by moods, habits, appetites, passions. A better class

51[25] In a current debate about the role of motives, C maintained a sceptical position. Comments on Edward Williams *An Essay on the Equity of Divine Government . . .* (1809), written in 1815, complain of those "Necessitarians" who discuss a motive as if it were "a *Thing*, that by impact communicated motion, instead of being a mere generic Term" (*SW & F—CC*). Cf *AR* (1825) 67: ". . . the Man makes the *motive*, and not the motive the Man".

are led, often without knowing it, by vivid impressions and a consequent
sensation of restlessness & dissatisfaction with the ordinary or existing
circumstances. And a few do not need motives except under extraordi-
nary pressures: for perfect Love shutteth out Fear,[26] and either contains
or supplies the place of Hope. Lastly, *Motives* are signs of Defect &
Imperfection—and are medicines for Disease not the Food of Health.
                                                          S. T. C.

52   II 350 | Lecture Introductory

That I believe God hath ordained nature in its present form, and estab-
lished it according to its present laws, for the single and express purpose
of shadowing forth that future perfect condition into which it is to be
brought: so that from man down to the lowest creature, and from the
animated creation down to the lowest plant, and from the vegetable cre-
ation throughout the elemental and inorganic world, every thing contain-
eth the presentiment of its own future perfection; hath been so consti-
tuted of God as to be prophetic thereof; and is bearing silent witness to
the redemption and restitution of all things which is yet to be; is in a
state of travail and great sorrow, groaning and wailing till it be delivered
of its immortal birth, in the day of the manifestation of the sons of God.
And herein lies the proper meaning of the word "Nature" (*natura*,
'about to be born'), that it is about to bring forth: not that it is any thing,
but that it is to become by bearing something.

Aids to Reflection[1]

53   II 351–3

* He [Adam] had nothing to desire, nothing to gain; there was provision
for all his wants, and satisfaction for all his desires: and no creature
could be more beneficently created, or better conditioned for standing in
the favour of God; because it was the great experiment, and the great
demonstration, to shew whether any creature in its creation-form can
stand; or whether there be not an absolute necessity that it should fall,
unless otherwise sustained.

* This and the preceding ¶ph. I acknowlege as having been derived
from my conversation, but then by only stating half of what I said M[r] I.
has rendered the opinion liable to great and obvious Objections. By not
explaining what a "Creation-form" as he most uncouthly words it, is,

---

51[26] 1 John 4.18 (var).
52[1] C draws attention to his own
work—*AR* (1825) 244—as the source of

Irving's speculative etymological analysis
of "Nature".

and wherein it consists, by referring it to no ~~idea~~ principle, he has con-verti~~ng~~ed a solving Idea into a bare Assertion, and provokes the question—whether it is compatible with Wisdom and Goodness—to create a creature incapable of standing for the mere purpose of proving ~~that~~ experimentally that what cannot stand must fall. I trust that I can affirm as sincerely as most men, that if only the Ventriloquist Truth makes her words audible, it is a matter of small anxiety to me whether the Voice appears to proceed from *my* mouth or from that of another.[1] But then it must be the *whole* Truth—or as in other instances besides this I ~~shall have~~ by uttering a Truth shall have occasioned the publication of Error.

54   II 353

. . . he [Adam] fell into transgression, subverted the end of his creation, defrauded the Christ of his faithful testimony, and threw off subjection to his Maker: and so the end of his creation, and of the creation of all things here below, was subverted.

Nay! according to Mr Irving (p 351) the end was *answered*![1]

55   II 354–66, referring to II 352–4

[In his exposition of the relationship between Adam and Christ, the Fall and Redemption, Irving describes Adam as potentially "the perfect type of Christ" (352) subjected only to a "test of obedience" coupled with a threat of death (352–3). God's "deeper purpose" reveals itself in the continuation of human life after Adam's lapse; it is "to permit the sin and to over-rule the Fall, to the destruction and extermination of sin" through Christ (353). The "one mighty plan" of God "is, to bring in the Christ through the avenues of sin and the jaws of death, and to establish all things by the method not of first creation, but of restitution" (354).]

N.B. The contents of this & the two preceding pages I neither grant nor deny: for in truth I do not understand them. All I know is, that I cannot express any article of my own faith, nor any opinion of mine, in these words. Nor can I recollect any thing, I have said or written, that could

---

53[1] Cf Truth as "divine ventriloquist" in *BL* ch 9 (*CC*) I 164.

54[1] Preceding **51** textus in the same paragraph: "The Lord, foreseeing and providing against the fall of man, and being thereby about to realize the great birth and manifestation of himself for ever, constituted Adam the type or 'figure,' but certainly not the reality, of 'Him that was to come' (Rom. V.): who was perfect in beauty, and completely accomplished in knowledge for his high place and vocation, not only as the regent of the lower world, but as the image of God, and after the likeness in which God should appear."

have suggested the matter of these pages. One thing, however, seems plain to me: viz. that after the assertion, l. 25 of p. 353, it is an inconsistency in Mr I. to ground his assertion of the actual infliction of everlasting torment on the fact of a Threat not half as clear & unmistakeable as this to Adam was.[1] Strike out the Word, God, and substitute the name of an Individual, and I tremble to think what the Judgement of every upright man would be respecting the character of that Individual as measured by the schemes, stratagems, saying & unsaying, here described and asserted. I should despise myself for a Slanderer if I attributed to Mr Irving the indirect proceedings which he does not hesitate to attribute to God!

In short, in my conversations with Mr Irving I have repeatedly endeavored to fix his attention on that main *hinge* on which my whole System turns, & without which it is worse than senseless, a rank fomes[2] of mischievous errors—viz. that what he calls Creation was the first Act of Redemption: which, of course, supposes an antecedent *fall* (antecedent in order of *Thought*, I mean, not in *Time*—For this Fall at least could not be in time, inasmuch as it was the origin of Time as *contra*distinguished from Eternity.[)] But this was not stuff for the Pulpit: & on this account, tho'.I fully believe not with his own consciousness, my friend always turned short off from my discourse on the Chaos, and the antecedents therein implied & presupposed, as so many hypertheological præterscriptural Sky-scrapers, the mere puff and pride of the Vessel,[3] which he was only too willing to suppose above his comprehension because he saw no motive and felt no impulse to make the attempt. From this one source all his errors & they have been most grievous errors, may be traced & have, in fact, been derived. Hence his ignorance respecting the Absolute, the abysmal Ground of the Trinity—his consequent utter misapprehension of the Trinity of itself, neither apprehending aright the unity or the distinctities—hence his ignorance of the subsistentces in the only-begotten W^{ORD} as the pleroma—and of the Father, as the I AM correlative to the ʽὮν, or HE IS, the Son εν τῳ κολπῳ

55[1] Irving p 353 lines 25–31: "And that they remained and died not, is the proof that God's purpose had not been defrauded altogether, yea, not defrauded at all; that, in fact, he had a far deeper purpose than shewed itself at the first—which was, to permit the sin and to over-rule the Fall, to the destruction and extermination of sin . . .".

55[2] The Latin word means "kindling-wood" or "tinder"; hence, in English medical usage, a substance in which diseases are harboured and breed.

55[3] "Hypertheological" and "praeterscriptural", "beyond theology" and "beyond scripture", do not appear in these senses in *OED*. A "sky-scraper" was, near the end of the eighteenth century, a triangular sail set above the royal yards as a jury rig. Such sails were set only in light airs, and the loftiness of the rig was a matter of pride to sailors.

τοῦ πατρος[4]—hence his fantastic notions respecting an all powerful Personage or Individual whom he calls the Holy Ghost.[5] But uninformed respecting the eternal Actualities & the eternal Realities, their Correlatives, he remains (if more *could* be) even more ignorant of the eternal Possibilities—& therefore of the *possibility* of a Fall, and of the necessary characters of a Fall actualized. Hence Matter, substantiated Matter (or Body in its physical sense as Matter filling a space) Body (in the narrower physiological sense, as Organ), Soul, Spirit—*every* thing! i.e. *systematically.*[6] I begin to fear that I ought to regret my intercourse with Mr I. on his own account. For if he had never been tempted out of the popular way of thinking, & guided wholly & exclusively by his honest feelings & the letter of Scripture, treating each subject as an integer, standing on its own grounds, and exerting its appropriate influences within its own sphere, disregarding its connections with other truths, otherwise than as *one* among others, and thus regarding Theology as a bag of Coins, each of which had a value for itself & might be put out to interest on its own account—he might by his Zeal and exalted disinterestedness and extraordinary eloquence have been the Benefactor of Thousands & Ten Thousands—giving them the medicines, to each what the disease needed, without troubling either the Patients or himself with any SYSTEM of rational Pathology grounded on more general principles of Physiology; and at all events would have avoided the offensive Errors into which a supposed System has seduced him.   *S. T. C.*

56   II 370–3

[Irving quotes Luke 8.6: "And some fell upon a rock; and as soon as it was sprung up, it withered away, because it lacked moisture."] In which words there is contained an important fact in the philosophy of natural history,—that the moisture is the only nourishment of the plant, the earth being but the bed for retaining the water, and conveying it to the roots of the plant . . .

Yet another Παραστησιοσμος, or dimidiation of Εστησῆ's discourse.[1] *Moisture* indeed is a *wide* word, sufficiently so to contain all the elements & conditions of Nutrition. But *Water* as pure Water, is the *medium* of Nutrition but no proper *part* of it: and Water, as a Compound, contains only two thirds ⟨⟨(i.e. Oxygen + Hydrogen)⟩⟩ of the ne food

55[4] John 1.18: "in the bosom of the Father".

55[5] C summarises objections that he has made throughout his annotation, as e.g. 1 above.

55[6] Cf **29** above, at n 12 and following.

56[1] A "perverted Coleridgeism" (cf **50** above) or "a halving of S. T. C.'s discourse".

universally necessary for *all* Vegetables, and only one half of the food indispendsable for the lowest animal.[2] Of the Vegetive Life the Hydrogen is the + or positive Material Factor, and Carbon (which Mr I. has passed over in silence) the − or negative material Factor, with Oxygen as its co-efficient. (Hence Carbonic Acid Gas[3] = Carb. + Oxyg. is the main nourishment of Vegetables.). But of animal Life Nitrogen with Hydrogen as its Co-efficient is the + or Positive Material Factor and Carbon with Oxygen as its Coefficient is the − or Negative Material Factor. So essential is Nitrogen to animal Sustenance that the Vegetables most nourishing to ⟨the⟩ Animal Life of Man contain it—ex. gr. the whole Family of Cole or Cabbage, Grain, Beans &c.[4] The Gluten of Wheat is a semi-animalized Substance.[5] It is a mistake, however, of small importance. Would that all my worthy Friend's Misconceptions of my Conversation had been equally harmless! S. T. C. = Ἐστησε.[6]

57   II 410, referring to II 410–24 | Lecture 1 pt 3 "The Schismatic"

[In a survey of ways in which Satan seeks to undermine religion, Irving analyses the "sectarian" character and contrasts it with the ideal of "the catholic Christian". The sectarian is one "who hath taken up with a part of the Divine word, and resolveth with himself that it is the whole of it" (410). The temptation to fix upon one congenial aspect of Christian doctrine is strong and has led to the formation of many dissenting congregations, but it must be resisted: "Now, brethren, the cure and remedy of all this, and the defeat of Satan under this disguise, is, to labour after the spirit of communion, to hunger and thirst for agreement, to desire peace and to ensue it. To surrender our own selfishness, our predilections for a party, and to seek the bowels of love towards all who love the Lord Jesus in sincerity and truth." (423)]

The pages from 410 to 4~~1724~~ sound, profitable, excellent.—

56[2] Chemical analysis proved plants to be composed of oxygen, hydrogen, and carbon; animals, of oxygen, hydrogen, carbon, and nitrogen ("azote"): see, e.g., a work C is known to have used, W. T. Brande *Manual of Chemistry* (1819). See also Levere esp pp 52–4, 194–200.

56[3] Carbon dioxide.

56[4] In OERSTED **10** (and n 1), however, C cites evidence of the presence of *equal* quantities of nitrogen in the bodies of graminivorous and carnivorous animals.

56[5] The gluten of wheat, described by

e.g. Brande *Manual of Chemistry* (1819) 364, interested C because of its high nitrogen content, nitrogen being associated especially with animals. A comment in BM MS Egerton 2800 f 155^v is explicit on this point: "Nitrogen—not unknown indeed in the vegetable world but yet known only as an alien, an antedated Animal in the ~~Wh~~ gluten of Wheat, which is almost an artefact of man by animal manures".

56[6] "Estēse": see ANNUAL ANTHOLOGY **10** n 3 for the meaning of this version of C's name.

58   ii 418–21

The last mentioned amongst these the fruitful causes of sectarianism is of too great importance, and in too frequent use with Satan, to be slightly passed over amongst the rest, of whose powerful influence it is the manifestation and continuance, in the midst of us: I mean, the number of our sects, which is our shame; for the Christian church was intended to be one: and of which the evil is, that we are all so full of our own peculiarities, and so nourish them in secret, if for certain ostensible ends we be forced to hide them in public, that it is hardly possible for any one born in their bosom not to be reared up with a great pride and favour for this which is our shame. . . . One is trained in the maxim, that all established churches are evil in principle, and only tolerated by Heaven's merciful eye; others are trained into the notion, that all creeds are impositions of ambitious churchmen, and restraints of Christian liberty; others are possessed with the notion, that infant baptism is a vile superstition, and not to be defended upon any ground of Scripture, history, or common sense; others again are taught, that ordination is of no avail unless by the hands of a bishop, and that all others are intruders into the vineyard. And the impurity of all other communions is spoken of as if their own were certainly pure.

My friend has omitted one cause or occasion of Schism, from which his own discourses are not free, and which is a prominent feature in the Ultra-calvinistic ~~Calvinist~~ Preachers and Divines—viz. the delight in stating and enforcing any doctrine, to which they attach a special importance, in assertions the most startling to the minds and most repulsive of the sympathies, of Christians educated into other associations, and accustomed to behold the truth (possibly common to both) in a different costume—Instead of becoming all things to all men,[1] salvâ fide catholicâ,[2] these Divines distinguish themselves by a boastful imperious reassertion in bare sharp and trenchant words of the ⟨very⟩ positions which, they know, excite the repugnancy of the dissentients, and in the form, which ha~~ve~~s given þ occasion and pretext to the rejection of the Doctrine. Ex. gr.—the doctrine, that God both made all men & redeems some, solely for his own glory.—This the Calvinist so states and clothes in such metaphors and phrases, ~~in common~~ familiar of necessity to his Hearer's memory as descriptive of ~~selfish~~ the motives of ambitious vainglorious men, as to have, perforce, the semblance of standing in direct contradiction and oppugnance to the other [? þ] Doctrine, that God is

58[1] 1 Cor 9.22.
58[2] "According to sound catholic faith".

Love and in transcendent Love & Goodness made and redeemed the
world.—Now I could almost pledge myself to set forth the former cal-
vinistic dogma without any disguise, much less suppression of the *truth*
therein, in ⟨such⟩ a form, that no christian would hesitate to adopt the
doctrine at once; and in many instances, with an expansion and clearing
up of his conceptions both of God and the Scheme of Redemption.

S. T. Coleridge

59   II 422–3

This is the spell by which Satan holds such multitudes of them [Dissent-
ers] chained in utter darkness or in twilight; as the spell by which he
binds the churchman is, *"that there is no salvation out of the church"
. . .

* which may be true, the error consisting in taking a part for the
whole—his portion of the Catholic Church for THE Church.—M^r I.
should, however, have prefixed the adjective, Romish, to churchman:
because the Protestant Sects in this Country opposing themselves to &
dissenting from, the English not the Romish Church, the term, Church-
man, ~~wh~~has its sense determined to the Clergy of the Establishment—
who hold no such doctrine, & whom Mr Irving did not intend to charge
with the error. Alas! too many are under a spell of a contrary character—
ultra-tolerance—i.e. toleration of errors as well as of erring *persons*.

60   III 1097 | Discourse 6

To the same great crisis of the destruction of all Anti-Christian power
for ever from the earth, doth the lxxxiii d Psalm refer, where all the
nations and peoples then known . . . take crafty counsel together against
thy people . . . saying, "Come and let us cut them off from being a
nation; that the name of Israel may be no more in remembrance." * And
the same mystery I take to be couched under Ezekiel's prophecy of Gog,
of the land of Magog, the prince of Moab, and Meshech, and Tubal,
who bringeth with him also Persia, Ethiopia, and Libya; Gomer, and all
his bands; the house of Togarmah of the north quarters, and all her
bands; and many peoples with them [Ezek 38.2–6].

* This, this is my grand objection to my friend's whole Scheme, *as
matter for the Pulpit*—. It is all, as Edward Irving's, or Hatley Frere's,
or Mr Drummond's, "I" *takes* it.[1] Now my "I" is as thoroughly con-

60[1] C refers to two of Irving's close as-
sociates. James Hatley Frere (1779–1866),
brother of C's friend John Hookham Frere,
was the author of *A Combined View of the
Prophecies of Daniel, Esdras, and S. John*
(1815). He met Irving shortly after his ar-

vinced, that they doid not *take* it *out of* the Texts, in the first instance; but out of their own fancies/ and thenat ⟨they only⟩ take out out[a] of their Bible what they had themselves put in. I may be all in the wrong. Who doubts it? But still, I contend, that the Press, not the Ministerial Pulpit, should be the Medium for the establishment of this. S. T. C.

61 II ⁻2–⁻1, referring to III 1192–8

[Irving advocates paying attention to the history of the church as illustrated in the three discourses he has just given, for "until we study and understand, and can give some account of the Lord's dealings with his church, his choosing her of his own free grace, his leading and guiding her in righteousness, after she hath been fairly set out by his mighty power; his afterwards leading her into temptation . . . and after long, long ages, his returning to her with the warmth of his first love, that none of his promises to his chosen ones might fail;—I say, until all these his dealings with the outward visible church be understood . . . it will never happen that we shall be able to bear his dealings with us as individuals . . ." (1194–5).]

p. 1192–1198.

If I know my own heart, I have every disposition to give the due weight to the arguments for the practical importance, or rather the indispensableness, of a lively watchful Attentions to the political events of the World as successive fulfilments of this or that supposed Prediction of the same, now in this now in that text of this, or that, or as third, 4th or 5th Prophet.—When an error in the Writings of a Man, whom I respect, flashes upon me, my first thought is to look about & into my own state of opinions, in order to discover if I can, whether it is ⟨not⟩ some Contrary error or defect in myself that has made me so quick in seeing the moat in my Brother's Eye.[1] And truly in this instance, I think, that something of the kind has had place. My position, insulated as it were,

---

[a] The repetition of "out" is probably not accidental

---

rival in London, and by early 1824 Irving had offered himself to Frere "as your pupil, to be instructed in prophecy according to your ideas thereof", as Irving said in the dedication of his *Babylon and Infidelity Foredoomed* (1825). In 1826, C described Hatley Frere as "a pious and well-meaning but gloomy and enthusiastic Calvinist, and quite swallowed up in the quicksands of conjectural prophecy": *CL* VI 557. Henry Drummond (1786–1860), wealthy banker,

politician, and religious enthusiast, was a friend of Hatley Frere and a founder of the "Irvingite" Holy Catholic Apostolic Church.

61[1] This sentence is a reformulation of C's "golden rule" as a reader, "Until you understand a writer's ignorance, presume yourself ignorant of his understanding": *BL* ch 12 (*CC*) I 232. The "moat" alludes to Matt 7.3–4, Luke 6.41–2.

& all my habits ⟨both⟩ of study and of life, have drawn my attention too exclusively to the invisible Church, to the communion of the Individual with the Spirit of Truth, in short, to Christianity as a ~~divine Philosophy and~~ Spiritual Light and at the same time an indwelling Energy from above. I have felt too little respecting the visible Church.—But still, while I earnestly ask for grace to fill up this chasm in my Christian Duties, I find myself wholly unable to reconcile my friend's Doctrines either with the ~~too~~ me palpable sense of the Scriptures, on which he grounds his Anticipations, or with our Lord's solemn declaration, that His Kingdom was not to be of this World.[2] For if the Supreme Power in every Body Politic be bound to act as Vice-roys of Christ, to take the Old & New Testament for ~~their~~ practical Law-book, political, civil and criminal;—and this as a Book of Law & State-policy, and not merely as far as the Bible contains the fundamental *principles* of all Legality; and if (as M[r] I. likewise asserts) the Kings and Rulers of the World are bound to receive the interpretations of this Book, and ⟨the⟩ applications of its Contents from the Pastors of the Church—it would be as [? a bad] rational to assert that George IVth is not King of Ireland because he governs by a Lord-Lieutenant, as to pretend that Christ's Kingdom is not a Kingdom of THE WORLD, i.e. of the Aggregate of civilized States.—My own System of Convictions on this point my honored Friend will find given at large in my, ''Aids toward determining the right *Idea* of the Constitution in Church, and State, with the essential Characters of the three Churches, the National, the Christian, and the Church of Antichrist''[3]—and will therefore have the opportunity of Ascertaining, wherein & how far my Convictions differ from his. S. T. *Coleridge*

62   III [+2–+3], referring to III 1193, completed in pencil

Christ in flesh, and Christ in us, that is the whole substance of our theology, theoretical and practical. But is that all? No, this lacketh the Holy Spirit, and the church which is his temple.

P. 1193. ''Christ in the Flesh: and Christ in us. Is that all?''

Now let me [be][a] permitted to restate & complete the position, thus: ''Christ, ~~th~~ who having taken the Humanity into his Divinity, became Flesh, and ~~as~~ dwelt among Men, a Man, and thus founded ~~his~~ the outward and visible Church as the Witness, and the representative of his Incarnation; and Christ, the Spirit of Truth, dwelling in the Faith⟨ful⟩,[b] and constituting the spiritual and invisible Church, the *center* of which,

[a] Word supplied by the editor   [b] Inserted in pencil

61[2] John 18.36.   **61**[3] *C&S* was published Dec 1829.

even Christ, is over*[a] all, by virtue of his omnipresence." or more briefly—"Christ, who dwelt among Men, and ~~the~~ his visible Church; and Christ, who dwelleth in the Faithful, and the invisible Church"— and then you may annex the *question*: & I will answer it.

IS THAT ALL?

Yes: and till you ~~t~~ can tell me of aught not included in this that is worthy of a place even in its neighborhood, I must persist in declaring, that this two-fold Christ in unity and these two Churches in union, *are* all!—all that remains for one who has ~~not~~[b] renounced the ~~W~~ deceits & vanities of the World, the Flesh and the Evil one!*[c]*—In these volumes I[d] seem to have had suggested to me a reason of Providence for the dim and grasp-eluding revelation of the H. G. as a distinct Δυναμις,[2] or Self-subsistence, in the New Testament. After the Councils of the Church had unfolded the Idea, & the H. Spirit was every where discoursed of as a distinct self-conscious Ens a Deo et Deus,[3] a Sect of Hagiopneumatists[4] arose—& in the middle Age the Followers of Francesco d'Assisi (the Franciscans) were concerned in the plan of a third Gospel, the Gospel of the Spirit, and S[t] Francis was to have been the Incarnation of the Holy Ghost—[5]

*[e]*P.S. ~~As~~ The improved Telescopes have resolved several supposed single Orbs into double Stars[6]—apply this to the fact—that in the Old

* Centrum quod ubique substat = Χριστος[1]

[a] Indicator and footnote added in pencil

[b] C has scribbled over "not" in pencil

[c] Full point in ink altered to ! in pencil

[d] "I", unsatisfactorily written in ink, is overwritten in pencil; the note then continues to the end in pencil

[e] A change of pencil, the writing lighter and smaller, perhaps indicating a later addition

62[1] "The centre which everywhere 'stands under' is Christ."

62[2] "Power", though C uses the term in connection with the Holy Ghost as equivalent to "miraculous Gifts" in FLEURY **100** at n 3.

62[3] A "being from God and [itself] God", as the Word in John 1.1.

62[4] "Holy-Ghost-ists", C's term formed from τὸ ἅγιον πνεῦμα, "the Holy Ghost".

62[5] As in LACUNZA **14**, C associates Irving with the heresy of certain Spiritual Franciscans of the thirteenth century. In accordance with the teachings of the mystic Joachim of Fiore or Flora (d 1202), they believed that they belonged to the third and

final period of history, associated with the Third Person of the Trinity, and that they were destined to convert the world. C would have found a full account of the Joachimites in e.g. J. L. Mosheim *An Ecclesiastical History* tr A. Maclaine (2 vols 1765) I 664–7, 680, 710.

62[6] C alludes to one of the triumphs of contemporary astronomy, William Herschel's cataloguing of over 800 double stars. The sustained metaphor of the telescope in this passage may, however, have been influenced by Irving, who on III 1195–6 says, "They cannot, with the telescope of his word discern the stars; how shall they expect to pry into the pores of their own flesh?"

Testament and the Apocryphal Wisdom of Solomon, the Second Dis-
tinctity in the One God is hidden in the third, viz. the Spirit, while in
the N. T.—especially in the writings of John & Paul, the Spirit, when
spoken of ~~with~~ as a person, seems to be, if not positively identified
⟨with,⟩ yet not clearly distinguished from, the Son—i.e. Christ, assur-
gent, and glorified.—The Telescope of the church has drawn out what
may, I doubt not, be fairly *inferred*, but cannot, perhaps, be coercively
proved from the declarations of the Evangelists and Apostles. And well!
for the Subjective, and the Objective may be made plain to Believers of
average Capacity; but the Objectively-Subjective requires a more steady
Vision and an ethereal atmosphere.

FRIEDRICH HEINRICH JACOBI
1743–1819

Ueber die Lehre des Spinoza in Briefen an den Herrn Moses Mendelssohn. Rev ed. [Anonymous.] Breslau 1789. 8°.

In an appendix to this edition Jacobi translates into German part of Bruno's *De la causa, principio et uno*. See **12**.

Bound as second with MAASS *Versuch über die Einbildungskraft* (Halle & Leipzig 1797). Rebound after C's death, the spine reading: "Maass Versuch | Mendelssohn über die Spinosa | MS Notes by S. T. Coleridge".

British Library C 126 d 15 (2)

Although C was interested in Jacobi as early as 1799 and was acquainted with some of his work then (*C Pantheist* 296–7), the first firm evidence of his possession of this volume occurs in a letter of Sept 1816 to the bookseller Thomas Boosey, requesting "all the works of the *Philosopher*, Jacobi, *except* his Briefe über die Lehre des Spinoza, which I have": *CL* IV 666. C drew upon this work in the *Biographia*, the *Statesman's Manual*, the 1818 *Friend*, the philosophical lectures, and the *Logic*.

MS TRANSCRIPT. VCL BT 21: transcript by EHC.

DATE. The majority of the notes possibly 1812–13, in conjunction with the annotation of SPINOZA, but more probably the summer or autumn of 1815, since the printing of *BL* began in Oct 1815, and *BL* is demonstrably indebted to this work at three points: the paraphrase of Job in ch 10 (*CC*) I 202; the passage quoted from Leibniz in ch 12 (*CC*) I 244–7; and an anecdote about Lessing in ch 22 (*CC*) II 140. The notes on the back flyleaves (**22**, **23**) appear to belong to the 1820s.

COEDITORS. Lore Metzger, Raimonda Modiano.

1   pp xxxviii–xxxix | Preface

* XXXIII. Wille ist reine Selbstthätigkeit, erhoben zu dem Grade des Bewusstseyns, welchen wir Vernunft nennen.

[* Will is pure spontaneity raised to that degree of consciousness which we call reason.]

* Ah! here lies the Difficulty! The Consciousness or Knowlege of a Thing does not affect the essence of the Thing. Now if Spontaneity be not Free Will (as who would attribute Free Will to a Plant, which how-

75

ever according to § 24 possesses Spontaneity = Selbstthätigkeit),[1] how can Consciousness render it so—So 0 + 0, were = 1.—/ N.B. I see the Sophism of this reasoning; but yet it holds good ad hominem

2   pp xliv–l

XLV. Wenn ich antworte, das Prinzip der Liebe sey dasselbige, von dessen Daseyn als Prinzip der Ehre wir uns schon versicherten: so wird man nur ein grösseres Recht zu haben glauben, in Absicht des *Gegenstandes*, den ich darstellen soll, dringend zu werden.

XLVI. Ich antworte also: der Gegenstand der reinen Liebe ist derjenige, den ein *Sokrates* vor Augen hatte. Er ist das Θειον im Menschen; und die Ehrfurcht vor diesem *Göttlichen*, ist was aller Tugend, allem Ehrgefühl zum Grunde liegt.

[45. If I reply that the principle of love is the same as the principle of honour, whose existence we have already ascertained, this constitutes all the more reason to believe in the urgency of the *subject* I intend to present here.

46. I answer as follows: The object of pure love is the same as that which a Socrates had in view. It is the "divine" in man; and it is the reverence for this *divine* [essence] that forms the basis of all virtue and all sense of honour.]

Here Jacobi's Eagle Wing seems to me to flag. The τό Θειον[1] is rather a synonyme than an explanation. Say that the Latter is impossible, as perhaps it is if we understand by explanation a full statement of preceding and co-existing Causes added to an exposition of its Ground—for "God is Love",[2] and therefore Love itself *must* ⟨be⟩ both Ground and Cause, consequently, uncaused and groundless and therefore ungroundable. But still Illustration is possible, both by exemplification, and by proving identity of essence in Modes of Being which have been ordinarily conceived of, as individual and disparate. *Ex. gr.*—Life—the characteristic Epithet of—the *living* God[3]—by which the God of Revelation is contra-distinguished from the Fate and mere τὸ Θεῖον of Greek Philosophy, and the thin abstractions of modern Δεισιδαιμονιὰ.—.[4] For it is actually a Fear, almost a Fright, at the Thought that God *lives*—that

1[1] Jacobi's Preface consists of 23 propositions arguing that man has no free will, followed by 29 defending the opposite position. In §§ 24–5 he states that among finite things one cannot conceive of an absolutely self-subsistent being, still less of a being that is "absolutely dependent". It is an absurdity to think of a being that is completely passive or subject to purely mechanical laws. Therefore each "mechanism is in itself only accidental, and

everywhere a *pure spontaneity* [*reine Selbstthätigkeit*] must necessarily form its basis".

2[1] "The Divine"—from textus.

2[2] 1 John 4.8, 16.

2[3] "The living God" occurs many times in AV, in both OT and NT, but see especially Simon Peter's declaration "Thou art the Christ, the Son of the living God" in Matt 16.16, John 6.69.

2[4] "Superstition." In classical Greek

instead of a logical x y z, ᵃ(which we are compelled by the mechanism of our Reason to postulate, as the ground unconditional of all things, or rather as [? ᴏɴ] the one absolute condition of unity of Thought—i.e. of Reason itself, still however ideal and but an ens logicum et hypotheticum)[5] there is a LIVING God—nay, (to utter the whole Truth so as to prevent the possibility of Mistake, even at the risk of seeming Irreverence, in the style of Luther or Zinzendorf),[6] that there is such a person alive, as God.—and that he has a living Son—and that there lives too a processional Person, the Spirit of and from the Father and the Son, and co-equal with both.[7] It is this δεισιθεότης,[8] this aversion to a LIVING JEHOVA GOD, originating in the heart-hardeneding & soul-blinding Worship of Mechanism, which is the essence of Idolatry & which generates Socinianism, most falsely called Unitarianism, instead of its true name, Unicism.[9]—Now where there is Life, there must be Time—and tho' God is not in Time, yet Time is with God[10]—and the perpetual antithesis, and synthesis of Time and Eternity, or rather the immanence of Time in Eternity, is the Intuition by and in which Love begetting is begotten. Et An Eternal Time is either a sublime Truth, or a blank Absurdity, according as the words are interpreted. Take all Rivers & Seas and the Ocean/ they exist all, at once—but for that very reason, the Rivers flow, and the Seas move in Tides, and the Ocean receives and restores— Even so is Time the filiation & consciousness, the outspoken *Word* of a living Eternity![11] Idolatry and Atheism are close ᴋ akin/ The former gives *Primacy* to Second Causes, the latter *eternity* to them. *S. T. C.*

ᵃ This opening parenthesis and its closing counterpart after "hypotheticum" are written in over original dashes

---

the word—lit "fear of (*or* reverence for) the gods (*or* the divinity)", or generally "religious feeling"—is mostly used in a derogatory sense. The Greek Fathers use it in both a neutral and an adverse sense, most often as "superstition"; it does not occur in Greek NT. For C's play on the word see n 8 below.

2[5] A "logical and hypothetical entity".

2[6] The context here makes it clear that C is referring to the blunt style of these reformers in religion, rather than to particular doctrines. Cf references to Nikolaus Ludwig, Count Zinzendorf (1700–60), as "a man of Genius, tho' somewhat extra-zodiacal" in EICHHORN *Apokryphischen Schriften* 11 and in conjunction with Luther, Calvin, Fox et al in *CN* III 3560.

2[7] The Holy Spirit, a "processional Person" in the sense of the Nicene Creed: "The Lord and giver of life, Who *proceedeth* from the Father and the Son, Who with the Father and the Son together is worshipped and glorified".

2[8] "Fear of God", coined by analogy with δεισιδαιμονία, n 4 above.

2[9] The doctrine that God is only one person. C's coinage, related to "Unicist" in Andrew FULLER 1 n 9 and "Unicity" in *LS* (*CC*) 176; cf "Modern *Unicism* absurdly called Unitarianism" in a letter of 25 Sept 1816 (*CL* IV 687).

2[10] Echoes John 1.1, "and the Word was with God, and the Word was God".

2[11] The underlying structure of the relationship between time and eternity here is

3 pp 25–7

[Jacobi presents himself in dialogue with Lessing.] Diese inwohnende unendliche Ursache hat, als solche, *explicite*, weder Verstand noch Willen: weil sie, ihrer transcendentalen Einheit und durchgängigen absoluten Unendlichkeit zufolge, keinen Gegenstand des Denkens und des Wollens haben kann; *und ein Vermögen einen Begriff vor dem Begriffe hervorzubringen, oder einen Begriff der vor seinem Gegenstande und die *vollständige* Ursache seiner selbst wäre, so wie auch ein Wille, der das Wollen wirkte und durchaus sich selbst bestimmte, lauter ungereimte Dinge sind.

[This immanent infinite cause has, as such, explicitly neither understanding nor will: for owing to its transcendental unity and universal absolute infinity it follows that it cannot have any object of thought or will; *and the power of producing a concept anterior to the concept, or a concept that is anterior to its object and *entirely* self-caused, and similarly a will that acted on volition and determined itself completely, [all these] are mere absurdities.]

* I never could see the force of this Reasoning, nor am I convinced that it was Spinoza's Meaning.[1] He admits an immanent Cause, or Ground, of which all Things, Minds included, are the Consequences—Now how is it more difficult to conceive this Cogitatio infinita[2] producing a collective Thought of the World, than the World itself—or why not, both as one? All that could be fairly deduced would be, that God's Thoughts were not as our Thoughts—i.e. not Anti- but Proto-types.[3] I do not be-

---

C's conception of the Trinity. The antithesis between eternity and time corresponds to that between the Father and the Son in the Trinity. The synthesis between time and eternity, the Father and the Son, is represented by the Holy Ghost, the embodiment of eternal love. The Son, who is identified with the Logos and the Word in C's scheme of the Trinity, represents the "essential Symbol of the Deity", by means of which God "manifest[s] himself to . . . all Creatures" (BÖHME 7) and eternity becomes manifest in the temporal world.

3[1] See Spinoza *Ethics* pt 1 prop 17 scholium: ". . . Therefore the intellect of God, in so far as it is conceived to constitute His essence, is in truth the cause of things, both of their essence and of their existence—a truth which seems to have been understood by those who have maintained that God's intellect, will, and power are one and the same thing. Since, therefore, God's intellect is the sole cause of things, both of their essence and of their existence . . . it must necessarily differ from them with regard both to its essence and existence . . .". Tr R. H. Elwes *The Chief Works of Benedict of Spinoza* (2 vols New York 1951). C's comments on the misrepresentation of Spinoza by Spinozists—and by Jacobi—are elaborated in SPINOZA.

3[2] "Infinite thought": see *Ethics* pt 1 props 16, 30, 31. C also associates the term with Spinoza in BÖHME **10** n 2.

3[3] The prefix "Proto-", "first", indicates priority in time, as in C's use of "archetype" (which also suggests point of origin) in *CL* II 1195 (13 Oct 1806): "But the Thoughts of God . . . are all IDEAS, archetypal, and anterior to all but himself alone . . .". The "antitype" is the "countertype" or correspondent other.

lieve, that Spinoza would have acknowleged the system attributed to him by Jacobi. To me it has appeared, that the peculiarity of Spinosism consisted in making *all* things proceed from the Essence, or Wisdom of God, necessarily:[4] even as the most orthodox admit certain Things to proceed—ex. gr. the properties of Space, and its Figurations, Circles &c—.   *S. T. C.*

I mean, that Spinoza does not, in my opinion, deny the Intelligence of God other than as the word implies Choice and Deliberation—or in short, *passivity* in any sense. His God is severely actus purissimus— Esse absolutum sine ullâ *Potentialitate*.[5]

4 pp 31–3

Ich [i.e. Jacobi]. . . . Was aber die unendliche Einzige Substanz des Spinoza anbelangt, so hat diese, für sich allein, und ausser den einzelnen Dingen, kein eigenes oder besonderes Daseyn. * Hätte sie für ihre Einheit (dass ich mich so ausdrücke) cine eigene, besondre, individuelle Wirklichkeit; hätte sie Persönlichkeit und Leben: so wäre Einsicht auch an ihr der beste Theil. *Lessing*. Gut. Aber nach was für Vorstellungen nehmen Sie denn Ihre persönliche extramundane Gottheit an? Etwa nach den Vorstellungen des Leibnitz? Ich fürchte, der war im Herzen selbst ein Spinozist.

[*I* [i.e. Jacobi]. . . . But as for the one infinite substance of Spinoza, it has no individual or distinct existence taken in itself and apart from particular things. * If its unity (if I may put it this way) had a peculiar, distinct, individual reality; if it had personality and life: then insight would also be its best constituent. *Lessing*. Good. But according to what sort of notions do you assume your personal extramundane God? According to those of Leibniz? I fear that Leibniz himself was a Spinozist at heart.]

* Here again I cannot agree with Jacobi, and wonder that Lessing should have yielded to it. If Insight or Intuition be the highest in the Finite because it passes out of the Finite & partakes of the Infinite, it is impossible that Sp. should not have regarded the Infinite as identical with it eminenter tho' not formaliter.[1] Nothing does Spinoza more zealously forbid, than the conception of God as an Abstraction or Aggregate

3[4] Cf *Ethics* pt 1 prop 16: "Now as the divine nature has absolutely infinite attributes (by Definition vi), of which each expresses infinite essence after its kind, it follows that from the necessity of its nature an infinite number of things (that is, everything which can fall within the sphere of an infinite intellect) must necessarily follow."

3[5] "Absolutely pure action—absolute Being without any *Potentiality*". For C's use of this variant of a scholastic phrase see BAXTER *Catholick Theologie* 1 n 2, *BL* ch 9 (*CC*) I 143.

4[1] "Eminently" not "formally": see BÖHME **12** n 1.

or mode of conception or perception. He is not a category, or to be categorically known.[2]—Now Space is not an ens reale,[3] but the universal Form (Handlungsweise) of sensuous Intuition/ (Anschauung.)[4] Consequently, if I take away the determination = limitation of a Circle or Square, in destroying the act I destroy all/ but suppose Space a reality, by removing the figure, ~~or~~ I should only ~~only~~ remove a negation/[5]

5　p 34

Uebrigens kenne ich kein Lehrgebäude, das so sehr, als das Leibnitzische, mit dem Spinozismus übereinkäme; und es ist schwer zu sagen, welcher von ihren Urhebern, uns und sich selbst am mehrsten zum besten hatte* . . .

[Furthermore I know no philosophical system that coincides with Spinoza's as closely as Leibniz's; and it is difficult to say which author tricked us and himself the most * . . .]

* This might not altogether groundlessly be said of Leibnitz; but surely, if ever Human Being was in earnest, totus et integer[1] in his Conviction of the Truth of his System, it was Spinoza.—[2]

6　p 35

Wenn Spinoza (*Epist.* LXII. *Opp. Posth.* p. 584 & 585.) unser Gefühl von Freyheit durch das Beyspiel eines Steins erläutert, welcher dächte und wüsste, dass er sich bestrebt, so viel er kann, seine Bewegung fortzusetzen: so erläutert Leibnitz dasselbe (Theod. §. 50.) mit dem Beyspiele einer Magnetnadel, welche Lust hätte sich gegen Norden zu bewegen, und in der Meinung stände, sie drehte sich unabhängig von einer andern Ursache, indem sie der unmerklichen Bewegung der magnetischen Materie nicht inne würde.

4[2] *Ethics* pt 1 prop 8 scholium 2. C makes a similar assertion in MENDELSSOHN *Morgenstunden* **11**.

4[3] A "real entity", as in *Logic* (*CC*) 69*.

4[4] *Handlungsweise*, "mode of procedure", "way of dealing with", properly "Tool" as in **15** below. This sentence adopts terms from Kant's first *Critique* with deliberate precision. A note in *BL* ch 12 (*CC*) I 289 shows how conscious C was of departures from Kantian usage elsewhere: "I take this occasion to observe, that . . . Kant uses the terms intuition and the verb active (Intueri, *germanice* An-

schauen) . . . exclusively for what can be represented in space and time. He therefore consistently and rightly denies the possibility of intellectual intuitions." For C's struggles with *Anschauung*, see also FICHTE *Bestimmung* **9**.

4[5] The illustration follows Spinoza *Ethics* pt 1 prop 11; C pursues a similar line of argument in KANT *VS* COPY C **24**.

5[1] "Whole and entire".

5[2] Similar tributes to the "pure spirit" of Spinoza (*CL* VI 893) recur throughout C's work, e.g. *BL* ch 24 (*CC*) II 285, *P Lects* Lect 13 (1949) 384–5.

[If Spinoza (*Epist.* LXII. *Opp. Posth.* pp 584 & 585) elucidates our sense of freedom through the illustration of a stone that thinks and knows that it strives as best it can to continue its motion, Leibniz explains the same thing (*Theod.* § 50) through the example of a compass needle, which desired to turn North, and was of the belief that it turned independently of any other cause, since it was not aware of the imperceptible movement of the magnetic material.]

And is Jacobi's Theory of Freedom, at all different? The Consciousness of *Spontaneity* is no more what we mean by the Free Will, than the Knowlege of the principle of Irritability.[1] Spontanëity in and of itself differs only from Compulsion, as a Necessity ab intra from an equal Necessity ab extra.[2] Freedom as only practically known can only be proved practically.

7   p 46

. . . ich nahm daher Gelegenheit für . . . die Cabbala, im eigentlichsten Sinne, aus dem Gesichtspunkte zu reden: dass es an und für sich selbst unmöglich sey, das Unendliche aus dem Endlichen zu entwickeln, und den Uebergang des einen zu dem andern, oder ihre Proportion, durch irgend eine Formel heraus zu bringen; folglich, wenn man etwas darüber sagen wollte, so müsste man aus Offenbarung reden. Lessing blieb dabey: dass er sich alles "natürlich ausgebeten habe wollte;" und ich: *dass es keine natürliche Philosophie des Uebernatürlichen geben könnte, und doch beydes (Natürliches und Uebernatürliches) offenbar vorhanden wäre.

[. . . therefore I took the opportunity of speaking from the perspective of . . . the Cabbala, in the strictest sense [of the word]: that it was in and of itself impossible to evolve the infinite from the finite or to develop the transition of the one to the other, or their proportion, by means of any formula; and, consequently, that if one wished to say anything about it one would have to speak from revelation. Lessing insisted that he "required everything to be natural"; and I [maintained] *that there could be no natural philosophy of the supernatural and that nevertheless both (the natural and supernatural) evidently existed.]

* This is a mere play on the word, little better than a pun. By natürlich Lessing meant vernunftmässig.[1] Substitute this, viz. *rationally*: and what becomes of Jacobi's repartee? That there can be no *rational* philosophy of the Super-natural?

6[1] C repeats a point made in 1, with the addition of a physical analogue to spontaneity in irritability, i.e. the bodily mechanism of muscular reactions (as opposed to sensibility, which depends upon the nerves): cf *TL* 39.

6[2] "From within . . . from without".

7[1] C asserts that Lessing's "natural" in textus meant "according to reason" and was misconstrued by Jacobi.

8   pp 46–7

Wenn sich Lessing eine *persönliche* Gottheit vorstellen wollte, so dachte er sie als die Seele des Alls; und das Ganze, nach der Analogie eines organischen Körpers. Diese Seele des Ganzen wäre also, wie es alle andren Seelen, nach allen möglichen Systemen sind, *als Seele*, nur Effekt.

[When Lessing wished to imagine a *personal* godhead, he conceived of it as the soul of the universe, and of the universe as analogous to an organism. This soul of the universe was therefore *as soul* only an effect, like all the other souls according to all possible systems.]

This with indeed most of the other essential Thoughts of Lessing has been adopted by Schelling: and ornamented with the splendid mysticism of Jacobi. According to Schelling the inexplicable *Indifference* becomes God, a living Person, by his manifestation in the Universe[1]—Thus tho' the Indifference (Entelechia universalis)[2] is the Ground, yet God as God is an *Effect*—tho' by making God & the Universe one, it may be called sui effectus,[3] or self-caused.

9   pp 106–7

[In a letter to Hemsterhuis—published here in both French and German versions—Jacobi imagines Spinoza's response to Hemsterhuis's *Aristée*:] *Spinoza.* Das *Seyn* ist keine Eigenschaft, ist nichts Abgeleitetes von irgend einer Kraft; es ist das, was allen Eigenschaften, Beschaffenheiten und Kräften zum Grunde liegt; das, was man durch das Wort Substanz bezeichnet; und vor welchem nichts gesetzt werden kann, sondern was Allem vorausgesetzt werden muss. . . . Das Denken, welches blos eine Eigenschaft, eine Beschaffenheit der Substanz ist, kann in keinem Sinne die Ursache der Substanz seyn. Es hängt ab von dem, worinn es sein Daseyn hat; es ist der Ausdruck davon und seine That; und kann unmöglich zugleich dasjenige seyn, was die Substanz in Handlung setzt.

[*Spinoza. Existence* is not an attribute, is not deducible from any power; it is that which constitutes the ground of all attributes, modes, and powers; that

---

8[1] C's generalisation may be based on such passages as the following, annotated in his own copy of J. F. W. Schelling *Einleitung zu einem Entwurf eines Systems der Naturphilosophie* (Jena and Leipzig 1799) i 59 (tr): "as these three steps are distinguishable in the *individual*, they must be distinguishable *in the whole organic nature*, and the gradation of the organisation

is nothing but a gradation of *productivity itself* . . .''. C gives a similar account of Schelling's theology elsewhere, e.g. *CL* iv 873–4; in Athenaeum **8** he complains that Schelling "overlooked the I AM in the Absolute—and then confounded the *Absolute* with *Nature*''.

8[2] "Universal actualisation''.

8[3] "Self-effected''.

which one denotes by the word "substance"; and before which nothing can be posited; rather it must be posited before everything. . . . Thought, which is merely an attribute, a property of substance, can in no way be the cause of substance. It depends on that from which it derives its existence [i.e. substance]; it is the expression of the same and its act; and it cannot possibly be at the same time that which substance sets in action.]

Wherein then does L'Etre, Das Seyn, differ from der Kraft,[1] except as an ens rationis,[2] an abstraction, or generalization?—This Spinoza solemnly denounces.[3] Must not then this "Be" or *Substance*, be a mere Mode of fixing our Thought, a sort of mental Word by & thro' which we represent to ourselves Power or Act generally? I can conceive das Leiden, or Passivity = το πασχειν,[4] as a specific Grade of action; but by no effort can I conceive or imagine action as a mode of passivity, no act having been presupposed.

10   p 109

Beydes gehört im Begriffe nothwendig zu einander; und es ist eben so unmöglich, dass das Denken . . . den Begriff oder die Vorstellung eines Gegenstandes hervorbringe, als es unmöglich ist, dass ein Gegenstand, oder eine Mittelursache, oder irgend eine Veränderung, das Denken im Nichtdenken zuwegebringe.

[Both belong necessarily to one another in concept, and it is just as impossible that thought . . . should produce the concept or presentation of an object as that an object or a mediate cause or any modification whatever should generate thought in the noncognitive.]

But is the modification of the Thought by an Object less incomprehensible than the production of the one by the other?

11   p 254

Daneben lehren mich Erfahrung und Geschichte, dass des Menschen Thun viel weniger von seinem Denken, als sein Denken von seinem Thun abhängt; dass seine Begriffe sich nach seinen Handlungen richten, und sie gewissermassen nur abbilden . . .

[Moreover, experience and history have taught me that man's action depends

---

9[1] Wherein does "Being" (French), "Being" (German) differ from "Power"?

9[2] "A thing of the mind [lit reason]", i.e. not a real thing.

9[3] In *Ethics* pt 1 prop 6 cor, and props 7, 34, Spinoza asserts that substances cannot be products, cannot owe their *being* to anything else.

9[4] The German *Leiden*, "suffering" or (usually in a religious context) "passion", is connected with the Greek *paschein*, "suffer", which is the root of "passion" and "passive". C also uses *paschein* this way in LUTHER *Colloquia* 1.

much less on his thinking than his thinking on his action; that his notions conform to his deeds and, in a sense, only reflect them . . .]

A plausible, but most dangerous, and, *I* think, sophistical, Doctrine. Who knows even in himself how many Myriads of Thoughts may have preceded & produced every Action? May not every Action be to the preceding Thoughts as Ganglions to the Nerves?—

12 p 284 | Extract from Giordano Bruno *Von der Ursache, dem Princip und dem Einem*

Der Begriff der Materie, als eines passiven Wesens, auf diese Weise gefasst, lässt sich mit dem Begriffe des höchsten übernatürlichen Prinzips, ohne Bedenken vereinigen, und nicht allein alle Philosophen, sondern auch alle Gottesgelehrte müssen ihre Stimme dazu geben. . . . Das erste und vollkommenste Prinzip fasset alles Daseyn in sich; *kann* alles seyn, und *ist* alles.

[The concept of matter interpreted thus as a passive thing can doubtless be reconciled with the concept of the supreme supernatural principle, and not only all philosophers but also all theologians must assent to it. . . . The first and most perfect principle subsumes all existence—*can* be everything, and *is* everything.]

It is doubtful Whether*ᵃ* to Bruno or to Jacob Behmen belongs the honor of daring to announce the *substantial* meaning of the (*verbally* by all X̄tns) acknowleged Truth, that God hath the *Ground* of his own Existence in himself, and that all things were created out of the *Ground*.[1]

13 pp 317–18 | ''Diokles an Diotime über den Atheismus''

In den letzten finsteren Jahrhunderten der Barbarey befanden sich Philosophie und Religion in einem so traurigen Zustande; *die Dummheit hatte mit den vortrefflichsten Ideen des Plato und Aristoteles einen so langwierigen und vielfachen Missbrauch getrieben; und dieser Missbrauch gieng zuletzt so weit, dass jeder Versuch, Hand an das daraus entstandene Gewirre zu legen, um es wieder in Ordnung zu bringen, Unsinn gewesen wäre.

[In the final dark centuries of barbarism, philosophy and religion were in such a pitiful state, *stupidity had misused the most excellent ideas of Plato and Aristotle so long and so variously, and this misuse went at last so far that any attempt to deal with the consequent confusion and restore order would have been senseless.]

ᵃ Certainly capitalised, but presumably by mistake, coming at the beginning of a line

12[1] C often affirmed the view that God was ''at once the Ground and the Cause'': see e.g. BÖHME **6** and **35**, FIELD **13**, *SM*   (*CC*) 32; see also *CN* III 4418 esp ff 11ᵛ–12, q below **21** n 6.

* Tis pity, that some one of the countless Despisers and Denouncers of the Schoolmen have not given a detailed proof of their Assertions, a full and fair scheme of the Scholastic philosophy, as far as it *was* philosophy.[1]—For it would be most unjust to bring forward those perversions of it to the defence of the superstitions of the Romish Church, which they were compelled to make in order to procure Toleration for the Philosophy itself.

14   pp 350–1 | Jacobi's commentary on Herder's *Gott*

Wirkliche Gedanken, *ausdrückliches* Bewusstseyn, *Verstand*, ist eine gewisse bestimmte Art und Weise, eine Modification (*modificatione modificatum*) des absoluten Denkens. Das absolute Denken selbst, *unmodifiziert*, (*infinita cogitationis essentia*) wird von der Substanz *unmittelbar* hervorgebracht; alle die verschiedenen Arten des Denkens aber, nur *mittelbar*; das heisst, sie alle können, *unmittelbar*, nur aus dem Endlichen fliessen, und müssen zur *erschaffenen*, keinesweges aber zur *unerschaffenen* Natur gerechnet werden.

[*Real* thoughts, *explicit* consciousness, *understanding*, is a certain particular kind and mode, a modification (*modificatione modificatum* [modified by a modification]) of absolute thought. Absolute thought itself, *unmodified* (*infinita cogitationis essentia* [the infinite essence of thought]), is produced by the substance *unmediated*; all the various modes of thought, however, are produced only *mediatedly*; that is, they all can proceed *unmediated* only from the finite, and must be classed with *created* nature but never with *uncreated* nature.]

But is there not an infirmity of Abstraction in this Consequence? How could Thought exist *essentially* by mere Limit, or Modification? An abstract Circle or Square hath indeed its whole essence in Limitation of Space: because Space itself is if not an abstract, yet a *form*, or mode of perception;[1] but an Orange—a globe of Water—in the former the figure expresses Power, in the latter negation—in neither essence. Add too, that the phantom, Time, is constantly intermingled in the argument, with that which is most opposite to Time tho' produced ⟨from it⟩ by imperfect memory, viz—division. In *our* mind we conceive Being as the Subject, Consciousness as a predicate—but why make it a dividuous Result or Effect? This were *irreligio[u]s*[a] [? Creation/Creatures].—

15   pp 352–3

Nach dem Zusammenhange deiner eigenen Begriffe . . . ist die Vorstel-

[a] Cropped

13[1] C himself attempted to give a fair account of the Schoolmen, notably in *P Lects* Lects 9 and 10 (1949) 265–311.   **14**[1] See **4** and n 5 above.

lungskraft nichts anders als Bewusstseyn; Bewusstseyn dessen, "was jeder Begriff voraussetzt, des *Seyns* oder *Seyenden;*" Bewusstseyn dessen, was allem, auch dem *Denken* seine Gesetze bestimmt . . .

[According to your own concatenation of concepts . . . the imaginative power is nothing but consciousness; consciousness of that "which every concept presupposes, of *being* or *existence*"; consciousness of that which determines the laws of everything including *thought* . . .]

assuredly, Daseyn = Existence, *Seyn* = Being, are abstracta abstractissima[1]—& to *hypostasize* Being, as a *something* prior in nature to Intelligence, Will, and Power, without Will, Intelligence and Power; and yet the ground and continent, or the e nihilo[2] creating cause of Intelligence, Will and Power, is not like the Mysteries of Theism merely above but against and below comprehension. Well does Butler (vide his Fragments found in his Memorandum Books) say:

> The Metaphysic's ~~is~~ but a puppet motion
> That goes with Screws, the *Notion of a Notion*:
> The copy of a copy, and lame Draught
> Unnaturally taken from a Thought:
> Turns Truth to Falsehood, Falsehood into Truth,
> By virtue of the Babylonian Tooth.[3]

All Heresies, religious or philosophical, arise from ~~turning~~ substantiating Abstraction/ mistaking the Tool or rather Handlung's-weise[4] ~~not~~ four[a] the Being—& then again abstracting.

16 p 353

Setzt das Denken deinem Gotte Augen ein? Und woher das Licht in diese Augen, ohne welches auch kein inneres Auge sieht? . . . In Wahrheit, ich verstehe dich nicht. Denn was ist Grundidee des Spinozismus, wenn nicht dieses, dass Gott das ausgedehnte Wesen selbst, das denkende Wesen selbst, das lebendige und handelnde Wesen selbst ist, und man deswegen ihm *unmittelbar*, eben so wenig Gedanken, als körperliche Bewegungen; eben so wenig ausdrückliches Bewusstseyn, als Figur und Farbe zuschreiben könne.

[Does thought give your god eyes? And whence the light in these eyes, without

---

a A slip for "for"

15[1] "The most abstract abstractions".

15[2] "Out of nothing".

15[3] Samuel Butler *Miscellaneous Thoughts* lines 93–6, 101–2, q against Hartley in *BL* ch 7 (*CC*) I 119; the reference

to "Fragments" suggests that C was using Butler's *Genuine Remains in Prose and Verse* ed Robert Thyer (1759) I 233.

15[4] "Mode of procedure" as in **4** above at n 4.

which not even the inner eye can see? . . . In truth, I do not understand you. For what is the basic concept of Spinozism if not this?—that God is the extended Being itself, the thinking Being itself, the living and acting Being itself; and that one can ascribe thoughts just as little to Him *unmediated* as one can ascribe bodily movements; specific consciousness just as little as form and colour.]

O! how much more rationally does St Paul ask—Shall he that made the Eye, not see? he that made the Ear, not hear?[1]—The Greek Philosophers ~~wisely~~ distinguished the Ground from the Thing, by saying, that the Former *was*, the other *had*, such and such Predicate/ Man *has*, God *is*, Wisdom.[2]

17 p 355

[Jacobi quotes Kant in a long footnote, ending with a reference:] Kants einzig möglicher Beweisgrund. S. 43. und 44.

102–103—[1]

18 p 408, pencil | Supplementary remarks on Spinozism

Er [Spinoza] musste eine unendliche Reihe von einzelnen Dingen, deren eins nach dem andern zur Wirklichkeit gekommen war, also, im Grunde, eine *ewige Zeit*, eine unendliche Endlichkeit annehmen. Das Ungereimte dieser Behauptung suchte er durch Gleichnisse aus der Mathematik zu vertilgen, und versicherte, es läge blos an unserer Imagination, wenn wir uns eine unendliche Reihe auf einander folgender . . . Dinge, als eine ewige Zeit vorstellen. Ich glaube aber, es war vielmehr Spinoza, der sich hier durch seine Imagination betrügen liess; denn die Folge, welche in den mathematischen Gleichnissen vorgestellt wird, ist keine objective und wirkliche, sondern eine subjective und blos idealische, die auch nicht einmal idealisch vorhanden seyn könnte, wenn ihr nicht eine *wirkliche* Succession in dem Subject, welches sie in Gedanken erzeugt, zum Grunde läge . . .

[Spinoza had to suppose an infinite series of individual things, of which one after another had attained reality—basically, that is, an *eternal time*, an infinite finite. He attempted to expunge the contradiction in this assertion with similes from

---

16[1] Ps 94.9 (var), q "Against Spinoza and Schelling" in HEINROTH **43**. Paul does not quote the verse, but C may have been thinking of the similar imagery in 1 Cor 12.16–17.

16[2] C refers presumably to the Platonists, e.g. to the distinction between "having knowledge" and "knowing" in *Theaetetus* 197. The distinction between having

and being is perhaps also implicit in C's use of Acts 17.28, "in whom we live and move and *have* our being": *BL* ch 12 (*CC*) I 277–8.

17[1] These are page references for C's edition of Kant *VS* II. The whole passage is quoted (in C's translation) in *BL* ch 10 (*CC*) I 201.

mathematics, and assured us that it lies within the power of our imagination to conceive of a series of consecutive . . . things as an eternal time. I believe, however, that it was rather Spinoza who here let himself be deceived by his imagination; for the succession that is demonstrated in mathematical analogies is not an objective and real one but rather a subjective and merely ideal one that could not even exist ideally if it were not founded on a *real* succession in the subject that conceives it . . .]

Who now makes "einem Sprung über sich hinaus",[1] if not Jacobi? He asserts a *personal* God, whose Thoughts are anterior to Things—now either these Thoughts have an actual Succession in the divine Mind, or else are simultaneous, and yet correspondent to and causative of Succession/ Now either of these Spinoza has ⟨as⟩ good right to predicate of his Gottes'-Gedanken, or "Modi Substantiæ eternæ"[2]—Again, Jacobi will not deny immortality, everlasting Life a parte post/[3] Why should not ⟨that⟩ which *is to* have an infinite Time have *had* an infinite Time, provided the Cause that acts per eternitatem a parte post, be conceived as acting a parte ante?—[4]

19   pp 410–11, pencil

Da Spinoza nun einmal Erfahrungsbegriffe von Bewegung, Einzelnen Dingen, Generation und Succession, zu Vernunftbegriffen erhoben hatte; so sah er sie zugleich von allem Empirischen—*gereinigt*. . . . Auch zu diesen Behauptungen hatten die Scholastiker ihm den Weg gebahnt. Mehrere Lehrer dieser Schule, um dem undenkbaren Begriffe *einer Schöpfung in der Zeit*, welcher allemal entsteht, wenn man die Reihe der Naturbegebenheiten will einen Anfang nehmen lassen, auszuweichen, nahmen zu einer Schöpfung von Ewigkeit her ihre Zuflucht. Wie Spinoza aus der Thatsache, dass die Dinge sich bewegten und gegenseitig veränderten, schloss, sie müssten sich von Ewigkeit her bewegt und verändert haben; so schlossen jene aus der Thatsache einer erschaffenen Natur, dass der unveränderliche Urheber derselben von Ewigkeit her erschaffen haben müsse.

[Since Spinoza had once raised the empirical concepts of motion, individual

18[1] "A somersault". C alludes to p 353 immediately following **16** textus: "Darum musste ich, wenn ich von dem Genusse dieses höchsten Wesens reden wollte, nicht nur diesen Genuss über allen Begriff erheben, sondern ausser allem Begriff kühn hinauswerfen. Mein scharfsinniger Freund Mendelssohn hatte Recht, dieses einen Sprung über sich selbst hinaus zu nennen. [If therefore I wanted to talk about the en-

joyment of the highest being, I must not only raise it above all concept but boldly place it beyond all concept. My shrewd friend Mendelssohn is right in calling this a somersault.]"

18[2] "God's Thoughts" or "Modes of eternal Substance".

18[3] "In a future sense".

18[4] "Through eternity in a future sense . . . in a past sense".

things, generation, and succession to concepts of reason, he saw them at the same time as *purified* of everything empirical. . . . The scholastics had paved the way even for these claims. Several thinkers of this school had recourse to the concept of a creation from eternity in order to avoid the unthinkable concept of *a creation in time*, which originates whenever one allows the series of natural events to have a beginning. Just as from the fact that things move and change in relation to one another Spinoza concluded that they must move and change from eternity, similarly the scholastics concluded from the existence of a created nature that its immutable author must have created it from eternity.]

I cannot see what Jacobi gains by all this—. He shows that an endless Time is undenkbar[1]—well! and so is as himself owns, a Creation in Time. "But the former is absurd"—Nay! replies Spinoza—that cannot be absurd, the contrary of which is clearly absurd— viz—an infinite cause ab eterno[2] uncausative, and a *beginning* of Time in Time.[3] Now whatever can be said to alleviate this, will much more alleviate the other—According to me Time *begins* perpetually, it being the necessary manifestation and *life* of Eternity, which implies Time as its Consequence even as Time implies Eternity as its Ground[4]—and I persevere in affirming with an intuitive certainty that the fault is in your Enthralment to your Senses, and sensuous Imaging, that you first *divide* time from Eternity, & by mincing it into moments oppose it, ως αλλο γενος,[5] and discontinuous to the Continuous, and then draw forth the absurdity which yourself had thus put in—

20   p 414

An Nachfolgern hierin hat es ihm nicht gefehlt, und noch giebt es mehrere sehr Achtungswürdige Philosophen unter uns, welche den Begriff einer *wirklichen* Schöpfung *wirklich* einzelner* successiver Dinge *von Ewigkeit her*, für einen möglichen Begriff halten.

[He [Leibniz] did not lack followers in this respect, and there are still several very estimable philosophers among us who hold that the concept of a *real* creation *from eternity* of *real*, individual,* successive things is a feasible concept.]

* The question rests on the meaning attached to the word "einzelner".[1]
In order to bring the point in dispute within Reimarus's demonstration[2]

19[1] "Unthinkable"—as in textus tr.
19[2] "From eternity".
19[3] For the substance of the argument C seems to be drawing on Spinoza's Letter xxix (to Meyer, 20 Apr 1663). Jacobi provides the reference to Spinoza's letter in a footnote on p 410.
19[4] See 2 and n 11 above.
19[5] "As of another kind".

20[1] "Individual"—as in textus tr.
20[2] The demonstration occurs in H. S. Reimarus (1704–68) *Abhandlungen von den vornehmsten Wahrheiten der natürlichen Religion* (Hamburg 1754) pt i "Vom Ursprunge der Menschen und Thiere" esp pp 50–9. In pp 57–9nn Reimarus quotes from works by Leibniz and Wolff, who shared the view that the concept of an infi-

of the impossibility, at least, irrationality of an infinite number (infinite a parte ante)[3] it would be necessary, me quidem judice,[4] to prove that every individual Thing is, and must be, likewise dividuous—not only distinct, but separate. Now this not only can not be *proved* a priori, or ex termino,[5] but seems to contradict our closer examination of the "forma nascendi, et existendi"[6] of the Things themselves: and thus the Notion would be reduced to an ειδωλον φαντασιας, the Creature des *Absehens*, nicht der wirklichen *Anschauung*[7]—not of positive Perception, but of non-perception—even as we see an empty Space, because we do *not* see the Air and Motes which fill it—.

21   pp 415–16

Ich habe schon . . . hinlänglich dargethan, dass der Begriff von Ursache, in so fern er sich von dem Begriffe des Grundes unterscheidet, ein *Erfahrungsbegriff* ist, den wir dem Bewusstseyn unserer Causalität und Passivität zu verdanken haben, und der sich eben so wenig aus dem blos idealischen Begriffe des Grundes herleiten, als in denselben auflösen lässt.

[I have already . . . sufficiently demonstrated that the concept of a cause, in so far as it is distinct from the concept of a ground, is an *empirical concept*, which we owe to the consciousness of our causality and passivity, and which can be just as little derived from as dissolved into the purely ideal concept of a ground.]

I believe the very Reverse: viz—that we trans-imaginate[1] our own Causality into the phænomena of Nature. Besides, to conjoin is not of necessity to confound the ideas of Ground and Cause—In a finite Intelligence I find a Cause, ~~without~~ that is not a Ground: but when I assume an infinite infinitely powerful Will, as das absolutes[a] Seyn,[2] or God, the Ground is likewise the Cause—and as these are in God *essentially* united, whatever must be predicated of the former cannot be incompatible with the latter—therefore as we must admit an eternal Grounding,

---

[a] A slip for "absolute"

---

nite number—whether infinitely small or infinitely great—was a pure fiction invented by mathematicians and had no basis in reality.

20[3] "Starting from the beginning".

20[4] "In my opinion, at least".

20[5] "From the end".

20[6] "The form of coming into being, and of being". The source of the phrase is not known.

20[7] "An 'image of fancy', the Creature 'of observation [looking outward], not of true intuition [looking inward]' ". For the significance of *Anschauung* see **4** n 4 above; *eidolon* occurs repeatedly as the antithesis of *idea* in C, e.g. *SM (CC)* 101.

21[1] To transfer or project by imagination—not in *OED*, though "imaginate" appears as an obsolete sixteenth-century usage. C uses "transimagine" in GREW **3**; for other compounds with the *trans-* prefix see DONNE *Sermons* COPY A **4** n 6.

21[2] "The absolute Being".

we cannot deny an eternal Causing[3]—Q.E.D.—P.S. Yet I am very far from asserting the *semperfuity*[4] of any created Being, and regard æviternity[5] as the incommunicable attribute of the Son of God and the Spirit proceeding thro' and from the filial Logos—and am fully persuaded that "Beginning" is the necessary Form under which Dependence must appear to all dependent Beings[6]—in other words, no Creature can conceive of God as his ground without conceiving of him at the same time as his Cause.

22   p +2, numbered "2" by C

Readers of my Logic, or the method of legitimate Thinking and Discoursing,[1] who yet expect to find short and easy ~~instruction~~ Receipts how to think without thinking at all—how to think without thought— how many! *Alas!*   S. T. C.—

In order to understand by the Rule you must first understand the Rule—and in order to ascertain this, it would be will[a] to know what you mean by Understanding in general—And this is one ~~of the~~ main Object of the present work.—

But who does not *know* this? Be it so. I say nothing to the contrary: and therefore I have not required you to *learn* what you ought to mean or should hereafter mean, but to know consciously what you actually, tho' without that ⟨reflective⟩ attention which constitutes distinct consciousness, always have meant by it. I know much that I do not understand; but to understand what I know (scire me scire)[2] is the end of all ~~speculative~~ *Science*, (for Instructions, of which this is not the end, may be called Arts, Methods, Rules, Ways, &c; but cannot be named Sciences) and the aim of all liberal Education, ⟨as far as the Intellect is concerned⟩. The very word implies it—for the mind is *educed*,[3] drawn forth, ~~and~~ or developed, in exact proportion as the consciousness is extended—[b]a truth of unspeakable Light [. . .] of human Life a [. . .]

[a] A slip for "well"

[b] The rest of the note is written vertically in the gutter; some words have been lost, or rendered illegible, in rebinding

21[3] See **12** n 1 above.

21[4] "Always-was-ness"—not in *OED*.

21[5] An obsolete equivalent to "eternity", *aeternitas* being an elided form of *aeviternitas*.

21[6] Cf *CN* III 4418 ff 11ᵛ–12: "That the matter of the Universe had no beginning is Atheism—that Beginning had no beginning, may be nonsense, at least like every form of an infinite series, utterly transcendent—but it does not alter the essential character of the dependent. Still all that has been, is, or will be, had, have, and will have, a Beginning, save God alone."

22[1] The *Logic*, for some state of which this note, pub *Logic* (*CC*) lxi, may have been intended.

22[2] "To know that I know".

22[3] For C's concept of education as "*educing* the faculties, and forming the habits" see *SM* (*CC*) 40, *C&S* (*CC*) 48.

23   p⁺3ᵃ

⟨A beautiful allegory of Persian Wisdom—its analogy to Prometheus—
to Satan or Lucifer—&c.⟩¹ Anahid, the Egyptian Nëith, the Greek
Athenè = Logos, Verstand²—Harut and Murat, who obtained permis-
sion to descend from heaven & become incarnate as Men,³ in order to
try the sensualᵇ nature & the possibility of its Subordination to the Spir-
itual—But they became sensually enamoured of bringing with them *the
holy Word* (Idea, Λογος πρωτογενης)⁴ by which they descended & were
enabled to re-ascend—But they became sensually enamoured of Ana-
hid, who gave them hopes of yielding herself to their embraces, on con-
dition of their communicating the Holy Word—. Instead of trying they
tempted.—⟨&⟩ They gave the Word to Anahid—which instantly was lost
to them, forgotten—and in the same instant, Anahid soared to the Morn-
ing Star (Phosphor)⁵ & with her harp strung with Sunbeams plays to the
spheres, the Goddess of Love & Order.—H. and M. = Reason &
Will.—

ᵃ This note is written in a larger hand than **22**
ᵇ The figure "35 = 2" written in the margin after these words is presumably a binder's mark; cf
"35 = 1" on MAASS ⁻3

23¹ C's interest in the Prometheus myth
in the versions of different cultures belongs
especially to the 1820s, with his own essay
On the Prometheus of Aeschylus read to the
Royal Society for Literature in 1825 (*SW &
F*), his assistance in HC's Prometheus proj-
ect (*CL* v 142–3), and references to Pro-
metheus in *AR* (1825) 277. Here Prome-
theus is identified with Lucifer (Satan) as
"Light-bearer": in *TT* 8 May 1824, C re-
fers to Prometheus as "the Redeemer and
the Devil jumbled together".

23² "Understanding". C names deities
identified with knowledge in different my-
thologies—the Greek Athene and Egyptian
Neithe corresponding to the Persian god-
dess Anahita, whom the Greeks identified

variously with Athene and Aphrodite
(Latin *Venus*, in n 5 below).

23³ In the second book of the Koran,
Harut and Marut are two angels sent to ad-
minister justice on earth. They fall in love
with a mortal woman, Zohara, who asks
them to tell her the secret name of God.
When they do so, she is carried up into
heaven as the planet Venus, but they are
imprisoned in a cave. RS's version of the
story in *Thalaba* iv names the angels Ha-
ruth and Maruth.

23⁴ The "first-born Word".

23⁵ "Phosphor", "Light-bringer", the
Greek equivalent to the Latin *Lucifer*
(above), is the planet Venus as Morning
Star.

Friedrich Heinrich Jacobi's Werke. Vols I–III (of 6). Leipzig 1812, 1815, 1816. 8°.

Columbia University Library

All three vols were cropped in rebinding, but the pages containing C's annotations were folded in to avoid mutilation. Columbia University Library bookplate in each vol.

CONTENTS. I 1–226 *Allwills Briefsammlung*; 227–324 *Zugabe. Sendschreiben an Erhard O***; 254–324 *Zufällige Ergiessungen eines einsamen Denkers*; 325–404 *Vermischte Briefe*. II 1–310 *David Hume über den Glauben, oder Idealismus und Realismus. Ein Gespräch*; 311–23 *Ueber die Unzertrennlichkeit des Begriffs der Freyheit und Vorsehung von dem Begriffe der Vernunft*; 325–411 *Etwas das Lessing gesagt hat. Ein Commentar zu den Reisen der Päbste*; 411–55 *Ueber das Buch ''Des lettres de Cachet'' und eine Beurtheilung desselben*; 455–501 *Einige Betrachtungen über den frommen Betrug und über eine Vernunft welche nicht die Vernunft ist*; 501–13 *An Herrn Friedrich Nicolai in Berlin*; 513–44 *An Herrn Laharpe, Mitglied der französischen Akademie zu Paris*. III [iii]–xxxvi "Vorrede"; 1–57 *Jacobi an Fichte*; 59–195 *Ueber das Unternehmen des Kriticismus, die Vernunft zu Verstande zu bringen*; 197–243 *Ueber eine Weissagung Lichtenberg's*; 245–460 *Von den Göttlichen Dingen und ihrer Offenbarung*; 461–568 *Briefe an Verschiedene*.

MS TRANSCRIPT. University of Vermont. W. G. T. Shedd's copy of the *Werke* with his transcript of C's marginalia written on slips of paper pasted in at the appropriate places in the text.

DATE. Sept 1816 to c summer 1817. C ordered these volumes on 4 Sept 1816 (*CL* IV 666) and evidently had them by him (at least) when he was preparing Vols I and II of *The Friend* (1818) from Dec 1816 to about May 1817. The small number of marginalia and the absence of connections between the annotations and the traces of the *Werke* in C's published works and notebooks is perhaps explained by the exceptional amount of writing he had in hand until the end of the lectures in 1819, and by his rapidly declining interest in Jacobi's work.

COEDITORS. Lore Metzger, Raimonda Modiano.

1   I 113 | Cläre to Sylli 29 Mar

Ach, Sylli! Warum hat allein die *Seele* Flügel! . . . Dein guter Plato spricht zwar von einem Schrinnen und Jucken an der Stelle der Flügel, welches ein Zeichen des Losklebens seyn soll. . . . Aber ich glaube fast, der gute Mann hat uns das nur zum Zeitvertreibe erzählt; denn, wenn es wahr wäre, wie lange hätten wir beyde, Du und ich, nicht schon andre als diese ärgerlichen Gänsefedern, womit wir so leidig zu einander kommen.

[Ah, Sylli! Why has only the *soul* wings! . . . Your excellent Plato, it is true, speaks of a smarting and itching of the wing area, which is supposed to be a sign of unfolding. . . . But I almost believe that this excellent man has only told us this for fun; for if it were true, would not both you and I have long had other quills than these exasperating ones that so inadequately bring us together?]

A modest conclusion verily: and a little characteristic of philos. *Square* (v. Tom Jones) who is a little ch. of F. H. Jacobi.[1] But the fault deserves to be *taken out* of F. H. J., and personified in novel or Drama, as the self-delusion of mistaking psychological notices for Conscience. akin to the preposterous position of invisible and imponderable Excitants (ex. gr. the Elect., Galvan., and Zōomagnetic) for the Excitable (Lebenskraft, anima vitalis, vital Principle.)[2]

2   II 107, pencil

Wie die den äusseren Sinnen sich offenbarende Wirklichkeit keines Bürgen bedarf, indem sie selbst der kräftigste Vertreter ihrer Wahrheit ist; so bedarf auch die jenem tief inwendigen Sinne, den wir Vernunft nennen, sich offenbarende Wirklichkeit keines Bürgen: sie ist ebenfalls selbst und allein der kräftigste Zeuge ihrer Wahrheit.

[Just as the reality revealing itself to the external senses needs no proof, because it is itself the strongest guarantee of its truth, similarly that reality which reveals itself to that deep inner sense which we call reason needs no proof; it too is in and by itself the strongest testimony of its truth.]

Is this consonant with fact? Is not Perception *demonstrably*, i.e. by historic facts which the senses themselves convey to every man who traces the process of Seeing, Hearing, &c in an infant, *an art* in which the particular acts are any thing rather than immediate? Is not every the most trifling act of Perception the result of an Enthymeme, Seclusion, Inclusion, Conclusion/[1] & the first (Seclusion, Theilen) an Act of Comparison—& therefore Urtheilen?—[2]

1[1] C's FIELDING annotations express his admiration for Fielding's work, in particular *Tom Jones*, where "the philosopher" Mr Square is one of Tom's two tutors. His position is summed up in *Tom Jones* bk 3 ch 3: "In morals he was a profest Platonist, and in religion he inclined to be an Aristotelian." Square, however, does not take Plato very seriously: he regards morality as a matter of theory only, and turns out to be one of the lovers of Molly Seagrim.
1[2] In N36 f 5 (29 Nov 1827), C makes a similar point: "Strange! that so many in-

genious men should ⟨not⟩ have detected the confusion in their minds between *the Life*, and the various agents that excite a Living Body to manifest its Life!" The sequence "Electric, Galvanic, Zōomagnetic" represents a rising series in the differentiation of life towards individuation, "zoomagnetism" being used as equivalent to "animal magnetism" or mesmerism. The terms "Life-force, vital spirit, vital Principle" are approximate synonyms.
2[1] An enthymeme is a syllogism in which one term is unexpressed—described

3 ii 208, pencil

Sie wissen, wir sind darüber eins geworden, dass zu unserm menschlichen Bewusstseyn . . . ausser dem empfindenden Dinge, noch ein wirkliches Ding, welches empfunden wird, nothwendig sey. *Wir müssen uns von Etwas unterscheiden.* Also zwey wirkliche Dinge ausser einander, oder Dualität.

[You know we have come to agree that our human consciousness . . . requires in addition to the percipient a real object that is perceived. *We must differentiate ourselves from something.* Hence two real, separate things, or duality.]

Ja! μ muss aber etwas wirklich unterschiedenes vorhanden seyn? Wenn Cogito, ergo sum, bündig ist—Hoc cogito, ergo est, wäre eine schlechte Logic.[1]

4 ii 217, pencil

[In the context of objections to the Kantian deduction of categories:] Ich bin alles, und ausser mir ist im *eigentlichen* Verstande Nichts. Und Ich, mein Alles, bin denn am Ende doch auch nur ein *leeres Blendwerk* von Etwas; *die Form einer Form* . . .

[I am the all, and nothing other than myself exists in the *actual* mind. And I, my All, am yet also in the end a mere *empty illusion* of something; *the form of a form* . . .]

Kant was analysing not Human Nature, but the speculative Intellect. And what, in all grace, can Speculation be but *Form*? What can a Thought be but a Thought? Of all men, Jacobi with his Faith of and in Reason ought to have been the last man to have made these Objections.[1]

more fully in *Logic* (*CC*) 56 as "a mere abridgment in the verbal stating of a syllogism, the mental process being taken as understood. . . . The omission is in the words only by which the mental process is conveyed." The sequence clusion, inclusion, conclusion is discussed in *Logic* (*CC*) 138.

2[2] *Theilen*, to divide or separate (into parts); *Urtheilen*, to judge, but literally to make a first discrimination. In *CN* iv 5123 f 106 (11 Feb 1824) C ascribes to Gassendi's *Syntagma philosophicum* the phrase "bene proponere" and explains it as "der richtige *Ur*theilen, the right placing of a thought before the Mind in its *original* or primary component *parts*, of Subject and Predicate".

3[1] "Yes! but must something really distinct be there? If 'I think, therefore I exist' is valid—then 'I think this, therefore it exists' would be a poor [piece of] Logic." C generally treated the Cartesian *cogito* as tautological, e.g. *Logic* (*CC*) 85.

4[1] Jacobi (pp 216–17) had objected to Kant's statement that "our senses teach us nothing at all about the properties of things" and that the understanding concerns itself not with things-in-themselves but with "*entirely subjective* intuitions" produced "according to *entirely subjective* . . . forms". Kant thereby, he argues, takes away all certainty from both sensibility and the understanding and "completely eradicates all claims to knowledge of truth". Kant's table of categories is a mere

5 iii 42–3, pencil

Ist das Höchste, worauf ich mich besinnen, was ich anschauen kann, mein leer und reines, nackt und blosses Ich, mit seiner Selbständigkeit und Freyheit: so ist besonnene Selbstanschauung, so ist Vernünftigkeit mir ein Fluch—ich verwünsche mein Daseyn. . . . Nie habe ich begriffen, wie man in Kants kategorischen Imperativ . . . etwas geheimnissvolles und unbegriefliches finden, und es unternehmen konnte, nachher, mit diesem Unbegreiflichen, die *Lückenbüsser* der theoretischen Vernunft zu Bedingungen der *Realität* der Gesetze der praktischen zu machen.

[If the highest thing upon which I can reflect, which I can intuit, is my empty and pure, naked and mere I, with its self-sufficiency and freedom: then reflective self-consciousness and rationality is a curse to me—and I curse my existence. . . . Never have I understood how one could find something mysterious and incomprehensible in Kant's categorical imperative and could subsequently use this mystery to turn the conditions of the *reality* of the laws of practical reason into a *convenient substitute* for theoretical reason.]

And what is Jacobi's Mystery? Is it not the Organ of spiritual Truth? And what is this but the *real* Ich, that shines thro' the *empiri⟨c⟩al* Ich[1]— the coincidence of which with the former is categorically demanded./ Kant's sublime Mystery is one and the same with Jacobi's unintelligible revealed mystery, the very revelation of which is most mysterious. Jacobi too often betrays a captious, envious, bissigen Geist.[2]

6 iii 195

Wahrheit, *Schönheit* und *Tugend*! Mit ihnen treten wir ins Reich des Göttlichen, des Unvergänglichen; ohne sie, ins Reich des Niedrigen, Verschwindenden, Gemeinen. So gewiss es etwas Wahres, Schönes und Gutes giebt; so gewiss giebt es einen Gott. Zu ihm führt alles, was über die Natur erhebt; der Geist des Gefühls; der Geist des Gedankens; unser inwendigstes Bewusstseyn. Sein Daseyn beruht uns nicht auf einem Wunsch; es ist das Sicherste und Gewisseste, aus dem unser eignes Daseyn hervorgieng: Unsterblichkeit beruht nicht auf einem müssigen Postulat; wir fühlen sie in unserm freyen Handeln und Wirken. Wir brauchen sie nicht zu erringen durch das Gute, weil sie uns mit demselben eigenthümlich angehört; wir können sie nur verlieren durch das Böse, und sie mit Kunst und List aus unsrer Erinnerung vertilgen.

"logical play with knowledge" (*ein logisches Erkenntnissspiel*) through which "the general human understanding . . . is mocked, as in Hume".

5[1] I.e. the necessary conjunction of "the *real* I" (the ideal I) with "the *empirical* I".

5[2] A "snappish" or "stinging" spirit.

[*Truth, Beauty,* and *Virtue!* With them we walk in the realm of the godly, the immutable; without them, in the realm of the low, the changing, the mean. As surely as there exists a true, a beautiful, or a good, there exists a God. Everything that rises above nature leads to him; the spirit of feeling, the spirit of thought; our most inward consciousness. His being touches us not whimsically; it is the surety and certainty from which our own existence stems: immortality rests not upon an idle postulate; we feel it in our free acts and works. We do not need to win it through the Good, because it already belongs to us originally; we can lose it only through evil, and through eradicating it by art and cunning from our memory.]

To kick at a dying or dead Lion is but an asine*a* Trick![1]

It is most remarkable, that neither Jacobi should have seen nor Schelling reminded him, that in a critical analysis of the *speculative* Intellect KANT *could* do no otherwise than ~~state~~ ground the Belief of Reason as ~~a Postulate~~ he did.—But in his Critique of the *Practical* Reason does he then represent this Faith as deriving its ~~force~~ Rights from "a lazy Postulate"?[2] O Shame to Jacobi! O Shame & double Shame to Schelling, his Antagonist! For he knew & had himself pointed it out.[3]

S. T. C.—

7 III ⁻1, referring to III 282

[Jacobi quotes Matthias Claudius's characterisation of Christ:] "Ein Erretter aus aller Noth, von allem Uebel; Ein Erlöser vom Bösen;—Ein Helfer, der umher ging und wohl that, *und selbst nicht hatte wo er sein Haupt hinlege!* um den die Lahmen gehen, die Aussätzigen rein werden, die Tauben hören, die Todten auferstehen *und den Armen das Evangelium gepredigt wird.* Dem Wind und Meer gehorsam sind, und—*der die Kindlein zu sich kommen liess, und sie herzete und segnete . . . . .*[b] der keine Mühe und keine Schmach achtete und geduldig war bis zum Tod am Kreuz, dass er sein Werk vollende;—der in die Welt kam die Welt selig zu machen, *und der darin geschlagen und gemartert ward und mit einer Dornenkrone hinaus ging!*"

---

[a] For "asinine"?   [b] Points of ellipsis thus in original

6[1] Schelling accused Jacobi of launching his attack on Kant's theory of knowledge when Kant was dying: see n 3 below.

6[2] "Einem müssigen Postulat"—in textus. C refers to Kant's claim that "the moral laws do not merely presuppose the existence of a supreme being" or the idea of immortality, but also "justify us in postulating" them. *C d r V* B662 tr Norman Kemp Smith; see also *Critique of Practical Reason* esp bk 2 ch 2 §§ 4–6, where the argument is that although such ideas cannot be proved in the sphere of theoretical knowledge, in the sphere of moral laws reason postulates them as originally legislative.

6[3] In SCHELLING *Denkmal* 54–61 (not annotated) Schelling said that after Fichte and others had challenged the critical philosophy, after Herder had published his *Metacritique*, and when Kant was close to death, Jacobi, no longer able to withhold "the fire burning inside him", directed upon Kant the attack that Hegel described as snappish, malicious, and false. See also 5 n 2 above.

["A deliverer from all ill, from all evil; a rescuer from wickedness;—a helper, who went around doing good, *and yet he himself had no place to lay his head!* around whom the lame walk, the lepers become cured, the deaf hear, the dead are raised, *and the Gospel is preached to the poor.* He whom the wind and the sea obey, and—*who allowed the children to come to him, and embraced them and blessed them* . . . he who despised no trouble and no shame and was patient unto death on the cross, in order to complete his work;—he who came into the world to make it holy, and *who there was beaten and martyred, and went out with a crown of thorns."*]

282, Ideal of Christ

8 III ⁻1, referring to III 314–15

Nach seinem Urtheil ist es eitel Prahlerei und Heuchelei mit *Unverstand*, wenn Jemand versichert, in Absicht aller Meinungen, diejenigen, welche *intolerant machten*, allein ausgenommen, tolerant zu seyn. Denn ein solcher sagt damit entweder: Er sey vollkommen gleichgültig gegen alle Wahrheit, und finde nur die Meinung von dem hohen Werthe derselben, und dem Vorzuge einer Ueberzeugung vor der andern unerträglich; oder er redet Unsinn. Was nicht *widersteht*, *besteht* auch nicht: jedes Widerstehen aber ist zugleich ein Angreifen. Was widerstehend besteht, schliesset aus. . . . Wer, dies erkennend, jedem seiner Mitmenschen, wie sich selbst—*die Befugniss der Intoleranz* zugesteht—der allein ist *wahrhaft* tolerant; und auf eine andere Weise *soll* es niemand seyn; denn eine wirkliche Gleichgültigkeit in Absicht aller Meinungen, da sie nur aus einem durchgängigen Unglauben entspringen kann, ist die schrecklichste Entartung menschlicher Natur.

[In his judgment it is vain boasting and *ignorant* hypocrisy if someone claims to be tolerant of all opinions excepting only those which *make him intolerant*. For such a person says by that either that he is completely indifferent to all truth and finds an opinion of the high value of truth, and of a preference for one conviction over others, unbearable; or else he talks nonsense. For that which does not *contradict* also cannot *assert* anything: every contradiction is at the same time an assertion. That which asserts by contradicting also excludes. . . . He who, knowing this, grants to each of his fellow men, as to himself, *the right to intolerance* is alone *truly* tolerant; no one *should* be tolerant in any other way. For a real indifference to all opinions is the most appalling debasement of human nature, since it can only spring from a thorough lack of faith.]

314. Toler. and Intolerance—¹

9 III ⁻1, referring to III 322 footnote

Es ist eine Bemerkung von Wichtigkeit, dass jeder unmittelbare Gegen-

---

8¹ See *Friend* (*CC*) I 96, where C agrees with Jacobi that "the only true spirit of tolerance consists in our conscientious toleration of each other's intolerance".

stand eines natürlichen Triebes, gleich dem Leben—das bei den unver-
nünftigen wie bei den vernünftigen Wesen die Prärogative, sich als
Selbstzweck zu setzen, oder *für sich zu seyn*, mit sich führt—um sein
selbst willen, und nicht wegen seiner Wirkungen . . . begehrt wird.

[It is an important observation that each immediate object of a natural instinct,
like life—which in non-rational as well as in rational beings entails the prerog-
ative of setting itself as *an end in and for itself*—is desired for its own sake and
not for its effects.]

322. Self-proposing or categorical Nature of every immed[iate][a] object
of a natural Instinct—

10 III ⁻1, referring to III 387

Er [der Naturalist] muss nie reden wollen auch von Gott und göttlichen
Dingen, nicht von Freiheit, von sittlich Gutem und Bösem, von eigent-
licher Moralität; denn nach seiner innersten Ueberzeugung sind diese
Dinge nicht, und von ihnen redend sagt er, was er in Wahrheit nicht
meint.

[He [the naturalist] must never speak of God and the divine, nor of freedom, of
moral good and evil, of true morality; for according to his innermost conviction
these things do not exist, and in speaking of them he says what in fact he does
not mean.]

387 Mem Schelling has right on his side: This is a most intolerant, in-
human, yea, *Dominican* Passage.[1]—What? the Herculean Intellect of
Kant[2] could deceive itself, & innocently—& not the ποιηται of Philos-
ophy, the εποπται φυσεως ὑλοζωικης?[3]

11 III 493, cropped | To J. G. Herder

Dass Sie, mein liebster Herder, das *Gesetz* der Lessingschen Expansion
und Contraction Gottes noch nicht einsehen, glaube ich gern. . . . Sie
[diese Idee] ist alt asiatisch. . . . Lässt Gott seinen Othem ausgehen, so

---

[a] Letters lost in binding

10[1] Schelling in *Denkmal* 17–18 (not
annotated) quotes this passage from Jacobi
and finds it most offensive in casting the
naturalist unfairly in the role of a liar who
denies all difference between right and
wrong, good and evil. C's view of the Do-
minicans as inhumane bigots appears in
e.g. Baxter *Reliquiae* COPY B **105** at n 1,
RS *Wesley* **48**.
10[2] In *Denkmal* 52, discussing Herder's
reply to Kant, Schelling refers to Kant as
"diesen *Herkules unter den Denkern*"—

"this *Hercules among thinkers*".
10[3] The "poets" of philosophy, the
"seers of hylozoic nature". For *epoptae*
see Böhme **47** n 5. Of the "hypothesis of
Hylozoism"—the view that matter (ὕλη) is
endowed with life (ζωή), or that life is
merely a property of matter—C was gen-
erally less tolerant than he appears to be
here, saying in *BL* ch 8 (*CC*) I 131–2 that it
is "the death of all rational physiology,
and indeed of all physical science".

werden die Dinge; zieht er ihn zurück, so *vergehen* sie. . . . Auch der Gedanke von einer wechselsweise einschlummernden und wieder erwachenden Gottheit findet sich bey ältesten Morgenländern.

[That you, my dear Herder, do not appreciate the *law* of the expansion and contraction of Lessing's God, I readily believe. . . . It [this idea] is an old Asiatic one. . . . As God's breath goes out, things *come into existence*; as it is drawn back things *disappear*. . . . The idea of a deity that alternately induces sleep and waking is also to be found among the earliest oriental peoples.]

Jacobi can never rise above the mechanical.*

* He seems always to have the Image of an Ocean before him, surging itself into forms. The begetting, the creating, these are above him.[1] Either the Allmight[2] has no distinct sense or is [? mat/most]*a*

---

a Remainder of note lost in cropping

11[1] Cf C's comments on Jacobi *Ueber die Lehre* **2**.

11[2] C uses "Allmight" of God also in Böhme **6** at n 5.

JOHANN JAHN

1750–1816

Appendix hermeneuticae seu exercitationes exegeticae. . . . Vaticinia de Messia. 2 vols. Vienna 1813, 1815. 8°.

The title given on the first page of the text of each volume is *Exercitationes exegeticae in vaticiniis Messiam promittentibus*.

Not located. Published from MS TRANSCRIPT (*a*).

MS TRANSCRIPTS. (*a*) VCL LT 50(j), in the hand of Mary Pridham Coleridge and initialled by her "M. C." The transcript is wrapped in a letter from DC to SC on which Mary Coleridge has written: "The notes from S. T. C. are furnished by Dʳ Wright—not LLOYD". (*b*) VCL LT 44: another transcript, by DC, evidently based on TRANSCRIPT (*a*) but provided with textus and textus tr; this version was used in *NTP* 135–9.

TEXTUS TRANSLATION. *NTP* 135–9, slightly modified.

DATE. Possibly Nov 1819 (4), though the date may be part of C's fabrication.

1 I 62 | Exposition of Mal 2.17–3.6 and 3.13–14

[Footnote to I 62:] . . . Ceterum si quaeritur, qualem illi antiqui Hebraei animo conceperint hunc legatum Jehovae et simul Jehovam: id unum responderi potest certum, non credidisse duos deos; cetera conjecturis nituntur . . .

[But if it be inquired what conception those ancient Hebrews formed of Him who was at once the messenger of Jehovah and Jehovah himself, this only can be replied with certainty, that they did not believe in two gods: all else rests upon conjecture . . .]

Why is it *necessary*, on what grounds of psychology is it *rational*, to demand an answer to the question, in what distinct Conceptions the more spiritual Israelites under the Law, and of the Prophetic Æra presented to themselves the Idea of the Word of God, that *was* (i.e. was not a mere verbal Abstraction) and yet was not a Creature contra-distinguished from God! The great *Idea* possessed all the Faithful, but before the coming of Jesus few, perhaps not One, possessed the Idea. Our Sailors—nay, whole Nations believe with equal liveliness their moral responsibility, and yet their predestination—how many Thousands without having once asked themselves, how the two are to be reconciled.[1]—

1[1] C makes a similar remark in a letter of 1810 to Thomas Poole (*CL* III 282): "There is a beautiful remark on this in Beattie's Immutability, concerning the

101

The Jehovah, the Jehovah *Word*, the Name, the Angel of the Presence (i.e. inseparably present) was a sacred *Tradition*, a treasured *Prophecy*[2]—a mysterious cypher in which all treasures of all knowledge were contained, but by Involution.

This view of the Doctrine of the Trinity, as a *Prophecy*, and like the great Prophecy of the Redemption, proceeding from dim Dawn to full Noontide, is a most important Analogy.   S. T. Coleridge.

Take an Acorn—and consider it in its successive growth as the Object of Watchful Attention.—It is *one*—but lo! it is becoming many—Nay, it still remains One—&c &c till at length the full Idea of the Oak is mastered—the original *Unity* becoming more & more intense, as the Distinctity becomes apparent.[3]

2 I 63

. . . hinc adventum legati divini, Hebraeis foederati, ad templum suum, cogitabant talem, qualis locis aliis non paucis memoratur adventus Jehovae, quo tamen non amplius significatur quam eminens quaedam operatio Jehovae. . . . Atque in hoc non errabant, sed id, quod erat praecipuum, negligebant, de adventu Messiae esse sermonem, et Messiam dici Dominum templi et legatum foederis, atque venturum, ut alias Jehova venturus dicitur.

[. . . hence the coming to his temple of the divine messenger, covenanted to the Hebrews, was thought of as similar to that which in not a few other places is mentioned as the coming of Jehovah, by which, however, no more is meant than some eminent operation of Jehovah. . . . And in this they erred not, but failed to discern what was of most importance, that the discourse was concerning the coming of Messiah, and that Messiah is called the Lord of the Temple and the Messenger of the Covenant, and that he would come, as elsewhere it is said that Jehovah would come.]

They erred in *this*: that the one series[a] of Instances could be easily rec-

---

[a] Transcriber first wrote "source" and crossed it out

---

faith of Sailors in Predestination, & yet equally in their free-agency & moral responsibility." C was probably combining Beattie's occasional illustrative use of sailors with the passage on fate and free will in which Beattie maintains that uneducated people in general display equally strong attachment to ideas of moral liberty and of fate: *An Essay on the Nature and Immutability of Truth* (1770; 2nd ed 1771) 354–5.

1[2] This sentence gathers together OT words and phrases associated with the prophecy of a messiah. The tradition that the Jehovah of the OT was the Word of the NT is alluded to elsewhere, e.g. BIBLE COPY B **11**; "the name of the Lord" appears in e.g. Exod 33.19; "the Angel of the Presence" in Isa 63.9 (var). There is a similar cluster of terms in BROWNE *Works* **39** and n.

1[3] C's defence of his coinage "distinctity" is quoted in a note to *C&S (CC)* 118–19 n 2. Cf his trinitarian use of the term in IRVING *Sermons* **39, 55**.

onciled with, & received their full & legitimate explanation out of the other, viz: the Jehovaship of the Messiah/ but the other not without the most outrageous laxity of interpretation reduced to the former.[1]

3 ɪ 104[a] | Exposition of Dan 9

[Jahn explains the prophecy in Dan 9.24–7 as an answer to Daniel's prayer in 9.4–19.]

And JOHN JAHN professes to *believe*, bonâ fide, this to have been a genuine Prayer!* of an *inspired* Prophet![2] and that Prophet the great DANIEL!!—Nay, John Jahn! by thy own sound and extensive Learning, and by all the flashings of shrewd *Sense*, that break forth from thy Comments, *I* profess, that I am *hard* of belief in this thy profession!— but I am fully persuaded, that thou art or wert, Philos. et Theol. &c. &c &c &c &c &c &c &c &c &c &c &c &c &c at VIENNA!!—[3]

S. T. Coleridge

* It has all the flaccid flabby verbosity of the Rabbinic *Romance*. Just like our *Agadoth* or early Volksmärchen, The Seven Champions &c.[1]

4 ɪ (perhaps flyleaf) referring to ɪ 234 | Exposition of Zach 10.12

. . . *nam corroborabo eos per Jehovam* (per me), *et in nomine eius* (meo) *ambulabunt, est effatum Jehovae. Ambulare venit pro agere*, adeoque *sensus est: in nomine meo agent, seu gerent bella. Maccabaeos prae reliquis omnibus in nomine Dei, seu ad tuendam religionem suam bella contra Syro-Macedones gessisse, monitione non indiget.*

[*For I will strengthen them through Jehovah* (through me) *and in his* (my) *name*

---

[a] In both MS TRANSCRIPTS this appears as the first note without a page reference; it seems likely that it was written on a flyleaf

2[1] The Jehovahship of Messiah cannot be reduced to "some eminent operation of Jehovah", but eminent operations of Jehovah can be explained in terms of the Jehovahship of Messiah.

3[1] C suggests that the popular narratives of different cultures share certain qualities of style. He offers as examples *Volksmärchen*, German "folktales"; children's stories such as "The Seven Champions" that C loved as a boy and always defended (e.g. *Lects 1808–1819—CC*—ɪ 278); and traditional Jewish narratives such as the *Haggadoth* (pl of *Haggadah*) and the "Specimens of Rabbinical Wisdom" that he translated in *Friend* (*CC*) ɪ 370–3.

3[2] Jahn does not actually "profess to *believe*". Without questioning the authenticity of the prayer, he notes (p 104) that many interpretations of Dan 9.24–7 have been offered, but many critics have neglected the connection of 24–7 with Daniel's speech in 4.19 and the occasion of the speech and the prophecy in 9.1–3. Jahn gives his own translation and exposition of 9.1–23.

3[3] C mocks the four lines of degrees and distinctions attributed to Jahn on the title-page, beginning "Philos. et Theol. Doct., Eccl. Metropol. ad S. Stephanum Viennae Canon. Capit."

shall they walk, said Jehovah [Zach 10.12]. *Walk* is for *act*, so the meaning is: they shall act, or wage war, in my name. That the Maccabees beyond all others waged their wars against the Syro-Macedonians, in the name of the Lord, or to defend their religion, needs not to be called to mind.]

234. et passim, imo, *ubique*[1]—the sad squinteyed application of great absolute truths & assurances to particular (sometimes inappropriate, but when appropriate, yet still *particular*) Instances. As if one were to apply the Laws propounded by Alpinus, Franklin, Oersted, Sir H. Davy, Faraday &c &c,[2] as of exclusive application to the steeple of St Bonifaces Church destroyed by Lightning in the Parish of Mudworth in the County of Rutland, Nov 9, 1819—[3]

Doubtless, the Maccabean Victories & Defeats were included in the prophecy, as far as the Prophecy included them: & no further. And verily the petty insurrection of a Province against a despot Overlord in defence of its own privileges or prejudices, are when tolerably successful, matters worthy of Record: ex. gr: those of *Biscay*, and of Catalonia against the encroachment & faith-breach of the Spanish Crown.[4] But was it necessary, that each should have been antedated some 3 or 4 hundred years by an especial Gazette in the Future Sense? Never can I attribute *Faith* in the highest Sense, viz: the Union of the finite individual Will with the Reason, and the willing Subjection of the individual UNDERSTANDING to the Reason, as the Representative of the Absolute Will, (as such therefore, the one UNIVERSAL Reason)—never can I attribute

---

4[1] "And here and there, indeed, *everywhere*".

4[2] This list of pioneers in the investigation of electrical phenomena begins oddly with Prospero Alpini (1553–1617), physician and botanist, whose discovery of the sexual differentiation of plants later provided Linnaeus with the basis for his comprehensive classification. Benjamin Franklin (1706–90) showed that lightning was electricity by flying kites in thunderstorms; Hans Christian Oersted (1777–1851), physicist and chemist, whose *Ansicht der chemische Naturgesetze* C annotated, founded the theory of electromagnetism; C's friend Humphry Davy (1778–1829), chemist, showed that chemical affinity was an electrical phenomenon; Michael Faraday (1791–1867), who began his career as assistant to Davy and made many fundamental discoveries in the theory of electricity, established the principle of electromag-

netic induction.

4[3] Apart from the name of England's smallest county, the details of this circumstantial example are C's comic invention.

4[4] Both the Basques (C uses "Biscay" in a collective sense) and the Catalans proudly resisted the assimilation of their ancient languages, laws, and customs. In the thirteenth and fourteenth centuries the Basques, as they lost some of their main strongholds to the growing power of the Castilians, forced the Spanish king to grant them democratic rights that they had traditionally enjoyed. The Catalans, although united with Aragon by marriage in 1137, rebelled against the mounting power of John II of Aragon in 1461–72; although the rebellion failed in the end, the Catalans declined to join the union of Aragon and Castile because of centralising policies of the Spanish king that would have destroyed their cultural identity.

Christian FAITH in this, its only legitimate sense, to the Man who confounds PROPHECY with PROGNOSTICATION, degrades the former into the latter, and places Moses, Isaiah, & Jeremiah, on the same Bench with Merlin and Nostradamus![5]   S. T. Coleridge—

5   II 219–21 | Exposition of Gen 3

[Footnote 9:] . . . Nunc ea in vicinia arboris dormiente, serpens more suo arborem conscendit, atque strepitu et sibilo occasionem somnio praebuit; evigilans mulier conspexit serpentem . . .

[Footnote 15:] . . . *vox vel sonitus Jehovae* potest quidem significare strepitum ambulantis, alias tamen denotat tonitrua, quae etiam h. l. intelligenda esse videntur, inprimis cum mox *timor* hominum commemoretur.

[Now she sleeping near the tree, the serpent after its manner climbed the tree, and by its noise and hissing gave occasion to a dream; the woman awaking saw the serpent . . .

. . . *the voice or sound of Jehovah* many indeed signify the noise of one walking, yet elsewhere it denotes thunderings; and this seems to be the meaning in these lines, especially since soon afterwards the *fear* of the man and woman is mentioned.]

P. 215–228.[1] ως εμοιγε δοκει[2] it is all over with a literal Interpretation, when the Interpreter is forced to play the Interpolator—ex. gr. to choose to assume, that Eve had selected the Forbidden Tree as the shady Bower for her Afternoon *Siesta*, fell asleep, and *dreamt* that she saw this & heard that!! and then that all the aweful Catcnation[a] of Words and Thoughts from v 11. to v 20 was *suggested* to Adam and Eve by a Peal of Thunder acting on an alarmed conscience—No! if an *historical* interpretation be any way practicable, it must still be as *mythic*[b] History— Adam and Eve must represent together with their Eden the *first* Race of Mankind[3]—and the primeval State viz: the horticultural or fructivorous—& must comprehend an indefinite & number of generations.—

[a] MS TRANSCRIPT (*a*) reads "Catination"
[b] The transcriber's original attempt at this word has been crossed through and is not legible

4[5] Merlin and Nostradamus are used as generic names for magicians, who are not to be confused with the prophets of the OT: cf C's similar use of their names together in EICHHORN *Alte Testament* **48**.
5[1] C's page numbers refer to the whole of the section devoted to an exposition of Gen 3.5–8, but the remainder of his note deals specifically with the textus supplied.
5[2] "As it seems to me, at least".
5[3] C offers such an interpretation in *AR* (1825) 250n–5n.

The History of the Hebrew Commonwealth, from the earliest times to the destruction of Jerusalem A.D. 72. Translated from the German [by Calvin Ellis Stowe] . . . with an appendix, containing a continuation of the history of the Jewish people to the time of Adrian. Vol I (of 2). Oxford 1829. 8°.

Pub May 1829 (*EC*). Revised from first American ed, Andover, Maine, 1828: see **2**.

British Library C 43 b 23

On I 25 a Hebrew word has been corrected in pencil, possibly by C. Passages are carefully marked in pencil in the margins of I 30, 31, 32, 33, 35: these marks do not appear to be C's. A few of the annotations have been slightly cropped in rebinding.

DATE. After May 1829, probably late 1829 after *C&S* had gone to press but before the publication of the 2nd ed of *C&S* with chapter divisions in Jan 1830 (**15** n 1).

A   p vii, pencil

History gives no knowledge of any people who have preserved a separate and distinct existence for so long a period, and at the same time maintained, <u>for substance</u>, most of their religious rites and customs.[1]?

1   I 31, pencil, slightly cropped

. . . he who alone is God . . . the God over all, who can neither be seen, nor represented by any image . . . this only true God was set forth by Moses, the mediator between God and the Hebrews, as their national and tutelar Deity.

See Gosp. of Joh[n] *I. 18.*[*][1]

[*] That the Word, the Son, the Icon (i.e. the living and substantive Image, the Divine Alterity), the Glory of the Father—all names of the same purport and implication was the Jehovah of Abraham, Moses and the Prophets,[2] that Christ was in the wilderness[3]—is not only positively

---

A[1] See **2** textus.

1[1] "No man hath seen God at any time; the only begotten Son, which is in the bosom of the Father, he hath declared *him*": an especially important text in C's trinitarian theology, as his gloss in IRVING *Sermons* **1** demonstrates.

1[2] Something has gone wrong with the syntax here—perhaps "was" should have been "as"?—but the basic position is clear. C suggests, as in JAHN *Appendix* **2**, that the Logos of the NT is one with the

asserted in the Writings of S[t] Paul,[4] but it is every where supposed as the ground of his reasoning. This mediatorial character in Jehovah is an additional argument.   S. T. [C.]

2   ı +3, pencil

Can the Translator be an Englishman?—the first page of the preface presents a *"for* substance":[1] and p 34. *obligated*!![2]

OXFORD!—[3]

Theological Seminary? Andover.

Calvin E. Stowe—not a Clergyman of the Established Church surely? And who is Professor Stuart?[4]

   The Book is *printed* by Tallboys of Oxford—But for whom?[5]

No *Oxford* Publisher—!—No London Publisher!

All this *looks* very like a *Purpose.*

Laughable!—& it is a Reprint of An American Work after all![6]—I should have remembered the proverb, Look before you leap—/

3   ı 56, pencil

As each tribe had its own magistrates and representatives, and administered its own affairs, each composed an entire political community, in some respects independent of the other tribes. . . . Hence it is evident that the Hebrew constitution authorized each tribe to provide for its own interest; or, if the strength of any one of them was insufficient for this

---

Jehovah of the OT. He lists other names of the Logos—"Icon" or Εἴκων, as in LEIGH-TON COPY B 11 and elsewhere; "Alterity" or "Otherness" as in *C&S* (*CC*) 84.

1[3] The period of Christ's temptation in the wilderness, recorded in Matt 4, Mark 1, Luke 4, is perhaps introduced here to emphasize his "mediatorial" humanity.

1[4] C is probably alluding to Col 1.13–20, in which Christ is "the image of the invisible God, the firstborn of every creature: For by him were all things created . . .". C quotes and discusses this passage in *SM* (*CC*) 44–5.

2[1] See A above.

2[2] Jahn p 34 reads: ". . . pagan religions obligated no man to worship this or that particular deity, much less all deities without exception". C objects to the same usage in 8 below.

2[3] On the title-page. See n 5 below.

2[4] The "Advertisement" of pp [v]–vi is signed by Calvin E. Stowe and dated from the Andover Theological Seminary 7 Nov 1828. Stowe (p vi) expresses his obligations to "Professor Stuart" of the Seminary, who encouraged Stowe's work and who wrote and signed the Preface (pp [vii]–x).

2[5] The imprint reads: "Oxford printed and published by D. A. Talboys".

2[6] A footnote to the Preface (p x) reads: "In this edition the whole has been thoroughly revised, and such alterations made as seemed requisite to render the Author's meaning clear and intelligible. The American edition indeed was so totally unfit for English readers as to make this absolutely necessary."

purpose, to unite with some of the other tribes and make common cause with them.

This may explain the neglect in providing a Successor to Joshua.[1] Yet as the result proved, it was a defect in the Mosaic Constitution: for which many causes might be assigned—the want of a central city being one. The want of a common Senate, or Amphyctyonic Council,[2] was severely felt likewise.

4 I ⁺4, referring to I 67,[a] pencil, cropped

It is worthy of remark, that the cloud which hung over the sacred tabernacle, and by its rising and setting determined the marches of the Israelites, did not supersede the necessity of another guide, who could conduct them to the secret fountains, the concealed wells, and the distant pastures of the desert.

P. 67. The great distinction of the Hebrew Religion did not consist in the want of a visible Symbol of their tutelar God—for the Sacred Fire, that preceded the Ark, in a column of flame, & (by day) of smoke, w[as] the Symbol of Jehovah[1]—but in this, that they were forbidden to identify the Symbol and the Power, whos[e] presence it signified. They dared not worship the Sign[.][2]

5 I 80–1, pencil, slightly cropped

As the Hebrews, in the course of time, became continually more obstinate in their idolatry, so each subsequent oppression of the nation was always greater and more severe than the preceding. So difficult was it, as mankind were then situated, to preserve a knowledge of the true God in the world; though so repeatedly and so expressly revealed, and in so high a degree made evident to the senses.*

* The question is and by thinking readers ever has been—*Could* this have happened, if the Hebrews had understood the Supreme Being by their Jehovah; if at any time the People had been brought to consider the

---

[a] Written above 15

3[1] The interval between Joshua's death and the rise of Samuel the prophet is recounted in Judges as six cycles of revolt, chastisement, and deliverance after Joshua had led the children of Israel across Jordan, and had captured Canaan and divided it among the tribes. St Paul summarises the period of leaderlessness in Acts 13.18–20, ending: "And after that, he gave unto them judges, about the space of four hundred years, until Samuel the prophet."

3[2] Usually "Amphictyonic", referring to the semi-annual representative assembly of confederated Greek states at Thermopylae and Delphi.

4[1] Exod 13.21–2.

4[2] Because of the prohibition against idols (Exod 20.4–5).

tutelary Gods of the surrounding Nations as non-entities; if in short it had not been considered by them as a question of superior Strength— which of the Gods was the mightiest? The answer is by another question—With the Records of Moses and the Book of the Law, read and expounded to them, how *could* they have been ignorant that the God of Abraham, Isaac and Jacob was the Creator of the Heaven and Earth, the alone God? The difficulty must be solved by the sensuality and unfaithfulness of their Learned Clas[s,] [P]riest and Genealogist.[1]—S. T. C.

6 I 89, pencil

* These times [i.e. the period of Judges] would certainly not be considered so turbulent and barbarous, much less would they be taken, contrary to the clearest evidence and to the analogy of all history, for a heroic age, if they were viewed without the prejudices of a preconceived hypothesis.

* What must we say then to those who urge the contrast between the number and excellence of the Artists who labored in the construction of the Ark &c under Moses, and the entire want of the most common Artificers under David, and the total dependence on the Tyrians?[1] Does not this argue an antecedent period of Barbarism?

7 I 98–9, pencil

Saul's great failing, and the source of all his errors, was, that he did not sufficiently give way to the theocratic nature of the Hebrew constitution. He thus rendered himself unfit to be the founder of a royal house, as his conduct could not be regarded as a pattern for the imitation of his successors.

God forgive me if it be an evil thought! But had I read the same account in any profane history I should not have scrupled to consider the deposition of Saul as the result of the theocratic Party's jealousy of their own diminishing influence. How much less heavy do these transgressions of Saul seem than those related of David!—

8 I 106, pencil, cropped

The rulers came with the whole army to Hebron, David <u>obligated</u> himself by an oath . . .

5[1] Cf Jahn p 46: "The *shoterim* (*genealogists, officers,*) are also mentioned with the elders . . .".

6[1] Exod 35.7 describes the building of the tabernacle under the direction of Moses; for the building of his temple, Solomon called in the Tyrians "as thou didst deal with David my father" (2 Chron 2.3).

Is this [gr]oss Vulgarism [so] naturalized [in] America, [t]hat even men of Learning adopt it?[1]

9 I 146–7, pencil, cropped

. . . he [Hezekiah] afterwards received from the same prophet [Isaiah] a divine promise of recovery, and of an addition of fifteen years to his life. For the confirmation of this promise, the king requested a miracle, and, accordingly, the shadow of the style went back ten degrees on the dial.

To convert clear predictions honorable to the sound Judgement and pre-science of the Sacred Augur & State-Censor [i]nto prodigies of prognos-tication,[1] irreconcilable with the [f]ree-agency of Man, by antedating an Oracle 3 or 4 [c]enturies is an easy contrivance, & of no rare occurrence [in] Greek & Roman History—but to do this when the Book itself de-clares the contrary—(*Here* end the Prophecie[s] of Isaiah (Ch. 40))[2]— & when all the following chapters by the clearest internal evidence prove themselves to have been delivered by an Exile to Exiles during the Cap-tivity—thi[s] is a flight above common![3]   S. T. C.

10 I 232, pencil

These . . . include the high priests of the Jews and Samaritans, who, as the chief magistrates of their people, are called kings, in the same man-ner as other rulers, by an historian who would not stop to inquire whether they really had the regal title, and mentions nothing respecting them but their splendid turbans (infulas).

Infula = a Turban?—!![1]

11 I 232, pencil, cropped | Continuing **10** textus

Though the meeting of Alexander with the Jewish high priest is passed over by historians, as *too trifling to be mentioned in comparison with so many other greater events, yet the whole narration of Josephus well corresponds with the impetuosity of temper, and superstitious trust in oracles, for which Alexander was remarkable . . .

8[1] Cf C's objection in **2**. The *OED Sup-plement* suggests that after the eighteenth century this use of the verb was "chiefly dialect and U.S. colloquial".

9[1] For C's objection to confusing proph-ecy and prognostication see JAHN *Appen-dix* **4**.

9[2] Not in Isa.

9[3] C alludes also in LACUNZA **61** to the "Deutero-Isaiah"—the "Chapters after the XLth" that were generally agreed by biblical scholars to be of later authorship—but the incident of the dial referred to in the textus is told in Isa 38 as well as in 2 Kings 20.

10[1] Primarily the woollen fillet worn by a priest, but also extended to include insig-nia of office and marks of distinction.

[* v]ery unsatisfact[or]y.

12 ɪ 233, pencil

. . . the principal thing mentioned, the royal protection of the Jewish religion and the exemption from tribute on the sabbatical year, certainly rests on good evidence. For stories, however exaggerated, have usually some truth at the bottom. . . . it is certain . . . that their religion was protected. If this was the case . . . there must have been some cause for it corresponding to the character of Alexander, and such a cause is alleged by Josephus.

The intimate connection of the Jews with Egypt and the great commercial Scheme which already occupied Alexander's mind, is the best and most probable solution of the favor shewn to the Jews. There may have been, no doubt, some historical ground for Josephus's narration; but it is so dresse[d] up, that "pars minima est ipsa puella sui.["]'[1]

13 ɪ 330–2, pencil, cropped

Had we all these writings, or at least the fifteen books of the learned Porphyɪy, they would throw great light on the obscurities of the Book of Daniel; for Jerome says of this opposer of the prophet: *"cujus impugnatio testimonium veritatis est, tanta enim dictorum fides fuit, ut propheta incredulis hominibus non videretur futura dixisse, sed narrasse praeterita." Praefat. Comment. in Dan. ["His attack is a testimony to the truth, for such is the fidelity of his utterances [to the facts] that unbelievers thought that he had not spoken of the future but had related events that were past." Preface to the Commentary on Dan.]

* But alas! where can we find the proofs of its Authenticity?[1] Were it but only one legitimate testimony for the existence [o]f the Book before the reign of Antiochus Epiphanes! The Talmudists themselves admit, that the visions were not compiled or brought together, till after the death of Antiochus.[2] It is undeniable, that infatuated as the Jews were in their predilection for the work, they did not venture to place it among the Prophets—which they must have done, had the Heads of the Synagogue possessed any temple copy or other equal evidence. Our Lord does not refer to the work as a prophecy[3]—but merely admonishes ⟨the⟩ Jews that

12[1] Ovid *Remedia amoris* 344: "A woman is the least part of herself" (LCL).

13[1] Through his reading of biblical scholarship and his debates with Edward Irving, C came eventually to consider the Book of Daniel as non-canonical, "a for-gery of the age of Antiochus Epiphanes" (PAULUS **43**). IRVING *Sermons* **20** n 3 gives further references.

13[2] I.e. after 163 B.C.

13[3] Christ alludes to Daniel in Matt 24.15 (also Mark 13.14): "When ye there-

when the profoundly politic, dispassionate & tolerant Roman Senate should repeat the insult to their religion spoken of in the Book of Daniel, the abomination of Antiochus Epiphanes,[4] they must not hope for the same passing away of the Storm; they might be sure, that their utter Ruin had been determined on.—

14   ɪ 378, pencil

Thus the Hebrews again had a king, and he at the same time held the office of high priest, as Zechariah had prophesied (vi. 9–15.) more than four hundred years before.*

* What? did Aristobolus I "build the Temple of the Lord"? For of the same Person, who was to be "a Priest on the Throne", Zechariah asserts, "he, even he shall build the temple of the Lord["].—[1]

15   ɪ +4, pencil

The Mosaic Institutes may be considered in two points of view—. First, as the initial part and means of a great mundane End, commensurate with the whole human race—Second—as a scheme of Polity, civil and ecclesiastical, for the furtherance of the interests of a particular Nation.[1]

And it is ~~very~~ not impossible, that the very defects of the Hebrew Constitution considered in the second point of view may be part of its excellence relatively to the first.—And so, I believe, the truth is. For if we try it wholly and exclusively as a National Code and Constitution, it must, I think, be allowed, that even in the Mosaic Sketch it contained the germs of its own decay and dissolution, without any adequate Antidotes. The system of Checks & Counter-checks is defective throughout; and neither cohesion nor unity sufficiently provided for. Nevertheless, notwithstanding, nay, because of these imperfections, it was the work of consummate Wisdom. It led gradually to the Loss of the Hebrew State, and the Salvation of Mankind.

---

fore shall see the abomination of desolation, spoken of by Daniel the prophet".

13[4] In his systematic persecution of the Jews, Antiochus Epiphanes defiled the Temple—the act associated with the "abomination that maketh desolate" prophesied in Dan 11.31.

14[1] Following up Jahn's allusion, C quotes Zech 6.12–13 to suggest that Aristobolus ɪ, who reigned 104 B.C., did *not* fulfil the prophecy.

15[1] Cf C's account of the Mosaic law in *C&S* (*CC*) 33–5, 37–40, where his chapter heading ". . . of the Hebrew Commonwealth" echoes Jahn's title. C's conclusion is "that not the principle itself, but the superior wisdom with which the principle was carried into effect, the greater perfection of the machinery, forms the true distinction, the *peculiar* worth, of the Hebrew constitution" (34).

N.B. The non-continuance of the Council of 72 after the death of Moses is a most remarkable Fact. It might have saved the Commonwealth[2]

15[2] Commenting on Jahn 45: "At the time of Moses, the larger collections of families were fifty-nine in number, the heads of which, together with the twelve princes of the tribes, composed a council of seventy-one members." C has added Moses to make a "Council of 72". Jahn observes that this council is not mentioned after the death of Moses.

JAHRBÜCHER DER MEDICIN

Jahrbücher der Medicin als Wissenschaft. Verfasst von einer Gesellschaft von Gelehrten und herausgegeben durch A. F. Marcus und F. W. J. Schelling. 3 vols (6 pts) in one vol. Tübingen 1805–8. 8°.

The title-page of I i (Ersten Bandes erster Heft) imprinted 1805; the general title-page of Vol I imprinted 1806. Bound as first with SCHELLING *Darlegung der wahren Verhältnisse der Naturphilosophie* (Tübingen 1806). Rebound in BM 1951.

British Library C 126 f 7 (i)

"S. T. C." label on the title-page of Vol I only.

The date and circumstances of C's acquisition of this volume are not recorded: it may have come in 1816–17 in response to his blanket order with the bookseller Thomas Boosey for all the works of Schelling and Steffens, Schelling being prominent in the *Jahrbücher* as joint editor and major contributor: *CN* III 4307 (Feb 1816), *CL* IV 665 (31 Aug 1816), 738 (14 Jun 1817). C praises Schelling's *Jahrbücher* aphorisms in SCHELLING *Denkmal* pp 131, 142–3, 164–5, and he mentions K. E. Schelling's essay in STEFFENS *Grundzüge* p ⁻12.

C annotated eight of Schelling's works and owned at least two others. He also annotated books by three other contributors to the *Jahrbücher*: C. A. Eschenmayer, Lorenz Oken (3 titles), and Heinrich Steffens (7 titles).

CONTENTS. I i (1805): 1–74 F. W. J. Schelling "Aphorismen zur Einleitung in die Naturphilosophie"; 75–88 F. W. J. Schelling "Allgemeine Anmerkung, die Lehre vom Verältniss des Endlichen zum Unendlichen betreffend"; 91–118 J. A. Schmidt "Ueber die speculative Tendenz der Erfahrnen"; 119–42 Ignaz Döllinger "Ueber den jetzigen Zustand der Physiologie"; 143–64 P. F. Walther "Historische Umrisse von Frankreichs naturwissenschaftlicher Cultur in näherer Beziehung auf Medicin und Chirurgie"; 165–206 F. W. J. Schelling "Vorläufige Bezeichnung des Standpunktes der Medicin nach den Grundsätzen der Naturphilosophie". I ii (1806): 3–36 F. W. J. Schelling "Aphorismen über die Naturphilosophe"; 37–57 C. A. von Eschenmayer "Appendix zu den Schriften über das gelbe Fieber"; 58–124 A. F. Marcus "Ueber die Anwendung des Eisens in der Medicin"; 125–60 "Anzeigen und Beurtheilungen einzelner Schriften". II i (1807): 3–46 K. E. Schelling "Ideen und Erfahrungen über den thierischen Magnetismus"; 49–75 P. F. Walther "Darstellung des Bichat'schen Systemes als erste Fortsetzung der historischen Umrisse von Frankreichs naturwissenschaftlicher Kultur"; [at this point, the first 6 pp of the following "Anzeigen" are included as pp 75–80 but are then displaced by Oken's essay] 75–94 L. Oken "Idee der Pharmakologie als Wissenschaft"; 94–114 "Anzeigen". II ii (1807): 121–58 F. W. J. Schelling "Aphorismen über die Naturphilosophie"; 158–90 K. E. Schelling "Weitere Betrachtungen über den thierischen

Magnetismus, und die Mittel ihn näher zu erforschen''; 190–224 [K. E. Schelling] "Grundsätze zu einer künftigen Seelenlehre''; 227–80 "Anzeigen''; 283–304 F. W. J. Schelling "Kritische Fragmente''. III i (1808): 3–113 A. F. Marcus "Versuch einer Theorie der Entzündung''; 113–24 Franz Baader "Ueber die Analogie des Erkenntniss und des Zeugungs-Triebes''. III ii (1808): 127–97 H. Steffens "Ueber die Vegetation''; 197–204 Franz Baader "Ueber Starres und Fliessendes''; 205–46 P. F. Walther "Von der Heilkraft der Natur''.

DATE. Between Aug 1816 and late Sept 1818, with notes made in at least two stages: **20** cannot have been written before Mar 1818, and there is an allusion to this volume in a notebook of 1820 (**18** n 1). The conjunction in time of three references to the *Jahrbücher* in C's annotations in SCHELLING *Denkmal* (acquired on or shortly before 30 Aug 1816) with five parallels in *SM* (*CC*) 18n, 24n, 29n, 83n, 98n implies a date at the end of Aug or early Sept 1816 for C's first reading.

COEDITOR. Raimonda Modiano.

1   p ⁻4

= equal to. N.B. Two other Notations are wanting in Metaphysics, one to express one in essence or kind, tho' perhaps of a different *degree* or dignity: the other to express the same as.—

2   I i 42 | Aphorisms 128–9

Jedes Ding ist in jeder Vollkommenheit . . . ewig: ewig nicht nur der Einheit nach, die begriffen ist in der göttlichen Einheit, sondern auch der Unendlichkeit nach. . . . Aber er [der Mensch] als das Ganze, und wie er in Relationen erscheint, ist nur, wie das Sonnenbild ist, wenn jene die dunkle Wolke im heitern Himmel wie aus Nichts schafft, und die durchsichtige Luft zu Wasser zusammenlaufen macht, um sich selbst in ihr wider zu strahlen. Sein Daseyn ist gesetzt und *dauert*, nur so lange die Verhältnisse der Positionen sich so gefügt haben, dass die Idea in ihnen widerleuchtet. Aber jene streben unaufhörlich nach der anfänglichen Freiheit; der Mensch vergeht, sobald jene Bedingungen vergehen, ohne dass deshalb etwas im All verschwände, wie der Regenbogen verschwindet, obgleich alle Elemente seiner Erscheinung bestehen, wenn nur ihre bestimmte wechselseitige Relation geändert ist.

[Each thing is in each perfection . . . eternal: it is eternal not only with respect to unity, which is contained in divine unity, but also with respect to infinity. . . . But he [man] as a whole, and as he appears in relationships, is just like the sun when it creates a dark cloud out of nothing in the clear sky, and makes the transparent air come together to form water in order to reflect itself in it. Man's existence is established and *lasts* only as long as the relations of the positions are so disposed that the idea is reflected in them. But they strive ceaselessly for their original freedom; man fades away as soon as those conditions pass away, though nothing in the cosmos disappears, as the rainbow disappears even though all elements of its appearance remain, if only their actual mutual relationship is altered.]

But whence these debasing Relations? Divine and permanent Positions should, methinks, have no other than divine and permanent Relations to each other.

3   ı i 49 | Aphorism 152

Das Phänomen der Dinge lässt sich beschreiben als beruhend auf einem Doppelbild. Das reine Compositum, oder die Relation für sich, wäre als ein blosses Ens imaginationis ohne alle Realität, und könnte nicht gesehen werden ohne das Positive, das in ihm wiederleuchtet. Mit dem Positiven der durchleuchtenden Idea verbunden, erzeugt es aber ein Doppelbild; wir sehen die Position mit dem, was an sich Nichts ist, dem blossen Compositum, zugleich also eine Mischung von Realität und Nichtrealität, ein wahres Scheinbild, das so wenig Wesentlichkeit hat, als das Spectrum solare, dessen Daseyn auf einem ganz ähnlichen Verhältniss beruht.*

[The phenomenon of things can be described as being based on a double image. The pure "composite", or the relation in itself, would, as a mere "construct of imagination", be without any reality and could not be seen without the positive which is reflected in it. However, combined with the positive of the illuminating idea it creates a double image; we see the positing with that which is in itself nothing, the mere composite, that is, a mixture of both reality and non-reality, a true phantom that has as little essentiality as the "solar spectrum" whose existence rests on an altogether similar relationship.*]

* All this is mighty plausible—but the minds, the percipient Foci—are they Nothings?

4   ı i 163

Auch ihm [dem Direktor der Pariser Medicinalschule] entstehen zuweilen abentheuerliche Projecte, z.B. jenes, die Materia medica in den verschiednen Hospitälern einmal ganz durchexaminiren zu lassen, und auf die Resultate dieser Versuche eine neue Theorie jener Doctrin zu gründen.*

[Occasionally he [the director of the Paris School of Medicine] also entertains extravagant projects, such as the one of having the materia medica thoroughly examined in the various hospitals and basing a new theory of that doctrine on the results of these experiments.*]

* If the Hospital Physicians & Surgeons could agree among themselves;

and keep the plan secret; and a cautious Judgement exercised in the selection of Patients for the different articles; it would be no bad scheme.

5 II i 39

* Täglich gewann ich über meine Somnambüle mehr Einfluss, so, dass ich gegen das Ende der Kur sie fast nur anzublicken brauchte, um sie in Krise zu versetzen.

[* I daily gained more influence over my somnambulist, so that towards the end of the cure I barely had to look at her to induce a state of crisis in her.]

* This merely betrays the influence of the Imagination—or rather of Fancy under the law of direct Association[1]

6 II i 91

Die elektrischen Inflammabilien sind daher stärkend für die Haut, die Leber und das Lymphsystem und die hieher gehörigen Sinnorgane, das Auge und die Nase, welche aber hier übergangen werden, und eben darum schwächend für die gegenüber stehenden Organe Epidermis, Knochen, Kreislauf, Gefühl, Ohr; so ist das Salz, die Säuren stärkend für den Magen und die homologe Lunge, aber schwächend für die andern Organe.

[The electrical inflammables are therefore strengthening for the skin, the liver and the lymphatic system and the sense organs belonging to it, the eye and the nose (which are not dealt with here, however), and for that reason weakening for the contrasting organs, epidermis, bones, circulatory system, touch, hearing. Hence salt and the acids are strengthening for the stomach and the homologous lungs, but weakening for the other organs.]

Oken seems to forget, that a medicine cannot be sent, like a letter, to the one place only, to which it is directed.

7 II ii 128 (misnumbered 130), pencil

[Footnote:] Spinoza in dem bekannten Brief über den Begriff des Unendlichen (*Opp. posth. Epp.* XXIX.) bedienet sich des Gleichnisses von den Ungleichheiten des Zwischenraums, der von zwey Kriesen verschiedner Mittelpunkte eingeschlossen ist. Die Unendlichkeit dieser Ungleichheiten ist eine schlechthin gegenwärtige, <u>actu daseyende</u> und beschlossene.

5[1] C invokes the *BL* distinction between imagination and fancy, in which fancy is "a mode of Memory" and therefore "must receive all its materials ready made from the law of association": *BL* ch 13 (*CC*) I 305.

[Spinoza in the well-known letter about the concept of the infinite (*Posthumous Works* Letter 29) uses the simile of the inequalities of the space enclosed by two circles with different centres. The infinity of these inequalities is present absolutely, by an existing and determined act.]

not actu reali:[1] for the demonstration holds only of the mathematical circle, that is, of an idea or Handlungsweise[2] of the Imagination[3]

8 II ii 130–1, pencil

Eben so kann nie die Position oder Substanz, welche das Ding ist, sondern allein das Abstraktum derselben getheilt werden;* alle Theilung ist darum eine lediglich imaginäre, die auf das Reale oder Positive keine Beziehung hat.

[In the same way, the positing or substance, which is the thing, can never be divided, but only the abstraction of it.* Every division is therefore merely imaginary, with no reference to the real or positive.]

* I agree ⟨with this,⟩ and could never see the infinite divisibility of matter in any other Light. But does not this do away the *proof* of the infinity § 130?[1]

* Does not the whole argument depend on the definition of matter, as filling space[2]—where there is a space to be filled, there is a space to be divided—ergo, &c?—all this expresses only a law of the Imagination, and the only apodictic or compulsory conclusion not that there can be end to the division of matter, but that from the properties of *Space* (i.e. modus imaginandi)[3] the end cannot be *imagined*.

7[1] Not "by a real act".

7[2] "Manner of proceeding": C uses this term as equivalent to "Universal Form" and "Tool" in JACOBI *Ueber die Lehre* **4** n 4, **15** n 4.

7[3] In KANT *Metaphysische Anfangsgründe* **5** C considers the value of geometrical illustrations that "present to the imagination a truth in itself not imaginable by an imaginable Substitute".

8[1] Aphorisms 127–30, to which **7** textus is a footnote. Schelling claims that matter and each of its parts are infinite and that this infinity must be carefully distinguished from "the imagined or empirical infinity which consists in the mere conglomeration [*Anhäufung*] of abstract finitudes". The original infinity of matter "has nothing in common with that which the imagination construes as infinite, and yet it is an unde-

niable conspicuous infinity": it does not arise out of "the *magnitude of* the confined *Space*", nor out of "*the aggregate of given parts*". Those who do not grasp the concept that matter is an infinite act "deny it on the ground that otherwise an infinite number must be taken as real or present". Yet they could have found ample evidence in mathematics that "there exists an infinity to which no number whatsoever, whether finite or infinite, . . . is commensurate". In mathematics "such an infinity is regarded as present with complete clearness [*Evidenz*] and is directly recognised".

8[2] In KANT *Metaphysische Anfangsgründe* **7** textus Kant defines matter as that which "fills space", arguing that " 'to fill a space' is a more precise definition of the concept of 'occupying a space' ".

8[3] "A way of imagining".

9 II ii 199, pencil

22. Alle scheinbare Beschränktheit in den sogenannten Aeusserungen der Seele in der Erscheinungswelt fällt demnach auf Rechnung des endlichen Organismus, auf welchen jene sich bezieht, nicht aber auf ihre Rechnung zurück.

[All apparent limitation in the so-called manifestations of the soul in the phenomenal world is therefore owing to the finite organism to which the limitation is referred, and not to its own account.]

§ 22. But what becomes of the Stetigkeit, in this transition of Souls into finite Organisms?[1] If the latter be Products, Creatures, or Reflexes of the Souls, to which they severally belong, how can the Defects in the Souls' Utterances be chargeable to *them*? Is the Shadow of Little ''My Lord'' answerable for his ~~happy~~ wry Side?—[2]

10 II ii 200–1, pencil

25. Was demnach in der Seele vorgeht, und was in ihr liegt, liegt von Ewigkeit her in ihr vorgebildet, und die scheinbare Befangenheit derselben in den zeitlichen Verhältnissen ist nur ein Schatten, der von dem endlichen Substrat, das sie in der Erscheinungswelt hat, auf sie fällt, ohne dass jedoch ihr Wesen dadurch verdunkelt würde.

[Therefore what goes on in the soul, and what is present in it, has been preformed in it from eternity, and the way it is apparently caught up in temporal relationships is only a shadow that falls on it from the finite substratum that it has in the world of phenomena, without its essence being darkened thereby.]

§ 25. It is this Shadow that almost provokes me in the Schellingians.[1]

9[1] Schelling describes ''the souls of individual things'' as simple substances, but at the same time ''members of the archetypal organism''. The word *Stetigkeit*, ''continuity'', appears p 194 in the following sentence: ''Als Einfaches zieht sich dasselbe vielmehr durch Alles hindurch, wie denn auch die Stetigkeit mit ein Grundgesitz des Einfachen ist. [As a simple substance it permeates all things, for continuity is likewise a basic law of simple substances.]''

9[2] This rather elliptical rhetorical question is concerned with the origin of evil: if the human being is a shadow of the divine, or if the finite individual is the product of an infinite soul (''My Lord''), where lies the responsibility for evil or deformity (the ''wry Side'')? The metaphor of the shadow appears also in **10** (and textus) and **12** below, and the figure here may include an allusion to Shakespeare's Richard III, who speaks bitterly of the way in which ''my shadow in the sun'' is a reminder of his deformity: *Richard III* i i 26.

10[1] In STEFFENS *Grundzüge der philosophische Naturwissenschaft* front flyleaf referring to p 172 C comments on this article by K. E. Schelling: ''It is the word, *Schein* [appearance], that most pozes me in the writings of the Schellingians: most intensely in the Essay on Psychology . . . by Dr K. Schelling. There seems to me a confusion of *seem* with Prætereunce or impermanence. . . . But I feel convinced, that I misconceive Steffens &c; and therefore,

The only points, concerning which we feel a living and real interest, I, Virtue, Guilt, Happiness, Pain—O! these are *Shadows*! Nothings—of which therefore Nothing need be said!

11 II ii 205, pencil

Die äussern Einwirkungen treffen nur unsern endlichen in der Erscheinungswelt befangenen Organismus. Sie sind aber weiter nichts, als die veranlassende oder Gelegenheit machende Momente, dass jener seine Seele auf diese oder jene Weise an sich repräsentirt. . . . Unsere Verhältnisse zur Aussenwelt sind uns angenehm und heilkringend, wenn sie die Veranlassung sind, dass die Repräsentationen unsers Organismus sowohl seiner geistigen als auch der leiblichen Seite nach seiner Seele adäquat sind,;*a* und umgekehrt sind die Eindrücke, welche unsern Organismus zu unadäquaten Repräsentationen seiner Seele bringen, ihm nothwendig zuwider, indem sie ihn in sich selbst entzweien.

[External effects act only upon our finite organism, which is limited to the phenomenal world. They are, however, nothing more than those moments that cause or create an opportunity, so that the organism can represent its soul in this or that manner to itself. . . . Our relations to the external world are pleasant and beneficial as long as the representations of our organism produced by them— both spiritual and physical—are adequate to its soul; on the other hand, those impressions that cause the organism to form inadequate representations of its soul are necessarily harmful, in that the organism is thereby divided against itself.]

But what is this "*unsere*"? This "*wir*"? what means dass *jener seine Seele* auf diese oder jene weise an sich räpresentirt?/[1] What do we gain by the intervention of this *Soul* between that which we mean by the word, "*I*", and God?—If it be a conception of this Soul (Begriff)[2] how can it be oblivious, vicious?/ Does this "I" *do* any thing or is it a mere result? If the former, to what purpose this multiplication of God? If the latter, it is a World of Lies—and the Soul, of which they are the necessary result, is the Father of Lies![3] And after all what are these numbered Paragraphs but bold *assertions*?

a Correction in ink, perhaps not by C, whose notes in this section are in pencil

according to my own golden rule . . . I conclude myself ignorant of their Understanding."
    11[1] "What is this 'our'? This 'we'?" What means "so that each one can represent its own soul to itself in this way or that"?—the last phrase from textus.
    11[2] "Concept"—from sec 32, p 201,

where Schelling describes the "successive manifestation of our soul in the form of both spirit and body" as "a constant self-oblivion and self-recollection", but observes also that the soul can be "forgotten and recollected only in so far as it is a temporal concept".
    11[3] If (as K. Schelling says) "one and

12 ɪɪ ii 206–7, pencil

44. Die Seele ist demnach für den Organismus, dem sie vorsteht, der
Spiegel der urbildlichen und der Erscheinungswelt, in gewissem Be-
tracht ist sie sein Ein und Alles. Aber für sich selbst ist die Seele nichts,
sondern was sie zu besitzen sich rühmen kann, verdankt sie ihrer Ver-
kettung mit dem urbildlichen oder göttlichen Organismus. Es ist mit ihr
in Beziehung auf die höchste Idee der nämliche Fall gegeben, wie mit
unserm Auge in Beziehung auf unsere Seele. Dieses letztere ist für un-
sern Organismus ein Spiegel für die Aussenwelt, aber für sich selbst
würde dasselbe nichts seyn, wenn es nicht durch seinen Antheil an un-
serm Organismus zugleich mit ein medium repräsentationis unserer
Seele wäre.

[For the organism over which it presides, the soul is accordingly a mirror of the
archetypal world and of the phenomenal world; in certain respects it is every-
thing to the organism. But in itself the soul is nothing, for what it can claim to
own it owes to its link with the archetypal or divine organism. The same is true
of it in relation to the highest ideas as is true of our eye in relation to the soul.
The eye is a mirror of the external world for our organism, but in itself it would
be nothing, if it were not, through its share in our organism, at the same time a
''medium of representation'' of our soul.]

No! first explain the *Eye*, & how an all-wise infinite *Soul* can *need* one/
& you have said something. Tho' even then you will have to prove the
eye to be self-conscious, in order to make it at all analogous. Shadows,
Reflections, Echoes I can understand—but self-conscious, sensitive
Shadows—Reflections *from* Nothing, of a Soul which does not perceive
them, which the Reflections themselves do perceive—tho' they are
nothings reverberated from nothing!—These are mysteries with a ven-
geance!—So again *unser* endliches Antheil.[1]—It ~~means~~ mourns, it re-
joices, hopes, fears, loves, hates—& yet it is nothing

13 ɪɪ ii 224

96. So wie sich die Seele in uns und mitten in dieser Welt der Erschei-
nung des Urbildlichen erinnert, so kann man sagen, wird sie sich auch
in der urbildlichen Welt dessen erinnern, was die Welt der Erscheinung

---

the same Soul . . . lies at the basis of our
temporal consciousness''—i.e. of every
''I''—should the ''I'' be seen as indepen-
dently active then it would be equivalent to
the archetypal Soul, i.e. to God, in which
case a multiplicity of individual selves
would amount to a multiplicity of Gods. If

the ''I'' is a mere result of the archetypal
Soul then it is reduced to the status of a
shadow (for which see **9** and **10** above).
The ''Father of Lies''—the Devil—is from
John 8.44 (var).

12[1] ''*Our* finite share''—based on tex-
tus.

ihrem Ideal Adäquates hervorgebracht hat. Zwar nicht wir als solche werden uns daher nach dem Tode unserer erinnern, dagegen wird sich die Seele dessen erinnern, was sie ihrem Ideal Adäquates an uns erkannte. Je nachdem also unsere Thaten auf dieser Welt gewesen sind, werden sie uns auch Zeugniss reden vor der Seele, und diess ist die Belohnung, die unserer wartet; die Strafe aber wird darinn bestehen, dass man vor der Seele der Vergessenheit anheimfällt, wenn man nicht gethan hat, das ihrem Ideal gleicht, denn nur dieses letztere ist beständig vor ihr gegenwärtig.

[Just as the soul in us remembers the archetypal world in the midst of the phenomenal world, one can say accordingly that it will also remember in the archetypal world what the phenomenal world has produced that is adequate to its ideal. This is not to say that we, as such, will therefore remember ourselves after death; however, the soul will remember what it recognized in us as adequate to its ideal. According to how our acts were in this world they will testify for us before the soul, and this is the recompense that awaits us; the punishment, however, will consist in becoming a prey to forgetfulness before the soul, if one has not done what is like the ideal, for only this latter is constantly present to the soul.]

Never surely was work written so utterly unsatisfactory, for both Head and Heart. What *we* are, or are to be; what the I is; is not even spoken of. But we are gravely told in the last ¶ph, that if we act virtuously, the Soul will remember a something of which *we*, while there was a we, *had* been likewise conscious *of*—While our Brother Nothings, who had not been virtuous, would be forgotten by this Soul!! Tho' how this unconcerned Soul can be said to *forget* what according to this hypothesis the never knew nothing at all about, I cannot even conjecture.—And what is the Basis of the Whole System—Mere Ipse dixits grounded on the mere assumptions of the Scheme of dead mechanical Emanation.[1]

14   ii ii 286, pencil

Nicht ein Objektiviren *ihrer selbst* ist die Vernunft, denn sie ist nichts für sich, dass sie sich objektiviren könnte. Sondern das Ewige ist *wesentlich* das Erkennen seiner selbst; und diese Selberbekräftigung des Absoluten, die sein Seyn ist, ist der ganze und einzige Inhalt der Vernunft.

[Reason does not consist in making *itself* objective, for it is nothing in itself, that could make itself objective. Rather, the eternal is *essentially* a recognition of oneself; and this self-affirmation of the absolute which is its being is the complete and only content of reason.]

13[1] A summary dismissal of K. E. Schelling's system. C found the "fruitful" heresy of emanation especially troubling: see LUTHER *Colloquia* **62** and n 2. An "ipse dixit" is an unproved assertion.

This is the Basis of the Schellingian Atheism, Σπινοσισμος πολυσαρ-κος,[1] or the *cloathed* Skeleton of Spinoza!

15 III i 29

Wir nehmen mit der Naturphilosophie an, dass der Magnetismus die Länge vorstellt, und der ersten Dimension entspricht, dass die Electricität als der zweyten Dimension entsprechend, die Breite hervorruft, und jene beschränkt.

Das Moment der Irritabilität, welches die Breite hervorruft, ist jenes, welches mit der Contraction bezeichnet wird.

Dic Wiederherstellung der Länge, und Beschränkung der Breite, ist jenes Moment der Irritabilität, welches mit Expansion bezeichnet wird.

Den Arterien, welche die Länge bilden, kommt die Expansion zu.

Den Venen im Gegentheile repräsentiren die Breite, und entsprechen der Contraction.

[We assume, with the *Naturphilosophie*, that magnetism represents length and corresponds to the first dimension, and that electricity, as corresponding to the second dimension, evokes breadth and limits length.

The factor of irritability that evokes breadth is that which is called contraction.

The re-formation of length and limitation of breadth is that factor of irritability which is called expansion.

Expansion belongs to the arteries, which form length.

The veins, on the contrary, represent breadth and correspond to contraction.]

There is some confusion in this. If the Veins represent Breadth, ⟨if Br.⟩ correspond to Contraction, and is = Electricity: & if the Arteries in their expansion form Length, and Length = Magnetism/ it may be asked—how then can the Veins, as belonging to the Reproductive Power, represent Magnetism, & how can the Arteriality or Irritability represent Electricity?[1]

14[1] "Well-fleshed Spinozism". Concerns about the atheistic tendencies of Spinozism are frequent in C's work: see e.g. JACOBI *Ueber die Lehre* 3, 14, 18. The connection between Spinoza and Schelling is also commonplace, as when C describes Schelling's system as "Plotinised Spinozism" in *CL* IV 883 (24 Nov 1818); cf the long analysis of Schelling's position in *CL* IV 873–6.

15[1] There is no confusion of terminology in Marcus's essay, but he and C worked with slightly different conceptual frameworks. As the textus indicates, Marcus identified magnetism with length and electricity with the control of length in breadth, contraction, and expansion. Both veins and arteries, in this system, belong to the "second dimension" of power represented by electricity. C makes a distinction, however, between the veins that function at a lower level as part of the "glandulo-venous System" and the arteries in the "musculo-arterial System": the phrases come from his note in STEFFENS *Beyträge* back flyleaf (referring to p 74). The correspondence of magnetism with reproduction, electricity with irritability, and chemical combining power with sensibility is outlined in *TL* 91–2.

16 III i 34–5[a]

Ausser der specifiken Beschaffenheit kömmt auch bey der Entzündung noch die Function des Organs in Betrachtung, wovon theils die Erscheinungen und das Eingreifen in verwandte Verrichtungen des Organismus abhängt. Dieses bezieht sich eben so wohl auf die Enzündungen, welche unmittelbar von der Dimension ausgehen, als auch auf jene, die sich zuerst in einem bestimmten Organe setzen. . . . Die Säfte überhaupt spielen bey der Entzündung eine äusserst wichtige Rolle, da sie die negative Seite der Irritabilität repräsentiren, und der Reproduction angehören.

Da alles nur im Gegensatze besteht, und bestehen kann, so müssen auch die mehr oder weniger oxydirten Säfte die Entzündung erhöhen oder vermindern helfen.

Wie es sich in diesem Betracht mit der Entzündung in der Dimension, der allgemeinen, verhält, eben so und noch bestimmter findet dieses in denen der Organe, den topischen Entzündungen, statt.

Daher ist die Entzündung in der Lunge eine ganz andere als in der Leber. Das Uebergewicht der Arteriellität in der Lunge setzt auch ein Uebergewicht in dem arteriallen Blute. Hierzu kömmt dann auch, dass in der Lunge der Oxydations-Process am lebhaftesten von statten geht.

[Aside from its specific nature, the function of the organ must also be considered as pertaining to inflammation, on which the appearances and the engagement of the organism in related functions partly depend. This applies as much to the inflammations that result directly from the dimension [of magnetism or electricity] as to those that settle at first in a specific organ. . . . The humours in general play an extremely important rôle in inflammation, as they represent the negative side of irritability and belong to [the dimension of] reproduction.

As everything exists and can only exist in opposition, the more or less oxidised humours must, accordingly, help increase or reduce the inflammation.

Just as here this is related to the inflammation in the dimension, it takes place likewise and even more precisely in the inflammations of organs, in the local inflammations.

Therefore inflammation of the lungs is altogether different from that of the liver. The preponderance of arteries in the lungs creates also a preponderance of arterial blood. Thus the oxidation process in the lungs is the most active of any anywhere.]

Hitherto most obscure and perplexed—a complete Tangle!

What is the Agent? What the matter acted on? are the visible particles susceptible of two or more distinct actions at the same [time],[b] dimen-

---

[a] This note begins at the foot of p 35, at the end of the section; it continues at the bottom of 34 and concludes at the top of 35

[b] Word omitted, presumably in haste

sional & organic? Above all, the magnetism in Life must needs be a far higher & more inclusive power than the Chemism[1] or Galvanism on the Metals—& this even in Vegetable Life. The terms, therefore, tend to mislead and must confuse. Hence, the few passages, I can understand, are flashes of Flame thro' Smoke.

17 III i 36

Nachdem wir nun das Wesen der Entzündung festgesetzt zu haben glauben, wollen wir versuchen ihre Charaktere anzugeben und zu erklären.

[After having, as we believe, determined the nature of inflammation, we should like to try to give an account of, and explain, its characteristics.]

Of which, I have not understood one word.

18 III i 51, pencil

Der äussere und der innere Organismus ist nur einer, und jede Veränderung, die sich in dem einen wie in dem anderen ergiebt, theilt sich gemeinschaftlich mit. Dem Grunde, worauf die Veränderung beruht, unterliegen beyde. Das, was die Cohäsions-Veränderung in dem einen bewirkt, bewirkt sie auch in dem anderen. Die sogenannte äussere Natur, wenn sie Krankheit im Organismus veranlasst, ist in diesem Falle den nämlichen Zuständen unterworfen.* Das Gewitter ist ein Fieber in der Atmosphäre, eben so wie es Fieber in dem Organismus giebt, den wir den unseren nennen.

[The external and the internal organism is one, and every alteration that takes place in the one or the other is mutually shared. The basis on which the alteration rests underlies both. That which brings about the alteration of cohesion in the one also effects it in the other. So-called external nature, on causing illness in the organism, is exposed to the same conditions in this case.* The thunderstorm is a fever in the atmosphere, in the same way that there are fevers in the organism that we call our own.]

* If not wholly false, it can be true only under multiform and manyifold exceptions & conditions: or every organized Being would be ill at the same time in the same district.[1]

19 III i 107

So wie das Nitrum die Lunge, so afficirt der Mercurius die Leber, der Moschus das Gehirn.

16[1] A variant of the Schellingian term *Chemismus* which C used as "Chemical Affinity" in *CN* III 4454 (c Oct 1818) and as "Galvanism" in *CL* IV 769, 808 (Sept 1817 and Jan 1818).

18[1] C gives a more extensive criticism of this passage in *CN* IV 4641 (30 Jan–5 Feb 1820).

[In the same way that nitre affects the lungs does mercury affect the liver, musk the brain.]

It is perplexing to think of the difference in the accounts of the German and the English Medical Writers as to the powers of Musk, & Animal Products generally.[1]

20 III ii [248], referring to III i 107 | **19** textus

p. 107.

Q. How are we to account for the glaring discrepance between the statements of the most experienced and celebrated German Physicians and those of the English Medical Writers, respecting the specific Powers of Musk, and other Animal Products over the nervous system? With the Germans Musk is to the Sensibility what Opium &c is to the Irritability and Mercury & Iron to the Reproduction. With us, it is little more than a chip in Porridge. Dr Bateman's account of his own case is the only one, I recollect, in which the specific powers of Musk as an excitant of Sensibility are attested.[1]

21 III ii [126],[a] pencil

Abstraction is to Generalization as the numeration below the Unit, as the fountain of both, is ⟨to⟩ the numeration above

$$
\begin{array}{c}
4 \\
3 \\
2 \\
\hline
1 \\
\hline
2 \\
3 \\
4
\end{array}
$$

[a] The blank verso of the half-title to Vol III pt ii

19[1] See **20** below.

20[1] Thomas Bateman (1778–1821), physician, one of the founders of the *Edinburgh Medical and Surgical Journal* (some volumes of which C annotated), contributor to Rees's *Cyclopaedia*, and one of the foremost authorities on skin diseases, read a paper to the Medical and Chirurgical Society of London on 31 Mar 1818 describing his own illness and the use of a musk "draught" in its treatment. He claimed that "the first dose of this medicine appeared to diffuse its stimulating effects through the whole frame, exciting a sort of electric tingling, even to the extremities of the limbs, and an immediate feeling of renovated strength": *Medico-Chirurgical Transactions* IX (1818) 228.

i.e. in abstracting you give the *character* of an integer to a component fraction of the integrality. You *super*individualize in order by means of an intenser Individity[1] to find the Genus or *common Form*. Hence abstraction is a necessary antecedent step to generalization. and hence the test of generalization, of its genuineness & philosophic truth, is given, when both acts are united in the common Base of another and higher Individual, and an *Ideal* is born. Where this is not the Offspring, the generalization is a mere technical artefact of the memory.[2]

22 iii ii 152–3

Schon *Arnim*, später *Winterl* und *Kastner*, endlich *Ritter* haben deutlich bewiesen, dass das frierende Wasser von dem flüssigen, noch mehr von dem kochenden, in Rücksicht der Spannung, verschieden ist. . . . Der Beweis, den *Ritter* führt, beruht vorzüglich auf der *oxydirenden* Eigenschaft des frierenden Wassers. Salzsäure, mit Wasser vermischt, ward durch das Frieren abgesondert, und in übersaure Salzsäure verwandelt. . . . Er schloss daraus, dass sich Sauerstoff aus dem Wassert abgesondert hatte, das Wasser also ein desoxydirtes seyn müsste.

[First Arnim, then Winterl and Kastner, and finally Ritter have clearly proved that freezing water is different from liquid water, and even more so from boiling water, with respect to tension. . . . The proof given by Ritter rests primarily on the *oxidising* property of freezing water. Muriatic acid, combined with water, was separated by freezing and transformed into hyper-oxidated muriatic acid. . . . He concluded from this that oxygen had separated itself from water, and hence that water had to be deoxygenated.]

Ritter did not know, that the Oxymuriatic (= Chlorine) was a simple substance, relatively to the Muriatic acid gas at least.[1] The experiment therefore proves Ice to be an Oxyde of Water—or a deutoxide of Hydrogen, supposed Water itself a protoxide.

23 iii ii 163, pencil

Die Nothwendigkeit des Wassers zum Gedeihen der Pflanzen ist allgemein bekannt, ja frühere Naturforscher, wie *van Helmont, Boyle, Bon-*

21[1] Possibly a slip for "individuality" or "individuity", the latter appearing in LUTHER *Colloquia* **1**.

21[2] C carefully distinguishes generalisation from abstraction but at the same time argues that generalisation must include abstraction, in *P Lects* Lect 5 (1949) 184–5, *Logic* (*CC*) 62–4.

22[1] Johann Wilhelm Ritter (1776–1810), early associate of the founders of German Romanticism—Novalis, Tieck, Schleiermacher, Schelling, the Schlegels—was the outstanding chemist among the *Naturphilosophen*. C's objection to Ritter is based on Humphry Davy's 1810 discovery that chlorine is an element, not a compound of muriatic acid gas and oxygen as French chemists believed.

net, Duhamel and *Tillet*, glaubten, das Wasser wäre das einzige Nahrungsmittel der Pflanze. Ein Irrthum, der durch die genauern Untersuchungen gänzlich widerlegt ist.*? Q͟ʸ**

[That plants need water to flourish is generally known; earlier naturalists, like van Helmont, Boyle, Bonnet, Duhamel, and Tillet, believed that water was the sole means of subsistence of the plant. An error which has been completely refuted by more exact investigations.? Q͟ʸ*]

* Substitute "Wachsthums"—for Nahrungsmittel:[1] and Van Helmont ⟨&⟩ Boyle's & assertion is *Doubtless* erroneous. But it may perhaps admit of a doubt whether the others may not be the stimulants, vital & chemical, & Water the sole Nutriment

24 p ⁺1 (i.e. of composite vol), referring to III ii 197

Du frägst: wie wir uns getrauen über die Vegetation etwas zu sagen, ohne über das Wesen des Lichts geredet zu haben? Hast du es gesehen, oder ist es nicht das Sehen selbst? Wo magst du es fassen, dass es dir durch Vergleichung klar werden könnte?

[You ask how we dare to say something about vegetation, without having spoken about the nature of light? Have you seen it, or is it not seeing itself? Where may you grasp it so that it could become clear to you by comparison?]

P. 197. There is a quackery in passages like these, very unpleasant to *my* feelings—this a metabasis eis allo genos,[1] without notice! Du fragst:[2]—o what do I ask? or concerning what? Light as an object—that somewhat, in the privation or absence of which Vegetables *blanch*, &c. And Steffens answers me as if I we had been conversing of *Subjective Light*—and asks me, is it not the same as Sight? Is not its Esse in the videre?[3]—I see a Herring, I see Milk—I slice the fresh Herring lengthways, and suspend the slips in a clear Phial of Milk—all this is *Seeing*. But in a hour or two I see the Vial shining, I see a luminous apparition and, if I darken the room, I can see other things by it within the sphere of a foot/. Now it is *this*, we̶ were talking of: and what sense is there in t̶e̶l̶l̶i̶n̶g̶ ̶m̶e̶ ̶t̶h̶a̶t̶ saying: Ist est[a] nicht das Sehen selbst?—[4]   S. T. C.

[a] A slip for "es"

23[1] I.e. substitute *Wachstumsmittel* (means of growth) for *Nahrungsmittel* (means of subsistence), reading "that water was the sole 'means of growth' ".

24[1] "Transition to another kind", an Aristotelian concept much cited by C, e.g. BAXTER *Reliquiae* COPY A **29** n 1.

24[2] "You ask"—the opening words of the textus.

24[3] "Is not its 'Being' in the 'seeing'?"—a variant of the Berkeleian formula "to be is to be perceived".

24[4] "Is it not Seeing itself?"—from textus.

25   pp $^+1-^+3$, referring evidently to III ii 198

Im Starren wie in Flüssigen oder Fliessenden, insofern sie beide blos nur solche sind; ist aber die Trennung des Stoffs und der Form gegeben, indem jenes die Form ohne den Stoff, dieses den Stoff ohne die Form darstellt. Nämlich das Starre zeigt und äussert zwar Kontinuität, aber keine Penetranz, Qualität, eindringende, andres auflösende oder in sich aufnehmende Subtilheit oder Zartheit; wogegen das Fliessende zwar mehr oder minder diese Penetrationskraft, aber keine Kontinuität äussert.

[In solid as in liquid or flowing things, in so far as they are both only such, the dichotomy of matter and form is given, in that the former represents form without matter, and the latter matter without form. For the solid shows and expresses continuity, it is true, but no penetration, quality, penetrating subtlety, or delicacy that dissolves other things or takes them up in itself; whereas what is flowing, while showing more or less of this power of penetration, displays no continuity.]

Ueber Starres und Fliessendes—[1]

What is Form but the Unity of the Stuff? How can there be a unity of the Form *and* the Stuff? I do not understand it. The *Stuff* of my finger is a + b + c + d + e + f: and the disposition of these into a finger *is* the form! But if the Writer means the forma formans,[2] what unity has this with the Carbon, Oxyg. Hydrog: Nitrogen, Phosph., Lime, more than a Bird with the materials of its Nest?—It is of the Writer's nomenclature, that I complain. The words, Stuff seems to mean *active power*— & then *continuity*—~~why~~ now I should have applied this term to the surface of a Fluid in preference to that of a Stone, if I made any difference/ —Altogether, the conception is wofully *cloudy*. Besides, it is not true in fact. Had B. resided in Malta, or the South of Sicily, he would have found the Sand-winds that blow from Africa, endued with as penetrating a power as a fluid—. The same with the lunar Caustic.[3]—B. should have begun with stating the conceptions—and then have selected appropriate expressions.—But this is the disease of Baader's mind. He never asks himself, whether his problems do not admit of other & plainer solutions. When the particles of Iron are exerting the force a = attraction of cohesion or a + a, they will of course be less disposed to exert the force c = attraction of combination or a + b./.—

25[1] "On Solids and Liquids"—the title of Baader's article.
25[2] "Forming form", as in *Logic* (*CC*) 80, where C's own translation is "formative" form.

25[3] Silver nitrate, produced in stick form for medical purposes, but also used as an indelible ink—therefore a "solid" with "as penetrating a power as a fluid".

The word, matter, materia, ὕλη,[4] is among the most obscure, and unfixed in the whole Nomenclature of Metaphysics—and I am afraid that the knot must be cut—i.e. a fixed meaning must be arbitrarily imposed on the word, as I have done in defining

Matter as mere *videri* ⟊ Spirit,

as quod agit et non apparet/ the Synthesis being *body*, quod est et videtur[5]—At all events, I would have preferred the terms, *Quantity* & *Quality*: thus:

Materia + Spiritus = Corpus. Ergo, Materia *est* in Corpore: Spiritus agit *per* Corpus[6]—Matter & Spirit$_1{}^a$ are Body: then Spirit$_2{}^a$ re-emerges in moments as a property or function of body, but in omni tempore and as a the *whole*, per totalitam immanentem it is Quality—Spirit potentialis.[7] Again, Materia *ens* in corpore = quantity.[8]—As B. states his position, it really amounts to little more than repeating in very inapt expressions that Fluids are fluid; and Solids are solid.

[b] ⟊ my mark for Antithesis: ⟊ for Contrariety.
Sweet ⟊ Sour: Sweet ⟊ Bitter. The others as in Algebra.[9]

26 iii ii 212, pencil

* Erst in diesen Tagen habe ich wieder einem sonst vollkommen wohl-gestalteten Kinde die Hasenscharte operirt, dessen Mutter schon meh-rere nicht mit Hasenscharten verunstaltete Kinder zur Welt brachte, welche aber in dem Anfange des 5ten Monathes ihrer Schwangerschaft im Felde durch einen Hasen lebhaft erschreckt wurde, und seit dieser Zeit das Bild des Hasenkopfes lange nicht mehr in ihrer Vorstellungs-kraft austilgen konnte.

[* I have, in the last few days, once again operated on the harelip of an otherwise perfectly well-formed child, whose mother had brought several other children

---

[a] The number originally written as a superscript has been printed as a subscript in order to avoid confusion with editorial matter

[b] C's footnote is squeezed into the space on p [+]1 above the beginning of the note itself

25[4] The usual Greek word for "matter".

25[5] "Matter as mere 'visibility' [lit to be seen, to appear] as opposed to Spirit as 'that which acts and does not appear'/ the Synthesis being *body*, 'which is and is seen' ". The distinction between matter and body was especially important to C as an improvement on Kant's system: cf *SM* (*CC*) 81–2; IRVING *Sermons* 29; KANT *Metaphysische Anfangsgründe* 8, 24.

25[6] "Matter + Spirit = Body. Therefore, Matter *is* in Body: Spirit acts *through* Body."

25[7] ". . . but 'in the whole time' and as the *whole*, 'through the abiding totality' it is Quality—potential Spirit."

25[8] "Matter [since it is] *being* [merely] in Body" is quantity.

25[9] A fuller list of C's symbols appears in JOANNES 4.

into the world who were not disfigured by harelips. However, she was startled by a hare in a field in the fifth month of her pregnancy and could not for a long time afterwards dispel the picture of the hare's head from her imagination.]

* But how many Children have been born Hare-lipped whose Mothers were never Harum-scarumed? How many whose Mothers never saw a Hare/.[1]

26[1] Though C was sceptical (as here) about some particular instances of what were popularly called "mother-marks" or "maternal impressions", he was not prepared to reject the theory altogether: see BATEMAN 1, KLUGE 32.

THOMAS JEFFERSON
1743–1826

Memoirs, Correspondence, and Private Papers of Thomas Jefferson, late President of the United States. Now first published from the original manuscripts. Edited by Thomas Jefferson Randolph. Vol IV (of 4). London 1829. 8°.

An incomplete copy comprising only the half-title, title-page, and pp 169–284, 453–541 (end).

New York Public Library (Rare Book Room)

Bookplate: "Lenox Library | Duyckinck Collection | Presented in 1878." Librarian's notes in pencil on p ¯2.

MS TRANSCRIPT. A transcript written by SC on loose sheets of paper in ink is contained within the volume.

DATE. After 1829.

1   recto of blank leaf preceding p 169, pencil

If such worthless materials deserved a series of comments, the sciolism, self-conceit, and uniform *one-sidedness* of this T. Jefferson's Mind & its Utterances would afford an opportunity of conveying many most concerning truths by the detection and exposure of as many counterfeits in Currency.—T. Jefferson is a Mind of the Genus, Pleonecta including the Soals, Plaice, Flounders & other *flat fish*, who have two eyes but both on one side—but never the *right* side.[1]   *S. T. C.*

2   pp 239–41, pencil | Letter to Thomas Leiper, 1 Jan 1814

But is our particular interest to make us insensible to all sentiments of morality? Is it, then, become criminal, the moral wish that the torrents of blood this man [Napoleon] is shedding in Europe, the sufferings of so many human beings, good as ourselves, on whose necks he is trampling, the burning of antient cities, devastations of great countries, the

---

1[1] Pleuronectes ("side-swimmers"), the generic name of the flat-fish to which belong halibut, sole, plaice, turbot, and flounder. The eyes are both on one side of the head but may be on either right or left. C had the name right in *AR* (1825) 395, where he refers to "a certain Order of Intellects, who, like the Pleuronectae in Ichthyology that have both eyes on the same side, never see but half of a subject at one time . . .".

destruction of law and order, and demoralization of the world, should be arrested, even if it should place our peace a little further distant? No. You and I cannot differ in wishing that Russia, and Sweden, and Denmark, and Germany, and Spain, and Portugal, and Italy, and even England,* may retain their independence.

* O monstrous!—The Offspring of England who had for centuries received *good*, if not from the 4 or 5 men of a Cabinet, or even the 4 or 500 of a Parliament, yet from England—& whose revolution was preventive, & conservative not emancipative—or only emancipative *a priori!*—this "*even*" expresses & owns a bitterness of unnatural hatred of the Anglo-Americans to their Mother Country the source of their Laws, Religion, Language, Arts—the country of Bacon, Newton, Shakespear, Milton &—that to a rightly-tempered mind is truly frightful. I have seen & read enough of vulgar abuse of America by English Scribblers, and loathed it and them/—but a betrayal of a hatred so fiendish I never have found occasion to accuse an English Man.[1]

S. T. Coleridge.

2A p 503, marked with a pencil line in the margin | Anas 2 Aug 1793

. . . that he had never repented but once the having slipped the moment of resigning his office, and that was every moment since; that *by God* he had rather be in his grave than in his present situation; that he had rather be on his farm than to be made *Emperor of the world;* and yet that they were charging him with wanting to be a King. That that *rascal Freneau* sent him three of his papers every day, as if he thought he would become the distributor of his papers; that he could see in this, nothing but an impudent design to insult him; he ended in this high tone.

[2]1 Related remarks in *TT* 28 May 1830 clarify C's position. He deplores reviewers' attacks on the Americans and says, "I, for one, do not call the sod under my feet my country. But language, religion, laws, government, blood,—identity in these makes men of one country."

JOANNES SCOTUS ERIGENA

c 810–860

De divisione naturae libri quinque, diu desiderati. Accedit appendix ex
Ambiguis S. Maximi graece et latine. [Fly-title to Pt 2:] S. Maximi
Scholia in Gregorium Theologum. [Edited by Thomas Gale (c 1635–
1702).] 2 pts (in one vol). Oxford 1681. F°.

British Library C 126 l 11

Inscribed "S. T. Coleridge" on the title-page, not in his own hand; with the
"S. T. C." label also on the title-page. Inscribed by John Duke Coleridge on
p ⁻2: "C" "Coleridge Heath's Court   1892   This book belonged to S. T. C".

CONTENTS. i [i–xiv] 1–312 *De divisione naturae*. ii [i–ii] 1–88 *Appendix ex
Ambiguis S. Maximi graece et latine*. [This "Appendix" consists of two works
of St Maximus Confessor (c 580–662): (*a*) *Ambigua*—addressed to John of Cy-
zius, prefaced with Erigena's dedication to Charlemagne (from which **3** textus
and some of the early *CN* extracts are taken); (*b*) *Scholia in Gregorium Theolo-
gum*, with Preface by Erigena. Translated by Gale. See also **3** n 1.]

DATE. C's first recorded reading of Erigena belongs to 1803 (*CL* II 949; *CN* I
1382), but the notes in this copy must have been made in the 1820s, possibly
1827 in conjunction with N35 (**3** n 1).

---

1   i 284 | Bk 5 para 36

In the next page, 285, we find the *Original* of the moral philosophy so
finely set to the music of Verse in Pope's Essay on Man—tho' probably
Pope received it from nearer Rills.[1]

2   i 285–6

Quae ratio docet non omnino vitia mala esse, sed illicita. * Si enim mala
essent, nequaquam in virtutes mutari possent, ceteraque similia, quae
cum contra naturam ex perversis motibus abusionis libera voluntate ra-
tionabilis naturae seipsam sponte sua captivantis videtur insurgere; uni-
versitatis tamen ordinationibus non sinuntur nocere, magis autem ornare
eas coguntur aeternis legibus divinae providentiae atque judicii ambita.

[This line of reasoning shows that vices are not altogether evil but are unlawful.
* For if they were evil they could by no means be changed into virtues. There

1[1] Textus **2** reminds C of the optimistic   *on Man* (1.294).
"Whatever is, is right" strain in the *Essay*

are other cases like this, of things which, though they seem to rise up in revolt against nature out of the perverse motions of the misuse of free will by rational nature herself voluntarily putting herself under constraint, yet are not permitted to do damage to the order of the whole but are, rather, under the influence of divine providence and justice, obliged to enhance that order.]

* The sophistry by which moral acts, ⟨i.e. Vitia⟩[1] which have their several *forms* or *names* from excess or defect, and their proper essence in the state of the Will, are here turned into *things*, transformable into other *things* (*in virtutes mutari possunt*);[2] and the inference, that there must therefore be something *Good* in *Vice*—just as if by *Vices* the writer had been thinking of sundry Bronze Images or Icons of the VICES, that had been melted down and forged anew into the Icons or bronze statues of the correspondent Virtues—& pronounced the Image ~~fine~~ good; when he meant only that the Bronze was good—this is to me highly interesting.—It instances ⟨the first stage in⟩ the true cycle of the famous controversy of the Realists and Nominalists.[3] First, the Δυναμεῖς included in but hidden and overlayed by, *Idolism*[4]—Such was the Realism of the Ante-Scholastic Thinkers, and of the first Schoolmen. 2. The Nominalists detected the errors, and having succee~~ding~~ed in resolving the larger number of these supposed Realities into Nomina, seu Entia Logica,[5] presumed the same of all: and lost [sight][a] of the Δυναμεις or denied their existence. 3. Lastly, came Ockham who carrying Nominalism into all its consequences was on the very brink of converting the Nomina into

---

[a] Word supplied by the editor

2[1] "Vices"—in textus.

2[2] "Can be changed into virtues"—the positive form of a negative statement in textus.

2[3] The Realist doctrine, drawn from Plato and the Plotinists by Erigena and widely disseminated by Remigius of Auxerre (c 841–c 908), held that "universals" have a real existence separate from the "particulars" in which they are embodied. The contrary position, Nominalism, holding that universals have no real existence but are logical entities—*nomina*, "names", not *res*, "things"—was established if not founded by Roscellinus (d c 1125) and refined by his first opponent, Peter Abelard (1079–1142), and later by William of Occam (n 6 below). The controversy between Realists and Nominalists, of crucial importance in the philosophical development of the doctrine of the Trinity, was also—C thought—"one of the greatest

and most important that ever occupied the human mind. They were both right, and both wrong. They each maintained opposite poles of the same truth: which truth neither of them saw, for want of a higher premiss. Duns Scotus was the head of the Realists; Ockham, his own disciple, of the Nominalists." *TT* 30 Apr 1830.

2[4] The Greek word *dynameis*, "powers", which in its singular form *dynamis* is the root of "dynamic" below. The doctrine of powers is central to C's mature thought, as in the physico-theological context of KANT *Metaphysische Anfangsgründe* **27**, **30**, **33**, and in the attempted definition in *Logic* (*CC*) 69*. Here C outlines what he held to be a recurrent historical pattern, whereby an original spiritual intuition is reified and worshipped in a material form, e.g. in Greek polytheism.

2[5] "Names, or Logical Entities".

Numina Rerum[6]—& thus prepared the way for the true i.e. the Dynamic Realism—~~and~~ which reducing the *Idola* Sensûs to the Nomina rerum finds the res ipsas, the entia verà realia, in the Δυναμεῖς, the Νόμοι, the 'Ιδέαι ἐνεργίκοι.[7] But alas! this third epoch is but in the Dawn./

S. T. C.

3 ii [ii]–[1] | S. Maximi Scholia in Gregorium theologum: Dedication

[Maximus is explaining a number of abstruse passages in Dionysius Areopagiticus:] Et iterum, ejusdem divinae videlicet bonitatis qualis sit reversio, id est congregatio per eosdem gradus ab infinita eorum quae sunt variaque multiplicatione usque ad simplicissimam omnium unitatem, quae in Deo est & Deus est; ita ut & Deus omnia sit, & omnia Deus sint.*

[And again [Maximus makes clear] what is the nature of the return of this divine goodness, that is, that it is the gathering together, through the same stages, from the infinite and varied multiplicity of the things that exist to the most simple unity of all, which is in God and is God; so that while God is all things, yet all things are God.*]

* How is it to be explained that J. Erigena with so many other Christian Divines and Philosophers should not have perceived, that pious words and scriptural phrases may disguise but can not transsubstantiate Pantheism—a handsome Mask that does not alter a single feature of the ugly Face, it hides?[1]—How is it to be explained that so comprehensive and subtle an Intellect, as Scotus Erigena, should not have seen, that his "Deus omnia et omnia Deus"[2] was incompatible with moral responsibility, and subverted all essential difference of Good and Evil, Right and

2[6] "Names into *Powers* of Things". The pun *nomen/numen*, not translatable directly into English—see e.g. BIBLE COPY B 33—turns upon the primordial potency, daemonic or divine, ascribed to a name.

William of Occam (or Ockham) (c 1300–c 1349), *Doctor invincibilis*, taught an extreme form of Augustinian and Scotist doctrine and was the principal advocate and exponent of Nominalism in the fourteenth century. C praised him for his definition of faith (*P Lects* Lect 9—1949—280–1) and placed him with Erigena and Duns Scotus among the "morning stars of the Reformation" (*TT* 6 May 1833).

2[7] Reducing the "*Idols* (*Shadows*) of Sense" to the "Names of things", the Dynamic Realism finds the "things them-selves, the truly real entities", in the "Powers, the Laws, the energic Ideas". The last word in Greek characters, not truly a Greek word, resembles the seventeenth-century "energic", for which *OED* cites three uses by C as a nonce-word.

3[1] The burden of C's objections to Erigena from 1803, when he described him in a letter to RS (*CL* II 954) as "clearly the founder of the School of Pantheism", to 1827, when a notebook entry (N35 ff 24–24ᵛ) sums up: "Briefly, Erigena's System is avowed Pantheism."

3[2] "God is all things, and all things are God"—in textus; also referred to in connection with Erigena in *Friend* (*CC*) II 80* (21 Sept 1809).

Wrong?—I can suggest no other solution, but the Innocence of his Heart and the Purity of his Life—for the same reason, that ⟨so many⟩ young men in the unresisted buoyance of their Freedom embrace without scruple the doctrine of Necessity, and ⟨only⟩ at a later ~~per~~ and less genial ⟨Period⟩ learn, and learn to value, their free-agency by its struggles to maintain itself against the increasing incroachments of ~~Society~~ Nature and Society.[3] It is a great Mercy of God that a good Heart is often so effective an antidote to the heresies of the Head. I could name more than ⟨one⟩[a] learned, ~~and~~ godly and religious Clergyman, who is a Pantheist thro' his Zeal for the TRINITY—without suspecting what nevertheless is ~~a most~~ demonstrably true, that Pantheism is but a painted Atheism and that the Doctrine of the Trinity is the great and only sure Bulwark against it. But these ~~m~~ good men take up the venomous thing, and it hurteth them not.[4]

               —S. T. C.

4   ii 88 (last page of text) and p ⁺1, pencil except for the last few words

Marks[1]

Common

= equal to, equivalent, the same as. N.B. This mark sufficient for geometrical purposes is too multivocal for philosophy, in which "equivalent" and "the same with" are very different conceptions.[2]

+ in addition to—placed before a single term it expressive[b] the Thesis or Positive Pole—

− less by:—or the antithesis, or Negative Pole—

÷ division   × multiplied into

---

[a] Word inserted in pencil   [b] A slip for "is expressive of" or simply "expresses"?

3[3] A recollection of C's own early Unitarian-necessitarian interlude and of his much longer struggle with pantheism before he was able to establish his trinitarian position.

3[4] Mark 16.18 (var).

4[1] This list with explanation of "Marks" represents a mature state of the system of signs that C used to convey graphically and unequivocally certain relations and functions that recurred in his exposition. The first five marks are the earliest and most stable of the system; the next set of three is, in the sense given here, unique; the last set of three C developed over a period of years. Their evolution may be traced through notebooks and marginalia, esp *CN* ii 2383–4; *CN* iii 4403; *CN* iv 4555; EICHHORN *Apocrypha* 2; SWEDENBORG *De equo albo* (1758) back flyleaves; also *Opus Maximum* i ff 193–4.

4[2] C may have been thinking particularly of Kant, whom he complained of for having "confounded" two meanings of the "equals" sign: KANT *Metaphysische Anfangsgründe* 2–5, *VS* COPY C 29.

Idiosymbolic,[3] or marks used by myself

⊙ = Identity, or Co-inherence of two in one previously to the Manifestation of the One, as two

○ = Indifference, or Mesothesis

⊕ = Synthesis

)(= disparate   Sweet)(Pungent

⋇ = opposed to   Sweet ⋇ Sour

⋇ = contrary to.   Sweet ⋇ Bitter.

ᵃ)(= disparate ⋇ in opposition to. ⋇ contrary to. Gold)(Silver: Sour ⋇ Sweet. Bitter ⋇ Sweet./*ᵇ*

---

5   p ⁺1, corrected and emended in pencil, footnote on ii 88

The whole tremendous difficulty of a Creation e nihilo—and if ex ali-quo,[1] how could it be Creation?—and not in all propriety of language—Formation or Construction?—this difficulty, I say, which appeared so gigantic to our Milton that he asserted the eternity of matter to escape from it, and then to ꜰ get rid of the offensive consequences reduces this matter to an Attribute of God, and plunges head over heels into Spinosism[2]—this difficulty, I repeat for the third time (the sad necessity of all Philo-parenthesists!)[3] arises wholly out of that Slavery*ᶜ* ⟨of the Mind⟩*ᵈ* to the Eye and ⟨the⟩ visual Imagination ⟨()or Fancy↙⟨)⟩,[4] ⟨under the influence of⟩ which ⟨the Reasoner⟩ must have a *picture* and mistakes surface for substance— ~~and~~*ᵉ* ⟨Such men—and their name is LEGION—⟩[5] consequently *demands* ⱥ *Matter*, as a *Datum*. As soon as this gross Prej-udice is cured by the appropriate discipline, and the Mind is familiarized to the contemplation of Matter as a *product↙* ⟨in time,⟩ the resulting

---

ᵃ⁻ᵇ On p ⁺1, in ink
ᶜ Capital S written in pencil over original lower-case letter
ᵈ Inserted in pencil—as are all the later insertions in this note
ᵉ Cancelled in pencil—as are all the later cancellations in this note except the next

4[3] Not in *OED*; C's coinage.

5[1] "Creation from nothing . . . from something". C's position on this theologi-cal issue is clarified in notes of 1815 on Edward Williams *An Essay on the Equity of Divine Government* (1809), where he ac-cepts the concept of creation out of nothing and observes that it is "a doctrine which Mosheim has proved peculiar to divine Revelation": *SW & F (CC)*.

5[2] C uses "Spinosism" here as equiva-lent to "pantheism"; he refers to the ac-count of the creation in bk VII of *Paradise Lost*, e.g. "the Earth,/ Matter unform'd and void" (232–3) and "I am who fill/ In-finitude" (168–9).

5[3] "Philo-parenthesist" is C's nonce-word for "a lover of parentheses". He of-ten mocked but also defended his habit of parenthetical digression, e.g. *CL* v 98–9.

5[4] The interesting redefinition of Fancy as "visual Imagination" here supports C's characteristic attack on the "despotism of the eye" as in *BL* ch 6 (*CC*) I 107, *Logic* (*CC*) 242–3.

5[5] Echoes the reply of the unclean spirit to Jesus, "My name is Legion: for we are many": Mark 5.9.

PHÆNOMENON of the equilibrium of the two antagonist Forces, Attraction and Repulsion, ~~as~~ ⟨*that*⟩ the Negative and ⟨*this* the⟩ Positive Poles of *Gravity/ ⟨()or the Power of DEPTH/()⟩ the difficulty disappears— and the Idea of CREATION alone remains.—For to will causatively with foreknowlege is to *create*, in respect of all finite products.—An absolute and coeternal Product ~~is either~~*a* (improperly so called) is either an Offspring, and the productive Act a *Begetting*, or a Procession. The WORD begotten, the Spirit proceeding.[8]   S. T. Coleridge

*b*N.B. Attraction, Repulsion, and Gravity as the Root and Unity of both, are only a more special formula of the Dimensions, Length, Breadth and Depth considered as Powers, η δυναμικως.†*c*[9]

* Centrality, or Vis centrificus[6] would be the preferable term. It is the same with the Mosaic Darkness, in Hebrew, the withholder or Holderin, *Inhibitor*.[7]—⚹ Light, as the distinctive *exhibitive* Power.

†*d* Several of the elder Logicians instead of the terms Length, Breadth and Depth use the far better terms, Linea, Superficies, Corpus.[10]

---

a Cancelled in ink in the course of first writing
b-c This afterthought, written in pencil, is crowded into the head of p +1 between the last section of 4 and the beginning of 5
d This footnote, written in pencil, is crowded into the head-margin of ii 88 (facing)

5[6] "Centrific force"—force that makes a centre. C's response (based on *Naturphilosophie*) to the Newtonian concept of gravity is that gravity is "not merely Attraction but a synthetic Power": BÖHME **79**.

5[7] In Hebrew, *choshek* (darkness) has as its related verb *choshak* (to be dark), which resembles but is not identical with *chosak* (to hold, keep back, withhold). In other expositions of the first chapter of Genesis, C similarly refers to the symbolic or "ideal" opposition of darkness and light: e.g. *CL* IV 767–76 (where C refers to Erigena), *CN* III 4418, BÖHME **139**.

5[8] In *CN* IV 5078 (c Dec 1823), C asserts that "the Church itself" observes a distinction between "the *begetting* of the Logos, the filial Deity, the Son, and the *Proceeding* of the *Spirit* from the Father and from the Son"; he alludes to the language of Articles 2 and 5 in the Articles of Religion.

5[9] "Or dynamically": C evokes the framework of the "compass of nature" here as in *TL, CN* III 4226, and the extended exposition of Genesis cited in n 7 above.

5[10] "Line, Surface, Body". The "elder Logicians" have not been identified.

SAMUEL JOHNSON
1649–1703

The Works of the Late Reverend Mr. Samuel Johnson, sometime Chaplain to the Right Honourable William Lord Russel. London 1710. F°.

British Library C 126 l 2

Inscribed by John Duke Coleridge on p ⁻4: "C" and "Coleridge Heath's Court 1892 S. T—C—". A note of two lines in ink on p 414 has been effectively erased (54A); a passage marked with what appear to be quotation marks, on p 409, is not included in the ANNEX as not conforming with C's usual practices; a few words in pencil on pp 412–13 are not in C's hand.

Some if not all of C's notes were written with Charles Lamb in mind: Lamb is addressed directly in 8. In his own copy, Lamb wrote C's remarks on Johnson as they are recorded in *TT* 15 May 1833 (the date of 53): E. V. Lucas *Life of Charles Lamb* (1905) II 318. Since the *TT* entry combined notes taken by HNC on separate occasions, and since *TT* itself was not published until after Lamb's death, it seems that HNC lent *TT* to Lamb in ms or page proof.

CONTENTS. Pp iii–xix "Some Memorials of . . . Johnson"; 1–52 *Julian the Apostate*; 53–116 *Julian's Arts to Undermine and Extirpate Christianity*; 117–235 *A Second Five Year's Struggle Against Popery and Tyranny*; 236–52 *Remarks upon Dr Sherlock's Book*; 253–8 *Reflections on the History of Passive Obedience*; 259–78 *An Argument Proving that the Abrogation of King James . . . was according to the Constitution of the English Government*; 279–93 *An Essay concerning Parliaments at a Certainty*; 294–322 *Notes upon the Phenix Edition of the Pastoral Letter*; 323–38 *A Confutation of . . . "A Letter Ballancing the Necessity of Keeping a Land-force in time of Peace"*; 339–99 *The Second Part of the Ballancing Letter, being an Occasional Discourse in Vindication of Magna Charta* (pp 378–99 appendixes added by publisher); 401–88 *Several Discourses upon Practical Subjects*.

DATE. May 1833. Dated in ms: 8 May 1833 (13), 15 May 1833 (53). The Reform Bill of 1832 is mentioned in 23.

1 p xvii, pencil

These several Propositions [as cited by Hampden in justification of "having abandon'd King *James*, and own'd King *William* and Queen *Mary*"] being maintain'd by Divines of Note, it is the less to be wonder'd that Mr. *Johnson* who oppos'd those Principles, and particularly in his Book about the Abrogation of King *James*, cou'd get no Church-Preferment, since he had such numerous and powerful Enemys among the Clergy, who represented him as a Republican, for maintaining that King *James* was dethron'd for Male-Administration, and that King *William* and Queen *Mary* were set up in his stead by Authority of Parliament.

Often have I had a wish whence I my reason almost forbad a Hope, that God would yet grant me an interval of sufficing Health & Power to execute my long fostered purpose of writing the history of Whiggery,[1] or the Principle (λογου αλογου)[2] of Compromise of Principles, from the first Whig, Lord Shaftesbury (Cromwell's Ashley Cooper & Dryden's Achitophel) to Earl Grey—ultimum Whiggorum.[3]—*Samuel Johnson, & Defoe.*—[4] *S. T. C.* N.B. King William (the Third) was no Whig; but an honest Man.[5]

[1] [1] The name "Whig", of uncertain origin, was given first to Scottish Presbyterians who marched on Edinburgh in 1648, then to the Covenanters who drove episcopacy out of Scotland, then to those who, with Johnson, tried to prevent James, Duke of York, as a Roman Catholic, from acceding to the throne. As "the name of a faction" (the definition given by the later Samuel Johnson in his *Dictionary*), it belongs as C suggests to the Restoration period. Under Queen Anne the name lost its rebellious colour and attached itself to the political party representing the well-to-do urban middle classes.

C projected a "history of Whiggism" in connection with his reading of ASGILL: it is outlined in *TT* 28 Jan 1832 and in a proposal for the publishers in *CL* VI 905 (7 May 1832).

[2] "Of illogical logic" or perhaps "of unreasonable reason". Cf the characterisation of Whiggism as "a compromise between two opposite *Principles*" and "*principle* unprincipled" in **43** and **52** below.

[3] Anthony Ashley Cooper (1621–83), 1st Earl of Shaftesbury (1672), in succession served Charles I in the field, abandoned his cause to side with the parliamentarians, led the opposition against Cromwell after being installed in his parliament, and was instrumental in the recall of Charles II. Rewarded with elevation in rank and responsibility, he fell into disfavour for supporting the Test Act (1673) and was dismissed from his offices; cajoled back into

the privy council, he was dismissed again for various subversive misdemeanours, not least his support of the Exclusion Bill (1680). Committed to the Tower on charges of high treason (1681), he was released by Charles and allowed to escape to Holland, where he died. Dryden's virulent portrait of him as "the false Achitophel" is in *Absalom and Achitophel* (1681) lines 150–99.

Charles Grey (1764–1845), Viscount Howick, later 2nd Earl Grey, prime minister of the Whig administration of 1831 that introduced a bill of parliamentary reform in that year without success and, after severe reverses in both Commons and Lords, succeeded in getting an altered bill passed in May 1832 (**46** below). Grey's name does not appear in C's *TT* proposal for a history but is present in *CL* VI 905 as "Lord Grey, who, I trust in God's Mercy, will be the last"—as here in Latin "the last of the Whigs".

[4] C considered Johnson "a very remarkable writer" to be "compared to his contemporary De Foe, whom he resembled in many points" (*TT* 15 May 1833). Defoe is named also in **8** and **45** below.

[5] In C's view "William the Third was a greater and much honester man than any of his ministers", virtually all of whom had corresponded with James II (*TT* 23 Jul 1827). C's criterion of whiggishness is readiness to compromise; hence, Johnson also is "no Whig" (**41**, **43**).

2 p xix, pencil

The title is modest enough—*Some* Memorials—but they are a meagre Substitute for a Life of Mr S.J.—a worthier subject of Biography than Dr S. Johnson—& this without denying the worth of the latter—but more thanks to Boswell than to the Doctor's own Works/—[1]

S. T. C.

Among my countless intentional Works, one was—Biographical Memorials of Revolutionary Minds, in Philosophy, Religion, and Politics.[2] Mr Sam. Johnson was to have been one/—I meant to have begun with Wickliff, & to have confined myself to Natives of Great Britain—but with one or two supplementary Volumes, for the Heroes of Germany (Luther & his Compeers) and of Italy (Vico)[3]

3 p 4, pencil | The Preface to the Reader

And St. Paul *himself was not for Passive-Obedience by any means, even when the lawful Magistrate persecuted him, if it were in an unlawful way; but he stood upon his Birthright. For did he not in one place awe the Centurion and Chief Captain, and make all the Soldiers vanish who were commanded to beat him, by telling them he was a* Roman?

Samuel Johnson is right; but might have made his Position more evident, had he made the difference between the Christian of St Paul's time and the Christian after Constantine that of Alien and Citizen.[1] The Alien is bound to consider Government in the Abstract, and in its universal Attributes—the defects of the particular government concern the *Citizen*, & native Member of the State.[2]

[2][1] The assertion that "Dr. Johnson's fame now rests principally upon Boswell" (*TT* 4 Jul 1833) is consistent with C's general hostility towards Johnson.

[2][2] This is the last reference to a project that C had had in mind for at least 30 years. It appears in *CN* I 1646 (Nov 1803) as a work on "Revolutionary Minds" including Aquinas, Scotus (probably Duns Scotus, not Erigena), Luther, Richard Baxter, Socinus, and George Fox; the names of Bruno, Böhme, and Spinoza immediately following may also have been part of the scheme. Certainly Bruno, Böhme, and Spinoza were central to the scheme in later forms, e.g. as part of the *Logosophia*: *CL* IV 589–90. By 1827 it had been retitled

Vindiciae Heterodoxae: NOBLE **14**.

[2][3] This is the only version of the project to include Johnson, Wycliffe, and Vico—all fairly recent enthusiasms. C annotated a copy of Robert VAUGHAN *Opinions of John de Wycliffe* (1828), and he had been introduced to Vico's *Scienza nuova* (3 vols Milan 1816) in May 1825 (*CL* v 454)—in fact, had not returned two vols of Vico by Oct 1833 (*CL* VI 965–6).

[3][1] The reign of Constantine the Great (c 288–337) was a turning-point for Christians, since Constantine as emperor made a point of integrating the Christians into the state and was himself baptised just before his death.

[3][2] C makes a similar point in **12** below.

4 p 16, pencil | Ch 2

Eumenius, in his Panegyrick to the same *Constantine . . .* tells him, "It was not the casual consent of Men, it was not any sudden effect of their Favour which made you a Prince. You gain'd the Empire by being born into the World; which seems to me the first and greatest Gift of the Gods, for one to come into the World Great, and to have that at home ready for him, which others can hardly attain with all the Toil and Labour of their whole Lives."*

* Here S. J. betrays the *Party*man/ as if the Flattery of a Court Orator (Eumenius) could be received as a proof that the Imperial office in Rome was hereditary. The very term, Imperator, contradicts it.[1]

5 p 17, pencil

[Of Nazianzen's Invective made upon the death of Julian and addressed to the soul of Constantius:] Now here is enough to shew that *Constantius* wou'd never have made *Julian* Caesar, nor have set up an Enemy of Christ over the Christians, if he had known him to have been such.

Tho' not amiss as a shrewd Nudge & Pinch of the *patristic* bigotry of the hot high-church Divines, yet as a matter of sober argument this, I cannot but think, an unhappy choice of Subject. It is absurd to assume the edicts of Constantine and Constantius to have been in the eyes of Julian's Contemporaries equivalent to what we mean by the Law & Constitution of the Realm/ The Christians were still a minority, tho' a very powerful & increasing portion of the Subjects of the Roman Empire/[1] Nazianzen's Invective (published, doubtless, after Julian's Death) would if published during Julian's Life, have been a seditious, nay, treasonable Libel—& no *Christian* Jury could without perjury have brought in a contrary verdict[2]—Probably, an addition to the Coronation Oath, to which Charles IInd would have consented in order to escape the Bill of Exclusion, imposed on the Successor by Act of Parliament, would have been a wiser measure than the *Exclusion*-attempt, which shocked the

4[1] C explains this point himself in **15** below.

5[1] Constantine and his son Constantius II (emperor 337–61) had opened Roman citizenship to Christians. Constantine's nephew Julian (332–63) during his brief reign as emperor moved to reverse Constantine's christianising policies and restore pagan worship.

5[2] Gregory of Nazianzus, or "Nazianzen" (329–89), who had been a fellow-student of Julian's at Athens, wrote two "invectives" against Julian; Julian's death was the occasion of the one cited here. The concepts of publication, libel, jury, and perjury are all somewhat anachronistic; C is addressing the contemporary implications of Johnson's argument.

prejudices of a large party among the Protestants themselves.[3] Then the Statute of Elizabeth (see, p. 6) would have *told*[4]—& *legally* justified James's after expulsion.

6 pp 18–19, pencil

He does not barely say, That if *Constantius* had known *Julian's* Religion, he wou'd not have made him *Caesar*; but he says, that he wou'd have disinherited his whole Family first, he wou'd have parted with his Empire, he wou'd have strip'd himself of all, and lost his Life rather than have done it. And accordingly we find, that as soon as *Constantius* understood his Error, he bitterly bewail'd it, which was just at his Death.

I object to the whole reasoning of this IInd Chapter, as essentially *papal* in its spirit—& making a Doxy, assumed to be *Ortho*-doxy, because it was S. Johnson's Doxy, under the name of *Religion* a sufficient reason for the dethronement of a legitimate King—& introducing *Law*, not simply as Law, but only because it happened, pro isto tempore,[1] to be *this* Religion.—Beyond all doubt, the Edicts of Julian & his Senate were as truly Roman Law as those of Constantine & Constantius/[2] & so if James had procured (as if he had not *hurried* & ~~been~~ let off the Blunderbuss of his bigotry when it was only primed, & before it was loaded, [as][a] he might have done [)], perhaps—he would have proceeded as lawfully as Elizabeth—& a rebellion against him as truly treason, as that of the D. of Northumberland & E. of Westmoreland against the imperial Virgin—[3]

---

[a] Insertion by ed

5[3] A section of the Coronation Oath of William and Mary, intended to secure the integrity of the Church of England against Roman Catholicism, had become crucial in the issue of the Catholic Emancipation Bill. See *C&S* (*CC*) 105; also **46** below. The Exclusion Bill, of which Johnson was "one of the most formidable advocates" (*TT* 15 May 1833), designed to preclude the accession of the Roman Catholic Duke of York, was passed by the Commons (with Shaftesbury's support) in 1680 but was rejected by the Lords and then killed by Charles's dissolution of parliament.

5[4] In the "Preface to the Reader" p 6 there is reference to "*that Statute* 13 Eliz. chap. I. *which makes it High Treason in her Reign, and Forfeiture of Goods and*

Chattels ever after, in any wise to hold or affirm, That an Act of Parliament is not of sufficient Force and Validity to limit and bind the Crown of this Realm, and the Descent, Limitation, Inheritance, and Government thereof".

6[1] "For that particular time".

6[2] C makes the same point in **5** above.

6[3] Sir Thomas Percy, 7th Earl of Northumberland (1528–72), and Charles Neville, 6th Earl of Westmorland (1543–1601), leaders of the "Northern Rising", a plot to release Mary Queen of Scots from her virtual imprisonment and (with help from Spain) to place her on the throne and restore England to the Roman Catholic religion.

7 p 18, pencil

[Quoting Gregory Nazianzen:] ". . . these three things he [Constantius] acknowledg'd were evil and unworthy of his Reign, The Slaughter of his Kindred, and his Declaring of the Apostate, and his Innovating in Matters of Faith. . . ." This is ten times more than if *Constantius* had actually excluded *Julian*. . . . But now he repents him upon his Death-Bed, where Mens Eyes are open, and they usually have their soberest Thoughts about them, that he had not done it, and reckons it in the number of those things which have blackned his Reign.

And those blind [? in/on] Acts S. J. seriously adduces! & a precious fellow this Constantius!! and his death bed Palinodia of 3 articles. Alas! 1. that he had murdered his kindred—2. that he had *not* murdered Julian! & 3. that he had been, ⟨he began to suspect, a little⟩ too hasty in deciding in favor of the Homoiousians against the Homo-ousians!!![1]

8 p ⁻1, referring to p 18 | **7** textus

P. 18.

The edifying death-bed Palinodia of Mr Sam. Johnson's *Christian Emperor Constantius*, in 3 clauses:

1. That (not to mention the ordinary routine of homicides incident to the assumption & maintenance of ~~the~~ imperial power) he had with one exception murdered all his ⟨male⟩ kindred.

2. That he had unwittingly made an exception, and (alas! alas!) had *not* murdered Julian.

3. That—perhaps—he began to fear, to suspect—that he had been— at least might have been somewhat over-hasty, and too vigorous, in deciding against the Homoousians ~~agai~~ in favor of the Homoiousians.

How much is it to be regretted, that so affecting a last Dying Speech and Confession should ~~have been~~ be historically grounded on, & prefaced by, an "And *it is said*"—"*On dit.*"—"It has been *reported*"— "ως λογος εστι."[1]—i.e. if Constantius did not happen to say so, it is what, in Sozomon's & Gregory Nazianzen's opinion,[2] he ⟨must have⟩

[7][1] At the synod of Rimini (359), called by Constantius, the Nicene Creed was reaffirmed against the Arians; but Constantius then forced the Western bishops, at a synod at Nice in Thrace, to subscribe to an Arianising creed in which the term *homoousios* ("of the same substance") was replaced by *homoiousios* ("of like substance"). The context of the debate is more fully explained in FLEURY **66** n 5.

[8][1] French "they say", Greek "as the story goes".

[8][2] Sozomen—Salmaninius Hermias Sozomen, a fifth-century historian who settled at Constantinople with intent to bring Eusebius's ecclesiastical history down to his own day but completed only nine books covering 323 to 425—is cited by Johnson (p 170) as an authority in his account of Constantius.

intended to say—at all events, *ought* to have said—& that Touch at the Trinity on the last Round of the Ladder[3]—Charles! dearest Charles! let it not have been ~~uttered~~ recorded in vain!—The two former clauses appertain to Newgate—But persons, who have never been in Newgate, may have been in Essex Street Chapel, not far distant—Alas! I am assured of this by my own experience—[4]   *S. T. C.*

"AND THIS WAS THE CONSCIENCE OF A DYING EMPEROR"!![5]

Think only what a grand high-minded Fellow Samuel Johnson (*M^r*) verily was (*his* treatment and Defoe's makes one feel the heterogenëity of William's own Character & that of his scoundrelly compromising Whig Ministers!)[6]—& then tell me whether you remember a more remarkable instance of the blinding, warping power of Party-Spirit even where it is the right & comparatively *righteous* Party!—

9   p 19, pencil | Ch 3

And here a Man may almost lose himself in the great variety of Instances which may be given of their Hatred and Contempt of *Julian* when he was Emperor: How they reproach'd him and his Religion to his very Beard, beat his Priests before his Face, and had done him too, if he had not got out of the way. . . . These things will better be seen in the History and Relation of the Matter of Fact; which I shall put into the best order I can, by giving an account of what was done in his Life-time, and then all that concerns his Death; and after that, how they us'd his Memory.

All this is an excellent Answer to the High Church quoters of the Precedents & Examples of the first Three or four Centuries of Christianity—but S. J. appears to quote them himself as Counter-precedents, examples to be followed. But surely these Christians were little better than our Crown & Anchor Patriots—and acted toward Julian, as our Radicals under Cobbett &c.—[1]

8[3] I.e. sec 3 in **7** and **8** above.

8[4] Though not criminal, they may be guilty of errors in religion. Christ's Hospital was in Newgate St; the "Essex Street Chapel" was the Unitarian church built in 1774.

8[5] This is not quoted from Johnson; perhaps C provided the quotation marks to give extra emphasis to his own exclamation.

8[6] William III eventually granted Johnson a bounty of £1000 and an annual pension of £300; during his reign, however, Defoe was fined, imprisoned, and pilloried.

9[1] The Crown and Anchor—where C had given his Philosophical Lectures and the last series of literary lectures in 1818–19—was a tavern in the Strand at which supporters of Burdett, Fox, and Cobbett gathered to advance the radical cause: see *EOT* (*CC*) II 306 n 5.

10   p 20, pencil

They did not only thus scoff at him [Julian], and deride him behind his back; but they took the freedom to reproach him and his Religion to his face. [Theodoret the historian gives as an instance of Julian's meek and tolerant behaviour towards the "blindness of bigotry" of a "Nobleman of Berea" who was excessively strict with his son for "warping towards the false Religion" which was Julian's own.] "I have not told this story in vain (says *Theodoret*) but was willing to shew, not only the admirable Freedom of this Divine Person, but also that there were very many who despis'd *Julian*'s Power and Authority."

No wonder that Gibbon as an Unfriend of the Christian Church selected Julian for his favorite Hero[1]—the wonder is, that a man like Johnson could have related this precious Passage without expressing his Contempt of Theodoret's factious Applause, & his reprobation of the Beræan's insolence, hard-heartedness & heart-hardening Bigotry and Fanaticism

11   p 22, pencil, marked with a line in the margin | Ch 4

And now I know no more than the Pope of *Rome*, what to make of all this, what they meant by it, or upon what Principles these Men proceeded. Whether the Laws of their Country allow'd them (which I am sure the Laws of our Country do not allow a Man to imagine) to offer Violence to their lawful Emperor, or whether old *Gregory* distinguish'd, and did not resist *Julian*, but only the Devil, which his Son so often tells us was in him; or how it was, I will never stand guessing. Only this we may be assur'd of, that none of these Bishops had ever been in *Scotland*, nor had learn'd to fawn upon an Apostate, and a mortal Enemy to their Religion.

Now in the spirit of these Sentences should all the foregoing have been written—i.e. not justifying the Christian Party but making the Passive Obedience-Divines ridiculous by the contrast of the words & actions of these admired Zealots with the tenets & pretences of their Admirers! But when will Partizans be cool enough to bear in mind, than[a] of two hostile Parties the probability is, that both are in the wrong.[b]

---

[a] A slip for "that"   [b] Here C has written "/\", and continued the note in the foot-margin with "/\"

10[1] Gibbon gives an extended and generally admiring account of Julian's character and career in *The Decline and Fall of* *the Roman Empire* chs 19–24: at the end of ch 22, for example, he writes, "Even faction, and religious faction, was constrained

The inadvertence to this truth was the occasion of Mr Fox's blundering Speeches at the commencement of the Anti-Jacobin War, by which he alienated all sober people, reduced his own followers to a hand-full, & enabled Pitt to raise that Panic of Property which rendered him irresistible.[1]

12   p 28, pencil | Ch 9

Has a Man no more Right nor Privilege after he is naturaliz'd, than when he was a Stranger, or Alien, or accounted an Enemy? Do not the same Laws, which forbid Men to invade other Mens Rights, enable them not withstanding to maintain and defend their own?

Now S. J. comes to the right *point*—the difference between the duties of Z, a pilgrim, an Alien, and the same Z, a Citizen, with all the obligations of a patriot.[1]

13   p 33, pencil, the last sentence marked with a line in the margin

For where is it said in the Word of the Lord . . . that we are to yield up our selves to Cut-Throats and Assassinates, which the *Papists* have ever been to poor *Protestants*? And how many hundred thousands they have massacred, I know not; but this I know, that they never did, nor ever will massacre more or less than just as many as they can.

This might be applied word for word to the Irish at the present time, 8 May 1833.[1]

14   p 81 | Answer to the Chapter of Passive Obedience

. . . the Bishop [Bilson] . . . says, *The Subject has no refuge against his Sovereign, but only to God, by Prayer and Patience:* But this is not the Case of Men who are under the Protection of the Laws, which were made on purpose to be a Defence and Refuge against all lawless Oppression whatsoever . . .

It is evident that the Laudensians[1] are guilty of the sophism of subsum-

---

to acknowledge the superiority of his genius, in peace as well as in war; and to confess, with a sigh, that the apostate Julian was a lover of his country, and that he deserved the empire of the world." Cf GIBBON in *CM* (*CC*) II 843–4.

11[1] "Panic of Property" is a phrase used more than once by C to account for the success of Pitt's repressive measures in the 1790s: *Lects 1795* (*CC*) 30–1, *C&S*

(*CC*) 131. C's analysis of Fox's behaviour during that time appears most fully in his "Letters to Charles James Fox" in the *Morning Post: EOT* (*CC*) I 376–90, 391–9.

12[1] See also **3** above.

13[1] See *C&S* (*CC*) 150–4, esp "the Irish massacre" in 153 and n 2.

14[1] Followers of abp William Laud (1573–1645) or, more broadly, members of the high-church party. Johnson is quot-

ing their conclusion in their premise. They first identify the Sovereign (i.e. the Individual, who is the Head of the State) and the Sovereign Power. Now this is true only in an absolute Monarchy. But when by the constitution of the Country the King is limited, there he is but a *part* of that Sovereignty, the whole of which indeed he *represents* as long as he *executes* its Will—i.e. in England, acts according to an *Act of Parliament.* D[r] Willis or the Keepers appointed by him might as wisely be brought in as rebels to the *Sovereign Power* because they confined George III[d] who was the *Sovereign.*[2] It is a droll *Pun.*

15 p 81

[Quoting Bishop Bilson:] *Theo.* If a Prince shou'd go about to subject his Kingdom to a foreign Realm, or change the form of the Commonwealth from Impery to Tyranny; or neglect the Laws establish'd by common Consent of Prince and People, to execute his own Pleasure: In these and other Cases, which might be nam'd, if the Nobles and Commons join together to defend their antient and accustom'd Liberty, Regiment and Laws, they may not well be counted Rebels.

Note! Impery (imperium) means *delegated* power. Imperat in distinction from jubet. Consulit Senatus, jussit Populus, imperavit Dux, vel Consul.[1]—Hence, says Gravina, the *Kings* among the ancients being held as arbitrary Monarchs, they took an *Oath*; but the Romans who submitted to Emperors would never suffer them to take this Oath, as it would imply that they were responsible to the Gods only.[2]

16 p 83

[Arguments in support of Hammond's position that *"Christ meddles not*

ing from Thomas Bilson (1546/7–1616), bp of Winchester *The True Difference between Christian Subjection and Unchristian Rebellion* (Oxford 1585), a defence of "the Princes lawful power to command"; Bilson had died before Laud was appointed in 1621 to his first bishopric.

14[2] Francis Willis (1718–1807), a successful "mad-doctor", was called in to care for George III in 1788 and attended him thereafter, assisted by staff and two of his sons—one of whom was called in in 1811 after his father's death.

15[1] A prince "governs", he does not "decree". "The Senate resolves, the People commanded, the Leader or Consul governed." The source of the formula is not

traced. It appears again (with the verbs in difference tenses), possibly written at much the same time as this, in HACKET *Scrinia* **47** n 4, where (as here) Gravina is named.

15[2] Giovanni Vincenzo Gravina *De romano imperio* sec 19, in *Opera* (Leipzig 1737) II 499–500. In c Oct–Dec 1804 C had copied out secs 19 and 20, in Latin (*CN* II 2225), at a time when he was reading Captain Ball's copy of Brougham's *Inquiry into the Colonial Policy of the European Powers* (1803) and cited Gravina as authority for his view that Brougham (II 19) in his "account of the Roman Governors & Governments is extremely incorrect": BM Egerton MS 2800 f 106.

with the Secular Government of this World":] (1.) The Scripture does not meddle with the Secular Government of this World, so as to alter it: for to alter Government is to overthrow the just Compacts and Agreements which have been made amongst Men, to which they have mutually bound themselves by Coronation-Oaths and Oaths of Allegiance . . .

Wherein does Scripture differ from Reason? I would answer: by *being* Reason, by acting on the Believer's mind as *Universal* Reason, having the same relation to our rational Understanding (Discourse of Reason)[1] as the living Air to our breathing Life. It is one with our Reason, but appears as distinct, a power from without, a Law—that which is diffused thro' all men, retracted, as it were, & presenting itself as a Unity independent of all—the Light beheld as a Sun. Reason essentially *objective*: but I might fear, that *my* Reason was merely subjective. Scripture warrants its Objectivity.

17 p ⁻2, evidently referring to p 84

. . . I shall now particularly examine those Texts of Scripture, which this author [Bilson] alledges; he begins with *Rom*. 13. 1, 2. *Let every Soul be subject to the higher Powers, for there is no Power but of God: The Powers that be, are ordain'd of God. Whosoever therefore resisteth the Power, resisteth the Ordinance of God; and they that resist, shall receive to themselves Damnation*. . . . If our Translators in this place had render'd the word ἐξουσίαι *Authoritys*, instead of *Powers*, as they were forc'd to do, I *Pet*. 3. 22. and ἐξουσία *Authority*, that is, a just and *lawful Power*, as they have render'd it in other places, and as it constantly signifies; they had effectually prevented the false Application of this Text.

P. 184[a]

Our translation of εξουσια in Rom. 13. by *Power* very judiciously censured. Beyond doubt, the word means not *Power* in the wide indefinite sense, but *a Power* lawfully delegated to or placed in, a Man or body of Men—an *Authority* ~~bestowed~~ committed, or right bestowed.— The Law has assigned to the King certain *prerogatives*—this *lawful* Prerogative is the ἐξουσια possessed by the Crown/ but an εξουσια under the conditions predetermined by the Law. See *Bracton*.[1]—So Sᵗ John—

[a] A slip for "84", where the pertinent textus is found

16[1] C was fond of quoting "discourse of reason" from *Hamlet* I ii 150 as a definition of Understanding: see e.g. *SM* (*CC*) 69, *Friend* (*CC*) I 156.

17[1] Henry de Bracton (d 1268), whose *De legibus et consuetudine Angliae* was the

He came to his own, & his own received him not. But to as many as did receive (n.b. here is the *condition*) to them he gave the *privilege* (εξουσιαν) to become the children of God[2]—τεχνα Θεου εν τῳ Υιῳ[a] Θεου = *Ideas* of God by resumption into the *Mind* of God, i.e. the co-eternal Word, the Supreme REASON, or the Supreme Being, or the Jehovah—for all three are Synonimes—.[3]

The *Absolute* Subject—

the *Absolute* Will, essentially causative of all *Reality*,

or true Being: = the one only Absolute Good.

The Good.

Deitas *relatively* Subjective	Deitas *relatively* objective
The Will as self-affirmed,	The Supreme Being
or Causa Sui[4]	= Reason, Mind.
The I AM	The Word,
The Holy One	The only-begotten Son.
The Father	The Jehovah.

Deitas objective in relation to the Subjective, Subjective in relation to the Objective.

The Spirit-Life = Love

eternally proceeding from the Good thro' the True

hence God = το αγαθον—The Father, Ο αγιος—The Son, ο αληθης. the Son Ἡ αγια Σοφια.[5]

The Good, *personal*, in the form of [? this][b] [Fo]r Truth is Wisdom.

18   p 111, pencil | An Answer to Jovian

For my part, I have read it [the statute 13 Car. 2. cap. 6] very often over, and cannot see any more in it than this, *That it is unlawful for both, or either of the Houses of Parliament, to raise or levy any War offensive or defensive against the King*; which was always Treason for any Subjects to do.

---

[a] Roman "U" for Greek "Y"   [b] The bottom outer corner of the leaf is dog-eared

---

first attempt to frame the whole of English law in a systematic and practical form. It does not appear that C knew Bracton's work at first hand; his acknowledged quotation from Bracton in Jan 1800 could have come from Milton's *Defensio pro populo Anglico*: *EOT* (*CC*) I 136–7 and n.

17[2] John 1.11–12 (var), AV reading "power (ἐξουσίαν) to become the sons of God". In the Greek, "children of God in the Son of God", the latter phrase is C's.

17[3] LEIGHTON COPY C 7 elaborates upon the relationship outlined here: "The Divine Idea [the Logos] assumed the form of Man, and thus became the Idea of the Divine Humanity = Jehova—and then the Individuality . . .".

17[4] "Deity . . . or Self-Cause".

17[5] "God is the good—The Father; The holy—The Son, the true. . . . The holy Wisdom."

Most true; but the Parliament under William and Mary with equal truth declared, that it *might* never the less be very *constitutional*.[1] As long as the Law was regnant, so long any resistance must be unlawful—

19 p 153, pencil | *Several Reasons for the Establishment of a Standing Army, and the Dissolving the Militia*

Neither is the Relation of Prince and Subject the same with that of a master and hir'd Servant; for he does not hire them, but as St. *Paul* saith, *They pay him Tribute*, in consideration of his continual *Attendance* and *Imployment* for the Publick Good.

an unhappy and inappropriate citation. Those to whom St Paul wrote, were conquered or vassal Provinces of *Rome*—and as such were *Tributaries*.[1] Taxes are not Tributes; but modes and accomodations of the circulation of the Wealth of a Community—not payed *to* the King, but *thro'* him. It has been by acts of their own, that our Kings have gradually exchanged the Lands & Revenues owned by them for a revenue supplied by a portion of the Taxes—but in this relation the Taxes are paid *to* him only as they are to a Clerk in the Custom House. Our King is as much *maintained* by the Nation as the Duke of Buccleuch, or of Devonshire—and no more.[2] What thanks they owe, the King owes—& no other.

20 p 153, pencil

But the fullest account of it in few words, is in Chancellor Fortescue, Chap. XIII. . . . *Ad tutelam namque legis subditorum, ac eorum corporum & bonorum, erectus est, & ad hanc potestatem a populo effluxam ipse habet, quo ei non licet potestate alia suo populo dominari.* For such a King . . . is made and ordain'd for the Defence or Guardianship of the Law of his Subjects, and of their Bodys and Goods; whereunto he receiveth Power of his People, so that he cannot govern his People by any other Power.

N.B. In our old Latin Law-Writers *Populus* must always be translated Nation.—Where the mere majority of Natives is meant, or the People in our present use of the term, *Plebs* is the Latin Equivalent.[1]

18[1] C refers to the Coronation Oath of William and Mary: **5** n 1 above.

19[1] The controversial text of Rom 13 is at issue, as in **17**; here the allusion is specifically to 13.6–7, "For this cause pay ye tribute. . . . tribute to whom tribute is due . . .".

19[2] These appear to be representative peerages without reference to contemporary individuals.

20[1] C had invoked this distinction in a letter of 1809 to Daniel Stuart (*CL* III 189) and in *C&S* (*CC*) 68; he echoes it again in **23** and **32** below, and in Macdiarmid **10** at n 2.

21   p 154, pencil

Render unto Caesar *the things which are* Caesar's, neither makes a *Caesar*, nor tells who *Caesar* is, nor what belongs to him; but only requires men to be just, in giving him those suppos'd Rights, which the Laws have determin'd to be his.

Merciful Heaven! Compare the manly, religious, book-learned Principles of the English Patriots of Charles II. James II. and William III[rds] reigns with the notions of *our* Reformers, from Earl Grey to M[r] Hume[1]—and while you groan at the contrast, ask—what Hope is there?—*Fuit* Anglia; Insula manet.[2]   S. T. C.

22   p 155, pencil

The Prayer [the Thanksgiving for the Fifth of November, eliminated by Laud] formerly ran thus: *To that end strengthen the hands of our gracious King, the Nobles and Magistrates of the Land, to cut off these* Workers of Iniquity (whose Religion is Rebellion, whose Faith is Faction, whose Practice is murdering of Souls and Bodys) and to root them out of the Confines of this Kingdom.*

✝ If instead of "these" the word "all" had been substituted, I see no reason why this Prayer might not have been retained, and fully vindicated against Archb[p] Laud's semi-romish *Literalism*. Laud was as truly a Papist as Bellarmin or any of the Jesuits.[1] Only it was not the Bishops of Rome or ⟨sundry of⟩ of their dogmata/ but for a joint-stock Company Pope, viz. the King & the Archb[p] of Canterbury. He was an Autopapist.[2]

23   p 155, pencil

. . . Magistrates themselves . . . when they turn Tyrants, do no less overthrow the Ordinance of God than the Seditious: and therefore their Consciences too are guilty, for not obeying the Ordinance of God, that is, the Laws which they ought to obey. So that the Threatenings in this place [Rom 13] do also belong to them: wherefore let the severity of this

21[1] C's contempt for "Lord Grey & his Gang" is expressed in **46** below; cf **1** and n 2 above. Joseph Hume (1777–1855) was a radical politician who advocated extending representation to the colonies in the Reform Bill of 1832.

21[2] "England *is no more*; [only] the island remains"—a play on Virgil *Aeneid* 2.325–6 "fuit Ilium, et ingens/ gloria Teucrorum".

22[1] C consistently used William Laud

(1573–1645), abp of Canterbury from 1633, as a representative and symbol of high-church tendencies in the C of E: see the LAUD titles annotated below, besides e.g. BAXTER *Reliquiae* COPY B **76** and n 1, QUARTERLY REVIEW **9**. Robert Bellarmine (1542–1621), eminent Jesuit controversialist, was canonised in 1930.

22[2] A "Self-Pope"—a pope unto himself, by analogy with an "autonomist", who seeks to be a law unto himself.

Command deter all men from thinking the Violation of the Political Constitution to be a light Sin.

Since the Reform Bill of 1832, following on the Bill for admitting Papists to political Power under the inauspicious Auspices of the Duke of Wellington & Sir Robert Peel, THE KING is extinct—We have *Statutes* in super-abundance—but no *Law*, no Constitution.[1] They have perished by the suicidal perjuries of George IVth & that precious *Plebs* personified, William IVth.—[2]

24 p 156, pencil

* Publick Laws are made by publick Consent; and they therefore bind every man, because every man's Consent is involv'd in them.

* But to consent implies a moral responsible Person, and therefore a moral obligation determining the consent, and therefore a Law antecedent to the Consent, which therefore rather *declares* & actualizes the Law thatn constitutes it. The whole Scheme of a compact is a mere fiction, or shall I say, an apologue, or allegory.[1] If my Great-grandfather consented without or against Right and right Reason, I am excused for following the bad example only as far [as] I cannot help myself—i.e. cannot do otherwise, without being hung or shot for it. But if he consented with good reason, the same good reason independent of his example obliges me.   *S. T. C.*

25 p 156, pencil

Power assum'd without a man's Consent, cannot bind him as his own Act and Deed.

Nonsense! It may rightfully bind him—as I was bound to learn As in præsenti, by the act and deed of my bum-brusher, Jemmy Bowyer.—[1]

23[1] The Reform Bill was passed in May 1832. The Catholic Emancipation Act had received the royal assent on 13 Apr 1829; the text of it is given in *C&S* (*CC*) 203–9. C's public response appears in his redefinition of "constitution" in *C&S* (*CC*) 19, 107–8.

23[2] George IV's "perjury" was his failure to honour the terms of the Oath of Allegiance and the Coronation Oath. See **5** and n 3 above. But George IV died in Jun 1830 and William IV gave assent to the Reform Bill of 1832. For the personification of *Plebs*, the mob, see **20** and n 1 above.

24[1] In a similar argument in *C&S* (*CC*) 14, C dismisses the "social contract" as "a pure fiction . . . an idle fancy. . . . at once false and foolish": cf his vehement denial of his own consent to the Reform Bill in **37** below.

25[1] James Boyer (1736–1814), the Christ's Hospital master to whom C paid memorable tribute in *BL* ch 1 (*CC*) I 8–11: other references to him are collected in BAXTER *Reliquiae* COPY B **112** n 3. *As in praesenti* is the phrase introducing a set of rules in Latin grammar, so familiar to generations of schoolboys that Addison could make a joke of it in *Spectator* 221 (13 Nov 1711).

26   p 157, pencil | *The Grounds and Reasons of the Laws Against Popery*

O! if at the Union we had had a Statesman of the Old English Breed/ a John of Gaunt,[1] who would have nothing to do for or against Transsubst[ant]iation, or the Dispute between Or*a* pro nobis, Sanctissima Maria! and Or*et* pro nobis, Maria![2] but waged war, body and Soul, against the *Pope* & that dilated Pope, an anti-national Clergy—!

27   p 197, pencil | *The Absolute Impossibility of Transubstantiation Demonstrated*

Here *Cartes* was beset . . . and therefore was put upon his Invention, which was first to contrive a way of solving the Appearances of Bread and Wine which are in the Sacrament, by a new Hypothesis of the Superficies. . . . [On being asked "whether he had bethought himself of a way to reconcile another part of his Philosophy with Christ's Body, being without local Extension upon the Altar"] *Cartes* stops short, and does not care to give any thing more concerning the Sacrament under his Hand, but offers to meet him if he pleases, and to tell him his Conjectures by word of Mouth.

Des Cartes was quite *in earnest* in his efforts to avoid a quarrel with the Court and the Priesthood. All the rest is the Superficies of his own invention—i.e. a copy of his Countenance.

28   p 199, pencil

Now therefore let the Papists give or take. Either the Bread is not transubstantiated; or if it be, by virtue of the self-same words the Priest is transubstantiated too. For every word in the Prolation with one breath . . . does operate as well as signify, and does what it says; and therefore if the word *Corpus* be effectual to make it a Body, then the word *Meum* makes it the Priest's Body. . . . For our Saviour visibly took Bread, and gave it the Office of representing him, and *made it the Figure of his Body* . . . He erected it as a standing Memorial to be us'd in *Remembrance or Commemoration of him.* . . . That he gave us the Bread by the name of his *Body*, Three of the Four Gospels witness. . . . But where did he ever say, That he himself wou'd always sacrifice himself by the Priest's Hands, and say, *Hoc est Corpus meum*, to the end of the World, by the Priest's Mouth?

The whole of this argumentation is valid and unanswerable against the

---

26[1] John of Gaunt (1340–99), Duke of Lancaster, immortalised as a patriot in Shakespeare's *Richard II*, esp II i 31–68.

26[2] Such disputes as the debate about the forms "*Pray* for us, most holy Mary" and "*Let* Mary pray for us"—referred to also in *C&S* (*CC*) 105—are hair-splitting that distracts Christian thinkers from more important issues.

Romish Doctrine of Trans[n], which identifies the Body spoken of (Hoc est corpus meum)[1] with the carnal material Body nailed to the Cross—From my Shield (for I hold Transsubstan[tia]tion in a certain sense)[2] these arguments fall off, like Straws

29   p 206, pencil | *The Way to Peace Amongst All Protestants*

In short, all the distance that is betwixt *English* Protestants, is occasion'd by little mistakes and misapprehensions about very little matters; and still they are so much of one mind even as to the matters in difference, that if the Conformists thought the Ceremonys Popish, they wou'd immediately turn Nonconformists; and if the Nonconformists did not apprehend them to be Popish, they wou'd never have scrupled them. So that they both of them plainly mean the same thing.

Alas! the Opposition of the present Dissenters rests on very different grounds—viz. Hatred of the Established Church *as* an established Church—and all thro' confounding the National Clerisy or Ordo trium Professionum[1] with the christian Church!!   S. T. C.

30   p 213, pencil | *A Letter from a Freeholder*

As for the good Disposition which is in the Conformists, to repeal those Laws with the first opportunity, that is always to be measur'd by Actions rather than Words; and therefore I shall give them an instance of it in the Bill for repealing the *35th* of *Elizabeth*, which pass'd both Houses of a *Church-of-England* Parliament, tho the Dissenters lost the benefit of that Pledg and Earnest of their Good-will, and are not ignorant which way it was lost.

Poor S. J. must have felt himself sadly put to it, with those infernal acts of Parliament Car. II., which the Popish Cabal had duped the high churchmen into carrying.[1] O passion of wrath and revenge! what a Fool art thou!—

28[1] "This is my body"—Vulgate version of words from Matt 26.26, Mark 14.22, Luke 22.19 included in the communion service.

28[2] FIELD **32** clarifies C's acceptance of transubstantiation in a symbolic sense.

29[1] In his definition of "clerisy" in *C&S* (*CC*) 46, 69, C does not describe the National Clerisy as an "Order of three Professions", but in *AR* (1825) 290n he states that "A Learned Order must be supposed to consist of three Classes": those "em-ployed in adding to the existing Sum of Power and Knowledge"; "those whose office it is to diffuse through the community at large the practical Results of Science"; and "the Formers and Instructors of the Second—in Schools, Halls, and Universities, or through the medium of the Press".

30[1] C refers not to the "Cabal" of 1667–73 but to a committee of the privy council formed by Charles II immediately after his restoration. Gilbert Sheldon, bp of London, was a member, and Clarendon

31   pp 214–15, pencil

By which it appears, that those men are the wretched Enemys both of the King and Kingdom, who wou'd fain persuade the King, that he has this *Dispensing Power* ["which can set aside as many Laws of the Land as he pleases"]; because therein they endeavour to persuade him, that Perjury is his Prerogative.

* A Dispensing *Power* must be somewhere; but it does not follow, that a dispensing *Authority* should be entrusted to any *part* of the Sovereignty.[1] So after bitter experience our Ancestors wisely decided. Where the Public Safety imperiously demands it, if you love your Country, you will do it; but having done it, you will then, if you love the Constitution of your Country, think it no shame to come to Parliament with a rope in your hand.—So said England to her Statesmen—

32   pp 298–9, pencil

One convincing Argument is as much as one thousand; and as the King has but one plain Title which is the Gift of the People, so there is but one plain Proof of it which is the Instrument of Conveyance of the Crown. . . . But after all this had pass'd in the Face of the sun, and been transacted by the greatest Authority upon Earth; I mean the *English* Community, which as King *Charles* the First says, *moulded* this Government and made it what it is . . . the King had a Throne given him by the only competent Authority that cou'd do it . . .

The Community, the People—this is either a real Unit, or a mere logical noun of multitude—a Singular for a *Plural*: just as it is indifferent, whether I say, bring in the Coal, or the Coals, in the Scuttle—bring in the Wood, or bring in the Logs.—Now an Army is an actual Unity/ a Parliament is an actual Unity—but except a mob be an exception, & and that however numerous, is but a fraction of the Community, what other moral Person did S. J. intend? I fear, that S. J. in the heat of Whiggism was staggering towards the Sovereignty of the *People*—i.e. confounding People with the *Nation*, a brute *Thing* (for a mere aggregate of Bodies tho' bodies of Persons is but a Thing, and most often a villainous ill-scented Thing as every one who has been in a Lobby Cram must have

dominated their proceedings. Charles's suspected inclination towards toleration of papists and sectaries aroused Anglican opposition, which was supported by parliament in a series of measures—the "Clarendon Code"—designed to restore the Church of England to the unquestioned position of the established church.

31[1] The distinction between power and authority is outlined in **17** above.

experienced) with an *Idea*, ~~tho~~ but not the less a real or rather actual existing *Power*, because an *Idea*.[1]

33   p 299, pencil

. . . *A Man may lawfully promise to do every thing which he may lawfully do.* I will give him an Instance to the contrary. It is certainly lawful for me, because our Saviour commands it, *If any compels me to go a Mile with him to carry his Burden, to go with him twain*: tho all such Precepts are to be taken with a Grain of Salt. But is it therefore lawful for me to promise this Man to be his Pack-horse all my Life, and to starve my Wife and Children in not providing for them, and in so doing to be worse than an Infidel? I trow not.

The Sophism of the Horse's Tail, unworthy of S. J.[1] No inference can be drawn from the legality of consenting to walk a few Yards with a Bully rather than quarrel with him, and that of promising to walk to York—It is clearly a metabasis εις αλλο γενος[2]—for a difference of degree may & often does constitute a difference of Kind. 32° of Heat is Frost—/   *S. T. C.*

34   p 301, pencil

For if his Subjects will not swear to Him, let us give the King his Oath again. . . . I am clearly for the old Law of Swearing every one above Sixteen at the Court-Leet, and not suffering any one that sets foot upon *English* Ground to be Unsworn above *Quarante jours*, which is the antient Common Law. And he that will not take the Oath ought to be treated as an Outlaw; for he ought [not] to live under a Government, who refuses to give it the customary and Legal Caution.

whether politic or no, this at least is *honest*; and I am thoroughly of S. Johnson's mind. Nay, I would have the custom restored at this present time/ the King's Oath being first recited, & then the Juror swearing on the condition of the royal Oath being faithfully kept./[1]

32[1] The "people" here are "a brute *Thing*" associated with the *plebs* of **20** and contrasted with the "*Idea*" of the Nation. In a letter written to James Gillman, Jr, in the margins of a copy of the 2nd ed (1830) of his *Church and State*, C laments "how few . . . have learnt to distinguish the PEO-PLE, which is a *real* living THING, from the Nation, which is an *actual* living IDEA!": *C&S* (*CC*) 233–4.
33[1] The "Sophism a gradibus contin-uis" which C describes in Andrew FULLER 2: "they go on pulling out hair by hair from the horse's tail . . . and then conclude with a shout that the horse never had a tail!"
33[2] "Transition into another kind", an Aristotelian formula.
34[1] In **46** below, C confirms his approval of Johnson's proposal that there be an oath for the subject corresponding to the oath taken by the monarch.

35 p 302, pencil, marked with a line in the margin

For it is all the Absolute Obedience in the world in the second instance; I mean, not in the performance of the first bare Command, but as that Command is inforc'd with a Penalty. For example, Suppose I liv'd under the Great *Turk*, and he for Will and Pleasure commanded me to break my Neck down a Precipice, and I on the other side, out of a natural tenderness for Life, desir'd to be excus'd; why there is the biggest Command in *Europe, Asia* or *Africa* lost. But if Passive Obedience come in the Black-Box, I must give up my willing Neck to the Bow-string, and there it is broke without Resistance, and the thing is done. And suppose this be practis'd upon 6666 Men, then you have a *Thebaean* Legion compleat. And Oh! . . . What a heavenly thing Slavery and Suffering is to some Men! But then it is always other People's Suffering and not their own, which so wonderfully edifys them.

It is rare indeed—an obscurity in S. J.'s writings—so rare, that I must suspect the fault to be in my own dullness.—But verily after a half a[a] dozen readings I do not understand this paragraph, with except[n] of the last witty sentences.   *S. T. C.*

N.B. Never despair! at the 7th reading I have made it out. If some word had been added to "*lost*" ex. gr. nullified and lost—so as to make its connection with command evident, I should have been less stupid.

36 p 302, pencil

N.B.—Asgill evidently formed his style on S. Johnson's Pamphlets—[1]

37 p 302, pencil

* What is done according to Law every body must abide by, because every body's Consent is involv'd in the making of every *English* Law . . .

* I dislike arguments grounded on fictions, tho' they may be fictions of Law. My consent involved in the Irish Emancipation or the later Reform Bill?—It is a damn'd Lie.[1]

---

[a] Passing from one line to the next, ms reads "a a"

36[1] Cf "Asgill evidently formed his style upon Johnson's, but he only imitates one part of it. Asgill never rises to Johnson's eloquence": *TT* 15 May 1833. The connection between Asgill and Johnson is also discussed in **1** n 1.

37[1] The phrase "fictions of Law" or "legal fictions" denotes propositions known to be false but conventionally accepted for practical reasons. C's rejection of the compact theory of law appears also in **24** above.

38   p 303, pencil

Are we in the case of those that are Slaves under the *Spaniard*, and
Slaves under the *French*, that often change their Master, but never their
Condition; that are Prize, and retaken, and Prize still? Let him answer
me to that. If not, why must our Vertue be taught us by their Necessity?
God help them, my soul pitys their Case, and I shou'd not readily know
what to do in it, because I never consider'd it. And perhaps it is like one
of those wherein our Saviour forbids Forecast, and wou'd have no man
premeditate, but promises help at a dead lift, *Dabitur in illa hora* ["It
will be given in that hour"].

Excellent! This *is* sound common sense. There are cases which can only
be judged of at *de præterito*—by a posthumous Rule.[1] The Rule is the
Epitaph—& will apply on the return of the *very same* thing under the
very same circumstances in the completed Cycle of the great Platonic
Year[2]—& not till then. Will it be right to set up an insurrection against
so & so?—Twenty years afterwards I will try to form an opinion. If you
are hung, I shall ⟨probably⟩ call it Rebellion, & you a well-meaning
Traitor.

39   pp 304–5, pencil

Now I can tell him that Allegiance is so obstinate a thing, that neither
Desertion nor Conquest, nor any thing in the world but what is intrinse-
cal to it, (that is Breach of Covenant or consent of both Partys) can
dissolve it: it is a Moral Duty, and Heaven and Earth may pass away
before Allegiance can pass away.

An Oath of Allegiance to a Conqueror implies the qualification of, as
long as no one conquers *you*. Louis 18th conquered Napoleon; & the
French who had fought for Napoleon according to their Oath of Alle-
giance swore the same to Louis—but when Louis allowed Napoleon to
reconquer *him*—why, then N. stood in the place of L. as L. had taken
the place of N.[1] The Light, the Oath, fell upon the *Place*, ~~which~~ and on

38[1] "From what has passed"—of
which C's phrase is a witty rendering that
leads into the following epigram.

38[2] According to ancient theory, a cycle
of human history coinciding with the cycle
of the motions of the heavenly bodies; one
figure suggested for the length of the cycle
is 28,500 years (*OED*).

39[1] Louis XVIII (1755–1824), as Count
of Provence, fled in 1791 during the Rev-
olution to Coblenz and after the death of

Louis XVII in 1795 was recognised as king
by the émigrés. After being hunted through
Europe by Napoleon and taking refuge in
England in 1807, he was restored to the
throne of France in Apr 1814 on the fall of
Napoleon. He immediately tried to restore
the old monarchy under the guise of con-
ciliatory policies, but his excesses allowed
Napoleon to return from Elba, whereupon
Louis and the royal family fled from Paris
to Ghent. After Waterloo he returned to

the *Figure* only *as*, and *while*, it occupied that Place.—I know no other Morality to suit such an Unmorality as Conquest.—Give me your money, or I'll blow out your Brains!—Swear that you will give me your money, or I'll blow out your Brains!—I confess, I see small difference between the two—& should scruple the latter as little or as much as the former. An oath extorted by violence is—the Air which the voice articulates, & all that a *Conqueror* has any right to demand.

40   p 305, referring to p 304, pencil

And therefore all honest men were for being rid of King *James* [ɪɪ] long before, and they were in the right. It was not such a puny thing as the after-clap of a Prince of *Wales*, which made them part with him. For tho the labour'd Discovery of that Fraud wou'd have done great Service to this Government, and ought not to have been spoil'd by being put into a strong Box, and let out again to disadvantage; yet we must have more than a supposititious Child to justify this Revolution. * For you must stop there; you may indeed set aside the Changeling, but that does not extend to Out the Father, who was Tenant for Life, because perhaps his Wife went forty weeks with a Cushion.

* p. 304.

as much perhaps as could be fairly expected from S. J.—tho' I should have been better pleased if he had scouted the story & ridiculed the Goodies[1] who needed to have their adhesion to William & Mary bolstered by such a mammock.[2]

41   p 304, pencil

But as for those that do not allow that he [James ɪɪ] Forfeited, and yet wou'd not assist him against an Invasion, as he proclaim'd it; and as for his Mercenarys that revolted from him, and pick'd his Pocket, what Reasons they had I know not. If he deserted, he was forc'd to desert; for the very ground he stood upon fell from under him, as I told more than forty people it wou'd be so, before ever the Prince of *Orange* embarqu'd; and because I lov'd my Country, was mightily pleas'd that it wou'd be a brave Dry *Dutch* War without any Blood-shed. And therefore as for

---

France with the allies and was again placed on the throne, but with greatly reduced authority.

40[1] Those who are good in a weak or sentimental way: cf C's usage in *TT* 20 Aug 1833.

40[2] In an image that consorts better with "Cushion" and "bolstered" than more recent versions, Johnson's *Dictionary* defines "mammock" as "a large shapeless piece". The textus alludes to the widespread rumour that the queen's pregnancy had been false, and the infant heir to James ɪɪ smuggled into her bed in a warming-pan.

those that forc'd away *James* the Just . . . They must never plead his Desertion in discharge of their Allegiance; for that is to make their Crime their Plea . . .

Excellent! manly—No! S. J. was no *Whig*[1]

42   p 305, pencil

But how came King *James* to be so abandon'd, as to be singl'd out and conquer'd by himself? We that knew he ceas'd to be a King, or perhaps of Right never was one, can give a fair account of this matter. But where were his Lieges all this while, that held him for their Natural Lord, and by Divine Right, and yet fail'd him? They that thought their Allegiance intire, and not dissolv'd by King *James* himself, ought by Law to have defended him . . . against all men both alive and dead: So that if old *Schomberg* shou'd chance to walk, for ought I know, by virtue of their Allegiance, they are bound to fight his Ghost. This is a Consideration which belongs to the Conquering Bishops and their inferior Clergy, and I leave it amongst them.

O that we had *now* an S. J. to fight for us

43   pp 305–6, pencil

S. Johnson was not a Whig: for a Whig implies a compromise between two opposite *Principles*: & S. J. was a man of *Principle*. Far rather would I call him a *Tory* in his right senses—who reverenced *the King* in the *Idea*, not in the *Idol*, and respected the latter only while it continued transparent, & did not intercept the Idea, which it was to enshrine.[1]

44   p 306, pencil

I have ever had a great Aversion to all *Maxims* of Government, true or false: for there always lies lurking this Deceit in Generals and Universals, that tho they be true for the most part, yet they are conceiv'd in terms large enough to be falsly apply'd; and then they become false, and are usually the Tools that dishonest Men go to work with. And I never saw a Man deal in transcendental Politicks which are over our heads, and avoid coming down to Particulars and to the Point, but with a purpose to deceive.

41[1] Clarified in **43** below.

43[1] The association of the Tory *ideally* with principles appears also in C's "Thoughts of an Honest Tory, of 1821" *EOT* (*CC*) III 262–3, and in the description in *C&S* (*CC*) 103 of "an old Tory Lawyer of the genuine breed, too enlightened to obfuscate and incense-blacken the shrine, through which the kingly Idea should be translucent, into an Idol to be worshipped in its own right".

This is admirable; & if S. J. had warned us not to confound *Maxims* with Principles, GENERALIZED past *experiences* with *Ideas*, in the light of which alone the Past can be safely applied to the future, these Remarks ~~might~~ would have merited the name of Wisdom.[1]

Reason in the Sense gives Mathematical *evidence*;

Reason in the Understanding gives logical *conclusion*;

Reason in the Reason gives Ideas, or Truth-powers,[2] or Truth actual—αληθειαι ζωοποιητικοι.[3]

Ŧ Neither of these three, the Antecessors, Conditionators, Guides ~~and~~ Interpreters of all Experience [? dare] be confounded with those more or less accurately generalized Precedents, called maxims, i.e. Regulæ Maximæ.—[4]

45 p 307, pencil

* The Reason why the Clergy were so zealous for Tyranny, was because it was a Tyranny on their Side; their own Interest and Strength to crush all other Protestants lay therein, and then according to the *Greek* and *Latin* wish to Enemys, Invasion so apply'd was a good thing, and the worse the better.

* A sincere Son and Lover of the Church of England I mourn over the truth of this charge made against the Churchmen of the Revolution, or rather from the Restoration even to the reign of George the 2ⁿᵈ. The same Topic is vigorously treated in Cato's Letters, by Gordon & Trenchard—**a* admirably by De Foe, *passim*[1]

46 pp 309–10, pencil

And again all *Englishmen* that have any tolerable knowledg of the Con-

---

a Not a further footnote indicator, but the sign of a later thought, rather like "P.S."

44[1] The distinction between maxims and ideas or principles or laws occurs frequently in C's work, e.g. *CN* I 1722, *TT* 24 Jun 1827, **52** below.

44[2] "Truth-powers", a formulation anticipated in **32** above, appears also in DONNE *Sermons* COPY B **60**.

44[3] "Life-making truths". The adjective is rare, but C could have coined it himself, without having encountered it in classical Greek texts, from the verb ζωοποιεῖν, which occurs in NT, e.g. John 6.63.

44[4] "Most important rules", C's usual etymology for "maxim", as in LEIGHTON COPY C **30** below.

45[1] *Cato's Letters*, by John Trenchard (1662–1723) and Thomas Gordon (d 1750), periodical essays chiefly on political subjects published 1720–3 in the *London Journal* and *British Journal*, and issued in collected editions from 1724. C read them at Christ's Hospital, and wrote later that the papers on "Liberty and Necessity" had generated in him "a rage for Metaphysics": N F° f 91ᵛ (9 Mar 1832).

It is not clear how familiar C was with Defoe's political tracts. He quoted from *Royal Religion: Being Some Enquiry after the Piety of Princes* (1704) in Apr 1809: *CN* III 3485, *CL* III 195.

stitution are sensible, that the Office of a King depends wholly upon the Law, both in its making and in its being; and that a King as he is impower'd by Law must act by Law: and therefore they must needs know at first sight, that a King whose Authority is antecedent to the Law, independent of the Law, and superior to the Law, as Dr. *Sherlock* says ours is, is an invented and study'd King, whom the *English* Law knows not; but is of Dr. *Sherlock*'s own making, and is a King of Clouts.

Excellent![a] Much as I dislike Lord Grey & his Gang for their transferring the deliberative & determining functions from the Parliament to the Mob before the Hustings, & thus degrading Representatives of the Realm into Delegates of the Rabble, yet I dislike ~~yea, d~~ far more, yea, detest them for nullifying the kingly office, by reducing the Coronation Oaths to Highgate Oaths.[1] For a genuine English King is the greatest possible Security for Freedom since ~~what~~ the Agent without or against Law is ipso facto *not* the King but some punishable Subject. It is the King, only while it is the Law—and on the other hand, the King is bound by the most solemn Oaths before God & to the Nation, to make abortive every projected Law, destructive of Freedom.—I agree with S. J. that every *Subject* on reaching the age of discretion ought to take the Oath of Allegiance, the King's Coronation Oath having been ~~forced~~ first recited to him/ & the Subject answering—The King having thus bound himself, I on my part swear that I will *return* faithful allegiance to him—&c &c.[2]

47   p 314, pencil

And therefore according to the Method of all <u>hir'd Politicks</u>, they must make sure of sinking three Kingdoms for fear of losing two . . .

i.e. venal Politicians—Politic*i*, not *ca*.[1]

48   p 315, pencil

The Sea is our Element; where our Shipping was lately more numerous than any Nation's in the World, and better built being of *English* Oak, and our Seamen Heart of Oak. Such a Strength, well manag'd and well apply'd, is fit to give Laws to all the World. . . . [We] shou'd have

---

[a] C has written "/\/\" beside this marginal word and has begun the body of the note in the foot-margin of p 309 with "/\/\"

46[1] I.e. to degrading and meaningless oaths. The phrase refers to an obsolete custom of Highgate pubs, by which a traveller had to swear "never to kiss the maid when he could kiss the mistress, never to drink small beer when he could get strong" etc, but with the nullifying clause "unless you like it best": *A Dictionary of Buckish Slang, University Wit, and Pickpocket Eloquence* (1811).

46[2] Johnson's proposal appears in **34** above.

47[1] Politic*ians*, not politic*s*—persons, not policies.

scorn'd *Dutch* Help to fight the *French* Fleet, and to go to War upon Crutches . . .

Another proof of my Assertion, that S. J. was *no Whig*;[1] but a genuine old English *Nationalist*, and *Kings*man, as long as the King represented the Sovereignty of the Nation by being himself Liege and Loyal thereto.

S. T. Coleridge/*

* Nothing can *reconcile* me to my wobbling name, Samuel;[2] but Dr Samuel Barrow, and the Rev^d Mr Samuel Johnson are Pound weights of palliative Consolation, to which sundry pennyweights are added by Dr Samuel Clark, and *D^r* Samuel Johnson.[3] I suspect, that before the Puritan Times Samuel was no *Christian* Name, but confined to Jews.[4]

49 p 315, pencil

But the Artillery of the World being chang'd since that time, we shall never be a warlike Nation more, till all our excellent Laws about Bows and Arrows which are wholly disus'd, be apply'd to the use of Fire-Arms. *

* There are scientific & veteran Officers in our army, who believe & contend that 20,000 old English Archers would even now play the devil with 30,000 Musketeers.

50 p 316

Knute, than whom there never look'd any thing liker a Conqueror, and who put an end to disputed Titles in the *Severn, at the desire of the*

48[1] See also **1** and **41** above.

48[2] Cf his expression of "Dislike & Disgust" for his Christian names, in a letter written to RS Apr 1804: "such a vile short plumpness, such a dull abortive smartness, in [the] first Syllable, & this so harshly contrasted by the obscurity & indefiniteness of the syllabic Vowel, & the feebleness of the uncovered liquid, with which it ends—the wabble it makes, & staggering between a diss- & a tri-syllable—& the whole name sounding as if you were abeeceeing": *CL* ii 1126.

48[3] C tendentiously prefers two comparatively obscure Samuels to two famous ones: on the one hand, Samuel Johnson "the Whig" and Samuel Barrow (b c 1625), to whose commentary on *Paradise Lost* C refers in Hartley COLERIDGE **51**; on the other, Samuel Clarke (1675–1729), mathematician and author of *The Scripture*

Doctrine of the Trinity, and Samuel Johnson (1709–84), the greatest critic of the late eighteenth century. In a note on the front flyleaf of Daniel WATERLAND *Vindication of Christ's Divinity*, C links Samuel Clarke and Dr Samuel Johnson as "overrated Men" of their respective generations.

48[4] Samuel is "rare as a christian name in the Middle Ages, though examples occur in 12th-century records, and the surnames *Samuel, Samwell* occur as early as 1273. Not all these were Jewish, though some may have been. After the Reformation *Samuel* became a favourite name, an early example being *Samuel* Daniel (1562–1619). It continued in general use after the Restoration, when many Biblical names went out . . .": *Oxford Book of Christian Names* ed E. G. Withycombe (2nd ed 1950).

English *Barons* sent his Army back to *Denmark*; for which see *Bracton's Englescheria*, the finest Point of Law in our *English* Constitution, almost in the same words, and exactly in the same sense as King *William* the First's Laws. [Johnson then quotes at length from Bracton *De Corona* and from Knyghton.]

I have long been persuaded, that our Sages of the Plantagenet Times had sounder and freer Judgements on English Liberty than the best Lights after the Reformation. While Popery reigned, the Lawyers felt themselves an antagonist Pole/

51   p 318 (misprinted 319)

[Johnson has been discussing honest critics who acquire the reputation of being madmen.] I have not Evidence for what I am now going to say, but am morally assur'd of it, that the Great *Wallop* was thus hinder'd from being made a Judg; of whom I will say the less, because his own Integrity in the worst of Times has eterniz'd him. . . . To pass by a hundred more of his Sayings, his comparing King *James*'s Declaration upon the very spot to the scaffolding of *Paul*'s Church, was so wise, so weighty, so seasonable, and so useful a Saying, that that new *Paul's* when it is built shall want Scaffolding again, before that Saying is forgot by the wise and honest part of this Nation.

I can *guess* what Wallop's Saying was; but I do not remember it, as preserved in any of our Histories. I would give a crown, poor as I am, to find it.[1]

52   p 320

The Whigs generally were Machievelian Moderès, by their party *principle* unprincipled—(i.e. for principles substituted *maxims*, generalizations of Experience under the guidance of Expedience)—*Compromisers*![1]—But of even the best of them, such as Bishop Burnet assuredly was,[2] the *character*, the Whig-mark, was—a *want* of positive faith in God, as the moral Governor. They might hope for his furtherance, but

---

51[1] Richard Wallop (1616–97), advocate, counsel in many celebrated anti-royalist cases including those of Titus Oates, Richard Baxter, and Samuel Johnson himself, *was* eventually made a judge (1696) in the Court of Exchequer. His *bon mot* unfortunately remains elusive.

52[1] This statement about the Whigs as "Moderates" takes up the arguments in earlier notes about their preferring maxims to principles (**44**) and their readiness to compromise (**43**).

52[2] In Gilbert BURNET *History of the Reformation* **7** C referred to him as "a Whig Bishop". C also annotated his *Memoires* and *Life of William Bedell* and in his early years had read and used Burnet's *History of His Own Time* (2 vols 1724, 1734).

never *trusted* ~~to~~ in him. Ex. gr. In the intended reform of our Liturgy—it sufficed, that the Ex-Archbishop Sancroft *might* have set up a real Church of E.,[3] to make Burnet congratulate himself on its abandonment.

53   pp 320–1

Secondly, That no body has a Right to defend these Rights, but they whose Rights they are. This necessarily follows from the former ["That the Rights of the Nation being invaded, may be defended"], for Rights must be a Man's to *Have* before they can be his to *Hold*. Besides, what has any body else to do with other Mens Rights?

First, I must be ~~as~~ensured as well as self-assured, that it IS "*mine both to have and to hold.*" 2. That my resistance, justified *in genere* by my Right, is proportioned *in gradu* to the value of the thing rightfully mine.[1] A gang of nightly House-breakers are forcing their way into the Chamber where my Cash, Plate, Jewels & Title-deeds are lodged—Fire!—bang! Off go mine & my man John's double-headed Blunderbuss at the Scumoundrels, & my Conscience cries, Huzza! Huzza! But a set of Striplings have got into my Apple-tree—my favorite Ripstone Pippins! Shall I let fly among them!—Yes, perhaps! with a large squirt, or a horse-whip—. And yet the golden Pippins and the golden Guineas were equally *mine to have & to hold.*—3. that[a] I *can* resist to any wise purpose—I must, if I can, skip out of the way of a tyrannical Cannon Ball, ⟨or throw myself flat, prostrate⟩ not, however rightful it may be, try to repel it with a Battledore—which, had the wrongous Missile been a Shuttle-cock, would have been discreet & laudable.

S. T. C.   15 May, 1833.

54   p 321

6thly. The Original Right which the People of *England* have to defend themselves, enables them to call for Assistance whenever they are beset and cannot help themselves, and to pray in Aid: And here this happy Revolution centers.

---

[a] Passing from one line to the next, C wrote "that that"

52[3] William Sancroft (1617–93), abp of Canterbury, was deprived of office as a Nonjuror in 1690, having refused to recognise William of Orange as king, though he had also resisted catholicising tendencies in James II. Gilbert Burnet did not like him and in his *History of His Own Time* (4 vols 1753) III 186–7 remarks upon his death:

"Sancroft had died a year before, in the same poor and despicable manner, in which he had lived for some years: He died in a state of Separation from the Church; and yet he had not the courage to own it in any publick declaration . . .".

53[1] "In kind . . . in degree".

Tho' my whole mind and heart are on S. J.'s side of the Argument—yet I see the Objection that might be started. If William's Troops were necessary, where is the proof that the Revolutioners *were* the People of England?

54A   p 414, where a note of two lines has been erased

As it is an Affront and Injury to God, so it is such an Injury to Man as cannot be repair'd; it robs a man of that which is most precious to him, and of which it is impossible to make him any Restitution. He that deprives a man of his Goods, "or his good Name," is capable of making him Satisfaction . . . but he that deprives a man of his Life, has for ever put it out of his power to make any manner of satisfaction for the wrong he has done.[1]

Annex

The following passages are marked as indicated.

A   p 324, marked with a line in the margin

For tho the Genius of a Hero, and personal Endowments make a great man, yet it is a great and considerable People alone, which makes a great King: and a Greatness built upon their Ruins, is a false and ruinous Greatness, and such Power is always Weakness.

This following Discourse was written some while ago, whereby some few expressions in it may seem less seasonable, and to have lapsed their time: but if it be worth reading, it comes out in time enough; if not, too soon.

B   p 326, with a pencilled check mark in the margin

In like manner a Standing Army was always a name of dread and horror to an *English* Ear, and signify'd the worst sort of Invasion, being intestine, and already got within us . . .

C   p 326, with a pencilled check mark in the margin

And lastly, this annual Army is to depend upon the regulation of an annual Parliament; but our Act is Triennial, and not over-easily obtain'd. However in a Parliament when it sits, the Land-Force will come into consideration in order *to be either increas'd, lessen'd, or quite laid aside as they shall see cause.*

D   p 347, with two pencilled crosses in the margin

This Preface likewise says, *England is now the Wonder of the World*; and it wou'd be a greater Wonder, if it shou'd just now be invaded: and I challenge

54A[1] This passage is included on the grounds that the erased note was probably C's, although the quotation marks are probably not.

any Man to name any imaginable State of Affairs, when it shall be fitter and safer and more necessary to lay aside an Army than now.

E   p 328, with a pencilled check mark in the margin

But they soon found their Error: *they saw that to live by one man's Will, became the cause of all mens Misery; and this constrain'd them to come to Laws,* as *Hooker*'s words are.

F   p 330, with a pencilled check in the margin

There never was such a Proposal in the World, unless that of Col. *Titus* to *Oliver*, and that I suppose is not in earnest either, that he wou'd kill himself lest somebody else shou'd, and lest it might be done by some vulgar Hand.

G   p 331, with two pencilled crosses in the margin

. . . so that, as Mr. *Selden* used to say, he that has but Two-pence in *England* is a King of that Two-pence.

H   p 331, with two pencilled crosses in the margin

And whensoever the nation has lost that noble Sense of Liberty, by which it has been so long preserv'd, it will soon make Fetters for it self, tho it shou'd find none at hand ready made.

I   p 337, with two pencilled check marks crossed through in pencil

Potestatem habet a populo effluxam ["He has a power that flows out from the people"], as *Fortescue* expresses it, speaking of an *English* King.

J   p 340, marked with a pencilled line in the margin

For his words upon Henry *the Seventh's initiating a Guard of 50 Archers, are these. "That [Guard]ᵃ of his Person, he only pretended as a Ceremony of State brought from the* French *Court; and yet it is strange that it went down so well with a* free People. For that Prince that will keep Guards about his Person in the midst of his own People, may as well double them into the pitch of an Army whensoever he pleases to be fearful; and so turn the Royal Power of Law into Force of Arms. *But it was the French Fashion, and the King's good hope to have all taken in the best sense."*

K   p 360, with a pencilled cross in the margin

The year following, tho *England* still lay under Oppression, yet the *Welsh* were resolv'd to bear the Tyranny no longer, but stood up for their Country and the maintenance of their Laws, and baffl'd several Armys first of the Prince and afterwards of the King.

ᵃ Square brackets in original

BEN JONSON
1572–1637

The Dramatic Works of Ben Jonson . . . printed from the text, and with the notes of Peter Whalley . . . Embellished with portraits, &c. Vol I (of 4). London 1811. 8º.

"Printed for John Stockdale, Piccadilly", and referred to as the "Stockdale Edition". The 4-vol set includes *The Dramatic Works of Beaumont and Fletcher* in vols II–IV. For a full description of this set, an account of the misbinding of forepages of Vol II referring to Beaumont and Fletcher with the forepages of Vol I, and the text of the marginalia in Vols II–IV see BEAUMONT & FLETCHER COPY B. Variant volume-numbers in title-pages, contents, and colophons show that Vol I was sometimes issued by itself with a title-page referring only to Jonson and that the 3 vols of Beaumont and Fletcher were similarly issued as a separate work.

British Library C 126 i 1

Inscribed by C on I ⁻3 (as on II ⁻3, III ⁻2): "S. T. Coleridge | 29 March, 1815 | Calne, Wilts. 4,,10.—'' "S. T. C." label on the title-page. C's notes on I ⁻3, ⁻2, xiv, xvi, xxxv have been marked with crosses in ink apparently at a later date, probably by family editors collecting text for *LR*; these crosses are ignored here. Some leaves in *Every Man Out of His Humour* were still unopened in 1987: I 65–8, 69–72. There is a note in pencil in another hand I 339, and a line through part of a word on I 297 that looks like a slip of the pen.

This is the edition that C used in preparing the lectures of Jan–Mar 1818, and the second series Dec 1818–Mar 1819: *Lects 1808–1819 (CC)* II 143.

SPECIAL ABBREVIATION. "H & S"—*Ben Jonson* ed C. H. Herford and Percy Simpson and (from Vol VI) Evelyn Simpson (11 vols Oxford 1925–52): I, II— "The Man and His Work"; III–VII—"The Plays" and "Entertainments and Masques"; VIII—"Poems and Prose Works"; IX–XI—"Commentary".

CONTENTS. [iii]–viii "The Life of Ben Jonson"; Vol II prelims bound in in error; [ix]–xxiii "The Preface" [to Peter Whalley's edition]; xxv–xliv "The Life of Benjamin Jonson" [by Whalley]; 1–42 *Every Man in His Humour*; 43–96 *Every Man Out of His Humour*; 97–144 *Cynthia's Revels*; 145–87 *Poetaster*; [189]–234 *Sejanus His Fall*; 235–82 *Volpone*; 283–326 *Epicoene*; 327–75 *The Alchemist*; 377–425 *Catiline His Conspiracy*; [427]–74 *Bartholomew Fair*; 475–517 *The Devil Is an Ass*; [519]–60 *The Staple of News*; 561–98 *The New Inn*; 599–633 *The Magnetick Lady*; 635–68 *A Tale of a Tub*; 669–90 *The Sad Shepherd*; 691–2 *Mortimer's Fall*; 693–721 *The Case Is Altered*.

DATE. 29 Mar 1815–c 25 Mar 1819, with intensive use during the series of lectures; and c Jun 1831 (**42**).

1 ı ⁻3

It would be amusing to collect from our Dramatists from Eliz. to Charles I. proofs of the manners of the Times. One striking symptom of general Coarseness (i.e. of *manners*, which may co-exist with great refinement of morals, as alas! vice versa) is to be ~~fou~~ seen in the very frequent allusions to the Olfactories and their ~~worst~~ most disgusting Stimulants—and these too in the Conversation of virtuous Ladies. This would not appear so strange to one who had been on terms of familiarity with Sicilian and Italian Women of Rank: and bad as they may, too many of them, *actually be*, yet I doubt not, thus the extreme grossness of their Language has imprest many an Englishman of the present Æra ~~with a or~~ with far darker notions, than the~~ir~~ ⟨same language⟩ would have produced in one of Eliz⁵ or James 1ˢᵗ˙ˢ Courtiers. Those who have read *Shakespear only*, complain of occasional grossness in *his* plays—Compare him with his Contemporaries, & the inevitable conviction is that of the exquisite purity of his imagination—[1]

2 ı ⁻2

The Observation, I have prefixed to the Volpone,[1] is the Key to the faint Interest, that these noble efforts of the intellectual power excite—with the exception of the Sad Shepherd—because in that fragment only is there any character, in whom you are morally interested.—On the other hand, the Measure for Measure is the only play of Shakespear's in which there are not some one or more characters, generally many, whom you follow with an affectionate feeling. For I confess, that Isabella of all Shakespear's female Characters interests me the least: and the M. for Meas. is the only one of his genuine Works, which ~~it~~ is painful to me.—[2]

Let me not conclude this Remark, however, without the thankful acknowlegement to the Manes of Jonson, that the more I study his writings, the more I admire them—and the more the study resembles that of an ancient Classic, in the minutiæ of his rhythm, metre, choice of words,

---

1[1] C's defence of Shakespeare against the common charge of grossness was always based on comparison with contemporaries, especially Beaumont and Fletcher: e.g. BEAUMONT & FLETCHER COPY B **49**, *Lects 1808–1819 (CC)* ı 117, 522.

2[1] **20** below.

2[2] In a note in SHAKESPEARE COPY A—the set used in preparing the literary lectures of 1808–12—ı 305, C enlarges on this remark: "This Play [*Measure for Measure*] . . . is to me the most painful, say rather, the only painful, part of his genuine Works. The comic & tragic parts equally border on the μισητεον [hateful]; the one disgusting, the other horrible . . .". Collier records an objection to Isabella in the 1818 lectures: *Lects 1808–1819 (CC)* ıı 245.

forms of connection, &c, the more numerous have the points of Admiration become.—I may add too, that both the Study and the Admiration cannot but be disinterested—for to expect any advantage to the present Drama were ignorance. The latter is utterly heterogeneous from the Drama of the Shakespearian Age—with a diverse Object and a contrary *principle*. The one was to present a model by *imitation* ⟨of real Life,⟩ to take from real life all that is what it ought to be, and to supply the rest— the other to *copy* what *is* and as it *is*—the best a tolerable, the most*ᵃ* a blundering, *Copy*.³ In the former the Difference was an essential Element—in the latter an involuntary Defect.—We should think it strange, if a Tale *in Dance* were announce[d], and the Actors did not *dance* at all! Yet such is modern comedy.⁴

3   I v, pencil

[In a long account, addressed to the Earl of Newcastle as possible patron, Jonson says that in a dream he found his cellar infested by a peculiar kind of mole:] ". . . this kind of mole is called 'a want,' which will destroy you and your family, if you prevent not the worsting of it in tyme."

This should have been explained. A mole is in some Counties called a *Want*.¹

4   I xii

The same observations can be extended to the generality of Shakespeare's and Fletcher's plays, where under exotic characters and story, the authors are continually glancing at domestic incidents, and comment on the times, skreened beneath the cover of antient or foreign fable. *
But Jonson was soon sensible, how inconsistent this medley of names and manners was in reason and nature; and with how little propriety it could ever have a place in a legitimate and just picture of real life . . .

* But did Jonson reflect that the very Essence of a Play, the very language in which it is written, is a Fiction to which all the parts must

ᵃ A slip for "worst"

2³ C's distinction between imitation and copy, appearing as early as 1804 in *CN* II 2211, was elaborated in *BL* ch 17 (*CC*) II 43 and in *Lects 1808–1819* (*CC*) I 83–4, 223–4 and nn.

2⁴ C makes an extended attack upon the fashionable comedy of his own time in "Satyrane's Letters" *BL* (*CC*) II 183–6, where he says that it aims only "to make us laugh by wry faces, accidents of jargon, slang phrases for the day . . ." (186).

3¹ In common use except in dialects of northern and north-east Midland counties (*OED*).

conform—Surely, Greek Manners in English is a still grosser improbability than a Greek Name transferred to English Manners.

5 I xiv

Kitely's wife then objects to him; "But what harm might have come of it, brother?" To whom Well-bred replies,

"Might, sister? so might the good warm clothes your husband wears be poison'd, for any thing he knows; or the wholesome wine he drunk, even now at the table." Kitely's jealous apprehension is immediately alarmed, and he breaks out in a passionate exclamation . . . imagining that he could feel the poison beginning to operate upon him. Nothing could be more in character, supposing the persons, as was the case at first, to have been natives of Italy.

Jonson's Personæ are too often not Characters but Derangements: the hopeless Patients of a Mad-doctor, rather than exhibitions of Folly betraying itself spite of existing Reason and Prudence. He not poetically but painfully exaggerates every trait—i.e. not by the drollery of the Circumstance but by the excess of the originating Feeling.

6 I xvi

In his design and exhibition of characters, Jonson was particularly happy in delineating those which are generally known by the name of characters of humour. . . . But as humour is the excess of a particular passion, and appropriate only to a single character, it hath from hence been thought, that Jonson's characters are only passions or affections personized, and not faithful copies from living manners. But to this we might reply, that far from being thought to build his characters upon abstract ideas, he was really accused of representing particular persons then existing; and that even those characters which appear to be the most exaggerated, are said to have had their respective archetypes in nature and life.

This degrades Jonson into a Libeller, instead of justifying him as a Dramatic Poet. Non quod verum est, sed quod verisimile,[1] is the Dramatist's Rule—at all events, the Poet who chooses transitory manners ought to content himself with transitory Praise—if his Object be Reputation, he ought not to expect Fame.[2] The utmost, he can look forward

---

6[1] "Not what is true, but what is truth-like"—has the appearance of truth, is plausible: Aristotle *Poetics* 1451ᵇ1.

6[2] The distinction between lasting fame and temporary reputation is elucidated by C elsewhere, e.g. *BL* ch 2 (*CC*) I 33.

to, is to be quoted by and to enliven the writings of, an Antiquarian. Pistol, Nym, &c do not please us as Characters, but are endured as fantastic Creations, Foils to the native Wit of Falstaff—I say *wit*: for this so often extolled as the Master-piece of Humor, contains and was not meant to contain, any humor at all/[3]

7   I xxxv

It is to the honour of Jonson's judgment, that the greatest poet of our nation had the same opinion of Donne's genius and wit; and hath preserved part of him from perishing, by putting his thoughts and satire into modern verse.

viz. Pope[1]

8   I xxxv

* He said further to Drummond, Shakspeare wanted art, and sometimes sense; for in one of his plays he brought in a number of men saying they had suffered shipwreck in Bohemia, where is no sea near by an hundred miles.

* I have often thought Shakespear justified in this seeming anachronism. In Pagan Times a single name of a German Kingdom might well be supposed to comprize a 100 miles more than at present.—[1]

9   I xxxvi

[Drummond's *Conversations* are cited for various anecdotes and opinions.] Petronius, Plinius Secundus, and Plautus, as he said, spoke best Latin, and Tacitus wrote the secrets of the council and senate, as Sueto-

6[3] C intends a negative: Falstaff *neither* contains nor was meant to contain humour. His rejection of the common conception of a "humour" character as outlined in the textus rests on the distinction between verbal wit, which arises "wholly [from] the Understanding and the Senses", and the higher quality of humour, though it is possible to find wit "passing into humor": *Lects 1808–1819 (CC)* II 117, 416–17, where, however, Falstaff illustrates both qualities.

7[1] Pope's *The Fourth Satire of Dr. John Donne . . . Versifyed*, originally written in c 1713, was published in greatly revised form in 1735 and was then included in the new Vol II of the octavo *Works* in the same year; *The Second Satire . . . Versifyed*, published anonymously in 1733, was also included in the 1735 *Works*.

8[1] The report of C's lecture of 5 Jun 1812 defends this celebrated solecism on other grounds: "He seemed to think that the want of geographical accuracy in speaking of the seacoast of Bohemia, and his anachronism in making *Julio Romano* live ages before he was born, were not the effect of ignorance, but a voluntary conformity to the old fable which he adopted for the foundation of his play": *Lects 1808–1819 (CC)* I 471.

nius did those of the cabinet and court; that Lucan taken in parts was excellent, but altogether naught; that Quintilian's 6th, 7th and 8th books were not only to be read, but altogether digested. That Juvenal, Horace, and Martial were to be read for delight, and so was Pindar, but Hippocrates for health.

These Notes of Drummond ought never to have been published. They are more disgraceful to himself than to Jonson. It would be easy to conjecture Jonson's Comments on them—how grossly he had been misunderstood, and what he had said in jest (as of Hippocrates) interpreted in earnest—But this is characteristic of a Scotchman/ He has no notion of a Jest, unless you *tell* him—*This is in joke/* still less of that shade of feeling, half and half—.

10   I 96, pencil | *Every Man Out of His Humour* Epilogue lines 27–9

> The throat of war be stopt within her land,
> And turtle-footed peace dance fairie rings
> About her court . . .

turtle-footed is a pretty word, a very pretty word: pray, what does it mean?[1] Doves, I presume, are not Dancers: and the other sort of Turtle, Land or Sea, Green-fat or Hawksbill, would, I should suppose, succeed better in slow Minuets than in the brisk Rondillo. The Pigeons indeed, and the Ring-doves, could not dance but with *a claw* (eclat)[2]

11   I 145 | *Poetaster* [Introduction] lines 1–2

> * Light! I salute thee, but with wounded nerves,
>   Wishing thy golden splendour pitchy darkness.

* There is no reason to suppose ~~Milton~~ Satan's address to the Sun in Par. Lost more than a mere coincidence with these Lines;[1] but were it otherwise, it would be a fine Instance, what usùrious Interest a great Genius pays in borrowing.

10[1] H & S (IX 482) glosses "*turtle-footed*" "slowfooted" and quotes the imitation of the phrase in Ford & Dekker *The Sun's Darling* v i: "And Turtle-footed Peace/ Dance like a Fairie through his realms".

10[2] In a set of ms notes sent to HNC for consideration in revising *LR*, Edward Coleridge referred to this annotation with the remark: "Wherever possible, these volumes, and all other remains of Coleridge would be greatly improved by omitting his puns, and pleasantries, and verbal corrections—": VCL S MS F 11.1.

11[1] C quoted these two lines from Jonson c Dec 1801, noting the parallel with *Paradise Lost* III 1–26: *CN* I 1059.

12   ɪ   146 | Prologue lines 15–20

> Here now, put case our author should, once more,
> Swear that his play were good; he doth implore,
> You would not argue him of arrogance:
> Howe'er that common spawn of ignorance,
> Our fry of writers may beslime his fame,
> And give his action that adulterate name.

[Whalley's note:] . . . it must be said, that our poet often takes care to acquaint the audience with his own good opinion of his works, and directs them to judge accordingly.

It would not be difficult to give a detailed pʏsychological proof from these constant outbursts of anxious Self-assertion, that Jonson was not a *Genius*—a creative Power.[1] Subtract that: and you may safely accumulate on his name all other excellencies of a capacious, vigorous, agile, and richly-stored Intellect.

13   ɪ   147 | ɪ i 59

> "While slaves be false, fathers hard, and bawds be whorish . . ."

[Whalley's note:] This line is not the most harmonious that might have been; and Mr. Theobald would render it more musical, by reading *sires hard*, instead of *fathers hard*: but Jonson has many others of the same rough cadence, and the authority of all the copies supports the present text.

a simple transposition would suffice—

> While Fathers hard, Slaves false, and Bawds be whorish,

14   ɪ   182–3 | v iii 492–509

CRIS[PINUS]. O—barmy froth—
CAES[AR]. What's that?
CRIS. —Puffie—inflate—turgidous—ventositous.
HOR[ACE]. Barmy froth, puffie, inflate, turgidous, and ventositous are
     come up.
TIB[ULLUS]. O terrible windy words.

12[1] C's assessment of Jonson often entails comparison with Shakespeare implicitly (as here) or explicitly, as in *Lects 1808–1819* (*CC*) ɪɪ 153: "He is not original in the same way that Shakspeare is original; but after a fashion of his own, Ben Jonson is most truly original." C's concept of genius is extensively developed in *BL*, e.g. in contrast to talent in *BL* ch 2 (*CC*) ɪ 31.

GAL[LUS]. A sign of a windy brain.

CRIS. O—oblatrant—furibund—fatuate—strenuous—

HOR. Here's a deal; oblatrant, furibund, fatuate, strenuous.

CAES. Now all's come up, I trow. What a tumult he had in his belly!

HOR. No, there's the often conscious damp behind still.

CRIS. O—conscious—damp.

HOR. It's come up, thanks to Apollo and Aesculapius: yet there's another; you were best take a pill more.

It would form an interesting Essay, t̶o̶ or rather series of Essays, in a periodical work, t̶o̶ were all the attempts to ridicule*a* new phrases brought together—to observe the proportion of*b* the words ridiculed that have been adopted and are now common (as Strenuous conscious &c)¹—& how far any grounds can be detected:—so that one might determine before hand, whether a word was invented under the conditions of Assimilability*c* to our Language. Thus much is certain, that the Ridiculers were as often wrong as right—and Shakespear himself could not prevent the naturalization*d* of Accomodation, Remuneration, &c—or Swift the *abuse* even of *Idea*.²

15   I 194-5 | *Sejanus* I 244-55

ARR[UNTIUS].   The name Tiberius,
    I hope, will keep, howe'er he hath foregone
    * The dignity and power.

SIL[IUS].   Sure, while he lives.

ARR. And dead, it comes to Drusus. Should he fail,
    To the brave issue of Germanicus;
    * And they are three: too many (ha?) for him

---

a C has overrun the edge of the page and the first letter appears on I 180

b This word appears on I 180

c The note having reached the foot of I 182, C wrote "Assim", and at the top of I 183 began "Assimilability" again

d This word overruns the page, "n" appearing on I 185

14¹ Both words are in the textus. For "strenuous" *OED* cites Marston *Antonio's Revenge* v i (1602) as first use, then Chapman's *Iliad*, Milton, and Pope's *Iliad*. For "conscious", as attributed to inanimate things, *OED* cites first Jonson *Poetaster* v i (but not this passage), then *inter alia* *Paradise Lost* VI 521.

14² Although Shakespeare made fun of the pretentious Latinity of "accommodate" (in *2 Henry IV* III ii 69–79) and "remuneration" (*LLL* III i 131–72), he also used "accommodation" and "remuneration" himself, in *Othello* I iii 238 and *Troilus* III iii 170 respectively. Swift's defence of the word "idea" occurs in his *Remarks upon a Book, Intituled, The Rights of the Christian Church Asserted*, where he mocks those writers who, in imitation of Locke, refer to the "idea" of a thing—Swift's example being the idea of a mousetrap.

To have a plot upon?

SAB[INUS]. I do not know
The heart of his designs; but, sure, their face
Looks farther than the present.

ARR. By the gods,
If I could guess he had but such a thought,
* My sword should cleave him down from head to heart,
But I would find it out . . .

*** This *anachronic* mixture of the Roman Republican, to whom Tiberius must have appeared as much a Tyrant as Sejanus, with the *James-and-Charles-the 1st* zeal for legitimacy of Descent, is amusing. Of our great names, Milton was, I think, the first who could properly be called, a Republican[1]—My recollections of Buchanan's Works are too faint to enable me to decide, whether the Historian is not a fair exception./[2]

16   I 200–1 | II 143–56

SEJANUS. Thou lost thyself, child Drusus, when thou thought'st
Thou could'st out-skip my vengeance; or out-stand
The power I had to crush thee into air.
Thy follies now shall taste what kind of man
They have provok'd, and this thy father's house
Crack in the flame of my incensed rage, *
Whose fury shall admit no shame or mean.
Adultery! It is the lightest ill
I will commit. A race of wicked acts
Shall flow out of my anger, and o'er-spread
The world's wide face, which no posterity
Shall e'er approve, nor yet keep silent: things
That for their cunning, close, and cruel mark,
Thy father would wish his . . .

* The more we reflect and examine, examine and reflect, the more

15[1] C may well have had in mind Johnson's notorious description of Milton as a "surly republican": *Lives of the English Poets* ed G. Birkbeck Hill (Oxford 1905) I 156. C himself comments on Milton's Republicanism as incorporating "highly aristocratic" ideas about government in *EOT* (*CC*) I 370 (Oct 1802).

15[2] C owned a copy of George Buchanan (1506–82) *Rerum Scoticarum historia* (1582), which he left behind at Allan Bank in 1810 and which finally came into J. H. Green's possession. *W Library* 754 (twice marked as C's), Green List 171. But in this context Buchanan is notable for his *De jure regni apud Scotos* (1579), "a textbook of the opponents of absolutism" (*DNB*). In DANIEL **20** (c Feb 1808) C said that only Buchanan, Knox, and Ralegh avoided a confusion of rights and duties that "occasioned a civil war".

astonished are we at the immense Superiority of Shakespear ~~to his~~ over his contemporaries—& yet what contemporaries! Giant Minds!—Think of Jonson's Erudition, & the force of learned Authority in that age—& yet in no genuine part of Shakespear is to be found such an absurd rant & *ventriloquism* as this & too, too many other passages ferruminated from Seneca's Tragedies, & the later Romans by Jonson. Ventriloquism, because Sejanus is a Puppet out of wc̄h the Poet makes his own voice appear to come.—[1]

17   ɪ 203 | ɪɪ 328–30

TIB[ERIUS]. Our edict shall forthwith command a court.
   While I can live, I will prevent earth's fury:
   Ἐμοῦ θάνοντος γαῖα μιχθήτω πυρί.

[Whalley's note:] This Greek verse, as the historians say, Tiberius had often in his mouth, and the poet thought it too memorable to omit it/:[1]

and to ~~make~~ render it more ludicrous makes it rhyme to fury

   While I can live, I will prevent earth's fury,
   Emoú thanóntos *geé*[a] michtheéto púri

18   ɪ 217 | ɪᴠ 156–66

LAT[IARIS]. This asses fortitude doth tire us all.
   It must be active valour must redeem
   Our loss, or none. The rock and our hard steel
   Should meet t' enforce those glorious fires again,
   Whose splendour cheer'd the world, and heat gave life,
   No less than doth the sun's.
SAB[INUS].   'Twere better stay
   In lasting darkness, and despair of day.
 * No ill should force the subject undertake
   Against the sov'reign, more than hell should make
   The gods do wrong. A good man should and must
   Sit rather down with loss, than rise unjust.

 * This is the boldest sophism, nay, transparent, that was ever brought

---

[a] Accent actually appears between "e" and "e"

16[1] A clear formulation of the objection C makes in other contexts, e.g. *BL* ch 22 (*CC*) ɪɪ 135 of WW—"two are represented as talking, while in truth one man only speaks"—and BEAUMONT & FLETCHER COPY B **66**, where the contrast between Shakespeare and his contemporaries is pursued on this ground.

17[1] H & S ɪᴠ 477, ɪx 609—"Milton translated the [Greek] line in *The Reason of Church Government* i ch 5, 'When I dye, let the Earth be roul'd in Flames'."

in defence of a Thesis supported by sophisms only.—The question is—Is ₦ it not just to resist a Tyrant? Answer—No!—Why not?—Answer—*Because* it is not just. −a = a.—

19   ɪ 224 | v 171–210

[The sacrifice to Fortune, who turns away her face, after which Sejanus mocks the priests and disrespectfully orders them to withdraw.]

This scene is unspeakably irrational. To believe and yet to scoff at a present miracle is little less than impossible.—Sejanus should have been made to suspect Priestcraft & a secret Conspiracy against him.

20   ɪ 235ᵃ | *Volpone*

This admirable indeed, but yet still more wonderful than admirable Play, is from the fertility and vigor of Invention, Character, Language and Sentiment the strongest proof, how impossible it is to keep up any pleasurable Interest in a Tale in which there is no goodness of heart in any of the prominent characters—After the 3ʳᵈ Act, this Play becomes not a dead but a painful weight on the Feelings.—F. C. Fathom, and Zelucco are instances of the same truth.¹—. Bonario and Celia should have been made in some way or other *principals* in the Plot—which the[y] might be, and the objects of Interest, without being made characters—in Novels the Person, in whose fate you are most interested, is often the least marke[d] character of the whole.

   If it were practicable to lessen the *paramouncy*ᵇ of Volpone, a most delightful Comedy might be produced, Celia being the Ward or Niece instead of the Wife of Corvino, & Bonario her Lover—

21   ɪ 283 | *Epicoene*

The Epicœne is to my feeling the most entertaining of old Ben's Comedies—and more than any other would admit of being brought out anew, if under the management of a judicious and stage-understanding Playwright; and ~~with~~ᶜ an Actor who had *studied* Morose might make his fortune.

   ᵃ I.e. the first page of text; the annotation is written through the Dramatis Personae, the Argument, and the Prologue.
   ᵇ C has underlined this word without leaving a mark on the paper: the mark of the dry pen remains
   ᶜ Deletion may not have been intended; only "wi" is clearly struck through

   20¹ The central figures in Smollett's *Adventures of Ferdinand Count Fathom* (1753) and John Moore's *Zeluco* (1786)—both unmitigated scoundrels.

22   I 286 | I i 157–9

CLER[IMONT]. He would have hang'd a pewterer's 'prentice once on a Shrove-Tuesday's riot, for being o' that trade, when the rest were quiet.

[Whalley's note:] The old copies read *quit*, *i.e.* discharged from working, and gone to divert themselves.

It should be *quit*, no doubt, but not, "i.e. discharged from working &c"—but quit, i.e. acquitted.[1] The Pewterer was at his holiday diversion as well as the other apprentices, and they as forward in the Riot as he. But he alone was punished, ~~not for~~ under *pretext* of the Riot, but in *fact* for his trade.

23   I 287 | I i 187–90

CLER. And this fellow waits on him now in tennis-court socks, or slippers soal'd with wool: and they talk each to other in a trunk.[a]*

* What does this mean? Of course, a note being *needed*, there is none.[1]

24   I 290 | II i 1 3

MOR[OSE]. Cannot I, yet, find out a more compendious method, than by this trunk, to save my servants the labour of speech, and mine ears the discord of sounds?

What does "Trunk" mean in this and the former scene? a large Ear Trumpet? [b]Or rather a Tube, such as passes from parlor to kitchen, instead of a bell?[c][1]

25   I 326–[327] | V iv 252

[Whalley's note at the end of the play:] Some criticks of the last age imagined the character of Morose to be wholly out of nature. But to vindicate our poet, Mr. Dryden tells us from tradition, and we may venture to take his word, that Jonson was really acquainted with a person of this whimsical turn of mind:* and as humour is a personal quality, the

---

[a] C has underlined these words with a dry pen, leaving a mark on the paper
[b–c] An afterthought, written in a larger hand than the first sentence

22[1] H & S prints "quit", and glosses it (x 9) "*quit*, acquitted" with a parallel from *Poetaster* v iii 381.

23[1] See **24** below.
24[1] H & S (x 10) glosses "*trunke*, speaking-tube".

poet is acquitted from the charge of exhibiting a monster, or an extrav-
agant unnatural caricatura.

* If Dryden had not made all additional proof superfluous by his own
Plays, this very vindication would evince that he had formed a false and
vulgar Conception of the nature and conditions of the Drama and dra-
matic Personation.[1] Ben Jonson would himself have rejected such a
Plea:

> "For he knew, Poet never credit gain'd
> By writing Truths,† but things like Truth, well-feign'd."
>
> Prologue 2nd to this Play[2]

† i.e. Facts—Caricatures are not less so, because they are found ex-
isting in real life—But Comedy demands Characters, and leaves Cari-
catures to Farce.[3] The safest & truest defence of old Ben were to call the
Epicœne the best of Farces. The defect in the Morose as in other of
Jonson's Dr: Personæ lies in this: that the accident is not a Prominence
growing out of and nourished by the *character* which still circulates in
it, but the Character rises out of the Accident—say rather, consists in
the Accident. Shakespear's ~~are~~ comic Personages have exquisitely char-
acteristic Features—however awry, disproportionate & laughable, yet
like his Bardolph's nose, still a Feature⟨s⟩. But Jonson's are either a man
with a huge *Wen*, having a circulation of its own, & which we might
[have] conceived amputated, and the Patient thereby losing all his *char-
acter*, or they are mere Wens instead of Men, Wens personified, or with
eyes, nose & mouth, cut out, mandrake-fashion.—

P.S. All the above, and more, will have been justly said, if and when-
ever the drama of Jonson is brought into "*comparisons of rivalry*"[4] with
the Shakspearian. But this should not be. Let its inferiority to the Shak-
spearian be at once fairly owned; but at the same time as ~~an~~ the infe-
rior⟨ity of an⟩ ~~yet~~ altogether different *Genus* of the Drama. On this

---

25[1] It is an important point in C's dra-
matic criticism that the greatest writers—
and Shakespeare most notably—create
their characters by looking into them-
selves, not by copying the world outside
them: e.g. *Lects 1808–1819* (*CC*) I 306.

His opinion of Dryden's plays was low,
and "vulgar" is an epithet used of them
elsewhere, e.g. of Dryden's reworking of
Shakespeare's *Tempest*, in *Lects 1808–*
1819 (*CC*) II 271.

25[2] The second "Prologue" (I 284)
lines 9–10 var.

25[3] This remark echoes the objection to
Jonson's characters in **5** above and C's de-
scription of "the greater number of Jon-
son's Comedies" as "Farce-plots" in *CN*
III 4486 para 6.

25[4] Source not identified.

ground, old Ben would still maintain his proud Height. He no less than Shakspear stands on the summit of his Hill, & looks round him like a Master: tho' his be Lattrig and Shaksp's Skiddaw.[5]

25A   I 332 | *The Alchemist*: footnote to I ii 25–7

DAP[PER]. What do you think of me,
    That I am a Chiause?
FAC[E]. What's that?
DAP. . . . As one would say, do you think I am a Turk?

[Whalley's footnote:] . . . The *Chiause*, as Dr. Grey observes from Sir Paul Ricaut's *State of the Turkish Empire*, were reckoned in the number of their militia . . .

26   I 333 | I ii 50, 54–8

FAC[E]. . . . a special gentle . . .
    That knows the law, and writes you six fair hands,
    Is a fine clerk, and has his cyph'ring perfect,
    Will take his oath o' the Greek Xenophon,
    If need be, in his pocket; and can court
    His mistress out of Ovid.

[Whalley's note on the Xenophon:] The 4to has *the Greek Testament*, which I should think the most eligible reading; as it is probable the clerk might carry a Testament about him, to administer oaths to his master's clients. But *Xenophon* is the reading of the folio of 1616, whose authority prevents me from altering the present text.*

* Probably, the meaning is: that meaning to give false evidence, he carried a Greek Xenophon to pass it off for a Greek Testament, & so avoid *perjury*—as the Irish by contriving to kiss their Thumbers instead of the Book.[1]

25[5] See also **12** and n 1 above. Skiddaw (3053 ft, only 60 ft lower than Helvellyn) and the homely Lattrig (1203 ft) were memorable landmarks to the north of Greta Hall. C described them in Sept 1800, in *CN* I 804 f 48: "spotty Skiddaw with his Chasms & ribs in sunshine looked in on me, and Latterig so so soft a pea green, its soft knobby Gavel End yellow/ it looked so

lovely—''.
26[1] In taking an oath the thumb was kissed instead of the Bible to avoid perjury: see e.g. *OED* sb *thumb* 6e, "thumb-kissing". *Misc C* is presumably correct in explaining "thumber" as "thumb-nail", but the word is not noticed in this sense in *OED*.

26A   I 357 | II i 1–2

Ṣ*U*R. Come on, sir. Now, you set your foot on shore
    In *novo orbe* [a new world] . . .[1]

27   I [376][a]

A fondness for judging one work by comparison with others, perhaps
altogether of a different Class, argues a vulgar Taste. Yet it is chiefly on
this Principle that the Cataline has been rated so low.—Take it and Se-
janus, as compositions of a particular Kind—viz. as a mode of relating
great historical Events in the liveliest and most interesting manner, and
I cannot help wishing that we had whole Volumes of such Plays. We
might as rationally expect the excitement of the Vicar of Wakefiedld
from Goldsmith's History of England, as that of Lear, Othello &c from
the Sejanus & Cataline.[1]

28   I 385–6, ink line in margin | *Catiline* I iv 505–12

* CAT[ILINE]. . . . . Sirrah, what ail you?
                                    (*He spies one of his boys not answer.*—)
PAG[E].   Nothing.
BES[TIAL].   Somewhat modest.
CAT. Slave, I will strike your soul out with my foot,
    Let me but find you again with such a face:
    You whelp—
BES. Nay, Lucius.
CAT.   Are you coying it,
    When I command you to be free, and general
    To all?
BES.   You'll be observ'd.
CAT.   Arise, and shew
    But any least aversion in your look
    To him that bourds you next, and your throat opens.

[Whalley's note to this last line:] The grossity of this image may be a

---

[a] Blank page facing the first page of text

26A[1] There is no obvious reason for
crossing through the name; the speech does
belong to Surly.
   27[1] Goldsmith's *The Vicar of Wakefield*
(written 1761–2, pub 1766) went through
more than 90 issues and editions by 1815.
His *History of England, from the Earliest
Times to the Death of George II* (4 vols

1771), a popular commissioned work, had
made c 12 issues by 1815. Green's library
included a copy of a 2-vol 1766 ed of *The
Vicar of Wakefield* (there were at least six
issues in 1766) and a copy of the *History of
England* (3 vols 1800), neither shown as
C's: *Green SC* (1880) 61, 689.

little shaded by restoring the true text, which former editors seem to have misunderstood. The first folio reads *bourds you next*, and that is the true word. To *bourd* is to joke, or to be familiarly merry with any one. . . . The Scots yet use *bourd*, in the sense of dallying and playing the wanton.

* This is either an unintelligible or (in *every* sense) a most *unnatural* passage—improbable if not impossible—at the very moment of signing & swearing such a Conspiracy for the most libidinous satyr. The very presence of the Boys is an outrage to probability. I suspect, that these Lines should be removed so as to follow the ~~third~~ 5th Line of the second Column, p. 38~~12~~—
> On this part of the House.—Sirrah! what ail you?
> P. Nothing. B. Aye, nothing—only somewhat modest—
> Cat. Slave, I will strike &c—[1] A total erasure, however, would be the best, or rather the only possible, amendment.

29 I 388 | II ii 115–16

SEM[PRONIA].   . . . He is but a new fellow,
  * An inmate here in Rome, (as Catiline calls him)

[Whalley's note quotes Sallust:] *Marcus Tullius inquilinus civis urbis Romae* ["Marcus Tullius a foreign-born citizen of the city of Rome"].

* A *Lodger* would have been a happier imitation of inquilinus.[1]

28[1] I.e. I iv 304–5, Catiline speaking:

Boy, see all doores be shut, that none
   approach us,
On this part of the house.

At this point C suggests transferring the later lines

               Sirrah! what ail you?
P. Nothing. B. Aye, nothing—only
   somewhat modest.
CAT. Slave, I will strike your soul out
   with my foot,
Let me but find you again with such a
   face:
               . . . Arise, and shew
But any least aversion in your look
To him that bourds you next, and your
   throat opens

before continuing

               Goe you, and bid
The Priest, he kill the slave I mark'd
   last night;
And bring me of his bloud, when I shall
   call him:
Till then, wait all without.

H & S (x 130) approves of C's opinion that "the episode here is both undramatic and repulsive" but makes no comment on C's proposed transition and points out that "The boys are heralded in line 172" and that "Sallust mentions the suspicion of such vice". See also BEAUMONT & FLETCHER COPY B **71**.

29[1] "Lodger", as H & S agrees (x 133) without quoting C, is here the better translation of *inquilinus* (a variant of *incolinus*) because Cicero is an outsider, "a meere upstart, / That has . . . no house".

30　ɪ 414 | ɪv vi 725–33, 746–54

CET[HEGUS]. I, at smock-treason, matron, I believe you;
　　And if I were your husband; but when I
　　Trust to your cobweb-bosoms any other,
　　Let me there die a fly, and feast you, spider.
LEN[TULUS]. You are too sour, and harsh, Cethegus.
CET.　　　　　　　　　　　　　　　　　　　You
　　Are kind and courtly. I'll be torn in pieces,
　　With wild Hippolytus, nay, prove the death
　　Every limb over, ere I'ld trust a woman
　　With wind, could I retain it. . . .
　　Can these or such be any aids to us?
　　Look they as they were built to shake the world
　　Or be a moment to our enterprise?
　　A thousand such as they are, could not make
　　One atom of our souls. They should be men
　　Worth heaven's fear, that looking up but thus
　　Would make Jove stand upon his guard, and draw
　　Himself within his thunder; which, amaz'd,
　　He should discharge in vain, and they unhurt.

What a strange notion Ben must have formed of a determined remorse-less all-daring Foolhardiness, to have represented it in such a mouthing Tamburlane and bombastic Tongue-Bully as this Cethegus of his!!![1]

31　ɪ 429–31 | *Bartholomew Fair* Induction 113–17, 127–31

SCRIV[ENER]. It is further covenanted, concluded, and agreed, That how great soever the expectation be, no person here is to expect more than he knows . . . neither to look back to the sword and buckler age of Smithfield, but content himself with the present. . . . If there be never a servant-monster i' the Fair, who can help it, he says, nor a nest of antiques? he is loth to make nature afraid in his plays, like those that beget tales, tempests, and such like drolleries, to mix his head with other men's heels; let the concupiscence of jigs and dances reign as strong as it will amongst you. . . .

[Whalley's note:] Our author, and who can help it, is still venting his sneers at Shakespeare. The servant-monster is the character of Caliban

---

30[1] Timur (d 1405), the Great Khan, conqueror and tyrant, familiar as a ranter on the English stage in Marlowe's *Tambur-* *laine* (1590) and Rowe's *Tamerlane* (1702).

in the *Tempest*: the *nest of antiques* is the clowns who dance in the *Winter's Tale* . . .

The best excuse that can be made for Jonson, and in a somewhat less degree for Beaumont & Fletcher, for these base and silly Sneers at Shakespear, is that his Plays were present to their minds chiefly as acted. They had not a neat correct *Edition* of them, as we have—so as by comparing the one with the other to form a just notion of the mighty mind that produced the whole.—At all events, & in every respect, Jonson stands far higher in a moral Light than B. & F.—He *was* a fair Contemporary—& in *his* way & as far as respects Shakespear, an Original—But B. & F. were always imitators, often borrowers, and yet sneer at him with a spite far more malignan[t] than Jonson—who has besides made noble Compensation by his Praises.—[1]

32　ɪ 440 | ɪɪ iii 30–1

JUST[ICE OVERDO]. I mean a child of the horn-thumb, a babe of booty, boy, a cut-purse.*

* Confirms what the passage itself cannot but suggest, the propriety of substituting Booty for Beauty in the first Act of Henry 4ᵗʰ first Part.— Falstaff. Let ~~us~~ not us that are &c./[1]

33　ɪ 440 | ɪɪ iii 59–60

KNOC[KHUM]. . . . I'll ha' this belly o' thine taken up, and <u>thy grass scour'd</u>, wench . . .

either "thee" or "thy tripes", guts or some other genteel Synonyme, "*grass-scoured.*"—"He is a *horse*-courser, Sir!"[1]

34　ɪ 441 | ɪɪ iv

It is not often that old Ben condescends to imitate a *modern*—But Master Dan Knockhum Jordan and his vapors are manifest Replicas of Nym and Pistol—[1]

31[1] On Jonson's talent see also **12** and n 1 and **25** above. Jonson's "noble compensation" was principally in his poem *To the Memory of My Beloved, the Author, Mr. William Shakespeare: and What He Hath Left Us*, prefixed to the First Folio.

32[1] *1 Henry IV* ɪ ii 24–5, "let not us that are squires of the night's body be called thieves of the day's beauty". C proposes this emendation also in SHAKESPEARE COPY

A ɪᴠ 96–7, COPY B 443.

33[1] C quotes Moon-calf in ɪɪ ii 34; Jordan Knockhum is described in "The Persons of the Play" as "A Horse-courser, and ranger o' Turnbull".

34[1] C is remarking upon the frequent repetition of the word "vapours" in Knockhum's speeches in this scene. H & S x 188–9 quotes this note and supports the connection C suggests with *1 Henry IV*:

35 I 442 | II v 81–2

QUAR[LOUS]. Nay, she is too fat to be a fury, sure some walking sow of tallow!
WIN-W[IFE]. An inspir'd vessel of kitchen-stuff!
QUAR. She'll make excellent geer for the coach-makers here in Smith-field, to anoint wheels and axletrees with.

* Good! but yet falls short of the Speech of Mr Johnes, M.P. in the Common Council, on the Invasion intended by Buonaparte—Houses plundered, then burnt, Sons conscribed, Wives and Daughters ravished, &c &c—"*but as* to *You, you LUXURIOUS Aldermen! with YOUR Fat will he grease the wheels of his triumphal Chariot!*["]"[1]

36 I 443 | II vi 35

COK[ES]. Avoid i' your satin doublet, Numps.

* This reminds me of Shakespear's "Aroint thee, Witch!["]"[1]—I find in several Books of that Age the word, Aloigne, and Eloigne thee—i.e. Keep your distance—! or Off with you!—I think it very probable, that aroiagne was a corruption of Eloigne, by the vulgar[2]

37 I 448, pencil | III iv 53–4

QUAR[LOUS]. How now, Numps? almost tir'd i' your protectorship? overparted, overparted?*

* An odd sort of propheticality in this Numps and Old Noll![1]

"*vapours* . . . performs in Knockhum's vocabulary all the function of 'humour' in Nym's". Of the likeness between Nym and Pistol and Knockhum, H & S observes, ". . . they are similar attempts to depict the contemporary roarer".

35[1] On 30 Jun 1803, the *Times* reported a speech given at a "Common Hall held at Guildhall" by "Mr. *Johnes* (late Member for Denbigh)" in favour of income tax. (The report confuses Thomas Johnes [1748–1816], MP for Cardiganshire, with Thomas Jones [1765–1811], MP for Denbigh until 1802, who was the actual speaker.) C may have seen an embroidered version of this speech, for the most extravagant expression reported by the *Times* is the following: "If the Country did not move in putting a stop to the career of this ambitious man, they must expect no more meetings like the present: instead of a Lord Mayor and Corporation, they would find Buonaparte and his sycophants on the Hustings in the body of the Hall; instead of respectable Tradesmen, it would be filled with Septemberizers with tri-coloured cockades . . .".

36[1] *Macbeth* I iii 6; *Lear* III iv 124.

36[2] For "aroint" *OED* notes that it was used only by Shakespeare and that the origin of it is unknown. In a notebook entry of c Oct 1812 C has proposed the same derivation as here: *CN* III 4166.

37[1] Both "Numps" and "Noll" are names equivalent to "fool", but "Old Noll" is also the nickname of the Protector, Oliver Cromweil (1599–1658).

38 i 453 | iii vi 49–51

KNOC[KHUM]. . . . I'll in, and joy Urs'la, with telling how her pig
works; two and a half he eat to his share; and he has drunk a pail-full.
He eats with his eyes, as well as his teeth.

a good Motto for the Parson in Hogarth's Election Dinner—who shows
how easily he might be reconciled to the Church of Rome—for he wor-
ships what he eats.[1]

39 i 472 | v v 67–75

BUS[Y]. . . . yet, I say, his calling, his profession is prophane, it is pro-
phane, idol.
"PUP[PET]. DI[ONYSIUS]. It is not prophane."
LAN[TERN]. It is not prophane, he says.
BUS. It is prophane.
"PUP. It is not prophane."
BUS. It is prophane.
"PUP. It is not prophane."
LAN. Well said, confute him with Not, still. You cannot bear him down
with your base noise, Sir.

[Whalley's note:] Mr. Selden (see his *Table Talk*) observes on this pas-
sage, that the author intended satirically to express the vain disputes of
divines, by Inigo Lanthorn's disputing with a puppet in Bartholomew-
Fair: *It is so, it is not so: It is so, it is not so . . .*

Add that it [is]*ᵃ* an imitation of the Quarrel between Bacchus ~~in~~ and the
Frogs in Aristophanes—κοαξ κοαξ κοαξ[1]

40 i 476, pencil | *The Devil Is an Ass* i i 40–3

SAT[AN].   What vice?
        What kind would'st th' have it of?
PUG.   Why any: Fraud,
        Or Covetousness, or lady Vanity,

ᵃ Word supplied by the editor, C having omitted it on starting a new line

38[1] The joke about transubstantiation
tends to confirm the connection between
this volume and Charles Lamb, as does the
allusion to Hogarth. In his essay "On the
Genius and Character of Hogarth" (1811)
Lamb mentions a copy of *The Entertain-
ment* (Plate 1 of Hogarth's *Election* series)
which he had "the happiness to have hang-
ing up in my parlour" as part of his
"choice collection of the works of Ho-
garth": *L Works* i 84. In the same essay, he
quotes C's tribute to Hogarth from the
1809 *Friend* (*CC*) ii 213.
    39[1] *Frogs* 209–68, selectively q *BL* ch 4
(*CC*) i 75–6. The Greek imitates the croak-
ing of the frogs: *koax, koax, koax.*

Or old Iniquity.

SAT.   I'll call him hither.

[Whalley's note:] The passage is wrong pointed, and the speeches seem improperly divided: it should be read thus:

> "Why any: Fraud,
> Or Covetousness, &c.["]

These vices were all personized, and usually made their appearance in the old plays.

> "I'll call him hither."

This should *probably be given to the master-devil, Satan.

* i.e. against all probability, and with a (for Jonson) *impossible* violation of Character. The words belong plainly to Pug and mark at once his simpleness & his impatience.

41   I 478, pencil | I ii 3–15

FITZ-DOTTREL. . . . But there's not one of these that ever could
    Yet shew a man the devil in true sort.
    They have their crystals, I do know, and rings,
    And virgin-parchment, and their dead men's skulls,
    Their raven's wings, their lights, and pentacles,
    With characters; I ha' seen all these. But—
 * Would I might see the devil. I would give
    A hundred o' these pictures to see him
    Once out of picture. May I prove a cuckold
    (And that's the one main mortal thing I fear)
    If I begin not now to think, the painters
    Have only made him.*a*

* Compare this exquisite piece of Sense, Satire, and sound Philosophy in 1616 with Sir M. Hales Speech from the Bench in the trial of a Witch, some 20 years after!/[1] Even such as the Poet : the Plodder./[2]

---

a C has marked the whole passage lines 9–14 with a pencilled cross in the margin

41[1] The reference is almost certainly to the famous trial of Rose Cullender and Amy Drury nearly *50* years later, in Mar 1662, when the women were convicted of witchcraft and Sir Matthew Hale (1609–76) affirmed his own belief in the existence of witches. A period of intensive reading about witchcraft in 1818 produced notes in *CN* III 4394, 4395, referring to Hales's judgment.

41[2] I.e. "as the Poet [is to] the Plodder".

42   I 484, pencil | II i

[The list of names at the beginning of the scene:] *Meer-craft, Fitz-dottrel, Engine, Trains, Pug.*

* enacted by Mʳ βαδμς of βιϱμινγάμ. *18275–1831.*[1]

43   I 484, pencil | II i 1–2

MEER[-CRAFT]. ∧ Sir, money's a whore, a bawd, a drudge;
    Fit to run out on errands: let her go.

∧ I doubt not, that "Money." was the first word of the line, & has dropt out. Read:

    "Money!—?—Sir! Money's a whore, a bawd, a drudge.["]

44   I 530 | *The Staple of News* II ii 12–14

BRO[KER]. From all the Spanish <u>mines</u> in the West-Indies,
    I hope; for she comes that way by her mother,
    But by her grandmother she's dutchess of mines.

Mints are the Mothers of Money, as Mines the Grandmother/ Add, that Spanish Dollars, or Pieces of Eight, were the most common coin at that time. See the song, p. 548.[1]

45   I 550 | IV iii 37–40

STAT[UTE].   H' has abus'd
    Your grace's body.
PEC[UNIA].   No, he would ha' done,
    That lay not in his power: he had the use of
    Ø̷f Your bodies, Band and Wax, and sometimes Statute's . . .

* I doubt the legitimacy of my transposition of the "of" from the 4ᵗʰ

42[1] "Mr Badams of Birmingham", whom C identifies with Meercraft the "Projector", fertile in get-rich-quick schemes, was John Badams (d 1833), a manufacturing chemist in Birmingham, who knew the Carlyles, the Montagus, and the Lambs. In 1829 he married Louisa Holcroft (b 1806); by that date also he was living in Enfield, outside London. He "took to drink, lost money by mining speculations, and died in Sept. 1833": *The Collected Letters of Thomas and Jane Welsh Carlyle* ed C. R. Sanders et al (Durham, NC, 1970–) III 95n. C's resentment was aroused by Badams's involvement in a scheme to make money for C by having his RSL annuity restored, c Jun 1831: *CL* VI 862n.

44[1] IV ii 95–116, sung by Madrigal, who introduces it with the line "The Sun is father of all metals, you know, Silver and gold . . .". The first stanza is as follows:

As bright as is the sun her sire,
Or earth her mother, in her best attire.
Or Mint, the midwife, with her fire,
Comes forth her grace!

(Of your bodies) to this̶e̶ preceding line—for tho' it facilitates the metre
and reading of the 4ᵗʰ line, and is frequent in Massinger, yet this dis-
junction of the preposition from its case seems to have been disallowed
by Jonson.

better, for the reason above assigned, read o' YOUR b̶o̶d̶i̶e̶s̶, the two
syllables slurred into one, o̶r̶ rather snatched or sucked up into the em-
phasized *Your*. In all points of view therefore Ben's Judgement is just—
for in this way the Line cannot be read as *metre* without that strong and
quick Emphasis on *your* which the *Sense* requires—: and had t̶h̶e̶ not the
sense required an emphasis on *your*, the tmesis of the sign of its cases,
"of," to, &c would destroy almost all boundary between the dramatic
verse and prose, in Comedy.—A lesson not to be rash in conjectural
amendments.   S. T. C.

46 I ⁻3,ᵃ referring to I 550 | **45** textus

See p. 550. It is worth noticing that Jonson uniformly prefers a slurring
of the signs of the Cases at the beginning of a line, so as to form but one
syllable with the noun pronoun or article, t̶h̶a̶n̶ to placing the sign at the
end of the preceding line, even where it would only make t̶h̶e̶ a last
trochaic of the 11-syllable dramatic blank verse line.—I think, judi-
ciously. Indeed, his verse throughout well deserves studying.—

47 I 551 | IV iv 34–5

P[ENNY-BOY]. JUN. I love all men of virtue, frommy princess,
    Unto my beggar here, old Canter . . .

fromme, = pious, dutiful/¹

48 I 558 | V iv

[A trial scene in which Penny-boy Senior appears to be mad.]

I dare not, will not, think, that honest Ben had the Lear in his mind in
this mock mad Scene—

49 I 564 | *The New Inn* I i 14–17

HOST. "A heavy purse makes a light heart."
    There 'tis exprest! first, by a purse of gold,

ᵃ Squeezed in between the acquisition inscription and the beginning of 1

47¹ The loss of a space between   conjectural" gloss (**45**) based on the Ger-
"from" and "my" has led C into a "rash   man adj *fromm*, "pious".

A heavy purse, and then two turtles, makes,
A heart with a light stuck in't, a Light-Heart!

makes frequent in old books, & even now used in some Counties for
Mates, a Pair.[1]

50 I 566 | I iii 72–4

HOST. . . . Instead of backing the brave steed, o' mornings,
To mount the chambermaid; and for a leap
O' the vaulting horse, to ply the vaulting house . . .

[Whalley's note:] For *play* which does by no means suit what follows,
we must read, I presume, *ply* the vaulting house.*

* vault*ing* house for domus fornic*ata*, vaults or Stews is a phrase not
like Jonson—I suspect that instead of ply for play we should read horse
for house—i.e. instead of leaping on the Stallion, to *play* the Stallion
yourself.[1]

*ᵃ*O' the vaulting Horse, to *play* the vaulting *Horse*. The punlet, or
pun-maggot or pun intentional, horse and house, is below Jonson:—and
vaulting house for vaulted too.—The jeu de mots below, on *Aqu*inas and
*Water*ings,[2] had a learned *smack* to season its insipidity.

51 I 566 | I iii 86–7

HOST.   . . . come, to read a lecture
Upon Aquinas at St. Thomas à Waterings . . .

[Whalley's note:] Antiently the place where criminals were executed, in
the county of Surrey.

Sᵗ Thomas Aquinas a witty Latin for Sᵗ Th. a watering[1]

ᵃ Having begun at the foot of the page, the note continues at the top

49[1] An ancient and dialectal use.
50[1] C objects to turning the Latin past participle "fornic*ata*" into an English present participle "vault*ing*". But the radical meaning of *fornix* is a vault or arch, and of *fornicatus* a vaulted (place); the special sense of *fornix* as "brothel" is from the vaulted places, cellars etc used in Rome for such a purpose. (The verb *fornicor*, to commit prostitution, to fornicate, is found only in ecclesiastical Latin.) Through this dislocated meaning "vaulting" is already a pun. H & S (x 303) glosses: "*vaulting*

house, or 'vaulting school', brothel" and quotes Dekker *The Seven Deadly Sinnes of London* IV.
50[2] **51** below. *Jeu de mots*, "play on words".
51[1] The "old place of execution on the Surrey side of the Thames. . . . It was situated at the second milestone of the Kent road, where is a brook; it was a halting-place for the pilgrims to the shrine of St. Thomas of Canterbury to water their horses": H & S x 303–4. Nevertheless C's notice of a pun on *aqua*, "water", stands.

52 ɪ 567 | ɪ v 7–8

[Whalley's note:]

> *Old Master* GROSS, *surnam'd* Ἀγελαστος,*
> *Was never seen to laugh, but at an ass.*

* Qʸ Is not this line some proof that Jonson read Greek accentually?—
With "surnamed" instead of "surnam'd" it would indeed make metre
as ăgĕlastōs; but it is not probable, that Jonson's Ear would have toler-
ated the jingling cacophony of lās and *ass*; and surnamed is a drawling
sound too. Therefore Agēlăstŏs.[1]

53 ɪ 570 | ɪ vi 140–3

LOV[EL]. Then shower'd his bounties on me, like the Hours,
    That open-handed sit upon the clouds,
    And press the liberality of heaven
    Down to the laps of thankful men! . . .

[Whalley's note:] It is pity so fine a passage should have been given with
such mistakes; but our comfort is, the emendation is as easy and obvi-
ous: for *Howres*, which conveys no idea, we are to read *like the Hours*;
the poetical goddesses presiding over the several seasons.

Like many other similar passages in Jonson, it is ειδος χαλεπον ιδειν,
a *sight* which it is difficult to make one's self *see*—a *picture*, ~~the~~ my
Fancy cannot *copy*, detached from the *words*.

54 ɪ 574 | ɪɪ v

Tho' it was hard upon old Ben, yet Felton, it must be confessed, was in
the right in considering the Fly, Tiptoe, Bat Burst, &c as Dotages.[1]—
Such a scene, as this, was almost enough to damn a new Play—and Stuff
is worse still, most abominable *Stuff*![2]

52[1] Ἀγέλαστος (unlaughing) is ac-
cented correctly, and no variant is re-
corded. But H & S (x 305), reading (as C
suspects) as though the word were intended
to be *agelástos*, cited *Cynthia's Revels* v xi
60 and the word "Philautía" for "the pro-
nunciation following the Greek accent".

54[1] Fly and Sir Glorious Tipto appear in
this scene, Bat Burst in ɪv ii. Owen Fell-
tham (c 1602–68) attacked "*Jug, Pierce,
Peck*, and *Fly*, and all/ Your Jests so nom-
inal" (but not using the word "Dotages")
in his *An Answer to the Ode of "Come*

leave the loathed Stage, &c"; the "Ode to
Himself" that Jonson appended "with iust
indignation . . . at the vulgar censure of his
Play" to *The New Inn*, which at first per-
formance (19 Jan 1629) was a disastrous
failure. See H & S vɪ 492–4, xɪ 339–40.
Whalley does refer to Felltham's attack
(ɪ xxxvi), but so cursorily that C may be
supposed to have had some more direct ac-
quaintance with it.

54[2] Nick Stuff, "The Ladies' Taylor",
appears only in ɪv iii; C puns on "stuff",
i.e. worthless matter.

54A I 583, pencil | III ii 96–8

HOST. . . . . It is a flame and ardour of the mind,
  Dead, in the proper corps, quick in another's:
  Transfers the lover into the Beloved.

55 I 583, pencil | III ii 165–70

LOV[EL]. . . . . So knowledge first begets benevolence,
  * Benevolence breeds friendship, friendship love:
  And where it starts or steps aside from this,
  It is a mere degenerous appetite,
  A lost, oblique, deprav'd affection,
  And bears no mark or character of love.

* Jonson has elsewhere proceeded thus far, but the ⟨part⟩ most difficult and delicate, yet perhaps not the least capable of being both morally and poetically treated, is the Union itself—& what even in this Life it can be—

JOHANN HEINRICH JUNG

"JUNG-STILLING"

1740–1817

Theorie der Geister-Kunde, in einer Natur- Vernunft- und Bibelmässigen Beantwortung der Frage: was von Ahnungen, Gesichten und Geistererscheinungen geglaubt und nicht geglaubt werden müsse. [Together with:] Apologie der Theorie der Geisterkunde veranlasst durch ein über dieselbe abgefasstes Gutachten des Hochwürdigen geistlichen Ministeriums zu Basel. . . . Als ersten Nachtrag zur Theorie der Geisterkunde. 2 pts (in one vol). Nürnberg 1808, 1809. 8º.

British Library C 126 h 7 (1, 2)

Monogram "C" of John Duke Coleridge on p ‾5. "S. T. C." label on titlepage verso. Letters in red crayon on the title-page appear to be binder's marks. The two pts—Pt i is pp xxviii 380, Pt ii is pp 76—were evidently bound together when C wrote his marginalia. The volume was later carefully rebound without cropping the annotations.

MS TRANSCRIPT. VCL BT 22 (incomplete).

DATE. Probably Apr–May 1819: the anecdote in **44** is recorded also in *CN* IV 4529.

COEDITORS. Lore Metzger, Raimonda Modiano.

1   i [v] | *Theorie der Geister-Kunde*

Das Titelkupfer ist das wahre Portrait einer Dame, die im 14ten Jahrhundert gelebt hat, sie hiess *Agnes*, war eine Prinzessin von *Meran*, und Gemalin *Ottonis* des 2ten Grafen von *Orlamünda*. . . . Ob nun diese, oder *Bertha von Lichtenstein* . . . die *wahre* weisse Frau sey, oder ob sie beyde erscheinen, das werde ich vielleicht einmal näher untersuchen.

[The frontispiece copperplate print is the true portrait of a lady who lived in the fourteenth century; she was named Agnes and was a princess of Meran and wife of Otto, the 2nd count of Orlamünde. . . . Whether, however, this one or Bertha von Lichtenstein . . . was the *true* white lady, or whether both appear, I shall perhaps investigate further some time.]

It is perhaps necessary, that the same total quantity of folly should exist in all ages; but differently distributed. If so, I should fairly infer, that all the Humdrummery of all the old Grannams[1] of the preceding Century had been condensed into this credulous *cock-sure*[2] Dotard of a Ghost-monger.

2   i 1, pencil, rubbed | § 1

Wenn man die Menschengeschichte, rückwärts, bis ins graue Alterthum durchdenkt, so findet man, dass sie immermehr mit den Einwürkungen, über- oder untermenschlicher, guter oder böser Wesen durchwebt ist.

[If one traces the history of mankind back into dark antiquity, one discovers that more and more it is interwoven with the influences of superhuman and subhuman, good and evil beings.]

How easily *a*[&] yet [? more truly] to put [not] "rückwärts" [but]*b* "vorwärts" l. 1. and "minder" for "mehr" l. 3, and "vom" for "ins", l. 2.[1]

3   i 2–3, pencil, badly rubbed | § 4

Kann die menschliche Einbildungskraft etwas erdichten, oder erschaffen, zu dem sie keinen Stof, keine Materie hat?—

[*Can the human power of imagination invent or create something for which it has no substance, no matter?—*]

* The confusion, stupidity, or rather brazen falseness of this § 4 [? is] unarguable. If by Ghosts of Men he means visible, but not Sensuous Images in the shapes of men, why should the numerous Apparitions (recorded by the same *faithful* Viewers) in dog or goat shape be ⟨not⟩ the Ghosts of Dogs and goats?[1]

4   i 2, pencil | Following 3 textus

Jeder vernünftige redliche Denker wird mir antworten, *Nein! sie kann sich durchaus kein Bild schaffen, von dem was nicht in die Sinne fällt.*

[Every reasonable thinker will answer me, "No! it cannot possibly create an image of something that is not perceived through the senses."]

a–b Badly rubbed, now almost illegible

1[1] "Grandmothers".

1[2] The word had rather recently acquired its derogatory sense, and C's underlining suggests also that he had deliberately chosen a vulgar expression; cf "cocksurety" in **37** below.

2[1] With these changes the sentence would read: "If one traces the history of mankind *forwards from* dark antiquity, one discovers that *less and less* it is interwoven with the influences of superhuman . . . beings."

3[1] Jung raises the question of an animal world of spirits in **5** textus.

Haud equidem imagines facere, sed eas tamen componere possum.[1]

5 i 3, pencil | Following **4** textus

Daraus folgt also unwidersprechlich, dass wir Menschen nie, von einer unsichtbaren Geisterwelt, von der Fortdauer unseres Wesens nach dem Tod, von guten und bösen Geistern, und von Gottheiten, von Ferne etwas geahnet hätten, wenn sich nicht dieses *Uebersinnliche* dem *Sinnlichen* offenbart hätte. Warum wissen wir nichts von einer *thierischen Geisterwelt?*—warum spricht man nicht vom wiederkommen freundlicher Hausthiere?—natürlicher Weise deswegen weil sich eine solche Welt nie den Menschen offenbart.

[Thus it follows irrefutably that we human beings would never have had the faintest notion of an invisible world of spirits, of the continuance of our existence after death, nor of good and evil spirits, nor of deities, had not this *supersensible* revealed itself to the *sentient*. Why do we know nothing about an *animal world of spirits*? Why do we never speak of the return of friendly domestic animals? Obviously, because such a world never revealed itself to men.]

i.e. we should never have seen Ghosts, if we had never seen Ghosts. True! but instead of this *you* infer, we should never have seen Ghosts had there not been Ghosts to be seen—which is not true, as every idle dream shews.

But ~~yet~~ you may reply, Dreams are Ghosts.—I answer—with all my heart—provided you will let me say, that Ghosts are Dreams.[1] And this one note, I conscientiously believe, contains the whole *Geisterkunde!*[2]

6 i 11, pencil | § 17

* Unter allen Völkern, Zungen, und Sprachen, gab es von Anfang der Welt an kein Einziges, welches *Ahnungen, Gesichte,* und *Geistererscheinungen* läugnete . . .

[* Among all nations, tongues, and languages, there was from the beginning of the world not a single one that denied *presentiments, visions,* and *apparitions* of spirits . . .]

* In all peoples, tongues and languages there have been Dreams: ergo, Dreams are *not* Dreams!!

4[1] "I cannot in fact create images, but I can still compose them."

5[1] This statement is consistent with other interesting analyses of ghosts as dreams, e.g. of Luther's vision of the Devil in *Friend* (*CC*) i 136–47, and of a vision of his own in *TT* 3 Jan 1823.

5[2] "Spirit-lore" or "ghost-lore"—from title.

7   i 20–1, pencil | § 29

Da man aber nun bey diesen Untersuchungen keine andere Kräfte ent-
deckte, als solche die der Materie eigen sind; oder wenn man Würkun-
gen verborgener Kräfte bemerkte, alsofort schloss, sie seyen auch ma-
teriel, nur nicht entdeckt, und man werde bey fernerem Fortschritt, auch
ihnen auf die Spur kommen . . . so sezte man als unwiderruflich vest,
es gebe durchaus keine andere als materielle Kräfte. *

[But since in the course of these examinations one discovered no other forces
than those proper to matter; or if, upon observing the effects of hidden forces,
one deduced immediately that they were also material, and only undiscovered,
and will in the course of future progress also be tracked down . . . thus one
established it as irrevocable that *absolutely no other powers than material pow-
ers exist.* *]

* But this was false Logic. To say that the universe consists of Matter
and Power is no more than to affirm, that it consists of manifestations
and Causes; but because matter (phænomenon) is the result of *Powers*,
does it follow that the Powers are material?[1] That is, that the *non*-
phænomenon is a phænomenon!!—

8   i 25, pencil | § 37

Wenn die Welt eine Maschine ist, die durch ihre anerschaffcne Kräfte,
allein, ohne andere Beyhülfe ihren Gang geht, wenn so gar Gott selbst
nicht mitwürkt, so haben auch weder gute noch böse Engel Einfluss auf
sie. . . . Ach mein Gott! welche eiskalte trostlose Vernunftweisheit ist
das!—sie weiss von keinem Vater im Himmel, und von keinem Erlöser
. . .

[If the world is a machine that through its innate powers pursues its course *by
itself* without other assistance, without even God himself acting upon it, then
also neither good nor bad angels have any influence upon it. . . . Oh my God!
what ice-cold, disconsolate, reasoned wisdom this is!—it knows of no Father in
Heaven, nor of a Redeemer . . .]

I am no friend, God knows! to the mechanic System, and hold it for
mere *Psilo*sophy;[1] but really I cannot see how or why the Christian Doc-

---

7[1] Jung goes on, in the sentences fol-
lowing the textus, to say that all matter is
subject to laws, that "the entire universe
consists of matter and its powers", and that
in consequence the universe is subject to
invariable laws.
  C often insisted that powers are ideal,
not material, and objected to the confusion,

common among the *Naturphilosophen*, be-
tween physical phenomena and the forces
they represent. See e.g. KANT *Metaphys-
ische Anfangsgründe* **11**, OKEN *Lehrbuch
der Naturgeschichte* **1**.
  8[1] C's coinage, "shallow philoso-
phy"—or "slender wisdom" in his own
glossing: *BL* ch 10 (*CC*) I 185 and n 1.

trine of Redemption depends on the existence of Angels ⟨more⟩ than on that of winged Serpents. Both may be true, for aught I know—or am concerned to know.

God's accredited Messengers (Angels) I receive and honor for the sender's sake, whether they be Bishops or Winds or Flames of Fire; but surely not every incidental allusion to the popular notions of the Jews that may occur in the New Testament (as the dispute between Michael & The Devil)[2] is to be made an essential article of Xtn Faith![3]

9 i 26 | § 38

* Die damaligen Sitten verglichen mit den heutigen, zeugen laut, dass der seelige *Jerusalem* rechte hatte, wenn er sagte: *lieber die spanische Inquisition, als herrschenden Unglauben.*

[* The morals of that time compared with those of today testify strongly to the fact that the blessed Jerusalem was right in saying, "rather the Spanish Inquisition than prevailing unbelief".]

* The proof? the proof?—Pity, that Jung had not read our Goldsmith's Dream in the Boar's-head Tavern on this point. (Goldsmith's Essays.)[1]

10 i 26 | § 39

Die Folgen des finstern *Aberglaubens fielen indessen stärker ins Auge*, als die Folgen des *mechanisch-philosophischen Systems* . . . daher grif man nun den Aberglauben mit den Waffen an, die die Philosophie an die Hand gab; man stürzte ihn vom Thron, aber auch mit ihm den seeligen beruhigenden Glauben des Christen.*

[The consequences of dark *superstition*, however, strike the eye more strongly than the consequences of the *mechanistic philosophical system* . . . therefore one now attacked superstition with the weapons supplied by philosophy; one dethroned it but along with it also the blessed, comforting Christian belief.*]

* No mode of reasoning is more captious (*verfänglich*) and less satis-factory than this of deducing from the supposed ground (= a) of the denial of some trifling point (= b) the necessity of denying (or even, as in *this* instance—the necessary Denial of) ~~the~~ C D E.—

8[2] Rev 12.7.

8[3] C wrote frequently in this vein on the subject of angels—"superstitious trash" he calls it in Hacket *Sermons* 16; cf Ox-lee **9, 10.**

9[1] Oliver Goldsmith "A Reverie at the *Boar's-head-tavern* in *Eastcheap*" (1760) *Collected Works* ed Arthur Friedman (Ox-ford 1966) iii 97–112. Goldsmith included this essay in collections of 1765 and 1766, and his essays were often reprinted; C's ed is not known. Goldsmith's essay denies that the human condition was any better in the past than it is in the present, and de-scribes the debaucheries of a monastery.

11 i 32–3, pencil | § 46

Die *menschlichen Sinnen* empfinden nur *die Oberfläche der Dinge* in *Raum* und *Zeit*. . . . Wir sind eingeschränkte Wesen, daher sind auch alle unsre Vorstellungen eingeschrankt: wir können uns keine *zwey Dinge*, geschweige *mehrere* zugleich vorstellen, daher mussten wir so organisirt seyn, dass uns alle *Dinge aussereinander* nähmlich in *Raum*, und *nacheinander* dass ist in *der Zeit* erscheinen. *Der Raum und die Zeit entstehen also blos in unsere Seele; ausser uns im Wesen der Natur selbst, ist keins von Beydens. Da nun alle Bewegungen in der ganzen Schöpfung in Raum und Zeit geschehen, ohne beyde keine Bewegung möglich ist, so sind auch alle Bewegungen in der ganzen Schöpfung blos Vorstellungsformen in unseren Seelen, die aber in der Natur selbst nicht statt finden. Folglich sind auch alle Weltsysteme, auch selbst das Co-pernikanische, blos Vorstellungsformen.*

[The *human senses* perceive merely *the surface of things* in *space* and *time*. We are limited beings, and therefore all of our representations are limited. We cannot form a representation of *two things* simultaneously, let alone *several*; hence we must be organized in such a way that all *things* appear to us *external to each other*, that is in *space*, and *in succession*, that is in *time*. Space and time originate therefore only in our soul; neither of them exists outside us in the being of nature itself. Since all motions in all creation occur in space and time, without either of which no motion is possible, thus also all motions in all creation are mental forms of representation, which do not, however, occur in nature itself. Hence all world systems, even the Copernican, are mere forms of representation.]

There is a strange *Tangle of Truth* and Sophism in this §. 46.—First, Time and Space are not *results* of the *Senses*; but the constitutive Forms of the Sense: or rather they are the Sense itself;[1] and the Laws thereof (namely, Geometry and Arithmetic) are Science, no less than Ethics and pure Logic. It is the Ptolemaic System, that was deduced from the *senses* by a senseless substitution of relative and perspective Phænomena for the Law of all sensuous Intuition explicative of these Phænomena—the substitution of the Problem for the Solution! The argument from God's perfection is weakness itself. God knows the scientific appearance of the Solar System is that which he has made *necessarily* ⟨not percipiently⟩ *appear* to a rational creature endowed with *Sense*. And should the Dynamic των μη φαινομενων[2] ever be raised into a Science, we might then say that Gods knows the Spiritual System according to the Laws, in

---

11[1] C is paraphrasing the Transcendental Aesthetic as given in the *Critique of Pure Reason*: see KANT *C d r V* **4**, *Logic*

(*CC*) 153 and n 3, and MAASS **2**.

11[2] "Of the non-phenomenal"—i.e. of that which is not manifest to the senses.

which he has manifested the same to his ⟨rational⟩ Creatures endowed with *understanding*. Even so with the *Will* as the Substance of Ontology—and who doubts that beyond all this and at once containing and transcending all these, there is a divine knowlege by which God knows all things, φαινομενα, δυναμικα, νουμενα, νοερα, or ουσια και τα υπερουσια[3] as God alone can know?—Jung confounds relation, as of A B C D E F to β in B, with the relation of A B & C to each other, each to each, each to all, and all to each.

12   i 38, pencil | § 53

. . . wir sehen es [das Licht] als eine Materie an . . . und es befindet sich auch in unserer Vorstellung in *Raum* und *Zeit*, und doch hat es Eigenschaften, die der Natur der ganzen übrigen Materie gerade entgegen stehen: *man bedenke nur die millionenfachen Durchkreuzungen der Lichtstralen aller leuchtenden und beleuchteten Körper, ohne sich untereinander in ihren geraden Richtungen zu verhindern.* Den Naturkündiger möcht ich sehen, der das aus den ewigen und unwandelbaren Gesetzen der Materie genügend erklären könnte.

[. . . we regard it [light] as matter . . . and it exists also in our mental representation in *space* and *time*, and yet it has properties that are diametrically opposed to the nature of all other matter: *one need only consider the millionfold crossings of the rays of light of all luminous and illuminated bodies without mutually interfering with their straight lines.* I should like to see *that* natural philosopher who could explain this satisfactorily on the basis of the eternal and unchanging laws of matter.]

Why not? We have only to state the particles as small enough, and at sufficient distances from each other: and the Understanding finds no difficulty whatever the Fancy may. Besides, is Matter necessarily corpuscular? Jung, at least, talks himself of material Powers or Forces—materielle *Kräften*.

13   i 86, pencil | § 107

Die sonderbare Erscheinung, *wenn Menschen sich selbst sehen, sich selbst erscheinen*, ist nicht selten. . . . Wenn mich jemand fragt, *wie es möglich sey, dass sich ein Mensch selbst erscheinen könne, oder wie dies sich selbst sehen in der menschlichen Natur gegründet sey?*—So antworte ich: dass nicht mehr dazu erfordert werde, als Engel und Geister zu sehen, wo keine sind. . . . so wie nun *fremde* Gestalten in der Einbildungskraft so lebhaft werden können, dass sie den äusseren sinn-

11[3] All things, "phenomenal, dynamic,   superessential".
noumenal, intellectual", or "essential and

lichen Eindrücken gleich sind, eben so kann auch die *eigene* Gestalt den nemlichen Eindruck machen.

[The strange phenomenon *when people see themselves, appear to themselves*, is not rare. . . . . When someone asks me *how it is possible that one can appear to oneself, or whether this seeing of oneself is possible in human nature?*—I answer thus: that this requires no more than to see angels and ghosts where none appear. . . . Just as *foreign* forms can become so vivid in the imagination that they resemble external impressions of the senses, similarly one's *own* form can also create the same impression.]

Not a false but an insufficient Solution.

14   i 92, pencil | § 115

Swedenborg kam mit einer Gesellschaft Reisender aus *England* zu *Gothenburg* an, hier sagte er, er habe von den Engeln erfahren, *dass es gegenwärtig in Stockholm in der und der Gasse brenne.* . . . . Den folgenden Tag erfuhren sie, dass sich die Sache genau so verhalten habe.

[When Swedenborg arrived in Gothenburg in the company of travellers from England, he said that he had learned from angels that *at that moment there was a fire in such and such a street.* . . . . On the following day they learned that this had been exactly the case.]

an incomparably better and fuller account of this in B. IV of Kant's Verm. Schrift.—[1]

15   i 103, pencil | § 124

[Jung tells a story about Böhm, a mathematician, who one afternoon, while enjoying the company of friends, had an irrational urge to go home. When he returned home, he experienced an equally irrational desire to move the bed from the place where it had always been. After moving the bed, he returned to his friends and stayed until ten in the evening, then went home with no anxiety and went to bed. In the middle of the night he heard a loud noise and woke to find that a beam from the ceiling had fallen in the place where his bed had originally been. Jung argues that a "mechanical philosopher" would explain the sequence of events as follows: during the previous night, Böhm must have heard the cracking of the beam; an obscure sense of danger was therefore aroused in him. But Jung rejects this explanation on the grounds that in fact

---

14[1] "Brief an [Fräulein Charlotte von Knobloch] über Swedenborg" in KANT *VS* IV 362–70 (not annotated by C). An account of Swedenborg and the fire also appears in *Träume eines Geistersehers*, which C annotated in all three copies: see esp KANT *VS* COPY C **16** and **17**.

Böhm's mind was free of anxiety and that when towards evening he felt the urge to go home, he tried to reason against it.]

Might or might not, according as the sensations were more or less similar to those, which the Body had experienced during its half-waking attention to the creaking of the Beam. The solution, true or false, is not at all invalidated by Jung's objections.

16   i 106–8, pencil | § 127

Der Kaufmann, bey dem ich ehmals von 1763 bis 1770 in Diensten war . . . erzählte mir öfters eine merkwürdige Ahnung, die er in *Rotterdam* gehabt hatte. . . . In *Rotterdam* war er nun mit seinen Geschäften fertig, er gieng also des Morgens zu dem Middelburger Marktschif . . . bestellte und bezahlte einen Plaz für sich. . . . Als er beynahe mit dem Essen fertig war, so kam der Matrose um ihn zu rufen; so wie der Mensch die Thür öfnete, und ihn der Kaufmann erblickte, so überfiel diesen eine unerklärbare Angst . . . *er dürfe nicht nach Middelburg reisen* . . . er muste dem Matrosen sagen, *er könne nicht mitfahren*. . . . [Man] erfuhr [gegen Abend], *dass der Blitz in das Middelbürger Marktschif geschlagen habe* . . .

[The merchant in whose service I was from 1763 until 1770 . . . told me frequently of a strange presentiment that he had experienced in Rotterdam. . . . He had finished his business affairs in Rotterdam, so that one morning he went to the market-ship of Middelburg . . . reserved and paid for a berth for himself. . . . When he had nearly finished his meal, the sailor came to call him; as soon as the man opened the door and the merchant caught sight of him, he was overcome by an inexplicable fear . . . *he must not travel to Middelburg* . . . he must tell the sailor that *he could not come along*. . . . It was learned [towards evening] *that lightning had struck the Middelburg market-boat* . . .]

It would be a hopeless task to reason on Anecdotes related by so credulous a Professor as Jung, and one so little disposed or qualified to cross-examine his Authorities, whether of first, second or tenth hand. In such cases the Fact most likely to escape Attention or slip out of the memory is that which contained the probable solution of the whole.—But even in this naked account, I see nothing unaccountable—i.e. nothing but what might have taken place under the known laws of Psychology—the contrary of which is a necessary Condition of our being permitted to have recourse to extra-natural Solutions. But men, like Jung, are for ever confounding *Occurrence* with Experience, ιδια και απαξ λεγο-μενα[1] with facts reproducible according to a Law or of precalculable

16[1] ''Private events and unique words''.

Recurrence. The ⟨oppressive & alarming⟩ Effect of an Atmosphere surcharged with Electricity on certain Temperaments is a fact of ordinary experience: & what more likely to increase & concentrate the *feelings* than the Sight of a Mariner as here stated? How much more charitable as well as rational would it not have been, to have admitted the difficulty and in many cases the impossibility, of distinguishing a super-nat. from a natural cause, so as to demonstrate the Negative as to the latter—i.e. in any *one* instance, taken by itself. As long as a man is convinced of the irrationality of the Ghost-theory, so long he is right in doubting, or attributing to known Laws, the stories and anecdotes pressed upon him as *Facts*. ᖆ A *Fact* is *one* thing, the narration of something *for a fact* is *another*.[2]

17   i 111, pencil | § 130

Wenn auch diese Haushälterin, ein drückend Vorgefühl von einem bevorstehenden Gewitter, und dem Einschlagen desselben hatte, *so konnte doch dies Vorgefühl unmöglich den Ort bestimmen, wo es einschlagen würde.*

[Although this housekeeper had an oppressive presentiment of an impending thunderstorm and lightning striking, *yet it is impossible that this presentiment could have determined the place where it would strike.*]

unmöglich?[1] Surely, nothing more likely.

18   i 131, pencil | § 138

Damit entfaltet sich auch ein Gesetz in seinem Gemüthe, dessen Formul ist: *Was du nicht willst das dir Andere thun sollen, das thue ihnen auch nicht.* . . . Bey weiterm Nachdenken kommt er nothwendig endlich dahin, wohin nun die Vernunft zu unsern Zeiten durch die philosophische Aufklärung gekommen ist, nähmlich zum *Deismus*, dann zum *Fatalismus*, dann zum *Naturalismus*, und nun zum *Atheismus*.

[Thus also a law becomes manifest in a heart whose maxim is: "Do not do to others what you do not wish others to do to you." . . . Upon further reflection one necessarily arrives finally at the point at which reason has arrived in our time through philosophical enlightenment—namely, at *deism*, then at *fatalism*, then at *naturalism*, and then at *atheism*.]

16[2] Cf KANT *C d r V* 5: "What do you mean by a *fact*, an empiric Reality, which alone can give solidity . . . to our Conceptions?" C also said that the proper subject of a supernatural tale is the mentality of a narrator who takes a "*Subjective* product (A saw the Ghost of Z) for an objective fact—the Ghost of Z was there to be seen": N43 ff 78–77ᵛ (20 May 1830).

17[1] "Impossible"—in textus.

Why so? And why *necessarily* so? The moral Rule, as a *Fact*, infers the very contrary. Remorse and Regret are diverse in *kind*: an[d] not merely different in *degree*.[1] Rem: = y, Reg: = x: not Rem. = x_3, and Regr: = x_1[a]—But this is inconceivable except on the assumption of Free Agency—and this again morally unrealizable without a God as the Identity of Holy Will and infinite Power.

19 i 134, pencil

Jedem Bild der Phantasie liegen *würkliche wahre* Ideen zum Grund . . .

[Each image of the imagination is founded on *real*, *true* ideas . . .]

What does Jung mean by *Ideas*?[1]

20 i 134, pencil

Alle, nur einigermassen cultivirte Völker, haben die Grundidee von Gott, von der Geisterwelt, und von der Unsterblichkeit der Seelen.

[*All peoples, even those only partly civilised, have a fundamental idea of God, of the world of spirits, and of the immortality of the soul.*]

I more than *doubt* this assertion. Pythagoras, Plato and a few others were not *the Greeks, das Volk*.[1]

21 i 143, pencil | § 141

Es kann durchaus keinen *blinden Zufall*, kein *bloses Ungefähr* geben; aus den allerkleinsten unbedeutendsten Vorfällen, entstehen gewöhnlich die allerwichtigsten Ereignisse; *kein Haar, kein Sperling fällt auf die Erde, ohne Gottes Willen*. An den Spieltischen, und bey den verbotendsten Handlungen und schrecklichsten Lastern ist das Geisterreich geschäftig.

[There is absolutely no such thing as *blind chance* or *mere accident*; from the minutest, most insignificant events spring usually the most important events; *no hair, no sparrow falls to earth without God's will*. At the gambling tables, and at the most illegal actions and hideous vices, the world of spirits is active.]

But reflect only on the innumerable Links of Causation that must inter-

---

[a] Written "$x^{(3}$ . . . $x^{(1}$"—printed "x_3 . . . x_1" to avoid confusion with footnote indicators

18[1] A distinction C insisted on, especially in relation to the theological issue of repentance, e.g. in *AR* (1825) 154, 257.

19[1] For a variety of meanings of "idea", and the sophisms involved in an unfastidious use of the term, see e.g. *SM* App E esp (*CC*) 100–6, 113–14.

20[1] "The people"—i.e. the common people, as C reads the sense of Jung's "peoples" in textus.

vene between the moment = a, when the Lottery numbers were presented in the dream, to the moment = Z, when the motion of the Muscle took place by which they were drawn![1]

22   i 162–3 | § 149

[Jung tells a story that he claims to have found confirmed in La Harpe's posthumous papers: how at a dinner of notables in 1788 Jacques Cazotte predicted the precise fate awaiting each one of them as a result of the Revolution—Condorcet, Chamfort, Nicolai, Malesherbes, and others—ending with the prophecy of his own death.]

This is, for thinkers, a most instructive Story; but for readers in general a most pernicious one. Not as causing or confirming Superstition: for S. like Reason, has no degrees: but as furnishing Irreligion with a powerful instance.

For it is not more clear that this was found among La Harpe's Papers after his Death, than that it is a made-up Romance,[1] to the construction of which just enough of Fact had existed, first to suggest the fable, & after some years to make the Writer, like Don Quixote in the Cave, doubtful whether there was not some truth in it[2]—enough in conjunction with so pious a purpose, to tempt him to pass it off for the truth—at least, to give it a *chance*, when there was no chance of his being questioned on the subject.—

23   i 165, pencil

[Jung reports Cazotte's prediction of the execution of the leading members of the nobility.]

This Story did La Harpe credit—for as all the ⟨other⟩ parties, who were ear-witnesses were dead when he invented it, and he would be dead when it was published, it ran no risk of detection—except by some one of Jung's Ghost-seers

21[1] C alludes to another of Jung's pieces of evidence, the account (i 117–20) of a dream that produced a winning lottery number.

22[1] The story appears in Jean-François de La Harpe (1739–1803) *Oeuvres choisies et posthumes* (4 vols Paris 1806), which is cited by Jung i 168. C may have known the work not at first hand but through reviews: see **28** n 1 below. It was revealed in 1817 that the editor of the work had suppressed the phrase at the end of La Harpe's report on Cazotte: "the prophecy is purely fictitious".

22[2] The cave in La Mancha to which the romance figure Montesinos retired to live out his life. When Don Quixote visited the cave he had a vision of Montesinos and other heroes (pt 2 ch 23). C drew attention to this episode when he lectured on Cervantes in 1818 and 1819: *Lects 1808–1819* (*CC*) II 156–66, 414–20.

24 i 167, pencil

Hier kommt Alles darauf an, *ob diese ganze Geschichte [von La Harpe]*
wahr, oder erdichtet, etwa nach der Erfüllung geschrieben ist?—Denn
dass alle Personen die bey dem Gastmahl waren, aus genaueste so ums
Leben gekommen sind, wie es ihnen hier *Cazotte* voraus sagt, das hat
seine vollkommene Richtigkeit; der Gastgeber, dem auch *Cazotte* nichts
weissagt . . . war der Einzige, der eines natürlichen Todes starb.

[This all depends on *whether this entire story [of La Harpe's] is true or fabri-*
cated, written after the event. It is perfectly true that all the persons that attended
the banquet had met with precisely the kind of death that Cazotte predicted; the
host, about whom Cazotte did not prophesy anything, . . . was the only one
who died a natural death.]

Strange that even this poor credulous man (credulous indeed who could
believe La Harpe!) should not have one gross improbability in this tale—
viz—that after the exact fulfilment of the prophecy in the first person/
none of the others should have recalled it to notice!

25 i 168, pencil | § 150

Ich frage jeden Wahrheitliebenden Kenner der Kunst, der *Ideale*, von
getreuen Copien der Natur zu unterscheiden versteht, *ob diese Erzäh-*
lung erdichtet seyn könne? Sie hat so viele kleine Nüanzen, und
Umständlichkeiten, die keinem Dichter eingefallen wären, und die er
auch nicht für nöthig gehalten hätte.

[I ask every truth-loving art connoisseur, who knows how to distinguish *ideal-*
ised from *exact copies of nature, whether this tale could have been invented. It*
has so many little nuances and minutiae that would not have occurred to any
poet, and that he would moreover not have considered necessary.]

The very contrary

26 i 169, pencil

Diese Sache vor seinem Tod bekannt zu machen, das war in der Zeit, in
der er starb, nicht rathsam, und noch weniger durften es die Gäste vor
der Revolution, und während derselben erzählen.

[In the age in which he died it was not advisable to make this matter public
before his death, and still less were the guests allowed to relate it before and
during the Revolution.]

Why not? Why not at their death?—

27 i 172, pencil | § 152

Diese Geschichte ist also gewiss und wahrhaftig wahr.

[*This story* [i.e. that outlined in **22** textus] *is therefore assuredly and actually true.*]

CAPITAL!

28 i 175, pencil

Was diese Donnerstimme bewürkt habe, das ist dem Allwissenden allein bekannt; es mag aber doch hin und wieder Nachdenken erregt haben. . . . Wahrscheinlich ist sie auch, wo nicht die nächste, doch wohl die entfernte, Ursache zu des *La Harpe* Bekehrung gewesen.*

[What the thunderer's voice may have effected, the All-knowing alone knows; it may nevertheless here and there have led to reflection. . . . Probably it was also, if not the immediate, then surely not the remotest cause of La Harpe's conversion.*]

* Here is (as Jung would say) a moral impossibility that it should be true. Would La Harpe not have made some *allusion*, at least, to it, in his ostentatious detailed account of his (I hope, not pretended) Conversion?[1]

29 p ⁺5, insertion in pencil, evidently referring to i 162–76

Strip even from La Harpe's story of Cazotte the drama and the drapery— & what is there in it, more than in Burk's historico-philosophical Prænunciations?[1]

The inward Schauen (Beholding) of the Somnambulists is demonstrably reducible to the Law by which on the suspension of the sensuous excitement ab extra,[2] thoughts and sensations translate themselves into sounds and images—not seldom, with a felicity truly prophetic.—The rapidity of change, by which sensations are transferred from one part of the Body to another, (absurdly supposed dependent on the attraction of

---

28[1] C's words suggest that he was familiar with La Harpe's account of his conversion in prison, when he happened to open the *Imitation of Christ* at the words "Me voici, mon fils, je viens à vous parce que vous m'avez invoqué" ("Here I am, my son, I come at your call"): *Oeuvres choisies et posthumes* i liv–lvi, but available to C also through the extensive quotations in reviews, e.g. *Monthly Review* LI (1806) 449–60 (conversion passage q 454–

5).

29[1] Statements before the fact, predictions: not in *OED*, but common in Latin. The "superiority of foresight" shown by Edmund Burke (1729–97) is assignable, C said, to the fact that "he referred habitually to *principles*. He was a *scientific* statesman; and therefore a *seer*. For every *principle* contains in itself the germs of a prophecy": *BL* ch 10 (*CC*) I 191–2.

29[2] "From without".

the Magnetizer's hand or Will) differs in degree only from the same effect produced in a waking Hypochondristiac. A̶ I succeeded myself in curing YY. by first delivering to Δ a paper containing what I should do[3]—& then made him acknowlege all sorts of pains & affections as having been or as then, experienced by him, in different parts of his body. What he did not instantly feel, he MOST DISTINCTLY remembered!—and doubtless, fully believed himself to remember. ⟨I then shewed him the paper, I had written./⟩ *S. T. C.*

30 i 179 | § 154

So erzählte ∧ dieser Pfarrer die Geschichte mit allen Umständen, ich hab den lieben Mann sehr gut gekannt, er war nicht fähig eine Unwahrheit zu sagen, und noch dazu in einer Sache, die allen seinen Grundsätzen widersprach.

[Thus the vicar told ∧ the story in all detail; I knew the dear man well, and he was incapable of telling an untruth, especially in a matter that contradicted all his principles.]

∧ observe the artifice in the omission of "*mir*"; & in the following *ich hab!*[1]

31 i 185–6 | § 159

*Wenn es viele, durch alle Zeiten fortgesezte, wahrhafte, Erfahrungen giebt, dass vernünftige, rechtschaffene fromme Menschen bezeugen, sie hätten Umgang mit Wesen aus der Geisterwelt . . . ist dann die Existenz der Geisterwelt . . . nicht eben so unwiderlegbar erwiesen, als die Existenz der elektrischen Materie, des Galvanismus, und des Magnetismus, und die Theilnahme, und Einwürkung dieser Kräfte auf die körperliche Natur?***

[*If continuously through all times there have been many true experiences of sensible, honest, pious people testifying that they had intercourse with beings from the world of spirits . . . is then the existence of the world of spirits . . . not proven as irrefutably as the existence of electricity, galvanism, and magnetism, and the participation of these powers in physical nature and their influence on it?**]

* O Lord! No! Nothing like it! The Electrical &c Fluids are mere hypotheses in behoof of a Theory of the electrical &c Phænomena.—Now

---

29[3] "Double U" and "D", William and Dorothy Wordsworth.

30[1] The "artifice" consists in not saying that the vicar "told the story *to me*" and yet using his close acquaintance with the vicar as tacit evidence of the vicar's reliability as witness to the story.

these are producible at demand: and it is *these* which we believe, and the hypothetical fluids are mere ways of *understanding* the phæ-nomena—not *believed* but *allowed* as *stop-gaps* till we get better. When Jung's rational, upright, godly *Eye*-witnesses of *invisible* creatures can excite Ghosts, as the Experimentalist excites the electric matter—*then* we may perhaps answer his question in the affirmative. Till then, it is a metabasis εις αλλο γενος.[1]   S. T. C.

---

32   i 261, pencil | § 191

Wenn der Geist zornig, oder auch sehr betrübt, wenn folglich eine Lei-denschaft in ihm herrschend war, so sprüzten Funken aus seinen Fin-gerspitzen. * Diese merkwürdige Erfahrung beweist meine Theorie vom Lichtgewand der Seelen: der Geist ist mit der ätherischen Hülle unzer-trennlich verbunden, diese Substanz würkt auf uns bald als *Licht*, dann als *Elektrizität*, oder als *Galvanismus*, und als *Magnetismus*, je nachdem sie durch die Umstände modifizirt wird.

[*When the spirit was angry or else very sad and consequently dominated by passion, sparks flashed from his fingertips.* * This curious experience proves my theory concerning the light-garment of souls: the spirit is inseparably united with the ethereal veil; this substance acts upon us sometimes as *light*, sometimes as *electricity*, or (that is to say) *galvanism*, and as *magnetism*, in accordance with its modification by circumstances.]

* But the *Skeleton* Finger and Thumb that scorched the Hymn Book!! Surely, never was a lamer Ghost-story ~~ever~~ re-narrated by a man in his senses![1]

---

33   i 266–7, pencil | § 196

Dass aber unser grosser Erlöser, auch dort noch, uns verborgene höchst weise Anstalten getroffen habe, wodurch auch dann noch Seelen geret-tet, und zum Licht geführt werden können, ob sie gleich nie *die* Seelig-keit erreichen werden, die denen bereitet ist welche hier in der Heiligung vollendet worden, das dünkt mir gewiss zu seyn.

[It seems certain to me that even there our great Redeemer made extremely wise provisions, not revealed to us, through which souls could yet be saved and

---

31[1] A "transition to another kind", an Aristotelian formula frequently invoked by C, e.g. BAXTER *Reliquiae* COPY A **29**, KANT *VS* COPY C **29**.

32[1] The textus here is part of Jung's commentary on a ghost story, published as an authentic account in 1759, in which, as

Jung relates p 244, the ghost burnt through the covers of a bible (including a psalter) as well as through the pages pointed out by its skeletal thumb and finger. Jung claimed personal acquaintance with the son of the ghost's victim.

guided to the light even though they could never attain *the* salvation granted to those perfected here in sanctity.]

The existence of a Purgatory after death cannot be an indifferent thing. Whether considered in its moral or its religious Bearings, it must needs be of vital importance. The practice of the Roman Church is a full Proof of this. The silence therefore of the New Testament is more than negative evidence against it. It is a strong presumption of its falsehood.[1] Jung himself is aware of its effect in tempting to Procrastination—*a*And then add the increased power of the Priests—that it converts the Hierarchy into Necromancers and Exorcists!—   *S. T. C.*

34 i 268–9, pencil | § 197

Bald nachher starb der junge Mensch, und nun harrte sein Meister auf seinen Besuch, und auf Nachricht aus der andern Welt. Etwa drey Wochen nach dem Tod des Gesellen, als der Meister . . . eben ins Bett gestiegen war, und noch darinnen sass, so bemerkte er gegenüber an der Wand einen bläulichen Lichtsschimmer, der sich zu einer menschlichen Figur bildete. Er fragte also ohne Furcht: *bist du es Johannes?*—der Geist antwortete vernehmlich, *Ja!*

[Soon afterwards the young man died, and now his master waited for his visit, and for news from the other world. About three weeks after the death of the journeyman, when the master . . . had just climbed into bed and was still sitting up in it, he noticed on the opposite wall a bluish glimmer of light that took on the shape of a human figure. He asked then without fear: "Is it you, John?"— The spirit answered audibly: "Yes!"]

There often take place fits of Slumber so brief and momentary as to escape the Slumberer's own consciousness. In these cases the Images and Sounds from the Brain blend with those from the Outward Senses, their distance being determined by their comparative vividness—just as reflected and transmitted Light, where a window fronts the fire-place. We see the Fire among the Bushes in the Garden, for instance—(supposing the window to overlook a Garden) and nearer and nearer as it grows darker & darker.[1] Now the impossibility of proving, that this Johannes was not a Dream or Brain-creature of this kind, amounts to a proof that it *was*/

---

a Here C has written "* *See above*" and continued in the head-margin with "*"

33[1] C's response to "the Romish figment of Purgatory" (*AR*—1825—302n) is generally based, as here, on the conviction that the NT contains all that is necessary to salvation.

34[1] C employs precisely this explanation in his account of Luther's vision of the Devil: *Friend* (*CC*) ɪ 144–5.

35   i 278, pencil | § 203

Ich bin vest überzeugt, dass noch nie jemand durch den Eindruck seiner Imagination gestorben ist . . .

[*I am firmly convinced that no one has yet died from the impact of his imagination . . .*]

Jung *wears out* his assertions: till the only answer, one feels disposed to return, is: "and I am as firmly convinced of the contrary."

36   i 280, pencil | § 204

Die Selbsterscheinungen sind also eine Art von Ahnungen, aber ohne ein entwickeltes Ahnungs-Vermögen, und ohne Mitwürkung der Engel.

[*Self-representations are thus a kind of presentiment, but without a developed faculty of presentiment and without the participation of angels.*]

I have myself had an experience of this Self-representation; but know no more of its cause, than that the position of the Eye is concerned—that some part of the face *not* seen by the Eye in its natural direction, *is* seen; and that probably the Law of Association by which any Part superinduces the Whole, does the rest. This Convulsion of the Eye is, doubtless, an effect & symptom of nervous Disease: & so may precede sudden death.[1]

37   i 280–1, pencil | § 205

*Eine der merkwürdigsten warnenden Erscheinungen, ist diejenige, die den Herzog von Buckingham betraf. * Sie ist auch gewiss wahr, und keine Erdichtung, oder sonst verschönerte Geschichte,* <u>wie ich aus sichern Quellen weiss</u> *. . .**

[One of the strangest apparitions serving as warning is the one met by the Duke of Buckingham. * It is also certainly true and is neither a fable nor an otherwise embellished tale, <u>as I know from reliable sources</u> . . .*]

* Poor Jung is Guaranté[1] general for the believableness of all Unbelievable Things! wie ich *weiss*[2]—he scorns aught below *Cock-surety!*[3]

36[1] In *TT* 3 Jan 1823, C similarly describes cases of "Self-representation" (including his own), accounting for them by "certain states of the nerves" that affect the operation of the eye so that it may "see a portion of the body, as if opposite to it".

37[1] An early form for "guarantee", i.e. a person who gives surety; now usually "guarantor".
37[2] "As I *know*"—from textus.
37[3] C echoes "cock-sure" from **1**, with a pun on "surety" and "guarantee".

38   i 288–9, pencil | § 208

Es ist traurig, dass man solche höchst wichtige Erfahrungen, wie die
Geistererscheinungen in der That sind, so verächtlich und wegwerfend
als eine entehrende Sache behandelt . . . prüfen soll man alles redlich
und genau, freylich wird man dann unter hundert Erzählungen neun und
neunzig Täuschungen finden, *aber wenn nun die Hundertste wahr ist,—
so ist der erscheinende Geist unser Bruder, bey dessen Schicksalen wir
nicht gleichgültig bleiben dürfen.*

[It is sad that one treats so contemptuously and deprecatingly as a disgraceful
matter such highly significant experiences as in fact the apparitions of spirits are
. . . one ought to check everything honestly and exactly; to be sure, one will
then find among a hundred tales ninety-nine frauds, *but if only the hundredth is
true, then the apparition is our brother, whose fate must not leave us indiffer-
ent.*]

According to Jung's own admission, 99 Believing Relators of Appari-
tions are lower than himself in judgement, and the power of distinguish-
ing Delusions from realities. Should he not have asked himself, whether
the 101 who believed yet less than he was not superior to him—and
[. . .]*ᵃ* to believe or rather saw into the delusion of the Whole, the [. . .]
[? right with]*ᵇ*

39   i 295, pencil | § 210

. . . das es keine leere *Vision* sey, was die Frau Pfarrerin sieht, *sondern
das sie würklich Wesen aus dem Geisterreich sehe, ist daher gewiss,
weil auch die Kinder den kleinen Engel bemerken.* . . . Auch das Weg-
springen der Klinke, die Verwundung der Verse, und der noch da lie-
gende Stuhl, sind Beweise für das würkliche Daseyn des unglücklichen
Geistes eines ehmaligen Pfarrers.

[. . . that it was no merely idle *vision* that the vicar's wife saw, *but a real being
from the realm of spirits, is certain from the fact that the children also noticed
the little angel.* . . . The flying-back of the latch, the wound in the heel, and the
chair still lying there are also proof of the real existence of the unhappy spirit of
a deceased vicar.]

! As if these very accidents might not have been the occasion of the
nervous derangement, producing the visa!¹

ᵃ Two or three words obscured by offsetting of the pencil writing on the facing page
ᵇ Words obscured by pencil offset

39¹ Latin *visa*, "things seen".

40   i 296, pencil | § 211

Ist er [der Geist] auf dem Wege der Heiligung aus der Zeit gegangen, und hat doch noch ein und anders an sich, das er nicht in die himmlischen Regionen mitbringen darf, so muss er so lang im *Hades* bleiben, bis er das alles abgelegt hat; allein er leidet keine Pein, ausser der, die er sich selbst macht.*

[If he [the spirit] has departed from life on the way to sanctity and still harbours something that he may not bring into the heavenly regions, then he is bound to remain in Hades until he has cast it all off; however, he suffers no pain except that which he inflicts upon himself.*]

* How do *you* know? Besides, can Hell itself present a hell more horrific, than a rational Soul not reconciled to its God and yet confined to itself—!!

41   i 308, pencil | § 217

. . . und da der Prof. *Oeder* weiter nichts sprach, so glaubte *Seidler* er wolle wieder einschlafen. . . . allein jezt fuhr *Oeder* auf einmal im Bette auf, schlug um, und neben sich, und rief mit einer fürchterlichen Stimme aus: *du musst hier weg, du hast mich lange genug beunruhigt.* . . . *Seidler* hörte dies alles mit an, allein er konnte nichts sehen.

[. . . and since Professor Oeder said nothing further, Seidler believed that he wished to go back to sleep. . . . only now Oeder rose up in bed, hit out in all directions, and called out in a terrible voice: "Be off with you, you have disquieted me long enough." . . . Seidler listened to all this, but he could not see anything.]

Evidently, the Night-mair.[1] Had it been otherwise, Oeder would not have called out to the Ghost, but have whispered it to Seidler.

42   i 310, pencil | § 218

Ist es nun wohl begreiflich, dass man auch diese Erscheinung einer Täuschung der Einbildungskraft zuschreibt? und doch geschieht es gegen *ᵃbesser Wissen und Gewissen, und gegen alle innere Ueberzeugung.ᵇ*

[Is it really conceivable to attribute even this apparition to a delusion of the

---

ᵃ⁻ᵇ Marked with a pencil line in the margin

41[1] As a particular kind of vision in sleep, the nightmare is strikingly described by C in notes for a lecture given in 1808 (*Lects 1808–1819—CC*—i 135–6) and in a notebook entry of Jan 1811 (*CN* iii 4046).

power of imagination? And yet this is done against all better knowledge and judgment, and against all inner conviction.]

How surely does Superstition betray the most benevolent disposition to Intolerance! What a presumptuous ⟨&⟩ uncharitable, as well as blind, assertion is not this!—

43   i 312, pencil | § 219

Dörien war also ein untadelhafter, braver, und rechtschaffener Mann, und doch war er nicht alsofort nach dem Tode glücklich. Wir wollen ja nicht lieblos über ihn urtheilen, er kann bald hernach seelig geworden seyn, sondern vielmehr untersuchen, *was ihn zu dieser traurigen Erscheinung veranlasst habe?*

[Dörien was an irreproachable, good, and honest man, and yet he was not happy immediately after his death. Let us rather not pass judgment unkindly on him; he may have become blissful soon afterwards; let us rather examine *what may have driven him to appear in this mournful manner.*]

I am almost tempted to call this Ghost-grounded Purgatory-doctrine[1] of Jung an accursed Seduction—that should be anathema maranatha[2] to all Protestants—

44   pp +1, +4[a], referring generally to the *Theorie*

The Seal was not put on the execution-warrant of Superstition (superstitûm, nihilo minus ob sensus apparentium assertio⟨nis⟩)[1] till Philosophy was retained as its advocate. For it could only be made conceivable by removing it from the Objective to[b] the Subjective—i.e. the Ghost was not to be seen, we admit; but still we contend that A. or B. saw the Ghost. But this again confounded the Sight with Dreaming—and all that remained for the advocate was to prove that it was a Dream of a particular or special Sort.—Let this be conceded. A species of Night-Mair— or the awakening of the sense of Touch.[2] Still what follows?—Coincidence, Fulfilment.—Aye but what proof that Fulfilment was not mere Co-incidence?—The conditions of experience—i.e. *anticipable* consequence, and reduction to a class—are wanting.—La Harpe's Story is a story composed by a Frenchman, or speaking in the superlative degree,

---

[a] Pp +1–+4 are unopened, leaving pp +2 and +3 inaccessible   [b] In ms "to to"

43[1] A point raised in **33** above.

43[2] I.e. subject to the most severe condemnation, C using the phrase from 1 Cor 16.22 (as he does also in LEIGHTON COPY C 13) in a conventional though incorrect way

(*OED*).

44[1] "Superstition—nothing but an assertion of appearances derived from sense".

44[2] **41** and n above.

by La Harpe![3] All the honest and German Stories are manifest dreams, marked by all the circumstances determinable a priori in a theory of Dreams.——. Anxiety, Cold, Pain—whatever tends to force the attention inward—then unconscious Slumber, for perhaps half a minute—or yet less. The Image *from* the Brain still present when the Images from the senses were not passed away, and when they re-commenced. Ergo, no conscious *Chasm*—Ergo, the Brain Image takes its place among the Eye Images—The same of the Ear.—But of ten thousand such incidents, an event is co-incident with *one*—& this is alone recollected.—The wonder for instance in the story of the King of Poland, Aug. 2nd and Field Marshal *Grum Cow*[4] is that a man in his wits like Jung (in his *senses* he was not) should have found any wonder in it.—O had he but taken to heart Nathan's incomparable answer to Daja, in Lessing's *wise* Drama!— "You reject such a solution as so strange and improbable!—not, I hope, as is too often the case, to believe something tenfold more improbable?—'"[5]

45 p ⁺5, pencil, rubbed

A more mischievous Book I have seldom met with. Alas! for poor Hu[man] Nature that so very silly a book could be [? published][1]

46 ii 18–19, pencil, rubbed | *Apologie der Geisterkunde*

". . . die Vernunft sey, wenn wir sie recht gebrauchen, eine uns von Gott geschenkte Führerin, die, wenn wir ihr folgen, uns aus den verworrenen, dunkeln Labyrinthen des Aberglaubens, so wohl als des Unglaubens, herausleite." . . . man lese doch die Stelle in der Geisterkunde *S.* 131. da heist es: *Die sich selbst überlassene nicht durch die*

44[3] The story commented on in **22–9**.

44[4] The story is told in i 270–3, immediately following **34** textus. When King Wilhelm I of Prussia held a farewell banquet for his friend King August II of Poland (1670–1733), he, knowing that August's life would be in danger if he drank too much, instructed his field marshal, Grumkow, to keep watch on August's wine. August ordered several bottles of champagne; Grumbkow, because of his own love of champagne, did not deny August's order and became so drunk himself that he broke a rib trying to make his way home and had to be carried in a sedan chair to receive August's final messages to Wilhelm. A few nights later, wakeful with the pain of his broken rib, Grumbkow saw the figure of King August enter his room and say, "My dear Grumbkow! at this moment I am dying in Warsaw." When news of August's death reached Berlin 40 hours later, it emerged that he had died at the exact time that Grumbkow had seen him—3 a.m. 1 Feb 1733.

44[5] *Nathan der Weise* I ii 83–6. C's reference to "*wise* Drama" puns on Lessing's title, *Nathan the Wise*.

45[1] This note is numbered here in sequence with notes on pt i since all the other notes on the back flyleaves have to do with pt i; but it should be noted that C expresses the same opinion of pt ii (**46**).

wahre geoffenbarte Religion geführte und erleuchtete Vernunft muss endlich dahin kommen, dass sie nach und nach, bey fernerem Forschen, von einer Stufe zur andern bis zum Naturalismus, und sogar zum Atheismus verfällt.

["... Reason, if we use her correctly, is a guide sent to us from God, who if we follow her leads us out of the confused, dark labyrinths of superstition as well as of disbelief." ... but just read the passage in the *Geisterkunde* p 131. It reads: "Reason left to itself and not guided and illuminated by true revealed religion is bound to come to the point at which further investigation leads it to decline step by step down to naturalism and even to atheism."]

This is the case with all shallow Enthusiasts. They explain their paradoxes into silly truisms. Thus: Jung explains his meaning into—that a darkened mislead*a* Reason will what? Be dark, and mislead. Note too the equivoque in the Word, Reason—now for the *scientific* power of the mind, and now for the *act* of arguing.—But the whole Book is bad were it only that it tempts to Contempt: hard to read & not despise the author.

47 ii 52

Müsste ich wieder nicht ehrwürdige Personen schonen, und dürfte ich die mir anvertrauten Papiere produziren, so würden die Herrn Verfasser nicht mehr zweifeln, und mich alberner Sagen beschuldigen. Ich hab einen ganzen Stoss Akten in Händen, in denen mehrere adeliche Personen von einigen Jahrhunderten her vorkommen, die in Duellen umgekommen, und an ungeweihten Orten begraben worden sind, und die nun noch die Beerdigung ihrer Gebeine verlangt, und erlangt haben.

[If I did not again have to protect respected persons and if I could produce the papers entrusted to me, the authors would no longer be sceptical and accuse me of [fabricating] foolish tales. I possess a whole pile of documents dealing with divers noble persons from several centuries, who died in duels and were buried in unhallowed sites and who yet demanded and obtained burial of their bones.]

It rests then on the Truth of these Stories: consequently, on the evidence of their truth: and this evidence Jung knew that he could not on moral and prudential grounds bring forward. How then could he *morally* bring forward the stories? Nay, ground thereon a disbelief in the solemn determinations of his own Church, and to the best of his power alienate the confidence of his fellow-members? And this on a bald bold Crede mihi, non autem Ecclesiæ?[1]

---

a I.e. "misled"

47[1] "Believe me, and not the Church."

48   ii 54–5

Man muss ja nicht denken, dass durch den Fortschritt der Aufklärung der Gespenster-Geschichten weniger geworden seyen; die Schande der Schwärmerey und des Aberglaubens womit man sie belegt, macht, dass man nicht davon spricht, und dann hält jede Familie solche Sachen gern geheim.

[There is no reason to think that through the progress of the Enlightenment the number of ghost stories has decreased; the ignominy of fanaticism and of superstition with which they are charged is the reason why one does not speak of them; and besides, each family prefers to keep such matters secret.]

But if these ghosty Occurrences have not diminished in frequency, and the comparative number of the Experti is still so mighty, how is this *Shame* possible? If I believe Jung, there are not fewer persons in Germany, who have had intercourse with the World of Spirits, than who have travelled into Spain, or seen Naples. Were this true, the one Witness would support the other as instantly and decisively in the former as in the latter case—or if not, it must be because they are themselves inwardly *uncertain* as to the outward reality of their own Experiences: and endeavor to make up for this sense of certainty by sensations and correspondent expressions of *positiveness*, as often as they can talk in a snug corner to such as are willing to listen and already want only an excuse for believing.[1]

48[1] The distinction between certainty and positiveness is invoked also in e.g.   Mendelssohn *Morgenstunden* 3, Blanco White *Practical Evidence* 11 n 2.

The Letters of Junius. London 1797. 8°.

British Library C 61 a 15

Autograph signature "S. T. Coleridge" on p ⁻1 (inside of original paper wrapper). The initials "STC" are written in ink on the title-page, not in C's hand. C has corrected a typographical error p 60.

DATE. Perhaps as early as 1802 or 1803, though both the hand and C's habits make a date after 1810 more likely; dated 1807 by HNC (*LR* I 248, evidence not cited).

SPECIAL ABBREVIATION. "Woodfall"—the first collected ed (2 vols 1772), corrected for the press by Junius and issued by the printer and editor of the *Public Advertiser*, Henry Sampson Woodfall (1739–1805).

COEDITOR. David V. Erdman.

1　p [i] | Title-page

Stat nominis umbra[1]

As he ~~adopted~~ never dropt the Mask, so he too often used the ~~poisoned~~ poisoned Dagger, of an Assassin.

2　p [vii] | Dedication to the English Nation

The whole of this Dedication reads, like a string of aphorisms arranged in Chapters classified by resemblance of subject, or a cento of Points.[1]

3　p viii

If an honest, and, I may truly affirm, a laborious zeal for the public service, has given me any weight in Your esteem, let me exhort and

---

[1]1 Junius's epigraph, from Lucan *Pharsalia* 1.135: *Stat [magni] nominis umbra*—"There stands the shadow of a [glorious] name"—refers to the anonymity (still secure) of the author, who said in his Dedication, "I am the safe depository of my own secret, and it shall perish with me" (vii–viii). For a summary and discussion of the circumstantial evidence that establishes "a respectable, if not a conclusive case" for identifying Sir Philip Francis (1740–1818) as Junius, see John Cannon ed *The Letters of Junius* (Oxford 1978) 539–72.

[2]1 This analysis was to be extended to other widely admired prose stylists as a sign of the depravity of the times—the "anglo-gallican fashion of unconnected, epigrammatic periods" condemned in *BL* ch 2 (*CC*) I 39, as in *Friend* (*CC*) I 20 and elsewhere.

conjure You, never to suffer an invasion of Your political constitution, however minute the instance many appear, to pass by, without a determined, persevering resistance.

Longer sentence & proportionably inelegant.

4 p xi

If you reflect, that in the changes of administration which have marked and disgraced the present reign, although your warmest patriots have in their turn, been invested with the lawful and unlawful authority of the crown, and though other reliefs or improvements have been held forth to the people yet that no one man in office has ever promoted or encouraged a bill for shortening the duration of parliaments, but that (who ever was minister) the opposition to this measure, ever since the septennial act passed, has been constant and uniform on the part of government.—

Long & as usual inelegant. Junius cannot manage a long Sentence: it has all the ins & outs of a snappish Figure-dance.

4A p xxv | Preface

Do you profess to govern according to Law; and it is consistent with that profession . . .?[1]

5 pp xxvii–[xxviii], 1–3 | End of Preface

an excellent preface; & the sentences not so snipt, as in the Dedication. The Paragraph from 24th to 26th page deserves to be quoted, as a masterpiece of rhetorical ratiocination in a series of questions, that permit no answer: or (as Junius says) which carry their own answer along with them.[1] The great Art of Junius is never to say too much, & to avoid with equal anxiety a commonplace manner, and matter that is not commonplace. If ever he deviates into any originality of Thought, he takes care, that it shall be such as excites surprize for its acuteness, rather than admiration for its profundity. *He* takes care? Say rather, that Nature took care for him. It is impossible to detract from the merit of these Letters: they are suited to their purpose, & perfect in their kind. ⟨They impel to action, not thought.⟩ Had they been profound or subtle in thought, or majestic & sweeping in composition, they would have been adapted for the closet of a Sidney, or for a House of Lords such as it was in the time of Lord Bacon;[2] but they are plain & sensible, whenever the Author is

---

4A[1] Woodfall also reads "is it".

5[1] For the text of this passage see ANNEX A.

5[2] As in *Friend* (*CC*) I 20, C looks to the Elizabethans and to the seventeenth century for rhetorical styles contrasting with the fashions of the late eighteenth century.

in the right, & ⟨whether right or wrong⟩ always shrewd, & epigrammatic ~~even when he is playing the Sophist;~~ & fitted for the Coffee-house, the exchange, the Lobby at the House of Commons, & to be read aloud at a public Meeting. ⟨When connected, dropping the forms of connection,⟩ Desultory without abruptness or appearance of disconnection, epigrammatic, ⟨antithetical to excess,⟩ sententious & personal, regardless of right or wrong, yet well-skilled to act the part of an honest warm-hearted man, & even when he is in the right, *saying* the Truth, but never proving it, much less attempting to bottom it—this is the character of Junius— and on this character, and in the mould of these writings, must every man cast himself, who would wish ~~to~~ in factious times to be the important & long remembered Agent of a Faction.—I believe, that I could ~~equal~~ do all that Junius has done, & surpass him by doing many things which he has not done: ex. gr. by an occasional induction of startling facts, in the manner of Tom Payne, & lively illustrations, & witty applications of good Stories, & appropriate anecdotes, in the best manner of Horn Took.[3] I believe, I could do it if it were in my nature to aim at this sort of excellence, or to be enamoured of the Fame, and immediate Influence, which would be its consequence & reward. But it is not in my nature. I not only love Truth, but I have a passion for the legitimate Investigation of Truth. The love of Truth conjoined with ~~the~~ a keen delight in a strict, & skilful, yet impassioned Argumentation, is my Master Passion/ and to it are subordinated even the Love of Liberty & all my public Feelings—& to it whatever I labour under of Vanity, ambition, & all my inward Impulses.

5A   p 5 | Letter 1

The management of the King's affairs in the House of Commons cannot indeed be more disgraced than it has been. . . . deliberate plans disconcerted, and a weeks preparation of graceful oratory lost in a moment, give us some, though not /andequate idea,[1] of Lord North's parliamentary abilities and influence.

6   pp 10–11

~~In~~ From this Letter all the faults & excellencies of Junius may be ex-

---

5[3] These remarks show a rare appreciation of the rhetorical skills of two prominent radicals, Tom Paine (1737–1809), author of the inflammatory *Rights of Man* (1791–2), and John Horne Tooke (1736–1812), a model to whom C addressed a sonnet in 1796: *PW* (EHC) I 150–1. It is

clear that C is here referring to Horne Tooke's political pamphlets and journalism, and not to his philological speculations.

5A[1] Woodfall reads "though not adequate".

emplified. The moral & political aphorisms are just & sensible, the irony ~~on~~ in which his personal satire is conveyed, is fine, & yet always intelligible: but it approaches too nearly to the nature of a Sneer/ the sentences are cautiously constructed without the forms of connection; the He, & It every where substituted for the who & which; the sentences are short, laboriously balanced, & the antitheses stand the test of analysis much better than Johnson's[1]—these are all excellences in their kind—where is the Defect? There is too much of each/ and there is a defect of many things, the presence of which would have ~~varied the~~ been not only valuable for their own sakes, but for the relief & variety which they would have given. It is observable too that every Letter adds to the Faults ⟨of these Letters,⟩ while it weakens the effect of their Beauties.

7   pp 20–1 | End of Letter 3

A capital Letter. Addressed to a private person, and intended as a sharp reproof of Intrusion its short sentences, its witty perversions & deductions, its questions, and its omission of connectives are all in their proper places—are *dramatically* good.

8   p 27, marked with a brace in the margin | Letter 5

For my own part, I willingly leave it [the subject] to the public to determine, whether your vindication of your friend [Granby] has been as able and judicious, as it was certainly well intended; and you, I think, may be satisfied with the warm acknowledgements he already owes you, for making him the principle figure in a piece, in which, but for your amiable assistance he might have passed without particular notice or distinction.

a long sentence & as usual inelegant & cumbrous

9   p 29 | End of Letter 5

a faultless Composition—with exception of the one long sentence.

10   p 30 | Letter 7

An academical education has given you an unlimited command over the most beautiful figures of speech. Masks, hatchets, racks, and vipers, dance through your letters in all the mazes of metaphorical confusion. These are the gloomy companions of a disturbed imagination; the melancholy madness of poetry, without the inspiration.

6[1] C's distaste for the commonly admired style of Samuel Johnson (1709–84) appears elsewhere: cf "the antithesis of Junius is a real antithesis of images or thought; but the antithesis of Johnson is rarely more than verbal" in *TT* 3 Jul 1833.

rhymes. Fancy had been better; tho' but for the rhyme Imagination is the fitter word.

11 p 30

Such a question might perhaps discompose the gravity of his muscles, but I believe it would little affect the tranquillity of his conscience.

a false antithesis. a mere verbal Balance. Far, far too many of these.[1]

11A p 31

It would have been more decent in you to have called this *d* dishonourable transaction by its true name . . .[1]

12 p 32 | End of Letter 7

with the exceptions marked in the margin a blameless Composition. Junius may be safely studied as a model for Letters that are truly *Letters*. Those to the Duke of Grafton, &c are small pamphlets in the form of Letters.[1]

13 p 34 | Letter 8

To do justice to your Grace's humanity, you felt for M'Quirk as you ought to do, and if you had been contented to assist him indirectly, without a notorious denial of justice, or openly insulting the sense of the nation, you might have satisfied every duty of political friendship, without committing[1] the honour of your Sovereign, or hazarding the reputation of his government.

an inelegant cluster of *"withouts"*

13A p 36

Otherwise, is it conceivable that his counsel should neglect to call in such material evidence?[1]

14 p 37 | End of Letter 8

Have you quite forgotten that this man was once your Grace's friend?

11[1] Cf **6** and n 1 above.

11A[1] Woodfall also reads "called this dishonourable".

12[1] Augustus Henry Fitzroy, 3rd Duke of Grafton (1735–1811), advanced from first lord of the treasury to first minister in Sept 1767, when Lord Chatham's incapacitating illness prevented him from continuing to lead his ministry. Between 18 Mar and 8 Jul 1769 Junius addressed five hostile letters to Grafton (Letters 8, 9, 11, 12, 15); C probably refers esp to 11, 12, and 15, all of which are long and detailed.

13[1] Woodfall also reads "committing".

13A[1] Woodfall also reads "is it".

Or is it to murderers only that you will extend the mercy of the Crown?
These are questions you will not answer, nor is it necessary. The char-
acter of your private life, and the tenor of your public conduct, is an
answer to them all.

Ne quid nimis.[1] Junius asks questions incomparably well; but—ne quid
nimis.

15   pp 38–40 | Letter 9

Perhaps, the fair way of considering these Letters would be ~~in~~ as a Kind
of satirical Poems—the short, and for ever balanced sentences constitute
a true metre; & the connection is that of satiric poetry, a witty logic, a
~~succession~~ association of ideas by amusing semblances of cause and ef-
fect—the sophistry of which the reader has an interest in not stopping to
detect—for it flatters his love of mischief, & makes the sport—.

16   pp 47–8 | Letter 12

The meanest of your predecessors had abilities sufficient to give a colour
to their measures. If they invaded the rights of the people, they did not
dare to offer a direct insult to their understanding; and in former times,
the most venal parliaments made it a condition, in their bargain with the
minister, that he should furnish them with some plausible pretences for
selling their country and themselves. You have had the merit of intro-
ducing a more compendious system of government and logic.

One of Junius's arts—& which gives me a high idea of his Genius, con-
sidering him as a poet & a satirist, is this: he takes for granted the exis-
tence of a character that never did, & never can exist, & then employs
his wit, & surprizes & amuses his readers with analysing & setting forth
its incompatibilities.—

17   pp 60–1 | End of Letter 14

Continual Sneer—continual Irony—all excellent, if it were not for the
''all''—but a countenance with a malignant smile in statuary fixture on
it, becomes at length an object of aversion, however beautiful the face,
and however becoming the smile. We are relieved from this by frequent
just & well expressed moral aphorisms; but then the preceding & follow-
ing Irony gives ~~it~~ them the appearance of proceeding from the Head, not
the Heart. This objection would be less felt, when the ⟨Letters⟩ were first
published—with considerable Intervals—but Junius wrote for Posterity.

14[1]   ''Never too much of anything'': Terrence *Andria* 61.

18   pp 107–8 | Letter 23

Let us consider you [the Duke of Bedford], then, as arrived at the summit of worldly greatness: let us suppose, that all your plans of avarice and ambition are accomplished, and your most sanguine wishes gratified, in the fear as well as the hatred of the people; Can age itself forget that you are in the last act of life? Can gray hairs make folly venerable? and is there period to be reserved for meditation and retirement? For shame! my Lord let it not be recorded of you, that the latest moments of your life were dedicated to the same unworthy pursuits, the same busy agitations, in which your youth and manhood were exhausted.

Sneer & Irony continued with such gross violation of good sense as to be perfectly nauseous.—The man who can address another on ~~his~~ the most detestable vices in a strain of cold continued Irony, is himself a wretch.—

19   p 114 | End of Letter 25

an excellent Letter.—

20   p 148 | Letter 35

To honour them [the Scots] with a determined predilection and confidence, in exclusion of your English subjects, who placed your family, and in spite of treachery and rebellion, have supported it, <u>upon the throne</u>, is a mistake too gross, even for the unsuspecting generosity of youth.

the words "upon the Throne" unfortunately placed for the harmonious effect of the Balance ~~weakens~~ "placed" & "supported".

21   pp 155–6, marked with a line in the margin and a bracket at the end

As to the Scotch, I must suppose your heart and understanding so biassed from your earliest infancy, in their favour, that nothing less than *your own* misfortunes can undeceive you. You will not accept of the uniform experience of your ancestors; and, when a man is determined to believe, the very absurdity of the doctrine confirms him in his faith. A bigotted understanding can draw a proof of attachment to the house of Hanover from a notorious zeal for the house of Stuart, and find an earnest of future loyalty in former rebellions. Appearances are, however, in their favour; so strongly indeed, that one would think they had forgotten that you are their lawful King, and had mistaken you for a pretender to the Crown. Let it be admitted, then, that the Scotch are as sincere in their present professions, as if you were, in reality, not an

Englishman, but a Briton of the North. You would not be the first Prince, of their native country, against whom they have rebelled, nor the first whom they have basely betrayed. Have you forgotten, Sir, or has your favourite concealed from you that part of our history, when the unhappy Charles (and he too had private virtues) fled from the open, avowed indignation of his English subjects and surrendered himself at discretion to the good faith of his own countrymen? Without looking for support in their affections as subjects, he applied only to their honour as gentlemen for protection. They received him as they would your Majesty, with bows, and smiles, and falsehood, and kept him until they had settled their bargain with the English parliament; then basely sold their native King to the vengeance of his enemies. This, Sir, was not the act of a few traitors, but the deliberate treachery of a Scotch parliament, representing the nation. A wise Prince might draw from it two lessons, of equal utility to himself. On one side, he might learn to dread the undisguised resentment of a generous people, who dare openly assert their rights, and who in a just cause are ready to meet their sovereign in the field. On the other side, he would be taught to apprehend something far more formidable;—a fawning treachery, against which no prudence can guard, no courage can defend. The insidious smile upon the cheek, would warn him of the canker in the heart.

13ᵗʰ *Par.*

22   A small slip of paper tipped in at pp 160/1, referring to pp 145–61 | End of Letter 35

This Address to the King is ~~more~~ almost faultless in composition; & has been evidently "tormented with the File".[1] But it has fewer beauties than any other long Letter of Junius; & utterly undramatic. There is nothing in the style, the transitions, or the sentiments, which represent the Passions of a man emboldening himself to address his sovereign personally. Like a Presbyterian's Prayer, you may substitute almost every where the third for the second Person without injury. The newspaper, ~~the~~ his closet, & his own person were alone present to the Author's ~~m~~ intuition & imagination. This makes the composition vapid. It possesses an Isocratic Correctness—when it should have had the force & drama of an oration of Demosthenes.[2] From this however the 13ᵗʰ paragraph, be-

22[1] An adaptation of Statius *Sylvae* 4.7.26: *Thebais multa cruciata lima*, "[my] *Thebaid*, tortured by endless polishing".

22[2] Isocrates (436–338 B.C.), orator and teacher of rhetoric, represents Attic prose in its most elaborate though somewhat attenuated manner; Demosthenes (384–322 B.C.), considered the greatest orator of his time, often achieved his greatest effects by the use of a few ordinary words.

ginning with the words—"As to the Scotch"[3]—& the two last paragraphs must be honorably excepted.[4] They are perhaps the finest passages in the whole of the volume.

Annex

The following passages are referred to in the marginalia.

A   Preface pp xxiv–xxvi, referred to in **5**

Some opinion may now be expected from me, upon a point of equal delicacy to the writer, and hazard to the printer. When the character of the chief magistrate is in question, more must be understood, than may be safely expressed. If it be really a part of our constitution, and not a mere *dictum* of the law, *that the King can do no wrong*, it is not the only instance, in the wisest of human institutions, where theory is at variance with practice.—That the sovereign of this country is not amenable to any form of trial known to the laws, is unquestionable. But exemption from punishment is a singular privilege annexed to the royal character, and no way excludes the possibility of deserving it. How long and to what extent, a King of *England* may be protected by the forms, when he violates the spirit of the constitution, deserves to be considered. A mistake in this matter proved fatal to *Charles* and his son.—For my own part, far from thinking that the King can do no wrong, far from suffering myself to be deterred or imposed upon by the language of forms in opposition to the substantial evidence of truth, if it were my misfortune to live under the inauspicious reign of a Prince, whose whole life was employed in one base, contemptible struggle with the free spirit of his people, or in the detestable endeavours to corrupt their moral principles, I would not scruple to declare to him,—"Sir, You alone are the author of the greatest wrong to your subjects and yourself. Instead of reigning in the hearts of your people, instead of commanding their lives and fortunes through the medium of their affections; has not the strength of the Crown, whether influence or prerogative, been uniformly exerted, for eleven years together, to support a narrow, pitiful system of government, which defeats itself, and answers no one purpose of real power, profit, or personal satisfaction to You?—With the greatest unappropriated revenue of any prince in Europe, have we not seen You reduced to such vile and sordid distresses, as would have conducted any other man to a prison?—With a great military, and the greatest naval power in the known world, have not foreign nations repeatedly insulted You with impunity?—Is it not notorious, that the vast revenues, extorted from the labour and industry of your subjects, and given You to do honour to Yourself and to the nation, are dissipated in corrupting their representatives?—Are You a prince of the house of Hanover, and do You exclude all the leading Whig families from your councils?—Do you profess to govern according to Law; and is it[a] consistent with that profession, to impart your confidence and affection to those men only, who though now perhaps detached from the desperate cause of the Pretender, are marked in this country by an hereditary attachment to high and arbitrary princi-

---

[a] Corrected by C in **4A**

22[3] See **21**.   22[4] See ANNEX **B**.

ples of government?—Are you so infatuated as to take the sense of your people from the representation of ministers, or from the shouts of a mob, notoriously hired to surround your coach, or stationed at a theatre?—And if you are, in reality, that public man, that King, that magistrate, which these questions suppose you to be, is it any answer to your people, to say, That among your domestics, you are good humoured;—that to one lady, You are faithful;—that to your children, You are indulgent?—Sir, the man who addresses you in these terms, is your best friend. He would willingly hazard his life in defence of your title to the Crown; and, if *power* be your object, would still show You how possible it is for a King of England by the noblest means to be the most absolute Prince in Europe. You have no enemies, Sir, but those who persuade You to aim at power without right, and who think it flattery to tell You, that the character of King dissolves the natural relation beween guilt and punishment.''

B Letter 35, last two paras, pp 160–1, referred to in **22**

These sentiments, Sir, and the style they are conveyed in, may be offensive, perhaps, because they are new to you. Accustomed to the language of courtiers, you measure their affections by the vehemence of their expressions; and when they only praise you indirectly, you admire their sincerity. But this is not a time to trifle with your fortune. They deceive you, Sir, who tell you that you have many friends whose affections are founded upon a principle of personal attachment. The first foundation of friendship is not the power of conferring benefits, but the equality with which they are received, and *may* be returned. The fortune, which made you a King, forbade you to have a friend. It is a law of nature, which cannot be violated with impunity. The mistaken Prince, who looks for friendship, will find a favourite, and in that favourite the ruin of his affairs.

The people of England are loyal to the house of Hanover, not from a vain preference of one family to another, but from a conviction, that the establishment of that family was necessary to the support of their civil and religious liberties. This, Sir, is a principle of allegiance equally solid and rational;—fit for Englishmen to adopt, and well worthy of your Majesty's engagement. We cannot long be deluded by nominal distinctions. The name of Stuart, of itself, is only contemptible;—armed with the Sovereign authority, their principles are formidable. The Prince who imitates their conduct, should be warned by their example; and, while he plumes himself upon the security of his title to the Crown, should remember, that, as it was acquired by one revolution, it may be lost by another.

PIERRE JURIEU
1637–1713

The History of the Council of Trent. In eight books. Whereunto is pre-fixt a discourse containing historical reflexions on councils, and particularly on the conduct of the Council of Trent, proving that the Protestants are not oblig'd to submit thereto. Written in French . . . and now done into English. London 1684. 8°.

Lacking title-page.

British Library C 43 a 1

DATE. Perhaps c 1823–4, or later. The hand is certainly "late", i.e. of Highgate date, and C alludes to a late-evolving doctrine in **8**.

1   pp iv–ix | Historical Reflections on Councils

In the first place the Reformed decline the jurisdiction of this Council [of Trent], as a Judge incompetent, because a Party. I easily foresee I shall be stop'd short here, and that it will be returned upon me, that the Churches being a Party, is the ordinary refuge of Hereticks. Had not the *Arians* as much right to tell the Council of *Nice*, you are a Party, and therefore can be no Judge in the Cause?

A Beech rises in a columnal Trunk to the height of 20 feet from the Ground—and there it divides into two, diverging as the Samian Y.[1] A River flows from its fountain ~~of the Rock~~ in one widening stream over a vast track of Country and thro' various soils, till it reaches a bed of rocks, over & between which it twists, foams, roars, eddies, for a while,

> "Shatters its waters abreast, and in mazy tumult bewilder'd
> Rŭshĕs dĭvīdŭŏus āll, āll rūshĭng ĭmpētŭoŭs ōnwārds,"[2]

till it is met by a vast compact breast-work of Rock, which divides the stream into two diverging Channels—and obtains the name of the Rock of Separation.—Which of the two Limbs shall call itself the Beech-tree

---

[1] The Greek capital letter upsilon, traditionally "Samian" because Pythagoras of Samos used it as an allegory of human life, illustrating the individual's choice between the easy path to ruin and the narrow way of righteousness.

[2] *Mahomet* lines 13–14 (var), the last two of 14 hexameters intended for a poem that in Sept 1799 C planned to write with RS: *PW* (EHC) i 330.

& retain the name of Trunk? Which of the two Streams, ~~shall~~ the South West, or the South-East, shall call itself *the* River?[3]—Is not the question palpably absurd?—What if the *Genie* or Naiad of the one Channel should with an angry sneer ask the Sister Naiad—Where were you & your Stream before Rock Separation?—Might not the latter—/ reply— Exactly where you were, Sister—To be sure, I have deposited a good deal of the mud & the filth which our waters had contracted during their long journey—I wish, Sister! you would make use of my Filtring Machine!— ~~To~~ In the same purpose was the answer of——to ~~the~~ his Catholic Neighbor who had asked him—Where was your Religion before Luther?—"Where was your Face before you washed it this morning?"[4]

S. T. C.

2   pp xii–xvii, xx–xxiii[a]

How great was then the injustice, to set up that Church [of Rome] for Judge of a Cause against which she had already given Judgment, and from which Judgment the Protestants had appealed? When there arise new and doubtful matters in a Church, there is no doubt but that Church hath a right to Judge of them, and to assemble her Councils to that end.

Here, I think, D[r] Jurieu's Reasoning grows weak, or disputable. The true point to be proved should have been, & this in the first instance— that a general Council may perhaps be the best attainable Judge of what is fittest or most expedient for the Church at any one particular time—in as much as, if fairly & impartially convened from all the several national Churches, it would be the best measure or criterion of the general Susceptibility of such and such innovations or Changes as should be submitted to it—but that a general Council is not, and without arrogation of a divine Attribute cannot be ♭ assumed to be, a competent Judge of the truth i~~t~~n itself, and of all truths, relatively to all ages, all future times.— Now if the Council of Trent, having decided as they did, had yet permitted the Doctors of the Church to have sought for and advanced new

[a] This long annotation is written in the foot-margins of a series of openings, missing pp xviii–xix

1[3] C returned to the metaphor of the divided river in discussions of the history of the Christian Church, e.g. in *CN* III 3872 (1810), *TT* 29 Apr 1823. A brief account of the Council of Trent is given in 2 n 1 below.

1[4] C associated this *bon mot*, which he encountered in 1810 in *A Preservative against Popery* (1738), with Sir Henry Wotton: *CN* III 3872 and n. It is repeated in an interesting variant form in *TT* 5 Jul 1834: "If a Romanist were to ask me the question put to Sir Henry Wotton, I should content myself by answering, that I could not exactly say when my religion, as he was pleased to call it, began—but that it was certainly some sixty or seventy years before *his*, at all events—which began at the Council of Trent."

arguments, or confirmations of the former, in the *World of Letters*, and in their Characters as Members of the Republic of Learning, for the assistance of a future age—then it would have been their duty, as Priests and Ministers of the Church for the time being to have submitted in peace & Charity to the Decision of the last Council/ the Council itself being fairly convened, & actually meriting the name of a General Council.—The sustainable objections of the Protestants to the Council of Trent are twofold—1ˢᵗ its *persecution* grounded in its undue arrogation of a right to decide ⟨on⟩ all truths for all times, in relation to the truth absolutely & not merely to the fitness for the time present & existing state of the Church—and secondly, that it was no general Council at all, but a *Papal* Conclave.[1]

3 pp xxix–xxxi

* If we may believe *Socrates*, there was nothing done in this Council [of Rimini] repugnant to the Faith of the Church. But he is not in this to be credited. He thought perhaps it would be a mighty service to the Church, to prevaricate in her behalf, and deny that this Great Council was of the number of those that favoured *Arianism*.

* After a careful weighing of the terms used, I ~~agree~~ am of the same opinion with Socrates, that the ~~Creed~~ Article respecting the Trinity agreed on in the Council of Rimini is orthodox—& by no means chargeable with Arianism.[1]—Nay, I am better satisfied with it, for omitting the inapplicable ~~&~~ term, Ομοουσιος—which ousia, as the noun abstract of

2[1] The Council of Trent, originally called by Pope Paul III in 1537 to meet the rising tide of Protestant revolt against the Roman Church, spanned a period of nearly twenty years 1545–63 but fell into three extended meetings with an interval of ten years between the second and third. Period I (1545–7), a very small assembly of some 35 delegates dominated by pro-papal Italian bishops, established several important matters of dogma, especially a decree on Justification and Merit designed to undermine the Protestant doctrinal position. Period II (1551–2), called by Pope Julius III and including stronger representation of the Protestant position, affirmed the doctrine of transubstantiation and repudiated the Lutheran, Calvinist, and Zwinglian eucharistic doctrines. The Council was suspended after only 18 months because of a revolt against Charles V and was not reconvened until after the death of the violently anti-Protestant Pope Paul IV. In Period III (1562–3), under the dominance of strong Jesuit forces, there was no hope of "conciliating the Protestants", and the decrees of the Council were confirmed in Jan 1564 and published by Pope Pius IV as the "Profession of the Tridentine Faith" (*ODCC*).

3[1] In LUTHER *Colloquia* **78**, C strongly denies that the Council of Ariminum (Rimini) held in 359 "was either Arian or heretical": it affirmed the Nicene Creed of 325. The "Socrates" referred to by Jurieu and C is Socrates Scholasticus (c 380–450), who wrote a continuation of Eusebius's *History of the Church* that was often published with it, e.g. in the Cambridge ed of 1683.

o ων, (the Platonic το οντως ων) is implicitly denied of the Absolute or Fontal Deity.[2] It is likewise an inconvenient because in the Latin it cannot be rendered—Consubstantial is no translation of omoousios—. So true is this that in order to have a word for υποσταϊσις, the proper word, namely, substantia, having been anticipated in the attempt to render ουσια, the Latin church introduced the unhappy word, Person—so surely does Error generate Error!—[3]

4 pp xxxii–xxxiii, pencil

It is apparent from all these Considerations, that tho the Council of *Trent* could be considered as a General Council, that would not bind us to believe it infallible, nor to submit blindly to its Decisions.

But to leave these general Arguments, and come up closer to the Council of *Trent*: We say it is a Council of the *Roman*, not of the Catholick or Universal Church; and that we can look on it as no other.

But the πρωτον ψευδος[a1] of the whole theory of Papal or Conciliar infallibility is the confusion between a Truth and an outward act.—The latter only is a possible subject of social compact or legislative Statute, or Synodic decree—because every *act* is necessarily a minute fraction—every Truth is the Whole in each.

5 pp xxxiv–xxxv

All the Churches of the *East*, *North*, and *South*, the *Greek* Church, the Church of the *Abyssins*, who possess all *Ethiopia*, which is a large share of *Africa*, and the Church of the *Russians*, are, say they [the Roman Catholics], Schismatical Assemblies; they have broken the bands of Union with the Head which is the Pope, and are no longer worthy of the name of Churches: for there are no true Christians but those that are subject to the Holy See, which is the band of Unity. This indeed is an excellent Principle.

     [a] Written ψευδος πρωτον and marked for transposition

[3²] " 'Of like substance' [*homoousios*]—which 'substance', as the noun abstract standing for 'the being' (the Platonic 'the thing that really *is*') . . .". Cf "All Beings are *Created*, save the Father . . . and the Father, the Son and the Spirit are the one only God. This was the confession of the Great Council at Rimini: and how the mere omission of the word, ομοουσιος, for Peace' sake, could render it heretical, only the Madness of Party can explain!": FLEURY **66** and nn 5, 6.

[3³] The linked problems of the translations for the Greek terms *hypostasis* and *ousia* and the concepts of substance and consubstantiality are further explored in FLEURY **56** and n. C's objections to "the unhappy word, Person"—referring especially to the "three persons" of the Trinity—are clearly expressed in CHANNING **1**, IRVING *Sermons* **1**.

[4¹] The "first error"—i.e. the fundamental one, from which others arise.

That the Party which in any of the fierce Conflicts de umbrâ asini,[1] which at once discredited yet characterized Christianity* had the worst of it, were wont at a very early period to appeal to the Roman Pontiff under some notion of his Primacy, it would be in vain to deny. The only ? is—was it attributed or conceded to the Pope as the Successor of St Peter and ⟨Inheritor⟩ of the supreme Pastorate delegated to Peter according to Matthew, Chapt. XVI. v. 18, 19; or as the Bishop of Rome, of the Imperial City, and who by the analogy of the pagan pontificate, on being Pontifex Maximus of Rome was the Universal High Priest of the Empire?—I think, on the latter account.[3]

* the two serpents in the cradle of the Xtn Hercules which the full-grown Man could not strangle![2]

6   pp xxxvii–xl

Not the *Lutherans* only, but all *Europe* agreed in it, that the Council of *Trent* was purely an *Italian*, a Papal Council. . . . Already we have taken notice with what heat and violence that Council acted against those over whom it pretended to be Judg.

In this article of Infallibility lies the strength & the weakness of the Roman Church—the latter aggravated by the uncertainty and dissension among themselves, in whom this gift resides. Hence they are afraid to alter any thing, however absurd, once decided by Council, Council convened by the Pope, Council convened & confirmed by the Pope; or the Pope with the Cardinals; or lastly, by the Pope alone. Had it been fixed in some one of these, many absurdities might be treated as such, or *infallibly* interpreted to the contrary of the literal sense of the words used by a previous defunct Infallibility. This is the vantage ground of the

5[1] "Concerning the shadow of an ass"—i.e. fierce conflicts on petty issues. The phrase is traditional: cf Erasmus *Adagia* I iii 52 in *Collected Works* (Toronto 1982) xxxi 279–81.

5[2] Before Hercules was eight months old Juno, jealous of Jupiter's fathering him on Alcmena, sent two large serpents into his cradle to devour him. Without fear he took them in his hands and crushed them to death. The "full-grown" Hercules could not kill the serpent-like Hydra without the help of his friend Iolaus (Apollodorus 2.4): C may be alluding to this legend, or comparing the power of the Church in its infancy with its later weakness, or—just possibly—referring to Luther, whom he calls "this Christian Hercules" in *Friend* (*CC*) I 140.

5[3] "And I say also unto thee, That thou art Peter, and upon this rock I will build my church. . . . And I will give unto thee the keys of the kingdom of heaven: and whatsoever thou shalt bind on earth shall be bound in heaven; and whatsoever thou shalt loose on earth shall be loosed in heaven"—Matt 16.18–19, a text invoked to establish papal authority. For C further on papal authority and the primacy of the bishopric of Rome, as based not on Petrine continuity but on historical accident, see FIELD **31** and n.

Protestants who attach & confine Infallibility to the Old & New Testament—which is thus always appellable yet always inviolate—thro' a succession of discordant Interpretations; & thus remains always in harmony with the reigning Philosophy of the Age.   S. T. Coleridge

7   p lxxi

These Ecclesiastical Immunities were things unknown to the Primitive times. The great and good Emperour *Constantine* did in Person, or by Commission hear and determine the Crimes of Ecclesiasticks, without excepting so much as Cases of Schism and Heresie.

! q.ᵛ *for nothing?*[1]

8   p 129

Above all, he [Catanea] laid great stress on this, that the Doctrine of *Dominico à Soto* overturned free Predestination, and established Predestination by the prescience of works; because if the efficacy of Grace depend on the Will of man, it is that Will which puts the difference betwixt the elect and the reprobate; a Sentiment confuted by all Divines.

Here lurks the πρῶτον ψεῦδος[1]—the confusion of the reflex conscious Will, the *accompaniment* of Works, and the essential Will, the *Rock & Antecedent* thereof.[2]

8A   p 350, pencil

[On the Eucharist.] One Friar *Amant* . . . went farther than all the rest, and said that according to the Doctrine of Cardinal *Cajetan*, the Bloud is no part of the substance of Man's body, but merely an Aliment . . .!!

7[1] The reasons for C's hostility towards Constantine the Great (c 280–337) are not known: Constantine summoned and presided at the Council of Nicaea (325), of which C on the whole approved: LUTHER *Colloquia* **78**.

8[1] "First error", as **4** n 1 above.

8[2] The doctrine of the "double will" is a fairly late development in C's thought: cf IRVING *Sermons* **29** at n 26.

IMMANUEL KANT

1724–1804

Copy A

Anthropologie in pragmatischer Hinsicht abgefasst. Königsberg 1798. 8°.

Nagoya University, Japan

Signed in ink on the title-page: "S. T. Coleridge". Bookplate of Sir James Mackintosh on p ⁻1, and inscription in pencil by him on the same page: "Given to me by Coleridge I think at the Lakes in 1801". Note by Mackintosh on p 4: "Coleridge's notes". A few marginal notes on pp 4, 9, 153, 156, apparently by Mackintosh. Some marginal lines and underlining in the text, not attributable.

DATE. Perhaps as early as summer 1800, certainly before Jan 1804.

COEDITORS. Kathleen Wheeler, Raimonda Modiano.

TEXTUS TRANSLATION. Mary J. Gregor tr *Anthropology from a Practical Point of View* (The Hague 1974). It may be noted that the text of the standard "Akademie" edition of Kant's work is that of COPY B, the 2nd ed (1800); section references here are those of the 1st ed (1798), but section numbers for the later ed, where they differ, are given in square brackets.

1   p 4, pencil, cropped | Pt 1 bk 1 sec 1

Es ist aber merkwürdig: dass das Kind, was schon ziemlich fertig sprechen kann, doch ziemlich spät (vielleicht wohl ein Jahr nachher) allererst anfängt durch Ich zu reden, so lange aber von sich in der dritten Person sprach, (Carl will essen, gehen u.s.w.), und dass ihm gleichsam ein Licht aufgegangen zu seyn scheint, wenn es den Anfang macht durch Ich zu sprechen; von welchem Tage an es niemals mehr in jene Sprechart zurückkehrt.—Vorher *fühlte* es bloss sich selbst, jetzt *denkt* es sich selbst.—Die Erklärung dieses Phänomens möchte dem Anthropologen ziemlich schwer fallen.

[But it is noteworthy that a child who can already speak fairly fluently does not begin to talk in terms of "I" until rather late (perhaps a year later); until then he speaks of himself in the third person (Charles wants to eat, to go for a walk, etc.). And when he starts to speak in terms of "I" a light seems to dawn on him, as it were, and from this day on he never relapses into his former way of speaking.—Before, he merely *felt* himself; now he *thinks* himself.—The anthropologist may find it rather hard to explain this phenomenon.]

236

[Sho]uld [th]is "I" [be] spoken [of at al]l—[prob]ably [it is] not
[. . . ? oly/ily/nly] [. . .] as [he un]ites it only [with that] which he ever
heard applied [to his] Self.[1]—The "αυτοσι ανηρ" was [an i]ntenser
'Εγω.—[2]

2   p 38, pencil | Sec 10 [12]

Er ist nichts weiter als eine hochtönende Tautologie: was er nämlich *auf
den Geheiss seiner moralisch-gebietenden Vernunft* will, das *soll* er, fol-
glich *kann* er es auch thun (denn das unmögliche wird ihm die Vernunft
nicht gebieten).

[It is only a high-sounding tautology: namely, what man wills *at the bidding of
his morally legislative reason*, he *ought* to do and consequently *can* do (for
reason will not command the impossible of him).]

Omnipotence of *Mind*

3   p 39, pencil

In der Regel ist alle Angewohnheit verwerflich.

[As a rule, all habits are objectionable.]

Mem.[1]

4   p 53, pencil | Sec 18 [21]

Je stärker die Sinne, bey eben demselben Grade des auf sie geschehenen
Einflusses, sich *afficirt* fühlen, desto weniger *lehren* sie. Umgekehrt:
wenn sie viel lehren sollen, müssen sie mässig afficiren. Im stärksten
Licht *sieht* (unterscheidet) man nichts, und eine stentorisch angestrengte
Stimme *betäubt* (unterdrückt das Denken).

[Given the same degree of action exercised on them, the senses *teach* less the
more they feel themselves being *affected*. Conversely, in order to teach a good
deal, they must be affected moderately. In a very strong light we *see* nothing
(distinguish nothing), and a stentorian voice *deafens* us (crushes thought).]

Idea
Mode
Sens[e]

1[1] See also COPY B 1 (on the same tex-
tus).
1[2] "The 'man himself' was an intenser
I." In ESCHENMAYER 5, C refers to this
paragraph as "one of the *very few* silly re-
marks of Immanuel Kant: all of which . . .
are to be found in his Anthropology".

3[1] With this early elliptical recognition
of the dangers of habit, especially in rela-
tion to the addiction to laudanum that was
soon to establish itself, cf *CN* I 1421 (c Jul–
Aug 1803)—a memorandum on habit that
he remembered as an "untreated subject 5
years ago" in *CN* III 3361 (Sept 1808).

5 p 109, pencil line in margin, note cropped | Sec 29 [39]

Dem Taubgebohrnen ist sein Sprechen ein Gefühl des Spiels seiner Lippen, Zunge und Kinnbackens, und es ist kaum möglich, sich vorzustellen, dass er bey seinem Sprechen etwas mehr thue als ein Spiel mit körperlichen Gefühlen zu treiben, ohne eigentliche Begriffe zu haben und zu denken.—

[For a man born deaf, his own speaking is the feeling of his lip, tongue, and jaw movements; and we can hardly conceive that in talking he does anything more than carry on a play of these feelings, without really having and thinking concepts.]

Unfai[r] & inconse[. . .]^{a1}

6 p 122, pencil, cropped | Sec 33 [43]

Dass Zeitalter der Gelangung des Menschen zum vollständigen Gebrauch seiner Vernunft kann in Ansehung seiner *Geschicklichkeit* (Kunstvermögens zu beliebiger Absicht) etwa ins zwanzigste, das in Ansehung der *Klugheit* (andere Menschen zu seinen Absichten zu brauchen) ins vierzigste, endlich das der *Weisheit* etwa im sechzigsten anberaumt werden; in welcher letzteren Epoche aber sie mehr *negativ* ist, alle Thorheiten der beyden ersteren einzusehen . . .

[As far as *skill* is concerned (dexterity in achieving whatever ends he has chosen), man reaches the full use of his reason around the age of twenty; in *prudence* (using other men for his purposes), around forty; and, finally, in *wisdom*, around sixty. In this final period, however, he uses his reason in a primarily *negative* way, to see into all the follies of the first two periods.]

[. . .]ver [. . .]dant [. . .]se

---

^{a} Reading doubtful. The words may not be in C's hand

5^1 "Unfair"—if that is the correct reading—perhaps in denying to deaf-mutes the possibility of forming concepts.

Copy B

Anthropologie in pragmatischer Hinsicht abgefasst. Zweyte verbesserte Auflage. Königsberg 1800. 8°.

British Library C 43 b 8

Inscribed on p ⁻5: "Lot 402"—i.e. in *Green SC* (1880). A short note in ink by J. H. Green is pasted to p ⁻2: "*Judgement* is, where the rule has been given, to apply it to the particular case *Wit* is to bring the particular under a general rule." Green has also written "Wit" in pencil at the top of p 153 and marked the definition of wit on that page; and on p 156 he marked the first paragraph and two other passages with his typically geometrical marginal pencil rule; against the second he wrote the note "See Quarterly Review N° 1850". Other marginal marks in this volume—pp 155, 207, 255—are identifiable as Green's from their resemblance to the note on p 156.

DATE. After 1817 if this was Green's copy.

COEDITORS. Kathleen Wheeler, Raimonda Modiano.

TEXTUS TRANSLATION. As COPY A.

1 p 4 | Bk 1 pt 1 sec 1

Es ist aber merkwürdig: dass das Kind, was schon ziemlich fertig sprechen kann, doch ziemlich spät (vielleicht wohl ein Jahr nachher) allererst anfängt durch Ich zu reden, so lange aber von sich in der dritten Person sprach, (Carl will essen, gehen, u.s.w.) und dass ihm gleichsam ein Licht aufgegangen zu seyn scheint, wenn es den Anfang macht durch Ich zu sprechen; von welchem Tage an es niemals mehr in jene Sprechart zurückkehrt.—Vorher *fühlte* es bloss sich selbst, jetzt *denkt* es sich selbst.—Die Erklärung dieses Phänomens möchte dem Anthropologen ziemlich schwer fallen.

[But it is noteworthy that a child who can already speak fairly fluently does not begin to talk in terms of "I" until rather late (perhaps a year later); until then he speaks of himself in the third person (Charles wants to eat, to go for a walk, etc.). And when he starts to speak in terms of "I" a light seems to dawn on him, as it were, and from this day on he never relapses into his former way of speaking.—Before, he merely *felt* himself; now he *thinks* himself.—The anthropologist may find it rather hard to explain this phenomenon.]

I am not disposed to deny this position; but the *fact* (3ʳᵈ Person vicè 1ˢᵗ in a Child) is too easily solved by mere imitation to be admitted as a *proof*.[1]

1[1] See also COPY A **1** (on the same textus) and n 2.

2   p 9 | Sec 2

Die Sprache des Staatsoberhaupts zum Volk ist in unseren Zeiten ge-
wöhnlich* pluralistisch (Wir N. von Gottes Gnaden u.s.w.). Es frägt
sich, ob der Sinn hierbey nicht vielmehr egoistisch, d.i. eigene Macht-
vollkommenheit anzeigend und eben dasselbe bedeuten solle, was der
König von Spanien mit seinem *Io el rey* (Ich der König) sagt. Es scheint
aber doch: dass jene Förmlichkeit der höchsten Autorität urspruünglich
habe *Herablassung* (Wir, der König und sein Rath, oder die Stände)
andeuten sollen.

[In our time, the head of state usually* speaks in the plural when addressing the
people (We . . . , by the Grace of God, etc.). The question arises: does not this
use of the plural pronoun really have an egoistic sense—that is, does it not in-
dicate his personal authority and intend the same thing as when the King of
Spain says *Io, el Rey* ("I, the King")? But it seems that this formality used by
the supreme authority was originally meant to indicate *condescension* (We, the
king and his council or the estates of the realm).]

* Rather, from a relique of Democracy retained by the policy of Augus-
tus, who merging in one the most important magistracies would be ad-
dressed not as a person but as a Proxy of the Majority— = Majestas.[1]
We, i.e. the Tribunes, the Pontif. Max. and the Princeps Sen./[2]

2[1] The politically significant derivation
of "majesty" from "majority" is one that
C used consistently from youth to age, e.g.
Lects 1795 (CC) 295, *C&S (CC)* 20.

2[2] Caius Octavius (63 B.C.–A.D. 14), re-
named C. Julius Caesar Octavianus on the
death of Julius Caesar in 44 B.C., became

the first Roman emperor and was known by
his honorary title, "Augustus". He was
virtually sole ruler, embodying the offices
of *tribuni plebis* (tribunes of the people),
pontifex maximus (high priest), and *prin-
ceps senatus* (first senator).

Critik der reinen Vernunft. 5th ed. Leipzig 1799. 8°.

"S. T. C." label on p [iv]. A fragment of a letter addressed in a copperplate hand "—— Coleridge Esqre.", on which C has written **1**, is tipped in at pp 876/7. A mark in the margin on p xxxix refers to a later note: see **3**. In this copy, pp 141–4 have by mistake been bound in between 132 and 133.

MS TRANSCRIPT. VCL BT 22.

DATE. Both the comparative scarcity of notes and C's reference to his "first perusal" (**4**) suggest an early date for most of these marginalia, between 1800 and 1808, possibly the intensive reading of Kant in the winter of 1800–1: *CL* II 676. References to the *Critique of Pure Reason* specifically do not occur before 1807–8: *CL* III 35, *CN* III 3346. One note (**2**), however, appears to have been written as a guide for someone else and from a more confident perspective, perhaps at the time of C's rereading of this work in conjunction with the philosophical lectures of 1818–19: *P Lects* Lect 13 (1949) 388–90.

COEDITORS. Kathleen Wheeler, Raimonda Modiano.

TEXTUS TRANSLATION. Norman Kemp Smith tr *Immanuel Kant's Critique of Pure Reason* rev ed 1933). It may be noted that the page numbers in C's copy correspond to those of the 2nd ed (1787) commonly cited as "B". Since this pagination is recorded in all standard editions, the titles of sections and subsections are omitted from headlines.

A p 43

Die beständige Form dieser Receptivität, welche wir Sinnlichkeit nennen, ist eine nothwendige Bedingung aller Verhältnisse, darinnen Gegenständen abstrahire, eine reine Anschauung, welche den Namen Raum führet. Weil wir die besonderen Bedingungen der Si*ff*nnlichkeit nicht zu Bedingungen der Möglichkeit der Sachen, sondern nur ihrer Erscheinungen machen können . . .

[The constant form of this receptivity, which we term sensibility, is a necessary condition of all the relations in which objects can be intuited as outside us; and if we abstract from these objects, it is a pure intuition, and bears the name of space. Since we cannot treat the special conditions of sensibility [C's correct emendation for the typographical error "morality"] as conditions of the possibility of things, but only of their appearances . . .]

B p 72

Es i̶s̶t̶ nicht auch nöthig, dass wir die Anschauungsart in Raum und Zeit auf die Sinnlichkeit des Menschen einschränken . . .

[This mode of intuiting in space and time need not be limited to human sensibility . . .]

1   pp 876/7, note tipped in,[a] referring to p 93

Alle Anschauungen, als sinnlich, beruhen auf Affectionen, die Begriffe also auf Functionen. Ich verstehe aber unter Function die Einheit der Handlung, verschiedene Vorstellungen unter einer gemeinschaftlichen zu ordnen.

[Whereas all intuitions, as sensible, rest on affections, concepts rest on functions. By "function" I mean the unity of the act of bringing various representations under one common representation.]

Cr. d. r. Vern.—p. 893

All intuitions, als sinnlich, beruhen auf *Affectionen*—die Begriffe also auf *Functionen*.[1]

If sinnlich here = sensual, empirisch,[2] how does this apply to the pure Intuitions, as the immediate products of the intuitive Act?[3] If not applicable, then *all* intuitions do not rest on *Affections*; & consequently, Functions are not contra-distinctive of the Understanding.—

2   p +1, referring to pp 129–69[b]

p. 129 to 169 comprehend the most difficult and obscure passages of this Critique—or rather the *knot* of the whole System.[1] If they are not comprehended, the whole Philosophy of Kant, as *Kant's* philosophy, remains unknown—. Perhaps, the best way of commencing the attempt to understand his specific meaning, after repeated perusal, of these pages, would be to draw up a scheme of those hypotheses, which are not Kant's meaning. For instance, it is clearly not the system of mere *Receptivity*, like that of Epicurus and Hartley[2]—it is not the System of innate Apti-

---

[a] The note is written on a fragment of a letter with a hole torn by the seal; paper not watermarked
[b] This note is written below **4** and was evidently added on another occasion

1[1] See textus.
1[2] Sensual, "empirical".
1[3] C here refers to the distinction drawn by Kant in the "Transcendental Dialectic" between "empirical intuition", which engages objects of experience through sensation, and "pure intuition", which, "even without any actual object of the sense or of sensation, exists in the mind *a priori* as mere form of sensibility" (p 35). For Kant the only two forms of pure intuition are space and time. The term *sinnlich* ("sensible") in Kant's usage can refer to both empirical and pure intuition, since "all our in-

tuition is sensible", i.e. pertains to sensibility (p 151). C observes correctly, however, that in p 93 Kant has in mind "empirical intuition" rather than "pure intuition", for he writes (immediately following the textus): "Concepts are based on the spontaneity of thought, sensible intuitions on the receptivity of impressions."
2[1] These pages contain the notoriously difficult "Deduction of the Pure Concepts of the Understanding", revised in this 2nd ed.
2[2] C's rejection of Hartley's associationism, partly on the ground that it denied

tudes or preformation, nor any form of pre-established Harmony[3]—and so on.—I have for a moment been inclined to understand it as something similar to that[a] Averroes—that all men participate *one* Understanding, each the whole, as—to use a very imperfect illustration—a 1000 persons may all & each hear one discourse of one voice.[4] At least, the difference between the original Unity of Consciousness, and empirical Consciousness is the great point, the germ—[5]

2A p 218

Alle Empfindungen werden daher, als solche, zwar nur *a posteriori*[1] gegeben, aber die Eigenschaft derselben, dass sie einen Grad haben, kann *a priori* erkannt werden.

[Consequently, though all sensations as such are given only *a posteriori*, their property of possessing a degree can be known *a priori*.]

2B p 219

. . . weil Apprehension nur eine Zusammenstellung des Mannigfaltigen der empirischen Anschauung, aber keine Vorstellung von der Nothwendigkeit der verbundenen Existenz der Erscheinungen, die sie zusammenstellt, im Raum und Zeit in derselben angetroffen wird.

[. . . for apprehension is only a placing together of the manifold of empirical intuition; and [C suggests "but"] we can find in it no representation of any necessity which determines the appearances thus combined to have connected existence in space and time.]

---

[a] For "that of", presumably

---

the mind any active powers, is usually dated by a letter of Mar 1801 to Thomas Poole (*CL* II 706); it is most fully developed in *BL* chs 6–7 (*CC*) I 106–28. About the same time, a letter to Wedgwood in Feb 1801 refers to Locke as founder of "the new Epicurean School" of atomic materialism (*CL* II 701): cf *SM* (*CC*) 108 and n.

2[3] Alluding to the controversy in contemporary biology between the preformationists and the epigenesists, Kant himself explicitly rejects what he calls "a kind of *preformation-system* of pure reason" (p 167) as a way of accounting for the Categories. One such system would be the doctrine of pre-established harmony identified with Leibniz: C's impatience with this doctrine is recorded in e.g. ESCHENMAYER **40** and n, *BL* ch 8 (*CC*) I 130–1.

2[4] C owed his knowledge of this doctrine of Averroes (1126–98) to Christoph Meiners, from whom he made a note in 1798–9, "The assertion of the Averroists that there is one speculative spirit in all men" (tr): *CN* I 374 and n.

2[5] Kant's distinction between empirical consciousness ("pure apperception") and the original unity of consciousness ("original apperception") appears particularly in the section entitled "The Original Synthetic Unity of Apperception" (pp 131–5), a section that in *BL* ch 9 (*CC*) I 153 C confessed to finding obscure but that he expounded carefully in *Logic* (*CC*) 70–9.

2A[1] C's correction here, as in **A**, **B**, and **2B**, is confirmed by later editions of Kant's text.

3 p 275

Ich bin mir meines Daseyns als in der Zeit bestimmt bewusst. Alle Zeit-bestimmung setzt etwas *Beharrliches* in der Wahrnehmung voraus. Dieses Beharrliche aber kann nicht etwas in mir seyn; weil eben mein Daseyn in der Zeit durch dieses Beharrliche allererst bestimmt werden kann.

[I am conscious of my own existence as determined in time. All determination of time presupposes something *permanent* in perception. This permanent cannot, however, be something in me, since it is only through this permanent that my existence in time can itself be determined.]

vide * in der vorrede pag. 39[1]

3A   pp 378–80, marked with a pencil line in the margin

Die Function der Vernunft bei ihren Schlüssen bestand in der Allge-meinheit der Erkenntniss nach Begriffen, und der Vernunftschluss selbst ist ein Urtheil, welches *a priori* in dem ganzen Umfange seiner Beding-ung bestimmt wird. Den Satz: Cajus ist sterblich, könnte ich auch bloss durch den Verstand aus der Erfahrung schöpfen. Allein ich suche einen Begriff, der die Bedingung enthält, unter welcher das Prädicat (Asser-tion überhaupt) dieses Urtheils gegeben wird (d.i. hier den Begriff des Menschen;) und nachdem ich unter diese Bedingung, in ihrem ganzen Umfange genommen, (alle Menschen sind sterblich) subsumirt habe: so bestimme ich darnach die Erkenntniss meines Gegenstandes (Cajus ist sterblich).

Demnach restringiren wir in der Conclusion eines Vernunftschlusses ein Prädicat auf einen gewissen Gegenstand, nachdem wir es vorher in dem Obersatz in seinem ganzen Umfange unter einer gewissen Beding-ung gedacht haben. Diese vollendete Grösse des Umfanges, in Bezie-hung auf eine solche Bedingung, heisst die *Allgemeinheit* (*Universali-tas*). Dieser entspricht in der Synthesis der Anschauungen die *Allheit* (*Universitas*) oder *Totalität* der Bedingungen. Also ist der transscenden-tale Vernunftbegriff kein anderer, als der von der *Totalität der Beding-ungen* zu einem gegebenen Bedingten. Da nun das *Unbedingte* allein die Totalität der Bedingungen möglich macht, und umgekehrt die Tota-

---

3[1] In his Preface (Vorrede), Kant asked that this sentence be altered as follows (tr): "But this permanent cannot be an intui-tion in me. For all grounds of determina-tion of my existence which are to be met with in me are representations; and as rep-resentations themselves require a perma-nent distinct from them, in relation to which their change, and so my existence in the time where they change, may be deter-mined." C's note records the page (xxxix) on which the substitute passage is given; C also marked the passage itself with a short horizontal line in the margin.

lität der Bedingungen jederzeit selbst unbedingt ist: so kann ein reiner Vernunftbegriff überhaupt durch den Begriff des Unbedingten, sofern er einen Grund der Synthesis des Bedingten enthhält, erklärt werden.

So viel Arten des Verhältnisses es nun giebt, die der Verstand vermittelst der Categorien sich vorstellt, so vielerley reine Vernunftbegriffe wird es auch geben, und es wird also *erstlich* ein *Unbedingtes* der *categorischen* Synthesis in einem *Subject, zweytens* der *hypothetischen* Synthesis der Glieder einer *Reihe, drittens* der *disjunctiven* Synthesis der Theile in einem *System* zu suchen seyn.

Es giebt nämlich eben so viel Arten von Vernunftschlüssen, deren jede durch Prosyllogismen zum Unbedingten fortschreitet, die eine zum Subject, welches selbst nicht mehr Prädicat ist, die andre zur Voraussetzung, die nichts weiter voraussetzt, und die dritte zu einem Aggregat der Glieder der Eintheilung, zu welchen nichts weiter erforderlich ist, um die Eintheilung eines Begriffs zu vollenden. Daher sind die reinen Vernunftbegriffe von der Totalität in der Synthesis der Bedingungen weningstens als Aufgaben, um die Einheit des Verstandes, wo möglich bis zum Unbedingten fortzusetzen, nothwendig und in der Natur der menschlichen Vernunft gegründet, es mag auch übrigens diesen transscendentalen Begriffen an einem ihnen angemessenen Gebrauch *in concreto* fehlen und sie mithin keinen andern Nutzen haben, als den Verstand in die Richtung zu bringen, darin sein Gebrauch, indem er aufs äusserste erweitert, zugleich mit sich selbst durchgehends einstimmig gemacht wird.

[The function of reason in its inferences consists in the universality of knowledge [which it yields] according to concepts, the syllogism being itself a judgment which is determined *a priori* in the whole extent of its conditions. The proposition, ''Caius is mortal'', I could indeed derive from experience by means of the understanding alone. But I am in pursuit of a concept (in this case, the concept ''man'') that contains the condition under which the predicate (general term for what is asserted) of this judgment is given; and after I have subsumed the predicate under this condition taken in its whole extension (''All men are mortal''), I proceed, in accordance therewith, to determine the knowledge of my object (''Caius is mortal'').

Accordingly, in the conclusion of a syllogism we restrict a predicate to a certain object, after having first thought it in the major premiss in its whole extension under a given condition. This complete quantity of the extension in relation to such a condition is called *universality* (*universalitas*). In the synthesis of intuitions we have corresponding to this the *allness* (*universitas*) or *totality* of the conditions. The transcendental concept of reason is, therefore, none other than the concept of the *totality of the conditions* for any given conditioned. Now since it is the *unconditioned* alone which makes possible the totality of conditions, and, conversely, the totality of conditions is always itself unconditioned, a pure concept of reason can in general be explained by the concept of the unconditioned, conceived as containing a ground of the synthesis of the conditioned.

The number of pure concepts of reason will be equal to the number of kinds of relation which the understanding represents to itself by means of the categories. We have therefore to seek for an *unconditioned*, first, of the *categorical* synthesis in a *subject*; secondly, of the *hypothetical* synthesis of the members of a *series*; thirdly, of the *disjunctive* synthesis of the parts in a *system*.

There is thus precisely the same number of kinds of syllogism, each of which advances through prosyllogisms to the unconditioned: first, to the subject which is never itself a predicate; secondly, to the presupposition which itself presupposes nothing further; thirdly, to such an aggregate of the members of the division of a concept as requires nothing further to complete the division. The pure concepts of reason—of totality in the synthesis of conditions—are thus at least necessary as setting us the task of extending the unity of understanding, where possible, up to the unconditioned, and are grounded in the nature of human reason. These transcendental concepts may, however, be without any suitable corresponding employment *in concreto*, and may therefore have no other utility than that of so directing the understanding that, while it is extended to the uttermost, it is also at the same time brought into complete consistency with itself.]

3B pp 382–3, marked with a pencil line in the margin

Nun geht der transcendentale Vernunftbegriff jederzeit nur auf die absolute Totalität in der Synthesis der Bedingungen, und endigt niemals, als bey dem schlechthin, d.i. in jeder Beziehung, Unbedingten. Denn die reine Vernunft überlässt alles dem Verstande, der sich zunächst auf die Gegenstände der Anschauung oder vielmehr deren Synthesis in der Einbildungskraft bezieht. Jene behält sich allein die absolute Totalität im Gebrauche der Verstandesbegriffe vor, und sucht die synthetische Einheit, welche in der Categorie gedacht wird, bis zum Schlechthinunbedingten hinauszuführen. Man kann daher diese die *Vernunfteinheit* der Erscheinungen, so wie jene, welche die Categorie ausdrückt, *Verstandeseinheit* nennen. So bezieht sich demnach die Vernunft nur auf den Verstandesgebrauch, und zwar nicht so fern dieser den Grund möglicher Erfahrung enthält, (denn die absolute Totalität der Bedingungen ist kein in einer Erfahrung brauchbarer Begriff, weil keine Erfahrung unbedingt ist,) sondern um ihm die Richtung auf eine gewisse Einheit vorzuschreiben, von der der Verstand keinen Begriff hat, und die darauf hinaus geht, alle Verstandeshandlungen, in Ansehung eines jeden Gegenstande, in ein *absolutes Ganzes* zusammen zu fassen. Daher ist der objective Gebrauch der reinen Vernunftbegriffe jederzeit *transscendent*, indessen dass der von den reinen Verstandesbegriffen, seiner Natur nach, jederzeit *immanent* seyn muss, indem er sich bloss auf mögliche Erfahrung einschränkt.

Ich verstehe unter der Idee einen nothwendigen Vernunftbegriff, dem kein congruirender Gegenstand in den Sinnen gegeben werden kann. Also sind unsere jetzt erwogene reine Vernunftbegriffe *transscendentale* Ideen.

[Now the transcendental concept of reason is directed always solely towards absolute totality in the synthesis of conditions, and never terminates save in what is absolutely, that is, in all relations, unconditioned. For pure reason leaves everything to the understanding—the understanding [alone] applying immediately to the objects of intuition, or rather to their synthesis in the imagination. Reason concerns itself exclusively with absolute totality in the employment of the concepts of the understanding, and endeavours to carry the synthetic unity, which is thought in the category, up to the completely unconditioned. We may call this unity of appearances the *unity of reason*, and that expressed by the category the *unity of understanding*. Reason accordingly occupies itself solely with the employment of understanding, not indeed in so far as the latter contains the ground of possible experience (for the concept of the absolute totality of conditions is not applicable in any experience, since no experience is unconditioned), but solely in order to prescribe to the understanding its direction towards a certain unity of which it has itself no concept, and in such manner as to unite all the acts of the understanding, in respect of every object, into an *absolute whole*. The objective employment of the pure concepts of reason is, therefore, always *transcendent*, while that of the pure concepts of understanding must, in accordance with their nature, and inasmuch as their application is solely to possible experience, be always *immanent*.

I understand by idea a necessary concept of reason to which no corresponding object can be given in sense-experience. Thus the pure concepts of reason, now under consideration, are *transcendental* ideas.]

3C   p 393, marked with a pencil line in the margin

Man sieht leicht, dass die reine Vernunft nichts anders zur Absicht habe, als die absolute Totalität der Synthesis *auf der Seite der Bedingungen*, (es sey der Inhärenz, oder der Dependenz, oder der Concurrenz,) und dass sie mit der absoluten Vollständigkeit von *Seiten des Bedingten* nichts zu schaffen habe.

[As is easily seen, what pure reason alone has in view is the absolute totality of the synthesis *on the side of the conditions* (whether of inherence, of dependence, or of concurrence); it is not concerned with absolute completeness *on the side of the conditioned*.]

4   p +1

Doubts during a first perusal—i.e. Struggles felt, not arguments objected.

1. How can that be called ein mannigfaltiges ὑλή,[1] which yet contains

4[1] The phrase, which C himself renders as "a confused Manifold" at the end of the note, is not Kant's, but C's paraphrase of Kant's position, e.g. in the introduction of

in itself the ground, why I apply one category to it rather than another? one mathematical form and not another? The mind does not resemble an Eolian Harp, nor even a barrel-organ turned by a stream of water, conceive as many tunes mechanized in it as you like—but rather, as far as Objects are concerned, a violin, or other instrument of few strings yet vast compass, played on by a musician of Genius.[2] The Breeze that blows across the Eolian Harp, the streams that turned the handle of the Barrel Organ, might be called ein mannigfaltiges, a mere sylva incondita,[3] but who would call the muscles and purpose of Linley[4] a confused Manifold?

5 p⁺2[a]

The perpetual and unmoving Cloud of Darkness, that hangs over this Work to my "mind's eye",[1] is the absence of any clear account of— was ist Erfahrung?[2] What do you mean by a *fact*, an empiric Reality, which alone can give solidity (inhalt) to our Conceptions?[3]—It seems from many passages, that this indispensible Test is itself previously

[a] This note is written in the same ink and hand as **4** but does not seem to be a continuation of **4**. See **2** n *a* above

the Table of Categories, p 102: "Transcendental logic . . . has lying before it a manifold (*ein Mannigfaltiges*) of *a priori* sensibility . . . as material for the concepts of pure understanding. In the absence of this material (*Stoff*) those concepts would be without any content (*Inhalt*), therefore entirely empty." The Greek word ὑλή— "matter" in philosophical contexts—is taken also in its primary sense as a forest or a confusion of trees and foliage—a sense which C plays upon in "sylva incondita" at n 3 below. For ὑλή/*sylva* see EICHHORN *Apocrypha* **19** and n 2.

4[2] "Aeolus's Harp", a stringed box "played" by the wind and named for the god of the winds, was celebrated soon after its invention in a footnoted stanza (I xl) of James Thomson's *Castle of Indolence* (1748), and became a common figure for the creative mind among poets of a later generation, notably C himself in *The Eolian Harp* (1795). The barrel-organ, like the harp, responds mechanically to natural forces and can be sounded without the aid of a skilled musician. Such appears to be C's point, but he may be combining the often elaborate barrel-organs of the eigh-

teenth century, which were generally operated by weights or clockwork, with the ancient "hydraulic organ" or hydraulis, run by water.

4[3] "A manifold, a mere unformed matter"—but for the pun see n 1 above.

4[4] Thomas Linley the younger (1756–78), one of the finest violinists in Europe in his day.

5[1] With the "Cloud of Darkness" cf the "cloud and darkness" of Exod 14.20 that stood between the Israelites and the Egyptians; the "mind's eye" is from *Hamlet* I ii 185.

5[2] "What is experience?"

5[3] See the passage q in **4** n 1 above, and cf e.g. Kant p 610 (tr), "nothing is an object *for us*, unless it presupposes the sum of all empirical reality [*empirischen Realität*] as the condition of its possibility". In NICOLAI **6**, C accuses Nicolai of not understanding this basic principle in Kant; here, he himself questions it. The concept of a "fact" occupied C considerably: it is defined in a philosophical context in the glossary in *SM* (*CC*) 113 as "A CONCEPTION, extrinsic and sensuous", or, alternatively, "a COGNITION".

manufactured by this very conceptive Power—and that the whole not of our own making is the mere sensation of a mere Manifold—in short, mere influx of motion, to use a physical metaphor.—I apply the Categoric forms to a Tree—well! but first *what* is this tree? How do I come by this Tree?[4]—Fichte I understand very well—only I cannot believe his System.[5] But Kant I do not understand—i.e. I have not discovered what he proposes for my Belief.—Is it Dogmatism?[6]—Why then make the opposition between Phænomena and Things in themselves—τα οντως οντα?[7] Is it Idealism? What Test then can I find in the ⟨different⟩ modifications of my Being to verify and substantiate each other? What other distinction between Schein and Erscheinung, Illusion and Appearance[8] more than the old one of—in one I dream to myself, and in the other I dream in common: The Man in a fever is only *outvoted* by his Attendants—He does not see their Dream, and they do not see his.[9]

[4] The "tree" may have been chosen as a playful reminder of ὑλή/*sylva*, above. To C's question Kant would reply that we can never know what the tree is in itself; we know only the appearance of the tree as given by our faculty of representation. C was not satisfied with Kant's distinction between appearances and things-in-themselves, objecting in the same way that for Schelling "experience" pertained not to empirical objects but only to the "Self-experience" of the mind: *CL* IV 875.

[5] See FICHTE General Note—*CM* (*CC*) II 594–5—for a summary of the evolution of C's opinion of Fichte.

[6] Kant takes up the question of dogmatism in the Preface, xxxv–xxxvi, saying that his *Critique* is not opposed to the dogmatic method, but (tr) "only to *dogmatism*, that is, to the presumption that it is possible to make progress with pure knowledge, according to principles, from concepts alone" (xxxv).

[7] "Things that really exist". The distinction between phenomena or "appearances", which are all we know, and things in themselves, which are unknowable, is fundamental to the *Critique*, e.g. p 164.

[8] Kant distinguishes sharply between an object viewed as *Erscheinung* (appearance) and *Schein* (mere illusion): "when I maintain that the quality of space and of time, in conformity with which, as a condition of their existence, I posit both bodies and my own soul, lies in my mode of intuition and not in those objects themselves, I am not saying that bodies merely *seem* [*scheinen*] to be outside me, or that my soul only *seems* to be given in my self-consciousness. It would be my own fault, if out of that which I ought to reckon as appearance, I made mere illusion" (p 69).

[9] The story of the madman "outvoted" by society, invoked by C in *BL* ch 12 (*CC*) I 262, appears to have been derived from Joseph Priestley *A Comparison of the Institutions of Moses with Those of the Hindoos* (Northumberland 1799) 303n.

Critik der Urtheilskraft. 3rd ed. Berlin 1799. 8°.

British Library C 126 h 6

"S. T. C." label on title-page verso. The note on Fulke Greville (2), written on a sheet of unwatermarked laid paper tipped in at pp 248/9, may not have been intended to have any connection with this *Critique*.

DATE. 6 Feb 1823 (1). Note 2 may well have been written much earlier: see 2 n 1 below.

COEDITORS. Kathleen Wheeler, Raimonda Modiano.

1   p⁻2

How ἑλ¹ is permitted to punish Maen by mocking & pretending to some ⟨of those⟩ *fashionable* Virtues ⟨of theirs⟩—Liberty, and Philanthropy, and Cosmopolitism in the French Revolutionists—then Loyalty, and Religion and Legitimacy & Godliness in theat accursed Austrian!,² & in the fiendish Austro-prusso-russian = Holy Alliance, which the King of England was audaciously counselled to *regret* that the English Constitution did not permit him openly to become a bound Eidgenoss of!!³

Highgate—6 Feby 1823.

2   pp 248/9, leaf tipped in

* Fulke Greville (Lord Brook) Sir P. Sidney's Friend and Fellow-student, whose works might, not inaptly, be described in Cowper's words (*Fragment on the old Oak at Yardley*) as

1¹ "Hell".

1² Klemens Wenzel Nepomuk Lothar, Prince Metternich (1773–1859). Since C does not refer to him elsewhere, the reasons for his strong distaste cannot be specified: Metternich's skill in diplomacy, however, had led many to see him as a temporiser, and the great influence that he exerted against national movements for independence in Europe after the Congress of Vienna—notably and recently against the Greek government, which the British government officially recognised in 1823—made him a figure of oppression.

1³ *Eidgenoss* (not in Kant), "confederate" or "ally". The declaration known as the "Holy Alliance"—a general statement of Christian principles by which governments were to be bound—was initiated by Alexander I of Russia and was signed by Russian, Prussian, and Austrian leaders on 26 Sept 1815. In England, the Prince Regent (George IV by the time C wrote this note) declined to sign on constitutional grounds but sent a courteous letter expressing his "entire concurrence" with the religious principles endorsed by the other rulers.

A Quarry of stout Spurs and knotted Fangs
That crooked into a thousand whimsies clasp
The stubborn Soil;[1]

but contain, however, chrystallized into ~~as many~~ a glittering chaos of needles, the substance of Tacitus, of Machiavel and the Italian Historians, and of the conversation of our own Elizabeth's hitherto unrivalled *Statists*.[2]

2[1] C wrote these lines from William Cowper *Yardley Oak* lines 117–19 in Lamb's copy of the works of Sir Fulke Greville in 1806 (GREVILLE **8**), and copied them into a notebook in Mar 1810 (*CN* III 3713). This note does not appear to have any connection with the work it is bound into, and it may have been written long before C wrote **1**.

2[2] Besides the Roman historian Tacitus (c 55–117) and the Italian statesman Machiavelli (1469–1527), who wrote a history of Florence, C's reference to "Italian Historians" would include Lodovico Antonio Muratori (1672–1750), whose *Annali d'Italia* C quoted in 1810 (*CN* III 3822). The long list of Elizabethan statesmen who were friends of Greville's includes Gabriel Harvey, Francis Bacon, and Sir Philip Sidney.

Grundlegung zur Metaphysik der Sitten. 4th ed. Riga 1797. 8°.

British Library C 126 e 9

Marked on p ⁻5 (p-d) "Lot 402"—i.e. *Green SC* (1880) 402—and on p ⁻1
"M.S. note by S. T. Coleridge pp 54–5".

DATE. 6 Dec 1803 (1): cf a series of notebook entries arguing with this work,
CN I 1705, 1710, 1717.

COEDITORS. Kathleen Wheeler, Raimonda Modiano.

TEXTUS TRANSLATION. T. K. Abbott tr *Fundamental Principles of the Meta-
physics of Ethics* (New York 1949).

1   p 54, pencil | Sec 2

Einer, der durch eine Reihe von Uebeln, die bis zur Hoffnungslosigkeit
angewachsen ist, einen Ueberdruss am Leben empfindet, ist noch so
weil im Besitze seiner Vernunft, dass er sich selbst fragen kann, ob es
auch nicht etwa der Pflicht gegen sich selbst zuwider sey, sich das Leben
zu nehmen. Nun versucht er: ob die Maxime seiner Handlung wol ein
allgemeines Naturgesetz werden könne. Seine Maxime aber ist: ich
mache es mir aus Selbstliebe zum Princip, wenn das Leben bey seiner
längern Frist mehr Uebel droht, als es Annehmlichkeit verspricht, es mir
abzukürzen. Es frägt sich nur noch, ob dieses Princip der Selbstliebe ein
allgemeines Naturgesetz werden könne. Das sieht man aber bald, dass
eine Natur, deren Gesetz es wäre, durch dieselbe Empfindung, deren
Bestimmung es ist, zur Beförderung des Lebens anzutreiben, *das Le-
ben selbst zu zerstören, ihr selbst widersprechen und also nicht als Natur
bestehen würde, mithin jene Maxime unmöglich als allgemeines Natur-
gesetz statt finden könne, und folglich dem obersten Princip aller Pflicht
gänzlich widerstreite.

[A man reduced to despair by a series of misfortunes feels wearied of life, but is
still so far in possession of his reason that he can ask himself whether it would
not be contrary to his duty to himself to take his own life. Now he inquires
whether the maxim of his action could become a universal law of nature. His
maxim is: From self-love I adopt it as a principle to shorten my life when its
longer duration is likely to bring more evil than satisfaction. It is asked then
simply whether this principle founded on self-love can become a universal law
of nature. Now we see at once that a system of nature of which it should be a
law to destroy *life by means of the very feeling whose special nature it is to
impel to the improvements of life would contradict itself, and therefore could

not exist as a universal law of nature; hence that maxim cannot possibly exist as a universal law of nature, and consequently would be wholly inconsistent with the supreme principle of all duty.]

* Strange Nonsense!—Self-love is not here supposed to impel the Will to the Prolongation of *Life*, as Life, but as the sum or instrument of pleasurable Feeling; & of course, with perfect consistency may impel a man to the destruction of Life, when Life is believed to be the Sum & Instrument of Pain & Evil. But Kant, & all his School, are miserable Reasoners, in Psychology & particular Morals—bad analysts of aught but Notions, equally clumsy in the illustration & application of their Principles—so much indeed as often to shake my Faith in their general System.   S. T. C.   Decemb. 6. 1803.   Keswick.

2   p 55, pencil | Continuing **1** textus

Ein anderer sieht sich durch Noth gedrungen, Geld zu borgen. Er weiss wol, dass er nicht wird bezahlen können, sieht aber auch, dass ihm nichts geliehen werden wird, wenn er nicht vestiglich verspricht, es zu einer bestimmten Zeit zu bezahlen. Er hat Lust, ein solches Versprechen zu thun; noch aber hat er so viel Gewissen, sich zu fragen: ist es nicht unerlaubt und pflichtwidrig, sich auf solche Art aus Noth zu helfen? Gesetzt, er beschlösse es doch, so würde seine Maxime der Handlung so lauten: wenn ich mich in Geldnoth zu seyn glaube, so will ich Geld borgen und versprechen, es zu bezahlen, ob ich gleich weiss, es werde niemals geschehen. Nun ist dieses Princip der Selbstliebe, oder der eigenen Zuträglichkeit, mit meinem ganzen künftigen Wohlbefinden vielleicht wol zu vereinigen, allein jetzt ist die Frage: ob es recht sey? Ich verwandle also die Zumuthung der Selbstliebe in ein allgemeines Gesetz, und richte die Frage so ein: wie es dann stehen würde, wenn meine Maxime ein allgemeines Gesetz würde? Da sehe ich nun sogleich, dass sie niemals als allgemeines Naturgesetz gelten und mit sich selbst zusammenstimmen könne, sondern sich nothwendig widersprechen müsse. Denn die Allgemeinheit eines Gesetzes, dass jeder, nachdem er in Noth zu seyn glaubt, versprechen könne, was ihm einfällt, mit dem Vorsatz, es nicht zu halten, würde das Versprechen und den Zweck, den man damit haben mag, selbst unmöglich machen, indem niemand glauben würde, dass ihm was versprochen sey, sondern über alle solche Äusserung, als eitles Vorgeben, lachen würde.

[Another finds himself forced by necessity to borrow money. He knows that he will not be able to repay it, but sees also that nothing will be lent to him, unless he promises stoutly to repay it in a definite time. He desires to make this promise, but he has still so much conscience as to ask himself: Is it not unlawful and inconsistent with duty to get out of a difficulty in this way? Suppose however that he resolves to do so, then the maxim of his action would be expressed thus: When I think myself in want of money, I will borrow money and promise to repay it, although I know that I never can do so. Now this principle of self-love or of one's own advantage may perhaps be consistent with my whole future welfare; but the question now is, Is it right? I change then the suggestion of self-love into a universal law, and state the question thus: How would it be if my maxim were a universal law? Then I see at once that it could never hold as a universal law of nature, but would necessarily contradict itself. For supposing it to be a universal law that everyone when he thinks himself in a difficulty should be able to promise whatever he pleases, with the purpose of not keeping his promise, the promise itself would become impossible, as well as the end that one might have in view in it, since no one would consider that anything was promised to him, but would ridicule all such statements as vain pretences.]

Who could believe that these pages were written by the same man, who could produce the two ¶ in pages 60 & 61?

2A　pp 60–1, marked with a pencil line in the margin

Hier sehen wir nun die Philosophie in der That auf einen misslichen Standpunct gestellet, der fest seyn soll, unerachtet er weder im Himmel, noch auf der Erde, an etwas gehängt, oder woran gestützt wird. Hier soll sie ihre Lauterkeit beweisen, als Selbsthalterin ihrer Gesetze, nicht als Herold derjenigen, welche ihr ein eingepflanzter Sinn, oder wer weiss welche vormundschaftliche Natur einflüstert, die insgesamt, sie mögen immer besser seyn als gar nichts, doch niemals Grundsätze abgeben können, die die Vernunft dictirt, und die durchaus wöllig *a priori* ihren Quell, und hiemit zugleich ihr gebietendes Ansehen haben müssen: nichts von der Neigung des Menschen, sondern alles von der Obergewalt des Gesetzes und der schuldigen Achtung für dasselbe zu erwarten, oder den Menschen widrigenfalls zur Selbstverachtung und innern Abscheu zu verurtheilen.

Alles also, was empirisch ist, ist, als Zuthat zum Princip der Sittlichkeit, nicht allein dazu ganz untauglich, sondern der Lauterkeit der Sitten selbst höchst nachtheilig, an welchen der eigentliche und über allen Preis erhabene Werth eines schlechterdings guten Willens, eben darin besteht, dass das Princip der Handlung von allen Einflüssen zufälliger Gründe, die nur Erfahrung an die Hand geben kann, frey sey. Wider diese Nachlässigkeit oder gar niedrige Denkungsart, in Aufsuchung des Princips unter empirischen Bewegursachen und Gesetzen, kann man auch nicht zu viel und zu oft Warnungen ergehen lassen, indem die menschliche Vernunft in ihrer Ermüdung gern auf diesem Polster ausruht, und in dem Traume süsser Vorspiegelungen (die sich doch statt der

Juno eine Volke umarmenlassen) der Sittlichkeit einen aus Gliedern ganz verschiedener Abstammung zusammengeflickten Bastard unterschiebt, der allem ähnlich sieht, was man daran sehen will, nur der Tugend nicht, für den, der sie einmal in ihrer wahren Gestalt erblickt hat.

[Here then we see philosophy brought to a critical position, since it has to be firmly fixed, notwithstanding that it has nothing to support it either in heaven or earth. Here it must show its purity as absolute dictator of its own laws, not the herald of those which are whispered to it by an implanted sense or who knows what tutelary nature. Although these may be better than nothing, yet they can never afford principles dictated by reason, which must have their source wholly *a priori*, and thence their commanding authority, expecting everything from the supremacy of the law and the due respect for it, nothing from inclination, or else condemning the man to self-contempt and inward abhorrence.

Thus every empirical element is not only quite incapable of being an aid to the principle of morality, but is even highly prejudicial to the purity of morals, for the proper and inestimable worth of an absolutely good will consists just in this, that the principle of action is free from all influence of contingent grounds, which alone experience can furnish. We cannot too much or too often repeat our warning against this lax and even mean habit of thought which seeks for its principle amongst empirical motives and laws; for human reason in its weariness is glad to rest on this pillow, and in a dream of sweet illusions (in which, instead of Juno, it embraces a cloud) it substitutes for morality a bastard patched up from limbs of various derivation, which looks like anything one chooses to see in it; only not like virtue to one who has once beheld her in her true form.]

Immanuel Kants Logik ein Handbuch zu Vorlesungen. [Ed Gottlob Benjamin Jäsche.] Königsberg 1800. 8°.

British Library C 43 a 10

Joseph Henry Green's copy: see **2**. Green has written two notes in pencil at the head of p ⁺2 which provided C with textus for his note **9**, and another note p ⁺4. Pencilled braces by Green appear in the margins of pp 4, 5, 6, 9, 148; there is a pencilled curlicue p ⁺1.

DATE. c 1822, in association with the *MS Logic* (**10** below).

COEDITORS. Kathleen Wheeler, Raimonda Modiano.

TEXTUS TRANSLATION. Robert S. Hartman and Wolfgang Schwarz tr *Kant's Logic* (New York 1974).

1 p ⁻5ᵃ

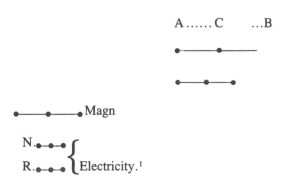

2 p ⁻4

Before I left Germany in 1799, I procured from the Nachdrückerᵇ or privileged Book-pirates a thin Octavo of two or at most 3 Sheets, under the name of Kant's Logic—doubtless, published by, or from the Notes of, one of his Lecture-pupils.¹ I highly approved of it, & found indeed

---

ᵃ The book was turned so that the writing is at right angles to the text in the volume
ᵇ A slip for ''Nachdrucker''

1¹ The first diagram, which recurs with variations several times in C's later mss and published writings, represents dynamic polarity; the second represents polarity in ''Magn[etism]'' and in Electricity. The letters should be N and P for ''nega- tive'' and ''positive'': the R is probably a slip.

2¹ A number of ''Logik''s, put together from the notes of students attending Kant's lectures, were circulating by 1800; even this Jäsche edition is considered to be a

nothing to complain of but that still two thirds of the little volume were an accomodation to the old Mumpsimus.[2] This book I have lost; & on receiving the present volume, borrowed from Mr Green, I was at first surprized at beholding my old acquaintance transformed or fatted up, into a goodly Octavo of 232 pages!—My surprize ceased when I turned over the leaves—& I rather felt disposed to thank the Editor for his moderation, as he might so easily by extracts from Kant's various Works have trebled the size.

3   p ⁻4

An advantage great beyond what a regular Scholar unacquainted with the English World as it is now is & has been for the last century can easily appreciate, did the old Logicians, Philologists and Philosophers possess—in that they had either to *ground* the pupil's mind on the appropriate import & use of terms, or might safely presume on readers so grounded by others—. The Self-conceit of ⟨well-cloathed⟩ Sciolism[1] and the consequent only not universal abuse & laxity of words, they had not to struggle with—[2]

3A   pp xx-xxi, marked with a pencil line in the margin | Jäsche's preface

Hierbey bleibt also die Logik *als solche* gänzlich aus dem Spiele; und es hat weder der Critik, noch der Wissenschaftslehre einfallen können — noch wird es überall einer Philosophie, die den transcendentalen Standpunkt von dem blos logischen bestimmt zu unterscheiden weiss, einfallen können—die letzten Gründe des realen, philosophischen Wissens innerhalb des Gebiets der blossen Logik zu suchen und aus einem Satze [a]der Logik, bloss als solchem betrachtet, ein *reales Object* herausklaben zu wollen.[b]

[Logic *as such*, therefore, is here not affected at all; and it could occur neither

[a-b] The pencil marks only this part of the text, at the top of p xxi

compendium and interpretation rather than a text authorized by Kant.

2[2] For the original of "Mumpsimus" as an adherent of old ways and an opponent of reform see BAXTER *Reliquiae* COPY A **44[b]** n 1. The "accommodation" that C notices seems to be to the syllogistic logic as handed down from Aristotle. Since he elsewhere calls Kant "the modern Aristotle, the founder of transcendental logic, and the first scientific analyst of the logical faculty"—*Logic* (*CC*) 268—he is perhaps thinking of the inclusion here of the syllo-

gistic materials in which Kant, like C, took a rather perfunctory interest (cf *TT* 23 Sept 1830).

3[1] Having pretentious superficiality of knowledge (*OED*). C complains of sciolism as a modern epidemic in e.g. *BL* ch 3 (*CC*) I 57.

3[2] C's recurrent complaints about the abuse of words led him to announce in *AR* (1825) vii that one of the goals of his work was to "direct the Reader's attention to the value of the Science of Words, their use and abuse".

to the *Critique* nor to the *Science of Knowledge*—nor will it ever occur to a philosophy capable of distinguishing the transcendental standpoint from the merely logical—to seek the last grounds of knowledge within the domain of mere logic and to pick from a proposition of logic, considered merely as such, a *real object*.]

3B   p xxi, marked with a pencil line in the margin | Continuing **3A** textus

Wer den himmelweiten Unterschied zwischen der eigentlichen (allgemeinen) Logik . . . und der Transcendental-Philosophie . . . bestimmt ins Auge gefasst hat . . . wird daher leicht beurtheilen können, was von *ᵃ*dem neuern Versuche zu halten sey, den Herr *Bardili* neuerdings (in seinem Grundrisse der ersten Logik) unternommen hat, der Logik selbst noch ihr *Prius* auszumachen, in der Erwartung, auf dem Wege dieser Untersuchung zu finden: "ein *reales Object*, entweder durch *sie* (die blosse Logik) gesetzt oder sonst überall keines setzbar; den Schlüssel zum Wesen der Natur entweder durch sie gegeben*ᵇ* oder sonst überall keine Logik und keine Philosophie möglich."

[Anyone who has firmly grasped and never lost sight of the world of difference that lies between (general) logic proper . . . and transcendental philosophy . . . can readily judge what is to be thought of the recent attempt undertaken by Mr. Bardili (in his *Ground-Plan of First Logic*) to determine a *prius* for logic, in the expectation of finding on this road: "a *real object*, either posited by *it* (mere logic) or else none that can be posited at all; the key to nature's essence, either given by *it* or otherwise no logic and no philosophy being possible at all."]

4   p 3, pencil | Introduction

Why might we not adopt the German allgemein, i.e. *all-common*?[1]

5   p 3, pencil

Alle Regeln, nach denen der Verstand verfährt, sind entweder *nothwendig* oder *zufällig*.

[All rules according to which the understanding proceeds are either *necessary* or *contingent*.]

Would not the Terms, Universal and Occasional, be better?[1]

ᵃ Pencil line begins here   *ᵇ* Pencil line ends here, at end of page

4[1] C may be responding to the use of the word on p 2 (where Kant says that "general"—*allgemein*—grammar "is the form of a language as such") or to its recurrence in the volume, as in **3B** and **6** textus. He did adopt it himself, e.g. as "*all-common-ness*" in Asgill **2**.

5[1] C sometimes used "universal" and "necessary" synonymously, e.g. "while the reason gives a necessity or universality to that determination under the condition of the rule", and "Whence then arise the nec-

6 pp 8–10, pencil

Allein richtiger hat *Home* die Aesthetik, *Critik* genannt, da sie keine Regeln *a priori* giebt, die das Urtheil hinreichend bestimmen, wie die Logik, sondern ihre Regeln *a posteriori* hernimmt, und die empirischen Gesetze, nach denen wir das Unvollkommnere und Vollkommnere (Schöne) erkennen, nur durch die Vergleichung allgemeiner macht. . . .

Die Logik ist eine Vernunftwissenschaft nicht der blossen Form, sondern der Materie nach; eine Wissenschaft A PRIORI *von den nothwendigen Gesetzen des Denkens, aber nicht in Ansehung besonderer Gegenstände, sondern aller Gegenstände überhaupt;—also eine Wissenschaft des richtigen Verstandes- und Vernunftgebrauchs überhaupt, aber nicht subjectiv, d.h. nicht nach empirischen (psychologischen) Principien, wie der Verstand denkt, sondern objectiv, d.i. nach Principien* A PRIORI, *wie er denken soll.*

[More correctly, Home has called aesthetics a *Criticism*, since it does not give, as logic does, rules *a priori* that sufficiently determine the judgment but takes up its rules *a posteriori* and generalizes, through comparisons, the empirical laws by which we cognize the less perfect and the perfect (the beautiful). . . . *Logic is a science of reason not only as to mere form but also as to matter; a science a priori of the necessary laws of thinking, not, however, in respect of particular objects but all objects generatim; it is a science, therefore, of the right use of the understanding and of reason as such, not subjectively, i.e. not according to empirical (psychological) principles of how the understanding thinks, but objectively, i.e. according to a priori principles of how it ought to think.*]

I consider this as so far false, that it is true in part only. The principles (as it were, the supporting Skeleton) of Beauty rest on a priori Laws, no less than Logic. The *Kind* is constituted by Laws inherent in the Reason, it is the *degree*, that which enriches the *formalis* into the *formosum*,[1] that calls in the aid of the senses.[2] And even this, the sensuous & sensual Ingredient, must be an *analogon* to the former.

It is not every Agreeable, that can form a component part of Beauty.[3]

---

essary, the permanent, the universal, or the truths having these attributes": *Logic (CC)* 97, 40.

6[1] That which enriches the "pure form" into the "shaped thing".

6[2] The counterpart to this statement appears in *BL* ch 10 (*CC*) I 171: "The first lesson of philosophic discipline is to wean the student's attention from the DEGREES of things, which alone form the vocabulary of common life, and to direct it to the KIND abstracted from *degree*."

6[3] C's most extended discussion of aesthetics, the 1814 essay *On the Principles of Genial Criticism*, argues that the "agreeable" and the "shapely" together constitute the "beautiful": *SW & F (CC)*.

7   pp 78–80, pencil | § 7 (B)

Nur die Schuld der Unwissenheit liegt demnach in den Schranken des
Verstandes; die Schuld des Irrthums haben wir uns selbst beyzumessen.
* Die Natur hat uns zwar viele Kenntnisse versagt, sie lässt uns über so
Manches in einer unvermeidlichen Unwissenheit; aber den Irrthum ver-
ursacht sie doch nicht.

[Only the fault of ignorance, therefore, is due to the limits of the understanding;
the fault of error we have to ascribe to ourselves. * Nature has indeed denied us
much knowledge, leaving us in inevitable ignorance about many things; but she
does not cause error.]

* Is the understanding then (Verstand) a separate agent from the Man
himself? How much more easy it would be to say, that Man errs, not by
the imperfection but by the misuse or non-exertion of his faculties! But
even this does not represent the case fully and fairly: for Nature compels
us in numberless instances to judge according to our present perceptions
modified by our past experience, and in these the limits and imperfection
of our faculties are ⟨sometimes⟩ necessitating Causes of erroneous
judgement—for this plain reason—that the sense of outwardness as a
sense of reality, is a Law of our Nature, & no conclusion of our Judge-
ment.—

8   pp 126–9, pencil | § 10

Unter Wahrscheinlichkeit ist ein Fürwahrhalten aus unzureichenden
Gründen zu verstehen, die aber zu den zureichenden ein grösseres Ver-
hältniss haben, als die Gründe des Gegentheils.—Durch diese Erklä-
rung unterscheiden wir die Wahrscheinlichkeit (*probabilitas*) von der
blossen *Scheinbarkeit* (*verisimilitudo*); einem Fürwahrhalten aus unzu-
reichenden Gründen, in so ferne dieselben grösser sind, als die Gründe
des Gegentheils.

[By probability is to be understood a holding-to-be-true out of insufficient rea-
sons, which, however, bear a greater proportion to the sufficient ones than the
reasons of the opposite. By this explanation we distinguish probability (*proba-
bilitas*) from *verisimilitude* (*verisimilitudo*), a holding-to-be-true out of insuffi-
cient reasons so far as these are greater than the reasons of the opposite.]

This appears to me obscurely stated. I do not question its truth, but it
requires much previous information & explanation to render it applica-
ble. As it is here given, it seems to be no more than that the Probable is
differenced from the Plausible by superiority in the *quality* of the
grounds; while the Plausible rests on the greater number of quantity. If
so, the far simpler Defin? would be—The Pr. is that which *is*, the Pl.

that which only *seems*, likely. But at the best, it is a mere Verbal, or Dictionary, Definition, better suited to Latin and English (or German) Dicts. under the words Probabilis & Plausibilis. I see indeed what Kant *meant*; but I squeak of the *words* in which his meaning is conveyed. But even with regard to the meaning, I cannot help suspecting that philosophic Probability and the mathem. doctrine of Chances are diverse, ἑτερογενη,[1] and therefore incommensurable. The mathem. is useful de quam plurimis to the Statesman, whether of a Kingdom or of an Life-insurance Association and assumes that we know nothing *de singulis*,[2] hence the Committees are obliged to recur to the philosophic Probability in the admission of each member.

9   pp +2–+3

[Pencil notes by Green at the head of p +2:]

⟨1⟩ Difference between an idea and an abstraction: I contains *in* it all it subordinates—A has all subordinates under it but the lower the subordinate in so much the more it contains than the superordinate—

⟨2⟩ *The idea* is *of necessity* involved in all the manifestations—the idea of the *whole* must necessarily involve yᵉ parts—it is the *efficient ground* which is presumed as yᵉ efficient cause of all its products—

If I understand the first ¶ph, there is some ambiguity in the word "contains" in the last line. Let the abstraction be   1. Thing
                                                         2. Organism
                                                         3. Animal &c
Is not the 2 still an Abstraction no less than 1., and 3. no less thatn its Superordinate 2? And how can ~~an~~ one Abstraction *contain* more than another when Abstraction is contra-distinguished from Idea by its not containing any reality?[1] Would it not be more accurate to say, that it increases in distinctness? Approaches more near to the point at which the ~~general~~ universal term passes into a *generic* term, and this becomes co-incident with an abstract (i.e. imperfect) Image, and differing from it only as the *term* is the same sign in the language of Intellect that the Image is in the language of the Sense?—Or might we not say, that each Subordinate becomes less *arbitrary* than [? t] its immediate Super-ordinate?—: Lambert, ~~from~~ in whose Letter to Kant the ¶ 1. originated, had no conception of ¶ 2.[2]—I should shew, first that Abstractions descend

---

8[1] "Of different kinds".
8[2] "In the greatest number of cases . . . in single cases".
9[1] C offers a closely related discussion of the distinction between abstractions and

ideas in *Logic* (*CC*) 62–4.
9[2] The paragraph numbers are those added by C to textus. He refers to the letter from J. H. Lambert (1728–78) to Kant, dated 3 Feb 1766, pub in *VS* II 6.

into Images, or total Impressions; but thant an Idea never passes into an Abstraction and therefore never becomes the equivalent of an Image; and that there is no interspace between Abstr. and Image for the Idea to occupy. Therefore I. and A. are *ipso genere* diverse,[3] and therefore likewise insusceptible einer ausein⟨an⟩dersetzung[4] by opposition or detail of opposite characters or attributes.

Heterogenes can not be opposed, the one to the other.—Ergo, opposita semper unigena.[5]

Opposites must be one in a suppositum—or a Thesis = Antithesis in the Prothesis. Two terms, that have no equation in a common Root, cannot stand in opposition to each other.

The modes of proof are convertible: and it is indifferent, which we take as the first.

10 ⁺5, pencil

After I have ceased dictating, I would be left with Watson & St./[1]

---

[3] Diverse "indeed in kind". The distinction between ideas and images is a recurrent theme, e.g. *SM* (*CC*) 100–2, *Logic* (*CC*) 63.

[4] "Of a discriminating analysis": C explains his interpretation of *auseinandersetzen* in *Logic* (*CC*) 255 and in Böhme **5**, where it is translated "explicate, develope, unfold".

[5] "Therefore, opposites are always of one kind" (see n 3 above)—a principle of polarity, for which see e.g. *Friend* (*CC*) I 94*.

[1] John Watson (c 1799–1827) and Charles Bradshaw Stutfield (fl 1822–53), amanuenses to C esp for the *MS Logic* Jan–Dec 1822: *Logic* (*CC*) xliv, liii–lv.

Die Metaphysik der Sitten in zwey Theilen. Erster Theil. Metaphysische Anfangsgründe der Rechtslehre. Zweyter Theil. Metaphysische Anfangsgründe der Tugendlehre. 2 vols. Königsberg 1797. 8°.

In C's copy the collective title-page and the part-title of Vol I have been bound with Vol II in error.

British Library C 43 b 5

Inscribed on p ⁻5 in each volume: "Lot 402"—i.e. *Green SC* (1880) 402; cf *Grundlegung*. Bibliographical note in pencil I ⁻1. On I xiv (Einleitung) Green has written in pencil: "Distinction of Legality & Morality".

DATE. Probably the summer (Jul–Sept) of 1809, when C's reading of this work was recorded in *CN* III 3558, 3560–2.

COEDITORS. Kathleen Wheeler, Raimonda Modiano.

TEXTUS TRANSLATION. Mary J. Gregor tr *The Doctrine of Virtue* (New York 1964).

1   II 14, and pp ⁺1–⁺2, referring to II 13–14 | *Tugendlehre* Intro § 4

Eben so ist es ein Widerspruch: eines anderen *Vollkommenheit* mir zum Zweck zu machen und mich zu deren Beförderung für verpflichtet zu halten. Denn darin besteht eben die *Vollkommenheit* eines andern Menschen, als einer Person, dass er *selbst* vermögend ist sich seinen Zweck nach seinen eigenen Begriffen von Pflicht zu setzen, und es widerspricht sich, zu fordern (mir zur Pflicht zu machen), dass ich etwas thun soll, was kein anderer als er selbst thun kann.

[In the same way, it is contradictory to say that I make another person's *perfection* my end and consider myself obligated to promote this. For the *perfection* of another man, as a person, consists precisely in *his own* power to adopt his end in accordance with his own concept of duty; and it is self-contradictory to demand that I do (make it my duty to do) what only the other person himself can do.]

* See p. 192.ᵃ

This seems at first view trifling—if not sophistical. For—it may be objected—if it be my Duty to make my own Perfectness my sole final end, to which all other ends are but means, how can it be otherwise than my Duty to make the moral Perfection of my fellow creatures the same? If to make them happy be the best means to this End in their case, so

---

ᵃ I.e. II ⁺1, the verso of the errata sheet which C has numbered in ms "192"

must it be in my own—therefore in both alike my final aim ought to be the realizing of the Kingdom of God on Earth, in myself & all others as far as & in proportion as they lie within my sphere of action & power—and it is my Duty to forward their & my own Happiness not for its own sake principally but as the means of Holiness—. All morality presupposes in the Subject the faculty of regarding itself as an Object—i.e. of placing the first in the ranks of the third Persons, & acting to all as one rank, Me, thee, Him.—.—. But yet Kant is in the right, ⟨&⟩[a] for this reason—that A versus B. C. D, etc can only supply the *means*; the best *means* in his power—what use B. or C will make of such means, he cannot anticipate—therefore these means become perforce A's ultimate end—But A versus A. has the *end* in his own management, & power—& must therefore contemplate that *end* as his exclusive *End* or *Aim*—& his Happiness only conditionally, as far as he finds it promotes that end.—Besides, A has no means of perfecting himself save by Habits of just & beneficent & generous Actions, & therefore—the Happiness of others must be his *End*—for if he thought of it as the means, his actions cease to be disinterested & contradict their own design—a beautiful Instance this of the importance of place & precedence—A + B = AB + BA—But B + A = − A + B − b. That is A is annihilated and B degraded & stripped of its better half—

2   II 39–40 | § 12c

* *Liebe* ist eine Sache der *Empfindung*, nicht des Wollens, und ich kann nicht lieben weil ich *will*, noch weniger aber weil ich *soll*, (zur Liebe genöthigt werden); mithin ist eine *Pflicht zu lieben* ein Unding.

[* *Love* is a matter of *feeling*, not of will, and I cannot love because I *will* to, still less because I *ought* to (i.e. I cannot be necessitated to love). So a *duty to love* is logically impossible.]

* If I say, I doubt this independence of Love on the Will,[1] and doubt even Love's being in its essence merely eine Sache der Empfindung, a mere matter of *feeling*, i.e. a somewhat *found* in us which is not of and from us/ Emp.-(= in sich)-Findung,[2] I mean only that my Thoughts are not distinct much less adequate on the subject—and I am not able to

[a] Obliterated by foxing stain

2[1] C recorded his dissatisfaction with Kant's analysis of the role of the will, especially in love, as early as 1803: *CN* I 1705. In notes associated with this reading of *Metaphysik der Sitten*, he directly contradicts Kant and asserts that love is always in part an act of the will: *CN* III 3562.

2[2] C explains this often-invoked etymology in *C&S* (*CC*) 180: "For all sensibility is a self-finding; whence the German word for sensation or feeling is Empfindung, *i.e.* an *inward finding*."

convey any grounds of my Belief of the Contrary. But the Contrary I *do* believe. What Kant affirms of Man in the state of Adam, an ineffable act of the will choosing evil & which is underneath or within the *consciousness* tho' incarnate in the *conscience*, inasmuch as it must be conceived as taking place in the Homo Νουμενον, not the Homo Φαινομενον³—something like this I conceive of *Love*—in that highest sense of the Word, which Petrarch understood—.⁴ See p. 193.*ᵃ*

3 p ⁺2, referring to II 41

Die Liebe des *Wohlgefallens* (*amor complacentiae*) würde also allein direct seyn. Zu dieser aber (als einer unmittelbar mit der Vorstellung der Existenz eines Gegenstandes verbundenen Lust) eine Pflicht zu haben, d.i. zur Lust woran genöthigt werden zu müssen, ist ein Widerspruch.

[Hence only the love that is mere *affection* (*amor complacentiae*) is direct. But a duty to this kind of love (which is a pleasure joined immediately with the thought of an object's existence) is a contradiction, since one would have to be necessitated to take pleasure in the object.]

P. 41.

This Subject/ of Love, as not only contra-distinguished from Lust, but as disparate even from the personal attachments of Habit and complex associations (sexual desire of A determined exclusively to B. by esteem negatively, & positively by accidents of association, by accidental freedom from other Attachment, and voluntary ⟨act of⟩ recalling of the form of B. become at length an *in*voluntary *Habit* of the Memory: which is the description of the complex passion which passes for *Love* in a vast majority of Instances)—in short, Love as different from Lust, from Friendship, from Affection of Habit, and from the result of all three united in the same Object—of Love therefore, as an *Element*/¹ ⟨this Sub-

---

ᵃ I.e. II ⁺2—p "193" in C's ms numbering

2³ In *Tugendlehre* pt 1 § 3 ("Aufschluss dieser scheinbaren Antinomie") Kant refers to man's double personality as a sensible being endowed with reason (*homo phaenomenon*) through which he "can be determined . . . to actions in the sensible world" and as a "being endowed with *inner freedom* (*homo noumenon*)", and states that moral obligations pertain only to man as *homo noumenon*. For Kant love relates exclusively to man's existence in the world of sense: for C it is connected with man's supersensible and free existence, i.e. his moral being. See 2 n 1 above.

2⁴ Although he annotated (lightly) two copies of Petrarch's Italian poetry, spoke highly of his Latin works, and lectured on him in 1818 (*Lects 1808–1819—CC*—II 86–7), C left no extended commentary on his writings. The reference to him as an authority on spiritual love is in any case conventional.

3¹ In a letter to HCR analysing the deficiencies of WW, C asserts that love is "no more a compound, than Oxygen, tho' like Oxygen, it has an almost universal affinity, and a long & finely graduated Scale of elective Attractions": *CL* III 305. This belief is

ject⟩ is one of the 4 5 or 5 6 Magna mysteria[2] of human Nature [?—]*a*
the Will, the Conscience, connate or adna[te]*a* (angebohrnes)[3] Evil =
original Sin, Identity, Coadunation or spiritual Marriage,[4] Growth and
Progression, and Love. There are two mighty mysteries to begin with
it—Action and Passion (or passive action)—and Love is a Synthesis of
these, in which each is the other—and as it is only *a* Synthesis, or one
of the Syntheses, of Action and Passion, other discoveries must be made
in order to know the principle that individuates this particular Synthe-
sis—for instance, we must master the principle of Individuation in gen-
eral, and then the principle of Personality—Action + Passion = Εγω +
Ουϰ εγω. Εγω = Εγω: Ουϰ εγω = ουϰ εγω—yet Ουϰ εγω = Εγω, and
Εγω = ουϰ εγω[5] by an *act* which is yet a passion = Love: Mysterium
finale.[6]

4   II 64, and p +3, referring to II 64 | "Ethische Elementarlehre" pt 1 § 1

Man kann diesen Widerspruch auch dadurch ins Licht stellen: /?dass
man zeigt, der Verbindende (*auctor obligationis*) könne den Verbunde-
nen (*subjectum obligationis*) jederzeit von der Verbindlichkeit (*terminus
obligationis*) lossprechen?; mithin (wenn beyde ein und dasselbe Subject
sind) er sey an eine Pflicht, die er sich auferlegt, gar nicht gebunden:
welches einen Widerspruch enthält.

a Obliterated by foxing stain

the outcome of many attempts to analyse
love by distinguishing it, as here, from re-
lated feelings: e.g. BROWNE *Religio* 22,
CN II 2130, 2556.

3[2] "Great mysteries".

3[3] Kant uses the word *angebohrnes*,
"inborn, inherent", in the title of *Tugend-
lehre* bk 1 ch 2 sec 1 § 13, in which he
defines conscience as an inner court of jus-
tice (see 4 n 2 below). In Introduction § 12
Kant also refers to conscience and other
moral qualities such as love of one's neigh-
bour and self-esteem as "originally" in
man in as much as he is a moral being. In
the philosophical letters of 1801 C had
sharply taken issue with Locke, in his ac-
count of the origin of ideas, for confusing
"innate" (born *in*) with "connate" (born
at the same time with) (*CL* II 691–3); here
he refines its implications further through
the prepositional prefix "ad-", perhaps
knowing that in physiological use "ad-
nate" meant "congenitally attached to".

3[4] Examples of C's use of "coaduna-

tion" are collected in AURELIUS 46 n 2.

3[5] Action + Passion = "I + Not-I. I
= I: Not-I = not I; yet not I = I, and I =
not-I". That is: Action may be considered
to be "I", and Passion (being acted upon)
as "Not-I"; nevertheless experience shows
us that "not-I" can become "I" and that
"I" can assume the condition of "not-I".
C's Greek terms suggest the threefold
movement proposed in Fichte's *Wissen-
schaftslehre* and summarised in *Logic* (*CC*)
87: (1) Εγω posits itself; (2) Εγω posits
non-εγω; (3) Εγω posits a limited εγω in op-
position to a limited non-εγω.

3[6] Love is "the final mystery". Cf the
passage from *Religio Medici* in BROWNE
Works 44 n 2, "There are wonders in true
affection, it is a body of *Enigmaes*, myster-
ies and riddles, wherein two so become
one, as they both become two"; and C's
comment in the letter to HCR: "One *and*
one = 2; but one cannot be multiplied into
one": *CL* III 305.

[We can also bring this contradiction to light by pointing out /?that the obligating subject (*auctor obligationis*) could always release the obligated subject (*subjectum obligationis*) from the duty (*terminus obligationis*)?. Therefore, if both are one and the same subject, then he would not be bound at all by a duty he imposes on himself, and this involves a contradiction.]

see p. 194[a]

p. 64.—This seems a confusion of juridical general Law ~~of M~~ with the Moral Law—For in the latter how & in what instance can the Auctor Obligationis release the Subjectum Obligationis[1] from the Obligation? Can the Law of Conscience release the Mind from obeying ~~its~~ a Law of conscience? Can God release a creature from the Obligation of obeying his Laws—i.e. infinite Wisdom permit Folly, Holiness Impurity?—[2]

5   II 71 | Pt 1 bk 1 § 1

Of Suicide.[1]

6   II 105 | Pt 1 bk 1 ch 2 sec 2 § 15

* (*Gebet* ist auch nur ein innerlich vor einem Herzenskündiger declarirter Wunsch).

[* (*Prayer* is also only an internal wish declared before a searcher of hearts).]

* I cannot suffer this to pass uncommented ~~es~~ especially as the same is re-asserted at large in the "Religion innerhalb den Grenzen der reinen Vernunft."—It takes for granted that Prayer is not an *act*, but a mere wishing[1]—O! who ever *prayed*, that has not an hundred times felt that

---

4[1] The "Author of the Obligation" and the "Subject of the Obligation", as in textus.

4[2] In his further elaboration of this figure Kant represents conscience as a court of justice within man, in which a lawsuit is conducted before a tribunal. Since the judge cannot be the same as the accused, conscience "will have to suppose someone other than himself to be the judge of his actions", either "a real person or merely an ideal one which reason creates for itself". Since this ideal person must have complete authority if he is to be "all-obligating", and since only God has the authority to present all duties as commands, "conscience must be conceived as the subjective principle of being accountable to God for one's deeds". Conscience therefore does

not release the mind from obeying the law; on the contrary, it leads man to regard "all his duties as divine commands". See § 13 "Von der Pflicht des Menschen gegen sich selbst, als den angebohrnen Richter über sich selbst".

5[1] C is merely translating Kant's heading.

6[1] Kant's view that prayer is "a merely *declared wish* before a being who needs no explanation of the inner disposition of a wishing man" appears in *Die Religion innerhalb der Grenzen der blossen Vernunft* (Königsberg 1794) 302, a passage not annotated by C. In Dec 1817 C told Green that Kant's "remarks on PRAYER in his RELIGION innerhalb d. r. V. are crass, nay vulgar; and as superficial even in psychology as they are low in taste" (*CL* IV 792); he

scarce an act of Life was so difficult as to determine to *pray*? Effective Resolve to Heart-amendment must have commenced, before true Prayer can be uttered—and why call words of Hypocrites or Formalists Prayers?—[2]

also exempts them from the praise given Kant in De Wette 7.

[6²] C adopts a similar position in Book of Common Prayer copy b 29 at n 9.

Metaphysische Anfangsgründe der Naturwissenschaft. 2nd ed. Riga 1787. 8°.

British Library C 126 h 8

DATE. ?1806–1819. Notes appear to have been made on three occasions, **30** being dated Jul 1811 with a reference to an earlier reading "some years ago" and a postscript dated Aug 1819 (as is **33**). The early date may be 1806: see **1** n 2.

COEDITORS. Kathleen Wheeler, Raimonda Modiano.

TEXTUS TRANSLATION. James Ellington tr *Metaphysical Foundations of Natural Science* (New York 1970). Italics have been added to the translation to correspond to italics in C's German text.

1   p 9, referring to pp 7–9 | Ch 1 explication 2 observation 3

Allein, was ist hier die Seite, nach der die Bewegung gerichtet ist? eine Frage, die mit der eine Verwandtschaft hat, worauf beruht der innere Unterschied der Schnecken; die sonst ähnlich und so gar gleich, aber davon eine Species rechts, die andere links gewunden ist; oder des Windens der Schwerdthohnen und des Hopfens, deren die erstere wie ein Propfenzieher, oder, wie die Seeleute es ausdrücken würden, *wider die Sonne*, der andere *mit der Sonne* um ihre Stange laufen? ein Begriff, der sich zwar construiren, aber, als Begriff, für sich durch allgemeine Merkmale und der discursiven Erkenntnissart gar nicht deutlich machen lässt. . . . Ich habe anderwerts gezeigt, dass, da sich dieser Unterschied war in der Anschauung geben, aber gar nicht auf deutliche Begriffe bringen, mithin nicht verständlich erklären (*dari, non intelligi*) lässt, er einen guten bestätigenden Beweisgrund zu dem Satze abgebe: dass der Raum überhaupt nicht zu den Eigenschaften oder Verhältnissen *der Dinge an sich selbst* . . . sondern blos zu der subjectiven Form unserer sinnlichen Anschauung von Dingen oder Verhältnissen, die uns, nach dem, was sie an sich seyn mögen, völlig unbekannt bleiben, gehöre.

[But what is here the side toward which the motion is directed? This question is related to the following one: upon what rests the internal difference of spirals which are otherwise similar and even equal, except that one species winds to the right and the other to the left? Or upon what rests the winding of pole beans and of hops, the former running around its pole like a corkscrew, or, as sailors would express it, *against the sun*, the latter running around its pole *with the sun*? The concept of this internal difference is one that indeed admits of being constructed, but as concept does not at all admit of being clarified by universal marks in the discursive mode of cognition. . . . I have elsewhere pointed out that since this difference admits indeed of being given in intuition, but does not at all admit of being brought to clear concepts and therefore of being intelligibly explicated (["given, not understood"]), it affords a good confirmative ground of proof for the proposition that space in general does not belong to the properties or relations of *things in themselves* . . . but belongs merely to the subjective form of our sensible intuition of things or relations, which must remain wholly unknown to us as regards what they may be in themselves.]

But there must be a cause ab extra,[1] why I see this Hop that, the Beans in the opposite direction.[2] What does this mean? We see nothing in itself, but only by its action on us modified by our own laws of Perception. K. should have shewn *how* our "subjective Form of sensuous Intuition" came to be called into action. To common minds the facts would appear instances in proof of the reality, = objectivity, of Space.—

2   p 20, pencil | Expl 5 prop 1 proof

Erster Fall. Da zwey Bewegungen *in eben derselben Linie und Richtung* einem und demselben Puncte zugleich zukommen.

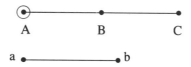

Es sollen in einer Geschwindigkeit der Bewegung zwey Geschwindigkeiten AB und ab als enthalten vorgestellt werden. Man nehme diese Geschwindigkeiten <u>für diesmal als gleich</u> an, so dass AB = ab ist, so sage ich, sie können <u>in einem und demselben Raum</u>, (dem absoluten oder dem relativen) an demselben Puncte nicht zugleich vorgestellt werden. Denn, weil die Linien AB und ab, welche die Geschwindigkeiten bezeichnen, eigentlich die Räume sind, welche sie in gleichen Zeiten durchlaufen, so würde die Zusammensetzung dieser Räume AB und ab = BC, mithin die Linie AC, als die Summe der Räume, die Summe beider Geschwindigkeiten ausdrücken müssen. Aber die Theile AB und BC stellen, jede für sich, nicht die Geschwindigkeit = ab vor; denn sie werden nicht in gleicher Zeit wie ab zurückgelegt. Also stellt auch die doppelte Linie AC, die in derselben Zeit zurückgelegt wird, wie die

1[1] "From without".

1[2] Kant uses the illustration of the hop and the runner bean elsewhere, but it seems   highly probable that it was from this work that C derived it to use in a letter of 1806 (*CL* II 1193) and in *Logic* (*CC*) 161.

Linie ab, nicht die zwiefache Geschwindigkeit der letztern vor, welches doch verlangt wurde. Also lässt sich die Zusammensetzung zweyer Geschwindigkeiten in einer Richtung *in demselben Raume* nicht anschaulich darstellen.

Dagegen, wenn der Körper A mit der Geschwindigkeit AB im absoluten Raume als bewegt vorgestellt wird, und ich gebe überdem dem relativen Raume eine Geschwindigkeit ab = AB in entgegengesetzter Richtung ba = CB, so ist dieses eben dasselbe, als ob ich die letztere Geschwindigkeit dem Körper in der Richtung AB ertheilt hätte (Grundsatz I). Der Körper bewegt sich aber alsdenn in derselben Zeit durch die Summe der Linien AB und BC = 2ab in welcher er die Linie ab = AB allein würde zurückgelegt haben, und seine Geschwindigkeit ist doch als die Summe der zweyen gleichen Geschwindigkeiten AB und ab vorgestellt, welches das ist, was verlangt wurde.

[*First Case*. Two motions *in the same line and direction* belong simultaneously to one and the same point.

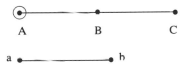

Let two velocities AB and ab be represented as contained in one velocity of the motion. Let these velocities be assumed for the time being to be equal, AB = ab; in this case I assert that they cannot be represented simultaneously at the same point in one and the same space (whether absolute or relative). For inasmuch as the lines AB and ab, which denote the velocities, are, strictly speaking, the spaces which are traversed in equal times; so the composition of these spaces AB and ab = BC, and hence the line AC (as the sum of the spaces), must express the sum of both velocities. But the parts AB and BC do not, individually, represent the velocity = ab; for they are not traversed in the same time as ab. Hence the double line AC, which is traversed in the same time as the line ab, does not represent the double velocity of the latter, as was nevertheless required. Hence the composition of two velocities in one direction *in the same space* cannot be represented intuitively.

On the other hand, if I represent the body A as moved in absolute space with the velocity AB and in addition I give to the relative space a velocity ab = AB in the opposite direction ba = CB, then this is the same as my having given the latter velocity to the body in the direction AB (Principle). But the body in this case moves in the same time through the sum of the lines AB and BC, their sum being equal to 2ab, and in this time it would have traversed the line ab = AB only; and yet its velocity is represented as the sum of the two equal velocities AB and ab, which is what was required.]

But this is a mere contradiction: two velocities in one, both being the same, is nonsensical confusion of abstracts with Concretes—Just as if I should say that two miles, one the right hand side of the road and the other on the left, were *contained* in the Mile in the middle of the road. Here seems a subreption of + in =; or A B = a b confounded with A B + a b.

3 p 21, pencil | **2** textus

Seven times have I read this "Erster Fall"[1] over; and am still in the Dark. If AB = ab, and if ab = BC, how can AB by itself, and BC by itself be *not* = ab? What does "sie" stand for?[a] For *both*? But what then is the meaning of "jede für sich"?[2]

4 p 21, pencil | **2** textus

* AB und ab = BC[b] (mithin —— Räume) die Summe &c—[c1]
* a certain colloquial carelessness of expression, with a neglect of the helps suppliable by punctuation and other marks not seldom renders Kant's sentences puzzling. Thus = so often contains the verb "ist" or "seyn",[2] that I was puzzled—whereas a mere AB und ab (= BC) would have made all plain.

5 pp ⁻4–⁻3, referring to pp 20–1 | **2** textus

P. 20. I have seldom been so much at a loss to discover, whether a passage has baffled my comprehension from my own Obtuseness or from the infinitesimal quantum of the meaning itself, as in this Erster Fall. After twice seven readings, I might say Spellings, it still seems to resemble a grave attempt to prove that you cannot ⟨conceive⟩ one Man's Pain or Pleasure on the quotient of the Pains or Pleasure of two men, ⟨viz. himself and another.⟩ How ⟨indeed⟩ *should* that which consists in ⟨a⟩ *degrees of a* & not in ~~the~~ an aggregate of partible quantities ⟨i.e. quantitas intensiva ✻ q. extensiva⟩[1] be conceived as made up of ⟨such⟩

---

[a] The note to this point is written in the head-margin, continuing down the outer margin. At "stand for" C has written "*", and continued the note with "*" below the first paragraph of **4** in the outer margin

[b] The formula "ab = BC" is circled by C

[c] The first sentence, "AB . . . Summe &c—", is written in the space between the body of **3** and the continuation of it and was therefore presumably written before **3**. The first sentence is preceded by "*", which is picked up by the remainder of **4** written in the foot-margin

3[1] "First case": in **2** textus.

3[2] In **2** textus, *sie* (they) and "individually" or "each for itself".

4[1] C is objecting to a specific passage in **2** textus, ". . . AB and ab = BC, and hence the line AC (as the sum of the

spaces) . . .".

4[2] I.e. "is" or "to be".

5[1] I.e. "intensive quantity as contrary to extensive quantity". The "contrary to" symbol is employed and explained in e.g. JOANNES **4**. The distinction itself comes

quantities? Now velocity is an *act* not a *thing*—an act, the degree of which is measurable only ⟨either⟩ by its effect, i.e. the force with which it impels ~~an~~ or impedes another Object—and which is here excluded—or by the *appearance*,—but the very word, appearance, implies a different space from that in which the body moves. But in this case I can find nothing more than—first, you cannot imagine two motions to be one motion, but only one motion twice as quick as another; but you can *fancy* one motion, ⟨which you do not see⟩ moving ~~with~~ in the opposite direction to another which you *do* see, with the same velocity, and you *know* that the latter will *appear* to move with the velocity of both.—But even so the consequence is *presented* intellectively, not pictorially.—I see, however, the nature of the service which Geometry may afford—it can present to the imagination a truth in itself not imaginable by an imaginable Substitute which being *einerley*, i.e. equal to or all *as* one with, the same as *if* it were the same as, the truth itself; Any consequences drawn from the one may with certainty be attributed to*ᵃ* other.[2] We do not always acquire hereby a better *in*sight into the truth; but we can always better make use of it.

P.S.*ᵇ* Had I read on to p. 26,[3] I should have found that I was in the right, and had understood p. 20, 21.[4] However, I do not regret this: for it gives me some confidence in my own ~~comprehensive powers~~ capability of what's what in questions of Lines &c—: and I still think Kant's Proof extremely confused and most obscurely expressed—still am in the dark as to the sentence (p. 21, l. 6) "Aber die Theile AB und BC*ɟ* stellen, jede für sich, *nicht* die Geschw: = ab vor: denn sie werden nicht in gleicher Zeit wie a b zurückgelegt."[5]—compared with the "Geschw: AB = Geschw: ab and BC = AB."[6]—Of course then BC = ab. . . . How then can it be said, that ⟨neither⟩ B.C. für sich, nor AB. für sich[7] is equal to ab?—

ᵃ A slip for "to the"   *ᵇ* The postscript is written in different ink and pen from the body of the note

from Kant, e.g. in this work, in Observation 2, p 26.

5[2] C's effort to interpret this work as proposing geometrical *metaphors* for natural laws is further recorded in **33** and **34** below.

5[3] C refers to Anmerkung 1 to Lehrsatz (Erklärung 5) (Observation 1 to Proposition of Explication 5) on the nature of geometrical construction and the sense in which Kant speaks of two velocities as one. Geometrical construction is based on the assumption that two combined motions are identical or are completely congruous with a third motion, not—which would be a mechanical explanation—that two motions actually produce a third motion. See **9** textus below.

5[4] I.e. 2 textus.

5[5] C is quoting **2** textus: "But the parts AB and BC . . .".

5[6] Here C paraphrases **2** textus, "Velocity AB = Velocity ab and BC = AB."

5[7] "For itself", alluding to the phrase

6 pp ⁻3⁻⁻2, referring to p 30 | Observ 3

Hat jemand Lust die gedachten drey Theile des allgemeinen phoronom-
ischen Lehrsatzes an das Schema der Eintheilung aller reinen Verstan-
desbegriffe, namentlich hiere der des Begriffs der *Grösse* zu halten, so
wird er bemerken: dass, da der Begriff einer Grösse jederzeit den der
Zusammensetzung des Gleichartigen enthält, die Lehre der Zusammen-
setzung der Bewegungen zugleich die reine Grössenlehre derselben sey,
und zwar nach allen drey Momenten, die der Raum an die Hand giebt,
der *Einheit* der Linie und Richtung, der *Vielheit* der Richtungen in einer
und derselben Linie, endlich der *Allheit* der Richtungen sowol, als der
Linien, nach denen die Bewegung geschehen mag, welches die Bestim-
mung aller möglichen Bewegung als eines Quantum enthält, wiewohl
die Quantität derselben (an einem beweglichen Puncte) blos in der Ge-
schwindigkeit besteht. Diese Bemerkung hat nur in der Transcendental-
philosophie ihren Nutzen.

[If anyone wants to connect the aforementioned three parts of the phoronomic
proposition with the schema of the division of all pure concepts of the under-
standing, namely, with that of the division of the concept of *quantity*, he will
observe the following. Since the concept of quantity always contains the concept
of the composition of the homogeneous, the doctrine of the composition of mo-
tions is at the same time the pure doctrine of quantity therein. And indeed this
doctrine according to all three moments furnished by space, namely, the *unity*
of line and direction, the *plurality* of directions in one and the same line, and
finally the *totality* of directions as well as of lines, according to which the motion
can take place, contains the determination of all possible motion as quantum,
although motion's quantity (in a movable point) consists merely in velocity.
This observation is useful only in transcendental philosophy.]

P. 30. The whole of Phoronomy[1] therefore consists in the demonstration
of the more per se evident fact, that one motion cannot be pictured as
two or more; but that you may picture two or more motions which shall
be equivalent to some one, or of which some one line of Motion shall
be the phænomenal exponent, perceived or imagined. Whether this does
not include or suppose a dynamic parents producing a common Off-
spring, i.e. whether Phoronomy does not clandestinely anticipate the 3
other branches as its *ground*,[2] we leave undiscussed at present: content
to derive this *logical* advantage, that a state of material existence may

---

jede für sich ("individually") in **2** textus,
noted particularly in **3**.

  6[1] Phoronomy, the subject of this sec-
tion of the work, is defined by Kant himself
on p 29 as "pure doctrine of the quantity of
motion".

6[2] The following three sections—"Dy-
namics", "Mechanics", and "Phenome-
nology"—treat the concept of matter from
the viewpoint of quality, relation, and mo-
dality.

be conceived prior to that by which xy is defined as filling (*erfüllend*) Space[3]—viz. ∴ᵃ as having *outward* relations, = relations to Space. I say "logical": because in Logic the mind itself being the Agent throughout does not take itself into question in any one part. It is a Teller which does not count itself; but considers all alike as *Objective*, because all alike is in fact *subjective*. —Now the Patient, required in all dynamic or generative act,ᵇ is in this instance, the mind's own recipiency or receptivity: consequently, left out of the Calculation—/—and Kant is justified in *prefixing* Phoronomy—and this indeed is the true sense of pure Geometry; or the Logic of the Constructive Imagination. Kant was in very *veryty*[4] a GREAT man! My only doubt at present is, whether *Motion* is not equally a product of the Mind with the rest—whether it need be ~~deemed~~ derived *empirically*, by any real difference from Figure, Space, & Time.[5]

7   p ⁻1, referring to p 32 | Ch 2 expl 1 observ

. . . die Materie hier nicht so betrachtet wird, wie sie widersteht, *wenn sie aus ihrem Orte getrieben* und also selbst bewegt werden soll . . . sondern wenn blos der *Raum* ihrer eigenen Ausdehnung *verringert* werden soll. Man bedient sich des Worts: einen *Raum einnehmen*, d.i. in allem Puncten desselben unmittelbar gegenwärtig seyn, um die *Ausdehnung* eines Dinges in Raume dadurch zu bezeichnen. Weil aber in diesem Begriffe nicht bestimmt ist, welche Wirkung oder ob gar überall eine Wirkung aus dieser Gegenwart entspringe, ob andern zu widerstehen, die hineinzudringen bestrebt seyn, oder ob es blos einen Raum ohne Materie bedeute, so fern er ein Inbegriff mehrerer Räume ist, wie man von jeder geometrischen Figur sagen kann, sie nimmt einen Raum ein (sie ist ausgedehnt), oder ob wol gar im Raume etwas sey, was ein anderes bewegliche nöthigt, tiefer in denselben einzudringen (andere anzieht), weil, sage ich, durch den Begriff des Einnehmens eines Raumes dieses alles unbestimmt ist: so ist *einen Raum erfüllen*, eine nähere Bestimmung des Begriffs: einen Raum *einnehmen*.

[. . . matter is not here considered as resisting *when it is driven from its place*

ᵃ Symbol for "therefore"   ᵇ A slip for "acts"?

6³ In "Dynamics" Kant defines matter as that which fills a space: see **7** textus below. There is therefore "logical advantage" in examining Phoronomy before being committed to that definition.

6⁴ C's idiosyncratic spelling of "verity", perhaps intended for intensification.

6⁵ Cf *CN* I 1771 (Dec 1803): "Of course, I am speaking of Motion psychologically, not physically—What it is in us, not what the supposed mundane Cause may be.—I believe, that what we call *motion* is our consciousness of motion, arising from the interruption of motion . . .".

and is thus itself moved . . . but only when the *space* of its own extension is to
be *diminished*. One uses the words "to occupy a space" . . . in order to indicate
thereby the *extension* of a thing in space. But there is not determined in this
concept what action, or whether any action at all, arises from this presence as it
resists other presences that try to press into it; or whether this concept signifies
merely a space without matter insofar as such a space is a sum total of several
spaces, just as one can say of every geometrical figure that it occupies a space
(it is extended); or even whether there is something in space necessitating an-
other movable to penetrate deeper into this something (attracting others). Inas-
much, I say, as all of this is undetermined in the concept of occupying a space,
"to fill a space" is therefore a closer determination of the concept "to occupy a
space".]

P. 32. A space occupying, or *taking up*, or (in the German phrase) *taking
in*, a space is so very near nonsense, that I hesitate in admitting its ⟨log-
ical⟩ legitimacy even as an abstraction. Geometrical figures have an *ob-
jective* reality, I grant; but then they are only *subjectively* objective, and
can not even be thought of but as theorems or products of ~~the~~ mind *in*
the mind. Now Matter must be that which appears and is contemplated
as *outward*. It is manifest as opposed to Spirit or Power, which is man-
ifest*ed*, cannot *appear* itself but is ⟨either self-⟩ known (= mind) or is
inferred from its representative.[1]—I do not therefore see the necessity
any more than I can admit the prop*é*riety, of giving the name, matter, to
a portion of empty Space, or of treating *a* space as an aggregate of
spaces, or of talking of "a *point* of space", the ⟨absolute⟩ negation of
Punctuality being the essential Character of Space. For I can readily
conceive a matter present ~~in~~ throughout a given space and, so far *taking
it in* or existing in it, without at the same time exclusively *filling* it—
which latter added to the former constitutes Body: i.e. Matter + Spirit
or rather perhaps M = Sp. + Sp. = Matter.

8 p 37, pencil; continued in pencil pp 36–7, and in ink pp +2–+5 | Expl 2 prop 2 note 1

?* Die expansive Kraft einer Materie nennt man auch *Elasticität*. Da
nun jene der Grund ist, worauf die Erfüllung des Raumes, als eine we-
sentliche Eigenschaft aller Materie, beruht, so muss diese Elasticität *ur-
sprünglich* heissen; weil sie von keiner anderen Eigenschaft der Materie
abgeleitet werden kann. Alle Materie ist demnach ursprünglich elas-
tisch.

[?* The expansive force of matter is also called *elasticity*. Now, since this force
is the basis upon which rests the filling of space as an essential property of all
matter, this elasticity must be termed *original*, because it cannot be derived from
any other property of matter. All matter is, accordingly, originally elastic.]

7[1] C elaborates this objection in **8** below.

* By Elastic I have always understood a tendency to re-expand combined with a *compressibility*—a passio motûs[1] followed by a re-action on itself, or a *suspensible* expansive force without destruction.[a] But Kant's πρωτον ψευδος[2] seems to me to lie in his definitions of *matter*, both the phoronomic and the dynamic: in the former assuming ⟨moveable⟩ *points* of Space = contrad. in terminis,[3] and then calling them *matter* = a misnomer: in the latter making repulsive expansion an essential property of *all matter* and thus confounding matter with Body, or at least with *material substance*.[b]

We must, in order to preclude all confusion and *equivocation, distinguish the terms Spirit (or power), Mind, Soul, Matter, Material Substance, and Body.[4]

Spirit = that which cannot *appear* but thro' the medium of a representative is manifested ⟨or inferred⟩

Mind = that which is self-known and may be inferred—but cannot appear. = Sp. self-known.

Soul = Spirit as the principle of Individuality. (Corollary. Rational Soul = Mind + Individuality.[)]

Matter: = that which simply appears, a subject having no other predicate than "to appear." Matter therefore is = φαινομενον ψιλον.[5] PHÆNOMENON.

Material substance = a subject, ~~mat~~ of which "to appear" is a predicate but not the only Predicable, so however that fixibility be denied—i.e. when the term is meant to be distinguished from Body:—but when from matter only, and namely so that all MS is M, but not all M. be MS; all Body be MS, but not all MS be B—then (—and this is the true order ~~of~~ in an ascending Series)—we may define

* By Equivocation I mean the confusion of two or more different Meanings in the same term.[c]

[a] Here C has written "Pass to the opposite page (36) Note *" and has begun the next paragraph with "*"

[b] Here C has written "Turn to the second blank Leaf, p. 1; at the end of this Volume = II p: 37", and resumed the note on p +3 with "II p. 37.—continued from the pencil note at p. 37, 36, and (again) 37.—"

[c] C's footnote is written on the otherwise blank p +2 opposite the place in the note it refers to

8[1] An "Experience of motion".

8[2] "Fundamental error": C's frequent use of this phrase is analysed in BAXTER *Reliquiae* COPY B 92 n 1.

8[3] A contradiction "in terms". See 7 above.

8[4] C made many attempts to desynony-mise these terms: in *BL* ch 12 (*CC*) I 234–5, he included most of them in a list of terms that "*include* all the difficulties, which the human mind can propose for solution"; *SM* (*CC*) 81 and n 2 give practical examples.

8[5] "Mere appearance".

Material Substance = Phænomenon Actuale,[6] o̶r̶ M + yx—An appearance, not adequately defined by the predicate, Apparency.
Body = Phænomenon actuale *ponderabile*, or perhaps Phænomenon reale.[7] M + yxz

In Physics we have no proper concern with Mind and Soul, which may therefore be removed: and Spirit we may take inclusively in MS and Body, as the yx and yxz which is + (*more than*) M.—But in Zöics[8] we must find a definition for Life as $Sp._2{}^a$—whether it be, 1. = Spirit containing in itself the power (or productivity) of the form in which it i̶n̶d̶i̶v̶i̶d̶u̶a̶l̶i̶z̶e̶s̶ ̶i̶t̶s̶e̶l̶f̶ ̶a̶n̶d̶ manifests itself—or—2.—the source of the manifesting form, in which it individualizes itself—or 3.—in which it manifests its own individuality. The problem or question is: whether the 3rd as containing the 1st and 2nd be affirmable of all Life; or whether each severally appertains to a kind of Life;—or whether the first implies the second, but not the third; and lastly whether the third be not Life = Soul, or the Link between Life and the Rational Soul, this latter being = Life + Mind + Individuality.—

But to return to Physics:—it is sufficient that we distinguish M. M_2. M_3.—M_3 or Body ⟨ = phænomenon reale,⟩ containing its own properties and capable of being contemplated as subsisting by itself. M_2 or Material Substance = phænomenon Actuale, having properties in itself, but only contemplable as [? s̶u̶b̶j̶] existing in *another* yet not as a property of the latter, but itself remaining another. Example. Electricity, and (in the theory of the French Chemists) Calorique.[9]

M_1 Phænomenon, sensu universali physico—T̶h̶e̶ ̶c̶o̶n̶d̶i̶t̶i̶o̶ ̶a̶s̶s̶u̶m̶p̶t̶i̶o̶ Conditio universaliter assumenda o̶f̶ Mundi sensibilis even as Spirit is the universal subpositum or subponendum. Mundi sensibilis hic subsumptio, ea co-assumptio sine quibus Mund. Sens. omnino non concipi potest.—[10]

---

a Written "Sp.$^{(2}$", and below "M$^{(1}$, M$^{(2}$"; printed "Sp.$_2$ . . . M$_1$, M$_2$" to avoid confusion with footnote indicators

8[6] "Actual appearance".

8[7] An "actual *weighable* Appearance", or perhaps a "real Appearance". For the distinction between actual and real see also KANT *VS* COPY C 8 and e.g. *C&S (CC)* 233–4.

8[8] C's coinage for "life sciences": in a letter of 1818 he proposes "Zoic" and "azoic" sciences, respectively those with and without "the presence of life": *CL* IV 863.

8[9] A term introduced by the French reformers of the chemical nomenclature in 1787 to denote a material substance (commonly thought of as an elastic fluid) to which the phenomena of heat and repulsion were attributed. See the succinct historical note about it in *CN* IV 5144n.

8[10] M_1—M in the prime sense, i.e. Matter—is "Appearance in a universal physical sense—the Condition universally assumed of the sensible World" even as Spirit is the universal "*sup*position or what is universally to be *sup*posed. This *sub*-

Matter = Verb impersonal of the sensible World = videtur)(est.
Materiaé = Participle = existens.
Body = Noun Substantive = ⟨Res, sive⟩ Phænomenon subsistens.[11]

Or we might (and perhaps still more aptly) treat Nature as a language the parts of speech of which are all Verbs, the infinitive moods however becoming Substantives,[12] or at least capable of being construed as such—and then we should have

Body = Verb substantive = subsistit
Material = Verb ~~transitive~~ mediæ vocis = existit, se manifestat
Matter = Verb impersonal = videtur[13] and construed *relatively* or interdependently as forming a sentenc~~ye~~
B = Noun Substantive, το ειναι, hoc Esse.[14]
M = Verb neuter
MS = Verb transitive

9 pp 39–40, pencil | Prop 3

Die Materie kann ins Unendliche zusammengedrückt, aber niemals von einer Materie, wie gross auch die drückende Kraft derselben sey, durchdrungen werden.

Beweis.

Eine ursprüngliche Kraft, womit eine Materie sich über einen gegebenen Raum, den sie einnimmt, allerwärts auszudehnen trachtet, muss, in einen kleineren Raum eingeschlossen, grösser, und, in einen unendlich kleinen Raum zusammengepresst, unendlich seyn. Nun kann für gegebene ausdehnende Kraft der Materie eine grössere zusammendrückende gefunden werden, die diese in einen engeren Raum zwingt, und so ins Unendliche; welches das Erste war. Zum Durchdringen der Materie aber würde eine Zusammentreibung derselben in einen unendlich kleinen Raum, mithin eine unendlich zusammendrückende Kraft erfodert,

---

sumption of the sensible world is that co-assumption [of elements] without which the Sensible World is altogether beyond conceiving."

8[11] Matter—that which "is seen" as distinguished from that which "is"; Material—that which "is existing"; Body—"a Thing, or a subsisting Appearance".

8[12] The primacy of the verb in C's speculations about universal grammar appears in e.g. *Logic (CC)* 16–19.

8[13] Body . . . "subsists"; Material (Verb "in the middle voice", i.e. reflexive) "exists, manifests itself"; Matter . . . "is seen (appears)".

8[14] "The being, this Being"—in both phrases the infinitive ("to be"), its status as a noun established in the Greek by the definite article, and in the Latin by *hoc* for want of a definite article in that language. For the special importance to C of the verb ειμί (I am) see IRVING *Sermons* 1 n 3.

welche unmöglich ist. Also kann eine Materie durch Zusammendrück-
ung von keiner anderen durchdrungen werden; welches das Zweyte ist.

*[Matter can be compressed to infinity; but it can never be penetrated by other
matter, regardless of how great the pressing force of this other may be.*

Proof
An original force whereby a matter endeavours to extend itself everywhere in
a given space it occupies must be greater when enclosed in a smaller space, and
must be infinite when compressed into an infinitely small space. Now, for any
given extensive force of matter there can be found a greater compressive force
that drives this matter into a smaller space, and so on to infinity; this was the
first point. But in order to penetrate the matter, its compression into an infinitely
small space would be required, and hence an infinitely compressive force would
be required; but such a force is impossible. Consequently, a matter cannot be
penetrated by the compression of any other matter; this is the second point.]

That the *fact* is as it would be if this were the case, I leave unquestioned:
but I do not see the self-evidence & absolute necessity of the Position,
or the utter *absurdity* of the contrary supposition. A high pressure of
danger will turn a Coward into a Hero; but a still higher will ⟨convert⟩ a
Hero into a Coward. To prove the *absence* of *all* analogy in matter to
this—the distance and faintness of the analogy we grant—we must first
prove the indestructibility of Matter, and next that Expansive Power =
Repulsion is—not a property, but—the *constituent* of matter,[1] which is
the same as Lambert's Matter = Solidity, which Kant rejects.[2] What if
the maximum of Resistance passed into Penetrability by the Law of Ex-
tremes meet?[3] I do not contend for the *minimum* of Probability; but
against the axiom of its blank impossibility. And so far Kant, I now see,
coincides with me: but I leapt into this criticism, before I had looked at
the *Anmerkung* that follows[4]—in the true spirit of a *Reviewer*![5]

9[1] Cf **11**, **16**, and **27** below for C's view
that Kant made his concept of matter unsta-
ble by representing repulsion and attraction
both as forces that constitute matter and as
"properties" of matter; this implies that
matter does not come into being by virtue
of the powers but already exists as a consti-
tuted entity, "as a datum, the subject of the
powers".

9[2] In ch 2 (pp 33–4) Kant contests Lam-
bert's notion (naming its author) that the
essential property of matter is solidity, ar-
guing that matter fills a space not by its
mere existence, but by a special moving
force, the force of repulsion.

9[3] For this favourite paradox see e.g.

BLANCO WHITE *Practical Evidence* **9** n 2.

9[4] Kant—anticipating C's objection—
explains in the Observation (pp 39–40) that
he has assumed from the beginning that the
more the expansive force would be com-
pressed, the more it would repel, and ex-
plains in what areas this assumption would
not apply. See also **10** textus below.

9[5] C's objections to the practices of re-
viewers are set out most systematically in
BL, but typical advice against their moral
effect appears in H. COLERIDGE **24**, where
he refers to "the constant itch to be witty—
which always implies a want of faith in the
interest of the Matter itself, of which he is
treating".

10   p 46 | Prop 4 observ 1

Durch den obigen Beweis aber ist dem Monadisten diese Ausflucht gänzlich benommen. Denn daraus ist klar: dass in einem erfülleten Raume kein Punct seyn könne, der nicht selbst nach allen Seiten Zurückstossung ausübete, so wie er zurückgestossen wird, mithin als ein ausser jedem anderen zurückstossenden Puncte befindliches gegenwirkendes Subject an sich selbst beweglich wäre, und dass die Hypothese eines Puncts, der durch blosse treibende Kraft, und nicht vermittelst anderer gleichfalls zurückstossenden Kräfte, einen Raum erfüllete, gänzlich unmöglich sey. Um dieses und dadurch auch den Beweis des vorhergehende Lehrsatzes anschaulich zu machen nehme man an, A sei der

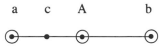

Ort einer Monas in Raume, ab sey der Durchmesser der Sphäre ihrer repulsiven Kraft, mithin aA der Halbmesser derselben, so ist zwischen a, wo dem Eindringen einer äusseren Monade in den Raum, den jene Sphäre einnimmt, widerstanden wird, und dem Mittelpuncte derselben A, ein Punct c anzugeben möglich (laut der unendlichen Theilbarkeit des Raumes). Wenn nun A demjenigen, was in a einzudringen trachtet, widersteht, so muss auch c den beiden Puncten A und a widerstehen. Denn wäre dieses nicht, so würden sie sich einander ungehindert nähern, folglich A und a im Puncte c zusammentreffen, d.i. der Raum würde durchdrungen werden. Also muss in c etwas seyn, was dem Eindringen von A und a widersteht und also die Monas A zurücktreibt, so wie es auch von ihr zurückgetrieben wird. Da nun *Zurücktreiben* ein Bewegen ist, so ist c etwas bewegliches, im Raum mithin Materie, und der Raum zwischen A und a konnte nicht durch die Sphäre der Wirksamkeit einer einzigen Monade angefüllt seyn, also auch nicht der Raum zwischen c und A, und so ins Unendliche.

[By the above proof, however, this subterfuge is completely taken away from the monadist. For from this proof it is clear that in a filled space there can be no point that does not itself on all sides repel in the same way as it is repelled, i.e. as a reacting subject, of itself movable, existing outside of every other repelling point; and it is clear that the hypothesis of a point filling a space by mere driving force and not by means of other likewise repulsive forces is completely impossible. In order to make this fact and thereby also the proof of the preceding

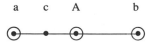

proposition intuitable, let it be assumed that A is the place of a monad in space, that ab is the diameter of the sphere of its repulsive force, and hence that aA is the radius of this sphere. Thus between a, where the penetration of an external monad into the space occupied by the sphere in question is resisted, and A, the centre of the sphere, a point c can be specified (according to the infinite divisibility of space). Now, if A resists whatever endeavours to penetrate into a, then c must resist both the points A and a, for if this were not so, they would approach each other unimpeded; consequently, A and a would meet in the point c, i.e., the space would be penetrated. Therefore, there must be something in c that resists the penetration of A and a, and thus repels the monad A as much as this something is repelled by the monad. Now, since *repulsion* is a motion, c is something movable in space, i.e. matter; and the space between A and a could not be filled by the sphere of the activity of a single monad, neither could the space between c and A, and so on to infinity.]

~~But~~ a = Raum, also "nicht bewegt", also an A nicht nähern kann. Der Beweis scheint mir das zum beweisende vorauszusetzen.[1]

11   pp [+]1, [+]3, referring to pp 45–6 | 10 textus

45. 46. I suspect my own dullness as the cause; but I cannot see the force of this demonstration against Leibnitz's Monad.[1] It strikes me as a mere petitio principii, and that a and c are reasoned on as points of matter, when by the hypothesis they are points of continuous space, therefore immoveable. For how can a point of *Space* approach nearer (nähern) to a contiguous point? and what should incline A (= the monad) to approach to a?

Besides, it is not clear to me that because the being repelled is a motion, therefore the repulsive power is of necessity moveable. The contrary seems involved in the very term, power—for if A exert no power beyond itself, how can it repel or attract? Does not Kant seem to adopt the very principle which he has before confuted, p. 33, as assumed by Lambert—viz—that repulsion = solidity, and ⟨that⟩ solidity is identical with matter?[2] It seems very unfair first to admit attraction and repulsion as two distinct powers added to matter, and not implied in it; and then to reason on these powers as being themselves Matter.[3] Doubtless, no *power* can be the subject of an intuition, einer

---

10[1] But "a = space, therefore 'not moved', therefore cannot approach A. The proof seems to me to presuppose what is to be proved."

11[1] According to Kant, Leibniz's explanation of matter is contradictory in that it relies on both a mechanical and a dynamical concept of matter. A monadist assumes that "matter consists of physical points

each of which (for this reason) has no movable parts"; yet he claims that matter "fills a space by mere repulsive force". "Accordingly, he would compound matter from physically indivisible parts and yet allow it to occupy space in a dynamical way" (p 44).

11[2] See **9** n 2 above.

11[3] See **9** and n 1 above.

sinnlichen Anschauung[4]—and if Kant wished to expose the conse-
quences of all *Realism* in Philosophy, he might have taken a shorter
way. He justly observes, in the Preface, that Difficulties are not Doubts;[5]
but where the whole turns on the *conceivable*, may not one incon-
ceivable fairly balance & neutralize another—and is therefore any
consequence of Monadology more inconceivable or contradictory than
the existence of infinite finite quantities in even the smallest finite
Mass? In short, reject matter at once—or do not quarrel with it.—What
follows, makes Kant's intention plain enough; but I still think his first
proof a———c———A————————b. uncandid—:[6] for he had himself com-
pounded the unknown cause with the phænomenon/ for what is repul-
sion but the unknown Cause of the phænomenon, extension and sepa-
ration? And yet the Proof goes on the rejection of repulsion, as = the
unknown cause, and demands for it the construib(i)lity of a
phænomenon. Certainly, Leibnitz had no right to affirm *a power* not
material as the predicate of a matcrial point—& Boscovich therefore
philosophically rejects the Monad, and retains only the sphere of
power[7]—i.e. an unknown xyz, which construed as a sphere is capable
of affording a mathematical system of phænomena.

12 p 61, pencil | Prop 7 observ 1

Dass man die Möglichkeit der Grundkräfte begreiflich machen sollte, ist
eine ganz unmögliche Forderung; denn sie heissen eben darum Grund-
kräfte, weil sie von keiner anderen abgeleitet, d. i. gar nicht begriffen
werden können. Es ist aber die ursprüngliche Anziehungskraft nicht im
mindesten *unbegreiflicher*, als die ursprüngliche Zurückstossung.

[That the possibility of fundamental forces should be made conceivable is a quite
impossible demand: for they are called fundamental forces precisely because
they cannot be derived from any other force, i.e., they cannot be conceived. But
the original attractive force is not the least bit more *inconceivable* than the orig-
inal repulsion.]

11[4] "A sensible intuition". The signifi-
cance of this phrase is outlined in Kant
C d r V 1 n 3.

11[5] Kant answered a critic of the *Cri-
tique of Pure Reason* in his Preface (p xvii
n), "Thus Newton's system of universal
gravitation is well established, even though
it carries with it the difficulty that one can-
not explain how attraction at a distance is
possible. But difficulties are not doubts."

11[6] 10 textus above.

11[7] The atomic theory of Ruggiero Giu-
seppe Boscovich (1711–87) was attractive
to C because Boscovich described atoms as
points of force rather than as material ob-
jects. C became acquainted with Bosco-
vich's ideas at Cambridge, where he bor-
rowed his work *De solis ac lunae
defectibus* (1760): J. C. C. Mays "Cole-
ridge's Borrowings from the Jesus College
Library, 1791–94" *Transactions of the
Cambridge Bibliographical Society* VIII
(1985). See also *Lects 1795 (CC)* 216n,
CN III 3962.

Be it so in the present instance: and in a system which *begins* with Space and physical Powers defined ex~~pa~~haustively by effects and products solely relative to Space and manifestable in and by Space, so it must be. But I have learnt by experience not to suffer myself to be cowed by the *term*, Grundkraft,[1] and the impossibility of rendering the same comprehensible. The major of the Syllogism I fully admit—Grundkr cannot be explained. But I must look again and again before I admit the minor—A + B are Grundkräfte—and (of course) the Conclusion.

13 p 62, pencil

Der gemeinste Einwurf wider die unmittelbare Wirkung in die Ferne ist: dass eine Materie doch nicht da, *wo sie nicht ist*, unmittelbar wirken könne. Wenn die Erde den Mond unmittelbar treibt, sich ihr zu nähern, so wirkt die Erde auf ein Ding, das viele tausend Meilen von ihr entfernt ist, und dennoch unmittelbar; der Raum zwischen ihr und dem Monde mag auch als völlig leer angesehen werden. *Denn* obgleich zwischen beiden Körpern Materie läge, so thut diese doch nichts zu jener Anziehung. Sie wirkt also an einem Orte, wo sie nicht ist, unmittelbar: etwas was dem Anscheine nach widersprechend ist. Allein es ist so wenig widersprechend, dass man vielmehr sagen kann, ein jedes Ding im Raume wirkt auf ein anderes nur an einem Ort, wo das Wirkende nicht ist. Denn sollte es an demselben Orte, wo es selbst ist, wirken, so würde das Ding, worauf es wirkt, gar nicht *ausser ihm* seyn; denn dieses *Ausserhalb* bedeutet die Gegenwart in einem Orte, darin das andere nicht ist.

[The most common objection to immediate action at a distance is that a matter cannot directly act *where it is not*. When the earth directly influences the moon to approach it, it acts upon a thing many thousand miles removed from it, but nevertheless acts immediately; the space between it and the moon may be regarded as entirely empty, *for* although matter may lie between both bodies, this does not affect the attraction. Therefore, attraction acts directly in a place where it is not—something that seems to be contradictory. But it is so far from being contradictory that one can say, rather, that everything in space acts on another only in a place where the acting thing is not. For if the thing should act in the same place where it is itself, then the thing upon which it acts would not be *outside it*; for "outside" means presence in a place where the other thing is not.]

To the popular Objection, A thing cannot act where it is not, it seems to me sufficient to answer: A Thing is only where it acts. The Obj. confounds the punctual place (Ort) of a Thing with the Thing itself: or still more grossly ~~with~~ the limit of its relative visibility, i.e. its optical Image.

12[1] "Fundamental force": in textus.

14 p ⁺6, referring to p 66, corrected and revised in pencil | Observ 2

Newton sagt (*Cor. 2. Prop. 6. Lib. III. Princip. Phil. N.*) "Wenn der Aether, der irgend ein anderer Körper ohne Schwere wäre, so würde, da jener von jeder anderen Materie doch in nichts, als der Form, unterschieden ist, er nach und nach durch allmälige Veränderung dieser Form in eine Materie von der Art, wie die, so auf Erden die meiste Schwere haben, verwandelt werden können, und diese letztere also umgekehrt durch allmälige Veränderung ihrer Form, alle ihre Schwere verlieren können, welches der Erfahrung zuwider ist &*c.*" Er schloss also selbst nicht den Aether (wieviel weniger andere Materien) vom Gesetze der Anziehung aus. Was konnte ihm denn nun noch für eine Materie übrigbleiben, um durch deren Stoss die Annäherung der Körper zu einander als blosse scheinbare Anziehung anzusehen? Also kann man diesen grossen Stifter der Attractionstheorie nicht als seinen Vorgänger anführen, wenn man sich die Freyheit nimmt, der wahren Anziehung, die dieser behauptete, eine scheinbare zu unterschieben und die *Nothwendigkeit* des Antriebs durch den *Stoss* anzunehmen, um das Phänomen der Annäherung zu erklären.

[Newton says (Cor. 2, Prop. 6, Lib. III, *Princip. Phil. N.*): "If the ether or any other body were without weight, it would, inasmuch as it differs from any other matter in nothing but form, be able to be transformed little by little through a gradual change of this form into a matter of the kind that has the greatest weight on earth; and conversely, this latter by a gradual change of its form would be able to lose all its weight, which is contrary to experience, etc." Thus he did not even exclude the ether (much less other matters) from the law of attraction. What kind of matter, then, could remain for him, by whose impact the approach of bodies to one another could be regarded as mere apparent attraction? Therefore, if we take the liberty of substituting for the true attraction which he asserted, an apparent one, and of assuming the *necessity* of an impulse through *impact* in order to explicate the phenomenon of approach; then we cannot cite this great founder of the theory of attraction as our precursor.]

P. 66. Will it be a fire and faggot Heresy, if I avowed[a] that the logical force in this argument of the great, the ingent.[1] Newton is not as clear to my apprehension as I could wish.—"which is contrary to Experience"—is not this a positive put for a mere negative? Suppose the first Comet to have been descriptively predicted, by Seth: would Cain have been entitled to declare it *contrary* to experience?

The phrase supposes either an eternity of the mundus sensibilis,[2] or

[a] Cancelled in pencil

14[1] From Latin *ingens*, "great".

14[2] The "sensible world"—as in **8** above; the phrase is also prominent in the title of Kant's inaugural address *De mundi sensibilis atque intelligibilis forma et principiis* (in Kᴀɴᴛ *VS* ɪɪ).

that it was created at one moment, with all its existing powers in their now existing relations—consequently not only with the same elementary forces as at present, but with all their syntheses and composite powers. May we not read the Past in the Present? Must not for instan̶t̶ce the Powers of the System have been in a very different period & consequently state of evolution, when the Metals, Gold, Silver &c were formed, from the present? May not the present be truly the *Iron* Age? Newton was uneinig mit sich selbst,[3] because Matter was with him, ⟨in the 1ˢᵗ place⟩ᵃ corpuscula quotquot sunt, erunt, et fuêre[4]—and ⟨secondly,⟩ᵃ these ⟨were⟩ᵃ an inscrutable *Datum.*ᵇ But why need we say more: since the error common to Kant & the Newtonian, is that Gravity is the same power as Attraction.[5] Had Newton seen the distinction, he might then consistently have denied Gravity to be an *essential* property of Matter: if only there were any meaning in the words essential as so applied,[6] or if i̶t̶ᶜ "essential"ᵃ were equivalent to i̶t̶s̶ᶜ theᵃ earliest conceivable functions.

15 p ⁺6, referring to p 69 | Prop 8

Die ursprüngliche Anziehungskraft, worauf selbst die Möglichkeit der Materie, als einer solchen beruht, erstreckt sich im Weltraume von jedem Theile derselben auf jeden andern unmittelbar ins Unendliche.

Beweis.

Weil die ursprüngliche Anziehungskraft zum Wesen der Materie gehört, so kommt sie auch jedem Theil derselben zu, nämlich unmittelbar auch in die Ferne zu wirken. Setzet nun: es sey eine Entfernung, über welche heraus sie sich nicht erstreckte, so würde *diese Begrenzung* der Sphäre ihrer Wirksamkeit entweder auf der innerhalb dieser Sphäre liegenden Materie, oder blos auf der Grösse des *Raumes*, auf welchen sie

---

ᵃ Inserted in pencil   ᵇ Underlined in pencil
ᶜ Cancelled in pencil

14³ "At odds with himself". The phrase is Kant's (var) as he continues to discuss Newton's errors.

14⁴ "The sum total of the little bodies that are, will be, and have been".

14⁵ C noted in a letter to Tulk (12 Jan 1818) Kant's error in assuming two powers only, and mistaking attraction and repulsion for gravity itself, instead of recognising the two poles of gravity, gravity being the "tertium aliquid et majus": *CL* IV 808. C's objection to Kant's concept of gravity may owe something to Schelling's criticism of Kant for equating the force of at-

traction with gravity and for failing to see that gravity is a synthesis of attraction and repulsion. See SCHELLING *Einleitung zu seinem Entwurf eines Systems der Naturphilosophie* (Jena & Leipzig 1799) ii 315–17 and nn, and cf i 82–3 (neither annotated).

14⁶ In *BL* ch 18 (*CC*) II 62 C defines essence as "the principle of *individuation*, the inmost principle of the *possibility*, of any thing, *as* that particular thing". He himself uses "essential" deliberately in **30** below.

diesen Einfluss verbreitet, beruhen. Das Erstere findet nicht statt; denn diese Anziehung ist eine durchdringende Kraft, und wirkt *unmittelbar* in der Entfernung, unerachtet aller dazwischen liegenden Materien, durch jeden Raum, als einen leeren Raum. Das zweite findet gleichfalls nicht statt. Denn, weil eine jede Anziehung eine bewegende Kraft ist, die einen Grad hat, unter dem ins Unendliche noch immer kleinere gedacht werden können: so würde in der grösseren Entfernung zwar ein Grund liegen, den Grad der Attraction, nach dem Maasse der Ausbreitung der Kraft, in umgekehrtem Verhältnisse zu vermindern, niemals aber sie völlig aufzuheben. Da nun also nichts ist, was die Sphäre der Wirksamkeit der ursprünglichen Anziehung jedes Theils der Materie irgendwo begrenzte, so erstreckt sie sich über alle anzugebende Grenzen auf jede andere Materie, mithin im Weltraume ins Unendliche.

[*The original attractive force, upon which the very possibility of matter as such rests, extends itself directly throughout the universe to infinity, from every part of the same to every other part.*

Proof
Because the original attractive force, namely, to act immediately at a distance, belongs to the essence of matter, it also belongs to every part of matter. Now, let it be granted that there is a distance beyond which the force of attraction does not reach; *this limitation* of the sphere of its efficacy would rest either on the matter lying within this sphere or merely on the magnitude of the *space* in which its influence is spread. The first does not take place, for this attraction is a penetrative force and acts *directly* at a distance, in spite of all intervening matters, through every space as an empty space. The second likewise does not take place. For inasmuch as every attraction is a moving force having a degree, beyond which ever smaller degrees to infinity can be thought; in the greater distance there would indeed lie a cause for diminishing the degree of attraction in inverse proportion to the amount of the diffusion of the force, but never for completely destroying it. Now, since there is hence nothing which might anywhere limit the sphere of the efficacy of the original attraction of any part of matter, this attraction reaches out beyond all assignable limits to every other matter, and hence reaches throughout the universe to infinity.]

P. 69. This is a difficulty which Kant does not seem to have surmounted—a Power *acting immediately* thro' all Space as thro' empty Space, and which really acts still at the extremes—& yet decreasing in a proportion to the distance—is very, very strange!—

16   p 70, pencil | Note 2

Da alle gegebene Materie mit einem bestimmten Grade der repulsiven Kraft ihren Raum erfüllen muss, um ein bestimmtes materielles Ding auszumachen, so kann nur eine ursprüngliche Anziehung im Conflict mit der ursprünglichen Zurückstossung einen bestimmten Grad der Erfüllung des Raums, mithin Materie möglich machen; es mag nun seyn, dass der erstere von der eigenen Anziehung der Theile der zusammengedrückten Materie unter einander, oder von der Vereinigung derselben mit der Anziehung aller Weltmaterie herrühre.

[Since all given matter must fill its space with a determinate degree of repulsive force in order to constitute a determinate material thing, only an original attraction in conflict with the original repulsion can make a determinate degree of the filling of space, i.e., matter, possible. Now, it may be that the attraction involved in this determinate degree of the filling of space arises from the individual attraction of the parts of the compressed matter among one another or arises from the union of this compressed matter with the attraction of all the matter of the world.]

A confounded with its grandchild—i.e. the *constituent* Powers with the proper forces (or properties) of the Constitutum.[1]

17   pp 70–1, pencil | Continuing **16** textus

Die ursprüngliche Anziehung ist der Quantität der Materie proportional und erstreckt sich ins Unendliche. Also kann die dem Maasse nach bestimmte Erfüllung eines Raumes durch Materie am Ende nur von der ins Unendliche sich erstreckenden Anziehung derselben bewirkt, und jeder Materie nach dem Maasse ihrer Zurückstossungskraft ertheilt werden.

Die *Wirkung* von der allgemeinen Anziehung, die alle Materie auf alle und in allen Entfernungen unmittelbar ausübt, heisst die *Gravitation*; die Bestrebung in der Richtung der grösseren Gravitation sich zu bewegen, ist die *Schwere*. Die Wirkung von der durchgängigen repulsiven Kraft der Theile jeder gegebenen Materie heisst dieser ihre *ursprüngliche Elasticität*. Diese also und die Schwere machen die einzigen *a priori* einzusehenden allgemeinen Charactere der Materie, jene innerlich, diese in äusseren Verhältnisse aus; denn auf den Gründen beider beruht die Möglichkeit der Materie selbst: *Zusammenhang*, wenn er als die wechselseitige Anziehung der Materie, die lediglich auf die Bedingung der Berührung eingeschränkt ist, erklärt wird, gehört nicht zur Möglichkeit der Materie überhaupt, und kann daher *a priori* als damit verbunden nicht erkannt werden. Diese Eigenschaft würde also nicht metaphysisch, sondern physisch sein, und daher nicht zu unsern gegenwärtigen Betrachtungen gehören.

[The original attraction is proportional to the quantity of the matter and reaches to infinity. Therefore, the determinate degree of the filling of space by matter cannot in the end be brought about without matter's infinitely reaching attrac-

---

16[1] A (i.e. Attraction), a power continuously "constituting", confounded with the properties of the "thing constituted".

tion; such a determinate degree of the filling of space can then be imparted to every matter in accordance with the degree of its repulsive force.

The *action* of universal attraction, which all matter exercises directly on all matter and at all distances, is called *gravitation*; the endeavour to move in the direction of the greater gravitation is *weight*. The action of the universal repulsive force of the parts of every given matter is called its *original elasticity*. Therefore, this elasticity and the aforementioned weight constitute the only *a priori* comprehensible universal characteristics of matter, the former being internal, the latter involving an external relation; for the possibility of matter itself rests upon these two foundations. When *cohesion* is explained as the reciprocal attraction of matter insofar as this attraction is limited solely to the condition of contact, then such cohesion does not belong to the possibility of matter in general and cannot therefore be cognized *a priori* as bound up with matter. This property would hence not be metaphysical but physical, and therefore would not belong to our present considerations.]

But the Metaphysician must at least shew the possibility*ᵃ* of some product in some possible proportion: or of what is he talking? Now if the two opposite forces are equal, how comes it that they do not destroy or suspend at least each the other? This surely should have been explained out of the nature of one or both the forces, or the power of which these are the forces.[1] Besides, tho' in picturative[2] or geometrical construction they can only be represented as motions differenced only by being in opposite directions; yet in Metaph. Kant himself has introduced other most momentous differences, viz. that the one filleds, and the other only acts in the distance, &c.[3]—It seems strange to me that K. should not have suspected (*wittert*) some confusion here.

18   p 71, pencil | 17 textus, "Die Wirkung . . . *Elasticität*."

But the possibility of a greater and a less, in a Power acting immediately at infinite distances, is the point, I want to have proved and explained.

19   p 77, pencil | Observ 2

Ich sehe wol die Schwierigkeit dieser Erklärungsart, der Möglichkeit einer Materie überhaupt, die darin besteht, dass, wenn ein Punct durch repulsive Kraft unmittelbar keinen anderen treiben kann, ohne zugleich den ganzen körperlichen Raum bis zu der gegebenen Entfernung durch

---

ᵃ C wrote "possibilty"

17[1] Schelling similarly attacks Kant's treatment of matter as the product of two powers in SCHELLING *Ideen zu einer Philosophie der Natur* (Landshut 1803) pp 55–7 (not annotated), arguing that the conflict between opposite powers would have no permanence unless there existed a third factor as ground of the identity of the two powers. This third factor is a spiritual principle, higher than a power and free from all physical laws.

17[2] C's nonce-word, not in *OED*.

17[3] In textus.

seine Kraft zu erfüllen, dieser alsdenn, wie zu folgen scheint, mehrere treibende Puncte enthalten müsste, welches der Voraussetzung widerspricht, und oben (Lehrsatz 4.) unter dem Namen einer Sphäre der Zurückstossung des Einfachen im Raume, widerlegt waren. * Es ist aber ein Unterschied zwischen dem Begriffe eines wirklichen Raumes, der gegeben werden kann, und der blossen Idee von einem Raume, der lediglich zur Bestimmung des Verhältnisses gegebener Räume gedacht wird, in der That aber kein Raum ist, zu machen.

[I see well the difficulty of this mode of explicating the possibility of matter in general. This difficulty consists in the fact that if a point cannot directly drive another by repulsive force without at the same time filling the whole corporeal space up to the given distance by its force, then this space must, as seems to follow, contain several repulsive points. This fact contradicts the assumption, but this fact was refuted above (Proposition 4) under the name of a sphere of repulsion of the simple in space. * However, there is a distinction to be made between the concept of an actual space, which can be given, and the mere idea of a space, which is thought only for the determination of the relation of given spaces but which is in fact no space.]

* Exactly as I anticipated—Lehrs. 4 sets up a man of straw—What authorized Kant's assertion, that Leibnitz realized his Space so as to compose it of moveable points?[1] It is a shade on Kant's Character, this eagerness to detract from Leibnitz.

20 p 79, pencil

Wenn es also heisst: die zurückstossenden Kräfte der einander unmittelbar treibenden Theile der Materie stehen in umgekehrtem Verhältnisse der Würfel ihrer Entfernungen, so bedeutet das nur: sie stehen in umgekehrtem Verhältnisse der körperlichen Räume, die man sich zwischen Theilen denkt, die einander dennoch unmittelbar berühren, und deren Entfernung eben darum *unendlich klein* genannt werden muss, damit sie von aller wirklichen Entfernung unterschieden werde.

[When it is said, then, that the repulsive forces of the directly mutually driving parts of matter stand in inverse proportion to the cube of their distances, this means only that they stand in inverse proportion to the corporeal spaces which one thinks of between parts that nevertheless immediately touch one another, and whose distance must just for this reason be termed *infinitely small* in order that such distance may be distinguished from all actual distance.]

Qу What may the Cube of an infinitely small distance amount to? If more than = 0, wherein differs the infinitesimal from real distances?

19[1] This assertion, made pp 50–2, is the culmination of Kant's attack on Leibniz in   · Proposition 4: see also **10** and **11** above.

21   pp 80–1, pencil | General note

Wenn wir nach allen Verhandlungen derselben zurücksehen, so werden wir bemerken: dass darin *zuerst* das *Reelle* in Raume, (sonst genannt das Solide) in der Erfüllung desselben durch *Zurückstossungskraft*, *zweytens* das, was in Ansehung des ersteren, als des eigentlichen Objects unserer äusseren Wahrnehmung, *negativ* ist, nämlich die *Anziehungskraft*, durch welche, so viel an ihr ist, aller Raum würde durchdrungen, mithin das Solide gänzlich aufgehoben werden, *drittens* die *Einschränkung* der ersteren Kraft durch die zweyte und die daher rührende Bestimmung des *Grades* einer Erfüllung des Raumes in Betrachtung gezogen, mithin die *Qualität* der Materie unter den Titeln der Realität, Negation und Limitation, so viel es einer metaphysischen Dynamik zukommt, vollständig abgehandelt worden.

[If we review all our discussions of the metaphysical treatment of matter, we shall observe that in this treatment the following things have been taken into consideration: *first*, the *real* in space (otherwise called the solid) in its filling of space through *repulsive force*, *second*, that which, with regard to the first as the proper object of our external perception, is *negative*, namely, *attractive force*, by which, as far as may be, all space would be penetrated, i.e., the solid would be wholly abolished; *third*, the *limitation* of the first force by the second and the consequent perceptible determination of the *degree* of a filling of space. Hence we observe that the *quality* of matter has been completely dealt with under the moments of reality, negation, and limitation, as much as such a treatment belongs to a metaphysical dynamics.]

Honor and Thanks are due to Kant for this first attempt. Even tho' the success had been less than it is, the Attempt, the Idea, would have demanded the admiration and gratitude of every Philosopher.—The defects may all be traced to the *barren* Dualism of the Reflective System.[1]

22   pp 82–4, pencil | General observ

Denn es kann nach dem ursprünglich verschiedenen Grade der repulsiven Kräfte, auf denen die erste Eigenschaft der Materie, nämlich die, einen Raum zu erfüllen, beruht, ihr Verhältniss zur ursprünglichen Anziehung (es sey einer jeden Materie für sich selbst, oder zur vereinigten Anziehung aller Materie des Universum) unendlich verschieden gedacht werden; weil die Anziehung auf der Menge der Materie in einem gegebenen Raume beruht, da hingegen die expansive Kraft derselben auf dem Grade ihn zu erfüllen, der specifisch sehr unterschieden seyn kann;

21[1] Schelling, who often complained about the dualism of Kant's system, argued that Kant reduces matter to two forces because he operates from "the standpoint of reflection and *analysis*" without reaching the higher standpoint of synthesis: SCHELLING *Einleitung* i 81–2 (not annotated).

(wie etwa dieselbe Quantität Luft in demselben Volumen nach ihrer grösseren oder minderen Erwärmung mehr oder weniger Elasticität beweiset) . . .

[For according to the originally varying degree of repulsive forces, upon which rests the first property of matter, namely, that of filling a space, the relationship of this property to the original attraction (whether to the attraction of every matter of itself, or to the united attraction of all matter in the universe) can be thought of as infinitely diverse. This is because attraction rests on the mass of matter in a given space, while the expansive force of matter rests on the degree to which the space is filled; this degree can be specifically very different (as the same quantity of air in the same volume exhibits more or less elasticity according to its greater or lesser heating).]

But what determines the specific degrees, that at once limit and determine the Attraction: and thus constitute the specific Matters? And does the Attraction *wait* till the Repulsive Expansion has *made ready* the quantum of matter in each given Space?—So vain is the attempt to find in a *Science* the ultimate ground of any other Science. Even Schelling who (with the help of F. Baader)[1] had seen the inadequacy of Kant's *two* Powers as constituting Matter, and had supplied a third as the copula and realization of the two, has yet succeeded no better *in fact*: tho' by *stealing-in* the *empirical* Law of Polarity he has counterfeited a more successful appearance.[2]

23   p 82, pencil | Continuing **22** textus

. . . wovon der allgemeine Grund dieser ist; dass durch wahre Anziehung *alle Theile** der Materie unmittelbar *auf alle Theile* der andern, durch expansive Kraft aber nur die *in der Berührungsfläche* wirken, wobey es einerley ist, ob hinter dieser viel oder wenig von dieser Materie angetroffen werde.

[The general ground involved here is that by true attraction *all parts** of matter act directly *on all parts* of other matter; but by expansive force, only the parts *in the surface of contact* act, and thereby it is all the same whether behind this surface, much or little of this matter is found.]

* But what is meant by Theile, Particles, in a continuous Plenum? And

22[1] Franz Baader (1765–1841), philosopher, medical student, and student of science, two of whose essays were included in JAHRBÜCHER. Schelling refers to Baader's rejection of Kant's two forces in SCHELLING *Einleitung* ii 317n (not annotated).

22[2] This direct reference to Schelling reiterates points made in earlier notes (**14**,

17). Here C alludes to SCHELLING *Einleitung* ii 311 ff, esp 315–17 (not annotated). C's objections to Schelling's *Naturphilosophie* are developed in marginalia to Schelling's works; cf also *CL* IV 873–5, where C describes the "inconsistency Schelling has contrived to hide from himself" by "making all knowlege bi-polar".

if the Parts "behind the Plane of Contact" do not work, how do they resist the Attractive Power, which works immediately on all the Parts?—

24   p 83, pencil | Continuing **23** textus

Hieraus allein entspringt nun schon ein grosser Vortheil für die Naturwissenschaft, weil ihr dadurch die Last abgenommen wird, aus dem Vollen und Leeren eine Welt blos nach der Phantasie zu zimmern, vielmehr alle Räume voll und doch in verschiednem Maasse erfüllt gedacht werden können, wodurch der leere Raum wenigstens seine *Nothwendigkeit* verliert und auf den Werth einer Hypothese zurückgesetzt wird, da er sonst, unter dem Vorwande einer zu Erklärung der verschiedentlichen Grade der Erfüllung des Raums nothwendigen Bedingung, sich des Titels eines Grundsatzes anmassen konnte.

[From all this a great advantage arises for natural science, by its being relieved of the burden of building a world merely according to fancy out of fulness and emptiness. Rather, all spaces can be thought of as full and yet as filled in varying measure. By means of this, empty space at least loses its *necessity* and is reduced to the value of a hypothesis, since otherwise it might claim the title of a principle, under the pretext of being a necessary condition for the explication of the different degrees of the filling of space.]

True! but this is effected by destroying Matter in the former sense: what is not merely subjective being *Spirit*.

25   p 85, pencil

Ein *Körper*, in physischer Bedeutung, ist *eine Materie zwischen bestimmten Grenzen* (die also eine Figur hat).

[A *body*, in the physical signification, is *a matter between determinate boundaries* (and such matter therefore has a figure).]

a doubtful Definition, at best. A finds himself in the midst of Waters, unconscious of any Bounds or Figure. Would he therefore deem them incorporeal? A Fluid has no proper figure: is it therefore not body? But K. had anticipated the true nature of Body in the constitution of his Matter.[1]

26   pp 88–9, pencil

Eine Materie, deren Theile, unerachtet ihres noch so starken Zusammenhanges unter einander, dennoch von jeder noch so kleinen bewegenden Kraft an einander können verschoben werden, ist flüssig.

25[1] C's many attempts to formulate a distinction between "body" and "matter"—as in **8** above—arise from theologi-cal as well as philosophical imperatives: see Irving *Sermons* **29** n 12.

[*A matter whose parts, notwithstanding their strong cohesion among one another, can yet be displaced past one another by every moving force, however small, is fluid.*]

First, this is too much a mere description of a Fluid in terms invented to ~~describe~~ignate the fact. Secondly, I doubt if it would not apply equally well to the opposite—namely, a bason of powders in the maximum of laevigation.[1]—Schelling's is far better: a Fluid = that the parts of which are not distinguishable by figure.[2] But throughout this Work, Kant is less happy in his discriminative definitions than in any other of his Works. It could scarcely be otherwise in the systematic portion of the Volume from the πρωτον ψευδους[a] in the conception of matter;[3] but even in the empirical parts he is less felicitous than usual.

27 pp 103–4, pencil

Diese Nothwendigkeit [des specifischen Unterschieds der Dichtigkeiten] aber beruht darauf, dass die Materie nicht (wie blos mechanische Naturforscher annehmen) durch absolute Undurchdringlichkeit ihren Raum erfüllt, sondern durch repulsive Kraft die ihren Grad hat, der in verschiedenen Materien verschieden seyn kann, und, da er für sich nichts mit der Anziehungskraft, welche der Quantität der Materie gemäss ist, gemein hat, sie bey einerley Anziehungskraft in verschiedenen Materien dem Grade nach als *ursprünglich verschieden* seyn könne, folglich auch der Grad der Ausdehnung dieser Materien bey derselben Quantität der Materie und umgekehrt die Quantität der Materie unter demselben Volumen, d.i. die Dichtigkeit derselben ursprünglich gar grosse specifische Verschiedenheiten zulasse.

[But this necessity [the specific difference of densities] rests on the fact that matter does not (as the merely mechanical investigators of nature assume) fill its space by absolute impenetrability, but by repulsive force; this force has its degree, which can be different in different matters. And since the repulsive force has of itself nothing in common with the attractive force, which is proportional to the quantity of the matter, the repulsive force can with regard to one and the same attractive force be *originally different* in degree in different matters. And consequently the degree of the extension of the matters may as regards the same

---

[a] A slip for "πρωτον ψευδος"; C has written the genitive form instead of the ablative

26[1] I.e. ground as fine as possible. C makes a similar remark in a note to an article on fluidity by Baader, where he cites his own experience in Malta and Sicily as proof that some solids (in this case, sand in sand-storms) can be as penetrating as liquids: JAHRBUCHER **25**.

26[2] C refers to SCHELLING *Einleitung* ii

26 (not annotated): "The fluid in general must be defined as a mass *in which no part can be distinguished from another by figure.*"

26[3] The "fundamental error" referred to in **8** above, namely Kant's confusion of matter with body.

quantity of matter, and, conversely, the quantity of matter may as regards the same volume, i.e., density of the matter, admit originally of very great specific differences.]

Again and again Matter assumed as a datum, the *subject* of the powers/ tho' two of these powers are elsewhere taken as constituting matter![1] Meantime no attempt to shew the conceivability of a power existing in a continuous yet gradual scale of increments from $0 = -1$. up to the maximum of sensible reality, i.e. power realized and realizing.—These defects have been avoided and this deficiency supplied, I flatter myself, in the Logosophia.[2]—Let me not, however, fail to acknowlege, that a great Idea and worthy of Kant is contained in the construction of matter by two powers, the one universal and the same in all, the other gradative and differential, and thus in each degree the ground of a specialty in matter.[3]—Kant saw the Truth, but not in its totality, & hence misnamed and misapplied it. [? Mem]—*3na Polaritas*.[4]

28 p 105, pencil, referring to pp 104–5

* Dies ist nun alles, was Metaphysik zur Construction des Begriffes der Materie, mithin zum Behuf der Anwendung der Mathematik auf Naturwissenschaft, in Ansehung der Eigenschaften, wodurch Materie einen Raum in bestimmte[m] Maasse erfüllet, nur immer leisten kann, nämlich diese Eigenschaften als dynamisch anzusehen und nicht als unbedingte ursprüngliche Positionen, wie sie etwa eine blos mathematische Behandlung postuliren würde.

[* This is all that metaphysics can ever accomplish for the construction of the concept of matter, and hence on behalf of the application of mathematics to natural science respecting the properties by which matter fills a space in determinate measure—namely, to regard these properties as dynamical and not as unconditioned original positions, such, for instance, as a merely mathematical treatment would postulate.]

* If by "Metaphysik" we mean a *science*, and nothing else—i.e. a scheme of Thoughts, excluding omne quod *præter* Intellectum ⟨est,⟩ sit ne super, sitne sub[1]—then "Dies ist vielmehr als Metaphysik"[2]—can honestly, i.e. from its own stores, contribute to the Construction of the

27[1] See **9 n 1** above.

27[2] The reference to the *Logosophia* indicates that this is one of the later notes in the volume: C used this term to refer to a projected work c 1815–18 (*CL* IV 589, *CN* III 4440). If, as it seems, he has a completed ms in mind, it must be the *Opus maximum* dictated to J. H. Green 1818–19.

27[3] As e.g. in **22** textus above.

27[4] *Trina Polaritas*—"three term polarity". The general rule about great minds being wrong chiefly in not grasping the *whole* truth is articulated in *TT* 1 Sept 1832.

28[1] Excluding "everything that is *beyond* Intellect, whether above or below".

28[2] "This is far more than Metaphysics".

material world.—But if it include (and Kant's Grundkräfte clearly in-
volve)[3] Autonomy—then This is *not* all.—

29   pp 116–17, pencil | Ch 3 prop 2

*Erstes Gesetz der Mechanik. Bey allen Veränderungen der körperlichen
Natur bleibt die Quantität der Materie im Ganzen dieselbe, unvermehrt
und unvermindert.*

Beweis.

(Aus der allgemeinen Metaphysik wird der Satz zum Grunde gelegt,
dass bey allen Veränderungen der Natur keine Substanz weder entstehe
noch vergehe. . . .) In jeder Materie ist das Bewegliche im Raume das
letzte Subject aller der Materie inhärirenden Accidenzen: und die Menge
dieses Beweglichen ausserhalb einander die Quantität der Substanz.
Also ist die Grösse der Materie, der Substanz nach, nichts anders, als
die Menge der Substanzen, daraus sie besteht.

[*First law of mechanics: With regard to all changes of corporeal nature, the
quantity of matter taken as a whole remains the same, unincreased and undi-
minished.*

Proof
(In universal metaphysics there is laid down the proposition that with regard
to all changes of nature, no substance either arises or perishes. . . .) In every
matter the movable in space is the ultimate subject of all the accidents inhering
in matter, and the number of matter's movable parts extenal to one another is
the quantity of substance. Hence the quantity of the matter according to its sub-
stance is nothing but the multitude of the substances of which it consists.]

I turn coward at the thought of my own Courage, while I am about to
avow, that this "Proof" appears to me a mere Sand-rope of Assertions:
and the fundamental Position from the universal "Metaphysik" is either
Atheistic, ad normam Spinozæ,[1] and making Substance a Synonime of
God confounds or identifies God and the sensible World:[2] or is nugatory,
by applying y = a to Matter, which has no claim to y = a—i.e. to
substance in that sense. I do not, however, deny it as a necessary as-
sumption in common Mechanics; but will not let it be forced upon me,
in Cosmology. Indeed it is too near of kin to ultimate Corpuscles and
empty Spaces that *really are* and yet are really Nothing.

28[3] "Fundamental forces" as in **12**
above.
29[1] "In Spinoza's manner".
29[2] C's admiration for Spinoza was

generally held in check by his disapproval
of Spinozism, which he outlines briefly in
HILLHOUSE **1** at n 5.

30 pp 117–18, last paragraph in pencil | Observ

Dagegen kann das, was als Gegenstand des inneren Sinnes betrachtet wird, als Substanz eine Grösse haben, die *nicht aus Theilen ausserhalb einander besteht*, deren Theile also auch nicht Substanzen sind, deren Entstehen oder Vergehen folglich auch nicht ein Entstehen oder Vergehen einer Substanz sein darf, deren Vermehrung oder Verminderung daher, dem Grundsatze von der Beharrlichkeit der Substanz unbeschadet, möglich ist. So hat nämlich das *Bewusstseyn*, mithin die Klarheit der Vorstellungen meiner Seele, und, derselben zu Folge, auch das Vermögen des Bewusstseyns, die Apperception, mit diesem aber selbst die Substanz der Seele einen *Grad*, der grösser oder kleiner werden kann, ohne dass irgend eine Substanz zu diesem Behuf entstehen oder vergehen dürfte.

[On the other hand, that which is regarded as object of the internal sense can as substance have a quantity that *does not consist of parts external to one another* and whose parts are therefore not substances. The arising or perishing of this quantity, consequently, must not be the arising or perishing of substance; and the increase or diminution of such quantity is therefore possible without detriment to the principle of the permanence of substance. To wit, *consciousness* has a *degree* that may be greater or smaller without any substance needing to arise or perish. And hence the clarity of the representations of my soul has such a degree, and in consequence of this fact the faculty of consciousness, namely, apperception—and along with this faculty even the substance of the soul—has also such a degree.]

I never could see the force of this argument against Mendlesohn and others.[1] Who *knows*, that Consciousness, or rather the act of consciousness, is the sole faculty of the Soul?—To matter I count 2 opposite powers, as *essential*, attraction & repulsion & possibly, many other powers may exist as added to different sorts of matter—Why not various powers inhere in the substance, *I* or Soul? If so, may not the soul during feeble consciousness be vigorously exerted in some other power?—

S. T. C.[a]

[a] At the foot of p 117 C has written "Turn over"—i.e. to p 118

30[1] Kant attempts to refute Mendelssohn's proof of the permanence of the soul in *C d r V* pp 414–27, asserting (as in textus here) that the permanence of the soul and of consciousness, "regarded merely as object of inner sense, remains undemonstrated, and indeed indemonstrable" (p 415). MENDELSSOHN, in *Morgenstunden* pp 202–5 (annotated p 203), explains in what sense the proposition "I myself really exist" must have objective truth in spite of our immediate awareness of the changeability of our being, and argues that the ground of our existence and of the permanence of the soul must be sought in a free cause, a necessary being who exists objectively by virtue of being conceived of by a subject.

The above remark, made some years ago, is just as far*a* it goes; but it does ⟨not⟩ apply against Kant, who has merely attacked the *demonstrative* force of Mendlesohn's argument. The Soul *may* have such & such powers is widely different from "The Soul *has* them."

~~Aug~~ July 1811.

*b*True! But still Kant's argument is false and sophistical. By what right does he apply the term "Parts" to a Monad? Aug. 1819.

31 p +3, referring to p 118

Dagegen der Begriff einer Materie als Substanz der Begriff des Beweglichen *im Raume* ist. Es ist daher kein Wunder, wenn von der letzteren die Beharrlichkeit der Substanz bewiesen werden kann, von der ersteren aber nicht, weil bey der Materie schon aus ihrem *Begriffe*, nämlich dass sie das Bewegliche sey, das nur im Raume möglich ist, fliesst . . . und folglich die Quantität derselben nur durch Zertheilung, welche kein Verschwinden ist, vermindert werden könne. . . . Der Gedanke Ich ist dagegen gar *kein Begriff*, sondern nur innere Wahrnehmung, aus ihm kann also auch gar nichts . . . folglich auch nicht die Beharrlichkeit der Seele, als Substanz gefolgert werden.

[On the other hand, the concept of a matter as substance is the concept of the movable *in space*. Hence it is no wonder if permanence of substance can be proved of matter but not of the soul. This is because in the case of matter there follows from its *concept*, namely that it is the movable, which is only possible in space . . . [and] consequently, the quantity of matter can be diminished only by division, which is no disappearance. . . . The thought "I" is, on the other hand, *no concept* at all but only an internal perception. Therefore, from this thought nothing at all can be concluded . . . consequently, the permanence of the soul as substance cannot be concluded from the thought "I".]

p. 118. A strange mode of reasoning! Space = an intuition a priori; matter = the sensation accompanying a specific intuition & scheme of space—parts &c all modes of thought—all purely subjective—and then the proof is, that the indestructibility of material substance can be proved—how? because it is involved in the definition—and is not reality involved—& thus this prove that it is not subjective?—If matter be subjective, and the I or subject be evanescible, must not the thought, matter, be at least equally so?

32 p 121, pencil | Prop 3 observ

Auf dem Gesetze der Trägheit (neben dem der Beharrlichkeit der Sub-

---

a "as" omitted   *b* The remainder of the note is in pencil

stanz) beruht die Möglichkeit einer eigentlichen Naturwissenschaft ganz und gar. Das Gegentheil des erstern, und daher auch der Tod aller Naturphilosophie, wäre der *Hylozoism.*

[The possibility of a natural science proper rests entirely on the law of inertia (along with the law of the permanence of substance). The opposite of this, and therefore the death of all natural philosophy, would be *hylozoism.*]

Why so? Or rather *is* Nature in this sense capable of proper *Science.* It seems sufficient for all purposes to say—While A remains A, so and so will follow.

33   p $^-$5, evidently referring to pp 124 ff | Prop 4 proof

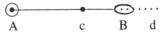

Es sey ein Körper A mit einer Geschwindigkeit = AB in ansehung des relativen Raumes gegen den Körper B, der in Ansehung eben desselben Raums *ruhig* ist, im Anlaufe. Man theile die Geschwindigkeit AB in zwei theile, Ac und Bc, die sich umgekehrt wie die Massen B und A gegen einander verhalten, und stelle sich A mit der Geschwindigkeit Ac im absoluten Raume, B aber mit der Geschwindigkeit Bc in entgegengesetzter Richtung *zusammt dem relativen Raume* bewegt vor: so sind beide Bewegungen einander entgegengesetzt und gleich, und, da sie einander wechselseitig aufheben, so versetzen sich beide Körper beziehungsweise aufeinander, d.i. im absoluten Raume, in Ruhe. Nun wahr aber B mit der Geschwindigkeit Bc in der Richtung BA, die der des Körpers A, nämlich AB, gerade entgegengesetzt ist, *zusammt dem relativen Raume* in Bewegung. Wenn also die Bewegung des Körpers B durch den Stoss aufgehoben wird, so wird darum die Bewegung des relativen Raums nicht aufgehoben. Also bewegt sich nach dem Stosse *der relative Raum* in Ansehung beider Körper A und B (die nunmehr im absoluten Raume ruhen,) in der Richtung BA mit der Geschwindigkeit Bc, oder, welches einerley ist, beide Körper bewegen sich nach dem Stosse mit gleicher Geschwindigkeit Bd = Bc in der Richtung des Stossenden AB. Nun ist aber, nach dem vorigen, die Quantität der Bewegung des Körpers B in der Richtung und mit der Geschwindigkeit Bc, mithin auch die in der Richtung Bd mit derselben Geschwindigkeit, der Quantität der Bewegung des Körpers A mit der Geschwindigkeit und in der Richtung Ac gleich; folglich ist die Wirkung, d.i. die Bewegung Bd, die der Körper B durch den Stoss im relativen Raume erhält, und also auch die Handlung des Körpers A mit der Geschwindigkeit Ac der Gegenwirkung Bc jederzeit gleich. Da eben dasselbe Gesetz (wie die mathematische Mechanik lehrt) keine Abänderung erleidet, wenn, anstatt des Stosses auf einen ruhigen, ein Stoss desselben Körpers auf einen gleichfalls bewegten Körper angenommen wird, imgleichen die Mittheilung der Bewegung durch den Stoss von der durch den Zug nur in der Richtung, nach welcher die Materien einander in ihren Bewegungen widerstehen, unterschieden ist: so folgt, dass in aller Mittheilung der Bewegung Wirkung und Gegenwirkung einander jederzeit gleich seyn (dass jeder Stoss nur vermittelst eines gleichen Gegenstosses, jeder Druck vermittelst eines gleichen Gegendrucks, imgleichen jeder Zug nur durch einen gleichen Gegenzug die Bewegung eines Körpers dem andern mittheilen könne.)

[

A   c   B   d

Let a body A be in motion toward the body B with a velocity = AB in relation to the relative space; the body B is *at rest* with regard to the same space. Let the velocity AB be divided into two parts, Ac and Bc, which are related to one another inversely as the masses B and A. Represent A as moved with the velocity Ac in absolute space but B with the velocity Bc in the opposite direction *together with the relative space*. Thus both motions are opposite and equal to one another; and since they mutually destroy one another, both bodies put themselves relatively to one another, i.e. in absolute space, in a state of rest. But, now, B *together with the relative space* was in motion with the velocity Bc in the direction BA; this velocity is exactly opposed to that of the body A, namely AB. Hence if the motion of the body B is destroyed by impact, then the motion of *the relative space* is not therefore destroyed. Hence after the impact, the relative space with regard to both bodies A and B (which now rest in absolute space) moves in the direction BA with the velocity Bc, or, what is the same thing, both bodies after the impact move with equal velocity Bd = Bc in the direction of the impacting AB. According to the foregoing, however, the quantity of motion of the body B in the direction and with the velocity Bc, and hence likewise the quantity of motion of B in the direction Bd with the same velocity, is equal to the quantity of the motion of the body A with the velocity and in the direction Ac. Consequently, the effect, i.e. the motion Bd, which the body B receives by impact in relative space, and hence also the action of the body A with the velocity Ac, is always equal to the reaction Bc. The very same law (as mathematical mechanics teaches) suffers no alteration when, instead of the impact upon a resting body, an impact of the body upon a moved one is assumed; similarly, the communication of motion by impact is distinguished from that by traction only in the direction in which the matters oppose one another in their motions. Because of all this there follows that in all communication of motion, action and reaction are always equal to one another (that every impact can communicate the motion of one body to another only by means of an equal counter-impact, every pressure by means of an equal counter-pressure, and, similarly, every traction only by an equal countertraction).]

August, 1819

A really formidable sum of puzzle and perplexity, and repetitions of reperusals, with groundless apprehension: that my utmost efforts had failed to understand the writer's meaning, would Kant have spared me, had he but commenced the work with the plain avowal—that not the truth of Nature, but the forms under which it may be *geometrically represented*, was its Object. *Power* or *Spirit* is not imageable, it being by its definition το μη φαινομενον—that which cannot appear immediately⸍ but by certain fictions of Abstraction we may produce adequate representatives in the imagination—namely, by converting ⟨per equationem⟩[1] all relations into relations of Space as measured by Time, or figures generated by Motion in Space.—Thus the Paradox, p. 124[2] that the Castle meets the Cannon Ball half way, means no more than—the same phænomenon ~~would~~ill result, if instead of the Gunpowder and the Gunner's aim you suppose so and so—and by the latter you may demonstrate the result geometrically, which you cannot do in the former⸍. Had I possess[ed][a] courage enough to have seen this at first, I might have spared all my notes—written at so many different and distant Times!!—

34   pp 127–8, pencil | Continuing **33** textus

In der Phoronomie, da die Bewegung eines Körpers blos in Ansehung des Raums, als Veränderung der Relation in demselben betrachtet wurde, war es ganz gleichgültig, ob ich den Körper im Raume, oder, an statt dessen, dem relativen Raume eine gleiche aber entgegengesetzte Bewegung zugestehen wollte; beides gab völlig einerley Erscheinung. . . . In der Mechanik aber, da ein Körper in Bewegung gegen einen anderen betrachtet wird, gegen den er durch seine Bewegung ein *Cautzalverhältniss* hat . . . da ist es nicht mehr gleichgültig ob ich einem dieser Körper, oder dem Raume eine entgegengesetzte Bewegung zueignen will. Denn nunmehro kommt ein anderer Begriff der Quantität der Bewegung ins Spiel, nämlich nicht derjenigen, die blos in Ansehung des Raumes gedacht wird und allein in der Geschwindigkeit besteht, sondern derjenigen, wobey zugleich die Quantität der Substanz (als bewegende Ursache) in Anschlag gebracht werden muss, und es ist hier nicht mehr beliebig, sondern *nothwendig* jeden der beiden Körper als bewegt anzunehmen, und zwar mit gleicher Quantität der Bewegung in entgegengesetzter Richtung; wenn aber der eine relative in Ansehung des Raumes in Ruhe ist, ihm die erforderliche Bewegung zusammt dem

[a] A hole in the paper

33[1] "Through equalisation".   **33**[2] I.e. textus.

Raume beyzulegen. Denn einer kann auf den anderen durch seine eigene Bewegung nicht wirken, als entweder bey der Annäherung vermittelst der Zurückstossungskraft, oder bey der Entfernung vermittelst der Anziehung.

[Inasmuch as the motion of a body was considered in phoronomy merely with regard to its space as a change of relation in space, it was all the same whether I wanted to ascribe the motion to the body in space, or instead ascribe to the relative space an equal but opposite motion; both gave fully the same appearance. . . . But in mechanics, a body is regarded as in motion toward another, respecting which it has a *causal relation* through its motion . . . [then] whether I want to ascribe an opposite motion to one of these bodies, or to the space, is no longer all the same. For now another concept of the quantity of motion comes into play, namely, not that which is thought merely with regard to the space and consists only in the velocity, but that whereby at the same time the quantity of the substance (as moving cause) must be taken into consideration. And it is here no longer optional but *necessary* to assume both bodies as moved, and indeed moved with an equal quantity of motion in an opposite direction. But when the one body is relatively at rest with regard to its space, then it is necessary to attribute the requisite motion to this body together with its space. For one cannot act on the other by this [first] one's own motion except by approach through repulsive force or by withdrawal through attractive force.]

Strange!—That in this manner the fact may be, nay, that in this manner only it can be, geometrically constructed, we may admit/ but surely K. must have forgotten that the primary and constituent Attraction and Rep. are not the only powers of *Bodies*—that a pound of Gunpowder is not = a pound of Wood-dust, & that a detached Body in free motion such as a cannon ball is not the same as a fixed body, a foot square of Rock for instance in a mountain of Granite. If it apply to free motion, there seems no reason why it should not apply to living Motion/ so that when John runs after Bill, and overtaking knocks him down, Bill has been moving with the same velocity towards John, and therefore might as well have been standing still.

But I do not understand Kant's drift—in one passage he represents his Laws, as mere geometrical equations, and then I comprehend him fully—in another as in the note overleaf[1] he seems to assert its bonâ fide objective Truth, and then I am all in the Dark again.

35 p 146, pencil | Ch 4 general observ

Denn, damit Bewegung auch nur als Erscheinung gegeben werden könne, dazu wird eine empirische Vorstellung des Raums, in Ansehung dessen das Beweglich sein Verhältniss verändern soll, erfodert, der

34[1] **33** textus.

Raum aber, der wahrgenommen werden soll, muss material, mithin, dem Begriffe einer Materie überhaupt zu Folge, selbst beweglich seyn.

[For in order that motion may be given even as appearance, there is required an empirical representation of space with regard to which the movable is to change its relation; but the space which is to be perceived must be material and hence, according to the concept of matter in general, must itself be movable.]

but not therefore *bodily*: and why may not this sensible (or rather, I should say, sensuous) Space be an adherent circumstance of Body?[1]

35[1] C reiterates the distinction he proposed between matter and body in **8**. The further distinction between "sensible" and "sensuous"—reviving Milton's coinage—is justified in e.g. *BL* ch 10 (*CC*) I 171–2: "to express in one word, all that appertains to the perception considered as passive, and merely recipient, I have adopted from our elder classics the word *sensuous*; because *sensual* is not at present used, except in a bad sense . . . while *sensitive* and *sensible* would each convey a different meaning".

Die Religion innerhalb der Grenzen der blossen Vernunft. 2nd ed rev. Königsberg 1794. 8°.

British Library C 43 b 4

DATE. Between 1818 and 1826. This work is named with others by Kant that "took possession" of C—apparently about 1802—"with a giant's hand": *BL* ch 9 (*CC*) I 153. The notes in this copy, however, plainly belong to a much later period. They reflect concerns of the 1820s, and 3 appears to belong to the period of the 1818–19 Lectures on the History of Philosophy.

COEDITORS. Kathleen Wheeler, Raimonda Modiano.

TEXTUS TRANSLATION. T. M. Green and H. H. Hudson tr *Religion within the Limits of Reason Alone* (Chicago 1960).

1 pp +4–+5, referring to pp 78–80 | Pt 2 sec 1 (b)

Wäre nun ein solcher wahrhaftig göttlich gesinnter Mensch zu einer gewissen Zeit gleichsam vom Himmel auf die Erde herabgekommen, der durch Lehre, Lebenswandel und Leiden das *Beyspiel* eines Gott wohlgefälligen Menschen an sich gegeben hätte, so weit als man von äusserer Erfahrung nur verlangen kann, (indessen, dass das *Urbild* eines solchen immer doch nirgend anders, als in unserer Vernunft zu suchen ist), hätte er durch alles dieses ein unabsehlich grosses moralisches Gute in der Welt durch eine Revolution im Menschengeschlechte hervorgebracht: so würden wir doch nicht Ursache haben, an ihm etwas anders, als einen natürlich gezeugten Menschen anzunehmen, (weil dieser sich doch auch verbunden fühlt, selbst ein solches Beyspiel an sich abzugeben,) obzwar dadurch eben nicht schlechthin verneinet würde, dass er nicht auch wohl ein übernatürlich erzeugter Mensch seyn könne. . . . Vielmehr würde die Erhebung eines solchen Heiligen über alle Gebrechlichkeit der menschlichen Natur der practischen Anwendung der Idee desselben auf unsere Nachfolge, nach allem, was wir einzusehen vermögen, eher im Wege seyn.

[Now if it were indeed a fact that such a truly godly-minded man at some particular time had descended, as it were, from heaven to earth and had given men in his own person, through his teachings, his conduct, and his sufferings, as perfect an *example* of a man well-pleasing to God as one can expect to find in external experience (for be it remembered that the *archetype* of such a person is to be sought nowhere but in our own reason), and if he had, through all this, produced immeasurably great moral good upon earth by effecting a revolution in the human race—even then we should have no cause for supposing him other than a man naturally begotten. (Indeed, the naturally begotten man feels himself under obligation to furnish just such an example in himself.) This is not, to be sure, absolutely to deny that he might be a man supernaturally begotten. . . . The elevation of such a holy person above all the frailties of human nature would rather, so far as we can see, hinder the adoption of the idea of such a person for our imitation.]

P. 79, 80.

This is, doubtless, the strongest Argument in support of the Socinian Scheme[1]—in truth, the only strong one. But as by a number of yet stronger Arguments, both scriptural & rational, Socinianism stands confuted, we must either say that the Example of Christ, commanded us to follow, has a peculiar meaning, and applies to the Actions rather than to the Agent (which would be, however, a hard Saying) or else deduce from the absence of the evil principle in the Nature of Christ ("he alone was born without Sin")[2] the existence of evil Beings, a world or kingdom of Darkness from without (= the Devil) whose power of acting on the Will of Christ was equal to that of the evil in the Heart of other men in their Will.—Now Kant expressly admits the *practical* equivalence of this, p. 72:[3] & this is, I think, a new and very strong positive argument for the *Reality* of the Devil—~~F~~ Of the possibility of such a Being, and that the Idea is not (as has been asserted) practically indifferent, I have a *series* of Proofs.—[4]

N.B. This Argument of the Socinians recoils on themselves: for who can deem a man invested with the power of working Miracles, and of prophecy, & above all, with an inspired certainty of a glorious Immortality as the immediate result of short sufferings, a fair *Instance* of what ordinary men may be expected to do?—2. N.B. by the bye, it may[a]

[a] C omits "be"

[1] C refers specifically to a contemporary form of Socinianism, Priestleian Unitarianism, which denied the divinity of Christ and which for a few years counted C among its followers. A brief history of Socinianism is given in BAHRDT **1** n 1; some commentary on C's published attacks on it appears in *BL* ch 24 (*CC*) II 245–6, *SM* (*CC*) 111 n 5.

[2] A paraphrase of Art 15 in the Articles of Religion.

[3] In p 72 Kant is not surprised that our "*invisible* adversary", the Devil, "who is known only through his operations upon us", is represented as "lying outside us,

and as an evil *spirit*". "From the practical point of view it is all one whether we place the tempter inside ourselves or outside: in the former case we are no less culpable than in the latter—we could not have been led astray by him unless we had been in collusion with him."

[4] C's interest in the problem of the sense in which the Devil and devils could be said to exist is apparent in the narrative about Luther's vision of the Devil in *Friend* (*CC*) I 136–42 and in several notes of c 1820–30, e.g. DONNE *Sermons* COPY B **32**, HILLHOUSE **1** n 7, LUTHER *Colloquia* **39, 91, 103**.

urged in favor of the interpretation, that Christ is proposed as the *Model for*, rather than an *Instance of*, Human Virtue, that God himself in his absolute Holiness is likewise held out for our Imitation/ "Be ye perfect, even as your Father in Heaven is perfect."[5]—the numerous Texts however that speak of Christ's having put on all innocent imperfections of Humanity, subjection to Temptations, &c, in short, that he became a Man in all respects, weigh down the scale in favor of the common Belief.—

1A   pp 89–90, marked with a pencil line in the margin | Sec 1 (c)

Nun ist das erstere ein Blick in eine *unabsehliche*, aber gewünschte und glückliche Zukunft, das Zweyte dagegen in ein eben so *unabsehliches Elend*, d.i. beydes für Menschen, nach dem, was sie urtheilen können, in eine selige oder unselige *Ewigkeit*; Vorstellungen, die mächtig genug sind, um dem einen Theil zur Beruhigung und Befestigung im Guten, dem Andern zur Aufweckung des richtenden Gewissens, um dem Bösen, so viel möglich noch Abbruch zu thun, mithin zu Triebfedern zu dienen, ohne das es nöthig ist, auch objectiv eine Ewigkeit des Guten oder Bösen für das Schicksal des Menschen *dogmatisch* als Lehrsatz vorauszusetzen, mit welchen vermeynten Kenntnissen und Behauptungen die Vernunft nur die Schranken ihrer Einsicht überschreitet.

[Now in the first experience we have a glimpse of an *immeasurable* future, yet one which is happy and to be desired; in the second, of as *incalculable a misery*—either of them being for men, so far as they can judge, a blessed or cursed *eternity*. These are representations powerful enough to bring peace to the one group and strengthen them in goodness, and to awaken in the other the voice of conscience commanding them still to break with evil so far as it is possible; hence powerful enough to serve as incentives without our having to presume to lay down *dogmatically* the objective doctrine that man's destiny is an eternity of good or evil. In making such assertions and pretensions to knowledge, reason simply passes beyond the limit of its own insight.]

2   pp 95–7, pencil

Da nun das Sittlich-Böse (Uebertretung des moralischen Gesetzes, *als göttlichen Gebotes, Sünde* genannt)* nicht sowohl wegen der *Unendlichkeit* des höchsten Gesetzgebers, dessen Autorität dadurch verletzt worden (von welchem überschwenglichen Verhältnisse des Menschen zum höchsten Wesen wir nichts verstehen), sondern als ein Böses in der *Gesinnung* und den Maximen überhaupt (wie *allgemeine Grundsätze* vergleichungsweise gegen einzelne Uebertretungen) eine *Unendlichkeit* von Verletzungen des Gesetzes, mithin der Schuld, bey sich führt,

1[5]   Matt 5.48.

(welches vor einem menschlichen Gerichtshofe, der nur das einzelne Verbrechen, mithin nur die That und darauf bezogene, nicht aber die allgemeine Gesinnung in Betrachtung zieht, anders ist), so würde jeder Mensch sich einer *unendlichen Strafe* und Verstossung aus dem Reiche Gottes zu gewärtigen haben.

[Now this moral evil (transgression of the moral law, called SIN when the law is regarded *as a divine command*)* brings with it endless violations of the law and so *infinite* guilt. The extent of this guilt is due not so much to the *infinitude* of the Supreme Lawgiver whose authority is thereby violated (for we understand nothing of such transcendent relationships of man to the Supreme Being) as to the fact that this moral evil lies in the *disposition* and the maxims in general, in *universal basic principles* rather than in particular transgressions. (The case is different before a human court of justice, for such a court attends merely to single offences and therefore to the deed itself and what is relative thereto, and not to the general disposition.) It would seem to follow, then, that because of this infinite guilt all mankind must look forward to *endless punishment* and exclusion from the kingdom of God.]

* We might as well conclude, that a Flea, that had presumptuously bit a Giant, must needs leave a gigantic Flea-bite. In answer to the whole §, Revelation forbids us as much to affirm a Justice in God unmodified by Mercy, as Mercy at variance with Justice—The attribute = Mercy-justice, consists in the acceptance of the Past, according to the *Total State* of the final Present. The *total Energy* of Will, this one act of the whole Being, which alone can produce this state, is Gospel *Faith*. By *Faith* we are justified.[1]—   S. T. C.

3   pp 210/11, note tipped in

The two weightiest Objections are these.[1] First, I have found by experience that the interest of an Audience (such namely as I can alone collect and in truth am te most likely to benefit) and with that the Spirit of the Lecturer *flag* under any but very short and occasional Narration, or detail of connected facts—however interesting and even amusing the very same Auditors would have found it in a Book.—The heaviest Lecture, the characters ef and biographies, anecdotes (or rather *ecdotes*)[2] of

2[1] Rom 3.28 (var). On the important subject of faith, C made many similar statements, e.g. DONNE *Sermons* COPY B 62 (a state of the will "or rather of the whole Man"), LEIGHTON COPY C 13 ("a *total* energy of the Soul"), *Friend* (*CC*) I 315 ("a *total* act of the soul").

3[1] This note, apparently bound into the volume by mistake, may be the draft of a letter. It discusses a proposed series of 14 lectures in which religious issues would be addressed, probably the Lectures on the History of Philosophy of 1818–19, in which Lect 11 was announced as taking up "the influence of the Calvinistic and Arminian controversy" though in the end C was cautious enough not to attack the subject directly: *P Lects* (1949) 312n.

3[2] The word "ecdote", not in *OED*, means "published account"—C correcting

R̶h̶ Corn. Agrippa, Reuchlin, and the Tuscan Platonists,[3] would probably be the most entertaining when published—

However, by reducing the proposed Course from 14 to 6 or 7 Lectures this might perhaps be in good measure obviated.

The Second.—I̶ ̶s̶h̶o̶u̶l̶d̶ ̶h̶a̶v̶e̶ ̶o̶f̶ *m̶o̶r̶a̶l̶* n̶e̶c̶e̶s̶s̶i̶t̶y̶ ̶(̶f̶o̶r̶ Must I not have to walking[a] over glowing embers? ŧThere are s̶u̶b̶j̶e̶c̶t̶s̶ convictions on which I may innocently be silent but could not innocently disguise/ ex. gr. I am walking with a Friend or Patron, who (I know) has r̶i̶g̶h̶t̶ ̶o̶r̶ w̶r̶o̶n̶g̶ an utter aversion to another Friend of mine which I lament but cannot overcome. I know that if I walk ŧ on the London Road, we must meet him. Surely, I may innocently take the Hamstead Road; but having taken the London Road not without duplicity and baseness pass by him unnoticed./. Now on the Subject proposed I must of *moral* necessity deliver opinions that would bring down a Swarm from opposite Hives—. The so called moderate Grotian and Paleyan Divines[4] and *thus almost all who will hear me* who have formed their notions of Christian Evidence from the Writers of this School I must offend by the proof that the Church of England and the great Founders of the Reformation held these opinions as scarcely less than heretical pravity, or half way between Popery and Pelagianism and even Socinianism—and that I am decisively and earnestly of the same opinion—/[5]

The ⟨Modern⟩ Calvinists I should offend bitterly by proving that Cal-

---

[a] A slip for "walk"

---

his own use of "anecdote" which he took in its strict sense of "unpublished account": cf DAVISON **10**.

[3] Cornelius Agrippa (1486–1535) and Johann Reuchlin (1455–1522), Hebrew scholars and writers on the Cabbala, are mentioned here as humanists engaged like the "Tuscan Platonists" Marsilio Ficino (1433–99) and Pico della Mirandola (1463–94) in the restoration of ancient learning. C discussed Agrippa and Reuchlin at some length in *P Lects* Lect 10, where he says that the doctrines of the Cabbala "were nearly the same as the lower Platonists' " (1949) 299. The source of C's information was J. C. Meiners *Lebensbeschreibungen berühmter Männer aus den Zeiten der Wiederherstellung der Wissenschaften* (1795–7). It is perhaps significant that in May 1826 C recommended that Dr de' Prati undertake "a series of critical & biographical Sketches of the most re-

markable revolutionary minds, in the manner of Meiners's Work", naming Cornelius Agrippa as a promising starting-point: *CL* VI 579.

[4] The liberal Church establishment of his day, whom C repeatedly attacked for their attention to worldly values: for Paley as representative of "the Grotio-Paleyan Scheme of Christian Evidence" see LUTHER *Colloquia* **80** and n 3.

[5] The specific issue here, "Christian Evidence", is the fashionable emphasis on miracles and other physical "proofs" of the divinity of Christ. C argues that Protestantism historically rests on spiritual truths, and that by dwelling on miracles Paley and his followers are little better than the superstitious Roman Catholics on one hand and rationalist sects such as the Pelagians (who reject the doctrine of original sin) and the Socinians (who reject the Trinity) on the other.

vin would have cried: Fire & Faggot, before he had read 100 pages of Dr Williams's Modern Calvinism[6]—and by declaring my conviction that it would be difficult to say which ~~have~~ stand at the greatest Distance from Luther, Calvin, ~~or~~ our Whitaker, Field, &c,[7] the hodiernal Evangelicals or their Antagonists with Mr Mant at their head[8]—Above all, the Missionary Society[9]—how would they recoil from the assertion, that Go ye ~~un~~into all nations, &c[10] means nothing more, than/ Preach the Gospel indifferently to ⟨Jews and Gentiles—⟩ all that will hear you, in whatever part of the Roman Empire the Hearer may have been—[? th]—that the ⟨pretended⟩ Missions of the Apostles, with the exception of St Paul and Peter recorded ~~in~~ in S or probably deducible from Scripture, are mere Fables, unsupported by any evidence that will stand the test of improved Historical Criticism—that even in the Apocalypse not only no reference is made that extends beyond the remotest Roman Colonies, but that the ~~Pagan World~~ extra-imperial World is spoken^a as still Pagan even at the conclusion of the Millennium[11]—so that the causa causarum[12] of the *utter failure* of the Japanese, Chinese, and Indian Mis-

---

^a "of" omitted

3^6 Edward Williams *A Defence of Modern Calvinism* (1812), attacked by C in *AR* (1825) 153–4 and in LEIGHTON COPY C **13**, where he makes the same point as he does here.

3^7 In *SM* (*CC*) 107 William Whitaker (1548–95), interpreter of the C of E in the strictest Calvinistic sense and author of *De authoritate scripturae* (1594), appears in a list of "names that must needs be . . . dear and venerable to a Minister of the Church of England . . . masculine intellects, formed under the robust discipline of an age memorable for keenness of research, and iron industry" with Richard Hooker, Richard Field, John Donne, John Selden, and Edward Stillingfleet. C annotated works of all these, but there is no record that he owned a copy of Whitaker's work.

3^8 The "present-day Evangelicals"—presumably the Methodists, who, at first within the C of E and with no intention of separating, had called themselves Evangelicals to identify their desire to revivify the teaching of the gospels. Richard Mant (1776–1848) in his Bampton Lectures of 1811 vindicated the evangelical character of Anglican preaching against the allegations of the Methodists that the C of E was

no longer evangelical, and attracted the official attention that set him in the way of rapid preferment to a bishopric in 1820. C regarded Mant as a representative of the "dregs of Grotianism . . . far worse than Unitarianism itself": *CN* III 4140n. Evangelicalism also continued within the C of E, with William Wilberforce as a prominent representative in the Clapham Sect.

3^9 Of several missionary societies founded in association with the Evangelical Revival, C is probably referring to the Church Missionary Society, founded in 1799 as the Society for Missions in Africa and the East. C was generally sceptical and sometimes abusive about them (e. g. of the British and Foreign Bible Society, DONNE *Sermons* COPY B **2** n 1), but in 1831 he expressed a willingness to defend and assist a missionary society: *CL* VI 1056. The Gillmans took in the *Evangelical Magazine* and *New Evangelical Magazine*, which carried regular reports about missionary activity.

3^10 Matt 28.19 (var)—Christ's final commission to his disciples.

3^11 C makes the same points in IRVING *Missionaries* **10, 14**.

3^12 The "cause of the causes".

sions (unless ~~eh~~ new *Christning* the Pantheon *All Saints* be success)[13] is that they were all Will-worship, entered on without any promise of Grace or special Assistance—just as the Monastic Life, the celibacy of the Clergy, Invocations of Dead Men, & the other Hay and Straw of Romanism.—

And again the Question, of so ~~much~~ near connection with the Bibliolatry[14] of the Day—Are all the Parts of all the Books of the Jewish Canon to be received as directly and expressly inspired by the Holy Ghost in the same sense & degree as the Law, and the Prophets? Is it necessary to Salvation that the affirmative should be believed? Does even a reference to any one Hagiographist or a quotation in the New Testament *prove* this to have been even the private opinion of the ~~Sacred Writ~~ Apostles or Evangelists?—Does it follow that Jude might not have made a moral application of a Legend in the Book of Enoch without implying the co-equality of that Book with the Canonical or even the *historical factity* of the Legend itself?[15] Or must we with the Romanists admit the Apocrypha, or the Alexandrine Canon, generally as differing from the Palestine,[16] because the Alexandrine Helenist*[a]* (probably, Apollos) the Writer of that most divine Epistle to the Hebrews appears to have received it[17]—Has not this indiscriminat[e]*[b]* and almost Judaizing Bibliolatry been one obstacle to our Success in our controversy with the ψeudo-catholic Romanists?[18]

4　pp ⁺2–⁺4, referring to 297 | Pt 4 § 4

Der Begriff eines übernatürlichen Beytritts zu unserem moralischen, ob

---

[a] A slip for "Hellenist"　　　*[b]* Final "e" omitted

3[13] All Saints' Day is the anniversary of the dedication of the Pantheon in Rome as a Christian church, the conversion taking place c 609, and the formal dedication 1 Nov 830.

3[14] "Idolisation of the Bible"—a term C was fond of: see CHILLINGWORTH COPY B 2 n 1.

3[15] Jude vv 14–15 quotes from Enoch by name. Tertullian thought this reason enough to include Enoch in the canon. See BIBLE COPY B **135** n 3. In the absence of "factuality" or "facticity" (both later coinages), "factity" is C's nonce-word.

3[16] The "Palestine Canon" of OT was in three sections: the Law (the Pentateuch), the Prophets (as in AV), and Writings or Hagiographia (variable, some now in the Apocrypha, some lost when they ceased to be copied); this was stable by c A.D. 100. By the "Alexandrine Canon" C means the Septuagint, the Greek version of OT, which arranges the order of the books, abandons the threefold division of the Hebrew Bible, and includes several books not found in OT which in the English Bible are called Apocrypha.

3[17] For Luther's view that Apollos was the author of the Epistle to the Hebrews see IRVING *Sermons* **5** n 4.

3[18] The "pseudo-"catholic Romanists are the Roman Catholics, not in C's opinion members of a truly "catholic" church—an opinion publicly expressed in *C&S* (*CC*) 141*.

zwar mangelhaften, Vermögen und selbst zu unserer nicht völlig gerei-
nigten, wenigstens schwachen Gesinnung, aller unserer Pflicht ein Ge-
nüge zu thun, ist transcendent und eine blosse Idee, von deren Realität
uns keine Erfahrung versichern kann.—Aber selbst als Idee in bloss
practischer Absicht sie anzunehmen, ist sie sehr gewagt und mit der Ver-
nunft schwerlich vereinbar; weil, was uns als sittliches gutes Verhalten,
zugerechnet werden soll, nicht durch fremden Einfluss, sondern nur
durch den bestmöglichen Gebrauch unserer eigenen Kräfte geschehen
müsste. Allein die Unmöglichkeit davon (dass beydes neben einander
statt finde), lässt sich doch eben auch nicht beweisen, weil die Freyheit
selbst, obgleich sie nichts Uebernatürliches in ihrem Begriffe enthält,
gleichwohl ihrer Möglichkeit nach uns eben so unbcgreiflich bleibt, als
das Uebernatürliche, welches man zum Ersatz der selbstthätigen, aber
mangelhaften Bestimmung derselben annehmen möchte.

[The concept of a supernatural accession to our moral, though deficient, capacity
and even to our not wholly purified and certainly weak disposition to perform
our entire duty, is a transcendent concept, and is a bare idea, of whose reality
no experience can assure us. Even when accepted as an idea in nothing but a
practical context it is very hazardous, and hard to reconcile with reason, since
that which is to be accredited to us as morally good conduct must take place not
through foreign influence but solely through the best possible use of our own
powers. And yet the impossibility thereof (i e., of both these things occurring
side by side) cannot really be proved, because freedom itself, though containing
nothing supernatural in its conception, remains, as regards its possibility, just as
incomprehensible to us as is the supernatural factor which we would like to
regard as a supplement to the spontaneous but deficient determination of free-
dom.]

P. 297. Half of the ingenuity which Kant has exerted in many single
pages ~~even~~ of this work would have enabled him to have given a ~~more~~
plausible elucidation & a more favorable Judgement on this Subject. He
has without any necessity adopted S⟨t⟩ Paul's metaphors of vicarious Sac-
rifice, Ransom &c, ⟨as the real doctrine: whereas they are⟩ evident meta-
phors, because the Customs from which they were drawn were perpet-
ually before his eyes, & because the doctrine expressed by them is
taught without them in the evangelists.[1]—Regeneration ~~by~~ thro' an act
and energy of the diseased Arbitrement aided & fostered by a supernat-
ural Will, or divine agency, which, in order to make this compatible
with the Laws of Spirit, was first united to Humanity—this is the Mys-

---

4[1] C uses Paul's account of redemption
as an illustration of the use of metaphor in
the NT and of the difference between met-
aphor and analogy in *AR* (1825) 319–26.

He regrets Irving's failure to free himself
from the "Debtor and Creditor Account"
of redemption in IRVING *Sermons* **11**.

tery in the unmetaphorical Language of Scripture—To explain this indeed impossible/ for a comprehension of the Free Will, and of the possibility of its becoming lamed and choosing evil is a pre-requisite—but these are in the very terms incomprehensible—i.e. causeless, unconditional, indetermined—else it could it[a] not be freedom—now all positive explanation consists in stating the precedents considered as causes or conditions—but there is another inferior sense of the word explanation,[2] in which it is possible—namely, the co-classing of this Object of Faith with analogous Objects or Facts of Experience—and tho' this does not increase our insight, yet it enlarges our view, and facilitates our belief, our rational belief: Whatever is real, must be possible—A is real, ergo possible—but B. ~~may be~~ appears analogous to A, therefore may be possible, may be real—and when to this is added a clear insight into the necessity of B = xyz, from the known tho' incomprehensible fact of a disease in man as a Vernunft-wesen unter Freiheit's Gesetzen,[3] it ~~would~~ amounts to a determi~~ning~~ngning Proof, of some thing the same nature with that of ⟨a⟩ clear and ~~honorable~~ weighty Testimony to the character of a Witness asserting on his own knowlege what the nature of the fact does not permit him to prove. Now such analogy is to be found I think in the undoubted Influence of Example, of Education, in short of all the administrants and auxiliaries of the Will—this influence Kant does not deny, but on the contrary makes the cultivation of certain qualities & habits important derivative Duties on this account—The will then may be acted on, not only by ourselves, in the cultivation of auxiliary Habits, but by the will of others—nay, even by nature, by the Breeze, the Sunshine, by the tender~~n~~ life & freshness of sensation, of convalescence, by shocks of Sickness forcing the attention backward in upon the state of our collective consciousness;—&c. &c.—(See that fine Sonnet, entitled Sin, p. 37 of Herbert's Temple).[4]—Why not then an influence of influences from the Son of God with the Spirit of God, acting directly on the Homo Νουμενον, as well as thro' the Homo Phænomenon?[5] This would make a just distinction between Grace to Redemption, and Providential

---

[a] The pronoun is repeated, C having changed lines and presumably lost track of the syntax

[4][2] Cf *TL* 35–6, "To *account* for Life is one thing; to explain Life another." There and elsewhere C invokes etymology to show that to "explain" a thing means "to unfold or spread it out": cf *Friend* (*CC*) I 477.

[4][3] "A being of reason under the laws of freedom". These are concepts from Kant, and the word *Freiheitsgesetzen* ("laws of

freedom") is actually used p 296.

[4][4] In *BL* ch 19 (*CC*) II 95–6, this sonnet is q as *The Bosom Sin*; C marked it in HERBERT 5.

[4][5] The "Noumenal (spiritual) Man" and the "Phenomenal (physical) Man", C adopting Kant's terms as in KANT *Metaphysik der Sitten* 2.

Aids—the direct action on the Noumenon would be the Grace, the Call—the influence on the Noumenon thro' the Homo phænomenon by the pre-arrangement of outward or bodily circumstances would be, as they are commonly called in pious language, Providences.—ΧΡΙΣΤΟΣ = Κοσμος επιστηματικος, Ανθρωπων;—Sensorium quasi commune? Idea totalis cogitationum omnium Modificatrix[6] Item—whether numerical Difference may not be an exclusive property of Phænomena—and Distinctness only belong to Noumena?—so that ο χριστοειδης χριστος γινεται[7]

4[6] "CHRIST is the sciential Universe for Men" (but the expected form of the adjective would be ἐπιστημονικός); "a sort of universal organ of sensation? A total Idea as one giving order to all thoughts".

4[7] "The Christ-like person becomes Christ".

Sammlung einiger bisher unbekannt gebliebener kleiner Schriften. . . .
Ed Friedrich Theodor Rink. Königsberg 1800. 8°.

British Library C 43 b 7

On p ⁻5, a pencilled note, "Lot 402", refers to *Green SC* (1880); on p 71 C has
corrected "Keinen" to "Keimen".

CONTENTS. [7]–23 "Neuer Lehrbegriff der Bewegung und Ruhe" (1758); 24–
33 "Gedanken bey dem frühzeitigen Ableben des Herrn Joh. Fried. v. Funk"
(1760); 34–55 "Versuch über die Krankheiten des Kopfes" (1764); 56–70
"Nachricht von der einrichtung seiner Vorlesungen in dem Winterhalbenjahre
v. 1765–1766" (1766); 71–80 "Von dem ersten Grunde des Unterschiedes der
Gegenden im Raume" (1768).

DATE. Undetermined: possibly c 1815, as JACOBI *Ueber die Lehre* (1 n).

COEDITORS. Kathleen Wheeler, Raimonda Modiano.

TEXTUS TRANSLATION. G. Kerferd and D. Walford tr *Kant: Selected Pre-
Critical Writings and Correspondence* (Manchester 1968).

1 p 71, pencil

Der berühmte *Leibnitz* besass viel wirkliche Einsichten, wodurch er die
Wissenschaften bereicherte, aber noch viel grössere Entwürfe zu
solchen, deren Ausführung die Welt von ihm vergebens erwartet hat.
Ob die Ursache darinn zu setzen: dass ihm seine Versuche noch zu un-
vollendet schienen . . . oder ob es ihm gegangen ist, wie *Boerhave* von
grossen Chemisten vermuthet, dass sie öfters Kunststücke vorgaben, als
wenn sie im Besitze derselben wären, da sie eigentlich nur in der Ueber-
redung und dem Zutrauen zu ihrer Geschicklichkeit standen, dass
ihnen die Ausführung derselben nicht mislingen könnte, wenn sie ein-
mal dieselbe übernehmen wollten, das will ich hier nicht entscheiden.

[The illustrious Leibniz enriched various departments of knowledge with many
genuine insights. But the world waited in vain for him to execute projects far
greater still. Whether the reason was that his efforts seemed too incomplete to
him . . . or whether it was with Leibniz, as Boerhaave suspects it was with great
chemists: that they often claimed the ability to perform certain undertakings, as
if they possessed the ability, whereas in reality they possessed only the convic-
tion and trust in their own skill that, once they wished to attempt the perfor-
mance of an undertaking, they could not but be successful: I do not wish to
decide here what the explanation is.]

Kant had a good deal of the Englishman in Him: and of all Peoples the

English are the least tolerant of Charlatanerie in any ~~both~~ut admitted Charlatans. Now that Leibnitz with all his acknowleged Genius & Merits had a *dash* of the Rosicrucian in his Compound, cannot be denied—[1]

---

[1] In JACOBI *Ueber die Lehre* **5**, C similarly suggests—it is not known on what basis—that Leibniz may not have been in earnest about the doctrines he published. In this context, "Rosicrucian" seems to be loosely used as a synonym for "charlatan", without reference to a specific set of esoteric beliefs.

Copy A

Im[m]anuel Kant's vermischte Schriften. Vol II (of 4). Halle 1799. 8°.

British Library C 126 e 7

A stray copy of Vol II, of unknown provenance and ownership. The copy of Vol I under this shelf-mark belongs with COPY C—the set that belonged to Joseph Henry Green—and has been transferred to that heading.

"S. T. C." label on title-page verso; typographical corrections by C on pp 331, 335, 456; an isolated ink-mark at the edge of p 473 does not appear to mark a particular passage.

CONTENTS. See COPY C headnote below.

MS TRANSCRIPT. VCL BT 22 (incomplete).

DATE. Apparently before 1816 (1 n 1); possibly 1810–11, in connection with notebook entries: *CN* III 3973, 3974, 4047.

COEDITORS. Kathleen Wheeler, Raimonda Modiano.

TEXTUS TRANSLATIONS. F. Goerwitz tr *Dreams of a Spirit-Seer* ed F. Sewall (1900); John T. Goldthwait tr *Observations on the Feeling of the Beautiful and Sublime* (Berkeley & Los Angeles 1959); Lewis White Beck ed *Kant's Latin Writings: Translations, Commentaries and Notes* (New York 1986).

1   II 344 and II $^{+}$1–$^{+}$2, referring to II 344 | *Träume eines Geistersehers* pt 2 ch 3

Wie? ist es denn nur darum gut, tugendhaft zu seyn, weil es eine andre Welt giebt, oder werden die Handlungen nicht vielmehr dereinst belohnt werden, weil sie an sich selbst gut und tugendhaft waren? Enthält das Herz des Menschen nicht unmittelbare sittliche Vorschriften, und muss man um ihn allhier seiner Bestimmung gemäss zu bewegen, durchaus die Maschinen an eine andere Welt ansetzen?* kann derjenige wohl redlich, kann er wohl tugendhaft heissen, welcher sich gern seinen Lieblingslastern ergeben würde, wenn ihn nur keine künftige Strafe schreckte . . .?

[What? is it good to be virtuous only because there is another world, or will not actions be rewarded rather because they were good and virtuous in themselves? Does man's heart not contain immediate moral precepts, and is it absolutely necessary to fix our machinery to the other world for the sake of moving man here according to his destiny?* Can he be called honest, can he be called virtuous, who would like to yield to his favourite vices if only he were not frightened by future punishment?]

* See the blank Leaf at the end of the Volume.^{a}

^{a} Note continues on pp $^{+}$1–$^{+}$2

p. 344. Let the Heart answer in silence to these Questions—a culti-
vated Heart, to which Vice in its ordinary shape is hateful on its own
account—. Will it not say—True! What I do, I would fain do well—it
is not any Hope of future Reward that impels me, nor any Fear of future
Punishment which keeps me in the Road—but the thought, that all, I can
do, is but a dream, and that not myself only but that all men & all things
are but Dreams, that nothing is permanent—which makes the mortality
of man a stupefying thought to me. I cannot conceive a supreme moral
Intelligence, unless I believe in my own immortality—for I must believe
in a whole system of apparent means to an end, which end had no exis-
tence—my Conscience, my progressive faculties, &c.—But give up
this, & Virtue wants all reason—. Away with Stoic Hypocrisy! I know
that in order to the idea of Virtue we must suppose the pure good will,
or reverence for the Law as excellent in itself—but this very excellence
supposes consequences, tho' not selfish ones—Let my maxim be capa-
ble of becoming the Law of all intelligent Being—well! but this sup-
poses an *end* possessible by intelligent Beings—For if the Law be barren
of all consequences, what is it but words? To obey the Law for its own
sake is really a mere sophism, in any other sense—: you might as well
put abra cadabra in its place.—I can readily conceive that I have it in
my nature to die a martyr, knowing that annihilation followed Death, if
it were possible to believe that all other human Beings were immortal,
& to be benefited by it—but any benefit that could affect only a set of
transitory Animals, whóat I could not deem myself worthy of any exer-
tion in my behalf, how can I deem others in of the same lot?—Boldly
should I say—O Nature! I would rather not have been—let that which is
to come so soon, come now—for what is all the intermediate space, but
sense of utter Worthlessness—. Far far below animals—for they enjoy a
generic immortality, having no individuation/ but man is truly & solely
an immortal series of conscious Mortalities, & inherent Disappoint-
ments—[1]

2 ii 426 | *Beobachtungen über das Gefühl des Schönen und Erhabenen* § 4

[Footnote:] Der Fanaticismus muss von *Enthusiasmus* jederzeit unter-
schieden werden. Jener glaubt eine unmittelbare und ausserordentliche
Gemeinschaft mit einer höhern Natur zu fühlen, dieser bedeutet den Zu-
stand des Gemüths, da dasselbe durch irgend einen Grundsatz über den
geziemenden Grad erhitzt worden . . .

1[1] C's *Theory of Life*, composed Nov–
Dec 1816 and reflecting his reading of
post-Kantian *Naturphilosophie*, proposes

increasing individuation as the key to the
hierarchy of forms in nature, admitting *de-
grees* of individuation even in the vegeta-

[Fanaticism must always be distinguished from *enthusiasm*. The former believes itself to feel an immediate and extraordinary communion with a higher nature; the latter means the state of the mind in which it has become inflamed by any principle above the proper degree . . .]

I dissent from Kant in this, & think that Fanaticism is only a species of Superstition, distinguished by its passion for proselytism[1]—it is born & lives only in a crowd of Sympathists! and what if one gives a false character to an Image, the other to a feeling? This is enough to make a species, not a genus.

3   II ⁻2, referring to 435–88 | *De mundi sensibilis* . . .

It is an interesting fact in philosophical History, i.e. the History of speculative Philosophy, that the "De Mundi Sensib. et intell. Form. et Prin." that Masterwork of profundity and precision, that model of steady investigation, clear Conception, and (as the Cambridge Mathematicians say) *elegant* Demonstration, was published 15 years before the Critique der reinen Vernunft—and produced no sensible effect on the philosophic Public.[1] The former work contains all the main principles of the Latter, and often more perspicuously expressed—yet all remained silent. The Critique der r. V. appeared—& the Universities of Germany *exploded*! What was the cause of this difference? Is it, that the same Thoughts appeared less strange, less paradoxical, in Latin than in the vernacular Tongue? Or that the ordinary proofs of the higher psychology are exposed more openly & expressly in the Crit. d. r. V. than in the former work?—Or lastly, that one's mother tongue however philosophized and technical still produces on us a liveliness of impression which a dead Language cannot produce?—However this be, the former work should always be studied & mastered previously to the study of the Critique d. r. V. & the works that followed it.—The student will find

ble and mineral kingdoms. Since the concept is here applied exclusively to human life, it seems likely that this note antedates the period of C's engagement with *Naturphilosophie*.

2[1] I.e. C objects that in Kant's distinction enthusiasm and fanaticism differ only in degree, not in kind. An extended account of his own version of the difference in kind—important because "the disease of the age is want of enthusiasm, and a tending to fanaticism"—is given in BIRCH 1.

3[1] *De mundi sensibilis*, Kant's "Inaugural Dissertation", was published in 1770, his first *Critique* in 1781. C's earliest reference to the former may be as early as 1800 (*CN* I 887), and he wrote about it with consistent enthusiasm, recommending it in a letter of Apr 1818—as he does here—as the best way to begin a study of Kant, and calling it "an invaluable Essay containing the *Germs* of all the great works published by [Kant] forty years afterwards": *CL* IV 851. Significantly, the letter calls this "Kant's only Latin work", suggesting that in 1818 C was not yet familiar with two other Latin essays in *VS* IV.

it a better auxiliary than 50 Vol. of Comments, from Reinhold, Schmidt, Schulz, Beck, Tieftrunk, &c &c &c.—[2]

3A II 439–40, marked off with short pen-strokes | § 1

Hinc patet; qui fiat, ut, *cum irrepraesentabile* et *impossibile* vulgo eiusdem significatus habeantur, conceptus tam *Continui* quam *Infiniti* a plurimis reiiciantur, quippe quorum, *secundum leges cognitionis intuitivae*, repraesentatio est impossibilis. Quanquam autem harum e non paucis scholis explosarum notionum, praesertim prioris, caussam hic non gero, maximi tamen momenti erit monuisse: gravissimo illos errore labi, qui tam perversa argumentandi ratione utuntur. Quicquid enim *repugnat* legibus intellectus et rationis, utique est impossibile; quod autem, cum rationis purae sit obiectum, legibus cognitionis intuitivae tantummodo *non subest*, non item. Nam hic dissensus inter facultatem *sensitivam* et *intellectualem*, (quarum indolem mox exponam) nihil indigitat, nisi, *quas mens ab intellectu acceptas fert ideas abstracta[s], illas in concreto exsequi, et in Intuitus commutare saepenumero non posse*. Haec autem reluctantia *subiectiva* mentitur, ut plurimum, repugnantiam aliquam obiectivam, et incantos facile fallit, limitibus, quibus mens humana circumscribitur, pro iis habitis, quibus ipsa rerum essentia continetur.

[Accordingly, *since the unrepresentable* and the *impossible* are commonly regarded as having the same meaning, and since representation of the concepts of *continuity* and *infinitude in accordance with the laws of intuitive knowledge* is clearly impossible, we see how it is that these concepts are rejected by the many. I am not here pleading the cause of these notions, rejected as they are by many schools. It is, however, of the utmost importance that those who follow this highly perverse line of argument should be warned that in so doing they fall into a most grave error. Whatever is *opposed* to the laws of understanding and reason is indeed impossible; but that which, being an object of pure reason, is merely *not subject* to the laws of intuitive cognition is not impossible. For this disagreement between the *sensitive* and the *intellectual* faculties (whose character I shall presently expound) shows no more than this: *the mind is frequently unable to follow in the concrete and to translate into intuitions abstract ideas which it has received from the intellect.* But this *subjective* inability very often gives a false

3[2] Contemporary popularisers of the critical philosophy: Karl Leonhard Reinhold (1758–1823), professor of philosophy at Jena; Karl Christian Erhard Schmid (1761–1812), who made a compendium of *C d r V* and compiled a dictionary of Kantian terms; Christopher Johann Schulz (1739–1805), who published with Kant's approval an exposition of *C d r V* (1784); Jacob Sigismund Beck (1761–1840), a student of Kant's and professor at Halle, who published several commentaries including *Grundriss der critischen Philosophie* (1796; tr into English 1797); Johann Heinrich Tieftrunk (1759–1837), editor of *Vermischte Schriften*, one of the foremost contemporary exponents of Kant's philosophy.

impression of some objective hindrance, and easily deceives the heedless into taking the limits circumscribing the human mind for those within which the very essence of things is contained.]¹

3B   II 487, marked with a marginal line | § 30

Ita autem statuimus, non propterea, quod eventuum mundanorum secundum leges naturae communes tam amplam possideamus cognitionem, aut supernaturalium nobis pateret vel impossibilitas, vel minima possibilitas hypothetica . . .

[We do not assume it [the order of nature] because of our possessing so wide a knowledge of cosmic happenings according to the common laws of nature, or because we perceive the impossibility, or the small hypothetical possibility, of the supernatural . . .]

3C   II 487, marked with a marginal line

Eandem ob rationem *miracula comparativa*, influxus nempe spirituum, sollicite arcemus ab expositione ᵃphaenomenorum, quia cum eorum natura nobis incognita sit, intellectus magno suo detrimento a luce experientiae, per quam solam legum indicandi sibi comparandarum ipsi copia est, ad umbras incognitarum nobis specierum et caussarum averteretur.

[For the same reason, we are careful to exclude *comparative miracles* from our exposition of phenomena; I mean the influence of spirits, since, as their nature is unknown to us, it would be greatly to the detriment of the intellect if it were diverted away from the light of experience—through which alone it has the means of judging between rival interpretations—to the shadows of forms and causes unknown to us.]

ᵃ Marginal line begins here

3A¹ This is the passage q by C in *BL* ch 12 (*CC*) I 288 and in *Logic* (*CC*) 243–4.

Copy B

Immanuel Kants vermischte Schriften. Vols I, II, III (of 4). Halle 1799. 8°.

University College, London

Autograph signature "H. C. Robinson" on the title-page of each volume, and his bookplate on the front p-d of each volume. The name "Field" is written in pencil on HCR's bookplate in Vols I and II; bookplate of Edwin Wilkins Field (HCR's literary executor) on III ⁻4. Brief booksellers' and librarians' notes appear on I ⁻3 (p-d), ⁺3, II ⁻5 (p-d), III ⁻5 (p-d). Someone other than C appears to have been responsible for emendations on I 155 and 580, and for the correction (in pencil) of a typographical error on I 465. Marked passages that could be C's are listed in the ANNEX.

CONTENTS. See COPY C headnote below.

DATE. c 1816. There is no record of the date when HCR lent these volumes to C; on 14 Jul 1816, the occasion of HCR's first visit to C at Highgate, C returned "*Kants Works*, Three Volumes *Miscellanies*, and Lamb brought me my other books from Calne": *CRB* I 185.

COEDITORS. Kathleen Wheeler, Raimonda Modiano.

TEXTUS TRANSLATIONS. *Dreams of a Spirit-Seer* (see COPY A Goerwitz); Stanley L. Jaki tr *Universal Natural History and Theory of the Heavens* (Edinburgh 1981).

1   I 31, pencil | *Gedanken von der wahren Schätzung der lebendigen Kräfte* pt 1 § 10

Diesem zu folge, halte ich dafür, dass die Substanzen in der existirenden Welt, wovon wir ein Theil sind, wesentliche Kräfte von der Art haben, dass sie in Vereinigung mit einander nach der [dem] doppelten umgekehrten Verhältniss der Weiten ihre Wirkungen von sich ausbreiten;* zweitens, dass das Ganze, was daher entspringt, vermöge dieses Gesetzes die Eigenschaft der dreyfachen Dimension habe. . . . Die Unmöglichkeit . . . einen Raum von mehr als drei Abmessungen uns vorzustellen, scheinet mir daher zu rühren, weil unsre Seele ebenfalls nach dem Gesetze der umgekehrten doppelten Verhältniss der Weiten die Eindrücke von draussen empfängt . . .

[As a result of this I consider that the substances in the existing world of which we are a part have essential powers of such a kind that in combination with one another they exert their influence according to double the inverse proportion of their distances;* secondly, that the whole that arises as a result has the property of three dimensions according to this law. . . . The impossibility of conceiving a space of more than three dimensions seems to me to rest on the fact that our soul also receives impressions from the outside according to the law of double the inverse proportion of distances . . .]

Where shall I find a man, at once a German Scholar, an Algebraist, and a Metaphysician to explain this to me? I cannot form a notion of Distance without have*a* pre-conceived Space—nor Space other than as of three Dimensions.[1]

2   I +1–+3,*b* referring to I 494 | *Allgemeine Naturgeschichte und Theorie des Himmels*
pt 3

[494] . . . [man muss gestehen,] dass die Entfernungen der Himmelskörper von der Sonne gewisse Verhältnisse mit sich führen, welche einen wesentlichen Einfluss in die verschiedenen Eigenschaften der denkenden Naturen, nach sich ziehen, die auf denselben befindlich sind, als deren Art zu wirken und zu leiden, an die Beschaffenheit der Materie, mit der sie verknüpfet sind, gebunden ist, und von dem Maass der Eindrücke abhänget, die die Welt, nach den Eigenschaften der Beziehung ihres Wohnplatzes zu dem Mittelpuncte der Attraction und der Wärme, in ihnen erwecket.

Ich bin der Meinung, dass es eben nicht nothwendig sey, zu behaupten, alle Planeten müssten bewohnt seyn. . . .

[502] Wenn man die Ursache der Hindernisse untersuchet, welche die menschliche Natur in einer so tiefen Erniedrigung erhalten; so findet sie sich in der Grobheit der Materie, darin sein geistiger Theil versenket ist, in der Unbiegsamkeit der Fasern, und der Trägheit und Unbeweglichkeit der Säfte, welche dessen Regungen gehorchen sollen. Die Nerven und Flüssigkeiten seines Gehirns liefern ihm nur grobe und undeutliche Begriffe, und weil er die Reitzung der sinnlichen Empfindungen, in dem Inwendigen seines Denkungsvermögens, nicht genungsam kräftige Vorstellungen zum Gleichgewichte entgegenstellen kann: so wird er von seinen Leidenschaften hingerissen. . . .

[503–4] In dieser Abhängigkeit schwinden die geistigen Fähigkeiten zugleich mit der Lebhaftigkeit des Leibes: wenn das hohe Alter durch den geschwächten Umlauf der Säfte nur dicke Säfte in dem Körper kochet, wenn die Beugsamkeit der Fasern, und die Behendigkeit in allen Bewegungen abnimmt, so erstarren die Kräfte des Geistes in einer gleichen Ermattung. Die Hurtigkeit der Gedanken, die Klarheit der Vorstellung, die Lebhaftigkeit des Witzes und das Erinnerungsvermögen werden kraftlos und erkalten.

a Perhaps a slip for ''having'' or ''I have''   *b* The note is written below **4**

1[1] In *Logic* (*CC*) 194–5* C cites the title of this essay, quotes the Latin epigraph to it, and states that ''This juvenile work of our modern Aristotle may be safely ranked among our most perfect specimens of scientific arbitration . . .''. He commends it similarly in *AR* (1825) 292–3n.

[. . . still one must admit that the distances of the celestial bodies [planets] from the sun embody certain relationships, which in turn entail a decisive influence on the various characteristics of thinking natures [beings] that are found there; whose manner of operating and feeling is bound to the condition of the material with which they are connected and [also] depends on the measure [intensity] of impressions which the [external] world invokes in them according to the properties of the relation of their habitat to [the sun,] the centre of attraction and heat.

I am of the opinion that it is not even necessary to assert that all planets must be inhabited. . . .

[502] If one looks for the cause of impediments, which keep human nature in such a deep abasement, it will be found in the crudeness of the matter into which his spiritual part is sunk, in the unbending of the fibres, and in the sluggishness and immobility of fluids which should obey its stirrings. The nerves and fluids of his brain deliver to him only gross and unclear concepts, and because he cannot counterbalance in the interior of his thinking ability the impact of sensory impressions with sufficiently powerful ideas, he will be carried away by his passions. . . .

[503–4] Because of this dependence, the spiritual faculties disappear together with the vigour of the body: when owing to the slackened flow of fluids advanced age cooks only thick fluid in the body, when the suppleness of the fibres and the nimbleness in all motions decrease, then the forces of the spirit too stiffen into a similar dullness. The agility of thought, the clarity of representation, the vivacity of wit, and the ability to remember lose their strength and grow frigid.]

P. 474.[1] I cannot see the force of this reasoning: rather seem to see that Kant, then a youth, had not known the different capacity of Heat in different Bodies. —For aught we know, the bodies of the Comets & their Inhabitants may be capacious of latent Heat[2] to a degree infinitely beyond those on our Heat[a]—or beyond a certain point may be insensible to Heat—or the Sun may not be Heat, but an occasioning cause of vibration, which may produce very different effects according to the nature of the media, they set in action—even as the same Ether vibrating $= \alpha$ produces Vision or Light, $= \beta$ sensation of Heat, $= \gamma$ sound/. It is possible at least, that the Body of a Cometarian[3] may have not only such a capacity for combined Heat, as to absorb all the Caloric of the Perihelion with no greater thermometric effect, & Sensation correspondent,

[a] A slip for "Earth"?

2[1] A slip for "P. 494".

2[2] This is the fairly recently introduced concept—anticipating the formulation of the law of conservation of energy—to which C alludes when he refers to "the heat in ice" as in *BL* ch 10 (*CC*) I 171. Cf Davy's explanation in *A Syllabus of a Course of Lectures on Chemistry* (1802) 51: "Bodies, in changing their states of existence . . . , absorb or give out that heat which, in consequence of its peculiar relation to the heat of temperature, is called *latent heat*, or caloric of combination."

2[3] The inhabitant of a comet; not in *OED*. Kant's subject is the possibility of life in outer space, the "plurality of worlds".

thatn we in our Summer Solstice; but may be so organized as gradually to expend this Heat, so as to keep an average warmth, till the new Perihelion refils it: even as Lamps draw from a reservoir of Oil.—Besides, Kant's own observations on the immense differences between man & man seems at variance with this hypothesis—for surely Newton was not only co-planetary, but compatriot with a multitude of Ideots—with Worms, Oysters &c—It would be not only interesting but instructive could we learn with what feelings Kant, as the Author of the Kritik d.r.V. reperused this passage (p. 502) of his youthful mind—such bold assertory materialism—how would he have smiled at the affinity between *thin* & intelligent, quick motion of a fluid and virtue!

Tho' Kant was but a youth when he wrote this extraordinary work, it still pains me to find such reasonings as from page 480 to 506[4]—and yet it[a] to encourage one—What a glorious answer do not the last years of Newton, Leibnitz, Milton & so many others, give to the assertion in p. 504—.[5] But the whole ground is groundless—. Not according to the Matter is the *body* even, much less the Soul; but according to the chemical, vital & rational powers, such is the matter[6]—The air, we breathe, is $\frac{4}{5}$ths probably a metal volatilized, which some chemical affinity will perhaps render malleable—Trace the dirt, & manure by the vegetable power transformed into the visible parts of Grass or Leaves—then by the vital part turned into flesh, blood, horn, ivory!—But this, as I have observed, is the deficiency of the admirable portion of his System—and the defect of the remainder.

3 I 503

Diese Grobheit des Stoffes und des Gewebes in dem Baue der menschlichen Natur ist die Ursache derjenigen Trägheit, welche die Fähigkeiten der Seele in einer beständigen Mattigkeit und Kraftlosigkeit erhält.

[The grossness of the stuff and of the texture in the build of human nature is the cause of that sluggishness which keeps the faculties of the soul in perennial dullness and feebleness.]

Does not a man live on the proud Oxen?—*His* vital power *humanizes* a

---

[a] A word omitted: "is"? "tends"?

2[4] In this section Kant treats matter as the ground from which the soul or mind originates and shows that the spiritual and mental powers of man depend on the properties of matter with which they are linked.

2[5] I.e. the last two sentences in textus.

2[6] C affirms that matter, constituted as it is by the interaction of dynamical powers which are entirely ideal, cannot be the source of any powers, either physical or spiritual.

trait, as a beast's *beastifies* it.—[a] The same worms may & often do serve for Food to Bird and Fish; but the Bird birdifies, and the Fish fishifies them. It is surprizing to find reasoning so weak even in Kant of 22 years' age!

4   1 [+1], referring to 1 513

Es ist zu glauben, dass obgleich die Vergänglichkeit auch an den vollkommensten Naturen naget, dennoch der Vorzug in der Feinheit des Stoffes, in der Elasticität der Gefässe, und der Leichtigkeit und Wirksamkeit der Säfte, woraus jene vollkommnern Wesen, welche in den entfernten Planeten wohnen, gebildet sind, diese Hinfälligkeit, welche eine Folge aus der Trägheit einer groben Materie ist, weit länger aufhalten . . .

[It is believable that although decay affects even the most perfect natures, nevertheless the advantage in the refinement of the stuff, in the elasticity of vessels, and in the lightness and efficiency of fluids of which those perfect beings that inhabit the more distant planets are composed, held up far longer this frailty, which is a consequence of the sluggishness of the cruder matter . . .]

p. 513. Kant would have made a still more delightful Mechanique Celeste,[1] a far more satisfactory Cosmogony, had he written with the present knowlege of Chemistry.—Ex. gr. he talks continually of coarser & finer sorts of Matter &c; whereas we have reason to believe, that Density is the exponent of Cohesion, and Cohesion in inverse proportion to Heat/ Gold, Platinum, Chrystal &c in Mercury may be [? d] subtle and mobile Fluids or Gasses, which may be animalized into [? p] Nerves & Fibres, [? The] exquisitely permeable by Electricity.[2]—One thing I find especially obscure—the first origination of a centre, why in one place rather than another. Nor can I conceive, how the chaotic Diffusive could subsist a single Hour, if not for ever[3]

---

[a] A change of pen at this point wrongly gives the impression of a change of hand

4[1] "Celestial Mechanics"—alluding to Laplace's *Traité de mécanique céleste* (1799–1825). In 1818, C referred to this work as "an unprincipled Plagiarism" from Kant: *CL* IV 808.

4[2] C refers as usual to the new chemistry as a dynamic science, a science of powers, supplanting Newtonian mechanism. In the scheme of the "compass of nature", the power that manifests itself as cohesion at the level of minerals (where it is associated with magnetism) may appear as density (in association with electricity) at the higher level of animal life. Cohesion is the subject of some notes of 1814–15 along with notes about the compass of nature, but the relationship of cohesion to density is not mentioned specifically: *CN* III 4223–6.

4[3] Kant's theory of the formation of the universe entails a chaos of elements (the *Zerstreuung*—e.g. p 315—that C renders "Diffusive") formed into a "central body" (the sun) "at the point of strongest attraction" (315).

326 *Immanuel Kant*

5 ɪɪ 77–9 | *Der einzig mögliche Beweisgrund einer Demonstration des Daseyns Gottes*
div 1 observ 1 § 3

Baumgarten führt die durchgängige innere Bestimmung, *in so fern sie
dasjenige ergänzet, was durch die im Wesen liegenden oder daraus fliessenden Prädicate unbestimmt gelassen ist, als dasjenige an, was im Daseyn mehr, als in der blossen Möglichkeit ist; allein wir haben schon
gesehen, dass in der Verbindung eines Dinges mit allen erdenklichen
Prädicaten niemals ein Unterschied desselben von einem blos Möglichen liege.

[Baumgarten defines the general inner determination *in so far as it complements that which is left indeterminate by the predicates within or issuing from
the essential nature, as that which is in existence more than in possibility; but
we have already seen that the difference between a thing and one that is merely
possible never lies in its connexion with all conceivable predicates.]

* Methinks, Baumgarten's Definition is just:¹ tho' it rather describes the
difference between the causative Ideas of God, & the Thoughts of Men,
than proves the reality of the Former. Degrees admit no generic definition: and what if Posse and Existere are but Degrees of Esse (Seyn)?² a
Thought possessing durchgängige innere Bestimmung, would be a
Thing κατ' εξοχήν: i.e. eminenter, or Ding in sich,³ such as would imply the Fiat. Facit et fit, creat et creatur.⁴ Yet Kant's Objection is valid
in all disquisitions, which instead of *grounding* on God aim to *deduce*
him: as those, which derive a God from the order of the material World,
not only confounding Certainty with Evidence, but mistaking for Evidence mere sensuous vividness.   S. T. Coleridge.

6 ɪɪ 77 | Continuing **5** textus

Ueberdem kann der Satz: dass ein mögliches Ding, als ein solches betrachtet, in Ansehung vieler Prädicate unbestimmt sey, wenn er so nach
dem Buchstaben genommen wird, eine grosse Unrichtigkeit veranlassen. Denn die Regel der Ausschliessung eines mittlern zwischen zwei
widersprechend entgegengesetzten verbieten dieses . . .

[Moreover the statement that a possible thing regarded as such is indeterminate
in respect of many predicates can, if the strict meaning is taken, cause a great

---

5¹ Alexander Gottlieb Baumgarten
(1714–62), cited in textus; author of works
on ethics, metaphysics, and aesthetics.
  5² What if "to be possible" and "to exist" are but degrees of "to be (being)"?
  5³ A *Thought* possessing "general inner

determination" (from textus) would be a
Thing "par excellence"—that is, "eminently", or "a thing-in-itself".
  5⁴ Erigena's definition of "the divine
nature": "it makes and is made, creates
and is created": *CL* ɪɪ 954.

mistake. For the rule of the exclusion of a mean between two contradictory opposites makes this impossible . . .]

Note here the difference between opposites and contraries. O. always have an Equator—C. never. ———|———.)(¹

7   ɪɪ ⁺2–⁺4, referring to ɪɪ 92–3ᵃ | Observ 3 § 3

Weil das nothwendige Wesen den letzten Realgrund aller andern Möglichkeit enthält, so wird ein jedes andere Ding nur möglich seyn, in so fern es durch ihn als einen Grund gegeben ist. Demnach kann ein jedes andere Ding nur als eine Folge von ihm statt finden, und ist also aller andern Dinge Möglichkeit und Daseyn von ihm abhängend. Etwas aber was selbst abhängend ist, enthält nicht den letzten Realgrund aller Möglichkeit, und ist demnach nicht schlechterdings nothwendig. Mithin können nicht mehrere Dinge absolut nothwendig seyn.

Setzet A sey ein nothwendiges Wesen, und B ein anderes. So ist vermöge der Erklärung, B nur in so fern möglich, als er durch einen andern Grund A, als die Folge desselben gegeben ist. Weil aber vermöge der Voraussetzung B selber nothwendig ist, so ist seine Möglichkeit in ihm als ein Prädicat, und nicht als eine Folge aus einem andern, und doch nur als eine Folge laut dem vorigen gegeben, welches sich widerspricht.

[Because the necessary Being comprises the ultimate real-ground of every other possibility, nothing else is possible except in so far as it is given by it as a ground. Any other thing, then, can exist only as a consequence of it; thus the possibility and existence of all other things depend upon it. Anything, however, that is itself dependent does not comprise the ultimate real-ground of all possibility, and consequently is not absolutely necessary. Hence it is not possible that more than one thing can be absolutely necessary.

Let us say that A is a necessary Being, B another. Thus by virtue of the definition B is possible only in so far as it is given through another ground A, as the consequence of this. Because, however, by virtue of the proposition, B itself is necessary, so its possibility is present in it as a predicate, and not as a consequence of something else, and nevertheless only as a consequence is the former true, which is a contradiction.]

The 92–93 page is that which I unwillingly halt at.¹ Because it is

ᵃ Written after **12**

6¹ The first figure illustrates visually the bipolarity of "opposites", their homogeneity, attraction, and bonding represented by the horizontal line—the "equator" possibly in the radical but exceptional sense of "that which equals or makes equal" (not in *OED* in this sense); but cf also the equatorial lines in the world-systems of *Naturphilosophie*, reflected in C's writings, e.g. in *CN* ɪɪɪ 4226. The figure)(here illustrates visually the heterogeneity, repulsion, and impermeability of "contraries". C used the symbol extensively, e.g. Joannes **4**.

7¹ copy c **10** has the same textus.

necessary, that there should be one, is it necessary that there should not be two, or many? Suppose matter to consist of elements, monads—it is[a] demonstrable, that all might not be eternal? And that the apparent Changes, and *Time*, their measure & consequence, might not be the result of Relations, and the vis representativa?[2]—of course, I am speaking of absolute *Demonstration*. In the court of common sense, much more of Conscience, it would not gain a Hearing.—If this be fully proved, that for any thing to be possible there must be a *one* something/ real,— & there cannot be more than one; all the rest follows inevitably.—A. There *must* be one; tho' there may be more. B. There must be one, and there can be one only.—B. urges, that it is contrary to the first Canon of sound Philosophy to assume many principles, when one is adequate: and that there can be but one Being, whose possibility is identical with (i.e. impossible without) its reality. A. replies, that the last assertion is a petitio principii, and boldly extends it to each & all the elementary monads—and while he admits the former rule in all other cases, yet here he hesitates—because of the World he has a realizing Experience, and may therefore use it as an Hypothesis: a *sub*-position/ while he charges his opponent with an Hypopoiēsis, or a *sub-fiction*—/—[3] This is retorted by B. who contends that monads, and elementary Particles are mere Fictions, insusceptible of [? a] rational [of] Deduction or ex[b] experimental Induction.—

Thus then, in the necessary existence of a "Τό Θεῖον"[4] both agree; but differ, as Polytheism and Monotheism—A contends for the Dii Immortales, απατερες, αμητρες, αει εοντες:[5] B. for the Ο θεος ὁ μονος, ο παυτοπατηρ.[6]—The Christian Faith, in all things bearing the marks of the Mediator and Reconciler, unites what is just in both, in the mystery-solving Mystery of the Tri-unity.[7]   S. T. Coleridge

---

[a] Error for "is it"?   [b] C presumably intended to delete "ex" but did not actually cross it through

7[2] "Representative force".

7[3] The etymological basis of this frequently invoked distinction is clarified by C himself in a note of 1809: "Hypothesis: the placing of one known fact under others as their *ground* or foundations. . . . Where both the position and the fact are imagined, it is Hypopœēsis not Hypothesis, subfiction not supposition": *CN* III 3587.

7[4] "The Divine": cf the distinction in **11** below.

7[5] A (i.e. Polytheism) contends for the "Immortal Gods, fatherless, motherless,

always in being".

7[6] B (i.e. Monotheism) contends for "The only god, the all-father"—the last word, not in Liddell & Scott or W. Bauer *A Greek-English Lexicon of the New Testament* (Chicago 1968), coined on the analogy of e.g. παντοκρατωρ, "all-ruler, omnipotent".

7[7] C used the term "Tri-unity" as other than a simple synonym of "Trinity", aware perhaps of seventeenth-century usage, as early as c May 1810 (*CN* III 3812). Cf Böhme 7—"one God, blessed over all!

8 ii 161, 160, pencil | Observ 5 § 2

Man hat Ursache zu glauben, dass diese Merkwürdigkeit ein Fall sey, der unter einer viel allgemeinern Regel stehen mag, nämlich, dass der stärkere Theil der Menschenarten auch einen grösseren Antheil an der Zeugungsthätigkeit habe, um in den beiderseitigen Produkten seine eigene Art überwiegend zu machen* . . .

[There is cause to believe that this peculiarity [that more boys are born than girls] is something that may well be due to a much more general rule; namely that the stronger part of human kind also has a greater share in conception, so that it causes its own kind to preponderate in the products of both parts* . . .]

* p. 160. If this were the Cause, should not the most vigorous men produce Boys rather*a* Girls? And yet it is a common saying, that any Weakling may beget a Boy, but that it must be a *man* to beget a girl.[1]— This, I know, is not uniformly the case—yet I think it probable, that the sex depends in part at *b*least on the excitement of the Imagination at the moment and that a woman intensely pleased + a girl.[2]

9 ii 219, rs in pencil on ii 220 | Div 3 § 2

Indessen haben wir einen berühmten Beweis [des Daseins Gottes], der auf diesen Grund erbauet ist, nämlich den so genannten Cartesianischen. Man erdenket sich zuforderst einen Begriff von einem möglichen Dinge, in welchem man alle wahre Vollkommenheit sich vereinbart vorstellt. Nun nimmt man an, das Daseyn sey auch eine Vollkommenheit der Dinge, also schliesst man aus der Möglichkeit eines vollkommensten Wesens auf seine Existenz. Eben so könnte man aus dem Begriffe einer jeden Sache, welche auch nur als die vollkommenste ihrer Art vorgestellt wird, z.E. daraus allein schon, dass eine vollkommenste Welt zu gedenken ist, auf ihr Daseyn schliessen.

[On the other hand we have a famous proof [of the existence of God] which is based on this principle, namely the so-called Cartesian. First of all one conceives an idea of a possible thing, which one imagines unites all true perfection. Now one assumes that existence is also a perfection of things and thus one deduces the existence of a most perfect being from its possibility. Precisely in this way one could deduce its existence from the concept of a something, which is also

---

a For "rather than"

b The note having reached the foot of p 161, C continued on p 160 with "(from the opposite page)"

Unity which *cannot* be *divided*! Tri-unity, which cannot *but* be *distinguished*."

8[1] C gives a Latin version of this proverb in COPY C **15**.

8[2] I.e. conceives a girl. For the conclu-

sion that, contrary to the popular doctrine of "maternal impressions", an influence of the mother upon the foetus cannot be shown, see KLUGE **32**.

only to be thought of as the most perfect of its kind, that is from the very fact that a most perfect world can be conceived.]

I cannot but think, that K. has here treated Des Cartes harshly, and attended to the *Letter* of his Argument to the exclusion of its *Spirit*. How often has K. himself been thus treated![1]

*a*Spite of all this, I suspect the Cartesian Proof to be essentially the same as Kant's:[2] which Tieftrunk treats in the same way.[3]

10   II ⁻4, referring to II 219–20*b* | **9** textus

P. 219–20. As I am not shaken in my Faith in Kant's Demonstration by the remarks of Tieftrunk (which seem to me to amount to no more than this, that if I think then it is true to me; but if I do not, then it ceases.[1] Now as I do think, and feel myself compelled to think on the subject, to me it is true) so neither am I convinced by Kant of the weakness of the Cartesian Proof.[2] It is not true, that we have a *clear intuitive Idea* (and upon this Des Cartes rests) of a perfect World, as we have of God

11   II ⁻4

It would gratify a not idle curiosity in me to learn, whether Schelling took the leading Idea of his Theology (I allude here to his "Untersuchung über das Wesen der Menschlichen Freyheit")[1] namely, the establishing an independent Ground of God's Existence, which is indeed God (τό Θεῖον) but not God himself ('Ο θεος) from Kant's "Einzigmögliche Beweisgrund" or from Behmen?[2] I mean, in the first instance. For that

---

a Note continues on II 220, in pencil   *b* This note is written below **11**

9[1] C makes a similar remark about the widespread misrepresentation of Descartes in NICOLAI **29**. Kant himself he represents as being misunderstood by some of his followers, e.g. HERDER *Kalligone* **9**, JACOBI *Werke* **6**.

9[2] C is probably referring here simply to Kant's exposition of "the Cartesian Proof", but cf the remark in *BL* ch 10 (*CC*) I 200, "I was pleased with the Cartesian opinion, that the idea of God is distinguished from all other ideas by involving its *reality*; but I was not wholly satisfied." The argument of Descartes is further considered in **12** below.

9[3] See **12** n 5 below.

10[1] C here refers to Tieftrunk's "Anhang zur Prüfung der Beweisgrundes" (II

230–46), and in **13** below he summarises Tieftrunk's objections to Kant's argument.

10[2] C alludes to **9** textus, though he might also have remembered Kant's argument against Descartes in *C d r V* (1799) 620–30.

11[1] Essay 5 in SCHELLING *Philosophische Schriften* (Landshut 1809) 399–511, on which C wrote more than 30 annotations.

11[2] The two Greek terms occur also in **7** above. In an annotation on Schelling's essay (pp 438–9) C said that "In truth, from p. 429. I find little but *Behmen*—which a Reader must have previously understood in order to understand." C also discusses Schelling's relationship to Böhme in *BL* ch 9 (*CC*) I 161–3 and BÖHME **74**.

he has profited by the Latter, is most evident. The very Terms of the System, as well as the System itself, pre-existed in the earliest Works of that extraordinary Enthusiast./.

12   II ⁺1–⁺2, referring to II 230–46 | J. H. Tieftrunk "Anhang zur Prüfung des Beweisgrundes"

P. 230. I cannot say, that I have been much edified by the "Anhang" of Herrn Tieftrunk der wahrhaftig nicht sehr tief getrunken zu haben scheint von seines Meisters Urquelle/[1] That the whole Argument is analytic, not synthetic, who could ever doubt?[2] And what need of so prolixly proving that which constitutes the very essence of the Problem? viz.—whether or no the reality of God's Existence does not form a unique Instance of the Analytic containing in itself that which in all other cases is peculiar to the synthetic: whether the ~~Idea~~ Thought does ~~it~~ not compulsorily bring with it the reality, the Idea involving the Ens *ideatum*.[3] Me judice,[4] this exquisite analysis is essentially the same, as the Demonstration of Des Cartes, afterwards illustrated by Mendelsohn[5]— only free from the error of taking Existence, as a Predicate, instead of the Position (Setzung) of all the Predicates/ & conducted throughout with more Science & scientific Arrangement. The Question (assuredly among the most interesting of all *scholastic* Problems) must rest for its solution pro or contra on the Fact—that we are *obliged* by the Laws of our human Nature, ~~as~~ quatenus intellectual[6] (& therefore not originating in its negations or limits) to identify the undeniable logical Form of a Reality, as the ground of all Possibility (= possibilitatum omnium fons et quasi possibilitas)[7] with its *actuality*, extrinsical & independent of human *Idioms*.[8] For *any* thing to be possible there must be a *some* thing real—that which would destroy all possibility, is itself impossible.— This is self-certain.[9] But tho' it is necessary, that there should be some

12[1] Johann Heinrich Tieftrunk (1759–1837), editor of this collection, "who truly does not seem to have drunk very deeply from the spring of his Master"—a play on the name *Tief-trunk* (loosely, "deep drunk").

12[2] Tieftrunk's contention II 234.

12[3] The "ideated Entity", "idealised Thing".

12[4] "In my opinion".

12[5] For "the Demonstration of Des Cartes" see **9** above. Moses Mendelssohn (1729–86), in his *Jerusalem*, and in his *Morgenstunden* ch 17, esp p 310 which C annotated (MENDELSSOHN *Morgenstunden*

19), pursues a similar line of argument.

12[6] "In so far as [it is] intellectual".

12[7] "The source—and, as it were, the possibility—of all possibilities".

12[8] Cf Kant's warning in *C d r V* (1799) 624n against the error of confusing a purely logical predicate with a real predicate of existence and of "arguing directly from the logical possibility of concepts to the real possibility of things" (tr).

12[9] A paraphrase of Tieftrunk's argument in "Anhang" pp 236–7: "All possibility presupposes something actual (a real); therefore there is a particular reality the destruction of which would also do

thing or things, does it follow, that such Thing ~~or Things~~ itself should be necessary? That it should be one only?—And this again would lead us to the old Question of an infinite Series, or the eternity of each Thing as self-grounded.—Is this merely incomprehensible, in which case it would be neither more or less objectionable than the counter-idea of a First Cause? Or is it *absurd*?—[10]

13   II ⁻3–⁻2, referring to II 230–46

p. 230–246. All Tieftrunk's Objections amount to this—1. If we do not choose to think, then we do not demonstrate the existence of an Ens Entium/[1] 2. and if we do, it is only the necessity of our Reason on which the conclusion is grounded and we have no corresponding Necessity of our Senses—in short, that we cannot think of God, as of a *Thing*. No, to be sure! Neither ought we. And how[a] it diminish the reality of a Truth to say, that that which, if it exists, can exist only as an Object of Reason, is by our Reason alone perceptible.[2] Surely, it is sufficient for all but madmen to have proved, that the Conclusion is inevitable except by the suspension of the concluding faculty—. But to say that after all it is only the mere form or law of our own Intellect that we affirm, is most unphilosophical—till it can be shewn, that a Table or a Tree[3] are for me any other than the Form of my Intuition & Understanding why should I prefer that which is the fallible Part of my Nature to that which never deceives me?—We live by *Faith*[4]—it is equally common to all our knowleges—& cannot therefore affect the plus and minus of Demonstration.—The true Objection to the argument is that to demonstrate that if any thing *is* either it or something else must always have been, is no demonstration of the existence of GOD: i.e. of a holy, self-comprehend-

---

[a] A word is omitted after this, perhaps "would" or "does"

---

away with all inner possibility in general. That, however, the destruction or negation of which annihilates all possibility, is absolutely necessary; *consequently something absolutely necessary exists.*" The same point arises in COPY C **8, 10**.

12[10] Recognising that "the human mind has no predilection for absurdity" (*Friend—CC*—I 430), C cites a maxim of Spinoza, "Where the Alternative lies between the Absurd and the Incomprehensible, no wise man can be at a loss which of the two to prefer" in *AR* (1825) 333.

13[1] Lit a "Being of Beings"—a Supreme Being.

13[2] Cf Tieftrunk's "Anhang" p 244

(tr): "In the case of sensory objects there is the connection with some one of our perceptions in accordance with empirical laws. But since the concept of the Creator is a pure concept of reason, and the object of this concept would therefore have to be known in a completely *a priori* manner, there is nothing left but to search in the concept itself to see whether it does not contain some condition that makes it necessary to posit its object."

13[3] I.e. any object of the senses, any object bounded by space and time.

13[4] Rom 1.17 (var, repeated in Gal 3.11, Heb 10.38).

ing, creative and arranging Will.[5] All we can or need say is, that the existence of a necessary Being is so transcendently Rational, that it is Reason itself[6]—and that there is no other form under which this Being is contemplable but that of a holy and intelligent Will—Admit this and all is solved—deny it, all is darkness—substitute any other Form, and we have a chaos of Absurdities—The deductio ad absurdum[7] in this case is no less demonstrative than in Geometry, for that originates in a Space of three dimensions, which a Sceptic might choose to question, as a mere subjective necessity of the Human Intuition—der menschlichen Anschauung—yea, and perhaps with much greater Plausibility.

14 ɪɪ 312–13, pencil, first two words in ink | *Träume eines Geistersehers* pt 2 ch 1

Es lebt zu Stockholm ein gewisser Herr *Schwedenborg*, ohne Amt oder Bedienung, von seinem ziemlich ansehnlichen Vermögen. Seine ganze Beschäftigung besteht darin, dass er, wie er selbst sagt, schon seit mehr als zwanzig Jahren, mit Geistern und abgeschiedenen Seelen im genauesten Umgange stehet, von ihnen Nachrichten aus der andern Welt einholet und ihnen dagegen welche aus der gegenwärtigen ertheilt, grosse Bände über seine Entdeckungen abfasst und bisweilen nach London reiset, um die Ausgabe derselben zu besorgen.

[There lives at Stockholm a certain Mr. Swedenborg, a gentleman of comfortable means and independent position. His whole occupation for more than twenty years is, as he himself says, to be in closest intercourse with spirits and deceased souls; to receive news from the other world, and, in exchange, give those who are there tidings from the present; to write big volumes about his discoveries; and to travel at times to London to look after their publication.]

It is singular, that Kant should not have known, or knowing not have noticed, the remarkable fact, that Swedenborg prior to a fever in his 40th year was a celebrated Naturalist, member of many learned Societies, and author of three Folio-Volumes—Tria Regna Naturæ—[1]

13[5] C insisted on the primacy of will in divine consciousness, affirming that "the supreme Reality, if it were contemplated abstractly from the Absolute Will, whose essence it is to be causative of all Reality, would sink into a Spinozistic Deity": *CL* vɪ 600, repeated in *C&S* (*CC*) 182.

13[6] For C's religious solution to the existence of God—at odds with Kant's—see *SM* (*CC*) 68 n 3: "By reason we know that God is: but God is himself the Supreme Reason. And this is the proper difference between all spiritual faculties and the bod-

ily senses;—the organs of spiritual apprehension having objects consubstantial with themselves . . . or being themselves their own objects, that is, self-contemplative."

13[7] "Deduction taken to absurd lengths", a variant of the traditional rhetorical strategy of *re*duction to the absurd.

14[1] Before turning his attention entirely to spiritual matters in 1747, Emanuel Swedenborg (1688–1772) had an even more spectacular career than C suggests. From the University of Uppsala he went to London and Germany for five years of scien-

15 iii 262 | *Das Ende aller Dinge*

In der *Apokalypse* (X. 5, 6.) "hebt ein Engel seine Hand auf den Himmel, und schwört bei dem Lebendigen von Ewigkeit zu Ewigkeit, der den Himmel erschaffen hat *u.s.w.*: *dass hinfort keine Zeit mehr seyn soll.*"

[In the Apocalypse (10.5–6) "the angel . . . lifted up his right hand to heaven, and swore by him that liveth for ever and ever, who created the heaven, etc. *that there shall be time no longer.*"]

Certain Translators render the words—The Time is not yet—which ~~is~~ seems indeed the Mouse of a parturient Mountain.[1] Yet the words certainly support if not demand this version—οτι χρονος ουκ εσται ετι, αλλα εν ταις ημεραις—[2]

Annex

A few passages in Vol I are lightly marked with a pencilled line down the margin, and the tables of contents in Vols II and III are marked with pencilled crosses at the items numbered 3, 4, 7, 8, and 9 in Vol II, and those numbered 1, 2, 3, 4, 8, 9, 10, 11, 12, 14, 18, and 19 in Vol III (see the Contents list to COPY C below). Since these markings are not inconsistent with C's practice, they are listed here, with the caveat that C was not the only person to annotate these volumes.

A i 466, pencil

Die Natur, ihren allgemeinen Eigenschaften überlassen, ist an lauter schönen und vollkommenen Früchten fruchtbar, welche nicht allein an sich Uebereinstimmung und Treflichkeit zeigen, sondern auch mit dem ganzen Umfange ihrer Wesen, mit dem Nutzen der Menschen, und der Verherrlichung der göttlichen Eigenschaften, wohl harmoniren.

[Nature, left to her general properties, is fertile in truly beautiful and perfect fruits which

tific research, and returned home to publish studies in algebra, the calculus, longitude, decimal measures, tides, docks, sluices, and saltrocks, and spent ten years studying mining and smelting and constructing a theory of creation. Appointed assessor of the Royal College of Mines in Stockholm in 1716, he was ennobled in 1719, and he continued in his appointment until 1747. The three works that C refers to as "The Three Kingdoms of Nature" are *Opera philosophica et mineralia* (3 vols 1734) which included *Prodromus philosophiae ratiocinatis de infinito, et causa finali creationis; Oeconomia regni animalis* (1740); and *Regnum animale* (1744–5). C anno-

tated all three of these (of the *Opera* only the *Prodromus*), but judging from the imprecise form of the title given and from the fact that none of the copies he annotated was in folio (though the second and third were in quarto), he may not have been familiar with them when he wrote this note.

15[1] An echo of Horace *Ars poetica* 139: "Parturient montes, nascetur ridiculus mus"—"the mountains labour, and an absurd mouse will be born".

15[2] C's Greek version—the wording of Textus Receptus—is literally "that [the] time will not be yet, *but* in the days [of the voice of the seventh angel . . . the mystery of God shall be finished]".

in themselves show not only concordance and perfection, but also well harmonize with the entire realm of their being, with the needs of man, and with the glory of divine attributes.]

B I 467, pencil

Nicht der ohngefähre Zusammenlauf der Atomen des *Lucrez* hat die Welt gebildet; eingepflanzte Kräfte und Gesetze, die den weisesten Verstand zur Quelle haben . . .

[It is not the haphazard concurrence of Lucretius' atoms that built the world; implanted forces and laws, which have the wisest Intellect for source . . .]

C I 471, pencil

Will man nun aber die Verfassung des Weltbaues, und den Ursprung der Bewegungen, von den allgemeinen Naturgesetzen ausnehmen, um sie der mittelbaren Hand Gottes zuzuschreiben . . .

[Should one, however, now except the constitution of the world-edifice [and the origin of motion] from the universal laws of nature in order to ascribe them to the immediate hand of God . . .]

D I 472, pencil

. . . und woher sind ihre Umläufe nicht vollkommen cirkelrund, wenn blos die weiseste Absicht, durch das grösste Vermögen unterstützet, diese Bestimmung hervorzubringen, getrachtet hat?

[. . . and why are their orbits not completely circularly round if only the wisest intention, supported by the greatest capability, had considered the production of this arrangement?]

Copy C

Im[m]anuel Kant's vermischte Schriften. 4 vols. Halle 1799 (I–III), Königsberg 1807 (IV). 8°.

Ed Johann Heinrich Tieftrunk (1759–1837), with his "Vorbericht des Herausgebers" (I i–cxxviii) and "Anhang zur Prüfung des Beweisgrundes" (II 230–46). Vol IV has a second title-page: *Sammlung einiger bisher unbekannt gebliebenen kleinen Schriften* (Königsberg 1807). IV 1–80 is a reprint or re-issue of the separate *Sammlung* (Königsberg 1800) of which C also annotated a copy.

British Library C 126 e 7 (Vol I only), C 43 a 9 (Vols II–IV)

Joseph Henry Green's copy, with his bookplate on III ⁻5 and IV ⁻5, notes in his hand I 602, 605, 608, 610, and passages marked in pencil apparently by him I 602, 608–10, III 38, 55, 56–7, 87, 155, 159, 161, 162, 163, 164, 187, 222, 254, 257–8, 364, 433, 441–2, 448–51, 453, 455–6. It is possible that **17A**, **21A**, **25A** are Green's, but the method of marking is consistent with C's practice elsewhere. C has corrected a typographical error on II 154. A figure "3" appears in ink on III ⁻1 and in pencil on III ⁻5. Three notes in German script, in pencil, in an unidentified hand, appear on III ⁺1, ⁺2, ⁺4; possibly in the same hand, but in ink, a bibliographical reference in Latin to a book published in 1797 appears on III ⁺2: C evidently wrote entries **23** and **24** after these notes had been written in the volume.

CONTENTS. Serial numbers of the marginalia written on any work or essay are shown in parentheses after the title. In the notes to *Vermischte Schriften* any particular work or essay is referred to by volume and item-number in the form "*VS* IV—8".

VOL I

    (i–cxxviii) "Vorbericht des Herausgebers" (COPY C **1**)

1 (1–282) *Gedanken von der wahren Schätzung der lebendigen Kräfte* (1747) (COPY B **1**)

2 (283–520) *Allgemeine Naturgeschichte und Theorie des Himmels* (1755) (COPY B **2–4**, COPY C **2–6**)

3 (521–74) "Geschichte und Naturbeschreibung der merkwürdigsten Vorfälle des Erdbebens, welches am Ende des 1755ten Jahrs einen grossen Theil der Erde erschüttert hat" (1756)

4 (575–610) "Die falsche Spitzfindigkeit der vier syllogisten Figuren bewiesen" (1762)

5 (611–76) "Versuch den Begriff der negativen Grössen in der Weltweisheit einzuführen" (1763)

VOL II

1 (1–54) *Untersuchungen über die Deutlichkeit der Grundsätze der natürlichen Theologie und der Moral* (1763) (COPY C **7**)

2 (55–229) *Der einzig mögliche Beweisgrund zur Demonstration des Daseins Gottes* (1763) (COPY B **5–11**, COPY C **8–15**)

2a (230–46) [Tieftrunk]: "Anhang zur Prüfung des Beweisgrundes" (COPY B **12, 13**)

DATE. Nov 1820 and Feb 1824, and probably also earlier. Dated in ms: 30 Nov 1820 (**4**), 2 Feb 1824 (**12**), 17 Feb 1824 (**24**).

COEDITORS. Kathleen Wheeler, Raimonda Modiano.

TEXTUS TRANSLATIONS. *Allgemeine Naturgeschichte*, see COPY B Jaki; *Träume eines Geistersehers*, see COPY A Goerwitz.

---

1 I xxxvi–xxxvii, pencil | Editor's introduction

[Tieftrunk, discussing the failings of contemporary metaphysics and Kant's aptitude to improve it, quotes the following passage from Kant:] "Wenn von verschiedenen Menschen ein Jeglicher seine *eigne* Welt hat, so ist zu vermuthen, dass sie *träumen*. . . . Denn wenn sie einmal, so

Gott will, völlig machen . . . die Augen aufthun werden, so wird Niemand von ihnen etwas sehen, was nicht jedem Andern gleichfalls bei dem Lichte ihrer Beweisthümer augenscheinlich und gewiss erscheinen sollte, und die Philosophen werden zu derselbigen Zeit eine *gemeinschaftliche Welt* bewohnen, dergleichen die Grössenlehrer schon längst inne gehabt haben; *welche wichtige Begebenheit nicht lange mehr anstehen kann*, wofern gewissen *Zeichen* und *Vorbedeutungen zu trauen ist, die seit einiger Zeit über dem Horizonte der Wissenschaften erschienen sind.*"

["If every one of different people has his *own* world, then one must presume that all of them *are dreaming*. . . . For when finally, God willing, they determine fully . . . to open their eyes, none of them can see anything that did not appear to all other persons just as evident and certain in the light of their own proofs, and at the same time the philosophers will inhabit a *common world*, the same that the great scholars had already possessed for a long time; *this important event can not be postponed much longer* insofar as certain *signs* and *forebodings that have appeared for some time on the horizon of sciences are to be trusted*."]

Kant overlooked one fatal difference between the Mathemat: and the Metaphys-ician, viz. the actual existence of a mathematical Public, and the non-exist: of a Metaphysical—or rather the intrusive existence of an every-body Court of Judicature, the *psi*losophical[1] Public.—

2   ı   305, pencil | *Allgemeine Naturgeschichte und Theorie des Himmels* preface

Herr *Wright* von *Durham* . . . hat mir zuerst Anlass gegeben, die Fixsterne nicht als ein ohne sichtbare Ordnung zerstreutes Gewimmel, sondern als ein System anzusehen, welches mit einem planetischen die grösste Aehnlichkeit hat, so dass, gleichwie in dicsem die Planeten sich einer gemeinschaftlichen Fläche sehr nahe befinden, also auch die Fixsterne sich in ihren Lagen auf eine gewisse Fläche, die durch den ganzen Himmel muss gezogen, gedacht werden, so nahe als möglich beziehen, und durch ihre dichteste Häufung zu derselben denjenigen lichten Streif darstellen, welcher die Milchstrasse genannt wird. * Ich habe mich vergewissert, dass, weil diese von unzähligen Sonnen erleuchtete Zone sehr genau die Richtung eines grössten Cirkels hat, unsere Sonne sich dieser grossen Beziehungsfläche gleichfalls sehr nahe befinden müsse.

[Mr Wright of Durham . . . gave me the first prompting to look upon the fixed stars not as a scattered swarming with no visible order, but as a system which has the greatest similarity with a planetary system, so that just as in this [system]

1[1] From C's coinage "psilosophy", "shallow" or "pseudo-"philosophy.   Other instances of C's use of the term are collected in DONNE *Sermons* COPY B **8** n 3.

the planets find themselves very close to a common plane, the fixed stars too are in their position related as closely as possible to a certain plane which must be conceived as drawn across the whole sky and, through their thickest crowding toward it, represent that bright streak which is called the Milky Way. * I have become convinced that because this zone, which is illuminated by uncounted suns, has very nearly the direction of a great circle, our sun must find itself very close to this great plane of reference.]

* To me the Milky Way has always had the figure of a ragged Bow or rather of a Hoop, that had sprung open, with a long ⟨& broad⟩ slit at one end, or *C* gap.¹ How often do I wish to have this Theory, namely that our Sun is somewhere near or on the Rim of this vast *Platter* of Stars, plained to me on the principles of Perspective.

3 ɪ 331–2, pencil | Pt 1

* Denn man siehet ihn [den Lichtstreif . . . der Milchstrasse] die Richtung eines grössten Cirkels, und zwar in ununterbrochenem Zusammenhange, um den ganzen Himmel einnehmen . . .

[* For one sees it [the band of light of the Milky Way] taking the direction of a great circle and doing so in an uninterrupted connection around the entire heavens . . .]

* My eyes are, perhaps, different from those of scientific Observers—I can only see a sort of Ribbon with a ragged edges and of unequal breadth, stretching in the form of an Arch, and ending in a divarication Ⱪ and as to its extension over the whole Cope of Heaven from Horizon to Horizon (if this be implied in the words, den *ganzen* Himmel einnehmen),¹—all, I can say, is that I never saw it.—   *S. T. C.*

4 ɪ ⁺1–⁺3, referring to p 331, reworking **3**, revised in pencil

Confessio Ignorantiæ¹

P. 331.—I am sadly puzzled with this and other descriptions of the Milky Way. I am almost driven to suspect that my eyes are different from other peoples'—for I have gazed at it a thousand times, but could never see any thing but a sort of Hoop that had *sprung* from the nails, that had joined its two ends—or a Ribbon of unequal ~~bre~~ width and with ragged edges, splitting or divaricating at one end into two unequal Legs or Branches—And as to its extending over the whole Cope of Heaven from one point of the Horizon to the opposite (if this be, as I suppose,

---

2¹ C makes a similar declaration about his own observation of the Milky Way in **2** and **4** below, as in Eschenmayer **44**: "But it is *not* a girdle, but ends in a gaping Slit."

3¹ From textus var: "taking in the *entire* heavens".
4¹ "Confession of Ignorance".

the meaning of "den ganzen Himmel einnehmen")—all *I* can say, is that I never saw it: and I am sure, it has not been from want of trying to do so.

So again, respecting the theory or hypothesis, that the Milky Way forms a system of Suns, each with its dependencies, on the same plane, in the shape of a Platter; & that our Solar System is somewhere near, (either on or within) the Rim. How I have *longed* to have this explained to me on the principles of Perspective! I can readily understand how by disappearance of the Interspaces the distant Fixed Stars would be compressed into a ribbon or hoop; but that Gap at one end, where the Strip splits into two straddling thighs—this I cannot account for on the said hypothesis.—   S. T. COLERIDGE.

Nay, worse and worse—for there is no end to my stupidity in these matters—it seems to me that if I suppose a city or vast Cluster of Houses built ⟨con⟩circularly² on a perfectly level Plain, and myself on the pavement in one ~~streets~~ of the Circles, the Houses nearest my eye would shut out the rest.—Imagine these to be Suns

*   *   *   *   *   *
•

A B C D E F

—how is the light from F to reach me placed near the A?—That this is mere stupidity, I am well convinced: for it was with no mock humility that I superscribed this, Confessio ignorantiæ. ⟨Indeed, I now see, where my Blunder lies.⟩*a*³

With somewhat greater confidence I dare acknowlege, that this representation of the Starry Universe fails to impress my mind with that super-superlative Sublimity, which Kant (p. 343, 344) and many other great Men consider it is calculated to inspire.⁴—To me it appears an endless repetition of the same Image: nor can I conceive, how the Thought of a blind Mare going round and round in a Mill can derive

---

a Insertion in pencil overtraced in ink

4² Not in *OED*: presumably for "in concentric circles".

4³ Perhaps in failing to consider that the stars are not disposed on a single plane?

4⁴ In these pages, Kant remarks upon the "magnitude of a planetary world in which the earth, as a grain of sand, is scarcely perceived", upon the greater magnitude of the Milky Way, and upon the yet greater magnitude of galaxies beyond it:

"There is here no end but an abyss of real immensity, in presence of which all the capability of human conception sinks exhausted, although it is supported by the aid of the science of number."

C himself invokes the conventional sublimity of the starry skies in his letter on "*the Vast*" to Thomas Poole (*CL* I 354), in *CN* II 2064, and in the conclusion to *BL* (*CC*) II 247–8.

Sublimity from the assurance, that there ⟨are⟩ 200 a^a million of such Mills, each with a dozen or more blind Mares pacing round and round. The admirable Variety yet Symmetry of a single Moss or Flower would both raise & gratify my imagination in a far higher degree. N.B. I well remember that ⟨some 20 years ago⟩ a valued and most valuable Old Friend, somewhat subject to sudden tho' brief Explosions of Anger & Impatience, was nearly for shooting me out of a Coach-door for making this ⟨same⟩^{b} remark—it was, he swore, such a d—n'd impudent Lie, which the very Dæmon of Paradox & Sophistry could alone have inspired—no wonder that I had pretended to think that one Shakspeare outweighed a score Sir Isaac Newtons—indeed, he expected to hear me profess Atheism in my next flight or^c bravado!—/ And yet, dear & honored P!^{5}— so I *did* think, & even so I continue to do.

S. T. C.—30 Novr. 1820.

5   i 352–3, pencil | Pt 2 ch 1

Ich nehme an: dass alle Materien, daraus die Kugeln, die zu unserer Sonnenwelt gehören, alle Planeten und Cometen bestehen, im Anfange aller Dinge in ihren elementarischen Grundstoff aufgelöset, den ganzen Raum des Weltgebäudes erfüllet haben, darin jetzo diese gebildeten Körper herum laufen. Dieser Zustand der Natur . . . scheinet nur der einfachste zu seyn, der auf das Nichts folgen kann. Damals hatte sich noch nichts gebildet. Die Zusammensetzung von einander abstehender Himmelskörper, ihre nach den Anziehungen gemässigte Entfernung, ihre Gestalt, die aus dem Gleichgewichte der versammleten Materie entspringet, sind ein späterer Zustand. . . . die Materie . . . hat in ihrem einfachsten Zustande eine Bestrebung, sich durch eine natürliche Entwickelung zu einer vollkommenen Verfassung zu bilden. Allein die *Verschiedenheit in den Gattungen der Elemente* träget zu der Regung der Natur und zur Bildung des Chaos das vornehmste bei, als wodurch die Ruhe . . . gehoben, und das Chaos in dem Puncten der stärker anziehenden Partikeln sich zu bilden anfängt. Die Gattungen dieses Grundstoffes sind ohne Zweifel, nach der Unermesslichkeit, die die Natur am allen Seiten zeigt, unendliche verschieden. Die von grösster specifischen Dichtigkeit und Anziehungskraft, welche an und vor sich weniger Raum

---

^{a} Correction in pencil ^{b} Insertion in pencil ^{c} Possibly in error for "of"

4^5 Thomas Poole, to whom C wrote on 23 Mar 1801: "The more I understand of Sir Isaac Newton's works, the more boldly I dare utter to my own mind & therefore to *you*, that I believe the Souls of 500 Sir Isaac Newtons would go to the making up of a Shakspere or a Milton": *CL* ii 709.

einnehmen und auch seltener sind, werden daher bei der gleichen Aus-
theilung in dem Raume der Welt zerstreuter, als die leichtern Arten
seyn.

[I assume that all [forms of] matter, of which the globes that belong to our solar
world, [that is,] all the planets and comets consist, have filled, [inasmuch as
they were] diluted into their elementary substance at the origination of all things,
the entire space of the world-edifice wherein now these [fully] formed bodies
are orbiting. This condition of nature, even if one considers it in and by itself
with no reference to a system, seems to be the only simplest one that can succeed
to the [mere] nothing. Nothing was yet developing at the time. The coalescence
of celestial bodies separate from one another, their separation proportionate to
the [mutual] attractions, their shape which arises from the balance of aggregated
material, are a later condition. . . . [M]atter has in its simplest state a tendency
to develop through natural development into a perfect constitution. But the *dif-
ference of the* [various] *kinds of elements* [which] tends to the stirring of nature
and to the shaping of the chaos, [is] the chief factor whereby the standstill . . .
is removed and the chaos begins its development at the point of the more
strongly attracting particles. The kinds of that elementary matter are without
doubt infinitely various according to the inexhaustibility which nature shows in
every respect. Those of greater specific density and attractive force, which in
and by themselves take up lesser space and are also rarer, become, owing to the
equal distribution [of matter] in space, more dispersed than those of the lighter
kind.]

Young as Kant was at the time he composed this work so demonstrative
of a grand scientific productive or rather constructive Imagination, still
it being posterior to the severely logical Critique on the Cartesian &
Leibnitzian Controversy,[1] I cannot but be surprized, at that he should
not have detected the contradiction between his Problem, according to
which he engages to construct the System of the Material Universe out
of matter indued merely with the two essential powers, Attraction &
Repulsion/ and this unendliche Verschiedenheit[2] of the primary parti-
cles.[a] For not to say, that there is somewhat of trick in the words, only
Attraction and Repulsion, when yet he intended to bargain for aboriginal
difference of degrees—by which he in fact he includes all possible Pow-
ers that can be manifested in the Relations of Space—for what can they
⟨be⟩ but degrees of retaining, producing and preventing nearness?—yet

---

[a] Here C has written "Turn to top of p. 352" and has continued his note there with "From p. 353."

5[1] Kant's critique of Leibniz's attack on
Descartes's theory of matter in *Gedanken
von der wahren Schätzung der lebendigen
Kräfte* (1747): see COPY B **1** n 1. Descartes
thought that corporeal objects could be de-
fined in terms of extension alone; Leibniz
considered that the material world could

not be adequately described in terms of ex-
tension and impenetrability but only in
terms of activity (force) and harmony.
5[2] "Endless variety". There are similar
objections to Kant's construction of matter
from two powers in KANT *Metaphysische
Anfangsgründe* **9, 11, 22.**

how is this consistent with primary Atoms? how can we think of comparative Density but as ⟨ = ⟩ paucity of Interspaces in a composite Body?

6   I 374, pencil | Ch 2

Dieser Raum mit dem Raume, in welchem nach unserer Voraussetzung alle Materie der Planeten ausgebreitet war, verglichen, ist dreissig Millionenmal kleiner als derselbe: also macht auch die Zerstreuung der planetischen Materien in diesem Raume eine eben so vielmal grössere Verdünnung aus, als die die Theilchen unserer Atmosphäre haben.

[This space compared with the space, in which according to our assumption all the matter of the planets was spread out, is thirty million times smaller than that; also, the dispersion of the planetary matter in that space entails an equally many times [greater] thinning out, than the thinness which the particles of our atmosphere have.]

I am really puzzled. In one page K. tells me of endless differences of Density, & from this derives his first centers: & in the next page assumes *all* the matter of *all* the Planets rarified to 30 million times thinner than the Air of our Atmosphere!—

7   II ⁻3, referring to II 42 | *Untersuchungen . . .* observ 3 § 3

Der Körper ist *zusammengesetzt*, was aber zusammengesetzt ist, ist *theilbar*, folglich ist ein *Körper* theilbar.

[The body is *composite*, but what is composite is *divisible*; consequently a *body* is divisible.]

p. 42.—For the life of me, I can see nothing but a palpable circle in this reasoning. A body is composite; but what is composite must be partible: ergo, a body is partible.—But why not? A body is partible; but what is partible, must be composed of parts: therefore a body is composite.—It is clearly an analytic judgement, tho' grounded on a ⟨previous⟩ *synthetic* one—& this a synthesis a posteriori. For mere extension does not contain the existence of partible extension—/

8   II ⁺1–⁺2, referring to II 83, revised in pencil | *Der einzig möglichen Beweisgrund . . .* div 1 observ 2 § 4

Alle Möglichkeit ist in irgend etwas Wirklichem gegeben, entweder in demselben als eine Bestimmung, oder durch dasselbe als eine Folge.

[All possibility is given in something real, either in the same as a determination, or through the same as a consequence.]

P. 83.—Better thus, perhaps: What supposes it is*a* own impossibility, is impossible—in other words, mere nonsense.—It is therefore and a fortiori impossible to deny all possibility: for if it were possible, then all possibility is *not* denied.—

~~But~~ Again: that which deprives a term of all ⟨its⟩ meaning, renders ~~it impossible~~ the Subject, represented by that term, an impossible Subject—⟨i.e. a Subject that is no Subject.⟩ But possibility has no meaning ~~exception~~ in relation to Existence (= the Actual) and as a *Mode* of Reality.

Real

+ Actual . . . . . − Possible.

(Here notice the Equivoque in the occasional use of the term Possibility, as the necessary Antecedent of any ⟨given⟩ Actual: ex. gr. in God is the *Possibility* of ~~all~~ human Existence. This is a mere figure of speech, by prolēpsis or anticipation of the antithetical Relation. I take a moment of time (say, at the Birth of Julius Cæsar) in which I put myself as not existing, and oppose (counterpone) myself as possible to Cæsar as Actual. But if not *actual*, wherein or on what account am I possible. The answer is: in God as the Ens realissimum.[1]—5 composed of 2 + 1 is a nothing. At the time of Cæsar wherein was I different from this *nothing*? and I was possible.—)

By denying all Existence we therefore deny all Possibility. But this is absurd—it is therefore absurd to deny that something exists.—But as ~~this both~~*b* the Premise, Conclusion, and Middle Term are ~~wholly~~ alike*c* indifferent to any particular Time, it is equally evident that something must have always existed.

Now it is highly *convenient*, and a Postulate of all sound Philosophy by the Canon de Causis non sine causâ multiplicandis,[2] that this Something ⟨or other,⟩ which it is necessary at each moment to suppose~~d~~, should be ~~itself~~ some one thing & itself a *necessary* Being—and to suppose oth-

---

a I.e. "its": C wrote "it is", then crossed out the "i" in "is" and inserted an apostrophe to form the possessive "it's" in his usual way

b First "this" was changed in ink to "both", and then "both" was crossed out in pencil

c Correction in pencil

8[1] "The most real Being".

8[2] "That causes are not to be causelessly multiplied"—a version of Occam's Razor (C refers to Occam in **10** below) perhaps especially associated with Kant, since C quoted Kant on this theme in *TL* 38n.

erwise is highly *unreasonable*. But that it is *impossible*, K. does not seem to me to have proved. On the conceivable hypothesis of the Stoics, viz. that God is an intelligent *Fate*, I my existence is necessary; but yet I am not a necessary Being, but a simply a necessitated one.[3]

9   II +3, evidently referring to II 83 | **8** textus

I have said that what deprives a term of all meaning renders the subject represented by that term, an *impossible* Subject. And so it is: for the Term is then itself the only Subject—and thus is no *Term* at all, but a mere Sound.—Now a Subject that is no Subject, and a Term that is no term, are, methinks, contradictions in *form*, by whatever means brought about: and I confess that I do not see the necessity of Kant's distinction—the purpose of which is much more intelligibly effected by shewing the difference between the conception, possibility, and *this* or *that* possibility. Whether *its* Existence be the a *Consequent* or not of the latter, *E*xistence is of necessity the *Antecedent* of both. For tho' no *Cause* should exist to actualize what on the supposition of a Cause would be possible, a *mind* must have *existed* to conceive it./

10   II +4–5, referring to II 92–3, corrections in pencil | Observ 3 § 3

Weil das nothwendige Wesen den letzten Realgrund aller andern Möglichkeit enthält, so wird ein jedes andere Ding nur möglich seyn, in so fern es durch ihn als einen Grund gegeben ist. Demnach kann ein jedes andere Ding nur als eine Folge von ihm statt finden, und ist also aller andern Dinge Möglichkeit und Daseyn von ihm abhängend. Etwas aber was selbst abhängend ist, enthält nicht den letzten Realgrund aller Möglichkeit, und ist demnach nicht schlechterdings nothwendig. Mithin können nicht mehrere Dinge absolut nothwendig seyn.

Setzet A sey ein nothwendiges Wesen, und B ein anderes. So ist vermöge der Erklärung, B nur in so fern möglich, als es durch einen andern Grund A, als die Folge desselben gegeben ist. Weil aber vermöge der Voraussetzung B selber nothwendig ist, so ist seine Möglichkeit in ihm als ein Prädicat, und nicht als eine Folge aus einem andern, und doch nur als eine Folge laut dem vorigen gegeben, welches sich widerspricht.

[Because the necessary Being comprises the ultimate real-ground of every other possibility, nothing else is possible except in so far as it is given by it as a

8[3] C remarks in *AR* (1825) 91 that "Of the sects of ancient philosophy the Stoic is, doubtless, the nearest to Christianity"; but the contrast is carefully drawn in *P Lects*

Lect 6 (1949) 219: "The Supreme Being they did indeed admit, a Will and an intelligent Being, but their notions of his personality were extremely weak . . .".

ground. Any other thing, then, can exist only as a consequence of it; thus the possibility and existence of all other things depend upon it. Anything, however, that is itself dependent does not comprise the ultimate real-ground of all possibility, and consequently is not absolutely necessary. Hence it is not possible that more than one thing can be absolutely necessary.

Let us say that A is a necessary Being, B another. Thus by virtue of the definition B is possible only in so far as it is given through another ground A, as the consequence of this. Because, however, by virtue of the proposition, B itself is necessary, so its possibility is present in it as a predicate, and not as a consequence of something else, and nevertheless only as a consequence is the former true, which is a contradiction.]

P. 92, 93. §. 3.[1] This do[? ne]es not give me the sense of full conviction. I read it, am silenced but do not feel satisfied. The Stomach of my Understanding does not reject it; but neither does it assimilate it. I read it again: and ask, is there not a Link missing? Ought not this § 3 to have been preceded by a proof of the impossibility of an infinite Regress? And I ~~agree~~ confess[a] with Occam, that an absolute Demonstration of this I have not yet met with:[2] and unless a necessary *Interest*[b] of Truth be admitted as a Part of Truth, ~~and~~ or one with the Truth (which, I think, may very rationally be demanded) I doubt, whether such a demonstration be possible.

Besides, in this argument of Kant's I suspect an equivoque in the term, necessary. G. may be necessary in relation to all possibility of H. J. K &c, and yet not *a* self-necessitated—. ~~In admitteding, I~~ That of necessity something must have at all times existed, ~~I grant~~ is one position; but that of necessity a one ⟨and the same⟩ necessary Being always exists, is another and if I mistake not a different position. This one and the same—I must either *find* at the outset, or *arrive* at, climb up to. In the first case, ~~all the~~ it is the Ground, the Co-present Ground, of all other not necessary things; ⟨it is⟩[c] the universal Subject, of which these are the

---

[a] Correction in pencil   [b] Underlined in pencil   [c] Insertion in pencil

10[1] This textus is the same as COPY B 7 textus.

10[2] For Occam on the impossibility of infinite regress cf TENNEMANN VIII ii 873 (not annotated). Tr: "The existence of God, [Occam] says, is an article of faith. It is neither certain in itself nor can it be clearly known from experience. The proofs contain no certainty, but only probability. Occam demonstrates this on the principle of the First Mover borrowed from Aristotle. This depends on the fact that everything that is moved is moved by some-thing, and that there is not an infinite series of causes. Neither of these is indisputable, for it is possible that an entity can move itself, and as for the second, Aristotle himself assumes an infinite series in the human race." There is still no collected ed of Occam, and editions of his separate works were rare. C wrote two marginalia on Tennemann's account of Occam, on VIII ii 879 and a more general note on p +7. C comments on Occam's nominalism in JOANNES 2 at n 6.

Predicates—and then I do not see how they Latter*ª* are *things* at all, or how I am to separate them (otherwise than by logical Abstraction)*ᵇ* from the Ground—and thus the World itself is the one necessary Being, the same tho' variously modifiable or self-modified.—In the second case, ~~it~~ in which I am to use the Jacob's Ladder, before I have any ~~other~~ better plea for stopping & calling the resting-place the *last*ᶜ Round,³ than my own weakness or weariness, I must prove the impossibility of an infinite Regress—and this is the previous Link of §. 3 which I complain of as missing.—If this could be proved, not only the Existence of God but the Fact of the absolute *Creation* of the World would be demonstrable—& a bonâ fide *Beginning* of Time—Genesis, Ch. I. V. I.⁴—And for *me*, and I will venture to add, for you, my dear Mʳ Green!⁵ who want no stronger demonstration of a thing than the evident and utter unreasonableness of preferring the only ⟨tho' not proveably impossible⟩ alternative, the missing Link could be easily supplied.⁶

11   ɪɪ 105, pencil | Observ 4 § 4

Der Beweisgrund von dem Daseyn Gottes, den wir geben, ist lediglich darauf erbauet, weil etwas möglich ist. Demnach ist er ein Beweis, der vollkommen *a priori* geführt werden kann. * Es wird weder meine Existenz noch die von andern Geistern, noch die von der körperlichen Welt vorausgesetzt.

[The proof of the existence of God which we give is simply constructed on the fact that something is possible. Accordingly it is a proof which can be given

---

ª Alteration in pencil   *ᵇ* Parentheses in pencil   *ᶜ* Underlined in pencil

10³ The image of Jacob's Ladder, from Gen 28.12, was a fruitful one for C, e.g. *CN* ɪv 4635 (c 1819–25): "The progress of human Intellect from Earth to Heaven not a Jacob's Ladder but a Geometrical Staircase with 5 or more Landing-Places . . .".
10⁴ Gen 1.1: "In the beginning God created the heaven and the earth."
10⁵ C addresses Green not only as owner of this copy of *VS* but also as his philosophical collaborator, as in other cases, e.g. HEINROTH **6, 13, 24**.
10⁶ In *CN* ɪv 5110, on 27 Jan 1824, C reviewed this annotation and **11** below. "Of Kant's only possible Demonstration &c [i.e. the title of this essay] I have given the sum and exposed the Quid pro Quo in the blank leaves at the end of his Tracts, Vol. II. (Mr. Green's Copy) viz—'Some-

thing must at all times have existed' for 'A some one and the same Thing must always have existed.' In order to the proof absolute of the latter, ⟨either⟩ the absolute *impossibility* of a Regressus ad infinitum [infinite regress] must be proved, the feasibility of which I doubt; or the utter unreasonableness of preferring a thing must be held equivalent to the impossibility of the thing—And *then* the existence of a necessary Being might be *enforced* vi Postulati [by the strength of the Postulate]; but it could scarcely be called a Proof a priori. . .". He then discusses **11** below. C's reference to "the blank leaves at the end of . . . Vol. II." may embrace not only **10** and **11**, but also **8** and **9** referring to ɪɪ 82–3.

absolutely *a priori*. * Neither my existence nor that of other spirits, nor that of the corporeal world is presupposed.]

* Surely, this is but a quibble. If it does not presupposes, it implies my knowlege of my existence, and my existence as proved in the knowlege of it. Possibility has no meaning but in relation to Existence; and Existence has no *meaning* (nihil noscibile)[1] but by relation to the Knowlege.

12   II 109, pencil | Div 2 observ 1 § 1

Ich will z.E., dass ein Raum durch die Bewegung einer gerade Linie um einen festen Punct umgränzt werde. Ich begreife gar leicht, dass ich dadurch einen Kreis habe, der in allen seinen Puncten von dem gedachten festen Punct gleiche Entfernungen hat. . . . Indessen entdecke ich, dass alle geraden Linien, die einander aus einem beliebigen Punct innerhalb dem Cirkel durchkreuzen, indem sie an den Umkreis stossen, jederzeit in geometrischer Proportion geschnitten seyn; imgleichen, dass alle diejenigen, die von einem Punct ausserhalb dem Kreise diesen durchschneiden, jederzeit in solche Stücke zerlegt werden, die sich umgekehrt verhalten wie ihre Ganzen.

[I want, for example, to have a space circumscribed through the movement of a straight line around a fixed point. I understand easily enough that through this I have a circle which has in all its points an equal distance from the imaginary fixed point. . . . I discover meanwhile that all straight lines that cross one another from any one point inside the circle, and thus press against the periphery, always intersect in geometric proportion; similarly, [I discover] that all those straight lines which cut through a circle from a point outside it are always divided into parts in such a way that they stand in inverse ratio to the whole lines.]

O my most unhappy unwise neglect of Mathematics at Jesus College, Cambridge! No week passes, in which I do not groan for it![1]
      S. T. Coleridge   Feb. 2. 1824

13   II 109, pencil | **12** textus

I now see that I puzzled my⟨self by⟩ mistaking the *position* of the extraperipheric Points relatively to the Periphery for their *Distance* from the Periphery.

14   II 122, pencil | Observ 2

*   . . . weil aller Entschluss eines Willens die Erkenntniss der Möglichkeit des zu beschliessenden voraussetzt.

11[1] "(Nothing knowable)".   Böhme **66**.
12[1] C expresses the same regret in

[* . . . because all decision of a will presupposes the awareness of the possibility of that which is to be decided.]

* N.b. This is predictable, or at least it is necessarily true, only of the *finite* will, the one *Pole* as it were of the + 0 −, the Intellect being the other Pole: not of the *Absolute* Will.[1]

15   II 160–1, pencil

Man hat Ursache zu glauben, dass diese Merkwürdigkeit ein Fall sey, der unter einer viel allgemeinern Regel stehen mag, nämlich, dass der stärkere Theil der Menschenarten auch einen grösseren Antheil an der Zeugungsthätigkeit habe, um in den beiderseitigen Produkten seine eigene Art überwiegend zu machen. . . . Es mag aber mit dieser Regel eine Beschaffenheit haben, welche es wolle, so kann man hiebei wenigstens die Anmerkung machen: dass es die Erweiterung der philosophischen Einsicht hindere, sich an die moralischen Gründe, das ist, an die Erläuterung aus Zwecken zu wenden, da wo es noch zu vermuthen ist, dass physische Gründe durch eine Verknüpfung mit nothwendigen allgemeineren Gesetzen die Folge bestimmen.

[There is cause to believe that this peculiarity [that more boys are born than girls] is something that may well be due to a much more general rule; namely that the stronger part of human kind also has a greater share in conception, so that it causes its own kind to preponderate in the products of both parts. . . . However, things may be as they will regarding this law; one can at least remark that it is a hindrance to the extension of philosophic insight to turn to the moral reasons (i.e. to the explanation from purposes) where there is still ground to suppose that physical reasons determine the consequences through a conjunction with necessary general laws.]

Nothing can be more just or judicious than Kant's *Rule*, not to fly to moral causes in physical facts; but his explanation of the greater number of male infants, say 19 to 18, is strangely unsatisfactory—If the "greater Share"[1] belongs to the male, why *now* & not the next time?

And the general Belief (which is *some*thing where our knowlege is nothing) tends to the contrary—

Vel Debilis fili*um* potest gigner*e*: non sine vigore gignitur fili*a*.—[2]

16   II 251, 250, pencil | *Träume eines Geistersehers* introduction

Er [Kant] bekennet mit einer gewissen Demüthigung, dass er so treu-

---

14[1] In C's view, Kant fails to discriminate between the finite human will and the divine will which is not opposed to reason but "is Reason itself", "a holy and intelligent Will" in COPY B 13.

15[1] In textus. Cf COPY B 9, which comments on the same textus.

15[2] "Even though a weak man can *sire* a *son*, it takes strength to sire a *daughter*." The Latin is apparently C's own.

herzig war, der Wahrheit einiger Erzählungen von der erwähnten Art nachzuspüren. * Er fand—wie gemeiniglich, wo man nichts zu suchen hat—er fand nichts.

[Kant confesses, with a certain humiliation, that he was naïve enough to trace the truth of some of the stories of the kind mentioned [i.e. reports of the supernatural]. * He found—as usual where it is not our business to search—he found nothing.]

* Turn to Kant's own Letter to a Noble Lady, Vol. IV p. 362–370:[1] and it will not be easy to convince yourself, that there is not some small sacrifice of truth to *point*, in this assertion. I cannot help thinking, that more sincerity would have led to a more useful result.[a] Ex. gr. the illegitimacy of the conclusion from Sw's knowlege of the fire at Stockholm, he being then at Gottenburg, 250 miles distant, to the truth of his Revelations generally &c.[2] But even in the letter in Vol. 4, written clearly under a *very very* different state of mind from this delightful Essay, there is a to me unaccountable ambiguity—in the phrase, können, had it in his power instead of, he *did* enquire.[3] [b]The truth seems to be—that Kant was not merely staggered but seriously impressed by the unexampled adequacy of Testimony for the three Wonder-stories, especially for that of the Fire: and in my opinion very much to his honor, both as a man and a philosopher. But after the receipt and perusal of Swedenborg's Works, and the consequent disappointment, he was vexed & angry with himself for his temporary indecision/ and (as happens when we are angry) did not do strict justice either to the object of his anger, viz. himself, nor to the occasion, viz. Swedenborg.

17   ii ⁻2–⁻1, referring to ii 250–1 | **16** textus

As pencil marks are treacherous memorials or rather Confidants that too

---

[a] Arriving at the bottom of the page, C has written "*s [plural] above", and has continued at the top of the same page with "*from below"

[b] The note continues on p 250, beginning "(from p. 251)"

16[1] The letter of 10 Aug 1758 "An Fräulein Charlotte v. Knobloch über Swedenborg" (*VS* iv—14) (not annotated). C's comment on Kant's treatment of Swedenborg in COPY B was apparently written before C had read *VS* iv.

16[2] The account of Swedenborg's accurately reporting a great fire at Stockholm while he himself was at Gothenburg is given by Kant in ii 315–16. It is one of the three anecdotes tending to demonstrate Swedenborg's supernatural gifts. Cf COPY

B 14.

16[3] Kant explains to Fräulein Knobloch (iv 366) that the man who reported Swedenborg's acts to him was in a position to investigate the validity of his statements: ". . . und die der Mann, welcher sie mir berichtet, unmittelbar an Stelle und Ort hat untersuchen können [and the man who related them to me had the opportunity of investigating them at the very place where they occurred]".

soon lose the power of being treacherous, I will transcribe the marginal note, from p. 250, 251: to the words—*er fand nichts*[1]—which, by the bye, are borrowed from Albinus's relation of the amour, which by rare felicity he had had the opportunity of witnessing ipso facto et momento, between two transparent water-insects. Vidi equidem—quid autem vidi? Omnino nihil!—[2]

Now whoever will turn to Kant's own letter to a Noble Lady, Vol. IV. of his Miscell. Works, p. 362–370, and evidently written under his first impressions, will not easily persuade himself, that in this—"he found nothing"—there is not some small sacrifice of truth to *Point*. I cannot help thinking that more sincerity would have led K. to a more profitable result: as for instance, to the danger and illegitimacy of concluding or expecting the credibility of a Revelation from the apparently adequate & satisfactory evidence in support of two or three unaccountable Facts. (First, that in this very statement I have myself confounded Fact with what is only a relation of a Fact: and 2[ndly] *unaccountable* absolutely with unaccountable by *me* or in the present state & extent of human knowlege: & 3[rdly] the very fact of two or three only (well-attested) relations of such facts, when if the conclusion had been just (i.e. Ergo: Swedenborg must have, as he solemnly asserts himself to have, an intercourse ad libitum, daily and hourly, with the world of Spirits) there ought to be two or three hundred at least: & cetera.)

But even in that very Letter there is a perplexing ambiguity from Kant's use of the words—from a man of sense, who had the means and opportunity of enquiring—instead of—who *did* enquire—which latter he must yet be supposed to mean. . The truth, I believe, is this: that Kant was at first (and in *my* opinion, much to his honor both as a man and a philosopher) not merely staggered but seriously impressed by the unexampled strength of the testimony for the 3 Wonder-stories, especially that of the Fire at Stockholm on the Saturday Evening, which Sw. accurately described at the very same time at Gottenburg, 250 English miles from Stockholm. But after his perusal of Swed[gs] anxiously expected Works and the ensuing woful disappointment our Philosopher was angry and mortified with himself for his temporary indecisions and so (as commonly happens in such cases) did not do strict justice either

17[1] "He found nothing"—from **16** textus, at the end.

17[2] "In the very instant of the act [lit "in the very act and instant"]. . . . Certainly I saw—but what did I see? Absolutely nothing!" "Albinus" is almost certainly a latinised name for Gilbert White, whose *Works, in Natural History* (2 vols 1802) C annotated in 1810. Though White describes the copulation of water insects (II 233), he does not mention transparency.

to the Object of his anger, i.e. himself, or to the occasion of it, i.e. the (at ⟨that⟩*ᵃ* time non-descript) Somnambulist, Swedenborg.[3]

17A   II 257, pencil | Pt 1 ch 1

Man findet in den Schriften der Philosophen recht gute Beweise, darauf man sich verlassen kann: dass alles was da denkt, einfach seyn müsse, dass eine jede vernünftigdenkende Substanz eine Einheit der Natur sey, und das untheilbare Ich nicht könne in einem Ganzen von viel verbundenen Dingen vertheilt seyn.?

[We find in the works of philosophers many good and reliable proofs that everything which thinks must be simple; and that every substance which thinks according to reason, must be a unit of nature; and that the undivisible Ego could not be divided among many connected things which make up a whole.?]

18   II 301 | Ch 3

Ferner sieht man daraus auch, dass, da die Krankheit des Phantasten nicht eigentlich den Verstand, sondern die Täuschung der Sinne betrifft, der Unglückliche seine Blendwerke durch kein Vernünfteln heben könne; weil die wahre oder scheinbare Empfindung der Sinne selbst vor allem Urtheil des Verstandes vorhergeht, und eine unmittelbare Evidenz hat, die alle andre Ueberredung weit übertrifft.

[Furthermore, as the disease of the visionary is not really to do with the reason, but with a disorder of the sense, it will be easily recognized that the unfortunate subject cannot remove the delusion by any reasoning; for a true or apparent impression of the senses precedes all the judgments of the reason, and carries with it immediate evidence far surpassing all other persuasion.]

Consistency, as a presumption, and Prophecy, or rather the Vis veridica,[1] as ⟨a Proof,⟩ *might* furnish a diagnosis. The one Swedenborg gave: the other he is related to have given.

19   II 572, pencil | *Briefwechsel* Lambert to Kant Nov 1765

Denn sonst würde *Wolf* sich von den *postulatis*, welche eigentlich dahin dienen, ganz andre Begriffe gemacht haben: so hatte er auch gelernt, man müsse nicht bei dem *allgemeinen*, sondern bei dem *einfachen* an-

---

ᵃ C wrote "time that" and inserted carets to indicate that the two words should be reversed

17[3] Since Swedenborg died before the advent of mesmerism, he could not have been described by his contemporaries as a "somnambulist", one experiencing a high degree of the mesmeric trance. C's scattered remarks on mesmerism are well represented by KLUGE and MESMER below.
  18[1] The "truth-telling force".

fangen, und AXIOMATA seyn von PRINCIPIIS verschieden, ungefähr wie Materie von Form &c.

[For otherwise Wolf would have gained quite a different idea of the *postulates* which serve this end; thus he had also learned that one must begin with the *simple*, not with the *general*, and that AXIOMS are different from PRINCIPLES rather in the same way that matter is different from form &c.]

—I should say the exactly contrary: if I understand Lambert's use of the terms, Matter and Form. According to my own sense, of Form, as the principium substantiale, and of Materia, as the Phænomenon individuum, I should *say* just the same as he does.[1]

20 II 573, pencil

Sodann glaube ich, man thue besser, *wenn man anstatt des einfachen in der Metaphysik, das einfache in der Erkenntniss aufsucht.* Hat man dieses alles, so kann es nachher so vertheilt werden, wie es nicht der Name der bisherigen Wissenschaften, sondern die Sache selbst mitbringt.*

[And then I believe one would do better *if one looked out for the simple in cognition instead of the simple in metaphysics.* If one has attained all this, it can afterwards be distributed in the way the matter itself brings with it, not in the way which the names of the sciences, as they exist up to now, require.*]

* What competent person can read this and from such a man as Lambert was, without feeling his obligation to Kant for his Critique of the faculties!—Thus, in this sentence, *die Sache selbst*[1] is the mere phænomenon.

21 II 574

. . . der Begriff *eines Dinges* ist der allerzusammengesetzteste den wir haben, weil er alle *Fundamenta divisionum et subdivisionum* in sich begreift.

[The concept of *a thing* is the most composite that we have, because it comprises in it all bases of division and subdivision.]

19[1] "Such is the influence of words, that on reading Lambert's first Letter to Kant, I believed myself to have found an anticipation of & an authority for, my thoughts; but I soon discovered, that he used the same terms in the contrary sense, meaning by Form what I mean by Materia, & vice versâ.—in short, that Lambert had fallen into the same error with Condillac, in confounding impressions (the subject of Physics or Psychology) with Notions or Thoughts (Begriffe) the proper subjects of Logic.—" *CN* IV 4764 (c Nov 1820 – 3 Jan 1821). C uses Latin terms for "essential principle", "matter", and "particular phenomenon".

20[1] "The thing itself"—from textus.

Qʸ whether the word, Thing, with the single exception of those sentences in which it is used as the Antithesis to a Thought, might not be struck out from our Discourse, or retained only as a more decorous Substitute for a Hem! or a pinch of Snuff, or sucking an Orange.

22 III ⁻5, pencil

    Ʒ a drachm

    Ʒ an ounce—

22A III [35], pencil

[Title:] Muthmasslicher Anfang der Menschengeschichte. ! ! !

[Presumed Commencement of Human History. ! ! ! !]

23 III 121–2, pencil | "Ueber das Gebrauch teleologischer Principien in der Philosophie"

Man hat auch nicht Ursache ihre Farbe, nachdem das, was die Sonne ihres Landes jedem Individuum der letzteren eindrückt, bei Seite gesetzt worden, für etwas anders, als die Brunette unter dem weissen Menschenschlag zu urtheilen. Was aber das Negerähnliche der Caffern, und, im mindern Grade, der Hottentotten in demselben Welttheile betrift, welche vermuthlich den Versuch der halbschlächtigen Zeugung bestehen würden: so ist im höchsten Grade wahrscheinlich, dass diese nichts anders als Bastarderzeugungen eines Negervolks, mit denen von der ältesten Zeit her diese Küste besuchenden Arabern seyn mögen.

[Nor is there any reason, leaving aside what the sun impresses on every individual in a country, to judge their colour as something different from that which the brunette is among the white races. But as regards the kaffirs' similarity to the negro and, in a lesser degree, that of the Hottentots in the same part of the world, which would, presumably, stand the test of hybrid conception, it is in the highest degree likely that these are nothing but the mixed progeny of a negro people with the Arabs who have visited the coast from ancient times onwards.]

Kant partook tho' in a much less degree the prejudice characteristic of the Naturalists of his Age against the use of the Mosaic Records as furnishing Bases for Anthropogony:[1] else this very conjecture concerning

23[1] *OED* Supplement cites a first use of "Anthropogony", the (study of the) origin of man, in 1868, and of "Anthropogeny", the study of the generation of man, in 1839. In a scheme for subdividing the study of man and his world, beginning with "Physiography, or methodical Description of the lifeless Bodies of the Planet" and ending with Logic and Language, C divides "4. Anthropology" into two parts, the second of which is "Anthropogony, or the Origin of the different Races as far as Facts and just Analogies render the same ascertainable or the subject of probable Conjecture": *CN* IV 5254 f 156 (c Sept 1825). C's aim in his own writings about

the Origin of the Hottentots as C = A + B, might have led him to prefer the 3 Noachidæ[2] to his 4[a] Aboriginal *Di*generations,[3] which Blumenbach, followed by all after Naturalists, improved into 5.—[4]

24 III +3–+5, referring to III 316–18 | "Von einem neuerdings erhobenen Ton in der Philosophie"

[Footnote:] . . . und da muss wohl bemerkt werden, dass von dem, was über alle mögliche Erfahrungsgränze hinausliegt, weder gesagt werden kann, es sey *wahrscheinlich*, noch es sey *unwahrscheinlich*. . . . Ist nun der Gegenstand gar kein Objekt einer uns möglichen Erkenntniss . . . so kann über die Möglichkeit derselben weder wahrscheinlich noch unwahrscheinlich, sondern gar nicht geurtheilt werden. Denn die vorgeblichen Erkenntnissgründe sind in einer Reihe, die sich dem zureichenden Gründe, mithin der Erkenntniss selbst, gar nicht nähert, indem sie auf etwas Uebersinnliches bezogen werden, von dem, als einem solchem, kein theoretisches Erkenntniss möglich ist. . . . In praktischer (moralisch-praktischer) Bedeutung aber ist ein Glaube an das Uebersinnliche nicht allein möglich, sondern er ist sogar mit dieser unzertrennlich verbunden. Denn die Summe der Moralität in mir, obgleich übersinnlich, mithin nicht empirisch, ist dennoch mit unverkennbarer Wahrheit und Autorität (durch einen kategorischen Imperativ) gegeben . . .

[. . . it must indeed be observed that one cannot say about [an object] that lies beyond all possible bounds of experience either that it is *probable* or *improbable*. . . . When, therefore, an object is not one of possible knowledge for us . . . it is not only that one cannot judge whether its possibility is probable or improbable, but one cannot judge anything about it at all. For the supposed grounds of knowledge belong to a series that does not come any closer to representing the sufficient grounds, therefore knowledge itself, in that they refer to something

---

[a] The "4" is repeated as the note continues at the top of III 122

race—in *CN* IV and *SW & F* (*CC*), and incidentally in the 1818–19 lectures on literature (*Lects 1808–1819—CC*—II 44–63) and philosophy (*P Lects* Lect 8—1949—254–5)—was to "reconcile the Kantean diagnostic of *Race* with the Mosaic Documents respecting the *Deluge*" (*CN* IV 4548, c Jun 1819).

23[2] Descendants of the three sons of Noah, as in BLUMENBACH **4** and n 3.

23[3] I.e. generations descending from two different sources (not in *OED*). In "Von den verschiedenen Racen der Menschen" *VS* II 607–32 and "Bestim-

mung des Begriffs einer Menschenrace" *VS* II 633–60, Kant speculatively described four races—all derived from a single root—that he identifies variously as Black, White, Yellow, and Copper-red, and as White, Negro, Hun, and Hindu. In *TT* 1 Jan 1823 and 24 Feb 1827, C reduces the number of Kant's races to three.

23[4] C comments approvingly on the "Pentad of Races"—Blumenbach's categories of Caucasian, Malayan, American, Ethiopian, and Mongolian—in BLUMENBACH **4** and *TT* 24 Feb 1827.

supersensible about which no theoretical knowledge as such is possible. . . . In the practical sense (the morally practical) a belief in the supersensible is not only possible, but is inextricably bound with it. For the sum of morality in me, although supersensible, therefore not empirical, is nonetheless given with unmistakable truth and authority (through a categorical imperative) . . .]

P. 317. In this admirable Essay (but what is there of Kant's not admirable!) I ~~re~~ am repeatedly regretting that this illustrious Thinker had not anticipated & enabled me to answer the Objection: Well! be it that *theoretically* I cannot arrive at a binding assurance of a given Truth, yet if by any other means it is once effected so that it be effected, what is to prevent me from making use of this assurance? What? Is the Categorical Imperative less imperative in my Reason than the *Phænomenon*, (not which but) the coincidence of which with the forms of the Understanding is the sufficing ground of our assurance of an external World? Do I ask more, than that the Moral Command and *involution* of the Truth should be a Surrogate for the Affection of my physical sensibility, in the eye &c?—[1]

[a]There is, however, besides this a very suspicious point in Kant's reasoning on the anthropomorphic defect in the attribution of Intelligence & Will to Deity—these implying an Einschränkung or Negation incompatible with the idea of God.[2] Essentially? Yes, says he. No! say I.—I have had occasion to notice the same "two faces under one hood"[3] in Spinoza—& that *he* had deluded himself by the merely formal intuitions of Geometry.[4] ~~It is~~ A mathematical Circle is, doubtless, formed by a negation of the Space not contained within the periphery: and in this sense (tho' even here it does not to me seem perfectly accurate) the circumferential line itself may be called a *negation*. But let it be a living & willing Circle-animal, and let the circumference be effected by a self-retraction at a given point, not in order to, but *in* the *act* & as constituting the act, of Self-consciousness: & then the same Circumference is a *Po-*

---

[a] There seems to be a change of pen here, the remainder of the note referring to a later passage in the text

24[1] Cf C's remark in COPY B 13 that our knowledge of the external world is at least as liable to be deceptive as our knowledge of spiritual matters; and the analogy in *BL* ch 12 (*CC*) I 242: "In short, all the organs of sense are framed for a corresponding world of sense; and we have it. All the organs of spirit are framed for a correspondent world of spirit; tho' the latter organs are not developed in all alike. But they exist in all, and their first appearance dis-

closes itself in the *moral* being."
24[2] C refers to Kant's long footnote on this subject, 25 textus.
24[3] Proverbial: *OED* records instances of this figure for duplicity from the fifteenth century.
24[4] E.g. in a long note of 1810, *CN* III 3869. C also comments on the danger of applying geometrical analogies to metaphysics and moral philosophy in COPY B 13.

sition, a positive Perfection—an unqualified Reality.[a]—So in the Note, p. 325, fully sympathizing with Kant's contempt for the affected *quality* tone (*vornehm*)[5] of pseudo-mystics, as a privileged Class, persons of distinction that look down with a smile of nausea at your vulgar *Operatives* in Philosophy, I cannot help startling at a *Begriff* von Gott von uns selbst *gemacht*[6]—and I confess, that Kant's, as explained p. 324,[7] is but an unsufficing *Mach*-werk,[8] a *pretence* to an x y z belief—the effective reality of which I doubt, whether it be even *possible*. I feel the liveliest conviction, that no religious man could retain the distinction between the Divine Will, and the unknown Something which is to answer the purpose of a Will—a non-intelligence that performs the functions of an Intelligence—Nor do I see wherein this differs from a moral & modest Atheism.—   17 Feb? 1824.—

25   III ⁻4, referring to III 323–6n

[C refers to a long footnote in which Kant denies the attribution of Understanding and Will to the deity.] Ich habe aber von einem andern Verstande, der etwa ein Anschauungsvermögen wäre, nicht den mindesten Begriff; folglich ist der von einem Verstande, den ich in dem höchsten Wesen setze, völlig sinnleer.—Ebenso: wenn ich in ihm eine andere Realität, einen *Willen*, setze, durch den er Ursache aller Dinge ausser ihm ist, so muss ich einen solchen annehmen, bei welchem seine Zufriedenheit (*acquiescentia*) durchaus nicht vom Daseyn der Dinge ausser ihm abhängt; denn das wäre Einschränkung (*negatio*). Nun habe ich wiederum nicht den mindesten Begriff, kann auch kein Beispiel von einem Willen geben, bei welchem das Subjekt nicht seine Zufriedenheit auf dem *Gelingen* seines Wollens gründete, der also nicht von dem Daseyn des äusseren Gegenstandes *abhinge*. Also ist der Begriff von einem Willen des höchsten Wesens, als einer ihm inhärirenden Realität . . . entweder ein leerer, oder . . . ein anthropomorphischer Begriff. . . . Mache ich mir aber vom *ens realissimum* den Begriff als *Grund* aller Realität, so sage ich: Gott ist das Wesen, welches den Grund alles dessen in der Welt enthält, *wozu wir Menschen einen Verstand anzunehmen nöthig* haben. . . . Wenn daher Einer von den Kraftmännern . . . sagt: "er verachte denjenigen, der sich seinen *Gott zu machen* denkt;" so

---

[a] The last five words are written askew to avoid overwriting a calculation in ink (correctly multiplying 286 × 7) that must have been there before the note was written, and that may be in C's hand

24[5] C alludes to Kant's note, **25** textus, where *vornehm*, "refined", is used pejoratively as "affected". Kant used the word also in the title to his essay.

24[6] A "*concept* of God *made* by ourselves"—in **25** textus.

24[7] **25** textus.

24[8] I.e. a bad job, a poor piece of work.

gehört das zu den Eigenheiten ihrer Kaste, deren Ton (als besonders Begünstiger) *vornehm* ist. Denn es ist für sich selbst klar: dass ein Begriff, der aus unserer Vernunft hervorgehen muss, von uns selbst gemacht seyn müsse. Hatten wir ihn von irgend einer Erscheinung (einem Erfahrungsgegenstande) abnehmen wollen, so wäre unser Erkenntnissgrund empirisch . . .

[I have not the least concept of another Understanding that might be like a faculty of intuition; therefore, the concept of an Understanding that I attribute to the supreme being is completely empty.—Likewise, if I attribute to him another reality, a *Will*, through which he is the cause of all external things, I must assume a Will such that his contentment ("acquiescence") is entirely independent of the existence of external things; for [otherwise] this would be limitation ("negation"). Again I have not the least concept, and can give no example of a Will, by means of which the contentment of the subject would be based on the *success* of his volition, who would not depend, therefore, on the existence of external things. The concept of a Will in the supreme being as something inherent in his reality is then either empty or . . . anthropomorphic. . . . If however, I take the concept of an *ens realissimum* as a *ground* of all reality, I am saying: God is the being who contains the ground of all beings in the world, *for which* men *must acquire an Understanding.* . . . If one of the men of power . . . says: "he despises him who thinks he is *making a God for himself;*" this belongs to the peculiarities of the class of those whose tone (especially patronising) is *affected.* For it is clear in itself that a concept that must arise from our reason must be produced by ourselves. If we wanted to obtain it from some appearance (some object of experience), then the ground of knowledge would be empirical . . .]

p. 323–326—viz. *the Note.*[1]

I do not clearly see by what right Kant *forbids* ⟨us⟩ to attribute to God Intelligence and Will, because we know by experience no Intelligence or Will but the human Understanding (?), the human Volition (?) and these subsist under relations ⟨and limitations⟩ not attributable to God: while yet he allows us to attribute ⟨to him⟩ the notion of a *Ground*, tho' our experience furnishes no instance of an *infinite* Ground, or an *absolute* Ground, more than of an infinite Understanding, or of an absolute Will.—Not to mention, except by the ? affixed, the petitio principii in the confusion of all intelligence with that of the Understanding, of Will (Arbitrium) with the faculty of Volition (Voluntas), and of all Will with *human* Volition.—[2]

25[1] C had copied part of this footnote into one of his notebooks in Dec 1804: *CN* II 2316 and n.

25[2] In analyses of the will, C began at least as early as Jan 1804 to insist on distinctions between "Volition & Free Will or Arbitrium" (*CN* I 1827); *BL* ch 12 (*CC*) I 293 quotes the three-way distinction (1812 *Omniana*) between will, choice, and volition.

26   III 357, pencil | "Ueber ein vermeintes Recht . . ."

Admirably reasoned as this Essay is, I yet regard it but ⟨as⟩ one of the rich purple Patches of the Robe of Casuistry which is to be the *substitute* for that *singleness of Heart* which fails not to give to its possessor what he should say in the moment of the occasion

26A   III 401, pencil | "Von der Macht des Gemuths . . ."

In einigen Familien ist das Altwerden erblich, und die Paarung in einer solchen kann wohl einen Familienschlag dieser Art begründen. Es ist auch kein übles politisches Princip zu Beförderung der Ehen, das gepaarte Leben als ein langes Leben anzupreisen? . . .

[In some families, longevity is hereditary, and mating into such a family can well establish a family characteristic of this sort. It is hardly a bad political principle for the promotion of marriage to extol the paired life as a long life? . . .]

27   III 411–13, pencil | § 3

Der Anwandelung des Appetits zum Wassertrinken (dem Durst), welche grossentheils nur Angewohnheit ist, nicht sofort nachzugeben und ein hierüber genommener *fester Vorsatz* bringt diesen Reiz in das Maas des natürlichen Bedürfnisses, des den festen Speisen beizugebenden flüssigen, dessen Genuss in Menge im Alter selbst durch den Naturinstinkt geweigert wird.

[By not giving way at once to a desire to drink (thirst) which is largely a habit merely, and by a *definite resolution* on this subject, this desire will be brought within the limits of the natural necessity of the liquid to be taken with solid food, whereas drinking any considerable amount is refused in old age simply by the natural instinct.]

The only error in the above is its not being carried still farther, i.e. to the prohibition of all Fluid as an *accompaniment* of solid food, and of Water even as the *Follower*. Where it can be done, Invalids and elderly persons should have the Wine &c in another Room, so that during the latter part of the Dinner, made Dishes, Pastry &c, in which they should not partake, and in the change from the Dining Room to the Wine-Parlour a full ¼ᵗʰ of an Hour may pass.

28   IV ⁺1,ᵃ referring to IV 123–72 (i.e. the whole essay) | *Principiorum primorum cognitionis* . . .

123–172. This *Degree* Essay, 1755, for admission as Member of the Philosophical Faculty, is a worthy *Dawn* of the Kantéan Day. Nothing

---

ᵃ This note is written in ink on the lower half of the page, following **32** but the Insight into the *equal* necessity of the supposed *Contrary*, & the consequent Conversion of Contraries into Opposites,[1] was wanting to have made the young Immanuel the founder of the System of the *Prothetic*, as the antecedent Identity of the Thetic & Anti-thetic—or rather of the + and minus *Antitheta.*—[2]

29 IV +2–+3, referring to IV 267–8 | *Monadologia physica* § 1

Prop. I. DEFINITIO. Substantia simplex, Monas* dicta, est quae non constat pluralitate partium, quarum una absque aliis separatim existere potest. [Footnote *:] Quoniam instituti mei ratio est, non nisi de ea simplicium substantiarum classe commentandi, quae corporum primitivae sunt partes, me inposterum terminis, *substantiarum simplicium, Monadum, elementorum materiae, partium corporis primitivarum*, tanquam synonimis usurum in antecessum moneo. [Footnote ends.]

Prop. II. THEOREMA. Corpora constant monadibus.

Corpora constant partibus, quae a se invicem separatae perdurabilem habent existentiam. Quoniam autem talibus partibus compositio non est nisi relatio, hinc determinatio in se contingens, quae salva ipsarum existentia tolli potest, patet, compositionem omnem corporis abrogari posse, superstitibus nihilo secius partibus omnibus quae antea erant compositae. Compositione autem omni sublata, quae supersunt partes plane non habent compositionem, atque adeo pluralitate substantiarum plane sunt destitutae, hinc simplices. Corpus ergo quodvis constat partibus primitivis absolute simplicibus, h.e. monadibus. . . .

Prop. III. THEOREMA. Spatium quod corpora implent est in infinitum divisibile, neque igitur constat partibus primitivis atque simplicibus. [By the use of a geometrical diagram, Kant shows that by continual division of a line one never comes to primary parts that can be divided no further: that is, that space is infinitely divisible and does not consist of simple parts.]

[Prop. I. DEFINITION. A simple substance, called a Monad,* is one that does not consist of a plurality of parts of which one cannot exist separately from another. [Footnote *:] Since it is my purpose to discuss only that class of simple substances which are parts of primary bodies, I give notice in advance that I shall use the terms *simple substance, Monads, elements of matter, primary parts of bodies* as synonyms from now on. [Footnote ends.]

28[1] Cf "he alone deserves the name of a Philosopher, who has attained to see and learnt to apply the difference between Contraries that preclude, and Opposites that reciprocally suppose and require, each the other": *CN* III 4326 (c 1816–17).

28[2] I.e. Kant would have formulated the polar logic in which opposites entail a prior unity, the prothesis in the logical pentad or tetractys, such as C uses in e.g. IRVING *Sermons* 2.

Prop. II. THEOREM. Bodies consist of monads.

Bodies consist of parts with a possibility of continued existence when separated one from another. Since however the composition of such parts is nothing but a relationship, hence a determination in itself contingent, which can be removed without ending their existence, it is clear that the composition of a body can be completely dismissed, and leave all the parts no otherwise than they were when in composition. But when all composition is removed the remaining parts have no composition and so are deprived of plurality of substance; they are simple. Therefore any body consists of absolutely primary parts, that is, monads.

Prop. III. THEOREM. The space that bodies fill is infinitely divisible, and therefore does not consist of primary and simple parts.]

P. 267.

It is scarcely worth the while to comment on Tracts, which the Author himself had perhaps forgotten; and the sentiments of which he had either outgrown, or stated more advantageously in later works. But the definition and the following Theorem in this page seem to me note-worthy from their Spinosistic Consequences of a one only Substance—or substantia unica.—Definitio *impossibilitat* definitum.—Ergo non datur Monas, nisi Universum,[1] would compleat the Enthymeme.

In the third Prop. and its Theorem as likewise in Kant's doctrine of mutual and equal approximation of the Ball and the Nine-pin, I more than suspect a Sophism,—μεταβάσιν, ἡγοῦν, εἰς ἄλλο γένος[2]—which I can only account for in the Founder of the Critical Propædia[3] from his predilection for Geometry. In his Metaphysische Anfangsgrunde zur Natur-wissenschaft there are several instances of $=$, equal to, or the same *as*, confounded with, $=$, identical, or the same, or the same *with*.[4] In other words, an adequate *Substitute* quoad Calculum seu demonstrationem geometricam[5] is passed off for the ⟨Principal or the⟩ Thing itself.—In the above instance of the infin. divis. of Space there appears to me to lurk a sophism in the position, You can *imagine* another & another line &c. Now this I deny. You may indeed repeat the former image or act of imagining with the adjunct of the *Thought*, another, or halved. But this of itself would be a *Transit*ⁿ *into another kind*, μετα-

---

29[1] "The definition renders impossible what is defined.—Therefore, the Monad is not produced, unless it be universal."

29[2] "Actually, a transition into another kind"—an Aristotelian formula used by C a few lines further on, and in many other places, e.g. *Logic* (*CC*) 90. The "Ball and the Nine-pin" are concrete specifics substituting for the demonstration that follows the textus here, very much like "the Paradox . . . that the Castle meets the Cannon

Ball half way", in KANT *Metaphysische Anfangsgründe* 33.

29[3] I.e. preliminary or introductory discipline, as in C's remark to HCR in 1812 that "Kant's writings are not metaphysics, only a propaedeutic": *CRB* I 70.

29[4] See KANT *Metaphysische Anfangsgründe* 2–5, esp 4.

29[5] An adequate substitute "in so far as it is a calculation or a geometrical demonstration".

βάσις εἰς ἄλλο γενος: & besides this, it is a Thought referring to an Image which is unimageable, therefore a Thought empty of Thought, or at best a petitio principii. The point to be proved is tacitly subsumed in, and in order to, the Proof.—

30 IV 354–5, pencil | "Versuch . . . über den Optimismus"

Nun behaupte ich, dass Realität und Realität niemals als solche können unterscheiden seyn. Denn wenn sich Dinge von einander unterschieden, so geschieht es durch dasjenige, was in dem einen ist, und in dem andern nicht ist. Wenn aber Realitäten als solche betrachtet werden, so ist ein jedes Merkmal in ihnen positiv; sollten sich nun dieselben von einander als Realitäten unterscheiden, so müsste in der einen etwas positives seyn, was in der andern nicht wäre, also würde in der einen etwas negatives gedacht werden, wodurch sie sich von der andern unterscheiden liesse, das heisst, sie würden nicht als Realitäten mit einander verglichen, welches doch gefordert wurde. Demnach unterscheidet sich Realität und Realität von einander durch nichts, als durch einer von beyden anhängenden Negationen, Abwesenheiten, Schranken, das ist nicht in Ansehung ihrer Beschaffenheit (*qualitate*), sondern Grösse (*gradu*).

[I maintain, then, that reality can never be distinguished from reality as such. For if things are different from one another, then it is so because of that which is in the one and not in the other. If, however, realities are regarded as such, then each feature in them is positive; if these then are to be distinguished as realities there would have to be something positive in the one which is not in the other; that is, something negative must be thought of as being in the one, by means of which it can be distinguished from the other, that is, they would not be compared with one another as realities, which is, however, what was required. Hence what distinguishes reality from reality is only negations, absences, limitations belonging to both, that is, not with reference to their nature ("by quality") but to magnitude ("by degree").]

This page is worth noticing as an instance of the false conclusions inevitable on the Logic of Dichotomy: to the exchange of which for that of Trichotomy Kant owed his after-greatness.[1] Here Reality is opposed to Non-entity—i.e. 0—of course can have no degrees or distinctions. But that quod opponitur, *ponitur*—now non-entity non *poni* potest/[2] of course, it is at once + A and − A: i.e. the major of the Syllogism is a contra-diction in terms.

30[1] C repeats this opinion, with the added view that Richard Baxter anticipated Kant, in BAXTER *Reliquiae* COPY B **130** and in *Logic* (*CC*) 241.

30[2] That "which is opposed (is opposite), is *placed*"—non-entity "cannot *be placed*".

31 IV 382–4, pencil, referring to 379–82 | "Ueber Schwärmerey . . . ."

Wider diesen Unfug ist nun nichts weiter zu thun, als den animalischen
Magnetismus magnetisiren und desorganisiren zu lassen, so lange es
ihm und andern Leichtgläubigen gefällt, der Policey aber es zu empfeh-
len, dass der Moralität hiebey nicht zu nahe getreten werde, übrigens
aber für sich den einzigen Weg der Naturforschung durch Experiment
und Beobachtung, die die Eigenschaften des Objects äussern Sinnen
kenntlich werden lassen, ferner zu befolgen. Weitläuftige Widerlegung
ist hier wider die Würde der Vernunft, und richtet auch nichts aus; ver-
achtendes Stillschweigen ist einer solchen Art von Wahnsinn besser an-
gemessen, wie denn auch dergleichen Ereignisse in der moralischen
Welt nur eine kurze Zeit dauern, um andern Thorheiten Platz zu
machen.

[Against this sort of mischief nothing can be done but to allow animal magnetis-
ers to magnetise and de-organise as long as pleases them and other credulous
persons, but to advise the police [to watch] that [the laws of] morality are not
infringed. For the rest, one ought oneself to pursue the only way to natural sci-
ence by experimentation and observation, which make clear the properties of an
object to the external senses. Extensive refutation is against the dignity of reason
and does not achieve anything. Contemptuous silence is more suited to such a
kind of madness, for such events in the moral world last but a short time and
make place for other follies.]

If among Mesmer's Partizans[1] there be any who place the observations
of Animal Magnetists, even those most conducted ad normam experi-
mentalem,[2] on a par with experiments (in the proper sense of the word)
respecting physical Magnetism and Electricity, to such persons this Es-
say is a fit and fair Reply. Or if any Mesmerists have indulged a kind
and degree of confidence inconsistent with a just appreciation of the dif-
ference between such Observations and proper experiments; if on the
authority of insulated Facts or Notices they have grounded a general
Theory and then employed the theory to support the credit of the Facts;
they are to be referred to the Principles or Criteria of Dialectic (i.e. Ju-
dicial Logic) and the Doctrine of Probability, to be taught better. And
for these too, supposing them to reject this ~~admission a~~ admonition,
lachendes (nicht aber verachtendes) Stillschweigen ist, ich gebe zu, bes-
ser angemessen als Widerlegung.[3] But if the notices respecting the ef-

31[1] Friedrich Anton Mesmer (1734–
1815), whose controversial treatment of
patients through mesmerism or "animal
magnetism" led to hypnosis therapy. C's
interest in mesmerism is reflected in many
annotations, esp KLUGE and MESMER.

31[2] "By the standards of scientific ex-
periment".
31[3] "Laughing (but not disdainful) si-
lence is, I admit, more appropriate than
refutation"—constructed from textus.

fects of magnetic Treatment have no higher rank claimed for them, than is claimed for empirical Medicine generally, I can more easily descry in this Essay the pride of the Man of Science, than the considerateness of the Philosopher. The introduction, however, is excellent and has its own permanent value, independent of its application.

32   IV   ⁺1, referring to IV 383–414, pencil | Review of J. G. Herder *Ideen zur Philosophie der Geschichte der Menschheit*

⟨P.⟩ 383–414. A perfect *model* of a Review! Kant takes the ground with all the ease and courtesy of a Gentleman and a Veteran, places his mortal strokes with so sure yet so light a hand, compliments the fallen Antagonist so handsomely, and finally inters him with all military Honors! O poor Herder! thou art defunct as a Philosopher: and all thy Metacritics & Calligones ~~are~~ only prove thee a spiteful resentful Ghost![1] Go, go, poor Ghost! and keep company with Ajax and Dido![2]

S. T. Coleridge

33   IV   ⁺4, pencil

Religion asserted, as necessarily revealed: ~~and~~ with the grounds of the belief, that the ⟨Scheme of⟩ Revelations (recorded in ~~the Old and New Testaments~~ the Bible) ~~are~~ is the only ~~ones~~ of universal Validity.

or,

RELIGION asserted, as necessarily [? A] Revelation: with the grounds of the Belief, that the system of revelations recorded in the Bible is alone of universal Obligation: by   S. T. Coleridge[1]

34   IV   ⁺4–⁺5, pencil

Instance of sesquipedalian Scholastic Words.

Quod si prædefinitionibus tuis incompossibilitaveris res ipsas ita prædefinitas—[1]

For as the renowed Salamancan, Doctor Quimboraca,[2] in his *Lux lucifer in Toletani cujusdam elucidationes Dunsii Scoti Commentariolo-*

32[1] Herder attacked Kant in *Verstand und Erfahrung. Eine Metakritik zur Kritik der reinen Vernunft* (1799) and *Kalligone*—also known as *Die Metakritik der Urtheilskraft*—in 1800. C refers to these works scornfully in HERDER *Briefe* **11**, *Kalligone* **1**.

32[2] Both Ajax and Dido took their own lives; but C seems to refer to them simply as representatives of the dead.

33[1] The projected "Assertion of Religion" was announced in similar terms in *AR* (1825) 152.

34[1] "But if by your predefinitions you incompossibilitate the very things you have so predefined—".

34[2] An author as Rabelaisian as the title that follows. The name presumably means—if anything—"Five-bottle", from *quin-* + *borachio* (Spanish for wine-skin or bottle).

rum in Magistri Petri Lombardi Sententias[3] has thus in few words tho' many syllables expressed it.

Annex

In Dr Williams's Library, among the papers of Henry Crabb Robinson (Bundle 1.II.35), there is a scrap of paper—possibly removed from this book—headed in HCR's hand "Coleridge on Kant". C's holograph note refers to *VS* III—5, from which the textus following is supplied.

A III 95 | "Einige Bemerkungen zu Jacobs Prüfung . . ."

Wenn ich aber doch . . . einsehe, dass wir von der körperlichen Natur nichts anders erkennen, als den Raum . . . das Ding im Raume ausserdem, dass auch Raum *in ihm* (d.i. es selbst ausgedehnt) ist, keine andere Wirkung als Bewegung . . . folglich keine andere Kraft, oder leidende Eigenschaft, als bewegende Kraft und Beweglichkeit (Veränderung äusserer Verhältnisse) zu erkennen giebt; so mag mir *Mendelssohn*, oder jeder anderer an seiner Stelle doch sagen, ob ich glauben könne, ein Ding nach dem *was es ist*, zu erkennen, wenn ich weiter nichts von ihm weiss, als das es etwas sey, das in äusseren Verhältnissen ist . . .

[If, however, I admit that we know nothing regarding physical nature except space . . . and furthermore concerning the thing in space, which is space *in itself* (i.e. is itself extended), we can attain no knowledge of its action other than its motion . . . consequently of no force or passive quality other than moving force and movability (change of external relations); let then Mendelssohn or anybody else in his stead tell me if I can believe that a thing is known according to *what it is*, when I know nothing further about it except that it is something that exists in external relations . . .]

P. 95

But would not Mendelssohn question the meagre limit of the word "Erkennen", as arbitrary?[1] Opium is ein körperliches Ding[2]—Do we know nothing of it but Space and Motion? Or do we attach Figure and Motion to it by any other Logic, than that by which we predicate its specific Qualities?—If Body in general be meant, it suffices to reply, that this ⟨is⟩ a mere non-ens, or generic Term.

34[3] *Light-bringing* (also, punningly, Satanic) *Light on the Elucidations of a Certain Toletanus of the little Commentaries of Duns Scotus on the Sentences of Peter Lombard*. Peter Lombard (c 1100–60) wrote celebrated *Sententiae*, and Joannes Duns Scotus (c 1264–1308) did write *Commentarii* on them (though the diminutive form is scarcely warranted unless C simply wanted to increase the number of syllables in the word); but the trail runs faint with "Toletanus", though he might be the Al-

phonsus de Vargas, abp of Toledo, who wrote on Aristotle. Cf the facetious title of C's "Historie and Gests of Maxilian" (*Blackwood's* Jan 1822).

ANNEX[1] In *Morgenstunden* ch 3 (1790) 59, Mendelssohn distinguishes three kinds of knowledge or cognition (*Erkenntniss*), and defines truth as "every cognition . . . that is affected by the positive powers of the soul".

ANNEX[2] "A bodily thing": textus.

JOHN KENYON

1784–1856

Rhymed Plea for Tolerance. In two dialogues. With a prefatory dialogue, &c. [Anonymous.] London 1833. 8°.

British Library C 126 d 16

"S. T. C." label on title-page verso; John Duke Coleridge monogram "C" on p ⁻4. Inscribed on the title-page, presumably by Kenyon, "To S. T. Coleridge Esqᵉ—with the Author's respect and regards." A note in the same hand, adding a new stanza to the text, is tipped in at pp 24/5, and a line is emended in pencil p 114. Inscribed on p ⁻2 in another, unknown hand, "From the Author". C has corrected typographical errors on pp 13, 16, 17, 46, 74, 82, 115, incorporating some but not all of the errata on the last page of text.

DATE. c 3 Jan 1834: *Table Talk (CC)* I 454 and n 1

1 p ⁻1 and title-page

I renounce and utterly abjure all "Tolerance" and "Toleration": and would erase the words from the Vocabulary of the Philosopher and Moralist.[1]—The Magistrate is exclusively concerned with "ers", "ists", "ans", "aries", &c—Robb*ers*, Murder*erers*,[a] Burglar*ists*, Incendiar*ies*; the Philosopher, Theologian, in short, every thinking Citizen, in his individual character, exclusively concerned with "isms", "ities" &c—Calvin*ism*, Lutheran*ism*, De*ism*, Christian*ity*, Infidel*ity*.—Now I will not *tolerate* any *isms* or *ities*, which I clearly see & steadfastly believe to be, Falsehoods, truth-precluding, perhaps, & mischievous, Falsehoods—ex. gr. those of Socinianism—but the "An" has no meaning for me. I recognize no such person as a Socini*an*.[2] Vice versâ—the Socini—the Luther—the De- or *Athe*- are sounds without meaning for the *Magistrate*—and he would have to condemn or Acquit John Nokes & or

---

[a] A slip for "Murder*ers*"

---

[1] Cf the essay on tolerance in the 1818 *Friend*, in which C declares "that as far as opinions, and not motives; principles, and not men, are concerned; I neither am *tolerant*, nor wish to be regarded as such": *Friend (CC)* I 96.

[2] The same distinction between individuals and creeds is invoked in the controversial passage in *BL* ch 24 *(CC)* 245–6 in which C denies that Unitarianism is Christianity but will not say that Unitarians are not Christians.

E. Style of being— —*an*, or *ist*.[3] You are an "*an*"—what I don't know. Away with you!—

2   pp vi–vii | Preface

But be it remembered, that had such a spirit [of toleration] been more fully poured into earlier or later ages, Christ and Socrates had not died by hemlock and the cross,* nor Servetus and Latimer by fire; nor would contempts and hatreds, more or less intense, stand up, as now, for bourns between sect and sect.

* But, my dear Mr K.,[1] is it complete *Tolerance*, on *your* part, of the innocent, even if erroneous, PERSUASIONS, or, of the deep Feelings & Interests vitally permeating these Persuasions, of ten times ten thousand, yea, and that again decupled, of your Countrymen, of which Number I, S. T. C. am a humble *One*—thus to couple together, as Creatures of the same kind and order, & as Animals belonging to the same Kennel, Christ and Socrates? Nay, even Servetus and Latimer have no one *fusing* or *uniting* point of character, but the common circumstance of Fire & Faggot.[2]

3   p vii

And let her [an established Church] so do [extend her toleration], not to gather in those without the fold, but to improve those within it; and to make, as nearly as possible, professions of faith and truth of fact coincident. To effect this, she should no longer hesitate to erase from her articles of faith and from her liturgy all clauses damnatory of other creeds, or shades of creed.

Buy why? if the very purpose & occasion of the Creeds be to warn against such or such Errors?—Only let them be so worded, as not to include *Persons*: & why should not *Errors* be fore-warned. ?

4   pp viii–xi

. . . if the damnatory clauses of our Liturgy and of our Church articles

---

1[3] I.e. presumably, since the magistrate in his official capacity knows nothing of Lutheran*ism*, de*ism*, or athe*ism*, the allegiances of the individual must be meaningless to him. (The names are representative, as John Doe.)

2[1] Through their common acquaintance with Thomas Poole, C and Kenyon became friends during the period of C's residence with the Morgans in 1814–15: *CL* IV 916, VI 1032. This work was Kenyon's first published volume of poetry.

2[2] As a member of the C of E, C objects to Kenyon's lumping together Michael Servetus (1511–53), who wrote against the Trinity, and Hugh Latimer (c 1485–1555), a Protestant martyr in the Marian persecutions.

be indeed not of general credence; then it requires small argument to show that they should no longer be suffered to remain.

If, as I suppose, the excellent Author refers to the Athanasian Creed, he might have called for its immediate expulsion from the Liturgy, it deforms, on many & more valid grounds—1. as pseudo-Athanasian, the work of a ignorant as well as bigotted Monk, half a century later than the Death of the truly good Athanasius; 2. as therefore without Church Authority.[1] It is the Creed of no Council or Synod: 3. for its confusing Tautology: 4. because it is virtually *heretical* by omission of an absolutely essential Article, the subordination of the Filial Word, *as* God—& not *per accidens*,[2] in the Incarnation.—5. because its determination in the Eutychean & Nestorian Controversy is controvertible,[3] & of very doubtful accordance with the best Catholic Divines, & being without even the shadow of a Scripture Text to support its dogmas, is (as indeed the whole Creed is) most offensively presumptuous. Myself a zealous Athanasian, who hold the doctrine of the Tri-unity not only to be an important article of Christianity;[4] but *to be* Christianity—not only not to contradict Reason or Religion; but to *be* the Reason & the Religion—denounce this Creed, as the great Dedecus, et Infortunium[5] of the Established Church: and its continuance without a remonstrance the opprobrium of its Bishops, and Dignitaries, since the time that Bull and Waterland *fixed* this Article for the whole Catholic Church, Romish & Protestant./[6]

---

[1] The traditional attribution of the Creed to Athanasius (c 296–373) had been disproved in 1642 (see LUTHER *Colloquia* 78 n 2); Daniel Waterland, to whom C refers below, argued in his *Critical History of the Athanasian Creed* (1723) that St Hilary of Arles (403–49) was the actual author.

[2] "By chance", adventitiously.

[3] A theological dispute that arose in the fifth century: Nestorius (d c 451) was identified with the doctrine of two Persons (divine and human) in Christ; Eutyches opposed Nestorianism by arguing that there were "two natures before, but only one after" the Incarnation (*ODCC*). The Athanasian Creed appears to have been composed before this controversy began.

[4] C often used "Tri-unity" as a more precisely defined concept than "Trinity"—e.g. in IRVING *Sermons* 1, *LS* (*CC*) 62. In *AR* (1825) 169–70 he wrote, "I am clearly convinced, that the scriptural and only true Idea of God will, in its developement, be found to involve the Idea of the Tri-unity."

[5] "Disgrace, and Misfortune".

[6] "A Clergyman in full Orders, who has never read the works of Bull and Waterland, has—a duty yet to perform": *AR* (1825) 308n. C may be referring to the English theologians as authorities on the Trinity, George Bull notably in *Defensio Fidei Nicaenae* (1685) and Daniel Waterland in *A Vindication of Christ's Divinity* (1720); or as Church historians writing on the Creeds, as in the work by Waterland cited in n 1.

5   p 3 | Prefatory Dialogue

>   *A.*—'Tis true, of all that ink satiric page
>   Few dip the pen from purely virtuous rage.
>   'Tis true, each stroke erased not honest quite,   *?**
>   And blackened leaves, not few, must turn to white . . .

>   * Is't true, your pen here wrote not *English quite?*
>   Th' Ellipsis flickers like a Farthing Light!—

6   p 6

>   These are the vile—but his a viler part,
>   Who makes his prey some woman's breaking heart,
>   And pours on penitence his caustic in,
>   Till the seared frailty hardens into sin.

"*pours in on*" would border on ολιπολοπ[1] english even in the natural sequence of the words; but in verse, and thus dislocated, it demands the Surgeon.

7   p 8

>   Virtue stands firm, and smiles in temperate might.

lifts her head in Light.[a]

8   p 10

>   * Some muck-worm prelate, earthly gains made sure,
>   Who leaves a bloated million from the poor;
>   * Some title-hunting judge, whose slanting sight
>   Can blink a tyrant wrong, or wrest a right . . .

* I cannot recall from the history of the last 50 years any one name of Judge or Bishop, to whom this dread charge can even on grounds of common Report, be probably applied.—Whom can Mr K. mean?—

---

[a] C's suggested emendation is written in directly below the words it would replace

6[1] "Slipslop", alluding to Mrs Slipslop—"a mighty affecter of hard words" and ancestor of Mrs Malaprop—in Fielding's *Joseph Andrews.*

CARL ALEXANDER FERDINAND KLUGE
1782–1844

Versuch einer Darstellung des animalischen Magnetismus, als Heilmittel. 2nd ed. Berlin 1815. 8°.

British Library C 126 i 11

"S. T. C." label on p [2] (half-title verso). Monogram of John Duke Coleridge on p ⁻4. A letter from Leonard Horner, in response to *CL* VI 709–10, is bound in at pp 128/9. On p 500 there is a small pencil mark—possibly C's—in the index against the word *Wahrnehmen* ("perceive").

DATE. C read this book more than once (5), the first reading occurring perhaps shortly after his "conversion" to qualified belief in the effects of animal magnetism, i.e. between 8 Apr and 8 Jul 1817: *SW & F* (*CC*). A reference to a periodical in 7 suggests a date after May 1817. At least one later reading can be dated c Dec 1827, when the letter from Horner found its way into the volume, probably as a bookmark.

COEDITORS. Lore Metzger, Raimonda Modiano.

1 pp ⁻1 and ⁺1,[a] cropped

S. T. C.'s Judgement after a careful and unbiassed Perusal of this Book.

Allowing the least possible to Fancy and Exaggeration, I can yet find nothing in the Cases collected by Dʳ Kluge that requires any other conclusion but this— that under certain conditions one human Being may so *act[b] on the body as well as on the mind of another as to produce a morbid Sleep, from which the Brain awakes while the organs of sense remain in stupor. I speak exclusively of the *intellectual* phænomena of An. Mag.[1] That the same vis ab extra[2] may act medically, there is no reason to doubt—any more than of the effects of Opium. Thus the modus agendi[3] in the first instance, the instrument thro' which the Magnetiser operates, is the only mystery: and on this neither Kluge nor any of his Predecessors have thrown a ray of Light. Their Somato —or brevi-

---

[a] Inside front and back of original paper wrapper
[b] The corresponding asterisk is within the body of footnote † below, at "The act"

1[1] Animal Magnetism.   **1[3]** "Manner of acting".
1[2] "Force from without".

371

tatis et euphoniæ causâ[4] †Somosphere[5] is a mere translation of the Fact into an unmeaning Image—. It is but the substitution of the word, Fluid, for Dr Reil or Dr Kluge.[7]　　　　　　　　　　　　　S. T. C.

~~Di~~ Contra-distinctions are best exemplified at their first presentation to the Reader's mind by *extremes*: provided, the examples are stated *as* extreme Cases.—Now Dr Kluge's Work cannot indeed be declared an extreme case, and yet it is not a fair instance of the *Average* of German Reasoning &c where new facts are concerned.—Still however it contrasts ~~strongly~~ characteristically with the manner, in which an English Physician would have treated the subject. The second or theoretical Section, unsatisfactory as it is, is by far the best.[8] The first is inferior; but this is the fault of the *man*, Kluge, and not of the *German*. Had it been written as many a German would have written ⟨it,⟩ it would have been the best—and would have shewn the German character in ~~its~~ one of its points of superiority—But Kluge seems to have constructed his references out of some Work of general Bibliography ⟨and to have known the

† a ~~ner~~ sphere supposed to be filled by a nervous fluid to an undefined distance round the Body. An *atmosphere* with Σωμα = Body for αθμὴ Halitus or Breathing.[6] The act* however is a discovery of great importance as well as curiosity: and it is far from my intention to detract from either.—[a]

[a] Here C has written "(Turn to the other Cover, at the end of the Book)" and has continued his note on p $^+$1

1[4] "For the sake of brevity and euphony".

1[5] According to Kluge, the nerves are conductors of a fine irritable substance, a fluid that builds around the nerves a sensible atmosphere (*sensibel Atmosphäre*) by means of which the vital current (*Lebensstrom*) acts at a distance (p 212 § 177). Kluge discusses the "sensible atmosphere"—C's "Som(at)osphere", below —esp in pp 210–14 §§ 175–80 (cf **11, 12**), pp 232–3, 256–7 (cf **21**).

1[6] C's etymology, suggesting that "somatosphere" is formed by analogy with "atmosphere", is not quite correct: ἄσθμα (C's ἀθμή is formed from German *Athmen*) and *halitus* both mean breath, but ἄτμος in "atmosphere" means vapour.

1[7] In pp 210–11 § 175 (**11** below) Kluge cites Johann Christian Reil (1759–1813) as one of the first scientists to advance the theory of a sensible atmosphere around the

nerves, a theory later verified by Humboldt (§ 176).

1[8] Kluge's treatise is divided into two main parts, *Theoretischer Theil* (pp 1–308) and *Praktischer Theil* (pp 309–503), each part being subdivided into three sections. C probably refers to the first and second sections of the *Theoretischer Theil*: "Entdeckungsgeschichte des animalischen Magnetismus" (pp 15–80), on the history of the earliest discoveries and interpretations of the phenomena of animal magnetism up to Mesmer and his followers, and "Uebersicht der magnetischen Erscheinungen" (pp 81–204), on the relationship between magnetiser and patient and the different degrees of magnetic influences (see **6–8** below). The third section, "Beleuchtung der magnetischen Erscheinungen" (pp 205–308), includes the theory of the magnetic fluid.

~~books~~ *Titles* only of the Books—⟩—the facts ⟨likewise⟩ are *alluded* to only, ~~not~~ or if given, ⟨yet not detailed,⟩ much less *weighed, or so stated as to enable the *Reader* to weigh them.[11] Very rarely either rank, character, or previous habits are particularized.—But worst of all, and without comparison *bad*, is the third part, which in an English work would probably have been the best—viz. the kinds of Diseases, ~~to~~ in which An. Magnetism has been found successful, and the particulars of the cures.[12]—The impression, which it must leave on a judicious Reader, is that of Doubt, whether *any* cures have been performed other than accidentally, by mere disturbance of the nervous system: as the [. . . . .]*c*

* *a*Ex. gr. the magnetizing of Trees, and the Amulets.[9] I have heard better evidence from Grannams in favor of Purses and Coffins from the Fire, and winding-sheets on tallow candles:[10] and yet *b*how easily might the former (the Apple-trees) have been brought to the Test. The [. . .] had the grace not to mention.

2 [p 1] half-title, pencil

I am in the habit of making marginal observations into books, I read—a habit indulged by the partiality of my friends. For the last 20 years there is scarce a book so bepenned or bepenciled, but some one or more instances will be found noticed by me of the power of the visual and its substitution for the conceptual.[1] Yet I remember few more striking than the scornful and pertenacious disbelief of An. Mag. compared with the eager belief of Electricity—the main cause of this difference being, I am persuaded, this only that [? Electricity] exhibited a flash of Light.[2]

a This footnote is written at the head of the page, preceded by ''* 1. 22.''—i.e. line 22 of the ms
b The rest of the footnote is written around the outer margin
c Cropped

1[9] Kluge discusses the method of magnetising trees (to which cures are attributed in **39** and **40** textus) in pp 416–23 §§ 328–37; there is a passing reference to the amulets p 24.

1[10] Popular superstitions propagated by ''grandmothers''—C uses ''grannams'' in the same way in JUNG **1**. These particular omens of good fortune or death are repeated in *Logic* (*CC*) 187 and n.

1[11] Kluge's treatise is primarily a work of reference with exhaustive documentation; each brief paragraph is followed by a long list of the titles and authors on which his observation is based.

1[12] *Praktischer Theil* third section: ''Bestimmung der Fälle, in welchen die Anwendung des animalischen Magnetismus angezeigt ist'' (pp 424–42, **41–43** below), in which Kluge analyses the kinds of diseases that are most affected by animal magnetism.

2[1] C indeed often writes of the ''despotism of the eye'' and the consequent neglect of concepts insusceptible of visualisation: *BL* ch 6 (*CC*) I 107; JOANNES **5**.

2[2] Although formerly a disbeliever himself, C wrote against ''the contemptuous rejection of animal magnetism, before and without examination'' in Jul 1817, arguing

3 p 8 | § 7

Ganz ausgezeichnet in seinen Wirkungen ist aber der animalische Mag-
netismus. Bei ihm ist . . . ein bleibender Uebergang und eine innige
Beimischung eines unmittelbar auf das Nervensystem und von da auf
den ganzen Organismus belebend wirkenden Fluidums. Der Körper . . .
erhält von aussen her einen wirklichen Zuwachs der ihm beiwohnenden
Lebenskraft.

[Animal magnetism is truly excellent in its effects. It brings with it . . . a per-
manent transfusion and an intimate admixture of an animating fluid that acts
immediately upon the nervous system and through it upon the whole organism.
The body . . . receives from outside a true increase of its inherent vital energy.]

An ominous § for the Introduction of a simple Statement of *Facts.* An
intimate Admixture of life-infusing Fluid, to and with the Vis vitæ[1] im-
manent in the Body!!

4 p 14 | Blank space after § 12

Mem. In Hoffman's Works (Folio, Vol. 3, p. 49, 50:) there are two
cases that approach to Natural Magnetopathia[1]—and evidence the cura-
tive power of Sleep—among other things, as a regular daily Purgative
of Scybala[2] &c.

5 p 52, pencil | § 44

Einige Schüler *Mesmers* machten indess von animalischen Magnetismus
einen weisern Gebrauch. Sie schlossen sich im Jahre 1784 einander an,
und bildeten in den verschiedenen Provinzen und Hauptstädten Frank-

---

not for belief but for fair consideration: BM
Add MS 36532 ff 5, 7–12. Here also, he
sees belief in animal magnetism as a victim
of the prejudice against invisible (therefore
possibly spiritual) forces.

3[1] "Life-force", as in **42** below.

4[1] Friedrich Hoffman (1660–1742) in
Opera omnia physico-medica (6 vols Halle
1718–40) iii 49–50 describes the cases of
two women (one aged 12, the other 24)
seized by recurrent "ecstatic catalepsy".
Their bodies became rigid, their eyes fixed
upon some pleasing image—of God, an-
gels, heaven, the Saviour, eternal life, ac-
cording to their later accounts. Between
trances both were free of symptoms and in
all respects normal. Though many reme-
dies were tried, none succeeded in arousing

them from their ecstatic states, and even-
tually both were cured "spontaneously".
A copy of this edition of Hoffman is in
Gillman SC (1843) 505.

"Magnetopathia"—magnetic cure (not
in *OED*)—on the analogy of homoeopathy,
hydropathy, allopathy, all early-nine-
teenth-century coinages in which the sec-
ond element (from πάθος, suffering) is
vaguely taken to mean relief from, or cure
of, suffering or disease.

4[2] "Rounded masses of faeces". Hoff-
man does not use the term but reports that
although the women took no solid food
during their trances they excreted daily and
the 12-year-old girl "evacuated copious
and very hard faeces every day".

reichs . . . magnetische Gesellschaften. . . . Hier wurden nun unter dem Beiseyn hinzugetretener Aerzte hülfsbedürftige Kranke unentgeltlich magnetisirt. Man theilte sich alsdann die gemachten Entdeckungen und Fortschritte einander wechselseitig mit, liess auch die Curgeschichten öffentlich drucken . . .

[Some of Mesmer's students meanwhile made a wiser use of animal magnetism. They assembled in 1784 and formed magnetic societies in various provinces and main cities of France. . . . Here ill persons in need of help were magnetised free of charge under the care of supervising doctors. They communicated their discoveries and advances to one another and also had the histories of their cures publicly printed . . .]

At the first perusal of this Book I read this Chapter without complaint: for I took for granted, that the third Section would ~~have~~ contain a full well arranged Selection of attested Cures, with all the particulars of each. But I have been disappointed in toto; and cannot help concluding, that either An. Mag. *medically considered*, is a wretched Cause, or Dr Kluge a wretched Advocate—or that each is *palliated* at the expence of the other. § 349. is the only satisfactory §^{1}—for tho' even this is but an assertion, it is a *definite* one/ and even here how many questions remain unanswered—as did the Epileptic Fits return? &c

6   p 102, pencil | § 94

Zu den, schon beim ersten Grade (§. 90.) im Voraus erwähnten . . . Erscheinungen gesellen sich nun noch folgende:—Die Wärme nimmt mehr zu und verbreitet sich, dem Gefühle des Kranken nach, von dem Magen aus, wie von einem Centralpunkte, über den ganzen Körper.

[The following phenomena now join those previously mentioned in connection with the first [magnetic] grade (§ 90) . . . the heat increases further and spreads, according to the patient's impression, from the stomach, as from a central point, over the whole body.]

α This sensation is the first noticeable effect of the nitrous Oxyd of Davy, when inhaled.[1] N.B. Have any experiments been made as to the state of the Blood during the different magnetic Grades?

5[1] In § 349 (p 433) Kluge discusses the application of animal magnetism to epilepsy, convulsions, and other nervous disorders, for which animal magnetism proved effective when all other remedies had failed. The "most dreadful convulsions magically disappeared through manipulation, and the unspeakable suffering of the patients instantly gave way to tranquillity and serenity".

6[1] Humphry Davy discovered in 1799 that nitrous oxide when "respired . . . produced effects analogous to those produced by drinking fermented liquors,—usually a transient intoxication, or violent exhilaration": *Elements of Chemical Philosophy* (1812) 258. C and RS were two of the first to inhale "laughing gas" experimentally

7	pp 164–5 | § 137

Vermöge dieser genauen Kenntniss seines innern Körpers bestimmt der Clairvoyant nicht nur sehr treffend den Sitz und die Beschaffenheit seiner Krankheit, sondern es entwickelt sich auch zugleich in ihm ein Instinkt, welcher ihn die zu seiner Wiederherstellung nöthigen Heilmittel wissen lässt. *Heinecken's* Kranke sagte: "Ich sehe das Innere meines Körpers, alle Theile schienen mir gleichsam durchsichtig und von Licht und Wärme durchströmt; ich . . . bemerke genau die Unordnungen . . . und denke aufmerksam auf Mittel, wodurch dieselben gehoben werden können, und alsdann kommt es mir vor, als ob mir Jemand zuriefe: dieses oder jenes musst du gebrauchen."

[By virtue of his precise knowledge of the inner workings of his body, the clairvoyant not only determines accurately the location and nature of his disease but at the same time develops an instinct which permits him to know the remedies necessary for his recovery. Heinecken's patient said: "I see the inside of my body, all of its parts appear to me equally transparent and suffused with light and warmth; I . . . notice the disturbances exactly . . . and think carefully of the means by which they can be removed, and then it seems to me as if someone cried out: You must use this [remedy] or that."]

The descriptions given by many, nay, by the most, of the Inside-seers, recorded in the Archives of An. Mag., & ~~the~~ in Nasse and Kieser's Magazin for An. Mag.[1] are so wild & cataphysical[2]—& all of them speak the language of Dreams so characteristically, that much stronger evidence, and instances far more decisive than have hitherto been produced, are wanting to make me a Believer on this point.[3] I am persuaded, that it is the Imagination at once producing and beholding.[4] This

---

under Davy's supervision; C's account of his sensations, printed in Davy's *Researches, Chemical and Philosophical; Chiefly Concerning Nitrous Oxide* (1800), is included in *SW & F* (*CC*). There is a further reference to nitrous oxide in **45** below. C's alpha (α) refers to Kluge's footnote indicator "a" (which falls at the end of the textus) and indicates the appropriate textus.

7[1] Kluge gives many case histories from journals (or "archives" as C puts it) on animal magnetism such as Lorenz Boeckmann's *Archiv für Magnetismus und Somnambulismus* (Strasbourg 1787, 1788) and Reil's *Archiv für Physiologie*. The magazine on animal magnetism to which C refers specifically is *Archiv für den thierischen Magnetismus* ed Dietrich Georg

Kieser (1779–1862), Christian Friedrich Nasse (1778–1851) et al. It is cited again in **28** below.

7[2] *OED* ascribes "cataphysical"— against nature, unnatural—to De Quincey (1839) but notes Jeremy Taylor's "cataphysics".

7[3] C's lifelong interest in dreams is reflected in many of his writings, and the "Language of Dreams" is explicitly the subject of a note of c May 1818: *CN* III 4409.

7[4] C knew that the royal commission appointed to investigate animal magnetism in 1784—of which Benjamin Franklin was a member—had concluded that most of its effects, including its cures, were produced by the imagination. The commissioners

will not appear wonderful to those who know how very large a share the plastic Memory has even in our waking Perceptions. In omnem actum Perceptionis influit Imaginatio efficienter, says Wolff.[5] Besides, if several undoubted Clairvoyants of the Fifth Grade[6] see what neither does or can exist, *then* none of them see by *objective* vision.

8   pp 178–9 | § 149

Tardy's Patientin bemerkte z.B. in einer ihrer Krisen, dass sie vor eilf Jahren ein Geschwür am Herzen gehabt, und dass dieses vor neun Jahren wieder verschwunden sei.* Während einer andern Krise, welche sie Nachmittags hatte, bemerkte sie, dass eine grosser Wurm, von welchem sie die Beschwerden in ihren Eingeweiden herleitete, gegen Mittag in ihren Magen gekommen sei, dort Nahrung zu sich genommen, und sich dann in den Zwölffingerdarm zurückbegeben habe, woselbst er noch zum Knaule zusammengerollt liege . . .

[Tardy's patient remarked, for example, in one of her crises that eleven years earlier she had had a growth on her heart and that nine years earlier it had disappeared.* During another crisis, which she had during the afternoon, she remarked that a large worm, to which she attributed the discomfort in her intestines, had entered her stomach near noon, had fed there, and then had returned to the duodenum, where it still lay coiled up . . .]

* What can this prove, unless Tardy had afterwards dislodged and eliminated this duodenal Inmate, that dined always at the Ordinary or Cook's Shop, by Oil of Turpentine or other Anthelmintic?[1] Other Clairvoyants have seen Warts on the apex of their Hearts—curdled Blood in their Veins—& what not?—Do not all these Images bear the very character & impression of *the* DREAM?

---

may have intended thus to discredit animal magnetism; refining their speculations, C can take their findings as evidence of the power of imagination. Kluge gives a short account of the commission pp 58–60.

7[5] "Into every act of perception imagination flows effectively", a variant of the statement recorded early in 1801 (*CN* I 905) with the reference "Wolff. Annot. in Psych. rat. §§. 24. vide Pl. 76."—i.e. Christian Wolff *Psychologia rationalis* sec 1 ch 1 § 24 (Frankfurt and Leipzig 1734) 20, as q in Ernst Platner *Philosophische Aphorismen* (2 vols Leipzig 1793) I 76. Although C annotated PLATNER, the passage is not marked in his copy. C uses the formula again, e.g. *Friend (CC)* I 146, *Lects*

1809–1819 (CC) II 208.

7[6] In pp 81–204 Kluge distinguishes seven magnetic grades or states: the higher the grade the farther the magnetic state is from the sensory world. (The first grade is mentioned in **6** textus, the fourth in **23** textus.) In the fifth grade the relationship between magnetiser and patient is "innerly", and clairvoyants attain an inner self-consciousness and intuition that enable them to locate their disease in the body and establish the remedy for it (pp 160–77); these C calls "Inside-seers".

8[1] Medicine used "against worms": *OED* records instances of the word from the seventeenth century onwards.

9   pp 206–7, pencil | § 169

Wenn die Erfahrung lehrt, dass der Mensch nur durch eine Ueberlegenheit an Kraft fähig wird, auf Andere magnetisch zu wirken . . . wenn man sich von alle dem überzeugt hat, so kann man mit der grössten Wahrscheinlichkeit daraus folgern, dass das hier Wirkende entweder jenes Wesen selbst sei, welches mit der Benennung des *nervenbelebenden Princips* bezeichnet wird, oder dass es doch wenigstens sehr nahe mit ihm in Verwandtschaft stehe.

[Since experience teaches us that only through a superiority of power does a man become capable of acting magnetically upon others . . . being convinced of all this, one can with the greatest probability deduce that what is active here must either be that essence itself which is denoted by the term *nerve-energising principle*, or that it must at least be closely related to it.]

Had not *Kluge* his theory in mind in laying so much stress on die Ueberlegenheit an Kraft?[1] At least Mr Tiek informed me that Dr Wolfart was a weak sickly man (schwach im Körper, und kränklich.)[2] Besides, Kraft is such an indefinite term—Force is distinct from Power, Power still more so from Strength[3]—and then of Mind, of Will, of Health, of Nerve, of Muscle, &c. All that can be said, methinks, is that to have magnetized B. proves a ~~relatively~~ Superiority in A. *at the time*—and of some sort or other. But it might be a superiority of *Effort* only, A. energizing, B. yielding or passive. For observe, the ? is twofold; 1. medical, in which Kluge is probably right, only that he should have said "sollte" instead of "fähig zu"[4]—2. theoretical or historical/ Is it practicable, however inexpedient it may be?

10   pp 209–10, pencil | § 173

Die Seele ist nach *Autenrieth* der dynamische Indifferenzpunkt aller Arten von Thätigkeit des Organismus. . . . Wie sich unter Magneten, die

---

9[1] "The superiority of power"—from textus (var).

9[2] Ludwig Tieck (1773–1853), whom C had met in Rome in 1806, when visiting London in Jun–Jul 1817 met C at Green's and then came to visit him in Highgate. C told J. H. Frere on 27 Jun 1817 how he had discussed animal magnetism with Tieck, the topic having been raised by Tieck when he noticed K. C. Wolfart's *Mesmerismus* (i.e. MESMER) "among my books", and C learned that Tieck "had been on a Brother's footing with Dr Wohlfart . . . from Childhood": *CL* IV 745. It was on this oc-

casion that Tieck expressed his opinion of Wolfart, an opinion that C repeats in MESMER 7.

9[3] The distinction is important in C's "polar" or "dynamic" philosophy, according to which force is a *manifestation* of a power. The further distinction between power and strength appears in a letter of 1803 to RS in which C wistfully remarks that he suspects himself of having "*power* not *strength*": *CL* II 959.

9[4] I.e. "should man act" for "does man become capable of acting": textus.

in verschiedener Richtung nebeneinander liegen und jeder für sich einen Indifferenzpunkt hat, ein vielleicht in keinem liegender ideeller Indifferenzpunkt bilden muss, der durch die Lage und Stärke aller bestimmt wird, also auch die Seele. . . . Doch entsteht die Seele nicht durch die Vereinigung aller Theile des Körpers und wird nicht vernichtet durch das Auseinanderweichen dieser Systeme; denn sie hat Freiheit und Bewusstseyn ihrer Willkühr, welches jeder Maschineneinrichtung fehlt. Dies Ursprünglich-Thätige, welches die Seele im Bewusstseyn ihrer Freyheit ausübt, begründet die Hoffnung ihrer Fortdauer nach Zerstörung ihrer Werkzeuge.

[According to Autenrieth the soul is the dynamic point of indifference of all kinds of activity in the organism. . . . Just as in magnets which are placed side by side facing in different directions, each having its own point of indifference, an ideal point of indifference must form which perhaps resides in none of them but is determined by the position and strength of all, so it is with the soul. . . . But the soul does not originate from the fusion of all parts of the body and is not destroyed when this system falls apart; for the soul has freedom and consciousness in its power, and this is lacking in a mechanism. In this originally active [power] which the soul—conscious of its freedom—exercises, lies the hope of its permanence after the destruction of its organs.]

§ 173. The Soul = the common point of Indifference of a number of magnets aggregated in different Directions, and which therefore may not fall in either. Consequently, it is a mere ideal relative result. But the Soul does not arise out of the bodily Organs, nor cease when they are dissolved—because it has free will, and consciousness—i.e. because it is not analogous to the Indifference-point of different Magnets. Blessed Logic!!—The Punctum Indifferentiæ[1] of a single magnet may be conceived as the Punct. originationis, amphoteric;[2] but of many it is = 0.[3] Suppose the centre of gravity in a System of Suns were (as Herschel imagines to be the case in some Systems) to fall in neither of the Suns[4]— yet what is it to solve? It presupposes its own effect, namely, the arrangement, as its own cause and condition!

11 p 211, pencil | § 175

Die Erscheinung der Empfindlichkeit mancher Theile, in welchen auch das schärfste Auge keine Spur eines Nervens entdecken konnte . . .

10[1] The "Point of Indifference"—recurrent in textus.

10[2] "The Point of origination, partaking of both values [i.e. + and −]".

10[3] I.e. the Point of Indifference of many [magnets] grouped together is of zero value.

10[4] Sir William Herschel (1738–1822) concluded from his study of double stars that they revolve about a common centre which is not located in either star, and he held a similar view of the centre of gravity of globular clusters.

brachte ihn [Reil] auf die Idee, dass die Nerven nicht Behälter, sondern blosse Leiter eines feinen, reizbaren Wesens seyn müssten . . .

[The phenomenon of a response in many parts when not even the sharpest eye could discover a trace of a nerve . . . led him [Reil] to the notion that nerves are not containers but mere conductors of a fine irritable substance . . .]

The ocular as degree—itself a deduct—an inference differing in the degree—not kind of clearness from that of a Soul, &c.

12   p 212, pencil | § 177

Der verdienstvolle *Rudolphi* versuchte zwar, ob es nicht möglich sei, die Humboldtschen Erfahrungen durch das dem Metalle entströmende galvanische Fluidum zu erklären, ohne dass man erst nöthig habe, eine besondere Nervensphäre anzunehmen; allein die bis jetzt hierüber aufgestellten Gründe sind keineswegs überzeugend, wie dies auch *Reil* zum Theil schon dargethan hat.

[The deserving Rudolphi did indeed try whether it were not possible to explain the experiences of Humboldt by the galvanic fluid flowing outward from the metal, without needing to postulate a particular nerve-sphere; however, the grounds established thus far in this matter are by no means convincing, as Reil has already demonstrated to some extent.]

This is so obvious and seems so probable, that Dr Kluge ought at least to have given Reil's proofs of the contrary.[1]

13   p 222, pencil | § 185

Einzelne Verbindungsäste können in dieser Ganglien-Kette fehlen, ohne Störung der Funktion, weil noch genug andere Verbindungen übrig bleiben, was nicht möglich wäre nach der gewöhnlichen Ansicht;* denn was den Ursprung giebt, kann nicht fehlen, ohne dass nicht auch das fehlt, was von ihm entspringen soll.

[Individual connecting branches can be missing in this chain of ganglia without interfering with its function, because enough other connections remain, which

---

12[1] In Reil's *Archiv für Physiologie* (1796) III 188–200 Carl Asmund Rudolphi has an article entitled "Etwas über die sensible Atmosphäre der Nerven", to which Reil appended a note objecting to Rudolphi's denial of a sensible nerve sphere (pp 200–1). Reil points out that Rudolphi's arguments failed to convince him that the idea of a sensible nerve sphere is without ground. He explains that by such a sensible sphere he does not mean an elastic fluid that surrounds the periphery of the nerves but a capacity within the nerves to transmit sensibility to adjoining parts which are not nerves. He goes on to refute Rudolphi's claim that because only a fifth of the surface of the skin is nerves, the whole skin is not therefore irritable, i.e. that only part of it responds to direct contact. Kluge (p 213) provides titles and page references for this material.

would not be possible according to the common view;∗ for if the originator does not exist, that which should originate from it must also not exist.]

∗ I do not perceive the logical force of this reasoning. What applies to the one case seems equally applicable to the other—unless the words "einzelne Verbindungs-äste"[1] do not refer to the Sympathetic Nerve,[2] which latter is taken as wanting in toto. Then indeed "the *sole* Source cannot be *wholly* wanting" without &c.

14 p 227, pencil, slightly cropped | § 189

Bei den Rindern machen die Organe, welche zur animalischen Sphäre gehören, gleichsam nur eine dünne Rinde für eine ungeheure Höhle aus, die mit lauter Eingeweiden angefüllt ist. Höher hinauf wird das Cerebral-System immer überwiegender . . . bis endlich im Menschen das vegetative und animalische Leben im Gemeingefühle und Selbstbewusstseyn einen Schlussstein findet, der es zur Einheit der Individualität und Persönlichkeit auffasst.

[In oxen the organs that belong to the animal sphere form as it were only a thin crust for an enormous cavity which is filled with nothing but bowels. The cerebral system becomes ever more predominant higher up . . . until finally in man the vegetative and animal life culminate in gregarious instincts and self-consciousness, the keystone that unites individuality and personality.]

After the writings of Kant is it not strange, that a Germa[n] Scholar shou[ld] thus confound the focus of a mirror wi[th] the perceptiv[e] power, to which it supplies onl[y] the condition of perception?[1]

15 p 229, pencil | § 191

. . . ohne Eingeweide würde der Mensch schwerlich Leidenschaften haben.∗[a]

[. . . without bowels, man would scarcely experience any passions.∗]

∗ How often has Jacob Behmen's Assertion that before the Passions were let loose by the Fall men had no Bowels, been picked out for ridi-

---

[a] In the outer margin C has written "*see below*", and he has written the note in the foot-margin below the previously written **16**

13[1] "Individual connecting branches" —in textus.

13[2] The name given to the largest cord in the sympathetic nervous system, running up the front of the spine. C's point is that if this were included among the "individual connecting branches", and if it were to fail, then the whole system—of which it is the trunk rather than a branch—would fail.

14[1] In C's world-view, as revealed in e.g. *TL*, what human beings have in common with plants and lower animals is only the *condition* of their distinctively human powers, which are divine in origin. The physical faculties supply terms and boundaries for human powers, as the Kantian categories describe the conditions governing human experience.

cule by such as had, perhaps, never attempted to read a 100 pages of his Works consecutively![1]

16 p 229, pencil

An diesem Pole der vorwaltenden Körperlichkeit liegen die Gefühle, welche am stärksten ausgesprochen und durch eine entschiedene körperliche Lust oder Unlust bestimmt sind; an jenem die mehr edlen, geistigen Gefühle. Beide werden im Gehirne aufgenommen, welches für die höheren Seelenkräfte das Organ ist, auf welches diese Kräfte beschränkt sind, für die Sinne und Gefühle aber der Spiegel, in dem alle Thätigkeit und Metamorphose des ganzen Organismus aufgesammelt wird.

[To this pole of predominating corporeality belong the feelings that are most strongly expressed and determined by a definite desire or aversion; to the other pole belong the nobler, more spiritual feelings. Both are received by the brain. It is the organ to which the powers of the soul are limited; but for the senses and feelings it is the mirror in which the whole organism's activity and metamorphosis are collected.]

a pretty phrase; but what does it mean? And these higher Soul-Powers— *what* do they reflect? The *grins* and *gestures* of Passion? This is all, that a Looking-Glass can do.

17 p 230, pencil

Die Nerven-Actionen diesseits des Apparats der Halbleitung sind bewusstlos, und die Vernunft im Gehirne bekommt auf diese Art ein entschiedenes Uebergewicht. Allein der Apparat der Halbleitung ist ein bedingter Isolator, der unter veränderten Umständen ein Conductor werden . . . kann.

[The nerve impulses on this side of the apparatus of the weak conductor are unconscious, and in this way reason gains a decided predominance in the brain. But the apparatus of the weak conductor is a limited insulator, which can become a conductor . . . under different circumstances.]

Merciful Heaven! what can the Man have been thinking of?—What? is *Reason* = a Fluid containing Consciousness, capable of accumulation by Insulators and of transfusion by Conductors?

18 p 241, pencil | § 204

Auf einem sehr sicheren . . . Pferde reitend, hatte er bereits die Hälfte des Weges . . . zurückgelegt, als mit einem Male das Pferd . . . unruhig ward . . . und aller Mühe ungeachtet nicht weiter zu bringen war. . . .

15[1] Böhme *Aurora* ch 17, not annotated in C's copy; but C seizes upon scientific corroboration of Böhme's remark.

Am andern Morgen erfuhr er, dass in der vergangenen Nacht eine Brücke . . . beim Darüberfahren eines Reisewagens eingebrochen, und die ganze Reisegesellschaft dabei ums Leben gekommen sei.

[Riding on a very sure-footed . . . horse, he had already covered half the distance . . . when suddenly the horse . . . became restless . . . and despite all effort could not be brought to move on. . . . The next morning he learned that the preceding evening a bridge . . . had collapsed as a coach passed over it, and the whole party of travellers had lost their lives.]

Surely, there is no such great difficulty in supposing the Smell of a graminivorous Animal to have been affected at that distance. Thus, Bullocks tremble at a considerable distance from a Slaughter-House, which they had never seen, and Mules in Sicily smell water a full half mile off to my own knowlege.[1]

19   pp 246–7, pencil | § 205

[To support the assumption of a sensible sphere surrounding the body, Kluge cites the case of a girl, both deaf and mute, whose highly developed telepathic sense enabled her to perceive a fire in a nearby manor house and on another occasion to anticipate correctly the unexpected arrival of her brother. In his long footnote (pp 246–9) Kluge cites a quantity of evidence and many authorities for such manifestations.]

Pity, that no one of these Philosopherists[1] has informed us what this compound Fluid of LIFE(!) is to do,[2] when the distant Object first dips into it: ex. gr. suppose the deaf and dumb Girl's Zöosphere[3] to extend a furlong in every direction, and the fire to have broke out just at its limited—How was this Fluid affected by the Fire. If this be answered, then I ask in what way did her *Brother* from Petersburg affect the Fluid, and so as to ~~be~~ produce a fraternal modification thereof?—A subtle fluid—elastic, expansible, expansive, repulsive, attractive, rarifiable, condensable, capable of vibrations, penetrative, & what not—take any or all of these qualities and properties, & whatever else is compatible with the word, *Fluid*—and then answer my Question. If you can not, what do I gain by the supposition, but a picture with the words under it—The Life-fluid as magnified a million times—Novalis seriously asks, from its as-

18[1] C visited Sicily in Aug–Nov 1804 and again in Sept–Oct 1805.

19[1] A contemptuous term, apparently C's coinage, for would-be philosophers.

19[2] C similarly rejects the materialist hypothesis of a nerve-fluid or magnetic fluid in **1** above, and in **22**, **25**, and **38** below.

19[3] Not in *OED*. Strictly "animal-sphere", the zone in which animal magnetism operates, but in the context perhaps "life-sphere". Cf "soma(to)sphere" in **1** above and **25** below, and "Neuro-sphere" in **20** and **28** below; and Kluge's terms *Lebenssphäre* (**20** textus), *vegetative Sphäre*, and *sensibel Sphäre* (**22** and **25** textus).

serted analogy to á Light, whether it does ⟨not⟩ split itself into colors![4] All this, I confess, puts *me* in a *brown* Study, with *black* Thoughts, *blue* Devils, &c.

20   pp 254–5, pencil | § 206

Endlich geben die beim animalischen Magnetismus beobachteten Erscheinungen den stärksten Beweis für die Wirksamkeit der Lebenssphäre; indem sie zeigen, dass der Magnetiseur auch ohne alle Berührung, selbst aus einer bedeutenden Ferne, durch sein blosses Wollen auf den Kranken influiren kann (§. 161).

[Finally, the phenomena observed in animal magnetism provide the strongest evidence of the efficacy of the vital sphere by demonstrating that the magnetiser can influence the patient without any contact, and even at a considerable distance, merely through his will power (§ 161).]

I should have taken this fact for a strong Objection to the dependence of this actio in distans[1] on a Neurosphere. For according to Kluge himself, it must bear some proportion in its extent to that of a single nerve, = $\frac{4}{5}$ of a Paris Line.[2]—Take it then at a 100,000 times that extent, still it would fall wofully short of the distance required by several of the Facts (Statements, at least). But the inference from ⟨the two ends of a⟩ divided nerve to the whole Body is not substantiated by any one of the facts that *ought* to be if the supposition were just. A violent passion that drives the Blood into the face ought surely to have some effect on a person standing face to face, not 3 inches off. And yet A might [? join/form] faces, and B. remain as cool as a Cucumber.

21   p 256 | § 207

Ehe ich diesen Gegenstand verlasse, bleibt mir noch eine Frage zu beantworten übrig, die man als Einwurf gegen das Gesagte aufstellen könnte: warum nämlich die Erscheinungen, welche auf einen sensibeln Wirkungskreis des thierischen Körpers hindeuten, sich nicht bei allen,

19[4] Friedrich von Hardenberg, known as "Novalis" (1772–1801), a copy of whose *Novalis Schriften* ed Ludwig Tieck and Friedrich Schlegel C owned (see HARDENBERG). Novalis's question about the life-fluid is not traced.
20[1] "Action at a distance".
20[2] Cf Kluge's statement in § 176 (pp 211–12): "He [Alexander von Humboldt] found that the metals proved effective even without touching a nerve or muscle, even when held at a distance of $\frac{5}{4}$ of a Paris line.

Likewise, in the case of nerves that were cut whose endings were placed at a distance of $\frac{5}{4}$ of a [Paris] line, the stimulation of one end nevertheless caused violent contractions in the muscle at the untouched end, whereas all reaction ceased when a glass plate was put between the nerve endings." A Paris foot being 12.785 English inches, a Paris line—one-twelfth of a Paris inch—is 0.0888 English inches, and $\frac{5}{4}$ of a Paris line is 0.111 English inches.

sondern nur bei einigen Individuen, und auch bei diesen oft nur zu gewissen Zeiten, äussern.

[Before leaving this subject one question remains to be answered which could be posited as an objection against what has been said: namely, why the phenomena that point to a sensible sphere of the animal body do not manifest themselves in all but rather only in some individuals and even in them often only at certain times.]

So that this sensitive Sphere is 9999 times useless for once that it is perceptible consequently capable of being of any service!

22 pp 258–9, pencil

Die Sensationen, welche wir durch diese Sphäre erhalten, gelangen zwar immer zu den verschiedenen Herden des Ganglien-Systems, werden aber von hier aus blos auf die gesammte vegetative Sphäre reflectirt, woselbst sie, wenn sie stark sind, Veränderungen veranlassen, die durch den Apparat der Halbleitung (§. 185.) dem Gehirne als Gemeingefühle überbracht, und in den allerwenigsten Fällen von den übrigen Gemeingefühlen unterschieden werden. Im normalen Zustande sind überdies die Wahrnehmungen durch unsere übrigen Sinne auch viel zu stark . . . mangeln uns aber die Sinne für die Ferne, so wird unsere Aufmerksamkeit mehr auf uns selbst und auf die nächsten Umgebungen gerichtet, und daher das Wahrnehmen durch die sensibel Sphäre schon bestimmter. Influirt nun noch der Wille auf das Ganglien-System (§.192.), so kann die Wahrnehmung an Deutlichkeit gewinnen, und, wenn das Ganglien-System durch eigene Körperbeschaffenheit, oder durch magnetische Einwirkung potenzirt wird, sogar bis zu Klarheit der gewöhnlichen Sinnesanschauung gesteigert werden.

[Although the sensations which we receive through this sphere always reach the different centres of the nervous system, they are transmitted from there only to the total vegetative sphere, where if they are strong they effect changes that are conveyed to the brain as general feelings through the apparatus of the weak conductor (§ 185) and only in the rarest cases are distinguished from other general feelings. Moreover, in normal conditions perception through the other senses is much too strong . . . if, however, we lack the senses for distance, our attention is directed towards ourselves and the nearest surroundings, and thus the perception through the sensible sphere is already more precise. If, in addition, the will also acts on the nervous system (§ 192), then the perception gains in clarity, and when the nervous system is activated through its own condition or through magnetic influence, the perception can even be raised to the clarity of a normal sensory intuition.]

An Evasion this. Surely the Sphere Ⓐ so vehemently potenziated as to agitate the whole frame and suspend the consciousness of a, ought to act perceptibly on the vegetal Life and vegetal Organs of b,[1] the spheres being as Ⓐ Ⓑ—: perceptible to C at least, if not to b himself.—Besides, suppose Ⓐ to extend a hundred yards, and that a is one of a crowd of persons within a space of about the same extent, how does each preserve its individuality? The persons would all alike hear the same *Sound*— why should they not participate in these impulses? Whether ab corpore or ad corpus,[2] whether the Fluid around each is as Water from a Spring in the centre, or as Water filling up the same area from rills ab extra,[3] the Fluid is the same in both instances/ therefore the S̶ Life-fluid of the Somatospheres and o̶f̶ the s̶p̶h̶e̶r̶e̶ ̶o̶f̶ ̶L̶i̶g̶h̶t̶ ̶f̶r̶o̶m̶ ̶a̶ ̶C̶a̶n̶d̶l̶e̶,̶ Light-fluid of a Candle-sphere ought to act alike, so far ⟨as that⟩ all within either should be similarly affected by the same Object, on the *rule*, exceptions from disease allowed for.

23   p 270 | § 214

Mit dem vierten Grade . . . geht der magnetisch Schlafende in die Zustände des Nachtwandlers über. . . . Wird unter diesen Umständen das Ganglien-System auch potenzirt, so, dass seine mannigfach zerstreuten Herde aus dem Verhältniss der Selbstherrschaft in das der Abhängigkeit von einem mächtiger gewordenen Centralpunkte treten . . . dann geht der Schlafende aus dem Zustande des Nachtwandelns in den rein magnetischen Zustand über . . .

[In the fourth [magnetic] grade . . . the magnetised sleeper passes into the state of somnambulism. . . . If under these circumstances the nervous system is also activated so that its variously dispersed centres pass from the state of autonomy into one of dependence on a more powerful central point . . . then the sleeper passes from the condition of somnambulism into that of pure magnetism . . .]

Whether potenzirt means a transfer of Power from Organ[a] to another, or an exciting into a *manifest* (actual) force a power already existing latently—in either case it seems to me an ill-chosen term.[1]

24   p 271

Die sonst bewusstlose, nur in der Bildung sich verwirklichende Idee, gelangt nun, noch innerhalb des Ganglien-Systems, zum Bewusstseyn, und der Instinkt reifet jetzt zum Willen (§. 188).* Das aus der sonst

[a] For "one Organ"

22[1] "Vegetal" here, as in HEINROTH 38, represents the lowest form of life present in the human being, "insect" and "animal" life rising above it.

22[2] "From the body or to the body".

22[3] "From without".

23[1] C brought "potenziate" into Eng-

lish from German in *BL* ch 12 (*CC*) I 287 and n, "to express the combination or transfer of powers"; he uses it and various cognates in **22** above and also e.g. BAXTER *Reliquiae* COPY B 99, IRVING *Sermons* 29 after n 25.

gleichgeltenden Masse des Ganglien-Systems nun zum Brennpunkte des Ganzen erhobene und zu einem Sensorio potenzirte Sonnengeflecht (§. 184.) wird ein neuer Gegensatz dem Sensorio des Cerebral-Systems; das Gehirn hört dadurch auf, absoluter Centralpunkt des Organismus zu seyn . . .

[The otherwise unconscious idea, realisable only in the formative process, reaches consciousness while still within the nervous system, and instinct now matures into will (§ 188).* The solar plexus, raised up out of the evenly constituted mass of the nervous system [to be] the focal point of the whole, and potenziated to a sensorium, becomes a new antithesis to the sensorium of the cerebral system; the brain thereby ceases to be the centre of the organism . . .]

* Wessen? Des Ganglion-System's? Ist Bewüsstseyn eins mit der Ichheit? wird das G. S. ein *Ich*?[1] If so, what becomes of the Soul's *I*? Are there two, or three *I*s, that of the Solar Plexus, the Cerebral I, and the I of the Soul?

25   pp 281–2, pencil | § 220–1

. . . der Somnambul bekommt in den höhern Graden mittelst seiner Sinnorgane durchaus keine Anschauungen, sondern nimmt Alles mit der ganzen Oberfläche seines Körpers wahr . . .
   § 221. Mittelst seiner sensibeln Sphäre nimmt also der Somnambul die Umgebungen wahr . . .

[. . . in the higher grades the somnambulist develops no intuitions whatsoever through his sensory organs, but perceives everything with the entire surface of his body . . .
   § 221. The somnambulist, then, perceives his surroundings by means of his sensible sphere . . .]

It is even painfully wonderful (would, I could call it strange too) that men of sense, science, learning and experimental knowlege, such as Dr Kluge evidently is, should attach such immense importance to the supposition of a nervine Somasphere/[1] Suppose it to exist, yet its extension must be bounded by the nervous spheres of every other sphere—10 yards would be too much for any fair analogy from any ascertained galvanic ⟨or x y z⟩ atmosphere/ and what could it effect after all? What could it as *a fluid* represent to the focal point but its own modifications as more or less elastic, more or less condensed, attracted from & thither, or repelled. But if it, the nervous Somatosphere, be itself, sentient—

24[1] "Whose? The nervous system's? Is consciousness one with I-ness? Is the nervous system an *I*?" above; but here the emphasis is on "nervine", with which cf "Neuro-sphere" in **20** above.
   25[1] For "Soma(to)sphere" see **1** (at n 5)

what has the Fluid to do with it? What connection has thinness with Thought?[2]—I have heard indeed ~~the~~ a question put to children (what did *Thought* do?) which attributed to it a water-making property under certain clinical conditions: but never of a Thought-making Water.

26   p 280,[a] pencil, referring to p 281

Es geht ihm [dem Somnambul] aber hierin eben so, wie es dem Blindgebornen mit den Farben geht; dieser bekommt durch sein verfeinertes Gefühl zwar auch Notiz von der Verschiedenheit der Farben, und sagt z.b., die Scharlachfarbe unterscheide sich von der grünen so,* wie sich der Trompetenton von dem einer Flöte unterscheidet; allein so richtig dies Verhältniss auch immer ausgedrückt ist, so bekommt er dadurch noch keine Anschauung und richtige Vorstellung von der Farbe an sich . . .

[In this respect he [the somnambulist] has much the same experience as a person born blind has in relation to colours; it is true that the latter perceives the difference in colours through his more finely developed sense and says, for instance, that scarlet differs from green just as* the sound of a trumpet differs from that of a flute; however, no matter how correctly this relationship is expressed, it does not lead him to an intuition and accurate representation of the colour as such . . .]

* p. 281.
    How smoothly a ben trovato[1] passes into a grave fact, the ground of an argument!! If this remark ever was made by a Blind Man, it is far more probable that it was suggested by the association of soldiers with the *word*, Scarlet.[2]

27   p 282

Hat aber der Blindgewordene schon einmal früher in seinem Leben mittelst des Farbensinnes eine wirkliche Anschauung der Farben gehabt, so wird er dann durch sein Gefühl nicht allein von dem Verhältnisse derselben Notiz bekommen, sondern es wird sich nun auch gleichzeitig mit dieser Notiz die jedesmalige, richtige Vorstellung der Farbe reproduciren. In diesem letzteren Verhältnisse steht gerade der Somnambul, der durch seine Herzgrube nicht blos vom Gesichts-, sondern auch von allen übrigen Sinnes-Eindrücken Notiz bekommt . . .

---

[a] All the marginal space on p 281 having already been taken up with the first part of **25**, C wrote **26** on p 280

25[2] C similarly mocks the materialist attribution of thinness to thought in MESMER **1, 12**.

26[1] A "witty invention".

26[2] The example was made famous by Locke in *An Essay Concerning Human Understanding* bk 2 ch 4 and bk 3 ch 4 § 11.

[But if a person who has become blind has earlier in his life once truly perceived colour through his sense of colour, then through his senses he will not only become aware of the relationship but, simultaneously with this awareness, will reproduce the actual, correct conception of colour. Exactly in this latter condition the somnambulist finds himself when he becomes aware not only of visual but also of other sense impressions through the pit of his stomach . . .]

N.B. Wherein lies the *essential* distinction between Seeing, and visual Notice-taking, Hearing and auditual Notice-taking, &c?[1] Does the absence of coloured Images in the Blind-born's Dreams prove more than this: that the conditions of Light ab intra require the previous exercise of those ab extra[2] in order to awaken and evolve them?

28 pp 282–5

a Again, *how* is a *notice*, be the kind what it may, taken of a unopened Letter pressed on the Pit of the Stomach? Or a Card unknown to the Magnetiscur, taken up from a heap of Cards in the Dark, and slipt under the Bed clothes from the knees upward, in a pitch-dark Room?[1] How, I say, is this explicable on the hypothesis that Perception is always passive, by an action or reflection of a Medium from the Object perceived? Kluge's own statement of the conditions, under which Touch can be ⟨substituted for⟩ Sight, confutes him/ For how did the Patient learn *at once* that a, (= affection of the Neurosphere) was ~~the~~ correspondent ~~of~~ to y (reflected Light of such or such a color)? Suppose (it is a fair analogy) the sense of Hearing suddenly and for the first time given to a person born deaf; that you tell him, in a dark room, or ~~with~~ having bound up his eyes, "Your Brother is arrived"—What will he hear but a "vox: et præterea nihil"?[2] Till the Sound, Brother, &c, has been repeatedly *associated* with the Sight-image, Brother &c? If the cases related by Van Ghert, Tritschler, and others (Archiv des Magn. by Keiser, Nasse and Eschenmeyer, 1816, 1817)[3] are *Facts*, I see no other solution but an *act* of Perception immediate—in short, a recurrence to the Platonic Theory of Sight.—[4]

27[1] In textus, *Notiz bekommt*, translated as "becomes aware".

27[2] "From within . . . from without".

28[1] C offers typical tests of the powers of clairvoyants, of which Kluge and other writers on animal magnetism give many examples. The case of the letter pressed to the pit of the stomach is in Kluge p 192; the patient fell asleep according to the instructions in the unopened letter.

28[2] "A voice, and nothing more"—the Spartan's comment on eating a nightingale: Plutarch *Moralia* 233A.

28[3] Both contributed articles to *Archiv für den thierischen Magnetismus* (see 7 n 1 above): P. G. van Gheert "Tagebuch einer magnetischen Behandlung" in II (1819) i 3–188, ii 3–51; Johann Christoph Salomon Tritschler "Sonderbare, mit glücklichen Erfolg animal-magnetisch behandelte Entwickelungskrankheit eines drey-zehnjahrigen Knaben" I (1817) ii 51–137.

28[4] See e.g. *Theaetetus* 156D–E: "As soon, then, as an eye and something else whose structure is adjusted to the eye come within range and give birth to the whiteness

29   p 283

[Footnote:] Fast dieselbe Idee habe ich auch in *Schubert*'s Ansichten von der Nachtseite der Naturwissenschaft ausgesprochen gefunden. Es heisst hier nämlich (p. 363.): "Während die Einwirkungen äusserer näher Gegenstände, welche durch's Auge gesehen werden, zwar viel stärker sind, als die, welche vermittelst des Gemeingefühls zu uns gelangen, sind doch auch diese, zugleich mit jenen, immer vorhanden. Das Gemüth hat in der Erinnerung die Einwirkungen der nahen Gegenstände, welche durchs Auge geschahen, mit der gleichzeitigen Wirkung derselben aufs Gemeingefühl so vereint, dass jetzt . . . in der Seele die gleichnamigen Vorstellungen, welche ehedem zu derselben Zeit durch das Sehen erweckt wurden, zugleich hervortreten . . ."

[I have found almost the same idea expressed in Schubert's *Views on the Dark Side of Natural Science*. It runs (p 363): "Whereas the impressions of nearby external objects which are perceived by the eye are much stronger than those conveyed by ordinary sensation, the latter are always present conjointly with the former. The mind, in recollecting the impressions of nearby external objects obtained through the eye, unites them with their simultaneous effect on ordinary sensation to the extent that now . . . the corresponding representations, which formerly were awakened at the same time through sight, emerge in the soul jointly . . ."]

The quotation from Schubert is no sufficient answer to the objection below:[a] for the contemporaneous impressions on the Eye and the Sense General or Gemein-gefühl are both from Light: which in the Somnambulist's case is not present. Or tho' the *materia* of the Neurosphere moved by the same law of *recti-lineal* radiation as *Light*—how would it apply to the *vermicular* motion of *Sound*?[1] Not to mention, that recollection of X by means of a *never-noticed*, tho' always co-present Y, is more plausible as a Co-efficient than as a Principal: if ⟨indeed⟩ it can be admitted *at all*, and if Schub: have not confounded the reproduction of X by co-presence of non *eo* tempore consciti Y,[2] with a reprod. of X by a Co-present, of which the Person never *had* been conscious at *any* time.

[a] I.e. the beginning of **28**, which is written at the foot of pp 282 and 283 and continues in the footmargins to p 285

together with its cognate perception . . . then it is that, as the vision from the eyes and the whiteness from the thing that joins in giving birth to the colour pass in the space between the eye becomes filled with vision and now sees, and becomes, not vision, but a seeing eye . . .": tr F. M. Cornford. Cf 184D on the mind "*with* which we perceive all the objects of perception *through* the senses as instruments".

29[1] I.e. C inquires whether the "matter" of which the hypothetical neurosphere is composed can be acted upon to the same effect by light, which travels in straight lines, and by sound, which travels in sinuous "wormlike" waves.

29[2] "The not-at-*that*-time-noticed Y".

30 p 285 | § 222

Ein jeder wird wohl schon die Erfahrung an sich gemacht haben, dass man Dinge wahrnehmen kann, ohne in dem Augenblicke des Wahrnehmens sich ihrer ganz deutlich bewusst zu seyn. . . . Eben so sind mehrere Erfahrungen vorhanden, dass im Zustande des Somnambulismus Erinnerungen von solchen in der Aussenwelt ehemals stattgehabten Vorgängen hervortreten,* die weder während ihres Geschehens, noch späterhin im Zustande des Wachens zum klaren Bewusstseyn gelangten
. . .

[Everyone has probably had the experience of perceiving things without being clearly conscious of them at the moment of perception. . . . Similarly there have been many experiences of memories emerging, in the state of somnambulism, of past events that occurred in the external world,* which reached clear consciousness neither during their occurrence nor afterwards in the state of wakefulness . . .]

* I often meet with a Sophism that is really *ingenious*—namely, an Objection to an asserted Law or Agent is quietly anticipated, and introduced as one of its Effects or Accidents—in order to use it afterwards as an answer to some other objection more glaring perhaps, but not more unanswerable. Ex. gr. "Among the numerous extra ordinary instances of the Omnipotence of Love ~~we~~ Naturalists have long observed with admiration the griefs and Crosses of Oysters."—Then afterwards—"As Oysters are softened into sorrow by disappointment in Love, why should we ~~not give likewise~~ refuse our belief to the Statue of Pygmalion?"[1]

31 p 288 | § 224

Die Somnambule nimmt die Nerventhätigkeit des Magnetiseurs auf; das Nervensystem des letzteren verlängert sich und findet sein peripherisches Ende im Körper der erstern. . . . Die Persönlichkeit der Somnambule wird aufgehoben und der des dominirenden Magnetiseurs untergeordnet. Der Wille des Magnetiseurs wirkt nun bestimmend auf die Somnambule (§. 160.), so wie auch die Gefühle desselben unwillkührlich der Somnambule überbracht werden (§. 139.).

[The somnambulist absorbs the nervous activity of the magnetiser; the nervous system of the latter is lengthened and finds its peripheral end in the body of the former. . . . The personality of the somnambulist is suppressed and subordinated to that of the magnetiser. The will of the magnetiser has a determining

---

30[1] The first part of C's illustration appears to be an allusion to the line in Sheridan's play *The Critic* III i "An oyster may be crossed in love." The second refers to Ovid's story of Pygmalion, the sculptor who fell in love with his own statue of a woman; Aphrodite turned the statue into a real woman, and Pygmalion married her.

effect on the somnambulist (§ 160), just as the feelings of the magnetiser are involuntarily transferred to the somnambulist (§ 139).]

In short, Dr K. begins by pretending to substitute a nervous atmo- or rather Somo-sphere for the Soul and ends by turning the nervous Sphere into a Soul.

32   p 291, pencil

Die von den Weibern . . . so eifrig in Schutz genommene Behauptung, dass bei der, in der Gebärmutter eingeschlossenen . . . Frucht, eine exaltirte Einbildungskraft der Mutter . . . Einfluss auf die Bildung der Frucht . . . haben könne, war von jeher immer ein Gegenstand des Streites unter den Aerzten. Auf der einen Seite glaubte man das Factum durch Erfahrungen hinreichend erwiesen zu haben, und auf der andern Seite zeigte man wieder die Nichtigkeit aller dieser Erfahrungen, weil das schärfste Auge noch keine Spur eines Nervens entdeckt hatte,* der von der Mutter zur Frucht übergegangen wäre und eine solche Seelenwirkung hätte möglich machen können.

[The belief . . . so vigorously defended by women, that the foetus in the womb . . . could be affected by the mother's overexcited power of imagination . . . has always been a subject of dispute among doctors. On the one hand the fact was thought to have been adequately demonstrated through experience, but on the other hand all these experiences have been proved inconsequential, since even the sharpest eye has discovered no trace of a nerve* joining the mother and foetus which might have made such an influence of the soul possible.]

* This is not the main argument against the belief; but the *limited* number of the sorts of mother-marks, whereas they ought to be as various as the occasions acting on, and the forms excited in, the imagination of the mother: at least, in some proportion.[1]

33   pp 298–9, pencil | § 227

Wie die Sonne nicht stärker scheint beim heitern Himmel, als beim bewölkten, und dennoch dort Licht und hier Dunkelheit herrscht, eben so verhält es sich auch mit der Seele; der Körper giebt <u>uns</u> ihre Strahlen bald möglich rein, bald hüllet er sie in Dunkel, oder bricht sie auch nach andern Gesetzen, und giebt <u>uns</u> statt eines reinen, ein vorworrenes Bild.* . . . Alle anderweitige Ausbildung des Geistes ist blos durch den Körper bedingt, und daher auch nur für diese Körperwelt und ihre Gesetze im Raume und in der Zeit berechnet, und muss dereinst in Nichts zerfallen, sobald diese irdischen Formen zerbrechen; doch jenes höhere

32¹ Cf C's scepticism about maternal impressions in JAHRBÜCHER **26** above.

Streben, über Raum und Zeit hinaus, sich dem ewig, einzig Wahren und Wahrhaften anzunähern . . . ist alleiniges Eigenthum des Geistes, woran der Körper keinen Antheil hat . . .

[Just as the sun shines no stronger in a clear than in a cloudy sky and yet light prevails there while here darkness rules, so it is with the soul: the body gives us its rays sometimes perfectly clearly, at other times obscures them in darkness or refracts them according to other laws and gives us a blurred image instead of a clear one.* . . . All further training of the spirit is conditioned merely by the body and therefore counts only for this corporeal world and its laws in space and time, and must some day disintegrate into nothingness as soon as these earthly forms fall to pieces; but that higher striving to approach, beyond space and time, that which is eternally and alone true and truthful . . . is the sole property of the spirit, in which the body has no part . . .]

* In reading the works of the later Germans, who all adopt more or less the phraseology of the Natur-philosophen, I am weary of asking—What then does *ich, wir, uns,* mean?[1] It is evidently used as a different Somewhat from the Soul: and then I ask, What is the Soul without this Ich, wir, uns?—What is ⟨the subject,⟩ or is there any *Subject,* of moral amenability? A shifting centre? A Focus as transferable as the Flash of a Looking-glass in a Boy's hand?—Wherein exists the Conscience? Not in the Soul: denn die Seele ist und bleibt stets dieselbe. Not in the I: denn das Ich ist nicht—*evenit, non est.* Aber *im Geiste?*[2] Pity that this Spirit, that is not the Soul, has not been more clearly explained—and how, being (as they affirm) the opposite *Pole* of the Body, it can exist separately so bald die irdischen Formen des Körpers zerbrechen?[3]

34 p 299

If any sense can be made out of Kluge's Notions, it must be on the supposition, that the I is a Reflection of the total Organismus, analogous to the Image collected in a cylindrical Glass[1]—If so, it must be called a Feeling, ein Gefühl, nicht aber eine Anschauung.[2]

33[1] *"I, we, us"*. For C's objection to this evasive mannerism in the writing of the *Naturphilosophen* see e.g. ESCHEN-MAYER **3**, HEINROTH **17** and **18** (where he uses the same figure of the mirror), and JAHRBÜCHER **11**.

33[2] Not in the Soul—"for the Soul is and always remains the same"; not in the I—"for the I does not exist—*it happens, it does not exist.* But *in the Spirit?*"

33[3] "As soon as the earthly forms of the body fall to pieces"—from textus (var). If the body and soul are opposites they must share the same essence and cannot exist separately, as C observes in e.g. HEINROTH **41**.

34[1] Of C's many references, literal and metaphorical, to mirrors and the phenomena of reflection, this may be the only one to a cylindrical mirror of the type that was popular both for experiments in optics and for distorting effects in the visual arts (esp in anamorphoses). It is not clear whether C's analogy includes the property of distortion.

34[2] "A feeling, but not an intuition".

35   p 300, pencil | § 228

Dass die Lebenskraft (das feinste Produkt der Organisation und sonach der Uebergang des Körperlichen zum Geistigen) diese Geistesberührung bewirkt, lässt sich vermuthen; dessen ungeachtet ist aber nicht einzusehen, wie dieses, wenn auch noch so ätherische, dennoch immer nur körperliche fluidum der Träger des Geistigen (des Gedankens) werden kann.

[It can be surmised that the vital energy (the finest product of the organism and thus the bridge from the corporeal to the spiritual) effects this contact with the soul; for all that, however, it is incomprehensible how this fluid, which be it never so ethereal is still always corporeal, can become the bearer of the spiritual (of thought).]

Just *as* easily ⟨as,⟩ and not a whit *more* easily than, its *sensation*. The μετάβασις εἰς ἕτερον γενος[1] is as gross in the one as in the other.— Material Objects are *words*: & such Questions seem to me equivalent to—How can we dine on the *word*, Venison? Or Jack Tar's contempt of the French for calling a Hat Chapeau? There is some sense in nicknaming a knife *Cut*eau; but d—n'd fools! to call a Hat *Shappo*![2] ⟨or the Spaniard's admiration of the Spanish Language—for calling Vino, Vino, and Pane Pane instead of Wine and Bread.⟩[a3]

36   p 301, pencil

. . . geht aber der fromme *Jung* noch weiter, und will er hierbei auch äussere, für unsere Sinne wirklich wahrnehmbare Erscheinungen aus der Geisterwelt geltend machen, so kehrt er nach meiner Ueberzeugung gerade hierdurch zum Materiellen wieder zurück, und seine Behauptung zerfällt, als dem Geistigen widersprechend, in sich selbst.

[. . . when however the excellent Jung goes still further and wishes thereby also to validate external phenomena from the spirit world as really perceptible through the senses, he thereby returns, in my opinion, precisely to the realm of matter, and his assertion collapses as contradictory to the spiritual.]

Why so? as the Νουμενα to the τα οντα, why not the Φαινομενα to the Νουμενα?[1] The question is—Is it so? ⟨*really:*⟩ not—*Can* it be so? i.e.

a Insertion in ink

35[1] The "transition to another kind", as in JUNG **31** and n 1.

35[2] A joke that C uses also in *CN* III 3542, 4237 (1809, 1814).

35[3] This comic illustration appears also in undated notes on the danger of equivocal terms: BM MS Egerton 2801 f 140.

36[1] "As the *Noumena* [are related] to the 'existence', why not the *Phenomena* to the *Noumena*?" For the Kantian distinction between noumenon and phenomenon see KANT *C d r V* **5** n 7, *Metaphysik der Sitten* **2** and n 3; also LACUNZA **19** and n 2.

logically. If I can conceive a Ghost communing with a Man, I can conceive the Ghost capable of assuming a form and a voice wherewith to commune. Let a man's fancy once get into the *Possibles* of Logic, and stop him who can.—He will in a twinkling, "at one bound high overleap all Bound", and "of Impossibility make slight work".—[2]

37   p 310, pencil | Epigraph

> Grau, Freund, ist alle Theorie,
> Doch grün des Lebens goldner Baum.
> *Göthe.*

[All theory, my friend, is grey,/ But green is life's golden tree.]

A golden Tree, that is green, must be a Tree made of Gold Leaf seen by transmitted Light, and *grau* for stets älternde,[1] or supperer-annuating (*verb neuter*) in a *half* abstract sense is not well put in antithesis to grün with Baum.[2]—Better perhaps Doch grün des Lebens Baum mit immer goldncm Früchte[3]

38   p 314 | § 233

Dass beim Magnetiseur in physischer Hinsicht ein *Uebergewicht an Energie*, in Beziehung auf den Kranken, die erste Bedingung ist, lässt sich aus den schon (§. 60–72.) angeführten Erfahrungen sehr leicht entnehmen.

[It can readily be deduced from the previously cited (§§ 60–72) experiences that in relation to the patient the magnetiser's primary physical prerequisite is a *preponderance of energy*.]

As far as I can learn, these assertions are by no means grounded on or generalized from Facts, but are the obvious consequences of Kluge's own Hypothesis—viz—that there is a magnetic fluid, the transfer of which from one body to another is the cause and agent of the magnetic phænomena; and 2—that this Fluid is the same with the Fluid of Life— or that there *is* a Lebensfluidum, & that this is the agent in Magnetism.[1]

36[2] Beginning perhaps from an echo of Swift's familiar "Digression Concerning Madness" in *A Tale of a Tub*—"But when a Man's Fancy gets *astride* on his Reason"—C passes from *Paradise Lost* IV 181 (var)—"At one slight bound high overleap'd all bound"—to *Coriolanus* V iii 60–2 (var)—"murd'ring impossibility, to make/ What cannot be, slight work".

37[1] " 'Grey' for 'constantly aging' ".

37[2] In antithesis to "green" with "Tree".

37[3] "But green is the tree of life with ever-golden fruit".

38[1] On *Lebensfluidum* see **19** above; see also *Lebenskraft* in **42** and **44** below.

39   p 422, pencil | § 336

Mir ist z.B. ein Fall bekannt, wo ein schon seit geraumer Zeit an einer Contractur des Kniegelenkes leidender Mann <u>dadurch</u> völlig geheilt wurde, dass er sein Knie während einiger Wochen täglich eine Stunde mit einem magnetisirten Baume durch Schnüre in Verbindung setzte.

[I know, for example, of a case in which a man who had been suffering for a considerable time from the contracture of his knee joint was completely cured <u>by</u> connecting his knee with cords to a magnetised tree for an hour daily over several weeks.]

Where is the proof of this *"dadurch"*?

40   p 423, pencil | § 337

Die Wirkung eines magnetisirten Baumes soll stärker und dabei doch angenehmer seyn, als die Batterie. Hellsehende Somnambuls* wollen einen solchen Baum schon in einer Entfernung von 30 Schritten durch einen eigenthümlichen Geruch erkannt . . . haben.

[The effect of a magnetised tree is said to be stronger and at the same time more agreeable than that of a battery. Clairvoyant somnambulists* claim to have recognised such a tree at a distance of thirty paces by its peculiar scent.]

* So only not everywhere throughout this work. "Clear-seeing (*clair-voyant*) *Somnambulists*"—how many?—and out of how many that were tried? in how many different places, or all at Strasbourg? Under what Magnetisers? Mesmerists, Spiritualists, or Psychosomatists?[1]—Altum silentium![2] Indefinite even to the want of an article!—

There are two cases possible, of which if the first be affirmed, the condemnation lights on Kluge, as a wretchedly injudicious Compiler; if the second, on magnetists and An. Mag. itself—1. The "Harmonics" established at Strasburg and elsewhere have made and published a series of pre-arranged Experiments[3]—Say for instance that 12 powerful Magnetisers take each a patient laboring under some one disease or of the same class of Diseases:—12 other in some other large Town another

40[1] Kluge outlines three different "schools" of animal magnetism pp 54–5; cf C's classification into three warring sects in *CL* IV 745 (27 Jun 1817): "Materialists" (Wolfart, Mesmer, "the French Magnetists"); "Spiritualists or Theosophists"; "Anti-theorists, or pure Experimentalists". The correspondence of two terms in the letter with two in the marginal note identifies the "Psychosomatists" of this note with the "Anti-theorists" of the letter.

40[2] "Deep silence!"

40[3] The "Harmonics" of Strasbourg formed one of the magnetic societies set up by Mesmer's followers under the direction of the Marquis de Puységur (1751–1825). Kluge discusses their aims and methods on pp 51–6, listing the publications of their cures in various journals in a bibliographical note on p 52.

Disease—& so on—& give the results?—2. No such plan has been adopted/ but mere hap-hazard Cases of apparent success!

41   pp 430–1, pencil | § 345

Vermöge dieses eigenthümlichen Wirkens wird der animalische Magnetismus bei denjenigen dynamischen Krankheiten anzuwenden seyn, welche entweder in einem absoluten Mangel, oder in einer abnormen Vertheilung der Lebenskraft (§ 195–198.) ihren Grund haben . . .

[By virtue of this peculiar effect, animal magnetism will be practicable in those dynamic diseases that are caused either by an absolute deficiency or by an abnormal distribution of vital energy (§§ 195–8) . . .]

But *what* diseases? How named? Medical men in general, and German Physicians in particular, are only too prodigal of Nosological Terms on all other occasions.—Must we not suspect, that this is an hypothetical Assertion? viz.—the preceding Theory being admitted, it follows that such and such cases are most adapted to the magnetic Cure?—So again §. 347, what can sound more promising to a large class of Sufferers?[1] But unfortunately ¾ths of the number are excluded by the last paragraph of §. 348.[2] So that cases of long continuance, and all in which the use of narcotics and stimulants has been either cause or consequence, being excepted, few remain that might not be better cured by a Tour, or Exercise, or the blue Pill.[3]

42   p 433, pencil | § 348

Wienholt überzeugte sich durch häufige Erfahrung, dass der animalische Magnetismus bei schon veralteten Nervenübeln und sehr eingewurzelten hysterischen Beschwerden nur in den allerwenigsten Fällen etwas leistete . . . es erfolgten entweder gar keine Reactionen, oder doch nur so schwache, dass sie die Krankheit nicht entscheiden . . . konnten. Am allermeisten war dies der Fall, wenn solche Personen schon mehrere Jahre hindurch an den Gebrauch reizender Arzneikörper gewöhnt waren.*

[Wienholt convinced himself through frequent experience that in cases of advanced nervous diseases and deep-rooted hysterical complaints, animal magnetism only rarely accomplished anything . . . there resulted either no reactions whatever or only such weak reactions that they could not be decisive for the

---

41[1] In § 347 (p 431) Kluge asserts that in diseases that cause nervous exhaustion and for which the most potent medicines prove worthless animal magnetism can effectively awaken new life.

41[2] See the last sentence of **42** textus below.

41[3] A mercurial antibilious pill much in vogue in the early nineteenth century; here, apparently, a placebo.

disease. . . . This was most frequently the case when such persons had already been accustomed to the use of stimulants for many years.*]

* Could the most zealous Anti-materialist wish a more decisive confutation of all the jargon of Lebens-kraft,[1] and its transmission—Whatever it be, that is transmitted (if indeed there be any thing) it can only be a stimulus, not the vis vitæ, or subjectum stimulabile.[2]

43 pp 439–40, slightly cropped | § 355

Nach so vielen, sprechenden Thatsachen kann man wohl den animalischen Magnetismus mit allem Rechte als das erste unserer Heilmittel betrachten, da wir ausser ihm noch keines besitzen, was so mit Leben uns erfüllte, und in so inniger Verbindung stände mit dem Geistigen in uns.

[Surely after so many telling facts animal magnetism can be rightly regarded as our foremost remedy, since besides it we possess none that so fills us with life and is so intimately connected with our spirituality.]

I must confess a deep disappointment. Eith[er] Kluge has betrayed his cause in this last section, or the cause is as ludicrously opposed to these words "das erste &c",[1] as the pretended Confidence of our advocate in his concluding senten[ce] to the Jury when he has few or no witnesses in his Behalf.—I expected a list of Diseases, with documents of Cures & the Particulars—instead of which—nervous Folks are nervous & affected, & violent pains that most [. . .] of themselves go away while the Magnetiser is manipulating!—It is in truth a most lame and impotent Conclusion.

44 pp [443–4] (Index part-title and part-title verso), pencil

All the influences, which have come to our knowlege as material, ~~from~~ ponderable or imponderable, are mere excitants, the magnetic in this respect differing not at all from the commonest Drugs: of which see a decisive proof, p. 433, l. 4.[1]—Absurdly therefore is it named vital power, or Lebens-kraft, or even nerven-belebende Princip.[2]—For this must needs be the correlative—i.e. excitability.[3] But how can this be

42[1] "Life-force". C translates it as "vital power" in **44** below.

42[2] "Life-force, or the subject susceptible to stimulation".

43[1] From textus—"foremost" in tr.

44[1] **42** textus above.

44[2] "Nerve-energising principle": **9** textus.

44[3] This is a key term in the medical system of John Brown, or "Brunonian" medicine, in which C was especially interested in 1799: *CN* I 388, 389; also *CN* III 3827. Kluge (p 211) refers to Brown as a precursor of the school of animal magnetism.

conceived in an immaterial somewhat, the essence of which must be activity? The grand Eureka, that might well deserve an hundred Hecatombs, would be the resolution of excitability into Perception; but this seems impossible without again resolving Perception into *Sensation*— which would be an explanation in circulo.[4]—The least objectionable Thesis would be that Life consists in the Indifference or rather the Prothesis of Sensation and Perception,[5] whose sole Object is its own relations—yet still Pain would be as much an ens irrationale, semper presuppondum[6] as in any other Theory./ It would be more to the Purpose to begin with PAIN, under the form of Hunger, Yearning, or the Fire that is to be quenched—and thus we should go back to Samothrace, and its Axieros, Axiokersa, and Axiokersos.[7]

45   p [504] (last printed page), pencil

From the facts as given in this book, it may (I think) be deduced, as highly *probable* at least that in certain states of mind, [? uniting/namely] those of the will and attention concentered to one Object, the human Body transpires a virus[1] in its *form* more analogous to the Galvanic Effluence than to any other datum of our present experience;[2] but in its medical effects most nearly resembling those of Opium but without its constipative powers, besides the differences produced by its very different *form*—Something between Opium and the Nitrous Oxyde,[3] participating of both, and differenced from both by its Locability (in which it resembles Electricity) would explain all the facts that have [been][a] fairly ascertained.   S. T. C.—

44[4] "Circular" explanation.

44[5] I.e. using the logical pentad (as in IRVING *Sermons* 2 at n 1), life may be considered as the original unity out of which sensation and perception are generated as opposites.

44[6] "An irrational thing, always presupposed".

44[7] In SCHELLING *Ueber die Gottheiten von Samothrace* (1815) pp 16–17, 60–3, C encountered the theory that the names of these gods of the Samothracian mysteries denoted "hunger" or "yearning": BÖHME **140** n 4.

45[1] I.e. gives off an influence? C does not appear to use "virus" in its normal sense of poison or offensive substance.

45[2] In § 179 (p 212) Kluge admits that he is uncertain about the identity of the magnetic fluid: some have attributed it to a chemical process in the animal body, others to a principle similar to the world soul of the ancients and comparable to light or to the magnetic, electrical, and galvanic fluids.

45[3] C's own experience with nitrous oxide is mentioned in **6** above.

RICHARD PAYNE KNIGHT
1751–1824

An Analytical Inquiry into the Principles of Taste. 3rd ed. London 1806. 8°.

Henry E. Huntington Library

Inscribed "STC" on the title-page, not in C's hand; and also on the title-page "Sara Coleridge Feby 1849. From Hartley." On p ⁻3 (p-d) there is a pencilled account of C's annotations, in an unknown hand: "This book belonged to S. T. Coleridge—Poet—& contains many notes in his own writing also his Initials in own Handwriting on Title page and also name in own Handwriting of *Sara Coleridge* from 'Hartley'—(her brother)". Another pencilled note on p ⁺4 (p-d) also refers to the volume as "Coleridge's copy". A typescript copy of a librarian's letter, inserted loose in the volume, accurately identifies the different hands in it.

Besides C's two notes, a series of some forty other notes, mostly in pencil, are in WW's hand: for the ingenious suggestion that these were written by WW at C's dictation in Mar or Apr 1808, see E. A. Shearer and J. I. Lindsay in *HLQ* I (1937) 63–99, esp 64–7, 95–9. Since sustained marginal annotation by WW is rare, and since the matter under discussion is germane to C's reflections upon poetic taste and imagination, the notes in WW's hand are printed in the ANNEX.

DATE. Between Jan and Apr 1808. C quoted from this work in the first lecture of the series given at the Royal Institution, on 15 Jan 1808: *Lects 1808–1819* (*CC*) I 31–4. If this copy is the one originally given to the Wordsworths by the Beaumonts, which DW had just begun to read 9 Jul 1806 (*WL—M 2*—II 54), C's notes in it may have been made during his stay with the Wordsworths at Coleorton from late Dec 1806 to Apr 1807; if, as seems more likely, this copy was C's own, both his and WW's notes may have been made during WW's visit to London, Feb–Apr 1808, but C must have read it—or read in it—before 15 Jan. *W Library* includes only one copy, listed as C's.

1   p 176 | Pt 2 ch 2 § 48, marked with a line in the margin

The Gothic architects varied the proportions of their columns from four, to one hundred and twenty diametres, and contrasted the ornaments and the parts with equal licence; and though a column so slender, employed to support a vaulted roof of stone, may offend the eye of a person, who suspects it to be inadequate to its purpose, and therefore associates ideas of weakness and danger with it; yet to those who know it to be sufficient, it will appear extremely light and beautiful; as is proved by the columns

400

of the cathedral of Salisbury, which are of this proportion, and which have been universally admired for many centuries.

I have opened the Book on this Page: and this single Period contains an absolute Demonstration that Mr Knight is just ⟨as⟩ ignorant *in head* of Taste, and its Principles, as the Author of Priapus &c must needs have been ignorant *in heart* of Virtue & virtuous feelings.[1]

S. T. Coleridge.

2   p 470 | Pt 3 ch 3 § 38

In the lower orders of society, where there are no such objects of habitual attachment ["objects of property or possession"], but where

> The modest wants of every day
> The toil of every day supplies—

the parental affections generally die away, as in the brute creation, with the necessities for their exertion, and the habits of continued intercourse, which those necessities produced.

God Almighty! what blasphemy against human nature! and what a LIE!

Annex: Wordsworth's Marginalia

W1   pp 93–5, pencil | Pt 1 ch 5 § 31

There are other privations, however, which it is surprising that he [Virgil] has omitted; since they make themselves most sensibly, and in some instances, most painfully felt throughout all the animal creation; and when personified as powers, and described in poetry, are as truly sublime, as any of the other powers, which he mistook for sensations.

> Close by the regal chair,
> Fell Thirst and Famine scowl
> A baleful smile upon their baffled guest.

There is scarcely a page in this book without a gross error. Thirst *personified* as a power may be tolerated but when thirst is made to scowl a smile, every well disciplined Imagination revolts at the Picture. Thirst considered nakedly as animal sensation has nothing sublime in it nor has Hunger or the sexual appetite, or any other of our animal appetites. But to understand this subject we must ask ourselves, what Powers may the mind receive from the strong domination of one of these ⟨appetites⟩, thirst for instance. Suppose a becalmed Mariner, or rather take the instance of tired traveller, in a parched country, upon a sultry day. Let

---

[1] Knight's first publication had been *An Account of the Remains of the Worship of Priapus Lately Existing in Isernia; to Which Is Added a Discourse on the Worship of Priapus, and Its Connexion with the Mystic Theology of the Ancients* (1786).

him hear unexpectedly a sound which he imagines to be that of trickling water, while a raging thirst is upon him, then ask what will be the effect of that sound upon his mind while he is yet uncertain whether it gives an assurance of water being within his reach, and after his doubts have passed away. The depth of interest with which he hears this sound which under the circumstances would either ~~of been~~ have been missed or slightly regarded, is a sublime state of mind. And therefore the sensation of thirst is an efficient cause in the production of the sublime as it calls forth the modifying power of the Imagination. There is an under consciousness of the sensation of thirst while the mind is affected by a power in the sound never felt but in similar circumstances.

W2   p 122, pencil | Pt 2 ch 1 § 29

> These softer moments, let delight employ,
> And <u>kind embraces snatch</u> the <u>hasty</u> joy.
> Not thus I loved thee, when, from Sparta's shore,
> My <u>forced</u>, my <u>willing</u>, <u>heavenly</u> prize, I bore;
> When first entranced in Cranae's isle I lay,
> Mix'd with thy soul, and all <u>dissolved</u> away!
> POPE'S ILIAD, iii. 549.

What detestable stuff! Kind emb—/

W3   pp 123–4, pencil | **W2** textus continued, referring to *Paradise Lost* IX 1026–32 and Pope's *Iliad* III 549–54

Adam's argument, in this case, is certainly more pointed and logical, than that of the young Trojan; but pointed and logical argument is not what the case required. The rapturous glow of enthusiastic passion, with which the latter addresses his mistress, would have much more influence upon the affections of an amorous lady, though it may be less satisfactory to the understanding of a learned critic.

What a Booby; Milton is describing sinful appetite the evidence & seal of the highest guilt: what had this to do with the rapturous glow of enthusiastic passion! his versification is perturbed like the feelings of our degraded parent. Contrast the movement of the verse ~~with~~ here with those passages when it is really his aim to describe rapturous admiration & so forth—Sweet is the breath of morn &c[1] ~~of plural joy~~—Or when he describes to Raphael his nuptials with Eve, though there is more perturbation than to the Angel appeared consistent with his dignity as a sinless creature and accordingly he warns Adam against it.[2]

W4   pp 125–6, pencil | § 32

"Let us figure to ourselves," says Dr. Blair, "a savage, who beholds some object, such as fruit, which raises his desire, and who requests another to give it to him . . ."

What means all this parade about the Savage, when the deduction as far as just ~~made~~ may be made at our own fire sides, from the sounds words gesticulations

W3[1] *Paradise Lost* IV 641 ff.   **W3**[2] *Paradise Lost* VIII 510–643.

looks &c which a child makes use of when learning to talk. But a Scotch Professor cannot write three minutes together upon the Nature of Man, but he must be dabbling with his savage state with his agricultural state, his Hunter state &c &c.

W5   p 129, pencil | § 33

. . . but a variety of flexible terminations is absolutely necessary to make words, so arranged, intelligible; and, in these, all the polished languages of modern Europe are defective: wherefore it is impossible that they should ever rival those of the Greeks and Romans in poetical diction and expression.

it is so far from being impossible that the writings of Shakespear and Milton infinitely transcend those of the Greeks and for reasons which might easily be given

W6   p 130, pencil

. . . but Milton, and other epic and moral writers in blank verse, who viewed nature through the medium of books, and wrote from the head rather than the heart, have often employed this inverted order merely to stiffen their diction, and keep it out of prose . . .

Milton wrote ⟨chiefly⟩ from the Imagination which you may place where you like in head heart liver or [? reins/veins]. *Him* the Almighty Power hurled headlong &c—see one of the most wonderful sentences ever formed by the mind of man.[1] The instances of imaginative and impassioned inversion in Milton are innumerable. Take for instance the first sentence of his Poem. Of Mans first Disobedience &c[2]

W7   p 197, pencil | Ch 2 § 74

Novelty will, indeed, make mountainous scenery peculiarly pleasing to the inhabitant of a plain . . .

that is a shallow remark

W8   p 199, pencil | § 75

But, nevertheless, the <u>Creator</u> having formed the one [animals] regular, and the other [trees] irregular, we habitually associate ideas of regularity to the perfection of the one, and ideas of irregularity to the perfection of the other . . .

Here Mr Knight forgets the Horatian precept, nec Deus intersit &c.[1]

W9   p 248 | § 124, quoting Blair, who quotes Pope's *Eloisa*

["]. . . Hide it, my heart, within that close disguise,
Where, mix'd with God's, his loved idea lies:

W6[1] *Paradise Lost* I 44–6.
W6[2] *Paradise Lost* I 1–16.
W8[1] Horace *Ars poetica* 191–2: "Neither should a god intervene, unless a knot befalls worthy of his interference."

> O write it not, my hand—the name appears
> Already written—wash it out my tears.

. . . when from her heart she passes to her hand, and tells her hand not to write his name, this is forced and unnatural; a personified hand is low, and not in the style of true passion; and the figure becomes still worse when, in the last place, she exhorts her tears to wash out what her hand had written . . .''

This is no doubt a villainous Couplet, though not for the reason assigned by the stupid Scotch Doctor. 1000 instances might be adduced in which the Hand is apostrophized with dignity and genuine passion. The meanness of the passage lies in this that the ⟨several⟩ apostrophes ~~are~~ arise not from the impulse of passion; ⟨they are not⟩ abrupt, interrupted and revolutionary but formal, and mechanically accumulated.—The versification also is wretched in the Extreme, the pauses being exactly in the middle of the lines, utterly unsuited to the perturbed state of feeling intended to be express'd, and producing a see saw or balance of sound which could not have existed if the Author had written from genuine ~~feeling~~ passion, but which well accords with the ~~adulterate~~ spurious stuff here substituted for it.

W10   pp 319–20 | Pt 3 ch 1 § 3

The great author, indeed, already so often cited, asserts that *the nearer tragedy approaches the reality, and the further it removes us from all idea of fiction, the more perfect is its power*; and he has illustrated this position by an example stated with his usual brilliancy and eloquence. "Choose," says he, "a day to represent the most sublime and affecting tragedy we have; appoint the most favourite actors; spare no cost upon the scenes and decoration; unite the greatest efforts of poetry, painting, and music; and when you have collected your audience, just at the moment, when their minds are erect with expectation, let it be reported that a criminal of high rank is on the point of being executed in an adjoining square, in a moment the emptiness of the theatre would demonstrate the comparative weakness of the imitative arts, and proclaim the triumph of real sympathy."

This is wretched trifling on the part of Burke whose book on the sublime is little better than a tissue of trifles.[1] The instance ~~used~~ adduced to illustrate this position has no tendency so to do. Supposing that it were possible to represent a Tragedy in such a manner that the delusion during the representation would be perfect, then suppose when it is proposed to repeat this tragedy that at the same time an event resembling it in its main outline, or at least the catastrophe of such an event is to be exhibited in the ⟨public⟩ execution of some King, princess or other eminent person. We ~~have~~ are then to ask to which spectacle the people would repair~~; but~~. But there is in the essentials of the case no similitude; for whatever may be our sensations when the attention is recalled to a scenic representation how farsoever we may then lose sight of its being a mimic show, we know perfectly at the time, when[a] we are going to see it, or when assembled at

---

[a] MS reads "when when", ending one page and beginning the next with the same word

W10[1] Edmund Burke *A Philosophical*   (1756).
Inquiry into the Sublime and the Beautiful

the Theatre in expectation; that it is nothing better or worse. It is possible, that the mind during the representation of a tragedy may have fits of forgetfulness ~~that it~~ & deception and believe the fiction to be the reality, but the moment you suppose it in a condition to make a choice of this kind, all sense of delusion vanishes. Therefore however perfect according to Burkes notion of perfection a tragedy may be unless you suppose the delusion indestructible the cases can admit of no comparison, nor if you do can they admit of any ~~for there are~~ thing identical, both becoming realities. But these absurdities are too gross for notice.

W11   pp 331–4, corrections and postscript in pencil | §§ 14–15

It is observed, by the great father of philosophical criticism, that the radical difference between tragedy and comedy is that the one exhibits the characters of men superior, and the other, inferior to those of ordinary nature; that is, tragedy displays the energies, and comedy, the weaknesses of humanity: for, in tragedy, it is not the actual distress; but the motives, for which it is endured; . . . [which] awaken all the exquisite and delightful thrills of sympathy. . . . but . . . as [comedy] is purely selfish, it awakens no sympathy; nor is it ever employed except to excite ridicule or aversion. . . . 15. * All the distress of dramatic fiction is known and felt, at the time of its exhibition, to be merely fiction: but the sentiments, excited by it, are really expressed; and expressed, too, with all the truth and energy, which real feelings could inspire; accompanied with all the graces of emphasis, tone, and gesture; which can convey those feelings to the soul of the spectator, with the full force, and vivid freshness of real nature.

This is rashly asserted. The most extravagant Arabian Tale that ever was formed, if it be consistent with itself and does not violate our moral feeling, subdues the mind to a passing belief that the events related really happened. In reading Hamlet or Lear ⟨also⟩,[a] though we are frequently sensible that the story is fictitious, yet in other moments we do not ⟨less⟩ doubt ~~less~~ of the things having taken place than when we read ⟨in History⟩ about Pompey or Julius Cæsar, we question the truth of the general story. Yet in Lear and Hamlet we have the ~~almost~~ unrealizing accompaniment of Metre. Nevertheless we believe: Our situation at a Theatre is undoubtedly very different, and the question before me now is to determine whether (as there can be no doubt that ⟨we⟩ have ⟨various degrees of⟩ continuous belief in the truth of fictitious stories in verse) ~~can~~ whether by the helps which representation supplies the delusion ⟨can⟩ be carried still further, and we may we be[b] made to believe even for a moment that the scene before us is not the representation of a transaction, but the transaction itself, is not a shadow or reflexion but a substance. In our attempt to answer this question let us first ~~ans~~ ask if there be any thing in the representation of a play that will tend to strengthen or prolong the first species of delusion which undoubtedly exists ⟨in reading it⟩, viz that of the facts represented or feigned having actually occurred. I believe the answer will be no; the Playhouse, the Audience, ~~the persons of the Actors,~~ the lights, the scenes all ~~tend~~ interfere with that ~~delusion~~ception and above all the ⟨persons⟩ gestures, and voices of the Actors which so immediately tell us that it is M^r or Mrs Such a One. ~~and~~ These matters

---

[a] Insertion in pencil   [b] Presumably a slip for "we may be"

of fact, ~~are~~ while consciously before us, are insuperable bars to the Imagination. ⟨Here then is a mighty loss; &⟩ If ~~then~~ during the progress of the Piece another species of delusion were not ⟨in its stead⟩ occasionally superinduced ⟨and by the very reason which⟩ had destroyed the ~~first~~ former, viz that the scene before us*[a]* a *reality* I do not see how it is possible that we should be *affected* to the degree ~~that~~ to which a fine tragedy exquisitely represented often does affect us. Whence is it that after the first inexperience of Childhood and youth has ceased we are so languidly moved by ⟨the representation of⟩ imaginative Tragedies, such as Lear, Macbeth & Hamlet, and the most languidly by those parts which are most imaginative, whence but because it is utterly impossible here to approximate to either species of delusion: there is such a disproportion ~~between the means and the end~~*[b]* the Powers of Nature, Storms &c, and the means employed to represent them ⟨and in like manner, with respect to the supernatural agencies.⟩ But ~~by~~ in the looks the gestures, and tones of a genuine actor, aided by the knowledge of Nature displayed ⟨in the words⟩ by the Poet, there is no such disproportion or unfitness; and the representation I confess appears to me not only to approach to reality but often for a short while to be wholly merged or lost in it. The scenery and machinery with which our ~~modern~~ modern theatres are decorated may heighten the delusion for simple minds, but they produce a contrary effect in those that are cultivated and so far are injurious to their pleasure. Stage Suns & Moons and stage thunder and lightning, are ludicrous to the refined Spectator; nor does he ⟨even⟩ look with much pleasure on the groves of Arden in As You Like it; yet still if Jacques and Orlando be exquisitely represented, the imperfect consciousness which the Spectator may have of the presence of these scenic helps as they are intended to be, may not ~~re~~ materially impair, nay perhaps may in some instance assist the delusion which the skill of the Actors is I think enabled to produce. The fact, I think is, that we *know* the thing to be a ~~dee~~ representation, but that we often *feel* it to be a reality. Though to this is to*[c]* referred but a small portion of the pleasure which fine acting gives.

I have said above that the Machine the Scenes the Actors &c [? ~~nem~~] destroy that sort of delusion with which the mind is overcome in reading a good fictitious narration, and this being taken away, on the opening of the piece by such obtrusive images, is it ever likely to be restored by the same agency. ~~I do not see how it is possible~~ To lose the man in the impersonation ~~seems~~*[d]* is indispensable to the highest pleasure ~~given~~ given by acting & it seems.*[e]* ~~And if we forget the Actor &c~~ it seems much more easy to pass into a delusion that the things ~~they are~~ represented are actually performed, than that such forgetfulness of the Actors ~~profession names~~ persons & names &c should take place and ~~terminate merely in~~*[f]* have no other effect than to impression a belief that they are ~~enjoyed in a whole as the representation is of some thing that actually occurred.~~*[g]* the whole is

---

[a] "us" in pencil

[b] WW appears first of all to have intended to insert the following phrase after "between", then to have made the cancellation; "between" should not have been cancelled

[c] For "to be"?

[d] Cancelled in pencil

[e] The note here runs down the right margin; WW indicates in the left margin the words by which it is to be connected with the text

[f] The foregoing cancelled and replaced by "have no . . . impress" in pencil

[g] The foregoing cancelled and replaced by "the whole . . . Story." in pencil. For sense, "they are" should have been included in the cancelled passage

merely a mode of telling a true Story. ⟨B̶u̶t̶ The senses have too strong impressions made on them for the imagination to have liberty to c̶r̶e̶a̶t̶e̶ rest in[a] that species of faith.⟩ I̶t̶ An acted play approaches too nearly to the reality to affect us i̶n̶ in that manner, t̶h̶a̶t̶ ̶i̶s̶ ̶a̶s̶ ̶a̶ ̶m̶o̶d̶e̶ ̶m̶o̶d̶e̶ ̶o̶f̶ ̶t̶e̶l̶l̶i̶n̶g̶ ̶a̶ ̶s̶t̶o̶r̶y̶,̶[b] and therefore I think no other supposition will account for the degree to which we are affected, saving that of short fits of belief that the scene before us is a [? r̶e̶l̶i̶a̶b̶l̶e̶] real affliction, or action.

[c]The above is happily illegible, as it is very confused; but it would be easy to give it development.[d]

W12   p 341, pencil | § 25

. . . the Achilles of Homer is the image of a perfect man, such as came from the hands of the Creator, with every faculty of mind and body formed upon the same scale . . .

monstrous!

W13   p 342, pencil | § 26

No character can be interesting or impressive in poetry, that acts strictly according to reason: for reason excites no sympathies, nor awakens any affections; and its effect is always rather to chill than to inflame.

this is grossly false

W14   p 348, pencil | § 30

We all know, from the first drawing up of the curtain, that Othello is to kill his amiable and innocent wife, and afterwards to kill himself: but we know likewise that Othello is an actor, and Desdemona an actress . . .

We *know* it no doubt but do ⟨we⟩ in every part of the piece, *feel* it. If we do what is the meaning of those phrases with which we consummate our praise of a good actor; that he was *lost* in the character; he appeared and *became* the very man?

W15   p 349, pencil | § 31

. . . for the pity, which we feel in contemplating the wants or miseries of a mendicant, or a maniac, how much soever it may affect us, does not, I believe, ever engender love of any kind, either towards its object, or any other.

monstrous assertion!

W16   p 354, pencil | § 38

Whatever tends to exalt the soul to enthusiasm, tends to melt it at the same time; whence tears are the ultimate effect of all very sublime impressions on the mind . . .

What nonsense this is, even on the writers own principles. Of the actions of his

---

[a] "Create" cancelled and replaced by "rest in" in pencil   [b] Cancellation in pencil
[c-d] Insertion in pencil

great exemplar Achilles, or of the sentiments of that hero, which Knight would ~~even here~~ pronounce most indicative of Enthusiasm is there one in a 100 that has any thing to do with tears?

W17   p 358, pencil | § 41

Fiction is known to be fiction, even while it interests us most; and it is the dignified elevation of the sentiments of the actors or sufferers, that separates the interesting, or the pathetic, from the disgusting, or the ridiculous.

this is false it is not *felt* to be fiction when we are most affected

W18   p 362, pencil | § 44

Throughout the poem [*Paradise Lost*], the infernal excite more interest than the celestial personages, because their passions and affections are more violent and energetic.

See page 342 from which it appears that characters acting according to reason as the Blessed Spirits must do can excite *no* interest.[1]

W19   p 363, pencil | § 46

Every energetic exertion of great and commanding power; whether of body or mind; whether physical or moral; or whether it be employed to preserve or destroy, will necessarily excite corresponding <u>sympathies</u>; and, of course, appear sublime . . .

of dread no doubt as well of participation, and the ignorance of this truth is the cause that Mr Knight attempting to ~~soar~~ make his way through the heights & depths of the sublime, ~~presents in a ludicr~~ is just as able to accomplish his purpose as a Bird would be to fly with one [? ~~with~~] wing & no more

W20   p 364, pencil

* Fear is the most humiliating and depressing of passions; and, when a person is under its influence, it is as unnatural for him to join in any sentiments of exultation with that which inspires it, as it would be for a man to share in the triumph or the feast of the lion, of which he was himself the victim and the prey.

this is again utterly false, he talks of fear in the abstract instead of contemplation in the concrete, that is involved in images, and coexisting with other modes of sensation.

W21   p 366, pencil | § 48

Even in dramatic exhibitions, we find that splendid dress, rich scenery, and pompous ceremony are absolutely necessary to support the dignity of tragedy . . .

Was this the case in Shakespears time, to an intellectual mind such a substitute as he got who asked for *bread* and received a *stone*.[1]

W18[1] I.e. **W13** textus.   **W21**[1] Matt 7.9.

W22   p 367, pencil | § 49

Darkness, vacuity, silence, and all other absolute privations of the same kind, may also be sublime by partaking of infinity; which is equally a privation or negative existence: for infinity is that which is without bounds, as darkness is that which is without light, vacuity that which is without substance, and silence that which is without sound. In contemplating each, the mind expands itself in the same manner; and, in expanding itself, will of course conceive grand and sublime ideas, if the imagination be in any degree susceptible of grandeur or sublimity.

Where then is the rapture &c the only allowed test of the sublime[1] caused by contemplation of darkness, vacuity & silence &c

W23   p 367, pencil | § 50

All the great and terrible convulsions of nature . . . impress sublime sentiments by the prodigious exertions of energy and power, which they seem to display: for, though these objects are, in their nature terrible . . . , it is not this attribute of terror that contributes, in the smallest degree, to render them sublime.

—What nonsense?

W24   pp 367–8, pencil | § 51

As far as feeling or sentiment is concerned, and it is of feeling or sentiment only that we are speaking, *that* alone is terrible, which impresses some degree of fear.

Here Mr. K— comes on his readers in full strength. Let us put this distinction between knowing & feeling which he forgot in the case of scenic represenation, to the test in this case. He has done it for use himself at the end of the sentence where he says, he cannot feel the sentiment which danger inspires till he either is or *imagines* himself to be within it. He therefore admits that the knowledge of danger being producible by an Object may in imagination pass into the *feelings*, or in other words actually impress him with fear.

W25   p 368, pencil | § 52

There is no image in poetry wrought up with more true sublimity and grandeur than the following of Virgil [*Georgics* I 328–31]; but that it should be quoted as an instance of terror being the cause of the sublime is to me most unaccountable.

Here again is a gross mistake, though we do not feel the same degree or perhaps kind of fear when we are reading of a thunder storm as when we are in the midst of one, does it follow therefore that we have no sense of fear at all. How are we enabled to sympathize with power producing change with pain sorrow ruin extinction of life &c but by some degree of fear; whaty are these images selected else?

W22[1] Knight's criterion p 336: "those enthusiastic raptures, which Longinus justly states to be the true feelings of sublimity".

W26   p 370, pencil | § 55

[Of travellers in a storm at sea] . . . the moment when they feel the actual pressure of fear, all sympathy with the cause that produces it, and, consequently, all relish for the sublimity of it, is at an end.

What an extravagant assertion

W27   p 371, pencil | § 56

Even in the inanimate objects of nature, if a general character of barrenness pervade the whole, even the grandest scenery . . . no sooner is the first impression of surprise passed, than we begin to find more matter of disgust than delight in the prospect.

this proves Mr Knight to be without Imagination, and therefore to what purpose does he write

W28   p 377, pencil | § 61

Fear, therefore, which is humiliating and depressive in one degree, must be proportionally so in another; and consequently, in every degree, the opposite of sublime.

as wisely might he say that the heat ~~heat~~ which if my hand were thrust into the fire would inevitably cause most acute pain would do the same if I held it at a reasonable distance. A certain quantity of laudanum would poison me, a less degree cure me of pain.

W29   p 387, pencil | § 74

. . . wild beasts and birds of prey are more frequently and more generally employed as the materials of sublime imagery in poetry, than any of the domesticated kinds: but still their sublimity of character arises entirely from their being energetic, and not at all from their being destructive . . .

if their sublimity arise *entirely* from their being destructive what nonsense to say what follows—[1]

W30   p 388, pencil | § 76

No person, I believe, ever felt any sublime emotions on viewing a swarm of bees wrangling in the air; but Virgil's description of it, though strictly true, is sublime in the extreme . . .

This is too childish for comment

W31   p 392, pencil | § 82

Virgil's description of the materials employed by the Cyclops in forming the thunder-bolts of Jupiter . . . all men feel to be extremely sublime; at the same time that they are obliged to own that no chimera of a madman ever presented a

W29[1] Textus continues ". . . for, where equal energy can be displayed in the exertion of beneficent qualities, it will be more sublime because more interesting . . .".

more incoherent picture than *three rays of twisted showers, three of watery clouds, three of red fire, and three of winged south winds; with terrific lightnings, sound, fear, anger, and pursuing flames mixed up in the work.*

I for one feel it to be extremely ludicrous W W

W32   p 393, pencil | **W31** textus continued

But the poet [Virgil] never meant to produce a picture; but merely to express, in the enthusiastic language of poetry, which gives corporeal form and local existence to every thing, those energetic powers, which operate in this dreadful engine of divine wrath.

how *dreadful* & to whom

W33   p 394, pencil | § 83

For if a certain degree of want of light and clearness produce a comparative degree of sublimity, it necessarily follows that a total want of them would produce the superlative degree of it . . .

did you learn this logic from Aristotle, Mr Knight.

W34   pp 400–1, pencil | § 87

Our blank verse, though used as an heroic metre, and appropriated to the most elevated subjects, is, like the Greek iambic, too near to the tone of common colloquial speech to accord well with *such flights* . . .

What nonsense does this Prater pour out. Let him read the ~~chara~~ sixth Book of Paradise lost and he will find that almost every line gives the lie to this libel— But it is little less than blasphemy in me to think of comparing this trash of Virgil, with the chariot of the Messiah, or his advance toward the rebel Angels; or with the first shock of the [? ~~encountering~~] encountering armies

W35   p 401, pencil | § 88

. . . but in no good writer, is there any confusion or indistinctness of imagery . . .

Whoever dreamt that there was, when he is good?

W36   p 401, pencil

. . . Gray's admirable imitations of the Greek lyric style:

> She wolf of France, with unrelenting fangs,
> That tear'st the bowels of thy mangled mate,
> From thee be born, who o'er thy country hangs,
> The scourge of Heaven. What terrors round him wait!
> Amazement in his van, with flight combin'd,
> And Sorrow's faded form, and Solitude behind.

very sublime indeed, amet tua Carmina Meavi!¹

W36¹ WW quotes a mocking line from   Virgil *Eclogues* 3.90 (misspelling the

W37   p 402 | § 88

> Close by her regal chair
> Fell <u>Thirst</u> and Famine scowl
> A baleful smile upon their baffled guest, &c.

What sort of a figure would Mr Knight make of Thirst.

W38   p 402 | § 89

The imagery of Milton . . . is often confused and obscure; and so far it is faulty: but, nevertheless, I can find neither confusion nor obscurity in the passage, which has been so confidently quoted as an instance of both.

> He above the rest,
> In shape and gesture proudly eminent,
> Stood like a tower: his form had yet not lost
> All <u>its</u> original brightness, nor appear'd
> Less than Archangel ruin'd, and th' excess
> Of glory obscured . . .

You Rogue *her*[1]—this little blunder lets out the whole secret, if any there has been; viz that Knight ~~has no~~ is incapable of the slightest relish of the appropriate grandeur of Miltons Poetry.

W39   pp 404–5, pencil | § 90

The imagery in the description of the allegorical personage of death by the same great author [Milton *Paradise Lost* II 666–73] must, however, be admitted to be indistinct, confused, and obscure; and, by being so, loses much of its sublimity . . .

~~The ideas interdict~~ This author confounds ~~indistinctness~~ indeterminateness, with dimness or inadequacy of ~~percept~~ communication. He perceives in the Fell Thirst of Grey an instance of this latter; but here in Milton is no inadequacy or dimness but the utmost liveliness in conveying the Idea which was that of a shape so perpetually changing upon the eye of the Spectator ~~that~~ and so little according ⟨in any of its appearances⟩ with Forms to which we are accustomed that the poet cannot without hesitation apply the ⟨familiar⟩ word shape ~~factual as it is~~ to it at all—in like manner with substance The Phantom had a *likeness* to a head & to a kingly crown but a likeness only—all which beautifully accords with [? ~~what death~~] our notions concerning death

W40   p 404, pencil

Ten furies may have collectively more strength than one; because the mechanic strength of many individuals may be concentered into one act or exertion; but this is not the case with fierceness.

that is false because the fierceness of one may animate that of another.

---

proper name): "Let him . . . love your songs, Maevius".

W38[1] The line should read "All her original brightness . . . .".

W41   p 406, pencil | § 92

. . . neither the evidence of sense, nor the deductions of analogy can set any boundaries to physical probability: whence he [Homer] . . . does not say that the Aloidae actually did pile mountains upon mountains; but only that they aimed at it . . .

Yet the battles of Achilles with the River he encounters are not a whit less extravagant

W42   p 408, pencil | § 93

Virgil has perhaps hurt the effect by making them actually engage in the mighty attempt instead of merely designing or aiming at it . . . and Claudian has quite spoiled it by making his giants complete the attempt, in which he has been followed by Milton in his battle of the angels . . .

The fact is that as far as Physical Power goes Homers Achilles His Giants and his Jupiters and Neptunes are contemptible Creatures compared with the angels of Milton, as is strikingly illustrated by the close of the fourth Book of Paradise Lost, where the Poet does not trust them to a conflict in this visible universe, for the whole would have gone to wrack before them.[1]

> Hæc quicunque legit [? tantum] cecinisse putabit
> Me mortem [. . .] Virgilium culicis.[2]

W42[1] *Paradise Lost* IV 992–4: "the Starrie Cope/ Of Heav'n perhaps, or all the Elements/ At least had gone to rack", i.e. if Gabriel and Satan had come to blows.

W42[2] The couplet, apparently WW's or C's, is extremely difficult to decipher; but it appears to allude to *Culex* (*The Gnat*), one of the minor poems doubtfully attributed to Virgil. Tr: "Whoever reads this will think that I have sung only of the death of [. . .], Virgil of the death of the gnat." The name of the insignificant person whose death Milton wrote about is unfortunately almost illegible, but it is certainly not either Edward King (*Lycidas*), or Hobson, the University Carrier, whose death was the occasion of two comic poems that C regularly refers to as examples of Milton's slighter work, e.g. in MILTON *Poems* 33 n 1. The word might be "Mansi", alluding to Milton's poem *Mansus*: though it is a tribute to Milton's friend Giovanni Battista Manso (c 1560–1645) and not an elegy for him, it makes much of his great age and ends with references to death.

BERNARD GERMAIN ETIENNE DE LA VILLE SUR ILLON
COMTE DE LA CÉPÈDE
1756–1825

LOST BOOK

Les Ages de la Nature et histoire de l'espèce humaine. 2 vols (in one). Paris 1830. 8°.

Not located; marginalia not recorded.

Green SC (1880) 419: "several MS. notes by S. T. Coleridge, some of which are unfortunately cut into by binder".

MANUEL LACUNZA Y DIAZ

1731–1801

The Coming of Messiah in Glory and Majesty. By Juan Josafat Ben-Ezra, a converted Jew [i.e. Manuel Lacunza]. Translated from the Spanish, with a preliminary discourse, by the Rev. Edward Irving, A.M. 2 vols. London 1827. 8°.

British Library C 126 i 7 (Vol II). Annotations from the lost Vol I are printed from MS TRANSCRIPTS and *LR* IV 399–415.

"S. T. C." label on title-page of Vol II, and John Duke Coleridge's monogram on II ⁻2. The original 2-volume set was probably presented to C by Edward Irving on publication, with Vol I inscribed by Irving as affectionately as he had inscribed IRVING *For Missionaries* two years earlier and was to inscribe *Sermons* in the following year. C is mentioned respectfully as a mentor I lxxv, lxxvii.

MS TRANSCRIPTS. (*a*) BM C 43 b 20, Vol I only, incorrectly described in *Green SC* (1880) 29 as having "several MS. notes inserted in S. T. Coleridge's autograph". Twenty-eight annotations have been copied in an unidentified hand on slips of paper tipped in to the text at the appropriate places, all but four of them referring to Irving's 194-page Preliminary Discourse. The authority of these notes is enhanced by corrections in C's hand (**15**) that suggest that he himself supervised the transcription. These annotations are not included in *LR*; it is possible that the notes selected for *LR* were removed from this transcript. A marginal cross that appears without a note on I xxxv may designate a lost note or marked passage.

(*b*) Cornell Wordsworth Collection: Healey 2625. In two unidentified hands on 48 pp, a transcript of 22 annotations from Vol I and 52 from Vol II. This transcript omits some notes that are in MS TRANSCRIPT (*a*) and includes one note (**12**) that is not.

Since MS TRANSCRIPT (*b*) can be compared both with (*a*) and with the holograph annotation of Vol II, it has been possible to reach some conclusions about the fidelity of the transcripts and to adopt the following policies. Cancels and interlinear insertions in the MS TRANSCRIPTS are taken for scribal errors and are not indicated in the text. Marginal crosses marking the textus are represented by asterisks: they may be facsimiles of C's original, and at least they indicate approximately the location of the note in C's own copy. The transcriber of (*b*) occasionally added C's initials in parentheses as an editorial insertion; these have been consistently ignored here. MS TRANSCRIPT (*a*) is used as the copy-text, with variant readings from (*b*) recorded in textual notes; in the few places where (*b*) offers a more plausible reading, its adoption is indicated in the textual notes. MS TRANSCRIPT (*b*) is followed in **12**, of which there is no record in (*a*). The annotations found only in *LR* are printed from that source, with ''(*LR*)'' given in the headline.

DATE. c 12 Apr to c late Dec 1827, or a little later, as indicated by dated notes **2, 18, 48, 98**.

COEDITOR. James Boulger.

1   I [front flyleaves] (*LR*)

Christ the WORD.

The Scriptures — The Spirit — The Church.

The Preacher.

Such seemeth to me to be the scheme of the Faith in Christ. The written Word, the Spirit and the Church, are co-ordinate, the indispensable conditions and the working causes of the perpetuity and continued renascence and spiritual life of Christ still militant. The Eternal Word, Christ from everlasting, is the *prothesis* or identity;—the Scriptures and the Church are the two poles, or the *thesis* and *antithesis*; the Preacher in direct line under the Spirit, but likewise the point of junction of the written Word and the Church, being the *synthesis*. And here is another proof of a principle elsewhere by me asserted and exemplified, that divine truths are ever a *tetractys*, or a triad equal to a *tetractys*: 4 = 1 or 3 = 4 = 1. But the entire scheme is a pentad—God's hand in the world.[1]

2   I [front flyleaves] (*LR*)

It may be not amiss that I should leave a record in my own hand, how far, in what sense, and under what conditions, I agree with my friend, Edward Irving, respecting the second coming of the Son of Man.[1] I. How far? First, instead of the full and entire conviction, the positive assurance, which Mr. Irving entertains, I—even in those points in which my judgment most coincides with his,—profess only to regard them as probable, and to vindicate them as nowise inconsistent with orthodoxy.

[1][1] C had published views about the logical relationship of the triad, the (Pythagorean) tetractys, and the pentad in *AR* (1825) 171n–175n. These figures are pervasive in his mature work, e.g. **45** and **49** below, IRVING *Sermons* **2**, *CN* IV 4829. The hand, of course, symbolises 5 = 1.

[2][1] For comparable general statements see **18, 27, 98** below. The principal texts are in Matt 24 in reply to the question ''what shall be the sign of thy coming, and of the end of the world?''; the phrase ''the coming of the Son of man'' occurs in vv 27, 37, 39.

They may be believed, and they may be doubted, *salva Catholica fide*.[2] Further, from these points I exclude all prognostications of time and event; the mode, the persons, the places, of the accomplishment; and I decisively protest against all parts of Mr. Irving's and of Lacunza's scheme grounded on the books of Daniel or the Apocalypse, interpreted as either of the two, Irving or Lacunza, understands them.[3] Again, I protest against all identification of the coming with the Apocalyptic Millennium, which in my belief began under Constantine.[4] II. In what sense? In this and no other, that the objects of the Christian Redemption will be perfected on this earth;—that the kingdom of God and his Word, the latter as the Son of Man, in which the divine will shall *be done on earth as it is in heaven*,[5] will *come*; and that the whole march of nature and history, from the first impregnation of Chaos by the Spirit, converges toward this kingdom as the final cause of the world. Life begins in detachment from Nature, and ends in union with God. III. Under what conditions? That I retain my former convictions respecting St. Michael, and the ex-saint Lucifer, and the Genie Prince of Persia, and the re-institution of bestial sacrifices in the Temple at Jerusalem, and the rest of this class.[6] All these appear to me so many pimples on the face of my friend's faith from inward heats, leaving it indeed a fine handsome intelligent face, but certainly not adding to its comeliness.[7] Such are the convictions of   S. T. Coleridge, May, 1827.

P.S. I fully agree with Mr. Irving as to the literal fulfilment of all the prophecies which respect the restoration of the Jews. (*Deuteron.* xxv. 1–8.)[8]

---

[2] "According to sound Catholic faith". The phrase occurs also (var) in IRVING *Sermons* **58** at n 2.

[3] C's chief objection to both Irving and Lacunza is the preoccupation with "particular Predictions" and their literal deciphering of symbolic elements as historical prognostications. See **47** (on Irving) and **79** (on Lacunza) below; see also n 4 for the basis of these "predictions" in Dan and Rev.

[4] In the reign of Constantine the Great (c 288–337), as C points out in JOHNSON **3**, the Christian became for the first time a *citizen* of a state.

The millennial controversies of C's day inevitably turned on interpretations of prophecies in "the Dream-book compiled under the name of Daniel" (IRVING *Ser-*

mons **20**) and the "Symbolic Drama" (below, **47**) of Revelation—both, in C's view, inappropriate for literalist interpretation.

[5] Echoing the Lord's Prayer as in Matt 6.10.

[6] The class consists of events recorded in the Bible that Irving treats allegorically but C interprets otherwise, generally as "Rabbinical fabling" (**27** below). The war in heaven, the conflict between Michael and Satan, and the fall of the rebel angels (Rev 12.7–9) are said to refer to "the apostate Hierarchy before the Flood" in IRVING *Sermons* **1** at n 19; cf JUNG **8**. The "Genie Prince of Persia" is Michael in Dan 10.13.

[7] C uses the same image in IRVING *Sermons* **25**.

[8] The *LR* reading is mistaken. C perhaps means Deut 26.18–19: "And the Lord

It may be long before Edward Irving sees what I seem at least to see so clearly,—and yet, I doubt not, the time will come when he too will see with the same evidentness,—how much grander a front his system would have presented to judicious beholders; on how much more defensible a position he would have placed it,—and the remark applies equally to Ben Ezra (that is, Emanuel Lacunza)—had he trusted the proof to Scriptures of undisputed catholicity, to the spirit of the whole Bible, to the consonance of the doctrine with the reason, its fitness to the needs and capacities of mankind, and its harmony with the general plan of the divine dealings with the world,—and had left the Apocalypse in the back ground. But alas! instead of this he has given it such prominence, such prosiliency of relief, that he has made the main strength of his hope appear to rest on a vision, so obscure that his own author and faith's-mate[9] claims a meaning for its contents only on the supposition that the meaning is yet to come!

3 I xxii | Translator's Preliminary Discourse

[Irving anticipates attacks upon this book from what he calls "the British Inquisition":] I mean those who set principle, who set truth, who set feeling, who set justice, who set every thing sacred up to sale. * I mean the ignorant, unprincipled, unhallowed spirit of criticism, which in this Protestant country is producing as foul effects against truth, and by as dishonest means, as ever did the Inquisition of Rome.

* It would have been better to have substituted the more comprehensive Term (inclusive of that here adopted viz. Criticism, and which might have been afterwards named in the unfolding of the larger and fuller Phrase) "the Anonymous Press in all its various names & departments of Newspapers, Magazines & Reviews, conducted in the mask of pretended *Boards* of Criticism wherein the writer of each portion of slander assuming the 'Majestic Plural' dishonestly gives to an individual judgement the authority of a Synod. The anonymous press I mean, which availing itself of every weapon in the vast armoury of human weakness

---

hath avouched thee this day to be his peculiar people, as he hath promised thee . . . And to make thee high above all nations . . . in praise, and in name, and in honour; and that thou mayest be an holy people unto the Lord thy God . . .". Irving endorsed the hypothesis by which Lacunza interpreted many of the OT prophecies, namely (II 9) that "This Christian church,

regarded chiefly in its active part, this executive kingdom of God, this administration of the vineyard of God, shall one day return back to the Jews, from whom it was taken; who shall be called in mercy to occupy that place which they lost by their unbelief."

2[9] Cf "faith-mate" in **86** below: not in *OED*.

& wickedness hath produced in this Protestant country and is weekly, daily yea hourly producing as &c''.[1]

4 I xxvi

First of the prophecies of Daniel. I see no sufficient reason to depart from the commonly received interpretation of the great statue, and sub-division of the four monarchies; while I can easily perceive the clue which has led our author into his interpretation, that the Babylonian and Persian do together compose but one of the kingdoms,* and that the fourth is the Gothic kingdom, or system of power which hath obtained in Europe since the sixth century, and obtaineth unto this day.

It does appear to me with so broad a light evident that the monarchies of Daniel are the Assyrian, Medo-Persian, Persian & Greek, that I am per-plexed how to reason with our Divines, who make the 4th either the Ro-man or the existing European. S. T. C.[1]

PS The mixed armies of Alexander's Successors, Greeks, and Asi-atics, Greeks and Egyptians, Greeks and Numidians &c so admirably answer to the Iron and Clay of the Seer.[2]

5 I xxviii

Upon which territorial aspect of the prophecies I may here observe in passing, lest it should escape me in another place, that I know not how it is possible for those prophecies which respect the latter times of Egypt, and Moab, and Ammon, &c. to be accomplished, *if you make them to respect the races of the inhabitants who are all intermingled and lost; but if you make them to respect the territories of these people, with such of the antient descendants as are there found, they are capable of an exact accomplishment.

I see no other objection to this territorial scheme but the difficulty of connecting such judgements with the moral causes assigned for them. It is not easy to see the propriety of thus addressing the Britons in the age of Caractacus for instance.[1] By your incestuous community of wives &c

---

3[1] C's distaste for the system of anony-mous reviewing is most coherently and persuasively developed in *BL*, esp ch 3 (*CC*) I 48–68.

4[1] At issue are the prophecies about four kingdoms in Dan 2.31–45 (associated also with the four beasts of Dan 7). C alludes to them in BIBLE COPY B **70** and in H. MORE *Theological Works* **5**.

4[2] Daniel interprets Nebuchadnezzar's dream, in which an image made in part of gold, silver, and brass has "His legs of iron, his feet part of iron and part of clay" (Dan 2.33).

5[1] Caractacus, who led the British resis-tance to the Romans, was captured A.D. 51 and taken to Rome.

you have become an abomination to the Lord and he has commanded me to take up a burthen against Britain, and some thousand of years hence, the descendants of a Gothic race who at that time will be the inhabitants of the Island shall be plagued with pestilence, fire and a profligate tyrant (Charles II)[2]

6 I xxx

And it is manifest that, if in emblematical visions, such as those of Daniel and the Apocalypse, you will interpret the periods literally, you may as well interpret the other parts literally, and insist on literal beasts of the character there set forth, and a literal throne, and so of the rest, which no one will be so foolish as to require. And why require it in one part and not in another? The word time, rather than year; and times, rather than two years; and the dividing of time, rather than half a year; were evidence to me that there was a mystery under it: but when I find it in the midst of an emblematical vision I can have no doubt thereof, according to all rules and canons of interpretation.

This is a sensible remark: tho if a man possessed the hardihood of those *critical* dreadnoughts the German Neologists,[1] he might pretend that the Archimager[2] or the Poet who assumed his name and character adopted this phrase instead of 3½ y. only to give an appropriate astrological colouring to the language.[3] That y 3½ meant three years and a half and *nothing more* M.ʳ Irving would not dignify with the bare name of a possible interpretation and yet there have been learned men, and such as have believed themselves convinced Christians, who have been smitten with the judicial blindness of finding the Maccabaic revolution as the main import.[4] Be this as it may one thing would be wonderful, if any thing in Apocalyptic Interpreters were wonderful—the fierce *confidence* of assertion on a point on which of a score of Interpreters (every one)[a] sports a different conjecture. I will so far shield myself under their authority as to speak out *my* mind boldly i.e. that the fact which staggers

[a] Possibly a transcriber's suggested insertion

5[2] C's views of Charles II are consistently hostile, as in "heartless Brotheller" in HOOKER **1**.

6[1] The "German Neologists" are identified in IRVING *For Missionaries* **1** and n 1. For "dreadnought"—a person who fears nothing—*OED* records uses in 1827 (early 1827 is the date of these marginalia) and by Walter Scott in 1832.

6[2] "Archimager", anglicised form of *archimagirus* (chief cook) in Juvenal 9.109. For C's questioning of the authenticity of Dan, and of the authorship of the book as we have it, see IRVING *Sermons* **20** and n 3.

6[3] Dan 7.25: ". . . and they shall be given into his hand until a time and times and the dividing of time".

6[4] The Maccabaean revolt against Antiochus Epiphanes began in 168 B.C.

me as to the Danielicity (authenticity?)[a] of the book of Daniel and more than any other argument keeps me from being of the same mind as the great Bentley, who wished the Church were fairly rid of it,[5] is the admitted general expectation of the Messiah about the time of our Lord's birth which the Jews grounded on Daniel's prophecy & which it would be difficult to assign to any other origin.[6] On the other hand it is singular that no *such* reference to these prophecies should occur in the new Testament, not even in the 1st Chap of Matthew nor in the Epistle to the Hebrews.

7 I xxxii

Next with respect to the Apocalypse, for the above mentioned are the only two visions of Daniel which he treateth at large, I must begin by observing that I perfectly concur with his idea that the title of this book "The Revelation of Jesus Christ,"* is to be understood in an active, not in a passive sense, to signify as it doth in all the epistles "the revealing of Jesus Christ," or the manifestation of his promised coming.

It is evident to me that this title refers to the prophecy in the 17 Chap. of Lukes Gospel which was current as a detached κηρυγμα under the title of Αποκαλυψις η μεγαλη Ιησου Χριστου, & which was the true basis of the Apocalypse of John the Theologian.[1]

8 I xxxvi

Against both of which perversities St. Peter, in the end of the first chapter of his second epistle, maketh strong debate: insisting against the former class, that no prophecy of the scripture is of any private application,* that is, neither to private men, nor particular ages, nor particular events, but hath an outstanding application to events yet to come, being spoken by the Holy Ghost for the profit of the Catholic Church; while against the spiritualizers, who were not then in being, he deals an antic-

---

[a] Apparently the transcriber's query

6[5] Richard Bentley (1662–1742), who published *Proposals for a New Edition of the Greek Testament* (1720) but did not complete the task. C alludes—probably on the basis of evidence from Francis Wrangham's biography of Bentley—to his having been "perplexed and gravelled" by Christ's reference to Daniel (Matt 24.15): see LUTHER *Colloquia* **20** and n 1.

6[6] Dan 7.13–14. For C's view that there is no earlier prophecy of the Second Coming see IRVING *Sermons* **20** esp at n 3.

7[1] The suggestion that Luke 17.20–37 was a detached "proclamation" (*not* a sermon: cf **45** below) is consistent with the view of Eichhorn, Gratz, Schleiermacher, and others that Luke was made up of a number of fragmentary drafts rather than being conceived and written as a single work. The wording of the title "The great Revelation of Jesus Christ" (repeated by C in **87** below) occurs, without μεγαλή (great), in Gal 1.12 and Rev 1.1.

ipative blow, by directing the Church to look to the "sure word of prophecy, as unto a light shining in a dark place . . ."

On this fine text that I should sooner have expected from Paul than from Peter, I would ground my apprehension[a] to Mr. Irving's whole scheme. The other text is mistranslated, the free rendering is we have the word of Prophecy βεβαιοτερον more sure i.e.[1]

9 I xxxvi

We have first the vision of Christ in emblematic form as the Shepherd and Bishop of the churches; and then we have his epistles to the seven churches of Asia, *which I have no doubt were seven actual churches, as Babylon, and Egypt, and Jerusalem, were actual places . . .

The mere *names* suffice to demonstrate the contrary every one being symbolical 4, 5 out[b] the same staringly so.[1]

10 I lxvii

. . . the Lord maketh this same forgetfulness of his coming to produce cruelty from one member of his house to another, saying, "But, and if that evil servant shall say in his heart, My Lord delayeth his coming, and shall begin to smite his fellow-servant, and to eat and drink with the drunken; the lord of that servant shall come in a day when he looketh not for him, and in an hour that he is not aware of. And shall cut him asunder, and appoint him his portion with the hypocrite; there shall be weeping and gnashing of teeth."

But surely this may, nay on many grounds *must* be understood of the call by Death.[1] M.[r] Irving seems to forget or rather never to remember that Parables are *Parables* not to be interpreted literally or in what respect would they differ from Historical Narratives? What possible dif-

---

[a] A transcriber's error for "objection"?

[b] Both transcripts read "4, 5 out the same", presumably meaning "4, if not 5, out of the same"

8[1] The "fine text" is 2 Pet 1.20–1, paraphrased by Irving in textus. The "other text"—2 Pet 1.19—is "mistranslated" through Irving's omission of "more" in AV "We have also a more sure word of prophecy"; C corrects this by quoting the Greek word, translating it "more sure", and ending his comment with the abbreviation for "that is".

9[1] The "seven churches which are in Asia" to which (Rev 1.11) St John's letter is addressed: in Ephesus, Smyrna, Pergamos, Thyatira, Sardis, Philadelphia, and Laodicea. Of these, all but Smyrna and Sardis are identified as actual churches: on the level of fact, at least, Irving is correct, C mistaken. There is further speculation about the symbolic names of cities in **70** below.

10[1] The text under discussion is Luke 12.45–51.

ference can it make to the man who died last month? That is the coming of the Lord to him.

11   I lxxx (*LR*)*[a]*

Now, of these three, the office of Christ as our prophet is the means used by the Holy Spirit for working the redemption of the understanding of man; that faculty by which we acquire the knowledge on which proceed both our inward principles of conduct and our outward acts of power.

I cannot forbear expressing my regret that Mr. Irving has not adhered to the clear and distinct exposition of the understanding, *genere et gradu*, given in the Aids to Reflection.[1] What can be plainer than to say: the understanding is the medial faculty or faculty of means, as reason on the other hand is the source of ideas or ultimate ends. By reason we determine the ultimate end: by the understanding we are enabled to select and adapt the appropriate means for the attainment of, or approximation to, this end, according to circumstances. But an ultimate end must of necessity be an idea, that is, that which is not representable by the sense, and has no entire correspondent in nature, or the world of the senses. For in nature there can be neither a first nor a last:—all that we can see, smell, taste, touch, are means, and only in a qualified sense, and by the defect of our language, entitled ends. They are only relatively ends in a chain of motives. B. is the end to A.; but it is itself a mean to C., and in like manner C. is a mean to D., and so on. Thus words are the means by which we reduce appearances, or things presented through the senses, to their several kinds, or *genera*; that is, we generalize, and thus think and judge. Hence the understanding, considered specially as an intellective power, is the source and faculty of words;—and on this account the understanding is justly defined, both by Archbishop Leighton, and by Immanuel Kant, the faculty that judges by, or according to, sense.[2] However, practical or intellectual, it is one and the same under-

---

[a] This note does not appear in either of the MS TRANSCRIPTS and may have been constructed by HNC, as editor of *LR*, from **12** and other notes

11[1] C's exposition "in kind and in degree" is in *AR* (1825) 200–28. Irving's mistake would be all the more galling to C since readers might attribute it to him too: in I lxxv Irving writes, "The method of intellection hath only to do with the pure reason, and therefore is imperfect to a being like man. Yet, forasmuch as the pure reason is the noblest part of man, the truth, in whatever way conveyed, must contain the food of pure reason, which my dear friend, my kind and honored instructor, Mr. Coleridge, hath well proved it to contain, in his invaluable book, entitled 'Aids to Reflection;' from whom also I received the first idea of the prophetic growth of God's word: as what have I not received from him?"

11[2] C alludes to Leighton's phrase "natural reason, judging according to sense", which is in the textus of LEIGHTON COPY C **12**. In his note on that passage (at n

standing, and the definition, the medial faculty, expresses its true character in both directions alike. I am urgent on this point, because on the right conception of the same, namely, that understanding and sense (to which the sensibility supplies the material of outness, *materiam objectivam,*)[3] constitute the natural mind of man, depends the comprehension of St. Paul's whole theological system. And this natural mind, which is named the mind of the flesh, φϱόνημα σαϱϰός, as likewise φυσιϰὴ σύνεσις,[4] the intellectual power of the living or animal soul, St. Paul everywhere contradistinguishes from the spirit, that is, the power resulting from the union and co-inherence of the will and the reason;[5]—and this spirit both the Christian and elder Jewish Church named, *sophia*, or wisdom.

12 I front flyleaves, referring to I lxxxii | **13** textus

The *natural* mind of Man (by St Paul called the mind of the Flesh,[1] and the Physical instinct in contradistinction from the spirit or spiritual mind, or unity of the Will & Reason—The natural mind, I say) consists of sense and understanding, to which the sensibility supplies the matter of *outness* = *materiam objectivam.* The Sense is the immediate, the understanding the medial faculty or the Faculty of *Means*; even as the Reason is the Power of proposing *Ends*, that is *Ends* truly so called, *ultimate* Ends. Particulars, Things of nature, or the world of the Senses are only by defect of language entitled Ends, i.e. Relatively Ends as links in a chain of purposes. B is an end in relation to A: but it is at the same moment a *means* to C: and the whole Chain from A to Z is but the collective *means* to some ultimate true *End.* Now every ultimate end must of necessity be an *Idea* i.e. that which can have no adequate and integral correspondent in outward *Nature* even were it only that in Nature there is neither a *First* nor a *Last.*[2] The Understanding is either practical or theoretical, that is, it may be considered either as an organ of Action or of Thought. But the same definition, comprises both. It is *the faculty of means*;—as an intellectual Power, the Understanding is the faculty of *words*; but words are *means, mediators* the means to wit by

---

5) C makes the same statement about Kant, referring to *C d r V* (1799) 75.

11[3] *"Objective material".*

11[4] "The mind of the flesh", as likewise "natural intelligence" (the "natural mind" of C's phrase just above). The latter phrase is not in NT; the former, central to C's thought, is glossed in LEIGHTON COPY B 15.

11[5] C refers to Paul's distinction elsewhere, notably in IRVING *Sermons* 27 at n 7, where the significant text appears to be 1 Cor 15.

12[1] Rom 8.6: see **11** n 4.

12[2] The view of nature as a realm of process, of becoming rather than being, is expressed esp in C's etymology of the word in *AR* (1825) 244, cited in IRVING *Sermons* 52. The same assertion appears in **11** above.

which we refer particulars to several kinds in General. By them we *generalize* and thus *conceive*, think. On the same Ground the Understanding is by Archbishop Leighton & Emmanuel Kant most correctly defined "the Faculty that judges according to sense".[3] Hence when the understanding is enlightened by a superior power, and made the instrument and minister of the spirit it proceeds and can only proceed by Symbols.[4] For as all the products of the understanding & therefore all *words* are generalized from Sense, it is only by a *Symbolical* use of words that they can be made to express things *above* sense. But symbols are grounded on the Prophetic character of all God's works; without prophecy Symbols would have no import or ground of truth: & without Symbols prophecy would be dumb.[5]   S. T. C.

P.S. The existing state of Theology in the Scotch Church, that scheme of Faith, namely, from which Asgill drew his wild, but legitimate, nay, inevitable conclusion,[6] exhibits an awful example of the determination to build up a religion without Symbols and with none but dead prophesies; that is, prophesies which have ceased to be prophesies, and which (on the principles of these Divines) should take their place among historical narratives of past miracles—[7]

13   I lxxxii

And, as I said, it is by this peculiar part or property alone that his word holdeth mastery over the intellect of man; the mind of God in this differing from the mind of man, and by this having authority over it; in that

12[3] See **11** n 2.

12[4] C describes the symbolic operation of the understanding similarly in LUTHER *Colloquia* **5**. The classic account of the symbol is *SM* (*CC*) 28–31.

12[5] In this statement, C's views about the state of mind that produces symbols and about the state of mind that produces prophecy coincide. Cf his interesting note on prophecy in EICHHORN *Alte Testament* **38**, and his account of the prophecy itself as a cypher in which all knowledge is contained by involution in JAHN *Appendix* **1**, **4**.

12[6] The "Scotch Church" is Irving's, but C represents John Asgill (1659–1730) as a precursor in "a Scheme of Religion without Ideas" (ASGILL **1**). In a famous pamphlet pub 1700—the seriousness of which has never been determined—Asgill argued that under the terms of "the covenant of eternal life revealed in the Scrip-

tures" a Christian should be able to be "translated" to immortality without passing through death. C satirised Asgill's title as "[An] Argument against the base & cowardly Custom of *Dying*" in a letter of 1832: *CL* VI 905–6.

12[7] This statement is clarified by C's letter to H. F. Cary, 25 May 1827, in which he says, "Now in every scheme of Organization Successive (and the great Scheme of Revelation is eminently such) every integral part is of necessity both prophecy & history, save the last or consummating Fact, which will be only History, and the initial which can only be prophecy: but of all the intervening components of the Scheme every part is both at once—i.e. Prophecy in relation to what follows and History in relation to that which had preceded. Now in this sense of the word I believe the whole Bible to be prophetic": *CL* VI 684–5.

it is prophetic, and doth take instruments upon the dark future, as well as upon the past and the present. The human mind is historical, and it is observant of the present, and it is metaphysical, that is, independent of place and time, but it is not prophetical. I say not that in any kind it doth at all approach to the mind of God, *but that in all other kinds it can ape it, and steal from it, and make a fashion of withstanding it, and doth withstand it, and suppose that it has triumphed over it; but in the dark arcana and mysteries of the future, it can make neither pretence nor debate against the holy word.

See the Mss Note on the blank leaf at the head of the Vol.[1] Of the natural mind of man, as far as he is himself & no more (but unless, above himself he can erect himself how mean a thing is man!)[2] of man thus limited, and of all the faculties apprehensive & comprehensive which he can *include* in himself as *his* detached property (sibi unius proprium)[3] M.r Irving's assertion is correct. Otherwise I shall remind him that all Science is necessarily prophetic, so truly so, that the power of prophecy is the test, the infallible criterion, by which any presumed Science, is ascertained to be actually & verily science. The Ptolemaic Astronomy was barely able to prognosticate a lunar eclipse; with Kepler and Newton came Science & Prophecy.[4] Luther was inclined to think that a large portion even of the scripture political & territorial burthens God revealed to the Seers, the sacred Tribunes & Ephori[m] of the Hebrew commonwealth thro' the medium & instrumentality of their moral science enlighten'd by the Ray, from the Word, their hearts having been purified & enkindled by the H. Spirit & on Luther the same prophetic light fell, if not with the vertical & unrefracted Rays vouchsafed to the old Prophets & the Apostles.[5]

14 I xciv, the note mistakenly bound in at xc/xci

* By this high authority we are informed that our present spiritual dispensation, which is wont to be interpreted as complete in itself, without any bud or promise of another, is as much preparatory to another, as was

13[1] I.e. **12**.

13[2] A quotation from Samuel Daniel *Epistle to the Lady Margaret, Countess of Cumberland*, often invoked by C: cf LEIGHTON COPY C **7** n 14.

13[3] C seems to be using *proprius* in a double sense, therefore "his unique property peculiar to himself".

13[4] In *C&S (CC)* 118–19 C uses the revolutionary astronomy of Kepler and Newton similarly to illustrate the role of ideas in science.

13[5] C may be thinking of the passage "Of Christ's Coming", which he annotated with specific reference to Irving and Lacunza: LUTHER *Colloquia* **21**. C repeatedly praises Luther as a successor to Paul, and at times refers to Irving as a successor to Luther, e.g. LUTHER *Colloquia* **36**, AR (1825) 372–3n, *C&S (CC)* 142–3*.

the Mosaic, which the Jews thought perfect in itself: or rather, to speak more exactly, the dispensation from Abraham to the present time is one dispensation, which is incomplete and inexplicable but by the belief of another dispensation of glory about to follow. Our Lord here expressly declareth to Nicodemus, that all which he taught him, concerning the regeneration of the Spirit, and his own lifting up, and the light unto the Gentiles, was a part of the earthly things, and no part of the heavenly things; or in other words, that the spiritual dispensation under which we live is but the unfolding and completing of the ritual and prophetic dispensation, and can no more be separated from it, than the exposition can be separated from the text, or the resolution from the perplexed riddle.

My brave friend will be charged I fear with conspiring with the Romish *Religieux*[1] to revive the old Franciscan heresy, of the 3 dispensations, to the Gospel of the Father from Moses to the Apostles 2nd the Gospel of the Son (now existing) and 3d the Gospel of the H. Ghost shortly to supersede the Christian Religion, as the Christian had superseded the Mosaic. The plot of the Mendicant orders it is asserted was to have made St Francis the H. Ghost incarnate.[2]

Certainly, our Lord's application of the epithet earthly to the mystery of regeneration is very remarkable.[3] Whether it will support all that Mr Irving builds upon it is another matter.

15 I CV

Here then is an intermediate function of the priestly office intervening between the atonement and the intercession, or rather I should say the first part of the intercessory office, which is to put into his censer the incense of his own merits, and in virtue thereof to obtain not only the forgiveness of our sins which appertaineth to his death, but likewise the gift of the Holy Ghost which appertaineth to the power of his resurrection. . . . It belongeth not to this but to another place to speak of the Holy Ghost; yet was it necessary to say so much in order to express a most important part of the priestly office of Christ which is not sufficiently attended to, but which is, I think, in scripture the most frequently insisted upon under this form of expression, "He baptizeth with the Holy Ghost."

Mr Irving has here set me an example, & in fact has shamed me in my own eyes. I have long entertained the same conviction viz. that the

---

14[1] Monks; members of the monastic orders.

14[2] This is the heresy of the Joachim-ites, alluded to and explained in IRVING *Sermons* **62** and n 5.

14[3] In textus, referring to John 3.12.

Church doctrine of the Holy Spirit is true indeed included (*implicita*)[1] in the philosophical Idea of the Trinity & legitimately deducible from sundry passages in the Holy scriptures; but not to be found *in* them, explicitly or as the proper and primary import of the words. But tho' I have long entertained this opinion and have recorded it in my MSS. Day-Books, I have lacked courage to make known & promulgate the same.[2]

P.S. The poverty of the Latin Language which offered but one word for the two distinct Greek words ousia and hypostasis and therefore exchanged the latter for προσωπον and rendered it by *persona* has tended greatly to obscure the clarity of the Idea of the Trinity and even to distort its practical application.[3] Θεος[4] = the absolute Will, the Abysmal Good, is the Identity of the Godhead and asserts the place of the Prothesis in the Logic of finite verities (See Blank leaf)[a5] The Father is the Ipseity the Son the Alterity, the Spirit the Community.[6] The Spirit selfmovent (αυτοκίνητον) the Son self subsistent, the Father self affirmed. Three self subsistences of which the Father alone is self originated; the Father is the Personeity, the Son the Person, the Spirit the Personal Life of the Godhead proceeding from the Father and the Son, εκπορευομενον και περικυκλομενον.[7] The Son and the Father live in us in the spirit. It is the Spirit of the Father and of the Son. The Son Baptizeth with the Spirit, & the Spirit Baptizeth to & into the Son. The apparent incongruity or contradiction in terms, of instrument (instrumentum et materia, *materia instrumentalis*)[8] and agent is only the necessary mark or character of an *Idea*. An equivalent self-contradiction will be found in the expression of every Idea or "no Idea can be expressed but by two ⟨Cl⟩auses ⟨or Positions⟩[b] that verbally *negative* each other—"[9]

---

[a] This reference, omitted in (*b*), may be the transcriber's suggestion
[b] The two insertions in angle brackets are in C's hand

15[1] "*Implicitly*".

15[2] The "MSS. Day-Books" were the new series of notebooks begun 5 Jul 1827 with N33 and collectively referred to as "Fly-Catchers", being generally small and intended as a day-by-day record of passing thoughts. The first entry in N33 explains C's reluctance to publish the opinions recorded there, alleging the difference between the *order* of thoughts as they arise spontaneously and as they are presented for instruction; as he says (f 5ᵛ), "in conceiving the thoughts [the thinker] is a *Nature* who works in continuous Articulation, and an unbroken series of *embryonic* formulations", whereas by preparing them for publication he "*becomes* the Logos" achieving the "conditions of distinct Vision and

lucid Order".

15[3] This lament over the terms in the Latin creed echoes IRVING *Sermons* 1 at n 4. *Persona*, lit "mask"—of which πρόσωπον is the Greek equivalent—but generally "person".

15[4] "God".

15[5] 1 above. For "Abysmal Good" cf IRVING *Sermons* 15 n 5.

15[6] There is a similar analysis of the Trinity in IRVING *Sermons* 3.

15[7] "Proceeding from and encircling"—the latter participle related to the concept of perichoresis (BÖHME **103** and n), and both repeated in **58** below.

15[8] "Instrument and matter, *instrumental matter*".

15[9] The quotation marks are puzzling:

⟨1⟩ ᵃBefore Abraham *was* ⟨2⟩I am.[10] The Soul ⟨1⟩is *all* ⟨2⟩in every part &c.

16   ɪ cix

But the system whereof our author sheweth the orthodoxy puts this whole subject in a worthier point of light, and gives body and substance to the whole, by presenting us the royal Judge coming to execute judgment by visible acts upon the earth, and after having consumed those who will not return from their rebellion, proceeding to judge the world in righteousness and the people with equity; establishing that law of holiness triumphant which is now trampled under foot, and by its sweet influences, producing all love, and unity, and blessedness amongst men.*

Would that my Friend had explained the compatability of this with the "νόμῳ τελείῳ τῆς ἐλευθερίας."[1]—His intellectual opponents exclaim, what would such a law be but Superfine Chinese? An absolute despotism in which the very perfection of the Monarch must act to the reduction of the subject to Automatons? I do not join in the exclamation, but I should like to hear the answer from such a man as Edward Irving!

17   ɪ cxiii, textus marked with a short line in the margin

So much and much more if space permitted, have I to say upon the prejudice which the priestly office of Christ hath undergone, through that oblivion of his kingly and judicial office which hath come over the church, by reason of her neglect, unbelief, and spiritual annihilation of those large portions of scripture which make known his second advent and set him forth as a Priest, not upon his cross, but upon his throne, not humbled and rejected of men, but ruling in righteousness from sea to sea, and from the river to the ends of the earth.

It is much to be regretted that M͏ͬ Irving has not adopted a word more expressive of his real meaning than *Spiritualizing*. The divines against whom E. I. remonstrates *notionalize*.[1]

ᵃ Both transcripts use superior numerals, here given in angle brackets to avoid confusion with footnote indicators

---

no source has been traced, and they may be inserted for emphasis, or intended as a loose paraphrase of the statement in *BL* ch 9 (*CC*) ɪ 156, "except in geometry, all symbols of necessity involve an apparent contradiction".

15[10] John 8.58.

16[1] Jas 1.25 (var): "With the perfect law of liberty".

17[1] Although the textus for this passage is clearly marked, C's note appears to refer to a passage near the bottom of the page below the textus for **18**: "It is one of the evil fruits of our spiritualizing whatever will spiritualize, and neglecting the rest, to have spread abroad the notion that the spirit

18 ɪ cxiii

In all that I have said, I have confined myself to that first province of his priestly power which concerneth the regeneration and sanctification of the soul; and I have now to treat and enlarge upon the two other provinces thereof, which our modern theology, though making such a parade of the written word, and the written word only, hath almost suffered to drop out of the mind and memory of the church. I mean the redemption of the body, and the redemption of the earth on which we dwell.

Now so far in all the deep & concerning Points which M.ʳ Irving has most ably maintained against the current dogmata of both Churches, his own & ours, in all the great moments of his Warfare; I am his fellow combatant & prepared to fight under his banner. Up to this stone he & I are one. Shall we differ then respecting our Lord's Kingly office? Scarcely I trust.—Or of Christ's 2ⁿᵈ coming to possess his Kingdom? I have no foreboding of dissent on this either. It is the personal coming, to the coming of Jesus, & the erection of an earthly monarchy, an imperial Theocracy, under Jesus, as the visible head & Sovereign, that my fear points. Fears that I shall find myself called on to withstand him to attack his positions & despoil him of his Faith? O no! no! no! but that I may not be able to partake of it! There will be no [? unitency/ uniting/ resistency],ᵃ but a yearning & a predisposition. If reason does not hold me back, my Will will project me at all events Daniel & the Apocalypse shall not part us   12 April 1827

19 ɪ cxxvi

The word of God took flesh of the Virgin Mary, passive humanity he took, obnoxious to every temptation, and begirt with every sinless infirmity. And that holy thing which was born of her was the seed of the regenerate world. . . . But he had to descend into the still lower depth of the grave, and wrestle against Satan in his strongest hold. . . . Behold, he doth bear flesh into the presence of the Holy Father. And the Father counts not the divinity of his Son dishonoured by flesh, but rather clothed with new honour, and he sits down at the right hand of the majesty on high.

If I erred not in my estimation of the advantage that would have accrued

---

ᵃ (*b*) reads "unitency", (*a*) is obscure

---

operateth upon the soul primarily and upon the body only in a very inferior degree . . .''. C habitually distinguished between ideas and notions, the latter being "the depthless abstractions of fleeting phenomena'': *SM* (*CC*) 23, cf 113. "Notionalize" is C's nonce-word.

to my Luther-hearted Friend, had he adhered systematically to my analysis of the natural mind of man, as restated in the blank pages at the head of this volume*a* & if he had squared his terminology therewith;[1] with how much deeper emphasis do I regret that he has not availed himself of the views respecting Flesh & Blood in the corpus νουμενον*b* as contradistinguished from the corpus φαινομενον! (See the Conclusion to the Aids to Reflection)[2] nay that he seems never even to have adverted to it! One consequence of this oversight is that M͏r Irving's Words are equally capable of conveying a most vital & soul-mastering *Idea* & a most death-doing, light-quenching *Idol* (εἴδωλον)[3] & alas more likely to excite the latter than the former, in the minds of the average of his readers. But I fear there is a heavier charge to which my friend, in the onrush of his eloquence has exposed himself—that of using visual images of Spiritual essences, without letting his reader know whether he intends them in their proper Sense, or as mere popular phrases, in an argument where the whole character & tendency of his tenets depends on the ascertainment of this point. Does M͏r Irving seriously & literally attribute a local *seat* to God & that in the same Seat or throne a flesh & blood man Jesus to wit is sitting on his right hand? Can he reconcile this I will not say with Reason & natural piety, but with St John's declaration Θεον ουδεις εωρακεν πωποτε?[4] But if he does not mean this what does he mean? The very root of the argument is *in* this. If this be for *us* (whatever it may have been for the Apostles) only figures of speech—then for us (whatever it may have been for the Apostles) all that follows of his coming again from the clouds must be only figures of speech.

20 ɪ cxxviii

And hath any soul, or any body of men, save the Virgin's Son, had presentation to the Father? I trow not. And hath any of them dared to present a prayer to the Father direct?* I trow not. When shall they be presented unto the Father? When their bodies are delivered from the power of the grave, for while there, they are underlying his curse. And

---

a (b) reads "the end of this volume"   *b* (a) reads in error νομενον

19[1] **11** and **12** above. For Irving as "Luther-hearted" see **13** n 5 above.

19[2] *AR* (1825) 386–402 discusses among other things the role of "invisible Energy" in the formation of the body, though it does not explicitly discriminate between the "phenomenal" body—the body in its physical appearance—and the

"noumenal" or spiritual body; cf **36** below, and IRVING *Sermons* **27**.

19[3] *Eidolon*, or idol, described also in *SM* (*CC*) 101 as "the antithesis not the synonyme" of "Idea".

19[4] John 1.18: "No man hath seen God at any time".

when shall that be? At his coming. . . . And do the sojourners on the earth present their prayers directly to the Father? I trow not; not without a Mediator . . .

To whom is the Lord's prayer addressed? The followers of Swedenborg are the only religious party as far as I know, in whose scheme of belief this is no difficulty, for according to them, the Lord's Prayer is a Prayer addressed to our Lord as well as taught by him.[1] Christ (so Swedenborg everywhere maintains) is our Father which is in the Heavens.—The strongest scripture text in favour of this position is our Lords answer to Philip & indeed the whole of the first Chap. of John's Gospel.[2]

21   1 cxlviii

This ["the Prince of Peace"] is the last syllable of his name, and ariseth to the highest pitch of honour and dignity. It addeth the awful attribute of sovereignty, the singular majesty of royal power, to the wonderfulness of working, the wisdom of counsel, the almightiness of power, the graciousness and propriety of Father.

It is but justice to my friend when I say that the main obstacle of Prejudice to the attentive consideration of his Scheme in the minds of men generally & that which would but for the Baron's personal relations of his travels in the Spirit-World ensure the Swedenborgian New Jerusalem a preferance over M! Irving's Interpretation of the same prophecies,[1] is to be found in the wide influence of the Cartesian Dualism i.e. assumption of two essentially *heterogeneous* constituents of man, Body & Soul; a notion which was first introduced by Des Cartes and the influence of which with its many mischievous effects in Science & Theology has

20[1] In Matt 6.9–13. As the next sentence indicates, C is making a general reference to Swedenborgian doctrine rather than alluding to a specific text. C's interest in Swedenborg was encouraged by Charles Augustus Tulk (1786–1849), a founding member of the Swedenborg Society though never a member of the New Church, whom C appears to have met in 1817: *CL* IV 767. Of C's annotated copies of Swedenborg's works seven titles survive.

20[2] C presumably means John 1.49–51, the dialogue between Christ and Nathanael, who was brought to him by Philip. Nathanael declares his belief in Christ as "the Son of God" and "King of Israel"; "Jesus answered and said unto him, Because I said unto thee, I saw thee under the fig tree, believest thou? thou shalt see greater things than these. . . . Verily, verily, I say unto you, Hereafter ye shall see heaven open, and the angels of God ascending and descending upon the Son of man."

21[1] This too is a general reference to Swedenborg's work; as an example, *The True Christian Religion*, which C annotated, combines anecdotes about the spirit-world as "memorabilia" with an interpretation of the OT prophecies and Rev as foretelling a "New Jerusalem" on earth, not as the founding of a religious sect but as the direct communion of God with true believers. Swedenborg interprets the Second Coming as a coming "not in person but in the word": *True Christian Religion* ch 14 § 776 (1819) II 528–30.

long survived the School in which it originated. M.ʳ Irving is not aware how much the exposition of his Scheme has lost thro' his inadvertence to the truths asserted & set forth in the *Conclusion* of my 'Aids to Reflection' & in the Chap. on Descartes &c in the 1.ˢᵗ Vol of my Biographia Literaria[2] See Blank leaf On the constitution &c of the Natural man prefixed to this Vol.[3]

22   I cliii, marked with short lines in the margin

We say that the day of the Lord . . . is the period during which this manifestation will be made. We interpret the conflagration of the earth to be its purification or baptism with fire, and not its annihilation. We doubt whether annihilation be an idea contained in the scriptures at all; for we perceive that the second death is not annihilation; nor are wicked men annihilated; nor is Satan, nor is death, nor is αδης [Hades], the place of separate spirits, which are all cast into a lake of fire. We believe that our Lord shall reign a certain limited time with his enemies under his feet, that is in a state of subjection; and afterwards that he shall reign for ever, with his enemies under the dominion of the second death.

But what is the office of Fire? Is it not to resolve composite bodies into their primary most simple constituents—to cleanse metals i.e. simple bodies to destroy *figure*ᵃ symbolically individually? Why then may we not hope, that the subjects which have resisted the cleansing of Fire may lose all individuality in its intense energy, but evil disindividualized ceases to be *evil*. Analogy from the central fire & Volcanic.

23   I cliv, marked with short lines in the margin

. . . this hell of the second death, with all that are doomed to abide therein, shall serve the opposite purpose to all God's intelligent and unfallen creatures, of demonstrating to them the horrors of disloyalty and disobedience to the great King, the fearful fruits of sin, the indestructible horrors of death, the passive and impotent misery of those who disobey the will of the Highest; the awful stability of the laws of heaven, and the indefeasible sovereignty of the word of God. But if these theorists destroy the earth, or make of it their hell . . . if they carry off the race of redeemed men to mingle with, and be lost amongst the countless myri-

---

ᵃ (*b*) reads "figures", and both transcripts continue "(symbolically individually", suggesting that C made an oblique stroke which looks like a parenthesis

21[2] C comments on Cartesian dualism or "the Corpuscular School" in *AR* (1825) 386–92 (recommended also in **19** above) and in *BL* ch 8 (*CC*) I 129–31.
21[3] I.e. **12** above.

ads of the unfallen angels, the whole end and termination of the glorious mystery of redemption is lost.

Indeed indeed this will not solve the problem! Still evil & that in its most terrific & aggravated form will exist in the empire of God—nay, be eternal. But this is impossible. What had a *beginning* & not *from* God must have an ending & *by* God.

When I have the opportunity of conversing with my Friend respecting the Nature of Life, & the essential attributes of *Divine* life (the H. Spirit) I doubt not with Grace assisting, to render this less incomprehensible to him & to shew the consonance of my views with Scripture

24 I clviii, marked with a pencil line in the margin

But it is argued by the objectors, that after the ascension he was glorified into a much higher and more honourable condition, of which it would be as it were a great reduction, to come back to the earth again and rule over it. . . . But if, which alone is proper to this argument, it be meant that as the Son of man, he entered into any other reward than to be head of the present church, and to wait to be made the head of the heathen, and of the world, and of the blessed universe, I must regard it as an hypothesis till I can find it proved from scripture. I know it is loosely held amongst the people, and the ministers of the people, but this is not conclusive evidence to a Christian or a minister of Christ.

An admirable ¶ph worthy of gravest consideration. Let my friend steer between both extremes & he will assuredly anchor in the desired haven. Hitherto the orthodox in ✠ to the infrasocinian scheme[1] have been in too great danger of losing the Son of Man in the co-eternal Son of God. Let us now contemplate him as both; but distinctly. The *peril* of Idolatry is infinitely diminished by the union; but the possibility of it is not done away. We must not attribute to the Son of Man attributes incompatible with Humanity; or the non-absolute, even in its highest perfection. If Edwᵈ Irving shall, as I trust he will apportion to the Acts of the Son of God before the World & in the World, before man & *in* the humanity, the due & constant quantity of attention, & bring into harmony therewith his present scriptural convictions, respecting the Son of Man he will establish in full the claim which *I* made for him to the name of Luther redivivus.[2]

24[1] C's symbol probably means in "opposition" to, though it does not occur among his usual devices, as in JOANNES **4**. The word "infrasocinian" ("below the So-cinian") is not in *OED*, but evidently refers to a position absolutely denying the divinity of Christ.

24[2] "Luther reborn", as in **13** n 5.

25 I clxi

* It is against reason that such a holy thing should be upon the earth; it is still more against reason that he should be trodden down by the wicked things of the earth. And yet so it was, in order to set reason at nought, and demonstrate her inability to attain unto any part of the mystery of divine love.

This is the sort of sentence, of too frequent occurrence in this Discourse, to which I so impatiently object. What is my friend's object in all this reasoning, but to set forth the perfect & exalted *Reason* of this economy that sets Reason at nought!!! What predilection can Irving have for the term Reason? What prejudice against Understanding? that he should prefer the ambiguous, the almost sure to be misconceived former to the safe & wholly unobjectionable ⟨latter⟩ term.[1] These passages always strike me as if his Amanuensis (some Pupil of the modern Calvinist School who had stolen into my friend's good opinion) had by a *pious* fraud had interpolated what my friend was dictating, with bits & scraps out of his own favorite Divines, & that my Friend in the ardor of preaching had read them straight forward without adverting to their dissonance from his own style of thinking & expressing his Thoughts.

26 I clxiii

And that they may sing with exultation during the millennial age, "And we shall reign with thee over the universe," as now the church in heaven singeth perpetually, "And we shall reign with thee upon the earth."*

O Dear Friend, the Universe is a big Word! It does not suit the mouth of conjecture.

27 I clxxiv

In all these marginal notices since those on the 1st part of this Pre-Discourse I have written in the character of a convert to M.r Irving's main κηρυγμα or tenet.[1] The Second personal coming of the crucified Son of Mary. What I object therefore is not objected against the doctrine but in support of it indirectly, at least by removing this or that obstacle, this or that unnecessary difficulty in the way of its reception. On this account & in this spirit I object to the protrusion of a (necessary, I admit, but nevertheless a) *dim* and *shadowy Idea* in no part of scripture asserted for its own sake or as the proper & primary end and purpose of the text, an

---

25[1] See **11** n 1 above.
27[1] Irving's "Preliminary Discourse" runs to 192 pp. The Greek κήρυγμα, asso-ciated with κῆρυξ (messenger) in **45** below, C translates "testimony" in EICHHORN *Neue Testament* COPY A **1**.

Idea which there is no sure grounds for supposing to have *originated* in Revelation but which we have strong grounds to believe imported by the returning Captives from Persia, an idea which[a] almost be described as oscillating between a dogma and a mythos.[2] I object I say to the expediency of protruding this into the foreground of the argument, among or rather at the Head of the most solemn, certain & express articles of Faith & facts of revealed history. Of those who *think* at all, there is probably no man who is in the habit of thinking half as freely as the author of the present Annotations, that goes equally far ⟨in the disposition⟩ to vindicate the *objective* existence of the Devil, or that attaches so much importance to the primordial *Fall* (ἀπόστασις) of the Spirits.[3] My whole system of Divinity is distributed into στάσις, ἀπόστασις, μέταστασις & ἀναστάσις.[4] But still I would not make a hypothesis however rational *co-ordinate* with the firm foundations & *corner-stones* of the Faith revealed.   S. T. C.[b]

Were my sense of the importance equal to my sense of its certainty to my *doubtless* conviction of the truth, there would be no position on the truth of which I would more readily stake my life & reputation, than on the Satan in the Prologos of Job, being no evil personage at all (& this is the primary sense of the Hebrew Satan & doubtless its sense in this not improbably *most* ancient book extant) Circuitor or Minister of Police and public Accuser (combine the French Minister of Police & our Attorney General in one Functionary) the Repeating angel. He acts throughout strictly *in character*. He no where calumniates Job, in no point exceeds his King's express commission; but only (as the Dramatic propriety demanded) replies to the King's question in the appropriate & very far from unreasonable answer. In all my rounds of Inspection I have detected nothing amiss in Job, but yet I dare not assert the positive integrity of his principles, or his inward righteousness, since hitherto he has been beyond all men preserved from Temptation. This may not be as amiable as the reply which the Sacred Dramatist would have given to the excusing or guardian Angel, but as surely it is neither malignant nor

---

[a] After this word a verb is missing: "may", "can", "might"?
[b] (b) gives initials, (a) gives them in parentheses

27[2] Cf **80** below, "Nor do I remember any allusion to such a Belief, as a Fall of Rebel Angels . . . till after the return from the Captivity . . .".

27[3] Concerning C's interest in the sense in which the Devil and fallen spirits could be said to exist see KANT *Religion* **1** n 4.

27[4] *Stasis, apostasis, metastasis,* and *anastasis,* lit "state" or condition, "fall from state", "change of state", "raising of state". These terms appear in a philosophical context in *CN* III 4449, but here they suggest a religious progression: innocence, fall, conversion, resurrection.

slanderous. He performs his part & *exit*. Then come poor Job's devils, viz. his Wife & his kind friends & comforters. It absolutely bewilders me to explain to myself how a man of Irvings Genius & Free spirit can possibly immolate so evidently true & genuine an interpretation to the Idol of Rabbinical fabling.[5] Warburton too received without thinking about it the same fancy. But he saw clearly that *then* the Book could not have been written before the Captivity, & was thus led to the *monstrous* figment of its having Ezra for its author!![6]

28   ı cxciv | End of the translator's Preliminary Discourse

O my God and King! my Head, the Head of thy Church, the Head of the worshipping universe! unto whom, with the Father and blessed Spirit, be honour and glory for ever and ever. Amen.

Conclusion. O Almighty God, Absolute Good! Eternal I am! Ground of my Being, Author of my existence, & its ultimate End! Mercifully cleanse my Heart enlighten my Understanding & strengthen my Will, that if it be needful or furtherant to the preparation of my soul & of thy Church for the Advent of thy Kingdom, that I should be led into the right belief respecting the Second Coming of the son of Man into the World, the Eye of my mind may be quickened into quietness & singleness of Sight.

29   ı 35 | Pt 1 ch 1 sec 1

This which I read with my eyes, I said, taking into my hand the holy Bible, is certain, and of faith divine. GOD himself is he who speaketh herein. That which I read in other books, be they what they may, is neither of faith, nor can be. Because, verily, in them speaketh man, not God. Because, verily, some say to me one thing and some another. Why, in fine? Because, verily, they tell me things very wide, very foreign, and sometimes very adverse from that which is clearly and expressly told me in the holy Bible. Finding then between God and man, between God who speaks, and man who interprets, a great difference and even contradiction, to which of the two should I give credit? To man, and cease from God: or to God, and cease from man?

27[5] C's interpretation of Job 1–2 here is repeated in GREW **25** and in *TT* 29 May 1830. Irving describes Satan as "stand[ing] up before God" against us, as he did "against patient Job" (clxxvi).

27[6] In his exposition of Job in *The Divine Legation of Moses* (1741), William Warburton concludes (ıı 541) that the author "could scarce be any other than the great EZRA himself, who was a *ready Scribe in the law of* MOSES, and had *prepared his Heart to seek the Law of the Lord, and to do it, and to teach in* Israel *Statutes and Judgments*". C dismisses this "*monstrous* figment" again in *TT* 29 May 1830.

Language of this sort has been repeated by one good man after another so long that there must be one would think something in it. And yet what sad trifling it does seem *to me* to be! After all the *interpretation* of the Scripture is that which passes into the mind, & is the proximate immediate object of our apprehension & consequently of our belief. But when we *read* an interpretation given by another, say Lightfoot, Hammond, or Cocceius under the name of a Comment we exclaim with J. J. Ben Ezra alias Emanuel Lacunza, this is but a man that speaketh.[1] But when we take our own[a] interpretation silently & without any visual or individual separation of the words from the Scriptures, words before our eyes.—O then it *is* Scripture itself, the very utterance of the Holy Spirit; & it is God who speaketh, tho' it is only Tim Titling in the one case & Jack Robinson in the other—in the one all *my* eye,[2] in the other it is another man's eyes & we prefer the former to the latter & find an excuse for it perhaps in the very circumstance that they had a learned Spectacles between them & the printed text. Tis I says the fly with my little eye that *rightly* do spy![3]—What then is the criterion? I know but one way, first to determine the true character and purpose of the Sacred Scriptures collectively, & then to draw up a code of canons of Interpretation *a priori* as abstracted from our reading-experience collectively & established[b] each canon by its evident reasonableness & applying these with due consideration of the distinctive character of the Sacred Book which is to be interpreted to abide by the result. To conclude, It does not become me to use the minatory language, in which my reverend[c] Friend, as an ordained Minister of Christ, warns his degenerate fellow servants, but I will dare make known the impression on my mind, that the Wounds (If I may thus express my friends sense of the dissent of his hearers from *his* view of the personal coming of the Son of Man) will not granulate healthily or be closed smoothly, till he has sloughed his diableries, & other like dead proud flesh of the popular Mumpsimus from the living texture of his Theology.[4] In plain English—all parts of his belief must

[a] There is a hole in the paper in (*a*); the word is supplied from (*b*)

[b] There may be a preposition missing here: "in", "for"?

[c] (*b*) reads "revered"

29[1] C annotated copies of the works of both Johannes Cocceius (1603–69) and John Lightfoot (1602–75): the Cocceius has not been located; Lightfoot is pub below. The name of Henry Hammond (1605–60) appears in conjunction with the names of Baxter, Milton, and Jeremy Taylor, in spite of doctrinal differences, in Baxter *Reliquiae* copy B 1 n 2.

29[2] All "my eye and Betty Martin", i.e. nonsense—a phrase C used punningly ("my I") in *BL* ch 9 (*CC*) I 159*. Cf Meckel 1 and n 3.

29[3] A variant on *Cock Robin*: " 'Who saw him die?' 'I', said the Fly, 'with my little eye, I saw him die.' "

29[4] An elaborate medical metaphor: the body of Irving's theology will not heal and

be homogeneous, either the very[a] letter throughout, in the principle of plenary *dictation* of[a] an Infallible informer—or the letter every where subordinate to the *Spirit*, i.e. to the known general purpose of the Writer, with distinction of manifest argumenta ad hominem;[5] of sentences *in ordine*[6] from those that contain the writers final object &c. the Supernatural light shining thro' the Human flesh-panes, but not removing the waving lines or even every tiny speck, knot, or bulb of temporary & individual[b]

30 I 40 | Sec 2

The real presence of Christ in the Eucharist, I add, counts years of possession, even for as long as the church hath been invested by Christ himself; for it is clear from constant and universal tradition, and likewise from all ecclesiastical history, that the church has always believed, taught, and practised it, as a thing received from the Apostles, and found written in the scriptures themselves.

It is interesting to observe, how quietly the good Jesuit passes over the actual contra-distinguishing tenet of his Church viz the Transsubstantiation to take his stand on a doctrine which Berengarius & after him the Reformers with the single exception of Zuinglius maintained as zealously as himself![1] But thank God! in holding with a firm gripe the doctrine of the Real Presence they did not forget that our Saviour had warned them that *his* words on this Subject were *Spirit* & that in all things the Spiritual is the only *reality*.[2] To say that the *real* flesh & blood

---

[a] Hole in the paper in (*a*); reading supplied from (*b*)
[b] Annotation ends thus in both copies

---

be healthy until he has cast off belief in devils and other bits of wilful ignorance. C uses "mumpsimus" (stubborn resistance to reform) elsewhere, e.g. in KANT *Logik* **2**.

29[5] Arguments improperly directed towards a particular person or persons rather than towards general truths.

29[6] "In [due] order".

30[1] Berengar of Tours (999–1088) challenged the doctrine of transubstantiation, was excommunicated, and recanted, although the sincerity of his recantation has always been doubted, and C's *Lines Suggested by the Last Words of Berengarius* in *PW* (EHC) I 460–1 assumes that he was un-

der compulsion. Ulrich Zwingli (1484–1531) departed more radically from orthodoxy by interpreting the Eucharist as purely symbolic.

30[2] The general doctrine of the "Real Presence" holds that the body and blood of Christ are actually present in the sacrament. C refers to John 6.32–65, Christ's teaching that he himself is "the bread of life" and that "Whoso eateth my flesh, and drinketh my blood, hath eternal life", and particularly 6.63: "It is the spirit that quickeneth; the flesh profiteth nothing: the words that I speak unto you, *they* are spirit, and *they* are life."

of Christ is taken in the Eucharist is to contradict the presence of the phenomenal—i.e. the F. & B. of the senses whose Esse is necessarily = Percipi.[3]

31 I 42

These truths, the church hath faithfully and constantly preserved from the beginning, always believed them, taught them, publicly and universally practiced them, in all parts, and at all times, without interruption, and without any substantial alteration. Of which these are the five principal: 1. The Apostles' creed. 2. The seven Sacraments. 3. The Hierarchy. 4. The perpetual virginity of the most Holy Mother of Messiah. 5. The scripture itself, as we now possess it, without more variety than is indispensable in the versions from one tongue to another.

An untricking[a] Jesuit would have been a miracle. Thus the 7 Sacraments. What as Sacraments in the very same sense of the term, sacrament as the first Christians applied to Baptism & the Lord's Supper?[1] The importance attached to the 4th Article is very amusing   [b] how cleverly Lacunza must have managed to put aside his tenet affirm[c] our obligation to interpret the words of Scripture literally—Christ's mother came to him & his *Brothers*.[2] Was there no such term as Son in Law among the Jews? Is there a hint given of any Children of Joseph by a different Mother? The [d]3rd Art. is a monstrous Falsehood, if the whole church be meant. See Eusebius.[e3]

32 I 43 | Sec 3

All the errors which are attributed to Origen . . . are certainly to be attributed to no other principle than this; That he inclined his understand-

---

[a] (*a*) reads "untriking", (*b*) has changed "unthinking" to "untricking"

[b] Both transcripts leave a space as for a missing or unintelligible word

[c] For "and affirm" or "to affirm"?

[d] In (*a*) the number looks most like a 3, but the letters are certainly not "rd" but "th"; (*b*) has "3rd"

[e] This is the last annotation in Vol I recorded in (*b*)

30[3] "To be (being) is the same as to be perceived". "F. & B." is "flesh and blood".

31[1] The Church of England distinguishes Baptism and the Eucharist as "two Sacraments ordained of Christ our Lord in the Gospel" from the five lesser sacraments of Confirmation, Penance, Orders, Matrimony, and Extreme Unction.

31[2] Luke 8.19, "Then came to him his mother and his brethren . . .". This and other NT passages referring to the brothers

and sisters of Christ have been variously interpreted, and C's solutions are traditional.

31[3] Eusebius *Ecclesiastical History* bks 2–6 gives lists of the numerous bishops of Rome, Alexandria, and Jerusalem, and describes the quarrels over succession in the various sees and the disputes for leadership among the various centres of authority in the early Church. C's edition has not been identified.

ing, not indeed to that which the scripture says, but to something else very remote, which it saith not; so that every word must have another occult sense . . . and the scripture became in his hands nothing better than a book of enigmas.

For which he alleged that text of St. Paul, *For the letter killeth, but the spirit maketh alive*, 2 Cor. iii. 6. . . . Proceeding upon a principle so false as was this, drawn from his understanding of *the letter killeth*— what wonder that he erred? The wonder would have been if he had not erred.

This is absolutely wonderful! Was it possible to find a passage so decisively disproving Lacunza's *literal Scheme*?[a]

33 1 67 (*LR*) | Ch 5 art 2 sec 2

Eusebius and St. Epiphanius (Euseb. lib. 3. hist. et St. Epiph. haeresi. 28.) name Cerinthus as the inventor of many corruptions. That heresiarch being given up to the belly and the palate, placed therein the happiness of man. And so taught his disciples, that after the resurrection, before ascending to heaven, there should be a thousand years of rest, during which, to all who had deserved it, the hundred-fold mentioned in the gospel, should be rendered. . . . And what appeared most important, each would be master of an entire scraglio, like a Sultan . . .

I find very great difficulty in crediting these black charges on Cerinthus, and know not how to reconcile them with the fact that the Apocalypse itself was by many attributed to Cerinthus.[1] But Mr. Hunt is not more famous for blacking than some of the Fathers.[2]

34 1 73–4 (*LR*) | Sec 4

. . . read St. Jerome upon Isaiah, who, speaking of Dionysius, thus expresses himself: "Against whom a very eloquent man, Dionysius Alexandrinus, a father of the church, wrote an elegant work, to ridicule the Millenarian fable, the golden and gemmed Jerusalem on the earth, the renewal of the temple, the blood of victims, the rest of the sabbath, the cruel rite of circumcision . . . slaughter of the vanquished, with the death of the sinner a hundred years old."

If the book of St. Dionysius had contained nothing but the derision

---

[a] This is the last annotation recorded in (*a*)

33[1] The sect of the Alogi (c 170) ascribed authorship both of John and of Rev to Cerinthus (fl c 100).

33[2] Henry "Orator" Hunt (1773–1835), a great demagogue of C's day, spent the last years of his life quietly attending to his business of manufacturing shoe-blacking.

and confutation of all we have just read, it is certain that he doth in no way concern himself with the harmless Millenarians, but with the Jews or judaizers.

Lacunza, I suspect, was ignorant of Greek: and seems not to have known that the object of Dionysius was to demonstrate that the Apocalypse was neither authentic nor a canonical book.[1]

35   ɪ 85 (*LR*) | Art 3 sec 3

The ruin of Antichrist, with all that is comprehended under that name, being entirely consummated, and the King of kings remaining master of the field, St. John immediately continues, in the xxth chapter, which thus commenceth:—*And I saw an angel come down from heaven. . . . And when a thousand years are expired, Satan shall be loosed out of his prison.*

It is only necessary to know that the whole book from the first verse to the last is written in symbols, to be satisfied that the true meaning of this passage is simply, that only the great Confessors and Martyrs will be had in remembrance and honour in the Church after the establishment of Christianity throughout the Roman Empire.[1] And observe, it is the souls that the Seer beholds:—there is not a word of the resurrection of the body;—for this would indeed have been the appropriate symbol of a resurrection in a real and personal sense.

36   ɪ 108 (*LR*)[a] | Ch 6 sec 7

Now this very thing St. John likewise declareth . . . to wit, "that they who have been beheaded for the testimony of Jesus, and for the word of God, and they who have not worshipped the beast," &c. these shall live, or be raised at the coming of the Lord, which is the first resurrection: that they shall be blessed and holy who have part in the first resurrection; that the rest of the dead are not raised then, but after a long time, signified by the name of a thousand years . . .

Aye! but by what authority is this synonimizing "or" asserted? The Seer not only does not speak of any resurrection, but by the word ψυχας,

---

[a] *LR* italicises quotations from the Bible in the textus

34[1] Dionysius the Great (d c 264), whose work is known mostly from quotations in Eusebius and Athanasius, demonstrated that John and Rev were not written by the same author and so questioned the authenticity and canonicity of Rev: Eusebius 7.24, 25. In Nov 1827 C commented on Dionysius in FLEURY **53–56**.

35[1] This interpretation is given more expansive treatment in **36**.

souls, expressly asserts the contrary.[1] In no sense of the word can souls, which descended in Christ's train (*chorus sacer animarum et Christi comitatus*) from Heaven, be said *resurgere*.[2] Resurrection is always and exclusively resurrection in the body;—not indeed a rising of the *corpus* φανταστικόν,[3] that is, the few ounces of carbon, nitrogen, oxygen, hydrogen, and phosphate of lime, the *copula* of which that gave the form no longer exists,—and of which Paul exclaims;—*Thou fool! not this*, &c.—but the corpus ὑποστατικὸν, ἢ νουμενον.[4]

But there is yet another and worse wresting of the text. Who that reads Lacunza, p. 108, last line but twelve,[5] would not understand that the Apocalypt had asserted this enthronement of the souls of the Gentile and Judæo-Christian Martyrs which he beheld in the train or suite of the descending Messiah; and that he had first seen them in the descent, and afterward saw thrones assigned to them? Whereas the sentence precedes, and has positively no connection with these souls. The literal interpretation of the symbols c. xx. v. 4, is, "I then beheld the Christian religion the established religion of the state throughout the Roman empire;—emperors, kings, magistrates, and the like, all Christians, and administering laws in the name of Christ, that is, receiving the Scriptures as the supreme and paramount law. Then in all the temples the name of Jesus was invoked as the King of glory, and together with him the old afflicted and tormented fellow-laborers with Christ were revived in high and reverential commemoration," &c. But that the whole Vision from first to last, in every sentence, yea, every word, is symbolical, and in the boldest, largest style of symbolic language; and secondly, that it is a work of disputed canonicity, and at no known period of the Church

---

36[1] Lacunza has omitted this word ("souls") in eliding his quotation of Rev 20.4: "and I saw the souls of them that were beheaded . . .".

36[2] *"The holy multitude of souls and Christ's company . . . to rise"*.

36[3] The "fantasy-body"—φανταστικόν (imagined) from φαντάζω rather than "phaenomenal" (apparent) from φαίνομαι (as in **19** above).

36[4] The body "substantial, or spiritual". C frequently invokes, as here and IRVING *Sermons* **29**, the distinction in 1 Cor 15 between the celestial and terrestrial body, or the natural and spiritual body.

36[5] At this point Lacunza quotes Rev 20.4; since C quarrels with Lacunza's quoting out of context, it is worth giving several sentences: "I suppose that you have the whole of the xxth chapter of the Apocalypse before you, and that you will actually consider it with more attention. Among other things, you will find in it this very remark, which of its own accord starts out before our eyes: That those beheaded for the testimony of Christ and the word of God, and who have not worshipped the beast, &c. not only rise at the coming of Christ, but that they reign with him a thousand years. *And they lived and reigned with Christ a thousand years.* This evidently supposes, that this same Christ will reign throughout the whole of that space of time, during which there shall be visible thrones, and certain ones sitting on them with the office and dignity of judges. *And I saw thrones, and they sat upon them, and judgment was given to them.*"

could truly lay claim to catholicity;—but for this, I think this verse would be worth a cartload of the texts which the Romanist divines and catechists ordinarily cite as sanctioning the invocation of Saints.

37 ɪ 110 (*LR*) | Sec 8

You will say nevertheless, that even the wicked will be raised incorruptible to inherit incorruption, because being once raised, their bodies will no more change or be dissolved, but must continue entire, for ever united with their sad and miserable souls. Well, and would you call this incorruption or incorruptibility. Certainly this is not the sense of the apostle, when he formally assures us, yea even threatens us, that corruption cannot inherit incorruption. *Neither doth corruption inherit incorruption.* What then may this singular expression mean? This is what it manifestly means. That no person, whoever he may be, without any exception, who possesseth a corrupt heart and corrupt actions, and therein persevereth unto death, shall have reason to expect in the resurrection, a pure, subtile, active, and impassible body.

This is actually dangerous tampering with the written letter.

Without touching on the question whether St. Paul in this celebrated chapter (1 *Cor*. xv.) speaks of a partial or of the general resurrection, or even conceding to Lacunza that the former opinion is the more probable; I must still vehemently object to this Jesuitical interpretation of corruption, as used in a moral sense, and distinctive of the wicked souls. St. Paul nowhere speaks dogmatically or preceptively (not popularly and incidentally,) of a soul as the proper *I*. It is always *we*, or the man.[1] How could a regenerate saint put off corruption at the sound of the trump, if up to that hour it did not in some sense or other appertain to him? But what need of many words? It flashes on every reader whose imagination supplies an unpreoccupied, unrefracting, *medium* to the Apostolic assertion, that corruption in this passage is a descriptive synonyme of the material sensuous organism common to saint and sinner,—standing in precisely the same relation to the man that the testaceous offensive and defensive armour does to the crab and tortoise. These slightly combined and easily decomponible stuffs are as incapable of subsisting under the altered conditions of the earth as an hydatid in the blaze of a tropical sun. They would be no longer *media* of communion between the man and his circumstances.

A heavy difficulty presses, as it appears to me, on Lacunza's system, as soon as we come to consider the general resurrection. Our Lord (in

37[1] E.g. ("we") 1 Cor 15.19, 59, 51, 52, 57; ("man") 15.23, 45, 47.

books of indubitable and never doubted catholicity) speaks of some who rise to bliss and glory, others who at the same time rise to shame and condemnation. Now if the former class live not during the whole interval from their death to the general resurrection, including the Millennium, or *Dies Messiæ*,[2]—how should they, whose imperfect or insufficient merits excluded them from the kingdom of the Messiah on earth, be all at once fitted for the kingdom of heaven?

38   I   118 *(LR)* | Ch 7 sec 3

It appears to me that this sentence, being looked to attentively, means in good language this only, that the word quick, which the Apostles, full of the Holy Spirit set down, is a word altogether useless, which might without loss have been omitted, and that it were enough to have set down the word *dead*: for by that word alone is the whole expressed, and with much more clearness and brevity.

The narrow outline within which the Jesuits confined the theological reading of their *alumni* is strongly marked in this (in so many respects) excellent work: for example, the "most believing mind,"[1] with which Lacunza takes for granted the exploded fable of the Catechumens' (*vulgo* Apostles') Creed having been the quotient of an Apostolic *picnic*, to which each of the twelve contributed his several *symbolum*.[2]

39   I   127 *(LR)* | Ch 9

The Apostle, St. Peter, speaking of the day of the Lord (2 Pet. iii. 10.) says, that that day will come suddenly, and adds, that in it there shall be a deluge of fire so great and devouring, that the elements themselves shall dissolve, and the earth and all the works which are upon the face of it shall be burned up and consumed.

There are serious difficulties besetting the authenticity of the Catholic Epistles under the name of Peter; though there exist no grounds for doubting that they are of the Apostolic age.[1] A large portion too of the difficulties would be removed by the easy and nowise improbable sup-

37[2] The "Day of Messiah", the Second Coming, as in BUTLER *Vindication* 1 and several notes below: **39, 59, 74, 89**. In Jul 1827 C annotated RHENFERD, which contains an article on this phrase, treating it as an erroneous translation of the Greek in 2 Pet 3.8–10: ". . . one day is with the Lord as a thousand years. . . . the day of the Lord will come like a thief in the night . . .".

38[1] C is quoting his own *Frost at Midnight* line 24: *PW* (EHC) I 241.
38[2] LUTHER *Colloquia* **23** suggests sources of C's knowledge of the history of the Apostles' Creed, and *Colloquia* **90** refers specifically to the tradition of the *symbolum*. In BAXTER *Catholick Theologie* **9** C reiterates his view of the Creed as intended for candidates for baptism (catechumens).
39[1] For C's view that 1 Pet was written

position, that Peter, no great scholar or grammarian, had dictated the substance, the matter, and left the diction and style to his *amanuensis*, who had been an auditor of St. Paul. The tradition which connects, not only Mark, but Luke the Evangelist, the friend and biographer of Paul, with Peter, as a secretary, is in favour of this hypothesis. But what is of much greater importance, especially for the point in discussion, is the character of these and other similar descriptions of the *Dies Messiæ*, the *Dies ultima*,[2] and the like. Are we bound to receive them as articles of faith? Is there sufficient reason to assert them to have been direct revelations immediately vouchsafed to the sacred writers? I cannot satisfy my judgment that there is;—first, because I find no account of any such events having been revealed to the Patriarchs, or to Moses, or to the Prophets; and because I do find these events asserted, and (for aught I have been able to discover,) for the first time, in the Jewish Church by uninspired Rabbis, in nearly or altogether the same words as those of the Apostles, and know that before and in the Apostolic age, these anticipations had become popular, and generally received notions; and lastly, because they were borrowed by the Jews from the Greek philosophy, and like several other notions, taken from less respectable quarters, adapted to their ancient and national religious belief. Now I know of no revealed truth that did not originate in Revelation, and find it hard to reconcile my mind to the belief that any Christian truth, any essential article of faith, should have been first made known by the father of lies,[3] or the guess-work of the human understanding blinded by Paganism, or at best without the knowledge of the true God. Of course I would not apply this to any assertion of any New Testament writer, which was the final aim and primary intention of the whole passage; but only to sentences *in ordine ad* some other doctrine or precept, *illustrandi causa*, or *ad hominem*, or *more suasorio sive ad ornaturam, et rhetorice*.[4]

---

by "some one of his [Peter's] Scholars" after his death see EICHHORN *Neue Testament* COPY B **32**. 1 and 2 Pet, with Jas, 1 John, and Jude, called "general" epistles in AV because unlike Paul's epistles they are not addressed to a particular person or church, were also called "catholic" because of their universal application and probably also to endorse them as canonical. Authorship and date of all are still in question, but the view of the early Church—of Origen, Irenaeus, Clement of Alexandria—that Jas, 1 Pet, 1 John, and Jude come from the apostolic period is generally accepted.

39[2] The "Day of Messiah", the "last Day", as **37** n 2 above.

39[3] The Devil, as in John 8.44.

39[4] Terms from logic and rhetoric: "in order towards" some doctrine; "for the purpose of illustration"; "directed towards the interest of the listener"; "in a persuasive manner, or for embellishment, and rhetorically".

40   ɪ 145 (*LR*) | Pt 2 phenomenon 1 sec 6

Third characteristic. *The kingdom shall be partly strong, and partly brittle.* This was verified, according to some, when the Roman empire was divided into the eastern and western empires: according to others . . . in the time of the civil wars between Marius and Sylla, between Caesar and Pompey, between Augustus and Antony; when the Roman empire was a divided kingdom.

Fourth characteristic. *They shall mingle themselves with the seed of men: but they shall not cleave one to another.* This was verified, according to some of them, when Caesar and Pompey were reconciled and made friends; and that the friendship might last, Pompey gave Caesar his daughter in marriage. The same thing afterwards did Augustus by Antony; and notwithstanding these unions, division and discord went on.

How exactly do these characters apply to the Greek Empire under the successors of Alexander,—when the Greeks were dispersed over the civilized world, as artists, rhetoricians, *grammatici*, secretaries, private tutors, parasites, physicians, and the like!

41   ɪ 153 (*LR*) | Sec 8

For to them [the servants of Christ] he thus speaketh in the gospel: ''And then shall they see the Son of man coming in a cloud with power and great glory. And when these things begin to come to pass, then look up, and lift up your heads; for your redemption draweth nigh.'' Luke xxi. 27, 28.

I cannot deny that there is great force and an imposing verisimilitude in this and the preceding chapter, and much that demands silent thought and respectful attention. But still the great question presses on me:— *coming in a cloud!* What is the true import of this phrase? Has not God himself expounded it? To the Son of Man, the great Apostle assures us, all power is given in heaven and on earth.[1] He became Providence,— that is, a Divine Power behind the cloudy veil of human agency and worldly events and incidents, controlling, disposing, and directing acts and events to the gradual unfolding and final consummation of the great scheme of Redemption; the casting forth of the evil and alien nature from man, and thus effecting the union of the creature with the Creator, of man with God, in and through the Son of Man, even the Son of God

---

41[1]   Matt 24—referred to below—esp 24.30.

made manifest. Now[a] can it be doubted by the attentive and unprejudiced reader of St. Matthew, c. xxiv, that the Son of Man, in fact, came in the utter destruction and devastation of the Jewish Temple and State, during the period from Vespasian to Hadrian, both included;[2] and is it a sufficient reason for our rejecting the teaching of Christ himself, of Christ glorified and in his kingly character, that his Apostles, who disclaim all certain knowledge of the awful event, had understood his words otherwise, and in a sense more commensurate with their previous notions and the prejudices of their education? They communicated their conjectures, but as conjectures, and these too guarded by the avowal, that they had no revelation, no revealed commentary on their Master's words, upon this occasion, the great apocalypse of Jesus Christ while yet in the flesh. For by this title was this great prophecy known among the Christians of the Apostolic age.[3]

42   I 253 (*LR*) | Phenomenon 3 sec 14

[Of the Woman seated on the Beast (Rev 17), here interpreted as symbolising the Rome of the future.] Never, oh! our Lady! never, oh! our Mother! shalt thou fall again into the crime of idolatry. That certainly is not the fornication here announced of thee. Thy faith shall not fail . . .

Was ever blindness like unto this blindness? I can imagine but one way of making it seem possible, namely, that this round square or rectilineal curve—this honest Jesuit, I mean—had confined his conception of idolatry to the worship of false gods;—whereas his saints are genuine godlings, and his *Magna Mater*[1] a goddess in her own right;—and that thus he overlooked the meaning of the word.

43   I 254 (*LR*) | Sec 15

The entire text of the apostle is as follows:—"Now we beseech you, brethren, by the coming of our Lord Jesus Christ, and by our gathering together unto him, that ye be not soon shaken in mind, or be troubled, neither by spirit, nor by word, nor by letter as from us, as that the day of Christ is at hand. . . ." [2 Thess 2.1–10]

---

[a] Thus in *LR*, but perhaps "nor" in ms

41[2] Vespasian (ruled 70–9) was responsible for the destruction of the Temple A.D. 70; Hadrian (ruled 117–38), by building a shrine to Jupiter on the site of the Temple and by systematic suppression of Jewish religious practices, precipitated revolts by the Jews 132–5 A.D.

41[3] The theory outlined in **7** (n 1) above.

42[1] "Great Mother", a name applied in classical mythology to the earth-goddess Cybele, and here by C to Lacunza's Rome.

O Edward Irving! Edward Irving! by what fascination could your spirit be drawn away from passages like this, to guess and dream over the rhapsodies of the Apocalypse? For rhapsody, according to your interpretation, the Poem undeniably is;—though, rightly expounded, it is a well knit and highly poetical evolution of a part of this and our Lord's more comprehensive prediction, *Luke* xvii.[1]

44 i 297 (*LR*) | Phenomenon 5

On the ordinary ideas of the coming of Christ in glory and majesty, it will doubtless appear an extravagance to name the Jews, or to take them into consideration; for, according to these ideas, they should hardly have the least particle of our attention.

In comparing this with the preceding chapter I could not help exclaiming: What an excellent book would this Jesuit have written, if Daniel and the Apocalypse had not existed, or had been unknown to, or rejected by, him![1]

You may divide Lacunza's points of belief into two parallel columns;—the first would be found to contain much that is demanded by, much that is consonant to, and nothing that is not compatible with, reason, the harmony of Holy Writ, and the idea of Christian faith. The second would consist of puerilities and anilities, some impossible, most incredible; and all so silly, so sensual, as to befit a dreaming Talmudist, not a Scriptural Christian. And this latter column would be found grounded on Daniel and the Apocalypse!

45 ii ⁻3–⁻2

The Prothesis or Identity is $1 = 2$, ~~and~~ both at once, & in the same Relation. Sum: the co-inherence of Being and Act, the Noun-Verb, or Verb Substantive.

The Indifference is *either* Thesis or Antithesis; or both at the same time but not in the same relation. Ex. Infinitive Mood. ⟨*Immergere* Heroem in lacu non poterat servare eum a morte.[1] Here Immergere is a Noun to the verb poterat, but a Verb to the Noun Heroem.⟩[a]

[a] This afterthought is squeezed into the space left by the setting out of the "Prothesis" diagram

43[1] I.e. Luke 17.24–37.

44[1] C's note is written clearly against the textus cited, but it makes a general point about Lacunza's argument, and may refer especially to the fact that while "Phenomenon 3" (i 177–266) was concerned with Antichrist, "Phenomenon 4", ending

i 297, is an account of the battle of St Michael and the Dragon based on Rev 12.7–9.

45[1] "*To dip* the Hero in the lake could not save him from death"—as in IRVING *Sermons* 2 and n 2.

1 Prothesis
THE WORD

	4	3
2 Thesis	Indifference	Antithesis
The Written Word	Spirit	Church

5
Synthesis
The Preacher.[2]

The Synthesis or Composition, the Compound of Thesis & Antithesis, defines itself. Ex. The Participle.

1. ~~Ad~~ Noun-Verb. 2. Noun. 3. Verb. 4. Infinitive Mood. 5. Participle—These are the 5 essential Parts of Speech, found in all languages. The non-essential are the modification of 2 by 3 = Adnoun, and the Mod. of 3 × 2 = Adverb.

Thus in both lines, the Vertical and the Horizontal, the Spirit is the Copula or Medium of Union.

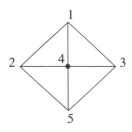

Vertical.		Horizontal
1, 4, 5.		2, 4, 3
1 Eternal Word		2. Wr. word
4 Spirit		4 The Spirit
5 Preacher		3 Church.

[a]⟨P.S. Preacher is not a happy name for κηρυξ. Herald, Ambassador, even Messenger, would be more expressive of the function, character, and authority by Delegation.[3] The Eternal Word thro' and by the Spirit

---

[a] The postscript is written partly in the space left around the diagram, and partly over it

45[2] Cf the simpler pentad of **1** above, and n 1.

45[3] C refers to term 5 above. The primary sense of κήρυξ is "herald"; it is

may fit the Individual to be a Teacher, a Discourser; but without supplying the place of the Church by miracles, or that the place of the written word by miraculous inspiration, he cannot be a Herald, an Ambassador/.—⟩

*On the opposite page the philosophic Pentad, or 5 essential forms of Noetic (or ideal Logic) applied to the Gospel Economy. N.B. Thesis and Antithesis mutually demand each the other. Neither can be suppressed without excluding the Indifference or common term of Both. In Romanism & modern Protestantism the Spirit has been quenched, the one hiding the Scriptures, the other acknowleging no Church.

46 II ⁻2–⁻1

I would not give a groat for a man, whose Heart does not sometimes betray his Judgement. The honest delight of finding a cöincidence of Sentiment on a subject of grave concern to all and of keenest interest to himself, in a quarter where it was least expected—this delight, characteristic of noble minds, whose passionate Love of Truth ~~precludes~~ soars above all petty pride of original discovery, prevented ~~the~~ my fervent Friend from *feeling* and a fortiori from seeing the prolixity και φυλλομανιαν¹ of the worthy Jesuit. While embracing a powerful Co-adjutor where he might ~~more with~~ rather have been prepared to meet the charge of a bigotted Adversary, ~~as to~~ there was no room in Mr Irving's Soul for Criticism.—Still however for the advantage of the Public it is matter of regret, that Lacunza's work had not been pruned down into a single Volume. To every fresh subject, almost to every Objection and to every Reply thereto, Lacunza has a garrulous* introductory ¶ph, not seldom a Chapter.—I hope, however, that Mr Irving will take muster of all his grounds, arguments and evidences, and reduce them to a systematic logical form—& thus supply the Religious Public with a check and circulable Synopsis of this great Pleading.   S. T. Coleridge

* Nevertheless, a sound Logician and for a Theologian a remarkably clear-headed Man.

---

a Squeezed in above **46**

---

translated as "preacher" only three times in NT, even though AV many times renders the cognate verb κηρύσσω as "preach" because to preach was to proclaim or herald the Gospel.

46¹ Prolixity "and running [wildly] to

leaf". The Greek noun *phyllomania* (lit "leaf-madness") appears in English as early as 1670 as a botanical term for the condition of a plant producing excessive leafage without seed or fruit.

47 ɪɪ ⁻1 and half-title

Surely, it ought to supply a presumption in favor of *my* view and Interpretation of the Apocalypse in my Friend's Mind, that Lacunza ~~ignorant of~~ not aware of any such scheme, and with so keen a disposition to discover particular predictions, and prognostics in the Book that he might have ~~read~~ pored on the contents for half a century without ⟨its⟩ once crossing his Brain even as ⟨a⟩ stray thought, should yet have found himself compelled to take the *negative* side of my theory—viz. that it is impossible ~~by~~ on my sound principles of interpretation to force the words, either allegorically, symbolically or literally, into any tolerable Shew of coincidence with any of the Events or Characters to which they have been applied by Divines from Augustine to his own time—/

In short, the longer I think and the more I reflect on the subject, the more scriptural does the Belief of Christ's reign on the Earth appear to me—and I cannot help auguring, that the millenarian tenet stripped of all its rabbinical figments will not be overthrown, if it ever be overthrown, without an earthquake Shaking of ~~the~~ sundry other now universally received opinions respecting the 1ˢᵗ Century of the Xtⁿ Church, and a strange revolution in the minds of the educated Classes as to the rank and character of the Hebrew Oracles! Nay, this doctrine blown abroad from the awakening Trumpet of my friend's eloquence & thus brought into general discussion with all its mighty Satillitium[1] of Scripture Proofs and strong Arguments from the analogy of ~~the~~ Faith (like the production of a missing Bone in a Mammoth Skeleton—proved by its fitting and filling the evident vacancy)—the forcible vindication, I say, of this Doctrine may be one of the means of accelerating that reign of Infidelity, the ~~arr~~ coming of which ~~is to~~ as the precursor of the Messiah King forms so prominent a part of the Doctrines. "When the Son of Man cometh, shall he find Faith in the Earth? I say unto you, Nay!—"[2] —But likewise the more shaken I am in my hitherto contempt & rejection of the Doctrine & the stronger I feel its attractive force drawing me towards my friend's Belief—the more lively does my conviction become, that the Apocalypse is ~~its~~ the most formidable Obstacle t in his way, and that the greatest service, that could possibly be rendered to the Millenarian Scheme, would be ~~rendered by the~~ to reduce this book to the same rank with Hermes, and Esdras[3]—tho' as a Symbolic Drama it

---

47[1] I.e. *satellitium*—"retinue, company"; but as applied figuratively to the conjunction of planets (as in the only use cited by *OED*) implying an accidental, occasional, or unstable association.

47[2] Luke 18.8 (var)—the answer being

added.

47[3] I.e. among the apocrypha. *The Shepherd of Hermas* was included in C's copy of NT Apocrypha (Bɪʙʟᴇ *NT Apocrypha*) though it is no longer counted among the canonical apocrypha. In the Ge-

must ever soar as much above them as the Eagle above the Bat and the Owl. I know indeed no Poem ancient or modern, unless it be the Paradise Lost, that can be compared with it either in the felicity of its Structure, or the sublimity of the parts.   S. T. Coleridge—

48 II half-title[a]

(Dec. 20 1827.—Since the above was written, the effect of Lacunza's Proofs has become weaker/. There is one other possible solution of the passages adduced by him—viz. that all the predictions, whether Threats or Promises, are conditional—& the Moral Conditions, tho' not always expressed, must always be understood. Shall God *force* his inestimable Gifts on Swine that prefer the Trough to the Lord's own Table? or at once by miracle make machines of righteousness out of them?)

49 II half-title verso and title-page

The Kingdom of God is within you.
Thy Kingdom come![1]

These are the Texts, on which I should ground my Belief in respect of the Coming of the Messiah in his kingly and judicial Character—or (which *I* should prefer) concerning the manifestations of the Son of Man as the SON OF GOD.[b]

Here the Identity of the S. of M. and the S. of G. is Christ. Consequently

Prothesis
———
Christ

Thesis	Indifference	Antithesis
———	———	———
Individual	Church	Genus

Synthesis
———
Kingdom

[a] Written in the middle of the page in the space left between parts of **47**
[b] Written in swash capitals

---

neva Bible and later English versions 1 and 2 Esdras were placed in OT as Ezra and Neh, 3 and 4 Esdras being renamed 1 and 2 and published with OT Apocrypha.
49[1] Luke 17.21; and Matt 6.10, Luke 11.2 (in the Lord's Prayer).

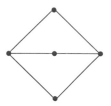

Now Christ is either behind the Cloud i.e. governs his Church as *Providence*—Or he stands in the Cloud rendered transparent or ~~rent~~ opened & repelled as a luminous Halo by the glory of his Epiphany.[2]

In like manner the Church is either visible & circumscript: or invisible and diffused.

As Christ & the Church, so the Kingdom—if they visible, it visible,—and vice versâ.

The question therefore will be—to what quantity, intensive *or* extensive, or intensive *and* extensive must *the Kingdom within*, = the Spiritual Christendom amount according to the Law of Spirit, in order to manifest it in a phænomenon or *outward*?—and whether here too Extremes do not meet,[3] and an evanescent minimum produce the same result as the maximum? (When Ch. cometh, shall he find Faith on earth?)[4]—Or, far rather both—viz. the Number of the Departed in the Faith complete, and the Unfaith of the existing World likewise at its predetermined Maximum?—

An aweful fact would it be if the same line should represent the increase and varying Quantity of real and nominal Christianity by merely reversing its position? If ▽ represented faith, largest as nearest its base—(i.e. the Apostolic Age); and ∧ the number of nominal Christians, inversely as the Faith!—

50 ɪɪ 11–12, pencil | Pt 2 phenomenon 6 sec 5

* 1. Jesus Christ founded his church in Jerusalem, and for the time being, of Jews only: but as he, according to the orders of his divine Father, had to depart immediately *into a far country, in order to receive a kingdom to himself and return* (Luke xix. 12.) he chose in his stead one of

49[2] The "cloud" is in Luke 21.27— "And then shall they see the Son of man coming in a cloud with power and great glory"—of which C said in N35 f 21 (c Oct 1827): "The most comfortable view of this & similar passages . . . is—that the whole prophecy is addressed to the Disciples as to the outward and visible *Church*—and that the Kingdom of God means the *establishment* of Christianity as the acknowleged Religion of the Empire . . .".

49[3] For this favourite aphorism of C's— "Extremes meet"—see BLANCO WHITE *Practical Evidence* **9** n 2.

49[4] Alluding to Luke 18.8, as in **47** at n 2.

the twelve apostles, St. Peter, whom he appointed his vicar upon earth, leaving with him all the keys of the house, and commending to his care, fidelity, and vigilance, the preservation, the enlargement, the instruction, and good government of the whole family, for himself and for his lawful successors till he should return.

* Were it not ascertained by the fact—(and what is actual, must be possible) it might well have been deemed little less than impossible, that a passage of Scripture containing a gentle & most delicate but nevertheless piercing expression of our Lord's knowlege of Peter's character and his *fears* concerning him in his pastoral functions should ~~have~~ be perverted, into a grand credential & writ of instauration of this Peter, as Prince of the Apostles, and the Vice-gerent of God on Earth and sole Vicar of the co-eternal Son of God!!—   S. T. C.

51 II 17–18, pencil, footnote in ink | Sec 6

"Why regard you this as marvellous? 'If the first fruit be holy the lump *mass* is also holy, and if the root be holy so also are the branches.' All those fruits having been to God so holy and acceptable, which at different times the house of Jacob hath offered to him from the whole lump better *"mass"*, to wit, the patriarchs, so many prophets and just men . . . and above all, Messiah himself; the whole house of Jacob, which is the lump mass from which all these precious fruits were taken, ought to be regarded as holy, as consecrated to God, and his inheritance . . .''

Lump is a most lumpish word.[1] But the whole ¶ph. seems to me but crazy Logic, a Simile being handled as Square[2]—i.e. as if, because the Apostle calls the Jewish Church an olive Tree, what⟨ever⟩ is true of a Tree might be asserted of the Jewish Church.*

* Besides—Lacunza has misunderstood Sᵗ Paul. Not the Jewish People but the Divine Covenant with its Consequents, the Revelations, Moral Code, Sacred Hymns, above all the interest in the Messiah, are the Olive with its Root and Fatness.[3] Mʳ Irving overlooked the lurking Popery in all this—Latet anguis in herbâ.[4] The doctrine of Works, and ~~the~~ of supererogation, is at the bottom.[5] The superabundant Righteous-

51[1] "Lump" is the AV translation of φύραμα in Rom 11.16 (as quoted in textus).
51[2] Alluding to the maxim in logic *simile non est idem*, "nothing like is the same"—or, as C himself translates it, "no likeness goes on all fours", "no simile quadrates": *Logic* (CC) 132, 143.
51[3] See Rom 11.17–24, the figure of the

wild olive tree (the Gentiles) whose broken branches can be grafted into "a good olive tree" (the Jewish Church). The figure continues through **52**.
51[4] "A snake lurks in the grass"—Virgil *Eclogues* 3.93.
51[5] The Roman doctrine of supererogation is explicitly rejected by the Articles of

ness, and Treasure of Merits, of the Patriarchs were the heir-loom of their descendants—who were born to a fortune. These merits were the fat sap, which shot forth the branches, and on which the Branches fed— and of the same accumulated surplus Merits of the Patriarchs, Prophets, and Holy Men from Abraham to John the Baptist the Gentile Grafts now partook! Need I say, how contradictory all this is to Paul's Doctrine?

52 II 19–20

Then, when the proper and natural branches of the same tree shall be wholly restored (as it is certain they shall be); when they shall be as it were inserted anew, according to nature, by the same wise, omnipotent, and beneficent hand of the God of Abraham, what fruits will it not be in their power to give, and what fruits will they not give.*

* This again is quite a gratuitous Assertion, without any ground in the Apostle's words.[1] St Paul argues from the Divine Goodness, and not from any præsumption of the spiritual superiority and fruitfulness of the Converted Jews over the Gentiles. If (reasons St Paul) so great a Blessing accrued to the World from God's repudiation of the chosen people, what may we not expect from his goodness as likely to accrue to the word[a] from their reconciliation and re-espousal to him? M[r] Irving's notion that the Gentiles in their turn will be rejected and the Jews received instead has as little foundation in Scripture as in reason and the great purposes of the Gospel Dispensation—utterly incongruous with this *Ride and Tie* Scheme—which reminds one of the Gentleman and Lady in a Dutch Weather-glass.[2]

53 II 20–1

If they are now worthy of wrath for their unbelief, for their obstinacy, and for your sakes; likewise are they worthy of mercy for the righteousness of their fathers, for the promises made to their fathers, for the merits of their fathers.

---

[a] Presumably a slip for "world"

Religion of the C of E: Art 14 asserts that "Voluntary Works besides, over and above, God's Commandments, which they call Works of Supererogation, cannot be taught without arrogancy and impiety"— citing Luke 17.10.

52[1] Rom 11.17–25, as in **51**.

52[2] *Ride and tie* is a way for two travellers to share a horse: one rides ahead and then ties up the horse for the one who has been walking, setting off again himself on foot; C alludes to it also in *Omniana* (1812) no. 89. The figures in a weather-glass similarly take turns coming out, one for fair weather and the other for rain: C uses them to suggest his own susceptibility to weather in a letter of 1803, *CL* II 976.

Was not I in the right?*ᵃ¹* Mʳ Irving was so carried away by the delight of finding his own millennary scheme in a Catholic Writer, that he could see nothing else. A few harmless tags of Romanism, ex. gr. the ~~over~~ - grandiloquence about the Virgin Mary, he admits—but not worth quarrelling with in such a Saint as Ben Ezra (i.e. the Jesuit Lacunza)— whereas in fact the very worst tenets of popery are to be found in this Work and ought to have been pointed out and their falsehood exposed.

54   ɪɪ 23 | Sec 7

[Rom 11.1–8:] "God hath not cast away his people which he foreknew. Wot ye not what the scripture saith of Elias? how he maketh intercession to God against Israel, saying, Lord, they have killed thy prophets, and digged down thine altars . . ."

The manner, in which Malachi introduces the clause respecting Elias, renders it in the highest degree probable that he referred to some prophetic work no longer extant—and from which, perhaps, some other of the notions respecting the advent of the Messia current among the Jews in our Saviour's time were taken or inferred.¹

55   ɪɪ 26 | Sec 8

* It would follow, in the second place, that as because of the incredulity of the Jews God called the Gentiles, made them to enter to his supper and occupy the place of the incredulous; (accomplishing punctually what Moses had already said, and what St. Paul observeth: "I will provoke you to jealousy by them that are no people, and by a foolish nation will I anger you." Rom. x. 19.) so, a time being arrived in which the Gentiles have ceased to believe, God shall return and call the Jews . . .

* And yet Sᵗ Paul expressly asserts, that the restoration of the Jews waits, till *the fulness* of the Gentiles comes in!¹ How indeed else could the many and magnificent Prophecies of the whole Earth serving the Lord be fulfilled.

56   ɪɪ 28–30

Let us, however, come to the examination of the promises, and we shall see that there is nothing contrary to them in that which hath been said.

ᵃ Written in the margin opposite textus and marked "I"; the note resumes in the foot-margin with the same symbol "I"

53¹ In **46**.

54¹ Mal 4.5—an utterance by the last of the prophets in the last two verses of OT— is the first direct reference to Elijah (Elias)

as the forerunner of the Messiah (cf Irving *Sermons* **28** n 7), and is carried over into Matt 11.14, 17.10–13.

55¹ Rom 11.25.

The first, "Thou art Peter, and upon this rock I will build my church; and the gates of hell shall not prevail against it." Matt. xvi. 18. The second, "But I have prayed for thee, Simon, that thy faith fail not." Luke xxii. 32. The third, "Lo, I am with you alway, even unto the end of the world." Matt. xxviii. 20.

If I were asked to select the *most* impudent pretension, that had come to my knowlege, it would be *this* of founding the whole enormous powers and prerogatives of the Bishop of Rome on the two texts, Matt. xvi. 18: and Luke 12 xxii. 32./ or (more correctly) on the unproved and improbable Tradition, ⟨by which the Texts are rendered applicable to the Papacy,⟩ of St Peter's having been Bishop of Rome, or in any special apostolic Relation to the Roman Christians. What? the whole Basis of the Faith? What? the only Gate to the Temple? What? the one and only Key to the Door of Salvation? on a Tradition, a vague, not to say contradictory, Rumor—and not one word in Scripture, not a hint from any Apostle, confirming the same, or informing Christians of so momentous a point, a point according to their Pope's own teaching, essentially, indispensably necessary to Salvation/ "Thou art Petr*os* ⟨(Rock*er* or Rockman)⟩ and upon this Petr*an* (Rock) I will build my Church"[1]—Now I should say that the "petran" (rock) referred to the Truth which Peter had just affirmed, viz. that Jesus was the Son of God.[2] But suppose Peter himself—how easy, & how necessary, to have added, "the Bishops of Rome: for they shall be thy Peter's Successors, and in them his privileges & functions shall survive"—P.S. By the bye, the text itself tends to confirm my suspicion respecting the origin of our Revision of the first of the 4 Gospels.[3] s. t. c. Cephites ✳ Paulists.[4]

---

57   II 39–42 | Sec 9

[Lacunza recounts the reviling of the Jews by fathers and doctors of the early Church, and intends a reconciliation. As "the holy doctors . . .

56[1] Matt 16.18 (var), which C intends as a gloss using—in the way of the Greek original—two forms of the word πέτρος (a masculine noun playing upon the Greek proper name Πέτρων) and πέτρα (of which C's "Petr*an*" is accusative). Πέτρος means a stone, πέτρα a rock, or mass of rock; C's distinction between Peter as "rockman" and *petra* as a massive foundation stone turns upon the masculine and feminine forms of the word.
56[2] Matt 16.16.
56[3] C's theory about the composition of the first four gospels appears e.g. in BIBLE COPY B 80, where he describes Matt as addressed "to Palestine Jews" and designed "to bring the facts [of Christ's life] into a striking reference to & connection with, the Sacred Books of the Hebrews".
56[4] "Peterites as opposed to Paulists", those who hold that Peter rather than Paul was the founder of the Church. The Greek *Petros* was considered equivalent to the Aramaic *Cephas*, as in John 1.42, "thou shalt be called Cephas, which is by interpretation, A stone".

spake, without abating of the truth, all the evil possible" of "the ancient spouse of God", the religion of the Jews, so] the most prudent fathers did not explain themselves, nor even so much as touch upon many truly delicate and critical points, regarding the consequences which must naturally follow . . .

An instructive, tho' softened and dulcified, Sketch of the Economia dispensatoria Veritatis[1] common to all the Fathers, but especially characteristic of the ~~Latin~~ Fathers and Doctors of the Latin Church from Tertullian to Augustine, from Augustine to Bellarmine, and from Bellarmine to D[r] Doyle and Charles Butler, Esq[re][2] who

> Leaves the FULL LIE on Milner's Gong to swell,
> Content with Half-truths that do just as well![3]

I wish, it had remained—this *Management* of Truth, i.e. Lying for Truth's sake—the exclusive accomplishment of the ~~Romanish~~ Rabbis! But alas! our own Bishops, and among them the brightest Stars of our Establishment, Jer. Taylor, Stillingfleet, Tillotson, present only too many proofs of their having graduated in the same School![4] In fact, it is inevitable where ever Truth is not contemplated an Absolute, and consequently as an End in itself; but as a *Means* to an *end*, i.e. to the Good—~~therefore~~ having a contingent and derivative Value but no inherent Worth. It is most true, that THE GOOD is deeper than the TRUE, ~~and~~ in order of thought antecedent, and in dignity precedent—but equally sure is it, that the True stands to the Good in filial subordination, not in servile Subjection. The two most uncommon things in the World are the Love of the Good for itself, and the Love of the True for itself: and the Latter is more uncommon than the Former. S. T. Coleridge.

57[1] "The managerial economy of Truth"—i.e. "this *Management* of Truth", below.

57[2] An anticlimactic roll-call of theologians from the great patristic writers Tertullian (c 160–c 220) and Augustine of Hippo (354–430) to the Jesuit controversialist Robert Bellarmine (1542–1621), and so to C's contemporaries James Warren Doyle (1786–1834), Roman Catholic bp of Kildare and Leighlin and champion of the Irish Catholics, and Charles Butler (1750–1832), a Roman Catholic lawyer who became engaged in controversy with RS and with Blanco White: see the General Note on Charles BUTLER in *CM (CC)* I.

57[3] *Sancti Dominici Pallium* lines 39–40, *PW (EHC)* I 450, from C. BUTLER *Book of the RC Church* 1.

57[4] Pillars of the C of E in what C regarded as its best period, the seventeenth century: Jeremy Taylor (1613–67), whose *Polemicall Discourses* (1674) is C's most copiously annotated book; Edward Stillingfleet (1635–99), whose "masterly" *Origines sacrae* C also commented on; and John Tillotson (1630–94), whom C dismisses as an Arminian in a note on Jeremy TAYLOR *Polemicall Discourses* i 739.

58   ɪɪ   42–6

The Good, the True, and the Beautiful are = the Root, the Stem, and the Flower of the Celestial Lily. But this is to be taken as only an illustration by way of similitude from the world of the Finite, or Non-absolute. In ~~the~~ propriety of Language, ~~such~~ the Absolute subsists totally in each of the Three, and the Three are *One*.

The Good = the Good, the True, and the Beautiful in the Form of the Good—i.e. the Absolute Will

The True = the True, the Good and the Beautiful in the Form of the True—i.e. the Absolute Reason (τοῦ Λόγου).[1]

The Beautiful = the Beautiful, the Good & the True in the Form of Beauty—i.e. Absolute Love.

The Idea of the Beautiful doth perhaps require a deeper Sabbath of the Mind that is to contemplate the same, than even the Idea of the True—a Jubilee Sabbath! Even in the translucency of its Reflex Images multiplied, as the Solar Disk in the Dew-drops, in the forms and motions of the Creatures we may satisfy ourselves of the affinity of Beauty with Life, with Community, with the *paraclete* functions. (Hence is the Beautiful in Greek το καλον, from καλεῖν—and with especial propriety is it το παρακαλοῦν—ο παρακλητης.[2] No less is it always πνευματικὸν τὶ, ὃ αει μενει και εκπορευεται[3]—remains yet proceedeth. Even in moveless objects, a Rose for instance, there is a circling Act subjectively excited. The Soul in beholding it περιχωρει καὶ κατακυκλοῖ ἐν ἑαυτῇ.[4] Hence the scriptural assertions of the *Beauty* of Wisdom—Wisdom, Sancta Sophia, being the distinctive name of the Holy Ghost./[5] The Father τὸ ἄγαθον; the Son, τὸ ἀληθες; the Spirit, η σοφια.[6]

59   ɪɪ   45

"The true sense seems to me to be what Theophilactus and Rupertus point out, that the kingdom of God is the name for that condition of

---

58[1] "Of the Logos": C adapts the Christian Trinity to the Platonic Triad.

58[2] In Greek "the beautiful, from 'to call' . . . 'to summon, call to one's side', the *paraclete* (AV 'Comforter')''. Originally παράκλητος in the passive sense "one *called* to another's aid", hence "advocate", the word acquired an active sense in Christian use as "helper" or "intercessor". The derivation of καλόν (beautiful) from καλεῖν (to call) has no authority.

58[3] "A spiritual thing, which ever re-

mains and proceeds".

58[4] "Goes around and circles about in herself".

58[5] "Holy Wisdom", an irregular combination of Latin adjective with Greek noun. *Sophia* (Wisdom) appears to have been applied in medieval theology to the Holy Ghost, as C says, but to have been used by the Greek Fathers of the Logos: Bɪʙʟᴇ *NT Gospels* **3** n 1.

58[6] "The Father the good; the Son, the true; the Spirit, wisdom".

things, in which God, after having put all enemies under his footstool (when he shall reign, as saith St. Paul), shall be all in all.''

Hah! if this were all, St Paul says! But Christ too resigned his power, that the *Father* alone may reign.[1]

Q^y Does not this refer to the Seculum Futurum, or *3rd* Epoch, in contradistinction from the *Dies Messiæ*, or 2nd?[2]

60   II 48–9 | Phenomenon 7 sec 2

Now it is certain from the scripture itself (Ezra ii.) that those who returned from Babylon to Jerusalem in these three parties, hardly made the amount of forty and two thousand and six hundred men; which is as much as to say that they were only a very small portion of the tribes of Judah and Benjamin (which, *a few years before the captivity, in the time of king Jehoshaphat, could furnish one million one hundred and three-score thousand soldiers . . .)

* a *few* years!—not a very appropriate epithet for the difference between 912 and 590! Lacunza must have confounded Jehoshaphat with Josiah, in some transient deliquium of the Memory[1]—or has Mr Irving mistaken years for centuries—read años for cien años?[2]

61   II 52–3

That permission of Cyrus, announced by the Holy Spirit two hundred

---

59[1] C continues the text that Lacunza has cited, 1 Cor 15.25, 28: "For he [Christ] must reign, till he hath put all enemies under his feet. . . . And when all things shall be subdued unto him, then shall the Son also himself be subject unto him that put all things under him, that God may be all in all.''

59[2] C gives a more detailed account of this scheme of epochs in Jeremy TAYLOR *Polemicall Discourses* i 813–21: "The Rabbis of best name divide into two or three periods. . . . The first was the Dies expectationis, or Hoc Sæculum . . . the second, Dies Messiæ—the time of the Messiah, i.e. the Millennium. The third, the Sæculum Futurum, or Future State: which last was absolutely spiritual & celestial.—But many Rabbis made the Dies Messiæ part, i.e. the consummation of this World, the ⟨conclusive⟩ Sabbath of the Great Week, in which they supposed the

Duration of the Earth, or World of the Senses, to be comprized. But all agreed that the Dies or Thousand Years of the Messiah was a transitional State during which the Elect were gradually defecated of the Body and ripened for the final or spiritual State—/.''

60[1] The dates 912 and 590 are the notional dates respectively for the beginning of the reign of Jehoshaphat and for the destruction of Jerusalem and the beginning of the captivity. The reign of Josiah began in 641; this narrows the "few years" from 322 to 51 years. But a "swoon" or "eclipse" of memory—C had copied from Jeremy Taylor in 1796 "deliquium, or a kind of Trance" (*CN* I 186)—cannot be assumed in Lacunza: 1,160,000 is the total of Jehoshaphat's men as given in 2 Chron 17.14–18 (cited by Lacunza).

60[2] I.e. read "years" for "centuries". Irving did not misread the Spanish original.

years before,* (Isa. xlv.) was without doubt, convenient and even necessary . . .

* Less boldly but more safely say—The ~~permissive~~ [? ~~Captor~~] Patron and Restorer promised by the H. S. through the prophet Isaiah 200 years before ~~its~~ the application ⟨of the promise⟩ to, and ⟨its⟩ fulfilment in, Cyrus—nominally—The Chapters after the XLth consist*s* of Isaian Oracles, i.e. inspired Comments, and specializing Verifications of Prophecies first announced by Isaiah, which were delivered by Prophets of the Captivity in Chaldea, except a very few that appear to have been delivered immediately after the return of the Exiles in Jerusalem. s. t. c.[1]

62 ii 53 | Sec 3

From the whole of this history, which we have related, there result these truths. . . . 2dly. That of the two tribes of Judah and Benjamin, which Nebuchadnezzar carried into Babylon, there did return only a slender portion to the land of their fathers; the most part remaining in Chaldea, in the same servitude.*

* Where are we to find the authority for this assertion? The number of Jewish Families carried into Chaldea by Nebuzar-adar is, if I recollect aright, no where stated—nor yet the number of the common people left in the Land. During the 40 or more years preceding this event many and powerful Causes of Depopulation had been at work. I would have inserted a parenthetic (it is probable) after "return".

63 ii 54–5

Let us now see shortly, some of the promises which were made in behalf of the house of Abraham, and we shall easily deduce whether they were accomplished in the coming up out of the captivity of Babylon. [Lacunza quotes passages from Isaiah, Jeremiah, Baruch, and Ezekiel.]

Where the object of the Preacher is to enlarge the views and direct the faith of Believers, the O. T. Prophecies offer abundant materials and an appropriate theme, but I can hardly conceive a more indiscreet *hysteron-proteron*, than that of selecting them as the fittest arguments for the conversion or conviction of learned Infidels, which nevertheless is an approved measure with the theological Debutants in our universal Pulpits & in their Lecture-courses—and the Subject must be treated in a very different way from that hitherto adopted to produce any desirable effect on a learned Jew—an animal of rare occurrence, I admit, but still to be

61[1] Isa chs 40–55, the Deutero-Isaiah described also in Jahn *History* **9**.

met with, often enough to supply proof, that the species is not altogether extinct.[1]

64 II 58–9

If, then, you see that the first part of the prophecies, which is the dispersion of Israel, hath been accomplishing itself to the letter,* why should their reunion and settlement in the land of their fathers, which the same prophecies announce with all the advantages as you have seen, be understood in another sense, making God to speak in a different manner?

* This well-put and well-worded Argument is so evidently unanswerable, that I could not help regarding an attempt to answer it as indicating a deadness in the Sense of Truth. Even if the so called and falsely so[a] called *spiritual* Interpretation of these express and most definite Predictions were admissible, yet I do not see what would be won by it.[1] The state described in these prophecies is as little realized in the members of the Christian Church morally, intellectually or spiritually, as in the Jews temporally and nationally.

To Lacunza's very plausible argument there is but one fair answer possible—that the Promises were all expressly *conditional*, & that the conditions were not complied with. What? should God force the bread from heaven, the fruits of Paradise, on those who preferred the Stie and the Trough?[2]

65 II 59

Yes, friend Christophilus, when the dispersion of the holy people, caused by God's hand, is entirely concluded; when the troubles of the children of Israel are finished; when their exile, their dispersion, and their captivity have come to an end; then shall all these wonders be accomplished,—all these annunciations, and all these mysteries, which now are so hard to be understood. Unless we would wholly offend the veracity and the omnipotence of God, we cannot doubt that as he hath promised, so he will fulfil it. *

---

[a] Resumed at the top of the page with "*from below/*"

63[1] C may well have had in mind his friend Hyman Hurwitz, founder of the Jewish Academy in Highgate and master there until 1821: see HURWITZ.

64[1] This is Irving's way of describing his and Lacunza's "prophetical" method of reading the Bible (I lxxxix–xciv), in which elements of the narrative are treated as "emblems", so that the history of the Jewish nation is interpreted as "a great type and emblem of the history of the spiritual and elect church which hath been from the beginning of the world" (I xc).

64[2] C puts the same question in **48** above.

* a more convincing Chain of Reasoning I have never read than the preceding Chapters. Indeed as long as the Author keeps at a distance from Daniel and the Apocalypse, he generally commands my Belief, and always my Respect. S. T. C.

66 II 59, 374 (last page), and ⁺3 | **65** textus

See Mss Note p. 374 and on the Cover of this Volume.[1]

* The true solution of the problem may, I think, be stated thus: OBJ. The Promises have not been performed. RESP. Who are the Plaintiffs? Not the Jews: for the Promises were conditional: and the~~y~~ir failure was and continues to be the Jews' own Act. OBJ. But the removal of the hardness of their hearts forms an express part of the promise & prediction. RESP. True! but by means congruous with the Divine Holiness, and therefore compatible with the moral freedom of the Individuals. What events, what series of accumulative evidences, ⟨may suffice to such an effect, salvo arbitrio;⟩[2] and after *what* lapse of time these are possible consistently with the laws of the natural & those of the spiritual world; or simply that *some* time the effect ~~will~~ must take place; God may know, by a knowlege that supposes no coercive superseding of human *free-agency.*[a]

And ~~how~~ what grounds can you pretend for asserting, that it will not be so? The Jews are still in existence & in no danger, that I know of, of extirpation. This is no *proof* of their future fulfilment of those promises; but it effectively prevents you from proving the contrary. OBJ. But sundry parts of the Promise have become impossible, others inappropriate. RESP. What is impossible, there can be no right to claim—least of all, by the only rightful Complainants in the~~se~~is case, the Jews:—for it is their own act, ⟨that has made the literal fulfilment impossible.⟩ If the substantial import of the Promise be ~~complied~~ carried into effect, God will have done ~~all~~ his part; even tho' out of the Stones of the Wilderness (i.e. the darkest and most uncivilized Tribes of the Gentile World) Children should be raised up to Abraham.[3]—Briefly,

the Theologians, whom Lacunza opposes or rather assaults and rides over, forget that if the *mere* letter killeth ⟨the Spirit,⟩ the Spirit giveth life to the Letter[4]—which is impossible, if it begins by destroying it. On the other hand, Lacunza himself in the heat of onset overlooks the im-

---

[a] Here C has written "(*turn* to the *Cover*)", and on II ⁺3 "continued from p. 374."

66[1] I.e. the passage following, which is written on those pages at the end of the volume.
66[2] "In sound judgment".

66[3] Matt 3.9, Luke 3.8 (var)—"of the Wilderness" added.
66[4] 2 Cor 3.6 (var).

portant fact, that the Promises of Jehova to the Jewish Nation have all of them, the nature of a *Covenant*, ⟨to the performance of which two parties are necessary.⟩ I dare not be sure, that the Fathers & the Commentators who followed in their track, looked so far onward: or I should judge, that the ultimate Ground of their repugnance to the literal interpretation of these prophecies was the difficulty they felt of reconciling the possible reception of ~~the M~~ Christ as their Messiah by the Jewish church with *their* (the Fathers') notion of the Redemption of Mankind by the Cross. For with *them* the Lamb sacrificed, the Church crucified, from the foundation of the World was but a metaphor for the foreknowlege & predeterminism of the Event. S. T. C.

67 II 61

Jeremiah in his two chapters, l. and li. speaks the same as Isaiah, with more diffuseness and at greater length; that is, he casteth a glance at that Babylon of Chaldea, dischargeth upon her a tempest of lightning, gives her to wit of the commandments of God, which pertained to her directly; after which, he passeth onward, until he is brought in spirit to another Babylon, so named by similitude, not by propriety; from whence, finally, he draws forth into freedom all the captives, as well of Judea as of Israel; and not only makes them free, but just, holy, entirely reconciled to their God, and restored with great privileges to the honour and dignity of his people; he planteth them anew in the land promised to their fathers, and promiscth to them from God that they shall not come again to be ruled over by any power upon the earth.

* It would, I suspect, pose the honest Jesuit to defend his hypothesis against his own arguments, p. 58: line 1–9.[1]

68 II 61–4

[With regard to Isa 50.3:] If the prophet speak here of the ancient Chaldea Babylon, it is certain that nothing of the kind was accomplished upon her, when the nation of the north under Darius and Cyrus came against her. That nation far from destroying Babylon, far from reducing her and all Chaldea to a solitude and desert, did no other remarkable thing than place upon the throne of Nebuchadnezzar, Darius the Mede,* and afterwards Cyrus the Persian.

* I should demand better evidences than I have yet seen, of the *Authenticity* of the VI first Chapters, i.e. the biographical preface to the proph-

67[1] I.e. **64** textus.

ecies, of Daniel; and even of the *competence* in point of historical infor-
mation, of the Compiler; before I consented to interpolate History with
this anachronical Darius the Mede[1] in compliment to the accidental cir-
cumstance that the Masters of the Law who made the last additions to
the Hebrew Canon in the time of Alexander the Great or soon after,
found a fragment of the traditional memorabilia of Daniel in corrupt
Hebrew and equally corrupt A Chaldaic—& this more probably a Trans-
lation than ~~the~~ part of the original Work—from the omission of sen-
tences necessary to the sense of the context; á which are preserved in the
far larger Greek, and ~~in~~ from the occurrence of apparent mistranslations
in passages, which in the Greek contain the undoubted sense intended
by the Writer.[2] N.B. I do not say, that the Greek ⟨Copy⟩ is the original/.
In short, I will not suppress my conviction. From motives of prudence—
no selfish prudence either, but from the fear of giving offence to the
weak in faith—I tried for a while the plan of *negative* falsehood, con-
cealing my doubts & my *no* doubts/ but a dearth and a dryness came
upon my spirit—difficulties, objections, scruples started up in every
page almost of the Scriptures, even the most unsuspected—all of which
vanished, or sunk into insignificance, as soon as I had liberated my mind
from the thraldom of Fear & again read my bible in the breezy open air
and sunshine of my ~~spirit~~ nature. I no longer walked as thro' a Jungle,
with "wicked whispers" of unbelief haunting me.[3] With Freedom came
Love; and with Love & Freedom came Faith. I will not therefore (I re-
peat) suppress my conviction, that this Darius the Mede is neither more
or less than one of the usual blunders that characterise the traditions of
the Vulgar, & taken in conjunction with the licentious differences in
different Mss Copies of the same Story sufficiently distinguish á the tra-
ditional from the historical.   S. T. C.—

69   II 65 | Sec 5

First key. The apostle St. Peter writing from Rome to all the churches
of Asia, concludeth his first epistle in these words, *"The church that is

---

68[1] The authenticity of Dan 1–6 and the
date of the whole book are considered in
IRVING *Sermons* **20** n 3. Darius the Mede,
named in Dan 5.31, 11.1 and elsewhere, is
"anachronical" as outside the time-frame
of the composition of the book: Darius the
Great d 485 B.C.

68[2] The book, as now included in OT,
is written in Hebrew and Aramaic, the Ara-
maic section being 2.4–7.28. Three books
presented in Septuagint as additions to Dan
and now relegated to OT Apocrypha are
written in Greek—The Song of the Three
Holy Children, The History of Susannah,
and Bel and the Dragon. The Septuagint
version of Dan, including these three,
would be "the far larger Greek" ms that C
here refers to as a conjectural entity. C
wrote two notes on Eichhorn's discussion
of Dan: EICHHORN *Alte Testament* **48, 49**.

68[3] *AM* line 246: when the mariner tried
to pray "A wicked whisper came, and
made/ My heart as dry as dust."

in Babylon elected together with you saluteth you.'' What meaneth this? St. Peter certainly did not write from the Euphrates, but from the Tiber, not from Chaldea, but from Rome. In St. Peter's time, ancient Babylon no longer existed, and was almost as much forgotten as it is now. Of what Babylon then speaketh he? Of Rome itself.

* Here Lacunza's Romish Delusions blinded his Judgement. Babylon was not only a great City in the time of Sᵗ Peter but centuries afterwards there was a celebrated Jewish University there, & a very powerful Colony under one of their princely Houses. There is not the slightest ground for doubting that Babylon meant Babylon, and that Sᵗ Peter performed his proper functions among his countrymen as the Apostle of the Circumcision.[1]

70 II 66–9

Second Key. After some years . . . St. John wrote his Apocalypse; and in the xvith, xviith, xviiith, and xixth chapters, he speaks expressly and by name of Babylon, prophesying against her things nowisc ordinary.* And to the end that none might disallow the Babylon of which he speaks; that no one might equivocate by thinking that he spoke of the old Babylon, which no longer existed, he sets down so many signs and characteristics, that it is absolutely necessary to recognize her, however repugnant it may be to our inclination. [Lacunza proceeds to juxtapose references to Babylon in Jer and Rev.]

* Aye—but mark the difference. John the Theologian did not mean Babylon by Babylon—not because no such city was then [in] existence—for this is not true. Jerusalem, Alexandria, and Babylon were at that time ranked as the three spiritual Metropolises of Jewdom—but because Sᵗ John expressly ~~says,~~ informs us, that he used the word Babylon enigmatically—And on her forehead was written the enigmatic name, Babylon/ ονομα μυστηριον a Hebraism for ονομα μυστηριωδες which ⟨last word⟩ our Version has ridiculously made part of the printed inscription/[1] Neither does John mean the *City* of Rome, otherwise than as Rome was the Symbol of Gentile Idolatry and military Despotism./ But this is a wide subject: and I must refer to my own continuous Commentary on the Apocalypse[2]—only remarking—that it seems strange logic to con-

69[1] The view of modern scholars is that the "Babylon" of 1 Pet 5.13 probably *is* Rome. As a Jew, Peter is (in contrast to Paul) "the Apostle of the Circumcision" in Gal 2.7–8.

70[1] "A name mystery . . . for a mystery-like name". The Greek reads ὄνομα γεγραμμένον, Μυστηριον, Βαβυλων, which AV renders "a name written, MYSTERY, BABYLON . . ." (Rev 17.5). C comments on this passage also in BIBLE COPY B **140**.

70[2] In spite of C's lifelong interest in Rev, no such "continuous Commentary"

clude from the circumstance of John's having borrowed the imagery for the destruction of an avowed Symbolical City from ~~the~~ Isaiah's anticipations of the Capture & destruction of Babylon, that therefore Isaiah's Babylon was only symbolical.

The City ~~of~~ and Temple of Jerusalem are the apocalyptic *Symbol* of the Law of Moses, or the Jewish Religion—the imagery ~~is~~ was here supplied by the history of the Siege & Destruction of Jerusalem. Therefore *Josephus's* Jerusalem was meant symbolically!![3]

Jeremiah passionately calls on his Countrymen to quit the idolatrous City[4]—Did not the result, viz. the poor feeble Handful that had religious & patriotic principle enough to prefer the Land of their Fathers, shew ~~with~~ what abundant reason there was for his efforts on this head. Could ~~thise~~ venerable Statesman, ~~and~~ the Holy Sage, employ too strong language: when the strongest proved of so little avail with his degenerate Brethren? so far, however, I can go with Lacunza, as to think it not improbable, that in the instance of Babylon the Prophets—such a succession of wise and enlightened Statesmen the World never saw before or since—contemplated the system of universal Monarchy in general, with its constant accompaniments of Sensuality and sensual Idolatry.

71 II 71 | Sec 7

Let us conclude then that those two great fortresses, unto which the interpreters of scripture betake themselves, (to wit, Babylon with her captives, and what is competent to, or what is not competent to the christian church,) are in reality two fortresses which partake much of the perspective, and being seen from a certain distance, put on a great appearance, and beget I know not what fear, but disappear both of them as we draw nigh and reconnoitre them.

Well! in the preceding Chapter the Jesuit has tied a knot like a second Ulysses; whether he has been equally successful in untying it—that is another question![1]—Contemplating the whole Bible, and the whole his-

---

survives, though after Irving's translation of Lacunza had impelled C to make a detailed and systematic study of the book together with the related prophecies—see e.g. *CL* VI 550, 557–8, 570 (Feb–Mar 1826)—many observations, interpretations, and queries appear in the Notebooks.

70[3] C is responding sarcastically to Lacunza's "prophetical" method of reading the Bible, which leads to his treating the history of the Jewish nation—as recorded

by e.g. Josephus—"symbolically": cf **2** n 8 above.

70[4] Jer 51.6–9, cited by Lacunza.

71[1] In BM MS Egerton 2800 f 188ᵛ C refers similarly to "The Ulyssean Knot"— i.e. a conundrum named for the Cyclops episode in *Odyssey* bk 9, in which Odysseus/Ulysses tells the Cyclops that his name is "Oudeis", "No-man". The ms further explains the problem as "the Idea that constantly recurs in all spiritual Gene-

tory of the chosen race from Abraham, as one continued prophecy, every event and every permanent character being more or less prophetic & typical,[2] I attach no such momentous importance to this or that particular Chapter—& consequently, find little or no difficulty in the point here mooted.

72   II 72

And that with so much power and evidence, that we have seen some modern Rabbis, by the force of arguments compelled to allow, that Messiah according to the scriptures ought to have come many ages ago, but that he has delayed his coming on account of the sins of his people.*

* Neither should I hesitate in conceding to a Jew, that the Messiah (in *his* sense of the word) has not yet come; if only I can prove to him, that *He* has come who will hereafter appear as Messiah—i.e. King Anointed of the Most High.—[1]

73   II 73–4

How is it possible for a Man of so much sensibility no less than of vigorous Sense, and so familiar with the Prophets, the Psalms and the Epistles of Paul, as Mr Irving, to pass from these and from all the strong *healthy* conclusions soundly and logically deduced from them to Daniel and the Apocalypse without *feeling* the discordance of the Books themselves, and without being startled at the diverse quality and character of the arguments, he has conjured out of them? In Lacunza, who from the circumstance of his Church imposing the belief of the canonicity and inspiration of the Apocrypha had had his feelings blunted by Custom, and the habit from childhood of reading the coarse stuff as Scripture dictated by the Holy Ghost, this Want of Tact is less inexplicable, and (I must add) more excusable.

74   II 76–9, pencil, continued in ink | Phenomenon 8 sec 2

[The text is Rev 12, esp 12.1, "a woman clothed with the sun".] This woman (continues the sacred text) was pregnant, and as the hour of delivery drew nigh endured great affliction, anguish, and pain, which manifest themselves openly by the wailing and groans which she uttered:

---

sis, in which the One repeats itself entire in Another, without ceasing to be itself (i.e. Generation) so that I = II. and yet each is = I''.

71[2] C alludes to *Lacunza's* declared method, as q in **2** n **8** above, and not to his own.

72[1] "Messiah"—an Aramaic word of which Χριστος (Christ) is the Greek equivalent—means "anointed". Cf *Unctus* in **90** below.

"And she being with child cried, travailing in birth, and pained to be delivered." Rev. xii. 2. . . . Immediately a great battle shall be joined between St. Michael and the dragon . . . and, the dragon being conquered, the woman, or the church, shall bring forth her sons with less affliction: "and she brought forth a man child" . . .

The Woman is doubtless the *Jewish* Church, but not the less *the Church*—The man-child is theocracy—which instantly that its *condition* was given, and the moral Law & the son of Man as the Legislator and Executive Head was snatched up to the throne of God—i.e. exists only as Providence till the Time come for the Kingdom on Earth, or Dies Messiæ, when a pure Theocracy will become visible & *a Fact*ᵃ—Armageddo (i.e. Mageddo-water, the vale & lake at the foot of Mount Carmel, the Lacus Thrasymenus of Jewish History), was a proverbial expression for utter destruction, extirpation.[1] Christianity supersedes Judaism, but adopts & retains the essentials, but it will extirpate Paganism throughout the Roman Empire. This is the true sense and the only sense of the passage in the Apocalypse.

75 II 78 | Sec 3

All the time that this instruction continues, they are with propriety said to be in the womb of the mother; who, as saith Augustine, "with suitable food nourisheth those whom she beareth in her womb, and rejoicing brings them full of joy to the day of their birth." This day of birth is no other than the day of baptism; after which the church recognizeth them for her children, as those who are already the children of God by the regeneration of the Spirit. (S. August. de Symb. ad catecum).

* Rather a mal a-propos Metaphor, if used within Hearing of an acute Anti-pædobaptist:[1] who might ask, what was the usual *prognosis* respecting Childenren brought to the light on the 8ᵗʰ Day or even Week after their Conception?

ᵃ From here, beginning with the dash, the note continues in ink

74[1] Armageddon—only in Rev 16.16—possibly "Ar Magedon", "mount of plagues" or "mount of Megiddo". Megiddo, about ten miles SE of Mount Carmel on the westerly flank of the broad valley of the river Kishon, was the site of the battle in which the Pharoah Necho defeated and killed Josiah (2 Kings 23.29). The "valley of Megiddo" in e.g. 2 Chron 35.22 and "the waters of Megiddo" in Judges 5.19 (the Song of Deborah) provide slender authority for C's topographically unaccountable "vale & lake at the foot of Mount Carmel". By making "Armageddo" the Jewish equivalent of Hannibal's crushing defeat of the Romans at Lake Trasimene (217 B.C.) C implies confidence in the connection between Armageddon and Megiddo. No source has been traced for this speculation.

75[1] One who is opposed to infant baptism.

76   ɪɪ 79

In fact, the text says, that the woman shall flee into the wilderness after having brought forth, and that in the wilderness she shall remain forty and two months, or one thousand two hundred and three score days, that is, the exact time of the persecution of Antichrist* . . .

* This again is merely a symbolic time; signifying the *work*-days of the Christian religion, preceding the Sabbath or Messianic Day—Whatever length of time these may comprehend—as 6 to 7, so 42 to 49.

77   ɪɪ 80–1

This is the clear and palpable order of all this prophecy. How then do we suppose the church in the time of Antichrist, and under the terror of his persecution, suffering great pains and straits in order to bring forth new children, and fleeing after their birth into the wilderness?

If any one can reconcile all these things in an easy and intelligible manner, I will subscribe to his opinion . . .

The Wilderness is the World—the Eagle wings the Providence of God (see Deuteromy*a*) which will wonderfully sustain the Jewish Church in the wilderness of the wide world during their exile & dispersion. [1]—The Dragon was, doubtless, the Roman Emperors, as the Delegates & Viceroys of the Prince of this World—Heaven is the Supreme Power in the State—the Stars the Magistrates, Proconsuls &c—Allusion is likewise made to the Delators, or Informers—this being the prime attribute of the Evil One, Đ that he is a Devil, Diabolus—i.e. a slanderous Informer. [2]

78   ɪɪ 85 | Sec 6

[On Rev 12.1, "clothed with the sun, and the moon under her feet".] For what new ornament, brightness, or splendour, can the light of the moon bring in the presence of the sun, or to a person clothed and girt about with the sun? If it be to denote, as some think, a shoe corresponding to the richness of the vesture, in that case, the expression *under the feet* seems not to be appropriate, since the shoe is not only under the feet, but to clothe and entirely cover them: it ought, in this case, to be said, *upon the feet*, which denotes another thing much inferior to the shoe itself.

a A slip for "Deuteronomy"

77[1] C answers Lacunza's challenge to interpret Rev 12.14 by reference to the miraculous provision of manna in Deut 8.

77[2] This view of the Devil is given more expansive treatment in **27** above.

This is one of the few passages as to which allegorical interpretation (as ✳ to[1] symbolical) is in its right place. Many significancies may be imagined in the Lunar subpeditry;[2] but the most obvious & natural is, placed above sublunary Change. It may, however, mean the direct Light of Revelation (the Sun) opposed to the reflected Light of the Understanding.

79   II 91–3

[Rev 12.5:] "And she brought forth a man child, who was to rule all nations with a rod of iron: and her child was caught up unto God, and to his throne." . . . Two principal points we have here to consider. First, who is this man child . . .? Secondly, what mystery is contained in this child's being presented before the throne of God so soon as it was born? These two mysteries have been as it were two most lofty and insuperable walls, which have stopped the progress of all interpreters of the Apocalypse . . .

The two lofty and insuperable Walls that (*not* stop *the*; but) prevent *all* progress of the Interpreters of Daniel and Apocalypse are first, their own deep-rooted prepossession by a false assumption, that the Apocalyptic Vision contains a series of particular Predictions no where else to be found in the Scriptures, by the decyphering of which they expect to prognosticate; and secondly, their utter want of all poetic Genius, and all ~~of~~ Eye, Taste and Tact for Poetry generally, with a total ignorance of the character and canons of Symbolic Poesy *in specie*.[1] Hence, they forget—if men can be said to forget what they had never learnt, that the Apocalypse is a POEM, and a Poem composed by a *Hebrew* Poet, after the peculiar type of Hebrew Poesy. So in this fine passage. The Woman is evidently the ⟨Jewish⟩ Church, patriarchal, mosaic and prophetic; but as evidently the *Ideal* Church. The Child is, doubtless, Theocracy impersonated in the Infant Messiah, as He in whom the Theocracy is hereafter to be realized on earth, and by whom it is actually dispensed during the interim (i.e. the six work days, or 42 weeks) in Heaven, and as PROVIDENCE.

80   II 105–9

[Rev 12.7–9:] "And there was war in heaven. . . . And the great dragon was cast out, that old serpent, called the Devil, and Satan, which de-

---

78[1] As "contrary" to, as in JOANNES 4. C writes about the difference between symbolic and allegorical readings in *SM* (*CC*) 28–31 and *AR* (1825) 198–9.

78[2] "The moon's under-footedness": *OED* has "subpedital" ("shoe") but not this.

79[1] "In its own kind", i.e. distinc-

ceiveth the whole World: he was cast out into the earth, and his angels were cast out with him.''* . . . . The [literal] interpreters of the Apocalypse . . . [suppose] that when Satan, abusing his liberty and the gifts of the Creator, raised rebellion in heaven against God, and drew over to his side . . . the third part of the angels, he was opposed by St. Michael. . . . Whereupon they waged with one another a great dispute, which naturally passed into a true battle, wherein St. Michael and his faithful companions conquered Satan and his rebels, and cast them from heaven to earth, that is to hell.

* Idolatrous Heathenism was no longer the Religion of the State—and found refuge almost exclusively among the lowest classes & in ~~the~~ obscure village-clowns—Pagani, whence Paganism.[1]—Mem. To trace, if I can, the mythos, on which Milton has found⟨ed⟩ the plot and machinery of his Paradise Lost, to the earliest Authorities—Are there any distinct notices of such a Belief (in its present shape, and as the origin of Evil[)], earlier than the Christian Æra? Are we to consider it as a monotheistic Version of the War of the Giants against the Gods, & derived from the Greek Mythology?[2] Or is it not rather to be looked for in the Titanic Gods of the Samothracian Mysteries—the Throes of the Planet in its ⟨first⟩ efforts to organize itself imagined as the struggles of the Infernal Trinity, Axieros, Axiokerses, &c/ against the Sun?[3] Or in Persia? or India, the Birth-place? Or finally, Egypt. If the last, it could not have passed out of ~~an~~ its original physiological purport, if it existed even in this, in the time of Moses/—if we may judge from the employment of the Serpent in the Mythos of the Fall[4]—Nor do I remember any allusion to such a Belief, as a Fall of Rebel Angels previous to the Creation of Man till after the return from the Captivity?[5] It would likewise be interesting to trace, if possible, the transition of the Story from physical to metaphysical. Unfortunately, I know not to what Work I can turn for the requisite information. Hypothetically, it would be easy enough to give the rise and progress of the Fable. Finite tho' mighty Beings, invis-

tively. C's consistent view of Rev as a symbolic poem appears also in **35, 47** above.

80[1] The derivation of "pagan" from *paganus* (villager, rustic) is standard; C uses "clown" in the equivalent Shakespearean sense.

80[2] The unsuccessful rebellion of the Giants against Zeus—an episode in Greek mythology to which C alludes as a more fruitful *idea* than Steffens's, in STEFFENS *Geognostisch* p 250.

80[3] These Samothracian divinities are invoked also in KLUGE **44**.

80[4] C's analysis of the serpent in the myth of the Fall appears esp in *AR* (1825) 250–4n.

80[5] C has made the same assertion in **27** above (at n 2); he takes up the issue of the existence and fall of "angels" many times, e.g. OXLEE **9, 10**.

ible to man, and these evil—As soon as the Jews ~~ad~~ abandoned their older & wiser opinion, that the Gods of the Heathen were non-entities, and began to attribute real Being to them, this first ingredient was furnished.—But finite Beings could not create themselves, and God could not have created them evil—therefore, there must have been a Fall—the Mythologies of Greece, Egypt, Persia and India supplied the rest; and perhaps the Apocalypse & Daniel may account for its universal adoption by the Christian Churches.

81   II   106

We know truly, from the same scriptures, that there are good and <u>bad</u> <u>angels</u> . . .

I doubt it

82   II   107 and ⁺1, referring to II 106–7

That the dragon and his angels, notwithstanding their being deprived for ever of the grace and friendship of God, have some access real or personal to him. . . . It is clear, from the second chapter of Job; it is clear from verses 19 and 21, of the xxiind chapter of the first book of Kings; it is clear from the 31st verse of the xxiind chapter of the Gospel by St. Luke; and it is evident from this very passage of the Apocalypse, verse 10.

See the blank leaf ad finem.[1]

P. 106. It is impossible not to respect Lacunza's good sense and sound ~~n~~ Judgement generally—and often where I most disagree with him. Something too may be fairly allowed to his prudence & fear of scandalizing weak minds. In his own mind, I suspect, that he would not consider the mere incidental use of popular language, or references to generally received notions for the purposes of illustration or ornament, no where forming the direct object or primary end of any passage, as sufficient grounds for raising such notions into articles of Faith—especially, when they clearly originated in Gentile Creeds. I at least find no passage in the New Testament, from which the obligation to believe in personal self-conscious disembodied Beings incomparably more powerful than Man, yet evil and in rebellion against ~~g~~ God, can be fairly concluded—Evil & malignant Spirits indeed are so spoken of in the Gospel, that we cannot but suppose that the Speaker intended the belief of them—but this I should be ready enough to do, even without the author-

82[1] "Towards the end", i.e. II ⁺1,   written. where the whole of the ensuing note is

ity of Revelation. But Spirits are not necessarily self-conscious individual Souls—or is Fever *a* Soul? Yet our Lord *rebuked* the Fever just as he had before rebuked the Spirit of Madness.[2]   S. T. C.

83   II 108

From this council or judgment after the last seal of the book was opened . . . there are seen to go forth immediately seven angels "to whom were given seven trumpets," at whose sound, and at whose successive voices, come to pass in succession, those seven horrible plagues which are mentioned in the eighth, ninth, and part of the tenth chapters.

The Jewish War, historical *and* symbolical.

84   II 108

A little afterwards are seen to proceed out of the same council other seven angels . . . to whom it is said "go your ways and pour out the vials of the wrath of God upon the earth." (xv and xvi.)

The Overthrow of Paganism, symbolical and not historical

85   II 110

He [the dragon] presents himself at those gates seeking audience; and claiming with that pride and audacity which is his proper character, that entrance should be given to him as heretofore, in order that he may propound and make good his accusations. You do not think, Sir, that this is any of those vain phantasms which the imagination conjures up.!!* Besides being a thing most natural, and to which, from any other quarter, no repugnancy is found, you shall see it all made clear in the following article.

* Was Lacunza joking? Scarcely. Yet that a man of his powers of intellect should have meant all this in good earnest, is inconceivable & almost incredible!!

86   II 117–18

There is no doubt that that most ancient prophet, "the seventh from Adam," Enoch, is still alive, as well as Elias, without our knowing the determinate place where either of them at present is.* . . . The interpreters of the Apocalypse, excepting some few, commonly judge or sus-

---

82[2] Luke 4.39, 4.35. The argument, "were it certain, that all Souls are Spirits, it does not follow that all Spirits are Souls", appears also in IRVING *Sermons* 27.

pect, that those two witnesses [of Rev. 11.7–14] shall prove to be Elias and Enoch.

* Extraordinary Feat of Cabbalistic Logodædaly—this Conversationion of the first instance of early and premature Death into an exemption from Death! But Elias, or Elijah?—Aye, Elijah! I could say something on this head—and something more and of more importance respecting Elias[1]—and when I find—I trust that I write this in lowliness of heart, and with love-yearning after the support of a Faith's-Mate—I will not, as I was about to do, call it a necessary support: for it has pleased God that I should stand alone[2]—when I find that Light which attests the presence of the Word in whom is Life I shall say it, and of "fit audience"[3] seek fit counsel.   S. T. C.

87 ii 119–21

Returning now to our two witnesses, considered as two moral bodies, we say, in few words, that from them will come forth those martyrs . . . still wanted to complete the number of the joint-heirs of the kingdom. . . . Nevertheless, following the allusion, which appears so clear, to the going forth from Egypt, there is easily to be seen a great resemblance and proportion between Moses and Elias, and it is not easy to find any between Aaron and Enoch. If you ask me, who that second wing shall be, or can be, according to the scriptures; I answer truly that I do not know.

Eichhorn with full consent adopts Herder's hypothesis, that the Witnesses are the Priest Jesus & Ananas, whose murder by the Idumæans Josephus narrates in the 5 Chapt. Book IV. of his Jewish War.[1] Had it been the Apocryphal Esdras,[2] that Herder was commenting on, I might perhaps have thought it a plausible & lucky Conjecture/ but even if the

86[1] What C had to say is probably contained in IRVING *Sermons* **28**, esp "that the passage in Kings is a poetic Paraphrase of the Fact, that Elijah departed . . . in the act of prophesying". The separation of "Elias" and "Elijah" here is puzzling, but may simply indicate that C was thinking of separate texts in which the prophet is given one name or the other.

86[2] The phrase recalls C's personal motto, based on his initials and signifying "He hath stood": see ANNUAL ANTHOLOGY **10** n 3 and *CN* iii 3325—"I am not a God, that I should stand alone."

86[3] ". . . fit audience find, though few": *Paradise Lost* vii 31.

87[1] Josephus *Jewish Wars* 4.3.9 ff and 4.4.3 ff. C alludes to a passage that he annotated in EICHHORN *Apocalypse* COPY A **19**, where he called the interpretation "wild and improbable". The text under discussion is Rev 11.3: "And I will give power unto my two witnesses, and they shall prophesy a thousand two hundred and threescore days, clothed in sackcloth."

87[2] I.e. 1 and 2 Esdras (as in **47** n 3 above).

symbolical character of the Apocalypse so admirably sustained from the first to the last verse had not ~~furnished~~ rendered the interpretation a priori improbable, I could not easily reconcile the investing of two unconverted Jews with such high and mysterious attributes with an Elder of the Church of Ephesus in John the Evangelist's Life-time.[3] My own belief is that the outward Profession of Christianity itself represented by the two sacramental Signs is intended; in short, that the two Witnesses are ~~the~~ Baptism and the Eucharist so personified—If, as is highly probabl~~y~~e, the matter and substance of this sublime poem, the prophecies I mean entitled κατ' εξοχην, Αποκαλυψις η μεγαλη Ιησου Χριστου,[4] preserved in an abridged form in Luke XVII.,[5] were received from St John, the Angel in C. XXII. 8. 9. who is one ~~of them that still keep the sayings~~ τῶν τηροῦντων τους λογους βιβλιου,[6] i.e. still alive, my interpretation would find a strong confirmation in the Epistle of John. ~~I~~ In the Epistle there are 3 Witnesses, because the whole Religion, the inward & spiritual as well as the outward & visible, is meant.[7] In the Apocalypse the latter only—consequently, the third witness is omitted.

S. T. C.

88   II 144–5 | Phenomenon 9 sec 2

. . . although the Lord did not reveal to them the particular and determinate secret which they desired to know, that is, the precise time of the restitution of the kingdom to Israel, he doth yet evidently confirm them in the substance of that mystery. That which they inquired was, if the kingdom of Israel, which according to the prophets ought to be restored by Messiah, would be restored immediately in those times or not.

The worst and weakest part of Lacunza's Scheme of Argument is his blindness to the impropriety of supposing a whole Race undergoing a sudden *transmentation*, μετανοια,[1] from invincible prejudice and hardness of heart to all that is holy and amiable, as the poles of a magnetic

---

87³ The two Jews are the priests Jesus and Ananas (above); the Elder is the suppositious author of Rev (C having rejected Eichhorn's attribution: see H. MORE *Theological Works* 4). In **7**, **70** above, he calls the latter "John the Theologian" to distinguish him from "John the Evangelist", following the arguments of Dionysius of Alexandria as reported in Eusebius *Ecclesiastical History* 7.25.

87⁴ "Pre-eminently, the great Revelation of Jesus Christ"—as in **7** above.

87⁵ Luke 17.20–37, e.g. 29–30: "But

the same day that Lot went out of Sodom it rained fire and brimstone from heaven, and destroyed them all. Even thus shall it be in the day when the Son of man is revealed."

87⁶ Rev 22.9 (var): "of them that keep the sayings of the book".

87⁷ 1 John 5.7: "For there are three that bear record in heaven, the Father, the Word, and the Holy Ghost: and these three are one."

88¹ Lit "a change of mind", conversion or (AV) "repentance".

Compass are reversed (have been at least) by a flash of Lightning. If this overwhelming of the moral freedom contains nothing contradictory to the moral attributes of the Deity, it might be done at any moment—and what ⟨can⟩ Lacunza or any other Millennarian conceive of a Kingdom of the Son of Man on earth & while the Subjects are still in bodies, beyond what any Nation, the Isle of G. Britain for instance, would exhibit and effect supposing that every individual from the Sovereign to the Cottager was an actual regenerate Christian?

89   II 182–3, pencil | Phenomenon 10 sec 3

Therefore we may well hope, without any fear, that the prophecies we speak of, with innumerable others of the like kind, shall be fully verified according to the letter, in the second time of Messiah, because in the first they could not have a place.

Now this second time being arrived . . . there shall happen among other things the elevation of mount Zion above all the mountains and hills . . . "and the Lord shall reign over them in mount Zion . . ."

If the Dies Messiæ[1] be an historical Event, to which we are required by H. Script. to look onward; if that fulfilment and consequent cessation of the *Nature* in Man, τοῦ γενίκου,[2] asserted by Jesus in answer to the Law-case, which the Saducees mooted, belongs to this Epoch; & lastly, if the Dies Messiæ shall be introduced by the convulsive revolutions in the Earth itself, as declared by Sᵗ Peter, or whoever was the Writer of the two Catholic Epistles under that name;[3] *if*, I say, these three *ifs* are conceded—where is the impossibility, that an immense Mountain comprizing all climates and soils may form the Metropolis of the Planet?

S. T. C.

90   II 186 | Sec 4

The truth of this notice, without recurring to the ancient history of the Assyrians, is to be discovered most clearly from the xxixth chapter of Ezekiel himself; "Son of Man, (says the Lord to this prophet) Nebuchadrezzar king of Babylon caused his army to serve a great service

89[1] "Day of Messiah" as in **37** n 2 above.

89[2] The adjective—"generic", "proper to the kind"—is an Aristotelian term not in NT Greek, though C thinks of it in connection with Matt 22.23–32, esp 30: ". . . in the resurrection they neither marry, nor are given in marriage, but are as the angels of God in heaven".

89[3] 2 Pet 3.10: "But the day of the Lord will come as a thief in the night; in the which the heavens shall pass away with a great noise, and the elements shall melt with fervent heat, the earth also and the works that are therein shall be burned up." C discusses the authorship of the "Catholic Epistles" in **39** above.

against Tyrus; *every head was made bald, and every shoulder was peeled: yet had he no wages, nor his army, for Tyrus, for the service that he had served against it: therefore thus saith the Lord God, Behold, I will give the land of Egypt unto Nebuchadrezzar king of Babylon . . .''

* Query. Does not this passage help to explain the Unctus iste exscindetur: et non erit illi, of Daniel,[1] and determine the sense to Cyrus, and the Scythian Expedition in which he was cut off, *and had no wages for his service?*—[2]

91   II 194 | Sec 7

Verse 4. ''There is a river, the streams whereof shall make glad the city of God, the holy place of the tabernacles of the most high.'' [Ps 46.4]

Verse 4, a fine *Hexameter*.

Thêre ĭs ă / River, the / flowing where/of shall / gladden the / City[1]

92   II 197–8

I say the end of the world, by which I understand the end of the sojourners, of generation and corruption; for I am not of opinion that the world, that is, the material bodies or celestial globes which God has created,* (amongst which one is this earth of ours in which we dwell) is to have an end, or to return to the chaos or the nothingness from which it came forth . . .

* ? Fused, vitrified, flashed or blown from within, so as to produce a peripheric surface of many hundred, perhaps thousands times greater than the present—and a lenticular point in each hemisphere, acting as a burning glass, and directed inward on the reprobate in the Hollow of the Globe—whom Tertullian & the Righteous will see as plain as Bees in a glass Bee-hive![1] Forgive me, O my God! that I have spoken in scorn! But to behold the glory of thy truth thus perverted & made the dream of a Dreamer was gall and vinegar to me: & my spirit was embittered.

90[1] ''The Anointed one will be cut off: and it will not be his''—not Vulgate, but C's Latin version of Dan 9.26.

90[2] The quotation is from Ezek 29.18 (in textus) but is applied to the death of Cyrus—in whose reign Dan is set—in 528 B.C. in a campaign against the Scythians.

91[1] A verse included (with the same variation of ''flowing'' for ''streams'') in a set of hexameters in 1799: *CL* I 533.

92[1] C objects to the image of God as a glassblower, creator of ''celestial globes'' which he then uses to become a ''Searcher of Hearts'': *CL* III 6. In a similar context, C uses the figure of a popular scientific curiosity, the glass beehive—''I, whose whole Being has been like a Glass Beehive before you for 15 years''—in a letter to Poole in 1813: *CL* III 437. The presence of Tertullian here is a little puzzling: perhaps C alludes to his scrutiny of the human soul in *De testimonio animae*.

93 ɪɪ 208

But if we cast our eyes upon that former Jerusalem which the Babylonians destroyed in the life-time of Jeremiah, we find houses and palaces of the kings of Judah, and we find idols in thousands, upon the terraces and the most lofty places of almost all the houses of the iniquitous Jerusalem.

I quite agree with Lacunza, that Jeremiah's image[1] is sufficiently fulfilled in such a destruction of Jerusalem, as rendered it necessary to build a new City with new walls, temple &c—tho' on the same S̶p̶ Plot. If I threaten that I will so smash a China Dish or Porcelain Vase, that it shall not be repairable either by Cement or rivet, and do so—have I not fulfilled the threat, because I afterwards permit another less costly Dish or Vase to be placed on the same Shelf where the former had stood?

S. T. C.

94 ɪɪ 241 | Pt 3 ch 5 sec 1

From this certain and undeniable principle, combined with sacred history, it follows legitimately that our terraqueous globe is not now as it was in its first times, or the times of its youth. Consequently that there has happened in it, in times very remote from the present, some great and extraordinary accident. . . . This accident can have been nothing else, let philosophers say as they please, than the universal deluge of Noah, whereby, as saith the apostle St. Peter,* "the world that then was, being overflowed, perished;" and as saith Christ himself, "the deluge came and took them all away." Matt. xxiv. 39.

* And this it is impossible that it can have been, if the Mosaic (our only) account be accurate? What? an ark floating quietly on the surface? What? an olive-tree with its brittle boughs uninjured at the bottom of an aqueous Tempest that convulsed and disorganized universal Nature!— If we may guess and make fancies, it would be far easier to suppose the Ante-diluvian Earth to have had a Ring like Saturn's—& this to have dissolved.

95 ɪɪ 241

To me it appears that no other [cause] can be pointed out, than the very omnipotent hand of the Creator, who, in his wrath against all the earth, corrupted to the last degree, caused it suddenly to move from one pole to the other, inclining its axis 23½°, and causing it to point with one of

93[1] Jer 52.4–14.

its extremities towards the star which we now call the polar star, or towards the extremity of the tail of the lesser bear.

All false in science & ~~impossible~~ irreconcilable with the facts.

96　ɪɪ 247 | Sec 3

That fire which is so oft announced against the great and terrible day of the Lord, cannot, according to the scriptures, be a universal fire to cover all our globe, as did the waters in the time of Noah, nor such as shall consume and reduce it to smoke and ashes, as so many have imagined.

It would be more consonant with recent discoveries to suppose the conflagration to arise from certain convulsive Earthquakes letting in the water on immense Masses of unoxydated Metals, such as Potassium, Sodium, Alumium, Calcium &c—the final Result of which might be the cloathing of the Planet with a new and more fertile Soil/.[1]

97　ɪɪ 249 | Sec 4

Now begin the thousand years of St. John, at the beginning of which the imprisonment of the devil must take place,* with all the circumstances which are written expressly throughout the xxth chapter of the Apocalypse . . .

* Were there but this one passage to support Lacunza's Scheme, this passage would suffice to overthrow it.—Where should the barbarous innumerable Multitude of Gog & Magog come from, at the close of such a period?[1]—This of itself determines the Millennium to be the period from Constantine to the Advent of the Messiah.[2]

98　ɪɪ ⁺2

Finally, my Judgement at this present 17 May 1827 is—that I can receive all the essential parts of Lacunza's Belief, after I have removed every f supposition grounded on the *misinterpreted* (if, which I greatly doubt, & canonical) Books, Jer^h/ and Daniel and the Apocalypse. And high time it is, that a clear Exposition should be given of the Second Coming of our Lord and the Days of the Kingdom, as grounded wholly

96[1] C's note appears to support the current theories of the "Wernerian" school of geology, which taught, as C says in *TL* (1848) 67, "the original fluidity of the planet" but also described different phases in the evolution of the earth that were the consequences of catastrophes. "Alumium" was the name originally given to aluminium by C's friend Humphry Davy.

97[1] Rev 20.7–8: at the end of the thousand years, Satan is to be loosed upon "the nations which are in the four quarters of the earth, Gog and Magog, . . . the number of whom is as the sand of the sea".

97[2] C's assertion also in **2** above at n 4.

on the prophets, evangelists, and the Epistles of Paul and Peter—and the compatibility of the Result with Right Reason, and its positive Consonance with the most legitimate Interpretation of existing Nature, physical & moral, vindicated.[1]—The title and substantial Idea of the whole might be comprized in the Title—Of the Fulfilment and Supersession of Nature in True Being.   S. T. Coleridge
                                Grove, Highgate/

98[1] In a notebook entry of 23 Jun 1827 (N26 ff 126ᵛ–127ᵛ) C expresses his conclusions about Lacunza in similar terms: "Either the Coming of the Messiah in Glory, preceded by a revolution scarcely less tremendous than that effected by the Deluge, is an article of faith; or the Prophets are merely Poets, and the Apostles & their Converts a set of Simpletons who mistake high-flying Odes for Divine Oracles . . .".

MALCOLM LAING
1762–1818

The History of Scotland, from the Union of the Crowns on the Accession of James VI. to the Throne of England, to the Union of the Kingdoms in the Reign of Queen Anne. 2nd ed rev. With a preliminary dissertation on the participation of Mary, Queen of Scots, in the murder of Darnley. Vol III only (of 4). London 1804. 8°.

Cornell University (Wordsworth Collection)

Bookplate of Sir James Graham Domville, Bt. On p ⁺4, in an unidentified hand, "Mⁿ Rhind|Kinloss"; and see MS TRANSCRIPT below.

MS TRANSCRIPT. On p ⁻4, in an unidentified hand, is written, "This pencil note by S. T. Coleridge copied in ink on the next flyleaf." The transcript (on p ⁻2), in the same hand, is copied with only slight variations from C's original.

DATE. Possibly c 1823, when C was reading Scottish history with the purpose of writing a biography of Robert Leighton: *CL* v 299–301. C refers to Laing in BAXTER *Reliquiae* COPY B 37.

1   III ⁻4, pencil

It is much to be regretted, that in this excellent work written (in other respects) in the true spirit of History the term, Religion, should always and ostentatiously be used in an odious sense, so that in almost every instance you may substitute the word Superstition, or Fanaticism, or Bigotry. This is not candid: nor is it a sufficient excuse that what the Scotch Presbyterians & English Puritans *called* Religion was superstitious ⟨or⟩ fanatical, and in both cases bigotted. Least of all, was it wise or even politic: for it will tend to exclude the work from a large party of Readers, who most need the sound political maxims with which the work is replete. How much more philosophical would it have been to have appropriated the language to the fact: viz. that the principle of Religion in all the jarring parties was leavened with, and in too many individuals superseded by, Fanaticism, Formality, and Hypocrisy.

S. T. C.

MARY LAMB
1764–1847

Mrs Leicester's School: or, the history of several young ladies, related by themselves. [By Mary Lamb, with contributions by Charles Lamb. We do not know what edition C used: all nine editions of 1809–25 were anonymous, and C's one note was written on a flyleaf now detached from the volume.]

Cornell University (Wordsworth Collection)

A name—possibly "Henry Gillman"—has been scribbled over, at the top of the leaf.

MS TRANSCRIPT. VCL LT 72.

DATE. About 1820 (1 n 2)?

1

It at once soothes and amuses me to think—nay, to *know*—that the Time will come when this little Volume of my dear and well-nigh oldest Friend's, dear Mary Lamb, will be not only enjoyed but acknowleged as a rich Jewel in the treasury of our permanent English Literature—and I cannot help running over in my mind the long lost*a* of celebrated Works of celebrated Writers, astonishing Geniuses!! Novels, Romances, Poems, Histories and dense Political Economy Quartos, which compared to ~~this~~ Mʳˢ Leicester's School will be remembered as often and prized as highly as Wilkie's & Glover's Epics and Lord Bolingbroke's Philosophics compared with Robinson Crusoe!!¹ Do you not think, Sir! (I declare, *I* do) that Sir Walter Scott is equal to Shakespear? (said Mʳ Terry, the Dramatizer of "the Northern Enchanter's" History-hashes)² I know,

---

a A slip for "list"

1¹ I.e. Mary Lamb's work will have the enduring popular success of *Robinson Crusoe* when many of the more pretentious works of her contemporaries have been forgotten. C's examples are Richard Glover's *Leonidas* (1737), William Wilkie's *Epigoniad* (1757), and (probably) Pope's *Essay on Man* (1733–4), which is addressed to Bolingbroke—or possibly Boling-

broke's own political and philosophical essays, e.g. *Letters on the Study and Use of History* (1752).

1² The actor Daniel Terry (c 1780–1827) was a close friend of "the Northern Enchanter" Walter Scott, and adapted several of his works for the stage, notably—for Covent Garden—a musical *Guy Mannering* (1816), *The Heart of Midlothian*

Sir! that some think him inferior to Lord Byron in genius—and certainly Lord [Byron]*a* is a stupendous creature—but not equal to—the Bard of Avon, or the Northern Inchanter (interruptively I (S. T. C.) replied)—but you, I am sure, will rank him on a par with *Milton*.—

M*r* G.[3] "Don't you think Lord Byron nearer to Dante, Sir!"

S. T. C.——~~I was~~ Sir! I was talking Nonsense, not ~~blasphemy!~~*b*

---

a Word lost in repair to corner of leaf
b Word heavily deleted in ink, probably not by C

(1819), and *The Antiquary* (1820). C probably met him at the Highgate home of the comedian Charles Mathews: in Apr 1820 Terry and Mathews tried to arrange a meeting between C and Scott (*CL* v 39).

1[3] Gillman?

WILLIAM LAUD

1573–1645

The History of the Troubles and Tryal of The Most Reverend Father in God, and Blessed Martyr, William Laud, Lord Arch-Bishop of Canterbury. Wrote by himself, during his imprisonment in the Tower. To which is prefixed the diary of his own life . . . and subjoined . . . the arch-bishop's last will; his large answer to the Lord Say's speech concerning liturgies; his annual accounts . . . and some other things relating to the history . . . [ed Henry Wharton]. London 1695. F°.

Sion College Library

Bookplate of Sion College Library on p ⁻5 (p-d), together with signature "Ri. Chiswell" (the publisher of the volume); the initials "S" and "C" are written on either side of the "London" imprint on the title-page. There is a pencilled cross to the far right of the margin on p 247.

CONTENTS. Preface [by Wharton]; 1–69 Laud's Diary; 71–443 History of the Troubles and Tryal; 443–4 A short Supplement to the preceeding History [from Rushworth]; 444–6 A Larger Supplement [from Heylyn]; 447–53 The Speech . . . upon the Scaffold; 454–7 The Arch-Bishop's Last Will and Testament; 458–69 Several Passages of Arch-Bishop Laud's Conference with Fisher the Jesuit; 470–513 The Answer . . . to the Speech of the Lord Say and Seal; 515–64 Arch-Bishop Laud's Annual Accounts; 565–6 Note by Wharton; 567–606 Rome's Masterpiece; 607 The Examination of Henry Mayo; 608–16 Letters.

DATE. Aug–Sept 1823. In mid-Aug C was trying to acquire a biography of Laud either on loan from his publishers (*CL* v 294) or on approval from a bookseller (*CL* v 295), in order to write an account of Leighton and his times for the work that eventually became *AR*. This copy was borrowed from Sion College Library, as a notebook entry shows: *CN* IV 4991, and cf G. BURNET *Memoires* headnote. By 9 Sept, C claimed to have completed his collation of this work ("Wharton") and others (*CL* v 300); fragmentary notes upon it survive in BM Egerton MS 2801 f 237, and extensive notes for the project as a whole are pub in *SW & F* (*CC*) and in *CN* v 5015–57 passim.

1   p 92, pencil | *History of the Troubles* ch 3 art 1

[Of the "Custom in *Scotland*, of Fasting on the *Lord's-Day*":] it is against the Practice of the whole Church of *Christ*. . . . the same general Tradition hath in all times accounted it unlawful to Fast upon that Day. . . . Nor is there any thing more clear in all Antiquity. [Laud then cites

486

in evidence and quotes, among others, Tertullian and Sts Ignatius, Hilary, Ambrose, and Augustine.]

Trash and Stuff indeed![1] Could Laud be ignorant that the Church of Scotland generally was far more disposed to rank even the early Fathers among the corrupters of the Faith, than as binding Authorities? that long before Chillingworth it held that the Bible was the only Code of Christians?—[2]

1[1] C echoes a phrase from earlier in the text, where Laud, objecting to the description of his theological opinions as "this stuff", indignantly retorts that "*this Stuff* . . . was once (and in far better times of *the Church*) valued at a better rate" (91).

1[2] C simply uses a variant of the rallying-cry popularly associated with William Chillingworth's *Religion of Protestants, a Safe Way to Salvation* (1638)—"the Bible only is the religion of Protestants". Two annotated copies of CHILLINGWORTH *Works* are recorded in *CM (CC)* ii.

The Second Volume of the Remains of the Most Reverend Father in God, and Blessed Martyr, William Laud, Lord Arch-Bishop of Canterbury. Written by himself. Collected by the late learned Mr. Henry Wharton . . . [Together with] an historical account of all material transactions relating to the University of Oxford, from Arch-bishop Laud's being elected Chancellor to his resignation of that office. 2 pts in 1 vol. London 1700. Fº.

Sion College Library

On p ⁻5 (p-d): "bought (wᵗʰ yᵉ Approbation of yᵉ revⁿᵈ Rowland Sandiford M.A. President) at yᵉ College Expence ie out of Cash in hand on yᵉ Library Account S.IX.28*'". Bookplate of Sir Philip Sydenham, Bt.

CONTENTS. i Preface; 1–60 Answer to the Speech of . . . Lord Viscount Say; 61–84 Speech Delivered in the Star-Chamber . . . June, 1637 . . . Concerning Pretended Innovations in the Church; ii 1–217 Historical Account . . . Relating to the University of Oxford.

DATE. Aug–Sept 1823: see LAUD *History* headnote.

1 p ⁺5, pencil, referring to i 12–13

. . . there is of late a Name of Scorn fastned upon the Brethren of the Separation, and they are commonly called *Round-heads*, from their Fashion of cutting close and rounding of their Hair: A Fashion used in *Paganism* in the times of their Mournings. . . . [In the shoulder-note Laud writes that the Grecians and Romans wore long hair; that "Rounding of the Head was sometimes a sign of superstitious sorrowing, so was it . . . an effeminate and luxurious Fashion"; that harlots had their hair cut, and that "rounding of the Head was a mark of Servitude and Vassallage".] "But whether our *Round-heads* do it for Superstition, or for Luxury, or out of any Base and Servile Condition, I cannot tell; though I think there need be little Question, but that many of them are guilty of all three, their Hypocrisy being not a Robe large enough to hide all of them . . ."

Of the unconscionably conscienceless good (i.e. self-complacent) Consciences: 1. Danger in private life when their Intimate is of a frank disp.—even to the confounding of the self-cond. before God, and the acknowlegement before men.

2. In state—
Lord Eldon's remark that the Ref. would have been an evil without the Rev.[1]—applied in the comparison between a R.h. & a Cav—p 12–3—P[t i]

2 i 15, pencil

Nay, yet farther, if this Reason be true, universally true, (as 'tis here given) [that if "that which was both before and under the Law concerning the Priesthood can give no Rule . . . to the Ministry under the Gospel, then can it give no Rule in any thing else"] then it reaches to, and thorough the whole Law. No part of it can give any Rule to Men, or things under the Gospel. For if no Rule to things, then none to Men, who must do or leave undone; and if so, then the *Moral* Law can give no Rule to Men under the Gospel, more than the *Ceremonial* or the *Judicial* Law. For the whole Law was before the Gospel, and here said, without any distinction, to be of another Nature, and so unable to give a Rule.

Tho' this Sophistry is too pitiful to require an answer—it might have been asked—what one Moral Law do we *of necessity* derive from the Pentateuch? Would Laud dare affirm, that Christ's Commands needed or could receive an additional sanction from Moses? Can a perfect Obligation be further perfected? Or is our Obligation to obey Christ not perfect *per se*, so that if t any of our Lord's Commands had not been anticipated by Moses, we might have treated it, as a Proclamation compared with an Act of Parliament?

3 i 67, pencil

There are Times when *Persecutions* were great in the *Church*, even to exceed Barbarity it self: Did any *Martyr* or *Confessor*, in those Times, *Libel* the *Governours?* Surely no; not one of them to my best *Remembrance* . . .

?Tertullian? Greg. Naz. in Julianum?[1]

1[1] John Scott, 1st Earl of Eldon (1751–1838), Chancellor 1801–6 and 1807–27, was an obstinate opponent of Catholic Relief. His view that without the Revolution of 1688, which firmly established the Protestant succession and ensured the primacy of the Protestant Church in England, the Reformation would have been an evil for the country had been most recently expressed—though not in the words C gives—in a speech in the House of Lords on 21 Jun 1822, on the occasion of the second reading of the Roman Catholic Peers Bill: Hansard.

3[1] C offers two obvious exceptions to Laud's general rule: Tertullian (c 160–

4   p +4, referring to i 68

Our main *Crime* is (would they all speak out, as some of them do) that we are *Bishops*; were we not so, some of us might be as *passable* as other Men.

And a great trouble 'tis to them, that we maintain that our *Calling of Bishops* is *Jure Divino*, by Divine Right. . . . And this I say in as direct *opposition* to the *Church of Rome*, as to the *Puritan Humour*.

And I say farther, that from the *Apostles times*, in all Ages, in all Places, the *Church* of *Christ* was governed by *Bishops*: And *Lay-Elders* never heard of, till *Calvin*'s new-fangled Device at *Geneva*.

Now this is made by these Men, as if it were *Contra Regem*, against the King, in Right or in Power.

But that's a meer *ignorant shift*; for our being *Bishops, Jure Divino*, by Divine Right, takes nothing from the *King's Right or Power over us*.

The danger of taking justification of certain disputable or at least disputed things on too high grounds as *jure divino* &c, when ~~that~~ a justification sufficient for all men of candor & common sense may be derived from Experience, Congruity with other existing Institutions &c—Vide p. 68—a divine right of a Bishop to do what by divine Right a King may forbid him to do—nay, must have authorized *him* to do!

5   p +4, pencil

77
78
79
83
84[1]

Annex

On i 77–84 passages are marked in pencil on the pages listed on p +4 (**5**).

A   i 77

One thin[g] sticks much in their Stomachs, and they call it an *Innovation* too. And that is *Bowing, or doing Reverence at our first coming into the Church, or at our nearer Approaches to the Holy Table, or the Altar*, (call it whether you

---

c 220) whose "daring defiance" he had remarked upon as early as 1810 (*CN* III 3891); and St Gregory of Nazianzus (c 329– c 390). Tertullian defended the early Christians against charges brought by the Roman governors in his *Apologeticus* (197); St Gregory of Nazianzus composed two famous invectives against the Emperor Julian, his former schoolmate.

5[1] See ANNEX.

will) in which they will needs have it, *That we worship the Holy Table, or God knows what.*

B i 78

And were the *times* such, as should beat down *Churches*, and all the *curious carved work thereof, with Axes and Hammers*, as in *Psal.* 74.6 (and such *Times* have been) yet would I *Worship* in what place soever I came to *Pray* . . .

C i 79

To this I Answer, That 'tis no *Popery* to set a *Rail* to keep *Prophanation* from that *Holy Table* . . .

D i 83

Why, But then my *Lords*; what is this *Mystery of Iniquity*? Truly, I cannot certainly tell, but as far as I can I'll tell you.

E i 84

I humbly crave *Pardon* of your *Lordships* for this my *necessary length*, and give you *all* hearty thanks for your *Noble Patience*, and your *Just and Honourable Censure* upon these Men, and your *unanimous dislike* of them, and *defence* of the *Church*.

GEORGE LAVINGTON
1684–1762

The Moravians Compared and Detected. By the author of The Enthusiasm of Methodists and Papists Compared [i.e. George Lavington]. London 1755. 8°.

The Viscount Emlyn

Inscribed on p ⁻4: "Robert Southey. Keswick. June 6. 1807." and Southey's Bewick bookplate on p ⁻5. Inscribed on p ⁻5: "Purchased at the Sale of Southeys Library by John Montgomery Trahern for five guineas! Sir R. Inglis Bart. bid up to £4.0.0. if I recollect aright. J. M. T. June 7. 1854." Below the bookplate in Trahern's hand: "The MS. notes are in the hand writing of Southey's brother in Law S. T. Coleridge Feb. 14. 1859"; and below this: "This vol. with the autograph of Robert Southey & the original notes of his Brother in Law Sam. Taylor Coleridge is presented to S. F. Earl of Cawdor by J. M. T. April 27. 1859". The same page bears the press-mark M. R. D. 3 and the note at the head: "Bought in by Lᵈ E @ the Stackpole sale at £400."

DATE. After Jun 1807, when RS acquired this book, C spent only two extended periods in Keswick, May–Oct 1810 and Feb–Mar 1812; he must have made his notes at one time or the other.

1 p ⁻4

It is with religious Sects as with certain Characters in common Life: the worst comes out first. The first fervors of Zeal impel both Teachers & Disciples to deduce Consequences from their main principles with a *straight-forward down-rightness*, and to obtrude them on the attention with a hardihood of profession, and in such Language as heated feelings naturally suggest—i.e. glowing, and sensuously material. From the same cause, almost all enthusiastic Sects in attempting to spiritualize matter are sure to materialize Spirit, the body playing them a trick which they themselves do not suspect.—But in a generation or two, at least where ever they are not persecuted, the natural operation of Sympathy, & the craving to be sympathized with, commences—what has been found offensive to others, becomes gradually so to the Sectary himself—& at last nothing remains but a Costume perhaps, and a more regulated mannerism of morals & religious *Cult*—while to fool-hardy Extravagances succeeds Shrewdness, Caution, & all the prudential qualities that make a *warm man*, & padlock the Chest which they are sure to fill.—   S. T. C.

2   pp ⁻4–⁻2

It would be well for most Sects, if only the *names* of their founders remained, their works having perished. For the attempts to explain away, what from consistency they dare not disavow, involves them in worse inconsistency, nay, has (as among the Quakers) ended in an absolute misology, or determination neither to talk or think on the disputed parts of their Faith/ the consequence of which is, generally speaking, an entire ignorance of the true grounds of *all* Faith. Thus—I doubt not, but that few *English* Moravians exist, who would not shudder at the Language & Tenets of Zinzendorf, if they were even now presented ⟨to⟩ them under any other name/ For I confess, there seems no possibility of favorably interpreting many parts: tho' he has been grossly misunderstood in more.[1]—His Doctrines of the Godhead assuredly resolve themselves into a fantastic Atheism (for his sleeping Propator is no better than Hesiod's Chaos)[2] branching out into a gross material Polytheism—and never sure on earth or since Adam was a more unlucky attempt made to spiritualize Sensuality by sensualizing in a the grossest & most objectionable forms the most awful Conceptions of Spirit. Yet the amiable & truly Christian Conduct of the Moravian Church shews us, how acceptable to God *it is to believe with the Heart* how strange so ever the chimæras of the Brain may be.[3] Of one fact I ~~should~~ much wish to be informed—whether the presence of the Elders is actually required at the

---

2[1] Nikolaus Ludwig, Count Zinzendorf (1700–60), founder of the Herrnhuter, established Moravian communities in Europe, the West Indies, and North America. In SOUTHEY *Wesley* p 351, C wrote that were it not for the practice of lots and the interference of the Church in marriages, "I should prefer the Moravian to all other Churches, to the C. of E. in *actual*, to all but the C. of E. in form & in *professed* Faith".

2[2] Describing Zinzendorf as "a man of Genius tho' somewhat extra-zodiacal", C in EICHHORN *Apocrypha* 11 had actually expressed approval of the doctrine of the "sleeping Propator" (in Church Latin, "forefather")—i.e. the idea that God "was unknown to the Jews . . . & was first

revealed by Christ". The same assertion— "[I] say with Luther and Zinzendorf" that Christ first "declared himself a Son . . . and then revealed the Father"—appears in WATERLAND *Vindication* pp 269–71. "Chaos" in Hesiod's *Theogony* is the origin of all things, good and bad.

2[3] C's firm conviction, expressed in e.g. his tribute to mystical writers in *BL* ch 9 (*CC*) I 152—"They contributed to keep alive the *heart* in the *head* . . . and enabled me to skirt, without crossing, the sandy deserts of utter unbelief." Cf also his response to a scatterbrained servant, in *CL* IV 783: "Never mind, Kitty! we shall leave our Heads where our Skulls lie—it is our Hearts only that we shall take with us to the other World!"

consummation of marriage—for words & passages in an individuals writings may lie inert or be reasoned away.—but a practice, a regular Rite, *burns in*, & belongs to every member of the Society.[4]—One other Remark I will add of a general nature—that among the leading errors common to all religious Enthusiasts this is not the last or least—that they always consider the Soul of man exclusively in reference to itself & to God—i.e. as if every man were always alone—and pass over that large portion of human nature which refers to the action of Man on Man—as sympathy, modesty & innocent Shame, not from guilt or any sense of guilt, but simply because something is referred to which is proper to solitude or in which no sympathy can be expected, or from recalling things in one state of mind which could only take place under a state of feeling altogether different—i.e. when we cannot sympathize even with our past Selves.—The Ignorance & consequent Contempt, of this beautiful part of our nature, (which Milton has given even to the Angel Raphael when he blushed at one of Adam's Questions)[5] and the gross confusion of it with guilty Shame & false Shame, was the ground of the very worst & most offensive part of Zinzendorf's Hymns & Sermons— and under the virtue of "retrenching all to Innocence"[6] he has not merely stripped, but absolutely *fleed*[7] his Disciples—taken off the covering which nature has inwoven with our moral Life.—

What the present Liturgical Language of the Moravians is, I know not; but I suspect, that their Theology still remains Idolatrous, even ~~in~~ after a more pernicious sort than that of the Romanists. Z's sophistry concerning the 2nd Commandment proves the importance of my fundamental Distinction between contingent & necessary Presence, as the sole Basis of all religious Adoration—[8]   S. T. C.

---

[4] Lavington's work does not answer this question, though—as C noticed—it does imply that elders were present by claiming that the Moravians annulled marriages that did not satisfy this requirement (p xi), and again that they considered marriages legal only when they were consummated in the presence of the Elders (p 112).

[5] *Paradise Lost* VIII 618–19, when Adam asks how spirits express love.

[6] Lavington quotes extensively from Zinzendorf's works: his *Hymns*, his *Maxims* ed Gambold, and his *Sermons and Discourses* ed Rimius. In his summing-up, p 144, Lavington writes, "And the *Moravians' Advocate*, Mr. *Gambold*, tells us, 'The *Brethren* are intent to retrench all to

Innocence; and yet, notwithstanding, they are no *Cynics*, or *Adamites*.' "

[7] I.e. flayed.

[8] C objects to arguments presented in defence of the Moravian practice of praying to the Son alone. They affirm that God the Father "was an unknown Being before the Incarnation of Christ" (p 9); Frey swears that he has heard Zinzendorf say that "as to praying to God the Father, it is no whit better than praying to a wooden, or stone God" (9); Rimius, as a spokesman, is quoted as saying, "To avoid *Idolatry*, People ought to be taken from the *Father and H. Ghost*; and conducted to the *Son*, with whom alone we have to do" (19–20).

C's "fundamental distinction" is clearly

3 pp 62–3

[Quoting Andrew Frey *True and Authentic Account* p 20:] "At their Merry-meetings, an Uproar, as if a Mad-house had broke loose,—Musicians heightening their Mirth with all manner of *wanton Tunes*;—their *Orgia* lasting till One or Two in the Morning, with the most indecent Levities; Increase of Wantonness, Tumults, Rioting.—The *Wounds of the Saviour made a Cloak for all Manner of Licentiousness.*—Not conforming to Lewdness shows a Man to be no humbled Sinner, and so void of Respect to the *Elders* . . .''

And in truth wherever the principles of a Sect are *efficiently* wicked, we then do hear chiefly of their actions and by these actions the principles are attacked & exposed—ex. gr. the Jacobins in France. Whenever therefore as in Epiphanius and Rimius & the present Author,[1] we find nothing but opinions & wild words held up to our abhorrence, or at least only reports of horrid enormities done in secret among the Initiated into the highest Mysteries, we may be pretty certain, that the Sect is harmless.—Who are stricter in their Lives, than the Calvinist Methodists? Yet what horrible consequences have been drawn from their doctrine of Faith without works, and charged on its Adherents. But Andrew Frey— *I suspect* old Andrew Frey!—How comes the Pun of "Merry Andrew" in a Letter supposed to be a translation from the German?—In the original it would be Hans Würste = Jack Sausage—and this would be no pun on Andrew, or Andreas.[2]—Besides, what do his charges amount

formulated in ROBINSON **3**, where C first establishes the difference between necessary presence (omnipresence) in an invisible object of worship, and "an accidental Presence (ergo, Absence elsewhere)" of a visible object; he then continues, "Now the *essence* of Idolatry consists in destroying the essence of all Religion, viz—the sense of necessary Presence by attributing it to a creature, or vice versâ, by attributing accidental & creaturely Presence to the Creator."

3[1] Either Lavington himself or Andrew Frey, whose diatribes against the Moravians are quoted extensively, as are the accounts of Heinrich Rimius in *A Candid Narrative of the Rise and Progress of the Herrnhuters* (1753)—a book C annotated. Lavington's method is to compare statements made about the Moravians with ancient accounts of heretics, esp the writings of St Epiphanius (c 315–403) against the Gnostics.

3[2] The pun appears not in Lavington's work but in one of his major sources, which C must have known directly or through reviews. In *A True and Authentic Account of Andrew Frey* (1753), Frey—an American who returned to Philadelphia after leaving the Moravians—publishes as the occasion of his work a letter that the Moravians had been circulating in Pennsylvania to discredit him, in which the ostensible author writes, "Many of us are concerned for *Andrew*. I am ready to believe that he has been treated as a *Merry-Andrew* should be treated . . .". As C points out, the German word for a buffoon, *Hanswurst*, would not be a pun on the author's name. Frey's work appeared first in German editions in 1748 and 1749.

to?—Black *words*, that frighten one, are his *colours*; but what are the *figures*? Truly, a grand *Romp* on a birth-night—music, which he calls *wanton tunes*—an attribute of a Tune which I have often indeed heard but could never understand—and that the only definite action, which he adduces, is a practical Joke, not very uncommon at rustic wakes and merry-meetings, and which may easily excite the *indignation* of the Stomach; but verily does not belong to the Court of Conscience.[3] I should never have delivered over the offender to the Prince of the Air,[4] unless for a few minutes that he might sweeten himself. Our good Bishop is indeed more merry than indignant at the *crime*. In what state of mind Andrew Frey was, and how competent a witness, see p. 52 of his Pamphlet—.[5] Such a man would both see and hear every thing, he chanced to dream of—in other words, the man was *crazy*—

S. T. C.

4   pp 66–7

'Tis remarkable that they bear a particular Spite to the *seventh Commandment*, for prohibiting Adultery. *"Count Zinzendorf, in a Sermon preached in London, publicly set forth, That the seventh Commandment could oblige us no more in the New Testament, because it was at a Time when one Man had five or six Wives."* Excellent Reason! Therefore it follows of Course, that it can be *no Adultery* to make use of other Women, or other Men's Wives, under the *Gospel Dispensation*; seeing it allows but *one Wife."* [The quotation is from H. Rimius *A Candid Narrative* (1753).]

There can be no doubt, from the particular Sanctity ascribed to marriage by the Moravians, that the Count Z's meaning was no more than this: that the moral obligation to marriage fidelity among Christians is not founded on the 7th Commandment delivered to the Jews; but on the purer & loftier morality of the Gospel Dispensation. In this sense the Count's Argument is a just one. To him who may have as many wives as he can

---

[3][3] Frey describes (q Lavington p 62) ". . . Revellings on *Birth-Days*,—a perfect Scene of *Gluttony, Drunkenness, and Debauchery*,—throwing one another on the Floor, and struggling with many filthy and gross Indecencies,—one Brother [i.e. Church member] *breaking Wind* over another's *Tea-Cup*, &c."

[3][4] The Devil, as in Eph 2.2.

[3][5] Frey (p 52, q Lavington p 64) makes grotesque assertions about the morality of the Moravians: "The Spirit of the *Evites* (conforming to our first *Parents* in their State of *Nakedness*) daily gets ground among them.—'Tis now *notorious*; though their *Doctrine* doth not expresly declare for a *Communitas Corporum* [Community of Bodies].—The abovementioned *principal Class* rejoice with great Rapture over the *Venereal Energy*.—Nothing can exceed their very *Children* in *Wickedness and Impudence*."

keep, the 7th Commandment is but the 8th & 10th Commands enforced in one most important instance.[1] Thou shalt not steal nor covet another's goods. Christianity founds it on the nobler & more more[a] mysterious necessity of exclusive Love. There is nothing common between Polygamy with the power of Divorce, and the marriage union of one Christian man with one Christian woman. They are essentially different States: and a Law applying to one cannot be immediately applicable to the other.   S. T. C.

5   p 68

They are set free from *all Law* by their *Marriage with Christ*. "The *Magistrate*, says the *Count*, may and must use Laws;—but when we consider our *Saviour's* ruling of the Heart, the Souls who are his *Bride*; here *we can't think of Law*. For (as he most ingeniously argues) how strange would it be between *Husband and Wife*, to have it set down how much each should do in their common Concerns, or how far they should yield to and gratify one another? This could not be called a *happy Match*."

Surely, nothing can be more innocent or just. The Count has said wisely, the outward morality which is producible by mere prudence, I entrust to the care of magistrates/ & therefore it is, that I have avowed that the strict Discipline & multitude of Officers in our Society, is not a religious but a civil and temporal Discipline. In matters of *Virtue* (i.e. the root, the fountain) we cannot think of *any* outward Law, no, not of the divine Law, as far as it is outward, i.e. grounded on threatenings or promises. But that the Count did not therefore hold Law superfluous is demonstrated by the watchful Discipline & multiplied Magistracy of the Moravians—in addition to the Laws of the Country.

6   p 69

[Quoting Zinzendorf] " 'Tis a *false* Charge against us, that we *make void the Law*. For we insist on those Things which are inculcated in a *legal* Method; and the Word *Law* is not rightly understood. By *Rom*. vii. it appears, that one's *Husband* is one's *Law*. But the *Saviour* is our Husband, and henceforth *he is the Law*."

i.e. we *insist* upon them at *all events*; but at the same time we teach, that

---

[a] C repeats the word as he begins another line

[4][1] The seventh, "Thou shalt not commit adultery", enforces the eighth, "Thou shalt not steal", and the tenth, "Thou shalt not covet thy neighbour's house . . . thy neighbour's wife . . . nor any thing that is thy neighbour's."

unless they flow from the new fountain, they are of no avail to a Christian's Sanctification. And is not this orthodox? is it not Sᵗ Paul's and Sᵗ James's Doctrine?[1]— Nay, has not even the Epicurean Horace said the same thing? "I have not robbed, or murdered—Well! and you have not been hung or sent to the Gallies. You have had your appropriate Reward."[2]   S. T. C.—

6[1] I.e. according to C's interpretation of Rom 7, cited in textus, esp 7.6, "But now we are delivered from the law, that being dead wherein we were held; that we should serve in newness of spirit, and not in the oldness of the letter"; and Jas 1.22, 25, "But be ye doers of the word, and not hearers only. . . . whoso looketh into the perfect law of liberty, and continueth therein, he being not a forgetful hearer, but a doer of the work, this man shall be blessed in his deed."

6[2] Horace *Epistles* 16.46–8.

WILLIAM LAW
1686–1761

A Serious Call to a Devout and Holy Life. Adapted to the state and condition of all orders of Christians. 10th ed. London 1772. 8°.

Not located; marginalia published from an appendix to C. M. Ingleby "On Some Points Connected with the Philosophy of Coleridge" *Transactions of the Royal Society of Literature* 2nd ser IX (1870) 433. According to Ingleby, the annotated copy had the "Autograph" of WW in it. A copy of this edition is included in *W Library*.

DATE. Probably between Jun 1809 and Mar 1810, while C was living with the Wordsworths at Grasmere.

1 pp 166–7 | Ch 14

[Law writes in favour of early rising to prayer.] If you consider devotion only as a *time* of so much prayer, you may perhaps perform it though you live in this daily indulgence [sleeping in]: but if you consider it as a *state* of the heart, as a *lively fervour* of the soul, that is deeply affected with a sense of its own misery and infirmities, and desiring the Spirit of God more than all things in the world, you will find that the spirit of indulgence, and the spirit of prayer, cannot exist together.

The thought that haunts me whenever I read this excellent book is the spirit of religious selfishness or rather *selfness* that pervades it. Generosity in *act* is everywhere enforced, and even in principle; but still the habit of the imagination is purely about *my* soul, *my* heart, the Spirit of God for *me*, etc. etc. This never, never can be the natural state of a human being; it makes every movement of the mind too much an act of full *consciousness*. Even in common life we instinctively dislike *self-conscious* folks—no odds, whether humility or pride.

LAW MAGAZINE

The Law Magazine; or, Quarterly Review of Jurisprudence, for January, 1830; and April 1830. Vol. III. London 1830. 8°.

Not located. Marginalia printed from *NTP* 216–18.

CONTENTS. [Jan] 1–71 Review of the "Real Property" Report, 1829; 72–117 Life of Lord Hardwicke; 117–25 The Negotiability of Promissory Notes; 125–31 The Effect of the Bankrupt Act; 131–9 On Resulting Trust of Land; 140–51 Review of Wellesley's *View of the Court of Chancery*, 1830; 152–8 Review of Cary's *Commentary* on Littleton, 1829; 158–80 Medical Jurisprudence: Insanity; 180–99 Mercantile Law: Of the Contract of Sale; 200–9 Review of *The Life of a Lawyer*, 1830; 210–59 Digest of Cases; 259–65 List of Cases; 266–73 Questions on Registration; 273–9 Outline of a Plan for a General Register; 280–2 Decisions on Lord Tenterden's Act; 282–3 The Patent Laws; 283–91 Review of *Quarterly Review* article on Welsh Judicature; 291–301 Events of the Quarter; 301–2 New Publications; [Apr] 305–40 Review of Greene's *Report of the Trial of James Forbes* [et al], 1823; 341–54 Conveyancing; 355–69 On the Requisites of Deeds; 370–4 Letter from J. J. Park; 375–81 On the Tenant's Right to Dispute his Landlord's Title; 382–7 Remedies on Bonds and Covenants; 388–96 Review of *Juridical Letters*, 1820; 396–505 Review of the Second Common-Law Report; 506–71 Digest of Cases; 571–8 List of Cases; 578–80 Abstract of Public General Statutes; 581–94 Administration of Justice in India; 595–[602] Events of the Quarter.

DATE. 1830–4.

COEDITOR. David V. Erdman.

1   p 97 | Life of Lord Hardwicke

In framing his judgments Lord Hardwicke appears always to have been anxious to bring the case within the scope of some broad general principle. This, however, he never effected by means of forced interpretations or fanciful analogies. He was always careful to support his opinion by the authority of legal precedents, in the selection and application of which he was particularly happy.

I am too well aware of my incompetence to set any value on my own opinion; but in reading, some years back, Atkyn's and Vesey's Reports (23 Vol.) and afterwards, Sir James Burrows, and (while I was at Malta) Robinson's Admiralty Reports,[1] I was exceedingly impressed with the

---

1[1] J. T. Atkyns *Reports of Cases Argued and Determined in the High Court of*   *Chancery, in the Time of Lord Chancellor Hardwicke* (3 vols 1781–2); Francis Vesey

measureless superiority of Lords Hardwicke and Mansfield and of Sir W. Scott to Lord Eldon, on the score of solid and comprehensive principle.[2]

2 p 102

His [the lawyer's] profession . . . gives him habits of thought uncongenial to those of a statesman; and it is to no purpose to argue that none but weak and plastic minds suffer themselves to be influenced by habit.

Better thus—none but soft and fictile minds yield to the impressions of habit. Influences excite, modify, temper, contemper, &c., but can rarely be said to *mould.*

Is there any authority for the use of this word in a passive sense?[1] *Qu.* fictile! "Soft" would have been better than "weak."

3 p 108

Some obloquy has been cast upon Lord Hardwicke because he disposed of the church patronage belonging to his office with a view rather to increase his own political influence, than to forward obscure merit or to further the interests of religion. This accusation is undoubtedly just; but whether the fault be a very venial or a highly criminal one is a question likely to be decided by different persons in very different ways: no one, at all events, will deny that it is a very common one.

—by the Venialists, I presume, in Change-Alley, or in the Hells, or at Windsor.[1] The denizens of Newgate would be ashamed of such a sentiment. But Lawyers are sorry moralists, and both they and the men in office are in whimsical wise contemptuously jealous of literary men.

Reports of Cases Argued and Determined in the High Court of Chancery [1789–1817] (20 vols 1795–1822); Sir James Burrow *Reports of Cases Argued and Adjudged in the Court of King's Bench during the Time of Lord Mansfield's Presiding* . . . (4th ed 5 vols 1790); Sir Christopher Robinson *Reports of Cases Argued and Determined in the High Court of Admiralty [1798–1808]* (6 vols 1799–1808).

1[2] Cf C's emphasis on the importance of principle to politicians in *BL* ch 10 (*CC*) I 191–2. Philip Yorke, 1st Earl of Hardwicke (1690–1764), was Lord Chancellor 1737–56; William Murray, 1st Earl of Mansfield (1705–93), was Lord Chief Justice 1756–88; William Scott, Lord Stowell (1745–1836), was judge of the High Court of Admiralty 1798–1828; his brother, John Scott (1751–1838), 1st Earl of Eldon, was Lord Chancellor 1801–27. C would have read about Hardwicke in Atkyns (n 1 above), about Mansfield in Burrow, and about Sir William Scott in Robinson, and about Eldon in Vols XVIII and XIX of Vesey.

2[1] *OED* gives examples from Evelyn (1675) and Carlyle (1837) of "fictile" as "capable of being moulded".

3[1] I.e. such quibbles belong to the hypocrisy of stock markets, debtors' prisons, and the court.

4 p 112

But unhappily his cupidity led him to regard the increase of his fortune as primary object of ambition; and though to accomplish it he never descended to employ means inconsistent with the strictest integrity, there cannot be a doubt that he sacrificed to it a species of fame which it was in his power to earn, and which it was incumbent on him to deserve. Had he not been deterred by avarice from effecting the reform of the Court of Chancery, he might have left behind him a smaller inheritance to his children, but he would have transmitted to them the glory of being descended from a disinterested benefactor of his country.

The Devil! What? an infamous prostitution of his immense patronage to his own dirty interests, "not inconsistent," &c. I will even risk the scorn of the Biographer[1] by asking him, in what chapter of the New Testament he found Avarice, a foible: or base breach of a sacred trust, a very venial fault!

4[1] Unidentified.

GOTTFRIED WILHELM VON LEIBNIZ
1646–1716

Theodicee, das ist, Versuch von der Güte Gottes, Freyheit des Menschen, und vom Ursprunge des Bösen. 5th ed rev Johann Christoph Gottscheden. 2 vols in 1. Hanover & Leipzig 1763. 8°.

Yale University (Beinecke Library)

Inscribed on p ⁻2: "From the Library of Thomas De Quincey, with holograph note by him underneath one holograph of Samuel Taylor Coleridge on opposite board. Ja: Braidwood Edin. 31ˢᵗ Aug. 1866. A most interesting memorial of two great men, in connection with the not less great Leibnitz whose work has been the occasion of their remarks." Extract from bookseller's catalogue pasted in p ⁻2. In 1988 the work was still (as De Q says in 1 n 3) unopened after I ii 304, with the following exceptions: I ii 345–8, 369–76; II 449–57, 793–802.

CONTENTS. (Note that pagination is in two series that do not correspond to the division into 2 vols.) I i [i–x dedication and preface]; 1–60 Des Hrn. von Fontenelle Lobschrift auf den Freyherrn von Leibnitz; 63–106 Vorrede des Verfassers; 107–12 J. P. Uz *Theodicee: ein Gedicht*; ii [new series in pagination] 1–96 Abhandlung von der Uebereinstimmung des Glaubens mit der Vernunft; 97–228 Des Versuchs von der Güte Gottes, von der Freyheit des Menschen, und vom Ursprunge des Bösen, Erster Theil; 229–432 Zweyter Theil; II 435–670 Dritter Theil; 673–712 Vortheidigung der guten Sache Gottes; 713–30 Gedanken über die Schrift des Herrn Hobbes, von der Freyheit, der Nothwendigkeit, und dem ungefähren Zufalle; 731–90 Anmerkungen über das Buch vom Ursprunge des Bösen; 791–7 Einige Beylagen zu der Fontenellischen Lobschrift; 797–800 Beschreibung des Leibnizischen Rechenkastens; 801–2 Beschreibung eines besondern arithmetischen Instruments; 803–24 Des Herrn von Leibnitz Rechnung mit Null und Eins; 825–38 Vernünftige Grundsätze von der Natur und von der Gnade; 838–52 Neues Lehrgebäude von der Natur und Gemeinschaft der Substanzen; 853–64 Erläuterungen des Neuen Lehrgebäudes von der Gemeinschaft der Substanzen; 865–908 Neueste Zugabe zu dieser fünften Auflage der Theodicee (1763).

DATE. C took a copy of the *Theodicee* (possibly the *Essais de Théodicée*— Amsterdam 1710—listed as his in *W Library*) to Malta in 1804 and read at least some of it during the voyage: *CN* II 1993 and n. This annotated copy, however, appears to have been De Q's own—he writes of its being "returned" to him (1 n 3)—and C did not meet De Q until 1807. The most likely period for the loan of the volume is 1809, when De Q first visited and then settled in Grasmere while C was living with the Wordsworths and producing *The Friend*.

TEXTUS TRANSLATION. E. M. Huggard tr *Theodicy* (1951).

1 p ⁻3 (p-d)

I confess, that the careful Perusal of this Work has lowered that veneration for Leibnitz which I had formed from some Essays & scattered passages of his Works.[1] There seems a petitio principii predominant throughout. What is best is best. But the Universe is the best—Therefore it is the best.—[2]

2 ɪ ii 45–6 | § 37

Wenn nun gleich noch so viel Wahrscheinlichkeiten vorhanden wären, dass dieser grosse Wohlthäter des menschlichen Geschlechts einen Diebstahl begangen hätte: würde nicht alle Welt über dergleichen Anklage lachen, so wahrscheinlich sie auch immer seyn möchte?

[Be there never so many witnesses or appearances of every kind tending to prove that this great benefactor of the human race [i.e. God] has just committed some larceny, is it not true that the whole earth would make mock of the accusation, however specious it might be?]

This takes for granted the truth of a metaphysical God—now these arguments are brought to invalidate this ɪn supposed Truth. But the ? is, not whether if God be, these be fair arguments against his goodness; but whether to the ?, Is there a God? there be not arguments on the negative.

3 p ⁺3, referring to ɪ ii 85 | § 76

Denn in diesem Falle würde sie dasjenige seyn, was die Alten *Scindapsus*, oder ein *Blitri* (Clem. Alex. Strom. 8.) das ist, leere Worte ohne Verstand, genennet.

[It would be in that case what the ancient Schools called *Scindapsus* or *Blityri* (Clem. Alex., *Stromateis*, 8), that is, words devoid of meaning.]

p. 85 *Scindapsus* et *Blitri*: at in Notis ad ᵃ in verbo Titivillitium—[1]

ᵃ Long space in ms

[1][1] C's early letters fairly frequently refer to various readings of Leibniz—notably, in the winter of 1800–1, *CL* ɪɪ 676—but they seldom mention texts specifically. An interesting letter of 1818, however, contains instructions for a course of reading in Leibniz that may reflect C's own: "... Noveaux Essais, & his Nova Logici Repertio, in Dutens' Edition, & his French Letters—His Theodicee I would pass over at present" (*CL* ɪᴠ 851). "Dutens" is Leibniz *Opera omnia* ed Louis Dutens (6

vols Geneva 1768), to which C apparently had access although it is not listed in the Gillman, Green, Southey, or Wordsworth library catalogues.

[1][2] A note by De Quincey follows: "N.B. The above note from Mʳ Coleridge, who, out of 908 pp. ᴏf which this work contains, could have read only 305—all after that being uncut when he returned it to me."

[3][1] "Also in the Notes to . . . at the word *Titivillitium*": C refers to the inci-

4   I ii 134 | Pt 1 § 26

Ferner muss man auch wohl bedenken, dass das moralische Böse in der
That nur deswegen ein so grosses Uebel sey; weil es eine Quelle vieles
physikalischen Uebels, und zwar in einer solchen Creatur ist, die das
grösste Vermögen hat, dergleichen Uebel anzustiften. Denn ein böser
Willen ist in seinem Bezirke dasjenige, was das böse Urwesen der *Ma-
nichäer* im Weltgebäude seyn würde: und die Vernunft, die ein Ebenbild
der Gottheit ist, giebt den bösen Gemüthern grosse Mittel an die Hand,
viel Böses zu verursachen. Ein einziger *Caligula* oder *Nero* hat viel
mehr Schaden gethan, als ein Erdbeden. Ein böser Mensch hat seine
Lust daran, dass er Jammer und Verderben anrichtet: und dazu findet er
mehr als zu viel Gelegenheit. Allein da Gott geneigt ist, so viel Gutes
hervorzubringen, als nur möglich ist, und hierzu alle mögliche Wissen-
schaft und Macht hat; so kann unmöglich ein Fehler, eine Schuld oder
Sünde in ihm seyn: wenn er aber die Sünde zulässt, so ist es bey ihm
lauter Weisheit und Tugend.

[It is again well to consider that moral evil is an evil so great only because it is
a source of physical evils, a source existing in one of the most powerful of
creatures, who is also most capable of causing those evils. For an evil will is in
its department what the evil principle of the Manicheans would be in the uni-
verse; and reason, which is an image of the Divinity, provides for evil souls
great means of causing much evil. One single Caligula, one Nero, has caused
more evil than an earthquake. An evil man takes pleasure in causing suffering
and destruction, and for that there are only too many opportunities. But God
being inclined to produce as much good as possible, and having all the know-
ledge and all the power necessary for that, it is impossible that in him there be
fault, or guilt, or sin; and when he permits sin, it is wisdom, it is virtue.]

This §, in my opinion, contains the Falsum Magnum,[1] on wͨh all the
Theodices have struck: & with them the first Principle of morality. I
mean the subordination of moral to physical Evill: in consequence of
which the latter in reality constitutes the true evil of the former—now as
the latter is evidently avoidable by omnipotence (every healthy Butterfly
proves it) the former becomes unintelligible—. Archbishop King has
fallen into the same error, & expressed it more [? simply].[2]

dence of the rare word (meaning "a very
small trifle", "a bagatelle") in Plautus
Casina II v 39, glossed as meaningless by
Gronovius from the second-century epit-
ome of *De verborum significatu* by Sextus
Pompeius Festus, e.g. in *M. Acci Plauti
quae supersunt Comoediae . . .* (Leipzig
1760) i 248n (tr) "Titivillitio has no mean-
ing, like βλιτυρί [*blituri*, the sound of a
harp-string] and σχινδαψός [*skindapsos*, a
four-stringed musical instrument] among
the Greeks." We do not know what edition
of Plautus C used.

4[1] "Great Error".

4[2] William King (1650–1729), abp of
Dublin, author of the well-known *Origin of*

5 I ii 274 | Pt 2 § 129

[Quoting Bayle's response to Leibniz *Reply to the Questions of a Provincial:*] "Die Zulassung eines gewissen Uebels ist als dann nur zu entschuldigen, wenn man demselben nicht abhelfen kann, ohne eine grössers Uebel einzuführen. Allein sie kann bey denenjenigen nicht entschuldiget werden, die so wohl wider dieses Uebel, als wider alle andere, die aus dessen Unterdrückung entstehen könnten, ein kräftiges Mittel in Händen haben."

Der Satz ist wahr: allein wider die Regierung Gottes kann er nicht angeführet werden. Die höchste Vernunft nöthiget ihn, das Böse zuzulassen. Erwählte Gott dasjenige nicht, was im Ganzen und schlechterdings das beste wäre: so würde dieses ein grösseres Uebel seyn, als alle besondere Uebel, die er durch dieses Mittel verhindern könnte. Diese schlimme Wahl würde seine Gütigkeit, oder seine Weisheit übern Hausen werfen.

["The permission of a certain evil is only excusable when one cannot remedy it without introducing a greater evil; but it cannot be excusable in those who have in hand a remedy more efficacious against this evil, and against all the other evils that could spring from the suppression of this one."

The maxim is true, but it cannot be brought forward against the government of God. Supreme reason constrains him to permit the evil. If God chose what would not be the best absolutely and in all, that would be a greater evil than all the individual evils which he could prevent by this means. This wrong choice would destroy his wisdom and his goodness.]

But does L. take das beste[1] for granted? $A = A : X = A$.

Evil, originally pub in Latin in 1702. C mentions him also in PARR **1**.

5[1] "The best", from textus.

ROBERT LEIGHTON

1611–1684

Copy A

The Expository Works and Other Remains of Archbishop Leighton, some of which were never before printed. Revised by Philip Doddridge, D.D. With a preface by the Doctor. 2 vols. Edinburgh 1748. 8°.

Not located. Marginalia published from MS TRANSCRIPT.

This copy was lent to C by a Bristol acquaintance, William Brame Elwyn (1774–1841), early in Apr 1814. C in turn began to recommend Leighton to others. An interesting unpublished letter from Hannah More to William Wilberforce, dated 13 Apr 1814 and now held in the Manuscripts Dept of the Perkins Library, Duke University, gives some account of the circumstances of C's introduction to Leighton as well as to Hannah More herself: "I found him very eloquent, entertaining and brimfull of knowledge. Added to this he seemed to have great reverence for Evangelical religion and considerable acquaintance with it. . . . Another thing pleased me, there is at Bristol a very accomplished man a Mᵣ Elwyn who has been very wild and an infidel. Colridge told me he had sat up till 4 that morning reading ArchBp Leighton which Mᵣ Elwin whose favorite Author he is become, lent him!''

The editions of Leighton used later in association with *AR* are COPY B and COPY C. A table showing the distribution of marginalia in all three copies is included in the headnote to COPY C.

CONTENTS. I v–vi "The Publisher to the Reader''; vii–xxii "Preface by Philip Doddridge'' (dated 26 Apr 1748); I 1–552, II 1–382 *A Practical Commentary upon the First Epistle of St. Peter*; 383–464 *Meditations Critical and Practical, on Psalms iv. xxxii. and cxxx*; 464–544 *Expository Lectures on Psalms xxxix. Isaiah vi. and Romans xii*; 545–59 *Letters* [8 in number]; 560–76 *Rules and Instructions for a Holy Life*.

MS TRANSCRIPT. University of Texas (Humanities Research Center): letter of 22 May 183[?5/8] from Alfred Elwyn to Edward Moxon in response to HNC's request for copies of C's marginalia. The letter identifies the edition, describes the volumes, and gives an unusually scrupulous transcript "copy[ing] . . . the peculiarities of his [C's] handwriting''. Elwyn describes 1 as written "in a large, clear, open hand'', and he adds, "The whole of the notes are in the first volume. And it is strange that for twenty four years, they should have been preserved without an erasure, all being in pencil. I fortunately learnt from Mrs Jameson, that a solution of gum arabic will make them indelible. May it be so, for with such memorials near me, I feel more under the spirit of the man, and as if my admiration and veneration for his genius and character, had a fellowship and sympathy with the individual himself." The transcript ends: "These are the whole.—May they be of interest." The Humanities Research Center contains also SC's copy of the marginalia, taken from Elwyn's letter.

DATE. Apr 1814 (1).

COEDITOR. John Beer.

1 "On one of the fly-leaves"

Surely if ever Work not in the sacred Canon might suggest a belief of Inspiration, of something more than human, this it is. When Mr. E. made this assertion, I took it as an hyperbole of affection, but now I subscribe to it seriously, & bless the Hour that introduced me to the knowledge of the evangelical apostolical Archbishop Leighton.[1]

S. T. Coleridge April 1814.

2 I 70 | *A Practical Commentary*: 1 Pet 1.6

Can we deny that it is Unbelief of those things that causeth this Neglect and Forgetting of them? The Discourse, the Tongue of Men and Angels cannot beget divine Belief of the Happiness to come; only he that gives it, gives Faith likewise to apprehend it, and lay hold upon it, and upon our believing to be filled with Joy in the Hopes of it.

Most true! Most true!

3 I 75 | 1 Pet 1.7

In spiritual Trials that are the sharpest and most fiery of all, when the Furnace is within a Man, when God doth not only shut up his loving Kindness from its Feeling; but seems to shut it up in hot Displeasure, when he writes bitter things against it, yet then to depend upon him, and wait for his Salvation, this is not only a true, but a strong, and very refined Faith indeed, and the more he smites, the more to cleave to him. Well might he say, *When I am tried I shall come forth as Gold.* Who could say that Word, *though he slay me yet will I trust in him*? though I saw, as it were, his Hand lifted up to destroy me, yet from that same Hand would I expect Salvation.

Bless God O my soul! for this sweet and strong Comforter. The Honey in the Lion.[1]

[1][1] C adopted Elwyn's judgment whole-heartedly, e.g. in his letter of c 27 Apr 1814 to Cottle: "If there could be an inter-mediate Space between inspired & unin-spired Writings, that Space would be oc-cupied by Leighton": *CL* III 479n; cf *C*

Talker 308, *CL* v 198. For Elwyn see head-note.

[3][1] An allusion to Judges 14.8–18, Samson's riddle of the honeycomb in the carcase of a lion.

4 ɪ 82 | 1 Pet 1.8–9

This natural Men may discourse of, and that very knowingly, and give a Kind of natural Credit to it, as to a History that may be true; but firmly to believe, that there is *divine Truth* in all these Things, and to have a Persuasion of it stronger than of the very Things we see with our Eyes, such an Assent as this, is the peculiar Work of the Spirit of God, and is certainly saving Faith.

Lord I believe! Help thou my unbelief.[1] My natural reason acquiesces. I believe enough to *fear*—O grant me the Belief that brings sweet *Hope*.

5 ɪ 83

[Faith] causes the Soul to find all that is spoken of him in the Word, and his Beauty there represented, to be abundantly true, makes it really taste of his Sweetness, and by that possesses the Heart more strongly with his Love, persuading it of the Truth of those Things, not by Reasons, and Arguments; but by an inexpressible Kind of Evidence, that they only know that have it.

Either this is true or Religion is not *Religion* i.e. *adds* nothing to Human Reason, non religat.[1] Grant it, grant it me O Lord.[2]

6 ɪ 131, paragraph marked | 1 Pet 1.13

[Leighton glosses the phrase "gird up the Loins" as a reference to the custom of tucking up long garments for labour or walking. He takes it in general as an allegory for mental preparation.] Gather up your Affections, that they hang not down to hinder you in your Race, and so in your Hopes of obtaining; and do not only gather them up, but ty them up, that they fall not down again, or if they do, be sure to gird them straiter than before. . . . We walk through a World where there is much Mire of sinful Pollutions, and therefore cannot but defile them; and the Crowd we are among will be ready to tread on them, yea our own Feet may be intangled in them, and so make us stumble, and possibly fall. Our only safest Way is to gird up our Affections wholly. . . . And we may also learn by the foregoing Doctrine, that this is the Place of our

---

4[1] Mark 9.24, quoted also in C's letter to Cottle 27 May 1814: *CL* ɪɪɪ 499.

5[1] "Does not reunite". Cicero derived *religio* from *relegere* (to read again), but modern etymologists, with C, prefer the derivation given by Augustine and others—*religare* (to bind again). C elaborates upon the position expressed here in a letter of the same period (*CL* ɪɪɪ 479) and in notes of 1823 associated with the composition of *AR* (BM MS Egerton 2801 f 234ʳ, pub *SW & F*—*CC*).

5[2] I.e. grant me faith that (as in textus) "causes the Soul to find all that is spoken of him in the Word".

Trial and Conflict, but the Place of our Rest is above: We must here have *our Loins girt*, but when we come there, we may wear our long white Robes at their full Length without Disturbance, for there is nothing there but Peace; and without danger of Defilement, for *no unclean thing is there*, yea the Streets of that new *Jerusalem* are pav'd with pure Gold. To him then, that hath prepared that city for us, let us ever give Praise.

In the whole course of my studies I do not remember to have read so beautiful an Allegory as this: so various & detailed and yet so just and natural

7   I 133–4 | 1 Pet 1.14

There is a Truth in it, that all Sin arises from some kind of Ignorance, or, at least, from present Inadvertence and Inconsideration, turning away the Mind from the Light; which therefore, for the time, is as if it were not, and is all one with Ignorance in the Effect; and therefore the Works of Sin are all called *Works of Darkness*. For were the true Visage of Sin seen at a full Light, undress'd and unpainted, it were impossible, while it so appear'd, that any one Soul could be in Love with it, but would rather fly it, as hideous and abominable.

This is the only (defect shall I say 'no' but the only) omission I have *felt* in this divine Writer—for him we understand by feeling—*experimentally*, namely, that he doth not notice the horrible Tyranny of *Habit*[1]— the trembling Devils *believe*.[2] What the Archbishop says is most true of beginners in Sin: but this is the Fore-taste of Hell, to see and loathe the deformity of the wedded vice, & yet still to embrace it & nourish.[3]

8   I 134

. . . our Apostle . . . he calls those Times wherein Christ was unknown to them, the *Times of their Ignorance*. Though the Stars shine never so bright, and the Moon with them in its full, yet they do not all together make it Day, still it is Night till the Sun appear.

How beautiful and yet how simple & as it were unconscious of its own beauty.

9   I 136–7

You were running to Destruction in the Way of Sin, and there was a

---

[1] As his correspondence makes clear, C's introduction to Leighton came at a time when he was desperately trying to give up opium: *CL* III 476–9, 489–92. Cf **12** below.

[2] Jas 2.19 (var).

[3] Cf "To know & loathe, yet wish & do" in *CL* II 984 (1803) and in *The Pains of Sleep* (*PW*—EHC—I 390).

Voice, together with the Gospel preached to your Ear, that spake into your Heart, and called you back from that Path of Death to the Way of Holiness, which is the only Way of Life. He hath sever'd you from the Mass of the profane World, and pick'd you out to be Jewels for himself . . .

Oh, how divine! surely, nothing less than the Spirit of Christ could have inspired such thoughts in such language. Other divines, Donne & Jeremy Taylor, for instance, have *converted* their worldly gifts, and applied them to holy ends; but here the gifts themselves seem unearthly.[1]

10 ɪ 152 | 1 Pet 1.18–19

As in Religion, so in the Course and Practice of Mens Lives, the Stream of Sin runs from one Age into another, and every Age makes it greater, adding somewhat to what it receives, as Rivers grow in their Course, by Accession of Brooks that fall into them, and every Man when he is born, falls like a Drop into this main Current of Corruption, and so is carried down with it, and this by Reason of its Strength, and his own Nature, which willingly dissolves into it, and runs along with it.

In this single period we have Religion (the Spirit), Philosophy (the Soul) and Poetry (the Body and Drapery[)] united,[1] Plato glorified by St Paul and yet coming as unostentatiously as any speech from an innocent girl of fifteen.

11 ɪ 163 | 1 Pet 1.20

It was doubtless the fit time; but notwithstanding the Schoolmen offer at Reasons to prove the Fitness of it, as their Humour is to prove all things, none dare I think conclude, but if God had so appointed, it might been either sooner, or later . . .

The true Spirit of modern Philosophy i.e. Psilosophy.[1]

12 ɪ 211 | 1 Pet 2.1–2

. . . the Infant is not cloyed nor wearied with daily feeding on the Breast, but desires it every Day, as if it had never had it before; this the Child of God hath an unchangeable Appetite for the Word, 'tis daily new to him, he finds still fresh Delight in it; thus *David* as before cited, *My Soul breaketh for the Longing it hath for thy Judgments at all Times.*

9[1] C also contrasts Leighton and Taylor in Howɪᴇ **8**.

10[1] Cf the same figure in *BL* ch 14 (*CC*) ɪɪ 18 and n.

11[1] "Shallow philosophy", C's frequent usage, e.g. *BL* ch 3 (*CC*) ɪ 67n, *CL* ɪᴠ 922 (where C's own translation is "slender wisdom").

And then *Psal. i*. This Law was *his Meditation Day and Night*. Whereas a natural Man is easily surfeited of it, and the very Commonness and Cheapness of it makes it contemptible to him.

Oh that this divine man had adverted more to the fiendish Tyranny of Habit[1]—but he wrote always from his Heart, & his Heart was too pure to be fully aware.

13   ɪ 213

If any one's Head or Tongue should grow apace, and all the rest stand at a Stay, it would certainly make him a Monster; and they are no other, that are knowing and discoursing Christians, and grow daily in that, but not at all in Holiness of Heart and Life, which is the proper Growth of the Children of God.

Father in Heaven have mercy on me! Christ, Lamb of God have mercy on me![1] Save me Lord! or I perish.[2] Alas, I am perishing.

14   ɪ 219 | 1 Pet 2.3

A well furnished Table may please a Man, while he hath Health and Appetite; but offer it to him in the Height of a Fever, how unpleasant would it be then? Though never so richly decked, 'tis not only then useless, but hateful to him: But the Kindness and Love of God is then as seasonable and refreshing to him, as in Health, and possibly more; he can find Sweetness in that, even on his Sick bed.

To the regenerate; but to the conscious Sinner a Source of Terrors insupportable. [a]S. T. C. i.e. Sinful, tormented Culprit.[1]

15   ɪ 231 | 1 Pet 2.4–5

These things hold likewise in the other Stones of this Building, chosen before Time; all that should be of this Building are fore-ordain'd in God's Purpose, all written in that Book before-hand, and then in due Time they are chosen, by actual calling according to that Purpose, hewed out and sever'd by God's own Hand out of the Quarry of corrupt Nature. Dead Stones in themselves as the rest, but made living, by his bringing them to Christ, and so made *truly precious*, and accounted precious by him that hath made them so.

[a] *LR* omits the rest of this note

12[1] See **7** above.

13[1] A variant of the Agnus Dei in the Communion service. C uses the Greek version of "Lord have mercy" in COPY B **17** below.

13[2] Matt 8.25 var.

14[1] For C's use of his initials, see ANNUAL ANTHOLOGY **10** n 3.

Tho' this is not only truth, but a most important Truth—it would yet have been well to have obviated the apparent carnal consequences.[1]

16   I 237

All Sacrifice is not taken away, but it is changed from the offering of those things formerly in use, to spiritual Sacrifices.

Now these are every Way preferable; they are easier and cheaper to us, and yet more precious and acceptable to God.

Still understand to the regenerated to others they are not only[a] easy & cheap but unpurchaseable and impossible too. O God, have mercy upon me.[1]

17   I 251 | 1 Pet 2.6

Though I be beset on all Hands, be accused by the Law and mine own conscience, and by Satan, and have nothing to answer for myself; yet here I will stay, for I am sure in him there is Salvation, and no where else.

"Here I will stay": but alas! the poor Sinner has forfeited the power of *Willing*. Miserable *wishing* is all he can command. Oh, the dreadful Injury of an irreligious education! To be taught our Prayers & the awful Truths of Religion in the same tone, as we are taught the Latin Grammar and too often inspiring the same sensations of Weariness and disgust,—

---

[a] Possibly a transcriber's error for "not only not"

15[1] Peter describes members of the Church metaphorically as "lively stones" composing a "spiritual house". C appears to object especially to Leighton's phrase "the Quarry of corrupt Nature" as over-looking, in his opinion, the spiritual quality in all *human* nature that sets it apart from the rest of the creation.

16[1] See **13** above.

Copy B

The Genuine Works of R. Leighton, D.D. Archbishop of Glasgow: with a preface by Philip Doddridge, D.D. A new edition, with corrections and additional letters. To which is now prefixed, the life of the author, by the Rev. Erasmus Middleton. 4 vols. London 1819. 8°.

Not located. James Gillman's copy, listed in *Gillman SC* (1843) 454; C mentions its not belonging to him in *CL* v 205. Marginalia published from MS TRANSCRIPTS and *LR* IV 156–83 (which conflates COPY A and COPY B). For the distribution of marginalia in the three copies, see headnote to COPY C.

CONTENTS. I ix–x Preface by the Rev. Henry Foster; xii–xxxvi "Preface by Dr. Doddridge"; xix–xxxvi "Life of Robert Leighton, D.D., Archbishop of Glasgow" by Erasmus Middleton; I 1–507, II i–354 *A Practical Commentary upon the First Epistle General of St. Peter*; 355–429 *Expository Lectures on Psalm XXXIX; on Isaiah VI; and on Romans XII*; 431–51 *Charges, &c. to the Clergy of the Diocesan Synod of Dunblane*; 452–64 *Seven Letters*; 465–80 *Rules and Instructions for a Holy Life*; III 1–226 *Eighteen Sermons*; 227–63 *An Exposition of the Creed*; 264–333 *An Exposition of the Lord's Prayer*; 334–400 *An Exposition of the Ten Commandments*; 415–18 *A Short Catechism*; 419–533 *Ten Sermons, from the Author's Manuscripts*; IV [vii]–xv "Preface by the Publisher of the Latin Edition [of *Praelectiones theologicae* (1693)]", James Fall; 17–257 *Theological Lectures*; 259–327 *Exhortations to the Candidates for the Degree of Master of Arts in the University of Edinburgh*; 329–426 *Meditations Critical and Practical, Psalms IV. XXXII. and CXXX.*; 427–55 *A Sermon, preached to the Clergy*; 457–84 *Letters*.

MS TRANSCRIPTS. (*a*) VCL S MS F 2.2; watermark "H 1822": John Watson transcript of 13 annotations, without textus; and at the end of the ms a note in C's hand (**28**). (*b*) VCL LT 54: SC transcript of **32** with textus and **33** textus, the corresponding annotation not being recorded here or elsewhere.

DATE. From about summer 1819 to at least Jul 1823, and probably with some additions from early Nov 1823 to the publication of *AR* in May 1825. Two notebook entries referring to this edition in c Jan 1822 are *CN* IV 4853–4; it was also in Jan 1822 that C broached with Murray the possibility of a collection of "The Beauties of Archbishop Leighton": *CL* v 200.

COEDITOR. John Beer.

1   I 9–13, referring to 9–16 | *A Practical Commentary*: 1 Pet 1.2

Ver. 2. *Elect, according to the foreknowledge of God the Father, through sanctification of the Spirit, unto obedience, and sprinkling of the blood of Jesus Christ*. [Leighton observes that this verse describes both the state and the causes of election, in which all three persons of the Trinity are active, since "eternal election" is attributed to God the Father and election in a second sense, "effectual calling", to the Holy

Spirit, while justification of the elect is achieved by the purifying blood of Christ. Leighton insists that no mortal is without "the natural pollution" of sin, and that no mortal effort can purge it: "There is nothing in religion further out of nature's reach, and out of its liking and believing, than the doctrine of redemption by a Saviour, and a crucified Saviour, by Christ, and by his blood, first shed on the cross in his suffering, and then sprinkled on the soul by his Spirit."]

That the doctrines asserted in this and the two or three following pages[1] cannot be denied or explained away without removing (as the modern Unitarians) or (as the Arminians) unsettling and undermining the foundation of the Faith,[2] I am fully convinced; and equally so that nothing is gained by the change, the very same logical consequences being deducible from the tenets of the Church Arminians,[a] scarcely more so from those which they still hold in common with—[b]Luther, Zuinglius, Calvin, Knox, Cranmer, and the other Fathers of the Reformation in England, and which are therefore most unfairly entitled Calvinism, than from those which they have substituted.[3] See this proved in my Mss notes to Taylor's letter on Original Sin,[4] Nay, the shock given to the

---

[a] MS TRANSCRIPT reads "Armenians"
[b] Long dash in MS TRANSCRIPT, possibly indicating an illegible name

[1][1] On pp 13–14 Leighton concentrates on the term "obedience", which he takes to consist "in the receiving Christ as our Redeemer" and in the "entire rendering up of the whole man to this obedience". He asserts that such obedience can be made possible only by "grace renewing the hearts of believers" and changing "their natures".

[1][2] For C at this time, the "foundation" involved belief in the Trinity (rejected by Unitarians) as well as in the doctrines referred to at the end of this note, original sin with redemption and "change of Heart" as its consequences. Cf *AR* (1825) 190–1. For C's frequent attacks on "modern Unitarians" see *LS* (*CC*) 111–12, *BL* ch 24 (*CC*) II 245–6, *AR* (1825) 205n. He uses the term "Arminian" interchangeably with "Grotian" (Grotius having been a follower of Arminius) to refer loosely to an episcopal high-church party associated with Laud or with Laudian principles: see n 4 below, and cf *C&S* (*CC*) 135 and n.

[1][3] In the history of the Church, Arminianism arose as a reaction against Calvin-

ism, and the two names are commonly used to denote contrasting beliefs. C here emphasises, however, the common ground that Arminian doctrine shares with the "Fathers of the Reformation"—Luther, Zwingli, Calvin, Knox, and Cranmer. In *AR* (1825) 156–7 he says, ". . . the Doctrines of Calvin on Redemption, and the natural state of fallen Man, are in all essential points the same as those of Luther, Zuinglius, and the first reformers collectively." Modern Calvinism C believed to have less in common with original Calvinism than had Arminianism: see n 11 below and COPY C 13.

[1][4] C records in several places his horror at Jeremy Taylor's "Arminian" minimising of the significance of original sin, and his emphasis on the sinner's responsibility for repentance, e.g. *Friend* (*CC*) I 434, BAXTER *Reliquiae* COPY A 49. The notes he refers to here are probably the eight annotations on *An Answer to a Letter from the Bishop of Rochester Concerning the Chapter of Original Sin, in the "Unum necessarium"*, in J. TAYLOR *Polemicall Dis-*

moral sense by these consequences is (to *my* feelings) aggravated in the Arminian[a] Doctrine by the thin yet dishonest disguise. Meantime the consequences appear to me, in point of Logic, legitimately concluded from the terms of the premises. What shall we say then? Where lies the fault? In the original doctrines expressed in the premises? God forbid! In the particular deductions logically considered? But these we have found legitimate. Where then? I answer in deducing *any* consequences by such a process, and according to such rules! The rules are alien and inapplicable, the process presumptuous, yea, preposterous. The error, τὸ πρῶτον ψεῦδος,[5] lies in the false assumption of a *logical* deducibility, at all, in this instance, First because the terms, from which the conclusion must be drawn [b](termini in Majore[c] præmissi a quibus scientialiter, et scientifice demonstrandum erat),[6] are accommodations, and not scientific—i.e. proper and adequate not per *idem*, but per quam maxime simile or rather quam minime *dissimile*.[7] Secondly, because the truths in question are *transcendent*, and have their *evidence*, if any, *in the Ideas* themselves, and for the *Reason*; and do not and cannot *derive* it *from* the *conceptions* of the understanding which cannot comprehend the truths but is to be comprehended in and by them: Vide I John: v: 5.[8] Lastly, and chiefly, because these Truths, as they do not originate in the intellective Faculty of Man, so neither are they addressed primarily to our Intellect; but are substantiated *for us* by their correspondence to the wants, cravings, and interests, of the Moral Being, for which they were given, and without which they would be devoid of all meaning—vox et præterea nihil.[9] The only conclusions therefore that dare be drawn from them must be such as are implied in the origin and purpose of their revelation; and the legitimacy of all conclusions must be tried by their consistency with those Moral interests, those Spiritual necessities, which are the proper *final cause* of the truths of our Faith therein. For *some* of

---

[a] MS TRANSCRIPT reads "Armenian"

[b] Square brackets in the original are given as parentheses to avoid confusion with editorial matter

[c] MS TRANSCRIPT reads "Massore", using a long "s"

---

courses i 896–910, particularly the last: ". . . Deny original Sin, & you will soon deny free will—Then virtue & vice—and God becomes Abracadabra—a sound!!'' C quotes Taylor on original sin in *AR* (1825) 251–6, and quotes one of his own notes on Taylor p 275.

1[5] "The fundamental error": see BAXTER *Reliquiae* COPY B **92** n 1.

1[6] "The terms in the major premise, from which philosophically and scientifi-

cally the demonstration was to be made''.

1[7] Not "through [being] *the same*'', but "through [being] in the greatest degree similar'' or rather "in the least degree *dissimilar*''.

1[8] Not 1 John, but John 1.5, "And the light shineth in darkness; and the darkness comprehended it not.''

1[9] "A voice and nothing more'', a Spartan's comment upon eating a nightingale: Plutarch *Moralia* 233A.

the Faithful these truths have, I doubt not, an *evidence* of Reason; but for the whole household of Faith their *certainty* is in their *Working*.[10] Now it is this, by which in all cases we know and determine Existence in the first instance. That which *works* in us or on us, *exists* for us. The shapes and forms that follow the working as its results or products, whether the shapes cognizable by sense or the forms distinguished by the intellect, are after all but the *particularizations* of this working; as it were its proper names, as John, James, Peter, in respect of human nature they are all derived from the relations, in which finite beings stand to each other; and are therefore heterogeneous and except by *accommodation* devoid of meaning and purpose when applied to the working in and by which *God* makes his existence known to us, and (we may presume to say) specially exists for the Soul in whom he thus works. On these grounds, therefore, I hold the doctrines of original Sin, the redemption therefrom by the Cross of Christ and change of Heart as the *consequent* without adopting the additions to the doctrines inferred by one set of Divines, the modern Calvinists,[11] or acknowleging the consequences burthened on the doctrines by their Antagonists. Nor is this my Faith, fairly liable to any inconvenience if only it be remembered, that it is a Spiritual Working, of which I speak, and a Spiritual Knowlege—not thro' the medium of *Image*, the seeking after which is *Superstition*, nor yet by any *sensation*, the watching for which is *Enthusiasm* and the conceit of its presence Fanatical Distemperature.[12] "Do the will of the Father and ye shall *know* it.[''']—[13]

2   I 157 | 1 Pet 1.22

Seeing you have purified your souls in obeying the truth through the Spirit.] Here is, 1. The chief seat or subject of the work of sanctification, *the soul.* 2. The subordinate means, *truth.* 3. The nature of it, *obeying of truth.* 4. The chief worker of it, the *Holy Spirit.*

For the *first*, the chief seat of sanctification, *the soul*: It is no doubt a work that goes through the whole man, renews and purifies all, Heb. x.

1[10] The emphasis on the "working" of the spirit here may be derived from the textus, e.g. p 16: ". . . and so [sanctification] comprehends justification, as here, and the first working of faith, by which the soul is justified. . . . The spirit or soul of a man is the chief and first subject of this work, and it is but slight false work that begins not there . . .".

1[11] For C at this time the phrase "modern Calvinists" had specific reference to Edward Williams: see COPY C **13** n 2 below, and *AR* (1825) 153–4, where his objection is that Williams and his party conceived of the human will as "absolutely passive, clay in the hands of a Potter".

1[12] C's distinction between enthusiasm and fanaticism is fully worked out in BIRCH **1**; these two are further related to superstition in BAXTER *Reliquiae* COPY A **51**.

1[13] John 7.17 (var).

22. 2 Cor. vii. 1. But because it purifies the soul, therefore it is that it does purify all. There impurity begins, Mat. xv. 18. not only evil thoughts, but all evil actions come forth from the heart, which is there all one with the soul; and therefore this purifying begins there, *makes the tree good that the fruit may be good.*

We must distinguish the Life and the Soul;[1] tho' there is a certain Sense in which the Life may be called the Soul—i.e. The Life is the Soul of the *Body*. But the Soul is the life of *the Man*, and Christ is the Life of the Soul. Now the Spirit of Man, the spirit *sub*sistent, is deeper than both, not only deeper than the Body and its life but deeper than the Soul, and the Spirit descendent and *super*sistent[2] is higher than both—In the regenerated Man the height and the Depth become one—the Spirit communeth with the Spirit—and the Soul is the Inter-ens or Ens-intermedium[3] between the life and the Spirit—the Participium not as a Compound however but as a Medium indifferens[4] In the same sense, in which heat may be designated as the indifference between Light and Gravity,[5] and what is the reason? The Spirit in its presence to the understanding abstractedly from its presence in the Will—nay, in many during the negation of the latter.—The Spirit present to Man but not appropriated by him is the Reason of Man—The Reason in the process of its identification with the Will is the Spirit—[a]

3 1 158[b] | 1 Pet 1.22

The chief point of obedience is believing; the proper obedience to truth is, to give credit to it; and this divine belief doth necessarily bring the whole soul into obedience and conformity to that pure truth, which is in the word . . .

This is not quite so perspicuous and single-sensed as Archbishop Leighton's sentences in general are. This effect is occasioned by the omission of the word "this," or "divine," or the truth "in Christ." For truth in

[a] Here MS TRANSCRIPT reads "*See Note D3ᵈ*", but no such note is given
[b] Not in MS TRANSCRIPT; supplied from *LR*

2[1] Cf **5** below; and for further development of this theme see COPY C **7**.

2[2] "Standing *over*", C's coinage by analogy with "subsistent" above, and perhaps contrasted with "superstition" in **1**.

2[3] The "Inter-being" (or being *between*) or "intermediary Being".

2[4] The "Partaker" as an "indifferent Midpoint".

2[5] In the method of analysis of the natural world that C learnt chiefly from German *Naturphilosophen* such as Heinrich Steffens (*Grundzüge der philosophischen Naturwissenschaft*—Berlin 1806—64), light and gravity are polar powers, with heat the product of their meeting in equilibrium. The same statement appears in e.g. BÖHME **79**.

the ordinary and scientific sense is received by a spontaneous, rather than chosen by a voluntary, act; and the apprehension of the same (belief) supposes a position of congruity rather than an act of obedience. Far otherwise is it with the truth that is the object of Christian faith: and it is this truth of which Leighton is speaking. Belief indeed is a living part of this faith; but only as long as it is a living part. In other words, belief is implied in faith; but faith is not necessarily implied in belief.[1] *The devils believe.*[2]

4 ɪ 166 | 1 Pet 1.23

Hence learn, 1. That true conversion is not so slight a work, as we commonly account it. It is not the outward change of some bad customs, which gains the name of a reformed man in the ordinary dialect; it is a new birth and being, and elsewhere called *a new creation.* Though it be but a change in qualities, yet it is such a one, and the qualities so far distant from what they before were, that it bears the name of the most substantial productions . . .

I dare not affirm that this is erroneously said; but it is one of the comparatively[a] few passages that are of service as reminding me that it is not the Scripture, that I am reading. Not the qualities merely but the root of the qualities is trans-created.[1] How else could it be a Birth? a Creation?

5 ɪ 170 | 1 Pet 1.24

This natural life is compared, even by natural men, to the vainest things, and scarce find they things light enough to express it *vain*; and as it is here called *grass*, so they compare the generations of men to the leaves of trees. But the light of Scripture doth most discover this, and it is a lesson that requires the Spirit of God to teach it aright. *Teach us,* says Moses, Psal. xc. 12. *so to number our days that we may apply our hearts unto wisdom*; and David, Psal. xxxix. 4. *Make me to know my life, how frail I am.* So Ja. iv. 14.; and here it is called *grass.* So Job xiv. 1, 2. *Man that is born of a woman is of few days, and full of trouble. He cometh forth like a flower, and is cut down.*

It is the fashion to decry Scholastic distinctions as useless subtleties or

---

^a MS TRANSCRIPT reads "comparitively"

3[1] There is a longer exposition of the distinction between faith and belief in BLANCO WHITE *Letters* 1.
3[2] Jas 2.19 (var), alluded to also in COPY A 7 at n 2.

4[1] Apparently C's coinage, given as a nonce-word in *OED*. For other compounds with the prefix "trans-" see DONNE *Sermons* COPY A 4 and n 6.

mere phantoms—entia logica vel etiam verbalia solum.[1] And yet in order to secure a safe and Christian interpretation to these and numerous other passages of like phrase and import in the old Testament it is of highest concernment that we should distinguish the Personëity or Spirit as the Source and principle of personality, from the person itself as the particular product at any one period and as that which cannot be evolved or sustained but by the Co-Agency of the System and circumstances in which the Individuals are placed.[2] In this latter sense it is that *Man* is used in the Psalms, in Job, and elsewhere—and the term made synonimous with Flesh—That which constitutes the Spirit *a Man* both for others and for itself *is* the *Man* and to this the elements and elementary powers contribute its *bulk* (το videri et tangi)[3] wholly, and its phænomenal *form* in part, both as co-efficient, and as conditions Now as these are under a Law of variety and incessant change—τα μη οντα αλλ'αει γινομενα[4]—so must all be to the production and continuance of which these are indispensable on this hangs the doctrine of the Resurrection of the Body as an essential part of the doctrine of immortality—on this the Scripture (and only true and philosophical) sense of the Soul, Psyche or Life as resulting from the continual assurgency of the Spirit thro' the Body, and on this the begetting of a new Life, a regenerate Soul, by the descent of the divine Spirit on the Spirit of Man.[5] When the spirit by sanctification is fitted for an incorruptible Body, then shall it be raised into a world of Incorruption, and a celestial Body [shall burgeon][a] forth thereto the germ of which had been implanted by the redeeming and creative word in this world.[6] Truly has it been said of the Elect—They fall asleep in Earth but awake in Heaven. So S͏t Paul expressly teaches and as the passage (Cor: I—xv) was written for the express purpose of rectifying the notions of the converts concerning the

---

[a] Space in MS TRANSCRIPT; words supplied from *LR*

5[1] "Things that exist in logic or rather only in words". C often had occasion to defend "Scholastic distinctions", e.g. the use of "subjective" and "objective" in *BL* ch 10 (*CC*) I 172, and of "aureity" in *TL* 29.

5[2] An important distinction that appears elsewhere in C's writings, e.g. IRVING 11, "that divine Humanity which is the *Ground* of the humanity or spiritual Personëity in every Person".

5[3] "The [capacity] to be seen and touched".

5[4] "Things that do not exist but are always becoming": cf C's observation that *natura* is a future participle, as implied in his definition of "nature" as "Natura, that which is *about to be* born, that which is always *becoming*" in *AR* (1825) 244, also *CL* VI 897.

5[5] Cf the distinction between life and soul in 2.

5[6] The issue of the nature of "body" and the doctrine of a "twofold" body (based on 1 Cor 15.40–4) are prominent in marginalia to LUTHER *Colloquia*, e.g. 40, and IRVING *Sermons*, esp 27, 29.

Resurrection all other passages in the N. T. must be interpreted in harmony with this.[7] But John likewise describing the same great event, as subsequent to and contra-distinguished from the partial or Millenniary Resurrection which (whether we are to understand the Apostle symbolically or literally) is to take place in the present world—beheld a new Earth and a new Heaven as antecedent to or co-incident with the appearance of the New Jerusalem—i.e.—the state of Glory, and the Resurrection to life everlasting.[8] The Old Earth and its Heaven had passed away from the face of him on the Throne, at the moment that it gave up the Dead.[9]

6 I 174–5 | 1 Pet 1.25

Ver. 25. But the word of the Lord endureth for ever. . . . with respect to those learned men that apply [the Prophet's words] to God, I remember not that this *abiding for ever* is used to express God's eternity in himself.

No! nor is it here used for that purpose but yet I cannot doubt but that either the Word, o Λογος εν αρχη,[1] or the divine promises in and thro' the incarnate word, with the [upraising][a] influences proceeding from him are here meant—and not the written ρηματα, or Scriptures.[b2]

7 II 242–31[c] | 1 Pet 4.14–16

And thus are reproaches mentioned amongst the sufferings of Christ in the gospel, and not as the least; the railings and mockings that were darted at him, and fixed to the cross, are mentioned more than the very nails that fixed him. And, Heb. xii. 2. the *shame* of the cross, though he was above it, and despised it, yet that shame added much to the burden of it . . .

I understand Leighton thus: that though our Lord felt it not as *shame*,

---

[a] Conjectural; MS TRANSCRIPT reads "graising", *LR* "gracious"

[b] Here MS TRANSCRIPT reads "See Note 6.", but Note 6 is missing from the sequence, which passes from 5(**6** in this volume) to 7(**11**)

[c] Not in MS TRANSCRIPT; supplied from *LR*

5[7] 1 Cor 15, esp 40–4 and 51, "Behold, I shew you a mystery; We shall not all sleep, but we shall all be changed".

5[8] See Rev 21, esp 1–4: "And I saw a new heaven and a new earth. . . . And I John saw the holy city, new Jerusalem, coming down from God. . . . and there shall be no more death . . .".

5[9] From Rev 20.11–13 (var).

6[1] "The Word [who was] in the beginning"—from John 1.1 (var).

6[2] The distinction between the Word and spoken or written words appears also in a notebook entry of c 14 Mar 1826 (*CN* IV 5338): see BÖHME **145** n 1. The same Greek words are used with different meanings, however, in *AR* (1825) 25n (omitted from 1831 on).

nor was wounded by the revilings of the people in the way of any correspondent resentment or sting, which yet we may be without blame, yet he suffered from the same as sin, and as an addition to the guilt of his persecutors, which could not but aggravate the burden which he had taken on himself, as being sin in its most devilish form.

8 II 293*ᵃ* | 1 Pet 5.5

This therefore is mainly to be studied, that the seat of humility be *the heart*. Although it will be seen in the carriage, yet as little as it can; as few words as may be concerning itself; and those it doth speak must be the real thoughts of the mind, and not an affected voice of it differing from the inward sense; otherwise humble speech and carriage only put on without, and not fastened in the inside, is the most refined and subtile, and indeed the most dangerous kind of pride. And this I would recommend as a safe way: ever let thy thoughts concerning thyself be below what thou utterest: and what thou seest needful or fitting to say to thy own abasement, be not only content (which most are not) to be taken at thy word, and believed to be such by them that hear thee, but be desirous of it; and let that be the end of thy speech, to persuade them, and gain it of them, that they really take thee for as worthless and mean as thou dost express thyself.

Alas! this is a most delicate and difficult subject: and the safest way, and the only safe general rule is the silence that accompanies the inward act of looking at the contrast in all that is of our own doing and impulse! So may praises be made their own antidote.

9 III 20–1*ᵇ* | Sermon 1, on Jas 3.17

. . . *They shall see God*. What this is we cannot tell you, nor can you conceive it: but walk heavenwards in purity, and long to be there, where you shall know what it means; *for you shall see him as he is*.

We say; ''Now I see the full meaning, force and beauty of a passage,—we see them through the words.'' Is not Christ the Word—the substantial, consubstantial Word, ὁ ὢν εἰς τὸν κόλπον τοῦ πατρός¹—not as our words, arbitrary; nor even as the words of Nature phenomenal merely? If even through the words*ᶜ* a powerful and perspicuous author—(as in

---

ᵃ Not in MS TRANSCRIPT; supplied from *LR*   ᵇ Not in MS TRANSCRIPT; supplied from *LR*
ᶜ For ''words of''?

9¹ John 1.18, ''Which [i.e. who] is in the bosom of the Father''. For the special significance of this verse to C see BIBLE COPY B **119** n 1, and *AR* (1825) 308n.

the next to inspired Commentary of Archbishop Leighton,—for whom God be praised!)—I identify myself with the excellent writer, and his thoughts become my thoughts: what must not the blessing be to be thus identified first with the Filial Word, and then with the Father in and through Him?

10 III 63*ᵃ* | Sermon 5, on Isa 60.1

In this elementary world, light being (as we hear) the first visible, all things are seen by it, and it by itself. Thus is Christ, among spiritual things, in the elect world of his church; *all things are made manifest by the light*, says the apostle, Eph. v. 13, speaking of Christ, as the following verse doth evidently testify. It is in his word that he shines, and makes it a directing and convincing light, to discover all things that concern his church and himself, to be known by its own brightness. How impertinent then is that question so much tossed by the Romish church, how know you the scriptures (say they) to be the word of God, without the testimony of the church? I would ask one of them again, how they can know that it is day-light, except some light a candle to let them see it? They are little versed in holy scripture, that know not that it is frequently called light; and they are senseless that know not that light is seen and known by itself. If our gospel be hid, says the apostle, it is hid to them that perish; the god of this world having blinded their minds against the light of the glorious gospel, &c. no wonder if such stand in need of a testimony. A blind man knows not that it is light at noon-day, but by report: but to those that have eyes, light is seen by itself.

On the true test of the Scriptures. Oh! were it not for my manifold infirmities, whereby I am so all unlike the white-robed Leighton, I could almost conceit that my soul had been an emanation from his! So many and so remarkable are the coincidences, and these in parts of his works that I could not have seen—and so uniform the congruity of the whole. As I read, I seem to myself to be only thinking my own thoughts over again, now in the same and now in a different order.

11 III 68

The author of the epistle to the Hebrews calls him [Christ] απαυγασμα "the brightness of his Father's glory, and the character of his person", Heb. i. 3. And under these expressions lies that remarkable mystery of the Son's eternal relation to the Father, which is rather humbly to be

---

ᵃ Not in MS TRANSCRIPT; supplied from *LR*

adored than boldly to be explained, either by God's perfect understanding of his own essence, or by any other notion.

Certainly not by a transfer of a notion, and this too a notion of a faculty itself but notional and limitary to the supreme Reality.[1] But there are *Ideas* which are of higher origin than the notions of the understanding and by the irradiation of which the understanding itself becomes a human understanding. Of such veritates verificæ[2] L. himself in other words speaks often, surely there must have been an intelligible propriety in the terms, Logos, Word, begotten before all Creation[3] adequate Idea or Icon &ᶜ;[4] or the Evangelists and Apostolic Penman would not have *adopted* them. They did not *invent* the terms, but took them and used them as they were taken and applied by Philo and both the Greek and Oriental Sages.[5] Nay, the precise and orthodox, yet frequent use of these terms by Philo and by the Jewish authors of that traditional Wisdom degraded in after times but which in its purest parts existed long before the Xtn Æra, is the strongest extrinsic argument against the Arians, Socinians, and Unitarians, in proof that Sᵗ John must have meant to deceive his readers, if he did not use them in the known and received sense.—To a Materialist indeed, or to those who deny all Knowleges not resolvible into notices from the 5 Senses these terms as applied to Spiritual beings must appear inexplicable or senseless—But so must *Spirit* itself. To me (why doᵃ I say, to me?) to Bull, Waterland, to Gregoryᵇ Nazianzen, Basil, Athanasius, Sᵗ Augustin the terms Word and Generation have appeared admirably yea most awfully pregnant and appropriate:[6] but as the Language of those who knew that their minds are placed with their backs to Substances and which therefore they can

ᵃ MS TRANSCRIPT reads "no"

ᵇ MS TRANSCRIPT has a comma here between the two parts of the name

11[1] C objects both to the attribution to God of mere *understanding* and to the assumption that the transcendent could be apprehended by that limited faculty.

11[2] "Truth-making truths".

11[3] As in e.g. John 1.14, or in the words of the Nicene Creed, "begotten of his Father before all worlds".

11[4] In COPY C 7, C expands upon the connection between "Word" and "Icon" (εἰχων): "The Logos is the substantial-Idea ⟨= Εἰχων⟩ in whom all Ideas are contained and have Being: it is the Idea of God."

11[5] C's knowledge of the significance of "logos" etc to Philo Judaeus (c 30 B.C.–

c A.D. 40) and the "Greek and Oriental Sages" may come from his reading of Eichhorn: see EICHHORN *Neue Testament* COPY A 32, *Apocrypha* 23.

11[6] C invokes great defenders of Trinitarianism capable of using such terms as "word" and "generation" symbolically to describe the spiritual relationship between the first two persons of the Trinity. Cf his strong objection in 1805 to Samuel Horsley's definition of "generation" (in a theological context) as "The inducement of a Form on a pre-existing material": *CN* II 2444.

name only from the correspondent *Shadows*—Yet not (God forbid) as if the Substances were the same with the *Shadows*[7]—which yet Leighton supposes in this his censure—for if he did not he then censures himself and a number of his most beautiful passages—These and 2 or 3 other sentences (slips of human infirmity) are useful in reminding me that Leighton's Works are not inspired Scriptures.

[a]*Postscript.* On a second consideration of this passage, and a revisal of my marginal animadversion—yet how dare I apply such a word to a passage written by a minister of Christ so clearly under the especial light of the divine grace as was Archbishop Leighton?—I am inclined to think that Leighton confined his censure to the attempts to "explain" the Trinity—and this by "notions,"—and not to the assertion of the adorable acts implied in the terms both of the Evangelists and Apostles, and of the Church before as well as after Christ's ascension; nor to the assent of the pure reason to the truths, and more than assent to, the affirmation of the ideas.

12   iii 73

The preceding Sermon excellent in parts, is yet on the whole the least excellent of Leighton's Works—and breathes less of either his own character as a Man, or the character of his religious philosophy, the Style too is in many places below Leighton's ordinary Style—in some places even turbid, operose, and *Catachres*tic ex gr. to trample on Smilings with one foot and on frownings with the other[1]

13   iii 121[b] | Sermon 9, on Rom 8.7

The reasonable creature, it is true, hath more liberty in its actions, freely choosing one thing and rejecting another; yet it cannot be denied, that in acting of that liberty, their choice and refusal *follow the sway of their nature and condition.

* I would fain substitute for "follow," the words, "are most often determined, and always affected, by." I do not deny that the will follows the nature; but then the nature itself is a will.

---

[a] The postscript is not in MS TRANSCRIPT; supplied from *LR*
[b] Not in MS TRANSCRIPT; supplied from *LR*

11[7] Using the allegory of the cave from Plato *Republic 7,* C defends the Trinitarians' use of the language of this world to describe a transcendent realm.
12[1] The example comes from iii 69, where Leighton says that the true Christian "can generously trample upon the smilings of the world with the one foot, and her frownings with the other".

14   III   121*ᵃ* | Continuing **13** textus

As the angels and glorified souls, (their nature being perfectly holy, and unalterably such) they cannot sin, they can delight in nothing but in obeying and praising that God, in the enjoyment of whom their happiness consisteth . . .

If angels be other than spirits made perfect, or, as Leighton writes, "glorified souls,"—the "unalterable by nature" seems to me rashly asserted.

15   III   121*ᵇ*

The mind Φρονημα] some render it the prudence or wisdom of the flesh. Here you have it, the carnal mind, but the word signifies, indeed, an act of the mind, rather than either the faculty itself, or the habit of prudence in it, so as it discovers what is the frame of both those.

I doubt. Φρόνημα signifies an act: and so far I agree with Leighton. But φρόνημα σαρκός is "the flesh" (that is, the natural man,) in the act or habitude of minding—but those acts, taken collectively, are the faculty—the understanding.[1]

How often have I found reason to regret, that Leighton had not clearly made out to himself the diversity of reason and the understanding![2]

16   III   194 | Sermon 15, on Ps 119.32

The heart is taken generally in scripture, for the whole soul, the understanding and will, in its several affections and motions; and the speech being here of an enlarged heart, it seems very congruous to take it in the most enlarged sense.

Leighton I presume was acquainted with the Hebrew Language but he does not appear to have studied it much—His observation on the heart, as used in the Old T. shews that he did not know that the ancient He-

---

ᵃ Not in MS TRANSCRIPT; supplied from *LR*   *ᵇ* Not in MS TRANSCRIPT; supplied from *LR*

15[1] The Greek phrase is from the text for this sermon, Rom 8.7—lit "the mind of the flesh" as C has it in *AR* (1825) 231 glossing "the understanding"; AV "the carnal mind", with marginal alternative "the minding of the flesh"; Art IX of the Articles of Religion in BCP renders it as "the lust of the flesh". There is an extended discussion of the phrase as C found it in John Webster's *Displaying of Supposed Witchcraft* (1677) in *CN* IV 4618 (c Oct 1819); cf HOOKER **28**, LACUNZA **11**, LUTHER **46**.

15[2] C published several explanations of this distinction, e.g. *SM* (*CC*) 59–62, *Friend* (*CC*) I 154–61, *AR* (1825) 207–11, 215–28.

brews supposed the Heart to be the Seat of intellect and therefore used it exactly as *we* use *the Head*[1]

17   III 196[a]

A narrow enthralled heart, fettered with love of lower things, and cleaving to some particular sins, or but some one, and that secret, may keep foot a while in the way of God's commandments, in some steps of them; but it must give up quickly, is not able to run on to the end of the goal.

One of the blessed privileges of the spiritual man (and such Leighton was,) is a piercing insight into the diseases of which he himself is clear. Ἐλέησον Κύριε![1]

18   III 204 | Sermon 16, on Rom 8.33–4

The great evidence of thy election is love. Thy love to him gives certain testimony of his preceding eternal love to thee, so are they here designed, they that love God; thy choosing him is the effect and evidence of his choosing thee. Now this is not labourious, that needs to be disputed, amidst all thy frailties; feel the pulse of thine affection, which way beats it, and ask thy heart whether thou love him or not, in this thou hast the character of thy election.

Know you not, that the redeemed of Christ and he are one, they live one life, Christ lives in them, and if *any man hath not the Spirit of Christ, he is none of his*, as the apostle declares in this chapter? So then, this we are plainly to tell you, and consider it, you that will not let go your sins to lay hold on Christ, have as yet no share in him.

But on the other side: the truth is, that when souls are once set upon this search, they commonly wind the notion too high, and subtilize too much in the dispute, and so entangle and perplex themselves, and drive themselves further off from that comfort that they are seeking after; such measures and marks of grace, they set to themselves for their rule and standard; and unless they find those without all controversy in themselves, they will not believe that they have an interest in Christ, and this blessed and safe estate in him.

To such I would only say, are you in a willing league with any known sin?

a Not in MS TRANSCRIPT; supplied from *LR*

16[1] C's statement is correct according to modern authorities: see HEINROTH **40** and n 1.

17[1] "Have mercy, O Lord!"—as in Septuagint Ps 6.3, Matt 15.22 etc. The words are more familiar in reverse order (as in e.g. Matt 17.15) from the transliterated title "Kyrie eleison" in the Commu-

An admirable antidote for such as too sober and sincere to pass off feverous sensations for Spiritual realities have been perplexed by Wesley's[a] Assertions—that a certainty of having been elected is an indispensable mark of Election.[1] Whitfield's Ultra-Calvinism is Gospel gentleness and Pauline sobriety compared with Wesley's Arminianism[b] in the outset of his career.[2] ⟨But the main and most noticeable difference between Leighton and the modern Methodists is to be found in the uniform *Self*ishness of the latter Not do you wish to love God? Do you love your neighbour?—⟩ Do you think O how near and lovely must Christ be or but are you certain, that Christ has saved you, that he died for *you*—you—you—you yourself on to the end of the Chapter—this is Wesleys *Doctrine*.

19 III 507 | Sermon 7, on Isa 30.15–19

The preceding (VIIth) Discourse admirable throughout, Leighton throughout![1] O what a contrast might be presented by publishing *this* and some discourse of some Court Prelate or Divine (South for instance)[2] preached under the same State of affairs—and printing the two in columns.—

20 III 518[c] | Sermon 8, on Jer 14.7–9

This eighth Sermon is another most admirable discourse.[1]

---

[a] MS TRANSCRIPT reads "Wesly's"   [b] MS TRANSCRIPT reads "Armenianism"
[c] Not in MS TRANSCRIPT; supplied from *LR* (see **23** n 1)

---

nion service. For C's self-reference see COPY A **13**.

18[1] E.g. John Wesley *Sermons on Several Occasions* (1825) I 108 (Sermon 10): "It all resolves into this: Those who have these marks are children of God: But we have these marks: Therefore we are children of God." But cf SOUTHEY *Life of Wesley* (1820)—annotated by C—in which Wesley's retreat from this position is given in his own words: SOUTHEY *Wesley* I 295, II 181–2.

18[2] C's views on the conventional contrast between Calvinism and Arminianism are expressed in **1** at n 3 above. For C's opinion of the differences between Wesley and Whitefield, the best source is his notes in SOUTHEY *Life of Wesley*, a book he reread (apparently several times) in the 1820s.

19[1] *LR* assigns this note to III 104, i.e. Sermon 7 in the first series of sermons, but the order of entries in the MS TRANSCRIPT identifies it clearly as belonging to the second series: see CONTENTS in headnote.

19[2] Robert South (1634–1716), chaplain for a time to Clarendon (1660) and to the Duke of York (1667). There are records of C's reading—on the whole, approvingly—his *Sermons* (1737) in 1797 and 1810: *CN* I 319–28, III 4003–4, 4008. C quoted South in an epigraph for *Friend* (*CC*) I 176.

20[1] In *LR* IV 177, which is the only source for this note, it is presented as the last sentence of an annotation that combines **23** and **27** (see **23** n 1), and as a comment on I 107. Given its association with

21 IV 96^a | Lecture 9 "Of the Pleasure and Utility of Religion"

For that this was his fixed purpose, Lucretius not only owns, but also boasts of it, and loads him [Epicurus] with ill-advised praises, for endeavouring, through the whole course of his philosophy, to free the minds of men from all the bonds and ties of religion . . .

But surely in this passage *religio* must be rendered superstition, the most effectual means for the removal of which Epicurus supposed himself to have found in the exclusion of the *gods many and lords many*,[1] from their imagined agency in all the phænomena of nature and the events of history, substituting for these the belief in fixed laws, having in themselves their evidence and necessity. On this account, in this passage at least, Lucretius praises his master.

22 IV 105^b | Lecture 10 "Of the Decrees of God"

They always seemed to me to act a very ridiculous part, who contend, that the effect of the divine decree is absolutely irreconcilable with human liberty; because the natural and necessary liberty of a rational creature is to act or choose from a rational motive, or spontaneously, and of purpose; but who sees not, that, on the supposition of the most absolute decree, this liberty is not taken away, but rather established and confirmed? For the decree is, that such an one shall make choice of, or do some particular thing freely. And, whoever pretends to deny, that whatever is done or chosen, whether good or indifferent, is so done or chosen, or, at least, may be so, espouses an absurdity.

I fear, I fear, that this is a sophism not worthy of Archbishop Leighton. It seems to me tantamount to saying—"I force that man to do so or so without my forcing him." But however that may be, the following sentences[1] are more precious than diamonds. They are divine.

---

^a Not in MS TRANSCRIPT; supplied from *LR*   ^b Not in MS TRANSCRIPT; supplied from *LR*

---

23 and 27, however, and the order of entries in the MS TRANSCRIPT, it seems more likely that it refers to Sermon 8 of the second series of sermons than to I 107 and Sermon 8 of the first series.

21[1] C uses this phrase from 1 Cor 8.5 to characterise pagan polytheism, a form of "superstition" and not "religion" proper as he defines it, e.g. in COPY A 5.

22[1] Continuing textus, pp 105–6: "But, in a word, the great difficulty in all this dispute is, that with regard to the *origin of evil*. Some distinguish, and justly, the substance of the action, as you call it, or that which is physical in the action, from the morality of it. This is of some weight, but whether it takes away the whole difficulty, I will not pretend to say. Believe me, young gentleman, it is an abyss, it is an abyss never to be sounded by any plummet of human understanding."

23 iv 107 | Lecture 11 "Of the Creation of the World"

Whoever looks upon this great system of the universe, of which he himself is but a very small part, with a little more than ordinary attention, unless his mind is become quite brutish within him, it will, of necessity, put him upon considering whence this beautiful frame of things proceeded, and what was its first original; or, in the words of the poet, "From what principles all the elements were formed, and how the various parts of the world at first came together*." [Leighton's footnote*:] ——Quibusque exordia primis

Omnia, et ipse tener mundi concreverit orbis.

Vir. Ecl. vi.

The Lines in p. 107,[1] noted by me are one of a myriad instances to prove how rash it is to quote single sentences or assertions from the correctest writers, without collating them with the known system or express convictions of the Author. It would be easy to cite 50 passages from Archbishop Leightons Works in direct contradiction to the Sentence in question which he had learnt in the Schools when a Lad, and afterwards had heard and met with so often that he was not aware that he had never sifted its real purport[2]

24 iv 113[a]

For, that this world, compounded of so many, and such heterogeneous parts, should proceed, by way of natural and necessary emanation, from that one first, purest, and most simple nature, nobody, I imagine, could believe, or in the least suspect: can it possibly be thought, that mortality should proceed from the immortal, corruption from the incorruptible, and, what ought never to be so much as mentioned, even worms, the vilest animalcules, and most abject insects, from the best, most exalted, and most blessed Majesty? But, if he produced all these things freely, merely out of his good pleasure, and with the facility that constantly attends almighty power; how much more consistent is it to believe, that this was done in time, than to imagine it was from eternity?

[a] Not in MS TRANSCRIPT; supplied from *LR*

23[1] *LR* assigns this note to iii 107, adding it as a postscript to a note (**27**) on a textus inappropriate to it. (Note **20** above is also incorporated into the *LR* version.) It is only in Vol iv that p 107 contains a "single sentence" quoted out of context.

23[2] The quotation, from Virgil *Eclogues* 6.33–4 (var), is part of an account of the formation of the world, sung by Silenus; C draws attention to the inappropriateness of Leighton's supporting his Christian views by reference to those of Silenus.

It is inconceivable how any thing can be created in time; and production is incompatible with interspace.[1]

25   IV   152[a] | Lecture 15 "Of Regeneration"

The Platonists divide the world into two, the sensible and intellectual world; they imagine the one to be the type of the other, and that sensible and spiritual things are stamped, as it were, with the same stamp or seal. These sentiments are not unlike the notions, which the masters of the cabalistical doctrine among the Jews, concerning God's *sephiroth* and seal, wherewith, according to them, all the worlds, and every thing in them, are stamped or sealed; and these are probably near akin to what Lord Bacon of Verulam calls his *parallela signacula* [corresponding marks], and *symbolizantes schematismi* [symbolic figures]. According to this hypothesis, these parables and metaphors, which are often taken from natural things to illustrate such as are divine, will not be similitudes taken entirely at pleasure; but are often, in a great measure, founded in nature, and the things themselves.

I have asserted the same thing, and more fully shown wherein the difference consists of symbolic and metaphorical, in my first Lay Sermon;[1] and the substantial correspondence of the genuine Platonic doctrine and logic with those of Lord Bacon, in my Essays on Method, in the Friend.[2]

26   IV   201[b] | Lecture 19 "That Holiness Is the Only Happiness on This Earth"

Even the philosophers give their testimony to this truth, and their sentiments on the subject are not altogether to be rejected: for they, almost unanimously, are agreed, that felicity, so far as it can be enjoyed in this life, consists solely, or at least principally, in virtue: but as to their assertion, that this virtue is perfect in a perfect life, it is rather expressing what were to be wished, than describing things as they are.

And why are the philosophers to be judged according to a different rule? On what ground can it be asserted that the Stoics believed in the actual

---

[a] Not in MS TRANSCRIPT; supplied from *LR*   [b] Not in MS TRANSCRIPT; supplied from *LR*

24[1] *CN* IV 4853 refers to this passage and elaborates the complaint about Leighton's "taking Eternity as a *sort* of Time . . . [whereas] it would be more convenient to consider Eternity as the Antitheton of Time . . .'". C makes the same point about the unthinkability of a creation in

time in JACOBI *Ueber die Lehre* **19**.
25[1] *SM* (*CC*) 59–93 (App C), esp 79. The distinction between symbol and metaphor plays an important part in *AR* (1825) 198–200, 311–28.
25[2] *Friend* (*CC*) I 482–95.

existence of their God-like perfection in any individual? or that they meant more than this—"To no man can the name of the Wise be given in its absolute sense, who is not perfect even as his Father in heaven is perfect!"[1]

27 IV 201–2

Doth religion require any thing of us more, than that we live soberly, righteously, and godly in this present world? Now what, pray, can be more pleasant or peaceable than these? Temperance is always at leisure, luxury always in a hurry: the latter weakens the body and pollutes the soul, the former is the sanctity, purity, and sound state of both. It is one of Epicurus' fixed maxims, "That life can never be pleasant without virtue."

This assertion in these words has been so often made from Plato's times to ours that even Wise men repeat it without perhaps much examination whether it be not equivocal—or rather (I suspect) true only in that sense in which it would amount to nothing—nothing to the purpose at least— This is to be regretted for it is a mischievous equivoque to make good a synonime of pleasant or even the genus of which pleasure is a species— It is a grievous mistake to say that bad men seek pleasure because it is *good*—No! like children they call it good because it is pleasant—Even the useful must derive its meaning from the good not *vice versâ*.[1]

28 IV 214[a] | Lecture 20 "Of Our Happiness . . ."

It would be quite silly to ascribe to the church a decisive power, as if, when a book were first presented to it, or brought out of any place, where it had been long concealed, it could immediately pronounce whether that book was a divine authority or not. The church is only a witness with regard to these books we acknowledge, and its testimony extends no farther than that they were received, in the first ages of Christianity, as sacred and divinely inspired, and as such handed down from age to age, to the church that now is; and he that would venture to discredit this testimony, must have a heart of lead, and a face of brass.

There is no occasion to dispute so fiercely about the inward testimony of the Holy Ghost: for I am persuaded that those who talk about it, understand nothing more by it, than that the Holy Spirit produces, in the hearts of men, that faith whereby they cheerfully and sincerely receive

---

[a] In C's hand

26[1] The last clause echoes Matt 5.48.   comment on the same saying in *AR* (1825)
27[1] C's point here is amplified in his   38–43.

these books, and the doctrine contained in them, as divine; because such a faith either includes, in the very notion of it, or at least is necessarily connected with, a religious frame of the mind, and a sincere disposition to universal obedience.

It is certain that the Fathers of the Latin Church to the time of Jerom gave the name of canonical and ~~extended~~ the attribute of inspiration to all the Books, "which the use of God's Church approved as profitable, and containing matter of good instruction["]—for instance, the Book of Wisdom—.[1] On the other hand the Greek Fathers did not unanimously receive all those found in the Hebrew—ex. gr. the Book of Esther. And tho' Origen, as might be expected from his great Learning, and ~~the~~ other Greek Fathers following his authority, paid greater attention to the difference between the Books existing in Hebrew, and those either written in Greek, or now extant only in Greek Translations from the Hebrew, yet I do not find that they confined the notion of inspiration to the Hebrew Canon exclusively/ And even if they had attributed a higher grade of inspiration to this than to the Wisdom and Ecclesiasticus, yet let it not be forgotten that different degrees, nay *sorts*, of Inspiration were affirmed of different parts of the Hebrew Scriptures—: Inspiration κατ' εξοχην[2] to the Pentateuch—a somewhat inferior to the Prophets—and a lower to the Hagiographa—: indeed so much lower, that Philo assigns little more to the Historians and Sententiaries than he claims for parts of his own Writings[3]—⟨In what sense the Scriptures are the Rule of our Faith, see Field p. 365, whose authority, I see, bears me out in my assertion of the necessity of a right Idea of God as an antecedent Criterion/ "the infinite excellency of God as that whereby the truth of the heavenly doctrine is proved".⟩[4]

28[1] Richard Field *Of the Church* (1635) 381. C's account of the biblical canon here is taken from Field bk 4 chs 22–4; cf C's annotated FIELD in *CM* (*CC*) II.

28[2] "Eminently".

28[3] The chapters of Field that C drew upon for this note do not contain the reference to Philo Judaeus, which must come from another source or at least from another part of Field's work. C had extensive knowledge of scholarly debates about the canon: see e.g. BIBLE *Apocrypha* **4** n 4, KANT *Religion* **3** at nn 14–17.

28[4] Field begins with the phrase quoted by C but goes on to other "rules": "Thus then we see, how many things, in severall degrees and sorts, are said to be rules of our faith. The infinite excellency of God, as that whereby the truth of the heavenly doctrine is proved. The articles of faith, and other verities ever knowne in the Church, as the first principles, are the canon, by which wee judge of conclusions from thence inferred. The Scripture, as containing in it all that doctrine of faith, which *Christ* the Sonne of God delivered. The uniform practice, and consenting judgement of them that went before us, as a certaine and undoubted explication, of the things contayned in the Scripture."

29   IV   225*a* | Lecture 21 "Of the Divine Attributes"

In like manner, if we suppose God to be the first of all beings, we must, unavoidably, therefrom, conclude his unity: as to the ineffable Trinity subsisting in this Unity, a mystery discovered only by the sacred scriptures, especially in the New Testament, where it is more clearly revealed than in the Old, let others boldly pry into it, if they please, while we receive it with an humble faith, and think it sufficient for us to admire and adore.

But surely it having been revealed to us, we may venture to say,—that a positive unity, so far from excluding, implies plurality, and that the Godhead is a fulness, πλήρωμα.[1]

30   IV   245*b* | Lecture 24 "Before the Communion"

Ask yourselves, therefore, what you would be at, and with what dispositions you come to this most sacred table?

In an age of colloquial idioms, when to write in a loose slang had become a mark of loyalty, this is the only L'Estrange vulgarism I have met with in Leighton.[1]

31   IV   252*c* | "An Exhortation to the Students, upon Their Return to the University after the Vacation"

Study to acquire such a philosophy as is not barren and babbling, but solid and true; not such an one as floats upon the surface of endless verbal controversies, but one that enters into the nature of things; for he spoke good sense, that said, "The philosophy of the Greeks was a mere jargon, and noise of words."

If so, then so is all philosophy: for what system is there, the elements and outlines of which are not to be found in the Greek schools? Here Leighton followed too incautiously the Fathers.

32   IV   441–2*d* | "A Sermon, Preached to the Clergy"

For these incongruous honours, to speak it in a word, raising some from contempt, teach them to contemn and insult over their brethren; to say nothing of their affronting of higher quality, yea, of princes and kings

---

a Not in MS TRANSCRIPT; supplied from *LR*   *b* Not in MS TRANSCRIPT; supplied from *LR*
c Not in MS TRANSCRIPT; supplied from *LR*   *d* This note is recorded in MS TRANSCRIPT (*b*) only

29[1] "Pleroma", "fulness", occurring 12 times in AV; cf C's use in COPY C **50** below, IRVING *Sermons* **55** at n 4.

30[1] C associated slangy prose with Sir Roger L'Estrange (1616–1704), who he believed had introduced slang into English literature: AURELIUS **62**.

themselves, while they pretend to be the only supporters of their crowns. And if this their insolency in advancement devolve them back again into contempt, and their honour become their shame, they may thank themselves for it.

I fancy that had he been present at the preaching of this sermon Archbishop Laud would have glanced on Archbishop Leighton with much the same sweet expression as Archangel Satan did on Archangel Michael over the body of Moses.[1]

33   IV   465ᵃ | Letters No 4

I thank you for the notice of your capuchin; but I almost knew that he was not here before I looked. It is true the variety of his book refreshes us, and by the happy wording, the same things not only please, but sometimes profit us; but they tell us no new thing, except it may be some such thing as, I confess, I understand not, of essential unions and sleeps of the soul; which because I understand them not, would rather disorder and hinder than advance me; and therefore I begin to be unwilling to look over these and such like, unless I could pick out here and there such things as I am capable of, and not meet with those steep ascents which I dare not venture on: But dear *a-Kempis* is a way to it, and oh! that I could daily study more and attain more sublime humble devotion there drawn to the life . . .ᵇ

Annex

LR IV 157 prints an annotation (referring to I 2) which does not appear in COPY A but may be associated with COPY B. BM MS Egerton 2801 f 188 is either a copy of such a note in COPY B or the original from which HNC took it into *LR*. (Textus is not provided in the ms.) HNC has added a sentence at the end that does not appear in the ms. C refers to this note in *CN* IV 4909 f 70 (29 Jul 1822): see also a close parallel in *CN* IV 4854 (c Jan 1822). The note appears in much revised form in *AR* (1825) 326–7 in the COMMENT to Spiritual Aphorism 19 as "Synopsis of the Constituent Points in the Doctrine of Redemption, in Four Questions, with Correspondent Answers". Since this comes immediately after the newspaper extract (p 325n) dated 4 Dec 1824, the note may have been written as late as c Feb 1825.

BM MS Egerton 2801 f 188, referring to I 2

. . . this first chapter is much on that [subject, i.e. *faith*], persuading them of

---

ᵃ This note is recorded in MS TRANSCRIPT (b) only
ᵇ MS TRANSCRIPT ends here, and there is no record of C's note

32[1] A playful allusion to Jude 1.9: "Yet Michael the archangel, when contending with the devil he disputed about the body of Moses, durst not bring against him a railing accusation, but said, The Lord rebuke thee."

the truth of that mystery they had received and did believe, *viz.* their redemption and salvation by Christ Jesus; that inheritance of immortality bought by his blood for them, and the evidence and stability of their right and title to it.

Note to Leighton Vol. 1 p. 2.

By the blood of Christ I mean, that I contemplate the Christ, first as Christus Agens,[1] the Jehovah Christ, God the Word; and secondly, as Christus patiens;[2] the ⟨God⟩ incarnate. In the former ⟨(i.e. as Chr. Agens)⟩ He is, relative to the human *intellect*, Lux lucifica, Sol intellectualis; relative ad *Existentiam* humanam, he is the Anima animans, Calor fovens.[3] In the latter, i.e. as Christus Patiens, he is Vita vivificans, Principium Spiritualis (id est, veræ, τῆς ὄντως οὐσῆς) Reproductionis in vitam veram.[4] Now *this* Principle or Vis Vitæ vitam communicans, considered in formâ passivâ, assimilationem patiens,[5] at the same time it excites the soul to the vital act of assimilating—*this*, I say, is the Blood of Christ, really (vere seu spiritualiter)[6] present thro' Faith & actually (actu) partaken by the Faithful. *ᵃOf this the body is the continual product, that is, a good life—the merits of Christ acting on the soul, redemptive.ᵇ*

ᵃ⁻ᵇ This sentence appears only in *LR*

ANNEX[1] "Christ acting".

ANNEX[2] "Christ suffering", i.e. "being acted upon".

ANNEX[3] As "Christ Acting" he is, "relative to the human *intellect*, light-making Light, intelligible Sun; relative to human *Existence*, he is the animating Soul, the cherishing Heat".

ANNEX[4] As "Christ Suffering" he is "life-giving Life, the Principle of Spiritual (that is, of true, or really existing) Rebirth into true life".

ANNEX[5] This "Life-Force communicating life", considered "in its passive form, undergoing assimilation".

ANNEX[6] "Truly or spiritually".

Copy C

The Whole Works of Robert Leighton, D.D. some time Bishop of Dunblane, afterwards Archbishop of Glasgow. A new edition, carefully corrected. To which is prefixed a memoir of the author, by George Jerment, D.D. 4 vols. London 1820. 8°.

The Advertisement, dated London Aug 1819, states that this edition is to replace *The Works . . . a New and Enlarged Edition* (6 vols 1805–8). In the 6-vol edition first appeared Jerment's "The Life of Bishop Leighton, in a new form; with a delineation of his character, and a critical review of his works", dated from Weston-place, 30 Aug 1807.

British Library C 126 h 1

"S. T. C." label on the title-page verso of each volume. John Duke Coleridge's monogram "C" on I ‾4. A note by EHC dated 16 May [? 1890/1896] is inserted in Vol I on a slip of paper. On II 157 (**34A**) C has corrected one misprint, but his minute marking of the text elsewhere does not support his statement that the volumes were "grievously" and "miserably misprinted" (*CL* v 200, 291).

No other set of annotations by C was as explicitly dedicated to a literary project as those in this copy of Leighton, which was presented to C by the publisher John Murray in Jan 1822 to allow him to prepare a collection of "The Beauties of Archbishop Leighton": *CL* v 200, 205. After examining the marked copy in Jun or Jul 1823, however, Murray decided against the project "on a ground, which he knew as well when the Proposal was first made by me & to a certain degree encouraged by him—namely, the existence of a Reprint of Leighton's Works" (*CL* v 282). The later history of the project, which became *Aids to Reflection* and was published by Taylor and Hessey, is given in the Introduction to *AR* (*CC*).

CONTENTS. I [sig a] "Advertisement"; i–lxxv "Life of Archbishop Leighton" by George Jerment; lxxv–lxxxix "Character of Archbishop Leighton"; ix$_2$–xxii$_2$ (second series paged to follow the 8 unfoliated pages of prelims—title-page, contents, advertisement) "Dr Doddridge's Preface"; xxiii$_2$–xxiv$_2$ "Preface to the London Edition of 1777" by Henry Foster; 1–436 *A Practical Commentary upon the First Epistle General of St. Peter*; II 1–381 *A Practical Commentary* cont; 383–452 *Meditations Critical and Practical, on Psalms IV, XXXII, and CXXX*; 453–64 *A Fragment on part of the Eighth Psalm*; 465–535 *Expository Lectures on Psalm XXXIX, Isaiah VI, and Romans XII*; III 1–84 *Lectures on the First Nine Chapters of St. Matthew's Gospel*; 85–461 *Sermons* [32 in number]; 462–80 *A Sermon Preached to the Clergy*; IV 1–37 *An Exposition of the Creed*; 37–106 *An Exposition of The Lord's Prayer*; 107–74 *An Exposition of the Ten Commandments*; 175–9 *A Short Catechism*; 181–359 *Theological Lectures* with (181–6) "Preface by the Publisher of the Latin Edition" by James Fall; 361–403 *Exhortations to the Candidates for the Degree of Master of Arts in the University of Edinburgh*; 404–12 *A Modest Defence of Moderate Episcopacy*; 413–30 *Charges to the Clergy of the Diocesan Synod of Dunblane*; 431–44 *Letters* [numbered 1–8, being the *Charge* and *Seven Letters* of COPY B]; 445–59 *Rules and Instructions for a Holy Life*.

DATE. Jan 1822 – early May 1825, probably in great part during the major re-working of the first half of *AR* (1825) from early Nov 1823 to late Mar 1824.

COEDITOR. John Beer.

PRESENTATION OF ANNOTATED AND MARKED PASSAGES. In the following transcript C's true marginalia and the passages he wrote in COPY C for inclusion in *AR* (1825) are both treated as marginalia and are given whole numbers (e.g. **1, 4, 10, 14**). Marked passages, whether or not labelled for a certain section of aphorisms, and whether or not they were actually included in *AR* (1825), are treated as submarginalia and are given lettered serial numbers (e.g. **2A, 4B**); C's usual practice of running a line down the margin and putting other symbols such as "Spir." or "M.X." somewhere near the middle of it has been regularised, with the symbols normally placed at the beginning or end of the passage in question. Notes simply instructing the printer are also treated as submarginalia (e.g. **8A, 10B**).

DISTRIBUTION OF MARGINALIA. Contents are given in the order in which they appear in COPY C, with the order for all three editions indicated by arabic numerals. The entry numbers for the marginalia are given in parentheses.

	COPY A	COPY B	COPY C
Commentary on 1 Pet	1 (**2–17**)	1 (**1–8**, ANNEX)	1 (**4A–37C**)
Meditations on Ps 4, 32, 130	2	12	2 (**38–38A**)
Expository Lectures on Ps 39, Isa 6, and Rom 12	3	2	3
Lectures on Matt 1–9			4 (**41–41D**)
Sermons		6, 9, 13 (**9–20, 32**)	5 (**42A–42D**)
Expositions of the Creed		7	6 (**42E–48**)
A Short Catechism		8	
Theological Lectures		10 (**21–31**)	7 (**48A–56C**)
Exhortations to Candidates for MA		11	8 (**56D–59**)
Defence of Moderate Episcopacy			9
Charges to the Clergy of Dunblane		3	10
Letters	4	4, 14 (**33**)	11
Rules . . . for a Holy Life	5	5	12

1 ɪ ⁻2, pencil

Apology for the Life of Archb L.[1]—or if it were permitted me to trifle on such a theme—
Apology for *A* Life of Archb. L.? Nevertheless, the Word is appropriate—and without using it as Watson did in his Apology for the Bible, in a sense which his readers were sure to *mis*understand[2]—~~yet~~ there is in the act of giving the countenance of his Name and his Virtue to the abhorred plans and measures of Lauderdale, Sharp, and the Royal Brothers that which ~~needs~~ asks an Apology[3]—and ~~yet if the Life of Leighton~~ that which his Life *asks*, what other Life can hope to *receive*? Abstine a Fabis. Worship the Echo.[4] For inobservance of these precepts, Verulam ⟨is⟩ a Beacon of Smoke, and a Mist ~~floatings~~ before Leighton's Pillar of Flame.[5]

1[1] C's original plan to write an improved biography of Leighton as an introduction to his selection of "beauties" from his works had by Sept 1823 become a plan for a much longer "apology" (*CL* v 299–300). Although he worked on it while on holiday at Ramsgate, it was still unfinished in Nov 1823 and had been abandoned by Mar 1824 (*CL* v 306, 345). An account of the project is given in *AR* (*CC*); some draft materials appear in *SW & F* (*CC*).

1[2] In his *Apology for the Bible, in a Series of Letters, Addressed to Thomas Paine* (1796), Richard Watson, bp of Llandaff (1737–1816), intended "apology" in the sense of "a defence" (in response to Paine's attacks) but might have been misunderstood to mean an acknowledgment of faults. C intends "apologia" in the sense of "praise for", while admitting that some aspects of Leighton's life do require justification. C also refers scathingly to Watson's work in *SW & F* (*CC*).

1[3] Charles Maitland, 1st Earl of Lauderdale (1616–82), and abp James Sharpe (1613–79) were responsible for several oppressive ecclesiastical measures culminating in the Act of Supremacy (1669), which declared that the government of the Church was an inherent right of the Crown. In BM MS Egerton 2801 f 255, C refers to them as "the Apostates—Lauderdale and Sharp" and as instruments of "the perjured Charles". Leighton supported the Act of Supremacy. The "Royal Brothers"

Charles ɪɪ and James ɪɪ were objects of C's contempt: cf HACKET *Scrinia* 14 n 4.

1[4] Two Pythagorean or Neopythagorean maxims. The first, "Keep away from beans", is generally interpreted as meaning "Keep away from politics"; C's acceptance of this interpretation is recorded by De Q in his essays about C's plagiarism: *De Q Works* ɪɪ 142–3. The second, recorded by C as early as 1803, is, as he admits in *SW & F* (*CC*), "one of least obvious interpretation", but he seems to have thought of it as complementary to the first maxim: Keep away from politics, and attend to the divine. Such an interpretation would be consistent with tradition. Rendering the maxim as a whole as "When the winds blow, worship the noise", Thomas Stanley (*History of Philosophy*—1701—411) adds the gloss of Iamblichus: "an exhortation to Divine Wisdom; for it implieth that we ought to love the similitude of Divine Nature and Powers: and when they make a reason suitable to their efficacies, it ought exceedingly to be honoured and reverenced". We do not know where C encountered these maxims, but there are many possibilities, e.g. the 1673 Latin and Greek edition of Hierocles' commentary on Pythagoras by John Pearson (whose *Exposition of the Creed* was important to C), in which they appear among the "Symbola Pythagorae", with the Greek ἤχω (*echo*) translated into Latin as *sonum*, "sound".

1[5] Cf *BL* ch 9 (*CC*) ɪ 152, where C,

2 ₁ ⁻2

We might compare Leighton in his appearance and character as ⟨an⟩ Archbishop of the short-lived Protestant Episcopal Church of Britain, or (the Scoto-anglican Church by Law established under the ~~re~~ Stuart Dynasty)[1] to the bright Star in Cassiopeia;[2] but with this difference, that in the ~~one~~ latter instance the Star ~~diminished~~ disappeared, the Constellation remaining, in the former the Constellation vanished, no longer numbered among the Heavenly Houses, while the Star remains ∅ in undiminished Magnitude, and unwaning tho' solitary Splendor.

2A ₁ xlvi–xlviii, pencil | "Life of Archbishop Leighton"

[Leighton to "a friend, when our Author was Principal of the University of Edinburgh":] ". . . I have sent you two little pieces of history,/. wherein it may be you will find small relish, but the hazard is small; and however I pray you do not send them back to me at all, for I have enow of that kind. The one is from a good pen, and an acquaintance and friend of yours, *Paulus Nolanus*, ~~ᵃand his~~ whose life of *Martin* of *Towers* I think you will relish, and I believe it is not in your *Vitae Patrum*: the other, *Valerius Maximus*, I conceived would cloy you the less, because it is of so much variety of selected examples, and the stages are so short, you may begin and leave off where you will, without wearying. But when all is done, there is one only blessed Hisstory wherein our souls must dwell and take up their rest; for amongst all the rest we shall not read, ~~Venite ad me, omnes lassi et laborantes, et ego vobis requiem prestabo.~~ '*Come unto me, all ye that labour*, &c.']ᵇ . . . That he felt as a stranger and pilgrim on the earth, even while he filled the highest seat in the university, and was panting for immortality, is evident from the following extract:—

'Sɪʀ,

[ᵃOh! what a weariness is it, to live amongst men, and find so few men, and amongst Christians, and find so few Christians;]ᵇ . . .

ᵃ⁻ᵇ Marked with a pencil line in the margin

adapting the imagery of Exod 13.21–2, commends the mystical writers: "If they were too often a moving cloud of smoke to me by day, yet they were always a pillar of fire throughout the night, during my wanderings through the wilderness of doubt . . .". C means that because of their involvement in politics and consequently imperfect attention to the divine, neither Bacon nor even Leighton is a perfect guide in spiritual affairs.

2[1] There were two periods of episcopacy in the Church of Scotland, both under the Stuarts: 1610–38, 1660–90. Leighton was one of the first Scottish bishops appointed by Charles ɪɪ at the Restoration.

2[2] "Tycho's Star" in the constellation Cassiopeia—so called because of the careful observations of Tycho Brahe (1546–1601)—appeared with extraordinary brilliance in Nov 1572 but over 18 months gradually diminished and disappeared.

*a*Therefore good night is all I add; for whatsoever hour it comes to your hand, I believe you are as sensible as I, that it is still night; but the comfort is, it draws nigh towards that bright morning that shall make amends . . .' ''*b*

3 I lxx–lxxii, pencil

A quality still more valuable belongs to our Author's works; a quality which it is easier to conceive and feel, than to express or describe. The word **unction* conveys the best idea of it.

* That this is the word; which in a metaphoric sense has been, and still is, employed for the expression of this quality, we know; but that the word primâ facie conveys the *best* idea of it, or that without being itself explained, both physically and historically, it conveys *any* idea of it at all, I neither know nor believe. On the contrary, Unction seems to me a low word, akin to *Slang:* and to which nothing reconciles me but the high Authorities for its use which have made it respectable, and the frequency of its application which secures its intelligibility.[1]

4 I lxxi, pencil

Even some evangelical discourses, are chargeable with dryness. They may be compared to stale bread; wholesome and nutritive, but not the most palatable. Indeed, frigid <u>orthodoxy</u>, whether in a minister, or in the hearers of the Gospel, is fervently to be deprecated.

Why, *Or?*?

4A I 3–4, marked with a pencil line | *A Practical Commentary:* 1 Pet 1.1

By that which is spoken of him in divers passages of the Gospel, he is very remarkable amongst the Apostles, both for his graces, and his failings; eminent in zeal and courage, and yet stumbling oft in his forwardness, and once grossly falling. And these by the providence of God being recorded in Scripture, give a check to the excess of *Rome's* conceit concerning this apostle. Their extolling and exalting him above the rest, is not for his cause, much less to the honour of his Lord and master Jesus Christ, for he is injured and dishonoured by it; but it is in favour of

---

a–b Marked with a pencil line in the margin

3[1] C objects to the cant use of a term honourably derived from 1 John 2.20, "But ye have an unction from the Holy One, and ye know all things." As C observes in LUTHER *Colloquia* **2**, "Every man among the Sectaries, however ignorant, may justify himself in scattering Stones and Fire-Squibs by *an Unction of the Spirit.*"

themselves. As *Alexander* distinguished his two friends, that the one was a friend of *Alexander*, the other a friend of the *king*, the preferment which they give this Apostle, is not in good will to *Peter*, but in the desire of *primacy*. But whatsoever he was, they would be much in pain to prove *Rome's* right to it by succession. And if ever it had any such right, we may confidently say, it has forfeited it long ago, by departing from St. *Peter's* footsteps, and from his faith, and retaining too much those things wherein he was faulty: namely,

His unwillingness to hear of, and consent to, Christ's sufferings,— his *Master, spare thyself*, or *Far be it from thee*,—in those they are like him; for thus they would disburthen and exempt the Church from the cross, from the real cross of afflictions, and, instead of that, have nothing but painted, or carved, or gilded crosses; these they are content to embrace, and worship too, but cannot endure to hear of the other. Instead of the cross of affliction, they make the *crown* or *mitre* the badge of their Church, and will have it known by prosperity, and outward pomp; and so turn the Church militant, into the Church triumphant, not considering that it is *Babylon's* voice, not the Church's, *I sit as a queen, and shall see no sorrow*.

Again, they are like him in his saying on the mount at Christ's transfiguration, when he knew not what he said, *It is good to be here*: so they have little of the true glory of Christ, but the false glory of that monarchy in their seven hills: *It is good to be here*, say they.

Again, in their undue striking with the sword, not the enemies, as he, but the faithful friends and servants of Jesus Christ. But to proceed.

We see here *Peter's* office or title,—*an apostle*; not *chief bishop*. Some in their glossing have been so impudent as to add that beside the text; though in chap. v. ver. 4. he gives that title to Christ alone, and to himself only *fellow elder*; and here, not *prince of the apostles*, but *an apostle*, restored and re-established after his fall, by repentance, and by Christ himself after his own death and resurrection. (see John xxi.) Thus we have in our Apostle a singular instance of human frailty on the one side, and of the sweetness of Divine grace on the other. Free and rich grace it is indeed, that forgives and swallows up multitudes of sins, of the greatest sins, not only sins before conversion, as to St. *Paul*, but foul offences committed after conversion, as to *David*, and to this Apostle; not only once raising them from the dead, but when they fall, stretching out the same hand, and raising them again, and restoring them to their station, and comforting them in it by his *free Spirit*, as *David* prays; not only to cleanse polluted clay, but to work it into vessels of honour, yea, of the most defiled shape to make the most refined vessels, not vessels of honour of the lowest sort, but for the highest and most honourable services, vessels to bear his own precious name to the nations; making the most unworthy and the most unfit, fit by his grace to be his messengers.

4B 1 5, marked with a pencil line | *AR* 61, Moral Aphorism 1

And what this apostleship was *then* . . . the ministry of the word in ordinary is *now*, and therefore an employment of more difficulty and excellency than is usually conceived by many, not only of those who look upon it, but even of those who are exercised in it;*ᵃ*—to be ambassadors for the greatest of kings, and upon no mean employment, that great treaty of peace and reconcilement betwixt him and Mankind. *V*. 2 Cor. v. 20.

4C 1 6, marked with a pencil line | *AR* 61–2, Moral Aphorism 2

Though Divine truths are to be received equally from every minister alike, yet it must be acknowledged, that there is something (we know not what to call it) of a more acceptable reception of those who at first were the means of bringing men to God, than of others; like the opinion some have of physicians whom they love.

5 1 7, marked with a pencil line

At the best, a Christian is but a stranger here, set him where you will, as our Apostle teacheth after; and it is his privilege that he is so; and when he thinks not so, he forgets and disparages himself; he descends far below his quality, when he is much taken with any thing in this place of exile.

But this is the wisdom of a Christian, when he can solace himself against the meanness of his outward condition, and any kind of discomfort attending it, with the comfortable assurance of the love of God, that he hath called him to holiness, given him some measure of it, and an endeavour after more; and by this may he conclude, that he hath ordained him unto salvation.

Election—mark of*ᵇ*
    Leighton most wisely avoids all metaphysical views of Election relatively to God: and confines himself to the practical—to the doctrine as it must bear on every Man who thinks at all.—[1]

ᵃ Pencil line begins
    ᵇ Written in pencil in the outer margin beside the second paragraph of textus; the rest is written in ink in the foot-margin

5[1] The same remark is made in BM MS Egerton 2801 f 171ᵛ, in a form closer to the   version in *AR* (1825) 158.

6   I   9–10, pencil, textus marked with an ink line | 1 Pet 1.2

The use and end of sprinkling were *purification* and *expiation,* because sin merited death, and the pollutions and stains of human nature were by sin. Such is the pollution, that it can be no manner of way washed off but by blood. (Heb. ix. 22.) * Neither is there any blood able to purge from sin, except the most precious blood of Jesus Christ, which is called (Acts. xx. 28.) the *blood of God.*

* The spiritual i.e. the true and real import of the *Blood* of Christ, which is likewise the Blood of *God*—that sense in which it is capable of being conceived as an Agent in á moral Subjects and an operative Cause of their Justification—I have shewn in a Note on this passage in Mʳ Gillman's Copy of Leighton's Works (Middleton's Edition)¹

6A   I   10, marked with a pencil line

The soul (as the body) hath its life, its health, its purity, and the contrary of these,—its death, diseases, deformities, and impurity, which belong to it as to their first subject, and to the body by participation.

7   I   10–15, marked with a pencil line, annotation in ink with corrections in pencil

Some who have moral resolutions of amendment, dislike at least gross sins, and purpose to avoid them, and it is to them cleanness enough to reform in those things; but they consider not what becomes of the guiltiness they have contracted already, and how that shall be purged, how their natural pollution shall be taken away. Be not deceived in this: it is not a transient sigh, or a light word, or a wish of *God forgive me*; no, nor the highest current of repentance, nor that which is the truest evidence of repentance, amendment; it is none of these that purify in the sight of God, and expiate wrath; they are all imperfect and stained themselves, cannot stand and answer for themselves, much less be of value to counterpoise the former guilt of sin. The very tears of the purest repentance, unless they be sprinkled with this blood, are impure; all our washings without this, are but washings of the blackmoor, it is labour in vain. Jer. ii. 22. Job ix. 30, 31. There are none truly purified by the blood of Christ, who do not endeavour after purity of heart and conversation; but yet it is the blood of Christ by which they are all made fair, and there is no spot in them. Here it is said, *Elect to obedience;* but because that obedience is not perfect, there must be sprinkling of the blood too. There is nothing in religion further out of nature's reach, and out of its liking and believing, than the doctrine of redemption by a

6¹   COPY B ANNEX.

Saviour, and a crucified Saviour,—by Christ, and by his blood, first shed on the cross in his suffering, and then sprinkled on the soul by his Spirit. It is easier to make men sensible of the necessity of repentance and amendment of life (though that is very difficult,) than of this purging by the sprinkling of this precious blood. Did we see how needful Christ is to us, we should esteem and love him more.

The Logos is the substantial-Idea ⟨= Εικων⟩*a* in whom all Ideas are contained and have Being: it is the Idea of God.[1] The Divine Idea assumed the form of Man, and thus became the Idea of the Divine Humanity = Jehova[2]—and then the Individuality—εγενετο σαρξ.[3] The Word was incarnate, and became the Divine *Ideal* of Human Kind, in which alone God loved (or could love) the World.[4] Hence, &c—[5]

Above all, remember that the *Potential* can neither have Being nor worth except in relation to and by Virtue of a co-existing *Actual*.[6] Every step is progressive only as it approximates—has value therefore not in or for itself, but in its relation to Another—but to what other? A Thought that never can be realized, & corresponds therefore to no Reality—but this is no *Thought* at all but a mere attempt to think an impossibility. But in the Word, in the Jehova, in Christ, the Actual is perfected in all its forms, the Universal, the General, and the Individual—and therein and thereby the Human Race, and each individual Man, has a potential Reality, a relative Worth—the whole Church is thus in the most strict & philosophic use of words the *Body* of Christ[7]—for all *Body* is but the Potentiality of the *Actual*, i.e. ⟨of⟩ the power or property *in actu*[8] in ~~its~~ each moment. ⟨2.⟩ the ~~Spirit~~oul is the Life of *the Man*: ⟨1⟩ †The Life is the Soul of the *Body:*[b9] ⟨3.⟩ and Christ is the Life of the Soul, ~~i.e. of~~ and

---

a The hyphen in ''substantial-Idea'' and the insertion are in pencil, as is a curved line around ''substantial-Idea''

b C has revised the order by inserting numbers but has not marked the first two items for transposition

---

7[1] Cf COPY B **11** at n 4, where C uses the phrase ''Idea or Icon''. C objected to the translation of ειχων as ''image'', e.g. in Col 1.15: ''Who is the image of the invisible God, the firstborn of every creature'' (AV): cf BIBLE COPY B **131** at n 4.

7[2] C argued steadily that the Jehovah of OT was the Word of NT, or ''Jehovah-word'': cf BIBLE COPY B **11**.

7[3] ''Became flesh'' or ''was made flesh'' (AV): John 1.14. C comments further on the translation in e.g. *AR* (1825) 380n.

7[4] An allusion to John 3.16–17.

7[5] C perhaps intended to pass from this point to the paragraph marked on p 21 beginning ''Hence much joy ariseth . . .'' (in **8A** below).

7[6] Cf C's invoking of this Aristotelian distinction in HUGHES **1**.

7[7] C takes up the words of Paul, 1 Cor 12.27, ''Now ye are the body of Christ, and members in particular.'' For C's scrupulous discrimination among meanings of the word ''body'', see IRVING *Sermons* **29** and n 12.

7[8] ''In the act'', ''in action''.

7[9] Cf COPY B **2**.

the Soul is the Indifference of the Life and the Spirit, the *Inter*-Ens as it were, or Ens intermedium,[10] as Heat is the Indifference of Light and Gravity.[11] It is in this sense of the human Soul, as the Inter-ens and *Participium*[12] (as it were) of the Life and of the Spirit, that we can understand the words "even to the *dividing* of Soul and Spirit"—[13]

> Unless above himself he can
> Erect himself, how poor a thing is Man!
> DANIEL.[14]

7A　I 14, marked with a pencil line | *AR* 62, Moral Aphorism 3

The exactest knowledge of things, is, to know them in their causes; it is then an excellent thing, and worthy of their endeavours who are most desirous of knowledge, to know the best things in their highest causes; and the happiest way of attaining to this knowledge, is, to possess those things, and to know them in experience.

7B　I 15–16, marked with a pencil line and altered in pencil

The spirit or soul of a man is the chief and first subject of this work, and it is but slight false work that begins not there; but the *spirit* here, is to be taken for the Spirit of God, the efficient, rather than for the spirit o[f] man, the subject of this sanctification. And therefore our Saviour in that place prays to the Father, *that he would sanctify his own by that truth*; and this he doth by the͟at concurrence of his spirit with tha͟te word of truth which is the life and vigour of it, and makes it prove *the power of God unto salvation to them that believe. ªIt is a fit means in itself, but it is a prevailing means, only when the Spirit of God brings it into the heart. It is a sword, and *sharper than a two-edged sword*, fit to divide, yea, *even to the dividing of soul and spirit*; but this it doth not, unless it be in the Spirit's hand, and he apply it to this cutting and dividing. The word calls, but the Spirit draws, not severed from that word, but working in it, and by it.

It is a very difficult work to draw a soul out of the hands and strong chains of Satan, and out of the pleasing entanglements of the world, and

---

ª From here onward marked in the margin with a pencil line

7[10] The "intermediary Being", as in COPY B **2** at n 3.

7[11] Also in COPY B **2** at n 5.

7[12] "Partaker", as in COPY B **2** at nn 3, 4.

7[13] Heb 4.12 (var), q thus by Leighton I 16, in **7B** below.

7[14] Samuel Daniel *Epistle to the Lady Margaret, Countess of Cumberland* lines 95–6; noted in ANDERSON COPY A **4** as "A noble Poem in all respects". C used these lines as a motto in *Friend* (*CC*) I 100, and quoted them twice in *AR* (1825) 5, 112.

out of its own natural perverseness, to yield up itself unto God,—to deny itself, and live to him, and in so doing, to run against the main stream, and the current of the ungodly world without, and corruption within.

The strongest rhetoric, the most moving and persuasive way of discourse, is all too weak; the tongue of men or angels cannot prevail with the soul to free itself, and shake off all that detains it. Although it be convinced of the truth of those things that are represented to it, yet still it can and will hold out against it, and say, *Non persuadebis etiamsi persuaseris* [You will not persuade [me] even though you should have persuaded me].

The hand of man is too weak to pluck any soul out of the crowd of the world, and to set it in amongst the select number of believers. Only the Father of Spirits hath absolute command of spirits, *viz.*, the souls of men, to work on them as he pleaseth, and where he will. This powerful, this sanctifying Spirit knows no resistance; works sweetly, and yet strongly; it can come into the heart, whereas all other speakers are forced to stand without. That still voice within, persuades more than all the loud crying without; as he that is within the house, though he speak low, is better heard and understood, than he that shouts without doors.

8 ɪ 19

* 2. It is most absurd to give any reason of Divine will without Himself.

*[a] It is absurd to ask *any* reason *for* the will of God, which is one with Reason itself. God is the Identity of Will and Reason—eternal Reason, Will absolute.[1] But then I draw a very different consequence from Leighton's.[2]

8A ɪ 20–3, marked with lines in pencil overtraced in ink | *AR* 63–5, Moral Aphorism 5

[b]III. The Connexion of these, we are now for our profit to take notice of; that *effectual calling* is inseparably tied to this eternal *foreknowledge* or *election* on the one side, and to *salvation* on the other. These two links of the chain are up in heaven in God's own hand; but this[c] M.5[d]

[a] In the margin beside the textus C has written "see above"; the note is written in the head-margin

[b] Pencil line begins here

[c] Ink line begins

[d] "M.5", repeated as this paragraph runs on to p 21, indicates that the paragraph was to be taken into *AR* as Moral Aphorism 5

8[1] C's repeated assertion: cf BUNYAN COPY B **16**, KANT *VS* COPY B **13**.

8[2] Leighton argues (ɪ 19) that God's foreknowledge "is no other than that . . . decree of election, by which some are appointed unto *life*, and . . . predestinate to the way to it"; C believed in the freedom of the will.

middle one is let down to earth, into the hearts of his children, and they laying hold on it, have sure hold on the other two, for no power can sever them. If, therefore, they can read the characters of God's image in their own souls, those are the counter-part of the golden characters of His love, in which their names are written in the book of life. Their believing writes their names under the promises of the revealed book of life,—the Scriptures, and so ascertains them, that the same names are in the secret book of life which God hath by himself from eternity. So that finding the stream of grace in their hearts, though they see not the fountain whence it flows, nor the ocean into which it returns, yet they know that it hath its source, and shall return to that ocean which ariseth from their eternal election, and shall empty itself into that eternity of happiness and salvation. M.5

This ¶ph. omitted] Hence much joy ariseth to the believer; this tie is indissoluble, as the agents are, the Father, the Son, and the Spirit: so are *election*, and *vocation*, and *sanctification*, and *justification*, and *glory*. Therefore in all conditions, believers may, from a sense of the working of the Spirit in them, look back to that election, and forward to that salvation: but they that remain unholy and disobedient, have as yet no evidence of this love; and therefore cannot, without vain presumption and self-delusion, judge thus of themselves, that they are within the peculiar love of God. But in this, *let the righteous be glad, and let them shout for joy, all that are upright in heart. . . .*[1]

M.5 The perfect blessedness of the Saints is awaiting them above; but even their present condition is truly happy, though incompletely, and but a small beginning of that which they expect. And this their present happiness is so much the greater, the more clear knowledge and firm persuasion they have of it. It is one of the pleasant fruits of the ungodly, *to know the things that are freely given them of God*, 1 Cor. ii. 12. Therefore the Apostle, to comfort his dispersed brethren, sets before them a description of that excellent spiritual condition to which they are called.[2] M.5

M.5 If *election, effectual calling* and *salvation* be inseparably linked together, then, by any one of them a man may lay hold upon all the rest, and may know that his hold is sure; and this is the way wherein we may attain, and ought to seek, that comfortable assurance of the love of God. Therefore *make your calling sure*, and by that, your *election*;

8A[1] The following paragraph in Leighton (omitted from textus here) became Moral Aphorism 4: see **8B**.

8A[2] This paragraph, though clearly marked and twice labelled "M.5.", is not included in *AR*; it was perhaps missed by the printer.

for that being *a*done, this follows of itself. We are not to pry immediately into the decree, but to read it in the performance. Though the mariner sees not the *pole-star*, yet the needle of the compass which points to it, tells him which way he sails: thus the heart that is touched with the loadstone of Divine love, trembling with godly fear, and yet still looking towards God by fixed believing, points at the love of election, and tells the soul that its course is heavenward, towards the haven of eternal rest. He that loves, may be sure he was loved first; and he that chooses God for his delight and portion, may conclude confidently, that God hath chosen him to be one of those that shall enjoy him, and be happy in him for ever; for that our love, and electing of him, is but the return and repercussion of the beams of his love shining upon us. M.5 . . . *b*Although from present unsanctification, a man cannot infer that he is not *elected*; for the decree may, for part of a man's life, run (as it were) underground; yet this is sure, that that estate leads to death, and unless it be broken, will prove the black line of reprobation. A man hath no portion amongst the children of God, nor can read one word of comfort in all the promises that belong to them, while he remains unholy. M.5

8B I 21, marked with a line in pencil overtraced in ink | *AR* 62, Moral Aphorism 4

M.4 It is one main point of happiness, that he that is happy doth know and judge himself to be so; this being the peculiar good of a reasonable creature, it is to be enjoyed in a reasonable way; it is not as the dull resting of a stone, or any other natural body in its natural place; but the knowledge and consideration of it, is the fruition of it, the very relishing and tasting its sweetness.

9 I 23–6, marked with a line in pencil overtraced in ink; note in pencil corrected in ink | *AR* 65–7, Moral Aphorism 6 and prefatory remark

M.6 If any pretend that they have the Spirit, and so turn away from the straight rule of the holy Scriptures, they have a spirit indeed, but it is a fanatical spirit, the spirit of delusion and giddiness: but the Spirit of God, that leads his children in the way of truth, and is for that purpose sent them from heaven to guide them thither, squares their thoughts and ways to that rule whereof it is author, and that word which was inspired by it, and sanctifies them to obedience. *He that saith I know him, and keepeth not his commandments, is a liar, and the truth is not in him.* 1 John ii. 4.

a Opening bracket inserted here in pencil, and in the gutter "cf 65"—i.e. the corresponding page in *AR* (1825); these markings are presumably not C's

b Leaving a gap of 10 lines at the beginning of the paragraph, C marks off in ink the following sentences

M.6   Now this spirit which sanctifieth, and sanctifieth to obedience, is within us the evidence of our election, and the earnest of our salvation. And whoso are not sanctified and led by this Spirit, the Apostle tells us what is their condition. Rom. viii. 9. *If any man have not the Spirit of Christ, he is none of his.*

δ Let us not delude ourselves: this is a truth, if there be any in religion; they who are not made Saints in the state of grace, shall never be Saints in glory, δ

The stones which are appointed for that glorious temple above, are hewn, and polished, and prepared for it here; as the stones were wrought and prepared in the mountains, for building the temple at *Jerusalem.*

Introduction to M.6.*[a]*

~~I select these ¶phs because they (at once) break shatter & precipitate~~*[b]* the only Draw-bridge*[c]* between the fanatical and the orthodox Doctrine of Grace and the Gifts of the Spirit. In scripture the term, Spirit, as a power or property seated in the human soul, never stands singly, but is always *specified* by a genitive case following—this being an Hebraism for the adjective which the Writer would have put if he had *thought*, as well as *written*, in Greek.—It is the Spirit of Meekness (a meek Spirit) or the Spirit of Chasity,*[d]* & the like.[1] The moral Result, the specific Form ~~of~~ and Character, in which the Spirit manifests its presence, a presence which is to be, & may safely be, inferred from its practical Effects; but of which an immediate Knowlege & Consciousness is *impossible*: and every Pretence to such Knowlege is either Hypocrisy or fanatical Delusion.   ~~S. T. C.~~*[e]*

9A   I 28–9, marked with a pencil line

It is also a loss even to those that oppose errors and divisions, that they are forced to be busied in that way: for the wisest and godliest of them find (and such are sensible of it) that disputes in religion are no friends to that which is far sweeter in it; but hinders and abates it, *viz.*, those pious and devout thoughts, that are both the more useful and truly delightful.

---

[a] Phrase in ink   *[b]* Cancelled in ink; "hatter" of "shatter" overtraced in ink
[c] "b" overtraced in ink   *[d]* A slip for "Charity"? *LR* (1825) prints "Chastity". See n 1 below
[e] Deleted with an ink stroke

9[1] "Spirit of Meekness" occurs in 1 Cor 4.21, Gal 6.1. Neither "Spirit of Chastity" nor "Spirit of Charity" occurs in AV, though there are many other combinations with "spirit" (of grace, of prophecy, of wisdom etc). C makes a similar point about Hebrew syntax in *AR* (1825) 363.

10 I 29–33, marked with a line in pencil partly overtraced in ink | *AR* 82–4, Moral Aphorism 7

*a*T And from our sense of this peace, or reconcilement with God, arises that which is our inward peace, a calm and quiet temper of mind. S *b*This peace which we have with God in Christ, is inviolable; but because the sense and persuasion of it may be interrupted, the soul that is truly at peace with God, may for a time be disquieted in itself, through weakness of faith, or the strength of temptation, or the darkness of desertion, losing sight of that grace, that love and light of God's countenance, on which its tranquillity and joy depends. *Thou didst hide they face*, saith *David, and I was troubled*. But when these eclipses are over, the soul is revived with new consolation, as the face of the earth is renewed and made to smile with the return of the sun in the spring; and this ought always to uphold Christians in the saddest times, *viz*., that the grace and love of God towards them, depend not on their sense, nor upon any thing in them, but is still in itself incapable of the smallest alteration.

T. The proper and natural Effect, and in the absence of all disturbing or intercepting forces the certain and sensible accompaniment, of Peace (or Reconcilement) with God, is our own inward Peace, a calm and quiet temper of Mind. And where*c* there is a consciousness of earnestly desiring, and of having sincerely striven after, the former, the latter may be considered as a *Sense* of ~~the same~~ its presence. In this case, I say, and for a Soul watchful, and under the discipline of the Gospel, the Peace ~~within it~~ a man's Self may be the medium, thro' which the assurance of his Peace with God ~~and the Organ~~ is conveyed, and the Organ, as it were, of its spiritual Perception. ~~But be it~~ ⟨We will not therefore condemn this mode of speaking, tho'⟩ ⟨we dare not greatly recommend it. Be it,⟩ that there is truly and in sobriety of speech, ~~sufficient~~ enough of just Analogy ⟨in the subjects meant,⟩ to make this use of the words, ⟨if less than proper yet⟩ something more than metaphorical,[1] ~~tho' less than proper~~ still we must be cautious not to transfer to the Object the defects or the deficiency of the Organ, which must needs partake of the imperfections of the imperfect Beings, to whom it belongs. Not without the co-assurance of other Senses and of the same Sense in other men dare

a First sentence marked with a curved ink line and a letter "T" (for "Theological"?) in the left margin, corresponding to the letter at the beginning of C's note. "S" in the right-hand margin refers to the second sentence (see n 2 below)

b Pencil line in the right-hand margin begins

c C has here written "(turn over [)]" and has continued the note p 30

10[1] The distinction between metaphor and analogy plays an important part in *AR*,   esp *AR* (1825) 198–200, 311–17.

we affirm that what our Eye beholds is verily there to be beheld. Much less may *a*conclude from the negatively, & from the privation of inadequacy or suspension or interruption affections of the Sight to infer the non-existence, or absence, or departure departure or changes of the Thing, or even identify the changes itself. The Camelion darkens in the shade of him, that bends over it to ascertain its colors. In like manner but with yet greater caution, ought we to think respecting a tranquil habit of the inward life, considered as a spiritual *Sense*, as the medial Organ in and by which our Peace with God, and the lively Working of his Grace on our Spirit, is perceived by us. This Peace, which &c p. 29, last line but 4.[2]

10A I 31, marked with ink brace, but additions and annotation in pencil | *AR* 84, last paragraph of Aphorism 7

M.VII.*b* A holy heart, that gladly entertains grace, shall find that it and peace cannot dwell asunder: while

An ungodly man may sleep to death in the lethargy of carnal presumption and impenitency; but a true, lively, solid peace he cannot have. *There is no peace to the wicked, saith my God*, Isa. lvii. 21.

to follow "alteration" p. 30, l.11.[1]

10B I 34, marked with a line in pencil overtraced in ink | 1 Pet 1.3–4

1. Nature cannot raise itself to this [i.e. grace], any more than a man can give natural being to himself. Sp. 2. It *c*The conformity of the mind to the mind that was in Christ, is not &c is not a superficial change; it is a new life and being. A moral man in his changes and reformations of himself, is still the same man. Though he reform so far, as that men, in their ordinary phrase, shall call him *quite another man*, yet, in truth, till he be born again, there is no new nature in him. . . . *d*But the Christian, by virtue of this *new birth*, can say indeed, *Ego non sum ego*, I am not the same man I was. Sp.

10C I 35–6, marked with a line in ink; inserts in pencil, partly overtraced in ink | *AR* 84, Moral Aphorism 8

M.VIII . . . they Worldly Hopes are not living, but lying hopes; and dying hopes; they die often before us, and we live to bury them, and see

---

a In turning the page between "may" and "conclude", C may have inadvertently omitted a pronoun—"we"?

b In ink

c Here C has written "∧" in pencil and marked the insert in the foot-margin in ink with "∧ Insert"

d Two sentences omitted by ed

10[2] C's note provides the first part of the aphorism, which then returns to the second sentence of textus: cf note *a*.
10A[1] I.e. the end of **10** textus.

our own folly and infelicity in trusting to them; but at the utmost, they die with us when we die, and can accompany us no further. But ~~this hope~~ But the lively Hope, which is the Christian's Portion, answers expectation to the full, and much beyond it, and deceives no way but in that happy way of far exceding it.

M.VIII.   A *living hope*, living in death itself! The world dares say no more for its device, than *Dum spiro spero* [while I breathe I hope]; but the children of God can add, by virtue of this living hope, *Dum exspiro spero* [while I am dying (breathing my last) I hope].

11   I 36, marked with a line in ink, immediately following **10C** | *AR* 85, Moral Aphorism 9, C's annotation printed as a footnote

M.IX.   It is a fearful thing when a man and all his hopes die together. Thus saith *Solomon* of the wicked, Prov. xi. 7., When he dieth, then die his hopes; (many of them *before*, but at the utmost *then*, all of them;) but *the righteous hath hope in his death*, Prov. xiv. 32.

* One of the numerous proofs against those who with a strange inconsistency hold the Old Testament to have been inspired throughout, and yet deny that the doctrine of a future State is taught therein. ~~I grieve to hear that this Warburtonian Whimsy is in great favor and acceptance with many of our Church Dignitaries.~~ [1]

11A   I 38–9, marked with a line in pencil overtraced in ink | *AR* 85–6, Moral Aphorism 10

* *As he that taketh away a garment in cold weather, and as vinegar upon nitre, so is he that singeth songs to a heavy heart*, Prov. xxv. 20. M.X. Worldly mirth is so far from curing spiritual *[a]*grief, that even worldly grief, where it is great and takes deep root, is not allayed but increased by it.*[b]* A man who is full of inward heaviness, the more he is encompassed about with mirth, it exasperates and enrages his grief the more; like ineffectual weak physic, which removes not the humour, but stirs it and makes it more unquiet/. *[b]*But spiritual joy is seasonable for all estates: in prosperity, it is pertinent to crown and sanctify all other enjoyments, with this which so far surpasses them; and in distress, it is the only *Nepenthe*, the cordial of fainting spirits: so, Psal. iv. 7, *He hath put joy into my heart.[c]* This mirth makes way for itself, which other

[a–b] Separately marked with a pencil line
[c] According to the marking the aphorism was first intended to stop here

11[1] C refers to William Warburton *The Divine Legation of Moses* (1737–41), which argued that the Jews had no concept of an after-life. For his plan to answer Warburton see *CN* IV 4708, q T. FULLER *Life Out of Death* **1** n 2.

mirth cannot do. These songs are sweetest in the night of distress.   M.X.

* The Note (to be printed at the end of this Aphorism) you will find in page 10, Slip III.[1]

11B   I 41, marked with pencil lines in both margins | *AR* 87, Moral Aphorism 11

Plotinus thanked God that his soul was not tied to an immortal body.

11C   I   41, marked with a pencil line | *AR* 87, Moral Aphorism 12

For as divines say of the knowledge of God which we have here, that the negative notion makes up a great part of it,—we know rather what He is not than what He is, infinite, incomprehensible, immutable, &c. so it is of this happiness, this inheritance; and indeed it is no other than God. We cannot tell you what it is, but we can say so far what it is not, as declares it is unspeakably above all the most excellent things of the inferior world and this present life. It is by privatives, by removing imperfections from it, that we describe it, and we can go no further, than this,—*Incorruptible, undefiled, and that fadeth not away.*[1]

11D   I 50, marked with a pencilled brace in the margin

Faith is an humble, self-denying grace; it makes the Christian nothing in himself and all in God.

11E   I 52, marked with a line in pencil, partly overtraced in ink | 1 Pet 1.5

You see what it is that the Gospel offers you, and you may gather how great both your folly and your guiltiness will be, if you neglect and slight so great salvation when it is brought to you and you are intreated to receive it. This is all that the preaching of the word aims at, and yet, who hearkens to it? How few lay hold on this eternal life, this inheritance, this crown that is held forth to all that hear of it!

   *a*Sp.   Oh! that you could be persuaded to be saved, that you would be willing to embrace salvation! You think you would; but if it be so, then I may say, though you would be saved, yet your custom of sin, your love to sin, and love to the world, will not suffer you: and these will still hinder you, unless you put on holy resolutions to break through them, and trample them under foot, and take this kingdom by a hand of violence, which God is so well pleased with. He is willingly overcome

---

a Ink line in the margin begins here

11A[1] C's "Note", the ms of which is not preserved, is printed in *AR* (1825) 86 as the second paragraph of Moral Aphorism 10.

11C[1] In *AR* (1825) 87, C in fact uses from Leighton's text only the italicised words (which he changes slightly).

by that force, and gives this kingdom most willingly, where it is so taken; it is not attained by slothfulness, and sitting still with folded hands; it must be invaded with strength of faith, with armies of prayers and tears; and they who set upon it thus, are sure to take it.

11F ɪ 54, pencil, marked with a line in the margin | 1 Pet 1. 6

A man is not only unknown to others but to himself, that hath never met with such difficulties, as require faith, and Christian fortitude, and patience to surmount them. How shall a man know whether his meekness and calmness of spirit be real or not, while he meets with no provocation, nothing that contradicts or crosses him? *a*Standing Water, whatever mud there may be at the bottom, will be clear at top, while it remains untouched.[1]

11G ɪ 55, marked with a line in pencil overtraced in ink | *AR* 88, Moral Aphorism 13

M.XIII.   It is not altogether unprofitable; yea, it is great wisdom in Christians to be arming themselves against such temptations as may befal them hereafter, though they have not as yet met with them; to labour to overcome them before-hand, to suppose the hardest things that may be incident to them, and to put on the strongest resolutions they can attain unto. Yet all that is but an imaginary effort; and therefore there is no assurance that the victory is any more than imaginary too, till it come to action, and then, they that have spoken and thought very confidently, may prove but (as one said of the *Athenians*) *fortes in tabula*, patient and courageous in picture or fancy; and, notwithstanding all their arms, and dexterity in handling them by way of exercise, may be foully defeated when they are to fight in earnest.

11H ɪ 55, marked with a line in pencil overtraced in ink | *AR* 88, Moral Aphorism 14

m.XIV   ~~For~~ [the word of God speaks to men, and therefore it speaks the language of the children of men: thus, Gen. xxii. 12, *Now I know that thou fearest God, seeing that thou hast not withheld thy son, thine only son from me.*

11I ɪ 56–7, marked with a line in pencil overtraced in ink; corrections in ink and pencil |
    AR 91, Moral Aphorism 15

m.Aph.XV.   Seek not altogether to dry up th*i*/*se* stream ~~the stream of Sorrow~~*c* of Sorrow, but to bound it, and keep it within its banks. ~~Grace~~

---

a Here C has written "/\" and marked the insert in the foot-margin with "/\"

b C's square brackets in pencil

c Written in pencil, cancelled in ink; the interlinear insertion in ink

11F[1] The inserted sentence is from Leighton ɪ 55 (var).

Religion[a] doth not destroy the life of nature, but adds to it a life more excellent; yea, ~~grace~~ it doth not only permit, but requires some feeling of afflictions. m.XV. There is an affected pride of spirit in some men, instead of patience, suitable only to the doctrine of the *Stoics* as it is usually taken,̷. they strive not to feel at all the afflictions that are on them,̷. [b][but this is to *despise the correction of the Lord*, which is alike forbidden with fainting under it. Heb. xii. 5. We should not stop our ears, but *hear the rod, and him that hath appointed it*, as the Prophet speaks, Mic. vi. 9.] Where there is no feeling at all, there can be no patience. XV.

N.b. the dotted lines signify *Omit*.[1] Thus after "that are on them".— there is to follow "Where there is no feeling".

11J ɪ 66, marked with a pencil line | 1 Pet 1.7

It is a hard task, and many times comes but slowly forward, to teach the heart, by discourse and speculation, to sit loose from the world at all sides, not to cleave to the best things in it, though we be compassed about with them, *though riches do increase*, yet *not to set our hearts on them*, Psal. lxii, 10., [c]*not to trust in such uncertain things* as they are, as the Apostle speaks, 1 Tim. vi. 17.[d] Therefore God is pleased to choose the more effectual way to teach his own the right and pure exercise of faith, either by withholding or withdrawing those things from them. He makes them relish the sweetness of spiritual comfort, by depriving them of those outward comforts whereon they were in most danger to have doated to excess, and so to have forgotten themselves and him.

12 ɪ 71–86, textus pp 71–2 marked with a pencil line; annotation corrected in part in pencil | 1 Pet 1.8–9 | *AR* 200, Spiritual Aphorism 8; C's comment, much revised, follows on 200–28

Faith elevates the soul not only above sense, and sensible things, but above reason itself. * As reason corrects the errors which sense might occasion, so, supernatural faith corrects the errors of natural reason, judging according to sense. . . .

This natural men may discourse of, and that very knowingly, and give a kind of natural credit to it, as to a history that may be true; but firmly to believe that there is *divine truth* in all these things, and to have a

---

[a] "Religion" is added twice, once in pencil and once in ink
[b] C has drawn a dotted brace in the margin, represented here by square brackets in colour
[c–d] An omission marked with pencilled dots in the margin

11I[1] See textual note *b*.

persuasion of it stronger than of the very things we see with our eyes,—such an assent as this, is the peculiar mark of the Spirit of God, and is certainly saving faith.

The soul that so believes, cannot choose but love.*a*

* It is of the highest importance to a right belief, and one among the most efficacious Preventives of fanaticism on the one hand and of ⟨the⟩ *Minimifidian* Heresy[1] ~~of the Ultra-Socinians~~ on the other, to be aware of the difference, yea, the diversity of Reason and of Understanding—(*See Coleridge's Elements of Discourse*)[2] and of no small expediency to be aware likewise, that our very best Writers, even Lord Bacon himself who has incomparably layed open the nature of this difference in his Novum Organum,[3] do most unhappily confound the words, using Reason for Understanding, and sometimes tho' less often Understanding for Reason. In consequence of this confusion of the two terms, Bacon was under the necessity of adopting fantastic and mystical phrases for *Reason*, as contra-distinguished from the Understanding—ex. gr. Lumen Siccum; Visio lucifica; and the like.*b*[4]

So in this sentence (p. 71) Leighton by Reason means the Understanding, and adds the definition of the word—namely, the faculty *judging according to Sense*: which is word for word the same with Kant's definition of the Understanding.[5] Reason on the contrary is the Power and

---

a Final sentence marked with "X" in the margin

b Here C has written "/\" near the top of the outer margin of I 73 and has continued the note in the foot-margin with "/\"

12[1] The position of one who believes as little as possible—C's coinage, defined by him in *AR* (1825) 207 in contrast to "Ultrafidianism" (also his coinage): "its object is to draw religion down to the Believer's intellect, instead of raising his intellect up to religion". Cf BLANCO WHITE *Practical Evidence* 2 n 2.

12[2] For the relationship of this projected work to C's *Logic* see *Logic* (*CC*) xxxix–li; while *AR* was in the press, C expected the *Elements of Discourse* to follow close behind it. The important distinction between reason and understanding is outlined in *Logic* (*CC*) 66–70, but C also gave it extended attention in *AR* (1825) 200–28 and in *Friend* (*CC*) I 154–61.

12[3] C expounds this unconventional reading of Bacon in *Friend* (*CC*) I 488–93, with reference particularly to *Novum organum* bk 1 aphs 39–44, 49.

12[4] "Dry light" and "lucific vision", as C translates these phrases in *AR* (1825) 208. The first appears in *Novum organum* bk 1 aph 49 and in *De augmentio scientiarum* bk 1 ch 1; the second does not appear actually to be Bacon's, though C may be recalling *Experimenta lucifera*, "light-bearing experiments", from bk 1 aph 99.

12[5] C was probably thinking of the statement about the understanding at the beginning of the Transcendental Analytic in the *Critique of Pure Reason*. C's German text, *C d r V* (Leipzig 1799) 75, reads "Dagegen ist das Vermögen, den Gegenstand sinnlicher Anschauungen zu *denken*, der Verstand." Tr Norman Kemp Smith: "The faculty, on the other hand, which enables us to *think* the object of sensible intuition is the understanding." Cf C's definition in *Friend* (*CC*) I 177*.

the Substance of universal, necessary, self-evident & supersensual Truths.[6] The Judgements of the Understanding are binding only in relation to the objects of the Senses contemplated under the forms of the human Understanding—Hence we may say the *human* Understanding *per antithesin*: for "God's Thoughts are not as our Thoughts"[7]—but there is no *human* Reason in this sense—there neither is nor can be but one Reason, one & the same in all—even "the Light that lighteth every *man*",[8] both the individual Sense and individual Understanding of each individual Person—& by which Light alone he becometh a *person*. Beasts partake of Understanding (the Dog, the Elephant, and above all the Ant) but not of Reason.[9] Hence too Lord Bacon wisely & in strict consequence confines proper Logic, as the for~~man~~l science of the Understanding, to forensic purposes, & to the Relations of Man to Man, and to Nature only in relation to Man.[10] ~~S. T. C.~~ I have only to add, that when *the Will* is sub~~ordinated~~jected to the Reason, and reduced to harmony therewith, and thus becomes one with the ⟨Divine⟩ Will; ~~of~~ and when the Understanding and the Sense are subordinated to the Reason, ~~which~~ in concert with the Will, there ~~thenceforward the~~ results an Identity, or Co-inherence, of *Speculative Insight* (i.e. Truth) and of practical Impulse and Authority (i.e. the Good, or Love): ⟨and⟩ th*é*is Result is Faith, which is a *total* energy of the Soul in reference to ultimate ends, and to the proper Objects of her highest Gifts and Faculties—and to all other things relatively and in subordination to these.[11] Therefore St Paul's Whether ye eat or drink, or whatever ye do, do it *in Faith*.[12] Without Faith we act piecemeal—and our actions are pledges of the temporary *mood*, not of the *whole Man*. It is assuredly the safest way (on all serious subjects, at least) to use the same word at all times in one and

12[6] C's interpretation of the Kantian distinction, repeated var in *AR* (1825) 208; cf other formulations in *Friend* (*CC*) I 154–61, 177*; *SM* (*CC*) 59–62.

12[7] Isa 55.8 (var). *Per antithesin*, "on the contrary".

12[8] John 1.9.

12[9] This observation is given expanded treatment in *Friend* (*CC*) I 154–61 and in *AR* (1825) 210–14, 234–42.

12[10] C is perhaps referring to Bacon's practice in general, rather than to a particular statement in his work; Bacon does, however, make a distinction between conventional syllogistic logic and Baconian inductive logic—"proper Logic", as C says

here—in "Distributio operis" ("The Plan of the Work") and describes ideal logic again in *De augmentis* bk 5 ch 1: Bacon *Works* (1740) I 12, 137–8; ed Spedding IV 23–6, 405–7.

12[11] C planned to write on faith in an essay "supplementary" to *AR*: *CL* VI 533, 534; cf *CL* V 434–5 and the "Essay on Faith" in *SW & F* (*CC*). Other marginalia support the definition given here, e.g. DONNE *Sermons* COPY B 62, JAHN *Appendix* 4.

12[12] C appears to be thinking of 1 Cor 10.31: "Whether therefore ye eat, or drink, or whatsoever ye do, do all to the glory of God."

the same Sense.[13] Therefore tho' I do not question any man's Right to speaking an of his Understanding, ⟨when⟩ enlightened by Reason, and applied to truths of Reason, as *his* Reason, meaning thereby his reason-*ing* or reason-appropriating Faculty; or again to use the word, Understanding, for the human mind integrally, or for the *Man* himself, especially contemplated as an *intelligent* Creature; yet I should hold it inexpedient to exercise that Right. I should think it in all respects better to understand by the human *Mind* the Soul considered exclusively in its intelligential Character, and as consisting of, 1. the SENSE, that is, the intuitive and imaginative Power; and 2. the Understanding, or the Power of Reflecting and Judging.[14] The Soul itself I define, as a Subject-Object, i.e. a Subject having itself as its Object, in other word,[a] a Self-conscious Being, consisting of Life, Sense, Understanding, and Will—to which in consequence and by necessity of its *finite* nature we must add Sensibility. Lastly, by the Body in relation to such a Soul—and I confess, a finite soul utterly bodiless is to me inconceivable—I mean, the sum of the *Organs* of all these Constituents, con in part the an efficient cause and in part a consequence of their limitation, and the medium of its[b] intercommunion with whatever the embodied soul is capable of communing with, by virtue of its Sensibility.[c][15] Still, however, the Great Question recurs—Are the Soul's ⟨objects⟩[d] conditioned by its *Sensibility*? Is it incapable of any other Objects than those supplied by the Senses, i.e. the Organs of Sense, or the Sense + the Sensibility in the several specific Relations to the exciting Causes? [e]⟨Thus the Light, whatever it may be in itself, is *for us Light* only under the condition of the Eye—as the Organist of Light and thus the Organ of Vision.⟩[16] He,

[a] A slip for "words"

[b] Cancelled in pencil

[c] Some corrections in pencil appear towards the end of this sentence, so incomplete and tentative that they have been disregarded: "soul is capable of communing with, . by virtue of its Sensibility/.". The significance of the numbers—usually a device for rearranging the parts of a sentence—is obscure here

[d] Inserted in pencil

[e] Inserted in pencil, beginning at the head of l 82 and continuing down the outer margin

12[13] One of the themes of *AR*, announced as the first of the "Objects of the present volume" in *AR* (1825) vii.

12[14] Among C's attempts to define "Mind" in distinction from "Spirit", "Soul" etc, *Logic* (*CC*) 252 comes closest to C's formulation here, giving mind the role of "vicegerent" to the soul.

12[15] Cf the concept of the soul as intermediary between "Life" and "Spirit" in 7

above (at n 10).

12[16] The eye is C's recurrent analogy for the organs of spirit. As he says in *Logic* (*CC*) 146, it must pre-exist to make *seeing* possible; cf *Omniana* § 174 in *SW & F* (*CC*); *BL* ch 7 (*CC*) I 123. It is also, interestingly, Locke's analogy for the understanding on the first page of his *Essay*: "The understanding, like the eye, whilst it makes us see and perceive all other things,

who affirms this, is (if he reason consequently) a *Materialist*. He who denies it, admits by necessary implication the reality of supersensual & supersensuous Objects, i.e. Verities that partake neither of Sense nor of Sensibility. But*a* Now*b* there are Truths of Reason; ⟨Truths,⟩ that have their substance & reality in Reason—i.e. they *are* Reason![17] As there are doubtless numberless Objects, so there are numberless Truths, beyond & *wholly out of*, the sphere of the human Soul—&*a* which ⟨, therefore, as⟩*b* individually*a* ⟨Truths⟩*b* it can neither believe or disbelieve. But to speak of *individual*ᶜ Truths ⟨, Truths⟩*b* capable of being believed, and consequently *ap*prehended, as *above* Reason, is mere absurdity. They are *therefore*ᶜ Mysteries, *because*ᶜ they are wholly and solely *Reason* itself. They are not indeed to be *understood*—for their *Sub*stans is in themselves.[18] Better to say, that they ⟨belong not to the Senseṡ—⟩ transcend the Sense; and *supersede* the Understanding, & involve the Reason. But FAITH, we have said, comprehends the *Life & Will* of the Soul, as well as the Presence and Illucence of *Reason*.[19] The concluding Sentences therefore of this Extract are in perfect conformity to Reason, and follow out of the very nature & Definition of Faith, as declared in this Note.   S. T. C.

PS. It would lead me too far and too deep to carry on this speculation into a Commentary on the words of Milton in the Archangel Raphael's Address to Adam—

> "whence the Soul
> "Reason receives; yet Reason is her *Being*."[20]

or it would not be difficult to evince the sound philosophy of the beautiful passages in Leighton immediately following the Extract above given, and their entire freedom from every taint of Enthusiasm or Mys-

---

a Cancelled in pencil   *b* Inserted in pencil   *c* Underlined in pencil

---

takes no notice of itself": *An Essay Concerning Human Understanding* ed A. C. Fraser (New York 1959) I 25.

12[17] Cf *Friend* (*CC*) I 156: "Thus, God, the Soul, eternal Truth, &c. are the objects of Reason; but they are themselves *reason*."

12[18] C's point depends upon an etymological distinction: *substans*, "substance", means literally "standing under"; substance therefore cannot be "understood", and is not accessible to the understanding.

Cf C's play with "substance" and "subject" in *AR* (1825) 386–7.

12[19] "Illucence", not in *OED*, appears to be C's coinage for "light *in*" or "the containing of light", by analogy with "translucence", "light *through*" or "the conducting of light". The common metaphor "the light of reason" is implicit here.

12[20] *Paradise Lost* V 486–7 (var); also q *Friend* (*CC*) I 156, *BL* ch 10 (*CC*) I 173–4. Cf ANDERSON COPY B 27.

ticism. I refer to the ¶phs on what the Archbishop calls the *uniting* act of Faith and the assimilative power of Contemplation, so sublimely stated by the philosophic Apostle[21]

12A   I 73, pencil, marked with a pencil line

Now <u>faith</u> [believes this report, and beholds this picture, and so] lets in the love of Christ to the soul. But further, it gives a particular experimental knowledge of Christ, and acquaintance with him: it causes the soul to find all that is spoken of him in the word, and his beauty there represented, to be abundantly true; makes it really taste of his sweetness, and by that possesses the heart more strongly with his love, persuading it of the truth of those things, not by reasons and arguments, but by an inexpressible kind of evidence, which they only know who have it.

13   I 88–94, marked with lines in pencil overtraced in ink, annotation in ink corrected in pencil | 1 Pet 1.10–12

* This is the very life of divine faith, touching the mysteries of salvation, firmly to believe their *revelation* by the Spirit of God. This the word itself testifies, as we see; and it is really manifest in it; it carries the lively stamp of Divine inspiration, but there must be a spiritual eye to discern it. He that is blind, knows not that the sun shines at noon, but by the report of others; but they that see, are assured they see it, and assured by no other thing, but by its own light. To ask one who is a true believer, How know you the Scriptures to be Divine? is the same as to ask him, How know you light to be light? . . .

The Spirit of God within, brings evidence with it, and makes itself discernible in the word; this all arguments, all books and study cannot attain unto. *It is given to believe*, 1 Phil. i. 29.

* On this evidence the Fathers of the four first Centuries, on this the great Reformers of the Church, on this the Founders and Martyrs of the Church of England mainly rested the divine authority of the Scriptures. And with this too the most eminent Divines of our Church before the Restoration were content. (See "THE CHURCH", by Dr Field, Dean of St Paul's in the reign of James the First.).[1] Of those who regarding this

---

12[21] The "philosophic Apostle" is Paul, cited by Leighton I 75. Writing of the Christian's love of God, Leighton says that faith persuades us of our "interest" in Christ "by that particular *uniting* act which makes him our God and our Saviour" (73), and that the Christian ideally contracts "a likeness to God in all his actions, by conversing with him, by frequent contemplation of God, and looking on his beauty" (74).

13[1] E.g. bk 4 ch 19 "Of the rules we are to follow, and the helpes wee are to trust to, in interpreting the Scriptures" in

as enthusiastic or evasive have essayed other modes of proof that are to force the belief on the unbelieving by dint of argument and history, I have read every Writer of any Note: & it is now many years since I have seen or heard a new argument in substance or even in form. May I, ⟨speaking exclusively of my own mind & experience,⟩ state the result, without offence?—and without It has been uniformly a restless and as it were insurrectionary Activity Bustle of Thought, and a logical Scepticism respecting the arguments and train of reasoning that which for at the time I found it it was not always in my power to keep distinct and at harmless distance from á doubting or nascent *misgiving* respecting the thing to be proved. I was under the temptation of transferring my dissatisfaction with from the Advocate to the Cause—and generally closed the Volume in under a Disorder, or at best a Languor, of Feeling, the only, but I thank God, the efficacious Cure for which I found in the Scriptures themselves. I am not ignorant of the danger of this Avowal in an Age and Country, where He who will not swear by Grotius must expect to be considered as under bonds to Calvin—or, worse still, as an Upholder of that "Modern Calvinism", (Vide of which (Vide (the late) Dᴿ Williams's Work under this name) is the accredited Exposition and Vindication) which with all due respect to the late Dʳ Williams, its Archaspistes,[2] I am persuaded that Calvin himself would have welcomed with an Anathema Maranatha.[3] But impolitic as the confession may be, such, I confess, has been most often the *immediate* result from the perusal of the Works in question. An other & less fugitive one is a haunting temptation to write a brief Essay under the title of "Christianity defended against its Defenders."   *S. T. C.*

13A   ɪ 94, marked with an ink line

The Apostle, speaking of Jesus Christ as the foundation of our faith, calls him *The same, yesterday, and to-day, and for ever*. Heb. xiii. 8. *Yesterday*, under the Law, *to-day*, in those primitive times, nearest his incarnation, and *for ever*, in all succeeding ages. And the resemblance holds good between the two cherubim over the mercy-seat, and the two testaments: *those* had their faces toward one another, and both toward

---

Richard Field *Of the Church* (Oxford 1635) 372–3; and see Fɪᴇʟᴅ.

13² "Archaspistes", lit "chief shieldbearer", i.e. champion: a term C adopted as early as 1803 (*CN* ɪ 1565). Edward Williams (1750–1813), author of *A Defence of Modern Calvinism* (1812) attacked by C in

e.g. *AR* (1825) 153–4. C's detailed comments on another work by Williams appear in *SW & F (CC)*.

13³ 1 Cor 16.22: "If any man love not the Lord Jesus Christ, let him be Anathema Maranatha."

the mercy-seat; and *these* look to one another in their doctrine, agreeing perfectly, and both look to Christ, the true mercy-seat, and the great subject of the Scriptures.

14 I 95–100, marked with ink lines

* 1. This their [i.e. the prophets'] diligence disparages not their extraordinary visions and revelations, and that which is added, that the Spirit of Christ was in them, and did foretel the things to come.

*a*It was their constant duty, and they being sensible of their duty, made it their constant exercise, to search into Divine mysteries by meditation and prayer; yea, and by reading such holy writers as were already extant in their times, as Daniel ix. 3. x. 11.*b* For which cause, some, taking the word actively, conceive *Daniel* to be called there a *man of desires*, because of his great desire, and diligent search after the knowledge of those high things. *a*And in this diligent way they constantly waited for those revelations which sometimes when it seemed good unto the Spirit of God, were imparted unto them.

"Prophecy resideth not (say the *Hebrew* doctors) but in a man who is great in wisdom and virtue, whose affections overcome him not in any worldly things, but by his knowledge he overcometh his affections continually; on such a man the Holy Spirit cometh down, and his soul is associated to the angels, and he is changed to another man." Thus *Maimonides.*b

* Prefix as title or heading to the ¶.ph following[1]—That ⟨as⟩ the Revelations occasionally vouchsafed to the Hebrew Prophets did not supersede their diligence, so neither did their diligence disparage their extraordinary Revelations. The busy discursation of ~~the question~~ Thoughts, the Question and Answer of the fleshly Understanding (Φρονημα Σαρκος),[2] the Catechist of the Senses respecting the Creed and Ordinances of Sense—~~all~~ these with the accompanying Volitions already ~~hushed~~ controlled and ~~stilled~~ awed ~~by~~ by the ~~stedfastness of Contemplation,~~ energy of Attention ~~it needs only~~ the first Touch of the Finger of the Spirit, its lightest pressure on the Pulse, ⟨will suffice⟩ for their total suspension. And this alone, this temporary entrancement of the dividual Self is alone needed, to raise the devout Meditations of a profound and fervid Intellect into Visions in which Time and the Subjects of Time take

a–b Marked with an ink line in the margin

14[1] C refers presumably to the first sentence of the textus, intending it as a title to that which follows; it was not, however, used in *AR* (1825).

14[2] Rom 8.7: see COPY B **15** n 1.

on them the nature ~~of Space~~ and ~~the~~ privilege of ~~Objects and the Objects in Space,~~ Space distant yet present. The *Valleys of Vision* (Isaiah, XXII. 5) are as sunny Glades and sudden Openings in the sacred Grove of Meditation.[3] But they are in its inmost recesses, ~~and~~ its central depths— and the Paths, that lead thereto, undiscoverable save by Light from Above—yea, there is no Path but for the ~~chosen~~ Feet of them whom the Most High hath chosen to bring back tidings of Salvation to Zion— ~~no~~ the Path ~~but~~ is in the same moment made and shewn by the luminous Tracts of the Angel Guide that goeth before them. O! Wisdom and Holiness are so excellent, ~~so~~ and marvellous in themselves, and so impossible without the fellowship of supernatural Grace, that we need not be perplexed or offended if their own effects and proper Workings pass indistinguishably into those of the miraculous Power that meets & perfects them, & whose Descent gave wings to their Ascending—even as the vaporous ~~and~~ electric ~~Shaft~~ Stem that ⟨half-detached⟩ stretches down from the Cloud, like ~~the mighty~~ an Arm of Aidance, and the upbooming Water-shaft from the Ocean, like an Arm upraised in fervent Supplication, in the same moment descend and rise and meet—behold! it is one ~~dread and~~ vast continuous Pillar uniting Earth with heaven; and who shall determine the point of Junction, who shall say, here ⟨the⟩ work of Heaven begins, here the lower Element has found its Zenith?[4]

14A　ɪ 107, marked with a pencil line | 1 Pet 1.13

The firmest thing in this inferior world, is, a believing soul.

15　ɪ 110–11, marked with a line in pencil overtraced in ink, and with a pencilled cross; note in pencil | *AR* 92, Moral Aphorism 16, with C's footnote

M.Aph.XVI　As excessive eating or drinking both makes the body sickly and lazy, fit for nothing but sleep, and besots the mind, as it cloggs up with ~~filthy~~[a] crudities the way through which the *spirits should pass, bemiring them, and making them move heavily, as a coach in a deep way; thus doth all immoderate use of the world and its delights, wrong the soul in its spiritual condition, makes it sickly and feeble, full of spiritual distempers and inactivity, benumbs the graces of the Spirit, and fills the soul with sleepy vapours, makes it grow secure and heavy in spiritual exercises, and obstructs the way and motion of the Spirit of God, in the soul. Therefore, if you would be spiritual, healthful, and vigorous, and enjoy much of the consolations of Heaven, be sparing and

---

[a] Cancelled in ink; in pencil in the margin "δ filthy"

14[3] This passage may be considered an early version of the allegory about different kinds of mystics in *AR* (1825) 382–6.

14[4] The figure of the waterspout recurs in C's poetry, e.g. *Osorio* ɪɪɪ i 29–31: *PW* (EHC) ɪɪ 551.

sober in those of the earth, and what you abate of the one, shall be certainly made up in the other.   Aph.XVI.

*ᵃ Technical phrases of an exploded Philosophy or Physiology will yet retain their places, nay, acquire universal currency & become Sterling in the language, when they at once represent the feelings and give an apparent solution of them by visual images ~~familiar to or~~ᵇ easily managed by the Fancy. Such are many terms & phrases from the now obsolete *Humoral* Physiology, as in this Extract. In Leighton's Time it was still dominant—yet the metaphors are far more popular, than any description would be from the Theory now culminant.¹

15A   ɪ 119, marked with a line in pencil overtraced in ink | 1 Pet 1.14–16 | *AR* 93, Moral Aphorism 17

. . . ᵻIt is a most unseemly and unpleasant thing, to see a man's life full of ups and downs, one step like a Christian, and another like a worldling; it cannot choose but both pain himself and mar the edification of others.   M.Aph.XVII.

15B   ɪ 122, marked with a line in pencil overtraced in ink; corrected in pencil | *AR* 93–4, Moral Aphorism 17

Aph.XVII *continued* What though the polite man count thy fashion a little odd and too precise, it is because he knows nothing above that model of goodness which he hath set himself, and therefore approves of nothing beyond it: he knows not God, and therefore doth not discern and esteem what is most like Him. When courtiers come down into the country, the common home-bred people possibly think their habit strange, but they care not for that, it is the fashion at court. What need, then, that the [godly]ᶜ Christian should be [so tender-foreheaded, as to be]ᶜ put out of countenance because the world looks on holiness as a singularity; it is the only fashion in the highest court, yea, of the King of Kings himself.

16   ɪ 124–5, pencil | 1 Pet 1.17

* No wonder, then, that the Apostle, having stirred up his Christian brethren, whatsoever be their estate in the world, to seek to be rich in

---

ᵃ The asterisk is overwritten in ink, the note being in pencil   ᵇ Cancelled in ink
ᶜ C uses square brackets to designate words to be omitted, without crossing the words through

15¹ C's point about the evolution of language is illustrated both by the terms to which he draws attention in the textus— terms that reflect the exploded medical doctrine of the humours—and by his own word "culminant", a term drawn from astronomy.

those jewels of faith, and hope, and love, and spiritual joy, and then, considering that they travel amongst a world of thieves and robbers,—no wonder, I say, that he adds this, advises them to give those their jewels in custody, under God, to this trusty and watchful grace of godly fear . . .

Spiritual[a]

* Substitute—Is a man rich in the precious Gems of Faith, and Hope, and Love, and Spiritual Joy, all set in the virgin gold of Innocence—& dare we wonder, that he is admonished to appoint godly Fear, as the trusty Warden of the Jewel Office? Seeing too, that they are Crown-jewels given in pledge—& which the Sovereign of Heaven will redeem with eternal Bliss!/[1]

16A I 126, marked with a line in pencil overtraced in ink

Spir. When he looks up to God, and considers the truth of his promises, and the sufficiency of his grace and protection, and the almighty strength of his Redeemer, these things fill his soul with confidence and assurance; but when he turns his eye downward again upon himself, and finds so much remaining corruption within, and so many temptations, and dangers, and adversaries without, this forces him not only to fear, but to despair of himself; and it should do so, that his trust in God may be the purer and more entire.

17 I 127, marked with a line in pencil overtraced in ink; annotation in pencil

Spir.[b] But he that hath assurance of salvation, why should he fear? If there is truth in his assurance, nothing can disappoint him, not sin itself. It is true; but it is no less true, that if he do not fear to sin, there is no truth in his assurance: it is not the assurance of faith, but the mispersuasion of a secure and profane mind. Suppose it so, that the sins of a godly man cannot be such as to cut him short of that salvation whereof he is assured; yet they may be such as for a time will deprive him of that assurance, and not only remove the comfort he hath in that, but let in horrors and anguish of conscience in its stead. Though a believer is freed from hell, (and we may overstrain this assurance, in our doctrine, beyond what the soberest and devoutest men in the world can ever find in themselves, though they will not trouble themselves to contest and dispute with them that say they have it,) so that his soul cannot come there;

---

[a] This word is written in ink; the passage to be inserted (C's note) is marked with an ink line
[b] "Spir." superimposed in ink over the first word of the pencilled note

16[1] Neither textus nor note was in the end used in *AR*.

yet some sins may bring as it were a piece of hell into his soul for a time, and this is reason enough for any Christian in his right wits to be afraid of sin.

This extracted in the Defence of Leighton against the charge of Calvinism./[1]

17A I 128, marked with lines in pencil

This fear is not cowardice; it doth not debase, but elevates the mind; for it drowns all lower fears, and begets true fortitude and courage to encounter all dangers, for the sake of a good conscience and the obeying of God. *The righteous is bold as a lion.* Prov. xxviii.1. He dares do any thing but offend God; and to dare do that, is the greatest folly, and baseness, and weakness in the world. From this fear have sprung all the generous resolutions and patient sufferings of the saints and martyrs of God: because they durst not sin against Him, therefore they durst be imprisoned, and impoverished, and tortured, and die for Him. . . . Fear not, but fear; and therefore fear, that you may not fear. This fear is like the trembling that hath been observed in some of great courage before battles.

17B I 142, marked with a line in ink | 1 Pet 1.20 | *AR* 294, Spiritual Aphorism 14

Spir.   As in great maps, or pictures, you will see the border decorated with meadows, and fountains, and flowers, &c., represented in it, but in the middle you have the main design; ~~thus~~ so is ~~this~~ it ~~foreordained~~ with the[a] redemption [b]of the moral & intelligential Being in Man amongst the works of God: all His other works in the world, all the beauty of the creatures, and the succession of ages, and things that come to pass in them, are but as the border to this as the main-piece. But as a foolish unskilful beholder, not discerning the excellency of the principal piece in such maps or pictures, gazes only on the fair border, and goes no further, thus do the greatest part of us[c] . . . as to[d] this great work of God, [e]the redemption of ~~Human~~ Personal Nature, and the re-union of the Human with the Divine by and thro' the Divine Humanity of the Word.

[a] C has written his revisions above the three words without cancelling them
[b] Here C has written "∧" and has introduced the inserted phrase in the outer margin with "∧"
[c] Here the ink line ends
[d] "as to" is written in the margin before "this great . . .", C neglecting to cancel the two intervening lines
[e] Here C has written "∧", and in the foot-margin has marked his addition with "insert ∧"

17[1] Intended probably for the "Apology" described in **1** n 1 above.

17C   ɪ 144, marked in ink | 1 Pet 1.21

Spir.   A man may have, while living out of Christ, yea, he must, he cannot choose but have a conviction with him, that there is a God; and further he may have, even out of Christ, some kind of belief of those things that are spoken concerning God; but to repose on God, as his God and his salvation, which is indeed to believe in Him, this cannot be but where Christ is the *medium* through which we look upon God . . .

17D   ɪ 148, marked with a line in ink | 1 Pet 1.22 | *AR* 94, Moral Aphorism 18

When, after variances, men are brought to an agreement, they are much subject to this, rather to cover their remaining malices with superficial verbal forgiveness, than to dislodge them, and free the heart of them. This is a poor self-deceit. As the philosopher said to him, who being ashamed that he was espied by him in a tavern in the outer room, withdrew himself to the inner, he called after him, "That is not the way out; the more you go that way, you will be the further within it:" so when hatreds are upon admonition not thrown out, but retire inward to hide themselves, they grow deeper and stronger than before; and those constrained semblances of reconcilement are but a false healing, do but skin the wound over, and therefore it usually breaks forth worse again.

17E   ɪ 171–2, marked with a line in ink | 1 Pet 2.1–2 | *AR* 94–5, Moral Aphorism 19

* M.Aph.XIX.   The stream of custom and our profession bring us ~~hither~~ *ª*to the Preaching of the Word, and we sit out our hour under the sound ~~of this word~~; but how few consider and prize it as the great ordinance of God for the salvation of souls, the beginner and the sustainer of the Divine life of grace within us! And certainly, until we have these thoughts of it, and seek to feel it thus ourselves, although we hear it most frequently, and let slip no occasion, yea, hear it with attention and some present delight, yet still we miss the right use of it, and turn it from its true end, while we take it not as *that ingrafted word which is able to save our souls*. James i. 21.   M.XIX

Thus ought they who preach to speak it; to endeavor their utmost to accommodate it to this end, that sinners may be converted, begotten again, and believers nourished and strengthened in their spiritual life; to regard no lower end, but aim steadily at that mark. Their hearts and tongues ought to be set on fire with holy zeal for God and love to souls, kindled by the Holy Ghost, that came down on the apostles in the shape of fiery tongues.

And those that hear, should remember this as the end of their hearing,

---

ª Here C has written "∧", and in the foot-margin has marked his addition with "insert ∧"

that they may receive spiritual life and strength by the word. For though it seems a poor despicable business, that a frail sinful man like yourselves, should speak a few words in your hearing, yet, look upon it as the way wherein God communicates happiness to those who believe, and works that believing unto happiness, alters the whole frame of the soul, and makes a new creation, as it begets it again to the inheritance of glory. Consider it thus, which is its true notion; and then, what can be so precious?   M.XIX

* *Heading.* Of the Worth and the Duties of the Preacher.

17F   I   175–6, marked with a line in ink | *AR* 96, Moral Aphorism 20

M.Aph.XX   The difference is great in our natural life, in some persons especially; that they who in infancy were so feeble, and wrapped up as others in swaddling clothes, yet, afterwards come to excel in wisdom and in the knowledge of sciences, or to be commanders of great armies, or to be kings: but the distance is far greater and more admirable, betwixt ~~the weakness of these new-born babes,~~ the small beginnings of grace, and our after perfection, that fulness of knowledge that we look for, and that crown of immortality which all they are born to, who are born of God.   M.XX

But as in the faces or actions of some children, characters and presages of their after-greatness have appeared, (as a singular beauty in Moses's face, as they wrote of him, and as Cyrus was made king among the shepherds' children with whom he was brought up, &c.) so also, certainly, in these children of God, there be some characters and evidences that they are born for Heaven by their new birth. That holiness and meekness, that patience and faith which shine in the actions and sufferings of the saints, are characters of their Father's image, and shew their high original, and foretel their glory to come; such a glory as doth not only surpass the world's thoughts, but the thoughts of the children of God themselves. 1 John iii. 2.   XX

17G   I   182, marked with a line in ink | *AR* 99, Moral Aphorism 21

M.Aph XXI.   . . .†The most approved teachers of wisdom, in a human way, have required of their scholars, that to the end their minds might be capable of it, they should be purified from vice and wickedness. *a*For this reason, the philosopher judges young men unfit hearers of moral philosophy, because of the abounding and untamedness of their passions, granting that, if those were composed and ordered, they might be admitted.*b* And it was Socrates's custom, when any one asked him a

a–b C has drawn his ink lines around the text and made a dotted line in the gutter to exclude this passage question, seeking to be informed by him, before he would answer them, he asked them concerning their own qualities and course of life.

17H   I 184–5, marked with a line in ink | 1 Pet 2.1–2

As the milk that infants draw from the breast, is the most connatural food to them, being of that same substance that nourished them in the womb; so, when they are brought forth, that food follows them as it were for their supply in the way that is provided in nature for it; by certain veins it ascends into the breasts, and is there fitted for them, and they are by nature directed to find it there. Thus, as a Christian begins to live by the power of the word, so, he is by the nature of that spiritual life directed to that same word as its nourishment. To follow the resemblance further in the qualities of milk, after the monkish way that runs itself out of breath in allegory, I conceive, is neither solid nor profitable, and to speak freely, the curious searching of the similitude in other qualities of milk, seems to wrong the quality here given it by the Apostle, in which it is so well resembled by milk, namely, the simple pureness and sincerity of the word; besides that the pressing of comparisons of this kind too far, proves often so constrained ere they have done with it, that by too much drawing, they bring forth blood instead of milk.

17I   I 187–8, marked in ink | *AR* 99–100, Moral Aphorism 22

M.Aph.XXII   To seek no more than a present delight, that evanisheth with the sound of the words that die in the air, is not to desire the word as meat, but as music, as God tells the prophet Ezekiel of his people, Ezek. xxxiii. 32. *And lo, thou art unto them as a very lovely song of one that hath a pleasant voice, and can play well upon an instrument; for they hear thy words, and they do them not.* To desire the word for the increase of knowledge, although this is necessary and commendable, and, being rightly qualified, is a part of spiritual accretion, yet, take it as going no further, it is not the true end of the word. Nor is the venting of that knowledge in speech and frequent discourse of the word and the divine truths that are in it; which, where it is governed with Christian prudence, is not to be despised, but commended; yet, certainly, the highest knowledge, and the most frequent and skilful speaking of the word, severed from the growth here mentioned, misses the true end of the word. If any one's head or tongue should grow apace, and all the rest stand at a stay, it would certainly make him a monster; and they are no other, who are knowing and discoursing Christians, and grow daily in that respect, but not at all in holiness of heart and life, which is the proper growth of the children of God. Apposite to their case is Epictetus's comparison of the sheep; they return not what they eat in grass, but in wool.   M.Aph.XXII

17J   I 190, marked with a line in ink

. . . ⨍In the judging of this growth, some persons conclude too rigidly against themselves, that they grow not by the word, because their growth is not so sensible to them as they desire. But 1. It is well known, that in all things that grow, this principle is not discerned in *motu, sed in termino*, not in the growing, but when they are grown. 2. Besides, other things are to be considered in this: although other graces seem not to advance, yet if thou growest more self-denying and humble in the sense of thy slowness, all is not lost; although the branches shoot not up so fast as thou wishest, yet, if the root grow deeper, and fasten more, it is an useful growth. He that is still learning to be more in Jesus Christ, and less in himself, to have all his dependence and comfort in Him, is doubtless a growing believer.

On the other side, a far greater number conclude wrong in their own favour⨍.

17K   I 196, marked with a line in ink | 1 Pet 2.3

No unrenewed man, ~~hath any of those in truth,~~ no, ~~not~~ not the highest kind of temporary believer,[a] doth in truth possess any of the Graces properly *Christian*. He ⱨHe cannot have so much as a real lively assent to the general truth of the promises; for had he that, the rest would follow. But as he cannot have the least of these in truth, he may have the counterfeit of them all; not only of assent but of application; yea, and a false spiritual joy arising from it; and all these so drawn to the life, that they may resemble much the reality: to give clear characters of difference, is not so easy as most persons imagine; but doubtless, the true living faith of a Christian, hath in itself such a particular stamp, as brings with it its own evidence, when the soul is clear and the light of God's face shines upon it. Indeed, in the dark we cannot read, nor distinguish one mark from another; but when a Christian hath light to look upon the work of God in his own soul, although he cannot make another sensible of that by which he knows it, yet he himself is ascertained, and can say confidently in himself, "This I know, that this faith and taste of God I have is true; the seal of the Spirit of God is upon it;" and this is the reading of that *new name in the white stone, which no man knows but he that hath it*, Revel. ii. 17.

---

[a] Here C has written "⋀" and has introduced the inserted phrase in the margin with "⋀"

17L 1 205, marked with a line in ink | 1 Pet 2.4–5 | *AR* 100, Moral Aphorism 23

M.Aph.XXIII   In times of peace, the Church may dilate more, and build as it were into breadth, but in times of trouble, it arises more in height; it is then built upwards: as in cities where men are straitened, they build usually higher than in the country.

17M 1 210–11, marked with a line in ink

Incense can neither smell nor ascend without fire; no more doth prayer, unless it arise from a bent of spiritual affection; it is that which both ~~makes it smell,~~ gives it fragrancy, and sends it heavenwards/.

17N 1 225, marked with a line in ink | 1 Pet 2.6

Spiritual Aph. 1.   What one says of wisdom, is true of faith, *Many would seek after it, and attain it, if they did not falsely imagine that they have attained it already.*

17O 1 226, circled in ink | *AR* 101, Moral Aphorism 24

M.Aph.XXIV.   Where there is a great deal of smoke, and no clear flame, it argues much moisture in the matter, yet it witnesseth certainly that there is fire there; and therefore, dubious questioning of ~~a man concerning himself,~~ is a much better evidence, than that senseless deadness which most take for believing. Men that know nothing in sciences, have no doubts. He never truly believed, who was not made first sensible and convinced of unbelief.   M.Aph.XXIV

17P 1 261, marked with a line in ink | 1 Pet 2.9 | *AR* 103–4, Moral Aphorism 27

M.Aph.XXVI   . . . ~~i~~It is a base, poor thing for a man to seek himself, far below that royal dignity that is here put upon Christians, and that priesthood joined with it. Under the Law, those who were squint-eyed were incapable of the priesthood: truly, this squinting out to our own interest, the looking aside to that, in God's affairs especially, so deforms the face of the soul, that it makes it altogether unworthy the honour of this spiritual priesthood. Oh! this is a large task, an infinite task. The several creatures bear their part in this; the sun says somewhat, and moon and stars, yea, the lowest have some share in it; the very plants and herbs of the field, speak of God; and yet, the very highest and best, yea, all of them together, the whole concert of Heaven and earth, cannot shew forth all His praise to the full. No, it is but a part, the smallest part of that glory, which they can reach.

18   I 297 | 1 Pet 2.13–24

* If you look on those great monarchies in Daniel's vision, you see one of them built up upon the ruins of another; and all of them represented by terrible devouring beasts of monstrous shape. And whether <u>the Roman empire be</u> the fourth there, as many take it, or not, yet, in the things spoken of that fourth, as well as of the rest, it is inferior to none of them, enlarging itself by conquests in all parts of the world.

* A striking instance of Leighton's Candor, & how little he ~~partook of~~ had to do with those to whom the question was put—Will ye *lie* for God?[1]—He was too sound & clear-sighted a Scholar to decide with the ordinary dogmatism ⟨against Porphyry⟩ on this point.[2]

18A   I 311–12, marked with a line in ink | 1 Pet 2.17 | *AR* 104, Moral Aphorism 28

M.XXVII.   The Jews would not willingly tread upon the smallest piece of paper in their way, but took it up; for possibly, said they, the name of God may be on it. Though there was a little superstition in this, yet truly there is nothing but good religion in it, if we apply it to men. Trample not on any; there may be some work of grace there, that thou knowest not of. The name of God may be written upon that soul thou treadest on; it may be a soul that Christ thought so much of, as to give His precious blood for it; therefore despise it not.

[a]Last line of Aph. XXVII.[1]

18B   I 313, marked with a line in ink | *AR* 104–5, Moral Aphorism 29

[b]*The sluggard*, says Solomon, *is wiser in his own conceit, than seven men that can render a reason*, Prov. xxvi. 16; and not finding others of their mind, this frets and troubles them. They[c] M.Aph.XXVIII. Too many take the ready course to deceive themselves; for they look with

---

[a] Written on p 312 against the last line of textus
[b-c] Marked with a line for inclusion, then the line cancelled

18[1] C adopted this phrase (based on Job 13.7) from Bacon *Advancement of Learning* bk 1 § 3: Spedding ed I 436, III 267; *Works* (1740) I 30.

18[2] Porphyry's views on the Book of Daniel, expressed in bk 12 of a lost treatise *Against the Christians*, are preserved in long quotations in Jerome's *Commentary on Daniel*. Porphyry identified the fourth kingdom of Dan 7 as the Greek kingdom after Alexander; Jerome, disagreeing, identified it as the Roman empire. Jerome's "has been by far the most popular traditional view": H. H. Rowley *Darius the Mede and the Four World Empires in the Book of Daniel* (Cardiff 1964) 7.

18A[1] Referring to this aphorism in its original rather than its eventual numbering, C is simply indicating for the printer where the passage ends.

both eyes on the failings and defects of others, and scarcely give their good qualities half an eye, while, on the contrary, in themselves, they study to the full their own advantages, and their weaknesses and defects, (as one says,) they skip over, as children do the hard words in their lesson, that are troublesome to read; and making this uneven parallel, what wonder if the result be a gross mistake of themselves!

18C   I 398, marked with a line in ink | 1 Pet 3.3–4 | *AR* 105, Moral Aphorism 30

It is not impossible that there may be in some an affected pride in the meanness of apparel, and in others, under either neat or rich attire, a very humble unaffected mind; using it upon some of the aforementioned engagements, or such like, and yet, the heart not at all upon it. *Magnus qui fictilibus utitur tanquam argento, nec ille minor qui argento tanquam fictilibus*, says Seneca: Great is he who enjoys his earthenware as if it were plate, and not less great is the man to whom all his plate is no more than earthenware.

18D   I 411–12, marked with lines in ink | 1 Pet 3.8 | *AR* 102, Moral Aphorism 26

Sometimes it *a*is from a ~~profane~~ supercilious disdain of all these things; M.Aph.XXX *b*and many there be among these of Gallio's temper, who *care for none of these things*, and who account all questions in religion, as he did, but matter of words and names. And by this all religions may agree together. But that were not a natural union produced by the active heat of the spirit, but a confusion rather, arising from the want of it; not a knitting together, but a freezing together, as cold congregates all bodies, how heterogeneous soever, sticks, stones, and water; but heat makes first a separation of different things, and then unites those that are of the same nature.*c* . . .

And though we have escaped this, yet, M.Aph.XXX concluded. *d*much of our common union of minds, I fear, proceeds from no other than the aforementioned causes, want of knowledge, and want of affection to religion. You that boast you live comfortably to the appointments of the Church, and that no one hears of your noise, we may thank the ignorance of your minds fords that kind of quietness.

18E   II 2, marked with a pencil line | 1 Pet 3.10

And if we consider it, it must indeed be of very great consequence how we use the tongue, it being the main outlet of the thoughts of the heart, and the mean of society amongst men in all affairs civil and spiritual; by

---

a The first marking begins here   *b* The second marking begins here
c Next paragraph omitted here   *d* The ink marking begins here

which men give birth to the conceptions of their own minds, and seek to beget the like in the minds of others.

18F ɪɪ 3–5, marked with lines in pencil, partly overtraced in ink | *AR* 105–6, Moral Aphorism 31

M.aph.31ˢᵗ ‡They who have attained to a self-pleasing pitch of civility or formal religion, have usually that point of presumption with it, that they make their own size the model and rule to examine all by. What is below it, they condemn indeed as profane; but what is beyond it, they account needless and affected preciseness: and therefore are as ready as others to let fly invectives or bitter taunts against it, which are the keen and poisoned shafts of the tongue, and a persecution that shall be called to a strict account.   M.Aph.31ˢᵗ

N.b ⟨The remainder of aph. 31 from ''account'' you will⟩ print from the Slip./Slip IV. p. 5:—[1]

*ᵃ*But the other kind—detraction, is more universal amongst all sorts, as being a far easier way of mischief in this kind, and of better conveyance. Railings cry out the matter openly, but detraction works all by surprises and stratagem, and mines under ground, and therefore is much more pernicious. The former are as the *arrows that fly by day*, but this, *as the pestilence that walketh in darkness*, (as these two are mentioned together in Psalm xci. 5, 6.), it spreads and infects secretly and insensibly, is not felt but in the effects of it; and it works either by calumnies altogether forged and untrue, of which malice is inventive, or*ᵇ* Aph.31. Nor will it be any excuse, that the slanders thus dispersed are not the *inventions* of Malice. Rather, it is ~~No m~~ And not ~~the less so that~~ characteristic of the Detraction here condemned to work by the advantage of real faults, of which it is very discerning, and these are stretched and aggravated to the utmost. It is not expressible how deep a wound a tongue sharpened to this work will give, with a very little word and little noise. ²—aph.31 *ᶜas a razor*, as it is called in Psal. lii. 2., which with a small touch cuts very deep,—taking things by the worst handle, whereas charity will try about all ways for a good acceptation and sense of things, and takes all by the best. This pest is still killing some almost in all

---

ᵃ⁻ᵇ Marked for omission with ink dots in outer margin; in the gutter, in pencil, ''print from Slip IV p.5, instead'', with a pencil line marking passage to be omitted

ᶜ⁻ᵈ The pencil line for inclusion resumes

18F[1] The ms ''slip'' is not preserved. The Aphorism as published continues with a revised version of C's insertion ''Nor will it be any excuse . . .'' and picks up Leighton's text again at ''by the advantage''.

18F[2] The Leighton text ends here in *AR* (1825) 106.

companies; it *casteth down many wounded*, as it is said of the strange woman, Prov. vii. 26. And they convey it under fair prefacing of commendation; so giving them poison in wine, both that it may pass the better, and penetrate the more. This is a great sin, one which the Lord ranks with the first, when he sets them in order against a man, Psal. 1. 20: *Thou sittest and speakest against thy brother.*[d]

18G II 5–6, marked with pencil lines | Continuing **18F** textus

III. *Vain fruitless* speeches are an evil of the tongue, not only those they call *harmless lies*, which some poor people take a pleasure in, and trade much in, light buffooneries and foolish jestings[a] . . . [b]They are in this *world of evil*, in the tongue; if no other way ill, yet ill they are, as the *Arabian* deserts and barren sands, because they are fruitless.

18H II 7–8, marked with a line in pencil overtraced in ink, insertion in pencil | *AR* 106–7, Moral Aphorism 32

m.Aph.32 It all true Remedy must begin at the heart; otherwise it will be but a mountebank cure, a false imagined conquest. The weights and wheels are *there*, and the clock strikes according to their motion. Even he that speaks contrary to what is within him, guilefully contrary to his inward conviction and knowledge, yet speaks conformably to what is within him in the temper and frame of his heart, which is double, *a heart and a heart*, as the Psalmist hath it, Psal. xii. 2.

19 II 9, pencil

* None that know the weight of that name [God], will dally with it, and *lightly lift it up*; (as that word translated *taking in vain*, in the third commandment, signifies;) they that do continue to *lift it up in vain*, as it were, to sport themselves with it, will find the weight of it falling back upon them, and crushing them to pieces.

* It has occurred to me, that the intent and purport of the Third Commandment was to forbid incantations, magical spells, et numinum per nomina Conjurationes.[1]

19A II 9–10, marked with a line in pencil overtraced in ink | *AR* 107–8, Moral Aphorism 33

M.Aph.33 It is an argument of a candid ingenuous mind, to delight in the good name and commendation of others; to pass by their defects,

---

[a] First marginal line ends   [b] Second marginal line begins

19[1] ''And the Conjuring Up of spirits by invocation''. C's interest in the connection   between *nomen* and *numen* is outlined in JOANNES **2** n 7.

and take notice of their virtues; and to speak and hear of those willingly, and not endure either to speak or hear of the other; for in this indeed you may be little less guilty than the evil speaker, in taking pleasure in it, though you speak it not. *ª*He that willingly drinks in tales and calumnies, will from the delight he hath in evil hearing*ᵇ* &c ~~And this is a piece of men's natural perverseness, to drink in tales and calumnies; and he that doth this, will readily, from the delight he hath in hearing,~~ slide insensibly into the humour of evil speaking. It is strange how most persons dispense with themselves in this point, and that in scarcely any societies shall we find a hatred of this ill, but rather some tokens of taking pleasure in it; and until a Christian sets himself to an inward watchfulness over his heart, not suffering in it any thought that is uncharitable, or vain self-esteem, upon the sight of others' frailties, he will still be subject to somewhat of this, in the tongue or ear at least. So, then, as for the evil of guile in the tongue, a sincere heart, *truth in the inward parts*, powerfully redresses it; therefore it is expressed, Psal. xv. 2., *That speaketh the truth from his heart;* thence it flows. Seek much after this, to speak nothing with God, nor men, but what is the sense of a single unfeigned heart. O sweet truth! excellent but rare sincerity! he that *loves that truth within*, *ᶜ*and who is himself at once THE TRUTH, and THE LIFE, He alone can work it there*/*! *ˢ*Seek it of him. M.Aph.33

20 II 11 | *AR* 108, Moral Aphorism 33

* He that spares speech, *favours his tongue* indeed, as the Latin phrase is, "*favere linguae*";*ᵈ* not he that looses the reins and lets it run.

*ᵉ It is characteristic of the Roman Dignity and Sobriety that in the Latin *to favour the* tongue (favere linguæ) means *to be silent*. We say, Hold your tongue! as if it were an injunction, that could not be carried into effect but by ~~dint~~ manual force, or the pincers of the Forefinger and Thumb! And verily—I blush to say it—it is not Women & Frenchmen only that would ⟨rather⟩ have their tongues bitten than bitted, and feel their souls in a strait-waistcoat, when they are obliged to remain silent.[1]

ᵃ⁻ᵇ In pencil, overtraced   *ᶜ* The insertion is in ink
ᵈ In the printed original the Latin phrase is in square brackets as a quotation
ᵉ The indicator corresponding to the asterisk is in pencil both here and in textus

20[1] In a letter to his nephew Edward Coleridge, who had objected to the aphorism based on this note—whether to the etymology or to the sneer against "Women & Frenchmen" is not clear)—C admitted that "the whole §§ph. might be omitted without loss—it is but a *witticism*" (*CL* VI 566); he retained it, however, in the revised *AR*. The Latin idiom was well known, e.g. through Horace *Odes* 3.1.2; C would have found it also in his annotated BEAUMONT & FLETCHER COPY B I 224.

20A II 12, marked with a line in pencil

He is wise that hath learned to speak little with others, and much with himself and with God.

20B II 12–13, marked with a line in pencil, partly overtraced in ink, insertions in pencil | *AR* 108, Moral Aphorism 34

. . . their chief good [that of the discourses] is the warming of the heart; ^{*a*}stirring up in it love to God, and remembrance of our present and after estate, our mortality and immortality; and extolling the ways of holiness, and the promises and comforts of the Gospel, and the excellency of Jesus Christ; and in these sometimes one particular, sometimes another, as our particular condition requires, or any occasion makes them pertinent. Therefore in conversation ~~these discourses~~, M.Aph.34 ^{*b*}seek not so much either to vent thy knowledge, or to increase it, as to know more spiritually and effectually what thou dost know. And in this way those mean despised truths, that every one thinks he is sufficiently seen in, will have a new sweetness and use in them, which thou didst not so well perceive before/.^{*c*} (for these flowers cannot be sucked dry,) and in this humble sincere way thou shalt *grow in grace and in knowledge* too.   M.Aph.34.

20C II 18, marked with a pencil line | 1 Pet 3.11

For in this [that particular good of our calling] some deceive themselves; they look upon such a condition as they imagine were fit for them, or such as in their eye when they look upon others, and they think if they were such persons, and had such a place, and such power and opportunities, they would do great matters, and in the mean time they neglect that good to which they are called, and which they have in some measure power and place to do.

20D II 24, marked with a pencil line | 1 Pet 3.12

The wisest knowledge of things is, to know them in their causes; but there is no knowledge of causes so happy and useful, as clearly to know and firmly to believe the universal dependence of all things upon the First and Highest Cause, the Cause of causes, the Spring of being and goodness, the wise and just Ruler of the world.

20E II 25, marked with a line in pencil, insertions in pencil

Not any one man in all kind of sins; that is impossible; It is true, that

---

^{*a*} Pencil line indicates a beginning here, but does not continue beyond one line of print
^{*b*} Ink line begins, ending at end of paragraph   ^{*c*} Pencil line indicates ending here

there is a concatenation of vices ~~sin~~, and one disposes and induces to another; but yet one vicious ~~ungodly~~ man is commonly more versed in and delighted with some one kind of sin, another with some other.[a] He forbears none because it is evil ~~and hateful to God,~~[b] but as he cannot travel over the whole globe of wickedness, and go the full circuit, he walks up and down in his accustomed way of sin.

20F II 25, marked with lines in pencil and ink, corrections in pencil and ink | *AR* 108–9, Moral Aphorism 35

To be abridged. [c]M.Aph.35. The good ~~godly~~ man hates the evil he possibly by temptation hath been drawn to do, and loves the good he is frustrated of, and, having intended, hath not attained to do. The sinner, who hath his denomination from sin as his course, hates the good which sometimes he is forced to do, and loves that sin which many times he does not, either wanting occasion and means, so that he cannot do it, or through the check of an enlightened conscience, possibly dares not do; and though so bound up from the act, as a dog in a chain, yet the habit, the natural inclination and desire in him, is still the same, the strength of his affection is carried to sin. So in the weakest *sincere* Christian ~~godly man,~~[d] there is that predominant ~~sincerity and~~[e] desire of holy walking, according to which he is called a *righteous person*, the Lord is pleased to give him that name, and account him so, being upright in heart, though often failing.

20G II 40, marked with a pencil line

. . . our ordinary babblings, that heart nonsense, which, though the words be sense, yet, through the inattention of the heart, are but as impertinent confused dreams in the Lord's ears . . .

20H II 40, marked with a pencil line

It is a supernatural work, and therefore the principle of it must be supernatural. He that hath nothing of the Spirit of God, cannot pray at all: he may howl as a beast in his necessity or distress, or may speak words of prayer, as some birds learn the language of men; but pray he cannot.

20I II 41–2, marked with lines in pencil

This is no small piece of our misery here: these wanderings are evidence to us, that we are not at home. But though we should be humbled for

---

[a] Pencil line ends here   [b] C uses parentheses and a symbol to indicate omission
[c] In pencil   [d] The cancellation and insertion are in ink
[e] C uses pencilled parentheses to indicate omission

this, and still be labouring against it, yet should we not be so discouraged, as to be driven from the work.[a] . . . Strive against the ~~miserable~~ evil that is within thee, but cast not away thy happiness. Be doing still. It is a froward childish humour, when any thing agrees not to our mind, to throw all away. Thou mayest come off, as Jacob, with *halting* from thy *wrestlings*, and yet obtain *the blessing* for which thou wrestlest.

20J II 42–3, marked with a line in pencil, corrections in pencil

~~Fervency; not to seek coldly; that~~[b] Coldness in Prayer presages refusal. There must be fire in the sacrifice, otherwise it ascends not. There is no sacrifice without incense, and no incense without fire.[c] . . .

But in this there must be some difference between temporal and spiritual things. That prayer which is in the right strain, cannot be too fervent in any thing; but the desire of the thing in temporals may be too earnest. A feverish distempered heat diseases the soul; therefore in these things, a holy indifferency concerning the particular, may, and should be, joined with the fervency of prayer. But in spiritual things, there is no danger in vehemency of desire/: [d]*Covet* these, *hunger and thirst* for them, be incessantly ardent in the suit; yet even in these, in some particulars, (as with respect to the degree and measure of grace, and some peculiar furtherances,) they should be presented so with earnestness,[e] ~~as~~ so <u>that</u> withal it be with a reference and resignation of it to the wisdom and love of our Father.

21 II 52–8, marked with a line in ink | *AR* 111–12, Moral Aphorism 36

M.Aph.36   Your blessedness is not,—no, believe it, it is not where most of you seek it, in things below you. How can that be?Ʌ It must be a higher good to make you happy. Ʌ

Ʌ Every Rank of Creatures, as it ascends in the Scale of Creation, leaves Death behind it, or under it.[1] The Metal at its height of Being seems a mute Prophecy of the coming Vegetation, into a mimic Semblance of which it́ christallizes. The Blossom & Flower, the Acmè of Vegetable Life, divides into correspondent Organs with reciprocal functions, and by instinctive motions and approximations seems impatient of théat fixture, by which it is differenced in kind from the flower-shaped Psyche,

---

[a] The pencil mark ends here; several subsequent sentences not marked
[b] C uses pencilled parentheses to indicate omission
[c] The text to this point is marked off with an enclosing line; C's marking resumes on II 43 with the marginal note "continued from p. 42, 'fire'."
[d-e] Marked for omission with encircling lines and dots in the margin

21[1] The account of the scale of nature that follows is a condensed and lyrical version of the "scientific" survey in *TL* 67–86.

that flutters with free wing above it. And wonderfully in the insect realm
doth the Irritability, the proper seat of Instinct, while yet the ~~but~~ nascent
Sensibility is subordinated thereto—most wonderfully, I say, doth the
muscular Life in the Insect, and the musculo-arterial in the Bird, imitate
and typically ~~repr~~ rehearse the adaptive Understanding, yea, and the
moral Affections and Charities of Man.[a] ⟨Let ~~it~~ us carry ourselves back,
in spirit, to the mysterious Week, the teeming Work-days of the Creator:
as t⟨h⟩ey rose in vision before the eye of the inspired Historian of "the
Generations of the Heaven & the Earth in the days that the Lord God
made the Earth and the Heavens."[2] And⟩ Who, that ⟨hath⟩ watche~~thed~~
their ways with an understanding heart, ~~can~~ could contemplate~~d~~ the filial
and loyal Bee; the home-building, wedded and divorceless Swallow;
and above all the manifoldly intelligent ~~Commonwealths of~~ Ant-tribes
with their Common-wealths, and Confederacies, their Warriors, and
Miners, ~~and~~ their Husband~~men~~-folk, that fold in their ⟨tiny⟩ flocks on
the honeyed Leaf, and their Virgin Sisters ~~in whom~~ with the ~~unsleeping~~
holy Instincts of Maternal Love, ~~lives d~~ burns detached and in self-less
purity[3]—and not say to himself, Behold the ~~protended~~ Shadow of ap-
proaching Humanity, ~~in the kindling Morn Sunrise of~~ the Sun rising
from behind, in the kindling Morn of Creation! Thus all lower Natures
find~~ing~~ their highest Good in semblances and Seekings of that which ~~h~~
is higher and Better. All things strive to ascend, and ascend in their
striving. And shall men alone stoop? Shall his pursuits and desires, ~~that~~
~~are~~ the *reflections* of his inward life, ~~but~~ be like the reflected Image of a
Tree on the edge of a Pool, that grows downward, and seeks a mock
heaven in the unstable element beneath it, in neighbourhood with the
~~oozy~~ slim water-weeds and oozy bottom-grass that are yet better than
itself and more noble, ~~they~~ in as far as Substances that appear as Shad-
ows are preferable to Shadows mistaken for Substance! No! it must be a
higher good to make you happy. While you labor for any thing below
your proper Humanity, you seek a happy Life in the region of Death.
Well saith the moral Poet—

> unless above himself he can
> Erect himself, how mean a Thing is Man![4]

21A   II 53, marked with a line in ink | 1 Pet 3.13 | *AR* 113, Moral Aphorism 37

M.Aph.37.   There is an imitation of men that is impious and wicked,
which consists in taking the copy of their sins. Again, there is an imita-

---

[a] C has written "Turn to the side Margin", where the insertion that follows is written

21[2] Gen 2.4 (var).

21[3] C takes up the examples of bees and

ants again in *AR* (1825) 210–14.

21[4] Samuel Daniel, as **7** at n 14 above.

tion which though not so grossly evil, yet, is poor and servile, being in mean things, yea, sometimes descending to imitate the very imperfections of others, as fancying some comeliness in them; as some of Basil's scholars, who imitated his slow speaking, which he had a little in the extreme, and could not help. But this is always laudable, and worthy of the best minds, to be *imitators of that which is good*, wheresoever they find it; for that stays not in any man's person, as the ultimate pattern, but rises to the highest grace, being man's nearest likeness to God, His image and resemblance, *ᵃ(and so, following the example of the saints in holiness, we look higher than them, and consider them as receivers, but God as the first owner and dispenser of grace,)ᵇ* bearing His stamp and superscription, and belonging peculiarly to Him, in what hand soever it be found, as carrying the mark of no other owner than Him.

21B   II 57, marked with a line in pencil overtraced in ink | *AR* 113, Moral Aphorism 38

M.Aph.38   . . . ꝉThose who think themselves high-spirited, and will bear least, as they speak, are often, even by that, forced to bow most, or to burst under it; while humility and meekness escape many a burden, and many a blow, always keeping peace within, and often without too.

21C   II 60–1, marked with a line in pencil | 1 Pet 3.14

Spiritualᶜ   . . . Luther calls Persecution, *malus genius Evangelii, the evil genius of the Gospel.* And we, being forewarned of this, as not only the possible, but the frequent lot of the saints, ought not to hearken to the false prophecies of our own self-love, which divines what it would gladly have, and easily persuades us to believe it. Think not that any prudence will lead you by all oppositions and malice of an ungodly world. Many winter blasts will meet you in the most inoffensive way of religion, if you keep straight to it. Suffering and war with the world, is a part of the godly man's portion here, which seems hard, but take it altogether, it is sweet: none in their wits will refuse that legacy entire, *In the world ye shall have trouble, but in me ye shall have peace*, John xvi. *ult.*

21D   II 65, marked with a line in pencil

Spiritualᶜ   Lay it [happiness] higher and surer, and, if you be wise, provide such a peace as will remain untouched in the hottest flame, such a light as will shine in the deepest dungeon, and such a life as is safe even in death itself, that life which is *hid with Christ in God.* Col. iii. 3.

ᵃ⁻ᵇ Marked for omission with dotted lines in the margin   ᶜ In ink

22   II 73–4, pencil, marked with a line in the margin | 1 Pet 3.15

* That Fear [of God], as greatest, overtops and nullifies all lesser fears: the heart possessed with this fear, hath no room for the other. It resolves the heart, in point of duty, what it should and must do, that it must not offend God by any means, lays that down as indisputable, and so eases it of doubtings and debates in that kind—whether shall I comply with the world, and abate somewhat of the sincerity and exact way of religion to please men, or to escape persecution or reproaches: no, it is unquestionably best, and only necessary, *to obey Him, rather than men*, to retain His favour, be it with displeasing the most respected and considerable persons we know; yea, rather to choose the universal and highest displeasure of all the world for ever, than His smallest discountenance for a moment. It counts that the only indispensable necessity, to cleave unto God and obey Him. If I pray, I shall be accused, might Daniel think, but yet, pray I must, come on it what will. So, if I worship God in my prayer, they will mock me, I shall pass for a fool; no matter for that, it must be done: I must call on God, and strive to walk with Him. This sets the mind at ease, not to be halting betwixt two opinions, but resolved what to do. *We are not careful*, said they, *to answer thee, O king—our God can deliver us*, but if not, this we have put out of deliberation, *we will not worship the image*. Dan. iii. 16. As one said, *Non oportet vivere, sed oportet navigare* [It is not necessary to live, but it is necessary to sail], so we may say, It is not necessary to have the favour of the world, nor to have riches, nor to live, but it is necessary to hold fast the truth, and to walk holily, to sanctify the name of our Lord, and honour Him, whether in life or death.

* N.b.—This for the first Extract of the Moral and Prudential.[1]—The Fear of the Lord is the Beginning of Wisdom[2]—were it only, that it nullifies all lesser fears.

22A   II 75–6, marked with a line in pencil partly overtraced in ink | *AR* 113–14, Moral
Aphorism 39

M.Aph.39   Our condition is universally exposed to fears and troubles, and no man is so stupid but he studies and projects for some fence against them, some bulwark to break the incursion of evils, and so to bring his mind to some ease, ridding it of the fear of them.[a] . . . Aph.39

---

[a] Two long sentences (omitted here) marked for omission with ink dots in margin

22[1] "Moral and Prudential" was a cat-
egory for aphorisms to be used in *AR*, men-
tioned in a letter of 8 Aug 1823 (*CL* v 290).

It was eventually abandoned.
22[2] Ps 111.10, Prov 9.10.

Thus, men seek safety in the greatness, or multitude, or supposed faithfulness of friends; they seek by any means to be strongly underset this way, to have many, and powerful, and trust-worthy friends. But wiser men, perceiving the unsafety and vanity of these and all external things, have cast about for some higher course. They see a necessity of withdrawing a man from externals, which do nothing but mock and deceive*a* those most who trust most to them; but they cannot tell whither to direct him. The best of them bring him *into himself*, and think to quiet him so, but the truth is, he finds as little to support him there; there is nothing truly strong enough within him, to hold out against the many sorrows and fears which still from without do assault him. So then, though it is well done, to call off a man from outward things, as moving sands, that he build not on them, yet, this is not enough; for his own spirit is as unsettled a piece as is in all the world, and must have some higher strength than its own, to fortify and fix it. This is the way that is here taught, *Fear not their fear, but sanctify the Lord your God in your hearts;* and if you can attain this latter, the former will follow of itself.   Aph.39

22B   ii 79, marked with a line in pencil, alterations and insertions in ink

Take heed, respect the Great Person you have in your company, who lodges within you. ~~the~~ It is a Holy Spirit/: THE HOLY is his Name.[1] *Grieve Him not*; it will turn to your own grief if you do, for all your comfort is in His hand, and flows from Him. THE COMFORTER is his Title.[2] If you be but in heart dallying with sin, it will unfit you for suffering outward troubles, and make your spirit low and base in the day of trial; yea, it will fill you with inward trouble, and disturb that peace which, I am sure, you who know it, esteem more than all the peace and flourishing of this world. Outward troubles do not molest or stir inward peace, but an unholy, unsanctified affection doth. All the winds without, cause not an earthquake, but that within its own bowels doth.

23   ii 80–1, marked with lines in pencil and in ink; note in ink | *AR* 114–15, Moral Aphorism 40

*b*There is a word or two in the Hebrew for *idols*, that signify withal *troubles*,† and terrors‡*c* And so it is certainly: all our idols prove so to us; they fill us with nothing but anguish and troubles, with unprofitable

---

a Here, at the top of p 76, C repeats "Aph. 39."
b–c Pencil line in margin begins at *b* but *b–c* marked for deletion; ink line begins at *c*

22B[1] Cf "whose name is Holy", Isa 57.15.   **22B**[2] The Holy Ghost is "the Comforter" in John 14.16, 26 etc.

cares and fears, that are good for nothing, but to be fit punishments of that folly out of which they arise. *ª*The ardent love or self-willed desire of prosperity, or wealth, or credit in the world, carries with it, as inseparably tied to it, a bundle of fears and inward troubles.*ᵇ*

ᶜ† *"Tigrim,"ᵈ* Isa. xlv. 16. from *"Tszus."* arctavit, hostiliter egit [He/it pressed, acted in a hostile manner].

‡ *"Miphletzeth,"* 1 Kings xv. 13. from *"Phalatz,"* contremiscere, et [to tremble all over, and] *"Emim,"* Job xv. 25. from *"Aim,"* formidabilis, terrificus [formidable, terrifying].*ᵉ*

* To be transposed, thus:

The too ardent Love or self-willed Desire of Power or Wealth or Credit in the World is, an Apostle hath assured us, Idolatry.[1] Now among the Words or Synonimes for Idols in the Hebrew Language there ~~are two~~ is one that in ~~their~~ its primary sense signif~~y~~ies ~~the one~~ Troubles†, ~~the~~ other ⟨two that signify⟩ *Terrors*.‡.[2]

24 ɪɪ 82–6, marked with a line in ink, insertions in ink | *AR* 115–17 and n, Moral Aphorism 41

. . .~~a~~ A regardless contempt of ~~them were~~ infidel writings is usually the fittest answer; *Spreta vilescerent* [Things that are despised become worthless]. But where the holy profession of Christians, is likely to receive either the main or the indirect blow, and a word of defence may do any thing to ward it off, there we ought not to spare to do it.

Christian prudence goes a great way in the regulating of this;/. ~~for holy things are not to be cast to dogs.~~ Some are not capable of receiving rational answers, especially in Divine things; they were not only lost upon them, but religion dishonoured by the contest. ⋀ᶠ But we are to answer every one that *inquires a reason*, or an account; which supposes something receptive of it. We ought to judge ourselves engaged to give it, be it an enemy, if he will hear; if it gain him not, it may in part convince and cool him; much more, should it be one who ingenuously

ᵃ⁻ᵇ Marked in ink in the margin

ᶜ⁻ᵉ Marked in pencil in the margin

ᵈ In the printed original "Tigrim" and the five other transliterated Hebrew words are in square brackets; quotation marks are substituted here to avoid confusion with editorial matter

ᶠ C adds "insert" in the margin

23[1] Col 3.5: "Mortify therefore your members which are upon the earth; fornication, uncleanness, inordinate affection, evil concupiscence, and covetousness, which is idolatry."

23[2] C's footnote indicators correspond to Leighton's. This note was further revised before it appeared in *AR* (1825) 114–15.

inquires for satisfaction, and possibly inclined to receive the truth, but is prejudiced against it by false misrepresentations of it . . .

∧¹ Of this sort are the vulgar Railers at Religion, the foul-mouthed Beliers of the Christian Faith and History. ~~It is degrading to the majesty and injurious to the character of our Faith to make Christianity~~ Impudently false and slanderous Assertions can be met only by Assertions of their impudent and slanderous falsehood: and ~~how can the~~ christians will not, must not condescend to this. How can ⟨mere⟩ Railing be answered by them who are forbidden to return a railing answer. Whether or on what provocations such Offenders may be punished ⟨or cöerced⟩ on the score of Incivility, and Ill-neighborhood, and for the Abatement of a Nuisance, as in the case of other Scolds and Endangerers of the public Peace, must be trusted to the Discretion of the civil Magistrate. Even so there is a danger of giving them ~~an~~ importance—~~that they~~ flattering their vanity by attracting attention to their works, if the punishment be slight; and if severe, of spreading far and wide their reputation as Martyrs, as ⟨the Smell of a⟩ Dead Dog∫ at a distance is said to change into that of Musk.² Experience hitherto seems to favor the plan of treating these Bêtes puantes and *Enfans* de Diable,³ as their four-footed Brethren, the *Skink* and Squash, are treated*ᵃ by the American Woo, nen, who turn

* About the end of the same Year (says Kalm)⁴ another of these Animals ⟨(Mephitis Americana)⟩ crept into our cellar; but did not exhale the smallest Scent, *because it was not disturbed. A foolish old Woman, however, who perceived it, at night, by the shining, and thought, I suppose, that it would set the world on fire, killed it: and at that moment its stench began to spread.*

We recommend this anecdote to the consideration of sundry old Women, on this side of the Atlantic, who tho' they do not wear the appropriate garment, are worthy to sit in their Committee-room, like Bickerstaff in the Tatler, ~~not~~ under the Canopy of their Grandam's Hoop-petticoat.—⁵

ᵃ On p 85 at the end of C's insert: "*See the Slip N° I." A leaf tipped in at pp 84/5 is headed: "Slip N° I. Note answering to *, Vol. II. page 85."

24¹ This long insertion is printed as para 3 of Aphorism 41; para 4 in that text takes up Leighton again, as indicated at the end of C's note ("On the other hand . . .").

24² A curiosity recorded and applied by C in *CN* I 1234 and in *Omniana* (1812) § 156.

24³ "Stinking Beasts and Children of the Devil". From Kalm (n 4 below) I 273.

24⁴ Pehr Kalm *En resa til Norra America* 3 vols (Stockholm 1753–61) tr J. R. Forster as *Travels in North America* (Warrington and London 1770–1); the English edition provides C's information about the American skunk "(Mephitis Americana)" on I 277.

24⁵ *Tatler* 116, 5 Jan 1709, conducts a mock trial of the newly fashionable widely

their backs upon the ~~skulking~~ fetid Intruder, and make appear not to see ~~them~~ him, even at the ~~risk~~ cost of suffering him to regale on the favorite viands of these animals, the brains of a stray Goose or crested Thraso of the Dung-hill.[6] At all events, it is degrading to the majesty and injurious to the character of Religion to make its safety the plea for their punishment, or at all to connect the name of Christianity with the castigation of Indecencies that properly belong to the Beadle, and ⟨the perpetrators of which⟩ would have equally deserved his Lash, tho' the Religion of their fellow-citizens thus assailed by them had been that of Fo or of Juggernaut.[7]

On the other hand, we are to answer &c p. 82.

25 II 87–90, marked with lines in ink; changes and note in ink | *AR* 117–18 and n, Moral Aphorism 42

M.Aph.42. ~~It~~ Truth needs not the service of passion; yea, nothing so disserves it, as passion when set to serve it. The *Spirit of truth* is withal the *Spirit of meekness*. The Dove that rested on that great Champion of truth, who is The Truth itself, is from Him derived to the lovers of truth, and they ought to seek the participation of it. Imprudence makes some kind of Christians lose much of their labour, in speaking for religion, and drive those further off, whom they would draw into it.[a] . . . Aph.42 The confidence that attends ~~this hope,~~ a Christian's Belief makes the believer not fear men, to whom he answers, but still he fears his God, for whom he answers, and whose interest is chief in those things he speaks of. The soul that hath the deepest sense of spiritual things, and the truest knowledge of God, is most afraid to miscarry in speaking of Him, most tender and wary how to acquit itself when engaged to speak of and for God.*

* Note: To the same purpose are the two following Sentences from Hilary.

Etiam quæ *pro* religione dicimus, cum grandi metu et disciplinâ dicere debemus. Hilarius de Trinit. Lib. 7.[b]

Non relictus est hominum eloquiis de Dei rebus alius quam Dei sermo. Idem.[1]

[a] One sentence (omitted here) marked for omission by ink dots in the margin
[b] C has written at the foot of p 87 "turn over" and has continued on II 88

hooped petticoat; Bickerstaff causes a sample, "in its form not unlike the Cupola of St. *Paul's*", to be hoisted as a canopy over the courtroom.

24[6] A Cock; "Thraso" is a name for a braggart, from a character in Terence.

24[7] "Fo" is a Chinese name for Buddha (cf HEINROTH 34 n 2), "Juggernaut" a title of Krishna, casually used by C and his contemporaries to represent heathen religion: cf *SM* (*CC*) 65.

25[1] The second sentence, "It was not

The latter, however, must be taken with certain *Qualifications & Exceptions*: as when any two or more Texts are in apparent contradiction, and it is required to ~~give~~ state a Truth that comprehends & reconciles both, and which, of course, cannot be expressed in the words of either. Ex. gr. the filial subordination (*My Father is greater than I.*)[2] in the equal Deity (*My Father and I are one.*)[3]

26   II 93–6, marked with lines in ink | 1 Pet 3.16 | *AR* 118–19, Moral Aphorism 43

It is a fruitless verbal debate, whether Conscience be a faculty or habit, or not. [a]As in other things, so in this, which most of all requires more solid and useful consideration, the vain mind of man feedeth on the wind, loves to be busy to no purpose, *magno conatu magnas nugas* [by a great effort [to produce] great fooleries]. How much better is it to have this supernatural goodness of conscience, than to dispute about the nature of it; to find it duly teaching and admonishing, reproving and comforting, rather than to define it most exactly! *Malo sentire compunctionem, quam scire ejus definitionem* [I would rather feel the prick of conscience than know its definition].

When all is examined, Conscience will be found to be no other than the *mind of man, under the notion of a particular reference to himself and his own actions.**

* ~~This and~~ the preceding ¶ph. in which L. follow[b] Thomas[1] ~~a Kempis, are scarcely worthy of his Candour: for t~~The ~~letter of this particular~~ Definition seems to say all and in fact says nothing—for if I asked, How do you define the *human mind*? the answer must at least *contain*, if not consist of, the words, ''a mind capable of *Conscience*.'' For Conscience is ~~not~~ no synonime of Consciousness, ~~but~~ nor any mere expression of the same as modified by the particular Object. On the contrary, a Consciousness properly human (i.e. *Self*-consciousness with the sense of moral responsibility), presupposes the Conscience, as its Antecedent Condition and Ground.[2] Lastly the sentence, ''It is a fruitless verbal

---

[a] The three sentences following not marked for inclusion   [b] A slip for ''follows''

---

left to the eloquence of men [to discourse] about the things of God beyond the word of God'', is indeed from St Hilary of Poitiers *De trinitate* 7.38. The first, ''Even what we say on behalf of religion we ought to say with great fear and restraint'', has not been traced in Hilary's works, though the attribution appears also in C's original notebook entry of 1807: *CN* II 3098.

25[2] John 14.28.

25[3] John 10.30 (var).

26[1] Thomas à Kempis (c 1380–1471), mystic, by tradition author of the *Imitation of Christ*, Leighton's favourite devotional writer, invoked by C as an ''ascetic Spirit'' in Howie **8**.

26[2] C makes this same point in e.g. Irving *Sermons* **9** and in Reimarus **1**. In BM

Debate,''[3] is an assertion of the same complexion with the contemptuous Sneers at Verbal Criticism by the Contemporaries of Bentley.[4] ~~For one instance of actual *Logomachy*.~~ In Questions of Philosophy or Divinity, that have occupied the Learned & have been the subjects of successive Controversies, ⟨for ~~any~~ one instance of mere Logomachy⟩ I could bring ten instances of *Logodædaly*, or verbal Legerdemain, which have perilously confirmed Prejudices, and withstood the Advancement of Truth, in consequence of the neglect of *verbal debate*—i.e. strict discussion of Terms.—In whatever Sense, however, the term, Conscience, may be used, the ~~last sentence of this Extract (p 94)~~ following Aphorism is equally true and important. It is worth noticing likewise, that Leighton himself in ~~the~~ a following page (97) tells us, that A good Conscience is the *Root* of a good Conversation. And then quotes from Sᵗ Paul a text, Titus I. 15, in which the Mind and the Conscience are expressly distinguished.[5]   S. T. C.

26A   ɪɪ 94, marked with a line in pencil overtraced in ink │ *AR* 120, Moral Aphorism 44

Aph.44   . . . ~~‡~~If you would have a good conscience, you must by all means have so much light, so much knowledge of the will of God, as may regulate you, and shew you your way, may teach you how to do, and speak, and think, as in His presence.

26B   ɪɪ 97, marked with a line in pencil overtraced in ink │ *AR* 120, Moral Aphorism 45

M.Aph.~~9~~45.[a] To set the outward actions right, though with an honest intention, and not so to regard and find out the inward disorder of the heart, whence that in the actions flows, is but to be still putting the index of a clock right with your finger, while it is foul, or out of order within, which is a continual business, and does no good.[b] Oh! but a purified

[a] "9" in ink overwritten with "4" in pencil   [b] The pencil line in the margin ends here

MS Egerton 2801 f 252, he refers specifically to this "aphorism on the equivocal meaning of the term, Consciousness", affirming "the identity or co-inherence of Morality and Religion, as the Transcendant containing both *in* and *as* one, that which our elder Divines meant by the Seed of Election in the Soul, and which Sᵗ Paul calls the Root"—cf below at n 5.

26[3] Beginning of textus.

26[4] In the controversy about the letters of Phalaris in the 1690s, the great classical scholar Richard Bentley (1662–1742) correctly maintained that the letters were spurious; on the opposite side, however, were Boyle, Temple, and Swift (who mocked Bentley as a pedant especially in *The Battle of the Books*). In *TT* 15 Jun 1830, C remarked, "The effect of the Tory wits attacking Bentley with such acrimony has been to make them appear a set of shallow and incompetent scholars." C annotated a biography of Bentley: see Wrangham.

26[5] Titus 1.15: "Unto the pure all things are pure: but unto them that are defiled and unbelieving is nothing pure; but even their mind and conscience is defiled."

conscience, a soul renewed and refined in its temper and affections, will make things go right without, in all the duties and acts of our callings.

26C   ɪɪ 99, marked with a line in pencil; corrections and insertion in ink

~~Thus often it~~ Even in respect of the World the advantage of a good Conscience is oftentimes most evident ∧ ~~is even~~ most evident ∧ to men; the victory of innocency, silent innocency, most strongly confuting all calumny, making the ungodly, false accusers hide their heads. Thus, without stirring, the integrity of a Christian, conquers; as a rock, unremoved, breaks the waters that are dashing against it.

26D   ɪɪ 106, marked with a pencil line | 1 Pet 3.18

There can be no higher example [of greatness than Christ]. Not only are the sons of adoption sufferers, but the *begotten*, the *only begotten Son*, the Eternal Heir of glory, in whom all the rest have their title, their sonship and heirship, derived from, and dependent on His; not only all the saints, but the King of saints.

26E   ɪɪ 109, marked with brackets in pencil

Whereas the soul perplexed about that question [of Christ's suffering], finds no relief in all other enjoyments; all propositions of lower comforts are unsavoury and troublesome to it. Tell it of peace and prosperity; say, however the world go, you shall have ease and pleasure, and you shall be honoured and esteemed by all; though you could make a man sure of these, yet, if his conscience be working and stirred about the matter of his sin, and the wrath of God which is tied close to sin, he will wonder at your impertinency, in that you speak so far from the purpose. Say what you will of these, he still asks, What do you mean by this? Those things answer not to me. Do you think I can find comfort in them, so long as my sin is unpardoned, and there is a sentence of eternal death standing above my head? I feel even an impress of somewhat of that hot indignation; some flashes of it, flying and lighting upon the face of my soul, and how can I take pleasure in these things you speak of? And though I should be senseless, and feel nothing of this all my life, yet, how soon shall I have done with it, and the delights that reach no further. And then to have *everlasting burnings*, an eternity of wrath to enter to! How can I be satisfied with that estate?—All you offer a man in this posture, is as if you should set dainty fare, and bring music with it, before a man lying almost pressed to death under great weights, and should bid him eat and be merry, but lift not off his pressure: you do but mock the man and add to his misery.

27   II 112, pencil, marked with a pencil line

* And though it was simply in the power of the Supreme Law-giver to have dispensed with the infliction, yet, having in His wisdom purposed to be known a just God in that way, following forth the tenor of His Law, of necessity there must be a suffering for sin.

* This, this is the point on which Leighton's Views seem to me short of his wonted Spiritual Insight. I dare not arraign the positions contained in these five lines as false; but I *s* rather saw,*a* my burthened Heart complains of them as inadequate, wanting in the *veriness*[1] of this precious Mystery of Love.

27A   II 114, marked with a line in ink

Look about thee, tell me what thou seest, either in thy possession or in thy hopes, that thou esteemest most, and layest thy confidence on. Or, to deal more liberally with thee, see what estate thou wouldst choose, hadst thou thy wish; stretch thy fancy to devise an earthly happiness. These times are full of unquietness; but give thee a time of the calmest peace, not an air of trouble stirring; put thee where thou wilt, far off from fear of sword and pestilence, and encompass thee with children, friends, and possessions, and honours, and comfort, and health to enjoy all these; yet, one thing thou must admit in the midst of them all; within a while thou must die, and having no real portion in Christ, but only a deluding dream of it, thou sinkest through that death into another death far more terrible. Of all thou enjoyest, nothing goes along with thee but unpardoned sin, and that delivers thee up to endless sorrow. *Oh that you were wise* and *would consider your latter end!*

27B   II 116–18, marked with a line in pencil and in ink | *AR* 121–3, Moral Aphorism 47

M.Aph.47*b*   God hath suited every creature He hath made, with a convenient good to which it tends, and, in the obtainment of which it rests and is satisfied. Natural bodies have all their own natural place, whither, if not hindered, they move incessantly till they be in it; and they declare, by resting there, that they are (as I may say) where they would be. Sensitive creatures are carried to seek a sensitive good, as agreeable to their rank in being, and, attaining that, aim no further. Now, in this is the excellency of Man, that he is made capable of a communion with his

---

a A slip for "say"?

b This notation is repeated at the top of the next page, p 117, as a guide to the *AR* printer

27[1] I.e. actuality, truth: not C's coinage, but perhaps a revival of a somewhat outmoded usage. *OED* lists the word as obsolete, giving an example from 1574.

Maker, and, because capable of it, is unsatisfied without it: the soul, being cut out (so to speak) to that largeness, cannot be filled with less. Though he is fallen from his right to that good, and from all right desire of it, yet, not from a capacity of it, no, nor from a necessity of it, for the answering and filling of his capacity.

Though the heart once gone from God, turns continually further away from Him, and moves not towards Him, till it be renewed, yet, even in that wandering, it retains that natural relation to God, as its centre, that it hath no true rest elsewhere, nor can by any means find it. It is made for Him, and is therefore still restless till it meet with Him.

It is true, the natural man takes much pains to quiet his heart by other things, and digests many vexations with hopes of contentment in the end and accomplishment of some design he hath; but still the heart misgives. Many times he attains not the thing he seeks; but if he do, yet he never attains the satisfaction he seeks and expects in it, but only learns from that to desire something further, and still hunts on after a fancy, drives his own shadow before him, and never overtakes it; and if he did, yet it is but a shadow. And so, in running from God, besides the sad end, he carries an interwoven punishment with his sin, the natural disquiet and vexation of his spirit, fluttering to and fro, and *finding no rest for the sole of his foot*; the *waters* of inconstancy and vanity *covering the whole face of the earth.*[a]   M.Aph.47 . . .

M.Aph.47   These things are too gross and heavy. The soul, the immortal soul, descended from heaven, must either be more happy, or remain miserable. The Highest, the Increated Spirit, is the proper good, *the Father of spirits*, that pure and full good which raises the soul above itself; whereas all other things draw it down below itself. So, then, it is never well with the soul, but when it is near unto God, yea, in its union with Him, married to Him: mismatching itself elsewhere, it hath never any thing but shame and sorrow. *All that forsake Thee shall be ashamed*, says the Prophet, Jer. xvii. 13; and the Psalmist, *They that are far off from Thee, shall perish*. Psal. lxxiii. 27. And this is indeed our natural miserable condition, and it is often expressed this way, by estrangedness and distance from God.[1]

27C   II 120–1, marked with lines in ink | *AR* 152–3, Spiritual Aphorism 1

Spir.Aph.1[b]   Common mercies of God, though they have a leading faculty to repentance, (Rom. ii. 4.) yet, the rebellious heart will not be led

---

[a] The next paragraph (omitted here) marked for omission by dots in the margin

[b] This notation is repeated at the top of the next page, p 121, as a guide to the *AR* printer

27B[1]   C adds a paragraph of his own to this text in *AR* (1825) 123.

by them. The judgements of God, public or personal, though they ought to drive us to God, yet the heart, unchanged, runs the further from God. Do we not see it by ourselves and other sinners about us? They look not at all towards Him who smites, much less do they return; or if any more serious thoughts of returning arise upon the surprise of an affliction, how soon vanish they, either the stroke abating, or the heart, by time, growing hard and senseless under it!*ᵃ* . . . ⱡLeave Christ out, I say, and all other means work not this way; neither the works nor the word of God sounding daily in his ear, *Return, return*. Let the noise of the rod speak it too, and both join together to make the cry the louder, *yet the wicked will do wickedly*, Dan. xii. x . . . *Spir.Aph.*1.

28   II 130–6 | 1 Pet 3.19–21

Other misinterpretations I mention not, taking it as agreeable to the whole strain of the Apostle's words*, that Jesus Christ did, before His appearing in the flesh, speak by His Spirit in His servants to those of the foregoing ages, yea, the most ancient of them, declaring to them the way of life, though rejected by the unbelief of the most part.

[Footnote*:] Thus I then thought, but do now apprehend another sense, as probable, if not more, even that so much rejected by most interpreters: the mission of the Spirit, and preaching of the Gospel by it, after His resurrection, preaching to sinners, and converting them, according to the prophecy which He first fulfilled in person, and after, more amply, in His apostles. That prophecy I mean, Isa. ɪx. ɪ Ch. 42.v.7.*ᵇ* and 61.1.¹ The Spirit came upon Him, and it was sent from Him on His apostles, to preach to *spirits in prison; to preach liberty to those captives*, captive spirits, and therefore called *spirits in prison*, to illustrate the thing the more, by opposition to that spirit of Christ, *the spirit of liberty*, setting them free. And this is to shew the greater efficacy of Christ's preaching, than of Noah's: though he was a signal preacher of righteousness, yet only himself and his family, eight persons, were saved by him; but multitudes of all nations by the Spirit and preaching of Christ in the Gospel; and that by the seal of baptism, the resurrection of Christ being represented in the return from the water, and our dying with Him, by immersion; and that figure of Baptism is like their Ark.

ᵃ The next sentence (omitted here) marked for omission by dots in the margin
ᵇ "Ch." and "v." are written above the figures

28¹ C corrects the text to cite the scriptural references plainly intended by Leighton.

It surprizes me that L. should have preferred this Second thought to his first; which is every way the more plausible. But it puzzles me, I confess, how such a Mind could have been satisfied with either! In what part of Scripture is "Spirits" or Pneumata, used for human Beings, or incarnate Souls?[2] I cannot doubt, that the Apostle, Peter (as elsewhere JUDE, v. 9.)[3] refers to some Rabbinical Tradition, now lost unless perhaps some relic or echo should lurk in some Cabalistic MSS.—It would be quite in the same Spirit with the Fable of the Dispute between the Devil and Michael (one of[a] Cabalistic Names of the Messiah)[4] if the Messiah Futurus, as the Angel of the Presence,[5] had been represented as explaining or *heralding* (εκηρυξεν is Peter's word)[6] the divine purpose to the avenging Spirits, to whom the Human Race had been assigned for destruction, and who had become impatient of the restraint, and the Curbing-in, during the delay necessary for the preparation of the Ark—and thus interfering for the salvation of the Eight Souls,[7] and in them for the temporal new Creation of the Human Race δι' υδατος,[8] at that time even as now δι' υδατος αντιτυπου[9] for the new Creation of the Hu-

---

[a] "The" omitted at the turn of the page

28[2] C takes up issues raised by both the Greek and AV texts of the passage in question, 1 Pet 3.19–21: Christ is described as "quickened by the Spirit", "By which also he went and preached unto the spirits in prison; which sometime were disobedient, when once the longsuffering of God waited in the days of Noah, while the ark was a preparing, wherein few, that is, eight souls were saved by water. The like figure whereunto even baptism doth also now save us . . .". Both Greek and English versions distinguish between πνεύματα ("spirits") and ψυχαί ("souls"), a distinction important to C and, he claims, to Paul, esp in 1 Cor 15: see IRVING *Sermons* **27** n 7.

28[3] Differing from both interpretations offered by Leighton, C will suggest that Peter is alluding to an old story of which few traces remain, as Jude does in the text cited: "Yet Michael the archangel, when contending with the devil he disputed about the body of Moses, durst not bring against him a railing accusation, but said, The Lord rebuke thee."

28[4] It is chiefly in commentaries on the Book of Daniel that the archangel Michael is identified with the Messiah. Bp Horsley is quoted in D'Oyly and Mant's Bible (**39**

n 1 below) commenting on Dan 10.13 and asserting simply that Michael is "a name for our Lord Himself". It was evidently a matter of contemporary controversy: in *Introduction to the New Testament* III (Cambridge 1801) 391, J. D. Michaelis asserts, "Michael cannot denote Christ, for Michael is the name of a created angel"; but his translator and annotator Herbert Marsh observes that some interpreters "appeal to the composition of the Hebrew word Michael, which signifies, 'Who is like God' . . .". The source of C's assertion about a cabbalistic tradition has not been traced.

28[5] The phrase "the angel of his presence" appears in Isaiah's prophecy of the Messiah ("Future Messiah" in C's Latin): Isa 63.9. Cf C's similar reference in JAHN *Appendix* **1** at n 2.

28[6] In 1 Pet 3.19 (q n 2 above), where the verb is rendered "preached" in AV but could mean "heralded", "announced", as C says. No precedent has been traced for C's speculation.

28[7] 1 Pet 3.20, q n 2.

28[8] "By water", from 1 Pet 3.20, q n 2.

28[9] "By the antitype of water", that is, by that which fulfils what was foreshadowed by water in the earlier story.

man Race to Life Eternal—This and this alone or something tantamount would solve all difficulties, and answer equally to the words of the Text, and to the thread and purpose of the Apostle's Reasoning.—For on what ground of Reason or Scripture rests the Assumption, that the Writers of the Apostolic Age should never make use of Parables, Apologues or traditionary Tales for the purpose of illustration or persuasion? That they did, is certain from the ninth of Jude,[10] and next to certain from the Epistle (or rather Oration) to the Hebrews both from the first Chapter (the delivery of the Law on Sinai by *Angels*, which was the tradition of the Jewish Church in Alexandria)[11] and from the allusions to the different Martyrdoms of the Faithful, XI. 33–38.[12] And had not Christ himself set them the example?—Indeed, if the contrary be still insisted on, with what consistency can we persevere in rejecting the Second Book of the Maccabees from the Canon—which however all Men of Learning are agreed in considering as a Romance—and the Author himself passes it for little better.[13]—But the 35th v. of Hebrews XI. beyond all doubt refers to the Mothers of the Seven Martyrs.[14]

28A II 143, marked with an ink line

The saints are usually the scorn and contempt of others, yet are they, ~~by that love the Lord carries towards them,~~[a] the very arches and pillars of states, and kingdoms, and families, where they are, yea, of the world/. . .

29 II 146, marked with an ink line | 1 Pet 3.21

The full and clear distinction of the godly and the wicked, being reserved for their after-estate in eternity, it needs not seem strange, that in

---

[a] Omission indicated by parentheses and a symbol in the margin

---

C echoes the words used at the beginning of 1 Pet 3.21.

28[10] Cited above at n 3.

28[11] C's assertion also in BIBLE COPY B **135** n 1.

28[12] E.g. Heb 11.33–4: "Who through faith subdued kingdoms, wrought righteousness, obtained promises, stopped the mouths of lions, quenched the violence of fire, escaped the edge of the sword, out of weakness were made strong, waxed valiant in fight, turned to flight the armies of the aliens". Cf n 14 below.

28[13] 1 and 2 Macc are among the Apocrypha of the English Bible, though they are accepted as canonical by the Church of Rome. In calling 2 Macc a "Romance" C

probably alludes to the concluding verses, in which the author refers to the artful "fashioning" of his story. The "Mant and D'Oyley" Bible that C refers to in **39** below is typical in its commentary, referring to the "extravagant and fabulous particulars" of 2 Macc.

28[14] C echoes the common view that the latter part of Heb 11.35—"others [women] were tortured, not accepting deliverance; that they might obtain a better resurrection"—refers to a martyrdom recorded in 2 Macc 7, the torturing of seven brothers before their mother's eyes, and of the mother herself after them, "to compel them to taste of the abominable swine's flesh" (2 Macc 7.1).

many things it appears not here. One thing, above all others most griev-
ous to the child of God, may take away the wonder of other things they
suffer in common, that is, the remainders of sin in them while they are
in the flesh: *though there is a spirit in them above it, and contrary to it,
which makes the difference, yet, sometimes the too much likeness, es-
pecially in the prevailings of corruption, doth confuse the matter, not
only to others' eyes, but to their own.

*ᵃ The Body of each man i̶s̶ does perhaps represent & be the result of
the moral qualities, good and evil, of his progenitors—nay, in as much
as the Stimulability is conditioned by the Stimulants, and the World &
Man are reciprocally each as the other, of the whole Race, of the civi-
lized Portion positively, of the Savage indirectly & negatively. On this
Idea I ground a distinction between Original & Hereditary Sin—& be-
lieve both.[1]   S. T. C.

30 ɪɪ 146–7 | **29** textus

* When I consider how nearly impossible a spotless innocence i̶n̶ is
during the union of the Soul with the present Body, I sometimes tho'
never without reverential trembling ask whether in each r̶e̶g̶e̶n̶e̶r̶a̶t̶e̶d̶
Soul elect to regeneration there may notᵇ some Sin or sinful tendency in
some mode proper to that Soul, and which is more peculiarly Spiritual,
and original—i.e. self-originated, or having its origin in the timeless
Will—while other weaknesses and their continuance, may be results of
the present Organization of the Body, and which as far as they are (as
many as are known of them) condemned by the Soul, and contrary to its
maxim = regula maxima,[1] will of themselves cease, and die with the
⟨mistuned⟩ instrument of which they are the Discords. Now the Con-
quest of the Soul thro' Christ over this Spiritual Evil can be known to
God only, and never ascertained by the Soul itself in her present state—
& yet the general Consideration may supply an additional ground of

---

ᵃ The annotation is written in the head-margin; the same asterisk in textus also corresponds to that at
the beginning of **30**, written in the foot-margin
ᵇ "be" omitted

29[1] *AR* (1825) 291–4 carries an ex-
tended discussion of the distinction be-
tween the doctrine of original sin which
"gives to all the other Mysteries of Reli-
gion a common Basis" and "the mon-
strous fiction of Hereditary Sin, Guilt in-
herited"—but there C evidently intends
"hereditary sin" in a different sense. The

central text for C's views on original sin is
AR (1825) 251–87.
30[1] "Greatest rule, highest exam-
ple"—C's customary etymology for
"maxim", which he carefully differenti-
ated from "principle" or "idea": cf
Friend (*CC*) ɪ 425, *C&S* (*CC*) 84, *TT* 24
Jun 1827. Cf Nɪᴄᴏʟᴀɪ **25** n 1.

Comfort both to the sincere Striver after Holiness, and to the Surviving of Friends of those who have died a premature or sudden death/.

31 II 152

That Baptism hath a power, is clear, in that it is so expressly said, *it doth save us*: what kind of power, is equally clear from the way it is here expressed; not by a natural force of the element; though adapted and sacramentally used, it only can wash away the filth of the body; its physical efficacy or power reaches no further: but it is in the hand of the Spirit of God, as other sacraments are, and as the word itself is, *to purify the conscience, and convey grace and salvation to the soul, by the reference it hath to, and union with, that which it represents. It saves *by the answer of a good conscience unto God*, and it affords that, *by the resurrection of Jesus from the dead.*

* and (L. should have added) *as* a *word*, or visual Language.

32 II 152–5 | Continuing **31** textus

Thus, then, we have a true account of the power of this, and so, of other sacraments, and a discovery of the error of two extremes: † (1.) Of those who ascribe too much to them, as if they wrought by a natural inherent virtue, and carried grace in them inseparably. (2.) Of those who ascribe too little to them, making them only signs and badges of our profession.

*†ᵃ but Leighton will have Baptism—the visible physical immersion in water, or rather the Water itself after ~~the~~ its sacramerdotal consacration[1]—a co-agent in the purifying of the conscience, in the working of Faith, and in the Conveying of Christ into the Soul, and a partaker of the *Spiritual* efficacy.[2] Now this I humbly yet firmly hold to be unscriptural and contrary to Scripture/ precluded by the Spirit of the New Testament throughout and contradicted even by the Letter in more than one express Text.[3] As well might it be said, that the Word, Water,

---

ᵃ C has written two indicators, as referring to textus of both **31** and **32**

32[1] The irregular spelling (C himself uses "consecrated" in the postscript below) is either a slip, C perhaps thinking of the late Latin *consacrare*, or a deliberate emphasis by etymology on the process of making something holy, "sacred".

32[2] Leighton's commentary continues on the same text, 1 Pet 3.21: "The like figure whereunto even baptism doth also now save us (not the putting away of the filth of the flesh, but the answer of a good con-

science toward God,) by the resurrection of Jesus Christ". C objects especially to the statement in the textus of **33**, in which Leighton ascribes spiritual efficacy to the water used in baptism rather than to the active participation of the Holy Spirit. C's views on baptism, and specifically his opposition to infant baptism, are outlined in *AR* (1825) 354–76.

32[3] C may have in mind the text under discussion here, 1 Pet 3.21 (q n 2 above);

had the property of Water in removing the filth of the flesh, as that the Sign, Water, had the efficacy of the B̶ Repentance (μετανοια)[4] and Belief signified thereby.—*ᵃ*P.S. It is well worthy of Observation, that Leighton's assertion of a Power in the Baptismal Water *as* that *Water*, which is not the same with the power of God acting spiritually in the Baptism, and yet by reason of which it may be *truly* said (i.e. in the literal sense of the words) to sanctify, and justify and so to save—& in like manner o̶f̶ in the consecrated Elements of the Eucharist—this his assertion, I say, is left by him a mere and naked assertion, an απαξ λεγομενον,[5] without any inference drawn therefrom in the subsequent Comment—nay, with so entire a præterition[6] of the dogma, that all that follows might well seem to imply an ignorance of the same or to have been intended for its confutation. The dangerous propinquity of this dogma to the Doctrine and Narrations of the Zoo-magnetists of the Post-kantean Physiosophic School has been elsewhere noticed by me, in reference to the miracles of the Second Century.[7]   S. T. C.—

33   ii 153

The mistake on both sides [between those who ascribe too much to sacraments, as if they "carried grace in them inseparably", and those who ascribe too little to them, "making them only signs and badges of our profession"], arises from the want of duly considering the relative nature of these seals, and that kind of union that is betwixt them and the grace they represent, which is real, though not natural or physical, as they speak; so that, though they do not save all who partake of them, yet, they do really and effectually save believers, (for whose salvation they are means,) as the other external ordinances of God do. Though they have not that power which is peculiar to the Author of them, yet, a power they have, such as befits their nature, and by reason of which,

---

ᵃ The postscript follows without paragraph break but with a change of ink and in a smaller hand

---

another important text, apparently alluded to in C's next sentence, is Matt 3.11: "I indeed baptize you with water unto repentance (μετάνοια): but he that cometh after me is mightier than I, whose shoes I am not worthy to bear: he shall baptize you with the Holy Ghost, and with fire".

32[4] See n 3.

32[5] "Unique utterance".

32[6] Or "preterition", passing by, passing over.

32[7] In CHILLINGWORTH COPY B **11**. The term "physiosophic" (referring to German *Naturphilosophie*) in conjunction with animal magnetism appears also in EICHHORN *Alte Testament* **18**. As this note suggests, C's principal writings on animal magnetism are generally concerned with the implications for miracles of the investigation of animal magnetism: BM Add MS 34225 ff 146–7, BM Add MS 36532 ff 5, 7–12.

they are truly said to sanctify and justify, and so, to save, as the Apostle here avers of Baptism.

Nay! the very contrary.

33A II 157

. . . yea, not a day ought to pass without a ¢Session of conscience within . . .

34 II 163–5, marked with lines in ink

We would willingly have all religion reduced to externals; this is our natural choice; and we would pay all in this coin, as cheaper and easier by far, and would compound for the spiritual part, rather to add and give more external performance and ceremony. Hence, the natural complacency in Popery*ᵃ* . . . Spir. But whither tends all this? Is it not a gross mistaking of God, to think Him thus pleased? Or, is it not a direct affront, knowing that He is not pleased with these, but ~~desires~~ calls for*ᵇ* another thing, to thrust that upon Him which He cares not for, and refuse Him what He calls for?—*ᶜ*that single, humble heart-worship and walking with Him, that purity of spirit and conscience which only He prizes;*ᵈ* . . . * Give me, saith He, nothing, if you give not this. Oh! saith the carnal mind, any thing but this Thou shalt have; as many washings and offerings as Thou wilt, *thousands of rams, and ten thousand rivers of oil;* yea, rather than fail, *let the fruit of my body go for the sin of my soul.* Mic. vi. 6. Thus we: will the outward use of the word and sacraments do it? then, all shall be well. Baptized we are; and shall I hear much and communicate often, if I can reach it? Shall I be exact in point of family-worship? Shall I pray in secret? *ᵉ** All this I do, or at least I now promise. Aye, but when all that is done, there is yet one thing may be wanting, and if it be so, all that amounts to nothing. Is thy conscience purified and made good by all these; †or art thou seeking and aiming at this, by the use of all means? Then, certainly thou shalt find life in them. ~~But does thy heart still remain uncleansed from the old ways, not purified from the pollutions of the world? Do thy beloved sins still lodge with thee, and keep possession of thy heart?~~ But does this World still lodge with thee? Or does a loveless self-seeking Pride keep possession

---

ᵃ First ink line ends here (five lines following being omitted)

ᵇ C has written his emendation above "desires" without cancelling that word

ᶜ⁻ᵈ Originally marked for omission by dots in margin, but restored by an ink line drawn around the words and straight line over the dots; rest of sentence omitted, as dots in margin direct

ᵉ C's footnote indicator is repeated: both refer to his note below

of thy Heart? Then &c Then art thou still a stranger to Christ, and an enemy to God. The word and seals of life are dead to thee, and thou art still dead in the use of them all. Know you not, that many have made shipwreck upon the very rock of salvation?[a] . . . There are still multitudes running headlong that same course, tending to destruction by the saddest of all the sad ways to it, through the midst of all the means of salvation; by the saddest way of all to it, through word and sacraments, and all heavenly ordinances, to be walking hell-wards! Christians and yet no Christians; baptized and yet unbaptized!

  * Mem.—Quote from the Friend, Vol. I, p. 86,[1] and *insert*, †

  † And have you tried ~~the~~ its goodness by the only test, ~~the~~ your God-likeness—which yet you cannot securely apply without having the true, tho' inadequate, Idea of God present to your Spirit?

35 ɪɪ 172–5 | 1 Pet 3.22

* A parcel of clay is made so bright, and set so high, as to outshine those bright flaming spirits, those Stars of the morning, that flesh being united to the Fountain of Light, the blessed Deity in the person of the Son.

* The blazing Ruby is, if I remember aright, $^{99}/_{100}$ pure Clay;[1] but alas! when we are speaking of an organized material *Body*, the identity being at no time other than the Continuance of the same *Form* (Stedfastness of Form in Flux of Parts) it is extremely difficult to attach a meaning to our words, or to satisfy our minds that we ~~mean any thing~~ have any meaning at all.[2] Leighton was too meek and single-hearted to permit me to suspect, that such passages as this are the Clay-hovels, in which his Philosophy lurks in disguise, as knowing herself outlawed & with a price set on her head, by Bigotry and purblind Superstition. What shall we say then? Even this: that Leighton was not at home in the Science of Symbols[3]—had looked at it from a distance, ~~though~~ feared that it would

***

[a] First ink line ends here, for omission of several lines, and resumes at "There are still"

34[1] C's page reference is to the 1818 *Friend*. The passage from *Friend*, (*CC*) ɪ 55–6, was expanded to become Introductory Aphorism 18 in *AR* (1825) 10–11, but neither the passage composed for insertion below nor the passage from Leighton was in the end used.

35[1] C's chief source for such chemical lore confirms C's statement without actually supplying a figure: W. T. Brande *Man-*

ual of Chemistry (2nd ed 1819) 330 analyses the ruby as composed of "nearly pure" alumina—the earth that is also the chief constituent of most clays.

35[2] For the significance of the concept of "body" see ɪʀᴠɪɴɢ *Sermons* **29** n 12.

35[3] C attempted to remedy this weakness by the sophisticated account of symbols in *AR* (1825), esp 198–9.

take him too far out of his road to visit it, and in the mistaken supposition that Edifice lay out of the broad practical High-way took a circuit, and passed it!—But I must not fear to add, that the mistook a ~~track~~ path hoofed by the Multitude, a Cattle-track, for the King's own High-way—which tho' narrow and winding over heights, command~~ing~~ed large & exalted views, and avoided the miry Ruts and too frequent Mal Aria[4] of the ~~Valley~~ Road in the bottom/.   S. T. C.

35A   II 199, marked with a line in ink[a] | 1 Pet 4.2–3 | *AR* 123–4, Moral Aphorism 48

M.Aph.49   Th~~ye~~ heart may be engaged in ~~thy~~ a little business as much, if thou watch it not, as in many and great affairs. A man may drown in a little brook or pool, as well as in a great river, if he be down and plunge himself into it, and put his head under water. Some care thou must have, that thou mayest not care. Those things that are thorns indeed, thou must make a hedge of them, to keep out those temptations that accompany sloth, and extreme want that waits on it; but let them be the hedge: suffer them not to grow within the garden.

36   II 208–10 | 1 Pet 4.4–5

. . . *they speak evil of you*; and what is their voice? * What mean these precise fools? will they readily say. What course is this they take, contrary to all the world? Will they make a new religion, and condemn all their honest, civil neighbours that are not like them?

* This Description and the Confirmation following[1] are of frequent recurrence in Leighton; but I fear that they do not hit the mark—or at best but the Rim of the Target. As far as I have seen, the sanctified methodistical manners, that alone excite the remarks and questions here attributed to the worldly-men, are really suspicious if not disgusting—and the Methodist is ~~si~~amply repaid for the occasional expressions of this disgust by the intense Sympathy & flatteries of the like-minded with himself. And after all, the dislike excited is of a very superficial character, and the martyrdoms of the⟨se⟩ Outsides of Godliness not very formidable—compared with the hatred in the depth, when not the Eye of the Thoughtless but the Heart of the World is touched/ Attack the doctrines

[a] A pencil line against the first line of the preceding paragraph on this page, and another on the paragraph ending at the top of p 201, may indicate that C intended to quote more

35[4] "Bad Air", from the Italian *mal'aria*: see *OED* "malaria".

36[1] Leighton goes on in the same vein, imitating the scoffers, and then writes (II 208), "He that is acquainted with the ways of holiness, can more than endure the counter-blasts and airs of scoffs and revilings; he accounts them his glory and his riches."

of Self-love, the slang of the Motive-mongers,[2] whether on the Stock-exchange, or St George's Church,[3] or at the Bethels & Ebenezers[4]—or at the table of Mr Wilberforce or Miss Hannah More[5]—& you will soon find out the difference.

36A II 211–21, marked in ink | 1 Pet 4.6 | *AR* 124, Moral Aphorism 49

M.Aph.50   It is a strange folly in multitudes of us, to set ourselves no mark, to propound no end in the hearing of the Gospel. The merchant sails not merely that he may sail, but for traffic, and traffics that he may be rich. The husbandman plows not merely to keep himself busy with no further end, but plows that he may sow, and sows that he may reap with advantage. And shall we do the most excellent and fruitful work fruitlessly, hear only to hear, and look no further? This is indeed a great vanity, and a great misery, to lose that labour, and gain nothing by it, which, duly used, would be of all others most advantageous and gainful: and yet all meetings are full of this!

37   II 215–17

. . . that *you may be judged according to men in the flesh, but live according to God in the spirit.*

I have not been able to satisfy my mind altogether respecting the sense of this very difficult Text. One thing, however, seems evident: that it was written under a very strong persuasion and expectation of a very speedy Approach of the End of the World and the re-appearance of Christ, and in the belief that the Christians existing at that time would not die, but be transfigured. It seems likewise that the Writer of this Epistle supposed that the Converts or the Elect who had died or who should die during the brief Interim between Christ's Ascension and his Second Coming or ~~glor~~ triumphant Descent, were comparatively so small a number as to form a mere exception to the Rule.—And where is the Harm of this Interpretation—when the Apostolic Writer himself has put us on our guard by declaring that he had no revelation on this point—

36^2 C attacks two popular eighteenth-century approaches to moral philosophy, the "doctrine of self-love" associated with Helvétius and others (cf *Friend—CC*—I 424), and the concept of "motives", a term (used by Locke among others, and much used in the necessitarian debates of the 1790s by Priestley and Price) which suggests mechanical operations, and to which C preferred "moral impulses": *Friend* (*CC*) II 18.

36^3 I.e., by synecdoche, the business world or fashionable religion. C may be referring specifically to St George's, Hanover Square, a fashionable church completed in 1724.

36^4 Contemptuous shorthand for dissenting chapels.

36^5 Eminent evangelicals associated with one another in the Clapham Sect. For the link between Hannah More and C's reading of Leighton see COPY A headnote.

that it was a mere inference of his own/ and that those who interpreted the words of the Lord ~~in the~~ moré spirituali & propheticalo,[1] viz. that a thousand years are but a Lord's Day, were as much privileged as himself in the literal interpretation.[2] Harm indeed? Ought we not rather to consider such passages in the New Testament as providential—inasmuch as they enable us to answer the very startling & plausible Objection of the Infidels from the almost universal Mistake of the primitive Christians in this respect by proof positive, that they had, ~~no~~ & confessed that they had, no authority from Christ or from Inspiration for this Belief—which rested on an uninspired Comment, ~~an unre~~ mere tho' an apostolic Conjecture?

37A II 218, marked with a line in ink

Spiritual/   David did not disdain the fellowship of the saints, and that it was no disparagement to him, is implied in the name he gives them, Psal. xvi. 2, *the excellent ones*, the magnific or noble, *adiri*: that word is taken from one that signifies a robe or noble garment, *adereth, toga magnifica*; so he thought them nobles and kings as well as he; *[a]they had *robes royal*, and therefore were fit companions of kings. A spiritual eye looks upon spiritual dignity, and esteems and loves them who are *born of God*, how low soever be their natural birth and breeding.

* /\ A spiritual Eye looks upon Spiritual Dignity, and in the ~~Loves~~ Thoughts, Actions, and Affections of *the Excellent ones* ~~beholdeth~~ contemplates their Robes of Royalty, and in the Fellowship of Saints beholds a Congress of Kings.

37B II 219, marked with a large pencil cross in the margin

Consider with thyself, whether thou hast any knowledge of the growth or deficiencies of this spiritual life; for it is here but begun, and breathes in an air contrary to it, and lodges in a house that often smokes and darkens it.

37C II 220, marked with a pencil cross in the margin

A slothful, unstirring life, will make a sickly, unhealthful life. Motion purifies and sharpens the spirits, and makes men robust and vigorous.

---

[a] Although he did not delete the words that follow, C intended to replace them with his own, as the annotation indicates

37[1] "In a spiritual and prophetic way".
37[2] Though the interpretation might be disputed, C appears to be thinking of verses from 2 Pet, possibly 1.20 ("no prophecy of the scripture is of any private interpretation") and 3.8 ("one day is with the Lord as a thousand years, and a thousand years as one day").

38 II 401–2 | Ps 4.5

The faith of Abraham was a sacrifice much dearer to God, not only than the ram which he actually offered, but even than his dearest son whom he had brought to the altar. *He was strong in faith*, says the Apostle, *and so he gave glory to God.*

Speaking of my own experience only, I do not hestitate to say, that this Sacrifice of Isaac[1]—unless I might consider the whole as taking place in a Vision: & even so yet if it is to be received as *exemplary*—is the most difficult passage in the sacred Scriptures. The moral difficulty is—What right had Abraham to conclude that it was God? The best solution, that I have found, is—that 1. it was *the Faith*, the unqualified Fealty that is exemplary; and 2. Abraham's numerous prior Experiences of intercourse with God, confirmed by the Results—

38A II 440–1, marked with lines in ink | Ps 130.3 | *AR* 125–6, Moral Aphorism 50

M.Aph.51   There have been great disputes one way and another, about the merit of good works; but I truly think they who have laboriously engaged in them, have been very idly, though very eagerly, employed about nothing, since the more sober of the schoolmen themselves acknowledge there can be no such thing as meriting from the blessed God, in the human, or, to speak more accurately, in any created nature whatsoever: nay, so far from any possibility of merit, there can be no room for reward any otherwise than of the sovereign pleasure and gracious kindness of God; and the more ancient writers, when they use the word merit, mean nothing by it but a certain *correlate* to that reward which God both promises and bestows of mere grace and benignity. Otherwise, in order to constitute what is properly called merit, many things must concur, which no man in his senses will presume to attribute to human works, though ever so excellent; particularly, that the thing done must not previously be matter of debt, and that it be entire, or our own act, unassisted by foreign aid; it must also be perfectly good, and it must bear an adequate proportion to the reward claimed in consequence of it. If all these things do not concur, the act cannot possibly amount to merit. Whereas I think no one will venture to assert, that any one of these can take place in any human action whatever. But why should I enlarge here, when one single circumstance overthrows all those titles: the most righteous of mankind would not be able to stand, if his works were weighed in the balance of strict justice; how much less then could they deserve that immense glory which is now in question! Nor is this to be denied

38[1] Gen 22.1–18.

only concerning the unbeliever and the sinner, but concerning the righteous and pious believer, who is not only free from all the guilt of his former impenitence and rebellion, but endowed with the gift of the Spirit. The interrogation here expresses the most vehement negation, and signifies that no mortal, in whatever degree he is placed, if he be called to the strict examination of Divine Justice, without daily and repeated forgiveness, could be able to keep his standing, and much less could he arise to that glorious height. "That merit," says Bernard, "on which my hope relies, consists in these three things; the love of adoption, the truth of the promise, and the power of its performance⸭."*a* This is the threefold cord which cannot be broken.   M.Aph.51

39   II   [536],*b* pencil

Mess*rs* Mant and D'Oyley entertain no doubt that there are myriads of Christians baptized in infancy who pass from the cradle to the grave without any remorse of conscience, or act of special Conversion toward God & without any reason or occasion for such[1]—They cannot deny the temptibility, *supposing* (alas! what a supposition!) nothing worse— but this they hold guiltless, blameless, on the same footing with the body's sensibility to pain.—Do these men treat their Maker and Redeemer as they expect to be themselves treated—What? if M. knew that his Betrothed was hourly feeling, tho' preventing it from passing into act, lust & desire to other men?—

40   II   +1, pencil*c*

Having explained and discriminated my plan and ~~purpose or~~ object, I must now state my Dative Case, Object of the Object—viz. Young Students *for* and *in* the Ministry—⟨2⟩ Educated men of all ages & professions who receiving Xtnty generally are not clear as to certain doctrines,

---

a Cancel and cancellation symbol in the margin in pencil; the Latin footnote answering to this asterisk is also marked in pencil for deletion

b Verso of the last page of text, with printer's imprint

c At the head of the leaf, in pencil, probably not in C's hand: "Leighton's Volume 2"

39[1] An assertion reiterated in *AR* (1825) 373n. Richard Mant (1776–1848), bp of Down, Connor, and Dromore, with George D'Oyly (1778–1846) published for the Society for Promoting Christian Knowledge a variorum edition of *The Holy Bible, with Notes Explanatory and Practical* (3 vols Oxford 1814). The reference here may be to the comment on Rom. 6.9–11 taken from Thomas Secker (1693–1768): "When the infants of believers are baptized, they are, by the solemnity which Heaven hath appointed, 'born again of water and the Spirit,' John iii.5, into a better state than that of nature. And till either sort of person forfeit their claim by wilful wickedness . . . they continue heirs of everlasting life": D'Oyly and Mant (2nd ed Oxford 1817–18) III.

or staggered by certain difficulties in the books of Scripture or in its external evidence, or who wish to see Religion as a total Scheme[1]—As for the wholly unawakened, in health & denying the very ground—their hour is not come/—for the opposite Class, I am persuaded that 100 pages of Leighton read conscientiously would avail more in the way of conviction than all the systematic Reasoning in the world—And yet I humbly hope that some preparation, some pioneering for the production of that susceptible state, in which L. & his Compeers can be fruitfully read by the great ends proposed in my work—viz. the toto genere diversity[2] of the Spiritual from the notional no less than from the carnal (Faith the *Substance*, the Spirit the Stasis itself)[3] from the *verily* and *indeed* of the Incarnation and Death on the Cross[4]—and the inward conviction that those Doctrines which the poor Heart craves and humbly moans for, are either Reason itself, or required by Reason, or at least agreeable to reason.—

41   III 3–4, pencil | Matt 1.1

The great diversity of the names from David to Joseph, (of them all indeed, save two,) has drawn several persons to take the one for the line of Joseph, the other for the line of Mary. * But the diversity of names ariseth not so much from the custom of that nation, of one person having divers names, (which commonly is answered in this,) though somewhat of that may be in it; but it is much rather from that, it seems, St. Matthew does deduce the legal succession in government (by Solomon), St. Luke the natural in birth (by Nathan).

* Now seriously it is aweful that such palpable and bungling Evasions as these, which if admitted would over rule all criteria of authentic History and vagabond Tradition should have satisfied such a mind as Leighton's! One of the most candid & learned Biblical Divines, I ever met with, tho' a Jew,[1] assured me that there was no fair way of reconciling the two Pedigrees—but that nothing was more common than such jarring Duplicates among the Jewish Families after the time of the Macca-

---

40[1] Apparently an early draft of the statement, in *AR* (1825) vi–vii, about the audience for whom the work was intended.
40[2] "The absolute diversity in kind".
40[3] *Substantia* and ὑπόστασις (*hypostasis*) being Latin and Greek equivalents, faith is the *sub*-stans (that which stands *under*), and spirit the "standing" (*stasis*): cf **12** above and n 18.

40[4] The syntax here is a little confusing: C may have intended to suggest that the corporeal insistence of the NT, if not further ratified by the spiritual, is in danger of being no more than a "carnal" truth.
41[1] Almost certainly Hyman Hurwitz (c 1775–1844), C's neighbour at Highgate and founder of a Hebrew school there: see HURWITZ headnote.

bees.[2] The Compiler of our Matthew had met with one, & ~~that~~ Luke another.

41A   iii 9, marked with a pencil line | Matt 2.1–2

Sure I am, to make them *three* to fit their number to their presents, and to make kings of them, and give them names, and then to wrangle about their burial-place, is to play the fool about the *wise men*.

41B   iii 20, marked with lines in ink | Matt 3.1 | *AR* 354–5, Spiritual Aphorism "On Baptism"

I will not here speak of the nature of Baptism, the combinement of preaching with it, their aspect each to the other, and concurrence to one excellent end; the word unfolding the sacrament, and the sacrament sealing the word; the word, as a light, informing and clearing the sense of the seal, and it again, as a seal, confirming and ratifying the truth of the word: as you see some significant seals or signets engraven, have a word about them expressing their sense.

But truly, the word is a light, and the sacraments have in them of the same light illuminating them; and this of Baptism, the ancients do particularly express by light. Yet are they both nothing but darkness to us, till the same light shine in our hearts; for till then, we are nothing but darkness ourselves, and therefore the most luminous things are so to us: noonday is as midnight to a blind man. And we use these ordinances, the word and the sacrament, without profit and comfort for the most part, because we have not of that Divine light within us; and we have it not, because we ask it not,/[a] are not often there where it is to be had, nor earnest suitors for it: for we have His word that cannot fail, that our Heavenly Father will give even this choice gift, this light, (for that is it,) His *Holy Spirit to them that ask it*. Then would word and sacrament be sweet to us, which now are so lifeless and unsavoury.

41C   iii 41, marked in the margin with a large pencil cross | Matt 5.1–12

The pure in heart, abridging themselves of sights and enjoyments that the world seeks after—sensual delights, *the lust of the flesh, the lust of the eyes, and the pride of life*,—shall have a better sight, and purer joy, suiting them; sweetest communion with God here, and ere long full vision: *for they shall see God*. So in the rest, it is clear.

---

[a] C has put "x" here, and encircled the remainder of the paragraph for omission

41[2] I.e. after the dynasty whose power extended from 168 B.C. to about 37 B.C., and whose history is recorded by Josephus and in the apocryphal 1 and 2 Macc; cf DAVISON **22**.

41D III 49, marked in the margin with a pencil cross | Matt 6.3

Then as to *Fasting*, which is a necessary help of Prayer; it does unclog and free the wings of the soul to mount to Heaven; and in some respects, it is a help to Alms too.

42 III ⁺2, pencil, referring to III 418–21

> 418.¹
> 420, 421 last & first line.²

42A III 418, marked with a line in pencil | Sermon 28, on John 21.22

Spir. Most men are beside themselves, never at home, but always roving. It is true, a man may live in solitude to little purpose, as Domitian catching flies in his closet. Many noisome thoughts break in upon one when alone; so that when one converseth with himself, it had need be said, *Vide ut sit cum bono viro* [See that he is with a good man]. A man alone shall be in worse company than are in all the world, if he bring not into him better company than himself or all the world, which is, the fellowship of God and the Holy Spirit.

42b III 419, marked with a pencil line

It is certainly a great error, to let our zeal run out from the excellent things of religion, to matters which have little or no connexion with them. A man, though he err, if he do it calmly and meekly, may be a better man than he who is stormy and furiously orthodox.

42C III 420, pencil

Some religious persons are perhaps weak persons, yet, in all ages, there have been greater, nobler, and more generous souls truly religious, than ever were in the whole tribe of atheists and libertines.

42D III 420–1, pencil, marked with a pencil line

All the sublimities of holiness may be arrived at, by ~~the~~ aᵃ deep and profound belief . . .

42E IV 2, marked with a line in pencil | *An Exposition of the Creed*

It is very hard to convince men of unbelief, directly and in itself.

42F IV 2, marked with a line in pencil

Are your consciences pure? Have you a living hatred and antipathy

---

ᵃ C's emendation is written above "the", which is not cancelled

42¹ The textus given as **42A** below.   42² **42D** below.

against all impurity? Then, surely, faith is there; for it is the peculiar virtue of faith to *purify the heart*, (Acts xv.9) and the heart so purified, is the proper residence of faith, where it dwells and rests as in its natural place. But have you consciences that can lodge pride, and lust, and malice, and covetousness, and such like pollutions? Then, be no more so impudent as to say, you believe, nor deceive yourselves so far as to think you do.

42G   iv 3, pencil, marked with a line in pencil

Sp. or Part 3.rd of the Extracts   Faith is either the doctrine which we believe, or that grace by which we believe that doctrine. Here, I conceive, it is both, met and united in the soul. As they say of the understanding in the schools, *Intelligendo fit illud quod intelligit* [By understanding it becomes what it understands], so, faith, apprehending its proper object, is made one with it.

42H   iv 4, marked with a line in pencil, insertion in pencil

~~As, in the Gospel,~~[a] Respecting the peculiar object of that faith which saves fallen man, it is all one whether we say it is Christ or the promises; for it is Christ revealed and held forth in the promises, that faith lays hold on. *In Him are all the promises of God Yea, and in him, Amen.* 2 Cor i. 20. So that it is all one act of faith that lays hold on Christ, and on the promises, for they are all one: he is in them, and therefore faith rests on them, because they include Christ who is our rest and our peace; as a man at once receives a ring and the precious stone that is set in it. This once rightly understood, any further dispute about placing faith in the understanding or in the will, is, possibly, in itself not at all needful: sure I am, it is no way useful for you.

42I   iv 5, marked with a pencil line

Whosoever they be who boast most in their own strength in any kind, and swell highest in conceit of it, they are yet but as a brittle glass in the hand of God: He can not only break it to pieces by the strength of His hand, but if He do but withdraw His hand from supporting it, it will fall and break of itself.

43   iv 6, indicators and insertion in pencil

The Son and the Spirit were, with the Father, authors of the Creation; but it is ascribed to the Father particularly, in regard of the order and

---

[a] First words not marked for cancellation, but caret inserted at this point

manner of Their working. * Whether natural reason may evince the creation of the world, we will not dispute . . .

* Here and throughout these volumes bear in mind that by "natural Reason", "human Reason", "the Reason of man" &c Leighton means, the power or faculty of ⟨Reason*ing*, i.e. of⟩ drawing conclusions from premises of Sense and Reflection.[1] In its highest and proper import, Reason does not *evince*, but *contain, present,* and affirm, Truths—T' αλη-θεα αχρονα.[2]

43A IV 7, marked with a pencil line

Quae scimus cùm necesse non est, ea in necessitate nescimus, says Bernard: The Things which we seem to know when it is not necessary for us to know them, we find, when necessary, that we know not.

43B IV 7, marked with a pencil line

What is it thou wouldst have done, that He cannot do if He think fit? And if He think it not fit, if thou art one of His children, thou wilt think with Him; thou wilt reverence His wisdom, and rest satisfied with His will. This is believing indeed . . .

44 IV 10–11, pencil

* This is that *great mystery of godliness, God manifested in the flesh*; the King of Glory after a manner divesting himself of his royal robes, and truly putting on *the form of a servant*, the Holy Ghost framing him a body in the virgin's womb.

* That this Text[1] refers to the miraculous *Conception* of Jesus, may be supposed but cannot be proved. It seems to me more in the spirit of St Paul's Writings in general, that the words simply express the same Doctrine as the first Chapter of St John's Gospel—"The Word became Flesh, and dwelt among us."[2]

45 IV 11, pencil

God was in Christ reconciling the world to himself. 2 Cor. iv. 19.

Considering the work to be done in this agreement . . . it was altogether needful that the Undertaker should be God and man. . . . * The

43[1] An important theme of *AR*, as noted in **12** above at nn 5, 6.

43[2] "Timeless truths": cf "eternal Ideas" in **50** below at n 4.

44[1] I.e. in the Apostles' Creed, ". . .

Jesus Christ his only Son our Lord, who was conceived by the Holy Ghost, Born of the Virgin Mary . . .".

44[2] John 1.14, "And the Word was made flesh, and dwelt among us".

mediation was not a bare matter of word, but there was such a wrong done as required a satisfaction should be made.

* It never ceases to be a *perplexer* to my mind, how such an Intellect as Leighton's could have consented with the Systematists in confounding St Paul's elucidations ⟨by various analogies⟩ of the beneficent *Effects* of the New Creation with a proper description of the mysterious Efficient itself.[1]

46 IV 13–16

That he died, and what kind of death, you see, is expressed. But as many particular sufferings of his body are not here mentioned, so, none of those of his soul, but all are comprehended in this general word, *He suffered.* . . . But surely, that invisible cup which came from his Father's hand, was far more bitter than the gall and vinegar from the hand of his enemies; the piercing of his soul, far sharper than the nails and thorns. He could answer these sweetly with, *Father, forgive them, for they know not what they do.* But those other pangs drew from him another kind of word, * *My God, my God, why has Thou forsaken me?*

* In order to console his Mother and the beloved Disciple^a our Lord quoted with a loud voice (*gave out,* as we now say) the 22nd Psalm, which having prophecied those very Sufferings which John and Mary were then beholding, with all the Liveliness and minute Circumstantiality of historic Detail, concludes by predicting the final Triumph and Universality of the Faith in the crucified Saviour.[1] You *see* the fulfilment of the one, the dolorous, Half of the Prophecy: can you doubt as to ⟨the⟩ fulfilment of the other half, full of Glory and Joy?—This sublime proof of wisdom in the exceeding propriety and efficacy of the Comfort given, and of ⟨the Giver's⟩ self-suspending Love and Sympathy even in the agony of his Suffering, forms the true interpretation of this Text, and not any reference to the hypostatic Union, or its hypothetical Eclipse, an Eclipse of which not even a Hint is to be found in Scripture, and by which no one Divine has been able to explain what is meant or ~~by it~~ to be understood. The Article of the Tri-unity, and of the proper Divinity of Christ, as the Incarnate Word, needs not such weak Props. It is built on^e and out of the Rock of Ages!

^{a} Written as "the beloved Disciple and his Mother" but marked for transposition by numbers over the words

45[1] This is the problem addressed by C's exposition of the use of metaphor by Paul in *AR* (1825) 198–200, 311–26.

46[1] This is consistently C's interpretation of Matt 27.46, Mark 15.34: cf IRVING *Sermons* **21**.

47 IV 14 and pp ⁻2–⁻1, referring to IV 14

Descended into hell.

See the blank leaf at the beginning of this Volume.[1]

P. 14. Descended into Hell (Hades)

I hold it *probable*, that this clause was *added* to the original Creed, after the *Spread* of the Gnostic Heresy or rather Heresies—and when the gnostics had become a powerful and numerous Sect.[2] But it is not *necessary* ⟨to suppose this.⟩ For even during the Life of Sᵗ John, the ⟨Gnostic⟩ Opinion had been taken up, that the Logos was instead of a Soul to the Body of Christ, and that his apparent Death consisted in a temporary withdrawing of the Logos from the Body—and [? in t] no less was the conceit already in bud and blossom, that the Body of Christ was a celestial Phantasma, in confutation of which Sᵗ John states on the evidence of his own Eyes that the Blood which flowed from the wound of the Javelin, was true and mere human Blood, consisting of Lymph (or Serum) and Crassament—(see Tertullian and Origen) and no celestial Ichor.[3] (These are Origen's own words who quotes the passage from the Iliad, in elucidation).[4] This the German, Lessius, for the first time about the middle of the last century converted into the monstrous Conceipt of the ½ oz of watry fluid sometimes found in the Præcordia, & which some Physiologists have supposed in all cases to follow and result from "*the Stimulus of Death*"[5]—a conceipt eagerly embraced by the Grotians and Minimifidian Quasi-Christians—to the sly merriment of the infidel portion of our learned Naturalists.[6]

47[1] I.e. IV ⁻2–⁻1, on which the remainder of this note is written.

47[2] C refers to the evolution of the Apostles' Creed in a similar way elsewhere, e.g. LUTHER *Colloquia* **23**. The chief source of his historical information about the Creed was John Pearson *An Exposition of the Creed* (12th ed 1741): see PEARSON. C's general opinion of the Gnostics is summed up in EICHHORN *Neue Testament* COPY B **5**; and cf *CN* IV 4626, cited n 3 below.

47[3] The text at issue is John 19.34: "But one of the soldiers with a spear pierced his side, and forthwith came there out blood and water." Towards the end of 1819, C made notes on a German article about the theological debate over this verse: *CN* IV 4626. K. G. Schuster's article in Eichhorn's *Allgemeine Bibliothek der biblischen Litteratur* IX 953–1104 supplied C with the Gnostic context and with several

useful references, including Tertullian *De carne Christi* (esp chs 5, 9: *Tertullian's Treatise on the Incarnation* ed Ernest Evans—1956—19, 37–9) and the Origen of n 4 below.

47[4] Origen *Contra Celsum* 2.36, quoting Homer *Iliad* 5.340: *CN* IV 4626.

47[5] "Lessius" is K. R. Less, in his *Auferstehungsgeschichte Jesu* (Göttingen 1779) 108. The theory is derived—without circumstantial particulars—from Schuster (n 3 above). C refers to this theory of "some modern Germans" in *TT* 6 Jan 1823. The phrase in quotation marks is John Hunter's, e.g. in the controversial chapter "Of the Living Principle of the Blood" in *A Treatise on the Blood, Inflammation, and Gun-shot Wounds* ed Everard Home (1794) 87. The "praecordia" is the area around the heart.

47[6] For "Minimifidian", "believing as little as possible", see **12** n 1 above. For

But, to return from this Digression, these Heresies were in existence in the Apostolic & succeeding Age, ~~whether~~ tho' the Name of Gnostic, and a separate Sect ~~might~~ay have been of later date.—Likewise, it is not impossible, tho' I readily admit ~~not~~ highly ⟨im⟩probable, that the Objection—~~of~~ Where is the proof, that this was not a case of Suspended Animation? might have been anticipated. Now ~~to~~ of all these Conceits of Misbelief or Scruples of Unbelief the Clause in question contains a renunciation—the sense being this—Whatever takes place in and for all Men by consequence of Death, that entire separation of the *Vital Principle*, whatever ⟨it⟩ be, from the Body, that took place in the Death of Jesus. That which happens to the invisible Adjunct of the living Body, and by which it lives, when the Individuals actually *die*, happened in the disanimation on the Cross. The *Body* of Christ was substantially, and indeed, and not merely phænomenally, the same as every other's Man's Body—as like to John's as John's to Peter. The invisible Adjunct likewise was of the same kind—and to the place or state of this Adjunct after its separation from the Body, in the case of every other Man from Adam to Christ, did it retire in the case of Christ himself. VERÈ *mortuus est*, is the whole and sole meaning of the Clause.[7] Previously to his Resurrection, he was as truly dead as a Man who had been dead six months, and his body already disorganized. Hence if it were Gospel Doctrine that the *rational* Belief of a future State rested ~~wholly~~ on the Resurrection, the Raising of Lazarus might be considered as supplementary by anticipation, and completory of the Evidence afforded by the Resurrection of Christ: in as much as the Criterion of Putridity had taken place in the former tho not in the latter instance.[8]   S. T. C.

47A IV 15, marked with ink lines

Were it as common to believe in him, as to repeat these words [the Creed], or to come to church and hear this gospel preached, then you would all make a pretty good plea on it. But believe it, it is another kind of thing to believe than all that, or than any thing that the most of us yet know. My brethren, do not deceive yourselves. That common highway faith will not serve. . . .*a* It is such a faith as endears Christ to the soul, unites it to him, makes Christ and it one, that makes all that is his to become ours.

a The rest of this sentence and the two sentences following (elided here) marked by dots and symbol for omission

"Grotians" see LUTHER *Colloquia* **4** n 1 and **80** n 3.

47[7] "He *really* died": cf DONNE *Sermons* COPY B **125** n 3, LUTHER *Colloquia*

23.

47[8] The story of Lazarus raised from the dead is in John 11.1–44.

47B ɪᴠ 26, marked in ink

We are gaping still after new notions, but a few things wisely and practically known, drawn down from the head into the heart, are better than all that variety of knowing that men are so taken up with.

47C ɪᴠ 27, marked in ink

Did we think of this Gospel which we preach and hear, *a*as of that by which we must be judged in the time to come, we should be more ruled by it in the present time. ~~that we must then be judged by it, we should be now more ruled by it.~~ But the truth is, we are willingly forgetful of these things; they are melancholy, pensive thoughts, and we are content that the noise of affairs or any vanities fill the ears of our minds, that we hear them not. If we be forced at some times to hear of this last judgement to come, it possibly casts our conscience into some little trembling fit for the time, as it did Felix; but he was not, nor are we, so happy as to be shaken out of the custom and love of sin by it. We promise it fair, as he did, some other time; but if that time never come, this day will come, and they who shun to hear or think of it, shall then see it, and the sight of it will be as terrible and amazing, as the timely thoughts of it would have been profitable. It is, no doubt, an unpleasing subject to all ungodly, earthly minds; but surely, it were our wisdom to be of that mind now, that then we shall be forced to be of: we shall then read, by the light of that fire which shall burn the world, the vanity of all those things whereon we now doat so foolishly.

48 ɪᴠ 28, marked with an ink line

Yea, the great design of God in the other great work, that of the first creation, was this second: He made the world, that out of it He might make this *elect world*, which is called His Church. The Son fell ~~on~~ asleep, ~~on~~*b* into a dead sleep, **~~indeed the sleep of death~~c* on the cross, that out of his side might be framed his Spouse, which is his Church.

* See Genesis II. The Hebrew word signifies *a Trance*[1]

---

a Here C has written a caret and has labelled his insertion in the head-margin "l. 8''; there is a second caret after "must then'', and the passage here cancelled (to show C's intention) has not been cancelled by him

b The two "on''s not cancelled; C's correction written over the words

c Words marked with parentheses for omission

48[1] C alludes to the creation of Eve in Gen 2.21–2, where, however, in the phrase "God caused a deep sleep to fall upon Adam'' the usual Hebrew verb for "sleep''—*yashen*—is used, rather than "trance'' (*radam*, as in Prov 10.5, Jonah 1.6). But *radam* in Ps 76.6 ("cast into a dead sleep'') and Dan 8.18, 10.9 ("I was in a deep sleep'') may have led C to suppose that the source word had been used of Adam.

48A IV 188, marked with a line in ink; cf IV ⁺1 **(58)** | *Theological Lectures*

. . . hHe that conveys the principles of virtue and wisdom into the minds of the lower classes of men, or the illiterate, whatever progress his disciples may make, employs his time and talents only for the advantage of his pupils; but he that forms the minds of magistrates and great men, or such as are intended for high and exalted stations, by improving one single person, becomes a benefactor to large and numerous societies.

48B IV 192, marked with a line in pencil

But it must be acknowledged, that the belief of these things [a "celestial life" of "riches" etc] is far from being common. What a rare attainment is faith, seeing that among the prodigious crowds of those who profess to believe, in this world, one might justly cry out, Where is a true believer to be found? That man shall never persuade me, that he believes the truth and certainty of heavenly enjoyments, who cleaves to this earth, nay, who does not scorn and despise it, with all its baits and allurements, and employ all his powers, as well as his utmost industry, to obtain these immense and eternal blessings.

49 IV 193, marked with pencil lines, annotation in pencil; cf IV ⁺1 **(58)**

Try an experiment, attended with no danger or expense. . . . For this purpose, I earnestly recommend to you, to be constant and assiduous in prayer. Nay, it is St. Paul's exhortation, that you *pray without ceasing.* 1 Thes. v. 17. So that Prayer may be, not only, according to the old saying, *Clavis diei, et sera noctis,* The key that opens the day, and the lock that shuts up the night; but also, so to speak, a staff for support in the day-time, and a bed for rest and comfort in the night; *two conveniences which are commonly expressed by one single Hebrew word. And be assured, that the more frequently you pray, with so much the greater ease and pleasure will your prayers be attended, not only from the common and necessary connexion between acts and habits, but also from the nature of this duty. For prayer, being a kind of conversation with God, gradually purifies the soul, and makes it continually more and more like unto Him. Our love to God is also very much improved by this frequent intercourse with Him; and by His love, on the other hand, the soul is effectually disposed to fervency, as well as frequency in prayer, and can, by no means, subsist without it.

* In what sense true?¹

49¹ Leighton invokes a famous crux, the fact that the same set of letters in Hebrew may (depending upon pointing) represent either of two different words—*matteh* ("staff") and *mittah* ("bed")—as seen in Gen 47.31 ("Israel bowed himself upon

49A   iv 195, marked with a pencil line; cf iv + 1 **(58)** | *AR* 22n (to Introductory Aphorism 29)[1]

This is what the schoolmen mean, when, in their manner of expression, they say, "That the will is carried towards happiness, not simply as will, but as nature."

It is true, indeed, the generality of mankind are not well acquainted with the motions of their own minds, nor at pains to observe them, but, like brutes, by a kind of secret impulse, are violently carried towards such enjoyments as fall in their way: they do but very little, or not at all, enter into themselves, and review the state and operations of their own minds; yet, in all their actions, all their wishes and desires, (though they are not always aware of it themselves,) this thirst after immortality exerts and discovers itself. Consider the busy part of mankind, hurrying to and fro in the exercise of their several professions, physicians, lawyers, merchants, mechanics, farmers, and even soldiers themselves; they all toil and labour, in order to obtain rest . . .

50   iv 196–9; cf iv + 1 **(58)**

And here it is to be, first of all, observed, that the transcendent and supreme end of all, is, the *glory of God;* *all things returning, in a most beautiful circle, to this, as the original source from which they at first took their rise.

* It is possible that the unripe age of Leighton's ⟨Pupils⟩ precluded it; but it is impossible not to regret that Leighton did not give a clearer & more distinct exposition of his Grounds—that he has*[a]* told us, what the exact meaning was which he attached to his fundamental terms—for instance, the *Glory* of God.[1] The right interpretation, I presume, is the manifestation of the Supreme Being, *as* the Supreme Being, in the Existent as existent. Thus: the Rays in their divergence from the Solar Unity (Apollo; from α not and polloi many)[2] are the Glory of the Sun, in the first & most proper sense—then the surrounding Clouds, pene-

---

a "Not" presumably omitted in error

---

the bed's head") and Heb 11.21 ("and worshipped, leaning upon . . . his staff"), both referring to the same event.

49A[1] The passage quoted from Leighton in *AR* in fact consists of a condensed version of several sentences preceding this marked textus, together with the first sentence of textus.

50[1] Cf a related note in Irving *Sermons* 15. "Glory" is one of a cluster of terms

associated with light and with the sun as source of light ("The earliest Symbol of the Tri-une God", as C says in Böhme **169**) that C, with biblical precedent, uses habitually in theological discussion—notably in *AR* (1825) 155, 197, 354.

50[2] The usual derivation for the name of Apollo, the sun god, is from ἀπόλλυμι, "destroy".

trated by the Rays and as it were, saturated with the Light, form a second Glory—~~th~~ viz. the ~~Reflection~~splendency of the Light, so that we behold the Light itself as well as the Objects *by* the Light—its *Glory* is spread out on the Earth.—The application of these to the Glory of God, is obvious. First, the Plerōma.[3] Host of Heaven unfallen—Ἰδέαι αἰώνιοι[a4] Second, moral and intelligential Creatures, capable of the Knowlege of God. Third, whatever unconsciously displays or is capable of displaying the Divine Attributes. To seek the *Glory* of God therefore is to seek all in all, ~~and~~ even to the filling of every Capacity in each. It is to seek whatever is good and seemly & perfect to the displacement & exclusion of all Evil, Disorder & Imperfection.

51 iv 196 | *AR* 32, Prudential Aphorism 1

Though I should not tell you, what is to be understood by the term *happiness* or *felicity* in general, I cannot imagine any of you would be at a loss about it. * Yet, I shall give a brief explication of it, that you may have the more distinct ideas of the thing itself, and the juster notions of what is to be further advanced on the subject. Nor is there, indeed, any controversy on this head; for all are agreed, that by the terms commonly used in Hebrew, Greek, and Latin to express happiness or felicity, we are to understand *that perfect and complete good, which is suited and adapted to intelligent nature.*

* An unhappy use of the term Happiness for that which excludes all Hap.—Good—Blessedness, Eupraxy.[1]

51A iv 198, marked with an ink line | *AR* 31, Prudential Aphorism 1

You will not, ~~I imagine~~, be offended, nor think I intend to insult you, ~~because~~ I ~~have~~ if once and again, with great earnestness and sincerity, I ~~wished~~ you and myself a sound and serious temper of mind; for, if we may represent things as they really are, very few men are possessed of so valuable a blessing. The far greater part of them are intoxicated either with the pleasures or the cares of this world; they stagger about with a tottering and unstable pace; and, as Solomon expresses it, *The labour of the foolish wearieth every one of them; because he knoweth not how to*

[a] A slip for αἰωνίαι

50[3] "Fulness", a term occurring 12 times in AV: cf C's use in COPY B **29** and n 1.

50[4] "Eternal Ideas": the adjective is used by Paul in 2 Cor 4.18.

51[1] A notebook entry of 1809 appears to be the first record of C's using the accepted root of the word to define "happiness" and to distinguish it from other conditions: *CN* III 3558. It is common in his work thereafter, e.g. *Op Max* III ff 42–3, *P Lects* Lect 3 (1949) 140–1.

go to the city: Eccl. x. 15:—the heavenly city, and the vision of peace, which very few have a just notion of, or are at pains to seek after. Nay, they know not what it is they are seeking. They flutter from one object to another, and live at hazard. They have no certain harbour in view, nor direct their course by any fixed star. But to him that knoweth not the port to which he is bound, no wind can be favourable; neither can he who has not yet determined at what mark he is to shoot, direct his arrow aright.

52 IV 200

We assert, then, that there is such a thing as human felicity. . . . But when I speak of human felicity, I am well satisfied you will not imagine, I mean such a happiness as may be had from human things, but that I take the term subjectively, and understand by it the happiness of man.*

* For the different senses of the useful & almost indispensable terms, Objective & Subjective, see Elements of Discourse by S. T. C.[1]

52A IV 201, marked with a line in ink | *AR* 32, Prudential Aphorism 2

. . . the whole human race must have been created in misery, and exposed to unavoidable torments, from which they could never have been relieved, had they been formed, not only capable of a good quite unattainable and altogether without their reach, but also with strong and restless desires towards that impossible good. Now, as this is by no means to be admitted, there must necessarily be some full, permanent, and satisfying good, that may be attained by man, and in the possession of which he must be truly happy.

53 IV 202, marked with a line in ink | *AR* 32–3, Prudential Aphorism 3

[a] . . . but *this* Book [the Bible] alone shews clearly, and with absolute certainty, what it [felicity] is, and points out the way that leads to the attainment of it.[b] This is that which prevailed with St. Augustine to study the Scriptures, and engaged his affection to them. * "In Cicero, and Plato, and other such writers," says he, "I meet with many things ~~wittily~~ acutely said, and things that ~~have a moderate tendency to move the passions~~ excite a certain warmth of emotion; but in none of them do I find these words, *Come unto me, all ye that labour, and are heavy laden, and I will give you rest . . .*"

[a–b] This portion of textus not marked

52[1] "Elements of Discourse" was one of the working titles of C's *Logic*, which was promised as forthcoming in *AR* (1825) 174*, 196. The definitions of "objective" and "subjective" appear in *Logic* (*CC*) 42; cf *BL* ch 10 (*CC*) I 172.

* The value of these writers, however, especially of Plato, in predisposing the mind to the reception of the Christian Faith, St Augustine himself elsewhere asserts on his own experience.[1]

54 IV 215

There are, indeed, very few demonstrations in philosophy, if you except mathematical sciences, that can be truly and strictly so called, and, if we inquire narrowly into the matter, perhaps we shall find none at all: *nay, if even the mathematical demonstrations are examined by the strict rules and ideas of Aristotle, the greatest part of them will be found imperfect and defective.

* Either these Demonstrations are not mathematical, or ~~Leighton~~ they must be strictly demonstrative. In either ~~Sens~~ case, it is plain that Leighton had not made himself Master of the Subject: as indeed few were, before the appearance of Kant's *Critique of the Pure Reason*.[1]

S. T. C.

54A IV 243–4, marked with a line in ink | *AR* 33–4, Prudential Aphorism 4

It is, ~~to be sure,~~ the wisdom of mankind to know God, and their indispensable duty, to worship Him. Without this, men of the brightest parts and greatest learning, seem to be born with excellent talents only to make themselves miserable; and, according to the expression of the wisest of kings, *He that increaseth knowledge, increaseth sorrow*, Eccl. i. 18. We must, therefore, first of all, consider this as a sure and settled point, that religion is the sole foundation of human peace and felicity. This, even the profane scoffers at religion are, in some sort, obliged to own, though much against their will, even while they are pointing their wit against it; for nothing is more commonly to be heard from them, than that the whole doctrine of religion was invented by some wise men, to encourage the practice of justice and virtue through the world. Surely then, religion, whatever else may be said of it, must be a matter of the highest value, since it is found necessary to secure advantages of so very great importance. But, in the mean time, how unhappy is the case of integrity and virtue, if what they want to support them is merely fictitious, and they cannot keep their ground but by means of a monstrous forgery! But far be it from us to entertain such an absurdity! For the first rule of righteousness cannot be otherwise than right, nor is there any thing more nearly allied or more friendly to virtue, than truth.

53[1] Augustine makes this point several times, notably *Confessions* 7.20, "the Platonists . . . taught me to seek for a truth which was incorporeal".

54[1] *Logic* (*CC*) 200–2, based partly on *C d r V*, clarifies C's conception of the nature of demonstration in distinction from merely physical proof.

54B IV 245–6, marked with a line in ink | *AR* 34–5, Prudential Aphorism 5

And it is, indeed, very plain, that if it were possible entirely to dissolve all the bonds and ties of religion, yet, that it should be so, would certainly be the interest of none but the worst and most abandoned part of mankind. All the good and wise, if the matter was freely left to their choice, would rather have the world governed by the Supreme and Most Perfect Being, mankind subjected to His just and righteous laws, and all the affairs of men superintended by His watchful providence, than that it should be otherwise. Nor do they believe the doctrines of religion with aversion or any sort of reluctancy, but embrace them with pleasure, and are excessively glad to find them true. So that, if it was possible, to abolish them entirely, and any person, out of mere good-will to them, should attempt to do it, they would look upon the favour as highly prejudicial to their interest, and think his good-will more hurtful than the keenest hatred. Nor would any one, in his wits, choose to live in the world, at large, and without any sort of government, more than he would think it eligible to be put on board a ship without a helm or pilot, and, in this condition, to be tossed amidst rocks and quicksands. On the other hand, can any thing give greater consolation, or more substantial joy*, than to be firmly persuaded, not only that there is an infinitely good and wise Being, but also that this Being preserves and continually governs the universe which Himself has framed, and holds the reins of all things in His powerful hand; that He is our father, that we and all our interests are His constant concern; and that, after we have sojourned a short while here below, we shall be again taken into His immediate presence? Or can this wretched life be attended with any sort of satisfaction, if it is divested of this Divine faith, and bereaved of such a blessed hope?

[Footnote, giving Greek version of phrase in textus*:] Φεῦ τι τούτων χάρμα μεῖζον ἂν λαβοίς.

55 IV 267

But the lively colours in which the image itself is drawn, are, says Nyssen, "purity, absence of evil, understanding, and speech†." [Footnote giving Greek version†:] Καθαρότης, κακοῦ ἀλλοτρίωσις, νοῦς, καὶ λόγος.

Reason and Understanding.[1]

55A IV 268, marked with an ink line; cf IV +1 (**58**) | *AR* 45–6, Prudential Aphorism 12

What, you will say, have I beasts within me? Yes, you have beasts, and

[1] For C's emphasis on this distinction see COPY B **15**.

a vast number of them. And that you may not think I intend to insult you, is anger an inconsiderable beast, when it barks in your heart? What is deceit, when it lies hid in a cunning mind; is it not a fox? Is not the man who is furiously bent upon calumny, a scorpion? Is not the person who is eagerly set on resentment and revenge, a most venomous viper? What do you say of a covetous man; is he not a ravenous wolf? And is not the luxurious man, as the prophet expresses it, a neighing horse? Nay, there is no wild beast but is found within us. And do you consider yourself as lord and prince of the wild beasts, because you command those that are without, though you never think of subduing or setting bounds to those that are within you? What advantage have you by your reason, which enables you to overcome lions, if, after all, you yourself are overcome by anger? To what purpose do you rule over the birds, and catch them with gins, if you yourself, with the inconstancy of a bird, are hurried hither and thither, and sometimes, flying high, are ensnared by pride, sometimes brought down and caught by pleasure? But, as it is shameful for him who rules over nations, to be a slave at home, and for the man who sits at the helm of the state, to be meanly subjected to the beck of a contemptible harlot, or even of an imperious wife; will it not be, in like manner, disgraceful for you, who exercise dominion over the beasts that are without you, to be subject to a great many, and those of the worst sort, that roar and domineer in your distempered mind?

55B   IV 273, marked with a pencil line

So that one of the ancients most justly called man, "God's favourite creature." And he spoke much to the purpose, who said, "God is neither a lover of horses, nor of birds, but of mankind."

55C   IV 274–5, marked with a line in ink | *AR* 46, Prudential Aphorism 13

Seneca tells us, "There is a settled friendship, nay, a near relation and similitude between God and good men; he is even their father; but, in their education, he inures them to hardships. When, therefore, you see them struggling with difficulties, sweating, and employed in up-hill work; while the wicked, on the other hand, are in high spirits, and swim in pleasures; consider, that we are pleased with modesty in our children, and forwardness in our slaves: the former we keep under by severe discipline, while we encourage impudence in the latter. Be persuaded, that God takes the same method. He does not pamper the good man with delicious fare, but tries him; he accustoms him to hardships, and," (which is a wonderful expression in a heathen) "PREPARES HIM FOR HIMSELF."

55D IV 284, marked with a line in ink; cf IV $^+$1 **(58)**

The Platonists divide the world into two, the sensible and the intellectual world: they imagine the one to be type of the other, and that sensible and spiritual things are stamped, as it were, with the same stamp or seal. These sentiments are not unlike the notions which the masters of the cabalistical doctrine among the Jews, held concerning God's *sephiroth* and seal, wherewith, according to them, all the worlds, and every thing in them, are stamped or sealed. And these are probably near akin to what Lord Bacon of Verulam calls, his *parallela signacula* [corresponding marks], and *symbolizantes schematismi* [symbolic figures]. According to this hypothesis, these parables and metaphors, which are often taken from natural things to illustrate such as are Divine, will not be similitudes taken entirely at pleasure, but are often, in a great measure, founded in nature and the things themselves.

56 IV 306–7; cf IV $^+$1 **(58)**

Nor is it possible for us to find it [i.e. true felicity] any where else, but in our union with that Original Wisdom and Goodness, from which we at first took our rise. Away, then, with all the fictitious schemes of felicity proposed by the philosophers, even those of them that were most artfully contrived; for even Aristotle's perfection of virtue, as well as what the Stoics fancied concerning their wise man, are mere fictions. They are nothing but dreams and fancies, that ought to be banished to Utopia. For, what they describe, is no where to be found among men, and if it were, it would not constitute complete felicity. So far, indeed, they are to be commended, that they call in the mind from external enjoyments to itself; but in this they are defective, that when the mind is returned to itself, they carry it no further, nor direct it to ascend, as it were, above itself. They sometimes, it is true, drop such expressions as these, "That there can be no good disposition of the mind without God;" and, That, in order to be happy, the soul must be raised up to divine things: they also tell us, "That the wise man loves God most of all, and for this reason is the most happy man." * But these expressions they drop only at random, and by the bye.

* A most illogical & uncandid way of treating the ancient Platonists & Stoics. How *at random*? And with what truth can it be said of Plato, Xenophon, Isocrates, Seneca, Epictetus, that they drop moral & religious truths only *obiter* or *by the bye*? This spirit of bigotry & detraction so unworthy of Leighton flows, in general, from the mean Conception of Christianity, as a System of *Teaching*—a mere Code of Prudential and Moral *Instruction*.

56A IV 317–18, marked with a line in ink | *AR* 46–7, Prudential Aphorism 14

If what we are told concerning that glorious city, obtain credit with us, we shall cheerfully travel towards it, nor shall we be at all deterred by the difficulties that may be in the way. But, however, as it is true, and more suitable to the weakness of our minds, which are rather apt to be affected with things present and near, than such as are at a great distance, we ought not to pass over in silence, that the way to the happiness reserved in heaven, which leads through this earth, is not only agreeable because of the blessed prospect it opens, and the glorious end to which it conducts, but also for its own sake, and on account of the innate pleasure to be found in it, far preferable to any other way of life that can be made choice of, or, indeed, imagined. Nay, that we may not, by low expressions, derogate from a matter so grand and so conspicuous, that holiness and true religion which leads directly to the highest felicity, is itself the only happiness, as far as it can be enjoyed on this earth. Whatever naturally tends to the attainment of any other advantage, participates, in some measure, of the nature of that advantage. Now, the way to perfect felicity, if any thing can be so, is a means that, in a very great measure, participates of the nature of its end; nay, it is the beginning of that happiness, it is also to be considered as a part of it, and differs from it, in its completest state, not so much in kind, as in degree.

56B IV 319–20, marked with a line in ink | *AR* 37–8, Prudential Aphorism 8

And if we seriously consider this subject but a little, we shall find the saying of the wise king Solomon concerning this wisdom, to be unexceptionably true: *Her ways are ways of pleasantness, and all her paths are peace.*

Doth religion require any thing of us more than that we live *soberly, righteously, and godly in this present world?* Now what, I pray, can be more pleasant or peaceable than these? Temperance is always at leisure, luxury always in a hurry: the latter weakens the body and pollutes the soul, the former is the sanctity, purity, and sound state of both. It is one of Epicurus's fixed maxims, "That life can never be pleasant without virtue." Vices seize upon men with the violence and rage of furies; but the Christian virtues replenish the breast which they inhabit, with a heavenly peace and abundant joy, and thereby render it like that of an angel. The slaves of pleasure and carnal affections, have within them, even now, an earnest of future torments; so that, in this present life, we may truly apply to them that expression in the Revelations, *They that worship the beast, have no rest day nor night.* "There is perpetual peace with the humble," says the devout A. Kempis; "but the proud and the covetous are never at rest."

56C IV 348–9, marked in ink | *AR* 2, Introductory Aphorism 4

It is the advice of the wise man, "Dwell at home," or, with yourself; and though there are very few that do this, yet it is surprising that the greatest part of mankind cannot be prevailed upon, at least to visit themselves sometimes; but, according to the saying of the wise Solomon, *The eyes of the fool are in the ends of the earth*. It is the peculiar property of the human mind, and its signal privilege, to reflect upon itself; yet we, foolishly neglecting this most valuable gift conferred upon us by our Creator, and the great ornament of our nature, spend our lives in a brutish thoughtlessness. Were a man, not only to turn in upon himself, carefully to search and examine his own heart, and daily endeavour to improve it more and more in purity, but also to excite others with whom he conversed, to this laudable practice, by seasonable advice and affecting exhortations, he would certainly think himself very happy in these exercises. Now, though, this expedient is never unseasonable, yet, it will be particularly proper on such an occasion as this, to try it upon yourselves; as you are not ignorant, that it is the great apostolical rule with respect to all who are called to celebrate the Divine mysteries, *Let every man examine himself, and so let him eat of that bread, and drink of that cup*. 1 Cor. xi. 28.

56D IV 372, marked with a line in ink | *Exhortations* | *AR* 47–8, Prudential Aphorism 15

"We are always resolving to live, and yet never set about life in good earnest*." Archimedes was not singular in his fate; but a great part of mankind die unexpectedly, while they are poŗring upon the figures they have described in the sand. O wretched mortals! who, having condemned themselves, as it were, to the mines, seem to make it their chief study to prevent their ever regaining their liberty. Hence, new employments are assumed in the place of old ones; and, as the Roman philosopher truly expresses it, "one hope succeeds another, one instance of ambition makes way for another; and we never desire an end of our misery, but only that it may change its outward form†." When we cease to be candidates, and to fatigue ourselves in soliciting interest, we begin to give our votes and interest to those who solicit us in their turn. When we are wearied of the trouble of prosecuting crimes at the bar, we commence judges ourselves; and he who is grown old in the management of other men's affairs for money, is at last employed in improving his own wealth. At the age of fifty, says one, I will retire, and take my ease; or the sixtieth year of my life shall entirely disengage me from public offices and business. Fool! art thou not ashamed to reserve to thyself the last remains and dregs of life? Who will stand surety that thou shalt live so long? And what immense folly is it, so far to forget mortality, as to think of beginning to live at that period of years, to which a few only attain!

[Footnote:] Victuros agimus semper, nec vivimus unquam.

[Footnote†:] Spes spem excipit, ambitionem ambitio, et miseriarum non quaeritur finis, sed schema tantum mutatur.

57   IV 396

If you, then, my dear youths, aspire to genuine Christianity, that is, the knowledge of God and Divine things, I would have you consider that the mind must first be recalled and engaged to turn in upon itself, before it can be raised up towards God: according to that expression of St. Bernard, "May I return from external things to those that are within myself, and from these again rise to those that are of a more exalted nature." But the greatest part of men live abroad, and are truly strangers at home: you may sooner find them any where than with themselves. Now, is this not real madness, and the highest degree of insensibility? Yet after all, they seem to have some reason in their madness, when they thus stray away from themselves, since they can see nothing within them, that, by its promising aspect, can give them pleasure or delight. Every thing there is ugly, frightful, and full of nastiness, which they would rather be ignorant of, than be at the pains to purge away; and therefore prefer a slothful forgetfulness of their misery, to the trouble and labour of regaining happiness. But how preposterous is the most diligent study, and the highest knowledge, when we neglect that of ourselves! The Roman philosopher, ridiculing the grammarians of his time, observes, "that they inquired narrowly into the misfortunes of Ulysses, but were quite ignorant of their own." The sentiments of a wise and pious man are quite different, and I wish you may adopt them.

~~The †~~Two grievous faults I find in these Exhortations—1. the disheartning, cheerless, monkish, anti-lutheran Gloom and Ascetic or rather Manichæan Morals:[1] 2. the indefiniteness of the contemptuous Declamation, Exh. after Exh. against Science, Learning, Philosophy, &c[2]— In common Candour, L. should have informed his Pupils beforehand that they were wasting their time & labor,—if his Contempt extended to

---

a Footnotes not marked

[1] C comments similarly on the "Manichaean" asceticism of the early Church in FLEURY **46**.

[2] C criticises Leighton's attitude in a similar way in **56** and **58**.

the whole of their academic Courses—& if not, then he ought after they were compleated, to have particularized what he thought unworthy of being further pursued.—

58   iv +1

    188. P.[1]
    193 S
    195. M.
    [? S] 196—Life of L.[2]
    268. *M*. 284. Sp.
    306 Life—Defect in Leighton—Commonplace Depreciation of the Greek & Roman Philosophers.
    368. *Life*—Railing against scientific & scholastic Theology—[3]
    373. Life—Ascetic Calumniation of Human Life—[4]

59   iv +2, pencil

    192[1]

58[1] With two exceptions, these page-references are associated with marginalia and sub-marginalia distributed through the sequence of pages in the text here: iv 188 is **48A**, iv 193 is **49**, iv 195 is **49A**, iv 196 is **50**, iv 268 is **55A**, iv 284 is **55D**, iv 306 is **56**. For iv 368, 373, see nn 3, 4 below.

The letters "P", "M", and "S" probably represent the scheme of arrangement sent to Hessey on 8 Aug 1823: "1. Philosophical and Miscellaneous. 2. Moral and Prudential. 3. Spiritual" (*CL* v 290). This had been changed by the end of the year.

58[2] For the aborted biography see **1** n 1 above.

58[3] I.e. iv 368, not marked in this copy: "As for you, young gentlemen, especially those of you that intend to devote yourselves to theological studies, it is my earnest advice and request to you, that you fly far from that infectious curiosity which would lead you into the depths of that controversial, contentious theology, which, if any doctrine at all deserves the name, may be truly termed, *science falsely so called*. And that you may not, in this respect, be imposed upon by the common reputation of acuteness and learning, I confidently affirm, that to understand and be master of those trifling disputes that prevail in the schools, is an evidence of a very mean understanding; while, on the contrary, it is an argument of a genius truly great, entirely to slight and depise them, and to walk in the light of pure and peaceable truth, which is far above the dark and cloudy region of controversial disputes."

58[4] I.e. iv 373, not marked in this copy: "Look about you, and see, whether there is any thing worthy of your affection, and whether every thing you see, does not rather excite your indignation and aversion. . . . how innumerable are the miseries and afflictions of various kinds, that seem alternately to re-echo to one another! Can it be any wonder, then, that a life of this kind should sometimes force, even from a wise man, such expressions of sorrow and concern as the following: 'O mother, why didst thou bring me forth, to be oppressed with afflictions and sorrows? Why didst thou introduce me into a life full of briers and thorns?' "

59[1] I.e. **48B**.

JOHN LESLIE
1766–1832

[ms] "Some Account of the Life of Josiah Wedgwood Esq. F.R.S. and A.S. Potter to Her Majesty & their Royal Highness[es] the Dukes of York & Clarence." Watermark 1794.

Keele University (Mosley Collection, Wedgwood Papers)

The ms comprises 53 leaves (7" × 9"), paginated 1–98, 98–104. Inscribed in ink on p 1: "Compiled by Mr John Le[s]lie, now Professor of Mathematics at Edinburgh, from a sketche drawn up by the late Mr Byerley, and written before 1800— | Josiah Wedgwood Augt 9 1815". Below this inscription, in pencil: "Notes by S T Coleridge". The ms includes brief pencilled annotations by Thomas Carlyle (1795–1881), of later date than C's. C's annotations, with the exception of **6**, are written on small slips of paper pasted into the ms; all were evidently written on a larger sheet (or sheets) and were then cut apart to permit their distribution through the ms.

Another ms among the Wedgwood Papers clarifies the history and status of the LESLIE annotations. On a visit to the Wedgwood house at Gunville in Feb and Mar 1803, C tried to use Leslie's text as a basis for "put[ting] the materials in order for the Life of Mr Wedgwood" (*CN* I 1347). He wrote a résumé of the first part of Leslie's biography, with a column of "Notes and Questions" on one side, which together make up the present ANNEX. Whether the notes that are now pasted into the later pages of the ms were similarly attached to an abridged version of this part of Leslie's narrative, or whether C—having abandoned the abridgment project—wrote his comments down on a larger sheet or sheets as he read is not clear, but the material in the ANNEX certainly antedates the notes in the ms. On 13 Mar 1803 C declared in a letter that he had had to abandon the project: "There is nothing to be done at present with Mr W.'s Life.—There are no materials at present—& whether any can be collected, seems doubtful. A most valuable work *might* be made, I have no doubt. But this, if ever, is for a future time.—": *CL* II 939.

DATE. Feb–Mar 1803.

1   Slip pasted in between pp 33 and 34, referring to pp 33–4

Among the first in England to perceive the advantage of forming canals was Mr Broad of Little Fenton, a person of easy fortune, fond of speculative schemes, & thence regarded by his neighbours as a Projector. . . . With Mr Wedgwood he held frequent conversations, & was eager to open his mind & to delineate the parts of his scheme. He proposed the canal to terminate at both sides of Harecastle, a low hill of two miles extent, on the confines of Cheshire. But the clumsy expedient of portage was happily superseded by the daring project of Brindley, to drive a mine & continue the canal under ground. In the year 1755, a survey was made & another by that able engineer in 1758; & it was intended to join the navigation of the Mersey, the Trent, & the Humber. His plan, however, presented difficulties so formidable, that its execution was delayed for several years & might have failed altogether, had it not been again resumed with intrepid zeal at a fortunate period when the general spirit, relieved from the pressure of war, was invigorated by the rapid extension of commerce. In 1765, Mr Wedgwood recalled the attention of the public.

There is, thro' this whole Life, such a strange disregard of Dates as to breed much confusion in my mind.—We do not hear of the plan of Canals till after the amputation of M^r W's leg; & now it is spoken of, as *resumed*, on the *restoration* of Peace—anterior to the amputation, as far as I can understand.[1]—⟨Likewise, a fuller account of Mr Bentley, on his first introduction to Mr W., would be interesting.—⟩[2]

2   Slip pasted in between pp 36 and 37, referring to p 37

For near a twelvemonth, he devoted to it [the plan for navigable canals] almost his whole time & attention; & while the bill was pending in Parliament, he gave a constant attendance in London, to watch & to urge its progress. At last, all the obstacles were removed, & the Act for cutting the Grand Trunk Canal passed, to the unspeakable joy of its enlightened promoters & the inestimable profit of the British nation. Within the space of eleven years, that famous canal, the parent of all the succeeding ones, was happily completed, extending from Liverpool on the west side of the island to Hull on the east. Of this Canal Company Mr Wedgwood was the first Treasurer, & continued, for more than twenty years, an active member of the Committee to superintend its concerns. Several memorials presented by him to the Committee & printed by their order bear ample testimony to his fidelity, his vigilance & penetration. At a late period, by the strict discharge of his trust, he was led to unveil certain practices which had gained footing to the prejudice of the proprietors of the Navigation, who, enlightened by his statements & inspired

[1] Leslie pp 28–30, last para of ANNEX below. The leg was amputated in May 1768; peace had been restored (after the Seven Years' War) in 1763.

[2] Thomas Bentley (1736–80), introduced to Wedgwood in Liverpool while Wedgwood was recuperating from the amputation, became his partner in Nov 1768.

by his counsels, had the courage to oppose the improper influence of a powerful & respectable nobleman.

p. 37

Again & again I must complain of this method of huddling facts together, by a clumsy classification that is most opposite to the spirit of biography—the memoirs should have been particularized—but the great error lies in running backward & forward from one date to another, the necessary effect of writing de rebus, instead of de homine[1]—making the catalogue of a museum, instead of following the events, ⟨thoughts, & actions⟩ of a ~~living~~ man's Life.

3 Slip pasted in between pp 38 and 39, referring to p 38

He married his cousin, Miss Sarah Wedgwood, from Cheshire; a lady in every respect worthy of his choice, indued with superior understanding, & blessed with the happiest mildest dispositions. With so amiable a companion, during thirty years passed in harmony & mutual endearment, he attained the purest connubial felicity. The smiles of a rising family, trained to virtue, varied & heightened his enjoyment.

Having fully ascertained the means of regularly producing the Queen's Ware, & having, by the invaluable acquisition of the Canal Navigation, removed the impediments which threatned to set limits to its consumption, he was desirous of procuring undisturbed leisure for prosecuting other improvements in pottery.

p. 38. Having fully &c.—This is an abrupt transition with a vengeance.

4 Same slip as **3**, referring to p 39

At no small expence, he had collected specimens of the different earths & stones; & few of those brought from foreign countries had escaped his examination. The various combinations of these substances might afford an endless diversity of products, but Mr Wedgwood judiciously escaped the labyrinth, by observing a methodical classification. He was accustomed to register the results of his experiments with care; so that, at any future time as occasion demanded, he could resume the ideas which they had furnished, & could see in the pieces deposited & arranged in the drawers of his cabinet sufficient, nay superabundant, employment for the remainder of his life.

2[1] Writing "about things" instead of "about a man".

p. 39. Mr W. was accustomed to register the results of his experiments. Are ~~these~~ such Memoranda extant?—

5 Same slip as **3**, referring to p 40

About the year 1766, he first produced the unglazed black porcelain, which he named *Basaltes* . . .

p. 40. It ⟨will⟩ seem~~s~~ strange in a life written under the inspection of M^r W's family, if the phrase "*about* the year &c" should so often occur.

6 p 44

[Quoting Erasmus Darwin *The Botanic Garden* II 297–300:]

> Gnomes! as you dissect with hammers fine
> The granite rock, the nodul'd flint calcine,
> ^a Grind with strong arm, the circling chertz betwixt
> Your pure Ka-o-lins & Pe-tun-tzes mixt . . .

Ld Jesus! *there's a couple of Lines*!!!![1]

7 Slip pasted in between pp 46 and 47, referring to p 46

At this time he introduced the *Terra Cotta*, being a compound of different coloured clays, most intimately & artificially combined to resemble granite, porphyry, or Egyptian pebble. With that substance, he imitated sacred urns, lamps, & other vessels of antiquity. It was likewise employed for some inferior subjects of modern origin.

Another valuable material soon offered itself to his invention:—This was a *White-Porcelain Biscuit* with a smooth wax-like surface.

p. 46. At *this* time—At what time?

At what time did that other valuable Material so politely "*offer itself to his Invention?*"

8 Slip pasted in between pp 50 and 51, referring to p 51

The demand for those elegant productions rapidly increasing, it was judged convenient to have the vases painted at Chelsea, where, from its vicinity to the capital, artists of superior skill could easily be assembled. This subordinate establishment was committed to the direction of Mr Bentley, who henceforth fixed his abode at Turnham Green. A few

---

^a C's note is written on the ms opposite this line and the next, the two lines marked with a brace

6[1] Beneath C's note, a note in pencil by Carlyle: "Oh S. T. C.!" A further note by Godfrey Wedgwood, identifying the two hands as C's and Carlyle's, and dated 22 Aug 1895, is pasted in between pp 44 and 45.

vases, finished at great expence & in the highest style, bid fair to survive the revolutions of empire & to convey to distant posterity a very favourable ⟨impression⟩ of the state of the arts in England.

p. 51. A few vases—why not particularize them?—

9   Slip pasted in between pp 52 and 53, referring to p 52

The influence of those extended manufactures was decisive. The public learned to judge & admire the fine models of antiquity. And if Mʳ Wedgwood's taste in the choice of subjects merited every praise, the original productions of his rich, yet correct, fancy procured him equal applause. The current of fashion rolled on with steady impulse. Artists in other departments caught the general spirit: Jewellers, silversmiths, & the various workers in metals now adopted the antique style. Every domestic article, whether calculated for convenience or splendour, was fashioned in all the sweetness & delicacy of form. The models of the English Etruria were imitated by the porcelain manufacturers on the continent. Attempts were even made to export them*ᵃ* to China; but of such indiscreet conduct Mʳ Wedgwood always disapproved. He well knew that, in several European states, the porcelain of the east is admitted on very easy terms, while the importation of English pottery is restrained by heavy imposts, amounting in many cases to a prohibition. Under such circumstances, therefore, he conceived it giving an undue advantage to those foreign rivals, since notwithstanding the mighty improvement lately effected in the composition of our earthen ware, this derived its principal value from the superior elegance of its forms.

p. 52.
    I do not understand the reasoning in this paragraph.—

Annex

The following, from another ms among the Wedgwood papers at Keele, is C's holograph abridgment (much of it direct transcription) of ff 1–16 (pp 1–32) of Leslie's biography, with memoranda towards revision. C wrote the text in two columns labelled "Facts" and "Notes & Questions". Since Leslie's text is the immediate source of all C's "Facts", editorial commentary on this material is slight and deliberately leaves most of C's queries unanswered. Answers may be found, however, in the *DNB* entry for Josiah Wedgwood, and in such standard works as Eliza Meteyard's *Life of Josiah Wedgwood* (2 vols 1865–6).

Wedgwood is the Name of an obscure Hamlet on the confines of Cheshire and Staffordshire, the *Seat of a long and respectable race of Yeomanry, bearing the

* still? or formerly?

ᵃ At this point, responding to C's objection, someone has added in pencil "the models", also writing on C's note, " 'them' = the models; and then it is logical"

same Name. Within the years [1600 and 1620?]*a* one Family of these Wedg-
woods removed* to the village of Burslem in Staffordshire; and from this Family
the several Families now settled in that Neighbourhood derive both their com-
mon Lineage, [and their hereditary trade of Pottery?]*a*

~~Thomas & Mary Wedgwood~~ Josiah Wedgwood, ~~the subject the [? source] the
present imperfect account~~ the subject of the following memoir, was born at
Burslem on the 12ᵗʰ of July, 1730: ⟨the son of Thomas & Mary Wedgwood;⟩ &
the youngest of thirteen children, the progeny of ~~Thomas and Mary Wedgwood~~
one marriage. His mother's maiden name was ~~Mary~~ Stringer. She was the
Daughter of a Clergyman, who resigned his Benefice during the †reign of
Charles the second from scruples of Conscience. ~~His Father,~~ Mʳ Thomas Wedg-
wood, his Father, possessed a small entailed Estate, and carried on a manufac-
tory of Earthen Ware. He was a presbyterian Dissenter.‡

Josiah Wedgwood lost his father ~~during~~ while he was yet an Infant. The eldest
Brother, named Thomas, succeeded to the paternal estate & to the charge of the
manufactory: only a ¶very slender provision was reserved for the younger Chil-
dren. He was bred & educati~~o~~ed among Dissenters, & received no other acquire-
ments than ~~a~~ those of Writing, Reading, and common Arithmetic; ⟨but like al-
most all men of Genius he ~~seems~~ is said to have ⟨given early indications of his
Talents, & to have⟩ displayed the same proportions of power, as a Boy among
Boys, and as a man among men.⟩*b* He was distinguished among his companions
by a characteristic liveliness both of manner & conception, was noticed for
warm & generous Temper, &\like alm\ost all rem\arkable m\en, held \the same
ra\nk appear\ to have \given earl\ indicati\ons of his \Talents. L\ike most L\ike al-
mos\ all men \of Genius,\to have h\ displaye\d in boyh\od as a b\y among \Boys,
& as \ man am\ong men, \the same \proportio\ns of power\& superi\rity which\ he
afterwa\rds evinc\d in man\ood as a \man susta\ned simila\ relation\ of intelle\c-
tual rank\ his schoolfellows §made him the Leader in all their Pursuits & Pas-
times.

About the age of fourteen he was bound apprentice to his Brother Thomas: &
applied to his Trade with the ardour & perseverance which seem to have been
constitutional with him: and often continued at his Labour beyond the allotted
hours. He learnt with his own hand all the processes performed in his Brother's
Manufactory, & found this opportunity of making himself acquainted with the
operations of the other Branches of Pottery established in the neighbourhood/
and by this well-directed & unremitted application acquired in a few years a
thorough knowlege of the whole Art of Pottery, as it then existed in England,

---

* as what? as Potters? were there Potteries at Wedgwood?

† at what part of his reign? on what occasion? from what scruples?

‡ were his Ancestors?

¶ would it be improper to state the sum & the particulars?

§ This is often said of remarkable men, as a Thing of course. Is there any
good evidence for it? The same fact was related ~~of me~~ even of *me* by one of my
school-fellows & I so far from Leader never played at all.—

---

a C's square brackets

b C wrote this passage at the end of the paragraph and marked it for insertion here; another, probably
earlier, version of the idea was tried out and deleted in the next sentence

rude indeed, compared with the state to which he himself afterwards raised it, & almost confined*a* to the narrow District around the village of Burslem.*b* ⟨The tract round Burslem is stiff & ill adapted for Tillage ~~in~~ during a rude state of Agriculture, but it afforded the ~~not~~ Potter both his means & his materials. A variety of coarse clays are to be found near the surface of the Ground; & ~~all~~ at moderate Depth, there is abundance of excellent pit-coal ~~at Burslem~~.⟩*c* At Burslem a rude species of Pottery was manufactured from time immemorial. ~~This is not only confirmed by~~ Of this fact the uniform tradition is of itself a sufficient Evidence; and in addition to this, in digging under the foundations of the oldest Houses fragments of coarse ware are often found, & traces discovered of Potters' kilns. The ~~technical~~ terms* of the Art still in use are evidently of German Derivation.

In the course of so many generations however it does not appear to have received any ~~new~~ sensible Improvement. Even down to the latter part of the 17th Century the Business was so †inconsiderable, that according to Dr Plot the principal sale of the articles made was "to poor cratemen who carried them at their Backs all over the country." The only sorts of Ware then known were the yellow, the red, the black, and the mottled, all produced from the natural varieties of the Clay. ⟨The glaze was produced by sprinkling powdered lead ore ~~over~~ upon the Pieces before Firing.⟩ About the year 1690 the first ~~step~~ improvement was ~~transplan~~ brought from Holland by two ingenious Brothers of the name of Ellers, who ~~set up~~ began a small work at Bradwall near Burslem, induced by a fine Bed of red Clay on that Estate, ~~of from~~ with which they made a pottery, imitating the oriental red Porcelain. They formed a fine glaze on their ware not by any previous application of fluxing substances, but by throwing into the kiln, when brought to its fiercest Heat, a quantity of common Salt. The volumes of pungent Smoke, which rose during this process, were considered as a [? nu] nuisance by the Neighbours, and they were driven away by the alarm raised against them in consequence; altho' shortly after the same ‡process was introduced by others

* might not the words be enumerated in a note, & the correspondent German Words. If the words are Anglo-Saxon, what can this prove but that Handicraftsmen ⟨in villages⟩ retain ~~more~~ old words, that have been dropped in towns? Is it not so in every village Trade? Does it not of course share in the provincial Diulect whatever it be.

† Were there not Potteries in other counties? The number of Potteries in the *kingdom* ought be inquired after. This would be a far better Test, what the extent of the Burslem trade was, than the fact of the Cratemen; which considering the then state of the Roads does not prove much.[1]

‡ was this a discovery of the Ellers? Or had it been part of the practice of the Dutch Potteries? Were there importations of Dutch Pottery to this Country?

a C wrote "confined almost" and marked the words for transposition

b The passage between *d* and *e* was originally written at the end of the paragraph and marked with a number 1 to precede the next sentence, which C marked "2" in ms

c The catch-phrase "Accordingly at Burslem a rude &c" follows in ms

ANNEX[1] *OED* gives Robert Plot's *Natural History of Staffordshire* (1686) as its first authority for the term "crateman"— "a man who carries a crate; a hawker of pottery".

whom they had employed, and it became so common that upon a Saturday, the common glazing Day, the whole Country was filled with Smoke, during 30 or 40 years ~~thereaft~~.

In 1720, a manufacturer, named Astbury, who had worked under the Ellers,* made ~~an~~ capital Improvement in the body of the ware itself. Having observed that Flint turns white by calcination he conceived & realized the idea of employing this material to †temper the clay. Hence that species of Pottery known by the appellation of white Stone ware, which came into pretty general use at home, and was exported in considerable Quantities to Holland & Germany. To conceal this Invention the Flint was at first pounded by the Hand in cellars & other private Apartments. But the Workmen, breathing in the fine dust, contracted dangerous pulmonary complaints; and from this, & other more common causes the ~~secret~~ process was suffered by degrees to ~~transpire~~ become public. Before the year 1740 mills were erected for grinding the calcined red Flint, & the operation was greatly facilitated by the addition of water. Near the same Period the pottery received other improvements, "tho' of small consequence. But it is ‡inexpedient to notice all the minute alterations which accident might introduce."[3]

Such was the State, in which M[r] Wedgwood found the art of Pottery.—[Here ought to come a simple Statement of what Pottery was, in all its Branches ~~at~~ in the first years of M[r] Wedgewood's Apprenticeship.][a] He perceived the Defects, & sought by meditation & experiments the means of removing them & the success of his First ¶Essays was sufficiently encouraging.

At this time §a severe Malady began to afflict him. A painful Disorder had fallen into his right Leg, first occasioned by the small Pox, & aggravated by neglect; & during one **half of the time of his Apprenticeship he was forced to sit at work with his leg stretched out before him on a Stool.—Yet under these

---

* N.B. Whither did these Ellers go?

† Why *temper*? Does it do nothing else—Temper is a very obscure word: for it signifies (besides all its moral meaning,) 1. to mingle, simply. 2. to qualify. 3. To soften 4. To harden.[2]

‡ Inexpedient? why? Surely, it must needs be interesting to those, who are likely to be at all interested in the work, to know the exact state of the art, as M[r] W. found it. It is not a novel, a fairy Tale, or poem, that ~~we~~ is here to be written. Besides, nothing is more instructive, in many & various ways, than minute histories of Improvements, in which every step is noticed/ it at once teaches Humility, & sharpens the inventive powers. Without something much more ~~clear~~ particular than this the words "Such was the State" come almost empty-handed to my understanding.

¶ are there no memoranda of any of these first Essays?—

§ At what time had M[r] Wedgewood the small Pox?—His bad Leg—had he it while he was at School?

** the latter Half?

[a] C's square brackets

ANNEX[2] Johnson's *Dictionary*, which C might well have consulted, distinguishes nine meanings of the verb, including all those mentioned by C as well as "moral" ones.

ANNEX[3] C quotes Leslie p 9 (var: Leslie wrote "accident or caprice").

seeming discouragements he discovered several happy contrivances; & even at this *early period he produced some specimens of that ware afterwards so much celebrated under the name of cream-coloured or Queen's Ware.

But his passion for experiment received no fosterage from his Master & Brother, who on the contrary reproved him for yielding to what he deemed idle curiosity; and who saw in "schemery & project-making"[4] any thing rather than the road to wealth or respectability. Various are the ways by which we impose upon ourselves & others in the attempt to conceal our own inferiority—we ~~name~~ call the qualities, we perceive in our superior, by the name of their ~~offen~~ faulty extreme, or we take [a]†advantage of some superficial resemblance to confound two qualities, which in their essentials are in direct opposition to each other. The perfect master & the man of genius both attempt innovation, the first from such an impatience of attaining the arbitrary end of ~~his Labour,~~ Labor in general, viz. wealth, as to ~~neglect be incapable~~ distaste all ~~of~~ the slow & ordinary means— the man of genius from such a passion for the ⟨immediate Object of his particular Labor, for the⟩ means & the ~~objects~~ advantages intrinsical & naturally connected with ~~them~~ it, as to convert them into an end, of themselves, & to become forgetful or careless of the arbitrary & common end. ~~All human Efforts~~ all perfect-makers are ⟨of the class⟩ of Alchemists ~~and can~~: A man of this sort would receive no delight from the discovery that Diamond is the element of Charcoal, but would waste a whole Life in the attempt to transmute charcoal into Diamonds —& that not for any use, ~~they~~ conceived to be inherent in Diamonds, but wholly from the charms of their arbitrary value. At the expiration of the ‡Term of his Apprenticeship he suggested various useful Reforms, pointed out modes for extending his concerns & desired to be admitted Partner in the Business. But his Brother was too cautious or too timid ~~to listen to~~; & rejected the Proposal. The consequence that[b] Mr Wedgwood engaged in partnership with Mr John Harrison, who was disposed[c] to transfer his capital from another ¶Trade to that of Pottery. The manufacture was accordingly begun at Cliffbank, in 1752—the 22ⁿᵈ year of Mr Wedgwood's age. Its success ~~was~~ fell short of the expectation of either party; & Mr W. finding his plans §extremely cramped, dissolved the contract at the expiration of two years. This ~~Business~~ Trial, however unsuccessful in other respects, ascertained Mr W's superior Talents, & spread his reputation—so that he found no difficulty in forming a new partnership with ⟨a⟩ Mr Whieldon, a gentleman who had acquired a considerable Fortune in the business of Pottery—&

* What period? Are there no memoranda of the month or year?—

[†] The Thought is just I believe; & valuable; tho' the expression is heavy, obscure, & perplexed—It is a fine Eel, wriggling thro' mud.

‡ what was the Term? Seven years.—

¶ What Trade?

§ By what? By the *dispositions* of Mr J. Harrison—? Or by the smallness of his Capital?

[a] The footnote indicator here corresponds to a long brace, with which C marks the passage from here to "arbitrary value" below

[b] For "was that"

[c] This word is repeated as C moves on to the second sheet

ANNEX[4] Not a quotation from Leslie; no source traced.

a manufactory was commenced in the village of Fenton—& this connection lasted 5 years—i.e. from Mʳ W.'s 24ᵗʰ to his 29ᵗʰ year.—Mʳ Wedgwood contracted to put in practice, for the joint Benefit, such secrets as he possessed, but without any Stipulation to reveal them. Six months were spent by him in preparing models, ~~model~~ moulds & the necessary Implements, his only Assistant a young man *who had acquired a casual knowlege of Modelling during an apprenticeship to a Potter.

His first ⟨new⟩ production was a new green ware with the smoothness & brilliancy of Glass, moulded into a variety of forms, as pine-apples, leaves, &c; & intended for Tea & Dessert Services. There was a very considerable Demand for it.—He manufactured likewise toilette vessels, snuff boxes, & numerous fanciful Toys, for mounting in metal, colored in imitation of Agates & precious Stones. These were offered to the Jewellers in London & Bath, "who †admired them as rare gems, & were not a little mortified to find so low a price set on them."[5]

But in the ‡midst of this fervid application an accidental Bruise on his Shin Bone occasioned a ¶return to an alarming Degree of the disorder in his Leg.— For many months he was confined to his chamber (*how many?*), and his robust body both emaciated & reduced to extreme weakness. Thus rendered incapable of personal superintendance (& personal exertion of any kind) Mʳ Wedgwood was under the necessity of communicating the knowlege of his mixtures to an intelligent workman. "His valuable §secrets were thus divulged";[6] & were eagerly adopted by the manufacturers in the Neighbourhood—His confinement however afforded him Leisure: & this Leisure he employed in reading, for which during the whole of his after life he retained a singular fondness. His Studies were encouraged & directed by the visits of his Brother in law, the Revᵈ Mʳ Willet, a man of extensive Learning & primitive ~~morals~~ manners.—How deeply Mʳ Wed. enjoyed such conversation, may be conjectured from a declaration of his, that it was then the height of his Ambition to obtain such a moderate competence as would enable him to devote the rest of his Days to Literature & Science.

In 1759 the Term of Partnership expired, & Mʳ W. erected on his own funds a small manufactory in his native village of Burslem. The productions of this small establishment were chiefly of the curious & ornamental kind—Vases for flowers, & for the decoration of Cabinets, Tea-services in several new & agreeable forms, with other ingenious Articles. They had a rapid sale both at home & abroad, & were ~~seen~~ soon imitated by the neighbouring manufactories.

* It would be pleasant to preserve his name.

† —why *mortified*? at their having been deceived?—I cannot perhaps tell why; but this way of relating the fact appears to me deficient in dignity—as if ~~the writer was enjoying~~ it were a sort of momentary *Trick* upon the Jewellers.

‡ in what year? Nothing gives such a confusion to Biography, as this dainty omission of Dates; because, forsooth, it makes no part of a rhetorical Period.—

¶ A *return*. When he was cured of it, is no where mentioned.

§ The secrets were *thus* only communicated. That they were divulged, must have arisen from the Dishonesty of "the intelligent workman"; which should not pass without one word at least declarative of the same.

ANNEX[5] C quotes Leslie p 12. ANNEX[6] C quotes Leslie p 13.

But on the recovery of his bodily strength, and the improvement of his capital, he took a complete set of Buildings, & engaged a larger number of workmen— & at the same time introduced into the ~~his~~ Pottery (& realized) the system of the subdivision of Labor—He borrowed some hints from the regulations, which Mr Bolton had introduced into his establishment at Soho, near Birmingham; & succeeded in previously convincing his workmen of the propriety & necessity of the measure. In this as in every other concern it was his habit & his creed to address himself to the understandings of his workmen by forcible plain good sense, & to their affections by ~~his~~ uniformly brotherly attention to their comforts & welfare.—at the same time he improved, with great ingenuity & perseverance, the Tools, machinery, & handicraft of the Pottery, which at that time *were few in number & still of the rudest kind. He invented & fashioned new gravers, new models, new moulds, new drying pans, and all the subordinate apparatus. He commonly passed the Day at the Bench beside his Workmen, instructing them individually, by his Voice & Example, & the first pattern of each piece came almost always from his own Hands. He spent his evenings in contriving tools, in designing forms, in fancying Ornaments, & in preparing for the general Business of the day following. These Thoughts frequently deprived him of his Sleep/ & all his after Life whatever ~~deeply~~ at all interested him, never failed to interrupt his Sleep. He believed however, that on awaking from short rest, after a night of meditation, his mind became more than ordinarily prompt & inventive.—He applied at the same time to chemistry, & examined the constitution of earthy substances & the properties of their Compounds.

On the accession of the present Queen Mr W. prepared a breakfast service with his utmost care & skill—of a yellow ground, decorated with laurel sprig, & other flowers coloured from Nature. The Queen very graciously received it & desired that the Fabric should bear her name, & without solicitation conferred on Mr W. the title of her Potter.—This Queen's ware became immediately fashionable, & had a large sale among people of rank & fortune.

Mr Wedgewood was thus encouraged to make the attempt to form large pieces calculated for dinner-services. Of this important Step the extreme Difficulty can hardly be conceived by persons unacquainted with the nature of the manufactory. After the composition of the †Biscuit, is perfectly ascertained, it might seem easy to make vessels of any moderate dimension. And so it is in the ordinary sorts of Pottery, which demand no nicety in the Firing. But in Porcelain, & the delicate Ware invented by Mr Wedgwood, the success depends chiefly in the nice management of the Kilns: for these required to be brought almost to the point of Semi-vitrification, & thus softened are apt to bend from their shapes, and if the fierce Heat be continued a few minutes too long, to run into a vitreous Mass. With large pieces of ware ‡*therefore*, the risk of destroying the forms is

* The number of Tools &c should be particularized in the former part of the work, where the State of Pottery is described anterior to M^r W's improvements.

† This should either be explained, or omitted, at present it is φωναῦτα συ-νετοισι,[7] i.e. One must be a potter to understand it.

‡ Such, no doubt, is the Fact; but I confess, I cannot see the *Logic* of this "*therefore*".

ANNEX[7] "Vocal to the wise"—a phrase from Pindar *Olympian Odes* 2.85, fre-quently used by C: BÖHME 9 n 5.

prodigiously increased. In overcoming this difficulty Mr W. incurred much vex-
ation, heavy expences & grievous Losses. Disaster succeeded disaster, one kiln
was pulled down, & another erected: a defect removed in one part only disclosed
more defects in another; at length however he succeeded; & his inflexible per-
severance was rewarded beyond his own most sanguine expectations. *Thus* did
the Queen's Ware, now better known by the name of Cream-coloured Ware
receive its last Improvement.—By many it was preferred to Chinese Porcelain,
which it excelled in lightness, cheapness, & elegance of Form. It became a sta-
ple article of Consumption, even among the middle Classes; the importation
from Holland †& France was discontinued; and some began to be exported. Yet
of this most valuable manufactory, tho' in the strictest sense his own, M^r W.
never claimed or enjoyed an exclusive privelege. His neighbours took advantage
of the Discovery, exempt from the toil & expence which it had cost—leaving to
Mr W. the advantage of the priority of the fabrics, established reputation, & a
more finished workmanship.

As the Potteries extended, the inconvenience of the bad roads was proportion-
ally felt, as most of the raw materials used in the manufacture were now brought
from places very remote; the chalk-counties‡, and Mr Wedgwood had begun to
draw a finer species of clay from Dorsetshire.—And Mr Wedgwood, by his in-
fluence & power of argument, the manufacturers & great Landholders were in-
duced to solicit an act of Parliament for a turnpike road four miles from Burslem
toward Liverpool—which was ¶obtained & the road immediately begun.—

§In reading Plumier's Book on the art of Turning he found a description of
the Engine Lathe for turning wood, ivory or metal into all possible variety of
Shapes, & eagerly conceived the project of adopting it to Pottery. Tho' ~~few ever~~
there were few in England, & those jealously kept secret, he however by assis-
tance of the *celebrated* **Mr Taylor he procured one to be constructed at Bir-
mingham—, not quitting the place till the machine was finished—& he brought
it home with him together with a person instructed in the manner of using it. His
first application of it was to the new porcelain, which being without glaze & of
a close texture, was well suited to receive a sharpness of work. He employed it
also for turning the vases which he then manufactured in Queen's Ware. Hence-

* *Thus*? How? The ways & means, which at last proved successful, are no
where stated.—

† Is it possible to procure any account of the Art of Pottery as it existed in
Holland & France, at the commencement of Mr Wedgwood's Improvements?
Did Mr W. derive any Hints from French or Dutch Potteries?

‡ What are these?

¶ In what year of Mr Wedgwood's Life. Dates & figures are almost as cau-
tiously avoided, as if it were a Poem.

§ Still the same abruptness from the omission of Dates. Instead of Dates the
Paragraphs are introduced with insipid commonplace general reflections, or gen-
eral affirmations.

** I never heard of him before.[8]

ANNEX[8] John Taylor of Birmingham, said by Eliza Meteyard (*Life of Josiah Wedgwood* I 287) to have been "at this date effecting a revolution in the small-ware branch of manufactures, such as buckles, buttons, and various light ornamental articles".

forth *the Engine Lathe came into general use & by the year 1763, when it was introduced, may be considered as an important epoch in the art of Pottery.

This year the ~~long~~ 7 years war ended, which had certainly not been without favorable effects on our rising establishments at home by obstructing the importation of Earthen ware †from the Continent: & ~~when~~ at the restoration of Peace the manufacture of Pottery had excelled the foreign Productions.

About this time, ‡the Disorder in his Leg which had never been radically cured relapsed; it was envenomed by a scorbutic taint, & mounted by degrees from the Shin-bone to the knee, & formed an Ancyclosis. On a journey to Liverpool he injured the sore by a Fall from his Horse, which confined him in Liverpool some weeks, during which time Mr Turner, his Surgeon, introduced to him, Mr Bentley—& the acquaintance soon improved into the ~~tenderest~~ strictest Friendship. A year or two afterwards his Leg was amputated at Burslem, tho' after his marriage ¶to his Cousin, Miss Sara Wedgwood, from Cheshire, & subsequent to the Birth of his eldest son, the present Mr John Wedgwood.

* Did Mr Wedgwood ~~dis~~ make it public? or was the secret betrayed by his Workmen?—These Things should not be omitted: for in other instances they throw light on Mr Wedgwood's character, his generosity or his equanimity.

† Were we not at war with Holland?[9] Besides, p. 23, this fact is accounted for wholly from the superiority of the Staffordshire Pottery.

‡ Is not the exact date attainable?

¶ Something, I think, should have been previously mentioned of the terms, on which Mr Wedgwood continued to live with his relations. One might suppose, that he had sent for an unseen Cousin.—

ANNEX[9] Holland was a neutral state in the Seven Years' War.

GOTTHOLD EPHRAIM LESSING
1729–1781

Gotthold Ephraim Lessings Leben, nebst seinem noch übrigen litterarischen Nachlasse. Ed. K. G. Lessing. 3 pts in 2 vols. Berlin 1793, 1795, 1795. 8°.

British Library C 126 c 12

Autograph signature "S. T. Coleridge" on title-page of Pts i and iii—i.e. the title-page of each bound volume. The volumes were rebound in uniform binding to make a set with LESSING *Sämmtliche Schriften*, with some loss to annotations in cropping.

At the foot of Vol I title-page, written upside-down in ink in German script, "Eingelegtes blatt", referring to the portrait—an instruction intended to be removed in rebinding. At the foot of Vol I pt i title-page, in pencil, and at the foot of pt ii title-page, in ink, "Ah—", an inscrutable jotting perhaps also to do with the binder.

CONTENTS. I i *Gotthold Ephraim Lessings Leben*; ii 1–88 "Ueber Lessings Philosophie und Theologie"; 89–100 "Anzeige seiner philosophischen und theologischen Bruchstücke"; 101–288 "Die Bruchstücke selbst"; 289–394 "Ueber Lessings poetisches und vorzügliches theatralisches Verdienst". II "G. E. Lessings Nachlass zur Deutschen Sprache, alten Literatur, Gelehrten- und Kunst-Geschichte", ed Georg Gustav Fülleborn.

DATE. Between 1816 and 1823? Although C may have acquired these volumes in Germany in 1798–9, when he began work on a life of Lessing, the marginalia are of rather later date: see e.g. **15**. In **14** C refers to his own observations on certain theological treatises of Lessing's that attracted his attention while he was annotating *Sämmtliche Schriften*, the notes on which date from c 1823.

COEDITOR. Lore Metzger.

1 I ii 21

Glaube war ihm Lernen, und Offenbarung Erfahrung, oder, wie es Herr Jakob in die Seele des Herrn Geh. Raths Jakobi denkt, sinnliche Evidenz oder anschauende Erkenntniss.

[For him faith meant learning, and revelation experience, or, as Mr Jakob considers it in the soul of Geheimrat Jacobi, sensuous evidence or intuitive knowledge.]

This is not a fair Criticism on Jacobi.[1] What was his Object? To prove,

1[1] Jacobi's position in *David Hume   über den Glauben oder Idealismus und*

that FAITH, which the Philosophers of his Day, held in contempt, was "sensuous Evidence", or Knowlege by immediate Beholding = Intuition?[2] No! But to prove that the sensuous Evidence itself was a species of Faith & Revelation: therefore, that the *Genus* could not despised[a], if any one Specie[b] were held in honor.

2 I ii 32

Doch Hr. Kant hat nunmehr systematisch erwiesen, dass der Mensch von dem Daseyn der Dinge nur durch seine Sinne oder Erfahrung überführt werden und von der Wahrheit der Dinge an und für sich unmöglich etwas zuverlässig erfahren könne; dass Verstand und Vernunft zu weiter nichts dienen und dienen sollen, als die sinnlichen Kenntnisse zu berichtigen; dass von dem Denkbaren auf das wirklich Existirende eben so sicher zu schliessen sey, als von einer entzückenden Romanheldin auf ein wirkliches Mädchen.

[But Mr Kant has now systematically demonstrated that man can know the existence of things only through his senses or experience and cannot possibly arrive at any certain knowledge of the reality of the things in and for themselves; that understanding and reason serve and should serve no other purpose than to correct the sense perceptions; so that it would be just as certain to make the connection between the conceivable and the actually existing as it would to make it between the charming heroine of a novel and an actual girl.]

All this is a most incorrect Statement of Kant's Doctrines. The Writer will not be contented, unless he has every thing in his *Intellect*: Kant has shewn, that the Intellect is not the whole of Human Being, nor the only Organ of Truth.[1] Does he, who draws our attention to a neglected Organ of Sense, circumscribe our means of Knowlege?— *S. T. C.*

3 I ii 36

Die Gränzen unseres Wissens, die Erkenntnisskraft nicht Eines Menschen, nicht Einer Generation, nicht Eines Landes, sondern aller Länder, aller Menschen und aller Zeiten, wie ein Tapezierer eine Stube

---

[a] For "be despised"   [b] For "species"

Realismus was that belief in the reality of things, being based on evidence of the senses, is unexplainable by reason and is to be regarded as a species of revelation.

[1][2] C liked to gloss the word "intuition" by the phrase "immediate beholding", which he ascribed to Hooker. See HOOKER **31** n 4, and cf JACOBI *Ueber die Lehre* 4, 20 (on *Anschauung, Ansicht*).

[2][1] This is a summary statement about the significance of Kant's *Critique of Pure Reason*, which C names as one of "the three greatest works since the introduction of Christianity" in SCHELLING *Philosophische Schriften* 1. In about 1812 he objected to Reimarus's treating the *Critique* "as if it were an investigation of the human Being, whereas, in fact, it is a Critik or Ordeal of the scientific Faculty alone, or the pure (i.e.) formal Reason": REIMARUS **5**.

ausmessen und mit ewig dauerhaften Möbeln ausputzen zu wollen: welch ein Einfall! . . . Anmassungen dieser Art macht die tägliche Erfahrung bald zu nicht.

[To want to measure up and fit out the limits of our knowledge, the intellectual power not of one man, not of one generation, not of one country, but of all countries, of all men, and of all times, like a paper-hanger measuring a room and fitting it out with everlasting furniture: what an idea! . . . Daily experience soon brings presumptions of this sort to nothing.]

I am sorry to say that this appears to me mere Calumny. Were our present State Eternity, then and then only could these Objections apply.

4 I ii 137, referring to ii 91–3, 119–37, or parts thereof

[The editor's notice (ii 91–3) quotes in Greek the Plutarch text under discussion: "Questiones conviviales" 4 in *Moralia* 668E. G. E. Lessing begins his uncompleted essay with the statement that Plutarch mentions in passing certain philosophers who had been called "Elpistics" (from the Greek word for "hope") because they had declared that hope was the strongest bond of life and that life was intolerable without it. He summarises (ii 119–33) his intended arguments against Heumann, who had identified the Elpistics with the Christians, and against Brucker, who had identified them with the Stoics. He declares (ii 133) his own view that the Elpistics were false prophets who claimed the name of philosophers, and then lists (ii 134–7) eight arguments in favour of this view, citing as an example of such a character Alexander in Lucian's "Alexander seu pseudomantis".]

The whole of these conjectures and arguments grounds itself on a presumption, which I hold at best very doubtful—viz—that any particular Sect ~~of~~ or Philosophy was meant—Why not writers on psychological and practical morality, of all or of no sect, who had distinguished themselves by panegyrics of Hope? This was compatible with all Sects, even the Stoic—as what was if ⟨not⟩ as what ought to be—ανθρωποις, if not τῷ σοφῷ[1]

5 I ii 164 | § 4 "Spinozisterei"

Ich mag mir die Wirklichkeit der Dinge ausser Gott erklären, wie ich will, so muss ich bekennen, dass ich mir keinen Begriff davon machen kann.

[Try as I may to account for the reality of things separate from God, I must acknowledge that I cannot form a clear conception of them.]

4[1] "For men [in general]'', if not "for the wise man".

Watch whether there be not a palpable Petitio principii in the word "Begriff"—.[1] To ask whether God has a Conception, or whether a Conception be in God—making already a *thing* out of ~~the~~ a Conception—and thus to shew that the World can be no way distinguishable from that Thing/[2] If A = A, then A = A—/ But make Creation an *Act*/[3] & instead of begreifen (conceive) use wissen (know) and the argument sinks undermined. In short, Lessing arbitrarily makes God's actions conceptions: and those Conceptions individual Things—and thus in his *compounding* of God loses God himself.

6   I ii 165

Das ist: in der Wirklichkeit ausser ihm muss etwas seyn, wovon Gott keinen Begriff hat. Eine Ungereimtheit! Ist aber nichts dergleichen, ist in dem Begriffe, den Gott von der Wirklichkeit eines Dinges hat, alles zu finden, was in dessen Wirklichkeit ausser ihm anzutreffen: so sind beide Wirklichkeiten Eins, und alles, was ausser Gott existiren soll, existirt in Gott.

[That is: in reality outside him there must be something of which God has no conception. An absurdity! If however there is nothing of that sort in the conception that God has of the reality of a thing and it contains everything pertaining to its external reality, then both realities are the same and everything that is supposed to exist external to God exists in God.]

Not ⟨at⟩ all!—that it *is* external—that being so, it is of necessity less perfect—this God knows.—I know myself writing—does it follow, that the writing & the knowlege of it are indistinguishable.

7   I ii 167, slightly cropped

Ihr selbst, die ihr Gott Begriffe von zufälligen Dingen beilegen müsst, ist euch nie beigefallen, dass Begriffe von zufälligen Dingen zufällige Begriffe sind?

[When you yourselves have to attribute to God concepts of contingent things, has it never occurred to you that concepts of contingent things are contingent concepts?]

5[1] A "begging the question" in the word "conception".

5[2] C's letter to Clarkson, 13 Oct 1806, is closely related to these annotations, especially in its views about "the difference . . . between THING and THOUGHT": "the Thoughts of God, in the strict nomenclature of Plato, are all IDEAS, archetypal and anterior to all but himself alone . . . and therefore . . . incomparably more *real* than all things besides, & which do all depend on and proceed from them in some sort perhaps as our Thoughts from those *Things* . . .": *CL* II 1194–5.

5[3] Cf in the same letter: "the human understanding never took an higher or more honorable flight, than when it defined the Deity to be—Actus purissimus sine *potentialitate*": *CL* II 1195.

Nie![1] but on the contrary to me it appears as gross ⟨an⟩ absurdity, a[s] if I should ⟨say⟩ that the Geometer's perception of an absurdity was an absurd perception.

8   I ii 191 | § 5 "Leibnitzisterei"

Leibnitz nimmt in seinen *Protogaeis* mit Burnet an, dass die Berge durch die Sündfluth entstanden. Ob das wahr sey, mag Gott wissen. Aber der Einwurf, den *Schmidt* dagegen, in der Vorrede zu diesem von ihm herausgegebenen Werke des Leibnitz, macht, ist herzlich elend. Nehmlich, dass die Berge von der Weisheit und Allmacht Gottes allzudeutlich zeigten, als dass sie ein Werk der Sündfluth seyn könnten.

[In his *Protogaeis* Leibniz assumes with Burnet that the mountains originated through the Flood. God knows whether that is true. But the objection which Schmidt makes to this, in the Foreword to this work of Leibniz which he brought out, is really wretched. Namely, that the mountains manifest God's wisdom and omnipotence far too clearly to be the product of the Flood.]

If by the Deluge be meant Noah's, Schmidt might have drawn a better biblical argument from the Olive Leaf.

9   I ii 243 | § 9

So viel fängt man ziemlich an zu erkennen, dass dem Menschen mit der Wissenschaft des Zukünftigen wenig gedient sey; und die Vernunft hat glücklich genug gegen die thörichte Begierde der Menschen, ihr Schicksal in diesem Leben vorauszuwissen, geeifert. Wenn wird es ihr gelingen, die Begierde, das Nähere von unserm Schicksal in jenem Leben zu wissen, eben so verdächtig, eben so lächerlich zu machen?

[This much we begin to recognise somewhat, that little has been gained by the man with the knowledge of the future; reason has, fortunately enough, contended against men's foolish desire to foreknow their fate in this life. When will reason succeed in making equally suspect, equally ridiculous, the desire to know the particulars of our fate in the life beyond?]

The difference is too gross! In the one we ask *particulars* interesting only to the Vanity or Cupidity of the Individual; but in revealed religion we ask—not for A. or B. or C. but the aweful Question/ Are we mere Bubbles? or progressive Realities?—Is there or is there not, a pre-established Harmony between final Happiness, & Duty?[1] Is it not shameful to compare this with gipsey questions

---

7[1] "Never!"

9[1] C adopts the famous phrase of Leib-

niz, upon which he comments directly in ESCHENMAYER **40** (and n 1).

10 I ii 244–5

Dieser Grund gegen die Astrologie ist ein Grund gegen alle geoffenbarte Religion. Wenn es auch wahr wäre, dass es eine Kunst gäbe, das Zukünftige zu wissen, so sollten wir dieses Kunst lieber nicht lernen.

[This argument against astrology is an argument against all revealed religion. Even if it were true that there was an art of foretelling the future, we would do well not to learn this art.]

I cannot suffer this to pass without some attempt to controvert it. The folly & impiety of Astrology, Cheiromancy, & all the hundred other modes of Fortune-telling consists in the anxiety to make the future the same as the present, & in the act of Rebellion against the All-wise, all-good, Regent of the Universe!—Is this to be compared with the simple Idea—"Death will not annihilate me. I shall be—& shall be that which it is best for myself & for the whole System that I should be."[a] And were I in lofty Stoicism to destroy the "Self", yet Benevolence would re-produce the "I".—

11 I ii 249 | § 11 "Gespräch über die Soldaten und Mönche"

A. Träumst du? der Staat! der Staat! das Glück, welches der Staat jedem einzelnen Gliede in diesem Leben gewährt.

B. Die Seligkeit, welche die Kirche jedem Menschen nach diesem Leben verheisst.

A. Verheisst!

B. Gimpel!

[A: Are you dreaming? the state! the state! the happiness which the state guarantees each individual member in this life. B: The bliss which the Church promises every man after this life. A: Promises! B: Dunce!]

This well deserved to have been carried on. If the Soldier is to be taken as the Support of the State, & this "State" as the very best for the well-being of all the Individuals included—all tyrannical States, that by the bye need most Soldiers, out of the question—all senseless wars, &c &c &c—then on the Monk's side you must put all superstition out of the question—& have mere Roger Bacons, Boscovichs, &c[1]

---

[a] There are no closing quotation marks in the original, and the quotation might therefore be considered as ending either earlier or later

[1] Roger Bacon (c 1214–c 1294), Franciscan, and Ruggiero Giuseppe Boscovich (1711–87), Jesuit, were both of them philosophers and scientists; for C they represent the RC Church establishment at its best. C noted that Roger Bacon was "thrown into dungeon" and Galileo persecuted "because he knew a little more than other people, and that of itself, if it was not impiety against the better Being, is

12 I ii 350

Eine Religion, die einen Christus gebildet, sollte nicht mehr einen so kahlen Reisenden, als der Lessingische *incognito* reisende Jude ist, hervorbringen? Wer das behauptet, der lästert den Vater und den Sohn, die jüdische und die christliche Religion.

[A religion which produced a Christ should no longer be able to produce such a paltry traveller as Lessing's incognito wandering Jew? Whoever maintains such a thing blasphemes the Father and Son, the Jewish and the Christian religion.]

What nonsense! Michaelis spoke of the present wretched State of the Jew~~ishs~~, not of the Jewish State[1]—so if a writer were blamed for introducing a learned philosophical Gypsy, he might as rationally be answered by referring to some great man born & bred in the North of Hindostan, before the expulsion of that Race.

13 II xv | iii Preface

Lessing hatte nemlich in frühern Zeiten den Plan, nach dem Beyspiele einiger Französischen Gelehrten, etwas über die Analogie der Deutschen und Griechischen Sprache zu schreiben. Ein dazu gehöriges Manuscript ist 1759 angefangen, und hat die Ueberschrift: *Ueber die Aehnlichkeit der Griechischen und Deutschen Sprache, zur Erleichterung der ersten, und Verbesserung der letztern.* Lessing scheint bey dieser Idee von keinem bestimmten Princip ausgegangen zu seyn; denn bald leitet er Griechische Wörter von Deutschen, z.B. δεινα von *den*, bald Deutsche von Griechischen, z.B. Ehre von εϱις, ab.

[Indeed, in earlier times Lessing had the plan, following the example of several French scholars, to write something on the analogy between the German and Greek languages. A manuscript pertaining to this was begun in 1759, and has the title *On the Similarity of the Greek and German Languages, for Making the Former Easier and Improving the Latter.* Lessing apparently arrived at this idea without proceeding from a definite principle; for sometimes he derives Greek words from German, e.g. δεινα [such a one] from *den* [the], sometimes German words from Greek, e.g. *Ehre* [honour] from εϱις [strife].]

Doubtless, Lessing meant neither to derive the German from the Greek,

---

always taken as impiety against the mob'': *P Lects* Lect 5 (1949) 182. C's knowledge of Boscovich's work is summarised in Böhme **14** n 1.

12[1] Johann David Michaelis (1717–91), theologian and orientalist, whose objection against G. E. Lessing's play *Der Juden*— that it gave an improbable picture of Jews

as noble and magnanimous—is attacked in turn in K. G. Lessing's text. C knew the scholarly work of Michaelis, having borrowed his *Introduction to the New Testament* tr Herbert Marsh (2 vols Cambridge 1793) from the Bristol Library Society in Jun 1796: *Lects 1795* (*CC*) 168, 175n.

or the Greek from the German; but to make it probable, that both Languages had a common Origin.[1]

14 ii xix, slightly cropped

Wenn er zuweilen, besonders bey kritischen Bemerkungen, gefehlt hat, so geschah es nicht aus Unwissenheit, sondern aus allzu grossen Scharfsinn.

[If he erred occasionally, especially in his critical comments, it happened not out of ignorance but rather out of all too great acumen.]

A very just remark: and applied (as I have had occasio[n] to observe more than once) to his theological Treatises even more than to his verbal Criticisms.[1]

14A ii 224 | "Altdeutscher Witz und Verstand" § 2

> Wer entbehrt der Ehre,
> Dem ist weder wohl noch wehre

["He who lacks honour is neither happy nor sad."][1]

15 ii 225

Aus Lehmanns *Florilegium.*

> Wenn alle Leute wären gleich,
> Und wären alle sämmtlich reich,
> Und wären all zu Tisch gesessen,
> Wer wollte auftragen Trinken und Essen?

[From Lehmann's *Florilegium.* "If all people were equal, And all of them were rich, And all were sitting at table, Who would serve food and drink?"]

In my youth I should have answered: "Take it by turns, to be sure!"—

16 ii 253 | "Anmerkungen über alte Schriftsteller: Homer *Odyssee*"

V. 10. Da Homer sagt ειπε και ἡμιν; auch uns, O Muse, sage ein Theil von allen diesen Dingen; scheint er nicht andeuten zu wollen, dass schon

---

13[1] C's own view, expressed in writings on "philosophical grammar", e.g. *Logic* (*CC*) 18, MATTHIAE **10**.

14[1] G. E. Lessing's "theological treatises" are assembled in *Sämmtliche Schriften* mainly in Vols v–vii, on which C wrote more than half his annotations in that collective edition, combining admiration with surprise at what seem to be uncharacteristic lapses, e.g. in *Sämmtliche Schriften* **8** below.

14A[1] C's plausible emendation produces a rhyme and alters the meaning to "He who lacks honour has neither happiness nor means of defence."

vor ihm oder mit ihm zugleich auch andre Dichter die Abentheuer des Ulysses besungen? (die Odyssee gehört allerdings unter die Νότους.)

[*Odyssey* 1.10. When Homer says, "O Muse, to us also say a part of all these things", does he not seem to mean to say that other poets before him or contemporary with him also sang of the adventures of Ulysses? (The *Odyssey* belongs anyway among the "Homecomings".)]

?—νοθους; = ἀντιλεγόμενα;[1]

17　ιι 272 | "Mimas"

(Dessen Fragmente in *Gale Opusc. Myth.* . . . .) Die letzten Worte bedürfen einer Verbesserung. Mimas redet von der Gedächtnisskunst, und sagt: . . . περι χαλκειας δε επι τον Ηφαιστον· περι δειλειας επι τον 'Επειον. Was ist das für ein Epeus, der wegen seiner Furchtsamkeit so berüchtigt wäre? Ich kenne keinen. Aber einen Epeus kenne ich wohl, der als grosser Künstler bekannt ist; ihn, der jenes

> *Instar montis equum, divina Palladis arte,*

baute,

> *—ipse doli fabricator Epeus.*

Und er baute dieses Pferd nicht allein, er war Mannes genug, sich auch selbst darein verschliessen zu lassen. Ich rette seine Ehre und lese so: Περι χαλκειας δε, επι τον Ηφαιστον και τον Επειον· περι δειλειας επι—Das Folgende fehlt.

[(Whose fragments appear in Gale *Opusc[ula] Myth[ologica]*. . . .) The concluding words need an emendation; Mimas speaks of the art of memory, and says, ". . . while [to remember] about bronze statuary [one should think] of Hephaestus, [to remember] about cowardice [think] about Epeus." Who is this Epeus, who was so notable for his cowardice? I know of none. But I know one Epeus well, who is well known as a great artist, he who built "the horse, like a mountain, by divine Pallas' art"—"himself the maker of the deception, Epeus". And he not only built the horse, but was enough of a man to have himself shut into it. I save his honour and read it so: "while [to remember] about bronze work [one should think] of Hephaestus and Epeus; but about cowardice—. The Rest is wanting."]

Instead of this violent alteration just read ξυ for δει, & you have the

---

16[1] Lessing meant that the *Odyssey* was one of a number of poems about the homecomings of the Greek heroes after the Trojan War. C, tempted no doubt by the ambiguous omission of a letter in the text (but a typesetter would be more likely to set τ for the single character στ in νόστους, "homecomings", than in mistake for θ), suggests "?—suppositious? i.e. disputed?"—implausible in view of Lessing's "when Homer" rather than e.g. "when the author".

natural antithesis to χαλκεια: as Vulcan in works of Brass, so Epeus in works of Wood.[1]

18 II 273–4 | "Heraclitus"[1]

Atlas οὗτος παραδεδοται φερων τον οὐρανον ἐπι των ὠμων· ὁ ἀδυνατον, ὑπο οὐρανου και αυτον ὀντα. Aber muss er nicht unter dem Himmel seyn, wenn er den Himmel tragen soll? Ich glaube, die Worte sind versetzt, und es muss heissen: ὑπο και αὐτου οὐρανον ὀντα, weil auch noch Himmel *unter* ihm ist.

[Atlas—"the tradition is that he supports the heavens on his shoulders; which is impossible, as he too is under the heavens". But must not Atlas be under the heavens if he is supposed to support the heavens? I believe the words are transposed and should read: "Heaven being also beneath him," because there is also heaven *beneath* him.]

Ingenious & a Conjecture not unworthy of Lessing but not quite necessary. For ὑπ' ουρανου[2] may mean & probably does, the same as our "under the Heaven."—Atlas ὑπ' ουρανου was himself a part of that Whole, which as an Agent external to it, he is supposed to support— This, of course, is impossible—like a man climbing on his own shoulders to take a wider prospect—Lessing had the *picture* before his fancy, the Greek the *meaning*. To support a weight we must be external to it— but Atlas was comprehended in it/. The passage is highly interesting in reference to the monotheism of the early Greek Sages—& might be cited against Warburton's assertion of their Spinosism,[3] taking~~en~~ as the identity (einerleiheit) of God and the World—but Spinoza asserts the contrary[4]—his System is "*one with*" not "*the same as*".—Spinoza it has been ever the *fashion* to calumniate/ even Leibnitz himself, who had been anticipated in all his main Ideas by Spinoza, and perhaps took them from him, sacrificed to Fear & Prudence, & joined the outcry against him.[5] Warburton was original in calumny only of Plato & all the theists of ancient Greece./

17[1] C suggests reading ξυλεία (woodwork) instead of δειλία (cowardice). But perhaps the wooden horse was a stock example of a cowardly trick, in which case no emendation would be needed.

18[1] This Heraclitus is not the pre-Socratic philosopher but the supposed author of a work on "Incredibilities" in Greek mythology.

18[2] "Under heaven"—in textus.

18[3] William Warburton (1698–1779) *The Divine Legation of Moses* (1738–41)

bk 3 § 4.

18[4] C notes (ARGENS 17 and n 1): "Spinozism does not consist in making Nature to be God; but in making God to be Nature."

18[5] C believed with Brucker and Jacobi that Leibniz "certainly borrowed from Spinoza" the idea of pre-establishd harmony: *BL* ch 8 (*CC*) I 130 and n. Leibniz dissociates himself from the Spinozists, of whom he speaks disparagingly, e.g. in *Nouveaux essais* bk 1 ch 1.

19 II 275 | "Diogenes Laertius"

[Lib. VI. Cap. I.] n. 3. Επωτωμενος δια τι ολιγους εχει μαθητας; εφη, ότι άργυρεα αυτους εκβαλλων ραβδῳ.

Dieses heisst in der lat. Uebersetzung: *interrogatus cur paucos haberet discipulos? Quod inquit, argentea illos virga non ejicio.* Casaubonus billigt die Negation. Ich finde auch ohne sie einen sehr guten Verstand. Ich glaube nehmlich, Antisthenes hat weiter nichts damit sagen wollen, als: *weil ich sie wegprügle.*

["Asked why he had few pupils, he [Antisthenes] said, 'Because I beat them away with a silver staff.' " Casaubon approves the negative. I can conceive very good sense without it. In fact, I believe that Antisthenes did not mean by this any more than "because I drive them away with blows".]

This does not satisfy me. I have not the work before me; but it would seem to mean that he repelled them by attacking their *Avarice*, and thus might furnish a parallel to Christ's conversation with the rich young man.[1]

20 II 281–2 | "Lucretius"

Lucrez versteht das Kunststück des malerischen Wohlklangs in einem hohen Grade; z.B. wenn er das Zittern der Glieder ausdrückt.

Lib. 6. v. 1188. *In manibus vero nervi trahier, tremere artus.*
——— v. 1213. Das allmählige Sterben.

> *Languebant pleraque morbo*
> *Et moriebantur.*
> Virgil.

Aen. VII. 76. Die Bewegung der Zunge ahmt die Bewegung der beschriebenen Sache nach:—

> *tunc fumida lumine fulvo*
> *involvi—*

Der langsame Gang nachgeahmt 634.

> *aut leves ocreas lento ducunt argento.*
> Ovid.

Metamorphos. I. 343.

> *Jam mare littus habet: planos capit alveus amnes:*
> *Flumina subsidunt: colles exire videntur:*

19[1] Matt 19.16–22, Mark 10.17–22, esp Matt 19.21: "If thou wilt be perfect, go and sell that thou hast, and give to the poor . . .".

> *Surgit humus: crescunt loca decrescentibus undis,*
> *Postque diem longam nudata cacumina sylvae*
> *Ostendunt—*

Diese Stelle ist schön und malerisch; sie würde aber noch weit malerischer seyn, wenn der Dichter seine Züge auch so geordnet hätte, wie die Dinge selbst in der Natur auf einander folgen. Die Hügel müssen eher wieder hervorzukommen scheinen, als die Flüsse in ihr Bette zurücktreten. Jenes ist das Zeichen der abnehmenden Ueberschwemmung, und in diesem ist schon keine Spur mehr davon. Dieses ist der Fehler, den Ovid fast in allen seinen Gemälden hat. Er ist reich an wahren und schönen Zügen; aber er wirft diese Züge unter einander, und entkräftet sie durch sein *hysteron proteron*.

[Lucretius has mastered to a high degree the art of making sound chime harmoniously with picture: for example, when he expresses the trembling of the limbs:
6.1188. "Relentlessly the sinews twitched in the hands, the limbs trembled."
6.1213. A gradual dying: "Most of them grew faint with disease, and died" [tr W. H. F. Rouse, rev M. F. Smith (LCL 1975)].
Virgil *Aeneid* 7.76. The movement of the tongue imitates the movement of the object described: "—then wreathed in smoke and yellow glare [they] beat out polished greaves from pliant silver" [tr H. Rushton Fairclough (LCL 1916–18)].
Ovid *Metamorphoses* 1.343. "Now the sea has shores, channels hold the level rivers; the floods subside, and hilltops spring into view; land rises up, the ground increasing as the waves decrease; and now at length, after long burial, the trees show their uncovered tops" [tr (adapted) Frank Justus Miller (LCL 1921)]. This passage is beautiful and painterly; but it would be far more painterly still if the poet had arranged his points in the order in which the things themselves follow one another in nature. The hills must have reappeared before the rivers returned to their beds. The former is the sign of the retreating flood and in the latter no trace of the flood remains. This is the mistake that Ovid makes in nearly all his pictorial passages. He is rich in true and beautiful touches; but he jumbles these together and weakens them by his putting the last before the first.]

The instances of imitative metre from Lucretius are striking: those from Virgil—well?—Why, I will dare to tell my own feelings—the first I find nothing in, and the second is a mere mechanical intentional artifice, that may be repeated by *Recipe*. The passage from Ovid—the first half ⟨(as to metre)⟩ is all it ought to be—⟨but⟩ the words from "crescunt" to "ostendunt" are at once poetry and appropriate music. Here I remember Johnson's criticism on imitative Harmony[1]—Like 9 10ths of his criti-

[1] Johnson *Rambler* 92 and 94. In the latter paper particularly, Johnson attacks the concept, arguing "that on many occasions we make the musick which we imag-

cisms, it is a mere sophism/ doubtless, a 100 Hexameters might be found, that begin with the same feet/ viz. a ~~m~~ long monosyllable & a cretico-molossus (–/◡◡ – – – –/) as "Et moriebantur"[2]—& yet no effect or a different effect.—What then? It is the coincidence of metre & meaning that's the merit. I think, Ovid might be defended against Lessing's Censure, by taking the first Line "Jam mare &c" as an annunciation of the *Whole*—& the three following as the *particulars*/ Indeed, I have exprest myself more diffidently than I ought—for "might be" read "*should* be defended".

21 II 295, slightly cropped | "Livius"

Lib. XXX. Kap. 34. Wenn Livius daselbst die Schlacht zwischen dem Scipio und Hannibal beschreibt, so sagt er unter andern: *Igitur primo impetu ex templo movere loco hostium aciem Romani. Ala deinde & umbonibus pulsantes, in summotos gradu illato, aliquantum spatii, velut nullo resistente, incussere, urgentibus & novissimis primos, ut semel motam aciem sensere.* Alles ist hier deutlich, bis auf die Worte: *Ala & umbonibus pulsantes.*

[When Livy describes (30.34) the battle between Scipio and Hannibal he says, among other things, "Consequently by the first attack the Romans at once dislodged the enemy's lines. Then beating them back with their shoulders and the bosses of their shields, being now in close contact with men forced from their position, they made considerable progress, as no one offered any resistance, while as soon as they saw that the enemy's line had given way, even the rear line pressed upon the first" [tr F. G. Moore (LCL VIII 1949)]. Everything is clear except the words *Ala et umbonibus pulsantes.*]

[Lessing goes on to suggest that *ala* cannot have its usual military meaning here—i.e. "wing" of an army—but that it might be the word for the rim reinforcing the top and bottom edges of the oblong shield.]

Might not Ala be an error for Alæ? or ala itself as a noun of multitude be nominative to incussere? only adding an "et" after pulsantes, or omitting it after deinde?[1]

22 II 298–9, cropped | "Seneca"

[Lib. I. cap. 1:] * *Stella* eine feurige Lufterscheinung, wie allenfalls der

---

ine ourselves to hear".

20[2] A slip—"Moriebantur" is a pyrrhico-molossus. A cretic – ◡ – (or amphimacer, as in *CN* I 373) is not used in dactylic hexameter.

21[1] C defends the meaning of *ala* as wing of an army, reading: "Then the wings (or wing), [both] beating them back with the bosses of their shields [and] being now in close contact . . .". Most modern editors and translators accept the text as Lessing quotes it, taking *ala* in another meaning as "upper arm".

Stern der Weisen aus dem Morgenlande könnte gewesen seyn, wenn der Weg nicht ein wenig zu weit wäre.

[* *The Star*, a fiery phenomenon of the atmosphere, as possibly the star of the wise men from the East might have been had the distance not been rather too great.]

* Much more probably the Star of S⟨t⟩ Matthew originated in some *astrological* inference.[1] Such a Planet in such a quarter of such a House (i.e.—one of the 12 Houses of the Star-mongers) might signify the Birth of a great Monarch, & in what country. The two or three Fantasts that still have faith in astrology, might quote this in their favor, and the [? Socinians] against the authenticity of the Chapters.

23 II 299 | Continuing 22 textus

Lib. I. cap. 3. Dass *Linea* auch die in einander laufende Gränze zweyer Farben bedeuten kann, das sehe ich nunmehr aus einer Stelle des Seneca, wo von dem Regenbogen die Rede ist: *Videmus in eo aliquid flammei, aliquid lutei, aliquid caerulei, & alia in picturae modum subtilibus lineis ducta.*

[That *linea* can also mean the merging boundaries between two colours I now see from a passage in Seneca, discussing the rainbow: "In it [a rainbow] we see some red, some yellow, some blue and other colours, drawn as in a picture, in thin bands" [tr Thomas M. Corcoran (LCL 1971)].]

Not Linea, but *subtilis* Linea, may: i.e. Linea quæ non est prorsus Linea/[1]

24 II 299

Bey den Alten muss der Fall nicht ungewöhnlich gewesen seyn, dass sich Leute selbst sahen; aber sie erklärten ihn aus einer Krankheit der Augen. *Quidam*, sagt Seneca, *hoc genere valetudinis laborant, ut ipsi sibi videantur occurrere, ut ubique imaginem suam cernant.*

[Among the ancients it cannot have been unusual for people to see themselves, but they explained this as a disease of the eyes. "Some people", says Seneca, "suffer from this kind of infirmity—they see their own reflection everywhere and seem to be running into themselves."]

Remarkable that this Disease prevailed & perhaps still prevails in the North of Scotland & in the Isles—[1]

22[1] I.e. the Star of Bethlehem, Matt 2.2.

23[1] Not "Line", but "*subtle* Line" may, i.e. "a Line that is not really a Line".

24[1] Cf C's likening of "political Nightmares" about the impending depopulation of the island of Britain to "a superstition, or rather nervous disease, not uncommon in the highlands of Scotland, in which men, though broad awake, imagine they

25 II 339 | "William Freke Esq"

Er hat 1693 zu London in 8. drucken lassen: *Select Essays tending to the universal Reformation of Learning* . . . . Aus dem Versuche wider die Astrologie will ich mir die zwey alten Verse merken, in welchen die Bedeutung und Kraft der zwölf Hänse(?) eingeschlossen ist:

> *Vita lucrum fratres genitor nati valetudo*
> *Uxor mors pietas regnum benefactaque carcer.*

[He published in 1693 in London in octavo *Select Essays* . . . . From the essay against astrology I wish to note the two old verses which contain the meaning and force of the twelve Jacks(?):

> Life, wealth, brothers, father, children, health,
> Wife, death, piety, kingdom, benefactions, prison.]

Strange that the Editor could not have corrected Hänse into Häuser[1]

---

see themselves lying dead at a small distance from them": *Friend (CC)* I 240. C is alluding to the phenomenon of "Second Sight" reported by visitors to the Highlands, e.g. Samuel Johnson, who "came away at last only willing to believe": *A Journey to the Western Islands of Scotland* (1785) 178 (a copy of this ed being in *Gillman SC*—1843).

25[1] I.e. "Jacks" into "houses".

Gotthold Ephraim Lessings sämmtliche Schriften, &c. 30 pts in 15 vols. Berlin 1784–98. 8°.

In this set, each volume has normally two title-pages, one for the series and one for the specific part; each volume contains two parts. Roman numerals in this entry refer not to volumes but to the separately paginated parts. The whole set has been bound uniformly with LESSING *Leben* and with *Freundschaftlicher Briefwechsel zwischen Gotthold Ephraim Lessing und seiner Frau* (Berlin 1789)—BM C 126 c 13—which is inscribed with C's name but was not annotated by him.

British Library C 126 a 1. The foot of x $^+$1, cut out of its volume, is in VCL (F 2.17): see **45**.

Autograph signature "S. T. Coleridge" on a title-page of the first part of each volume (showing that the parts were already bound in pairs when he acquired them; cf "this volume" in **8**). Also inscribed by C on vi $^+$4 (at the end of the third bound volume) in a style slightly different from the signatures at the beginnings of volumes: "S. T. Coleridge | Feb. 1813 | 71 Berner's Street Oxford S^t" (see **85** n 1); this leaf (vi $^+$4/$^+$5) may originally have been a front flyleaf to Pt v (the beginning of the third bound volume) or more probably to Vol i. In 1987 iv 125–8, 297–300, xxvii 173–6, 285–8, 477–80, xxviii 221–4, 237–40 were still unopened.

J. H. Green has written a memorandum on vi $^+$6: "Original Sin V 5 p 28 | Inspiration ib p 109 | Revelation necessary to Salvation ib p 39 | Doctrine before Scripture ib. p 19 | Internal Evidence p 20."—probably notabilia for his "Introduction" to *CIS* (2nd ed 1849, v–xliii), which included a few quotations from these annotations and which was written, as SC stated in her Advertisement, "in consequence of my consulting him on the subject of my Father's obligations to Lessing in the *Confessions of an Inquiring Spirit* [1840]". Green or another reader has also written notes in pencil on vi 29, 30, 87, 115, 237, xviii 226, 424, xxiv 328–9, xxix 302, 463. Bookseller's or binder's marks (in ink) appear on v 81, x 97, xv 449. C has corrected typos on vi 241, vii 186, xxvi 369. Many passages, some running on for several pages, are marked with pencil lines in the margins. Though some of these may be C's, many certainly belong to other readers, esp J. H. Green, and it is impossible to distinguish different hands. Instead of being presented in full entries as submarginalia or in an annex, pages so marked are here listed: v 19–20, 28–9, 39, 91, 97, 109, 121, 164, 165, 166; vi 16, 23, 36, 75, 80, 83, 86, 87, 88, 91, 94–9, 106, 108, 114, 115, 135, 138–9, 141, 233, 234, 247–8, 250–4, 274–8, 290, 295, 297; xvii 44, 68–9, 311; xxv 230, 231, 232, 233, 241, 243, 245, 303, 306, 336, 383, 387–8; xxvi 144, 282, 322, 343, 382; xxx 424–5, 426, 432–3, 439, 440.

Inscribed by John Duke Coleridge on i $^-$4: "This set of books belonged to S. T. Coleridge—then to J H Green—then to Ernest H Coleridge from whom I purchased them—I wish them so far as my wishes have any power to stay at

Heath's Court Coleridge June—1892''. A short personal note written by C on a back flyleaf of Pt x (fifth bound volume) was cut out by EHC, evidently for reasons of propriety, and is now in VCL (MS F 2.17): see **45**.

CONTENTS. (Capital Roman numerals are the numbers of parts, not volumes.) I [i–ii] Vorbericht; [1]–82 Sinngedichte; [83]–92 Epigrammata; [93]–304 Über das Epigram, und einige der vornehmsten Epigrammatisten; [305]–72 Lieder. II [i]–xxxii Vorbericht; [1]–34 Oden; [35]–82 Fabeln und Erzählungen; [83]–172 Fragmente; [173]–220 Gedichte; [221]–76 Zur Geschichte der Aesopischen Fabeln. III [1]–22 Vorbericht; [1]–275 Rettungen [Lemnius, Cochläus, Cardan, *Ineptus Religiosus*, Horace]. IV [1]–28 Vorbericht; [1]–308 Briefe. v [iii]–viii Vorrede; [1]–112 Bruchstücke über einige Fragmente der Wolfenbüttelischen Ungenannten; [113]–302 Durch die Fragmente der Wolfenbüttelischen Ungenannten veranlasste, einzeln gedruckte kleine Schriften. VI [1]–313 Kleine Schriften (cont). VII [iii]–x Vorrede; [3]–118 Theologische Aufsätze; [119]–322 Philosophische Aufsätze. VIII [iii]–vi Vorrede; [3]–116 Gesammelte Vorreden; [117]–[285] Beiträge zur Kenntniss der deutschen Sprache; [286]–[368] Vom Alter der Oelmalerey aus dem Theophilus Presbyter. IX [iii]–iv Vorrede; [1]–410 Artistische und antiquarische Schriften: *Laokoon*. X [iii]–xiv Vorrede; [1]–408 Artistische und antiquarische Schriften (cont). XI [iii]–xvi Vorrede; [1]–340 Artistische . . . Schriften (cont): *Briefe, antiquarischen Inhalts*. XII [1]–166 *Briefe, antiquarischen Inhalts* (cont); [167]–208 Entwurfe zur Fortsetzung der Briefe antiquarischen Inhalts; [209]–310 Zusätze zu den Briefen antiquarischen Inhalts; [311]–62 Zusätze zu der Abhandlung vom Alter der Oelmalerey. XIII [iii]–xii Vorrede; [1]–451 Einige Beyträge zur Litteratur, aus der Wolfenbüttelischen Bibliothek. XIV [1]–180 Einige Beyträge (cont); [181]–428 Beyträge zur Griechischen Litteratur. XV [v]–xvi Vorbericht; [1]–478 *Kollektaneen zur Litteratur* A–J. XVI [1]–478 *Kollektaneen zur Litteratur* K–Z. XVII [iii]–x Vorrede; [1]–384 Theologischer Nachlass. XVIII [1]–210 Fabeln; [211]–492 *Nathan der Weise*. XIX [1]–188 *Miss Sara Sampson*; [189]–238 *Philotas*; [239]–393 *Emilia Galotti*. XX [5]–190 *Der junge Gelehrte*; [191]–263 *Die Juden*; [264]–356 *Der Misogyn*. XXI [3]–158 *Der Freygeist*; [159]–252 *Der Schatz*; [253]–440 *Minna von Barnhelm*. XXII [i]–vi Vorrede; [1]–264 Theatralischer Nachlass; [265]–390 Beyträge zur Historie und Aufnahme des Theaters. XXIII [1]–40 Beyträge (cont); [41]–334 Auszug aus G. E. Lessings Theatralischer Bibliothek; [337]–400 Einige Recensionen vom Jahre 1751; 401–4 Zwei Erzählungen. XXIV [1]–416 Hamburgische Dramaturgie. XXV [1]–408 Hamburgische Dramaturgie (cont). XXVI [v]–xxvi Vorrede [by C. F. Nicolai]; [1]–388 Auszüge aus Lessings Antheil an den Litteratur-Briefen: 1759–1763; [389]–432 Lessings Einzige Recension in der Bibliothek der schönen Wissenschaften. XXVII [iii]–xvi Vorrede; [1]–52 Briefe an K. W. Ramler 1755–1779; [53]–78 Briefe an J. J. Eschenburg 1772–1780; [79]–486 Briefwechsel mit Fr. Nicolai 1756–1777; [487]–520 Anmerkungen zu Moses Mendelssohns . . . Briefwechsel mit G. E. Lessing. XXVIII [1]–356 Briefwechsel mit Moses Mendelssohn 1755–1780; [357]–466 Briefwechsel mit D. Johann Jacob Reiske 1769–1773. XXIX [1]–216 Briefwechsel mit Friedrich Wilhelm Gleim 1757–1779; [217]–306 Briefwechsel mit Conrad Arnold Schmid 1770–1780; [307]–408 Briefwechsel mit Johann Arnold Ebert 1768–1780; [409]–466 Briefwechsel mit Christian Gottlieb Heyne 1764–1779; [467]–476 Briefwechsel mit Joachim Heinrich Campe 1779–1780; [477]–499 Einzelne Briefe. XXX [1]–524 Briefwechsel mit . . . Karl Gotthelf Lessing.

DATE. c 1813–23, probably mostly c 1816. C did not date any of these marginalia, but a few scraps of internal evidence are imbedded in them: **8** refers to George IV and was presumably written after 1820; the reference to Estlin in **28** suggests a date after Jan 1814 (see **28** n 1); **76** refers to A. W. Schlegel's Shakespeare lectures, which were first delivered in 1811; **83** refers to the *Memoirs of the Life of Colonel Hutchinson* (1806), which C read with the Wordsworths in early 1807 but did not annotate until many years later (see HUTCHINSON). Some of the annotations are written in a noticeably large hand which may be of early date.

COEDITOR. Lore Metzger.

1 v ⁻2

I seldom take up a volume of Lessing without renewed indignation at Nicolai's miserable Judgement, ⟨or rather Lack of all Judgement,⟩—in the omission of all the Tracts & Fragments published by L./ & retaining only the remarks, sometimes scarcely intelligible, and always less interesting, without them.[1] Had they been extracts from common Books, there might have been some excuse for it; but being either most rare, or Mss. they are in fact a part of Lessing's Works.— Ө The omission of a single volume of those *mere* Letters/, just indeed what a sensible man would write; but assuredly not such as he would think fit for publication, would have included the whole—nay, one half of such a volume.[2]

S. T. C.—

2 v 12 | *Bruchstücke* 2

Sie [die Deisten] wollen die Freyheit haben, den Gott der Christen zu verlachen; und doch geduldet seyn. Das ist freilich ein wenig viel: und ganz gewiss mehr, als ihren vermeinten Vorgängern in der alten jüdischen Kirche erlaubt war. Denn wenn deren einer des Herrn Namen lästerte, (Levit. XXIV. 12.) so ward er ohne Barmherzigkeit gesteiniget, und die Entschuldigung half ihm nichts, dass er nicht den wahren Gott, den die Vernunft den Menschen lehre, sondern den Aftergott gelästert habe, wie die Juden sich ihn bildeten.

1[1] Christoph Friedrich Nicolai (1733–1811), bookseller and author, whose autobiography C also annotated (NICOLAI), was a friend of Lessing's and edited several parts of this edition: he is named as editor of XXVI–XXX, and according to the title-pages his family firm published XI–XII and XXVI–XXVII. C assumes that he was also responsible for V–VIII, for which no editor is specified: **29** below. C objects especially to the omission of the *Wolfenbüttel Frag-*ments (though later comments on them are published among the shorter works of V and VI), the essay on Wissowatius, and the extracts from Berengar of Tours (**85** below).

1[2] This remark is clarified in **29** below. Lessing's correspondence occupies pts XXVI–XXX—the two fattest vols in the set—and includes many letters *to* Lessing from Nicolai and others.

[They [the deists] desire the freedom to ridicule the Christian God and yet to be tolerated. That is surely more than was permitted to their alleged predecessors in the old Jewish religion. For when one of them blasphemed the name of the Lord (Lev 14.12) he was mercilessly stoned and could not be saved by the excuse that he had blasphemed not the true God of whom reason teaches man but, rather, the false God whom the Jews conceived.]

Smile-waking Sophistry! As if such philosophical Deists existed in the time of Moses, other than as he himself was one of them. As if it were possible, that such a rare, if at all existent, crime could have been the object of Legislation for a Horde of emancipated quasi-Negroes— ~~so~~ degraded & brutalized by a 500 years Slavery in Egypt.

3   v 51, pencil | *Bruchstücke* 4

Das Alte Testament weiss von keiner Unsterblichkeit der Seele, von keinen Belohnungen und Strafen nach diesem Leben. Es sey so. Ja, man gehe wenn man will, noch einen Schritt weiter. Man behaupte, das A. T. oder doch das Israelitische Volk, wie wir es in den Schriften des A. T. vor den Zeiten der Babylonischen Gefangenschaft kennen lernen, habe nicht einmal den wahren Begriff von der Einheit Gottes gehabt.

[The OT says nothing about the immortality of the soul or reward and punishment after this life. So be it. One could even go a step further if one wished. One could maintain that the OT, or at least the people of Israel as we are acquainted with them through the writings of the OT in the period before the Babylonian Captivity, did not have anything like a true concept of the unity of God.]

The *Law* of the *Land* does not teach [? á] it, any more than it teaches the existence of the Supreme Being. It takes both for granted, as being the universals of natural Religion/ but it confined the Θεῖον[1] to One Being, the God of their Fathers, thus precluding Polytheism/ but the Belief of Rewards & Punishments after Death rather required moderating than strengthening among so barbarous a Race—

4   v 54, pencil

. . . [man] füge hinzu: dass, so wie Moses selbst im Anfange seiner Sendung von dem Unendlichen keinen Begriff hatte . . . sich Gott zu ihm herabliess, und sich ihm nicht als den Unendlichen, sondern bloss als eine von den besondern Gottheiten <u>ankündigte</u>, unter welche der Aberglaube Länder und Völker vertheilt hatte.

[Let us add that as Moses himself had no idea of the Infinite at the beginning of his mission . . . God accommodated himself to him and <u>announced</u> himself not

---

3[1] The ''Divine''.

as the Infinite but only as one of the special deities among whom superstition had divided land and people.]

I cannot well imagine a clearer revelation, certainly no one more sublime, than the answer to Moses—"*I am*" hath sent thee.[1]

5   v 56, pencil

Die heiligen Bücher der Braminen müssen es an Alter und an würdigen Vorstellungen von Gott mit den Büchern des A. T. aufnehmen können, wenn das Uebrige den Proben entspricht, die uns itzt erst zuverlässige Männer daraus mitgetheilet haben.

[The sacred books of the Brahmins must be equal to the OT in antiquity and in noble conceptions of God, if the remainder corresponds to the samples that only now have been communicated to us by some reliable men.]

all Europe has been the Dupe of Dupes in this respect.

6   v 90, pencil

Seine Jünger haben diese Lehre getreulich fortgepflanzt. Und wenn sie auch kein andres Verdienst hätten, als dass sie einer Wahrheit, die Christus nur allein für die Juden bestimmt zu haben schien, einen allgemeinern Umlauf unter mehrern Völkern verschaft haben: so wären sie schon darum unter die Pfleger und Wohlthäter des Menschengeschlechts zu rechnen.

[His disciples have faithfully propagated this teaching. And even if they had no other merit than having given wider currency to a truth that Christ seemed to have destined for the Jews alone, they would for this have to be counted among the guardians and benefactors of mankind.]

How was it possible that Lessing could assert this, in the face of Go ye into all Nations &c/[1] the discourse with the Samaritan woman,[2] &c &c.

7   v 95–6, pencil

Z.E. die Lehre von der Dreyeinigkeit.—Wie, wenn diese Lehre den menschlichen Verstand . . . nur endlich auf den Weg bringen sollte, zu erkennen, dass Gott in dem Verstande, in welchem endliche Dinge *eines* sind, unmöglich *eins* seyn könne; dass auch seine Einheit eine transcendentale Einheit seyn müsse, welche eine Art von Mehrheit nicht ausschliesst?—Muss Gott wenigstens nicht die vollständigste Vorstellung von sich selbst haben? d.i. eine Vorstellung, in der sich alles befindet,

---

4[1] Exod 3.14 (var).   16.15; cited again in **60** below.
6[1] Paraphrasing   Matt   28.19,   Mark   **6**[2] John 4.7–26.

was in ihm selbst ist. . . . Folglich kann entweder Gott gar keine vollständige Vorstellung von sich selbst haben: oder diese vollständige Vorstellung ist eben so nothwendig wirklich, als er es selbst ist.—Freylich ist das Bild von mir im Spiegel nichts als eine leere Vorstellung von mir. . . . Aber wenn denn nun dieses Bild *alles*, alles ohne Ausnahme hätte, was ich selbst habe: würde es sodann auch noch eine leere Vorstellung, oder nicht vielmehr eine wahre Verdoppelung meines Selbst seyn?—*

[E.g. the doctrine of the Trinity.—What if this doctrine . . . were only intended to guide human understanding finally to the recognition that God, in the sense in which finite things are *one*, cannot possibly be *one*; that even his unity must be a transcendental unity, which does not preclude a kind of plurality? Must God at least not have the most complete notion of himself? That is, a notion in which everything exists that exists in him himself. . . . Consequently either God does not have a complete notion of himself, or this complete notion is just as necessarily real as he is himself. Certainly my image in the mirror is nothing more than an empty representation of me. . . . But what if this image contained *everything* that I myself have without exception: would it then still be an empty representation or rather a true duplication of myself?—*]

But *we* have a knowlege of our Existence without any such Duplique or Alter Ego. And is Existence, i.e. the position of attributes, susceptible of a Representation? Is it not a *Sense*, rather than a reflection? Viel mehr ein Gefühl, als eine Vorstellung?[1]

8   v ⁻1, vi ⁺1–⁺2, referring to v 115–26 | *Ueber den Beweis des Geistes und der Kraft*

Page 115 to p. 126. Year after year I have made a point of re-perusing the Kleine Schriften, as master-pieces of Style and argument. But in the Reasoning from 115 to 126 I feel at each re-perusal more and more puzzled how so palpable a *Miss* could have been made by so acute a mind.[1] He ought to have denied ⟨in the first instance & under *all* circumstances⟩ the possible consequence of a speculative conviction from a supposed miracle ~~presented to the Senses~~ having no connection with the doctrine ~~assertioned~~—ex. gr. A Man cut a grindstone in half with his thumb. I saw it with my own eyes. Therefore, there are three and only three Self-subsisting ~~Persononas~~ in the Unity of the Deity.—But L. having conceded this (p. 117, 118),[2] it is absurd to affirm, that the most unques-

7[1] "Much more a feeling than a representation".

8[1] These pages are part of an essay, *Evidence of the Spirit and Power*, occasioned by the publication of the *Wolfenbüttel Fragments*, in which Lessing considers the credibility of miracles and of historical evidence.

8[2] On p 117 Lessing writes that if he had lived at the time of Christ and had been a witness of his miracles with no reason to doubt their authenticity, then he would have believed what Christ said; on p 118 he expresses the difficulty of belief during the eighteenth century, when miracles no longer happen.

tioned and unquestionable historic evidence (ex. gr. that George the third was not the Son but the Grandson of George the Second, to ~~us~~ me who live under George the 4ᵗʰ)³ is in *no* degree a substitute for the evidence of my own Senses—that á the conviction produced by such BEST *possible* Confluence of Testimony bears *no* proportion to the conviction produced in me by the recollection (i.e. testimony of my memory) of my own experience.—*ª*As well—or ⟨with⟩ only one degree more of paradoxy—might Lessing have applied the same reasoning to the Eye-witness's ⟨own⟩ *recollection* of the Miracle compared with *the Seeing* it. ~~For~~ Of one thing I am sure that I have been as often deceived by my own memory as by any testimony that ~~is~~ was agreeable to the known Rules of Evidence, and the Canons of credibility.—Neither should I omit that there is a little *trickery* in the Chasm between "X cut a grindstone in half with his thumb": & "Ergo: The Deity is tri-personal." The major consists in the tacit presumption, that all superhuman power is derived from the God of truth—and that God will not bestow this power for purposes of imposition or error.—The defects of the argument are obvious—first, that the assumption is not warranted by the language of the very Revelation, in support of which it is hazarded.—2ⁿᵈ that as far as the *effect* (the conviction, namely, worked on the mind of the Beholder) ⟨is concerned,⟩ it is not the ~~one~~ in re verâ⁴ *Superhumanness* of the power displayed, but the belief of it, from the Beholder's ignorance of any human means adequate to the solution of the phænomenon—and no one will affirm that God will not permit the mistake of ~~an~~ the unusual for the præternatural—Lastly, there is no small difficulty in answering the objection—Will the God of Truth communicate truths unintelligible, & therefore for the receiver *not* truths but mere sounds but if intelligible, why not discoverable by the same Light of Reason that sufficed to teach us the existence & moral Attributes of God.—But tho' the argument is defective, it is not *absurd*.   S. T. C.

9 v 122–5

Ich leugne also gar nicht, dass in Christo Weissagungen erfüllet worden; ich leugne gar nicht, dass Christus Wunder gethan: sondern ich leugne, dass diese Wunder . . . seitdem sie nichts als Nachrichten von Wundern

---

ª Here, at the head of vɪ ⁺ 1, C has written: "*Note* on p. 115–126 *continued* from the blank leaf at the beginning of the volume"

8³ After ten years as Prince Regent during his father's illness, George ɪv reigned 1820–30.

8⁴ Not the "actual" or "matter of fact" *Superhumanness*.

sind . . . mich zu dem geringsten Glauben an Christi anderweitige Leh-
ren verbinden können und dürfen.

[I by no means deny that prophecies have been fulfilled in Christ; I do not deny
that Christ worked miracles; but I do deny that these miracles . . . , since they
are nothing but reports of miracles, . . . can and may bind me to the slightest
belief in Christ's other teachings.]

I cannot see the consequentness of this reasoning. If (as Lessing admits)
the sight of a Miracle or the present fulfilment of a known prior prophecy
would be the sufficient Ground of implicit faith in the assurances of the
Prophet and Thaumaturge, the Belief of such an Occurrence ⟨in proof of
such assurances⟩ on the strongest possible historical evidence must be
the ground of a *proportional* belief in these Assurances. Less indeed and
less impressive, but yet *a* ground. For suppose the historic evidence *not*
the best possible, the Belief would be *less*. Now what is capable of ⟨sen-
sible⟩ diminution must be a *sensible* quantity—. Belief would not be
rational Belief, if it did not bear some ratio to Knowlege: even tho' I
should grant what L. (*erroneously*, I think) assumes—that the *sight* of
an unusual phænomenon is = the knowlege of its being a miracle, i.e.
a supernatural phænomenon./

10　v　128 | End of *Ueber den Beweis* . . .

But all this takes for granted, that the History is an essential part of the
Religion. Now in orthodox Christianity the incarnation of the Logos in
Jesus Christ is *the Religion* itself. As far*ᵃ* morals & natural Theology are
concerned, Christ neither taught or pretended to teach, any thing *new*.
He in short did not *teach*—he *was*—the Religion—to be believed *in*, not
merely believed/

11　v　145–7, pencil | *Eine Duplik*

Will es denn Eine Klasse von Leuten nie lernen, dass es schlechterdings
nicht wahr ist, dass jemals ein Mensch wissentlich und vorsetzlich sich
selbst verblendet habe? Es ist nicht wahr, sag ich; aus keinem geringern
Grunde, als weil es nicht möglich ist.

[Will one class of people never learn that it is utterly untrue that a man ever
knowingly and intentionally deceived himself? I say it is not true for no less
reason than that it is not possible.]

Lessing too often (I had almost said, *habitually*) lets his Logical Acute-
ness master his psychological Insight, or *Empfindung*—what he might

---

ᵃ For "as far as"

find within.[1] At any one moment it may, *perhaps*, be impossible for a man wilfully to blind himself (& this I merely *"perhaps"*) but in a continuous Series of moments? O too, too often!—L. himself felt it, in the case of the interested Bigot—& turned *sharp round* not to contradict himself.—"Harry! thy Wish was Father to that Thought!"[2] Who of men is not at times the "Harry" of this Sentence?

12   v 154

Und doch, selbst die crudesten Begriffe von der Theopneustie angenommen, getraue ich mir zu beweisen, dass, wenn die Evangelisten einmal, einander widersprechende Nachrichten von der und jener bey der Auferstehung vorgefallnen Kleinigkeit hatten . . . dass, sag ich, der h. Geist ihnen diese widersprechende Nachrichten nothwendig lassen musste.*

[And yet even accepting the crudest notions of divine inspiration, I venture to prove that if the Evangelists ever had reports that contradicted each other about this or that minor occurrence at the Resurrection . . . that, I say, the Holy Ghost must have necessarily left them these contradictory reports.*]

* *lassen*—Ja!—*Dictiren* aber? Und das leztere ist der Begriff der Theopneustie.[1]

13   v 163

Die Religion ist *da*, die durch die Predigt der Auferstehung Christi über die heydnische und jüdische Religion gesieget hat: und diese Predigt soll gleichwohl damals nicht glaubwürdig genug gewesen seyn, als sie siegte?

[The religion is *that* which has triumphed over the heathen and Jewish religion through the teaching of the resurrection of Christ; and yet this teaching is supposed to have been not credible enough at the time that it triumphed?]

I cannot find that this was the Case in the degree that Lessing states: who thus plays into the Hands of the *Units*. Paul preached the Άναστασις[1] of the Human Race obtained by the *Cross* of Christ—His Resurrection was a necessary consequence of his divinity—"it was not *possible*, that he should know corruption"[2]—The Resurrection of Christ is no *analogy*

11[1] Though *Empfindung* is normally translated "sensation" or "perception", C justifies his own version, "Insight", etymologically: cf KANT *Metaphysik der Sitten* 2 n 2.

11[2] *2 Henry IV* IV v 91 (var). The "case of the interested Bigot" does not appear to be in *this* work of Lessing's.

12[1] C takes up terms from textus: "*leave*—Yes!—But *dictate*? And the latter is the notion of divine inspiration."

13[1] "Resurrection".

13[2] A fusion of texts from Acts 2.24, "Whom God hath raised up [i.e. Jesus],

to *our* Αναστασις; but a proof i̶t̶ of it by, & as far as it is a, proof of his Godhead.

14   v 184

Dass auch ἑτοιμαζειν im N. T. an mehrern Orten nichts als *destinare* heisst, davon hat *Grotius* bereits die Exempel gesammelt; nur sehe ich keinen Grund, es mit ihm einzig auf *destinationem divinam* einzuschränken.

[Grotius had already collected examples demonstrating that ἑτοιμαζειν in many places in the NT means no more than *destinare* [fix upon; intend]; only I see no reason for restricting it with him to *destinationem divinam* [holy purpose].]

Our english word "ordered" seems to me the true meaning of ἑτοιμα-σαν. On their return they ordered i̶t̶ such & such Articles[1]—just as if I met my Taylor in the Church-yard on Sunday morning, & told him—I shall be measured for a suit of clothes tomorrow—

15   v 188–9

Johannes sagt, dass Joseph und Nicodemus den Leichnam Christi so begraben, ganz so, *wie die Juden zu begraben pflegen.* Und Sie sagen mit Ihrem raren Einfalle: nein, nicht so, nicht ganz so; denn sie hatten nur die eine Hälfte der Salbung, die Salbung wider die Fäulniss vollzogen, und die andre Hälfte, des Wohlgeruchs wegen, war noch übrig, und wie billig, den frommen Weibern übrig gelassen worden, deren Nase so ekel ist.

O der trefflichen Harmonie, die zwey widersprechende Nachrichten, die wörtlich bey den Evangelisten stehen, nicht anders vereinigen kann, als durch Erdichtung einer dritten Nachricht, von der kein einziger Evangelist eine Sylbe sagt!

[John says that Joseph and Nicodemus buried the body of Christ, just *as the manner of the Jews is to bury.* And you say, in a rare moment of inspiration, no, not so, not entirely so; for they had completed only half of the anointing, the anointing against decay, and the other half, for the perfuming, was yet remaining and, as was fitting, had been left to the pious women, who are so easily disgusted by bad odours.

Oh, such splendid harmony that can reconcile two contradictory reports,

having loosed the pains of death: because it was not possible that he should be holden of it", and 2.31, "He seeing this before spake of the resurrection of Christ, that his soul was not left in hell, neither his flesh

did see corruption."

14[1] The text at issue is Luke 23.56, "And they returned, and prepared [Greek ἡτοίμασαν] spices and ointments . . .".

which are to be found verbatim in the Evangelists, in no other way than by the invention of a third report, about which no single Evangelist says a syllable!]

Considering the object & character of S[t] John's Gospel I can see no contradiction here—Joseph & Nicodemus buried Christ with all the usual forms—So we should say, that King William & the Queen buried Tillotson with all appropriate Honors[1]—Would that imply that his female friends did not lay him out, or prepare the funeral ornaments?—A minute Biographer would state the latter—an Historian would content himself with the former—

16   v 197

Wie? Maria [Magdalena] konnte bloss daher, weil sie von weiten den Stein vom Grabe abgewälzt sahe, blos daher schliessen, dass der Leichnam Christi nicht mehr darin befindlich sey? . . . Sie wollte mit ihren Gespielinnen ja auch den Stein vom Grabe wälzen. Sie war ja schon darum besorgt gewesen, wer ihnen wälzen hülfe. Und doch wollte sie den Leichnam Christi nicht verschleppen; sie wollte ihn nur salben. Und ihr fiel nicht erst ein, dass ihr andere in eben dieser Absicht wohl schon könnten zuvorgekommen seyn? Sie sahe nicht erst hin, ob es nicht so wäre? . . . Sie läuft, und sieht wirklich nicht erst in das Grab? Johannes wärc? Sie schliesst nur—wenn das anders schliessen heissen kann: der Stein ist weg; also ist auch der Leichnam weg? . . . Sie läuft, und sieht wirklich nicht erst in das Grab? Johannes will wirklich nicht, dass wir das dabey in Gedanken ergänzen sollen?

[What? Mary [Magdalene] could only—because she saw from afar the stone rolled away from the grave—conclude that the body of Christ was no longer to be found there? . . . She too wished, with her companions, to roll the stone from the grave. She had already been concerned about who would help her to roll it. And yet she did not want to bear away the body of Christ; she wanted only to anoint it. And it did not first occur to her that others had anticipated her in this very intention? She did not first look in to see if it were so? She merely concluded, if such can be called a conclusion, the stone is gone, so the body must be gone too? . . . She runs, and really does not look first into the grave? John really does not intend us to supply that in our mind?]

I cannot agree with Lessing. These Women were the appointed Persons—how could they suppose, that others had *volunteered* the Task without their knowlege to a Body taken down from a shameful Gallows? Any fearful woman, who on approaching her House had seen the Doors broke open, & knew the whole family to be absent, would act similarly.

15[1] John Tillotson (1630–94), abp of Canterbury, was buried in the chancel of his church of St Lawrence Jewry, and Burnet preached his funeral sermon.

17 v 239–41

[Lessing complains about those harmonists who wish to harmonise every syllable of the gospels. He comes back to the disharmonies centred upon Mary Magdalene, e.g. the reports of her vision.] Was Marcus den gesammten Jüngern (v. 10. 11.) melden lässt, ist augenscheinlich bloss und allein der Bericht der Maria Magdalena von der ihr besonders geschehenen Erscheinung. Denn Maria kömmt da ganz allein, erzählt ihnen ganz allein, dass der Herr lebe . . .

[What Mark has communicated to all the disciples evidently is purely and solely Mary Magdalene's report of the vision that appeared specially to her. For Mary comes all alone, tells them all alone, that the Lord lives . . .]

That man, methinks, will best answer these attacks, which in coarseness and captiousness harmonize the Pot-Orator of a Tap-room with a pettifogging Attorney's Clerk (O how unworthy of LESSING!) who best bethinks himself, how his own wife, sister, or servant maid would have done, looked and expressed themselves on a similar occasion.—Tho' half a dozen had been co-present, would not each have exclaimed—"He is risen! I have seen him!"—would either have said, *We?*—Scarcely. Yet Lessing himself could not held[a] the Harmonists more cheap than I do, or have been more jealous of the historic Exegesis, or in short a more sturdy Anti-Grotian—hodiernâ linguâ, Anti-Paleyian.[1]   S. T. C.

18 v 282–3

[*Eighth Contradiction.* The argument of this section turns on apparent discrepancies in the Evangelists' account of events following the Passion. Matthew (28.7) and Mark (16.7) seem to say that the disciples received divine instruction on Easter Monday to betake themselves immediately to Galilee; but Luke (24.29) states that Our Lord himself commanded them to remain in Jerusalem, apparently on Easter Monday too. The anonymous author whom Lessing is discussing attempts to reconcile these passages by attributing the instruction to remain in Jerusalem to Ascension Day. In support of this interpretation he adduces Acts 1.1–6. Lessing, however, demolishes this reading of the opening verses of Acts: the only satisfactory reference in the matter is Luke 24.33–53, which passage associates the injunction to remain in Jerusalem firmly with Easter Monday. We must rely on the evidence of these verses, otherwise nothing is clear or definite in the Gospels at all.

[a] For "hold" or "have held"?

17[1] "Anti-Grotian—in today's terms, Anti-Paleyian". For C's repeated reference to William Paley as the latest of the successors to Hugo Grotius see LUTHER *Colloquia* **80** n 3.

Ninth Contradiction. This section continues the subject of discrepancies in the account of Christ's appearances after the Resurrection. Matthew (28.16–20) narrates his appearance upon a mount; John (21) describes his visitation of the disciples on the shore of Lake Tiberias. Lessing insists that Matthew's silence in no way disproves the possibility of *additional* appearances. Christ's words on the mount, he continues, sound like his departing words; on the other hand, we know from the previous argument that the events of Ascension Day took place near Jerusalem. Hence the appearance on the mount comes after the events of Easter Monday, after the subsequent appearance in the presence of Thomas, and after the appearance beside Lake Tiberias. John calls the visitation at Tiberias the third appearance; this remark must signify the third *major* one to correspond with his own account. Matthew says (28.16) that the mount was the place to which the Lord had already directed the disciples; hence, by the probabilities of logical behaviour and narration, the appearance on the mount ought to be the first one of all—or at least the first in Galilee. And yet by virtue of the previous argument the appearance beside Tiberias was earlier. Lessing attempts to escape this dilemma by calling the whole situation *ein Rätsel* ("a riddle") rather than a "contradiction".]

The 8th & 9th are the only "Contradictions" that are of any moment. I would, I could solve them.—For they are far too important to be safely attributed to the natural & inevitable variations of the most veracious Witnesses. They consist of what eye-witnesses could not have either forgotten or confounded—

19 VI [1]

It is worth noticing that just a century before this Controversy,[1] the famous Baxter had supported the very same position, as Lessing's, in answer to an Infidel MSS to which B. himself gives a similar character as Lessing gave to the Fragments.—See Baxter's Own Life edited by Silvester—p. 153 of Part III.—[2]

19[1] The public controversy that followed Lessing's publication in 1774–7 of an allegedly anonymous ms in the Wolfenbüttel library, the *Fragmente eines Ungenannten* (Fragments of an Unnamed Author). These fragments were in fact part of H. S. Reimarus's *Apologie oder Schutzschrift für die vernünftigen Verehrer Gottes* (Apology or Defence of the Rational Worshippers of God), which criticised Christian doctrines by applying criteria of historical evidence. C's note is written on the flytitle of the "Kleine Schriften" that were Lessing's contributions to the debate, especially with Johann Melchior Goeze (1717–86).

19[2] BAXTER *Reliquiae* COPY B **105**, where Baxter replies to a professed infidel "that *Christianity* was proved true many years before any of the New Testament was Written", and C remarks upon the parallel between Baxter and Lessing and the "more than Dominican Virulence" of Lessing's chief opponent, Goeze.

20 VI 41–2 | *Lessings nöthige Antwort auf eine sehr unnöthige Frage*

Eigen ist es . . . dass eben derselbe [Augustin] behauptet, das *Symbolum* dürfe nicht geschrieben werden.

* *Sermone* 213 . . . *Nec ut eadem verba Symboli teneatis, ullo modo debetis scribere, sed audiendo perdiscere: nec, cum didiceritis scribere, sed memoria semper tenere et recolere.*

[It is strange . . . that the same person [Augustine] maintains that the Creed may not be written down. * "Sermon 213 . . . To master the exact words of the Creed you must on no account write them down but learn them thoroughly by hearing them said: nor must you write them when you have learned them, but retain them and keep going over them in your memory."]

* Lessing has violently perverted the plain meaning of this Passage, which does not imply a prohibition to write what himself & others not only wrote but published—but not to write it down, as a substitute for actually recollecting it. By writing any thing, as in a Mem: Book so far from impressing it on the memory we rather disburthen the memory of it.[1]

21 VI 93–5 | *Axiomata*

Endlich das *feste prophetische Wort*!—Woher der Beweis, dass unter dem prophetischen Worte auch alle historische Worte verstanden werden?

[Finally the *sure word of prophecy*!—Whence the proof that by the prophetic word all historical words are also to be understood?]

That St Peter *included* the Messianic *Prophecies* of the O. T. in this phrase,[1] it would be fantastic to deny. But I am strongly inclined to assert, that not ~~th~~ even the Books of the *Prophets* as we have them and as the Jews had them, are here meant; but the Collection made by the Priests before the Birth of our Lord, and entitled The Marks of the Messiah.[2] And secondly, I am disposed to believe, tho not to assert, that the Apostle meant ⟨likewise⟩ more than this—namely, the ~~sam~~ revival and continuance of the same Prophetic Word in the Disciples of Christ. So taken and collated with Acts of the Apostles, Ch. II. v. 16, 17, 18.[3] this

20[1] C repeats this observation—an interesting insight into his own use of note-books and marginalia—in **54** below.

21[1] 2 Pet 1.19.

21[2] Probably the "Similitudes" or "characteristics of the messiah" in the pseudepigraphical Book of Enoch chs 37–71. C refers to the "Marks of the Messiah"

also in EICHHORN *Alte Testament* **12**, SCHLEIERMACHER *Luke* **1**. 5.

21[3] Peter, speaking at the Pentecost, in Acts 2.16–18: "But this is that which was spoken by the prophet Joel; And it shall come to pass in the last days, saith God, I will pour out of my Spirit upon all flesh: and your sons and your daughters shall

text with the corresponding passages in Peter's first Epistle, Chapt. I, would supply a presumption in favor of the Authenticity of the two Epistles which Eichhorn would *viel zu gerne*[4] attribute to some Scholar of Sᵗ Paul's.—[5]

22 vi 113–15

Unartig genug, dass viele Protestanten den Beweis für die Wahrheit der christlichen Religion so führen, als ob die Katholiken durchaus keinen Antheil daran hätten! Ich dächte, wie nur das *gegen* das Christenthum gelten kann, worauf weder Katholik noch Protestant zu antworten weiss: so müsse auch nur das zum Christenthum gehören, was dem Katholiken und Protestanten gemein ist.*

[Bad enough that many Protestants conduct their proof of the truth of the Christian religion as if the Catholics had absolutely no share in it! I should think that just as only that is valid *against* Christianity which neither Catholic nor Protestant can refute, so only that ought to belong to Christianity which Catholic and Protestant have in common.*]

* God forbid! The first half of the Position is evident: for suppose an argument against Xty which the Catholic could but the Prot. could not answer, it would be an argument against Protestantism not against Christianity—But to infer from this, that that ~~alone is Christianity~~ which ⟨is⟩ common to *both* (and if ~~in this case~~ to two, then to all other denominations of Christians) is alone essential Christianity, is tantamount to the assertion that the only true Christian is he who believes the least, as long as he believes any thing that other Christians profess!—

23 vi 224–5 | *Anti-Goeze*

Wer fähig ist, eine Schriftstelle wieder besser Wissen und Gewissen zu verdrehen, ist zu allem andern fähig;* kann falsch Zeugniss ablegen, kann Schriften unterschieben, kann Thatsachen erdichten, kann zu Bestätigung derselben jedes Mittel für erlaubt halten.

Gott bewahre mich, dass ich zu verstehen geben, sollte, dass die Apostel zu diesem allen fähig gewesen, weil sie die Kirchenväter zu *einem* für fähig gehalten!

[He who is capable of distorting a piece of writing against his better knowledge

prophesy, and your young men shall see visions, and your old men shall dream dreams: And on my servants and on my handmaidens I will pour out in those days of my Spirit; and they shall prophesy''.

21[4] ''Much too readily''.

21[5] EICHHORN *Neue Testament* COPY B (annotated 1829) 32 takes up in a similar spirit Eichhorn's suggestion that 1 and 2 Pet were composed by a follower of Paul; C argues that they were composed after the death of Peter by one of *his* followers.

and conscience is capable of anything;* he can bear false witness, can forge documents, can invent facts, and can regard any means of substantiating them as permissible. God forbid that I should imply that the Apostles were capable of all this *simply* because the Church Fathers were capable of them.]

* This and thus worded and in this application is not only Sophistical, but something so much worse than Sophistry that I can never cease to regret that Lessing should have been seduced into it. Goeze's Assassinous Bigotry may extenuate, but cannot justify it.[1]

24 vi 313

It is now notorious that the justly celebrated Reimarus the elder, the best and greatest of the Defenders of the three articles of (so called) Natural Religion, the Unity and Attributes of God, as Creator and Providence; the moral responsibility of man; and the immortality of the Soul, or personal Consciousness in the future state, was the Author of the Wol: Fragments.[1] It is no mere interest of curiosity this—but a most important inference may, in my opinion, be drawn—viz. Either that a Priestleian Unitarian must declare all the grounds of nat. theology sophistical or insufficient—or like Reimarus, embrace Deism.[2]

25 vi +2

One cause of the Quarrels between young People, whether Friend with Friend, or Husband with Wife—provided, the parties are good-hearted—Viz—that taking a thorough good heart, as a thing granted & generic, they dwell on differences & imperfections, as the sole matters of Controversy—But when we have had long experience in Life, alas! alas! the having a thoro' good heart becomes the distinction—& the various errors & infirmities the things common & generic, & varying only to make Jack Jack, & Tom Tom—Hence Friendship[s][a] that survive or supervene 15 years from 20, promise to be lasting.—

26 vii -2

~~E Extremes~~

Disparates in the same Substantive—Ex. gr. THE DEFINITE. Let it be the *necessary* Definite, as in the demonstration of mathematical Figures, and in the ~~su~~ obedience therto we have our "perfect Freedom", and purest intellectual Joy—But of all states that are incompatible with a free or even emancipating Intellect, the *arbitrarily* Definite is the most so—

---

[a] Letter supplied by the editor, the word reaching the worn edge of the leaf

23[1] The circumstances of Lessing's dispute with Goeze are outlined in **19** nn 1, 2 above.

24[1] See **19** n 1.
24[2] C expands upon this remark in **26** below.

Hence it is scarcely possible for an expanding Mind to rest in Unitarianism, as taught by Priestley[1]—But one sense can be given—there is no Elbow-room (see ISAIAH—)[2] Atheism (as a transitional State) is far more congenial with the ever-restless Antennæ of our insect Spirits

27 VII 12–15 | *Leibnitz von den ewigen Strafen*

[Footnote, quoting Mosheim:] "Er [Soner] setzt zum Grunde, in Gott sey keine andere Gerechtigkeit, als diese, dass er seine Zusage halten müsse; in allen andern sey seine Macht unumschränkt. * Sehr wohl! So wird denn deutlich folgen, dass Gottes Gerechtigkeit gar nicht hindere, dass er den Gottlosen ewige Strafen auflegen könne."

["He [Soner] establishes that God's righteousness consists only in this, that he must keep his word; in all other respects his power is unlimited. * Very well! Then it clearly follows that God's righteousness does not prevent him from condemning the godless to eternal punishment."]

* Sophistry, Master Mosheim![1]—no other *justice*—i.e. nothing else, which we can rationally represent to our minds as analogous to what is called justice in *Man*. But Soner does not say that there is no other *any* thing, whereby the (in †itself unlimited) Power is directed and qualified. He does not say, there is no Wisdom, no Love, no Mercy. Soner's argument is this—. ~~The divine~~ *Justice*, in that ~~only~~ sense in which and in which alone it can be predicated of God, does not ~~require~~ the eternal punishment of Sinners: and his Love, Wisdom and plighted Mercy forbid it. Or—The ⟨Idea of the⟩ et. pun. of Sinners is not included in the idea of the divine *justice*, and it ⟨is⟩ excluded by (i.e. inconsistent with) the ideas of the Divine *Love & Wisdom*.   S. T. C.

† i.e. abstractly considered,—argumenti causâ, *sup*pono quod ponere absurdum foret.[2] Power subsisting singly, separately, un*qualified*— i.e. talis factus qualis de ~~pater~~ Deo predicari potest[3]—by the attributes of which it is the *Base*, is an impossible conception.

26[1] C writes from personal experience, having been a Unitarian and an admirer of Joseph Priestley (1733–1804) for several years from 1795. In 1805 he described Unitarianism as "the Religion of a man, whose Reason would make him an Atheist but whose Heart and Common Sense will not permit him to be so" (*CN* II 2448). He made public attacks upon Unitarianism in *SM* (*CC*) 99–100, *BL* ch 24 (*CC*) II 245–6, and *AR* (1825) 205n.

26[2] I.e. one interpretation only is acceptable. The biblical reference may be to Isa 28.19–20: ". . . it shall be a vexation only to understand the report. For the bed is shorter than that a man can stretch himself on it: and the covering narrower than that he can wrap himself in it."

27[1] Johann Lorenz von Mosheim (1694–1755), German theologian, mentioned in textus.

27[2] I.e. "for the sake of argument I make a supposition that it would be absurd to posit".

27[3] I.e. "made of such a quality as can be predicated of God".

28 VII ⁻3, referring to VII 62

Ich schliesse mit der nähern Anzeige der gleich anfangs erwähnten Ursache, warum ich wünschen könnte, dass sich Herr *Eberhard* gegen die ewigen Strafen der Lasterhaften, wenigstens nicht in einer Apologie des Sokrates möchte erklärt haben. Es ist diese, weil Sokrates selbst solche ewigen Strafen in allem Ernste geglaubt, wenigstens so weit geglaubt hat, dass er es für zuträglich gehalten, sie mit den unverdächtigsten ausdrücklichsten Worten zu lehren. Man sehe seine Rede zum Schlusse des *Gorgias* beim Plato, in welcher folgende Stelle schlechterdings keine Einwendung dagegen erlaubt. [Lessing here quotes *Gorgias* 525 B–C.]

[I conclude with a closer presentation of the reason (already mentioned at the beginning) why I wished that Mr Eberhard would not declare himself against the eternal punishment of the depraved, least of all in an apology for Socrates. It [the reason] is this: that Socrates himself believed quite seriously in these eternal punishments, at least believed in them to the extent that he found it useful to profess them in the most trustworthy and explicit terms. See his speech towards the end of the *Gorgias* of Plato, where in the following passage no objection against these punishments is allowed.]

62—Plato + Socrates versus Δ° Εσθλιν[1]

29 VII 79 | "Des Andreas Wissowatius Einwürfe wider die Dreieinigkeit"

[Note by the editor:] . . . [da] die hier in den Beiträgen eingedruckte lateinische *Antwort* des *Leibnitz* auf die Einwürfe des *Wissowatius* gegen die Dreieinigkeitslehre mehr für eigenliche Gelehrten ist . . . und, was er [Lessing] nun darüber sagt, ohne Wiederholung des Abdrucks der *Leibnitzischen* Antwort an diesem Orte verständlich ist: so mag auch er allein hier fortreden.*

[. . . [since] Leibniz's Latin "Reply" to Wissowatius's objections against trinitarianism, which is here inserted in the *Beiträge*, is more for true scholars . . . and since his [Lessing's] comments on it are here intelligible without reprinting Leibniz's reply, he may be allowed to continue by himself.*]

* Nicolai—the *provoking* Coxcomb! And this very man forced on the Public Volume after Volume of Lessing's Letters, which L. would have stamped his feet at the sight of ~~them~~ in pr[in]t![a1]

---

a Letters lost in hole in paper

28[1] The Greek letters spell "Dr Estlin", i.e. John Prior Estlin (1747–1817), a Unitarian minister at Bristol, a close friend from 1796 but alienated in 1814 by C's referring to Satan as a "sceptical Socinian" in one of his lectures: *CL* III 471–2, 477–8, 492.

29[1] C repeats the objection of **1**.

30 vii 93–5

Was haben sie [die Socinianer] denn auch je gründliches jenen Folgen
entgegengesetzt, die nothwendig aus ihrer Lehre fliessen, und die nie-
mand stärker gegen sie betrieben hat, als *Abbadie*? Nemlich, dass wenn
Christus nicht *wahrer* Gott ist, die mahometanische Religion eine un-
streitige Verbesserung der christlichen war, und Mahomet selbst ein un-
gleich grössrer und würdigerer *Mann* gewesen ist, als Christus . . . der,
wenn er sich selbst auch nie für Gott ausgegeben hätte, doch wenigstens
hundert zweideutige Dinge gesagt hat,* sich von der Einfalt dafür halten
zu lassen, da hingegen dem Mahomet keine einzige dergleichen Zwei-
deutigkeit zu Schulden kömmt.

[What have they [the Socinians] ever set up in essential opposition to the con-
sequences which necessarily follow from their teaching and which no one has
more vigorously pursued against them than Abbadie? Namely, that if Christ be
not the *true* God the Mohammedan religion was incontestably an improvement
on the Christian, and Mohammed himself was an incomparably greater and wor-
thier *man* than Christ . . . even if he never claimed to be God, Christ neverthe-
less made at least a hundred ambiguous statements* to let himself be so consid-
ered by the simple-minded, whereas Mohammed was not guilty of a single such
equivocation.]

* This is a mistake of Lessing's—A Persian or Arabian Man of Letters,
~~who has~~ and one of the Converts of the Missionaries at Calcutta, but
fallen aside to a sort of Arianism, and whose controversial tracts have
been lately re-printed by the Unitarian Society, has adduced several pas-
sages from the Koran similar and equivalent to the most express texts in
the Gospel of John/[1] the argument being—These high phrases ~~are~~ were
mere metaphors & mystic hyperboles in the mind & mouth of Mahomet,
who confessedly never affected divinity—why not in the case of the

30[1] The source of C's information is a
review in the *Monthly Repository* xviii
(Aug–Sept 1823) 473–9, 540–5, of two
tracts by Rammohun Roy (Rama Mohana
Raya): (1) *The Precepts of Jesus the Guide
to Peace and Happiness, Extracted from
the Books of the New Testament Ascribed
to the Four Evangelists. To Which are
Added, the First and Second Appeal to the
Christian Public in Reply to the Observa-
tions of Dr. Marshman, of Scrampore.* Re-
printed by the Unitarian Society 1823. (2)
*Final Appeal to the Christian Public, in
Defence of the "Precepts of Jesus."* Cal-
cutta 1812. The *Monthly Repository* gives
a full account of the controversy between
Rammohun Roy and the Baptist missionary
Joshua Marshman on the doctrine of the
atonement. Marshman attacked Rammo-
hun Roy as a heathen because he denied the
divinity of Christ. The fact that Marsh-
man's papers in the controversy were re-
published in England induced the Unitarian
Society to reprint Rammohun Roy's tracts.
The *Monthly Repository* quotes all the pas-
sages C refers to, discussing Christ's divin-
ity according to the Gospel of St John and
Mohammed's assertions of his divine mis-
sion (pp 540–1). The review comments on
Rammohun Roy's Arianism, citing his
tract "The Claims of Jesus" as an avowed
defence of the Arian hypothesis (p 544).

other oriental prophet?—But this plausible argument is grounded on a false assumption. The Koran was written & delivered piece-meal and at different periods of Mahomet's Life & at one period ~~of which~~ he meant to have passed himself for the paraclete, or Holy Ghost.—

31 VII 163–7 | *Pope ein Metaphysiker*

[Having outlined (VII 138–58) 14 propositions derived from Pope's *Essay on Man*, Lessing tests them against passages from the poem.]

> *On superior pow'rs*
> *Were we to press, superior might on ours:*
> *Or in the full creation leave a Void.*

Die Schöpfung nemlich ist ihm nur deswegen *voll*, weil alle Grade darin besetzt sind.

Und dieses ist ein Beweis mehr, dass zwei verschiedene Schriftsteller deswegen noch nicht einerlei Meinung sind, weil sie sich an gewissen Stellen mit einerlei Worten ausdrücken *Pope* hatte einen ganz andern Begriff von *leer* und *voll* in Ansehung der Schöpfung, als *Leibnitz*; und daher konnten sie beide sagen: *the creation is full*, ohne weiter etwas unter sich gemein zu haben, als die blossen Worte. . . . * Aus dem Vorhergehenden schliesst *Pope a priori*, dass nothwendig der Mensch in der Welt angetroffen werden müsse, weil sonst die ihm gehörige Stelle unter den Wesen leer seyn würde.

Leibnitz hingegen beweiset das nothwendige Daseyn des Menschen *a posteriori*, und schliesst, weil wirklich Menschen vorhanden sind, so müssen solche Wesen zur besten Welt gehört haben.

[That is to say, for him creation is *full* only because all its degrees are occupied.

And this is one further proof that two different authors are not identical in their opinions simply by virtue of the fact that in certain passages they express themselves in identical words.—Pope had a completely different conception from Leibniz of *empty* and *full* with regard to creation; and therefore both could say *the creation is full*, without having anything in common other than the mere words. . . . * From these premises Pope concludes *a priori* that man must necessarily be found in the world, because otherwise the place that belongs to him in the chain of being would be empty.

Leibniz, on the other hand, proves the necessary existence of man *a posteriori*, and concludes that because men really are present such creatures must have belonged to the best world.]

* Assuredly, this at least is a distinction without a difference. Pope premises, that God must have acted with the highest possible Wisdom/ if so, there must have been an interdependent Place for every class— ergo, for Man—ergo, if Man were not, a Link would be wanting.—The

only difference, is that Pope has omitted a known fact which it would have been needless for him to have added as a Philosopher, and ludicrous as a Poet: viz. that men do exist. The Syllogism is the same in both. All that exists exists as a necessary part & consequence of an infinitely wise Plan. Man exists. Therefore, Man is a necessary &c.—In the VIth thesis likewise Pope's meaning is evidently the same as that of Leibnitz, tho' as might be expected in a Poem, ⟨expressed⟩ with less precision.[1] For Pope evidently implies that God will not interfere in particular cases because such Interference would be incompatible with General Laws—in other words, that a continuous universal agency excludes the idea of particular Determinations. It is false, that Pope concedes, "dass Gott, der besten Welt *unbeschadet*," &c[2]—He could not but see the obvious consequence, that all human Providence and all motive for its exertion, nay, all Science, ~~m~~ would be precluded by the ~~occasional~~ Suspension of general Laws on every occasion of moral or physical Evil.—Mendelssohn and Lessing seem to forget,[3] that this very Preference of General Laws is not an assumption but a deduction from the fundamental Thesis, that God cannot act but with consummate Wisdom.—

32   vii 172

Dasjenige also, was *Pope* den Zusammenhang nennt, findet in unsrer Welt nicht Statt, und dennoch ist sie die beste, dennoch kann in ihr keine Lücke angetroffen werden. Warum dieses? Wird man hier nicht augenscheinlich auf das Leibnitzische System geleitet, dass nemlich, vermöge der göttlichen Weisheit, alle Wesen in der besten Welt in einander gegründet, das heisst, nach der Reihe der Wirkungen und Ursachen neben einander geordnet seyn müssen?

[What Pope calls the "great chain" does not occur in our world, and yet it is the best, yet it contains no lacunae. Why so? Does this not apparently lead us to the Leibnizian system, namely that by virtue of the divine wisdom all beings are ordered relative to one another in the best possible world—that is, they must be ordered in relation to one another according to the system of effects and causes?]

31[1] The sixth thesis derived by Lessing (vii 146) from the *Essay on Man* affirms that God works towards common rather than particular ends. Lessing goes on to discuss this thesis in **33** textus.

31[2] "That God, *without detriment to* the best world": C alludes to a passage on vii 164, where Lessing infers from Pope's *Essay* that there must exist imperfections in the world which God could have avoided without detriment to the best of all worlds if he had been willing to countermand his general laws by specific determinations.

31[3] C knew that the essay upon which he was commenting was the product of a collaboration between Lessing and Moses Mendelssohn (1729–86). This information he gathered from a biography of Lessing that he read in Germany in 1798–9: *CN* i 377 f 13.

It is clear to me, that Pope's gradual Degradation is no more than a Poetical Translation of Leibnitz's sufficient Causes—a visual metaphor, an allegorical picture of the same Thesis.

33 vii 175

Man sehe einmal nach, was er zu der angezogenen Stelle aus dem ersten Briefe

> *the first almighty Cause*
> *Acts not by partial, but by gen'ral Laws*

unmittelbar hinzusetzt:

> *Th' Exceptions few.* *

Der Ausnahmen sind wenig? Was sind das für Ausnahmen?

[Just consult the passage cited from the first epistle ". . . the first almighty Cause/ Acts not by partial, but by gen'ral Laws". He adds immediately, "Th' Exceptions few."* *There are few exceptions?* What kinds of exceptions are these?]

Why not suppose, that Pope purposely added this sentence, to preclude the charge of denying Miracles?

34 vii 179

[Immediately preceding **34** textus is the quoted text "Or partial ill is universal good,/ *Or change admits*, or Nature lets it fall."] Die Worte *Nature lets it fall* habe ich so erklärt, als ob sie eben das sagten, was der Dichter mit den Worten *Nature deviates* sagen will.

[The words "Nature lets it fall" I have explained as if they meant exactly what the poet wishes to express by the words "Nature deviates".]

Strange! Pope's meaning may be exemplified in *Mules*—Nature lets them *fall*—i.e. every Child has a Father, but not every Child a Son—

35 vii 180

Allein was für einen Sinn verknüpfen wir mit den Worten *Or change admits* . . . ? Kann nach *Popens* System . . . etwas anders die göttliche Weisheit entschuldigen, dass die Böses in der Welt zugelassen, als die Vollkommenheit des Ganzen, welches den besondern Theilen vorzuziehen gewesen, oder die Allgemeinheit der Gesetze, die Gott nicht hat stören wollen?

[Only what meaning do we connect with the words "Or change admits . . ."?

According to Pope's system, can anything excuse divine wisdom for admitting evil into the world except the perfection of the whole, which should have been preferred over the particular parts, or except the universality of the laws that God did not wish to disturb?]

This too is plain enough to an English Reader, tho' not happily exprest— It is either permanently a good on the whole or it is capable of being removed by exertions of our faculties, and as motives to such exertions are even therefore good.

35A vii 184

[Quoting Thomson *The Seasons*:]

. . . *these, as they change—are but the varied God.*

36 vii 218 | *Vorrede und Zusätze zu Carl Wilhelm Jerusalem's philosophischen Aufsätzen*

Tugend und Laster *so* erklärt; Belohnung und Strafe hierauf einge-schränkt: was verlieren wir, wenn man uns die Freyheit abspricht?* Etwas—wenn es Etwas ist—was wir nicht brauchen . . .

[If virtue and vice [arc] *thus* explained, reward and punishment thus limited: what can we lose if we are deprived of freedom?* Something—if it is some-thing—that we do not need . . .]

* ~~Lose~~ What do we lose? What, compared with which all other things are Dust & Rottenness—the sense of Justice & Holiness in God, Awe for the Conscience, Esteem, Indignation, & all moral Worth & all moral Beauty. These we should lose!— S. T. C.

37 vii 245–6 | *Ernst und Falk*

FALK. Glaubst du, dass die Menschen für die Staaten erschaffen werden? Oder dass die Staaten für die Menschen sind?

ERNST. Jenes scheinen einige behaupten zu wollen. Dieses aber mag wohl das Wahrere seyn.

[FALK. Do you believe that people are created for the state? Or that the state exists for the people?

ERNST. Some seem to assert the former. But the latter is probably the more ac-curate.]

Without the slightest reference to Kings or their right divine, who are themselves like all others parts of the State, not *the* STATE, I hold, that the former Position (to wit, that ⟨*the*⟩ Men were made for, i.e. have their final cause in, the State, *rather* than the State for *the* Men) is capable of being maintained in a weighty and even sublime sense. I say *rather*, because both may be true. Not only is the Whole greater than a Part; but where it is a Whole, and not a mere All or Aggregate, it makes each part that which it is.

38   vii 248

ERNST. . . . Als ob die Natur nicht auch die Mittel zweckmässig hervorbringen müssen! Als ob die Natur mehr die Glückseligkeit eines abgezogenes Begriffs—wie Staat, Vaterland und dergleichen sind—als die Glückseligkeit jedes wirklichen einzeln Wesens zur Absicht gehabt hätte!

[As if nature must not also produce the means purposefully! As if nature aimed more at the happiness of an abstract concept—such as state, fatherland, and the like are—than at the happiness of each real, individual being!]

Is it an impossible Conception, that a *perfectly organized* Corpus Politicum might (in, ⟨and *through*,⟩ that perfection) acquire a common *Sensorium*? even as the Corpus Naturale?[1] Is not this more than hinted, as the nature of the Future State, under Christ, our *Head*, by the Apostles, John and Paul?—[2]

39   vii 252–6

FALK. Wir nehmen also die beste Staatsverfassung für erfunden an; wir nehmen an, dass alle Menschen in der Welt in dieser besten Staatsverfassung leben: würden deswegen alle Menschen in der Welt nur einen Staat ausmachen? . . . Denn nicht wahr, jeder dieser kleinen Staaten hätte sein eigenes Interesse? und jedes Glied derselben hätte das Interesse seines Staats? . . . Diese verschiedene Interesse würden öfters in Collision kommen, so wie itzt . . .

[We shall suppose, then, that the optimum constitution has been discovered; we shall suppose that all the men in the world live under this best constitution; would therefore all the men in the world compose only one state? . . . For each of these small states would have its own interest, would it not? and each of its members would share the interests of his state? . . . These different interests would frequently come into collision, as now . . .]

The sole defect in this reasoning is in the *Premise*: that this is the best *imaginable*, i.e. *compossible*, State. Now what a single Individual *can*

38[1] "Political Body . . . Natural Body".

38[2] Paul in numerous places refers to Christ as "head" of the Church and of Christians as "members" of his body, e.g. Eph 5.23, 29–32. In the fourth gospel C is perhaps thinking of the parable of the vine, e.g. John 15.5: "I am the vine, ye are the branches: He that abideth in me, and I in him, the same bringeth forth much fruit".

be *absolutely* convinced of (i.e. by universal reason) all *may* be. I do not say, *can* be. For "*may*" refers to the nature of Things in their permanent relations & compatibilities; *can* to accidents of Time & Space. Only to an *infinite* Mind[a] are both the same. But the Interests of all States are *really* tho' not *actually* congruous: i.e. they are incongruous in consequence of errors concerning their own well-being.—Still Lessing's Idea of a Counterpoise to such errors pro tempore et pro tanto is a grand one:[1] only it must be a permeating not a *vascular* Influence. Yet I will not say, that even an additional Set of Vessels, tho' subject of course to all the essential Evils of *Vessels* (i.e. bodies, associations, &c) may not be beneficial at particular Times—as a new morbid action superinduced medicinally.[2] But ever are the permeating, *uncontainable*, Powers (as Public Opinion, the Press when free, &c) the only ones, which Theory can recommend as general Laws.—

40 VII 254

FALK. Viele von den kleinern Staaten würden ein ganz verschiedenes Klima, folglich ganz verschiedene Bedürfnisse und Befriedigungen, folglich ganz verschiedene Gewohnheiten und *Sitten, folglich ganz verschiedene Sittenlehren, folglich ganz verschiedene Religionen haben.

[Many of the smaller states would have completely different climates, therefore completely different needs and gratifications, therefore completely different customs and *manners, therefore completely different moralities, therefore completely different religions.]

* *wickedly* false! For *Sitten* can in this place mean *Morals* only, as distinguished from *Manners* = *Gewohnheiten*.[1]

41 VII 256

* ERNST. Ja ich begreife nicht, wie einerlei Staatsverfassung ohne einerlei Religion auch nur möglich ist.

---

[a] This word has an ink blot over it; C has written below it, in ink, "mind"

39[1] His idea "considering the times and in proportion to the magnitude", in VII 262–4, is that since a single state would be cumbersome to administer, there ought to be different states under the same set of laws, and that the differences that would unavoidably arise between such states could be counteracted by an elite "free of the prejudices of nationality and well aware at what point patriotism ceases to be a virtue". Lessing's speaker, Falk, identifies this elite with the Masonic order.

39[2] C may have been led to his medical analogy of a treatment in which one disease drives out another by the word "vascular", which commonly refers to the system of tubular vessels in the body rather than to "vessels" generally.

40[1] C was accustomed to seeing the term in ethical contexts, as in KANT *Metaphysik der Sitten*, but it does have the other meaning as well.

[* I simply do not understand how a uniform constitution without uniform religion is even possible.]

* Could Lessing have been ignorant, that every known mode of the Christian Religion co-exist under the same Constitution in Great Britain?—and every mode of Religion, Pagan, & Mahometa,[a] under the influence of that Constitution?

42   vIII 94–5, pencil | Preface to *Richardsons Sittenlehre für die Jugend in äsopischen Fabeln*

Roger Lestrange ist bei den Engländern der berühmteste Compilator Aesopischer Fabeln. . . . Seine Schreibart wird von seinen Landsleuten für eine der reinsten und meisterhaftesten gehalten . . .

[Englishmen regard Roger Lestrange as the most famous compiler of Aesop's fables. . . . His countrymen consider his literary style one of the purest and most distinguished . . .]

Mercy! whence could Lessing have derived this strange Information? Lestrange's *Slang* is indeed the master *Slang* of his age—unless Ned Ward & Tom Brown be thought his Corrivals[1]—and as to the "Reinheit",[2] it puts me in mind of the Hibernian, who spit *clean* in a man's Mouth, as he was gaping.   S. T. C.

43   vIII 232 | *Wörterbuch über Friedrichs von Logau Sinngedichte*

Indessen sollte man aus diesem Sinngedichte fast schliessen, dass der Dichter einen sehr schlechten Begriff von der Quadratur des Zirkels gehabt, und vielleicht weiter nichts, als ein Viereck darunter verstanden habe, das man innerhalb eines Zirkels beschreiben kann.

[One should, however, almost conclude from this epigram that the poet had a very poor conception of the squaring of the circle and perhaps understood by it nothing more than a square that can be described within a circle.]

More probably, no idea at all; but he had often heard about the squaring of the Circle, & took it for granted that it was something (whatever it might be) that great Mathematicians had done.   *S. T. C.*

---

[a] Presumably for "Mahometan"

42[1] C considered Sir Roger L'Estrange (1616–1704) the "Introducer" of slang into English prose, with Thomas Brown (1663–1704) and Edward Ward (1667– 1731) as his followers: AURELIUS **62** and n. Cf LEIGHTON COPY B **30** and n 1.
42[2] "Purity" or "cleanness", adapted from textus.

44 IX 121 | *Laokoon 7*

[Quoting Juvenal *Satires* 11.100–7:]

> *Tunc rudis & Grajas mirari nescius artes*
> *Urbibus eversis praedarum e parte reperta*
> *Magnorum artificum frangebat pocula miles,*
> *Ut phaleris gauderet equus, caelataque cassis*
> *Romuleae simulacra ferae mansuescere jussae*
> *Imperii fato, geminos sub rupe Quirinos,*
> *Ac nudam effigiem clypeo fulgentis et hasta,*
> *Pendentisque dei perituro ostenderet hosti.*

. . . Alles ist verständlich, bis auf die letzten zwey Zeilen, in welchen der Dichter fortfährt, noch ein solches getriebenes Bild auf Helmen der alten Soldaten zu beschreiben. So viel sieht man wohl, dass dieses Bild der Gott Mars seyn soll; aber was soll das Beywort *pendentis*, welches er ihm giebt, bedeuten?

["In those times the rude soldier, ignorant and unappreciative of Greek art, would break up cups made by great artists if they turned up as part of his share of the booty from the sack of cities, in order that his horse might exult in its trappings, or his engraved helmet display to the enemy about to die the likeness of the Romulean beast bidden by the fate of empire to grow tame, the twin Quirini beneath the crag, and the naked image of the god, gleaming and hanging [above him] with shield and spear." . . . Everything is clear up to the last two lines, in which the poet goes on to describe yet another such embossed figure on the helmets of the ancient soldiers. This much is obvious: that this is supposed to be a picture of the god Mars; but the epithet *pendentis* [hanging] given to him—what is that supposed to mean?]

what? if for "ac" we should read "aut"?[1] Else what is "nudam"? Either a *chased* Bas relief, or a mere figure (effigy) on the Top which of course would hang down over the *prostrate* foe.

45 X +1[a]

ὁ βωστεδ ατ α Μεςς οπενλι θατ η ἀδ ~~φιντγεϱδ~~ ——— οϝ βῶθ[1] This was the beloved [. . .] Boast of a woman's Favors!—[? Hateful] loveless! & yet their Favorite! *Her* Love[b]!—O!!!!!

---

[a] VCL S MS F2.17, in a small envelope with a note by EHC, dated 5 Jul 1890: "Fragment—cut out of Vol. 9. 10 of Lessing" (i.e. the vol containing pts IX and X)

[b] The last word written in oversize but not capital letters

44[1] C suggests reading "or" in place of "and" in the penultimate line of verse. In the same line, "nudam" is "naked".

45[1] Not Greek, but transliterated English, recording a painful private experience: "He boasted at a Mess openly that he

46 xv 400–1 | "Magister Hugo" [Hugh of St Victor]

Ein Scholastiker, von dem *Johannes Sarisberiensis* (*Metalogic*. L. IV. c. 13.) die Erklärung des Glaubens in geistlichen Dingen anführt: *fides est voluntaria certitudo absentium, supra opinionem, infra scientiam constituta.*

[A schoolman whose definition of faith in spiritual matters John of Salisbury adduces in his *Metalogicon* bk 4 ch 13: "Faith is a voluntary certitude concerning something that is not present, a certitude that is stronger than opinion, but falls short of science" [*Metalogicon* tr Daniel D. Mcgarry (Berkeley & Los Angeles 1955)].]

I far prefer Ricardus di St Victore[1] and the mystical Theologians, with whom join Luther, who difference proper Faith from Science by the sort and not by the degree of certainty. Voluntaria Certitudo,[2] however, is an apt phrase—i.e. an assuredness or habit of Certainty grounded in the Will or practical Reason, the speculative Reason assenting or at least not gain-saying.

47 xvi 118 | "Magnet"

Von den Aerzten, welche diese weitere Kraft des Magnets nicht einsahen, ob sie gleich seine Anziehungskraft vor Augen hatten, sagt er [Paracelsus]: "Sie haben alle weitere Erfahrung verlassen, und sich beholfen an ihrem Küchengeschwätz, das nicht einmal mit Ehren zu verantworten ist."

[Of the doctors who did not recognise this further power of the magnet, although they had its power of attraction before their very eyes, he [Paracelsus] said, "They have abandoned all further experiment and have betaken themselves to their kitchen gossip, which cannot even honourably be vouched for."]

The time will come when Paracelsus will be unanimously acknowleged not only, as now, the Prince of Blackguards and Puffers, but either as a Repository of the Arcana dispersed thro' Christendom by the abolition of the Samothracian— ~~or~~ Cabiric Mysteries, or as the greatest Physiologist since the Christian Æra.[1]   S. T. C.—

---

had ~~fingered~~—— of both". Given the conjectured dates of these marginalia, possibly an incident involving Charlotte Brent and her sister Mary Morgan, with whom C lived for most of the period 1811–16, and about whom he had ambivalent sentimental and sexual feelings: cf *CN* iii 1408.

46[1] C's knowledge of the theologian and mystic Richard of St Victor (d 1173)

was probably derived from Tennemann. His annotated copy, in the BM, contains a note in the section devoted to this pupil of Hugh of St Victor: W. G. Tennemann *Geschichte der Philosophie* (Leipzig 1798– 1817) viii i 270.

46[2] "Voluntary Certitude"—from textus.

47[1] This view of the historical role of

48 XVII 84–5 | *Die Religion Christi*

It is more than probable, that this Article was a mere fragment or Memorandum of Lessing's—perhaps for his Adam Neuser,[1] or for the author of the Wolfenbüttel Fragments[2]—written not in his own person, but as the plausible thoughts of a Deist—Otherwise, it would contradict his "Education of Mankind",[3] & his avowed Dislike of the Socinians—

49 XVII 86

§ 7. Die Religion Christi ist mit den klarsten und deutlichsten Worten darin enthalten;

§ 8. Die christliche hingegen so ungewiss und vieldeutig, dass es schwerlich eine einzige Stelle giebt, mit welcher zwey Menschen, so lange als die Welt steht, den nehmlichen Gedanken verbunden haben.

[§ 7. Christ's religion is contained therein [the gospels] in the clearest and most distinct words;

§ 8. The Christian religion, on the other hand, is so uncertain and ambiguous that there is scarcely a single passage that, since the beginning of the world, two people have connected with the same thought.]

Is it possible, that Lessing could have asserted this § 7 and 8, in earnest? Could he have re-perused either Matthew & or Luke (S[t] John out of the question) and persisted in these opinions? As sure as I ~~know~~ believe Lessing to be (what I mean by) *Lessing*, do I believe this impossible. The question is not here concerning the absolute metaphysical Deity of Christ; but whether he is represented by the Evangelists as more than mere man.[1]

50 XVII 95, pencil, marked with a line in the margin | *Historische Einleitung in die Offenbarung Johannis*

Der Märtyrer Justinus, der um 170. nach Christi Geburt schrieb, ist der erste von allen Kirchenlehrern, welcher der Offenbarung gedenket; und

---

the chemist and alchemist Paracelsus (1493–1541) as a medium for ancient beliefs is repeated in several contexts c 1818–19 and later, notably in the first lecture of the 1818 series, *Lects 1808–1819* (*CC*) II 56, but also in *P Lects* Lect 11 (1949) 322 and in T. FULLER *Holy State* 7. C's main sources of information about the Samothracian mysteries were FABER and SCHELLING *Ueber die Gottheiten von Samothrace* (Stuttgart & Tübingen 1815).

48[1] *Von Adam Neusern, einige authentische Nachrichten* (not included in this ed), a sympathetic account of Adam Neuser, who was imprisoned in 1572 for denying the divinity of Christ.

48[2] See **19** n 1 above.

48[3] *Die Erziehung des Menschengeschlechts*, included in pt V of this collection.

49[1] C's note, written at the end of this very short tract, responds not only to §§ 7–8 but to the general question with which the work begins: "Whether Christ was more than a man [*Mensch*] is a problem" (XVII 84).

das Merkwürdigste dabey ist, dass er sie dem Apostel Johannes beylegt
. . . [er sagt] *Es hat unter uns einen gewissen Mann, Nahmens Jo-*
hannes, gegeben, ᵃwelcher einer von den zwölf Aposteln Jesu Christi
gewesen.ᵇ Dieser hat in seiner Offenbarung geweissaget, dass die Gläu-
bigen tausend Jahre in Jerusalem zubringen würden.

[Justin Martyr, who wrote c A.D. 170, is the first of all the Church Fathers who
mentions the Revelation; and the curious thing about the matter is that he as-
cribes it to the Apostle John . . . [he says:] "There was among us a certain man
named John who was one of the twelve disciples of Jesus Christ. He prophesied
in his Revelation that the faithful would live a thousand years in Jerusalem."]

It seems to me no irrational Suspicion, that these words were interpo-
lated/ It does not look like the mode, in which in the year 170, a Father
would speak of so famous an Apostle; but exactly so as he would intro-
duce *a* John, a θεολογος,[1] the Author of a controverted Book—

51   xvii 112–13 | "G. E. Lessings so genannte Briefe an verschiedene Gottesgelehrten"

Ich will nicht hoffen, dass man mich hier zu *Schöttgen* verweisen wird,
welcher im Sohar und andern Midraschischen Büchern die deutlichsten
Spuren von allen christlichen Glaubensartikeln will gefunden haben.*

[I trust that I shall not here be referred to Schöttgen, who claims to have found
the most distinct traces of all Christian articles of faith in the Sohar and other
Midrashic books.*]

* I would, I could be sure of this! i.e. that no Doctrines closely resem-
bling those of the Trinity Redemption, Marriage of the Church with the
Word, existed among ~~the~~ a certain class of the Jewish Rabbins before
Christ. I have always feared in it a stronger argument in favor of a De-
istic Hypothesis, than against the Socinians

52   xvii 118–23, pencil

Die *Worte* des Irenäus sind: **Non enim per alios dispositionem nostrae*
salutis cognovimus, quam per eos, per quos Evangelium pervenit ad
nos, quod quidem tunc praeconaverunt, postea vero per Dei voluntatem
in scripturis nobis tradiderunt, fundamentum et columnam fidei nostrae
futurum. Diese Worte sollen sagen, dass die Schriften der Grund und
Pfeiler unsers Glaubens geworden? Gewiss nicht! Es müsste sodann

---

ᵃ⁻ᵇ Passage marked with pencil

50[1] A "theologian" or "divine"—the
Greek attribute in the title of the last book
of the NT, "The Revelation of John the Di-
vine", which C with other scholars as-
cribed not—as had been conventional—to
the Apostle John, but to "an Elder of the
Church of Ephesus in John the Evangelist's
Life-time": LACUNZA 87 at n 3.

schlechterdings *futuris* anstatt *futurum* und da der Syntax *Fundamentum
et columnam futuris* zu seyn, nicht wohl erlauben würde: so müsste die
Veränderung sich noch weiter erstrecken und es wenigstens heissen,
*fundamento et column*ae *futuris*; wenn Irenäus nicht lieber eine ganz
andre Wendung gewählt hätte, falls er das hätte sagen wollen, was man
mit einer lutherischen Brille so offenbar darin entdecken will. *Futurum*
beziehet sich auf *Evangelium*; und dass dieses sowohl *praeconatum*, als
scripturis traditum, der Grund und Pfeiler unsres Glaubens geworden,
ist der eigentliche Sinn des Irenäus.

[The *words* of Irenaeus are: *"But by no other means have we known of our
salvation but by those which are conveyed to us through the gospel, which were
made known at that time and later in truth by the will of God committed to us in
the scriptures, being the foundation and pillar of our faith." Do these words say
that the writings have become the foundation and pillar of our faith? Certainly
not! It must in this case simply be *futuris* ["being", ablative, modifying "scrip-
tures"] instead of *futurum* [accusative, modifying "gospel"] and since the syn-
tax would not allow *fundamentum et columnam futuris* ["they—the scriptures—
being the foundation and pillar"], the alteration must go still further and be at
least *fundamento et column*ae *futuris* ["by being in the foundation and pillar"];
as if Irenaeus had chosen an entirely different meaning and had wanted to say
what those wearing Lutheran spectacles so obviously want to discover in it.
Being refers to *gospel*, and the real meaning of Irenaeus is that this, as well as
made known and *committed to scripture*, is the foundation and pillar of our
faith.]

* Lessing's Logic forsook him here. Surely, Irenæus positively asserts,
that the Xtians had no other stable foundation of their Faith than the
Preaching of the Gospels in the Life-time of the Apostles, & their *writ-
ten* Sermons (as we should say, their *published* Histories & Discourses)
after their Death. But in the age of Irenæus the Apostles were dead:
ergo, the Apostolic Writings were then the sole foundation of Christian
Knowlege & Belief. This clearly contradicts, as far as *his* opinion
weighs, Lessing's assertion that the Christians were to learn it from the
Bishops immediately, who again derived [a]it as needed[b] from the Holy
Ghost. Besides, take Evangelium in Lessing's Sense, and the passage
amounts to this, that we learn that System of Faith which the Apostles
preached, by the System of Faith preached by the Apostles—i.e. it
amounts to that species of Nonsense, called a Truism or identical prop-
osition in a duplicate—that a man is a man is clear because a man is a
man—   *S. T. C.*

[a–b] Passage obscured by offsetting from facing page; someone has superimposed, in pencil, "it
made"

53 XVII ⁻2⁻⁻1, referring to XVII 119–20

P. 119. 120.

I cannot discover any Weakening of my Confutation in the Note, in Lessing's after Observations.[1] It does not follow, that Irenæus & the Catholic Church did not hold the Evangelium (= Gospel Doctrine) which the Apostles first preached, and then in obedience to the divine will committed to writing, in order to supply the preaching after their Death, fundamentum et columnam fidei[2]—because in controversies with Heretics Irenæus prudently began with proving the regular descent of the Dogma from Bishop to Bishop thro' the Catholic Church, and then proceeded to shew the very same doctrine in the Scriptures.[3] Had he begun with the latter, the Heretics might have either quoted another passage seemingly as favorable to ~~his~~ their side, as Irenæus's to his, or given a different interpretation/ But by always giving two arguments both of undoubted Strength, where the Heretics could give only one, he was sure of mastering them. It makes no difference in the sense of the passage, whether it be futurum or futuris—in the former it would agree with the Wine, in the latter, with the Vessels containing it—evangelium in scripturis, or scripturas evangelium nobis tradentes.[4]

Lessing appears to me to have mistaken precepts of the Fathers (plus justo sacerdotalia)[5] ~~intended for~~ addressed to the mass of Catholic Believers (ideotis)[6] for declarations concerning the Grounds, the existing Grounds, & Pillars of the Faith of the Church itself—now these were, first, the universal Tradition of the Churches—and 2. Ostensio e Scripturis:[7] in other words, the Scriptures interpreted according to the consonant Belief of the Church in all ages.—Even such is the doctrine of the Church of England herein honorably distinguished both from the Catholics who place their pretended Traditions & the Powers of the existing Church Hierarchs above the Scriptures, and from the Anti-episcopal Protestants who reject Tradition and Church Authority altogether.

S. T. Coleridge

53[1] I.e. Lessing's commentary in **52** textus.

53[2] The "foundation and pillar of faith", as in **52** textus.

53[3] C paraphrases an observation of Irenaeus q Lessing XVII 124 (and also VI 67), which he also uses in *CIS* 85: "Shew them that this and only this is the *ordo traditionis, quam tradiderunt Apostoli iis quibus committebant ecclesias* [course of that tradition which the Apostles delivered to those whom they entrusted with the churches], and which we should have been bound to follow, says Irenaeus, *si neque Apostoli quidem Scripturas reliquissent* [even if the Apostles had not left us any Scriptures]."

53[4] "The message in the scriptures" or "the message of the scriptures handed down to us".

53[5] "More accurately, statements about the priesthood".

53[6] "Ordinary people", "the uneducated mass" (properly *idiotis*).

53[7] "That which is shown from the Scriptures".

54 XVII 125

Denn eben das, was er *Regulam veritatis* nennt, nennt er an andern Stellen *veritatis Traditionem* oder *veterem Traditionem*. . . . Und wie hätte auch das Glaubensbekenntniss in der ersten Kirche überhaupt anders heissen können, als Tradition, da es gar nicht aufgeschrieben werden durfte, sondern . . . bloss aus öfterem mündlichen Vorsagen auswendig gelernt werden musste? So ward es noch zu den Zeiten des Augustinus in der Kirche damit gehalten; und was könnte uns verleiten zu argwohnen, dass es jemals anders damit gehalten worden.

[For it is precisely what he calls *Regulam veritatis* [the Rule of truth] that in other passages he calls *veritatis Traditionem* or *veterem Traditionem* [the Tradition of truth, ancient Tradition]. . . . And what else but tradition could the Creed have been called in the early Church since it was not permitted to be written down but . . . had to be memorised solely from frequent oral recitation? This was still the practice in the times of Augustine; and what could mislead us so as to doubt that it had ever been different?]

Why? that Irenæus, Tertullian, Augustin, &c &c, did write it down, and publish it. The command[1] was no other than Do not trust to your having it in writing, which is one way of unloading the memory and of forgetting a thing; but write it in your *heart*.

55 XVII 130

[Lessing quotes Clement as saying that the Bible contains many things besides the simple morals to be taught to children and childlike people.] . . . für wen ist denn alles übrige? Hierauf antwortet Clemens; für προσωπα ἐκλεκτα, für auserlescne Personen. Und wer sind ihm diese auserlesene Personen? [He quotes Clement as saying that they are all those who have time and ability to delve deeper.]

[. . . for whom then is all this that remains? To this Clement answers: for προσωπα ἐκλεκτα, for elect persons. And who are these elect persons?]

No!—but particular classes. St Paul's Epistles to which Clemens evidently refers, form the best commentary on this passage.

56 XVII 131

[Lessing says of Clement *Paedagogus* 3.12.97:] Ὀλιγα ταυτα ἐκ πολλων, δειγματος χαριν, ἀπ'αὐτων διεξελθων των θειων γραφων ὁ Παιδαγωγος, τοις ἀυτου παρατιθεται παισιν, δι' ὦν, ὡς ἐπος ἐιπειν, ἀρδην εκκοπτεται κακια, και περιγραφεται ἀδικια. Μυριαι δε ὁσαι ὑποθηκαι, ἐις προσωπα ἐκλεκτα διατεινουσαι, ἐγγεγραφεται

54[1] Matt 16.20; C alluded to the same view in LUTHER *Colloquia* 24.

ταις βιβλοις ταις ἀγιαις· ἀι μεν, πρεσβυτεροις· ἀι δε, ἐπισκο-
ποις· ἀι δε διαχονοις· ἀλλαι χηραις' περι ὡν ἀλλος ἀν ἐιη λεγειν
καιρος· πολλα δε και δι' ἀινιγματων· πολλα δε και δια παρα βολων
τοις ἐντυγχανουσιν ἐξεσιν ὠφελεισθαι.

[Such are a few injunctions out of many, for the sake of example, which the
instructor running over the divine Scriptures sets before his children; by which,
so to speak, vice is cut up by the roots, and iniquity is circumscribed. Innumer-
able commands such as these are written in the Holy Bible appertaining to cho-
sen persons, some to presbyters, some to bishops, some to deacons, others to
widows, of whom we shall have another opportunity of speaking. Many things
[also] spoken in enigmas, many in parables, may benefit such as may fall in with
them [tr William Wilson *The Writings of Clement of Alexandria* (1867–9) I 339–
40].]

I can find in this passage this meaning only: that besides the rules of
Duty applicable to and binding upon all Christians alike, there are like-
wise particular precepts for particular persons, as Bishops, Deacons,
Widows, Presbyters—& likewise too some more abstruse passages,
which require more than ordinary Learning & Study—

57 xvII 143

Wenn das Buch des Hermas hiernächst, von welchem Eusebius sagt,
dass es zum ersten Unterrichte in der Religion gebraucht worden, über-
haupt der heiligen Schriften mit keiner Sylbe gedenkt, worüber sich Hr.
Less selbst so sehr verwundert: was folgt daraus? Entweder waren die
Schriften des neuen Testaments damals noch nicht beysammen; oder sie
standen in dem Ansehen noch nicht, in welchem sie jetzt stehen, und
wurden zu dem Unterrichte in der christlichen Religion für entbehrlich
gehalten;—oder beydes.

[When after this Book of Hermas, of which Eusebius says that it was used for
the first religious teaching, does not even mention one syllable about the Holy
Scriptures, about which Mr Less himself was astonished—what follows from
this? Either the writings of the New Testament were at that time not yet assem-
bled, or they did not stand in the same regard that they do now and were consid-
ered unnecessary for instruction in the Christian religion—or both.]

Lessing has ⟨himself⟩ provided an answer to this in his (somewhat ex-
aggerated) statement, p. 129.[1]—See too p. 2. of the blank Leaf at the
head of this Volume.[2]

57[1] Discussing the fact that Clem-
ent's moral teaching was not based on the
Bible, Lessing in xvII 128–9 observes that
Christian *morality* is not the Christian *reli-* *gion*, and that one goes to the Bible for a
system of belief, not for practical morality.
57[2] I.e. **53** above.

58 xvii 146–9

Ihm [Clemens] sind die menschlichen Zeugnisse, eben die Zeugnisse der Propheten und Apostel, so lange sie unabhängig von der Regel der Wahrheit genommen werden; und die Stimme des Herrn, die allein gilt, die allein keine weitere Demonstration zulässt . . . ist, mit Einem Worte, das Glaubensbekenntniss.

[Clement accepts human testimony, including the testimony of the prophets and Apostles, as long as it is accepted as distinct from the principle of truth; and the voice of the Lord, which alone is valid, which alone admits of no further demonstration . . . is, in a word, the Creed.]

I have not Clemens by me, to examine the passage cited; but Lessing's interpretation of "the Word of the Lord" by the Creed seems most extravagant. The obvious meaning is the Word of Christ in our Heart—Let the same *mind* be in you as was in Christ Jesus—in short, the indwelling Word. "My Father and I will come, & we will dwell in you."[1] And what is or was this Creed, πιστις, fides, regula fidei, κανων της αληθειας, traditio,[2] of which Lessing so exalts? The Apostles' Creed, so called? Surely, L. knew that this was only the Creed of the Roman Church, at furthest, of the Western Churches—that the story of its origination is a mere Legend—that as appears by Eusebius & from various sources, the Eastern Churches had other, & from the Heresies which early disturbed them, far fuller Creeds—that Creeds were adapted to the necessities of the Time—that it is not improbable that "the Apostles' Creed" might be only the Creed of the Catechumens preparatory to the fuller Creed of Baptism,[3] at all events, there were moreany Creeds, i.e. Forms of Professions, some more, some less full, some more, some less explicit—/ if then Scripture were to be judged by its analogy with the Creed, by what analogy were the Creeds to be judged? Less L. ought to have proved, 1. that there did exist anterior to the Gospels & Epistles a *one Form*, a one Professio Fidei,[4] containing ⟨in all Languages⟩ the

58[1] Not a quotation but a paraphrase, perhaps of John 14.10, 16–17: "Believest thou not that I am in the Father, and the Father in me? . . . the Father that dwelleth in me, he doeth the works. . . . And I will pray the Father, and he shall give you another Comforter, that he may abide with you for ever; Even the Spirit of truth; whom the world cannot receive, because it seeth him not, neither knoweth him: but ye know him; for he dwelleth with you, and shall be in you."

58[2] "Faith [Greek], faith [Latin], rule of faith, canon of truth, tradition".

58[3] LUTHER *Colloquia* **23** n 1 and **90** n1 outline some of the sources of C's information about the history of the Apostles' Creed and explain the "Legend" of its composition: cf also BAXTER *Catholick Theologie* **9** n 1.

58[4] "Profession of Faith".

same Articles of Faith in the same words: and 2. to have produced & attested this one.—

59 xvii 149

Auf die fünfte Stelle des Clemens endlich brauche ich nichts zu erwiedern, als dieses, dass Clemens daselbst von den Gnostikern insbesondere, nicht aber von den Christen überhaupt, spricht. Der Gnostiker allerdings muss Schrift aus Schrift erklären und beweisen. Aber die Christen überhaupt haben das nicht nöthig; weil der Gnostiker selbst, so weit er sich über sie verstiegen hat, doch wieder zu ihnen herab muss, und wenn er die Schrift aus Schrift noch so apodiktisch erwiesen hat, doch nur auch durch das Glaubensbekenntniss apodiktisch überführen kann. Das ist der wahre Sinn folgender Stelle des Clemens die, wenn sie diesen Sinn nicht hätte, gar keinen haben würde. Ὄντως καὶ ἡμεῖς, auch wir, wir Gnostiker, ἀπ' αὐτων περι αὐτων των γραφων τελειως ἀποδεικνυντις ἐκ πιστεως πειθομεθυ ἀπωδεικτικως.

[Finally, on the fifth passage of Clement I need make no reply except that Clement says this of the gnostics in particular and not of Christians in general. The gnostic indeed must expound and demonstrate scripture from scripture. But the Christians generally do not need to do this; because the gnostic himself must still, however far he has risen above them, come down again to their level, and however apodictically he may have demonstrated scripture from scripture he can yet draw conclusions apodictically only from the Creed. This is the real meaning of the following passage of Clement, which if it did not have this meaning would have none at all. "So, consequently, we also", we too, we gnostics, "giving a complete exhibition of the scriptures from the scriptures themselves, from faith persuade by demonstration" [Clement tr William Wilson].]

Not having Clem. Alex., I dare not speak ⟨as⟩ other than a Querist, on the construing of a detached Sentence—but if πιστις[1] here meant the Creed, and not the gift of Faith, surely the Greek would demand εκ τῆς πιστέως;[2] I can see no glimmer of Sense, as Lessing renders the words; but if my Guess be just, a very fine one—viz—that the highest proof, Learning can give, & the Subject is capable of, does not exclude but unites & harmonizes with Faith. We believe in the Light thro' the Light.

60 xvii 150–5

Von diesem [Tertullian] nun muss ich Ewr. Hochwürden im Voraus bekennen, dass er es ist, von welchem ich zuerst eine richtigere Vorstellung von der wahren Quelle unsers Glaubens erlangt zu haben glaube

---

59[1] In textus, here translated "faith".
59[2] I.e. adding the definite article to say

not "from faith" but "from the faith" or "from the Creed".

. . . dass er es ist, welcher mich zuerst überzeugt, wie natürlich es sey, wenn sich die Apostel vor allen Dingen unter einander über ein gewisses Formular verglichen, um nicht allein selbst einerley zu glauben, sondern auch einerley zu lehren . . .

[I have to admit in advance, Your Reverence, that it is he [Tertullian] from whom I believe I first derived the right conception of the true source of our faith . . . that it is he who first convinced me that it would have been natural if the Apostles consulted one another above all on a given formulation, in order not only to believe uniformly but also to teach uniformly . . .]

Mercy! and so Lessing really did give credit to the fable of the Apostles clubbing to make a Creed?[1]—Yet Luke knew nothing of it: S[t] Paul knew nothing of it! For if true, it was a Fact of such pre-eminent Importance, that it is morally impossible that they should know & yet pass it over in silence. How is it conceivable, that S[t] Paul should not have appealed to it concerning the disputes on the Resurrection in the Corinthian Church—on a point declared vital, & essential by himself?[2] How could Peter have not only overlooked it, this supposed botteh "Foundation and Pillar"[3] of the Christian Temple, but have referred us to the surer Word of Prophecy![4]—Whether Prophecy here import, the Jewish Prophets, or the Gift of Prophecy among the first Christians, or Christ's Prophecies— or (as I believe) all inclusively—or lastly, the manifested spiritual might of Preaching only—it is still incompatible with Lessing's fundamental Faith-Compact, or federal Creed! Now it does not appear, that they always *literally* observed even our Saviour's own Formula, or adhered to the very words of his most solemn Command—Go ye, & baptize all nations in (or into) the name of the Father, the Son, and H. G.[5]—which by many has been supposed, & which doubtless had the best right, to be the one common Forma fidei[6] of all Christians!—If the so called Apostles' Creed be indeed the one Creed, by which alone the Scriptures could be tried, on what pretence could they have pronounced Paul of Samosata—Heretic?[7] The Creed itself must in this case have needed a tradi-

<hr>

60[1] The legend of the "Symbolum" or, as C says, "this fable of the Creed being a picnic contribution of the 12 Apostles" is outlined in LUTHER *Colloquia* 90 and n.

60[2] E.g. 1 Cor 15.13–14: "But if there be no resurrection of the dead, then is Christ not risen: And if Christ be not risen, then is our preaching vain, and your faith is also vain."

60[3] Quoting the controverted phrase of 52 textus.

60[4] 2 Pet 1.19 (var), q also in 21 above.

60[5] Matt 28.19 (var), cited also in 6 above.

60[6] "Form of faith".

60[7] The third-century bp of Antioch, deposed in 268 for heretical views that included the original unity of the Godhead— an issue that is not raised (as C indicates) in the Apostles' Creed. An account of his heresy is given by Eusebius in *Ecclesiastical History* 7.27–30.

tional, commentary, Creed to have established its actual meaning. In
what article of this Creed is *any* species of divine Worship of Christ
taught? Yet can we suppose that the Christian Churches should all chant
solemn Prayers to Christ, as to their God—carmina Christo, quasi
Deo[8]—without an express article of Belief—while they at the same time
not only admitted the 1. & 2. Commandment, but carried their horror of
Idolatry almost to superstition? The veriest modern Socinians, the least-
believing Psilanthropists, Priestley, Belsham, and Co. profess them-
selves able and *ready* to repeat the Apostles' Creed with a safe
Conscience[9] and might do so, if no *higher* Authority be in existence to
determine the true import of "his Son" and "our Lord".—How then,
& with what force or purpose, could Eusebius appeal to his baptismal
Creed, as precluding all disbelief of Christ's Divinity?[10] Assuming for
the argument's sake only the *common* faith of Arius & Athanasius, that
Christ was, in the belief of all Churches, the Δημιουργος[11]—by whom,
thro' whom, and for whom all things were created—and could they, the
destined & Zealous Oppugnants of polytheism, have dared to hold, to
profess, and in the most solemn offices of religion to act upon this Belief
unauthorized by the highest & only fundamental Authority? But this is
not the only Instance, in which our excellent Lessing's microscopic
Acuteness of Vision rendered him at once short- and narrow-sighted.[12]

61   xvii 169 | "Hilarius"

Es waren die Arianer, es war Constantius, auf Anstiften der Arianer, die
es ausdrücklich verlangten, dass der Streit von der Gottheit Christi *tan-
tum secundum ea, quae scripta sunt* [Hil. ad Constantium, lib. II. §. 8.]
ausgemacht werden sollte. Hilarius liess sich dieses sehr wohl gefallen.
. . . Er stellte dem Kaiser darinn vor, dass es unmöglich sey, Glaubens-
lehren aus blossen Schriftstellen auszumachen, wenn man nicht zugleich
eine gewisse Regel annehme, wie diese Schriftstellen verstanden wer-

---

60[8] "Songs to Christ, as if to God".

60[9] For these Unitarian leaders see LU-
THER *Colloquia* **35**. "Psilanthropist", a
believer in the "mere humanity" of Christ,
is a Coleridgean coinage: cf *OED*, *LS* (*CC*)
176 and n 4, *BL* ch 10 (*CC*) I 180 and n 2.

60[10] The creed presented at the Council
of Nicaea in 325 by Eusebius of Caesarea
(c 260–c 340) with the introductory words,
"As we received from the bishops before
us, both in our catechetical instruction and
when we were baptized . . . so also we
now believe and submit our belief to you":

J. N. D. Kelly *Early Christian Creeds* (3rd
ed 1972) 183. C would have encountered
the formula of Eusebius in Socrates Scho-
lasticus and other accounts of the Council
of Nicaea cited in LUTHER *Colloquia* **78** nn
2, 3.

60[11] "Demiurge": C uses the term to
denote the common factor in the teachings
of the most radically opposed sects, as the
Arians and Athanasians.

60[12] Cf C's objections in **8** and **11**
above.

den müssten. Und diese Regel war keine andere, als das Glaubensbekenntniss, davon er die Ueberzeugung in der Taufe angelobet und empfangen habe. Diese innere Ueberzeugung, sagt Hilarius, habe er, und bedürfe einer äussern aus der Schrift nicht: *penes me habeo fidem, exteriore non egeo.*

[It was the Arians, it was Constantius himself at the instigation of the Arians, who explicitly stipulated that the argument about the divinity of Christ should be settled only "according to what is written". Hilary pronounced himself well satisfied with this. . . . He told the emperor that it was impossible to decide on articles of faith from passages of scripture alone if one did not at the same time accept a certain rule as to how these passages were to be understood. And this rule was the Creed that he had promised to believe and accepted as his conviction at his baptism. This inner conviction he had, says Hilary, and he needed no external proof from scripture: "I have faith within me, and need none from without."]

But these Arians, especially Arius himself and his Contemporaries, Bishops & others, had been baptized. Did they ever renounce their baptismal profession? No! but they otherwise interpreted it. Hilarius must therefore have meant the spiritual Gift of Faith: for what are words but words—exteriora?[1]

62 xvii 239 | *Von der Art und Weise der Fortpflanzung und Ausbreitung der christlichen Religion*

Aber warum war es gleichwohl eine Schande, wenn die Griechen nicht allein selbst ein Handwerk trieben, sondern auch nur durch ihre Knechte treiben liessen?

[But why was it equally a disgrace that the Greeks not only plied a trade but also had it carried on only through their slaves?]

* easily solved. Had an old English Baron employed 300 Vassals in his fields, gardens or the tools appertaining, he is a Baron—; but if he employed them in making Lace, he becomes a Master Lace-manufacturer. In Italy it is no disgrace to a Nobleman even to retail the produce of his own Estate.   S. T. C.

63 xvii 243

Orosius, welcher (*lib.* VII. *c.* VII.) hinzusetzt, *ac per omnes provincias pari persecutione Christianos excruciari imperavit*, verdient keinen Glauben. Man kennet ihn als einen Schriftsteller, der immer aus seinen Quellen mehr schöpfte, als darin ist.

61[1] "Outward" or "external things".

[Orosius, who adds, "and he gave orders that the Christians should be persecuted and tortured in the same way in all the provinces", deserves no credence. He is known as an author who always draws more from a source than it contains.]

A strange way of getting rid of History! What more probable, nay, almost inevitable, than that the Xtn Religion should be proscribed after the Christians, as *Christians*, had been sentenced to horrid Deaths at Rome as Incendiaries? Doubtless, some of the Prophecies of John were even then in currency, concerning the downfall of Babylon, interpreted Rome—Some Papists had in their fanaticism prophesied the Destruction of London by Fire—when it took place, the Papists, as Papists, were believed the Incendiaries—and then what Laws followed or were reinforced.

64 xvii 248

Die Heiden bestraften die ersten Christen nicht sowohl wegen ihrer Religion, als wegen der Uebertretung der Gesetze. Die Heiden hatten keine Gesetze, welche die Gewissen banden, und dieses und jenes zu glauben befahlen. Aber sie hatten Gesetze, welche alle Zusammenkünfte, und besonders alle nächtliche Zusammenkünfte, bey schwerer Strafe untersagten.

[The heathen punished the first Christians not so much because of their religion as because of their transgression of the laws. The heathens had no laws that governed their consciences and commanded them to believe this or that. But they had laws that prohibited all assemblies, and especially assemblies held at night, upon severe penalties.]

But, Lessing, honest Lessing! whence could these midnight meetings have come if not from prior persecution? Is there one word commanding them in the Creed or apostolic Writings. This is Effect per Cause, if ever there was.

65 xvii 258–9

Plinius sagt von diesen Liebesmahlen, dass sie zusammen gekommen wären *ad capiendum cibum, promiscuum tamen et innoxium*. Ich finde keinen Ausleger, der dieses *promiscuus* erklären wollen; dass ich also zweifle, ob es viele gehörig verstanden. . . . Ich glaube, dass nicht sowohl alle Speisen unter einander damit gemeynet werden, als die Vermischung der Gäste selbst von allerley Stand, Alter und Geschlecht. Diese Vermischung war den Alten bey ihren Gastereyen . . . amstössig, so wären sie doch sonst von allem Frevel frey.

[Pliny says of these love-feasts that they were assembled "to take food, yet promiscuous and unharmful [food]". I can find no commentator who would explain this *promiscuus*; I therefore doubt whether many understood it properly. . . . I believe that it means not so much all the combination of foods, as the mixing of guests of every class, age, and sex. This mixing at parties was offensive to the ancients . . . even if the parties themselves were otherwise free of all offences.]

Cœna, dapes,[1] might *possibly* endure such an interpretation, as Lessing's; but never, never "cibus."[2] One or other of two meanings are of necessity conveyed in the words—1. either cibum promiscuum—"food common to all," tamen et innoxium—but yet innocent—or 2. (which, I doubt not, is Pliny's meaning) ad capiendum cibum—promiscuum tamen, *but such as ~~by~~ chanced to have been procured*, without any fixed or particular kind, and quite harmless—(not human Blood, or young Children, or any other abomination attributed to the Christians by their persecutors[)].—S[t] Paul furnishes the best commentary. Lessing like our Warburton, too fond of *finding out* things.[3]

66 xvii 340–3 | *Tertullianus de Praescriptionibus*

Es stehet geschrieben, sagen sie: *Suchet, so werdet ihr finden.* Lasst uns nicht vergessen, wenn der Herr diese Aufmunterung ergehen lassen. Ich glaube, es war im Anfange seiner Lehre, als noch alle zweifelten, ob er der Christ sey. . . . Damals war es Zeit zu rufen: *Suchet, so werdet ihr finden!* als derjenige noch musste gesucht werden, der noch nicht erkannt war. . . . [343:] Alle Worte des Herrn, die durch die Ohren der Juden zu uns gekommen, sind zwar für alle niedergeschrieben; doch da die meisten an gewisse Personen gerichtet sind, so können sie für uns die alte Kraft des Befehls eigentlich nicht haben, sondern nur nach Massgebung.

[It is written, they say, "Seek and ye shall find." Let us not forget on what occasion the Lord uttered this exhortation. I believe it was at the beginning of his teaching, when everyone still doubted that he was the Christ. . . . Then was the time to exclaim, "Seek and ye shall find!" when it was still necessary to seek him who had not yet been recognised! . . . All the words of the Lord that have come down to us through the ears of the Jews are indeed written down for

65[1] "Supper, banquet".
65[2] "Food".
65[3] William Warburton (1698–1779), bp of Gloucester, author of *The Divine Legation of Moses* (2 vols 1738–41), whose "perverted ingenuity" C also complains of

in Milton *Poems* 22. In Lessing *Leben* 18 he cites what he perhaps thought of as a typical specimen, Warburton's assertion that "the early Greek Sages" were all Spinozists.

everyone; but since most of them were directed at particular persons, they cannot really have for us the full force of a command, but only the power to influence.]

This is an ingenious and plausible mode of evacuating all the obligatory Precepts of the Gospel/ "Consider the Time, at which, the persons, to which, the circumstances, on which, such & such a precept was delivered"—then follows the Ergo: "this was very well for the Apostles and other Disciples; but *we* have nothing to learn from it".—The answer is: Christ was the World—the Light, that lighteth *every* man/[1] ~~the~~ and the burthen of the Proof lies on those who assert that such or such a Precept was merely temporary and personal—Either all are so—& then Christ is no longer *our* Teacher/ & or there must be rules establishable and established, by which we may safely and obviously distinguish the one from the other.—This may be done or rather Christ himself & the Evangelists have distinguished in several cases—as in the purchase of the Sword, in the precepts for Christians in the Jewish War, in the directions given to the 70—&c.[2]— ~~3.~~ Therefore where the Precept is expressed in universo,[3] we have presumptive reason that it was meant to be universal/ Of these latter the Rule of Distinction should be, but never has, and (I will venture to assert) never will or can be given: for in order to effect such a rule, it must be proved that such a precept was in genere[4] immoral & irrational, and rendered innocent by a *Dispensation*—i.e. a moral miracle = impossibility, & the very Thought blasphemy—. For the Laws of the material World, and the *mechanism* of the sentient and even intellectual World, are God's Creatures; but his moral Laws are himself, the Supreme Reason.—Just such Language as this of Tertullian did Eckius and his comrades hold to Luther[5]—and surely to the repetition of it from a Protestant it should be enough to reply—*Luther*! Great Britain ⚹ Spain!—[6]

67 xvii 345–7

Also ist zu suchen, was Christus verordnet. Es ist zu suchen, *wenn* wir es noch nicht gefunden; es ist zu suchen, *bis* wir es gefunden. Nun haben

---

66[1] John 1.9 (var).

66[2] The pragmatic advice about the sword appears in Luke 22.36 ("But now, . . . he that hath no sword, let him sell his garment, and buy one"), and Christ's instructions to the 70 disciples sent out to preach, in Luke 10.1–16; the text C interprets as "precepts for Christians in the Jewish War" has not been identified.

66[3] "In universal [form]".

66[4] "In kind".

66[5] Johann Maier von Eck (1486–1543), German Roman Catholic apologist, condemned Luther's new theses and led the resistance to Protestant reform.

66[6] Great Britain "as opposed to" Spain.

wir es aber ja wohl gefunden, wenn wir es geglaubt. Denn wie hätten wir es glauben können, wenn wir es nicht gefunden! . . . Darum suchen wir, um es zu finden; darum finden wir, um es zu glauben. Alles Suchen, alles Finden hört mit dem Glauben auf.

[Therefore what is to be sought is what Christ decreed. It is to be sought *so long as* we have not yet found it; it is to be sought *until* we find it. But we have surely found it if we have believed it. For how could we have believed it if we had not found it! . . . Therefore we seek in order to find it; therefore we find it in order to believe it. All seeking, all finding ends with belief.]

Now all this does but convince me, how very early the Papal *Spirit* began. ~~almost as~~ And this *Spirit* is the main Harm of the Doctrines, which (some more, & some less distant, from Tertullian's Age)[1] were but the inevitable Shoots and Developments, the manifestations and Constructions, of this Spirit.—It is certain, that the Gospels no less than the apostolic Epistles represent Xtn Faith as *a Process*, a gradual Process, even as ⟨that of⟩*a* an Oak from an Acorn/ The Acorn is the *principle* of sincere Faith—the main doctrines *common* to *all*, its Tap-Root and Trunk; the general Doctrines its Branches; to which, (as God grants, and the mind is willing & able) different Believers shoot out ~~different~~ various but not diverse, Boughs and Sprays—* Now to *search* the Scriptures is thro' the whole of this spiritual Vegetation as breeze and sunshine, whose Influences of To Day never supersede the Influences of Tomorrow. It is a continuous Process—*S. T. C.* If then Progression in Knowlege as well as Holiness be the doctrine of Christ (*vid. Epistle of Peter*)[2] then the doctrine of Tertullian and the Romanists must be that of Anti-Xst.

* Yea, and support themselves by numberless, and tho' not essential, yet feeding & fastn'ing, off-roots and radicles.

68 XVIII 295–7 | *Nathan der Weise* II iii

SALADIN. Hat seinen Reichthum dieser Mann aus Gräbern,
 So warens sicherlich nicht Salomons
 Nicht Davids Gräber. Narren lagen da
 Begraben!
SITTAH. Oder Bösewichter! . . .

a The top of the inserted phrase cropped

67[1] Tertullian (c 160–c 220), whose views are the subject of the essay that provides this and the previous textus (**66**).

67[2] 2 Pet 3.18, "But grow in grace, and in the knowledge of our Lord and Saviour Jesus Christ."

[SALADIN. If this man gets his wealth from graves, they were certainly not the graves of Solomon and David. Fools lay buried there.
SITTAH. Or knaves! . . .]

I cannot understand this Speech—Fools (ϴ rather *Crackpates*—) or *Villains*? Lessing's Creed, whether it were that of Deism at this time, or of Spinosism, to which in some sense or other he afterwards professed himself a Convert,[1] does not disturb either my Love or Admiration, neither injures him *with* ME as a Man or ⟨as⟩ a Philosopher—. But that any man could read David's Poems, or the Gnomonics attributed to Solomon, & yet deem the men crazed or scoundrels—that, *that* would exceed my charity—it would imply such a vulgar Bigotry of low unthinking Antichristianism, as would level Lessing with a Diderot, or Tom Payne.[2] But I trust, I misinterpret the words.—I know one who from a Socinian became a Deist, or rather a Pantheist—and then from his increased & enthusiastic admiration of the character of Moses, considered merely as a Lycurgus or Solon,[3] with rejection of all inspiration & miracle, was gradually led back to a Belief in Revelation, & after intense study declared, he could conscientiously subscribe all the *doctrinal* Articles of the Church of England.[4]

69　XVIII 308–10 | II v

TEMPELHERR. Sehr wohl gesagt!—Doch kennt Ihr auch das Volk,
　　　　　Das diese Menschenmäkeley zuerst
　　　　　Getrieben? Wisst Ihr, Nathan, welches Volk
　　　　　Zuerst das auserwählte Volk sich nannte?
　　　　　Wie? wenn ich dieses Volk nun, zwar nicht hasste,
　　　　　Doch wegen seines Stolzes zu verachten,
　　　　　Mich nicht entbrechen könnte? Seines Stolzes,
　　　　　Den es auf Christ und Muselmann vererbte:
　　　　　Nur sein Gott sey der rechte Gott!—Ihr stutzt,
　　　　　Dass ich, ein Christ, ein Tempelherr, so rede?
　　　　　Wann hat, und wo die fromme Raserey,

68[1] C is probably thinking of F. H. Jacobi's report of a conversation with Lessing in which Lessing said that if he followed anyone in his views on God, it was Spinoza: JACOBI *Ueber die Lehre* p 22—C annotated the dialogue, but not this page.

68[2] Notorious adversaries of Christianity, Denis Diderot (1713–84) especially for his controlling hand in the rationalist *Encyclopédie* from 1745 to 1772, and Thomas Paine (1737–1809) especially for his deistic *Age of Reason* (1794).

68[3] I.e. as a lawgiver, like the legendary Lycurgus of Sparta (c 600 B.C.) or Solon of Athens (c 640–c 558 B.C.). C invokes the same names in LUTHER *Colloquia* 35.

68[4] This general description might be said to fit WW (*W Life* II 104–7) or C himself as he describes his own development in e.g. *CN* II 2448, IV 5000.

Den bessern Gott zu haben, diesen bessern,
Der ganzen Welt als besten aufzudringen,
In ihrer schwärzesten Gestalt sich mehr
Gezeigt, als hier, als jetzt? . . .

[Very well expressed!—But do you also know the people that first practised this mockery? Do you know, Nathan, which people first called itself the chosen people? What though I did not hate this people but could not restrain myself from despising their pride? Their pride that they bequeathed to Christian and Moslem: that their God alone be the true God!—You are startled that I, a Christian, a Knight Templar, speak thus? When and where has the pious raving to possess the superior God, to impose this superior God as the best on the whole world, more shown itself in its blackest form than here and now? . . .]

But surely, there is an unphilosophical, nay, an *unhistorical*, Spirit in these Lines.—What is "the God" of a Religion, but the sum of its *practical* and *practised* Tenets?—Were not Polygamy, that certain *Dry-rot* of the moral Being, joined with unlimited Concubinism (th*e*at almost certain Cause of "παιδεραστιας"[1] & ⟨of⟩ all other sensual Denaturalizations) the uniform accompaniments, & allowals, of Mahomctans—Was not universal Conversion by the Sword its especial Command?—And shall one, who teaches Mcckness, Reverence of man as man, Love, Justice, and progressive Purity, be charged with "einer frommen Raserey" (= a pious madness) because he would press on his fellow-men "den bessern Gott"[2]—i.e. substitute worth*y*ier notions of the supreme Legislator?/ with ~~an~~ the idea*s* of whom the nature of supposed moral Obliga⟨tions⟩ ever ha~~ve~~s been, and for the mass of mankind ever must be, coincident?—All *have* the same God; but all do not *believe in* the same God/ unless Jehoram's Moloch = Mendelsohn's Jehovah.[3]—for the character of Nathan was meant by Lessing for his friend, Mendelsohn—the truly great, and almost unjudäic Jew!—[4]

70 xviii 355 | iii vii

NATHAN. . . . Denn gründen alle [Religionen] sich nicht auf
            Geschichte?
        Geschrieben oder überliefert!—Und
        Geschichte muss doch wohl allein auf Treu
        Und Glauben angenommen werden?—Nicht?—

69[1] "Of pederasty".

69[2] "The superior God"—from textus.

69[3] Jehoram, king of Judah, son of Jehoshaphat, associated with a lapse into idolatry in 2 Chron 21, though not explic-itly with Moloch.

69[4] Moses Mendelssohn (1729–86), well known to have been the model for the enlightened and tolerant Nathan. C annotated at least three of his works: see below.

Nun, wessen Treu und Glauben zieht man denn
Am wenigsten in Zweifel? doch der Seinen?

[For do not all [religions] base their creeds on history? Written or orally trans-
mitted!—And history must surely be accepted solely on the basis of trust and
faith?—Is it not so?—Then whose trust and faith does one doubt the least?
Surely one's own?]

Suppose a man utterly unacquainted with History, and with the Canons
of Historic Credibility—and supposing too an almost dormant state of
the logical and practical reason—in short, suppose a Mahometan utterly
incapable of making such a speech as this—& such a man *might* make
such a speech. If 2 + 2 = 3: 4 + 4 = 6.

71   xxiii 125, pencil | *Ueber das Lustspiel die Juden*

[Lessing introduces a letter from an unnamed Jew—actually his friend
Moses Mendelssohn.] "Man sagt, es sey Niederträchtigkeit bey den Ju-
den. Wohl! wenn Niederträchtigkeit Menschenblut verschont; so ist
Niederträchtigkeit eine Tugend."

["It is said that there is villainy among the Jews. Well! If villainy spares human
blood, then villainy is a virtue."]

No! No! No! This is a Jew-Ethic with a *vengeance*!

72   xxiii 125–6, pencil | Continuing **71** textus

* "Wie mitleidig sind sie [die Juden] nicht gegen alle Menschen, wie
milde gegen die Armen beyder Nationen! Und wie hart verdient das Ver-
fahren der meisten Christen gegen ihre Armen genannt zu werden!"

[* "How compassionate they [the Jews] are towards all people, how charitable
towards the poor of both nations! And how harsh the behaviour of most Chris-
tians towards their poor deserves to be called!"]

* How different must the German Jews be from the English, where yet
they are so far from being oppressed, that in many important points they
are favored by the Law! Besides, "das liederliche Gesindel"[1] is a con-
tradiction in Fact. No religious Sect on Earth have been or are so shame-
fully neglectful of the morals & education of their Poor. Compare them
with the Quakers.[2]

72[1] "The disorderly vagabonds": the
phrase is used by Lessing p 118 while de-
fending his characterisation of the Jews.
He argues that such Jews as he depicts are
not to be found in real life among the vag-

abonds who are encountered at fairs.
   72[2] The Quakers themselves, however,
are criticised for their devotion to com-
merce and neglect of learning in *LS* (*CC*)
185–91.

73 xxiii 165, pencil | *Von den lateinischen Trauerspielen, welche unter dem Namen des Seneca bekannt sind*

Er ist mit den poetischen Farben allzuverschwenderisch gewesen; er ist oft in seiner Zeichnung zu kühn; er treibt die Grösse hier und da bis zur Schwulst; und die Natur scheinet bey ihm allzuviel von der Kunst zu haben. * Lauter Fehler, in die ein schlechtes Genie niemals fallen wird!

[He uses poetic colours too lavishly; he is often too bold in his design; here and there he carries grandeur to the point of bombast; and nature seems in his works to have too much of art about it. * Nothing but errors that an inferior talent will never fall into.]

* The very symptom of a Pseudo-Genius! O Lessing! *Lessing!*

74 xxiii 165, pencil

Ist es billig, dass wir das, was seine Zeitverwandten in dem Munde des Herkules für schreckliche Drohungen hielten, für unsinnige Grosssprechereyen halten, und sie als solche, mit sammt dem Dichter, auspfeifen wollen?

[Is it fair that what his contemporaries considered as terrible threats from the mouth of Hercules we should consider unreasonable boastfulness and should therefore hiss at them as well as at the poet?]

But was not all this the case with the Greek Tragedians? Yet where in *them* do we find such cannon-mouthed Bombast? Such bloated Boa Contractors ending in a pointed Epigram-Tail!—

75 xxiii 171, pencil

> *si novi Herculem*
> *Lycus Creonti debitas poenas dabit.*
> *Lentum est, dabit; dat: hoc quoque est lentum; dedit.*

[If I know Hercules, Lycus will pay the penalty for [the murder of] Creon. "He will pay" is too slow. "He is paying the penalty now" is also too slow. He has paid it already.]

Yet how much better would it have been, had the metre permitted—Dabit? lentum est![1]—what follows is certainly *ludicrously* witty. But spite of a created *fine* Taste Lessing was "ein witziger *Kopf* ".[2]

75[1] "He will pay? It is too slow!" Lessing is quoting from Seneca's *Hercules furens* 642–4.

75[2] "A wit"—in a hearty, even vulgar, sense. Lessing uses this example from Seneca to make fun of a critic who claims that the line was the source of a line in Molière: "I'm dying, I'm dead, I'm buried!"

76 XXIII 283, pencil, marked with line in margin | *Geschichte der englischen Schaubühne*

[On *Gorboduc:*] Allein der Dichter hat von einer andern Seite desto grössere Vorzüge; die Richtigkeit der Empfindungen, die natürliche Deutlichkeit des Styls, die leichte Harmonie des Sylbenmasses, ertheilen seinem Stücke jene Würde, jene Genauigkeit, die der Tragödie so wesentlich ist, und doch von fast allen nachfolgenden englischen Trauerspieldichtern, entweder so wenig verstanden, oder so sehr vernachlässiget worden.

[But the poet has that much greater advantage in another respect; the justness of his feelings, the natural clarity of his style, the easy harmony of his metre, impart to his compositions that dignity, that precision, which is so essential in tragedy and yet which has been either so little understood or so much neglected by subsequent English tragedians.]

!!*Ohe! Satis*!!¹ what a Lesson to me never to criticize on aught but the Thoughts & Feelings of a Poem in another Language/ When a Lessing, a Schlegel, &c can make such gross Blunders. Schlegel, ⟨ex. gr.⟩ pronounces the style of the London Apprentice, Yorkshire Tragedy, Tit. Andron. &c quite Shakespear!!²

77 XXIII 285, pencil

[On *Gammer Gurton's Needle:*] "Doch *Hodge* findet die Nadel noch zu rechter Zeit in seinen Beinkleidern, und macht der Komödie dadurch ein Ende"—Wie viel Komisches in so einem Stücke seyn könne, und von welcher Gattung es seyn müsse, kann man gar leicht von selbst abnehmen.

["But Hodge finds the needle in his breeches just in time and thus brings the comedy to an end"—One can easily see for oneself how much that is comical such a piece may contain and of what genre it may be.]

And yet there is "viel Komisches,"¹ & Humour, & sweet Versification in this, our first Comedy.

78 XXIII 292, pencil

Diese zwey Freunde [Beaumont and Fletcher] sind als dramatische Dichter nicht zu trennen, indem sie alle ihre Werke gemeinschaftlich verfertigen.

76¹ "Ho! Enough!"
76² August Wilhelm Schlegel *Vorlesungen über dramatische Kunst und Litteratur* (3 vols Heidelberg 1809–11) III 232–9 (C mistakenly renames *The London Prodigal*).
77¹ From textus: "much that is comical".

[These two friends cannot be considered separately as dramatists since they collaborated on all their works.]

A mistake/[1]

79 xxiii 294, pencil

Er [George Chapman] war in der lateinischen und griechischen Sprache sehr erfahren, und seine Uebersetzung des *Homer* wird auch noch jetzt nicht ganz verachtet.

[He was well versed in Latin and Greek, and his translation of Homer is even now not altogether despised.]

lege:[1] admired by all men of genius.

80 xxvi 15 | Letter 4

Bolingbroke . . . gedenkt mit Beyfall eines Gelehrten, den man einst in der *Kirche, in seiner Kapelle . . . Gott auch dafür danken gehört, dass er die Welt mit Lexikonsmachern versehen habe.

[Bolingbroke . . . mentions with approval a scholar who was once overheard in his *chapel in the church . . . as he thanked God for having provided the world with lexicographers.]

* a curious instance of an error in the correction of a Blunder. Lessing had not heard of, or had forgotten, Christ Church College at Oxford— eines Gelehrten, ~~College~~ Ædis., *Christ's-kirche*, Socii—[1]

81 xxvi 120–1, pencil | Letter 41

[Lessing quotes Pope on Spenser's pastorals, pointing out that a division by months is liable to be unsuccessful "because the year has not that variety in it to furnish every month with a particular description, as it may every season".] Wenn Herr *Dusch*, wie man sagt, auch der Uebersetzer von *Popens sämmtlichen Werken* ist, so muss es uns viel mehr befremden, dass er sich dieser Anmerkung seines *Helden* nicht erinnern wollen. Wenn er es gethan hätte, so würde es in seinen Schilderungen vielleicht nicht von so vielen Gegenständen bis zum Esel, *mutatis mu-*

78[1] As C knew, John Fletcher (1579–1625) wrote a number of plays by himself both before and after Beaumont's death; he also had other collaborators. For C's two annotated copies of their collected corpus, see BEAUMONT & FLETCHER in *CM* (*CC*) i.

79[1] I.e. "[for 'not to be despised'] read".

80[1] "Of a learned man, fellow of Christ Church College". Lessing's letter criticises the translator of Bolingbroke for his errors, but he himself mistakes Bolingbroke's reference to a "studious man at Christ-church" for someone in a church. His letter gives both the German and English versions (xxvi 16).

tandis, heissen:—Noch blüht die schöne Rose nicht!—Nun blüht die schöne Rose!—Nun hat die schöne Rose geblüht!

Doch welche Bedenklichkeit kann Herr *Dusch* haben, sich selbst auszuschreiben! er, der Andere mit der allerunglaublichsten Freyheit ausschreibt?

[If, as is reported, Mr Dusch is also the translator of Pope's *Collected Works*, it is all the more surprising that he should not recall this remark by his *hero*. If he had done so, perhaps he would not repeat himself like a jackass in so many descriptions, mutatis mutandis: Not yet does the beauteous rose bloom!—Now the beauteous rose is blooming!—Now the beauteous rose has bloomed! Yet what scruple can Mr Dusch himself have to plagiarise! He who with the most unbelievable freedom plagiarises from others?]

This must have both appeared and been an irresistible Objection to Pope: and ⟨that⟩ it seemed so to Lessing is a proof how little he too had studied Nature with the faithful eye of a Lover.—O how sweet are the openings, the preparations, the prophecies of Nature—to a Dusch indeed, the Rose may always be the "beauteous Rose": but to a Poet?—And then the Labors & the Festivals of Man!—

82 xxvi 133, pencil

Und wer ist *Bournet*? Wenn hat ein *Bournet Archaeologias philosophicas* geschrieben? Ein *Burnet*, weiss ich wohl; und was braucht Herr *Dusch* den ehrlichen Schotten in einen Franzosen zu verwandeln?

[And who is Bournet? Whenever did a Bournet write *Archaeologiae philosophicae*? A Burnet I know well; and why need Mr Dusch transform the honest Scot into a Frenchman?]

Blunder versus Blunder!*

* L. confounds T. B. the Master of the Charter house with Burnet, the Whig Bishop.[1]

83 xxvi 164–5 | Letter 50

Mit wenig deutlichen Ideen von Gott und den göttlichen Vollkommenheiten, setzt sich der Schwärmer hin, überlässt sich ganz seinen Empfindungen, nimmt die Lebhaftigkeit derselben für Deutlichkeit der Be-

82[1] Thomas Burnet (c 1635–1715), master of Charterhouse, was the author of *Archaeologiae philosophicae* (1692) as well as of the famous *Sacred Theory of the Earth*, which appeared in English in 1684. The Scottish-born Gilbert Burnet (1643–1715), bp of Salisbury, was the author of the *History of the Reformation of the Church of England* (1679–81) and of the posthumously published *History of His Own Time* (2 vols 1724, 1734). C annotated three works by Gilbert Burnet and one by Thomas: see *CM (CC)* i.

griffe, wagt es, sie in Worte zu kleiden, und wird,—ein *Böhme*, ein *Pordage*.—

[With few clear ideas of God and divine perfection, the enthusiast sits down, surrenders utterly to his feelings, mistakes their vividness for clarity of concepts, dares to put them in words, and becomes—a Böhme, a Pordage.—]

Q.y Pordage? Can it be the man mentioned in the Life of Colonel Hutchinson?[1]—As to Böhme (= Jac'b Behmen) I should infer from this passage, that Lessing at the time had not read his Works. In some sense good or bad, a Visionary he was; but of blind fanatical Feelings he ought to [be][a] honorably acquitted[2]

84 xxviii 340–1, pencil, lightly cropped | Letter 65: Mendelssohn to Lessing, 1 Feb 1774

Für Ihr *intelligibile, intelligens* und *intellectus* werden sich die Herren höflichst bedanken. Sie müssen unter Ihren jugendlichen Aufsätzen noch einen finden, worin Sie diese Distinction mit vielem Scharfsinne aus einander gesetzt haben.

[You are hardly going to receive thanks for your *intelligibile, intelligens*, and *intellectus* [understandable, understanding, understood]. You will have to find among your youthful essays one in which you explicate these distinctions with great acumen.]

Mendelssohn's sneer grounds itself on his forgetfulness of the infinite & generic difference of a *creative* Intellect, whose Ideas are *causative* of Things, prior to them, & therefore more *actual* more per se stantes,[1] than their Effects, & human Images & Notion[s] which are the results, shadows, and relics of things.—[2]   S. T. C.

85 xxix ⁻2

When a poor poet, the purchaser of this expensive Edition, casts his eye over the huge number of uninteresting Letters (tho' exactly such as they should be) and then thinks of the number of Tracts & Articles omitted, which Lessing himself thought most valuable, both from their contents

---

a Word supplied by the editor

83[1] John Pordage (1607–81), author of *Theologia mystica* (1683); his name has not been found in Lucy Hutchinson's *Memoirs of the Life of Colonel Hutchinson* (1806) in the edition C annotated: see *CM* (*CC*) ii.

83[2] C's great admiration for Jakob Böhme (1575–1624) appears in the copious annotations to his *Works* (*CM—CC*—i) and

in published tributes, e.g. *BL* ch 9 (*CC*) i 146–7, *AR* (1825) 377–8, 385—the latter text especially interesting since it defends Böhme against such judgments as this of Lessing's.

84[1] "Standing for themselves".

84[2] A distinction invoked elsewhere, e.g. Jacobi *Ueber die Lehre* 3.

& their uniqueness or at least extreme scarcity—such as that of Wissowatius,[1] &c—may he not be pardoned for uttering an angry "Damn the book-making Prig!—or Master Nicolai—".[2] These two volumes, in which not a single Letter of any permanent Value (exclusive of the style)—nay, one of these Volumes would have contained the whole, & Berengarius to boot?—[3]

85[1] This edition includes Lessing's essay about Wissowatius (vii 65–102) but neither the work by Wissowatius that prompted it nor Leibniz's contribution to the controversy, as C complains in **29** above.

85[2] As C had done in **1** and **29** above.

85[3] The edition includes Lessing's commentary on a ms by Berengar of Tours discovered by Lessing (xiii 3–211), but not the ms itself.

JOHN LIGHTFOOT

1602–1675

The Works of the Reverend and Learned John Lightfoot D.D. late Master of Catherine Hall in Cambridge; such as were, and such as never before were printed. In two volumes. With the author's life, and large and useful tables to each volume. Also three maps: one of the Temple drawn by the author himself; the others Jerusalem and the Holy Land, drawn according to the author's chorography, with a description collected out of his writings. 2 vols. London 1684. F°.

Not located; marginalia printed from MS TRANSCRIPT.

Possibly HCR's copy, coming into his possession after C had written his marginalia in it, they being rather earlier in date than C's earliest acquaintance with HCR.

MS TRANSCRIPT. Dr Williams's Library, HCR papers Bundle I.V.3., 2.x.4: HCR transcript made on or about 24 Jun 1836 (*CRB* II 496). Two copies of notes 2–4 exist, and where they differ as to accidentals the version closer to C's usual practices (the same version in every case) has been followed.

CONTENTS. I Dedication; Preface [by George Bright]; i–xxxix "Some Account of the Life of . . . Lightfoot"; 1–147 *A Chronicle of the Times, and the Order of the Texts of the Old Testament*; [a made-up copy paginated 1–4, 205–6, 7–35, 236–687] *The Harmony, Chronicle and Order of the New Testament*; 691–8 "A Few, and New Observations, upon the Book of Genesis"; 699–725 "An Handful of Gleanings out of the Book of Exodus"; [727]–889 *A Commentary upon the Acts of the Apostles*; [891]–985 *The Temple Service as it stood in the Days of Our Saviour*; [987]–1031 *Erubhin or Miscellanies Christian and Judaical*; [1045]–2070 *The Temple especially as it stood in the days of our Saviour*; II Dedication; Preface [by John Strype]; 1–811 *Horae Hebraicae & Talmudicae, Hebrew and Talmudical Exercitations*; [title-page numbered 813, but text 1033–1355] Sermons and Discourses.

DATE. c Sept 1809. In c Sept 1809 C transcribed into N24 a passage from "The Publisher's preface to the Reader" (i.e. "Preface" in CONTENTS; this passage he used as motto to *Friend* No 10, 19 Oct 1809), and two passages from Vol II: *CN* III 3613–14 and nn, *Friend* (*CC*) II 134 (I 205).

COEDITOR. J. Robert Barth, S.J.

1   II 569 | Hebrew and Talmudical Exercitations: on John 9.2 "Who did sin, this man or his Parents?"

It is the opinion of the Pharisees Ψυχὴν πᾶσαν μὲν ἄφθαρτον μεταβαι-

707

νειν Qu: μενειν[1] δε εἰς ἕτερον σῶμα; τὴν τῶν ἀγαθῶν μονον, τὴν δὲ τῶν φαύλων ἀϊδίῳ τιμωρίᾳ κολαζεσθαι· *That the souls of all are immortal, and do pass into another body; that is those of the good only:* (observe this) *but those of the wicked are punished with eternal torments.* i.e. Every soul being essentially immortal passes from this body into another; but that the Souls of the good *abide* in this second (glorified) body, but that of the wicked are punished with an endless torment—i e of change from one evil body to another according to the analogy of the predominant bad passion—This is a mere conjecture, yet the words as they now stand involve *absolute* contradiction

NB: If any use be made of this to refer to the Text—"My brother by *gore*"[2]

An Anecdote

2　II 1044 | "A Sermon preached before the Staffordshire-Natives, at St. Mary Wolchurch London, Novemb. 22. 1660"

II. The chief cursed promoters and procurers of this backsliding, was that multitude of false Teachers of the *Jewish Nation*, that went about pretending to have the Spirit of *Prophesie* and *Revelation*; and <u>many of them working Miracles by the power of *Magick*</u>; so shaking the minds of men, and drawing them away from the Faith of the Gospel of Christ.

Socinian! you, who rest the main pillar of Christian Evidence on the Basis of Miracle! assist me in answering this objection of the Philosopher. You do not believe any magic, but that of imposture—Now how can *those* be competent evidences of *true miracles*, who could not distinguish imposture from Miracle? In the N:T: the Miracle is always acknowledged—the only difference asserted is this: from the nature of the doctrine this or that supernatural act was effected by a spirit of Evil, this or that by the good spirit—the Miracle as miracle (i e something achieved by a suspension or supernatural employment of the powers of nature) being the same in both—Now if the first were mere Jugglery, how could the persons so imposed on be competent witnesses of a miracle as distinct from juggling?[1]

[1] C questions the Greek text, proposing to substitute for the verb "pass into" (as Lightfoot translates it) the verb "abide".

[2] I.e. by blood. The source of this "text" has not been traced, unless it is one of C's own jokes, as when he refers to his brothers as "Relations by Gore" in a letter of 1799: *CL* I 528.

[1] Recognising the force of Hume's argument against miracles—to which C alludes in *CN* III 4381—and therefore deploring the tendency of the Church in his time to rely upon miracles as "evidences of Christianity" (this being the title of a famous book by William Paley), C consis-

3 II 1046

The Spirit of *Holiness* and *Revelation* are far different, therefore the one is not the cause of the other. . . . Now see what a cheat they are in *This* to themselves, (if they believe it themselves) and to others that believe it, in this argumentation, *I am holy, therefore I have the Spirit of Revelation* . . . 2. Consider the second *Adam*. He was holiness it self, yet had he not the Spirit of *Revelation* by that holiness. In *Christ* there were two things. *The holiness of his person*, by union with the *Godhead*, and *the Indowment of the Spirit upon his person*. He was so holy that he was not only without sin, but he was *impeccable, Rom.* VIII. 2. as we are a Law that cannot but sin, so he *contra*. Now this holiness of Christs person or nature is to a clean different end to what the guifts of the Spirit upon him were. His *person* was so holy, that he might perform the Law, satisfie justice, pay obedience, conquer Satan. But the *guifts* of the Spirit were to fit him for *Mediatorship*, to cast out Devils, to reveal the will of God, to work Miracles to confirm that Doctrine.

Who would not suppose that the writer was discoursing of some Carpenter work? He is *impeccable*. Then he was not tempted, and could afford no example to us. Dr L. is surely, very faulty in this strange mechanic material mode of representing sacred mysteries. Did he disbelieve the existence of a will an Arbitrium?[1] Perhaps the making of some compound according to laws of chemical affinity would be an exacter metaphor than Carpentery. Take a menstruum—pour in some—θεοτης[2] it combines & forms holiness—then add some gifts of spirit, & the result will be the grand πανφαρμακον—[3]

4 II 1047

Consider his [Christ's] own words, *Mark.* XIII. 32. *But of that day and that hour knoweth no man, no not the Angels which are in Heaven, neither the Son but the Father:* Some are ashamed to confess their ignorance of any thing, yet he doth it plainly. For the *Divine Nature* in

---

tently treated accounts of miracles sceptically and insisted that Christianity must be based on a more spiritual foundation. Among many statements on this subject, a letter of 1806, linking the argument from miracles with Socinianism and with Paley, may be the best gloss on this note: *CL* II 1189.

3[1] I.e. a will that makes decisions. Cf similar discrimination of different functions or possibly kinds of will in JURIEU **8** and MILLER **7**.

3[2] "Divinity", some of "the divine nature".

3[3] The Greek spelling of "panpharmacon" meaning panacea or cure-all, adopted in English by the seventeenth century. (Though the roots of the word are Greek, it is not a transliteration from the Greek.)

Christ acted not to the utmost of its power. Tis clear from this passage of *Christ*, that by his nature he had not the Spirit of *Revelation*, but he had it by the *immediate* guift of God. For it pleased not God so to reveal that day and hour to him, while he was here on Earth. So that by this example you may see much more the fallacy of that argument, *I am a Saint, therefore I have the Spirit of Revelation.* Whereas Christ himself could not say so.

And yet the only possible definition of the Divine Nature is Actus purissimus sine aliqua potentialitate[1]—This not granted Eternity would cease to be its attribute for Eternity is totius possessio simultanea.[2] I grieve that the excellent Author should so unnecessarily have *pawed* these high mysteries for the discourse, these parts excepted, is full of just acute, & very useful expositions   It would be well that some of our modern Saints would peruse it—The §§ dotted are most admirable.[3]

Annex

Passage cited in **4** n 3 above:

The Spirit of Revelation is given indeed to Saints, but means little that sence, that men speak of, but is of a clean different nature. The *Apostle* prays, *Ephes.* I. 17. *That God would give unto them the Spirit of Wisdom and Revelation in the knowledge of him.* And God gives this Spirit; but in what sence? Not, to foresee things to come, not to understand the *Grammatical construction* of Scripture without study, not to preach by the Spirit: but the Apostle explains himself, *vers.* 18. *The eyes of their understanding being enlightned, that ye may know what is the hope of his calling, and what the riches of the glory of his inheritance in the Saints.* So that the *Revelation* given to the Saints is this, that God reveals the experience of those things, that we have learned before in *Theory* from Scripture, a saving feeling of *the hope of his calling, and the riches of the glory of his inheritance.* Here let me speak of three things.
    I. To feel the experience of Grace is not by new Light, that was never known before, but by application of what was known before. As the Queen of *Sheba* first heard of the Fame of *Solomon*, then found by experience. Compare we our knowledge of Spiritual things to a Banquet, to your Feast this day. A man before Grace sees the banquet God hath provided for his people, hath by the word learned the nature and definition of *Faith, Repentance, Holiness, Love of God,* and *Love to God,* but as yet he does but see the banquet; when Grace comes, then he sees and tastes these things in experience and sence in his own Soul. He had a light before from the Word, now it is brought so near his heart that he feels

4[1] "Absolutely pure Act without any potentiality"—a scholastic formula frequently invoked by C, e.g. BAXTER *Catholick Theology* **1** and n 2.
    4[2] "Simultaneous possession of the whole"—eternity being by definition removed from temporal sequence.
    4[3] C must have used a row of dots to mark the passage that HCR identifies in his transcript as running from "the Spirit of revelation" to the end of the page (1047), i.e. the text in the ANNEX following.

warmness, he feels life and sence and operation of these things, is as it were changed into these things; as in II. *Cor.* III. 18. *We with open face beholding as in a glass the glory of the Lord, are changed into the same image from glory to glory.* Now this is not the Spirit of *Revelation* in that sence, that these take it in, but tis so called, because it is by a light and operation above natural light and operation. As *Common grace* is called grace, because 'tis above the ordinary working of nature, so this is called *revelation*, because above the work of common light.

2. How do men come to assurance of pardon and salvation? Not by the Spirit of *revelation* in their sence, not by any immediate whispers from Heaven, but another way. As in *Rom.* XV. 4. *Through patience and comfort of the Scriptures we have hope.* In Scripture is your comfort, and in your own conscience; and in them is your assurance. A Saint makes this holy *Syllogism.*

Scripture, Major, *He that repents, loves God, hath the pardon of his Sins.*
Conscience, Minor, *Lord, I believe, Lord, I love thee.*
Saint, from both makes the *Conclusion, Therefore I am assured of the pardon of my sins, and my Salvation.*

Thus *Christ* would bring *S. Peter* to assurance of his Estate after his denial, by this trial, *Lovest thou me? Not by any revelation that Christ loved him, but it was assurance enough, if he loved Christ. And here by the way let me speak one word for trial, whether we have the Spirit of Sanctification,* that we be not deceived in the rest. Never believe you have the Spirit of *Sanctification*, unless your heart be changed to love God. Among many signs this is the most sensible and undoubted. I say, unless the *heart be changed*, and changed *to love God. Change of heart* is the mother habit of all Graces. God speaks enough in *Ezek.* XXXVI. 26. *A new heart will I give you, and a new spirit will I put within you.* In that question about *perseverance* and *loss of grace*, as in the case of *David, Peter,* &c. we say, *That the Act may be suspended and lost for the present, but the Habit not.* Now by *habit* we mean not the particular seed of this or that Grace, but the change of the Heart, the *materia prima* of all graces. That is never unchanged back again: the *stone* is taken away. The heart indeed may freez into *ice*, as *Davids* and *Peters*, but never turn into *stone* again.

CHARLES LLOYD
1775–1839

Nugae Canorae. Poems by Charles Lloyd, author of "Edmund Oliver," "Isabel," and translator of Alfieri. 3rd ed. London 1819. 8°.

British Library C 45 a 22

Inscribed on p ⁻2: "From the Author", and below in pencil in an unidentified hand "preserve this". A pencil note on p ⁻5 (p-d): "MS Notes by Coleridge and at Page 145. Sonnet by Coleridge contains a Correction in his hand-writing." See **5C**.

At pp 169–74 Lloyd (in print) quotes extensively from C's introduction to the "Sheet of Sonnets" of Bristol 1796, only to say that "he totally differs from him [C] in the opinion given in the succeeding part of that composition".

DATE. c Oct 1819, presumably shortly after publication. Lloyd's Preface is dated Aug 1819 and his Dedicatory Sonnet 6 Sept 1819.

1   p 128, pencil | *Stanzas. Let the Reader Determine Their Title* st 1 lines 7–9

> while the haze
> Of twilight in the vale is lingering,
> *   The Oread from mountain top the sun-rise welcoming.

*

           ◡ — ◡ū ū — ◡ — ◡ — ◡ — ◡◡ !!!

as a *variety* of ◡ — ◡ —¹

2   p 131, pencil | St 8 line 9

> "To dream myself the only living thing, save thee!"

> To think myself the only Being alive.
> *Remorse.*¹

3   p 135, pencil | St 15 lines 6–9, st 16 line 1

> While others take a more fantastic course,
> And with <u>such</u> involutions sing and play
> 'Twixt sandy banks, or with a note more hoarse,
> O'er rocks and sparry beds, forgetful of their source,

> <u>That</u> one might deem they were without a law,

---

¹ C complains that line 9 is an extravagant departure from the iambic norm of the poem.

2¹ *Remorse* IV iii 20: *PW* (EHC) II 868.

/ These are not lyrical transitions; but the mere Orange-sucking of bewildered garrulity—really vexatious in a poem of so much merit.

4   p 135, pencil, lightly cropped | Continuing **3** textus: st 16 lines 2–9, st 17 lines 1–2

> Lawless as winds, if winds could be, or ere
> The Almighty architect impressed an awe
> On nature's wildest freebooters;—or were,
> Like as in sung of the crystalline sphere,—
> Involved in maze of such perplexity,
> *a*That e'en that skill which made *intention* clear,
> So intricate was it, one might deny
> The very law itself from its transcendency.

> When first, I say—I've <u>played</u> the truant long,
> From the theme I had espoused . . .

This *may* be *Sense*: it is certainly neither Gramma[r] nor Logic

4A   p 138, pencil | St 21 lines 5–8

> Strange melodies assigned
> To it, harsh discord seem to th' ears of all:
> Yet not a note doth breathe from it designed
> To give a pang: it <u>mayn't</u> be musical:—

5   p 138, pencil | St 22 lines 7–9

> . . . yet still if he
> Feels, while it floats around, as though a wing
> Protected him* with tremulous faint o'ershadowing.

* Him is in its effect on the ear more a rhyme to "wing", than "oershadowing".

5A   p 139, pencil | St 23 lines 6–9

> I seek communion, covet sympathy,
> E'en with their wildest moods:—they suit my woes—
> <u>I meant to say</u> when souls from agony
> A little respite feel . . .

5B   p 140, pencil | St 25 lines 7–9

> How little dreamt I *then* this shuddering,
> * From the heart's nice calculation, whence we infer
> Futurity, was my fate's harbinger . . .

---

a C has made a pencil line in the margin beside this and the next two lines

5C p 145, pencil | *Poems on the Death of Priscilla Farmer*: Sonnet "The piteous sobs that choak the Virgin's breath" (signed S. T. Coleridge) lines 12–14

> And from the Almighty Father shall descend
> Comforts on his late Eve~~ning~~, whose you~~ng~~thful breast
> Mourns with no transient love the Aged Friend.

6 p [259], pencil | Advertisement to the Translations

The Metamorphoses in the original are written in a style highly artificial: the Author, therefore, in his translation has rather preferred the adopting a smooth* and even versification, to the more loose, easy, and natural one, which latterly has been so much in vogue.

* verily, rather too good a joke!

M. LOEWE

fl 1822

A Treatise on the Phenomena of Animal Magnetism; in which the same are systematically explained, according to the laws of nature, &c. London 1822. 8°.

Yale University (Beinecke Library)

At the top of p ⁻1, apparently in C's hand: "A Treatise". Two names added to the list of subscribers in an unidentified hand.

DATE. Late 1822? Loewe's book was perhaps drawn to C's attention upon publication by his friend Hyman Hurwitz, whose name appears in the list of subscribers. The author's dedication is dated 12 Aug 1822, so publication must have been late in the year.

COEDITOR. Lore Metzger.

1 p ⁻2, pencil, overtraced

On the whole an able and well-written *Exposé* of the Physiology grounded on the Schellingian or Natur-philosophie. But the defect, which Schelling manages to hide from a careless survey, lies on the very surface in Mʳ Loewe's Exposition. From his introductory ¶phs. we are led to expect from the Scheme an explanation of Life, Mind, Will, Individuality; but one ~~at~~ after the other, these slip in quietly as old Inmates, ~~being mere~~ jam diu demonstrata,[1] and a God, and a Soul to boot; and instead of the Scheme accounting for these, these are in fact successively called in to account for all that is of main interest and importance in the Scheme. In short, the hardest and most important *Problems* of Physiology and Anthropology are converted into the Solutions: and of course, the Basis of the whole ⟨inverted⟩ Pyramid is the old Apex, Sic voluit Deus.[2]—which is very true & very pious but unluckily nothing to the purpose—i.e. the purpose of a Philosopher, which is *Insight*.

S. T. Coleridge

2 p 94, pencil | § 73

The name of a person includes his whole self. By pronouncing, or calling him by his name, the whole individual, who, in fact, is not com-

---

1[1] "Things long since demonstrated". 1[2] "God willed it so".

pletely asleep, necessarily awakes, the internal and complete conscious-ness of himself is recalled, and at the same time the disposition to self-preservation again comes into action . . .

This is pretty, I admit. The unity of man takes place in and thro' the co-instantaneous concurrence of all the special Brains, 36 of which live together in every single Skull.[1] Ex. gr. They all like a kennel of Fox-hounds, start up simultaneously at the Sound of their common name—one less than Dandy Dinmont's Terriery was gifted with.[2]/ But where lies the Camera obscura in which all these converge? Where the optic Cylinder, in which they form *one* consciousness?[3] Where is THE MAN

3 p 102, pencil | § 79

[Footnote:] That the functions of sight in some animals are supplied by other organs, which hitherto have remained unknown to us, is proved by the experiments made by Spallanzani, who deprived bats of their eyes by digging them out, and made the observation, that those animals would fly about in different apartments without hitting against any thing, and found their way, while flying, between threads drawn across the room, were it even by contracting their wings.

Probably, as far as the experiments can be relied on, from sense of Tem-perature, which is probably exquisite in Animals made to pursue their prey during the Night.

4 p 103, pencil | § 80

As the vital or original power is in general ever anxious about the pres-ervation of individuality, it is less to be wondered at, that magnetised persons should examine their own frame, in order to discover its faults;

2[1] The system of phrenology formulated by F. J. Gall and J. G. Spurzheim de-scribed the brain as "an aggregation of or-gans" (Spurzheim *The Physiognomical System of Drs. Gall and Spurzheim*—1815—166), but the number of organs identified ranged from 26 to 36 depending on the practitioner. The usual figure given by e.g. Spurzheim, Thomas Foster (*Sketch of the New Anatomy and Physiology of the Brain and Nervous System*—1815), and George Combe (*Essays on Phrenology*—Edinburgh 1819) was 33, but C may have preferred one of the variants of the system.

2[2] All the terriers bred by the Lowland farmer Dandie Dinmont in Walter Scott's *Guy Mannering* (1815) ch 22 were called either Pepper or Mustard. "Dandie Din-mont" has itself become the name of a ter-rier breed.

2[3] Literally "dark chamber", the cam-era obscura consists of a box or darkened room admitting light through one small hole only; the hole contains lenses which project an image of the external scene upon a screen or wall or sheet of paper at the fo-cal point. It was a favourite image for C: cf *BL* chs 3, 22 (*CC*) I 48*, II 128. By "optic cylinder" C appears to mean "telescope"; *OED* cites "optic tube" in a poetic context in 1827.

for what should restrain the inward man from searching into himself, since he is in a condition in which his perceptions are not governed by those laws to which the organs of sense are subject. The descriptions which such persons give are chiefly regulated by the degree of the cultivation of their minds.*

* In all the *well*-attested instances, that have come to my knowlege, the descriptions have been palpably the creatures of fancy, and bore all the distinctive characters of Dreaming—ex. gr. Warts on the Apex of the Heart; the Aorta choked up by co-agulated Blood; & the like.—[1]

4[1] C responds knowledgeably to Loewe's references to the "clairvoyant" phase of the experience of the patient under animal magnetism—the phase in which the patient appeared to be able literally to look within himself or (more often) herself and to describe the interior of the body. In his wide reading on animal magnetism, C would have found several case histories of clairvoyants, e.g. C. A. von Eschenmayer et al *Archiv für den Thierischen Magnetismus* I (Altenburg and Leipzig 1817) 135 ff; II (1818) 18. A comment specifically on "the Inside-seers" appears in KLUGE 7 and 8, with the case of the woman with warts on her heart.

MARTIN LUTHER

1483–1546

Dⁱˢ Martini Lutheri Colloquia mensalia: or, Dʳ Martin Luther's divine discourses at his table, &c. Which in his life time hee held with divers learned men (such as were Philip Melancthon, Casparus Cruciger, Justus Jonas, Paulus Eberus, Vitus Dietericus, Joannes Bugenhagen, Joannes Forsterus, and others) conteining questions and answers touching religion, and other main points of doctrine, as also many notable histories, and all sorts of learning, comforts, advises, prophesies, admonitions, directions and instructions. Collected first together by Dʳ Antonius Lauterbach, and afterward disposed into certain common places by John Aurifaber Dʳ in Divinitie. Translated out of the high Germane into the English tongue by Capt. Henrie Bell, &c. London 1652. F°.

British Library Ashley 4773

Inscribed in ink on p ⁻2: "EDWARD WHITE". Notations in ink on p ⁻3 (p-d) referring to pp 143, 228, 229; on p ⁻2 in pencil referring to p 143; and on p ⁺3 (p-d) referring to p 386, like the corrections to the text on pp 511 and 515, appear to have been written before C's notes, and may be White's, for his signature is written above the pencil note on p ⁻2. Notes in pencil on pp 37, 58, 63, 71, 79 (2), 114 (2), ⁺3—three of them overtraced in ink—do not appear to be in C's hand, although it is difficult to discriminate when pencilled notes are overtraced in ink in another hand. All these notes are very brief, and neither handwriting nor content is sufficiently Coleridgean to warrant their inclusion here. Three short pencilled notes on pp 217, 219, 244, which may have been C's, were deliberately erased and are no longer decipherable. Passages are marked with pencil lines, and in some cases with a pointing finger, on sig A3ᵛ, [C5ʳ], pp 22, 28, 29 (2), 35, 58, 60, 73, 79, 149, 319 (3), 324, 367, 421, 426. Some marks in the text could be C's: pp 48, 53, 138, 235, 306. None of these, however, is associated with any note of C's, and in view of the rather extensive marking in a hand or hands clearly not C's, these cannot confidently be ascribed to him.

Between p 208 and p 446, certain annotations have been marked with a large arabic number in the margin to make a series of 15 notes for the editor(s) preparing the selection of notes printed in LR IV 1–65. All but 3 of these indicators were copied into MS TRANSCRIPT (a).

More than 20 of Luther's disciples kept records of his informal conversation between 1529 and 1546. Selected passages from their notes, together with extracts from letters and certain published works, were edited, arranged according to topic, and published 20 years later as table-talk (Tischreden) by J. Goldschmidt (who Latinised his name as Aurifaber), Luther's secretary in the last year of his life. Henry Bell's English translation is at the same time an abridgment of Aurifaber's work.

A great admirer of Luther's German works, as his essays in *The Friend* (*CC*) I 132–4, 136–43 and occasional warm recommendations (e.g. *CL* IV 845–6) show, C carried this copy of the *Colloquia* away from Charles Lamb's library, apparently in Sept 1819. It was one of his favourite books in the later years of his life and is one of his most heavily annotated. (The annotations spilled over as extracts and notes in the later notebooks: *CN* IV 4594, 4599, 4600, 4664, 4665, 4671, 5326, 5393, 5415.) The book was still in his possession when he died. Lamb, to whom some notes, such as **59**, are directly addressed, tried at first to recover the volume, writing C a comical but also rueful letter about "Luster's Tables", as the maid called it (*LL* II 284–5). The occasion, and perhaps the writing of the letter, prompted more magnanimous remarks about C as a bookborrower in "The Two Races of Men" (*London Magazine* Dec 1820). Lamb originally gave as the reason for his concern the fact that the book did not really belong to him, but was "the property of a friend, who does not know its value"—probably the Edward White whose name appears in the book, if he is the same Edward White who was Lamb's East India House acquaintance (*LL* III 112).

MS TRANSCRIPTS. (*a*) MS facsimile. BM C 45 i 16 *Colloquia mensalia; or, the familiar discourses of Dr. Martin Luther at his table . . . Translated . . . by Captain Henry Bell. Second edition . . . [with] the life and character of Dr Martin Luther by John Gottlieb Burckhardt*, &c. (London 1791), with the heraldic bookplates of Henry Crabb Robinson and his executor, Edwin Wilkins Field, on p ⁻4 (p-d). A note in ink on the title-page in an unidentified hand reads, "This edition is nothing equal to that of 1652—great liberties are taken in this of omissions & alterations.—" Some account of the missing items is tipped in at pp 40/1. About half the copied notes have been written directly on the pages of text, the rest on slips of paper tipped into the volume. The transcript seems to be in the same hand as the transcript of LACUNZA Vol I. The transcription is not accurate, and nothing was copied pp 232–328; a number of notes, including the long notes on front and back flyleaves, are omitted.

(*b*) Marked copy. *Dⁱⁱ Martini Lutheri Colloquia mensalia* &c (London 1652). [Another copy.] Professor T. W. Baldwin, Urbana, Illinois. Inscribed on the front outside cover: "Olim e libris S. T. C. Ex dono Alexandri G[illman?]." Underlinings, question marks, and single words in black, red, blue, and violet pencil on pp 91, 132, 135, 136, 147, 159, 227, 257, 262, 288, 351, 390, 401, 402, 407, 426, 429, 447, 509, 510, 433 [i.e. 533], 541. There is no evidence for ascribing any of these marks to C, yet it may well have been a copy kept in the Gillman family and by family tradition said to have been C's.

DATE. Sept 1819 to Aug 1829: notes are dated 25 Sept 1819 (**57**), 11 Feb 1826 (**1**), 26 Jun 1826 (**32**), 10 Aug 1826 (**78**), 19 Aug 1826 (**95, 112**), Jul 1829 (**40, 50**).

1   p ⁻2

Mem. Sunday, 11 Febʸ 1826.—I cannot meditate too often, too deeply, or too devotionally on the personëity of God, and his personality in the WORD, ὑιῳ τῳ μονογενεῖ[1]—and thence on the *individuity* of the responsible Creature, that it is a perfection which not indeed in my intellect but yet in my habit of *feeling*, I have too much confounded with that complexus of visual image, cycles or customs of Sensations, & fellow-travelling-Circumstances (as the Ship to the Mariner) which make up our empirical *Self*—Thence to bring myself to apprehend livelily the exceeding Mercifulness and Love of the *Act* of the Son of God, in descending to seek after the prodigal Children, and to house with them in the *Stie*— Likewise by the relation of my own Understanding to the Light of Reason, and (the most important of all the truths that have been vouchsafed to me!) ~~of~~ to the Will that *is* the Reason, Will in the form of Reason I can form a sufficient gleam of the possibility of the subsistence of the human Soul in Jesus to the Eternal WORD, and how it might perfect itself so as to merit *glorification* & abiding Union with the divinity—and how this gave a humanity to our Lord's Righteousness ~~as~~ no less than to his Sufferings. Doubtless, As God, as the Absolute Alterity of the Absolute, he could not Suffer; but that he could not lay aside the Absolute, and by Union with Creaturely become Affectible, and a Second, but Spiritual, Adam, and so as afterwards to be partaker of the Absolute in the Absolute even as the Absolute had partaken of passion (τοῦ πάσχειν)[2] and infirmity in *it*—i.e. the finite & fallen Creature—*this* can be asserted only by one who (unconsciously perhaps) has accustomed himself to think of God, as a Thing—having a necessity of Constitution, that *wills* or rather *tends* & inclines to this or that because it *is* this or that—not of that which is that which it wills to be—. This necessity is truly *compulsion*—which is not in the least altered in its Nature by being assumed eternal, that by an endless remotion or retrusion of the Constituent Cause which being manifested by the Understanding becomes a foreseen *Despair* of a Cause./

2   p ⁻1, pencil, overtraced

One argument strikes me in favor of the tenet of Apostolic Succession in Ordination of Bishops and Presbyters, as taught by the Church of Rome, and by the larger part of the earlier Divines of the Protestant Church of England, which I have not seen, in any of the books on this subject[1]—Viz. that in strict analogy with other parts of Christian History

---

1[1] "His only begotten son"; cf John 3.16.

1[2] The Greek infinitive *paschein*, meaning "to suffer", "to endure", in opposition to acting, is etymologically the root of "passion" and "passive".

2[1] The question of the apostolic succession—the theory that the ministry of the

the Miracle itself contained a Check upon the inconvenient conse-
quences necessarily attached to all Miracles, *as* Miracles—*ª*narrowing
the possible claims to any rights not proveable at the Bar of universal
Reason and Experience.

Every man among the Sectaries, however ignorant, may justify him-
self in scattering Stones and Fire-Squibs by *an Unction of the Spirit.*[2]
The Miracle becomes perpetual, still beginning, never ending! Now on*ᵇ*
the Church Doctrine the original Miracle provides for the future recur-
rence to to*ᶜ* the ordinary and [. . .]*ᵈ* calculable Laws of the Human Un-
derstanding and Moral Sense:—*ᵉ*instead of leaving every man a Judge
of his own Gifts, and of his right to act publicly on that Judgement.—*ᵉ*
The initiative alone is supernatural; but all BEGINNING is necessarily
miraculous[3]—i.e. hath either no antecedent, or one ἑτέρου γενοῦς,*ᶠ*[4]
which therefore is not *its* but merely *an* antecedent—or an incausitive
alien Co-incident in Time,—as if for instance Jack's *Crepitus*[5] were fol-
lowed by a Flash of Lightning that struck and precipitated the Ball on Sᵗ
Paul's Cathedral. This would be a Miracle as long as no causative nexus
was conceivable between the Antecedens, the Noise and Odor of the
Crepitus, and the Consequens, the atmospheric Discharge.   *S. T. C.*

3   sig A4, pencil, overtraced | *The Epistle Dedicatorie*

One Post shall run to meet another, and one messenger to meet another,
to shew the King of *Babylon* his Citie is taken at one end; but this will
bee your glorie and wals inexpugnable, if you cleav in truth and practice
to God's holie service, worship and religion: That Religion* and Faith
of the Lord Jesus Christ, which is pure and undefiled before God even
the Father, which is to visit the fatherless and widows in their affliction,
and to keep your selvs unspotted from the world, *James* I.27 . . .

ª Dash not overtraced   *ᵇ* Thus overtraced, but perhaps originally "in"
ᶜ Second "to" not overtraced   *ᵈ* Cancelled letters erased: illegible
ᵉ Punctuation not overtraced   *ᶠ* Greek not overtraced

Christian Church has been derived in an unbroken line from Christ's Apostles—is not explicitly addressed by Luther in the *Colloquia*, and this note therefore cannot be attached to any particular passage. Luther's scorn for the idea emerges occasionally, e.g. p 300, in the chapter *Of Antichrist.*

2[2] In the figurative meaning recorded in *OED*, a spiritual influence acting upon a person.

2[3] As C says in *AR* (1825) 73, the realm of nature is the realm of unbroken sequence of cause and effect; first causes ("the initiative") and uncaused events belong to the realm of the supernatural.

2[4] "Different in kind".

2[5] "Fart".

* Few mistranslations (unless indeed the word used by the Translator of St James meant differently from its present meaning) have led astray more than this rendering of Thrēskeia (= outward or ceremonial Worship, Cultus, Divine Service &c) by the English, *Religion*.[1] St James sublimely says, What the *ceremonies* of the Law were to Morality, *that* Morality itself is to the Faith in Christ—i.e. its outward symbol, not the substance itself.

4 p 2, pencil, overtraced | Ch 1 *Of the word of God; or the holie scriptures, conteined in the Bible* "Proofs, that the Bible is the word of God"

That the Bible is the Word of GOD (said *Luther*) the same I prove as followeth: All things that have been, and now are in the world; also, how it now goeth and standeth in the world, the same was written altogether particularly at the begining, in the first Book of *Moses* concerning the Creation. And even as God made and created it, even so it was, even so it is, and even so doth it stand to this present daie. And although King *Alexander* the Great, the Kingdom of *Egypt*, the Empire of *Babel*, the *Persian, Grecian*, and *Romane* Monarchs; the Emperors *Julius* and *Augustus* most fiercely did rage and swell against this Book, utterly to suppress and destroie the same; yet notwithstanding, they could prevail nothing, they are all gon and vanished, but this Book from time to time hath remained, and will remain unremoved in full and ample manner as it was written at the first.

A proof worthy of the manly mind of Luther, and compared with which the Grotian, pretended Demonstrations from Grotius himself to Paley are mischievous Underminings of the Faith, Pleadings fitter for an Old Baily Thieves' Counsellor than for a Christian Divine.[1] The true Evidence of the Bible is the Bible—of Christianity is the living Face of Christianity itself, as the manifest Archeus[2] or Predominant of the Life of the Planet.

5 p $^-$3 (p-d)^a referring to p 4 | "Of the art of the school-divines in the Bible"

The art of the School-Divines (said *Luther*) with their speculations in the

^{a} A sheet of paper attached with sealing-wax

3[1] C repeats this objection in *AR* (1825) 15n, where he proposes the translation "outward service".

4[1] In his many statements on this topic, C habitually traced the contemporary reliance on the external evidence of miracles for the defence of the Christian religion to the work of the Dutch jurist and theologian Hugo Grotius (1583–1645): *CN* II 2640n conveniently documents his position and identifies his antagonists.

4[2] This Paracelsian term, for which C here provides his own translation, appears also in BÖHME *Works* **15**; cf *CN* III 4136 and n.

Holy Scriptures, are meerly vain and humane cogitations, spun out of their own natural wit and understanding. . . . They talk much of the union of the will and understanding, but all is meer fantasie and fondness. The right and true speculation (said *Luther*) is this: *Believ in Christ; do what thou oughtest to do in thy vocation*, &c. This is the onely practice in Divinitie.

P. 4. Chapter I.

Still, however, du theure Mann Gottes, mein verehrter Luther![1] Reason, Will, Understanding are words, to which real entities correspond: and we may in a sound and good sense say, that Reason is the Ray, the projected disk or image from the Sun of Righteousness, (ἥλιος, filius, Eλ υιος, i.e. God the Son)[2] an echo from the Eternal Word—"the Light that lighteth every man that cometh into the World".[3] And that when the Will placeth itself in a right line with the Reason, there ariseth the Spirit, thro' which the Will of God floweth into and actuateth the Will of Man, so that it willeth the things of God—and the Understanding is enlivened, and thenceforward useth the materials supplied to it by the Senses symbolically—that is, with an insight into the true *Substance* thereof.

6   pp 9–10 | "That the hereticks do contemn God's word"

The Pope (said *Luther*) usurpeth and taketh to himself the power to expound and to construe the Scriptures according to his pleasure; what hee saith, must stand and bee spoken as from heaven.

Therefore let us love and pretiously value the Divine Word, that thereby wee may bee able to resist the Divel and his swarm.*

* Often as I pray verse 16 of Psalm 71st (in our prayer-book version),[1]

5[1] "Thou dear man of God, my honoured Luther". C's frequent use of the epithet "dear man" for Luther may reflect a familiarity with the eighteenth-century collected edition of Luther's German works entitled *Des theuren Mannes Gottes, D. Martin Luthers sämtliche . . . Schrifften und Wercke* ed C. F. Boerner (Leipzig 1729–40)—a folio edition in 23 parts, usually bound as 12 vols (referred to in notes hereafter as "Leipzig ed"). The five "massive folios" (*BL* ch 10—*CC*—I 206) described as annotated by C in *W Library* probably belonged to this edition: see below, LUTHER *Schriften* headnote.

5[2] The word play here depends upon resemblances in sound between the Greek *hēlios* (sun), Latin *filius* (son), and Arabic-

and-Greek *El [h]uios* (God the Son). The symbolic connection between the Son and the Sun is traditional. C records the same "innocent" sequence of words in a ms note in Copy G of his *Statesman's Manual* (*LS—CC*—55–6 n 4), in connection with *The Works of the Great Albionean Divine . . . Mr Hugh Broughton* ed John Lightfoot (1662), which does not, however, appear to be a direct source. Cf also DONNE *Sermons* COPY B 17.

5[3] John 1.9 (var).

6[1] "Forsake me not, O God, in mine old age, when I am gray-headed: until I have shewed thy strength unto this generation, and thy power to all them that are yet for to come": BCP (differs from AV).

Ɨ my Thoughts especially revert to this subject—namely, the right appreciation of the Scriptures, and the in what sense the Bible may be called The Word of God—and how & under what conditions the Unity of the Spirit is translucent thro' the Letter/ which read, as the Letter merely, ả is the Word of this and that pious but fallible and imperfect Man. Alas for the Superstition, where the words themselves are made to be the Spirit!—O might I live but to utter all my meditations on this most concerning Point!

7 pp 12–13 | "Of the errors which the sectaries do hold concerning the word of God"

Bullinger said once in my hearing (said *Luther*) that hee was earnest against the Anabaptists, as contemners of God's Word, and also against those which attributed too much to the literal word, for (said hee) such do sin against God and his Almightie power; as the Jews did in naming the Ark, God. But (said hee) whoso holdeth a mean between both, the same is taught what is the right use of the Word and Sacraments.

Whereupon said (*Luther*) I answered him and said: *Bullinger* you Err, you know neither your self, nor what you hold; I mark well your tricks and fallacies: *Zuinglius* and *Oecolampadius* likewise proceeded too far in this your ungodly meaning: but when *Brentius* withstood them, they then lessened their opinions, alleging, they did not reject the literal Word, but onely condemned certain gross abuses. * By this your Error (said *Luther* to *Bullinger*) you cut in sunder and separate the Word and the Spirit . . .

* In my present state of mind and with what Light I now enjoy (may God increase it, and cleanse it from the dank mist into the Lumen Siccum[1] of sincere Knowlege!) I cannot persuade myself, that this vehemence of this dear Man of God against Bullinger, Zuinglius & Œcolampadius on this point could have had other origin, than his misconception of what they intended! But Luther spoke often (I like him & love him all the better *therefore*!)[2] in his moods and according to the Mood.—Was not that a different *mood*, in which he called James's Epistle *a Jack-straw-poppet*—and even in this work selects one verse as the *best* in the whole letter?[3] ⟨evidently meaning, the only verse of any great

7[1] The phrase "Dry Light", attributed to Heraclitus, is associated especially with Bacon, who thus glosses it: "HERACLITUS the Obscure said; the dry light is the best soul: meaning, when the faculties intellectual are in vigour, not drenched, or as it were blooded by the affections": Apophthegms no 241 (*Works*—1740—III 286).

Cf *CN* IV 5379 and n.

7[2] C quotes his own comic verse about Luther (**91** below), a verse which may in turn be an adaptation of a once well-known song or poem: C uses the phrase allusively in a letter of 1818, *CL* IV 868, and in Lamb's copy of DANIEL **1**.

7[3] The "one verse" is that q in **3** textus,

value.⟩—Besides, he accustomed himself to use the term, the Word, in a very wide sense when the narrower would have cramped him. When he was on the point of rejecting the Apocalypse, then *The Word* meant *the Spirit* ⟨of the Scriptures⟩ collectively

8 p 21 | "That God's word, is, and remain's God's word, whether wee believ it or not"

* Even so is it likewise with Baptizing of Children: I (said *Luther*) do not hold that children are without faith when they are baptized; for inasmuch as they are brought to Christ by his command, and that the Church praieth for them, therefore, without all doubt, faith is given unto them, although, with our natural sens and reason, wee neither see nor understand it.

* Nay, but dear honored Luther! that is *not* fair!—if Christ or Scripture had said in one place—Believe and thou mayst be baptized—and in another place, Baptize Infants—then we might perhaps be allowed to reconcile the two seemingly jarring texts by a "faith is given to them, although &c". But when ⟨no⟩ such text, as the latter, is to be found, nor any one instance as a substitute—then it is not fair.[1]

9 pp 25–7, pencil, overtraced | "That above and before all things, God's word must and shall bee preferred"

This Argument [that the apostles of Christ are better guides than St Paul, who was converted after the death of Christ] (said *Luther*) concludeth so much as nothing; for, although they were greater Apostles; yea, although they had been Angels from heaven, yet that troubleth mee nothing at all; * wee are now dealing about God's Word, and with the truth of the Gospel, that is a matter of far greater weight to have the same kept & preserved pure and clear; therefore wee (said *Luther*) neither care nor trouble our selvs for, and about the greatness of Saint *Peter* and the other Apostles, or how manie and great miracles they wrought: the thing which wee strive for is, That the truth of the holie Gospel may stand; for God regardeth not men's reputations nor persons.

* Oh that the dear Man, Luther, had but told us here what he meant by

---

Jas 1.27. Luther made the famous remark that the Epistle of James is "an epistle of straw" in the 1524 version of his preface to the NT: Leipzig ed pt 12 p 55. C's colourful adaptation, with its image of a straw doll, conflates the terms of the original, in which "S. Jacobs" is said to be "eine rechte ströherne Epistel".

8[1] C did not share Luther's opinion of

the importance of infant baptism, regarding it as a symbolic ceremony rather than as an essential rite. Although a notebook entry of 1828 (N37.95) expresses some dissatisfaction with the formulation of his own position in *AR* (1825) 354–76, the latter remains the best sustained statement of his view.

the term, Gospel?—That Sᵗ Paul had seen even Luke's, is but a conjecture grounded on a conjectural interpretation of a single Text, doubly equivocal—namely, that the Luke mentioned was the same with the Evangelist, Luke—and that the *evangelium*ᵃ signified a book:[1] the latter of itself improbable derives its probability from the undoubtedly very strong probability of the former.—If then not any Book, much less the four Books, now called the four Gospels, were meant by Paul, but the *contents* of those Books as far as they are veracious, and whatever else was known on equal authority at that time, tho' not contained in those books—if in short, the whole Sum of Christ's Acts and Discourses, be what Paul meant by the Gospel—then the argument is circuitous, and returns to the first point—What *is* the Gospel? Shall we believe *you*, & not rather the F̶ᵇ Companions of Christ by Eye & Ear witnesses of his A̶c̶t̶s̶ᵇ Doings and Sayings? Now I should require a good thumping Miracle to make ⟨me⟩ believe, that Sᵗ Paul had been guilty of such a palpable False Logic—and ɪ therefore feel myself compelled to infer, that by Gospel Paul intended the eternal truths known *ideally* from the Beginning, and historically realized in the manifestation of the Word in Christ = Jesus: and that he used the ideal immutable Truth as the Canon and Criterion of the oral Traditions/—ᶜEx. gr. a Greekᵈ Mathematician standing in the same relation of Time and Country to Euclid as Paul stood to Jesus Christ, might have exclaimed in the same Spirit—What do you talk to me of this, that, and the other intimate Acquaintance of Euclid's—? My object is to convey the sublime System of Geometry which he realized: and by that must I decide—&c &c. I ⟨⟨says Sᵗ Paul⟩⟩ have been taught by the Spirit of Christ—a teaching susceptible of no addition, and for which no personal anecdotes, however reverendly attested, can be a substitute.—But dearest Luther was a *Translator*—he could not, *must* not, see this.   S. T. C.

10 p 32, pencil, overtraced | "That God's word, and the Christian Church, is preserved against the raging of the world"

The Papists have lost the caus; with God's Word they are not able to resist or withstand us. . . . *The Kings of the earth stand up, and the*

ᵃ Underlining not overtraced

ᵇ Overtracing skips deletion

ᶜ The final "s" in "Traditions" and the punctuation after it are not overtraced

ᵈ Here C has written "(look opposite)" and has continued in the foot-margin of p 27, repeating "Greek"

9¹ 2 Tim 4.11–13.

Rulers take counsel together. . . . God will deal wel enough with these angrie Gentlemen, (said *Luther*) and will give them but smal thanks for their labor, in going about to suppress his Word and servants: he hath sate in counsel above these five thousand five hundred years, hath ruled and made Laws. Good Sirs! bee not so cholerick, go further from the wall, lest you knock your pates against it. . . . *Kiss the Son, lest hee bee angrie, and so yee perish*, &c. That is, take hold on Christ, or the divel will take hold on you. . . . This second *Psalm* (said *Luther*) is a proud Psalm against those fellows: It begins milde and simply, but it endeth stately and ratling. . . . It is a most excellent and a brave stately Psalm (said *Luther*) and I am much taken with it: above, it saith, *Habitator Coeli*, Hee that dwell's in heaven taketh our part, therefore take good heed what yee do. . . . I (said *Luther*) have now angred the Pope, about his Images of Idolatrie: O! how the Sow raiseth her bristles. I have given the Pope a gilded cup in his hand, hee must taste first of that, I have a great advantage against him: *For the Lord saith unto my Lord* . . . sheb limini, *sit on my right hand, until I make thy enemies thy footstool.* Hee saith; *Ego suscitabo vos in novissimo die* [I will raise you up on the last day]: and then hee will call and saie: Ho! *Martin Luther, Philip Melancthon, Justus Jonas, John Calvin*, &c. Arise, Com up: and God will call us by our names, as our Saviour Christ saith in Saint *John*'s Gospel; *Et vocat eos nominatim* [And he calls them by name]. Well on, (said *Luther*) let us bee of good comfort.

A delicious ¶. How our *fine* Preachers would turn up their Tom-Tit Beaks and flirt with their Tails at it.—But this is the way in which the man of *Life*, the Man of Power sets the dry Bones in Motion.

S. T. C.

11   p ⁻2, pencil, referring to ch 2 *Of God's Works*

p. 40. 42. 43.¹

11¹ Pp 40, 42, and 43 are unmarked, and no transcriptions from them appear among the extracts from Luther in *CN* IV. Since they contain no material strikingly connected with C's concerns, it is perhaps prudent to give the titles of all the articles on those pages: p 40 includes "That God made all things for mankinde", "That God's Creatures are used, or rather abused, for the most part by the Ungodlie", "The Chanceries of God, and of the Divel", and "That God, and not monie, preserv's the world"; p 42, "What it is that most displeaseth God", "God's cours when hee intendeth to destroie a Land", "That God punisheth, and no man can flie away from it", and "That God, if hee pleased, could purchase great store of monie and wealth"; p 43, "When God holdeth not his hand over us then are wee quite lost" and "That God's corporal gifts are but little regarded". Textus for pp 45 and 54, also cited on this page, are given in **12** and **13**.

12   p ⁻2, pencil, referring to p 45ᵃ | "That God hath hidden great gifts in small and contemned things"

I do much admire (said *Luther*) that God hath put such excellent Physick in dung and muck; for, yee know by experience, that swine's dung stint's the bloud; Hors dung serve's for the Plurisie; the dung of man-kinde healeth wounds and black botches; Asses dung is used for the bloudie flux, and Cow dung with preserved Roses serve's for the Epilep-sie or the convulsion of Children.

p. 45. Medicina merdacea.[1]

13   p 54, pencil, overtraced | "That out of the best come's the worst"

Out of *Abraham* came *Isaac* and *Ishmaël*: out of the Patriarchs and holy Fathers came the Jews that crucified Christ; out of the Apostles came *Judas* the Traitor; Out of the Citie *Alexandria* (where a fair illustrious and famous School was, and from whence proceeded manie upright and godlie learned men) came *Arrius* and *Origenes* . . .

Poor Origen! Surely, Luther was put to it for an instance and had never read the Works of that very best of the old Fathers, and eminently an upright and godlie learned Man.[1]

14   p ⁻2, pencil, referring to p 54 (**13** textus)

54.—Evil out of good, & worst out of best.—Item: Luther ignorantly uncharitable toward Origen and little Sparrows.—[1]

15   p 54, pencil, overtraced | "That God extolleth his mercie in us sinners through his benefits"

The Sparrows are the least birds, and yet they are very hurtful, and have the best nourishment; they have the whole year through the best daies, and do the greatest hurt. In Winter-time they lie in the Barns and Corn-houses; In the Spring they eat the Corn from the fields, also they eat the Plants, and other growth; In time of Harvest they have enough in the fields, and soon after, the Grapes and Fruits are their refreshments: *Ergò digni sunt omni persecutione* [therefore they all deserve to be perse-cuted].

ᵃ The textus is marked with a line in the right margin on p 45

12[1] "Excremental medicine".

13[1] The warmth of C's defence suggests that he himself was writing from first-hand exposure to Origen's work. The fact that he added Origen's name in ms annotations of the 1818 *Friend* (*CC*) ɪ 430 n 3 may indi-cate recent acquaintance, possibly through the account of Origen in Tennemann *Geschichte der Philosophie* vɪɪ (1809) 106–15.

14[1] See **15** below.

Poor little Philip Sparrows!*[a]* Luther did not know that they more than earn their good wages by destroying Grubs and other small vermin.

16   p 61, pencil, overtraced | "Where and how God is to bee found most certainly"

I have said it often, and do saie it still, (said *Luther*), Hee that without danger will know God, and will speculate of him, let him look first into the Maunger, that is, let him begin below, and let him first learn to know the Son of the Virgin *Marie* born at *Bethlehem*, that lie's and suck's in his mother's bosom; or let one look upon him hanging on the Cross; Afterwards hee will finely learn to know who God is. . . . But take good heed (I saie) in any case of high climbing cogitations, to clamber up to Heaven without this Ladder, namely, the Lord Christ in his humanitie . . . do but relie upon Him, and suffer not thy self to bee drawn from Him with thy wit, humane sens and reason, as then thou takest right hold of God.

mind this*[b]*

To know God as God (τον Ζηνα, the *living* God)[1] we must assume his *personality*—(otherwise what were it but an Ether, a Gravitation?) but to assume his personality we must begin with his *Humanity*/ this impossible but in History: for Man is an historic (not an eternal) Being. Ergo, Christianity of necessity *historical* and not philosophical only.

17   p 69, pencil, overtraced | Ch 3 *Of the Creation* "Of Adam's fall"

Miserable and lamentable was the Fall of *Adam*, (said *Luther*) who, from the state of Innocencie fell into such calamitie as is not to be uttered; for during the space of nine hundred years, hee saw God's anger in the death of everie humane creature.

This is sublime

18   p 103 | Ch 6 *Of the Holie Trinitie* "How the learned heathen have described God"

The Philosophers and learned Heathen (said *Luther*) have described GOD, that hee is as a Circle, the point whereof in the mid'st is everie where; but the Circumference, which on the outside goeth round about, is no where: herewith they would shew, that God is all, and yet is <u>nothing</u>.

---

[a] Exclamation mark very faint, and not overtraced

[b] Written at the end of the paragraph, and possibly not by C; the note proper, in C's hand, is written in the outer margin

16[1] C implies that there is a connection between Ζην, a poetic form of the name   Zeus, and ζῆν, the verb "to live".

What a huge difference the absence of a blank space which is nothing or next to nothing may make! The words here should have been printed God is All, and yet is no *Thing*. For what does Thing mean? Itself, viz. The *Ing*, i.e. inclosure, that which is contained within an outline, or circumscribed. So likewise to *think* is to inclose, to determine, confine and define. To think an infinite is a contradiction in terms, equal to a boundless Bound. So in German Ding, denken—in Latin Res, reor[1]

19   p 113 | Ch 7 *Of the Lord Christ* "All heresies and errors go against Christ"

Helvidius alleged, the mother of Christ was not a Virgin, so that (according to his wicked allegation) Christ was born in original sin.

What? Does Original Sin make its first entrance into a Woman on her Wedding Night? O what a Tangle of impure Whimsies has this Ebionite Tradition brought into the Christian Church.[1] I have sometimes suspected that the Apostle John had a particular view to this Legend in the first half of the first Chapter of his Gospel. Not that I suppose our present Matthew then in existence, or that supposing John to have seen the Gospel according to Luke that the Poem of the Infancy had been already prefixed to it.[2] But the Rumor might have been whispered about, and as the purport was to give a psilanthropic Explanation & Solution of the phrases, Son of God and Son of Man, so S[t] John met it by the true solution, namely, the eternal filiation of the Word—[3]

20   p 120 | "Of Christ's riding into Jerusalem"

This was a very strange kinde of riding for so powerful a Potentate, as the Prophecie of the Prophet *Zechariah* shewed, to the end the Scripture might bee fulfilled. . . . * But I hold (said *Luther*) that Christ Himself

---

18[1] Although the resemblance of words for "thing" and "think" in different languages was probably originally brought to C's attention by J. Horne Tooke Ἔπεα Πτεροεντα, *or, the Diversions of Purley* (1798, 1805) II 405–6, C developed his own theories about the significance of the resemblance: cf *CN* II 2784, III 3587 and n, *CL* IV 885.

19[1] The Ebionites, an early sect of Jewish Christians, believed that Christ was the human son of Mary and Joseph, and that the Holy Spirit entered him at the time of his baptism.

19[2] C's note reflects then current scholarly speculation about the textual history of the Bible, specifically the argument that Luke 1–2 was a late addition to that gospel: the issue of the dating of the "evangelia infantiae" or "Christopaedia" is developed at greater length in 1828 marginalia to PAULUS **2, 24**, and **25**.

19[3] John 1.32 gives an account of the descent of the Holy Spirit at the time of the baptism of Christ similar to that of Luke 3.21–3, which could be used by Ebionite or psilanthropic sects teaching the "mere humanity" of Christ. John, however, corrects this tendency by his insistence on the eternal and spiritual essence of Christianity ("In the beginning was the Word").

did not mention that Prophecie, but rather, that the Apostles and Evangelists did use it for a witness.

* Worth remembering, for the purpose of applying it to the text in which our Lord is represented in the first (or so called Matthew's) Gospel and by that alone, as citing Daniel by name. It was this text that so sorely, but I think very unnecessarily, perplexed and gravelled Bentley, who was too profound a Scholar & too acute a Critic not to see the spuriousness of the Books[1]

21   pp 120–3 | "Of Christ's coming"

The Prophets (said *Luther*) did set, speak, and preach of the second coming of Christ in manner as wee now do; wee know that the last daie will com, yet, wee know not what and how it will bee after this life, but onely in general, that wee which are true Christians shall have everlasting Joie, Peace and Salvation.

I regret that M[r] Irving should have blended such extravagances and presumptuous prophesyings with his support and vindication of the Milennium & the Return of Jesus in his corporeal individuality[1]—because these have furnished our orthodox Divines, both Church & Dissenting, with a pretext for treating his doctrine with silent contempt—Had he followed the example of his own Ben Ezra, & argued temperately and learnedly, the controversy must have forced the momentous question on our Clergy—Are Christians bound to believe whatever an Apostle believed—and in the same way & sense? ⟨I think, S[t] Paul himself lived to doubt the solidity of his own literal interpretation of our Lord's Words.⟩[a]

The whole passage in which our Lord describes his coming is so evidently & so intentionally expressed in the diction and images of the Prophets,[2] that nothing but the carnal Literality common to the Jews at that time & most strongly marked in the Disciples who were among the

---

[a] The insertion begins with "I think"; the continuation ("doubt the solidity") is written above the end of the note in the foot-margin. Because the head and outer margins of p 121 had already been used for **22–23**, **21** is continued in the head-margin of p 122 and the head- and foot-margins of p 123

20[1] The spuriousness of Daniel (a crucial text for those who, unlike C, believed that the Bible promised a "temporal Messiah") is a recurrent theme in C's biblical commentary: EICHHORN *Alte Testament* **48**; *TT* 6 Jan 1823, 30 Aug 1827; *CN* IV 4615n. The source of C's information about Bentley was almost certainly Francis WRANGHAM *The Life of Dr. Richard Bentley* (1822) 5n (a passage that C annotated), in which Wrangham gives several instances of Bentley's uneasiness about the Book of Daniel, and refers to NT allusions to it.

21[1] See C's annotations on LACUNZA *The Coming of Messiah in Glory and Majesty* tr Edward Irving (1827); Irving is also mentioned below, **99** and n.

21[2] Matt 24–5.

least educated of their Countrymen, could have prevented the symbolic import and character of the words from being seen.—Mem. The whole Gospel & the Epistles of John are a virtual confutation of this reigning error—& no less is the Apocalypse whether written by, or under the authority, of the Evangelist.[3]

The unhappy effect which S⟨t⟩ Paul's incautious language respecting Christ's Return produced on the Thessalonians, led him to reflect on the subject—and he instantly (II Ep. to the Thess.) *qualified* the doctrine/ and never afterwards resumed it; but on the contrary in the 15th of Corinthians substitutes the doctrine of immortality in a celestial state & spiritual body.[4]

On the nature of our Lord's future Epiphany or phænomenal Person, I am not ashamed to acknowlege that my Views approach very nearly to those of Emanuel Swedenberg.[5]

22   p 121 | "That Christ did preach out of a book"

[Title] That Christ did preach out of a book*

* As many notes, memoranda, cues of connection and transition, as the Preacher may find expedient or serviceable to him. But to read *in* a MSS Book, as our Clergy now do, is not to *preach* at all. Preach *out* of a Book, if you must; but do not read *in* it—or even *from* it. A read Sermon of 20 minutes will seem longer to the Hearers than a free Discourse of an Hour.   *S. T. C.*

23   p 121 | "Of Christ's descending into Hell"

My simple opinion is, (said *Luther*), and I do believ, that Christ for us descended into Hell, to th' end Hee might break and destroie the same, as in the 16 *Psalm*, and *Acts* 2. is shewed and proved.

Could Luther have been ignorant, that this clause was not intruded into the Ap. Creed till the VIth Century P.C.?[a1]

[a] The first sentence is written beside the subtitle of the paragraph, the second at the end of the paragraph

21[3] C eventually rejected the traditional view (which was also Eichhorn's) that St John the Evangelist was the author of Rev, attributing it to "an Elder of the Church of Ephesus": LACUNZA **87** and n 3.

21[4] Although Paul himself alluded to the Second Coming in 1 Thess 3.15–17, 2 Thess 2.2–3 contains a reassurance that the event is not imminent: ". . . be not soon shaken in mind, or be troubled, neither by spirit, nor by word, nor by letter as from us, as that the day of Christ is at hand". As

C observes, 1 Cor 15 describes "the glory of the celestial" (v 40).

21[5] Swedenborg believed, as did C, that the Second Coming was to be interpreted not as a personal, physical event, but as a spiritual manifestation, e.g. *True Christian Religion* (1819) II 528–31. It is not likely that C shared Swedenborg's belief that the agent of the millennium was Swedenborg himself: *True Christian Religion* (1819) II 531–2.

23[1] Although C is right about the evo-

The intention of the Clause was no more than—Verè mortuus est[2]—in contradiction to the hypothesis of a trance or state of suspended animation.

24 p 122 | "Whether those that did spread abroad and make report of Christ's wonderfull works, did write thereon or no, seeing Christ forbade them to do the same"

When Christ (said *Luther*) speaketh, as without His Office, then Hee speaketh as Hee is God, as when Hee speaketh of His Person, and saith, *All that is the Father's, the same also is Mine: Believ yee in God, so believ yee also in Mee*, &c. But when Hee speaketh according to His Office (as beeing sent from the Father) then hee speaketh as a Man or Servant, and not of His Person, as when Hee saith, *I am com that I may serv or minister*, &c. see here in this place, where Hee forbiddeth to spread abroad or to make known His works of wonder. There Hee speaketh as beeing sent from the Father, and doth well and right therein in forbidding them, to the end that thereby Hee might leav to us an Example, not to seek our own prais and honor, in that wherein wee do good; but wee ought to seek onely and alone the honor of God.

not satisfactory. Doubtless, the command was in connection with the silence enjoined respecting his Messiahship.[1]

25 p 147, pencil, overtraced | Ch 8 *Of the Holie Ghost* "Of the Holie Ghost"

. . . Doctor *Hennage* said to *Luther*, Sir! where you saie that the Holie Spirit is the certaintie in the Word towards God, that is, that a man is certain of his own minde and opinion; then it must needs follow, that all Sects have the II. Ghost, for they will needs bee most certain of their Doctrine and Religion.

Luther might have answered/ *positive*, you mean—not *certain*.[1]

26 pp 160–1 | Ch 9 *Of Sins* "Luther's describing of the spiritual government"

* But who hath power to forgive or to detein sins? Answer, The Apostles and all Church-servants, and (in case of necessitie) everie Christian. Christ giveth them not power over monie, wealth, Kingdoms, &c. but

---

lution of the Creed, the textual history of the creeds was not fully explored until after Luther's time, notably by the Dutch theologian G. J. Voss (1577–1649). "This clause" refers to "He descended into Hell". The source of C's information was John PEARSON *An Exposition of the Creed* (12th ed 1741) 225–52, a book which he annotated, and which he cites in DONNE

Sermons COPY B **125**.
   23[2] "He really died".
   24[1] Matt 16.20. Cf LESSING *Sämmtliche Schriften* **54** and n 1.
   25[1] This distinction, which appears in the Notebooks as early as 1803 (*CN* I 1410), was a lifelong favourite; *BL* ch 4 (*CC*) I 71 n lists numerous repetitions.

over sins and the Consciences of humane creatures, over the power of the Divel, and the throat of Hell.

* Few passages in the Sacred Writings have occasioned so much mischief, abject Slavishness, bloated pride, tyrannous Usurpation, bloody persecution with Kings ~~for the unwilling~~ even against their will—the Drudges, false soul-destroying quiet of Conscience, than this Text misinterpre~~tationed~~.[1] It is really a tremendous proof of ~~the~~ what the misunderstanding of a few words can do.—That even Luther partook of the delusion, & this ¶ph. gives proof. But that a delusion it is—that the Commission was confined to the Seventy whom Christ sent out to proclaim and offer the Kingdom of God, and refers exclusively to the gifts of miraculous Healing which our Lord at that time and for that especial Mission conferred on them—and that, per figuram Causæ pro Effecto,[2] Sins here mean Diseases, I have not the smallest doubt—

27   p 161 | Continuing **26** textus

For Christ laieth his Passion and Resurrection in the Apostles' mouths, and maketh subject unto them Hell, Death, and Damnation, together with Heaven, Life, and everlasting Salvation, insomuch that they are able to pronounce such a sentence, that the Divel himself must bee affraid thereof: and again, they are able to Absolv and make a humane creature free and loos from all his sins, if in case hee repenteth and believeth in Christ; and on the contrarie, they are able to detein all his sins, if hee doth not repent and believeth not in Christ.

If he be impenitent and unbelieving, his Sins are detained, no doubt— whether the Minister do or do not.[a]

In like manner if he sincerely repent (μετανοη)[1] and believe, his sins are forgiven, whether the Minister absolve him or not. Now if M + 5 = 5, and ~~M~~ 5 − M = 5, M = 0. Christ's Words refer to the Holy Spirit given to the Apostles—i.e. the miraculous powers: and Sins must be rendered Diseases.[2]

---

[a] Written in the inside margin beside the textus, ending "*See above*"; the note continues at the head-margin with *

26[1] John 20.22–3, q Luther p 160: "The spiritual Government (said *Luther*) consisteth in absolving and deteining of sins and sinners; As Christ saith, *Receiv yee the holie Ghost, whose sins yee remit, to them they are remitted; but whose sins yee retein, to them they are reteined*."

26[2] "According to the figure of cause for effect".

27[1] C here uses the verb where more commonly he cites the NT noun μετάνοια, "repentance", drawing attention to the roots of the word as in *AR* (1825) 127n: "Μετανοια ... compounded of μετα, *trans*, and νους, *mens*, the Spirit, or practical Reason".

27[2] As in **26** above. In the formula "M

28 p 163 | "That the forgiveness of sins proceedeth of grace without all works"

But *Adam* was creäted of God in such sort righteous, as that hee became of a righteous an unrighteous person; as *Paul* himself argueth, and withall instructeth himself, where hee saith, The Law is not given for a righteous man, but for the lawless and disobedient.

This follows from the very definition or idea of Righteousness—it is itself the Law—Πας γαϱ δικαιος αυτονομος.[1]

29 p 163 | "Of the acknowledgment of sins"

It can bee hurtful to none (said *Luther*) to acknowledg and confess their sins. . . . for the Scripture saith, God maketh the ungodlie righteous; there hee calleth us all, one with another, despairing and wicked wretches; for what will an ungodlie creature not dare to accomplish, if hee may but have occasion, place, and opportunitie? /\

with a lust within correspondent to the temptation from without.

30 p 163

A Christian's Conscience, methinks, ought to*a* a Janus bi-frons[1]—a Gospel-face ⟨retrospective &⟩ smiling thro' penitent tears on the Sins of the Past, and a Moses-face in frown and menacing looking forward frightening the harlot Will into a holy Abortion of Sins conceived but not yet born, perchance not yet quickened. The fanatic Antinomian reverses this: for the Past he requires all the horrors of Remorse and Despair till the Moment of Assurance/ thenceforward, he may do what he likes—for he cannot sin.

31 p 165 | "Everie man seeketh his own profit, seeing our nature is spoiled"

All natural inclinations (said *Luther*) are either against or without God; therefore none are good. . . .

a For "ought to be"

+ 5", "M" presumably stands for "Minister".

28[1] "Every righteous man is his own law." The phrase does not appear in NT, but C may be recalling Rom 2.14, "For when the Gentiles, which have not the law, do by nature the things contained in the law, these, not having the law, are a law unto themselves". The Epistle to the Romans contains Paul's most sustained statement about the relationship between "outward" law and "inward" righteousness, though the passage to which Luther alludes is from 1 Tim 1.9.

30[1] "Janus with two faces", traditional epithet and emblem, put to use in a different way in *CN* III 3294 and applied to Jeremy Taylor in *CL* III 541. C cites Ovid (probably meaning *Fasti* 1.65) as his source for the figure in *Friend* (*CC*) II 278; as a schoolboy he must have encountered it in Andrew Tooke's *Pantheon* (1771) 148–54, where the interpretation of the two faces as looking to past and future is preferred to other possibilities.

Experience also witnesseth the same; for wee see, that no man is so honest as to marrie a wife, onely thereby to have children, to love and to bring them up in the fear of God.

This is a very weak instance/. If a Man had been commanded to marry by God, being so formed as that no sensual delight accompanied—and refused to do so, unless this appetite & gratification were added—*then* indeed!—

32   pp 169, 168 | Ch 10 *Of Free-will* "Another discours of free-will"

Ah Lord God (saith *Luther*)! why should wee anie waie boast of our Free-will, as if it were able to do anie thing in divine and spiritual matters were they never so smal? . . .

I confess, that mankinde hath a Free-will, but it is to milk Kine, to build houses, &c. and no further: for so long as a man sitteth well and in safetie, and sticketh in no want, so long hee thinketh, hee hath a Free-will which is able to do somthing; but when want and need appeareth, that there is neither to eat nor to drink, neither monie nor provision, Where is then the Free-will? It is utterly lost, and cannot stand when it cometh to the pinch. But Faith onely standeth fast and sure, and seeketh Christ.

Therefore Faith is far another thing then is Free-will, nay, Free-will is nothing at all, but Faith is all in all.

Luther confounds Free Will with efficient *Power*—which neither does nor can exist, save where the finite Will is one with the Absolute Will.

That Luther was practically on the right side in this famous Controversy, and that he was driving at the truth, I see abundant reason to believe—But it is no less evident, that he saw it in a Mist, or rather as a Mist, with dissolving outline—and as he saw the Thing as a Mist, so he ever and anon mistakes a mist for the Thing. But Erasmus & Saavedra were equally indistinct; & shallow & unsubstantial to boot.[a1] But in fact,

---

[a] Here the note has reached the foot of p 169; C has written "turn opposite" (the head- and foot-margins of p 169 being already filled), and has continued at the foot of p 168 with "From p. 169."

32[1] Erasmus would come naturally to C's mind at this point. Luther refers to their controversy, and C will have known that Erasmus defended the doctrine of free will in his *Diatribe de libero arbitrio* (1524) and *Hyperaspistes* (1526). Saavedra—the Spanish statesman and moralist Diego de Saavedra Fajardo (1584–1648)—hardly seems to be in the same class, but C may have been thinking of his role as a popular-iser. The English translation of his book of moralised emblems, *The Royal Politician Represented in One Hundred Emblems* (1700), includes (II 281–6) a discussion of the freedom of the will in which Saavedra argues that free will extends only to the mind and body of the individual, who has no control over external circumstances and no influence upon the overwhelming will of God.

till the appearance of Kant's Kritique der reinen, and die der prac-
tischen, Vernunft the Problem had never been accurately or adequately
stated—much less solved.[2]   26 June 1826.—

33   p 174 | "Of the doctrine touching the free-will towards God"

Loving Friends (said *Luther*) our Doctrine (that Free-will is dead and
nothing at all) is grounded powerfully in holy Scripture. But I speak of
the Free-will towards God, and in causes touching the Soul.

It is of vital importance for a theological Student to understand clearly
the utter diversity of the Lutheran, ~~and~~ which is likewise the Calvinistic
denial of *Free* Will in the Unregenerate and the doctrine of the modern
Necessitarians[1] and (proh pudor!)[2] of the later Calvinists,[3] which denies
the proper existence of Will altogether. The former is sound, ~~m~~ scrip-
tural, compatible with the divine justice, ~~and even~~ a new, yea, a *mighty*
motive to Morality, & finally, the dictate of common Sense grounded
on common Experience. The former[4] the very contrary of all these.

34   p 187 | Ch 12 *Of the Law and Gospel* "That the use of the law is twofold"

Therefore (said *Luther*) this is now the first instruction concerning the
Law; namely, that the same must bee used to hinder the ungodlie from
their wicked and mischievous intentions. For the Divel (who is an Abbot
and a Prince of this world) driveth and allureth people to work all man-
ner of sin and wickedness; *for which caus God hath ordained Magis-
trates, Elders, Schoolmasters, Laws and Statutes to the end, if they

---

32[2] C refers repeatedly to Kant's eluci-
dation and solution of the problem of free
will, e.g. *P Lects* Lect 12 (1949) 364–5,
CN III 3583 and n. C's note in SCHELLING
Philosophische Schriften (Landshut 1809)
465 clarifies the argument as C saw it:
". . . all that we want is to prove the *pos-
sibility* of Free Will, or what is really the
same, a Will. Now this Kant had unan-
swerably proved by shewing the distinction
between Phænomena and Noumena, by
demonstrating that Time and Space were
Laws of the former only . . . and irrelative
to the latter, to which Class the Will must
belong." However, A. O. Lovejoy, in an
essay that makes use of this comment on
Luther, has argued that the defence of free
will is C's own deduction from Kantian
principles: "Coleridge and Kant's Two
Worlds" *Essays in the History of Ideas*
(Baltimore 1948) 254–76.

33[1] From the "pernicious Doctrine of
Necessity" (*CL* II 1037) which he attrib-
uted to Hartley, Priestley (and the Unitari-
ans), and Godwin, C appears to have extri-
cated himself early in 1801: *CL* II 706. His
brief allegiance to it is discussed in *C Pan-
theist* 174–7. C's view of "the difference
between a Calvinist and a Priestleyan Ma-
terialist-Necessitarian" is given at large in
A. FULLER **4**.

33[2] "Ah, for shame!"

33[3] C probably has in mind such expo-
sitions of doctrine as Edward Williams *Es-
say on the Equity of Divine Government*
(1809) and *Defence of Modern Calvinism*
(1812), both of which he read in 1815: *CL*
IV 547–8. In 1825 C represented Williams
as the spokesman of "Modern (or Pseudo-)
Calvinism": *AR* (1825) 153–4. Cf *C&S*
(*CC*) 135 and n 1.

33[4] Presumably an error for "latter".

can[not] do more, yet at least that they may binde the claws of the Divel, and to hinder him from raging and swelling so powerfully (in those which are his) according to his will and pleasure.

Secondly, wee use the Law spiritually, which is don in this manner; That it maketh the transgressions greater as Saint *Paul* saith; that is, that it may reveal and discover to people their sins, blindness, miserie and ungodlie doings wherein they were conceived and born; namely, that they are ignorant of God, and are his enemies, and therefore have justly deserved Death, Hell, God's Judgments, His everlasting Wrath and Indignation. Saint *Paul* (said *Luther*) expoundeth such spiritual Offices and works of the Law with manie words, *Rom. 7.*

* Nothing can be more sound or more philosophic than the contents of these two ¶phs. They afford a sufficient answer to the pretence of the Romanists and Arminians, that by the Law St Paul meant only the ceremonial Law.[1]

35 p 189 | "That to teach the doctrine of the law is not necessarie to salvation . . ."

From thence arose the continual dissention and strife which St *Paul* had alwaies with the Jews. And if *Moses* had not Cashier'd and put himself out of his Office, and had not taken it away with these words, (where hee saith, **The Lord thy God will rais up unto thee another Prophet out of thy brethren, Him shalt thou hear.*) Who then at anie time would or could have believed the Gospel, and forsaken *Moses*?

* If I could be persuaded that this passage (v 15 – v 19.^{a} XVIIIth Deuteronomy) referred to Christ; and that Christ, not Joshua & his Successors, was the Prophet promised; I must either become a Unitarian Psilanthropist, and join Priestley & Belsham[1]—or abandon to the Jews their own Messiah as yet to come, and cling to the Religion of John and Paul, without further reference to Moses than to Lycurgus, Solon and Numa all of whom in their different spheres no less prepared the way for the coming of the LORD, the desire of *the Nations*—[2]

^{a} C wrote "v" above each verse number

34[1] C makes the same statement about the "Arminian" party of Laud and Jeremy Taylor in *AR* (1825) 296, and a similar statement in BUNYAN COPY A 7. The disputed text is Rom 7.1: "Know ye not, brethren, . . . how that the law hath dominion over a man as long as he liveth?" C's observation is certainly supported by Taylor's use of the term "law" in *Unum necessarium. Or, the Doctrine and Prac-*

tice of Repentance: ΣΥΜΒΟΛΟΝ ΘΕΟΛΟΓΙΚΟΝ, *or a Collection of Polemicall Discourses* (3rd ed 1674) [557]–893.

35[1] I.e. teach the "mere humanity" of Christ, with Joseph Priestley and Thomas Belsham (1750–1829), who succeeded Priestley as minister of the Gravel Pit Unitarian Chapel at Hackney in 1794.

35[2] Hag 2.7 (var). As in LESSING *Sämmtliche Schriften* **68** at n 3, C invokes

36 pp 190–1 | "That Moses with his law, is a master of all hangmen"

It is therefore most evident (said *Luther*) that the Law can but onely help us to know our sins, and to make us affraid of death. Now sins and death are such things as belong to the world, and which are therein. Therefore it is clear and apparent, that the Law can do nothing that is lively, saving, celestial or divine; but what it doth or causeth, is altogether temporal; that is, it giveth us to know, what in the world is evil both outward and inwardly.

Both in Paul and in Luther (names I can never separate)—not indeed peculiar ⟨to⟩ these, for it is the same in the Psalms, Ezekiel & throughout the Scriptures; but which I feel most in Paul and Luther—there is one fearful Blank, the wisdom or necessity of which I do not doubt, yet cannot help groping and straining after, like one that stares in the Dark— And this is—*Death*. The Law makes us afraid of *Death*   What *is* Death? An unhappy Life? Who does not feel the insufficiency of this Answer? What analogy does immortal Suffering bear to the only Death which is known to us?

*a*Since I wrote the above, God has, I humbly trust, given me a clearer Light as to the true nature of the Death so often mentioned in the Scriptures[1]

37 pp 190–1 | "That it is a difficult thing in trials and temptations, to contemn the curs and the burthen of the law"

It is (said *Luther*) a very hard matter; yea, an unpossible thing for thy humane strength, whosoëver thou art (without God's assistance) that (at such a time when *Moses* setteth upon thee with his Law, and fearfully affrighteth thee, accuseth and condemneth thee, threatneth thee with God's wrath and death) thou shouldest as then bee of such a minde; *namely, as if no Law nor sin had ever been at anie time; I saie, it is in a manner a thing unpossible, that a humane creature should carrie himself in such a sort, when hee is and feeleth himself assaulted with trials and temptations, and when the conscience hath to do with God, as then

---

a A short line separates this afterthought from the preceding paragraph

---

the names of great pagan lawgivers, adding the legendary Numa Pompilius, said to have lived 751–653 B.C.

36[1] C expounds a theory of spiritual death in *AR* (1825) 316: ". . . besides that dissolution of our earthly tabernacle which we call death, there is another death, not the mere negation of life, but its positive Opposite. . . . Thus the regeneration to spiritual life is at the same time a redemption from the spiritual death."

to think no otherwise, then that from everlasting nothing hath been, but onely and alone Christ, altogether Grace and deliverance.

> * And Sin and Sorrow and the Wormy Grave
> Shapes of a Dream.
>
> Religious Musings.[1]

Yea, verily, Amen and Amen! For this short heroic Paragraph contains the sum and substance, the heighth and the depth of all true Philosophy—. Most assuredly, right difficult it is for us, while we are yet in the narrow chamber of Death with our faces to the dusky ⟨falsifying⟩ *Looking-glass* that covers the scant end-side of ∏ the blind Passage from floor to ceiling, right difficult for us so wedged between its walls that we cannot turn round nor have other escape possible but by walking backward, to understand that all we behold or have any memory of having ever beheld, yea, our very selves as seen by us, are but *shadows*—and when the forms, that we [? lived/loved], vanish, impossible not to feel as if real.[2]

38   pp 197–201 | "That the gospel requireth of us no works"

Nothing that is good proceedeth out of the works of the Law, except Grace bee present; for what wee are forced to do, the same goeth not from the heart, neither is it acceptable. The people under *Moses* were alwaies in a murmuring state and condition, they would needs stone him, they were rather his enemies then his friends.

A Law supposes a Law-giver, and implies an Actuator, and Executor—consequently, Rewards and Punishments publicly announced, and distinctly assigned to the Deeds enjoined or forbidden.—and correlatively in the Subjects of the Law there are supposed—1. Assurance of the Being, the Power, ~~and~~ the Veracity and ~~Cognitive~~ Seeingness of the Law-giver, in whom we here comprize the legislative, Judicial and executive functions; and 2. Self-interest, Desire, Hope and Fear. Now from this view, it is evident that the Deeds or Works of the Law are ~~in~~ themselves null and dead, deriving their whole significance from their attachment or alligation to the Rewards and Punishments, even as this ~~Ink and Paper~~

37[1] C recalls the Christian Platonism of *Religious Musings* (*PW*—EHC—ɪ 124), of which these are the last two lines.

37[2] Of C's many references to the figure of the looking-glass, the most revealing as far as this passage is concerned occurs in a recommendation of Luther in Jul 1826, *CL* vɪ 596: "Was it only of the world *to come*, that Luther and his Compeers preached? Turn to Luther's Table-talk: and see if the larger part be not of that other world which now *is*, and without the Being and the working of which the world *to come* would be either as unintelligible as Abracadabra, or a mere refraction & elongation of the world of Sense—Jack Robinson between two Looking glasses, with a series of Jack Robinsons in secula seculorum."

~~have their~~ diversely shaped & ink-colored Paper has its value wholly from the words or meanings, which have been arbitrarily ~~at~~ connected therewith—or as a Ladder, or flight of stairs, of a Provision-loft, or Treasury. If the Architect or Master of the House had ~~been~~ chosen to place the Store-room or Treasury on the Ground-floor, the Ladder or Steps would have been useless/. ~~and~~ The *Life* ~~and Efficacy~~ is divided between the Rewards & Punishments, ⟨on the one hand,⟩ and the Hope & Fear ⟨on the other:⟩—namely, the active Life or Excitancy ~~in~~ belongs in the former, the passive Life or Excitability ~~in~~ to the latter. Call the former the Afficients, the latter the Affections: the deeds being merely the signs or impresses of the former as the Seal on the latter as the Wax.—Equally evident is it, that the Affections are wholly ~~shaped~~ formed by the Deeds, which are themselves but the lifeless unsubstantial Shapes of the actual Forms (formæ formantes),[1] viz. the Rewards and Punishments.—Now contrast with this the process of the Gospel. Here the Affections are formed in the first instance not by any reference to Works or Deeds, but by ~~Joy~~ an unmerited Rescue from Death, Liberation from Slavish Task-work; by Faith, Gratitude, Love, and affectionate Contemplation of the exceeding Goodness and loveliness of the Saviour, Redeemer, Benefactor; from the Affections flow the Deeds, or rather the Affections overflow in the Deeds, and the Rewards are but a continuance & continued increase of the free grace in the *State* of the Soul and in the growth and gradual perfecting of the State, which are themselves Gifts of the same Free Grace, and one with the Rewards— for in the kingdom of Christ which is the Realm of Love & Intercommunity, the Joy & Grace of each regenerated Spirit becomes & thereby augments the Joys and the Graces of the others, and the Joys and Graces of all unite in each—Christ, the Head, and by his Spirit the Bond, or unitive Copula of all, being the Spiritual Sun whose entire Image is reflected in ~~myriads~~ every individual of the myriads of Dew-drops—/— While under the Law the All was but an Aggregate of Subjects, each striving after a Reward for himself and not as included in and resulting from, the State but as the stipulated Wages of the Task-work—as a Loaf of Bread may be the Pay or Bounty promised for the Hewing of Wood or the Breaking of Stones./

39 p 196, referring to p 197[a] | ''That wee must not dispute with the divel out of the law, but out of the gospel''

Hee (said *Luther*) that will dispute with the Divel out of the Law, the same is beaten down and taken captive; but hee that disputeth with him

---

[a] Written after **40**; written in the space available on p 196

38[1] ''Forming forms''.

out of the Gospel, overcometh him. The Divel hath the written bond against us, therefore let no man presume to dispute with him of the Law, or of sin.

Q^y I. II. III.

I. Abstractly from, and independent of, all sensible Substances, and the bodies, wills, faculties and Affections of Men, has the Devil—or would the Devil have—a personal Self-subsistence? Does He, or can he, exist as a conscious individual Agent or Person?—Should the answer to this q^y be in the negative: then

II. Do there exist finite & personal Beings whether with á composite and decomponible Bodies—i.e. embodied, or with simple and indecomponible Bodies, (which is all that can be meant by disembodied ~~wh~~ as applied to finite Creatures), so eminently wicked or wicked & mischievous in so peculiar a *kind*, as to constitute a distinct Genus of Beings under the name of Devils? ^{a}III. Is this second hypothesis compatible with the acts and functions attributed to the Devil in Scripture?—O to have had these three Questions put by Melanchthon to Luther, and to have heard his Reply!!!^{1} S. T. C.

40   p $^+$1, referring to pp 197–9, 201–2

Mem. In my Noetic or Doctrine & Discipline of Ideas = Logicè *Organon*^{1}—I purpose to select some four, or five or more instances of the sad effects of the Absence of Ideas in the use of words and in the understanding of truths, in the different departments of Life—ex. gr. the word *Body*, in connection with the Resurrection Men, Burk^2 &c—and the last instance will (please God!) be, the sad effects on the whole sys-

---

^{a} C probably meant a new paragraph here but has written straight on to save space

39^1 The name of Melanchthon is not arbitrarily chosen: it appears on the title-page of the *Colloquia* and occasionally in the text (cf **49** textus) as one of the "divers learned men" from whose conversations with Luther the contents were derived. Belief in a Devil or devils seemed to C generally polytheistic (*CN* III 4396) and a too easy solution to the problem of the origin of evil (*CN* III 3701); nevertheless, as J. Robert Barth says, the figure of Satan "puzzled Coleridge all his life" (*CCD* 119n).

40^1 The reference is to a version of the ever-expanding *magnum opus*. A (mostly cancelled) draft paragraph entitled "In-troduction to the Organon, or Logic of Ideas, more properly NOETIC" remains among C's papers: BM Egerton MS 2801 f 84.

40^2 To the resurrection men who provided anatomists with subjects by robbing graves, as to William Burke and his partner William Hare who did it by murdering 15 victims, "body" presumably meant no more than "corpse". This is a particularly topical illustration: Burke was executed 28 Jan 1829. C takes up the question of the meaning of "body" again (and offers his own definition of the term) in **91** below; cf IRVING *Sermons* **27, 28**, and DONNE *Sermons* COPY B **80, 126**.

tem of Christian Divinity/ Mem. Asgill's Book..[3] Religion necessarily as to its main & proper Doctrines consists of Ideas = spiritual truths that can only be spiritually discerned, and to the expression of which Words are necessarily inadequate—& must be used by accommodation. Hence the absolute indispensability of a Christian *Life*, with its conflicts & inward experiences—which alone can enable a man to answer to an Opponent, who charges this doctrine ~~not~~ as contradictory to another—Yes! it is a contradiction *in terms*; but never the less so it is—& both are true, nay, parts of the same truth.—But alas! besides other evils there is this—that the Gospel is preached in fragments, and ~~the~~ what the Hearer can recollect of the Sum total of these is to be his Christian Knowlege & Belief. But this is a grievous error.—First, labor to enlighten the Hearer as to the essence of the Christian Dispensation, the grounding and ~~ever~~ pervading Idea—and *then* set it forth,—in its manifold *perspective*, ~~and~~ its various stages, and modes of manifestation.—In this as in almost all other qualities of a Preacher of Christ Luther after Paul or John is the great Master. None saw more clearly than he, that the same proposition, which addressed to a Christian in his first awakening out of the Death of Sin was a most wholesome, nay, ~~cond~~ a necessary, truth, would be a most condemnable Antinomian Falsehood, if addressed to a secure Christian boasting and trusting in *his* faith—yes, in *his* own faith—instead of the faith *of* Christ communicated to him.—See p. 198.—[4]

I cannot utter how dear and precious to me are the contents of p. 197–199, to l. 17. of this work[5]—more particularly the Section headed— "How we ought to carry ourselves towards the Law's accusations".

S. T. Coleridge
July 1829.

40[3] A champion of John Asgill, C nevertheless described one of his tracts in 1827–8 as "the ablest attempt to exhibit a Scheme of Religion without Ideas, that the inherent contradiction in the thought renders possible": ASGILL **1**. Asgill argued that a Christian could be "translated" to immortality without dying: see LACUNZA **12** n 6.

40[4] Probably the section "How wee ought to carrie our selvs towards the *Law's* Accusations", in which Luther comments on the smugness of "seeming workers of Holiness" who "do think it an easie matter to believ; which maketh them quite ignorant of that which a contrite heart and a fearful Conscience doth; therefore they go on and proceed in so great secureness".

40[5] These pages contain the following sections: "Of the caus, why the Law was abolished", "That wee must not dispute with the Divel out of the *Law*, but out of the *Gospel*", "Of the Allegations of the *Antinomians*, that the *Law* should not bee preached", "The caus why the Gospel is now preached so clearly", "That the Gospel maketh no difference of Persons", and "How wee ought to carrie our selvs towards the *Law's* Accusations". The last of these is q **40** n 4.

Add to these the two last sections of p. 201:—the last "touching St Austin's opinion" especially.[6] Likewise, the first half of p. 202.[7] But indeed the whole of the 12th Chapter "Of the Law and the Gospel" is of inestimable value to a serious and earnest Minister of the Gospel. Here he may learn both the orthodox faith, and a holy prudence in the time and manner of preaching the same.

41 p 200 | "That it is a matter very difficult to distinguish rightly between the law and the gospel"

Not long since (said *Luther*) a learned Divine at *Wittemberg* made his complaint unto mee, and said, That by no means hee could make a right difference between the Law and the Gospel.

I answered him, and said, I believ you well; if you were able to do that, then I would hold you for a learned Doctor indeed. St *Paul* could never bring it so far, but it was said unto him . . . My Grace is sufficient for thee; that is, thou hast My Word and Command, hold thee thereon, and let that suffice thee.

The main reason is, because in this instance the Change in the Relation constitutes the difference of the Things. X considered as acting ab extra on the selfish fears & desires of men is *the* LAW: the same X acting ab intra as a new *nature* infused by Grace, as the Mind of Christ prompting to all obedience thro' Love, is the Gospel.[1] Yet what Luther says is likewise very true. Could we reduce the great spiritual truths or Ideas of our Faith to comprehensible *Con*ceptions,[2] or (for the thing itself is impossible) fancy, we had done so, we should inevitably be proud vain Asses.

40[6] The "last two sections" are entitled "That the preaching of the Law and Gospel is necessarie" and "Touching *St Austin's* opinion, of beeing justified by the *Law*". In the latter, Luther cites Augustine's view that fulfilling the law is sufficient for justification only "when the holie Ghost cometh thereto", and argues on the contrary that individuals must also call upon God's mercy, "For God hath decreed, that mankinde shall bee saved, not by the Law but through Christ."

40[7] One article, "Whether wee should preach onely of God's Grace and Mercie, or not?" occupies more than half of p 202. Luther advises a timely preaching that will prevent complacency and offer comfort in turn: "The Gospel is like a fresh, milde,

and cool aër in the extreamest heat in Summer-time, that is, a solace and comfort in the anguish of the Conscience; not in the time of Winter, when it is cold enough already, that is, in the time of peace, when people are secure, and intend to bee justified by their works."

41[1] *Ab extra*, "from without", and *ab intra*, "from within". The argument about the relationship of grace and law in this section of the *Colloquia* stems from Paul's analysis in the Epistle to the Romans.

41[2] The distinction between conceptions and ideas—the former being products merely of sense and understanding—came to be crucial to C: cf *C&S* (*CC*) 12–13 and n 1.

42 p 203 | ''Of the difference of the law and gospel''

But whereas Christ, and also St *Peter* and *Paul* in the Gospel do give many Commandments and Doctrines, and do expound the Law, the same wee must account of, as of all the other works and benefits of Christ.

See Mss Note, p. 200[1]

43 p 203 | Continuing **42** textus

And as to know His Works and Actions, is not yet rightly to know the Gospel, (for thereby wee know not as yet that Hee hath overcom sin, death and the Divel); Even so likewise, it is not as yet to know the Gospel, when wee know such Doctrine and Commandements, but when the voice soundeth, which saith, Christ is thine own with Life, with Doctrine, with Works, Death, Resurrection, and with all what Hee hath, doth, and may do.

most true.

44 p 205 | ''That St Paul had much trouble with the Jews about the law''

True it is, *Paul* for a certain time kept the Law, by reason of the weak, to win them; but in this our time it is not so, neither agreeth it any waie therewith: therefore the Antient Fathers said well . . . Distinguish the times, then may wee easily reconcile the Scriptures together.

Yea! and not only so but we shall reconcile truths, that seem to repeal this or that passage of Scripture with the Scriptures. For Christ is with his Church even to the end.—

45 p 205 | ''Of the Jews disturbances touching the law''

I verily believ (said *Luther*) it [the abolition of the Law] vexed to the heart the beloved St *Paul* himself* before his conversion, as it is written, *Acts 9.* wee see also *Romans 9.* that *Paul* was much troubled about the same, yea after his conversion.

* How dearly Martin Luther loved St Paul! How dearly would St Paul have loved Martin Luther! And how impossible, that either should not have done so!

46 p 205 | Continuing **45** textus

In this case, touching the distinguishing the Law from the Gospel, wee

42[1] I.e. **41** above.

must utterly expel all humane and natural wisdom, reason and understanding, which are arch-enemies to faith . . .

N.B. *All* Reason is above Nature. Therefore by Reason in Luther or rather in his Translator, you must understand the *reasoning* faculty:—[a] that is, the Logical Intellect, or the intellectual Understanding. For the U. is in all respects a medial and mediate Faculty—and has therefore two Extremities or Poles—the Sensual, in which form it is Sᵗ Paul's φϱονημα σαϱϰος;[1] and the intellectual Pole, or the hemisphere (as it were) turned towards the Reason/ ~~or~~ Now the Reason (*Lux idealis seu spiritualis*)[2] shines down into the Understanding, ~~p~~ which recognizes the Light, id est, *Lumen* a Luce Spirituali, quasi alieni~~gumen~~um aliquid,[3] which it can only comprehend ~~by~~ or describe to itself by ~~the~~ attributes opposite to its own essential properties. Now these being Contingency, and *Particularity, it distinguishes the *formal* Light (= *Lumen*) (not the substantial Light = Lux) of Reason by the attributes of the Necessary and the Universal. And by irradiation of this Lumen or *Shine*, the Understanding becomes a conclusive or logical Faculty—As such it is Λογος ανθϱωπινος.[4]

* For tho' the immediate Objects of the Understanding are Genera et Species, still they are *particular* Gen. et Sp.—

47   pp 206–7 | "Of the curs of the law"

When Satan saith in thy heart, God will not pardon thy sins, nor bee gracious unto thee, I pray (said *Luther*) how wilt thou then, as a poor sinner rais up and comfort thy self, especially when other signs of God's wrath besides do beat upon thee, as sickness, povertie, &c. And that thy heart beginneth to preach and say, Behold, here thou lyest in sickness, thou art poor and forsaken* of every one, &c. How canst thou as then know, that God is gracious unto thee? then thou must turn thy self to the other side . . .

* Oh! how true, how affectingly true is this! And when too Satan, the Tempter, becomes Satan, the Accuser, saying in my heart—This Sickness is the consequence of Sin or sinful infirmity—& thou hast brought

---

[a] The remainder of the note appears to have been added later, in a different ink and a larger hand

46[1] "The mind of the flesh" is the translation C preferred for this much-used phrase from Rom 8.7: cf Blanco White *Letters from Spain* 1 at n 2; *AR* (1825) 14, 231; *CN* iv 4618.

46[2] "The ideal or spiritual light".

46[3] "That is, *a Light* from the Spiritual Light, as something different in kind". For the distinction between *lumen* and *lux* cf Book of Common Prayer copy b **29** n 3.

46[4] "The logos pertaining to man"; thus *human* understanding.

thyself into a fearful dilemma—thou canst not hope for salvation as long as thou continuest in any sinful practice—and yet thou canst not abandon thy daily dose of this or that poison without suicide. For the Sin of thy Soul has become the Necessity of thy Body—daily tormenting thee, without yielding thee any the least pleasurable sensation, but goading thee on by terror without Hope. Under such evidence of God's Wrath how can'st thou expect to be saved?—Well may the Heart cry out—Who shall deliver me from the *Body* of this Death![1] from this Death that lives and tyrannizes in my body!—But the Gospel answers—There is a Redemption from the Body promised—only cling to Christ. Call on him continually, with all thy heart and all thy ~~Sen~~oul, to give thee strength, to be strong in thy weakness—and what Christ doth not see good to relieve thee from, suffer *in hope*.

It may be better for thee to be kept humble and ⟨in⟩ self-abasement. The thorn in the flesh may remain—& yet the Grace of God thro' Christ [? ~~prove~~] prove sufficient for thee. Only *cling* to Christ, and do thy best. In all love, and well-doing gird thyself up to improve & use aright what remains free in thee.[a] and if thou doest aught aright, say and thankfully believe, that Christ hath done it for thee. O what a miserable despairing Wretch should I become, if I believed the doctrines of Bishop Jer. Taylor in his Treatise on Repentance—or those I heard preached by Dr Chalmers![2] If I gave up the faith, that the Life of Christ would *precipitate* the remaining dregs of Sin in the crisis of Death, and that I shall rise a pure *capacity* of Christ, blind to be irradiated by his Light, empty to be possessed by his fullness, naked of merit to be cloathed with his Righteousness!—

[a] Here, at the foot of p 206, C has written "/\/\" and has begun the continuation of the note, in the foot-margin of p 207, with the same symbols

47[1] Rom 7.24, but with a poignant personal application to the physical and spiritual effects of C's addiction to opium.

47[2] C found both the right and left wings of the established Church, the "Arminians" and the Calvinists, severe towards the repentant but weak sinner. *Friend (CC)* I 433–4 puts Taylor's case and observes, "I could never read Bishop Taylor's Tract . . . without being tempted to characterize high Calvinism as (comparatively) a lamb in wolf's clothing, and strict Arminianism as approaching to the reverse." C also analyses Taylor's position in *AR* (1825) 301n–303n. Thomas Chalmers (1780–1847), a celebrated evangelical preacher who at one time had had Edward Irving as his assistant, preached in London from time to time, and visited C at Highgate in 1827 and 1830. Among Chalmers's published sermons, one on "Faith and Repentance" expresses the position that C found so distressing: "To repent of sin, is something more than to grieve for it. It is to turn from it. It is something more than to regret your sins—it is to renounce them. Repentance may begin with sorrow, but it does not end there. Sorrow of itself is not repentance; it only works repentance. And he alone fulfils this work, who gives up the evil of his doings, and enters with full purpose of heart on a life of new obedience": *Select Works* ed William Hanna (Edinburgh 1855) IV 294.

48   p 207 | "What God's righteousness is . . ."

The Nobilitie, the Gentrie, Citizens and Farmers, &c. are now become so haughtie and ungodly, that they regard no Ministers nor Preachers, and (said *Luther*) if wee were not holpen somwhat by great Princes and persons, wee could not long subsist; therefore *Isaiah* saith well, *And Kings shall bee their Nurses, &c.*

Corpulent Nurses too often, that overlay the Babe! Distempered Nurses, that convey poison in their Milk!

49   p 208 | Ch 13 *That only Faith in Christ justifieth before God* "Of Philip Melancthon's disputations . . ."

Philip Melancthon said to *Luther*, The opinion of S[t] *Austine* of justification (as it seemeth) was more pertinent, fit, and convenient when hee disputed not, then it was when hee used to speak and dispute; for thus hee saith, Wee ought to censure or hold, that wee are justified by faith, that is, by our Regeneration, or by beeing made new Creatures. Now if it bee so, then wee are not justified onely by faith, but by all the gifts and virtues of God given unto us. . . . Now what is your opinion, *(Sir)* do you hold, that a man is justified by this Regeneration, as is St *Austin's* opinion?

Luther answered, and said, I hold this, and am certain, that the true meaning of the Gospel, and of the Apostles is, *that wee are justified before God *Gratìs*, for nothing, onely by God's meer mercie, wherewith and by reason whereof, hee imputeth righteousness unto us in Christ.

True! But is it more than a dispute about words? Is not the regeneration likewise "*gratis*, only by God's meer mercie"? We according to the necessity of our imperfect Understandings must divide & distinguish. But surely Justification, and Sanctification are one Act of God—& only different perspectives of Redemption by, in, thro', and *for* Christ. They are one and the same Plant, Justification the Root, Sanctification the Flower—and (may I not venture to add?) Transsubstantiation into Christ the celestial Fruit!   S. T. C.

50   p 211 | "Melancthon's sixth replie", "Luther's answer"

Sir! you saie, *Paul* was justified, that is, was received to everlasting life, onely for mercie's sake. Against which, I saie, if the piece-meal or partial Caus, namely, our obedience followeth not; then wee are not saved, according to these words, *Wo is mee, if I preach not the Gospel*, 1 Cor. 9.

No piecing or partial Caus (said *Luther*) approacheth thereunto; For

Faith is powerful continually without ceasing; otherwise, it is no Faith. Therefore what the works are, or of what value, the same they are through the Honor and Power of Faith, which undeniably is the Sun or Sun-beam of this shining.

This is indeed a difficult question: and one, I am disposed to think, which can receive its solution only by the Idea, or the Act and fact of Justification by Faith self-reflected. But humanly considered, this Position of Luther's provokes the mind to ask—Is there no receptivity of Faith, considered as ~~an act~~ free gift of God, pre-requisite in the Individual? does ~~it~~ Faith commence by generating the receptivity of itself? If so, there is no difference either in kind or in degree between the Receivers and the Rejectors of the Word, at the moment preceding this Reception or Rejection: and a Stone is as capable a Subject of Faith as a Man?—How can obedience exist, where disobedience was not possible? Surely, two or three Texts from St Paul detached from the total organismus of his Reasoning ought not to outweigh the plain fact, that the contrary position is implied ⟨in,⟩ or an immediate Consequent of, our Lord's own Invitations & Assurances! Every where a something is attributed to the Will.   *S. T. C.**

* Mem. I should not have written the above Note in my present state of Light. Not that I find it false; but that it may have the effect of falsehood by not going deep enough.   July 1829

51   p 211 | ''Luther's answer [to Melanchthon's eighth reply]''

To conclude, a faithful person is a new Creature, a new Tree. Therefore all these speeches which in the Law are usual, belong not to this Case: As to saie, *A faithful Person must do good works*: neither were it rightly spoken, to saie, *The Sun shall shine: A good Tree shall bring forth good Fruit:* or, *Three and seven shall bee Ten*, &c. For the Sun shall not shine, but it doth shine by nature unbidden, it is thereunto creäted. Likewise, A good Tree bringeth forth good fruit without bidding: Three and seven are ten alreadie, and shall not bee &c.

This important ¶.ph. is obscure by the Translator's ignorance of the ~~Ger~~ true import of the German *soll*, which does not answer to our *shall*; but rather to our *ought*—i.e. *should* do this or that, is under an *obligation* to.[1]   S. T. C.

51[1] C's complaint is valid. The passage is taken from Melanchthon's Latin notes of 1536; Aurifaber's original *Tischreden*, giving both the Latin and German versions, translated the Latin *debet* with the German *soll*.

52 p 213 | "Of Luther's addition to the foresaid Melancthon's writing"

And I, my Loving *Brentius*, to the end I may better understand this case, do use to think in this manner, namely, as if in my heart were no Qualitie or Virtue at all, which is called Faith, and Love, (as the Sophists do speak and dream thereof) but I set all on Christ, and saie, My *Formalis Justitia*, that is, my sure, my constant and Compleat Righteousness (in which is no want nor failing, but is, as before God it ought to bee) is Christ my Lord and Saviour.

Aye! this, *this* is indeed to the Purpose! In this doctrine my Soul can find rest! I hope to be saved by Faith; not by *my* faith, but by the faith of Christ in me.

See the MSS Note written in the blank leaf at the end of a small Volume translated from Fenelon, belonging to my *all-dear-and-holy-names-in-the-name-of* Friend, Mʳˢ Gillman.[1]　　　S. T. Coleridge

53 p 214 | "Of the Nature of Faith"

The Scripture nameth the faithful, a people of God's Saints. . . . But here one may saie, The sins which daily wee commit, do offend and anger God; How then can wee bee holie? *Answ*. A mother's Love to her Childe is much stronger then are the Excrements and scurff thereof. Even so, God's Love towards us is far stronger then our filthiness and uncleanness. . . .

Yea, may one saie again, Wee sin without ceasing, and where sin is, there the holie Spirit is not: therefore wee are not holie, becaus the holie Spirit is not in us, who maketh holie. *Answer*. The Text saith plainly, *The holie Ghost shall glorifie mee*, &c. Now where Christ is, there is the holie Spirit. Now Christ is in the faithful (although they have and feel sins, do confess the same, and with sorrow of heart do complain thereover) therefore sins do not separate Christ from those that believ.

All in this page is true and necessary to be preached. But O! what need is not there of holy prudence to preach it aright, i.e. at right times, to the right ears! Now this is when the Doctrine is *necessary* and then comfortable; but where it is not necessary, but only very comfortable, in such cases it would be a narcotic poison, killing the Soul by infusing a stupor or counterfeit peace of Conscience—Now where there is are no Sinkings of Self-abasement, no griping Sense of Sin & Worthlessness, but perhaps the contrary—reckless Confidence & Self-valuing for good

---

52[1] FÉNELON **1**, in which C asserts, "Thus we see even our faith is not ours in its origin: but is the faith of the Son of God graciously communicated to us."

qualities supposed an overbalance for the Sins, there it is *not* necessary. In short, these are ⟨*not* the⟩ truths, that can be preached καιρως ακαιρως, i.e. in season and out of season.

In declining life or at any time in the hour of sincere humiliation, these ~~rig~~ truths may be applied in reference to past Sins collectively; but a ~~true~~ Christian must not, a true however infirm Christian will not, can not administer them to himself immediately after Sinning—Least of all immediately before! We ought fervently to pray thus:

Most holy and most merciful God! by the grace of thy holy Spirit make these promises profitable to me to preserve me from despairing of thy forgiveness thro' Christ, my Saviour! But o! save me from presumptuously perverting them into a pillow for a stupified Conscience! but give me grace so to contrast my Sins with thy transcendent Goodness, and long-suffering Love as to hate it with an unfeigned hatred for its own exceeding Sinfulness—

54 p ⁺2, referring to pp 214–15 | "Of the nature of faith"

This putteth mee in minde (said *Luther*) of a passage that happened in my youth time, namely, In the time of Shrovetide, (as was usual) my self and another Boie went about to sing before people's doors for Puddings. A certain Towns-man merrily disposed, came towards us (one daie) crying aloud, What will these whoreson Boies? and with such words hee ran towards us, having in his hand two Puddings, which hee offered unto us. But wee, bceing scared at his first feigned Gesture in running and calling, ran and flew from him, who, in truth, meant us no harm, but intended to do us good. And in that hee might not fail of his good purpose, hee called with a milde voice unto us, insomuch that at last, wee turned unto him and received his Puddings.

P. 215. first seven lines.

This merry Story of Luther's reminds me of the fellow who in the dusk of the evening without speaking a word robbed the inside passengers of a Stage Coach by terror of a huge Black Pudding—and having received the money from each in his hat, dropt the Hog-Sausage—with Heaven reward you, kind Gentlemen and Ladies! I did not expect a tenth part so much for it.—

55 p 217 | "That no man can teach purely and rightly of faith . . . except hee . . . hath run through the pikes"

Sᵗ *Paul* was well exercised in this Art [of teaching "pure and rightly touching Faith"]; hee speaketh more basely and vilely of the Law, then any arch-heretick can speak of the Sacrament of the Altar, of Baptism, or then the Jews have spoken thereof; For hee nameth the Law, an Office of death, of sin and of damnation . . .

Q.ʸ? *John X. 8.*[1]

56   p 220 | "How faith and hope are distinguished"

Faith and Hope (said *Luther*) are divers waies distinguished: First, in regard of the *Subject*, wherein every thing consisteth. For Faith is, and consisteth in a Persons understanding, but Hope consisteth in the Will. . . . Fifthly . . . Faith fighteth against Errors and Heresies; It proveth, censureth and judgeth the spirits and doctrines. But Hope striveth against troubles and vexations, and among the evil it exspecteth good.

Therefore (said *Luther*) Faith in Divinitie is the wisdom and providence, and belongeth to the Doctrine. But Hope is the Courage and Joifulness in Divinitie, and pertaineth to Admonition. . . .

Now like as wisdom or understanding is unprofitable and atchieveth nothing without Courage and Joifulness; Even so, Faith without Hope is nothing worth; for Hope endureth and overcometh misfortune and evil.

N.B. Luther in his Postills discourseth far better and more genially of Faith, than in these ¶phs—Unfortunately, the German[a] have but one word for Faith and Belief—viz. Glaube. And what L. here says, is spoken of *Belief.* Of *Faith* he spokeaks in the next Article but one—[1]

57   pp 226–7, pencil, overtraced | "That regeneration onely maketh God's children"

* The Article of our Justification before God (said *Luther*) is, as it useth to bee with a Son which is born an Heir of all his Father's goods, and cometh not thereunto by deserts; hee succeedeth (without any work or desets[b] in his Father's wealth.

* I will here record my experience. Ever when I meet with the doctrine of Regeneration and Faith and Free Grace simply announced—"*So it*

---

[a] A slip for "Germans"?   [b] Presumably a slip for "deserts"

55[1] Christ's explanation of the parable of the sheepfold, John 10.7–8: "Verily, verily, I say unto you, I am the door of the sheep. All that ever came before me are thieves and robbers: but the sheep did not hear them." C's point presumably is that Christ himself spoke harshly of the order that preceded him. There is further comment on this "astounding text" in *CN* IV 5393.

56[1] In the article to which C refers, "Of Faith, and the caus thereof" (220–1), Luther defines faith as "a Gift and Present of God in our hearts, that thereby we fasten and take hold on Christ". Faith in this sense is a recurrent theme in the postils (Leipzig ed pts 13–14), which C was reading Dec 1826 (*CL* VI 656); in fact, it is a theme in the very postil he mentions, the one on the marriage-feast at Cana (Leipzig ed pt 13 pp 349–54).

is"—then I believe; my Heart leaps forth to welcome it. But as soon as an explanation or reason is added, such explanations namely and reasonings as I have any where met with,—then my Heart leaps back again, recoils—and I exclaim, Nay! Nay! but not *so.*

S. T. Coleridge
25th of Septr 1819

58   p 227, pencil, overtraced | "Of objections against this, that faith onely justifieth"

Doctor *Carlestad* (said *Luther*) argueth thus: True it is, that Faith justifieth, but Faith is a work of the First Commandement, therefore it justifieth as a work. Moreover, All that the Law commandeth, the same is a work of the Law. Now Faith is commanded, therefore Faith is a work of the Law. Again, what God will have, the same is commanded; God will have Faith, therefore Faith is commanded.

Luther's *Answer*. St. *Paul* (said *Luther*) speaketh in such sort of the Law, that hee separateth it from the Promiss, which is far another thing then the Law. The Law is terrestrial, but the Promiss is celestial; God giveth the Law, to the end thereby wee may bee rouzed up and made pliant; for the Commandements do go and proceed against the proud and haughtie, which contemn God's Gifts, now a Gift or a Present cannot bee a Commandement.

Therefore wee must answer according to this Rule . . . Words must bee taken and understood according to the matter and business touching which they speak. . . . St *Paul* calleth that the work of the Law, which is don and acted through the knowledg of the Law by a constrained will without the holy Spirit, so that the same is a work of the Law, which the Law earnestly requireth and strictly will have don; it is not a voluntarie work, but a forced work of the rod . . .

And wherein then did Carlestad and Luther differ? Answer. Not at all, or essentially and irreconcileably, according as the *feeling* of Carlestad was. If he meant the particular Deed, the latter: if the total Act, the agent included, then the former.

59   pp 230–1 | Ch 14 *Of Good Works* "Of the love towards the neighbor"

* The Love towards the Neighbor (said *Luther*) must bee like a pure and chaste Love between Bride and Bridegroom, where all faults are connived, covered and born with, and onely the virtues regarded.

In how many little escapes and corner-holes does the sensibility, the *fineness*, (that of which refinement is but a counterfeit, at best but a Reflex) the geniality of nature appear in this Son of Thunder!—O for a

Luther in the present Age! Why, Charles! with the very Handcuffs of his prejudices he would knock out the brains (nay, that is impossible— but) he would split the skulls, of our *Cristogalli*—translate the word as you like—French Christians, or Coxcombs.[1]

60 p 232 | "That wee ought highly to regard the works of our vocation and calling"

Let *Witzell* know, (said *Luther*) that *David*'s wars and battles, which hee fought, were more pleasing to God, then the fastings and prayings of the best, of the honestest, and of the holiest Monks and Friers; much more then the works of our now ridiculous and superstitious Friers.

A cordial rich and juicy Speech, such as shaped itself ⟨into,⟩ and lived anew in, Gustavus Adolphuses.[1]

61 p 244, completed in pencil, overtraced | Ch 15 *Of Praier* "That praier is certainly heard"

God most certainly heareth them that praie in Faith, and granteth when and how hee pleaseth, and knoweth most profitable for them. Wee must also know, that when our praiers tend to the sanctifying of his Name, and to the encreas and honor of his Kingdom (also that wee praie according to his will) then most certainly hee heareth. But when wee praie contrarie to these points, then wee are not heard; *for God doth nothing against His Name, His Kingdom, and His Will.

* Then (saith the Understanding, το Φρονημα σαρκος)[1] what doth Prayer effect. If A − Prayer = 3, and A + Prayer = 3, Prayer = 0.— The attempt to answer this argument by admitting its validity relatively to God, but asserting the efficacy of Prayer relatively to the Pray-er or Precant himself, is merely staving off the Objection a single step. For this Effect on the Devout Soul is produced by an Act of God.—The true answer is, Prayer is an *Idea*, and Ens Spirituale, out of the cognizance of the Understanding.[a][2]

[a] Here C has written a note indicator in the outer margin and has continued the note in the foot-margin with the same symbol

59[1] "Charles" is Charles Lamb, who owned this copy of the *Colloquia* and with whom C carried on a friendly competition in puns. The second half of "Christogalli" signifies "French"; the pun in the first half involves "Christ-" as a prefix and the Latin *crista*, a cock's comb (whence "coxcomb", a dandified fool).

60[1] Gustavus Adolphus (1594–1632), King of Sweden, was for C a model of the Christian soldier (cf *CN* III 3845 f 123): he intervened in the Thirty Years' War on behalf of fellow-Protestants in Germany, and died on the field of battle.

61[1] "The mind of the flesh" as **46** n 1 above.

61[2] C's thinking about and practice in prayer underwent change in 1825–6 as he worked on an essay on the "philosophy of prayer" that was to be a supplement to *AR*

The spiritual Mind ~~contemplates~~ receives the answer in the contemplation of the Idea—[a]Life = Deitas diffusa.[3] We can set the Life in efficient[b] motion; but not contrary to the Form or Type.

62 p 245, pencil, overtraced

The Errors and false Theories of Great Men sometimes, perhaps most often, arise out of true Ideas falsified by degenerating into *Conceptions*[1]—Or the mind excited to action by an inworking Idea, the Understanding works in the same direction according to its kind; and produces a counterfeit, in which the mind rests.[c]

This I believe to be the case with the scheme of Emanation in Plotinus—God is made a first & consequently a *comparative intensity*—& matter the last—the whole there *finite*, & thence its conceivability.— But we must admit a gradation of intensities in Reality—[d2]

63 p 247 | Ch 16 *Of the Confession and Constancie of the Doctrine* [of Justification]

When Governors and Rulers are enemies to God's Word, then our dutie is to depart, to sell and forsake all wee have, to flie from one place to another, as Christ commandeth. Wee must make and prepare no uproars nor tumults, by reason of the Gospel, but wee must suffer all things.

Right!—But then it must be the lawful Rulers—i.e. those in whom the Sovereign or supreme power is lodged by the known Laws and Constitution of[e] the Country. Where the Laws and Constitutional ~~Rights &~~ Liberties of the Nation are trampled on, S the Subjects do not lose and

[a] Here an ink blot, evidently made by C; the writing continues in a watery brown ink
[b] The note is concluded in pencil, overtraced
[c] Here C has written a + and resumed the note in the foot-margin with the same symbol
[d] Four or five very faint words follow: "[? an onion peel with/that]"
[e] Here C has written "(*see below*)" and has continued the note in the foot-margin without an indicator but repeating "of"

(*AR*—1825—376n, *CL* VI 544–6), and this note indicates the general outline of his solution to the question. In Apr 1826 he wrote to Daniel Stuart about his new-found conviction of the efficacy of prayer: *CL* VI 577. "Ens Spirituale": "Spiritual Entity".

61[3] I.e. the idea that life is "Deity diffused".

62[1] Cf **41** and n 2 above.

62[2] In C's view, the Neoplatonic doctrine of emanation, "the most ancient, the most widely diffused and the most fruitful, of Heresies" (BÖHME **110** at n 2), erred in making the Creator continuous with the

creation. It is not enough to "admit a gradation of intensities in Reality"; God and Nature must be recognised as essentially different. The doctrine of emanation is propounded by Plotinus, e.g. in *Ennead* 5.2, "The Origin and Order of the Beings following on the First", and 5.4, "How the Secondaries rise from The First: and on The One": *The Enneads* tr S. MacKenna (rev ed 1956 repr 1966) 380–1, 400–2; C read the Latin translation by Ficino, *Plotini . . . operum philosophicorum omnium* (Basle 1580), in which the corresponding pages are 493–5, 516–19.

are not in Conscience bound to forego their right of resistance because they are Christians or because it happens to be a matter of Religion, in which their Rights are violated.—And this was Luther's Opinion.

64   p 247 | "That every Christian is tied to confess Christ"

Every Christian, specially those in Offices, should alwaies bee ready (when need requireth) boldly to stand up and confess his Saviour Christ, to maintain his Faith, and alwaies bee armed against the World, the Divel, Sectaries, and what els the Divel were able to produce. But no man will do this, except hee bee so sure of his Doctrine and Religion, as that, although I my self should plaie the fool, and should recant and denie this my Doctrine and Religion (which God forbid) hee notwithstanding therefore would not yield, but saie, If *Luther*, or an Angel from Heaven, should teach otherwise, *Let him bee accursed*.

[a]Well and nobly said, thou rare Black Swan![1] This, THIS is the Church. Where this is found, there is the Church of Christ—tho' but 20 in the whole congregation. And if there were twenty such in 200 different places, the ~~whole~~ Church would be entire in each. Without this no Church.

65   p 248 | "Of the constancie of Johannes Prince Elector of Saxon . . ."

In the year 1530. Emperor *Charls* the Fifth summoned a Diet at *Auspurg*, intending to bring the differences in Causses of Religion to an agreement; Hee practised at that time by all craftie means to draw the said Prince Elector from the Confession of the Gospel; but the Prince (dis-regarding all flattering friendships, malice and threatnings), would not yield, no, not the breadth of an hair, from the true Religion and Word of God, though hee was compassed with many eminent dangers, but on the contrarie, hee cheered up and comforted his Learned Divines (which hee brought with him to the Diet) as *Philip Melancthon*, Justus Jonas, *George Spalatine*, and *John Agricola*, and charged those of his Council to tell His Divines, That they should deal uprightly to the honor and prais of God, and that they should regard neither his person, his Countries, nor people.

Whether if a ~~Russian~~ popish Czar, should act as our James IInd acted, the Russian Greekists would be justified in doing with him what the English Protestants justifiably did with regard to James the IInd is a Knot,

[a] This note is squeezed in in the outer margin above the last part of **63** and surrounded with an irregular line

64[1] For Luther as swan see **83** and n 4 below.

I shall not attempt to ~~un~~ cut—tho' I guess, the Russians would, by cutting their Czar's Throat.[1]

66   p 248 | Continuing **65** textus

Therefore (said *Luther*) this Prince Elector held constant over God's Word, with an excelling Princely courage. . . . And hee sent for one of his chiefest Privie Counsellors, named Lord *John von Minkwitz*, and said unto him, You have heard my Father saie, (running with him at Tilt) that to sit upright on hors-back maketh a good Tilter. If therefore it bee good, and laudable in temporal Tilting to sit upright: How much more is it now prais-worthie in God's Caus, to sit, to stand, and to go uprightly and just?

Princely! So Shakespear wou'd have made a Prince Elector talk!—The Metaphor is so grandly in character!

67   p 249 | Ch 17 *Of Holie Baptism* "Of the holie sacraments"

God oftentimes (said *Luther*) hath altered His Sacraments and Signs in the world; for from *Adam*'s time to *Abraham*'s, the Church for Sacraments had Offerings and Sacrifices, insomuch that Fire came down from Heaven . . . which was a far more glorious sign, then those which wee have. Afterwards, *Noah* had for a sign the Rain-bow. *Abraham* thereupon had the Circumcision. The Circumcision stood and remained until Christ came. From the time of Christ, to this present daie, Baptism hath continued. *Signa sunt subinde facta minora, Res autem & facta subinde creverunt* [The signs continually became less, but the Facts and the actions continually grew].

A valuable Remark! As the Substance waxed (i.e. became more evident) the ceremonial Sign waned—*a*till at length in the Eucharist ~~it~~ the Signum united with the Significatum,[1] and became Consubstantial. The ceremonial Sign, viz. the eating the Bread and drinking the Wine, became a *Symbol*—i.e. a solemn instance and exemplification of the ~~m~~ *Class* of mysterious Acts, which we are, or as Christians *should* be, performing

---

a Here, in the space at the end of the paragraph, C has written "/\" and resumed the note in the foot-margin with the same symbol

65[1] On pp 247–8 Luther gives examples to show that integrity in matters of religious conviction is properly independent of political or worldly concerns. The English Revolution of 1688 was justified, in C's view, as a way of avoiding the confusion of aims implicit in a Roman Catholic regime or, as C says in *C&S* (*CC*) 129–45, a Church of Anti-Christ. In 1606 an attempt to establish a Roman Catholic tsar, Demetrius, in Russia had in fact been foiled by assassination.

67[1] "The Sign . . . with the Thing signified".

daily & hourly in every social duty and recreation.[2]—This is indeed to
re-create the Man in and by Christ. Sublimely did the Fathers call the
Eucharist, the extension of the Incarnation[3]—only I would have pre-
ferred the perpetuation & application of the Incarnation.   S. T. C.

68   p 249

No Credit is to bee given to a Seal that is set to a Blank paper, whereon
nothing is written; and again, A bare writing without a Seal is of no
force.

Metaphors are sorry Logic: especially Metaphors from human and those
too conventional usages to the ordinances of eternal Wisdom!

69   p 250 | ''Of baptisms power and operation''

Luther said, No; A Christian is wholy and altogether sanctified. . . .
Wee must take sure hold on Baptism by faith, as then wee shall bee,
yea, alreadie are sanctified. In this sort *David* nameth himself holie.

A deep thought!—Strong meat for *Men*—It dare not be offered for *Milk*.

70   p 276 | Ch 21 *Of Excommunication, and the Jurisdiction of the Church* ''An
admonition touching excommunication''

I would willingly proceed with the Excommunication . . . after this
manner: First, when I my self have admonished an obstinate sinner, then
I send unto him two other persons . . . if as then hee will not better and
amend himself . . . Then I will declare him openly to the Church, and
in this manner I will saie, Loving Friends, I declare unto you, how that
N. N. hath been admonished, First by my self in private, afterwards also
by two Chaplains; thirdly by two Aldermen and Church-wardens, and
those of the Assemblie; yet notwithstanding hee will not desist from his
sinful kinde of life. Wherefore I earnestly desire you to assist and ad-
vise, to kneel down with mee, and let us praie against him, and deliver
him over to the Divel, &c.

N.B. Luther did not mean, that this should be done all at once; but that
a day should be appointed for the Congregation to meet for joint consul-
tation, & according to the resolutions passed to choose & commission
such & such persons to wait on the Offender, & to exhort, persuade &

67[2] It is characteristic of C to discuss the
Eucharist as a symbol: *LS* (*CC*) 88, *TT* 20
May 1830, and esp C. BUTLER *Vindication*
1 at n 3.
    67[3] C echoes Jeremy Taylor *The Worthy*

Communicant (1674) 30, a page marked in
C's own copy: ''Consonant to which Doc-
trine, the Fathers by an elegant expression
call the blessed Sacrament, the extension
of the Incarnation.''

threaten him in the name of the congregation;—then if after due time allowed all this proved fruitless, *then* to kneel down with the Minister &c—. Surely, were it only feasible, nothing could be more desirable. But alas! it is not compatible with a Church National (whose Congregations therefore are neither gathered, nor selected) or a Church established by Law:[1] for Law & Discipline are mutually destructive of each other, being the same as involuntary & voluntary Penance.—

71 p 290 | Ch 22 *Of the Office of Preaching, and Ministers of the Church* "That wee must make a difference between the manner of life, and the doctrine"

The manner of life (said *Luther*) is as evil among us, as among the Papists; wherefore wee strive not with them by reason of the manner of life, but for and about the Doctrine.*

* This is a Remark of deep Insight, verum verè Lutheranum![1]

72 pp 291–2 | "That pride, presumption, and ambition do the greatest hurt in the Church"

Ambition and Pride (said *Luther*) are the ranckest poison in the Church when they are possessed by Preachers. * *Zuinglius* thereby was mis-led, who did what pleased himself, as his interpreting of the Prophets sheweth, which is stuffed full with presumption, pride, and ambition; hee presumed to contemn every man, yea also, the Potentates and Princes, for thus hee wrote, Yee honorable and good Princes, must pardon mee, in that I give you not your Titles: for the Glass-windows are as well illustrious as yee. In like manner *Grickle* and *Jeckle* behaved themselvs in proud and haughtie manner in the Convocation at *Muntzer*. To conclude, Ambition is a consuming fire.

* One might fancy in the Vision of Mirza Style[1] that all the angry, contemptuous, haughty Expressions of good and zealous Men, Gallant Staff-officers in the Army of Christ, formed a Rick of Straw and Stubble, which at the last day is to be divided into more ~~and~~ or smaller Haycocks, according ~~as~~ to the number of kind & unfeignedly humble and charitable Thoughts and Speeches that had intervened/ and that these were placed in a file, Leap-frog fashion, in the narrow road to the Gate of Paradise, and burst into flame as the Soul of the Individual approached—so that he must leap over and thro' them. Now I cannot help thinking, that this dear Man of God, heroic Luther, will find more op-

70[1] C invokes the distinction that he was to elaborate as the distinction between the National Church and the Church of Christ in *C&S* (*CC*) 113–28; cf also Bax- | TER *Reliquiae* COPY A 32.
71[1] "A truly Lutheran truth!"
72[1] A well-known Oriental allegory of human life in *Spectator* 159 (1 Sept 1711).

portunities of shewing his Agility, and reach the Gate in a greater Sweat, and with more Burn-blisters, than his Brother Hero, Zuinglius! I guess, that the Latter's Comment on the Prophets will be found almost sterile in these Tyger-Lilies and Brimstone Flowers of polemic Rhetoric, compared with the former's controversy with our Henry the 8th—Replies to the Pope's Bulls &c &c!—²

73 p 291 | **72** textus at "Glass-windows"

The joke is lost in the translation. The German for "illustrious" is "durchlauchtig" i.e. transparent or translucent.

74 p 291 | "Where honor should bee sought for"

When wee leav to God His Name, His Kingdom and Will, then will Hee also give unto us our daily Bread, and will remit our sins, and deliver us from the Divel and all evil. Onely His Honor Hee will have to Himself.

A brief but most excellent Comment on the Lord's Prayer!—

75 p 297 | "That St Paul diligently studied Moses and the Prophets . . ."

There was never any that understood the Old Testament so well as St *Paul*, except onely *John* the Baptist.*

* I cannot conjecture what Luther had in his mind when he made this exception

76 p 335 | Ch 27 *Of General Councils* "Whereto councils are profitable"

* I could wish (said *Luther*) that the Princes and States of the Empire would make an Assemblie, and hold a Council and an Union both in Doctrine and Cerimonies, so that everie one might not break in and run on with such insolencie and presumption, according to his own brains, (as already is begun) whereby many good hearts are offended.

* Strange Heart of Man! Would Luther have given up the Doctrine of Justification by Faith alone, had the majority of the Council decided in

72² C points out affectionately that Luther was probably more guilty than his contemporary Zwingli (1484–1531) of the faults with which he charges him. Luther's pamphlet *Contra Henricum Regem Anglicum* (1522) is remarkably abusive about "Henry, by God's disgrace, King of England". (For the work to which Luther was responding Henry had been rewarded by the Pope with the title "Defender of the Faith".) By "replies to the Pope's Bulls"

C may mean Luther's public response to the bull "Exsurge Domine" (1520) which threatened him with excommunication (Luther burnt the bull along with the papal decretals and a few volumes of canon law, and published a treatise justifying his position), or may refer more generally to Luther's notoriously rough handling of the Pope and papacy elsewhere, e.g. in the chapters *Of Antichrist* and *Of the Pope's Spiritual Laws* here, pp 298–328, 423–5.

favor of the Arminian Scheme? If not, by what Right could he expect Œcolampadius or Zuinglius to recant their convictions respecting the Eucharist[1] or the Baptists theirs on Infant Baptism, to the same Authority? Luther's arguments against the last mentioned Doctrine (p. 251–255) are so flimsy, one can scarce believe him in earnest.[2]

77 p 336 | "Of what councils ought to order"

In the year 1539, the 27 of *Januarie*, A book was sent to *Luther*, intituled *Liber Conciliorum*, which with great diligence, labor, and pains, was made and collected together: *After the reading of which, hee said, This book will defend and maintain the Pope, whenas in his own Decrees innumerable Canons are quite against him and this book. . . . Councils have power to make Ordinances onely concerning External things . . .

* The Wish therefore expressed overleaf[1] must be considered as a mere flying thought shot out by the mood & feeling of the moment, a sort of conversational Flying Fish that dropt as soon as the moisture of the Fins had evaporated.—This ¶ph. alone should be considered as Luther's genuine Opinion.

78 pp 337–9 | "Of the Council of Nice"

The Council of *Nice*, held after the Apostle's time, (said *Luther*) was the very best and purest; but soon after in the time of the Emperor *Constantine*, it was weakned by the *Arrians*; *for at that time, out of dissembling hearts they craftily subscribed, that they concurred in one opinion with the true and upright Catholick Teachers, which in truth was nothing so . . .

* What Arius himself meant, I do not know: what the modern Arians teach, I utterly condemn;[1] but the[a] great Council of Ariminum was either

[a] For "but that the"

76[1] An attempt to unite the German and Swiss reformers at the Colloquy of Marburg in 1529 foundered over the doctrine of the Eucharist when Zwingli, seconded by John Oecolampadius (1482–1531), rejected the Lutheran doctrine of consubstantiation. A note of Jun 1820 (*CN* III 3847 f 125) expresses C's dissatisfaction with both Lutheran and Zwinglian views.

76[2] In these pages, Luther defends infant baptism against the Anabaptists by such arguments as that Christ's injunction to the disciples to teach and baptise all nations included no restriction as to age (p 251). He sums up thus (p 254): "If God did not accept of the baptizing of Children, then (said *Luther*) Hee would not give unto them so much as a piece of the holy Ghost. To conclude, there could not have been one Christian Creature upon the face of the Earth in so long a time heretofore to this present daie." Cf **8** above.

77[1] **78** textus.

78[1] The First Council of Nicaea (325)

Arian or heretical, I could never discover—or descry any essential difference between its decisions and the Nicene—tho' I seem to find a serious difference of the Pseudo-athanasian Creed from both.[2] If there be a difference between the Councils of Nice and Ariminum, it perhaps consists in this: that the Nicene was more anxious to assert the equal divinity in the Filial Subordination, the Ariminian to maintain the filial subordination in the equal divinity.[3] In both there are three Self-subsistent, and only one self-originated—which is the substance of the Idea of the Trinity, as faithfully worded as is compatible with the necessari̶l̶yy inadequacy of *Words* to the expression of *Ideas*—i.e. Spiritual Truths that can only be spiritually discerned.[4]

S. T. Coleridge   18[a]August 1826—

79   pp 347–9 | Ch 28 *Of Imperial Diets* "Of the strength and profit of the confession and apologie of Augspurg"

* But (said *Luther*) wee brought with us a strong and mightie King, a King above all Emperors and Kings, namely, Christ Jesus the powerful word of God. Then all the Papists cried out, and said, O, it is insufferable, that so smal and sillie a heap should set themselvs against the Imperial power.

Luther every where identifies the Living Word of God with the Written Word; and rages against Bullinger, who contended that the latter w̶a̶s̶ is the Word of God only as far as and for whom it is the Vehicle of the

[a] Or perhaps "10th"

met chiefly to deal with the Arian denial of the true divinity of Christ. By "modern Arians" C probably means the Unitarians, earnestly regretting as always his own early Unitarian phase.

78[2]   C's views here reflect his concern with the defence of the doctrine of the Trinity. With regard to the essentially anti-Arian character of the Council of Ariminum (359) and its reinforcement of the conclusions of Nicaea, he shares the opinion of Daniel Waterland, whose book *The Importance of the Doctrine of the Holy Trinity Asserted, in Reply to Some Late Pamphlets* (2nd ed 1734) 330–3 may be a source of information here: cf *CN* III 3968. Another possible source is Socrates Scholasticus, to whose history of the Church C refers in JURIEU **3**, in a similar context: see n 3 below. Athanasius had been a leader of the

anti-Arian party at Nicaea, but the traditional attribution to him of the Athanasian Creed was disproved by the Dutch theologian G. J. Voss in 1642, whence C's habitual "Pseudo-Athanasian": cf BÖHME **33** n 1, *TT* 8 Jul 1827.

78[3]   This appears to be C's own conclusion, based on a study of documents which he could have found collected in *The Ecclesiastical History of Socrates Scholasticus*, a continuation of Eusebius pub in e.g. *The History of the Church* (Cambridge 1683) 199–394, where accounts of the councils of Nicaea and Ariminum appear on pp 215–27 and 271–5 respectively; or in Denis Petau *Dogmata theologica* (Antwerp 1700) II 40–2. For Petau, see **80** n 4 below.

78[4]   C repeated this definition in a note of later date, **40** above.

former.[1] To this Luther replies—My Voice, the vehicle of my Words, does not cease to be my voice because it is ignorantly or maliciously misunderstood. Yea (might Bullinger have rejoined) the instance were applicable and the argument valid, if we were previously assured, that all and every part of the O. and N. Testament is the Voice of the Divine Word. But except by the Spirit, whence are we to ascertain this?

Not from the Books themselves: for no one of them makes this pretension for itself, and the two or three Texts, which seem to assert it, refer only to the Law and the Prophets & no where enumerate the books that ~~are~~ were given by inspiration/ and how obscure the history of the formation of the Canon, and how great difference of Opinion respecting different Parts, what Scholar is ignorant of?

80 pp 349–51 | Ch 29 *Of the Books of the Fathers of the Church* ''That the Fathers of the Church . . . are not to bee valued for disputing''

Patres, quanquam saepe errant, tamen venerandi propter testimonium fidei [Although they are often wrong, the Fathers are to be revered for their witness of faith]. Wee honor *Jerom, Gregorie,* and others (said *Luther*) becaus in their writings wee feel, that they believed in Christ as wee do, like as the Christian Church from the beginning of the world hath had our Faith.

I am nearly if not wholly of Luther's mind respecting the works of the Fathers—those which appear to me of any value are valuable chiefly for those articles of Christum Faith which are, as it were, Ante Christum Jesum,[1] viz. the Trinity, and the *primal* Incarnation spoken of by John, Ch. I. v. 10.[2] But in the main I should go even farther than Luther: for I can not conceive any thing more likely than that a young man of strong and active intellect, who has no fears or suffers no fears of worldly Prudence to cry, Halt! to him in his career of Consequential Logic, and who has been innutritus et juratus in the Grotio-Paleyian Scheme of Christian Evidence,[3] and who ~~consi~~ has been taught (by ~~all~~ the men and books

79[1] Johann Heinrich Bullinger (1504–75) was a younger Swiss reformer greatly influenced by Luther but also involved in controversy with him (notably over the Eucharist). In describing the way Luther ''rages'' against him, C is probably thinking specifically of *Colloquia* pp 12–13, including the passage q as textus in **7** above.

80[1] ''Before Jesus Christ''.

80[2] ''He was in the world, and the world was made by him, and the world knew him not.''

80[3] The Latin means ''brought up in [probably deliberately with the punning second meaning 'without nourishment'] and sworn to''. Opposition to defences of the Christian faith based upon such external evidence as miracles is a recurrent theme with C, who often refers to Grotius as the founder of the tradition and to Paley as a popular contemporary spokesman of it: e.g. *CL* II 1189; *CN* II 2640; BAHRDT **2** n 2; BLANCO WHITE *Evidence* **1** n 1; *AR* (1825) 335–40, 397. His own projected

which he has ⟨been⟩ bred up to regard as authorities) to consider all inward Experiences as fanatical delusions—I say, I can scarcely conceive such a young man to make a serious study of the Fathers of the 4 or 5 first Centuries without becoming either a Roman Catholic or a Deist—. Let him only read Petavius and the different ⟨patristic and Eccl.-Historical⟩ Tracts and Volumes of Semler[4] & have no better Philosophy than that of Locke, no better Theology than that of Arminius and Bishop Taylor (Jeremy)[5]—and I should tremble for his Belief! Yet why tremble for a Belief which is the very Antipode of Faith? Better for such a mind to precipitate on to the utmost goal—for then perhaps he may in the repose of intellectual activity feel the nothingness of his prize or the *wretchedness* of it—then, perhaps, the inward yearning after a Religion may make him ask—Have I not mistaken the road at the Outset? Am I SURE, that the Reformers, Luther &c, collectively, were Fanatics?   S. T. C.

81   p 349 | "Of the book of *Cyprian*"

Luther reading *Cyprian, de singularitate Clericorum* (how spiritual persons should separate themselvs and abstain from women, and handling such foolish and childish things in his book) said, I doubt (said *Luther*) whether this bee *Cyprian*'s book or no . . .

Plain from this, that Luther was no great Patrician.[1] He was better employed.—

82   p 350

. . . the Holie Fathers said, in the fourth Petition in the Lords praier, wee praie not for corporal and temporal things, for it is against the sen-

---

Assertion of Religion was to be "Anti-Paleyo-Grotian" (*CL* v 134).

80[4] In the summer of 1810 C had referred to the work of Petavius (Denis Petau, 1583–1652) as "a sort of Scapula" to be consulted during the reading of patristic literature and the documents of Church history: *CN* III 3934. The work of reference that he had in mind was probably the six folio volumes of Petau's *Dogmata theologica* (1644–50), said to be the first attempt to treat the development of Christian doctrine from a historical point of view. C appears here to have more reservations about the value of the work, or perhaps simply a more highly developed sense of the limitations of a purely scholarly approach to re-

ligion. The prolific scholar and editor Johann Salamo Semler (1725–91), head of the theological faculty at the University of Halle and of interest to C as one of the early "neologic" divines in Germany (*CN* III 4399, 4401n), would have appeared in the same light.

80[5] See **47** n 2 above.

81[1] Many works attributed to St Cyprian (d 258) circulated for centuries before being rejected from the Cyprianic corpus. In prominent editions of his works before C's time, Erasmus admitted the *Libellus de singularitate clericorum* (1521) and John Fell rejected it (1682), but it was accepted in a later French ed (1718).

Gr. Trevethen sculp.

MARTINUS LUTHERUS ISLEBIUS THEOLOGUS VIXIT AN LXIII.
Obiit Islebii Anno 1546 Febr 18

Rome orbem domuit, Roman sibi Pap's subjecit ;
Viribus illa suis, fraudibus isto suis .
Quanto isto major Lutherus, major et illâ .
Totum illumq, una qui domuit calamo .

Rome tam'd the world: but Rome the Pope ore-aw'd:
The one by force, the other wrought by fraud :
Greater then both was learned Luther, when
Both this and that hee conquer'd with his pen .

ctor Martin Luther was born at Isleben, in ý Countie of Mansfield, in the Yeare 1483 the

2. Engraved portrait of Martin Luther from *Colloquia mensalia* (1652).
See LUTHER *Colloquia* **83** and n 4
Thomas Fisher Rare Book Library, University of Toronto; reproduced by kind permission

tence of Christ, where hee saith, *Take no care what yee shall eat,* &c. As though that commandment did not hinder the carping and ~~earing~~ for the daily bread.

/\ *anxiety*. Sit tibi *curæ*, non solicitudini, panis quotid.[1]

83   p 351 | "Of the four pillars of the Church [Ambrose, Jerome, Augustine, and Gregory]"

Even so was it with *Ambrose*, hee wrote indeed well and purely, was more serious in writing then *Austin*, who was amiable and milde. . . . *Fulgentius* is the best Poët, and far above *Horace*, both with sentences, fair speeches, and good actions, hee is well worthy to bee ranked and numbred with and among the Poëts.

Der Teufel![1] Surely the words should be reversed. Austin's mildness, he, the crudelis pater infantum!![2] And the super-horatian poetic Effulgence of Master *Foolgentius! O† Swan! Swan! thy critical Cygnets are but Goslings!

* I have, however, since I wrote this note, heard Mr J. H. Frere speak highly of Fulgentius.[3]

† Luther a german word for Swan.[4]

82[1] "Let your daily bread be a matter of care, not of anxiety." In denying that there is any contradiction between Matt 6.11 and Matt 6.25, C restores the distinction implicit in both the Latin and English versions of the latter.

83[1] "The Devil!"

83[2] "A cruel father to children": a variant of an epithet traditionally applied to Augustine, as e.g. Jeremy Taylor explains: ". . . it having been affirmed by S. *Austin*, that Infants dying unbaptized are damn'd, he is deservedly called Durus pater Infantum ['a hard father to children'], and generally forsaken by all sober men of the later ages . . .": "An answer to a Letter . . . concerning the Chapter on Original Sin, in the 'Unum Necessarium' " in ΣΥΜΒΟΛΟΝ ΘΕΟΛΟΓΙΚΟΝ. *Or, a Collection of Polemicall Discourses* (3rd ed 1674) 897. C uses the "durus" version in *AR* (1825) 368.

83[3] C thought highly of the literary taste of J. H. Frere, diplomat, poet, translator of Aristophanes, and an encouraging friend to C during the Highgate years: cf OMNIANA 24 n 1. For the dating of this postscript, it is worth noting that Frere made his home in Malta after 1820 but returned to England for a year in Sept 1825. Fulgentius (468–533) is not usually distinguished among the Fathers of the Church either for originality of doctrine or beauty of style.

83[4] "Luther" is not a German word for "swan", but C has been misled by an editor's collection of prophecies about Luther in *Colloquia* 534: "And specially (concerning *Luther*, and touching his powerful teaching and preaching) *John Huss* prophecied in the year 1415. (as hee was to be burned at Costnitz) and said, This daie yee rost a Goos, but one hundred years hence, yee shall hear a Swan sing, (*Huss* is called a Goos, and *Luther* a Swan) him yee shall not bee able to rost nor overcom . . .". The Bohemian reformer Huss did indeed pun on his own name, which in Czech means "goose", and Luther more than once told the story of his prophecy; C might have noticed it, for example, in his commentary on the Book of Daniel (Leipzig ed pt 12 p 35). The portrait of Luther at the beginning of the *Colloquia* prominently features a goose, as do a few of the earlier images of

84   pp 352–3 | "Of Luther's esteeming the Fathers and teachers of the Church"

Although it beseemeth not mee (said *Luther*) to censure the holie Fathers
. . . yet notwithstanding the more I read their Books, the more I finde
my self offended; for they were but men, and (to speak the truth) their
Reputes and Authorities did undervalue and suppress the Books and
writings of the sacred Apostles of Christ.

We doubtless find in the writings of the Fathers of the second Century,
and still more strongly those of the third, passages concerning the Scrip-
tures that *seem* to say the same as we Protestants now do—But then we
find the very same phrases used of writings not Apostolic, ~~an~~ or with no
other difference than the greater *name* of the Authors would naturally
produce—just as a Platonist would speak of Speusippus's books, were
they extant, compared with later Teachers of Platonism—He was Plato's
Nephew—had seen Plato—was his appointed Successor &c[1]—But in
inspiration the ~~two~~ early Christians made no *generic* difference, let
Lardner say what he will.[2] Can he disprove that it was declared *heretical*
by the Church in the Second Century to believe the written words of a
dead Apostle in opposition to the words of a living Bishop, seeing that
the same Spirit, which guided the Apostles, dwells in and guides the
Bishops of the Church?—This is certain—the later the age of the Writer,
the stronger the expression of *comparative* Superiority of the Scrip-
tures—the earlier on the other hand, the more we hear of the symbolum,
regula Fidei[3] = the Creed.

Luther recorded in R. W. Scribner *For the Sake of Simple Folk: Popular Propaganda for the German Reformation* (Cambridge 1981) e.g. p 220. See Plate 2.

This note, like the punning "Foolgentius" above, is a reminder that the book C was annotating belonged to Charles Lamb.

84[1] Cf *P Lects* Lect 5 (1949) 174–5. The principal source of C's information about Speusippus appears to have been Tennemann *Geschichte der Philosophie* (Leipzig 1798–1817) III 8–10.

84[2] C's early reading of Nathaniel Lardner was associated with his Unitarianism, and he praised him highly—though minute criticism followed his praise—in a letter to a Unitarian friend in 1802: *CL* II 821–4. Later he was to write of him as a dull though learned man: *CL* VI 894. The assumption that the earliest records were the most authoritative and the most truly in-

spired is the foundation of Lardner's best-known work, as its full title shows—*The Credibility of the Gospel History, or, the Principal Facts of the New Testament Confirmed by Passages of Ancient Authors Who Were Contemporary with Our Saviour, or His Apostles, or Lived near Their Time.* Lardner also makes explicit claims, e.g., citing the opinion of Tertullian, "The apostles have truly preached and written the doctrine they received from Christ. The apostolical men have also faithfully published in writing what they received from the apostles. All the gospels are therefore supported by the authority of apostles, yea, of Jesus Christ": *Works* (1788) II 260.

84[3] These are terms traditionally applied to the Apostles' Creed: "the symbol, the rule of faith". For *symbolum* esp see **90** below.

85 p 357 | Ch 31 *Of the Books of the Old and New Testaments* "Of Solomon's proverbs"

The third Book of *Hester* (said *Luther*) I bid adieu: those things which *Hester* dreamed of in the fourth book are fair and prettie knacks; as, *The Wine is strong, The King is stronger, Women strongest of all*; but the Truth is stronger then all these.

Ezra.[1]

86 p 362 | Ch 32 *Of Patriarchs and Prophets* "Of the Prophet Jonas"

This Historie of the Prophet *Jonas* is so great, that it is almost incredible; yea, it soundeth more strange then any of the Poët's Fables; and (said *Luther*) if it stood not in the Bible, I should take it for a lie . . .

It is quite wonderful that Luther who could see so plainly that Judith was an Allegoric Poem should ~~not~~ have been blind to the Book of Jonas being an Apologue, in which Jonas means the Israelitish Nation!—[1]

87 p 364 | "Of Adam"

For they entred into the Garden about the hour at noon-daie, and having appetites to eat, shee took delight in the Apple, * then, about two of the clock (according to our accompt) was the fall.

* Milton has adopted this Notion in the Par. Lost—not improbably from this book[1]

88 p 365 | "That David was an eloquent man"

Neither *Cicero*, *Virgil*, nor *Demosthenes* are to bee compared with *David* for eloquence, as wee see in the 119 *Psalm*, where hee divideth one sens and meaning into two and twentie sorts, onely that the words do differ, hee had a great gift, and was highly favored of God. . . . * *Moses* and *David* were the two highest Prophets, what *Isaiah* had, the same hee took out of *David*, and so did other Prophets likewise. Wee (said *Luther*) are sillie Scholars in comparison of them, wee have indeed a Spirit, but our Gifts are nothing so great.

* I have conjectured that the 119th Psalm might have been a form of

85[1] 1 Esdras 4.37–8 var. C is correcting the textual error of giving 3 Esther for 3 Ezra, the latter being the name by which the apocryphal 1 Esdras was known to Luther.

86[1] Luther's interpretation of the apocryphal Book of Judith as a work of imagination appears p 358. C refers to his own reading of the Book of Jonah as an "apo-logue", in which Jonah is the bigoted and rebellious representative of his nation, in *SM* (*CC*) 59, *AR* (1825) 255n, and BÖHME **180**.

87[1] *Paradise Lost* IX 739, "Meanwhile the hour of noon drew on." Modern commentary on Milton has not yet linked this passage with Luther.

Ordination—in which a series of Candidates in the open temple made their prayer & profession—before they went to the several Synagogues in the Country.[1]

89   p 365 | "Of the punishment of Shimei"

Som are of opinion (said *Luther*) that *David* dealt not well and uprightly, in that upon his death-bed hee commanded *Solomon* his Son to punish *Shimei*, who cursed and threw dirt at him in his flight before *Absalom*. But (said *Luther*) I saie, hee did well and right thereon; for the Office of a Magistrate is to punish the guiltie and wicked Malefactors. Hee made a vow, indeed, not to punish him, but that is to bee understood, so long as *David* lived.

O Luther! Luther! Ask your own heart! if this is not *Jesuit* Morality!

90   p 367 | Ch 33 *Of the Apostles and Disciples of Christ* "By whom the Childrens Creed was made"

I believ (said *Luther*) The words of our Christian Belief were in such sort ordained by the Apostles, who were together *and made this sweet *Symbolum* so briefly and comfortable.

*   It is difficult not to regret that Luther had so superficial a knowlege of ecclesiastic Antiquities—ex. gr. his belief in this fable of the Creed being a picnic contribution of the 12 Apostles, each giving one sentence as a Symbolum—whereas nothing is more certain than that it was the gradual Product of 3 or 4 Centuries.—[1]

91   pp 369–70 | Ch 34 *Of Angels* "What an angel is"

An Angel (said *Luther*) is a spiritual Creature created by God (without a bodie) for the service of Christendom, specially in the Office of the Church.

What did Luther mean by a Body?[1] For to me the word seemeth capable of two senses, universal and special. First, a Form indicating to A, B, C, &c &c the existence and finiteness of some one other Being demonstrativè—Hic—et disjunctivè—Hic et *non* ille.[2] In this sense God alone

88[1] No written elaboration of this conjecture by C is known.

90[1] A false etymology—tracing the Latin *symbolum* to the Greek συμβολή ("contribution") instead of to σύμβολον ("sign")—led to the legend recorded by Tyrannius Rufinus in 404 in his commentary on the Apostles' Creed. In English, "symbol" or "symbolum" retained for centuries the secondary meaning of a contribution (properly to a feast or picnic) or share or portion. It is now obsolete and was probably archaic in C's time, although Lamb uses it.

91[1] See **40** n 2 above.

91[2] "Demonstratively—*Here*—and disjunctively—Here and *not* there".

can be without body. Second, that which is not merely *Hic* distinctivè—but *divisivè*[3]—yea, a product divisible from the producent as a Snake from its Skin—a precipitate and death of living Power—and in this sense the Body is proper to *Mortality*, and to be denied of Spirits made perfect as well as of the Spirits that never fell from perfection, and perhaps of those who fell below Mortality, namely, the Devils.

But I am inclined to hold, that the Devil has no one body, nay, no body of his own; but ceaselessly usurps or counterfeits bodies—for he is an everlasting Liar[4]—yea, the Lie which is the colored Shadow of the substance that intercepts the Truth.—

92   p 370 | ''Of good and evil angels''

Many Divels are in woods, in waters, in wildernesses, and in dark poolie places, ready to hurt and prejudice people; som (said *Luther*) are also in the thick black clouds, which do caus hail, lightnings and thunderings, do poison the air, the pastures and grounds: when these things happen, then the Philosophers and Physicians do saie, It is natural, they ascribe it to the Planets, and shew I know not what reasons for such misfortunes and plagues as proceed and fall thereout.*

> *   ''The Angel's like a Flea
>   The Divels are a Bore''—
> No matter for that! quoth S. T. C.
> I love him the better *therefore*!

Yes, heroic Swan! I love thee even when thou gabblest like a Goose! *Thy* Geese helped to save the Capitol.[1]

93   p 371 | ''That the Angels are Lords Protectors''

Concerning Angels (said *Luther*) . . . I do verily believ, that the Angels already are up in Arms. . . . For (said hee) the daie of Judgment draweth near, and the Angels prepare themselvs for the Fight and Combate, and that within the space of a few hundred years they will strike down both Turk and Pope into the Bottomless pit of Hell.

—Yea! two or three more such Angels, as thyself, Martin Luther! and thy prediction would be, or perhaps have been, accomplished!

                                                     S. T. C.

91[3] ''*Here* distinctively—but *divisive-ly*''.
91[4] Cf John 8.44.
92[1] C plays with the notion that ''Luther'' means ''swan'', as in **83** above. Ac-cording to legend, sacred geese gave warning and saved the Capitol in Rome from an invasion by the Gauls.
The verses are pub *PW* (EHC) II 1009 and are alluded to in **7** above.

94 p 388 | Ch 35 *Of the Divel and His Works* "How wee ought to carrie our selvs in time of tribulation"

Cogitations of the Understanding do produce no Melancholie, but the cogitations of the Will caus sadness; as, when one is grieved at a thing; or when one doth sigh and complain, those are melancholie and sad cogitations, but the *understanding is not melancholie.

* Even in Luther's lowest Imbecillities ~~th~~ what gleams of vigorous good Sense! Had he understood the nature and symptoms of Indigestion, together with the detail of Subjective Seeing and Hearing, and the existence of mid-states of the Brain between Sleeping and Waking, Luther would have been a greater Philosopher; but would he have been so great a Hero?*a* I doubt it. Praised be God whose mercy is over all his works, who bringeth good out of Evil, and manifesteth his wisdom even in the follies of his Servants, his Strength in their Weakness![1]

95 p 389

Hee [the Devil] oftentimes tribulateth mee touching Praying; hee striketh cogitations into my brest, as did I neglect to praie diligently. . . . My earnest advice is (said *Luther*), that no man contemn written or described Praiers; for whoso praieth a Psalm, the same shall bee made throughly warm.

N.B. Expertus credo—[1]   S. T. C.   19 Aug. 1826.*

* PS. I have learnt to interpret for myself the imprecatory verses of the Psalms of my inward & spiritual Enemies, the old Adam, and all his corrupt Menials—& thus I am no longer as I used to be stopped or scandalized by such passages, as vindictive and anti-christian.

96 p 389 | Continuing **95** textus

The Divel (said *Luther*) oftentimes objected and argued against mee the whole caus which (through God's Grace) I lead; hee objecteth also against Christ; But better it were that the Temple brake in pieces, then that Christ should therein remain obscure and hid.

Sublime!

97 p 389 | "Of the whale the Divel"

In *Job* are two Chapters concerning *Behemoth* the Whale, that by reason

---

a Word written not in capitals, but in large letters

94[1] C copied the textus here into a note-book: *CN* IV 4594 f 36.   **95**[1] "I have tried it and I believe it": after Virgil *Aeneid* 11.283.

of him no man is in safetie. . . . These are colored words (said *Luther*) and figures whereby the Divel is signified and shewed. The Whale careth for no Ship, neither doth *Behemoth*: hee careth for no Art, for no wisdom nor power.

A slight mistake of Brother Martin! the Behemoth of Job is beyond Doubt neither Whale nor Devil; but the Hippopotamus, who is indeed as ugly as the Devil, and will occasionally play the Devil among the Rice-grounds. But tho' in this respect a Devil of a Fellow, yet on the whole is too honest a Monster to be a Fellow of Devils.

Vindiciæ Behemoticæ.[1]

98   pp 390–1 | Ch 36 *Of Witchcraft* "Of the power of witchcraft against Christians"

Certain it is (said *Luther*) that good and godlie Christians may bee bewitched; For our souls are subject to lies, but the same shall bee delivered. Nevertheless, the bodies must bee subject to the murthering stabs of the Divel.

It often presses on my mind as a weighty Argument in proof of at least a negative Inspiration, of an especial restraining Grace in the Composition of the Canonical Books, that tho' the Writers individually did (the greater number at least) most probably believe in the objective reality of Witchcraft, yet no such direct Assertions as these of Luther's, which would with the vast majority of Christians have raised it into an article of Faith, are to be found in either Testament. That the Ob, and Obim, of Moses are no authorities for this absurd Superstition, has been unanswerably shewn by Webster.[1]

98A   p 397 | Ch 37 *Of Tribulation and Temptation* "That heavie cogitations do sicken the bodie"

Heavie thoughts (said *Luther*) do inforce rhumes, when the soul is busied with grievous cogitations, and the heart troubled therewith, then the bodie must partake of the same. *Austine* said well, *Anima plus est ubi amat, quam ubi animus* [The soul is where it loves, not where it animates]. When cares, heavie cogitations, sorrows and passions do ex-

97[1] Luther uses "behemoth", "leviathan", and "whale" interchangeably as emblems of the Devil. C identified "leviathan" as the crocodile and "behemoth" as the hippopotamus (BIBLE COPY B 29 n 1), and he here playfully proposes "the case for Behemoth".

98[1] In 1819 C annotated a copy of John Webster *The Displaying of Supposed Witchcraft* (1677), and in his commendation of the work in *TT* 1 May 1823 47 cites the text he probably has in mind here, arguing after Webster (pp 120–2, 127–9) that in 1 Sam 28 the "Witch" of Endor is a mistranslation of the Hebrew *Ob*, "bladder". There are further comments on Luther's views about witchcraft in *CN* IV 4594.

ceed, then they weaken the bodie, which without the soul, is dead, or like a hors without one to rule it.

N B.

99   p 398 | "That every one hath his particular tribulations"

To conclude (said *Luther*) I never yet knew a troubled and perplexed man, that was right in his own wits.

A sound Observation of great practical utility. E. I.[1] should be aware of this in dealing with conscience-troubled (but in fact, fancy-vexed) women.

100   p 398 | "Of Luther's wish and desire in his sickness"

How willingly would I bee instructed of St *Paul* . . . what manner of tribulation his was at that time, it was not a Thorn in the flesh touching the inchast love hee bare towards *Tecla* (as the Papists dream)* O no! (said *Luther*) it was no sin that so pierced him, I know not what it was . . .

* I should like to know, how high up this strange ~~Tradition~~ Legend can be traced? The other Tradition has a less legendary character—viz. that St Paul was subject to epileptic Fits. The phrase "Thorn in the Flesh" is scarcely reconcilable with Luther's hypothesis—otherwise than as doubts of the *objectivity* of his Vision and of his after-revelations may have^a consequences of the disease—whatever that might be.[1]

S. T. C.

101   p 399 | "To have Patience in suffering"

Our Lord God doth like a Printer, who setteth the Letters backwards;

^{a} A slip for "have been"?

99[1] Edward Irving, a fashionable preacher in London for several years after his arrival from Scotland in 1822, was flatteringly attentive to C both in person and in print. C annotated three of his works: *For Missionaries* (1825), *Sermons* (1828), and the translation of LACUNZA. He began to have misgivings about Irving's interpretation of the apocalypse in 1826 (*CL* VI 557) and came eventually to doubt his sanity, but he paid tribute to his Luther-like spirit as late as 1830 in *C&S* (*CC*) 140n–143n.

100[1] In 2 Cor 12 Paul describes his "visions and revelations of the Lord" but adds that he was prevented from pride in these revelations by "a thorn in the flesh, the messenger of Satan to buffet me" (v 7). C believes the phrase to be too explicitly physical to justify Luther's conjecture of a spiritual malaise. The entry alludes to two other theories: the one Luther attributes (on what foundation is not known) to the Roman Catholic Church, that Paul was sexually attracted to his pupil Thecla, a legendary figure known only through the apocryphal *Acts of Paul and Thecla*; and the epilepsy hypothesis that is still dominant in interpretations of the passage.

wee see and feel well his Setting, but wee shall see the Print yonder, in the life to com: In the mean time wee must have patience.

a beautiful Simile! Add that even in this life the Lives, especially the Auto-biographies of eminent Servants of Christ, are the Looking-glass or Mirror, which reversing the types renders them legible to us.—

102 p 403 | "Of Luther's comfort which hee wrote and sent to Philip Melancthon, who laie very sick"

His lines were these following:

Indignus sum, sed dignus fui,

> *Creäri à Deo, Creätore meo.*
> *Doceri de filio Dei & spiritu sancto.*
> *Cui ministerium verbi credatur.*
> *Qui in tantis malis versarer.*
> *Cui praeciperentur ista credere.*
> *Cui sub aeternae irae maledictione interminaretur, nè ullo modo de his dubitarem. . . .*

That is,
To be

Although I am unworthie, yet nevertheless I have been was[a] worthie,

> ~~First, In that I am~~ Creäted of God my Creätor
> ~~Second, In that I am~~ taught of his Son and the Holie Ghost.
> ~~Third, In that I am~~ trusted with the Office of Preaching.
> ~~Fourth, In that I am~~ in such Tribulations.
> ~~Fifth, In beeing~~ earnestly commanded to believ the same.
> ~~Sixth, In that I am~~ sorely threatned (under pain of God's Wrath, Displeasure, and everlasting Damnation) in any case not to make doubt thereof.

This translation does not give the true sense of the Latin. The dignus fui has *here* the sense of dignuṡm me Deus habuit, or dignabar (*voce passivâ*) a Deo.[1] See Herberts Temple p. 107. "Sweetest Saviour! &c"[2]

---

[a] C has written "was" in above "have been"

102[1] "Dignus fui" means "I have been worthy" or "I was worthy", with the possible further implication "and I am no longer so". But C finds a "true sense" beyond this literal meaning: "God has held me to be worthy" or "I was considered worthy (*in the passive voice*) by God."

102[2] C recalls the beginning of the poem entitled "Dialogue": "Sweetest Saviour, if my soul/ Were but worth the having . . .": *The Temple* (1709) 107.

103   p 404 | "How those are to bee comforted that are in tribulation concerning faith"

Secondly, the chiefest Physick for that diseas (but very hard and difficult it is to bee don) is, that they firmly hold, such cogitations not to bee theirs, but that most sure and certain they com of the Divel, therefore they must use the highest diligence to turn their hearts upon other thoughts, and beat out such cogitations . . .

More and more I understand the immense difference between the faith-article of THE *Devil* (τοῦ Πονηροῦ)[1] and the Superstitious fancy of *Devils*—Animus Objectivus Magnetista et dominationem in τον Ειμι affectans—ουτος το μεγα Οργανον Διαβολου ὑπάρχει[2]

104   p 431 | Ch 44 *Luther's discours of Seducers and Sectaries that opposed him* "Of Luther's censure of Erasmus Roterodamus"

I truly advise all those (said *Luther*) who earnestly do affect the honor of Christ and the Gospel, that they would bee enemies to *Erasmus Roterodamus*, for hee is a devaster of Religion. Do but read onely his Dialogue *De Peregrinatione*, where you will see how hee derideth and flowteth the whole Religion/ . . .

Religion here means the vows and habits of the Religious or bound ~~by~~ to a particular Life—the Monks, Friars, Nuns, in short, the Regulars in contradistinction from the Laity and the Secular Clergy.[1]

105   p 432

* *Erasmus* can do nothing but cavil and flout, hee cannot confute. If (said *Luther*) I were a Papist, so would I easily overcom and beat him. For although hee flouteth the Pope with his Ceremonies, yet hee neither hath confuted nor overcom him; no enemie is beaten nor overcom with mocking, jeering and flouting.

* most true; but it is an excellent Pioneer and an excellent Corps of Reserve/ Cavalry for pursuit, and for clearing the field of Battle—And in ~~thise~~ first use Luther was greatly obliged to Erasmus—but such utter Unlikes can not but end in Dislikes: & so it proved twixt Erasmus &

103[1] "The Devil" not in NT but in patristic usage.

103[2] "A Spirit Objective, Magnetist, and aiming at mastery over the I Am—this constitutes the great Instrument of the Devil."

104[1] One of Erasmus's popular colloquies, "Peregrinatio religionis ergo", consisting of a dialogue between a pilgrim and one who stayed at home attending to his household, exposes the false claims made about shrines and pilgrimages. C's interpretation of the work as an attack upon the Roman Catholic establishment is a reasonable corrective to Luther's intemperate view of it.

Luther.[1] Erasmus (might the Protestants say) ~~attacked the Church~~ wished no good to the Church of Rome & still less to our party—It was with him *Rot her*! and Dam' us!

106 pp 442–3 | Ch 48 *Of Offences* "Of the offences which David erected"

David's example is full of offences, that so holie a man chosen of God, should fall into such great abominable sins and blasphemies; whenas before, hee was very fortunate and happie, of whom all the bordering Kingdoms were afraid, for God was with him.

If any part of the O. T. be typical, the whole Life and Character of David from his birth to his Death are eminently so. And accordingly the History of David & his Psalms which form a most interesting part of his History occupies as large a portion of the Old Testament as all the others. The Type is twofold—now of the Messiah, now of the Church, and of the Church in all its relations persecuted, victorious, backsliding, penitent.

N.B. I do not find David charged with any *Vices*: tho' with heavy Crimes. So with the Church. Vices destroy its essence—

107 p 442 | "Happie is hee, that is not offended at mee"

The same was a strange kinde of offence (said *Luther*) that the world was offended at him who raised the dead, who made the blinde to see, and the deaf to hear &c.

Our Lord alluded to the verse that immediately follows and compleats his quotation from Isaiah—I, Jehovah, will come & do this.[1] That he implicitly declared himself the Jehovah-Word[2]—this was the Offence.

108 p 443 | Ch 49 *Of the True Service of God* "Of an argument touching the service of God"

God will (may one saie) that wee should serv him free-willingly, but hee that serveth God out of fear of punishment and of hell, or out of a hope and love of recompence, the same serveth and honoreth God not freely;

105[1] That Erasmus was a "pioneer" in the Reformation is typically C's view: cf *P Lects* Lect 10 (1949) 305, *Friend (CC)* I 129–34.

107[1] The text upon which both Luther and C comment is Matt 11.5–6: "The blind receive their sight, and the lame walk, the lepers are cleansed, and the deaf hear, the dead are raised up, and the poor have the gospel preached to them. And blessed is he, whosoever shall not be offended in me." C accounts for the "offence" by referring to the prophecy in Isa 29.18–19, which foretells the same events as acts of God: "Therefore, behold, I will proceed to do a marvellous work among this people . . ." (Isa 29.14).

107[2] See JAHN *Appendix* 1 n 2.

therefore such a one serveth God not uprightly nor truly. *Answ.* This argument (said *Luther*) is Stoïcall, which the Block-Saints inferr, who reject the affections and inclinations of humane nature, and press here-upon, wee ought free-willingly to honor, to serv, to love and to fear God as the chiefest good onely, which is the prime end and final caus. . . . it hurteth him not, specially, if hee hath regard to God himself as the chie-fest and final caus, who giveth every thing *Gratìs*, for nothing, out of meer grace without our deserts.

A truly wise ¶ph. Pity, it was not expanded. God will accept our imper-fections, where their face is toward him, on the road to the glorious Liberty of the Gospel.

109 pp 446–7 | Ch 50 *Of Matrimonie* "That the most amiable companie and communion is among honest married people"

It is the highest grace and gift of God, to have an honest, a God-fearing houswifely consort, with whom a man may live peaceable, in whom hee may put in trust his wealth and whatsoever hee hath, yea his bodie and life, with whom hee getteth children. But God thrusteth many into the state of matrimonie before they bee aware and rightly bethink them-selves.*

* Alas! alas! this is the misery of it that so many wed and so few are christianly married! But even ⟨in⟩ this the analogy of Matrimony to the Religion of Christ holds good: for even such is the proportion of nominal to actual Christians—all *christened*, how few baptized!—But in true matrimony it is beautiful to consider, how peculiarly the marriage state harmonizes with the doctrine of Justification by free Grace thro' Faith alone. The little quarrels, the imperfections on both sides, the occasional frailties, yield to the one thought—there is Love at the bottom. If Sick-ness or other sorer Calamity visit me, how would the Love then blaze forth. The faults are there but they are not imputed/—The Prickles, the acrid rind, the bitterness or sourness, are transformed into the ripe Fruit—and, the foreknowlege of this gives the name and virtue of the ripe fruit to the fruit yet green on the Bough.

109A p 446 | "Next after Religion, Matrimonie is the principallest state"

* The state of matrimonie (said *Luther*) is the chiefest state in the world after Religion, but people (like the Beasts in the fields and the Dregs of the world) do shun and flie from the same, by reason of personal mis-haps, who while they intend to out-run the rain, do fall into the water. Wherefore go on with joie in the name of the Lord, and cast thy self

under the Cross, wee ought herein to have more regard to God's Command and Ordnance (for the sake of the Generation and bringing up of children) then to our untoward humors and cogitations, and when although this caus or reason were not, yet ought wee notwithstanding to consider, that it is a Physick against sin, and to resist in chastitie. I am angrie with the Lawyers (said *Luther*) who in every thing deal according to their Canons and Decrees in the strictest manner against their own consciences, they will not yield to God's Word, they maintain secret contracts against Natural, Divine and Emperial Laws, yet nevertheless they boast, that their Canons are upright. On the contrarie none should bee compelled to marrie, but it should bee free for every one, and left to their conscience, for bride-love may not bee pressed and forced.

110   p 447 | ''Of the causers and founders of matrimonie''

The causers and founders of matrimonie are chiefly God's Commandements, Institutions and Ordinances, it is a state instituted by God himself, visited by Christ in person, and presented with a glorious present, for God said, *it is not good that the man should bee alone*, therefore the wife should bee a help to the husband, to the end that humane Generation may bee encreased and children nurtured to God's honor, and to the profit of people and Countries, also ~~to shun whoring, and~~ to keep our bodies in sanctification., and mutual reverence; & [? could] and our Spirits in a state of Love and Tenderness; and our imaginations pure and tranquil. Matrimonie is well pleasing to God, for St *Paul* compareth the Church to a Spous or Bride and a Bridegroom. Therefore wee ought to take heed and beware, that in marrying wee esteem neither monie nor wealth nor great descents; ~~Nobilitie nor our leacherie~~ and so that the ⟨natural⟩ Desire should ~~originate in~~ be occasioned by our Love not ~~our~~ the imagined Love ~~from~~ originate in our Desire. In a word, matrimonic not only preserveth humane Generation, so that the same remaineth continually/; but it preserveth the generation *human*.

111   p 450 | ''Of secret contracts, how they were to bee punished''

In the *Synod* at *Leyptzik*, the Lawyers concluded, that secret contracters should bee punished with banishment, and bee disinherited. Whereupon (said *Luther*) I sent them word, that I would not allow thereof, it were too gross a proceeding. . . . But nevertheless I hold it fitting, that those which in such sort do secretly contract themselvs, ought sharply to bee reproved, yea also in som measure severely punished.

What a sweet union of prudence and kind nature! Scold them sharply, and perhaps let them smart a while for their indiscretion and disobedience/ and then kiss & make it up—remembering that young folks will be young folks & that Love has its own Law and Logic.

112 p 451 | "Touching the censure of the consistorie at Wittemberg, in a caus of matrimonie, where a husbandman got with childe the sister of his deceased married wife, and afterwards married her"

. . . the same marriage in this degree is not to bee suffered nor endured; therefore accordingly it is acknowledged void, and that those two persons bee separated the one from the other. Also by reason of their exercised leacherie, to terrifie others by their example, they shall bee laid in prison, and there remain certain weeks, and the begotten childe to bee brought up and maintained by the parents on both sides. And whereas the minister (without the advice and instruction of his lawful magistrate and spiritual superattendent) did permit that marriage in a prohibited degree, therefore hee shall also bee punished with eight daies imprisonment.

I look on this as a very doubtful case. Bp Jeremy Taylor justifies, nay, recommends such marriages. There is much & of much weight to be advanced on both sides.—If first Cousins may marry, *then* I should confidently decide, that a man may marry his Wife's Sister.[1] But as I do not approve of the former, neither dare I d give a positive opinion for the lawfulness of the latter.—Is it a mere whim?—But somehow or other I contemplate the man's marrying his deceased Wife's Sister with more tolerance than a Widow's marrying her Husband's Brother.

> S. T. C.
> 2̶0̶ 19 Aug. 1826.—

113 p 481 | Ch 59 *Of Allegories* "Of the insolent boldness of the sophists . . ."

The Presumption and boldness of the Sophists and School-Divines is a very ungodlie thing, which som of the Fathers also approved of and

---

112[1] The interpretation of Lev 18, which prohibits marriage within certain degrees of kinship, had been a recurrent matter of concern in the Church, although the Table of Kindred and Affinity in the BCP had been stable since the sixteenth century. In C's time the Church permitted marriage between cousins but did not allow a man to marry his deceased wife's sister; the latter connection was not in fact legal in England according to civil law until 1907. Jeremy Taylor discusses the prohibited degrees in *Ductor dubitantium or the Rule of Conscience in All Her General Measures* (1660) bk 2 ch 2 §§ 34–89, pp 229–42 "Of the Marriage of Cosen-Germans", in which he argues strongly in favour of permitting the marriage of first cousins. C's consistently austere views on the marriage of cousins were tried in 1826 when he discovered that his daughter was engaged to her cousin HNC (*CL* vi 589–91, 604): the marriage took place in 1829.

extolled; namely, of spiritual significations in the Holie Scripture, whereby shee is pitifully tattered and torn in pieces. . . . it is an Apish work in such sort to juggle with Holie Scripture: It is no otherwise then if I should discours of Physick in this manner: 1. The Fever is a sickness, *Rebarbara* is the physick. 2. The Fever signifieth the sins, *Rebarbara* is Jesus Christ. 3. The Fever is a fault and failing, *Rebarbara* is the strength against it. 4. The Fever signifieth Condemnation, *Rebarbara* the Resurrection. Who seeth not here (said *Luther*) that such significations are meerly juggling tricks? Even so and after the same manner are they deceived that saie, Children ought to bee Baptised again, becaus they had not Faith.

For the life of me I can not find the *Even so* in this sentence.—The Watchman cries, ~~past~~ Half past Three °clock—*Even so* and *after* the *same manner* the Great Cham of Tartary has a Carbuncle on his Nose!

114   p 483 | Ch 60 *Of the Legends of the Saints* "The Legends of St Christopher"

. . . *George* in the Greek tongue is called a <u>Builder</u>, that buildeth Countries and People with Justice and Righteousness . . .

A mistransl. for a Tiller or ⟨*Boor* from⟩ Bauer, Bauen/ the latter hath two senses, to build and to bring into cultivation.[1]

115   p 503 | Ch 70 *Of Astronomie and Astrologie* "How far wee ought to allow of astrologie"

And so long as Astronomie remaineth in her Circle whereunto God hath ordained her, so is shee a fair gift of God, but when shee will step out of her bounds, that is, when shee will Prophecie and speak of future things, how it will go with one, or what fortune and misfortune one shall have, (as the Astrologers use to saie) as then shee is not to bee justified. But *Chyromantiam* or Palmestrie, that is, to look in ones hands and to tell what shall happen, wee ought utterly to reject.

   True it is, the Sooth-saiers and Star-peepers are able to make known to an ungodly person, what death the same shall die, for the Divel knoweth the cogitations and enterprises of the ungodly . . .

Tho' the problem is of no difficult solution for reflecting minds, yet for the Reading Many it would be a serviceable Work, to bring together and

---

114[1] The error appears to have been Luther's and not the translator's. The name "George" is derived from the Greek γή, "earth"; although C's assumption that the translator had chosen the wrong one of the two possible meanings of "Bauer" is reasonable, the word in Aurifaber's German text is "Bauherr", which is unambiguously "a builder".

exemplify the Causes of the extreme and universal Credulity, that characterizes sundry periods of History (ex. gr. from A.D. 1400 to 1650)—and Credulity involves Lying and Delusion—for by a seeming paradox Liars are always credulous, tho' credulous persons are not always Liars. *Most often, tho'*.

116   p 503

. . . I am now advertised (said *Luther*) that a new Astrologer is risen, who presumeth to prove that the earth moveth and goeth about, not the Firmament the Sun, Moon nor the Stars, like as when one sitteth in a Coach or in a Ship and is moved, thinketh hee sitteth still and resteth, but the earth and the trees go, run and move themselvs. Therefore thus it goeth, when wee wean our selvs to our own foolish fancies and conceits. This foole will turn the whole Art of Astronomie upside-down, but the Scripture sheweth and teacheth him another Lesson, where *Josua* commanded the Sun to stand still, and not the earth. In the Stars (said *Luther*) is neither strength nor operation, they are but onely signs.

A similar but still more intolerant and contemptuous anathema of the Copernican System in Sir T. Brown, almost two centuries later than Luther.[1]

117   p 502[a] | **116** textus

It would be worth while to make a collection of the judgements of eminent men in their generation respecting the Copernican or Pythagorean Scheme. One Writer (I forget the name) inveighs against it as *Popery*, and a popish Stratagem to reconcile the minds of men to Transsubstantiation & the Mass.—For if we may contradict the evidence of our Senses in a matter of Natural Philosopher,[b] a fortiori, or much more may we be expected to do so in a matter of Faith.

---

[a] An afterthought written in the space at the end of Ch 69 at the foot of p 502, but clearly referring to **116** textus and ms note, on the facing p 503

[b] A slip for "Philosophy"

116[1] C often quotes Sir Thomas Browne's rejection of the Copernican system as madness, referring apparently to *Pseudodoxia epidemica* bk 1 ch 5 in *Works* (1658–9) i 13: *Logic* (*CC*) 148 and n 2.

Lost Book

"Luthers Samptliche Schrifften". 5 vols.

Not located; marginalia not recorded; title from *W Library*, identified as belonging to C. In a letter of 29 Dec 1826 and a notebook entry of Feb 1827 (*CL* VI 656, N17.174 f 100) C mentions his current reading of Luther's postils; on 21 May 1828 he refers to "my Remarks on the blank Leaf at the Beginning of Luther's Postills" (N37.77 f 66). If he read the postils in a volume of Luther's works from the set recorded as his in *W Library*, two editions are likely, but C's set must have been incomplete. The first, *Luthers Samptliche Schriften*, ed J. G. Walch, 24 pts (Halle 1740–50), has been associated with C since Hare supplied a reference from it for *BL* (1847) I 212n (cf *CN* I 385n, *BL—CC—*I 206n), but neither Hare nor SC suggested that C had used this particular edition. The second, ed C. F. Boerner, is entitled *Des theuren Mannes Gottes, D. Martin Luthers sämtliche . . . Schrifften und Wercke* (Leipzig 1729–40); it is a folio edition published in 23 pts, usually bound in 12 vols, and containing the postils as pts 13–14. A circumstance in favour of this edition is C's echoing of its title in LUTHER *Colloquia* 5, where he says, "du theure Mann Gottes, mein verehrter Luther!"

DAVID LYNDSAY
i.e. MARY DIANA DODDS
fl 1822

Dramas of the Ancient World. Edinburgh 1822. 8°. [Pseudonymous: the author, Mary Diana Dodds, took the name of a sixteenth-century Scottish poet.]

British Library C 126 h 10

Inscribed by C in pencil on p ⁻2: "E libris S. T. Coleridge". "S. T. C." label on title verso. John Duke Coleridge's monogram on p ⁻4. The pages of *The Plague of Darkness*, *Rizpah*, *Sardanapalus*, *The Destiny of Cain*, and *The Death of Cain* were still unopened in 1987, and *The Nereid's Love* unopened at pp 260–3, 266–71.

CONTENTS. 1–64 *The Deluge*; 65–90 *The Plague of Darkness*; 91–100 *The Last Plague*; 101–23 *Rizpah*; 125–76 *Sardanapalus*; 177–208 *The Destiny of Cain*; 209–56 *The Death of Cain*; 257–78 *The Nereid's Love*.

DATE. After mid-1822.

1   p 23 | *The Deluge*

FIRAOUN.   It hath been said
    Thou troublest our land, and hast been long
    A dreamer of like horrors, threat'ning men

troublĕ-ēst?ᵃ

2   p 24

NOAH.   To the God
  * Who rules, and is all things, think'st thou, Firaoun,
    Ought is impossible?

* Noah a Spinozist? This is something new.

3   p 57

CHASALIM.   MANKIND IS DEAD.—The waters have entomb'd*
    The last of human kind;—the mountain's top

ᵃ Written in the margin against line 2 of textus

782

Is cover'd;—on the summit of our tower,
We two, now watch alone!

* Smart work on my word! A score of Candles would scarcely have been snuffed out within the time!

4   p 57 | Continuing **3** textus

FIRAOUN.   Man,—thy wild words
            Will drive me to despair.

Sublimity of Bathos! A flatting-machine must have been employed.[1]

4[1] C refers sarcastically to the abrupt way in which, in this poem, all but two members of the human race have been eliminated. A flatting-machine or flatting-mill (C refers to it also in PAULUS **34** and **45**) was used to press gold or silver into thin sheets for minting; in Cowper's poem "The Flatting Mill" the machine is used to illustrate one of the functions of the poet.

GEORGE LYTTELTON, BARON LYTTELTON
1709–1773

The History of the Life of King Henry the Second, and of the Age in which he Lived, in Five Books: to which is prefixed, a history of the revolutions of England from the death of Edward the Confessor to the birth of Henry the Second. 3rd ed. Vol I (of 6). London 1769. 8°.

Not located; marginalia printed from MS TRANSCRIPT.

MS TRANSCRIPT. VCL BT 33, in the hand of SC.

DATE. Between 1804 and 1814, possibly 1807–9 (3 n 1).

COEDITOR. David V. Erdman.

1 I 1

The Kingdom of England, after having been harrassed by the invasions of the Danes, and subject successively to three kings of that nation, had been restored to the Anglo Saxons at the death of Hardicanute, by the election of Edward, surnamed the Confessor, one of the sons of King Ethelred by Emma of Normandy. This prince, who was fitter for a monastery than a throne, having reigned, under the direction of the great lords of his court, about four and twenty years, died without issue, in the year of our Lord one thousand and sixty six.

It sometimes happens that in works of great merit the first 3 or 4 pages are not only the worst of the whole work, but really very bad. So it is here. Let the reader be unassisted by any previous knowledge and I dare appeal to him whether the first leaf of this History is not almost inexplicable confusion, from the strange intermixture of the tenses.

2 I 10

The best expedient would have been, to have given the crown to Edgar, and made Harold protector;* but it was not then thought of; or at least we do not find that it was ever proposed.

* This which we know to be of great importance, & which therefore would be practicable, or rather what would follow of course, would to our ancestors have appeared at such a conjuncture a low shuffling about a name.[1]

2[1] Lyttelton's argument is that at the   death of Edward the Confessor in 1066

3 i 152–3

He did not enough consider, how much the design of detaching the clergy from any dependence upon their own sovereign, and from all ties to their country, was promoted by forcing them to a life of celibacy, but concurred with the see of Rome, and with Anselm, its minister, in imposing that yoke upon the English church, which till then had always refused it.

? whether Buonaparte really wishes the papal ordinance of the celibacy of the clergy to be retracted?[1] The present Pope is a pious good old man; but a mere monkish bigot at the same time.[2] It seems to me that Catholicism would gain far more than it would lose by giving up this point of discipline, which (they hold)*a* quite in the power of the Pope & dependent for its propriety on circumstances. I pray that it may not be abandoned: for should a milder and less war-enamoured Emperor succeed Napoleon, and the civic professions raise their heads again, the enforced celibacy of the Roman priesthood would infallibly multiply the number of converts to the Reformed in France among the Students of Theology. Indeed I question whether under a compleat toleration, and such a scanty provision for the established Faith as exists in France, the Catholic Religion could stand its ground, there being already three or four millions of Protestants in France only. The great obstacle at present is the general tendency to Socinianism among the Reformed Clergy in France.

4 i 177

Philip died not long afterwards, and, to expiate his sins, in the habit of a monk, which he took at the point of death; a very commodious method of renouncing the world when a man is just going out of it, and therefore frequently resorted to in those days by princes who had led wicked lives. Nay, so weak is the human mind, when loaded with guilt and fooled by superstition, that the same practice has continued in Roman-catholic countries even down to these times.

a The parentheses (in ms) may indicate words supplied by the transcriber

William of Normandy might have been appeased if his kinsman Edgar Atheling had been made King and Harold of Wessex been named Protector instead of King. C believes that succession by right of birth was less important in 1066 than it became later.

3[1] The revolutionary constitution of 1791 in France removed restrictions on the marriage of priests, and Pius vii (n 2 below) allowed marriages contracted during that period to be continued after the Concordat of 1802 that re-established the Roman Catholic Church in France. C's note must have been written while Napoleon was emperor (1804–14), and possibly before 1809, when the conflict between the emperor and the Pope led to the Pope's imprisonment. Such extensive notes are rare in C's books before 1807.

3[2] Pius vii (1740–1823, Pope from 1800); C cannot resist the pun on his name.

Aye, and to this very hour, at least in Palermo, few Nobles will die out of the Franciscan cowl, if they have wherewith to purchase it.[1] Yet perhaps a majority of these poor wretches have studied Voltaire, & from 20 to 40 or 50 years of age no small number are his converts. So little of permanent effect is produced by laughing a man out of his Faith promiscuously, without substituting any other.

5   I 187

For William, the son of Duke Robert, distinguished by the surname of Clito (used in that age by the Normans, as Atheling was by the Saxons, to denote a prince of the royal blood) had now attained to manhood . . .

? Is Clito taken from the Greek Κλεῖτος? as Atheling from Adel or Edel, which is possibly the same root with Αδρος, eminent in strength or vigour—tho' possibly, as nobleman was *Par* regis, a Peer, or Comes, a Count or Companion, & the highest were addressed as "my brother" by the Kings, as the others less related to royal blood are now cousins of the King, Adel might have come from Αδελφος—[1]

6   I 191

[Henry I of England had given over the son of the governor of one of his castles in France as a hostage; when the boy returned blinded to his father, Henry allowed the father to mutilate in a similar fashion *his* two hostages, the two daughters of Henry's own illegitimate daughter.] Ancient Rome would perhaps have admired him for this action, and the history of England has no other that comes up to the force of it: but, though the principle on which it was done demands veneration, and no ordinary mind could be capable of it, the deed raises horror; and one could wish, for Henry's honor, that he had found less direful methods to appease his injured servant, without inflicting on innocence pains that are only due to guilt, and in the persons of those whom the first and greatest of all laws, the law of nature, particularly obliged him to save and protect.

4[1] C lived in Sicily Aug–Nov 1804, and for part of that time—though records are scanty—in Palermo. His information may of course be hearsay.

5[1] C's note combines conventional etymological wisdom with fairly wild speculation. The titles "peer" and "count" are derived from the Latin *par*, "equal" (C says "*Equal* of the king"), and *comes*, "companion", respectively; the Saxon *atheling*, "of noble birth", is closely related to the German *edel*, "noble". C wishes, however, to trace the Anglo-Norman terms to Greek roots. As an epithet the Greek *kleitos* means "renowned", and as a name it is associated with Kleitos or Clitus, the close friend of Alexander the Great (who killed him in a state of drunkenness). C ignores the rough breathing on *hadros* in order to link it with "Adel or Edel", then changes his mind and offers *adelphos*, "brother", instead.

I can never conceive veneration compatible with horror. I venerate the principle of the elder Brutus, but so far from likewise feeling horror at the deed, I would (I trust) have done the same.[1] But *here* the principle is as false as the act was monstrous. It may be said "But Henry thought it right." Well! but I. who knows this? 2. and if so, who can say how far bad passions may not have influenced his reason in adopting the principle? an influence always to be suspected in glaring exorbitations of an erring conscience—and lastly, an Inquisitor's conscience prompts first to torture and then burn alive hundreds of women and children for mere words without meaning—by the utmost stretch of charity we may admit his principle as a *palliation* of his crime, but do we *venerate* it? This is not unworthy of notice, for much inquiry has been done to the morals of men by this rash confounding of actions: 1. by teaching a few Bigots to justify cruelty by the principle, and 2^{ndly} a thousand others to admit no regular guide but that of feeling, liking, and sympathy with the multitude—because, forsooth, we cannot act up to principle, for *principle*, forsooth, leads to such cruel unnatural deeds. In short, either the horror is unjust, and not necessarily arising out of a good and humane disposition, or (which is most often the case), the principle is as erroneous as its consequences are atrocious.

7 ɪ 228

It [the Anglo-Norman Constitution] had also this inherent and essential advantage, that the very service required of the military vassals necessarily put arms into the hands of almost all the considerable landholders. Nevertheless it was faulty in many points of great moment, and particularly in this, that the commons of England, till long after these days, were much overbalanced in property and power by the clergy and the nobles.

faulty not the right word. It was as good as the present, it being equally proportioned to the then relations of property and influence. We shall never think wisely if we do not distinguish the Government and the State = *status rerum in toto*.[1] The Government for such a State was good; but the State itself was imperfect and unripe. Lyttelton evidently *meant* what

---

6[1] The assassination of Julius Caesar was a controversial subject in C's period, and he expressed his position several times in print, notably in an essay in *The Friend* in which he refers to "the fervent admiration felt by the good and wise in all ages when they mention the name of Brutus": *Friend* (*CC*) ɪ 323.

7[1] The "state of things altogether" or "general state of affairs". C does not use this distinction in *C&S*, though he there points out that "state" may be used in a collective or limited sense, and that it should be distinguished both from "church" and "nation": *C&S* (*CC*) 22, 101*, 39–40.

I have here expressed; but lax words not only *originate* in *indistinct* conceptions, but *lead* to very false and dangerous notions. Is an instance required in the present case?—All the favor that *honest* men have shewn to Jacobinism and mock reforms of Parliament for 30 years past furnishes it.[2] Deny all other sense to the words Perfect and Imperfect, as applied to Government, but well or ill adapted to the *status rerum*, and transfer the abstract rule to the State, and we may be progressive without being seditious.

8 ɪ 228–9

It must be also observed, that the temper of the nation was, by the military genius of this constitution, so impelled to war, that, when they were not led out, to make it in foreign countries, they naturally fell into civil commotions: and thus a spirit of conquest, however improper to our insular situation, and destructive to that which ought to be the <u>sole ambition of England, the encrease of its trade</u>, was rather encouraged than restrained in our kings by their parliaments . . .

No!

[7²] C's reference is too vague to help very much with the dating of these notes: the call for parliamentary reform grew in strength during the 1770s and produced a series of abortive Reform Bills (starting in 1780) before the successful Bill of 1832.

JOHANN GEBHARD EHRENREICH MAASS
1766–1823

Versuch über die Einbildungskraft. Rev ed. Halle & Leipzig 1797. 8°.

Bound as first with JACOBI *Ueber die Lehre*.

British Library C 126 d 15(1)

Autograph signature "S. T. Coleridge" on the title-page, "S. T. C." label on title-page verso. On the title-page in pencil, and on p $^-$3 in ink, is written "35-1" (apparently a binder's memorandum); "35-2" appears on p $^+$3. On p $^-$3, in pencil, a drawing of a man's head similar to that in COWLEY **3**, but in profile.

MS TRANSCRIPT. VCL BT 21.

DATE. c 1815: the "philosophical chapters" 5–13 of *BL*, very much indebted to this work, were composed Aug–Sept 1815.

COEDITORS. Lore Metzger, Raimonda Modiano.

1 p $^-$3

$$
\begin{array}{l}
\quad 1{,}406 \\
\quad \underline{3{,}882} \\
\end{array}
$$

$$
2)\ \ 5288\ /\ \underset{\text{by }2}{2644}\ /\ \underset{\text{by }3}{1762\tfrac{3}{20}}
$$

$$
\begin{array}{l}
\quad 4544 \\
\quad 3882 \\
\quad \underline{1406} \\
3)\ \ 9832\ /\ 3277\tfrac{3}{10}\ /\ 2\ /\ 4{,}916
\end{array}
$$

Numbers for the next Lottery[1]

$$
\begin{array}{c}
2644 \\
\underline{4916}
\end{array}
$$

2 pp $^-$2–$^-$3

In Maass's introductory Chapters my mind has been perplexed by the division of things into matter (sensatio ab extra) and form (i.e. per- et

[1]¹ In *CN* II 2579n Kathleen Coburn quotes this marginal note and observes that the "play with figures . . . looks like a cal-culation of probabilities". For C's attitude towards lotteries see the same note and *The Friend* (*CC*) I 60 and n 2.

con-ceptio ab intra.)[1] Now as Time and Space are evidently only the Universals, ⟨or modi communes,⟩[2] of sensation and sensuous Form, & consequently appertain exclusively to the sensuous Einbildungskraft, (= Eisemplasy (πλαττειν εις εν)[3] which we call Imagination, Fancy, &c—all poor & inadequate terms, far inferior to the German Einbidldung) the Law of Association derived ab extra from the contemporëity of the impressions, or indeed any other difference of the characterless Manifold (mannichfaltige) except that of plus and minus of impinge[?nce/ment] becomes incomprehensible, if not absurd. I see at one instant of Time a Rose and a Lily—Chemistry teaches me that they differ only in ~~feu~~form, being both reducible to the same Elements—if then Form be not an external active power, if it be wholly transfused into the Object by the esenoplastic[4] or imaginative faculty of the percipient, or rather Creator, where & wherein shall I find the ground of my perception, that this is the Rose, and that the Lily?

[a]In order to render the creative activity of the Imagination at all conceivable, we must necessarily have recourse to the Harmonia præstabilita of Spinoza and Leibnitz:[5] in which case the automatism of the Imagination and Judgement would be Perception in the same sense, as a ⟨self-conscious⟩ Watch ~~as~~ would be a Percipient of Time, and inclusively of the apparent motion of the Sun and Stars. But as the whole is but a choice of incomprehensibles, till the natural doctrine of physical influx, or modification of each by all, have been proved absurd, I shall still prefer it:[6] & not doubt, that the Pencil of Rays forms pictures on the Retina ~~n~~ because I cannot comprehend how this Picture can excite a mental Fac-simile.

---

[a] Here the hand changes; the rest of the note may be a PS

2[1] "Sensation from without" and "perception and con-ception from within". C probably has in mind *Versuch* § 3 pp 5–6, where Maass differentiates between the representation of an object's sensory qualities and the representation of its form.

2[2] "Common modes".

2[3] C is glossing the German term for imagination by the Latin equivalent of its etymon, meaning "forming into one". C's introduction of "esemplastic" into English has been much commented on: see the full notes in *BL* ch 10 (*CC*) I 168n–70n.

2[4] A variant of "esemplastic".

2[5] Following Mendelssohn, Lessing, and Jacobi, C generally asserted that the theory of "pre-established Harmony" for which Leibniz is famous was derived from Spinoza: e.g. *BL* ch 8 (*CC*) I 130.

2[6] C refers to the scholastic theory of *influxus physicus*, according to which the body and the soul were believed to have a reciprocal influence upon each other through the transmission of physical particles from one substance to another. This theory, based on the system of Democritus, was the common solution given to the mind/body problem before Descartes. Leibniz consistently attacks the theory of mutual influence, arguing that thought and matter, as Descartes showed, cannot act on each other, and that their relationship is of a purely ideal nature, according to a divine scheme of universal harmony.

3 p 1, pencil

Es giebt unter unsern Vorstellungen zwei Hauptarten: Begriffe und An-
schauungen. Denn die Merkmale, wodurch ein Objekt vorgestellt wird,
müssen entweder individuelle oder gemeinsame seyn. Eine Vorstellung
aber, so fern sie gemeinsame Merkmale vorstellt, heisst ein *Begriff*,
und, sofern sie individuelle Merkmale vorstellt, eine *Anschauung*.

[Our perceptions fall into two main categories: concepts and intuitions. For the
signs that represent an object must be either particular or universal. Thus, we
call a representation a *concept* in so far as it represents general signs, and an
intuition in so far as it represents individual signs.]

Deceptive. The *mark* in itself is always individual [? tho']ᵃ by an act of
the understanding it may be rendered a Sign or general Term. The word,
''Vorstellung'' has been as often mischievous as useful in German phi-
losophy.[1]

4 pp 28–9

Wenn sich *B* mit *A* wirklich unmittelbar associirt, so ist nicht nöthig,
dass die ganze Vorstellung *B* mit der ganzen Vorstellung *A* schon zusam-
men gewesen sey, es braucht nur irgend ein Merkmal von *A*, etwa *m*,
mit irgend einem Merkmale von *B*, etwa *n*, zusammen gewesen zu seyn.
Wenn alsdann *A* gegeben, also *m* vorgestellt wird, so associirt sich damit
n, da beide schon zusammen gewesen sind . . . [Maass further applies
this rule to the common experience of being reminded of a friend at the
sight of a complete stranger. This, he explains, is determined by the fact
that at some time one has seen a third person whose appearance com-
bined certain features of the friend with those of the stranger.]

[If *B* is really immediately associated with *A*, it is not necessary that the whole
representation *B* be previously linked with the whole representation *A*; only a
characteristic of *A*, say *m*, be linked with some characteristic of *B*, say *n*. If then
A is given, that is, *m* is imagined, then *n* is associated with it since both have
already been linked.]

This seems to me a proof, that Likeness as co-ordinate with, but not
always subordinate to, Time exerts an influence per se on the Associa-
tion. Thus too as to Cause and Effect—they can not of course be *sepa-
rated* from Contemporëity, but yet act *distinctly* from it. Thus too Con-
trast: and even Order. In short, whatever makes ~~the~~ certain parts of a
total impression more vivid or distinct, will determine the mind to recall

---

ᵃ Blank space (or word rubbed out) in ms

3[1] ''Representation'': from textus.

these rather than others. Contemporëity seems to me the common condition under which all the determining Powers act rather than itself the effective Law.[1] Maass sometimes forgets (as Hartley seems never to have remembered) that all our Images are abstractions:—and that in many cases of Likeness the Association is merely an Act of Recognition.

5   p 29

Daher kann man das allgemeine Associationsgesetz auch so ausdrücken:

* *Mit einer gegebenen Vorstellung können sich alle, aber auch nur, diejenigen unmittelbar vergesellschaften, die mit ihr zu einer Totalvorstellung gehören*; oder, wie man auch sagt: *jede Vorstellung ruft ihre Totalvorstellung wieder ins Gemüth.*

[Therefore the universal law of association can be stated thus: *with a given representation, all those, and only those, representations can be immediately associated that are part of the same total representation*; or, to put it another way, *each representation recalls the total representation to the mind.*]

rather, is capable, under given conditions, of recalling: or else our whole Life would be divided between the Despotism of outward Impressions, and that of senseless Memory

* I object to this Law as becoming nugatory by its universality. Consider how immense the Sphere of a total Impression, from the Top of St Paul's—& how rapid the series of total Impressions.[1]

5A   pp 32–3, marked with a cross in pencil

Die Ursach, wodurch α bei der sich associirenden Einbildung hervorgebracht werden soll, ist irgend eine andre Nervenschwingung π, die sich dergestalt fortpflanzt, dass die erstre entsteht; π aber ist etwas von dem Eindrucke wesentlich Verschiednes, den *A* hervorbrachte, als die Oscillation α bei der Empfindung entstand.

[The cause by means of which α is produced in the associative imagination is some other vibration of the nerves π that is so propagated as to give rise to the former; and yet π is essentially different from the impression that produced [the object] *A*, since the oscillation α arose from sensation.]

5B   p 33, marked with a cross in pencil

Aber man könnte sagen: Die Nerven haben durch die Empfindung des

---

4[1]   Cf *BL* ch 6 (*CC*) ɪ 110: "Thus the principle of *contemporaneity*, which Aristotle had made the common *condition* of all the laws of association, Hartley was constrained to represent as being itself the sole *law.*" The account of theories of associa-

tion from Aristotle to David Hartley (1705–57) in *BL* chs 5–7 (*CC*) 89–128 enabled C to present imagination as a superior synthetic power of the mind.

5[1]   This note is repeated and expanded in *BL* ch 6 (*CC*) 111.

Gegenstandes *A* eine Disposition zu der Schwingung α erhalten; dürfen folglich nur überhaupt in Bewegung gesetzt werden, um α hervorzubringen.

[But one could say that the nerves, by means of the perception of the object *A*, acquire a predisposition towards vibration α; in general, therefore, they must only be set in motion to bring α forth.]

6 p 348, pencil

Am Ende des sechszehnten Jahrhunderts . . . machte auch *Hobbes* . . . grosses Aufsehen.

[At the end of the sixteenth century . . . Hobbes, too, caused a sensation.]

Qu!!   1650 [? &c].[1]

7 p 351, pencil

Bald nach Hobbes trat der grosse *Cartesius* auf . . .

[Soon after Hobbes appeared the great Descartes . . .]

Qu!!   Dec. died long before Hobbes[1]

6[1] Thomas Hobbes (1588–1679) published *Leviathan* in 1651.
7[1] Descartes died in 1650, Hobbes in 1679. Descartes' major works antedate those of Hobbes.

JOHN MACDIARMID
1779–1808

Lives of British Statesmen, &c. London 1807. 4º.

Not located; marginalia published from MS TRANSCRIPT.

MS TRANSCRIPT. VCL LT 51, in an unidentified hand, from the original in James Gillman's library (**10**).

DATE. Probably early to mid-1820s. Since this was Gillman's book, C's notes must have been written after he moved into the Gillmans' house in Apr 1816. The political theory of **10** has connections with *C&S*, which C began to write in 1825, but **9** must have been written before Jul 1825 (n 1).

COEDITOR. David V. Erdman.

1   p 70 | Sir Thomas More

[Footnote:] Picus of Mirandola, whom he so much admired, was distinguished for the freedom of his religious opinions. He was, during his whole life-time, persecuted* by the devotees of Rome, with charges of heresy, and saved from their hands probably by his rank.

* Utterly false. He was, or suffered himself, owing to his own superstition, to be *teized* by some Accusers of his 900 Theses, and his explanation of them. But this endured for a few years only, and never amounted to *persecution*. Innocent 8ᵗʰ who first approved & then prohibited the Discussion, at the same time expressly preserved the reputation of Picus as a faithful and dear Son of the Church, and Alexander VI. cleared him still more honorably. In fact, Count Mirandola was the *Idol* of his Age— and but for Savonarola's oath that he had seen him in *Purgatory*, or rather that Picus cloathed in flames had appeared to him and informed him that he was prevented from going immediately to Heaven by the crime of having delayed to become a Dominican Monk, he would probably have been beatified.[1]

2   p 132 | William Cecil, Lord Burleigh

The part which Cecil acted, during these renewed calamities of his early

---

1[1] The main source of C's information about Pico was the detailed life that he read in Göttingen in 1799, Christoph Meiners *Lebensbeschreibungen berühmter Männer aus den Zeiten der Wiederherstellung der Wissenschaften* (Zürich 1795–7) II 3–110: *CN* I 374.

patron, seems more reconcilable to prudence than to gratitude. It is said, that when Somerset, some time before his arrest, sent for him, and communicated to him his apprehensions, the secretary, instead of suggesting any means to avoid his impending dangers, coldly replied, "that if he was innocent, he might trust to that; and if he was otherwise, he could only pity him." Pity, indeed, if he really felt it, was all that he bestowed; for it does not appear that he interposed, either publicly or privately, to avert the destruction of his former patron. Yet when we consider the character of Somerset himself, we must allow that such an interposition would have been as imprudent, as it was likely to be unavailing. . . . Without benefiting his patron, he would probably have lost his fortune, his liberty, or his life; leaving behind him only the praise of unsuccessful generosity.

I know not whether John Macdiarmid Esqʳᵉ be an Irish or a Scotch Mac: but this paragraph exhibits the very *Mac* (as they say in Cumberland, for shape and fashion) of a Scotchman's Heart.[1]

3   p 162

Whitgift, the succeeding primate, taught by this example, proceeded to exercise severities, which Parker would not have ventured to commit, nor the queen, in the earlier part of her reign, have countenanced.

Is it not then singular, that Richard Baxter (in his Life) should have mentioned Whitgift among the good and wise Prelates of the early Church in contrast with their successors?[1]

4   p 266 | Thomas Wentworth, Earl of Strafford

At no period was the omnipotence of parliament a more established doctrine [than in the time of Henry VIII]. It was not enough that More con-

---

2[1] He was a Scot, and C habitually spoke scornfully of the Scotch, as J. P. Collier testified in his diary entry for 20 Mar 1832, when C's target was Sir James Mackintosh: "Coleridge had an intolerable and inexplicable aversion to anything Scottish; and I have heard him say more than once, 'When I speak of a Scotch rascal, I always lay the emphasis on Scotch'": *An Old Man's Diary* (1871) 62.

3[1] C may be thinking of a passage in BAXTER *Reliquiae* (1699) 440, not annotated in either of C's copies: "We know that when Parliament had cast out Bishops, Liturgy and Ceremonies, the generality both of Ministers and People, took it for granted that they were all bad, and so had more Light than their Forefathers had, before they ever studied their Controversies: I have asked many of them that have boasted of this Light, whether they ever read what *Cartwright, Bradshaw, Ames, Parker, Baynes, Gersome, Bucer, Didoclavius, Salmasius, Blondell, Beza, &c.* have said on one side; and what *Saravia, Bilson, Whitgift, Cavell, Downham, Burges, Hooker, Paybody, Hammond,* &c. have said on the other side; and they have confest they never thoroughly studied any one of them."

fessed its power to make or depose a king: he suffered for a treasonable offence, because he would not acknowledge its right to confer a supreme controul over men's consciences.

Q^y? Is not this a contradiction, this very King being an essential part of this omnipotent Parliament? And would Henry have endured such a doctrine as that his Vassals and Subjects had the right to depose him?

5   p 269

In this conjuncture . . . two expedients seem to have been requisite for the prevention of violent civil dissentions: the limitation of the royal prerogative by such accurate and insuperable barriers, as would for ever guard the persons and property of the subject from arbitrary encroachments; and the separation of the king's private expenditure from the disbursements of the public. . . . But of these expedients, the separation of the king's expenditure from that of the nation, however simple and obvious it may now appear, does not seem to have then occurred either to the prince or the people.

Now this appears to me one of those *plausible* silly remarks that even sensible men may sometimes fall on. At a second thought, however, a man of reflection would see, that this "*simple* and *obvious*" expedient involves one or other of two consequences. Either the two Houses of Parliament were to appoint, appropriate, and control the national expenditure: or they were not. If the latter, the separation would be nominal only—a mere powerless Act of Parliament! If they were, it would itself be and constitute such a limitation as the boldest Patriot at that time would not have thought of. With no greater patronage than the Crown *then* possessed, it would have reduced the King to a mere Stadtholder.

6   p 443

But his most dangerous enemy at court was the queen, whose influence over her husband was daily becoming more unbounded. Her inveterate antipathy to the Duke of Buckingham had been transferred to his creature, Laud; and, by a natural association, to the principal friend and supporter of Laud.

Q^y? Εϱως ψευδο = σωϰϱατιϰος ϰαϱολου ως ϰαι πατϱος Ιαϰωβου;[1]

6[1] "Query? The pseudo-socratic love of Charles as also of his father James?" C suggests that the queen's antipathy was based on sexual jealousy; he mentions Buckingham with similar distaste elsewhere, e.g. HACKET *Scrinia* **1, 6, 32**. He refers to the "Psoriasis Favoritistica" of James I in BM MS Egerton 2801 f 240^v; his views on homosexuality appear at large in ANDERSON COPY A **1** and n 6.

7   p 468

Strafford was aware that his life was in the hands of his enemies; that no chance of escape remained: but he was not prepared to expect so sudden a dereliction by his sovereign. . . . And when assured of the fatal truth, he raised his eyes to heaven, and laying his hand on his heart, exclaimed, "put not your trust in princes, nor in the sons of men: for in them there is no salvation."

Canting scoundrel—a hypocrite in his very last act! Nothing indeed can justify the measures of the H. of Commons, nothing palliate the baseness of the H. of Lords: unless it be the unvaried example of all their predecessors & the faithful imitation of the same submission to the stronger party by all their successors, spiritual and temporal. It was not this remorseless Apostate that suffered undeservingly/ he deserved a thousand deaths; but England, but Law and the everlasting principles and grounds of Law in the sense of public Justice that received a deadly wound: and every Bill of Pains and Penalties since then has been a fresh Hydra-Head sprouting from that wound. Thus is the cycle of retributive Providence compleated. What the Gracchi begin, a Blue-beard and an Heliogabalus finish.[1]

8   p 471

During this interval, the king, dissatisfied with himself, looked around for some expedient to save the life of Strafford. . . . Hollis advised that Strafford should petition his majesty for a short respite to settle his affairs. . . . Unfortunately the transaction was, in the meantime, represented to the queen, as if Strafford had bargained for his own life, by a promise to accuse her, and betray her counsels. Under this persuasion . . . she prevailed on the king to lay aside his intention of repairing to the house of lords; to convey his requests to them in a letter sent by the hands of the Prince of Wales; and even to abandon his whole proposal, by adding this cold and indifferent postscript, *if he must die, it were charity to reprieve him till Saturday.*

And such was the Man, so base and faithless to friend and foe, in public & in private life; whose chaste attachment to the Minion, Buckingham,

---

7[1] Bills "of Pains and Penalties" establish the punishments for crimes. C is commenting on the use of violent means for just ends: the Roman tribunes Tiberius Sempronius Gracchus (163–133 B.C.) and Caius Sempronius Gracchus (153–121 B.C.) used violent means on behalf of the Roman people, and in the end died by assassination; when violence is sanctioned by the just, it leads to the excesses of a Bluebeard or of the notoriously profligate emperor Heliogabalus (c 201–22).

inspired with horror and disgust the Queen, of whom he was uxoriously fond:[1]—yes! such was the Man, who under the name of a Martyr is still permitted to disgrace the most perfect Ritual of Christian Devotion, existing in Christendom, with a blasphemous application & parody of texts which had been written historically or prophetically concerning the merits and sufferings of the sinless Son of God, the Redeemer of the World![2]

9   p 472

In his address to the people from the scaffold, he assured them that he submitted to his sentence with perfect resignation. . . . He declared that, however his actions might have been misinterpreted, his intentions had always been upright: that he loved parliaments,* that he was devoted to the constitution and to the church of England: that he ever considered the interests of the king and people as inseparably united: and that, living or dying, the prosperity of his country was his fondest wish.

If aught could—but nothing can, nor dare we indeed desire, that any thing should—remove the superstition in favor of dying words, this fact and the similar fact in Charles' own scaffold scene are well-fitted to produce the effect. Both died with a lie in their mouths—Strafford with his love of Parliaments and devotion to the constitution by which the King was made dependent on them; and Charles with delivery of his Icon Basilike, as his own work![1]

10   pp 495 ff | Edward Hyde, Earl of Clarendon

The king, however, found reason, from this incident [Hyde's opposing the publication of a state paper drawn up by Colepeper], to respect the sentiments of Hyde still more than formerly, when he discovered that this opposition had proceeded from his objection to a statement of Cole-

8[1] See **6** and n 1 above.

8[2] In the special service in honour of Charles I added to BCP in 1662, and celebrated on the anniversary of his death, 30 Jan, the collect refers to "our martyred Sovereign" who "was enabled so cheerfully to follow the steps of his blessed Master and Saviour, in a constant meek suffering of all barbarous indignities, and at last resisting unto blood; and even then, according to the same pattern, praying for his murderers".

9[1] The authorship of *Eikon Basilike*, attributed to Charles I and published on or about the day of his death, is still a matter of controversy, with John Gauden (1605–

62) the most likely contender. Macdiarmid takes it for granted that Gauden was the author. C had changed his mind on the question by 1825, when he annotated one of Christopher Wordsworth's contributions to the debate, *"Who Wrote* EIKΩN BAΣI-ΛIKH?*" Considered and Answered* (2 vols 1824–5), which argued in favour of authorship by the king: on pp 174–5 C expressed his view that "internal evidence" proved it to be the work of Charles I, and added, "I believe the authenticity of the Εἰκὼν βασιλικὴ *notwithstanding* Dʳ W's [? argumentation] in its support." Cf *CL* v 477–8 (13 Jul 1825) and EIKON BASILIKE in *CM* (*CC*) II.

pepper's, affirming that the king, the lords, and the commons formed the three estates of the kingdom; whereas the king, in his opinion, should have been mentioned as the sovereign of the whole, and the bishops as the third estate.

This is a Tory Tenet, which it would be good policy in the Whigs to adopt; if indeed any party, deserving the name of Whigs in its right import, is still extant.[1] For a genuine Whig, according to my conviction, may be defined—A patriot who (considering *practical good sense*, in distinction from a theor*istic* predilection for strict logical *Consequence*, as the characteristic of the English People and the only appropriate interpreter of the English Constitution) acts in the spirit of *Compromise* with the Monarchy and the Major Barons to the advantage, *on the whole*, of the great Mass of Proprietors, landed, mercantile, and professional; and who giving its largest sense to the term, Property, so as to make it commensurate with its true ground and justifying definition, viz. a sphere of individual free-agency, and, therefore extending it to the lowest kind and degree of Property compatible with the Possessor's personal independence in the performance of his civic duties, judicial; (i.e. as a jury-man) municipal, and elective, includes actually or by probable reversion the whole effective male adult population; and yet so as that the accruing of civic (not natural) rights of the people, thus contradistinguished from the Populace (ut Populus a Plebe)[2] should be formally and functionally realized in such times and ways, and under such circumstances, conditions and limitations, as render the rights of the third class consistent with the co-existence of an effective Royalty & Aristocracy, nay, an additional safeguard to each against the other, and thus indirectly to both against its own encroachments.—This is the *Ideal*, by the light of which the genuine Whig (the proper ENGLISH *Publicola* sed et Patriota nihilominus)[3] guides and regulates his aims and efforts corrective and perfective, his regrets, fears, and wishes. And for the attainment of this by as close an approximation as wisdom dare expect from human imperfection, our Constitution had provided, and still prescribes, the sufficient means. Let only the House of Lords consist exclusively of bona fide Major Land-owners, of ancient families, or of men whose eminent merits and services entitle them to become the Founders of Fami-

10[1] In JOHNSON (annotated 1833) **1** and **43** C proposes a "history of Whiggery" with "Whig" understood to imply "a compromise between two opposite *Principles*".

10[2] "As populus [is distinguished] from mob": clarified in JOHNSON **20** as the difference between "Nation" and "majority of Natives".

10[3] "Friend of the people but nonetheless patriot also".

lies, but who on being raised to the Peerage should, as an indispensable accompaniment have, or be put in possession of *Lands* proportional; and the H. of Commons of two classes, the one, constituting a powerful and respectable minority in number, the representatives of the Minor Barons, i.e. the landed Proprietors, free-hold or copy-hold, not sitting with the Major Barons jure proprio,[4] nor yet included in their Estates and Dependencies; and of a majority (say two thirds) the representatives of Cities, Towns, and Sea Ports. The Cities and Boroughs, to whom the elective Franchise is entrusted, need not be more numerous than at present—if only (alas! the *one* oversight of our ancestors) the Franchise adhered to the thing originally meant & not to the *name* (Old Sarum, for instance)[5] when the thing had ceased—if from A − C it passed to B × C^a instead of remaining in A − C only because it was *ci devant* A × C^b!—These are the three proper *Estates* of the Realm, Change of Times having dis-estated the Church or identified it with the first or second as they now exist—namely, first, the Major Barons who sit jure proprio and form a House of their own: second, the Minor Barons, who sit by representatives: and thirdly, the Inhabitants of Towns &c, or the commercial, manufacturing, distributive, and professional Interests, who sit by their representatives in the same House with those of the Minor Barons. The two former Estates form the elements of Permanence in a nation, and bind the Present with the Past: the third is the element of Progression and Improvement, the former supplying the main nutriment of the commonweal, the latter its requisite stimulus. Call then A. E. I. Then, whenever as will oftenest happen, the interests of A. and E. coincide, their combined strength will suffice to counteract any attempted encroachment on the part of I, tho' I. is numerically the majority in the lower House: and when, as will sometimes happen, a real or supposed division of Interest takes place between A. & E, it is not less than a moral certainty that I will join with E to the efficient protection of E. against any novelty attempted by A: and should (as in the case of Corn Laws & the like) A and E combine against I, I by its numerical majority has the power of protecting itself. To connect, therefore, this long note with the text which occasioned it,—it is clear, I say, that the King is not an *Estate* of the Realm, but the Majesty of all three[6]—that

---

^{a} Thus in ms, but possibly B + C in original ^{b} Thus in ms, but possibly A + C in original

10[4] "In their own right".

10[5] A notorious borough with no inhabitants but two members of parliament (Horne Tooke was actually elected for Old Sarum in 1801).

10[6] All his life, C interpreted "majesty" as standing for "majority", on historical and etymological grounds: cf *C&S* (*CC*) 20 and n 1.

is, the Crown in its legislative character represents the Nation, its ancient Laws and Customs, ante-parliamentary as well as Parliamentary, and on his solemn oath alone (violent and extra-regular means not in question) does the Common-wealth depend for the continuance of its *super*-parliamentary Rights; while as the Executive Power, the Crown is the Agent and Trustee for all, chosen by the Nation not elected by the Estates, or more truly appointed by Providence, as the Copula of all the complex Causes, the grounds and acts and results of which constitute the National History.—Thus, my dear Gillman! without intending it I have left on record for you the sum of my political Religion, or the Constitutional Creed of S. T. Coleridge.[7]

11   p 520

It is not to be concealed that even Hyde encouraged the attempts of captain Titus and others, to remove Cromwell by assassination.

Nor ought it to be concealed that Hyde suborned assassins against an honester man than Cromwell the patriot Ludlow.[1] When to this detestable wickedness we add his hardening of Ch. I. in his prelatical superstition, his being an accomplice of the King's in the three contradictory treaties with three different parties at the same time neither of which the King intended to fulfil and his total abandonment of the religious Rights of the subjects to the fury of the Bishops after the Restoration[2] we must

10[7] C's final formulation of this elaborate theory of constitutional balance appeared in *C&S* in 1829: *C&S* (*CC*) esp 23–31.

11[1] Edmund Ludlow (c 1617–92), an eminent republican who fought for parliament in the Civil War and was one of the judges who signed the death warrant of Charles I, but later opposed Cromwell's government. At the restoration of Charles II he fled to the Continent, returning to England only briefly in 1689. His *Memoirs* (2 vols 1698) give circumstantial details of plots against his life from 1663 to 1669 but do not accuse Clarendon directly; historians of the rebellion generally assume that Charles II was ultimately responsible for these plots, however, and Clarendon as Chancellor before his own fall in the summer of 1667 may have been more directly involved. C repeats the charge in later notes in N38 ff 7ᵛ–8 and PEPYS II 55.

11[2] Clarendon's consistent position on episcopacy is the subject of **13** below; by

his "abandonment" of religious rights C refers to the repressive legislation of the Clarendon Code—in which Clarendon acquiesced, though he was not personally in favour of every part of it—which included the Act of Uniformity of 1662. Macdiarmid makes no reference to "three contradictory treaties", but C makes a similar statement about Charles I in HACKET *Scrinia* **45**: "Not a month before his Execution he signed three contradictory treaties with three different parties, meaning to keep neither. . . ." Charles was known for double-dealing and during the Civil War he had carried on secret negotiations (not "treaties") more or less simultaneously with Parliament, the Scots, and the Irish; in Dec 1747 he signed the "Engagement" with the Scots that led to the Second Civil War; in the last few months of his life he discussed with Parliament a treaty he never meant to honour and that in fact he never signed (the Treaty of Newport). Nevertheless C exaggerates.

attribute the high praise bestowed on Clarendon by Historians and the general Respect attached to his memory chiefly to the infamy of the rest of the Cavalier Faction canonizing Bad by incomparably Worse.

12   p 522

When the death of Cromwell, and the deposition of his son, enabled the active spirits to resume the business of framing constitutions, they shewed that their political sagacity had undergone no improvement. Without comprehending the distribution of powers, by which the authority of rulers is rendered at once effectual and innoxious; their crude discussions turned upon the eligibility of vesting the supreme power in one man, in a few, or in the people at large; and men seemed ready to lose their lives for theoretical governments, which were either pernicious or impracticable.

This at least cannot be said of Harrington's scheme:[1] nor should it be forgotten, that Cromwell's Scheme of Representation eulogized by Clarendon himself and which would have more than superseded the Revolution, owed its failure not to the ambition of Cromwell, but the narrow prejudices and persecuting Bigotry of the Presbyterians, who furthermore brought back the perjured popish Brotheller[2] without conditions and met their due reward.

13   pp 538–9

It would have been fortunate for the memory of Clarendon, if the same good sense and benevolence, which guided his civil policy, had governed his religious opinions. But, in these, prejudice triumphed over his better judgment; and we find him breathing sentiments, which, in a darker age, would have led him to promote the most cruel persecution. From his early youth, he had imbibed the maxim of *no bishop, no king*, as an infallible truth; and had conscientiously instilled, into the mind of his sovereign, the doctrine, that episcopacy is the only form of church government compatible with monarchy.

It is sad to think, how dangerous a poison the Tone and general Spirit of our modern Historians instils into the public mind, and (still worse) into the souls of the young men, whose talents, rank or connections destine them to a public Life:—a poison, slow indeed and lurking, and therefore

---

12[1] C read and commented respectfully on two political tracts included in James Harrington's *Oceana* (1700) while he was in Sicily in Oct 1804: *CN* II 2223 and n.

12[2] This is one of C's blunter remarks about Charles II, but cf also "brotheller, tyrant, and hireling of France" in *EOT* (*CC*) II 91.

the fittest to undermine the moral constitution. What an effect[a] must not the mere attachment of the honors of Virtue to wicked Statesmen only because they were much less wicked than others! "Conscientiously"! What? was Hyde a poor simple Recluse? must not the knowledge that this Tenet was despised as absurd and detested as base and ruinous by Falkland, Southampton,[1] and a majority of the great & good men who lived and died for the Monarchy have at least so far influenced an honest mind as to prevent him from persecuting with remorseless cruelty thousands, nay, myriads of men whose only charge was that of holding the same opinion respecting the Prelates (for the quarrel was not concerning Episcopacy, such as Arch-bishop Usher supported, but *Prelacy*)[2] as Falkland? If a Conscience seared by Party-passions and the assumption of Infallibility is to be the sufficient reason for calling actions conscientious, for Heaven's sake, say not an unkind word against the Massacre on S[t] Bartholomew's Day or the horrors of Bonner and Gardner!—[3]

The plausibility of the sophism, No Bishop, no King! rests wholly on the circumstance: that there is *some* truth in the Converse, viz. No King, no Prelate.

---

[a] SC notes at this point that a word appears to have been left out, either by C himself or by the transcriber

13[1] Lucius Cary, Viscount Falkland (1610–43), royalist hero, author of the posthumously published *Discourse of Infallibility . . . [with] Two Discourses of Episcopacy by Viscount Falkland and William Chillingworth* (1660); and Thomas Wriothesley, 4th Earl of Southampton (1607–67), highly respected advisor of Charles I and Treasurer of England under Charles II. Both were friends of Clarendon's: Macdiarmid outlines Southampton's disagreement with him on this point on pp 539–42 but does not specify Falkland's views—C may simply have added the name of Falkland as a royalist hero.

13[2] In *C&S* (*CC*) 124, C distinguishes between the "prelate" who has temporal power and the "bishop" who has spiritual power. James Ussher (1581–1656), abp of Armagh, was one of the episcopalian members of the Westminster Assembly appointed in 1643 to reform the English Church. An annotation by C in Jeremy

TAYLOR *Polemicall Discourses* (1674) i 1 clarifies his position here: "The Westminster Divines were confessedly not *Prelates*, but there were many in all other points orthodox and affectionate Members of the Establishment, who with Bedell, Lightfoot, and Archbishop Usher, held them to be Bishops in the primitive sense of the Term; & who yet had no wish to make any other change in the hierarchy than that of denominating the existing English Prelates *Arch*-Bishops . . .". Ussher published *The Original of Bishops* in 1644.

13[3] C refers to well-known instances of persecution of Protestants. Edmund Bonner (c 1500–69), bp of London, and Stephen Gardiner (c 1490–1555), bp of Winchester and Lord High Chancellor under Mary Tudor, were active in the Marian persecution. In the St Bartholomew's Day Massacre in France in 1572, 5,000–10,000 French Protestants died.

JAMES MACPHERSON
1739–1796
Lost Book

The Poems of Ossian, the Son of Fingal. Translated by James Macpherson, Esq. To which are prefixed, dissertations on the era and poems of Ossian. 2 vols. Edinburgh and London 1803. 12°.

Not located. Sold 24 Feb 1959 as Lot 121 in the William J. K. Vanston Sale, Parke-Bernet Galleries, New York; described in the sale catalogue as C's copy "with an autograph poem, 20 lines, written on the verso of title-page, and signed '*S. T. C.*, *March 20th*, 1805' ". The poem is not identified.

THOMAS ROBERT MALTHUS
1766–1834

An Essay on the Principle of Population; or, a view of its past and present effects on human happiness; with an inquiry into our prospects respecting the future removal or mitigation of the evils which it occasions. Rev ed. London 1803. 4°.

Preface dated "London, June 8, 1803." 1st ed published 1798.

British Library C 44 g 2

Inscribed by C on the title-page: "S. T. Coleridge E dono D. Stuart, Armigeri." RS has written short notes in pencil on pp 45, 64, 65, 93, 108, 141, 358, 364, 538, 539, including such salutes to Malthus as "fool" (p 64), "Ass!" (p 65), and "booby" (p 93, with which cf "this mischievous booby" in *S Letters*—Curry—I 357). C's notes were written to help RS with a review that duly appeared in the *Annual Review* for 1803 (1804) 292–301, adopting C's suggestions and incorporating some of his notes.

DATE. c 9–11 Jan 1804: *CN* I 1832, *CL* II 1026–7 and cf 1039, 1191.

1 p vi, pencil, marked with a pencil line in the margin | Preface

The main principle advanced is so incontrovertible, that, if I had confined myself merely to general views, I could have entrenched myself in an impregnable fortress; and the work, in this form, would probably have had a much more masterly air.

If by the main Principle the Author means both *the Fact* (i.e. that Population unrestrained would infinitely outrun Food) & the Deduction from the Fact—i.e. that the human race is *therefore not* indefinitely improvable/ a popgun would batter down this Impregnable Fortress. If only the Fact be meant, the assertion is quite nugatory/ in the former case Vapouring, in the latter a Vapour.   S. T. C.

2 p vii, pencil

Throughout the whole of the present work, I have so far differed in principle from the former, as to suppose another check to population possible, which does not strictly come under the head either of vice or misery; and, in the latter part, I have endeavoured to soften some of the harshest conclusions of the first essay.

And of course you wholly confute your former pamphlet & might have spared yourself the trouble of *making up* the present Quarto.[1] Merciful God! are we now to have a Quarto to teach us, that great misery & great vice arise from Poverty & that there must be Poverty in its worst shape, where ever there are more Mouths than Loaves, & more Heads than Brains!—The whole Question is this: Are Lust & Hunger both alike Passions of physical Necessity, and the one equally with the other independent of the Reason, & the Will?—Shame upon our Race, that there lives the Individual who dares even ask the Question!—   S. T. [C.][a]

3   p 6, pencil

There are many parts of the globe, indeed, hitherto uncultivated, and almost unoccupied; but the right of exterminating, or driving into a corner where they must starve, even the inhabitants of these thinly peopled regions, will be questioned in a moral view.

The stupid Ignorance of the Man! a moral View!— H to begin such a book as this without stating what a moral View is!— If it be immoral to kill a few Savages in order to get possession of a country capable of sustaining a 1000 times as many enlightened & happy Men/ is it not immoral to kill millions of Infants & Men by crowded Cities, by Hunger, & by the Pox?—

4   pp 8–10, pencil, footnote in ink; textus marked with a brace

Taking the whole earth instead of this island, emigration would of course be excluded; and supposing the present population equal to a thousand millions, the human species would increase as the numbers 1, 2, 4, 8, 16, 32, 64, 128, 256, and subsistence as 1, 2, 3, 4, 5, 6, 7, 8, 9. In two centuries the population would be to the means of subsistence as 256 to 9; in three centuries as 4096 to 13, and in two thousand years the difference would be almost incalculable.

Quote this Paragraph, as the first sentence of your Review: & observe that this is the sum & substance of 8 pages—& that the whole work is written in the same Ratio, viz.—8 lines of Sense & substance to 8 × 30 = 240 Lines of Verbiage and senseless repetition[1] and even ⟨of⟩ these 8

---

[a] Letter lost through cropping or wear of paper

2[1] The "former pamphlet", which C bought immediately before going to Germany in Sept 1798, was the anonymous 396-page octavo *Essay on the Principle of Population as It Affects the Future Improvement of Society, with Remarks on the* *Speculations of Mr Godwin, M. Condorcet, and Other Writers* (1798): *CL* I 417. The 1803 ed is 610 pp in quarto.

4[1] RS adopted this suggestion in his review: cf headnote above.

lines ~~might have been better expressed in two,~~ & all the ~~silly~~ Pomp
of Numerals & Ratios ⟨might have been⟩ cashiered, by substituting
~~an~~ Proposition which no one in his senses would consider as other
than axiomatic/ viz: Suppose, that the human race amount to a thou-
sand millions/ divide the square acres of food-producing Surface by
500,000,000, that is to say, so much to each married Couple, estimate
this Quotum as high as you like/ & if you will, even at a thousand, or
even at ten thousand acres to each family/ suppose Population without
check, & take the average Increase ~~of each Family~~ from two* Families,*a*

* ⟨For⟩ ~~H~~in this Statement I have supposed each Individual to marry
out of his Tribe—and you must therefore take the 49 million as belong-
ing to 2 Quota of Land—the conclusion is the same—. But do the sum
at once—find out the number of square Acres on the Globe (of Land) &
divide the number by 500,000,000.—I have myself been uselessly pro-
lix, and in grappling with the Man have caught his itch of Verbiage.—
Suppose a married couple to have six children (not half the number,
which they would have, if you suppose *all* checks to Population re-
moved) & suppose all their posterity to marry and each couple to in-
crease in the same proportion, and it is evideneet on the slightest reflec-
tion, that in a given number of Generations their Posterity would want
standing-room. *b*(That it must be so, the Rule of Multiplication would
enable a child to demonstrate; and a School boy, who has advanced in
Arithmetic as far as Compound Interest, may astonish his younger Sister
both by the Fact, and by the exact number of years, in which it would
take place.—) on the other hand ⟨let⟩ the productiveness of the Earth ~~to~~
be ~~as~~ increased beyond the Hopes of the most Visionary Agriculturist,
still the Productions take up room,—*c*if the present crop of Turnips ~~to~~
occupy one fifth of the space of the Turnip Field, ~~th~~ the increase can
never be more than quintupled/ & if you suppose two Harvests for one,
the increase ⟨still⟩ can not exceed ten: so that supposing a little Island of
a single Acre, and its productions occupying one fifth of its absolute
space, & sufficient to maintain two men and two women, four genera-
tions would outrun its *possible* ~~Increase~~ power of furnishing them with
Food—we may boldly affirm that a Truth so self-evident as this, was
never overlooked, or even by Implication contradicted.—What proof
has Mr Malthus brought, what proof can he bring, that any writer or
Theorist has overlooked this Fact, which would not apply (with rever-

---

a The deletion and insertion are in ink
b Parentheses inserted in the darker ink that begins at note *c*
c Written in darker ink from here to end of C's footnote

as 5 (which is irrationally small, supposing the human Race healthy, & each man married at 21 to a woman of 18) and in 12 generations the Increase would be, forty eight million, 828 thousand, one hundred & twenty five/—now as to any conceivable Increase in the Productions, or Improvement in the Productiveness of the 1000, or 10,000 Acres, it is ridiculous even to think of Production at all—in as much as it is demonstrable, that either already in this 12th generation, or *certainly* in a few generations more (I leave the exact statement to School-boys, not having Cockers Arithmetic by me & having forgotten the number of square Feet in an Acre)[2] the quotum of Land would not furnish Standing-room to the descendants of the first agrarian Proprietors.

---

ence be it spoken) to the Almighty himself, when he pronouned the awful command "Increase and multiply.—"[3]

5   pp 11–13 | Bk 1 ch 2 "Of the General Checks to Population, and the Mode of Their Operation"

Promiscuous intercourse, unnatural passions, violations of the marriage bed, and improper arts to conceal the consequences of irregular connexions, clearly come under the head of vice.

* It is to the last degree idle to write in this way without having stating[a] the meaning of the words Vice & Virtue. That these and all these are Vices in the present state of Society, who doubt?—So was Cœlibacy in the Patriarchal ages. Vice & Virtue subsist in the agreement of the habits of a man with his Reason & Conscience—and these can have but one moral guide, Utility or the Virtue & Happiness of Rational Beings. We mention this not under the miserable notion that any state of Society will render these actions ~~ration~~ capable of being performed with conscience & virtue, but to expose the utter ungroundedness of this speculation— adding however, that if we believed with Mr Malthus's ~~h~~ *warmest* partizans, that Man never will, ⟨in⟩ general~~ly~~, be capable of regulating the sexual appetite by the Law of Reason, & that ~~the~~ the gratification [of][b] Lust is a Thing of physical Necessity equally with ~~hun~~ the gratification of Hunger—a faith, which we should laugh at for its silliness if its wickedness had not pre-excited Abhorrence—nothing would be more easy than to demonstrate, that ~~ma~~ some one ~~in~~ or other of these actions,

[a] A slip for "stated"   [b] Word supplied by the editor

4[2] *Cocker's Arithmetick, Being a Plain and Easy Method* (1678), an improved version of *Cocker's Tutor to Arithmetic* (1664), reprinted many times as an introductory textbook. An acre is 43,560 square feet; C's "square acre" is a tautology.
4[3] Actually "Be fruitful, and multiply": Gen 1.22 etc.

whether Abortion, or the Exposure of Children, or artificial Sterility on the part of the Male, would become Virtues—a Thought, which we turn from with Loathing; but not with greater Loathing, than we do from the degrading Theory, of which it would be a legitimate Consequences[a]— and which by a strange Inconsequence admits the existence of all these Vices, and of all that mass of Misery, on account of which alone these Vices are Vices, in order to prevent that state of Society, in which admitting some one of these actions after the Birth of the second or third Child, the whole Earth might be imagined filled to its utmost extent with enlightened & happy Beings. M[r] Malthus is continually involving himself in the silly Blunder of the Quakers, who idolize words—for instance, I am talking to *you*; I & every body uses *you* to signify one person, & we all use it indiscriminately to men of all ranks & conditions/ *you* so understand it/ there is neither an intention of deceiving, or a possibility of being deceived; and yet ~~forsooth~~ I am guilty of A LIE and of FLATTERY, because, forsooth, some centuries ago the word "you" was only known as a Plural, and applied to ~~an~~ Individuals of high Rank from motives of Flattery.[1]—I am weary of confuting such childish Blunders.—all that follows to the 355th page[2] may be an entertaining farrago of [? opt] of quotations from Books of Travels, &c; but surely, very impertinent in a philosophical work—/—bless me 340 pages—for what purpose!—a phil. work can have no legitimate purpose but proof & illustration/ & 350 pages to prove an AXIOM! to illustrate a self-evident Truth!—It is neither more nor less than Book-making! —

[a] A slip for the singular

5[1] C is explaining the Quakers' preference for "thou" and "thee" as the second person singular.

5[2] C's figures are approximate, and he is probably referring to the end of Bk 2 "Of the Checks to Population in the Different States of Modern Europe" on p 351.

The Grounds of an Opinion on the Policy of Restricting the Importation of Foreign Corn; intended as an appendix to "Observations on the Corn Laws." London 1815. 8°.

Bound as second in *Ottery Tracts 1812–30*. A 48-page pamphlet, published Feb 1815 (*EC*).

British Library C 126 i 3(2)

Inscribed on the title-page "John Kenyon." and in pencil overtraced in ink "At Mrs Simpson's—30—Portland Place London—"

DATE. End of Mar – early Apr 1815? The Kenyons arranged to visit C at Calne 27 Mar 1815 (*CL* IV 557) and probably brought this pamphlet with them, knowing about local interest in the subject. C had drawn up a petition against the Corn Bill for the inhabitants of Calne earlier in the month: *CL* IV 555.

1   title-page verso

Mr Malthus's *first* Pamphlet

^a in Quarto he was forced to lug in his *Morals*[1]—Why not now examine whether by moral measures—enforcing the amelioration in the execution of "No Poor Laws—&c"—this Bill might not have been superseded—[2]

---

^a Starting a new line, C omits the capital letter

1[1] C refers—as in MALTHUS *Essay 2*—to the discrepancies between the 1798 and 1803 versions of the *Essay on the Principle of Population*: the volume grew in length because Malthus added "moral restraint"—voluntary abstention—to his list of ways of coping with overpopulation.

1[2] Malthus's *Essay* notoriously recommended the abolition of the Poor Laws by which parishes were required to support those who could not support themselves. Malthus argued that no one had a *right* to support that the community could not afford, and that the relief of real distress should be left to the charity of individuals; C appears to suggest that the moral implications of that position have been ignored in this pamphlet.

BERNARD DE MANDEVILLE
1670–1733

The Fable of the Bees: or, private vices, publick benefits. With an essay on charity and charity-schools. And a search into the nature of society. The third edition. To which is added, a vindication of the book from the aspersions contained in a presentment of the Grand-Jury of Middlesex, and an abusive letter to Lord C. 2 vols. London 1724. 8°.

Nagoya University Library

Bookplate of Joseph Henry Green, and of "Wiston Old Rectory". Note of inquiry from J. L. Hancy to W. G. Boswell-Stone 2 Oct 1902 pasted in, and letter from R. H. Hew of the Clarendon Press to Major Christopher Stone 15 Jun 1922 seeking information about this copy on behalf of F. B. Kaye, who published C's note in his ed of *Fable* (2 vols Oxford 1924) II 453.

DATE. Unknown, but after 1817 if the book belonged originally to J. H. Green. It appears in *Green SC* (1880) 457.

1   p $^-$1, referring to p 35

. . . in this *Enquiry into the Origin of Moral Virtue*, I speak neither of *Jews* or *Christians*, but man in his State of Nature and Ignorance of the true Deity; and then I affirm, that the Idolatrous Superstitions of all other Nations, and the pitiful Notions they had of the Supreme Being were incapable of exciting Man to Virtue, and good for nothing but to awe and amuse a rude and unthinking Multitude. It is evident from History, that in all considerable Societies, how stupid or ridiculous soever People's received Notions have been, as to the Deities they worship'd, Human Nature has ever exerted it self in all its Branches, and that there is no earthly Wisdom or Moral Virtue, but at one time or other Men have excell'd in it in all Monarchies and Commonwealths, that for Riches and Power have been any ways remarkable.

P. 35.—It is, perhaps, a piece of simplicity to treat of Mandeville's work, as other than an exquisite ~~p~~ *bon bouche* of Satire & Irony! But as there have been, and are, Mortals and man-shaped Mortals too, very plausible Anthropöeids, who have adopted his positions in downright *opake* Earnest, it may be worth while to ask—how? by ~~by~~ what strange changce there happened to start this premier species of Ouran Outangs,

811

yclept Man, these *Wise-Men* (p. 28.)[1] these Law-givers, who so cleverly took advantage of this *Peacock* Instinct of Pride and Vanity?

---

[1] P 28 of this text: "The Chief Thing therefore, which Lawgivers and other Wise Men, that have laboured for the Establishment of Society, have endeavour'd, has been to make the People they were to govern, believe, that it was more beneficial for every Body to conquer than indulge his Appetites, and much better to mind the Publick than what seem'd his private Interest."

PHILIP MASSINGER

1583–1640

The Plays of Philip Massinger . . . with notes critical and explanatory by William Gifford.

Includes J. Ferriar's "Essay on the Dramatic Writings of Massinger". [Edition not identified: either 4 vols London 1805 (8°) or the 2nd ed, 4 vols London 1813 (8°).]

Not located; marginalia published from *NLS* II 53–5, text based on a "copy . . . belonging to Mr. Gillman". *NLS* prints another note based on a ms now included in *Lects 1808–1819 (CC)* II 152.

DATE. About 1817? *Lects 1808–1819 (CC)* II 143 records C's occasional reading in Massinger from 1797 onwards. If this annotated copy belonged to Gillman, as *NLS* says it did, C's notes were made after he moved to Highgate, possibly in preparation for the 1818 lectures but also possibly later. The play specifically named here—*The Guardian*—is not mentioned in the lectures.

1

Two or three tales, each in itself independent of the others, and united only by making the persons that are the agents in the story the *relations* of those in the other, as when a bind-weed or thread is twined round a bunch of flowers, each having its own root—and this novel narrative in *dialogue*[1] such is the *character* of Massinger's plays—That the juxta-position and the tying together by a common thread, which goes round this and round that, and then round them all, twine and intertwine, are contrived ingeniously—that the component tales are well chosen, and the whole well and conspicuously told; so as to excite and sustain the mind by kindling and keeping alive the curiosity of the reader—that the language is most pure, equally free from bookishness and from vulgarism, from the peculiarities of the School, and the transiencies of fashion, whether fine or coarse; that the rhythm and metre are incomparably good, and form the very model of dramatic versification, flexible and seeming to rise out of the passions, so that whenever a line sounds im-metrical, the speaker may be certain he has recited it amiss, either that he has misplaced or misproportioned the emphasis, or neglected the ac-

---

1[1] Cf C's remark in *TT* 5 Apr 1833:   plays have the interest of novels."
"Massinger is always entertaining; his

813

celeration or retardation of the voice in the pauses (all which the mood or passion would have produced in the real Agent, and therefore demand from the Actor or [? emulator/translator]*ᵃ*) and that read aright the blank verse is not less smooth than varied, a rich harmony, puzzling the fingers, but satisfying the ear—these are Massinger's characteristic merits.

Among the varieties of blank verse Massinger is fond of the anapæst in the first and third foot, as:

"Tŏ yoŭr mōre | thăn mā|scŭlīne rēā|sŏn thāt | cŏmmānds 'ĕm ‖—"

The Guardian, Act i. sc. 2.²

Likewise of the second Pæon (◡–◡◡) in the first foot followed by four trochees (–◡) as:

"Sŏ grēēdĭlў | lōng fŏr, | knōw theĭr | tītĭll|ātiŏns."

Ib. ib.³

The emphasis too has a decided influence on the metre, and, contrary to the metres of the Greek and Roman classics, at least to all their more common sorts of verse, as the hexameter and hex and pentameter, Alchaic, Sapphic, &c. has an essential agency on the character of the feet and power of the verse. One instance only of this I recollect in Theocritus:

τα μῆ χᾱλᾱ χᾱλᾱ πεφᾱνται⁴

unless Homer's Ἄρες, Ἄρες, may (as I believe) be deemed another— For I cannot bring my ear to believe that Homer would have perpetrated such a cacophany as Ὦρες, Ἄρες.⁵

"In fēar | my chaasteetee | may be | suspected."⁶

Ib. ib.

ᵃ NLS prints these doubtful readings one above the other, joined by a brace

1² *The Guardian* I ii 45: (1805) IV 140, (1813) IV 144.

1³ The abbreviation means "same act, same scene". Ibid I ii 50: (1805) IV 140, (1813) IV 145.

1⁴ Theocritus *Idylls* 6.19, "What is not fair, seems fair"—a line famous for the change of quantity (the first syllable in χαλα being short the first time and long the second) dictated by the metre. Both this line and the one alluded to at n 5 are quoted in MATTHIAE II 955.

1⁵ *Iliad* 5.31 (repeated 5.455): "Ares, Ares, thou bane of mortals" etc. Like χαλα above, Ἄρες is found sometimes with a long vowel, sometimes with a short one. The phenomenon is not usually thought to require an explanation, but in his 1729 edition of the *Iliad*, Samuel Clarke introduced a note on this line in which he remarked that short syllables may be lengthened and that here the word would be pronounced as though it were Ὦ ῥες (O Ares).

1⁶ Massinger *The Guardian* I ii 41: (1805) IV 139, (1813) IV 144.

In short, musical notes are required to explain Massinger—metres in addition to prosody. When a speech is interrupted, or one of the characters speaks aside, the last syllable of the former speech and first of the succeeding Massinger counts but for one, because both are supposed to be spoken at the same moment.

> "And felt the sweetness *of 't*."
>> "*How* her mouth runs over"[7]
>>> Ib. ib.

Emphasis itself is twofold, the *rap* and the *drawl*, or the emphasis by quality of sound, and that by quantity—the hammer, and the spatula—the latter over 2, 3, 4 syllables or even a whole line. It is in this that the actors and speakers are generally speaking defective, they cannot equilibrate an emphasis, or spread it over a number of syllables, all emphasized, sometimes equally, sometimes unequally.

1[7] Ibid I ii 59: (1805) IV 140, (1813) IV 145.

COTTON MATHER
1663–1728

Magnalia Christi Americana: or, the ecclesiastical history of New-England, from its first planting in the year 1620. unto the Year of our Lord, 1698. In seven books, &c. 7 pts in one vol. London 1702. F°.

Henry E. Huntington Library

Inscribed on the title-page "Robert Southey. Nottingham. June 21. 1811." Small pencil marks by RS throughout; also pencilled notes about an error in binding, on i 2 and ii 3. C has corrected a typographical error on sig C2ᵛ, changing "Lymei" to "Lyncei". Entry from bookseller's catalogue pasted in on p ⁻4; librarian's note in pencil p ⁻5 (p-d).

CONTENTS. Each part has a separate fly-title and separate pagination: i *Antiquities*; ii *Ecclesiarum Clypei. . . . containing the Lives of the Governours*; iii *Polybius. . . . containing the Lives of Many . . . Divines*; iv *Sal gentium. . . . containing an account of the University* [pagination begins with p 125]; v *Acts and Monuments. . . . containing the Faith and the Order in the Churches of New-England*; vi *Thaumaturgus . . . Demonstrations of the Divine Providence in remarkable Mercies and Judgments*; vii *Ecclesiarum Proelia . . . reflecting the Afflictive Disturbances of which the Churches of New-England have suffered . . .*; Appendix. *Decennius Luctuosum. An History of . . . the Long War, which New England hath had with the Indian Salvages.*

DATE. Possibly late Feb 1812, when C was at Greta Hall with access to RS's books; and see **1** n 1.

COEDITOR. J. Robert Barth, S.J.

1   ii 37 | Sir William Phips

If such a Renowned Chymist, as *Quercetanus*, with a whole Tribe of *Labourers in the Fire*, since that Learned Man, find it no easie thing to make the common part of Mankind believe, That they can take a *Plant* in its more vigorous Consistence, and after a due *Maceration, Fermentation* and *Separation*, extract the *Salt* of that *Plant*, which, as it were, in a *Chaos*, invisibly reserves the *Form* of the whole, with its vital Principle; and, that keeping the *Salt* in a *Glass* hermetically sealed, they can, by applying a *Soft Fire* to the *Glass*, make the *Vegetable* rise by little and little out of its *Ashes*, to surprize the Spectators with a notable Illustration of that *Resurrection*, in the Faith whereof the *Jews* returning from the Graves of their Friends, pluck up the *Grass* from the Earth, using those words of the Scripture thereupon, *Your Bones shall flourish like an Herb* . . .

What shall we think of these stories, told & solemnly, with God invoked as the witness, affirmed for facts of their own knowlege, not by Quercetanus & his followers only, but by Kircher & still later chemists[1]— Was the Flower drawn on the inside of the Glass in the red & green oxymuriats of Cobalt, which disappears in the cold, revives by Heat?[2]

2 ii 61

The Persons [investigating the *"assault from Hell"* on a large number of New Englanders] were Men eminent for *Wisdom and Virtue.* . . . They did in the first Place take it for granted, that there are *Witches* . . . To satisfie them in which Perswasion, they had not only the *Assertions* of the *Holy Scripture* . . . but they had also an *Ocular Demonstration* in one, who a little before had been executed for *Witchcraft*, when *Joseph Dudley*, Esq; was the Chief Judge.

Of what? of his witchcraft? No: but of his being hung. The Jews had the same ocular demonstration of our Saviour's Blasphemy and Treason: they saw him *executed* for the said crimes—Alas! this precious Quid pro quo was not peculiar to the NEW-*England* Logicians.[1]

The "grand Contender", the blind roaring Cyclops *Thumper* that follows, not unlike the Polypheme of Ulysses, returns the old "Ουτις"— to the "Who? Who?" of Common Sense.[2]—*Whose* images? *Who* con-

---

1[1] "Of the flower apparitions so solemnly affirmed by Sir K. Digby, Kercher [i.e. Athanasius Kircher, 1601–80], Helmont &c. see a full and most interesting account in Southey's Omniana, with a probable solution of this chemical marvel": *Friend* (*CC*) I 516*. This note in the 1818 *Friend* tends to confirm the dating of the marginalia, since *Omniana*—a collaboration between RS and C—was published Oct 1812, and C may have directed RS to Erasmus Darwin's *Botanic Garden* (1791) I 48–9n for the cobalt "solution" given in RS's article 198, "Spectral Flowers", which quotes examples from Kircher, Paracelsus, Kenelm Digby, and others, including this passage from Cotton Mather: *Omniana* (1812) II 82–103.

1[2] C knew about the properties of cobalt from his reading and amateur experiments in chemistry. Compounds of cobalt were used in invisible (or "sympathetic") ink, and were known to produce the crystalline structures called "flowers of cobalt".

2[1] I.e. the fallacy of putting one thing *in place of* (not, as the phrase is more commonly used, in return for) another.

2[2] The allusion is to Ulysses' adventure with the Cyclops Polyphemus in *Odyssey* 9: Ulysses gave his name as *Outis*, "Nobody", so that when Polyphemus was asked who had put out his one eye, he replied, "Nobody". The "grand Contender" (source untraced) or *"Thumper"* of an illogical argument follows directly upon the textus: "There was one whose *Magical Images* were found, and who *confessing her Deeds*, (when a Jury of Doctors returned her *Compos Mentis*) actually shewed the whole Court, by what *Ceremonies* used unto them, she directed her *Familiar Spirits* . . .".

fessed the deed? *What* 12 Doctors returned a Compos Mentis?—*Who* were hurt?—Why, there was *one*—& it was *she*—and there was a jury of Doctors, and it was *they*—& all a Whole Court, and that was the Court—and the Hurts were done to *People*!—What a stammering tedious Paraphrase of Ουτις! Ουτις! *S. T. C.*

3   iii 21 | Mr. John Cotton

But inasmuch as very much of an *Athenian Democracy*, was in the Mould of the *Government*, by the *Royal Charter* . . . Mr. *Cotton* effectually recommended it unto them, that none should be *Electors*, nor *Elected* therein, except such as were *visible Subjects* of our Lord Jesus Christ, personally *confederated* in our Churches. In these, and many other ways, he propounded unto them, an Endeavour after a *Theocracy*, as near as might be, to that which was the glory of *Israel*, the *peculiar People*.*

* Scarce has this man escaped Persecution, but he sophisticates a charter of freedom by excluding from the rights of citizens all not visibly confederated with him in his Church! Persequi was not then a verb impersonal so far as respected a perpetual *Caret* of the first person S. and Pl. thro' all the moods & tenses.[1] In short, the doctrine of irrefragable Grace[2] sensibly made known & certain to the elect, what is it but Infallibility rescue[a] from Roman Monopoly, or Every Puritan his own Pope. Now infallibility assumed, Persecution becomes not only blameless, but a *Duty*.

4   iii 72, pencil, overtraced | Mr. Francis Higginson

It was a good Courage of Old *Cyprian*, to declare: *If any think to join themselves unto the Church, not by their Humiliation and Satisfaction, when they have scandalized the Brethren, but by their Great Words and Threats, let them know, that the Church of God will oppose them, and the Tents of Christ will not be conquered by them.* And no less was the good Metal in our *Higginson*.

In this and the following ¶s we find proofs that the modern Methodists

[a] For "rescued"?

[1] *Persequi*, to persecute; *Caret*, he or it lacks. Perhaps C means by this convoluted expression that persecution applies only to those who are not "of the first Person singular and plural", that is, the persecutor (I) and the persecutor's allies (we).

[2] Also called "irresistible grace", a concept bound up with the predestination controversies dating from the time of Augustine.

are close Copyists of the old furious Puritans, or rather Nettles from the same Seed.

5 iii 72, pencil, overtraced

. . . [Higginson] told that Man [a drunkard and swearer] before them all, *That he was not willing to give the Lord's Supper unto him, until he had professed his Repentance, unto the Satisfaction of the Congregation.* . . . The Wretch continued in an exorbitant Frame for a few Days, and at last roared out, *That he was damn'd, and that he was a Dog, and that he was going to the Dogs for ever.* So cried, and so he died: And this was *known to all People.*

O the blinding power of Bigotry! This instance (one of many score, no doubt) this shocking instance of pulpit murder, is related with triumph & jubilation, as rampant as old Knox's on the assassination of the Regent effected by his own pulpit anathemas. See Knox's History of the Reformation of the Church of Scotland.[1]   S. T. C.

6 iii 73, pencil, overtraced

This Faithfulness of Mr. *Higginson* was variously Resented: Some of the People disliked it very much . . . * But the better sort of the People generally approved it, as a Conformity to that Rule, Them that sin before all, Rebuke before all, that others may fear . . .

* Who does not see that wherever these pulpit Rebukes are tolerated, nay, deemed acts of Duty, a pure theocracy, or priestly Despotism must be the consequence? What is the power of having a man tried in my presence, & the privilege of actuating the verdict of a Jury by sentencing his Body to imprisonment, compared with the privilege, of inflicting

---

5[1] Though it was not actually an assassination, C may be referring to the death in 1560 of Mary of Guise, queen regent during the minority of her daughter Mary Queen of Scots. Knox takes considerable pleasure in the part he believes he played in bringing about her death. After recounting a story that circulated about the delight Mary took in the sight of the naked corpses of those slain by the French in an assault on Leith in 1560, Knox goes on: ". . . against the which John Knox spake openly in the pulpit, and boldly affirmed, That God should revenge that contumely done to his image, not only in the furious and godless soldiers, but even in such as rejoiced thereat: and the very experience declared, that he was not deceived; for within few days (yea, some say, that same day), began her belly and legs to swell, and so continued, till that God, in his wisdom, took her away from this world, as after we shall hear": John Knox *History of the Reformation of Religion within the Realm of Scotland* (Edinburgh 1790) 222. We do not know what ed C used, and none is noted in *Southey SC* (1844).

Infamy ad libitum on Kings & Governors in the name of the King of Kings?   S. T. C.

7 iii 183, pencil | John Eliot

There was a Godly Gentleman of *Charlstown*, one Mr. *Foster*, who with his Son, was taken Captive by *Turkish* Enemies. . . . Mr. *Eliot*, in some of his next Prayers, before a very solemn Congregation, very broadly beg'd, *Heavenly Father, work for the Redemption of thy poor Servant* Foster; *and if the Prince which detains him will not, as they say, dismiss him as long himself lives, Lord, we pray thee to kill that Cruel Prince . . .*

God forgive me if my feelings are uncharitable; but when I read this Prayer offered to the Almighty by a good & humble Christian in himself, I cannot but shudder at the presumptuous Spirit of Puritanism! How could these good men read the*[a]* our Lord's Reproof of*[b]* of the Disciples who would have called down Fire from Heaven!—*[1]*

7A iii 187, marked with a pencil line in the margin

. . . with what Fervour he uttered an Expression to this purpose, *Lord, for Schools every where among us! That our Schools may flourish! That every Member of this Assembly may go home and procure a good School to be encouraged in the Town where he lives! That before we die, we may be so happy as to see a good School encouraged in every Plantation of the Country.*

7B iii 210, marked with a pencil line in the margin

May the poor *Greeks*, *Armenians*, *Muscovites*, and others, in the Eastern Countries, wearing the name of *Christians*, that have little *Preaching* and no *Printing*, and few Bibles or good Books, now at last be furnished with Bibles, Orthodox Catechisms, and Practical Treatises by the Charity of *England . . .*

7C iii 210, marked with a pencil line in the margin

May sufficient Numbers of great, wise, rich, learned, and godly Men in the Three Kingdoms, procure well-composed *Societies*, by whose united Counsels, the Noble Design of *Evangelizing* the World, may be more effectually carried on . . .

---

[a] The article should have been cancelled when the change recorded in note *b* was made

[b] C wrote "the Reproof of our Lord's" and then marked the words for transposition

7[1] Luke 9.54–6, esp 56, "For the Son   but to save them."
of man is not come to destroy men's lives,

8   iv 128 | The History of Harvard-Colledge

. . . *Baccalaureus* being but a Name Corrupted of *Batualius*, which *Batualius* (as well as the French *Bataile*) comes *à Batuendo*, a Business that carries *Beating* in it . . .

Wranglers[1]

9   iv 131

Unto this brief Recitation of Occurrences relating to the *Colledge*, I shall only annex a few Passages, used by Mr. [Increase] *Mather*, when he gave the *Degrees*. . . . De verâ Nominis *Baccalaurei* Notatione, inter Peritissimos ambigitur. Nonnulli Verbum * à *Bacculo*, derivari volunt [On the true etymology of the word *Baccalaureus* scholars are in disagreement. Some would derive the word from *Bacculus* [*baculus*, a stick]] . . .

Verius forsan—viri bacculo potius quam lauro digni.[1]

10   iv 142 | Mr. John Brock

'Tis a vast Priviledge, for a Christian to be *Assured*, that the Lord will do this or that individual Thing for him. . . . but it is the *Holy Spirit* of the Lord Jesus Christ, that with a Singular Operation, does produce in a Christian this *Particular Faith*; which indeed is near akin to the *Faith of Miracles*. . . . Eminent was Mr. *Brock*, for this *Mysterious Excellency*.

It is a pity that some of our Saints should not from the swarm of miracles performed by the old and new Puritans compile & compose a Liber Conformitatum!—[1]

11   vi 70 | Ch 7 "Thaumatographia Pneumatica" Seventh Example

Mr. *Philip Smith*, aged about fifty years . . . a Deacon of the Church in *Hadley*, a Member of the *General Court* . . . a Man from *Devotion, Sanctity, Gravity*, and all that was honest, exceeding Exemplary. Such a Man was in the Winter of the Year 1684, murder'd with an hideous *Witchcraft*, that fill'd all those Parts of *New-England* with *Astonishment*.

8[1] The name given (with ranking, e.g. Third Wrangler) to candidates in the first class in the mathematical tripos at Cambridge. C appears to be offering evidence in support of Mather's etymology. According to *OED* ("bachelor") the etymology is still obscure.

9[1] "Perhaps more truly men better deserving the stick than the laurel"—the laurel being a symbol of honour, and *bacca lauri*, the laurel berry, being another possible source for the word *baccalarius*, "bachelor".

10[1] "Book of the conformed" or "of conformities". The reading is doubtful here, and might be *Confirmitatum*—for *Confirmatum*, "of the confirmed", hence a list of those who have the kind of assurance described in textus?

In order to any rational conviction of the miraculous nature of these ~~facts~~ quasi-*facts*, it would be a condition with me that a medical man of known science & philosophical temper, should have attended & examined & attested the case. Quid si hoc fuisset exemplum Syphilitidos deterrimæ diu celatæ—et lusus diabolici nil nisi comœdia dolosa ob ignominiam celandam, etiam post mortem?—[1]

12   vi 71 | Ninth Example

* *ᵃ*Four Children of *John Goodwin* in *Boston*, which had enjoy'd a Religious Education, and answer'd it with a towardly Ingenuity. . . . These were in the year 1688. arrested by a very stupendous *Witchcraft*. [Having been cursed by an Irish laundress, one after another of the children fell prey to "odd Fits": "Sometimes they were *Deaf*, sometimes *Dumb*, sometimes *Blind*, and often all this at once." The laundress, who used dolls stuffed with goat-hair and boasted about her pact with the Devil, was executed.]

* This is a most interesting account, & highly valuable as it throws unusual Light on the nature of the diseases mistaken for Witchcraft, and the state of mind of those who were the attendants and exorcists.

13   vi 73, marked with a short horizontal line

It was the Eldest of these Children that fell chiefly under my own Observation: For I took her home to my own Family, partly out of compassion to her Parents, but chiefly, that I might be a critical Eye-Witness of things that would enable me to confute the *Sadducism* of this Debauch'd Age.

how free from all Prepossession![1]

14   vi 73 | Continuing **13** textus

Here she continu'd well for some Days; applying *her self* to Actions of Industry and Piety: But *Nov.* 20. 1688. she cry'd out, *Ah, they have found me out!* and immediately she fell into her Fits; wherein *we* often observ'd, that she would cough up a Ball as big as a small Egg, into the

---

ᵃ C's asterisk is against the heading, "The Ninth Example"

11[1] "What if this were an example of a very advanced case of syphilis, long hidden—and the devil-play nothing but a sad masquerade for the purpose of hiding the shame, even after death?"

13[1] "Sadducism" is used in textus as synonymous with materialism; the word gained this meaning from the Sadducees' denial of the resurrection of the dead or the existence of angels.

side of her *Wind pipe*, that would near choak her, till by *Stroaking* and by *Drinking* it was again carry'd *down*.

evident Hysterics!—

15   vi 73

Moreover, one singular Passion that frequently attended her, was this: An *invisible Chain* would be clapt about her, and she in much pain and Fear, cry out when "*They*"*[a]* began to put it on.

invisible!

16   vi 73

A *Quaker's Book* being brought her, she could quietly read whole Pages of it; only the Name of GOD and CHRIST, she still skipp'd over, being unable to pronounce it, except sometimes, stammering a Minute or two, or more upon it. . . . But a Book against *Quakerism* "*They*"*[a]* would not hinder her from reading; but "*They*"*[a]* would from reading Books against Popery.

O *excellent*! Compare this with the narrations of Witchcraft given by several of the Quaker Memorialists.[1]

17   vi 74

A certain Prayer-Book being brought her, she not only could read it very well, but also did read a large Part of it over, calling it her *Bible*. . . . Only when she came to the Lord's Prayer now and then occurring in that Book, she would have her Eyes put out; so that she must turn over a new Leaf, and then she could read again.

O capital!—This whole case ought to be reprinted/ for at all events it would have a tendency to exorcize of this vile Superstition the Papists, the Quakers, the Church of England, & all the Arminian Sects.—

18   vi 77 | Twelfth Example

I will . . . single out one, that shall have in it much of *Demonstration*, as well as of Particularity.

It was on the Second of *May*, in the Year 1687. that a most ingenious,

---

[a] The square brackets of the original have been changed to quotation marks, to avoid confusion with editorial matter

16[1] For C's interest in the Quakers see MORE *Theological Works* **17** n 1.

accomplish'd, and well-dispos'd *young Gentleman*, Mr. *Joseph Beacon* by Name, about 5 a-clock in the *Morning* as he lay, whether sleeping or waking, he could not say, (but judg'd the latter of them,) had a View of his Brother then at *London*, although he was now himself at our *Boston*, distanc'd from him a thousand Leagues. . . . His [brother's] *Countenance* was very pale, ghastly, deadly, and he had a bloody Wound on one side of his Forehead. . . . Said *Joseph, what's the matter Brother! How came you here!* The Apparition reply'd, *Brother! I have been most barbarously and inhumanly murder'd by a debauch'd Fellow, to whom I never did any wrong in my Life.*

From this most plusquam demonstrative[1] Fact, we not ⟨only⟩ learn the truth of Apparitions, but likewise ⟨guess⟩ at what rate they travel, & that they are very fallible Beings. Bradley first measured the speed of Light—and if the Narrator or Letter-writer had but mentioned the day of the month as well as the month itself (april) of the Murder we should be able exactly to calculate how many miles an hour a Ghost can fly—/[2] Pity, that the Ghost was mistaken as to his escape to N. England.[3]

19 vi 78 | Thirteenth Example

The Natives of Heaven, as Dr. *Fuller* phraseth it, grudge not to guard those who are only Free Denizens thereof. The Excellent *Rivet* hath well express'd what is to believ'd of this matter, *That every one of them, who shall be Heirs of Salvation, hath . . . always one particular Angel with him, is a probable Truth, and not against the Scripture.*

What would the excellent Rivet have taught of a Louse who had asserted that he had always one man at least for his Lacquey to prevent his being combed out and cracked!—

20 vi 79 | *Sadducismus debellatus*

[The case of the "bewitched" daughter and niece of Samuel Paris, Pastor of Salem.] At length one Physician gave his Opinion *That they were under an Evil Hand.* . . . He had also an *Indian* Man-servant, and his Wife, who afterwards confess'd that . . . they had taken some of the afflicted Persons Urine, and mixing it with Meal, had made a Cake, and

---

18[1] "More than" demonstrative— mocking textus.

18[2] C is mistaken here: James Bradley (1693–1762), a meticulous and celebrated astronomer, was not the first to calculate the speed of light, nor was he associated particularly with that problem.

18[3] The ghost advised Beacon to take out a warrant for the arrest of his brother's murderer, who it said was trying to escape to New England. As it happened, the murderer made no such attempt: he was arrested; but he was not executed, thanks to the intervention of his friends.

bak'd it, to find out the Witch, as they said. After this, the afflicted Persons cry'd out of the *Indian* Woman nam'd *Tituba*, that she did pinch, prick, and grievously torment them . . .

N.B.

21   vi 79

In a short time after, other Persons who were of age to be Witnesses, were molested by Satan, and in their Fits cry'd out upon *Tituba*, and Goody O. and *S. G.* that they or spectres in their Shapes, did grievously torment them.

Poor Tituba!

22   vi 80

Her [Tituba's] Confession agreed exactly (which was afterwards verify'd in the other Confessors) with the Accusations of the Afflicted.

Very Observable! Poor Creature!—

23   vi 83

Can a more awful Instance be conceived of blind infatuated Belief than that the writer & transcriber of this 82 and 83 pages should have narrated as facts & evidences all the pages preceding!—[1]

24   vii 15 | Ch 3 "The First Synod of New-England"

. . . upon the Recommendation of *Alexander*, the Bishop of *Alexandria*, the Emperor singled out but Three Hundred and Eighteen [of 2048 bishops], who were all of them *Orthodox Children of Peace* . . . and that by the Emperor's happy chusing and heeding of these Three Hundred and Eighteen . . . the *Orthodox Religion* came to be Established.

If this be true or probable, it affords a strong argument for the Arians, who might fairly object to this celebrated Council—they were a *packed* Jury. Who need wonder, th in 318 Athanasians picked out of 2048 Bishops should report Athanasianism to be the orthodox Faith?

23[1] Pp 82–3 contain an analysis of the evidence in the preceding cases in the Salem witch trials and conclude "there was a going too far in this *Affair*"; that it rested on erroneous assumptions; that the number of cases increased rather than decreased after "witches" were executed; and that it seemed highly probable that innocent people had been executed. Mather attributes these conclusions to the "worthy Author, from whose Manuscript I have transcrib'd this Narrative" (83); C wonders how such rational conclusions are compatible with the credulity of the narrative.

25   vii 96, pencil, overtraced | Appendix

Have the *Quakers* ever yet Censured this their Author [Thomas Maule] for Holding-forth in his *Alcoran* . . . That the *Devil, Sin, Death, and Hell, are but Nothing, they are but a Non-Entity*: And . . . That *all Men who have a Body of Sin remaining in them, are* Witches?

Doubtless, poor TOM MAULE[a]1 meant these words in a mystic sense— God *is* & He only *is* together with those that have their being *in* Him. All true Entity is in Him included—but Death, Hell &c are neither in God nor with God nor of God—Ergo Non-Entity.

> Why at Tom Maule dost fret & foam?
> Thy own Book's but a mauling Tome.
> Add to thy name an R: for rather,
> A Mauler art thou than a Mather!
>   S. T. C.

26   iii 98, pencil

[In conversation with a Quaker, a minister asks leading questions and tries to argue the Quaker out of the *"Damnable Heresies"* of George Fox.]

What an ill-mannered Bigot does this Minister prove himself!—

---

[a] Double underlining not overtraced

251 Thomas Maule (1645–1724), resident of Salem, Quaker author of a pamphlet called *Truth Held Forth and Maintained*, for which he was imprisoned in 1695. He was a victim of laws directed specifically against Quakers "or any other blasphemous Heretics" who dissented from the prevailing orthodoxy of the New England Church. The very possession of writings by Quakers was punishable by fine.

AUGUST HEINRICH MATTHIAE
1769–1835

A Copious Greek Grammar. . . . Translated from the German by Edward Valentine Blomfield. 3rd ed. 2 vols. London 1824. 8º.

The 2 vols are paginated continuously.

Henry E. Huntington Library

Inscribed p ⁻2 "Edward Coleridge.—Eton College. 1825." and "Peter Balderston Macgregor September 16ᵗʰ 1884". These two signatures have been crossed out in ink; below them, the inscription "George Scott Merton Coll: 19/4/85" is in turn crossed out in pencil; the final inscription reads "D. O'Donovan Brisbane". Short notes by Edward Coleridge on I xiii, 115, and II 436 as well as underlining and marginal crosses or question marks on I xxiv, xxv, xxxvi, xxxvii, xl, xlii, l, 3, 4, 5, 6, 7, 9, 98, 99, 108, 109, II 844, 1032, 1033. There is a correction apparently by George Scott on II 825. Since C's notes are neatly written in ink, it is unlikely that he also made the large pencilled crosses on I xxxviii, xxxix, xliv, xlv. A typed slip by the Huntington librarian is pasted in at I ⁻6 and II ⁻4, and an extract from a bookseller's catalogue at I ⁺6.

DATE. Between 26 Jul and 6 Sept 1825, and possibly up to Jan 1826. On 7 Sept 1825 C wrote to Edward Coleridge, "I will return your Matthai as well worth your valuing, as the sum total of my Lucubrations on the philosophy of Language in detailed Application to the Greek Language can make it—" (*CL* v 493). He probably borrowed the book on the occasion of his taking Henry Gillman to Eton (21–6 Jul 1825: *CL* v 487n) and actually returned it 30 Jan 1826 (*CL* VI 549).

1   I xxxiv–xxxvii | Remarks to p 19 § 19

The *spiritus lenis* [smooth breathing] was an invention of the grammarians.* It denotes nothing more than the absence of the *spiritus asper* [rough breathing].

* I feel more inclined to express than I find myself to support, a doubt as to the truth of this Assertion. What if the Greek fineness and sensitive Subtlety of Ear, educated to exquisiteness by the Grammaticè,[1] had discovered the fact, that even the Vowels cannot be sounded without a slight, yet appropriate, modification by muscular energy? May not the Lenis have resembled the Breathing which the Latins in certain words

1[1] "Grammar", literally "Grammatical [art]".

827

substituted for the Aspirate, and expressed by an s? as sex, septem for ἑξ, ἑπτα.[2] The Digamma in its original by civilized Organs unpronouncible Harshness was, I doubt not, ng, the sound, we hear in the nang, nang of a vexed and angry infant—& probably the same with the primitive force of the Hebrew *Nain*.[3]

2 ɪ 15 | § 15

In some vowels, the mode in which the Romans expressed them, leads us to form a tolerably accurate judgment of the pronunciation of the Greeks: e.g. In Latin η is always expressed by a long *e*. Σειληνός, *Silenus*, ʼΑθῆναι, Athenae, as in Greek the long *e* of the Romans is expressed by η . . .*

* Yet Titus is found in Greek Writers both Τειτος and Τητος.[1] The Port-Royal prove that η was pronounced as A in Ale by the Aristophanic Sheep, βη βη.[2] So the French hear it: we are equally sure, that the Sheep say, Bah Bah—or the a in Mam*a*.

3 ɪ 18 | § 17

3. δ and θ are pronounced by the modern Greeks with an aspirate, yet so that it is less in δ, and more strong in θ, which latter is exactly expressed by the pronunciation of *th* in English.

We confound in writing two very distinct sounds for the ear, *thy Thigh*— δy θy or ƚy[1]

4 ɪ 20–1 | § 20

. . . the ancients pronounced every word which began with a vowel, with an aspirate which had the sound of our *w*, and was often expressed by β, or υ, and also γ. For this the figure of a double Γ was invented, Ϝ,

---

1[2] Greek *hex, hepta* ("six, seven"—as the Latin).

1[3] C has more to say about the digamma in **4** below. He believed that the digamma must have been pronounced originally as a double gamma, i.e. as "ng", and that the same primitive sound is found in the Hebrew letter ayin. There is a full explanation of his position in Hartley COLERIDGE **4** n 1.

2[1] C repeats this point in Hartley COLERIDGE **29**.

2[2] *A New Method of Learning with Facility the Greek Tongue . . . Translated from the French of the messieurs de Port-Royal* (1746) ɪ 6 cites Eustathius who quoted an ancient writer named Cratinus to prove that sheep say βῆ, βη, the long *e* of eta being said to be equivalent to the *e* in *fête* and *bête*. (No English equivalent is given.) C confuses this example with a later one (ɪ 11) in which it is pointed out that Aristophanes has a dog say αὐ, αὐ.

3[1] Besides the Greek letter theta (θ), C invokes two symbols—δ and ƚ—from a "universal" or phonetic alphabet (untraced) like that in John Hart's *Orthography* (1569) or F. Lodwick's *Essay towards a Universal Alphabet* (1686) to express the difference between the voiced and unvoiced *th*.

whence the name digamma, which was called Aeolic, because the Aeolians, of all the tribes, retained the greatest traces of their original language.

The space of this Margin will not suffice for the disproof of this Assertion. Had the Digamma *originally* expressed so so[a] soft a sound as w or u: why was it discontinued at so early a period? That it had, however, already been softened when the Iliad was composed, I do not doubt; and think it more than probable, that not only in different Dialects but in different words in the same dialect the Digamma had different substitutes, β, f, χ, w, u, s[1]—& that in some cases the primitive sound was rendered pronouncible by prefixing a Vowel, as in anguish, a*nghe*los.[2]

5 ɪ 64–5 | § 61

The parts of speech in Greek are:
1. Words which indicate the ideas of corporal substances found in space, *Nouns*. These are: 1. Either substantive . . . They express things or persons . . . 2. Or unsubstantive, which convey no perfect substantial idea, but must always be considered in connection with a substantive thing with which they are found; *N. adjective*.

There is one Error common to all Grammars, and the Queen-bee of a whole Hive of false notions, viz. that words correspond to *Things*: whereas they refer wholly to our *Thoughts* of Things and the mental Acts occasioned by or ensuing on the impression.[1] While *things* are present, men converse δεικτικως;[2] or talk from the mere habit of social communion, & even then address themselves to the Thoughts, in which they seek a sympathy with their own thoughts, or a confirmation of the Objectivity (= real *Outness*) of the Appearance.—This whole enumeration of the Parts of Speech is vulgar, *unthinking*, & below the book.

S. T. C.

6 ɪ 65 | § 63

Generally, every substantive has its determinate gender. . . . This determination of the gender of a substantive is founded probably in accidental

---

[a] C repeats the word in going from the end of one line to the beginning of the next

4[1] In C's list the first character is a Greek beta (*b*) and the third a chi (*ch* as in "loch"). For C's theory of the digamma see **1** and n 2 above.

4[2] C's phonetic transcription of the Greek ἄγγελος, "messenger".

5[1] This is a cardinal point in C's philos-ophy of language; cf similar remarks in the instructional letter written to James Gillman Jr in Oct 1826, *CL* vɪ 630.

5[2] "By pointing": C reserved *apodeixis*, "demonstration", for information acquired by logical processes, e.g. *Logic* (*CC*) 202.

resemblances, which certain ideas seem to bear to one of the two genders in nature.

Vix credo.[1] It is plausible: as common-place notions generally are. I hold the genders to be the metaphors of Grammarians—a mere copula technica[2] peculiar to languages, or rather to the state & period of the languages, in which the *most* general relations of Place are expressed by agglutinated Postpositions, named Cases.

7 ɪ 68–70 | § 66

Obs. 1. In the two first declensions the termination only of the nominative case is changed in the remaining cases, so that the number of syllables remains the same. In the third, on the contrary, the terminations of the other cases are affixed to the nominative, yet with some change. The first are called *parisyllabic*, the others *imparisyllabic*.
Obs. 2. The old grammarians reckoned ten declensions, five simple, and five contracted. . . . The new division [into three declensions] originates with J. Weller, or according to others, with Laurentius Rhodomannus.

It would, ως εμοίγε δοκεῖ,[1] be more simple to divide the Nouns into Pari- and imparisyllabic, with a supplementary for the parisyllabic with exception of the Dat. Plural—classing the Ionic Form under the Second, τειχος, τειχεος; and the Attic under the last.[2]

The τειχεος, τειχοῦς; and φιλέω, φιλῶ; are the mere Tobacco hoc, tobacco hic of Grammarians invented, one would think, to promote Stammering in boys.[3] Almost as wisely might we have ειμι, εμμι or εσω, ero,[4] or run the Castilian and Portuguese Dialects of the Spanish together. Surely, the differences in the 5th Declension are at least as striking as that between ας, ου, and ος, ου.[5] On the plan, I propose,

6[1] "I can scarcely believe it."
6[2] A mere "artificial link".
7[1] "As it seems to me, at least".
7[2] C attempts a simplification of Matthiae's scheme. *Teichos* ("wall") belongs to a large class of nouns with stems ending in e, which in the Attic dialect that the grammar books take as their standard merges with the vowel of the inflexional suffix; the dative plural, however, always has the extra syllable. The "Attic" declension (not peculiar to the Attic dialect) has second-declension endings with -ως instead of -ος. C's "last" is a slip for "first": the Attic declension belongs to the parisyllabic division.

7[3] C is complaining about the way in which students are drilled in reciting the alternative uncontracted and contracted forms of certain nouns and verbs as they appear side by side in the grammar books. "Tobacco hoc, tobacco hic" is the beginning of a schoolboy jingle.
7[4] Dialect variants of the verb "I am", and an active Greek form (see **10** n 28) invented by the grammarians to correspond to the Latin future "I shall be".
7[5] Masculine nouns of the first declension, ending in -ας or -ης, have the genitive ending -ου, borrowed from the second declension's mainly masculine -ος words, while the larger group of first-declension

each declension would be subdiv⟨id⟩ed into Masc. Fem. & Neuter: for which the Learner would be prepared by the ο, η, το.[6] But neither the Gr. Declensions nor Conjugations can be understood without a previous insight into the significant Letters, and ⟨the⟩ Breathings represented by the Letters—the Halitus in certain words being semi-articulated—as m and s, both of which suffered elision in the elder Latin. The Genitive was always υ, the Dative ι, the Accusative ν, or the *letter* ς. It may, however, bear a question, whether some of the Genitive Terminations are not the (now) Nominatives of Pronoun Adjectives. Grammarians forget, if indeed they ever knew, that there must have been a state anterior to Cases, as well as a state of the language posterior to them/. ex. gr. Italian & Modern Greek.[7]

8 ı 208–9, partly in pencil | § 169

The prepositions σὺν and ἐν, *whose final consonant is changed . . . into γ, λ, μ, ϱ, σ take ν again before the *syllablic augment*, e.g. ἐγγίγνομαι . . .

I[a] cannot tolerate this use of the personal Genitive, *whose*, for "of which." It neutralizes our poetry and stiffens our prose[1]—Why should we diminish the so scanty number of significant terminations in our language? But such is the Spirit of the Age—under a shew of Refinement to confound ⟨Things with⟩ Persons, in order to subordinate the latter to the former!—Varnish *vice* Polish!   S. T. Coleridge

9 ıı 448 | § 312

The vocative is used, as in English and Latin, in addressing an object.

[a] In pencil, as is the asterisk in the textus

---

feminines end in -α or -η in the nominative singular and -ας or -ης in the genitive. The variations in the stem vowels and in the genitive singular are the only marks distinguishing the first and second declensions. C would be right to imply that the differences between the nouns in Matthiae's third declension are more striking, but the old fifth declension includes only the more straightforwardly inflected nouns; greater variations come in the five declensions of contracted nouns (also in Matthiae's third declension).

7[6] I.e. by the declension of the definite article. The division by genders might not work very well with some classes of impari-

syllabic nouns. C proposed several schemes for learning Greek and Latin, and wrote lessons and exercises for his own children as well as for the Gillman boys: see CAMDEN headnote, *CN* ııı 4210 and n. No other outline of this system of Greek nouns appears to have survived.

7[7] Italian and modern Greek eliminated all and some (respectively) of the case endings in the course of their evolution from Latin and ancient Greek. C looks back to a state prior to the evolution of cases, the "prothesis" of a logical pentad (as in IRVING 2).

8[1] A frequent complaint: cf MILTON *Poems* 3.

The Cases may be defined generally as significant vocables, of two kinds: first, signs of Subject and Object = Nom. et Accus.—and 2. of the most general and comprehensive relations of *place* = Gen. and Dative.—The Vocative is no proper case; but expresses a mere accident of the Voice in calling to a distinct Subject—where the additional Quantity (intensio) of Sound on the first syllable is ~~con~~ equalized by the subtraction from (fall of the Voice in) the last Syllable. Dominus, Dómine.[1]

10　ɪɪ 449–64 | § 313

[In the section of the work that deals with syntax, Matthiae begins with the rules and conventions governing the nominative and vocative cases, and then turns to] what are called the *oblique cases* (i.e. those which must always be dependent upon other words), the genitive, dative, and accusative. The most extensive range among these cases belongs to *The Genitive*, which may stand not only with the predicate, but with any word of the proposition, and expresses in a certain degree a relation in general . . .

The original sign of the Genitive I apprehend to have ⟨been⟩ ὑ,[1] as expressive of ~~thate~~ perpendicular line to and from ᴀ 2 given points ⎰ , which we may generalize in the term, dependency—& it is not impossible, that the Rain imagined as lineѕ or threads of water from the Sky (i.e. Clouds) might have furnished the primary image, or at least the first application. Ὕω, pl*uo*.[2] Hence, the frequent translatability of the Greek Genitive by *de*,[3] and hence too the double use of our own of, ~~in~~ the Son of David wrote *of* (= concerning) trees and herbs. Still, however, it is necessary in philosophic grammar to keep the relation in space before the imagination, and to rem̃ber*a* that ⟨in⟩ c | c, the line c c may equally

$$\begin{array}{c} a \\ | \\ b \end{array}$$

express a flash of electric fire from the cloud, a, perpendicularly to the earth, b; or from the earth, b, to the cloud, a.—. The ὑ therefore will be capable of expressing every kind of *direct* connection, that at the same time implies a former contact with the point a, or b: and ⟨it is⟩ in this

---

a A conventional contraction: "remember"

9[1] The nominative and vocative "Lord, O Lord".

10[1] The Greek letter upsilon with a rough breathing, pronounced *hū*: C speculates that this "position"—as he calls such grammatical units in a letter of 1826 (*CL* ᴠɪ 633)—was the origin of genitive case endings in Greek, as iota and nu are said below and in **7** above to be the origins of dative and accusative ones.

10[2] The Greek and Latin for the verb "I rain".

10[3] Latin "down from" or, as below, "concerning".

γόνου ὑβρίσματα, 'insults offered to the brother', *injuria fratris. Id. Androm.* 1060. γυναικὸς αἰχμαλωτίδος φόβος, 'fear of the slave'. ἔχθος Κορινθίων, ἔχθρα Λακεδαιμονίων, φιλία Δημοσθένους, εὔνοια 'Αθηναίων *Thuc.* VII. 57. Comp. *Xen. Anab.* IV. 7, 20. Passages also occur, where substantives which are derived from verbs, or correspond to verbs which take the object in the dative, are constructed with the genitive. *Eurip. Or.* 123. νερτέρων δωρήματα, 'offerings of the dead, i. e. offered to the dead'. *Plat. Leg.* VII. *p.* 342. ἐν (τοῖς?) τῶν θεῶν θύμασιν. *Soph. Antig.* 1185. εὔγματα Παλλάδος, 'prayers to Pallas', *Thuc.* II. 79. ἡ τῶν Πλαταιέων ἐπιστρατεία, 'the march against the Platæans'. *Id.* I. 108. ἐν ἀποβάσει τῆς γῆς, 'in the act of landing on the coast'.

314.   *Obs.* 1. Sometimes one substantive governs two different genitives in different relations. *Her.* VI. 2. 'Ισιαῖος — Σαρδὼ νῆσον τὴν μεγίστην ὑποδεξάμενος κατεργάσασθαι, ὑπέδυνε τῶν 'Ιώνων τὴν ἡγεμονίην τοῦ πρὸς Δαρεῖον πολέμου, 'the leading of the Ionians in the war against Darius'. *Thuc.* III. 12. εἴ τῳ δοκοῦμεν ἀδικεῖν προαποστάντες διὰ τὴν ἐκείνων μέλλησιν τῶν εἰς ἡμᾶς δεινῶν, 'on account of their delay with respect to the harm'. *Plato Republ.* I. *p.* 150. ἔνιοι δὲ καὶ τὰς τῶν οἰκείων προπηλακίσεις τοῦ γήρως ὀδύρονται, when the genitive τοῦ γήρως is used *objectively*, 'the insults which the relations offer to old age'. *Isocr. Panath. p.* 249. Δ. ('Αγαμέμνων τοὺς βασιλεῖς ἔπεισε κινδυνεύειν καὶ πολεμεῖν) ὑπὲρ τοῦ μὴ τὴν 'Ελλάδα πάσχειν ὑπὸ τῶν βαρβάρων μήτε τοιαῦτα, μήθ' οἷα πρότερον αὐτῇ συνέπεσε περὶ τὴν Πέλοπος μὲν ἁπάσης Πελοποννήσου κατάληψιν, Δαναοῦ δὲ τῆς πόλεως τῆς 'Αργείων, Κάδμου δὲ Θηβῶν.

Obs 2. The following are abbreviated phrases, which cannot be explained by the above modes: ἅρμα ἵππων Νισαίων *Herod.* VII. 40. 'a chariot drawn by Nisæan horses', λευκῆς χιόνος πτέρυξ *Soph. Antig.* 114. 'a snow-white wing, a wing of snow'.

The following cases are especially to be noticed :

I. To words of all kinds other words are added in 315. the genitive, which show the respect in which the sense of those words must be taken; in which case the genitive properly signifies, 'with regard to'.

1. With verbs: in the phrases ὡς, ὅπως, πῶς, οὕτως ἔχει, 'to be qualified or endowed in any manner whatever', *se habere. Herod.* VI. 116. Ἀθηναῖοι δὲ, ὡς ποδῶν εἶχον, τάχιστα ἐβοήθεον ἐς τὸ ἄστυ, *ut sese habebant quoad pedes, i. e. quantum pedibus valebant,* 'as fast as they could run'. Thus also *Plat. Gorg. p.* 131. and elliptically *Æsch. Suppl.* 849. σοῦσθ᾽ ἐπὶ βᾶριν ὅπως ποδῶν *Herod.* IX. 66. ὅκως ἂν αὐτὸν ὁρέωσι σπουδῆς ἔχοντα. V. 20. καλῶς ἔχειν μέθης, 'to be pretty drunk'. I. 30. μετρίως ἔχειν βίου. *Eurip. Hipp.* 462. εὖ ἔχειν φρενῶν. *Soph. Œd. T.* 345. ὡς ὀργῆς ἔχω. *Thuc.* I. 22. ὦ ἑκάτερος τὶς εὐνοίας ἢ μνήμης ἔχοι, 'as each wished well to a party, or remembered the past'. II. 90. ὡς εἶχε τάχους ἕκαστος. Thus also *Plat. Gorg. p.* 13. πῶς τὰ ἄστρα πρὸς ἄλληλα τάχους ἔχει, and before, πρὸς αὐτὰ καὶ πρὸς ἄλληλα πῶς ἔχει πλήθους, 'as they stand in relation to each other with regard to number'. *Rep.* II. *p.* 221. τοσαῦτα λεγόμενα ἀρετῆς πέρι καὶ κακίας, ὡς ἄνθρωποι καὶ θεοὶ περὶ αὐτὰ ἔχουσι τιμῆς, τί οἰόμεθα ἀκουούσας νέων ψυχὰς ποιεῖν, *i. e.* ὡς ἅ. καὶ θ. αὐτὰ τιμῶσι. III. *p.* 267. ὅπως πράξεως ἔχει, *i. e.* ὅπως πράττει. *Gorg. p.* 53. οὐ γὰρ οἶδα, παιδείας ὅπως ἔχει καὶ δικαιοσύνης, *ignoro, quam sit doctus, quam bonus vir, Cic. Tusc. Qu.* v. 12. *Leg.* IV. *p.* 163. ναυπηγησίμης ὕλης ὁ τόπος πῶς ἔχει; 'how is the place with respect to timber for shipbuilding'? Thus *Plat. Lys. p.* 241. in Heindorf, §. 33. it is properly τοὺς οὕτως ἀγνοίας ἔχοντας, and *Leg.* IX. *p.* 17. it should be πῶς ἔχει συμφωνίας, not τῆς συμφ. *Xen. Cyrop.* VII. 5, 56. οὕτω τρόπου ἔχειν, *eo ingenio esse*[t].

---

[t] Hemsterh. ad Lucian. t. i. p. 228.   Valck. ad Herod. p. 263, 33. ad Eur. Hippol. 462.   Wessel. ad Her. p. 722, 36.   Fisch. iii. b. p. 72. 85. Toup. Em. in Suid. t. iii. p. 12.   Brunck ad Arist. Lysistr. 173.

respect ⟨that⟩ it differs specifically from the *iota*, as the sign of the Dative.[4] For this image of dependent connection becoming the prevailing thought, ~~it becomes~~ the verticality of the line ceases to be essential, & the direction may be imagined as horizontal—ex. gr. the imaginary line from a Ship to the shore, it had sailed from.—(When the remotion or distance becomes the predominant thought, the "of" in our language is intensified by aspirate or reduplication into *off*.) The ~~Father~~ Parent and *Off*-spring presenting all the conditions of this *original* attachment or coincidence, with separation, dependency &c, gave occasion to the term, Genitive.[5] But single Instances pro toto[6] lead to many mistakes, by narrowing the original generalization.—A Girl with a bird on a string, as an emblem of *property*, would supply one in a series of little pictures expressing the dependent (Gen.) Case.—. N.B. In the Genitive *absolute*,[7] the true philosophic parsing would be, to mention the radical & say, *it* was governed (i.e. had its relation determined by) the affixed Case-vocable: for the Case Absolute is analogous to the Conjunction, i.e. Preposition governing a whole Sentence considered as one indeclin able (because in all its parts already declined) word.—

On the other ⟨hand,⟩ the ι which I suppose with Blomfield to have been the original Dative[8] represents the horizontal, or perhaps (by combination with φ[9]?) the slant ascending line, accompanied with the idea, ⟨sometimes⟩ of a determinate commencing point; ~~and~~ but always of a determinate direction and *point toward which*. $\diagup$ b or a —— b. In the

a

Genitive the origin may be *a*, or ⟨may be⟩ *b*: in the dative this is ⟨either left unexpressed, or it is⟩ determined to *a* exclusively. The reason follows. Viz. that the idea of the continuing connection or colligation is omitted. It is an arrow from the ~~String~~ Bow to the Mark, not the Bird at the end of the Silk-thread, or the Lead at the

10[4] In *TT* 18 Mar 1827 C is reported as saying, "The genitive case denotes dependence; the dative, transmission."

10[5] The term, meaning in a broad sense "belonging to birth or generation" and associated with such words as "genitor", appears to have arisen as a mistranslation of a Greek word signifying "generic" (*OED*): the misconception is as old as the term itself and is not peculiar to C.

10[6] "Standing for the whole".

10[7] Matthiae discusses the genitive absolute II 457–8 as an instance of the geni-

tive's being used to signify "with regard to".

10[8] Edward Valentine Blomfield (1788–1816) was the translator of the work. C is recalling his "Remarks" in I xxxviii: "It is consonant with analogy to suppose, that the termination of the dative case was originally uniform. . . . Upon the whole I cannot but think, in opposition to Fabricius, Koen, and others, that the ι was the most ancient termination of this case."

10[9] With omega, as an iota subscript.

end of the Clock-pendulum. Hence our equivalent for the Dative, *to*, & *for*—i.e. either the direction or the mark. Hence ——b would sufficiently express the Dative; but the Genitive must have a——b:—another reason for preferring the name, *Dependent* Case, to Genitive, and for placing it last instead of second. The order, & names, I would recommend, are 1. Subjective. 2. Subjective vocativè. 3. Objective. 4 4 Post-objective (till I can hit on a better word, from τελος[10] in the *teleo*logical sense.) 5. Dependent. N.B. all words following a preposition except in in the Accusative are governed by the case interposed (ut instar præpositionis)[11] between the Prep. and the Radical—as παρ' οικου, παρα υ οικ[12] from *close off* the house./ παρα in παρεια, paries, par—*cheek* by Jole.[13] But even Accusatives are frequently governed by their own significationnt Affix, as after Verbs passive, the ν[14] itself meaning "as to" and superseding the necessity of the clumsy κατα.[15] So εις ν ναον[16] is literally "going["], the object of the *Go* (or Motion onward) being the Temple, avidum percussus arundine pectus &c.[17] The mistake of Grammarians may in great part be attributed to their ignorance of the necessarily wide & multifold import of the primitive significant Images, or Terms of a language.[18] The growth of language, ⟨as⟩ of all other growing things, is a process of developement, explication[19]—Sameness advancing towards Unity by a continued evolution of diffenrrences—from Chaos to κοσμος.[20]—From inadvertence to this the Grammar-makers *antedate* the distinctions, and support the anachronism by arbitrary subintelligiturs, ενεκα, κατα, περι, & the like.[21] One great use of Grammar is to teach Youths the habit of generalizing & analysing, by accustoming them to reflect on the multifold significancy of the simplest

10[10] The *telos* or "end proposed": in C's words above and below, "direction", "mark", "aim".

10[11] "Equivalent to a preposition".

10[12] C appears to be suggesting that before they became case endings the genitive ν and dative ι would have been placed between the preposition and the radical form of the noun.

10[13] C finds traces of the Greek preposition *para*, "beside", in *pareia*, "cheek", and in the Latin words "wall" and "equal".

10[14] The letter nu, a common ending for the accusative singular.

10[15] The preposition meaning "as to" or "in respect of".

10[16] Lit "to a temple". C would make

this accusative the direct object, deriving εις "to" from εἰμι "I go".

10[17] Ovid *Heroides* (*Epistles*) 9.161: "stricken with the arrow in his lustful heart" (tr Grant Showerman LCL 1914).

10[18] Given the exceptionally direct use of images in this note, C's comment in *AR* (1825) 314n is apposite: ". . . all radicals [belong] to one or other of three classes, 1. Interjections . . . 2. Imitations of sounds . . . 3. and principally, visual images, objects of sight".

10[19] Lit an "unfolding"—a point C makes elsewhere, e.g. BÖHME 5.

10[20] *Cosmos*, "order", "world", "universe".

10[21] The prepositions "on account of", "as to", "around".

forms of motion & position, in respect of Space & Time—as the constant accompaniments & therefore the natural exponents, of our actions and their Objects & Aims; and then by transfer (per metaphoram)[22] the allegories of our internal acts & experiences. Lastly, the main complaint, I make against Matthiæ's dissertation on the Cases, is its αναρτητον.[23] The differences should have been evolved *genetically* from the seminal Idea—Thus all the numerous sentences, cited by him as examples of the Genitive, may without difficulty be reduced to the general Conception of *subsisting dependency*, under the ~~several~~ two forms of proceeding from & belonging to; which latter again divaricates into the conceptions of property (= the Possessive) and finality or that which determines the direction of the Proceeding, expressed ~~in~~ by the words, *"in respect of"*, *"on account of,"* etc. In this last form the Genitive approaches to the 2nd power of the Dative.: the 1st power being direction (= *to*), the 2nd Aim or Mark (= *for*). The Latin Ablative I regard as a mere refinement, to compensate for the narrower use of the Genitive & occupying, as it were, the mid-ground or punctum indifferentiæ[24] between the Gen. and Dative. It exists only in the Singular number, and but in moderate proportion of the Nouns. The origin of the Dual and Plural Terminations, the ov, αι, ων and the final σ, has been the subject of a few fanciful guesses with me; but nothing more. Nescio.[25]

S. T. C.

P.S. To understand the Genitive after Verbs it is only necessary to bear in mind, that tho' the Verb Substantive (the Identity of Act and Being) polarizes into Noun and Verb,[26] the latter ~~is~~ expresses the abstraction of motion from the thing moved in different degrees in different words, more completely in one, less so in another. In other words, a Verb always contains a Noun; & ~~in~~ sometimes the Noun retains & exercises its nominal functions, especially where the Verb Substantive affixed is in its passive form, or neutral—i.e. *obscurely* active. The genitive following αρχω, μήνησασθαι, ληθεσθαι are in fact governed by αρχη, μνησις, ληθη.[27] Even in the V. S. there is an oscillation between

---

10^{22} "By a metaphor"—C drawing attention to the literal equivalence of "transfer" and "metaphor" as derived from Latin and Greek roots (respectively) meaning "carry across".

10^{23} "Incoherence", "lack of connection".

10^{24} "Point of indifference".

10^{25} "I do not know." No such speculations survive in written form.

10^{26} C alludes to the triad or pentad of grammar which appears also in e.g. a letter of 1829 to Hyman Hurwitz (*CL* VI 816–17), *Logic* (*CC*) 16–18, *TT* 18 Mar 1827, and LACUNZA **45**.

10^{27} I.e. these verbs—"I rule", "to remember", "to forget" (the last two examples given by Matthiae II 463–4)—govern the genitive because their cognate nouns govern the genitive. In *TT* 18 Mar 1827, C

the Active & Passive./ Where the Act predominates, as in the obsolete εω, ω, that is extent*a* only as a termination, we may render it by, I make me to be: while —ομαι, —σθαι, may be translated *"to suffer."*[28]

---

a A slip for "extant"?

---

is reported as saying, "It is absurd to talk of verbs governing."

10[28] The normal form εἰμί ("I am") was wrongly assumed by the grammarians to have superseded the hypothetical forms given by C. (Έω does exist as a present subjunctive.) The theory that the inflections of all Greek verbs arose from suffixing appro-priate forms of the verb "to be" was maintained by e.g. VINCENT *The Greek Verb Analysed* (passim), HERMANN 173. The future of the verb "to be" has passive (or middle) endings: ἔσομαι "I shall be" and ἔσεσθαι "to be going to be". C takes them as evidence of the "oscillation between the Active & Passive".

FRIEDRICH VON MATTHISSON
1761–1831

Copy A

Gedichte. [Carlsruhe 1792.]

This copy lacks the title-page.

Victoria College Library (Coleridge Collection)

MS TRANSCRIPT. VCL LT 45: EHC transcript.

DATE. On or about 10 Oct 1801.

1 p +4,ᵃ pencil

First Stone layed by Sara on Thursday, March 26th, 1801. So it re-mained, till Saturday noon, October 10th, 1801—when at between the hours of 12 and 2, William Wordsworth, & his Sister, with S. T. Cole-ridge built it—to wit, all the stone-work, with the foot-stones—we being all then in hope & prayer, that Mary with Tom Hutchinson had then already set off, & was setting off, from Gallow Hill, on their road to Grasmere.—God in heaven bless her—& him too.—[1]

October 10th—10 days before my Birth day—when I shall be 29 years old—Eheu! *vixi*!![2]   S. T. Coleridge

2 p +5,ᵇ pencil

Saturday ⟨Noon,⟩ from ¼ past 12, to 2—(Octob. 9̶ 10th 1801) Numbers, 1. 2. and 4. built up compleatly* the Seat, of which little Five[1] had layed the first stone so long back as ⟨Thursday⟩ March 26th, 1801.

Dear Mary! I wish, you may be on the road to us.—   S. T. C.ᶜ

* all but the Moss Cushion.—

ᵃ At the head of the page, in ink, possibly by C: "2"
ᵇ At the head of the page, in ink, possibly by C: "2" (cf **1** n *a*) and "36"
ᶜ The last sentence and C's initials are written between two wavy lines

1[1] C records the building of "Sara's Seat" (for Sara Hutchinson) at Dove Cottage; *DWJ* I 77 confirms the date of 10 Oct.

1[2] "Alas! *I have lived*!!" C makes the usual mistake about his birthday, which was actually 21 Oct; in *CL* II 766, he writes to RS, "Oct. 21. 1801.—The day after my Birth day—29 years of age!—Who on earth can say that without a sigh!"

2[1] Sara Hutchinson (as recorded in **1**), whose sister Mary must have been "Three" to the "1. 2. and 4." of WW, DW, and C.

Copy B

Gedichte. 4th ed. Zürich 1797. 8°.

University of Texas (Humanities Research Center)? Reported to be here, but not catalogued, and not located 1986 or later

Inscribed on p ⁻2: "Herbert Coleridge, for his love of Matthison's Muse, from his affectionate mother, Sara Coleridge, Augst 10th 1848."; "Edith Coleridge 1861"; "Bequeathed to Frances Patteson, by Edith Coleridge 1911." "Presented to Ernest Hartley Coleridge, by his cousin Arthur Duke Coleridge, October 1914. A. D. C. died, Oct. 29. 1913."

DATE. 9 May 1820.

1   p ⁻2

Sara Coleridge from her affectionate Father S. T. Coleridge

"Die Kinderjahre" p. 15–29; der "Schmetterling" p. 50; and the Alpenreise, p. 75; will be especial Favorites with you, I dare anticipate.

9 May, 1820. Highgate.

S. MAXWELL
fl 1823

The Battle of the Bridge; or, Pisa Defended. A poem, in ten cantos. . . . 2nd ed. Edinburgh & London 1823. 12°. The preface is dated 1 May 1823.

This work was first pub 1822 as *Chinzica; or, the Battle of the Bridge*, by Henry Stobert. No other record has been found of either Stobert or Maxwell, however, and it seems possible that both are pseudonyms.

British Library C 126 d 14

Inscribed in ink on the half-title: "To S. T. Coleridge Esqre From the Author". "S. T. C." label on title-page verso. John Duke Coleridge's monogram on p ⁻4. Unopened after p 37.

DATE. 1823.

1 p ⁻2

The metrical arrangement ◡ — |◡ — ◡ | — | — | — of far too frequent recurrence in modern Poems, of tetrameter Iambic. Ex gr.

> The Sun's | unclouded | Beams | ne'er leave/[1]

The sum total of the times in this metre ought be[a] 12, varied by 11. Now taking in the necessary pauses occasioned by the spondaic monosyllables, I find the above arrangement = 14 times at least, and sometimes (as when any of the three last word-syllables are emphatic) = 15; that is, iso~~me~~chronous to an Heroic, or Pentameter Iambic.—

2 pp 23–4 | Canto I xvi st 3

How long her thoughts in one dark maze,
(Held her in wild and) vacant gaze   Fix'd her wild eyes in
How long, ~~w~~With clasp/ed hands, and rais/ed eyes,
~~She seem'd to supplicate~~ How long she commun'd with the skies
How long, ~~with~~ how ferven~~ey~~tly she pray'd;
I know: ~~not; yet I mark'd~~ for I behold, the maid.

[a] For "to be"

[1] Canto 1 st 4 line 8.

839

Her tall form in the midnight wind,
Which toss'd her flowing hair behind,
I mark*ʹd*; and as the increasing blast
Drove the thick rain unheeded past;
*ᵃ*And as the frequent lightning stream'd,
She like a marble statue gleam'd.
I mark'd again: with calm, still air,
She's like an angel watching there.

A marble Statue she might seem,
~~That~~ And as the frequent Lightnings stream
Gives a new terror to the gleam.
Again I mark: with calm, still air
I see an Angel watching there.

ᵃ C has made an ink line in the margin beside this and the following three lines

JOHANN FRIEDRICH MECKEL, THE YOUNGER
1781–1833

System des vergleichenden Anatomie. Vol I (of 6 vols in 7). Halle 1821. 8°.

Flyleaf only, watermarked 1822, from Vol I, the volume itself not located. The other vols (II being in two parts) were published 1824, 1825, 1828, 1829, 1831, 1833.

New York Public Library (Berg Collection)

DATE. 12 Jan 1825 (1).

COEDITOR. Raimonda Modiano.

1 I, flyleaf, referring to I vii

Zuvörderst habe ich . . . das ganze Werk in einen allgemeinen und einen desondern Theil zerfällt. Der erste, welchen der vorliegende Band begreift, enthält die allgemeinsten Momente der thierischen Form und die Bildungsgesetze. Diese habe ich . . . am richtigsten so aufzufassen geglaubt, dass ich alle untergeordneten Betrachtungspunkte auf zwei, die *Mannichfaltigkeit* und die *Einheit* oder die *Analogie*, zurückführte.

[First of all, I divided . . . the entire work into a general and a special section. The first, which the present volume deals with, contains the most general characteristics of the animal form and the laws of development. These . . . I thought best to interpret by reducing all secondary aspects to two: *Variety* and *Unity* or *Analogy*.]

12 Jany 1825. It rather surprizes me to find in the work of a *German Physiologist* to the Fact, which was to be referred, laid down as the Principle, from which it is to be *deduced*: and thus the Problem itself metaphrased into its own Solution. That an organized Body is a Whole consisting of several and various Parts is the fact/ as fact of every man's knowlege. And what are we the *knowinger* for being told, that Manifoldness and Unity are the *Laws* of Plastic Life? i.e. that Animal-making is the way pursued by Nature in making Animals! And then still further to prove the vagueness of the Author's conception, he gives Relation and Analogy as two synonimes of Unity—"Unity *or* Relation *or* Analogy"!1—But page VI and 7 VII (i.e. the 2nd and third pages of the

---

1¹ Textus and I 6, where Meckel defines the law of unity as "das Gesetz der *Identi*- *tät*, der *Analogie* oder der *Reduction* [the law of *Identity, Analogy*, or *Reduction*]".

Vorrede) awakened my suspicions—[2]

> O these facts! these facts!
> Of *such* facts I'm aweary
> Light I can get none—
> For all my eye is mere eye!—
> My Eye and Betty Martin!
> And that's a fact for sartain![3]
>
> *S. T. C.*

2 ɪ flyleaf, referring to ɪ 11 | Bk 1 § 1

Die Erscheinungen der thierischen Form an und für sich, auf welche sich diese beiden Gesetze gründen, führen zu einer mehr oder weniger deutlichen Erkenntniss der *physischen* Kraft, welche das Daseyn der Organismus überhaupt, und der thierischen insbesondere, bedingt. Namentlich ist es unverkennbar, dass ihre Form aus dem Gesichtspunkte der Mannichfaltigkeit sowohl, als dem der Analogie betrachtet, eine Menge von Erscheinungen darbietet, welche mit denen der *Electricität* und des *Magnetismus* übereinkommen.

[The manifestations of the animal form in and for itself on which these two laws are based lead to a more or less clear perception of the *physical* force on which the existence of the organism in general, and of the animal organism in particular, depends. It is impossible not to see that its form, considered from the viewpoint of variety as well as from that of analogy, yields a multitude of phenomena which are in agreement with those of *Electricity* and *Magnetism*.]

Mem. How comes it, that Meckel in his Preface *cuviers* away at a great rate; but makes no mention of John Hunter, and (worse still) is silent respecting his obligations to Schelling, and H. Steffens—as ⟨to⟩ the potenziated Magnetism & Electricity of Organic Life? p. 11.[1]

1[2] In the Preface to which C refers, Meckel appeals repeatedly to facts, e.g. ɪ vii: "Einen fernen Grund fand ich in der Bemerkung, dass seit Cuvier's unsterblichem Werke in der That keines erscheinen war, worin den schon vorhandnen Thatsachen viele hinzugefügt . . . worden wäre [In addition, I observed that since Cuvier's immortal works no other has appeared that actually added many more facts to those already known]."

1[3] "All my eye and Betty Martin"—traditional for "nonsense"—a phrase which C often invoked (cf LACUNZA **29** n 2) and about which he supported the ingenious but apparently unfounded theory that it was a corruption of a Protestant oath:

CRB ɪ 114.

2[1] C protests against the praise given to the French scientist Georges Cuvier (1769–1832)—as q **1** n 2 above—and the neglect of German and English ones whom C himself admired: John Hunter (1728–93), "the profoundest . . . physiological philosopher of the latter part of the preceding century", as C called him in *Friend* (*CC*) ɪ 493*; F. W. J. von Schelling (1775–1854), leader of the *Naturphilosophen*; and his eminent follower Heinrich Steffens (1773–1845), whose pupil C himself said he longed to be: STEFFENS *Grundzüge* p ⁻12. C annotated several works by Schelling and Steffens, and drew on the work of all three men in his *Theory of Life*, composed in 1816.

"MEDICAL TREATISES"

"A Collection of Medical Treatises" in SC's description, including George Turner *A Brief and Distinct Account of the Mineral Waters of Piedmont, from the original of Scippius, and of the spaw from the best authors* (London 1733) and John Soame *Hampstead-Wells: or, directions for the drinking of those waters. Shewing, I. The nature and virtues. II. The diseases in which they are most beneficial. III. The time, manner, and order of drinking. IV. The preparation of the body requir'd. V. The diet proper to be used by all mineral water-drinkers. With an appendix, relating to the original of springs in general; with some experiments of the Hampstead Waters, and histories of cures* (London 1734).

Not located; annotation from MS TRANSCRIPT.

MS TRANSCRIPT. VCL BT 37.8: SC transcript.

DATE. 1819.

1 "Blank leaf at the beginning of the book"

It is a fact peculiarly honorable to the medical profession in Great Britain at least, that of all the learned classes it is the only one which within the last 40 or 50 years has manifestly improved not the art itself only, which may owe something to the recent discoveries in chemistry and experimental physics, but in the professors themselves. Subtract whatever in modern practice rests on chemical insight or the consequent saner notions of the materia medica, and let the cause be tried by superiority in plainness, openness, and good sense—and then compare the medical books, such as the Tracts in this volume, or any other of the myriads *ejusdem farinæ*,[1] from 1660 to 1760, with those from 1760 to the present year 1819—or again, tho' not so glaringly perhaps, those from 1760 to 1790 with those since the latter date—since Hamilton's and Abernethie's works—and the contrast is highly creditable to our physicians.[2]

1[1] "Of the same nature".

1[2] John Abernethy (1764–1831), an eminent London surgeon and writer on medical issues, is rather oddly paired with the Scottish doctor James Hamilton (1749– 1835), whose only contribution to medicine was his *Observations on the Utility and Administration of Purgative Medicines in Several Diseases* (Edinburgh 1805), which had gone into its eighth edition by

Now of our Statesmen, Divines, and Metaphysicians the contrary is the case.   S. T. C.

1826, and which C read in 1807: *CN* II 3173. Hamilton's work was certainly successful, and C and Gillman may have thought especially highly of it; there is also, however, the possibility that "Hamilton" was SC's mistranscription for "Hunter", i.e. John Hunter (1728–93), most of whose works were published post-humously, and whose name C habitually linked with that of his pupil Abernethy. C made his contribution to the debate about Hunter's work in the *Theory of Life* of 1816, on the whole defending Abernethy's *Enquiry into the Probability and Rationality of Mr. Hunter's Theory of Life* (1814).

MEDICO-CHIRURGICAL SOCIETY OF EDINBURGH

Lost Book

Transactions of the Medico-Chirurgical Society of Edinburgh. Instituted August 2. 1821. With plates. Vol II. Edinburgh 1826. 8°.

Not located; marginalia not recorded. *Gillman SC* (1843) 374 lists this work "With MS. notes by S. T. Coleridge."

MOSES MENDELSSOHN
1729–1786

Jerusalem oder über religiöse Macht und Judenthum. Frankfurt & Leipzig 1791. 8°.

British Library C 43 a 5(2). Bound as second with MENDELSSOHN *Morgenstunden*.

A few words are written in red crayon, in a German hand, on p 17.

DATE. c 1817, when C was reading JACOBI *Werke* and working on the 1818 *Friend*: see **1** n 1 below.

COEDITORS. Lore Metzger, Raimonda Modiano.

1   p 87, pencil | Pt 2

[Quoting Iselin in footnote to pp 85–8:] In Rüksicht auf die bürgerlichen Rechte sind alle Religionsgenossen einander gleich, diejenigen allein ausgenommen, deren Meinungen den Grundsäzen der menschlichen und der bürgerlichen Pflichten zuwider laufen. . . . [Sie] können nur Duldung erwarten, so lange sie nicht durch ungerechte und schädliche Handlungen die gesellschaftliche Ordnung stöhren. Wenn sie dieses thun, müssen sie gestraft werden, *nicht für ihre Meinungen; sondern für ihre Thaten.*

[With respect to civil rights all religious sects are equal except those whose views clash with the principles of human and civil duties. . . . [They] can expect toleration only so long as they do not disturb the social order by unjust and harmful actions. If they do this, they must be punished *not for their opinions, but for their deeds.*]

But is not the Propagation of principles subversive of Society itself an *Act*? Are there none but *manual*[a] actions? I am convinced that no Theory of Toleration is possible; but that the Practice must depend on Expedience & Humanity.[1]   *S. T. C.*

---

[a] The word is written on a crumpled part of the paper and has been written again above it in pencil, evidently by C

[1] Cf C's discussion of tolerance in *Friend* (*CC*) I 96–7. In this passage, which is not in the 1809 version of the essay, C agrees with Jacobi's definition of tolerance but does not cite Mendelssohn. Jacobi's view as paraphrased by C is "that the only true spirit of Tolerance consists in our conscientious toleration of each other's intolerance".

2 p 168

Nach einem ungeschriebenen Geseze, konnte keine Leib- und Lebens-
strafe verhängt werden, wenn *der Verbrecher nicht von zween unver-*
dächtigen Zeugen, mit Anführung des Gesezes, und unter Bedrohung
der verordneten Strafe gewarnt worden . . .

[According to an unwritten law, capital punishment could not be imposed unless
the criminal had been warned by two unimpeachable witnesses, citing the law
and threatening the prescribed punishment . . .]

But where is the proof of the *age*, of the authenticity, of this unwritten
Law. i.e. of this *Saying*?

Morgenstunden oder Vorlesungen über das Daseyn Gottes. Erster Theil [all published]. Rev ed. Frankfurt & Leipzig 1790. 8°.

British Library C 43 a 5(1). Bound first in the volume containing *Jerusalem*.

DATE. c 1812–16.

COEDITORS. Lore Metzger, Raimonda Modiano.

1 p⁻1

The unspeakable importance of the Distinction between the Reason, and the Human Understanding, as the only Ground of the Cogency of the Proof a posteriori of the Existence of a God from the order of the known Universe—.[1] Remove or deny this distinction, and Hume's argument from the Spider's proof that Houses &c were spun by Men out of their Bodies becomes valid.—[2]

2 pp 4–5, pencil | Ch 1

Da sich unsre Gedanken zu ihren Gegenständen gewissermassen eben so verhalten, wie Zeichen zum Bezeichneten; so haben einige diese Erklärung allgemein machen, und das Wesen der Wahrheit in die Uebereinstimmung zwischen Worten, Begriff und Sachen setzen wollen.

[Since our thoughts correspond to a certain extent to their objects in the same way as signs to things signified, some have tried to apply this explanation universally and to define truth as the agreement of words, concept, and things.]

Instead of Things and Matters of Fact put Ideas and the Verities of Reason on the one hand, and ⟨on the other⟩ the Perceptions and the Forms of Sense, under the conditions taught by Experience—and the corre-

---

[1] The distinction between reason and understanding, the cornerstone of C's philosophy, is expounded especially in *Friend* (*CC*) I 154–61 and *AR* (1825) 207–28; the connection between this distinction and proofs of the existence of God is made explicitly in *BL* ch 10 (*CC*) I 200–3.

[2] In Hume's *Dialogues Concerning Natural Religion* pt 7, one speaker demonstrates the absurd consequences of the argument from design by suggesting that it validates the ancient Indian theory "that the World arose from an infinite Spider, who spun this whole complicated Mass from his Bowels. . . . And were there a Planet wholly inhabited by Spiders, (which is very possible) this Inference wou'd there appear as natural and irrefragable as that which in our Planet ascribes the Origin of all things to Design and Intelligence . . .'': *The Natural History of Religion and Dialogues Concerning Natural Religion* ed A. Wayne Colver (Oxford 1976) 207. C alludes to this argument in *P Lects* Lect 13 (1949) 373.

spondence of Words to Conceptions, and of these to the Realities of Sense and Reason is no bad answer to the ? What is Truth?, i.e. relatively to the Human Mind.[1] Relatively to God the Question has no Meaning or admits but of one reply—viz. God himself. God is the *Truth*—i.e. the Identity of Thing and Thought, of *Knowing* and *Being*.[2]

P.S. I see no sufficient cause, why the Realities of Reason might not be called Things as well as the Realities of Sense, in this connection at least. If so, the coincidence of the Word, the Thought, and the Thing would constitute Truth, in its twofold Sense of Insight, and the adequate Expression of the same.

3   pp 28–9, pencil | Ch 2

Nicht, dass es dieser unvollständigen Induction an Ueberführungskraft oder Evidenz fehlen sollte; sie reicht vielmehr in vielen Fällen vollkommen zu, uns völlige Versicherung zu geben, und über allen Zweifel hinwegzusetzen. Ein jeder von uns erwartet mit ungezweifelter Gewissheit z.B., dass er sterben werde; ob gleich der Grund der Ueberzeugung blos unvollständige Induction ist.

[Not that this incomplete induction lacks persuasive power or evidence; in many cases, on the contrary, it completely suffices to provide full certainty and remove all doubts. Each of us expects with indubitable certainty, for example, that he will die, although the certainty is grounded only on incomplete induction.]

I do not at present recollect any German word fully answering to our ''Positiveness''—''I am positive''—but I suspect that my beloved Mendelsohn has here confounded Positiveness with CERTAINTY:[1] or rather the Twilight between both with the full Light of the Latter.   S. T. C.

4   pp 38–9 (misprinted 49), pencil

Wenn wir die Körper haben sich ausdehnen sehn, so oft sie dem Feuer näher gebracht worden sind, so setzen wir den Verbindungsgrund der Ausdehnung, in die beständigen Eigenschaften des Feuers; eignen dem Feuer eine Kraft zu, die Körper auszudehnen: und erwarten eben diesen Erfolg, von dem Feuer und den Körpern, von welchen wir es noch nicht erfahren haben. Der Grad der Gewissheit nimmt mit der Menge der beobachteten Fälle zu; und ist, wenn die Anzahl der Fälle sehr gross ist . . . von der vollkommnen Evidenz nur unmerklich unterschieden.

2[1] ''What Is Truth?'' is the title of this section of *Morgenstunden*.

2[2] C discusses the absolute as the identity of being and knowing elsewhere, e.g.

BL ch 12 (*CC*) I 285–6.

3[1] C made much of this distinction: cf 6 below, LUTHER 25 and n 1, *CN* III 3592n.

[Having seen bodies expand every time they are brought nearer to the fire, we connect the cause of the expansion with the constant properties of fire; we attribute to fire a power to expand bodies; and we expect from fire and bodies just that effect which we have never experienced before. The degree of certainty increases the more instances we observe; and when the number of instances is quite large . . . it is hardly distinguishable from complete evidence.]

and yet still in the Dark! Thus, the Heat that expands Iron, contracts Clay, even in its purest state, and after it has been deprived of all accidental moisture: & without any answering ponderable Results which might account for its Shrinking in magnitude by its diminution in Quantity.—It is possible, that Experiments have not been duly instituted, but I speak of our present knowlege as dependent on INDUCTION.

5   pp 38–9, pencil

Zwey Erscheinungen, die sich beständig begleiten, halten wir (<u>mit eben dem Rechte</u>)!! für die mittelbare oder unmittelbare Würkung einer gemeinschaftlichen Ursache; und erwarten die eine so oft wir die andere wahrnehmen. Die Farbe und das Gefühl des Brodts ist so oft mit diesem Geschmacke, mit diesem Einfluss auf die Nahrung unsers Körpers, verbunden bemerkt worden, dass wir mit Recht beydes für die Folgen einer innern Beschaffenheit des Brodtes halten . . .

[Two phenomena that constantly go together we regard (<u>with equal justification</u>)!! as the mediate or immediate effect of a common cause; and expect the one as soon as we perceive the other. We have so often observed the connection of the colour and feel of bread with its taste and nourishing impact on our body that we justifiably consider both to be the effect of an inner quality of bread . . .]

But surely this is a false Creation of a *Thing* out of an aggregate of *Effects*—and what more does the sane Idealist plead for, than 1. an X Y Z for the Objects, or Things in themselves—and 2. the analogy from the one thing known (Life, Consciousness) to the Unknown?

6   p 43, pencil | End of section

[Continuing the argument of **4** and **5** textus, Mendelssohn discusses ways in which various kinds of evidence from the senses may produce in the mind degrees of conviction amounting to certainty.]

* Still I find the confusion between a *sensation* & a *sense*. The *Sensation* I call Positiveness: the *Sense* Certainty—Now between these the difference is not only perceptible but I have an insight into their essential disparity.[1] In problems of the absolute Infinite the *sense*, or Insight, is directly opposed to the Sensation.—

6[1] See **3** n 1 above.

7   p 151, pencil | Ch 8 axiom 7

Wenn z.B. die Körper eben sowohl eine allgemeine Schwere haben, als nicht haben könnten; so kann der Satz: Alle Körper haben eine Schwere, nicht anders wahr werden, als in so weit diese, ohne Rücksicht auf Zeit und Ort, so und nicht anders, als das Beste erkannt und gebilligt worden ist . . .

[If, for example, matter can just as well have or not have universal gravity, then the statement "All matter has gravity" can be true only in so far as, thus and not otherwise, regardless of time and place, it [gravity] is recognised and confirmed as the best . . .]

How is Matter conceivable without or rather, what *is* Matter but, the synthesis of its essential component Powers, Attraction and Repulsion?[1] Take A. as Thesis and R. as Antithesis; and again Rep. as Thesis and Attraction as the Antithesis: the Synthesis, ⟨ = Gravity, is⟩ of ~~of~~ ideal (& therefore, if matter *exist*, no less of physical) *necessity*. Its existence has its *cause* in the *will* of God; but its essence has its ground in his Being or Nature.—

8   pp 200–1, pencil | Ch 12

. . . ich erkläre mich ausdrücklich: dass ich weder für den Menschen, noch für die Gottheit selbst eine andre Freyheit anerkenne, als die von der Erkenntniss und Wahl des Besten abhängt. Das Vermögen, diese Beste einzusehen, zu billigen und zu wählen, ist wahre Freyheit, und ein Vermögen, dieser Erkenntniss, Billigung und Wahl zuwider zu handeln, ist nach meinen Begriffen, ein wahres Unding.

[. . . I state my position clearly, that I recognise no other freedom either for man or for God himself than that which depends on the knowledge and choice of the best. The power to perceive, to sanction, and to choose this best is true freedom, and a power to act contrary to this knowledge, sanction, and choice is, in my opinion, an utter impossibility.]

But, dear and revered Mendelsohn! what were the result, if instead of applying this Position to God, and to good & wise men, you had considered it in its relations to wicked Intelligences? Satan & his Crew you perhaps would have non suited with a good-natured Smile of Unbelief; but Cæsar Borgia, or (for you are still alive in my mind, dear Mendelsohn!) Talleyrand, Buonaparte?[1]—Would it not end in reducing Guilt to innocent error?

7[1] The conception of matter as the synthesis of the powers of attraction and repulsion is discussed in a letter of Sept 1817 to C. A. Tulk (*CL* IV 775) and in KANT *Meta-physische Anfangsgründe* esp **9** and n 1.

8[1] C names unscrupulous empire-builders of the past and of his own day, the legendary Cesare Borgia (1476–1507) along

9 p 203, pencil

Wenn der sinnlich evidente Satz: *Eine Sinnenwelt ist würklich vor-
handen*, oder . . . der Satz: *Ich selbst bin würklich vorhanden*, objective
Wahrheit seyn muss; so werde ich, als Subject dieses Satzes, mit dem
Daseyn, als Prädicate desselben, in Verbindung stehen, und so wie ich
bin, mit allen meinen Individualbestimmungen, ohne dieses Prädicat,
nicht gedacht werden können . . .

[If the conspicuously evident statement "An external world really exists" or
. . . the statement "I myself really exist" must be objectively true, then I as
subject of this statement must be connected with existence, its predicate, and
that which I am, with all my individual characteristics, cannot be conceived
without this predicate . . .]

Not convincing to me. The "I" is assumed as the Material, and its Ex-
istence as the Form. Can any thing be more arbitrary? What if the I be
the phænomenon of the inner Sense? And *I*ing or Self-ponence[1] be as
Running, Writing &c?

10 p +3, referring to p 203

Nun ist das subjective Bewusstseyn von meiner Veränderlichkeit über
allen Zweifel hinweg, und es ist eben so unleugbar, dass ein Wesen,
welches sich seiner Veränderung bewusst ist, auch in der That veränder-
lich seyn muss. Ein unmittelbares Bewusstseyn belehrt mich, dass ich
vorhin anders gewesen, als ich jetzt bin: da aber die Zeitfolge in der
Denkbarkeit des Begriffs nichts vermindert; so kann das Gegentheil von
dem, was ich vorher gewesen, noch jetzt nicht aufgehöret haben, denk-
bar zu seyn. Der Wahrheitsgrund des obigen Satzes wird also nicht in
dem Materialen des Erkenntnisses, sondern in dem Formalen desselben;
nicht in der Denkbarkeit des Subjects, sondern in seiner Güte und Voll-
kommenheit zu suchen seyn. . . . [204:] Nun kann diese relative Güte
eines zufälligen Wesens auf keine andere Weise seinen Würklichkeits-
grund enthalten, als in so weit es dadurch einer freyen Ursache zur Ab-
sicht dienen, und sonach von demselben gebilliget werden kann. . . .
[205:] Diese freye Ursache kann selbst nicht zufällig seyn. . . . Wir
müssen also am Ende auf ein nothwendiges Wesen zurückkommen, bey
welchem dieser Wahrheitsgrund in der Denkbarkeit des Subjects selbst

---

with Napoleon and his notoriously corrupt
associate Talleyrand (1754–1838). Since C
appears still to link Talleyrand and Napo-
leon, this note may have been written
before 1814, when Napoleon abdicated

(6 Apr) and Talleyrand supported the Res-
toration party. Talleyrand later represented
France at the Congress of Vienna.
  9[1] I.e. placing oneself. Neither this
word nor "I" as a verb appears in *OED*.

lieget, zu einem Wesen . . . welches vorhanden ist, weil es gedacht werden kann.

[Since the subjective consciousness of my changeability is beyond all doubt, it is just as undeniable that a being who is conscious of its change must actually be changeable. An immediate consciousness informs me that a short while ago I must have been different from what I am now: but since the time sequence does not diminish the conceivability of the concept, the opposite of that which had previously been cannot yet have ceased to be conceivable. The ground of the truth of the statement mentioned above must be sought not in the matter of knowledge but in its form; not in the conceivability of the subject but in its goodness and perfection. . . . Now, this relative goodness of an accidental being can acquire its reality in no other way but in so far as it serves the purpose of a free cause and thus can be sanctioned by it. . . . This free cause cannot itself be accidental. . . . In the end we must therefore return to a necessary being whose reality lies in the conceivability of the subject itself, to a being . . . that exists because it can be conceived.]

P. 203.

Even here I believe myself to detect an equivocation—"That which I was (i.e. felt and did) yesterday, I am not to day—but the position in Time does not diminish the conceivability of the former state. Reverse the position—and the two States of Existence remain equally conceivable—Therefore, some other cause must be supposed, and this can be found only in the moral Determinants, or final Causes." Such is M's argument.

But (I reply) by *whom* is it conceivable? ~~Or far rather~~ At least *negatively*—i.e. not-*inconc*^le^? By *me*, who know and overlook but a few links of the vast Chain, and these but imperfectly? Be it so. The same would hold good of every ignorant person with respect to the works of a complex Machine. But by the Mechanist? But by an omniscient Mind? And can this be asserted by a Disciple of Leibnitz, Wolf, Baumgarten? and ⟨what becomes⟩ their favorite Principium indiscernibilium?[1] And after all, is this Denkbarkeit (conceivability) any thing more than the power of repeating the Conceptions, Lungs + Heart in the order, H. + L.?—

11   p ⁺8, referring to p 217 | Ch 13

. . . oder vielmehr, er [der Spinozist] spricht: der gesammte Inbegriff

---

10[1] "Principle of indiscernibles". Leibniz formulated the principle of the identity of indiscernibles, according to which there cannot be two things in the universe which are absolutely alike, in *Nouveaux essais* bk 2 ch 27 § 3, *Monadologie* 9, *IVme Lettre à Clarke* §§ 4 and 6 in *Opera omnia* ed Erdmann (1840) 277, 755–6. Christian Wolff (1679–1754) adopted Leibniz's principle, as did Alexander Gottlieb Baumgarten (1714–62), a disciple of Wolff. Mendelssohn was indeed indebted to all three philosophers, as C maintains.

unendlich vieler endlichen Körper, und unendlich vieler Gedanken, mache *Ein* einziges unendliches *All* aus, unendlich an Ausdehnung und unendlich an Denken: *Alles ist Eins.*

[. . . or rather the Spinozist says that the whole essence of infinitely many finite things and infinitely many thoughts constitutes *one* single infinite *whole*, infinite in extension and infinite in thought: *all in one.*]

217—This Spinoza repeatedly and earnestly guards against: viz. that God is the collective or gesammte Inbegriff.[1] M. did not understand Spinoza.—

12 p 218

Um uns diesem System so viel möglich zu nähern, lasset uns vor der Hand nicht rügen, dass Spinoza das Unendliche der Kraft nach, mit dem Unendlichen der Ausbreitung . . . zu verwechseln scheint. Aus unendlich vielen endlichen Gedanken setzet er das an Gedanken Unendliche gleichsam zusammen.

[In order to become as closely acquainted with this system as possible, let us not for the moment censure Spinoza for seeming to confuse infinite power with infinite extension. . . . From infinitely many finite thoughts he constructs, so to speak, the infinite in thought.]

All this is false as attributed to Spinozism. M. has confounded with it a quite different System, that of the Anima Mundi, non per se sed ex Harmoniâ omnium cum omnibus[1]—a mind the result of an organized Universe—in which God is a coeternal Effect: than which nothing can be more opposite to Spinoza's System.

13 p ⁺6, referring to p 219

Auch wir gestehen, dass eine solche selbstgenügende Substantialität bloss dem unendlichen und nothwendigen Wesen zukomme, und dass es selbst von diesem keinem endlichen Wesen mitgetheilet werde. Allein wir unterscheiden das *Selbstständige* von dem *Fürsichbestehenden*. Das Selbstständige ist unabhängig und bedarf keines andern Wesens zu seinem Daseyn. Dieses also ist unendlich und nothwendig; das Fürsichbestehende aber kann in seinem Daseyn abhängig, und dennoch, als ein von dem unendlichen abgesondertes Wesen, vorhanden seyn. Das

---

11[1] "Sum total". C makes the same observation in Jacobi *Ueber die Lehre* 4; his opinion is shared by the Spinoza scholar Harry Wolfson, who declares that "a conception of substance as merely the aggregate sum of the modes is contrary to all the uttered statements of Spinoza": *The Philosophy of Spinoza* (New York 1958) I 73.

12[1] "World Soul, [existing] not through itself but from the harmony of all things with all things".

heisst, es lassen sich Wesen denken, die nicht blos als Modificationen eines andern Wesens bestehen, sondern ihre eigene Bestandheit haben und selbst modificirt sind.

[We too admit that such a self-sufficient substantiality can be attributed only to the infinite and necessary being and cannot even be communicated by it to any finite being. Only we distinguish the *self-sustaining* from the *self-subsistent* being. The former is autonomous and needs no other being for its existence. It is, therefore, infinite and necessary; but the self-subsistent being can be dependent in its existence and still be one of the infinite separate beings; that is, one can conceive of beings that do not consist of modifications of another being, but have their own permanence and [capacity for] self-modification.]

P. 219. Would Mendelsohn have been able to give a distinct Conception of his Fürsichbestehende, that was yet not Selbstständige,[1] in any sense different from that in which Spinoza himself admits it—. Why dwell wholly on one of Spinoza's metaphors, Modification? Does he not admit, that God thinks the Human Soul as[a] abiding & progressive? Does he deny, that A is A and not B?—Above all, does he not establish an infinite Chasm between God and all finite things?[2]—Assuredly, the defect in Spinoza's System is the impersonality of God—he makes his only Substance *a Thing*, not *a Will*—a *Ground solely*, & at no time a *Cause*.[3] Now this Mendelssohn has left untouched—The Question which Sp. would put to M would be—"If God were to suspend his Power, would that, which now is, still continue to be—just as a House after the Death of the Builder?—"[4] If he answered, Yes! then indeed there would exist an essential difference between them respecting the aggregate of finite

---

[a] Possibly a slip for "is"

13[1] "Self-subsistent . . . self-sustaining": from textus.

13[2] Spinoza frequently emphasises the difference between the divine and human nature, and that between infinite substance and finite things. Cf his assertion that intellect and will do not belong to the essence of God (*Ethics* pt 1 prop 17 cor 2 scholium) and his statement that while individual things cannot be conceived without God, God does not belong to their essence (*Ethics* pt 2 prop 10).

13[3] This is C's reiterated objection to the system of Spinoza: cf "Spinoza in common with all the Metaphysicians before him (Böhmen, perhaps, excepted) began at the wrong end—commencing with God as an *Object*" in SPINOZA (annotated 1812–13) **5**, and "he saw God in the ground *only* and exclusively . . . and not likewise in his moral, intellectual, existential and personal Godhead" in the 1817–18 note on Spinoza in BM MS Egerton 1801 f 11: *SW & F (CC)*.

13[4] *Ethics* pt 1 prop 24 cor answers the question firmly in the negative: "From this it follows that God is not only the cause of things' beginning to exist, but also of their persevering in existing, *or* (to use a Scholastic term) God is the cause of the being of things." In his 1812–13 annotations on Crabb Robinson's copy of SPINOZA, however, C comments at length on the apparently contradictory crux of *Ethics* pt 1 prop 28, which describes the existence of finite individual things as contingent upon other finite individuals.

Existents. But then M. would be in opposition to all Philosophers, Jewish & Christian, as well as to Spinoza.—

14   p 220 | Following **13** textus

Eine Substantialität von dieser zweyten Gattung glauben wir mit Recht auch endlichen zufälligen Wesen zuschreiben zu können. . . . Will Spinoza diese, ihrer Abhängigkeit halber, nicht Substanz nennen; so streitet er bloss in Worten. Wird der Unterschied in der Sache zugegeben; so erdenke man für die Bestandheit abhängiger Wesen einen andern Nahmen, um einen Unterschied, der in der Sache liegt, nicht unbemerkt zu lassen; und der Zwist ist entschieden.

[We have reason to believe that a substantiality of the second order can be attributed to finite contingent beings. . . . If Spinoza does not want to call these substance, because of their half-dependence, then he is merely quarrelling with words. Once the difference in the object is admitted, one should invent a different name for the essence of dependent beings, in order not to leave unperceived a difference that resides in the object; and the dispute is settled.]

Ay! but here is[a] the Rub.

15   p 221

Anstatt zu beweisen, dass alles Fürsichbestehende nur Eins sey, bringet er [Spinoza] am Ende blos heraus, dass alles Selbstständige nur Eins sey.

[Instead of proving that all self-subsistent things are only one, Spinoza merely establishes in the end that all self-sustaining things are only one.]

Here M. and not Spin. plays with words. What does M. mean by Eins? Sp. meant by one, that which being conceived all other things are conceived in it: that which must be conceived, whenever one thing is conceived. Thus, my Thoughts & my Mind are *one*: not that I therefore think my Mind the mere Aggregate or generic Term of all my Thoughts—

16   p +8, referring to p 279 | Ch 15

[Opinions ascribed to Lessing:] Gott dachte sich von Ewigkeit her in aller seiner Vollkommenheit, d.h. Gott schuf sich von Ewigkeit her ein Wesen, dem keine Vollkommenheit mangelte, die er selbst besass.—

In den folgenden Sätzen suchte *L.* durch eine nicht unfeine Wendung, hieraus das Geheimniss der Dreyeinigkeit zu erklären; oder gar, wie er sich öfters in jüngern Jahren schmeichelte, metaphysisch zu demonstri-

---

[a] Word obliterated by a spot of ink; another spot of ink follows "here" in the ms line above

ren. Von dieser jugendlichen Anmassung . . . ist er freylich in der Folge zurück gekommen.

[God comprehended himself in all his perfection from eternity, i.e. from eternity God created a being who lacked no perfection that he himself possessed.

In the statements that follow, Lessing sought, through a not unskilful turn, to explain the mystery of the Trinity; or even, as he used to flatter himself in his younger years, to demonstrate it metaphysically. Afterwards he did, of course, revert to his youthful assumption.]

p. 279
I should like to hear, what the objections are to this metaphysical Proof of the eternal Filiation of the Logos, a self-comprehending Creator having been assumed. Not surely that the adequate & therefore substantial Idea of God would think a third Idea, and so on ad infinitum? This the co-existence of the Ideat[u]m[a][1] or Father would preclude: for we suppose a living Intelligence & supreme Wisdom, not a blind Power.

17   p +8, referring to p 296 and appendix p xxvi | Ch 16 and appendix

Der Sache muss ein Begriff entsprechen; jedes Object muss in irgend einem Subjecte dargestellt; jedes Vorbild in irgend einem Spiegel nach-gebildet werden. Sache ohne Begriff hat keine Wahrheit; Wahrheit, ohne dass irgend ein Wesen von ihr versichert sey, führt nicht den min-desten Grad von Evidenz mit sich, ist also keine Wahrheit.

[A concept must correspond to a thing; every object must be represented in some subject; every model will be reflected in some mirror. A thing without a concept has no reality; reality, unless some being is certain of it, carries not the least degree of evidence and is therefore no reality at all.]

p. 296. and p. xxvi. of the Anm. u. Zus.—[1]
M. does not defend Idealism: & yet every where I find the Idea iden-tified with the Ideatum, the Begriff (conceptio) with that, of which we have the conception.—I can not know A but by the Notion, a—if there were no percipient or thinking Beings, A would not be known—but this of itself proves only that A + a would not exist, not that A would not *be*. There may be other proofs of this; but M's is not.—

---

[a] Letter obscured by mend in paper

16[1] "Object" or, as C says in **17**, "that, of which we have the conception". C com-ments on the issue of filiation also in SPI-NOZA **17**, where in Latin he writes, "From infinite thought an infinite intellect ought to follow, nay an infinite will as well—and from these all else—which the most Holy Trinity sanctions."

17[1] "Anmerkungen und Zuzätze" [Re-marks and Addenda], i.e. the supplemen-tary pages iii–xxxv added to the text of *Morgenstunden*.

18   p ⁺7, referring to p 302

Alle Möglichkeiten also haben ihr idealisches Daseyn in dem denkenden
Subject, und von diesem werden sie als denkbar dem Gegenstande zu-
geschrieben. Eine nicht gedachte Möglichkeit ist ein wahres Unding.
. . . Also muss alles Würkliche nicht nur *denkbar* seyn; sondern auch
von irgend einem Wesen *gedacht* werden. Jeder Realexistenz entspricht
in irgend einem Subjecte eine Idealexistenz; jeder Sache eine Vorstel-
lung. Ohne erkannt zu werden, ist nichts Erkennbares; ohne bemerkt zu
werden, kein Merkmal; ohne Begriff kein Gegenstand würklich vorhan-
den.

[All possibilities thus have their ideal existence in the thinking subject, which
ascribes them to the object as conceivable. A possibility that is not conceived
[by a subject] is an utter absurdity. . . . Therefore all real things must not only
be *conceivable* but also must be *conceived* by some being. Each real existence
has a corresponding ideal existence in some subject; each thing has a corre-
sponding conception. Without being perceived nothing is perceptible; without
being observed there can really be no mark, and without a concept no object.]

302—Mend. evidently grounds his Position on the inherence of the
Thing in the Thought: for supposing them separate, & simply correspon-
dent, as my face to the Image in the Looking-glass, it is absurd to say
that my face would not exist or be if there were no Looking-glass. In-
stead of being an argument therefore from Realities, it is in fact only an
argument against them, in any other sense than as modes of mind. For
the whole amounts to no more than the impossibility of conceiving a
thing per se unconceived—i.e. conceived and not conceived. It would
have been far better therefore to have begun with the thesis—We can
attach no meaning to the term, *Thing*, *separated* from Thought—or that
all *possibility* (or by the bye, the German seems to have led M. into an
Equivoque, for I should have said, *Potentiality*) is the mere application
of Time and Space to Objects—I know Iron, I know Caloric—They are
now together/ & there is a Fluid. I withdraw the latter—there is a solid.
I apply to the Objects before me future Time—& imagine the same
space to both—and say, Fusion is a potentiality of this Iron.—But Time
& Space are forms of Perception—ergo, &c.—But a plain man would
answer: Tho' we cannot know any thing but by knowing it, yet having
thus known its existence we at the same time learn that it would have
been tho' we had not known it.

19   pp ⁺4–⁺5, referring to p 310 | Ch 17

An statt des Nothwendigen, setzte er [Cartes] das Unendliche, das voll-
kommenste Wesen. Es ist offenbar, dass das nothwendige Wesen keine

veränderliche Schranken haben, und also alle Vollkommenheiten in dem höchsten Grade besitzen müsse. In der Idee eines nothwendigen Wesens liegt also der Inbegriff aller vollkommenen Eigenschaften, die einem Wesen zukommen können. Nun, schloss *Cartes* weiter, nun ist die Existenz offenbar eine vollkommene Eigenschaft der Dinge; also schliesst der Begriff des Nothwendigen, auch die Vollkommenheit der Existenz mit in sich; also muss das Nothwendige auch würklich vorhanden seyn.

[In place of the necessary being he [Descartes] put the infinite, the perfect being. It is evident that the necessary being cannot have changeable bounds and therefore must possess all perfections in the highest degree. In the idea of a necessary being thus resides the essence of all perfect qualities with which a being can be endowed. Now, Descartes further concludes, existence is really a perfect quality of things; thus the concept of the necessary being must also include the perfection of existence; thus the necessary being must really exist.]

P. 310. I could never discover in the Cartesian Proof more than this: If I have a clear conception of a necessary Being, i e. that which cannot be thought of otherwise than as existing: then I must conceive his Existence.—But what compels me to assume a necessary Being? Whatever that be, must, methinks, have anticipated this Proof. If there be any thing at all, it must be either dependent or independent: if the former, there must be the latter, for omne quod dependet, dependet *ab* aliquo/[1] if the latter, it is of itself. What does the Cartesian Proof add to this; but a Verbal Interpretation of a Necessary Being?—or substitute "all-perfect"—"God has all perfections; but Existence is a Perfection; therefore, God exists." Yes! if it be first proved, 1. that every clear idea has its correspondent Ideatum or Reale,[2] and 2. that we have a clear *idea* of an all-perfect Being, and that what is so called is not a mere series of Ideas abstracted from this and that, and then asserted collectively. Otherwise, it would seem that the Position ought to run thus:—The Idea of God implies all perfections: ergo, Existence as being a perfection. Consequently, in the Idea of God I have the Idea of his Existence. But the BELIEF therefore? Does that necessarily follow?—I have a distinct Idea, whenever I chuse to have it, of a Chain of Mountains in the planet Jupiter 8 times higher than the Andes—the *Idea* of its being there is of course the *Idea* of its being there; but not the Belief— If But if by Idea be meant a clear perception of the Actuality of the Thing, then again it is a mere lazy Truism.—The thing to be proved is, not that the Idea of

19[1] "Everything that is dependent is dependent *on* something" (in fact the preposition is *from*, a reminder that "depend"

means literally "hang down from").
19[2] "Object" (as in 16) or "Realisation".

God involves the Idea of his Existence, but that the Idea of God contains in itself the Belief in that Idea. Now this seems to contradict the essential meaning of Belief: which is always a something added to, not contained in, an Idea or Conception.—Again, it would require proof that Intellect & Will were Perfections—i.e. positive Attributes, and not (as Spinoza believed himself to have demonstrated) the result of Limitation & Modification[3]—It would require Proof that the Universe is any thing but its constituent Laws—& that these Laws are not the necessary Being—

20 p 313

Wenn nun die Vereinigung aller bejahenden Prädicate oder Vollkommenheiten nichts Undenkbares ist, und zum Inbegriff aller Vollkommenheiten offenbar die Existenz mitgehört; so hat die Folge ihre Richtigkeit, dass von dem Begriffe des Unendlichen oder Allervollkommensten ∧ die Existenz unzertrennlich sey.

[If then the union of all affirmative predicates or perfections is not inconceivable, and if existence manifestly belongs to the essence of all perfections, it can be correctly inferred that ∧ existence is inseparably linked to the concept of the infinite or the supreme perfection.]

∧ der Begriff der Existenz, nicht die Existenz.[1]

21 p 315

Ein eingeschränktes Wesen kann, als Modification von mir selbst, gedacht werden, ohne dass ich ihm würkliches Daseyn zuschreibe. . . . Das nothwendige Wesen hingegen kann entweder nicht gedacht werden, entweder auch als Modification von mir selbst keine Wahrheit haben, oder ich muss es wenigstens als würklich vorhanden denken.

[I can conceive a limited being as a modification of myself without ascribing a real existence to it. . . . The necessary being, on the other hand, either cannot be thought of, can have no reality even as modification of myself, or else I must at least think of it as really existing.]

Still the same (to me almost in⟨con⟩ceivable) Sophism. The necessary Being cannot be a modification of my mind; but the Idea of a necessary Being may. Is a Poker and the Idea of a Poker the same?

19[3] According to Spinoza "finite existence involves a partial negation, and infinite existence is the absolute affirmation of the given nature . . ." (*Ethics* pt 1 prop 8). Will and Intelligence, Spinoza argues, do not appertain to the essence of God but "stand in the same relation to the nature of God as do motion, and rest, and absolutely all natural phenomena . . ." (*Ethics* pt 1 prop 32).

20[1] "The concept of existence, not existence".

22 p 315

Blosser Begriff ohne Sache kann dieses Wesen* schlechterdings nicht seyn; als blosse Modification von unserer Denkungskraft kann dieses Wesen nicht gedacht werden.

[It is utterly impossible that this being* should be merely a concept without an object; this being cannot be thought of as mere modification of our thinking power.]

Certainly not; but the *idea* of this Being may.—

23 p ⁺8, referring to appendix p vi, part of a note to p 77

6ᵗʰ page of the Anmerkungen excellent—[1]

23[1] In this discussion of the relationship of words to clear thinking, Mendelssohn admits that in every recollection there lies a separate concept even without language. One may recognise a melody, which is not given through language, even if one does not understand the notes and regardless of whether the melody is played in higher or lower notes, on the violin, the piano etc, which produce very different sensory impressions. What, then, is the value of words to abstraction and clear thinking? Mendelssohn suggests that words give boundaries to concepts which otherwise remain undetermined. They establish distinctions of mode, kind, degree, class, quality, relation etc. Language, therefore, is a splendid gift without which we could neither communicate nor grasp determinate concepts and develop clear thinking. He goes on to argue (p vii) that if a deaf-mute who acquired language could tell us about his previous mode of thinking, it would probably prove to be close to that of animals, i.e. mostly individual representations deprived of clearly defined concepts.

Lost Book

Philosophische Schriften. 2 vols. Carlsruhe 1780. 8°.

Not located; marginalia not recorded. ''With several marginal notes in the autograph of S. T. Coleridge'': *Green SC* (1880) 474.

BENEDETTO MENZINI

1646–1704

Poesie di Benedetto Menzini Fiorentino divise in due tomi. 2 vols. Nice 1782. 12°.

Victoria College Library (Coleridge Collection)

Inscribed on title-page of Vol I, apparently by Mrs C: "S. T. Coleridge Gretahall Keswick." Work described as part of "Green Bequest" by EHC on card in pocket pasted to I $^+$5 (p-d).

DATE. 1811–12? See **1** n 1.

1 II 2

> I stand alone, & nor tho' my Heart should break
> Have I, to whom I may complain or speak.
> Here I stand, a hopeless man and sad
> Who hoped to have seen my Love, my Life.
> And strange it were indeed, could I be glad
> Remembring her, my Soul's betrothed Wife/
> For in this World no creature, that has life,
> Was e'er to me so gracious & so good/
> Her Love was to my Heart, like the Heart-blood.[1]

1[1] *PW* (EHC) II 1010. Whether these lines were in fact composed by C or were transcribed or adapted from another source, they must refer to the separation from SH in 1810 and the difficult period that followed the quarrel with WW.

FRIEDRICH ANTON MESMER
1732–1815

Mesmerismus. Oder System der Wechselwirkungen, Theorie und Anwendung des thierischen Magnetismus als die allgemeine Heilkunde zur Erhaltung des Menschen von Dr. Friedrich Anton Mesmer. Ed Karl Christian Wolfart. [Bound with] Erläuterungen zum Mesmerismus von Dr. Karl Christian Wolfart . . . als zweiter Theil des Mesmerismus. 2 vols in 1. Berlin 1814, 1815. 8°.

British Library C 43 c 1

In Jan 1812, at the request of a commission appointed by the Prussian Government to investigate animal magnetism, Dr K. C. Wolfart, editor of ΑΣΚΛΕΠΕΙΟΝ [*Asklepeion*] (see KLUGE **9** n 2), wrote to Mesmer and invited him to lecture in Berlin. Mesmer, then aged 78, declined the invitation but asked Wolfart to come to Frauenfeld in Switzerland and observe his healing methods. Wolfart went to see Mesmer in Sept 1812, and in 1813 he acquired the long ms "Système des influences" which Mesmer had originally started in France and had been writing for many years. Wolfart edited the ms and entitled it *Mesmerismus*; his own book, the *Erläuterungen*, is a commentary keyed to passages in Mesmer's work. An additional note that may be associated with these vols is given under WOLFART.

DATE. c 1815–18, and possibly also later. C owned this book by 27 Jun 1817 (*CL* IV 745); the verse lines in **8**, however, belong to a poem of 1826 (**8** n 1).

COEDITORS. Lore Metzger, Raimonda Modiano.

1 I 51, pencil | Pt 1 sec 2 ch 1

Der *Zusammenhang* ist also ein Zustand der Zusammenfügung hinsichtlich seines Widerstandes gegen eine Gewalt, welche jene aufzulösen sucht.

Der Widerstand kommt von zwei Ursachen her:

1. von den wechselseitigen Strömen der feinen Materie, welche die Theilchen zu einander führt und sie zusammenfügt.

2. davon, dass zwei Theilchen, indem sie sich unmittelbar berühren, an dem Berührungspunkte einen umkreisenden Flutstoff ausschliessen.

[*Cohesion* is then a state of fusion [produced by] its resistance to a force that seeks to disintegrate it.

The resistance derives from two causes:

1. from the alternating currents of the fine matter that conducts the particles towards each other and unites them.

2. from the fact that two particles, by coming into immediate contact with each other, exclude a surrounding fluid at the point of contact.]

Would that M. or W.[1] had informed us, wherein identity differs from immediate contact. If the latter be only at one point; yet wherein does *this* one point and the other one point differ from *one only*: except, by the mind's own recollection of its own former position and circumstances of interspace &c? In short, Mesmer begins with the pure fiction of ultimate monads or absolute minnims—his System therefore is atomic with all the superadded difficulties of an absolute *Plenum*/[2] in consequence, his only resource is to *repeat* as often as he likes the phantom, thin fluid, adding to each the *word* (to the *image* he cannot) the particle *er*. Thin—thinner—yet thinner—thinner yet—&c &c—

2 ɪ 53, pencil | Ch 2

Die Sphäroidal-Gestalt (die kugelartige Kreisgestalt) der Urkügelchen, woraus die elastische Fiber besteht, lässt es zu, dass sie anfangen können, sich vom Ort zu rücken ohne sich zu trennen . . .

[The Spheroid form (the globular circle-shape) of the original small spheres, which constitute the elastic fibre, enables them to begin moving themselves from the spot without separating themselves . . .]

A reason lies hid in this position—but to be sought for not in the spheroid itself but in the cause of the Spheroid.

3 ɪ 59, pencil | Ch 4

Zu derselben Zeit und auf dieselbe Weise hat sich *der Mond* gebildet, der ebenmässig blos aus einem Theil der im Umlaufskreis der Erde sich befindenden ungleichartigen Materie zusammengesetzt wurde.

[At the same time and in the same manner *the moon* was formed, which was

[1][1] Mesmer or his editor Wolfart.

[1][2] As in his earlier works, Mesmer postulates the existence of a universal fluid which surrounds and permeates all bodies. Originally, matter which exists in a state of even cohesion fills all space, and "this is what is meant by the plenum in the universe". Matter is formed of primary particles ("Urtheilchen") or "ultimate monads", as C calls them, which, after a first universal push ("Universal Anstoss"), begin to move and enter into various combinations and relationships, the totality of which constitutes the universal fluid: *Mesmerismus* 10–12. C repeatedly referred to Mesmer's system as materialistic. Cf **7** and **17** below and the letter to Frere (27 Jun 1817) in which C speaks of three sects of animal magnetists and classifies Mesmer and Wolfart as materialists: *CL* ɪv 745.

equally composed from only one part of the dissimilar substances that are found in the earth's orbit.]

But why one moon only? It would be easier to fancy the Earth a confluence of Moons, and the Moon likewise—and so that the latter would have *set up* for herself, as a Sun's Moon, had she begun building a little further off.

4　ɪ 135, pencil | Sec 3 ch 4

Hier möge man die Natur und die Wirkungen des Spiegels wohl überlegen. . . . Wenn die Oberfläche eine ganz genaue regelmässige und glatte Ebene ist, so werden auch die Bilder wahr und regelmässig seyn; im Gegentheil werden sie krumm, gebrochen, verstümmelt, undeutlich seyn, wenn die Oberfläche des Spiegels ungleich, zerbrochen, dunkel . . . ist. . . . Eine ähnliche Affekzion kann entweder äusserlich in Bezug auf die äussere Oberfläche der Sinne, oder innerlich im Centralsensorium . . . statt finden. Dies kann durch physische Unregelmässigkeiten der Organe vorkommen, wie üble Bildung, Krankheiten; oder . . . durch die Verstimmung der Eindrücke durch Irrthümer, Vorurtheile, Leidenschaften, Gewohnheiten . . .

[Here one may well consider the nature and working of the mirror. . . . When the surface is a perfectly smooth and level plane, the images are accordingly faithful and uniform; on the contrary, they become twisted, broken, distorted, and unclear when the surface of the mirror is uneven, cracked, dark. . . . A similar action can take place either externally, on the outer surface of the senses, or internally, in the central sensory unit. . . . This may occur through physical anomalies of the organs, such as malformation or disease, or . . . through the disordering of impressions by errors, biases, passions, habits . . .]

This ¶ is a masterpiece of mock Analogy! To set forth (auseinandersetzen) its beauties in detail, would be *dull*—and useless to boot.—For observe,[a]

5　ɪ 343 | Pt 2 sec 2 appendix

[Animals typically give birth alone, eat the afterbirth, and sever the umbilical cord by biting it through.] Die menschlichen Mütter der Vorzeit, im Gegensatz mit den Thieren, obwohl sie die Aehnlichkeit der Geburtsorgane mit denselben erkennen konnten, kehrten sich, wahrscheinlich aus einem leicht zu begreifenden Ekel und Abscheu, nicht an das täglich vor ihren Augen vorkommende Beispiel, sondern erfanden und versuchten nach Willkühr andere der Nature fremde, vielmals unglückliche Methoden.

[a] Note breaks off thus, with no trace of erasure

[In contrast to animals, the human mothers of ages long past, although they could recognise the similarity of their birth organs to those of animals, took no note of the examples that daily occurred before their eyes, probably out of an easily understandable disgust and loathing; instead, they arbitrarily invented and tried unnatural and often unfortunate methods.]

The Disgust a proof that Instinct does not teach Women this practice, ergo, a *beastly* practice.

6   II ⁻1

The whole Logic of these two Volumes may be reduced to ~~this~~ one undeniable Truth; a[nd]*a* one not very improbable Conjecture. First, that if x y (the magnetic Agent or agency, for instance) which *is not* capable of acting on the sense of ~~Sight~~ vision *were* capable of so acting, then it would be visible—2ⁿᵈ that if visible, it would appear more like E Vitr. Ether[1] than any thing else—!—Ο θαυμαστον.[2]

7   II ⁻1, ⁺1

It is amusing to observe the neither very honest nor the very ingenious efforts of Dʳ Woolfart (?φιζζλε?)[1] to distill the ~~crude~~ dreggy Materialism of Mesmer into the hyper-alcoholic Spirit of Schellingianism, but alas! it will not do even for a child's *Picture-book* to the System der Natur-philosophie.[2]—It is however no sound Objection to the facts of Animal Magnetism, that its most successful Professors have been men of weak judgement. For the prevention of distraction of mind, and earnestness of Volition are ex hypothesi[3] the conditions of concentering and emitting the influence, even as Anger, ~~or~~ and the energy of self-defence

---

a Letters lost in binding

6[1] "Vitreous ether", i.e. transparent (and therefore scarcely "visible"): cf C's objections to Mesmer's ever more refined universal magnetic fluid in **1** above and in e.g. JUNG **31**, KLUGE **1**.

6[2] "O wonderful".

7[1] "Fizzle", to break wind quietly—a synonym for "woolfart". C's "Greek" is simply a transliteration of the English word, which he could not in propriety write for everyone to see.

7[2] Wolfart claims that it is a gross error to regard Mesmer's system as materialistic, arguing that the magnetic fluid is not a substance but a field of interaction between various bodies, and that Mesmer conceived

of matter not as an independent entity but as a manifestation of an original unity in the absolute (*Erläuterungen* 2–8, 20–3, 51–5). Wolfart repeatedly stresses the connection between the universal fluid and a divine creator, which, as C rightly comments, is hardly a conspicuous tenet in Mesmer's doctrines. Wolfart also points out that Mesmer's system is congruent with the principles of Schelling's *Naturphilosophie*, and that Mesmer's categories of "movement" and "matter" spell out in clearer terms what Schelling means by the infinite and the finite as two dimensions of the absolute (*Erläuterungen* 53).

7[3] "Upon this hypothesis".

are the conditions of the Gymnotus ~~be~~ accumulating its galvanism[4]—but this devotion of Thought, freedom from disturbing Doubts, and even from the activity of philosophic Inference, in short, Faith (as a unifying energy) are most likely to exist in weak & credulous, but sincere, sensitive[a] and warm-hearted Men.—Just such a man is Dr Wolfart—as I have been assured by one of his most intimate friends.—That friend, who admitted him to be a man of no vigor of intellect, and bodily too ein schwacher, kränklicher Mensch (feeble and sickly) spoke in the highest terms of his veracity, his disinterestedness—in short, as a man incapable of guile—And this friend likewise (Ludwig Tieck, the celebrated Poet and Critic) attested the fact of Wolfart's power of fixing the needle in the Mariner's Compass by pointing his finger on it, (See p. 92.) attested it as a frequent Eye-witness[5]—He likewise attested in answer to the same question—(What have you yourself seen?) the powers of Magnetism in each of the six Grades, with exception of the last or the *extatic*—Of this, however, he had no doubt: so many instances had been related to him by Physicians of eminence, men on whose honor and veracity he placed entire reliance, who had themselves been the Magnetisers.

I think it probable, that An. Magnetism will be found connected with a *Warmth-Sense*: & will confirm my long long ago theory of Volition as a mode of *double Touch*.[6]

8 ii iii (fly-title), pencil | Epigraph

[Wolfart takes as an epigraph a passage from Plato *Phaedrus* 270^d tr Schleiermacher:] Und glaubst du die Natur der Seele richtig begreifen zu können, ohne des Ganzen Natur?

Wenn man dem Asklepiaden Hippokrates glauben soll, auch nicht einmal die des Körpers ohne ein solches Verfahren.

[Then do you think it possible to understand the nature of the soul satisfactorily without taking it as a whole?

  a Running out of space, C wrote here "turn to the back", and continued his note on $^+$1

7[4] C refers to the electric eel, which he also discussed in a fragment of 1817 on animal magnetism: BM Add MS 36532 f 8. The capability of certain species of fish to emit electric shocks was widely discussed in the travel and scientific literature of the time: *Phil Trans RS* LXV (1775) contains three articles on *Gymnotus electricus*, the last by John Hunter (pp 94–101, 102–10, 395–407). KLUGE talks about the electric eel on a page bearing C's annotations (*Magnetismus* 241).

7[5] On Tieck's report of Wolfart cf KLUGE **9**, where C cites the same information. The experiment with the compass is described in *Erläuterungen* 92.

7[6] C's speculations about volition as a mode of double touch appear to date from 1801: *CN* I 1827 and n, II 2405; *Lects 1808–1819* (*CC*) I 136 and n 37; *BL* ch 12 (*CC*) I 293–4. What he means by "double touch" has itself been much debated: John Beer, quoting this note, puts it in the context of magnetic theory in *Coleridge's Poetic Intelligence* (1977) 81–7.

If we are to believe Hippocrates, the Asclepiad, we can't understand even the body without such a procedure [tr R. Hackforth].]

> And strait from Dreamland came a Dwarf: and *he*
> Must tell the cause, forsooth, and know the cure.[1]

9　II 78, pencil | § 40

Diese beiden Mittelpunkte bedingen eine innere Kugel, so wie eine dieselbe einschliessende peripherische Kruste, nicht minder in ihrem Innern die Zentralfeuer. . . . Es ist keineswegs dabei die Meinung, dass dieses Zentralfeuer als ein Feuer, wie er uns vermöge des Zutritts der Athmosphäre erscheint, zu betrachten sey. . . . Zum wirklich erscheinenden Feuer fehlt nur die Bedingung der athmosphärischen Luft: tritt diese durch die Erdklüfte hinzu, so bricht das Zentralfeuer aus, und dadurch hängen auch nothwendig alle Vulkane auf der ganzen Erdoberfläche zusammen.

[These two centres necessitate an inner sphere, as well as a peripheral crust enclosing the former, no less than they do the central fire in its interior. . . . This is by no means to say that this central fire should be regarded as the same fire that appears to us through the presence of the atmosphere. . . . For the fire really to appear only the condition of the atmospheric air is lacking: if this enters through rifts in the earth then the central fire breaks out, and thus all volcanoes are necessarily connected throughout the surface of the earth.]

!! Strange! Air, of sufficient purity to feed fire, finds its way thro' Caverns and Rifts four *thousand* miles perpendicular depth below the surface, the whole atmosphere, capable of sustaining fire, not exceeding forty miles in height!!!

10　II 89, pencil | § 45

. . . (hierin zugleich die Erklärung der Sonnenflecke, welche deutlich als abgesondert, beweglich und umtreibend <u>beobachtet worden sind</u>) . . .

[. . . (herein at the same time [lies] the explanation of sunspots, which <u>have been clearly observed</u> as detached, mobile, and drifting about) . . .]

by whom? W. is mistaken.[a] All the phænomena of the Solar Maculæ are explicable without the supposition of detached Bodies, either in Wilson's or Herschell's theory.[1]

---

[a] This first part of the note is written in the margin; the remainder, with a footnote symbol, appears at the foot of the page

8[1] C used these lines in "The Two Founts" *PW* (EHC) I 454–5, composed May 1826.

10[1] Sir William Herschel's paper "Observations tending to Investigate the Nature of the Sun" *Phil Trans RS* XCI (1801) 265–

11   ɪɪ 90, pencil | § 46

Das Eisen, als Eisen, hat diejenige innere Organisazion, welche das-
selbe gerade zu diesem Körper macht, und so muss auch ein Stäubchen
Eisen jene noch in ganz gleicher Art haben, wie der Stab, von welchem
man es trennte.

[Iron as iron has that inner organisation which forms it into just this body, and
thus even a dust particle of iron must still contain it [i.e. inner organisation] in
exactly the same way as the bar from which it has been detached.]

apply this to a *Fiddle*.

12   ɪɪ 154 | § 70

. . . so gelangt man für das thierische Leben, und höher für die geistigen
Eigenschaften im Menschen als *vermittelnde* Träger zu Flutreihen . . .
worin also die Lebens- und Geistesschwingung als höchstes, als reinstes
Licht sich zu offenbaren vermag, als das Element, in welchem der reine
*urthätige Ausfluss des Unerschaffenen und Ewigen als möglichst frei-
thätiges Leben erwacht . . .

[. . . thus one arrives at a series of fluids as *intermediary* transmitters for the
animal life and for the higher spiritual human qualities . . . in which the organic
and spiritual vibrations can manifest themselves as the highest, as the purest
light, as the element in which the pure, *primally active emanation of the uncre-
ated and eternal awakens as the most active life possible . . .]

*   Qʸ *Urfläthige?*[a][1]
Why, it is as plain as a Pike-staff!

Inner and Inner,
Thinner and thinner.
Our Thoughts are the *volatile* T——ds of our Dinner
And sententiâ meâ
The Soul's but a thin sort of Diupsorrhea![2]

[a] The remainder of the note appears at the foot of the page

318 provides detailed information on sun-
spots and concludes that "those appear-
ances which have been called spots in the
sun, are real openings in the clouds of the
solar atmosphere" (270); in a footnote on
the same page, Herschel cites Alexander
Wilson's paper "Observations on the Solar
Spots" *Phil Trans RS* ʟxɪv pt i (1774) 7–
11, which demonstrates that sunspots could
arise only in "vast photospheric excava-
tions".

[12.1] According to Grimm, in middle
high German the word *flätig* meant (1)
"pure, beautiful, clean" or (2) "sordid,
spoiled, dirty". In modern German only
the word *unflätig* survives, meaning "un-
clean". C evidently wants to alter Wol-
fart's expression "primally active" (*urthä-
tige*) to "primally dirty".

[12.2] "Elevated diarrhoea" or "diar-
rhoea of sublimities": C coins the word
from the Greek ὕψος (*hypsos*) which means
"high, sublime". "T——ds" is "Turds";
sententia mea, "in my opinion".

13 ɪɪ 155–7, pencil, marked in the margin in pencil

Wer das nun Gesagte ganz begriffen hat, der wird sich daraus den Schlüssel zu allem übrigen, was nur diesen Magnetismus noch betreffen kann, gar leicht entnehmen können; *a*und dass er ihn wirklich gefunden hat diesen Schlüssel in der klaren Erkenntniss, das wird er daran erkennen: dass ihm nichts was das Leben überhaupt, so wie die Erscheinungen des thierischen Magnetismus, auch die seltensten und vom Gewöhnlichen am meisten abweichenden, also auch . . . wunderbarsten Wirkungen insbesondere betrifft, räthselhaft erscheint, noch bleibt.

[He who has understood what I have just said will be able to gain quite easily the key to all the rest that may further pertain to this magnetism; and that he has truly found this key to clear understanding, he will recognise from the fact that nothing concerning life in general, as well as the manifestations of animal magnetism, even the rarest and most extraordinary, even . . . in particular the most marvellous effects, appears or remains mysterious.]

These ⟨Lines,⟩ and to the end of this ¶. ought to have suggested a suspicion in the Author's own mind, that he had duped himself by words: that is, had translated facts into general terms, and thus *passed off* the exponents and (perhaps) arbitrary *pictures* of the problem for its Solution. For what man of sound Understanding but would startle at the position, that a single discovery (and in its ⟨first⟩ Dawning too) should at once render the Discoverer omniscient? Yet no less must that Mind ⟨be,⟩ for which nothing in the universe of Nature remains enigmatic!!—The Mesmerists have a warning example in John Brown, and the first eulogists of the Brunonian System. A week's, nay, a single Day's Reading—and thenceforward nothing in Physiology or Pathology would remain a riddle. All and each taken up without residue into the Light of + and − Excitability, + and [? so] − Excitement![1]

14 ɪɪ 158–9, pencil | § 72

Und da bei der Mittheilung hier dasselbe statt findet, was beim Magnet, beim Feuer, beim Licht und beim Schall durch weiter schwingende

---

a From here to end of textus marked with a line in the margin

13[1] According to John Brown, a well-known Edinburgh physician (1735–88) and author of the popular work *Elementa medicinae* (1780), "excitability" is the property which distinguishes all living from dead matter, and "excitement" represents the effect of various external and internal stimuli on the excitability. When the exciting powers are too intense, the excitability is too rapidly consumed, and when the stimuli are weak, the excitability accumu-lates excessively. Thus all diseases, Brown claims, are either sthenic, arising from excessive excitement, or asthenic, caused by deficient excitement, a distinction which C seems to have in mind here. See *Elements of Medicine* in *The Works of John Brown* (3 vols 1804) e.g. ɪɪ 134–49, 179–81. For C's reading in John Brown and the interest he aroused in Germany cf *CN* ɪ 388, 389 and nn.

Bewegung in der Fortgesetztheit der Flutordnungen nachgewiesen worden; so ist es klar, dass der ursprüngliche Brennpunkt, von welchem die Wirkung des Magnetismus ausgeht, eben so wenig einen Abgang, einen Verlust an irgend etwas erleiden könne, als ein Bild, wenn es sich auch . . . in tausend und aber tausend Spiegeln wiederholt . . .

[And since in the transmission the same thing occurs here as was demonstrated with the magnet, with fire, with light, and with sound through the further oscillation in the continuity of the fluid orders, it is therefore clear that the original focal point from which the effect of the magnetism proceeds can be as little reduced or diminished as an image is even if it is reflected in thousands and thousands of mirrors . . .]

Yet this assertion is in direct contradiction to the experience of Weinholdt, Gmelin, Kluge, and other practitioners in Animal Magnetism.[1] Nay, the strongest argument hitherto adduced in proof of its being a physical Agent, is that the exhaustion of the Magnetiser is diminished by insulating himself and the patieneet, analogous to Electrization.

15 II 166–7, pencil | § 706

Magnetisirte Kranke haben oft die augenblicklichen entweder erhöhten oder anders gearteten Wirkungen empfunden, wenn ich, während sie von den Stralen der Sonne oder des Mondes berührt wurden, gegen diese Himmelskörper in ihrem Lichtstral magnetische Bewegungen gemacht hatte. Ich weiss, dass gerade dieses Vielen am unglaublichsten, ja als abgeschmackt vorgekommen [ist] . . .

[Magnetised patients have often felt instantaneous influences of a heightened or uncommon kind, when, while they were touched by the rays of the sun or moon, I produced in the rays of light [that touched the patients] magnetic vibrations counteracting the heavenly bodies. I know that just this has seemed to many as most unbelievable, even in bad taste . . .]

W. does not see the thing in the right view. Not any supposed impossibility in the *extent* of the influence, the fact of the influence itself to any extent being granted, but the exceedingly slight grounds, on which so extraordinary and a priori experience improbable an Assertion is hazarded—this constitutes the ludicrous part of the pretension. The fancies and fancied sensations of a few dreamy and nervous Females!!—

14[1] C brings to bear evidence from KLUGE's *Magnetismus* pp 83–5, where Kluge speaks of the loss of power (*Kraftverlust*) commonly experienced by a magnetiser after a session with a patient and cites works by Wienholt and Gmelin. Kluge also points out that when a magnetist is insulated by electrical bodies, his loss of power is diminished and his effect on the patient is much more intense (p 85).

16 II 169 | § 77

Wie fangen wir es gewöhnlicherweise an, unsere Gedanken andern mitzutheilen?—Da einmal der Gedanke doch unleugbar organisch im Gehirn in dessen feinster Thätigkeit *vermittelt* wird; so muss auch nothwendig, organisch betrachtet, jeder bestimmte Gedanke aus einer bestimmten Schwingung in einer . . . blos flutbaren und im Gehirn allein möglichen Organisazion bestehen . . . [Wolfart goes on to show how this vibration is transmitted to the will and speech organs of the speaker and finally reaches the fluid matter of the listener's brain, where it is converted into the message articulated by the speaker.]

[How do we normally communicate our thoughts to another? Since thought is undoubtedly an organic [product] of the brain, *transmitted* through its finest activity, any thought must, therefore, arise from a determinate vibration in a . . . purely fluid organisation that is possible only in the brain . . .]

Exquisite Logic! $x = y$; but $z = x$; therefore $z = y$. The only omissions are "*if*" $x = y$; and "*if*" $z - x$; and the *proof* that either is the case. An Ass = Plato; but Dr Wolfart = an Ass; therefore Dr W. = Plato: or vice versâ.

17 II 188 | § 85

. . . besonders muss darin das nicht übersehen werden, wie die eigentliche höhere Organisazion immer als beherrschend und gleichsam schöpferisch über und in den andern Organisazionen, worin sie sich erst verwirklicht, waltet.

[. . . particularly it must not be overlooked here how the properly higher organisation always governs dominatingly and, as it were, creatively over and in the other organisations in which it first realises itself.]

W. has breathed into Mesmer's crass Materialism a better spirit acquired from the Natúr-philosophy. But Mesmerism is susceptible of this better spirit: and it is well and amiable in Wolfart so to do.[1]

17[1] Cf **7** n 2 above.

JOHN MILLER
1787–1858

Sermons Intended to Show a Sober Application of Scriptural Principles to the Realities of Life. With a preface addressed to the clergy. Oxford 1830. 8°.

British Library C 43 b 11

Inscribed on p⁻2: "From the Author". George Whalley's original notes on this volume indicate that when he first examined it it was unopened from p 275 (of 475) onwards; by the time it was checked in 1987, however, only pp 275–8 remained unopened.

DATE. 12 Sept 1830 (4). Also recorded in N46, dated 12 Sept 1830: "Read and wrote long ~~MS~~ marginal Notes on good Mʳ Miller's Sermon on the fallen state of Man.—"

COEDITOR. J. Robert Barth, S.J.

1   pp xxv–xxvi, pencil | Preface

Yet such, from one cause or another, has our predicament become, that we most surely find the people *in effect* dictating divine truth to <u>the priest,</u>* rather than "seeking the law at his mouth;" . . .

* Tho' I am willing to understand this as a *figurative* expression, I yet must regret the introduction of the term, *Priest*. The Christian Church has and can have, only one *Priest*—even Jesus, the everlasting High Priest. We have Teachers, Preachers, Pastors, Ministers, & Bishops— and the National Church or Clerisy contains Curates, Vicars, Rectors, Parsons, Deans, Prelates. But Priests and Priest-Orders are Judaisms & Paganisms derived to us thro' Popery.[1] N.B. I speak of the meaning and general acceptation of the Word, without adverting to its possible etymology. It may be a corruption or correption of *Presbus, Presbyter*— but it is universally understood as = Ιερευς[2]

1[1] C alludes to his own formulation of the function of the National Church in *C&S* (1829); a fragment on the origins of the "priestly caste" is published with that work in *C&S (CC)* 229–30.

1[2] C is correct about both the etymology of the word and the different roles to which it could be applied, on the one hand the presbyter or "elder", on the other he who offers sacrifice.

2 pp 22–3 | End of Sermon 1 "The Ground of Mutual Regard Between Ministers and People"

I have but one complaint to make, relatively to the preceding discourse—that it stands alone, & is not followed by two or three others, unfolding the deeply interesting truths & principles here with beautiful simplicity stated into the *particulars*—especially, the two points—first, the duties & accordant feelings of a Christian Pastor toward his Flock— & secondly, the duties of a Congregation to such a Pastor, & consequently, the divine *Right* of the Pastor, which nothing can excuse him from enforcing ⟨on his flock,⟩ and openly insisting on, as a momentous part of the duties necessary to ~~their the~~ scripture-ground assurance of their Salvation—nothing, but the inward Consciousness that he has not himself fulfilled the duties, out of which the *Right* springs, as a Stem from the Root.

3 pp 23–4 | Sermon 2 "The Original, and the Fallen, State of Man"

> *God created man in his own image;*
> *in the image of God created He him.*

Such was the original condition of man's nature. It came from the hands of the Almighty pure and perfect.* Man himself has made it what it is.

* Negatively, and in respect to the existence of *Actual* Evil, of *positive* imperfection or rather *dis*perfection, this is doubtless *true*. Still it is a truth not necessarily conveyed by the Words of the Text—which have a far profounder Meaning—a meaning not to be opened out in the space allotted to a marginal Note. *Mem.* A far juster interpretation of this Text is given in the apocryphal "Wisdom of Solomon". "But God made man in his own image—to be the *Image* of his own Eternity made he Man."[1]—Of *the Eternal* there is but one *Image* possible—that is, the *Immortal*. See "Aids to Reflection"—[2]

4 pp 25–35

It is worse than unprofitable to be for ever ransacking the very depths and sinks of sinfulness, to overwhelm ourselves with more than real notions of individual depravity. Such is not (as I apprehend) the way of Scripture; nor is it fitted to do good.

3[1] Wisd of Sol 2.23 var.
3[2] C is probably alluding to the distinction between reason and understanding, esp *AR* (1825) 209, where he asserts that "Reason is pre-eminently spiritual, and a Spirit, even *our* Spirit, through an effluence of the same grace by which we are privileged to say Our Father!"

It is indeed a melancholy truth, that the modern Calvinists too generally reason on this subject much as a man would do who finding the centrifugal force in the planetary system should forget, that without the centripetal it could never have manifested itself, as actual—We cannot be made too sensible of the *potential* Evil, that not only is *in*, but which *is*, the Ground of our creaturely Being. But then we are no less bound to know that without the divine Good this very Evil could never have assumed *actual* Being. Whatever *actually* exists, *therefore* exists, because Redemption hath *begun* in it, because it is within the conditions of redeemability. But alas! in order to the full insight into this great truth, it is for the Many necessary, that the superstitious & most erroneous notions respecting the true New Testament Sense of the Devil, and the Evil Spirits, should be cleared away.[1]

I am not surprized, nor does it in the least detract from my respect and high estimation of Mr Miller's Head and Heart, that he has taken a very erroneous view of this subject—a view, incompatible with a full and adequate Conception of the Redemption of the World in and by the Word "that became flesh."[2] Yet I wonder that St Paul's declaration, that the first Adam was a *living Soul*, but the second a *life-making Spirit*,[3] had not occasioned a pause, a questioning, in his Mind. "Put on the *new* Man" says St Paul—not the *reformed* Man[4]—If the first Adam stood not, what ground of assurance to us of our Standing, if we are merely restored to his place? Without the life-making Spirit the living Soul must ever be in the same jeopardy, as the first Adam was. O! in the first Chapter of St John the estimable & most amiable Writer of these Discourses may, & I trust, *will* find a far nobler sense of restoration by and into Christ—who "came to *his own*"—a restoration to the "being τεχνα Θεου"[5] in the *Pleroma*, the living *Fullness* of the Godhead![6] The Work of Christ is verily and strictly a new *Creation*, not a MENDING.—But in order to an insight into this momentous truth it is necessary to have contemplated the 2nd v. of Gen. I as the product of the original Fall, and v. 3, 4, as the *commencing* Act of the Redemption! But alas! this, which

4[1] In DEFOE **14** (a note written c 1830) C asserts that "the existence of a Personal intelligent Evil Being, the Counterpart and Antagonist of God, is in direct contradiction to the most express declarations of Holy Writ!" For other statements on this theme see KANT *Religion* **1** n 4, LACUNZA **27, 29**.

4[2] John 1.14 var, C insisting on the translation of the Greek verb ἐγένετο in the active sense "became" as opposed to AV

"was made".

4[3] 1 Cor 15.45 var, q *AR* (1825) 209— the passage cited in **3** n 2 above.

4[4] Eph 4.24, q by Miller in textus **5** below.

4[5] Being "offspring of God" (as John 11.52); the phrase "came to his own" echoes John 1.11.

4[6] John 1.16: "And of his fulness have all we received, and grace for grace." Cf LEIGHTON COPY B **29** and n 1.

next to the Idea of the Tri-une God is the most momentous, most radical, pregnant and *concerning*, of *all* truths—this is *Metaphysics*—and that ominous word is the m~u~agic Anti-*Sesamè, to fling the door of the Mind in the face of the Reasoner, yea, to bolt and bar it against all entrance! Strange infatuation! Metaphysics—that is, μετα φυσικα, truths that transcend the evidence of the Senses![8]—And this is a terriculum[9] to a professed Believer in a God, a Redeemer, a responsible Will and a birth in the Spirit to him who saith, I am the Resurrection & the Life—the Life everlasting!—Infatuation indeed! Yet scarcely to be called strange, inasmuch as it may be easily explained by the bran, straw and froth which the Idols of the Age, Locke, Helvetius, Hume, Condillac, & their Disciples have succeeded in passing off for Metaphysics.[10] But is it not mournful that such common-place stuff scummed from the mere surface of the Senses should have superseded the Works of Luther, Melancthon, Bucer, yea, of Bull, Waterland, and Stillingfleet,[11] in the Libraries of the Clergy, even of those who have & use Libraries? I do not mention Richard Baxter, because—tho' of all Divines the nearest to the opinions of the serious Ministers of ~the~ our present Church, he is numbered among the Dissenters—with about as much right, as I might charge a man ~from~ with desertion whom I had thrown out of window in the hope of breaking his neck! But this I will say, that in Baxter's "Catholic Faith", and other of his Works, there is enough to *shame*, as well as supersede, whole Shelves of later Divines & Metaphysicians, French,

---

*Arabian Nights—Open Sesame! open.[7]

4[7] The magic word that opened the door of the robbers' den in the tale "Ali Baba and the Forty Thieves" in the *Arabian Nights*, to which C always refers with gratitude and affection, e.g. *CL* I 347, *TT* 31 May 1830.

4[8] C echoes the common misconception about the meaning of "Metaphysics": the title was applied by the medieval Schoolmen to Aristotle's work to signify everything that came "after the *Physics*" in the manuscript, rather than what is "beyond" or "above" nature.

4[9] "Bugbear".

4[10] A characteristic diatribe against the materialist and in some cases atheistic philosophers admired in C's day: cf *BL* ch 3 (*CC*) I 54: ". . . Bacon, Harrington, Machiavel, and Spinosa, are *not* read, because Hume, Condilliac, and Voltaire *are*"; the conviction that the name of philosophy had

been usurped "by physical and psychological Empiricism" in *LS* (*CC*) 170; and the attack on "Locke, Hartley, & Condillac" in the 1817 letter to Lord Liverpool (*CL* IV 760).

4[11] The great names of the Protestant Reformation and of the English Church about the time of Locke: Martin Luther and his loyal associates Philipp Melanchthon (1497–1560) and Martin Bucer (1491–1551); George Bull (1634–1710), author of *Defensio Fidei Nicaenae* (1685); Daniel Waterland (1683–1740), whose *Vindication of Christ's Divinity* (1719) C annotated; and Edward Stillingfleet (1635–99), author of *Origines sacrae* (1662) and of several pamphlets against Locke's *Essay*. In KENYON **4**, C mentions Bull and Waterland as having "*fixed*" the article of Trinity "for the whole Catholic Church, Romish & Protestant".

Scotch, & English.[12] God knows my heart! there may be & I trust are, many among our Clergy who love, prize and venerate our Church as earnestly and as disinterestedly as *I* do! But that any man, "on this side idolatry" can love & prize it more, or more sincerely, I it is not in my power to believe.—For those, however, who suppose like the Master of Trinity, he who wrote "Who wrote Eikon Basilikè?" that the character of our venerable Church is identified with that of those Diseases of the Age, Charles I., Laud, & Sheldon, I must submit to be scowled at, as an Alien and an Adversary.[13]

12 Sept 1830.   S. T. Coleridge

5   p 27

St. Paul, exhorting his Ephesian disciples to walk as persons who had learned Christ's power truly—so as to <u>regain</u>, through him, that better nature which had else been lost to them, speaks thus: "Put on the new man . . ."

No such word in S[t] Paul—No such thought *could* have entered his mind.[1]

6   pp 36–7

* Now, supposing men were naturally holy—what must be their universal conduct? We must needs find the awful name of the Divine Majesty accounted holy, and reverenced accordingly. If Christ hath, in his holy word, appointed any special ordinances, and bid us to observe and keep them; if God hath *ever* chosen an especial day unto himself for his own honour and service . . . must we not find such separate and chosen day for God's honour esteemed still as the "holy of the Lord," and "accounted a delight?"

* But if such had been the case, there could have been no reason or motive for an *especial* day. We should "pray always."[1]—It is at least injudicious to select ⟨the strict observation of⟩ a remedial ordinance, implying our corrupt *Nature*, as a distinctive character of an unfallen State. But the amiable Writer is discoursing on a mystery, the *idea* of which

4[12] C's admiration for Baxter (1615–91) is expressed also in his marginalia in two copies of *Reliquiae Baxterianae* and in *Catholick Theologie* (1675): *CM (CC)* I.

4[13] Christopher Wordsworth (1774–1846), whose *"Who Wrote* ΕΙΚΩΝ ΒΑΣΙΛΙΚΗ" *Considered and Answered* (2 pts 1824–5) C read and annotated c Jul 1825,

commenting on it also in a letter to Samuel Mence: *CL* v 477–8.

5[1] Cf **4** above at n 4.

6[1] Presumably an allusion to 1 Thess 5.17, the injunction to "Pray without ceasing", rather than to 2 Thess 1.11 though the AV verbal formula there is closer—"Wherefore also we pray always for you".

he had not mastered—which existed for him only in the consciousness and conscience of the *fact*—namely, that we are fallen Creatures. But wherein *the fall* consists, M͏ͬ M. does not appeared to have considered.

7 pp 43–5

While we are busy with inventions to destroy ourselves, the Almighty hath prepared a great discovery also; he hath "devised means that his banished be not expelled from him" for ever. *

* I cannot but think, that all the preceding parts of this Discourse might with great advantage have been compressed into a single paragraph. The first ¶ph. of Jer. Taylor's Letter on original Sin would for every christian Hearer have been abundantly sufficient.[1] As thorns do not produce Grapes, so neither does the Vine produce the poison-berries of the Night-shade. Moral Evil is over all—& the best men feel a will of the flesh opposing the Will of the Spirit. A source of Moral Evil, not accidental, but common to all men, is therefore a *fact*— He if any man deny it, he must be referred to his own conscience for the confutation. If he has a seared Conscience, all argument is *for him* useless. He must be made a *better* man, before he can be rendered a wiser.[2]—But the abuse of this fact, as a pretext of Self-delusion, is a most interesting point, & well worthy of a Preacher's exposure. These paragraphs therefore I highly admire—and only regret, that this so interesting subject had not been pursued more into detail, with instructions *how* we may and ought to avail ourselves of the fact of our corrupt Nature in our prayers and petitions to God for *Help* and *Mercy*. It is when we cry out for Mercy without ask⟨ing⟩ or truly desiring *Help*, that we are on the brink of a ruinous hypocrisy & delusion.

8 p 45

* We may yet be renewed after the image and likeness of God, at least in the particulars above mentioned.

* Most true!—and this, this is the poison of Modern Ultra-Calvinism—

7[1] It is difficult to be sure what passage C had in mind, since Taylor wrote in an epistolary form several defences of the controversial chapter rejecting the doctrine of original sin in his *Unum necessarium. Or, the Doctrine and Practice of Repentance* (1655). Four are included in the *Polemicall Discourses* (1674) that C annotated; of these, the most likely is the opening paragraph (pp 865–6) of *Deus justificatus* (1656), addressed as a letter to the dowager Countess of Devonshire. C addresses Taylor's teaching on original sin directly (but with reference chiefly to *Unum necessarium*) in *AR* (1825) 251–87.

7[2] C makes the same assertion in NICOLAI 7.

which represents the actual state of Man as *all evil*.[1] An *actual all*-evil is an impossibility—Evil cannot become *actual* but by participation of the Good. *Real*, fearfully real, it is—but Evil, solum *per se*,[2] is essentially *potential*.

8[1] C's objections to ''Modern Ultra-Calvinism'' and to its spokesman Edward Williams are glossed in LEIGHTON COPY C

13 and n 2 above.
8[2] ''In itself alone''.

JOHN MILTON

1608–1674

A Complete Collection of the Historical, Political, and Miscellaneous Works of John Milton: correctly printed from the original editions. With an historical and critical account of the life and writings of the author; containing several original papers of his, never before published. 2 vols. London 1738. F°.

University of Chicago Library

Daniel Stuart's copy (1). Donors' bookplate I ⁻10, II ⁻5. When these vols were rebound c 1961, the bookplate of an earlier owner, the Hon. George Frisbie Hoar of Worcester, Mass., was removed from I ⁻6 (then p-d), as was C's note on that page, i.e. 1 footnote. Inscribed in an unidentified hand at the head of I ⁻5 above C's note: "2 Vols. of Jefferies in Pall Mall: Feb: 1791". A few notes in pencil in an unidentified hand—possibly Stuart's—appear in *Areopagitica* I 143, 145, 147, 159, 160.

This is evidently not the copy bought by Lamb—apparently at C's request—in Oct 1802. C however had known of, and desired, this edition as early as Nov 1799, when he wrote to Southey: "I received from them [Lamb and Lloyd] in the last Quarter Letters so many, that with the Postage I might have bought Birch's Milton" (*CL* I 542).

CONTENTS. I i–xcvii An Account of the Life and Writings of John Milton, by T. Birch; 1–29 *Of Reformation in England*; 30–8 *Of Prelatical Episcopacy*; 39–75 *The Reason of Church-Government*; 76–102 *Animadversions . . . against Smectymnuus*; 103–34 *Apology for Smectymnuus*; 135–40 *Of Education*; 141–61 *Areopagitica*; 162–213 *The Doctrine and Discipline of Divorce*; 214–70 *Tetrachordon*; 271–94 *The Judgment of Martin Bucer concerning Divorce*; 295–308 *Colasterion*; 309–24 *The Tenure of Kings and Magistrates*; 325–59 *Observations on the Articles of Peace*; 360–444 *Eikonoclastes*; 445–544 *A Defence of the People of England*; 545–59 *A Treatise of Civil Power in Ecclesiastical Causes*; 560–81 *Considerations touching . . . Hirelings*; 582–4 *A Letter to a Friend*; 585–6 *The Present Means . . . of a Free Commonwealth*; 587–601 *The Ready and Easy Way to Establish a Free Commonwealth*; 602–6 *Brief Notes upon a Late Sermon*; 607–28 *Accedence commenc'd Grammar*. II 1–121 *The History of Britain*; 122–7 *Of True Religion*; 128–47 *A Brief History of Muscovia*; 148–52 *A Declaration*; 153–234 *Letters of State*; 235–617 *Opera omnia Latina*; Index.

DATE. 28 Mar 1808.

1 pp ⁻5–⁻3

Bought for Mʳ Stuart, 28 March 1808—price 3 guineas.¹ If G. Britain remain independent (and o! what Extremes of Guilt and Folly must combine in order to the Loss ~~of~~ even of her paramounce!) the prose Works of Milton will be more and more in Request. Hooker, Bacon, Harrington, Sidney, Jeremy Taylor, and these Volumes (to which I would add Sir T. Brown, if rich and peculiar Genius could wholly cover quaint⟨n⟩ess & pedantry of Diction) are the Upper House of genuine English Prose Classics.²—This present Century, among many worse things, which cast a gloom over its infancy, will be *notorious* in English Literature for the shameful Incorrectness, with which Booksellers, (too ignorant or too niggardly or both, to employ learned men in the business) have edited the various works of Bacon, Milton, & a number of other Works of great size/ ~~as tho²~~ The late Edition in 12 Vol Octavo of Lord Bacon, and Anderson's British Poets in 14 Vol:³ (thick Octavo, double column (each volume equal to two common Quartos, or even three)[)] are ~~not merely~~ absolutely *infamous* for their Errata; in the former ⟨there exists⟩ one error in every second, in the latter from 3 to half a dozen of the *worst** sort of blunders in every, page.⁴ This Edition of

ᵃ* "worst sort of blunders": i.e. those which substitute a *stupid sense* for an exquisite beauty. Of the self-conceit of ignorant Composi-

ᵃ The footnote, originally on 1 ⁻6, was removed from the volume in rebinding and is printed from a photograph

1¹ C had worked as a journalist for Daniel Stuart (1766–1846) on both the *Morning Post* and the *Courier*, and at this time, while he was lecturing in London, lived in rooms above the *Courier* office (the address at the end of this note). The political and patriotic content of the note suggests that it was written specifically for Stuart to enjoy.

1² C gradually developed the notion of a "classic style" in prose "more exclusively [than a popular style] addressed to the learned class"; in the 1818 lecture from which these phrases are taken (*Lects 1808–1819—CC*—II 231–43) he declares that "the great models of it in English are Hooker, Bacon, Milton, and Taylor, although it may be traced in many other authors of that age" (233). Sir Thomas Browne is there described (234) as a corrupter of the style, though valuable in his own way; Algernon Sidney is said to "afford excellent exemplars of a good modern practical style" (236). Sir James Harrington usually appears in C's writings not as a stylist but as a thinker—e.g. *BL* ch 3 (*CC*) I 54 and nn 2, 3—but he may be included in this list as a political writer interesting to Stuart.

1³ Francis Bacon *Works* (12 vols 1807), published by Jones; *not* the 10-vol Johnson ed (1803) used by C himself in 1807 (*CN* II 3174n).

C annotated three sets of "Anderson's British Poets", i.e. Robert ANDERSON ed *The Works of the British Poets* (13 vols Edinburgh and London 1792–5, with Vol XIV added 1807): *CM* (*CC*) I 37–87.

1⁴ In his prose "Historie and Gests of Maxilian" *Blackwood's* XI (1822) 5n, C mentions a folio Petrarch as "by the bye, the worst printed book in respect of blunders I know of, not excepting even Anderson's British Poets".

Milton therefore by the excellent and laborious *Birch*,[5] corrected with a care worthy of the praise of Milton himself, cannot but rise in value: and I dare prophesy, that in less than 20 years it will be sold at not less than ten guineas.—I greatly prefer this Folio to the Quarto Edition of Milton, which some have bought in order to have his prose works uniform with the 4to Edition of his poetical Works,[6] even for the opposite Reason— Admirable to the very height of Praise as[a] Milton's Prose works are, still they are "of a *party*" ~~to~~ in country, in religion, in politics, & even in *Morals*—(the Treatise in favor of Divorce)[7]—a party indeed, to which in all respects I cleave with head, heart and body—but yet it is a *Party*. But his Poetry belongs to the whole World/ It is alike the Property of the Churchman and the Dissenter, the Protestant and Catholic, the Monarchist and the Republican—and of every Country on Earth, except the kingdom of Dahomy, in Africa, for the *present* at least, and of France (as long as it shall be inhabited by Frenchmen) *for ever!*[8] A mine of Lead could sooner take wing and mount aloft at the Call of the Sun with the Dews and with the Lark, than ~~a~~ the witty discontinuous Intellect, and sensual Sum Total of a Frenchman could soar up to Religion or to Milton & Shakspear. It is impossible. ~~They~~ Frenchmen are the *Indigenæ*, the *natives* of this Planet—and all the Souls, that are not Wanderers *from* other Worlds, or destined *for* other Worlds, ⟨who are not mere⟩ Probationers ⟨here⟩ and Birds of passage—all the *very own* Children of this "*Earth*" enter into the wombs of Frenchwomen, from N. E. S. W. and increase the population & Empire of France. Russia* furnishes such

---

tors instances enough might be collected, from literary men, to make a volume—and a very entertaining one it would be.—

^{b}* I write this not from the accident of a war with Russia, but from an intimate knowlege of the Russian Character, gained from two years

---

^{a} C has written "*turn over*" and has continued the note on I $^-$4
^{b} This footnote appears on I $^-$3, opposite the footnote symbol

1[5] Thomas Birch (1705–66), editor of this collection as well as author of the biography included in it—the first scholarly biography of Milton.

1[6] I.e. the one-volume prose *Works* (1753) and Tonson's ed of *Poetical Works* (2 vols 1720).

1[7] I.e. I 162–213, *The Doctrine and Discipline of Divorce*.

1[8] In the remainder of this note C elaborates further on the lack of spiritual capacity in the French. The kingdom of Dahomey in West Africa was at this time a centre of the slave trade, with the active involvement of its black rulers; C would have felt his estimate of it justified by the fact that it eventually became a French colony. In his essays "On the Principles of Genial Criticism" C refers to a traveller's report "that in their whole language they have no word for beauty, or the beautiful": *BL* (1907) II 226.

large supplies of French Souls, that they probably will be commanded to abide where they arrive, and form a "ɴNew France"—a Nova Gallia—as we have a ɴNew England in America, & a Nova Scotia./ And alas! even G. Britain sends large ~~Supplies~~ Colonies thither. What are the greater part of the members of the two Houses of Parliament, especially the Whitbreads, & Roscoe-pamphet*ᵃ* Men,[10] but Souls passing thro' the Stomach & Intestines of England, like Misletoe Berries thro' those of the Thrush, or Nutmegs (in the Spice Islands) thro' those of the Eastern Pigeon, in order to be matured for germinating in France & becoming ⟨Frenchmen?⟩ some in the next—some in the following ⟨generation,⟩— And few (Mʳ Fox[11] for instance) may even take three or four generations, sinking in each into a nearer proximity, before the Soul is compleatly *unsouled* into a ~~Frenchman~~ proper Gaul—This Process is now so common, that every Englishman has cause for alarm, lest instead of singing with Angels, or ~~partakin danc~~ beating off imp-flies with his Tail among the Infernals, his ⟨Spirit⟩ should some 50 or a 100 years hence be dancing, crouching, and *libidinizing*, beneath the Sceptre of one of Napoleon's Successors.—I know no better way, by which he can assure himself of the contrary, and prove his *Election* either to be a happy angel hereafter, or at worst an honest English Devil, than by his being sincerely conscious, that he reads with delight, feels, understands, and honors the *following Works* of *Milton. This* being, it necessarily follows that he loves Sidney, Harrington, Shakspere, & the *Poet* Milton.

S. T. Coleridge.   *348, Strand.*

Intercourse with Russians, of all ages, & rank, and of both sexes.[9] The Russian is a thorough Frenchman, without the Frenchman's Wit.

ᵃ For "pamphlet"

1[9] C does not appear to mention such sustained association with Russians elsewhere, though his reference to "two years" of experience may suggest the Malta period.

1[10] Samuel Whitbread (1758–1815), MP; and William Roscoe (1753–1831), MP 1806–7. A *Courier* leader of 1811, attributed to C, refers to pamphlets published by each of them in 1808 as indistinguishable: *EOT* (*CC*) ɪɪ 322 n 18.

1[11] Charles James Fox (1749–1806), Whig leader and defender of the revolution in France long after most of C's contemporaries had lost faith in it.

Lost Book

Paradise Lost: a poem in twelve books. . . . From the text of Thomas Newton, D.D. London 1777. 12°.

Not located; marginalia not recorded. *Gillman SC* (1843) 334, ''With MS. Notes by S. T. Coleridge''.

Poems upon Several Occasions, English, Italian, and Latin, with translations . . . *viz*. Lycidas, L'Allegro, Il Penseroso, Arcades, Comus, Odes, Sonnets, Miscellanies, English Psalms, Elegiarum Liber, Epigrammatum Liber, Sylvarum Liber. With notes critical and explanatory, and other illustrations, by Thomas Warton. . . . 2nd ed. London 1791. 8°.

Harvard University (Houghton Library)

Inscribed in pencil on p ⁻4: "To S. T. Coleridge Esqʳ with the love, regard & esteem of his obliged and grateful friend J. Watson Octʳ 17ᵗʰ 1823." (The presentation was made in Ramsgate.) Above this inscription, Coleridge has written in ink: "I bequeath this Book to Mʳˢ Gillman—S. T. Coleridge, 28 June 1827." Title-page verso contains Mrs Gillman's inscription on her gift of the book to Robert Watson [? Cowen] 4 May 1854. Autograph signature "John Drinkwater 1921." on p ⁻5 (p-d). A stub only remains of pp ⁻1–⁻2, the main part of the leaf having been removed before C wrote **9**. A copy of Alice Snyder's letter in *TLS* 25 Aug 1927, identifying John Watson, is loose in the volume.

DATE. Shortly after 17 Oct 1823 (date of presentation), **20** being dated 22 Oct 1823; and possibly later (**12** n 2).

1   pp ⁻4–⁻3, pencil

Of Criticism ~~in general~~ we may perhaps say, that those divine Poets, Homer, Eschylus & the two Compeers, Dante, Shakespear, Spencer, Milton, who deserve to have Critics, κριται, are placed above Criticism in the vulgar sense, and move in the Sphere of Religion, while those, who are not such, scarcely deserve Criticism, in any sense.—But speaking generally, it is far far better to distinguish Poetry into different Classes: & instead of *fault*-finding to say, this belongs to such or such a class—thus noting inferiority in the *sort* rather than censure in the particular poem or poet. We may *outgrow* certain *sorts* of poetry (Young's Night-thoughts,[1] for instance) without arraigning their excellence *proprio genere*.[2] In short, the wise is the genial: and the genial Judgement is to distinguish accurately the character & characteristics of each poem, praising them according to their force & vivacity in their own kind—& to reserve Reprehension for such as have no *character*—tho' the wisest reprehension would be not to speak of them at all.

1[1] Edward Young *The Complaint, or Night Thoughts on Life, Death and Immortality* (1742–6); C refers to its "figurative metaphysics and solemn epigrams" in *BL* ch 23 (*CC*) II 211.
1[2] "In their own kind".

2   p [iii]

Most shamefully incorrect. The Errata in the Latin Quotations are so numerous & so whimsical, as to puzzle the ingenuity of the best Latinist.[1] I suspected, that this is one of old Lackington's pirate editions. The paper seems too bad for such respectable Publishers, as the Robinsons', who did not deal in this charta cacatilis.[2]

3   p [iii], pencil | Preface

* After the publication of the PARADISE LOST <u>whose</u> acknowledged merit and increasing celebrity might have naturally contributed to call other pieces of the same author, and of a kindred excellence, into a more conspicuous point of view, they long continued to remain in their original state of neglect and obscurity.

* Can Tom Warton have been guilty of this offence against prose English—? Whose instead of "of which".[1]

4   p iv, pencil

It was late in the present century, before they [Milton's early poems] attained their just measure of esteem and popularity. Wit and rhyme, sentiment and satire, polished numbers, sparking couplets, and pointed periods, having so long kept undisturbed possession in our poetry, would not easily give way to fiction and fancy, to picturesque description, and romantic imagery.

It is hard to say which of the two kinds of metrical composition are here most unfaithfully characterized, that which Warton opposes to the Miltonic, or the Miltonic asserted to have been eclipsed by the former. But a marginal note does not give room enough to explain what I mean.

4A   p xiv

In a Letter to Henry Oldenburgh, written in 1654, he says, "Hoc cum libertatis adversus inopinatum certamen, DIVERSIS longe et AMANIORIBUS omnino me studiis intentum, ad se rapuit INVITUM."[1]

2[1] C makes corrections to the Latin in **4A**, **4B**, and **43**, and to the Italian in **33A** and **33B**.

2[2] "Toilet paper"—to modernise C's habitual complaint about bad paper (based on Catullus's *cacata carta*), as in EICHHORN *Apocalypsin Joannis* COPY B **1** and n 2.

The imprint names G. G. J. and J. Robinson as the publishers; there is no evidence to substantiate C's attribution of the edition to the bookseller James Lackington (1746–1815) of the "Temple of the Muses", famous for its large stock and low prices.

3[1] A usage to which C objects also in MATTHIAE **8**.

4A[1] C corrects only one of several errors in this passage: *adversus* should be *adversariis*, and *amanioribus* should be *amoe-*

4B p xx

[Warton quotes from Cowley's Latin Hymn to Light:]

Te bibens arcus Jovis ebriosus
Mille formosus ~~removit~~novat colores,[1]
Pavo coelestis. . . .
Lucidum trudis properanter agmen:
Sed resistentum super ora rerum
Lǿenitųer stagnas . . .

[Drunken with draughts of thee Jove's bow, the beautiful, the heavenly peacock, removes [C suggest "renews"] a thousand colours. . . . But upon firm bodies standing in thy way gently thou settlest . . .]

5 pp [1], [xlviii] | *Lycidas* line 1

[Warton's note:] *Yet once more*, &c.[a] * The best poets imperceptibly adopt phrases and formularies from the writings of their contemporaries or immediate predecessours. An Elegy on the death of the celebrated Countess of Pembroke, sir Philip Sydney's sister, begins thus:

Yet once againe, my Muse.—

* This, no doubt, is true; but the application to particular instances is exceedingly suspicious. Why, in Heaven's name! might not "once more" have as well occurred to Milton as to Sidney? On similar subjects or occasions some similar Thoughts *must* occur to different Persons,[b] especially if men of resembling Genius, quite independent of each other. The proof of this, if proof were needed, may be found in the works of Contemporaries of different Countries in books published at the very *same time*, where neither *could* have seen the work of the other—perhaps ignorant of the language. I gave my Lectures on Shakespear two years before Schlegel *began* his at Vienna—& I was myself startled at the close even verbal Parallelisms.[1]   S. T. Coleridge.

[a] Warton used a closing square bracket to mark the end of the quoted lines and the beginning of his comment; this punctuation has been omitted here and in later notes, to avoid confusion with editorial matter
[b] The note, begun on p [1], is here resumed on p [xlviii] with "*note continued from opposite*"

---

nioribus. Tr: "This unexpected contest with the adversaries of liberty took me off against my will when I was intent on very different and altogether pleasanter studies."

4B[1] The *removit* reading is incorrect, and C's emendation plausible. Cowley, however, wrote *revomit*, "pours forth again". In the following lines C corrects

typographical errors: *lonitur* is not a Latin word.

5[1] C repeats the statement made in *BL* ch 2 (*CC*) I 34, anticipating charges of plagiarism from A. W. Schlegel's *Vorlesungen über dramatische Kunst und Litteratur* (1809–11), which, however, he certainly made use of in lectures of 1811–13: *Lects 1808–1819* (*CC*) I lxii.

6   pp 2–6 | Line 5

[Warton's note:] * *Mellowing year*. Here is an inaccuracy of the poet. The *Mellowing year* could not affect the leaves of the laurel, the myrtle and the ivy; which last is characterised before as *never sere*.

* If this is not finding fault for fault-finding sake, Maister Tummas! I do not know what it is. The young and diffident poet tells us, that the Duty to his Friend's Memory compels him to produce a poem before his poetic Genius had attained ~~to~~ its full developement, or had received the due culture & nourishment from Learning and Study. The faculties appertaining to Poetic Genius he symbolizes beautifully & appropriately by the Laurel, the Myrtle and the Ivy—all three berry-bearing Plants: and these Berries express here the *actual* state, degree and quality of his poetic Powers, as the Plants themselves express the potential—the Leaves of the Ivy are "never sere", both because this is the general character of Ivy and of Verse, and by a natural and graceful Prolepsis in reference to his own future productions—Now if Warton had THOUGHT instead of criticized, he must have seen that it was the Berries which were to be plucked, but that in consequence of their unripeness & ⟨the⟩ toughness of the pedicles he was in danger of *shattering* the Leaves in the attempt. It was the *Berries*, I repeat, that the more advanced Season was to have *mellowed*: & who indeed ever dreamt of *mellowing* a Leaf?! The Autumn may be said to mellow the *tints* of the Foliage; but the word is never applied to the Leaves themselves.   S. T. C.

7   pp 3–4 | Line 11

[Warton's note:] *To sing, and build the lofty rhyme*. . . . I cannot however admit bishop Pearce's reasoning, who says, "Milton appears to have meant a different thing by RHIME here from RIME in his Preface, where it is six times mentioned, and always spelled without an *h*: whereas in all the Editions, RHIME in this place of the poem was spelled with an *h*. Milton probably meant a difference in the thing, by making so constant a difference in the spelling; and intended we should here understand by RHIME not the *jingling sound of like Endings, but Verse in general*." REVIEW OF THE TEXT OF PARADISE LOST, Lond. 1733. p. 5.

I am still inclined to think Bishop Pearce in the right. It is the tendency of all Languages to avail them of the opportunities given by accidental differences of pronunciation and Spelling to make a word multiply on itself/ ex. gr. Propriety, Property; Mister and Master. [1]—Besides, we can

7[1] C himself made much of this sort of desynonymisation; for instance, he uses "propriety" in distinction from "property" in *C&S* (*CC*) 35.

prove that this was Milton's plan. In the *first* Edition of the Par. Lost in *Twelve* Books, called the Second Edition, Heè, Sheè are systematically thus distinguished from He, and She; and her, their from hir, thir—when they are to convey a distinct image to the mind, and are not merely grammatical adjuncts, such as would be *understood* in Latin.[2]

8   p 5 | Line 18

[Warton's note:] * *Hence with denial vain, and coy excuse.* The epithet coy is at present restrained to Person. Antiently, it was more generally combined. Thus a shepherd in Drayton's Pastorals,

> Shepherd, these things are all too coy for me,
> Whose youth is spent in jollity and mirth.

That is, "This sort of knowledge is too *hard*, too difficult for me, &c." . . . [Warton's note:] † *Together both*, &c. Here a new paragraph begins in the edition of 1645, and in all that followed. But in the edition of 1638, the whole context is thus pointed and arranged.

> For we were nurst upon the self-same hill,
> Fed the same flock by fountain, shade, and rill;
> Together both, ere the high lawns appear'd, &c.

*† Why, Warton! dear Tom Warton! wake up, my good fellow! You are snoring. Even in Drayton's Pastoral the "coy" is poorly explained into "*hard*"; but here it is evidently *personal*—excuse shewing coyness in the Sisters.—but this ⟨is⟩ nothing to the want of Tact, Taste, and Ear—yea, of Eye and sagacious nostril—evidenced in the preference given to the Edit. 1638—The ¶ph. begins anew with, Together &c— after shroud there should be a colon only.[1]

7[2] Richard Bentley's notoriously freely emended version of *Paradise Lost* in 1732 led several scholars to examine the text(s) more closely; in particular, the Jonathan Richardsons (father and son) in *Explanatory Notes and Remarks on Milton's Paradise Lost* (1734) cxxxi–cxxxii drew attention to the now famous correction among the errata to the first edition of *Paradise Lost* in 12 books (1674)—"Lib. 2. v. 414, for *we* read *wee*"—which suggested that Milton had "systematically" used two spellings of the personal pronouns in order to discriminate between ordinary and emphatic use, the latter being the usual occasion for the appearance of pronouns in

Latin. This principle was not, however, put into practice until Capell Lofft's edition of *Paradise Lost* appeared in 1792: R. G. Moyles *The Text of 'Paradise Lost': A Study in Editorial Procedure* (Toronto 1985) 85–6. C's own annotated copy of the 1777 ed, based on Thomas Newton's text, did not preserve the distinction.

8[1] Both 1638 and 1645 have a full stop after "shroud" in line 22 ("And bid fair peace to be my sable shroud./ For we were nurst . . ."), but 1645 and subsequent editions also begin a new paragraph with "Together" in line 25. In **9** below C elaborates on his interpretation of the effect that a colon would have at the end of line 22.

9   pp ⁻3–⁻1, ⁻2/⁻1 | **8** textus

P. 5. It is astonishing to me, that Warton should not have felt that the Couplet

> For we are nurst upon the self-same Hill,
> Fed the same flock by fountain, shade and rill!

is manifestly the Basis or Pedestal of the Stanza or Scheme of verse, ~~beginning~~ commencing with, "Begin then, Sisters,['] and that it is divided from the 8ᵗʰ line of the Scheme by a colon: i.e. a full stop intended but with the *cadence* revoked, as it were, by a sudden recollection of some appertaining matter, confirming, enforcing or completing the preceding thought. Then follows a Pause, during which the Thought last started & expressed generally, unfolds itself to the poet's mind—and he begins anew with the proof & exposition of it by the particulars.—

Another & for a poet's ear convincing, proof that the couplet belongs to the third Stanza is, that the 8ᵗʰ line like the first is *rhymeless* and was left so, because the concurring rhymes of the concluding Distich were foreseen as the compensation. Mem. This applicable to Sonnets viz. under what circumstances the Sonnet should be 8 + 6, 12 + 2, or 14.—[1]

10   pp 8–11 | Lines 37–44

> *But, O the heavy change, now thou art gone,
> Now thou art gone, and never must return!
> Thee, Shepherd, thee the woods, and desert caves
> With wild thyme and the gadding vine o'ergrown,
> And all their echoes mourn:
> The willows, and the hazel copses green,
> Shall now no more be seen
> Fanning their joyous leaves to thy soft lays.

* There is a delicate beauty of Sound produced by the floating or oscillation of Assonance and consonance, in the rhymes gone, return, ⟨caves⟩ o'ergrown, mourn, green/ seen, ⟨lays.⟩ Substitute flown for gone, in the first line: & if you have a Poet's Ear, you will feel what you have lost & understand what I mean.   ~~S.T.C.~~   I am bound, however, to confess that in the five last lines of this Stanza I find more of the fondness of a classical Scholar for his favorite Classics than of the self-subsistency of a Poet destined to be himself a Classic—more of the Copyist of Theoc-

9[1] C wrote remarkably little about the theory of the sonnet, but a late prose preface to a fragment of his own challenges the "Procrustean" convention of 14 lines: "What Is an English Sonnet?" *Blackwood's* XXXI (1832) 956.

ritus & *his* Copyist, Virgil than of the free Imitator, who seizes with a strong hand whatever he wants or wishes for his own purpose and justifies the seizure by the improvement of the material or the superiority of the purpose, to which it is applied.[1]

11 p 13 | Lines 56–7

[Warton's note:] *Ay me! I fondly dream!*
                           Had ye been there—for what could that have done?

So these lines stand in editions 1638, 1645, and 1673, the two last of which were printed under Milton's eye. Doctor Newton thus exhibits the passage.

> Ay me! I fondly dream
> Had ye been there, for what could that have done?

And adds this note: "We have here followed the pointing of Milton's manuscript in preference to all the editions: and the meaning plainly is, I fondly *dream of your having been there*, for what would that have signified?" But surely the words, *I fondly dream had ye been there*, will not bear this construction. The reading which I have adopted, to say nothing of its authority, has an abruptness which heightens the present sentiment, and more strongly marks the distraction of the speaker's mind. "Ah me! I am fondly dreaming! I will suppose you had been there—*but why should I suppose it*, for what would that have availed?" The context is broken and confused, and contains a sudden elleipsis which I have supplied with the words in Italics.

Had this been Milton's intention, he would have written *but*, as W. has done; and not for. Newton's is clearly the true Reading.

12 pp 13–14 | Line 63

[Warton's note:] *Down the swift Hebrus to the Lesbian shore*. In calling Hebrus SWIFT, Milton, who is avaricious of classical authority, appears to have followed a verse in the Eneid, i. 321.

> —VOLUCREMQUE fuga praevertitur Hebrum

["'and outstrips winged Hebrus in flight" *Aeneid* 1.317 tr H. Rushton Fairclough, LCL]. But Milton was misled by a wrong although a very antient reading. Even Servius, in his comment in the line, with an ag-

---

10[1] C's distinction between imitation   (*CC*) II 72 and n 4.
and copy is clearly formulated in *BL* ch 18

gravation instead of an apology, blames his author for attributing this epithet to Hebrus . . .

"Smooth" would have suited M's purpose even better than "swift", even tho' the latter had not been inappropriate, as poetically contrasting with the vehemence & turbulence of the preceding Lines.—Possibly, Milton was at this period of his life too predominantly a Poet to have read Servius.[1]

Mem. The Virgilian Line might not unhappily be applied to the Hon. M^r B****, who has made a more hasty "Cut and run" than his *fast* friend, H——r[2]—Volucremque fugâ prævertitur Hebrum—i.e.

> Prick'd from behind by Fear, his Legs his Bail,
> Outruns Swift HEBER following at his *Tail*.

13   pp 44–5 | *L'Allegro* line 23

[Warton's note:] *Fill'd her*, &c. Mr. Bowle is of opinion, that this passage is formed from GOWER'S SONG in the Play of PERICLES PRINCE of TYRE. A. i. S. i. . . .

> This king unto him took a phear,
> Who died, and left a female heir
> So BUCKSOME, BLITHE, and full of face,
> As heav'n had lent her all his grace. *

* Perhaps, no more convincing proof can be given that the power of poetry is from a *Genius*, i.e. not included in the common faculties of the human mind common to all men, than these so frequent "opinions,["] that this & that passage was formed from, or borrowed, or stolen &c from this or that other passage, found in some other poet or poem, three or 300 years elder. In the name of common sense, if Gower could write the lines without having seen Milton, why might not Milton have done so with tho' Gower had never existed? That Mr Bowle, or Bishop Newton, or Mr [? Cory] etc[1] should be unable to imagine the origination of

12[1] Maurus Honoratus Servius, the Roman commentator on Virgil, who flourished at the end of the fourth century, is cited by Warton in the textus.

12[2] Presumably the book collector Richard Heber (1773–1833), MP for Oxford University 1821–6. Resigning his seat early in 1826, he lived in exile on the Continent in order to avoid charges of pederasty: *S Letters* (Curry) II 402n. In *PW* (*CC*), J. C. C. Mays proposes Henry Grey

Bennet (1777–1836) as the most likely candidate for the Hon Mr B.

13[1] John Bowle (1725–88) and Thomas Newton, bp of Bristol (1704–82), are cited by Warton as authorities on Milton's sources, e.g. Bowle in textus here, Newton in **11** above. Warton does not mention a "Cory", and this is an uncertain reading; it might almost be "Gray" (Thomas), whom Warton does cite.

a fine thought, is no way strange; but that *Warton* should fall into the same dull cant—!!—

14   pp 64–6 | Lines 133–4

[Warton's note:]   *Or sweetest Shakespeare, fancy's child,*
                             Warble his native wood-notes wild.

. . . Milton shews his judgement here, in celebrating Shakespeare's *Comedies*, rather than his Tragedies. For models of the latter, he refers us rightly, in his PENSEROSO, to the Grecian scene, v. 97.   H.

be damn'd! *An Owl!*—
   H = Hurd: T = T[?~~om~~]¹
~~Good~~ H. thou Right Reverend Aspirate! what had'st thou to do with sweetest Shakespeare? Was it not enough to *merder*² the Prophets? But to be serious—if by Tragedies Hurd means "Songs of the Goat", and if there were any pagans that had to make such, they would have to look to the Ancient Greeks for Models.³ But what Shakespear proposed to realize was—an Imitation of human Actions in connection with sentiments, passions, characters, incidents and events for the purpose of pleasurable emotion; so that whether this be shewn by Tears of Laughter or Tears of Tenderness, they shall still be Tears of Delight, and united with intellectual Complacency. I Call such a Work a Drama: and then I will tell the whole Herd of Hurdite Critics, that the Dramas of Shakespear, whether the lighter or the loftier emotions preponderate, are all, this one no less than the other, MODELS with which it would be cruel & most unjust to the ~~names~~ manes either of Eschylus, Sophocles & Euripides, ⟨or of Aristophanes,⟩ to compare ~~their~~ TRAGEDIES of the former or the Comedies of the latter. Shakespere produced Dramatic Poems, not Tragedies nor Comedies.—If the Greek Tragedies, in as H. affectedly expresses it, "The Greek Scene" ~~is~~ be a Model for any ~~thing~~ modern, it must be for the Opera House.   *S. T. C.*

14¹ Warton announces in his Preface (xxv) that notes signed "H." are by Bishop Hurd (n 2 below). With "T", one might expect "Turd" here, esp with *merder* below; but the traces that are left of the deleted letters do not support that reading. "Tom" would be Warton himself, "dear Tom Warton" in **8**.

14² C's coinage from French *merde*, "shit", i.e. "beshit"; also, punningly,

"*murder*", with an allusion to Matt 23.37, "*thou* that killest the prophets". Richard Hurd, bp of Worcester (1720–1808), was the author of *An Introduction to the Study of the Prophecies Concerning the Christian Church* (1772).

14³ The conventional derivation of "tragedy" from the Greek "Hymn of the Goat" is explained by C in a lecture of 1808: *Lects 1808–1819 (CC)* I 44 and n 2.

15   p 76 | *Il Penseroso*

The first 60 Lines are (with unfeigned diffidence I add) in my humble Judgement not only inferior to to the Allegro, but such as many ~~cases of~~ a secondrate Poet, a Pygmy compared with Milton, might have written.

16   p 88 | Lines 145–50

[Warton's note:]   *And let some strange mysterious dream*
Wave at his wings in airy stream
Of lively portraiture display'd,
Softly on my eye-lids laid.

I do not exactly understand the whole of the context. Is the Dream to wave at Sleep's wings? Doctor Newton will have *wave* to be a verb neuter: and very justly, as the passage now stands. But let us strike out *at*, and make *wave* active.

—Let some strange mysterious dream
Wave his wings, in airy stream, &c.

"Let some fantastic DREAM put the wings of SLEEP in motion, which shall be *displayed*, or expanded, in an *airy* or soft *stream* of visionary imagery, gently falling or settling on my eye-lids." Or, *his* may refer to DREAM, and not to SLEEP, with much the same sense. In the mean time, supposing *lively* adverbial, as was now common, *displayed* will connect with *pourtraiture*, that is, "pourtraiture lively displayed," with this sense, "Wave his wings, in an airy stream of rich pictures so *strongly displayed* in vision as to resemble real *Life*." Or, if *lively* remain an adjective, much in the same sense, *displayed* will signify *displaying* itself. On the whole, we must not here seek for precise meanings of parts, but acquiesce in a general idea resulting from the whole, which I think is sufficiently seen.

A winged Dream upon a winged Sleep on the Poet's eye-lids! More Sacks on the Mill![1]—Warton must have written these notes in a careless hurry.

17   pp 88–9 | **16** textus

Explain the four lines as you will, and tinker them how you can, they will remain ~~an~~ confused and awkwardly arranged period. But the *con-*

16[1] Proverbial, usually but not invariably in the phrase "sacks *to* the mill", for piling weight upon weight or argument upon argument, as in Shakespeare *Love's Labour's Lost* IV iii 79.

struing I take to be this—and at his wings (*dewy-feather'd*) softly laid on my eyelids let some st. mys. Dream flow wavingly in aery stream of lively portraiture—*display'd* being a rhyme to "laid", and therefore not *quite* superfluous.   *S. T. C.*

P.S. If any conjectural Reading were admissible, I should prefer[a]

> Weave on his wings ~~in~~ its aery scheme (or *theme*)
> In lively &c.

18   p 93

[Warton's note at the end:] * Of these two exquisite little poems [*L'Allegro* and *Il Penseroso*], I think it clear that this last is the most taking; which is owing to the subject. The mind delights most in these solemn images, and a genius delights most to paint them.   H.

* I feel the direct opposite, almost painfully. But I suspect, that this contrariety would go thro' all my decisions in reference to Bishop Hurd's.

19   pp 152–3, pencil | *Comus* line 108

[Warton's note:] *And Advice with scrupulous head.* The manuscript reading, *And quick Law*, is the best. It is not the essential attribute of *Advice* to be *scrupulous*: but it is of *Quick Law*, or *Watchful Law*, to be so.   W.

Bless me! Who would have expected a remark so tasteless or so shallow a reason from Warton?[1]—It is not the essential character of Advice; but it is the very character, by which the God of Riot and Wassail would ridicule him.—And then the sound & rhythm—*Quick* Law—& the confusion of executive (Quick) with judicial Law (scrupulous). In short, the wonder is that it should be found in the Mss—as having occurred to Milton/

20   pp 155–7 | Line 140

[In a note on the line "From her cabin'd loop-hole peep", Warton refers at length to Milton's use of the "loop-holes" in the Indian fig-tree in *Paradise Lost* IX 1110:] Milton was a student in botany. He took his description of this multifarious tree from the account of it in Gerard's

---

[a] Here C has written "(*Turn* to the top of the page)"

19[1] Notes signed "W."—as Warton points out in his Preface (xxv)—are by Warburton. C has either forgotten the attribution or accepted Warton's selection of notes as implying his approval of them.

HERBALL, many of whose expressions he literally repeats. [Warton quotes extensively from Gerard and then from *Paradise Lost*.]

If I wished to display the charm and *effect* of metre & the *art* of poetry, independent of the Thoughts & Images—the superiority, in short, of *poematic* over *prose* Composition, the poetry or no-poetry being the same in both—I question, whether a more apt and convincing instance could be found, than in these exquisite lines of Milton's compared with the passage in Gerald,[1] of which they are the organized Version.—Shakespeare's Cleopatra on the Cydnus compared with the original in North's Plutarch is another almost equally striking example.[2]

S. T. C.—22nd Octr 1823. Ramsgate.

21   p 168, pencil | Lines 238–9

[Warton's note:]   *O, if thou have*
                    Hid them in some flow'ry cave.

Here is a seeming inaccuracy for the sake of the rhyme. But the sense being hypothetical and contingent, we will suppose an elleipsis of *shouldest* before *have*. . . . We find another instance below, v. 887.

> And bridle in thy headlong wave,
> Till thou our summons answer'd HAVE. *

Could W. have been so ignorant of English Grammar? His Brother would have flogged a Winchester Lad for an equivalent ignorance in a Latin Subjunctive.[1]

22   p 188 | Line 380

[Warton's note:] *Were all to ruffled.*— . . . * ALL-TO, or AL-TO, is, *Intirely*.

* Even this is not the exact meaning of to- or all-to/ which answers to the German *Zer*, as our *for* in forlorn to ver, pronounced fer.[1]

20[1] C means "Gerard", as q by Warton.

20[2] The speech by Enobarbus in Shakespeare *Antony and Cleopatra* II ii 198–226, known to have been based on a passage in Thomas North's translation of Plutarch's *Lives* that was reprinted in e.g. Shakespeare *Plays* (10 vols 1778—the "Johnson-Steevens Shakespeare") VIII 172n–3n.

21[1] Thomas Warton's brother Joseph (1722–1800), who contributed some notes to this edition, was headmaster of Winchester School (where he had himself been a pupil) from 1766.

22[1] Later linguistic scholarship confirms these observations: see *OED* "all" *adv* 14, 15, and "forlese".

23   pp 242–6 | Lines 892–5

> My sliding chariot stays,
> Thick set with agat, and the azurn sheen
> Of turkis blue, and emrald green,
> That in the channel strays . . . .

[Warton supplies a long note arguing that Drayton's *Polyolbion* was a source for the description of the chariot.]

L. 895. the word "strays" *needed* a Note—and therefore it is the only part of the sentence left unnoticed. First of all, Turquoises & Emeralds are not much addicted to *straying* any where; and the last place, I should look for them, would be in channels; and secondly, the verb is in the singular number & belongs to Sheen, i.e. Lustre, Shininess, as its nominative Case. It may therefore bear a question, whether Milton did mean the wandering flitting tints and hues of the Water, in my opinion a ~~much~~ more poetical as well as much more appropriate Imagery/. He particularizes one precious stone, the Agate, which often occurs in brooks & rivulets, and leaves the *substance* of the other ornaments as he had of the chariot itself undetermined, and describes them by the effect on the eye/ thick set with agate and that transparent, or humid, Shine of (turquoise-like) Blue, and (emeraldine) ~~Blue~~ Green that strays in the channel—For it is in the water immediately above the pebbly Bed of the Brook, that one seems to see these lovely glancing Water-tints.—N.B. This note in the best style of Warburtonian perverted ingenuity.

24   pp 250–1, pencil, marked with a pencil line in the margin | Lines 946–55

> * And not many furlongs thence
> Is your Father's residence,
> Where this night are met in state
> Many a friend to gratulate
> His wish'd presence, and beside
> All the swains that near abide,
> With jigs and rural dance resort;
> We shall catch them at their sport,
> And our sudden coming there
> Will double all their mirth and chear;[a]
> Come let us haste, the stars grow high
> But night sits monarch ∧ yet in the mid sky.

---

[a] Pencil line in margin ends here

* With all prostration of reverence at the feet of even the Juvenal,[1] Milton—I must yet lift up my head, enough to pillow my chin[2] on the Rose of his Shoe, & ask him in a timid whisper ⟨whether⟩ Rhymes and Finger-metre[3] do not render poor flat prose ludicrous, rather than tend to ~~elev~~dec-orate it, or even to hide its nakedness.—

25   p 272 | *On the Morning of Christ's Nativity* st 11 lines 115–16

> Harping in loud and solemn quire,
> With unexpressive notes to Heaven's new-born Heir.

[Footnote:] So in LYCIDAS, v. 176.

> And hears the UNEXPRESSIVE nuptial song.

The word . . . was perhaps coined by Shakespeare, As you Like it, A. iii. S. ii.

It is strange that *Milton* should have held it allowable to substitute the active Aorist *ive* for the passive adject⟨ive⟩ ible. It ~~is a~~ was too high ⟨a⟩ compliment ⟨even⟩ to Shakespear. What should we think of undescriptive for indescribable? Surely, no authority can justify such a Solecism.

26   p 274 | St 15 lines 141–8

> Yea Truth and Justice then
> Will down return to men,
>   Orb'd in a rainbow; and like glories wearing
> Mercy will sit between,
> Thron'd in celestial sheen,
>   With radiant feet the tissued clouds down steering:
> And heav'n, as at some festival,
> Will open wide the gates of her high palace hall.

XV. A glorious Subject for the Ceiling of a princely Banquet-room, in the style of Parmeggiano, or Allston.[1]   s. t. c.   Stanz. XXIII. I think, I have seen—possibly, by Fuseli.[2]

24[1] I.e. juvenile—"juvenal" was an acceptable variant in 1823.
24[2] The phrase comes from Milton himself: see **27** textus.
24[3] Metre that fulfils only the rudimentary requirement of the correct number of syllables, as counted on the fingers.
26[1] C is recalling especially pictures associated with his visit to Italy in 1806, when he met Washington Allston in Rome and made notes on his painting *Diana and Her Nymphs in the Chase* as well as on a Parmigianino in the Uffizi Gallery in Florence; both pictures are reproduced in *CN* II (Plates v, vi): *CN* II 2794, 2831, 2853 and nn. An exhibition of Allston's in Bristol was the immediate occasion of C's "Essays on Genial Criticism" in 1814.
26[2] Henry Fuseli (1741–1825), professor of painting at the Royal Academy

27 p 281 | Line 231

[Warton's note:] *Pillows his chin upon an orient wave.* The words *pillows* and *chin*, throw an air of burlesque and familiarity over a comparison most exquisitely conceived and adapted.*

* I have tried in vain to imagine, in what other way the Image could be given. I rather think, that it is one of the Hardinesses permitted to a great Poet. Dante would have written it: tho' it is most in the Spirit of Donne.

28 pp 286–7 | *The Passion*

[Note at the end of the poem:] *This subject the Author finding to be above the years he had, when he wrote it, and nothing satisfied with what was begun, left it unfinished.*

* I feel grateful to Milton that instead of preserving only the VIth and the first five lines of the VIIIth Stanza, he has given us the whole Eight. The true solution of 1st, 2nd, 3rd, 4th, V[th], and 7th Stanzas is, that Milton had not yet *un*taught himself the looking up to inferior minds,[a] which he had been taught to consider as Models. He did not yet dare to know, how great he was.

29 p 307, pencil, overtraced in ink by another hand | *At a Vacation Exercise* lines 1–4

Hail native Language, that by sinews weak
Didst move my first endevouring tongue to speak,
And mad'st imperfect words with childish trips,
Half unpronounc'd, slide through my infant-lips.*

* "Slide" seems to me not quite the right word. Perhaps "stumble" or "struggle" would be better? omitting "my"

["]Half unpronounced, stumble, thro' infant lips"

30 p 307, pencil, overtraced in ink by another hand | Lines 5–6

Driving dumb silence from the portal door,
Where he had mutely sat two years before . . .

[a] Written "minds inferior" and marked for transposition

1801–4, 1810–25 (and consequently for a short time, at the very end of his career, a colleague of C's close friend Joseph Henry Green, who lectured on the relationship between anatomy and the fine arts at the Royal Academy 1825–52). C refers to his work in general terms as early as 1794 ("all the Diableries, that ever met the Eye of a Fuseli": *CL* I 135). One of Fuseli's ambitious projects was the "Milton Gallery", his exhibitions, in 1799 and 1800, of paintings based on works by Milton; it included, as C says, a painting based on this part of the *Nativity* ode, now unfortunately lost: Gert Schiff *Johann Heinrich Füsslis Milton-Galerie* (Zurich and Stuttgart 1963) catalogue no 29.

* Well might He speak late who spoke to such purpose!

31 p 312, pencil | Lines 59–60

[Warton's note on the speech of the Sibyl who prophesies the future of the infant Substance, saying "For at thy birth/ The faery ladies danc'd upon the hearth."] This is the first and last time that the system of the Fairies was ever introduced to illustrate the doctrine of Aristotle's ten categories. It may be remarked, that they both were in fashion, and both exploded, at the same time. *

* exploded?—The Categories? Aristotle's *Table* of the Categories was corrected & improved, but even this not till long after the Date of this Exercise.[1]

32 p 314, pencil | Line 83

To find a foe it shall not be his hap . . .

[Warton's note:] *Substantia substantiae nova contrariatur* ["a new substance is opposed by substance"—i.e. cannot exist], is a schoolmaxim. *

* It is curious that in this purely logical Conception, or rather *form* of Conceiving, Spinoza re-edified the Pantheism of the old Greek Philosophy.[1]   *S. T. C.*

33 pp 318–20, pencil | *On the University Carrier* ("Here lies old Hobson")

[Note:] I wonder Milton should suffer these two things on Hobson to appear in his edition of 1645. He, who at the age of nineteen, had so just a contempt for,

> Those new-fangled toys, and trimming slight,
> Which take our new fantastics with delight.
>   H.

* It is truly edifying to observe, what value and importance certain Critics attach to a farthing's worth of paper. One *wonders*—another *regrets*—just as if the two poor Copies of Verses had been a Dry-rot, threating[a] the whole life & beauty of the Comus, Lycidas, and other

---

31[1] C is presumably referring to Kant's reformulation of the table of categories in the *Critique of Pure Reason* (1781).

32[1] Aristotle's maxim is that there can be nothing contrary to substances: *Catego-ries* 5 (3ᵇ24). Spinoza's definitions of substance in *Ethics* pt 1 def 3 and props 1–9 resemble Aristotle's and, in C's view, build anew a form of pagan pantheism.

work in their vicinity!—I confess, that I have read these *Hobsons* 20 times, & always with amusement/ without the least injury to the higher & very different Delight afforded by Milton's *poetry*.[1]—These are the Junior Soph's very learned Jocularity/.—   *S. T. C.*

And why should not Milton as well as other Cantabs ~~be pleased with repeat~~ like to chuckle over his old College Jokes, & crack them anew?

33A   p 327, pencil | Sonnet 2 lines 1–6

> Donna leggiadra il qui bel nome honora
> L'herbosa val di Rheno, e il nobil varco,
> Bene è colui d'ogni valore scarco
> Qual tuo spirto gentil non innamorøa,
> Che dolcemente mostra si di fuora
> De suȷo atti soavi giamai parco . . .[1]

[Tr Arthur Livingston: Beauteous lady, whose fair name honoureth the grassy vale and the noble gorge of the Reno, lightened of all burden of worth must be he who is not enamoured of thy gentle spirit: which sweetly revealeth itself in ever bounteous dispensations of its graciousness and of those charms . . .]

33B   p 330, pencil | Sonnet 4 lines 1–2

> Diodati, e te'l dirò con maeraviglia,
> Quel ritroso io ~~ch'ampor~~ ch'amor spreggiar soléa[a][1]

[Tr Arthur Livingston: Diodati—and I tell thee in amazement at myself—that same scornful I, who have always shown contempt for love . . .]

33C   p 335, pencil | Sonnet 8 lines 10–11

> The great Emathian conqueror did bade spare
> The house of Pindarus . . .

34   p 340 | Sonnet 13 *To Mr. H. Lawes on the publishing his Airs*

It is rather singular that the Compliment to ~~H. Lawes~~ a Musician by a the most musical of all poets ⟨&⟩ who ~~both~~ loved the Man, ~~and~~ as well

---

[a] "Ch'amor" is written as a correction in both the left and right margins of the page, as well as at the top of it

33[1] C uses the poems on Hobson in a similar way in *BL* ch 3 (*CC*) ı 61, where he scoffs at critics who condescend to Milton: "Admit, that the Allegro and Penseroso of Milton are not *without merit*; but repay yourself for this concession by reprinting at length the *two poems on the University*

Carrier!"
33A[1] C has noticed two typographical errors and corrected the first properly; the second should read *suoi*.
33B[1] Both *maraviglia* and *meraviglia* are accepted spellings; in *ch'amor* C is correcting a typo.

as his Art, should be the least musical of all the Sonnets—notwithstanding the sweetness of the three last lines.[1]   S. T. C.

35   p 376 | *Translation of Psalm VII* lines 1–6

> Lord, my God, to thee I fly,
> Save me and secure me under
> Thy protection while I cry,
> Lest as a lion (and no wonder)
> He haste to tear my soul asunder,
> Tearing, and no rescue nigh.

[Warton's note:] This is a very pleasing stanza, and which I do not elsewhere recollect.

*Q*ᵞ? A B A B B A. A more pleasing stanza might I think be constructed for a *shorter* poem by extending it to eight lines

> A B A B B A B A
> ire rage fire cage page sire wage lyre.

36   p 378 | *Translation of Psalm VIII*

a truly majestic composition.

37   p 378 | Line 1

> O Jehovah our Lord, how wondrous great . . .

Milton pronounced Jē hŏ vāh, as an amphimacer.   S. T. C.

38   pp 378–9 | Lines 7–8

> To stint th' enemy, and slack th' avenger's brow,
> That bends his rage thy providence t' oppose.

[Warton's note to line 7:] . . . Here is a most violent cesure in the last syllable of *Enemy*.

Milton's ear taught him that accent even with emphasis, provided the latter be slight, quickens the sound.—I doubt not, that Milton meant there should be no elision of the e final of the definite article, but intended thĕ ĕnĕmў for a dicretic or tetrabrach isochronous only to an emphasized Iambic. I find it easy to read the line so as to give it a good

---

34[1] In this text, p 342: "Dante shall give fame leave to set thee higher/ Than his   Casella, whom he woo'd to sing/ Met in the milder shades of Purgatory."

and striking metrical effect, by at once rapidly and yet emphatically pronouncing "the e'nemy" with a smart stroke on the "en".

S. T. Coleridge.

P.S. to the Mss on the page opposite.[a]

The two first lines of the 5th Stanza are more difficult.[1] Yet even here there needs only an educated ear. In the first line the two last feet properly read are almost spondees instead of iambics: the others, a trochee and a ~~dactyl~~ choriambic. Now count the four last syllables as equal to six breves, and you have the same number of times as in five Iambics, the spondaic character of the two last feet compensating for the quickened utterance of the 3 former.

39   p 385 | *Translation of Psalm LXXXII*

With a few alterations this Psalm might be adopted in a new church Version—or at least a revision of Sternhold.[1]

40   p 386 | Lines 23–4

But ye shall die like men, and fall
* As other princes *die.*

* *other?* Ought not this word to have been in italics. This is the only passage or verse in the Old Testament in which I can imagine any allusion to the fall of the Spirits—the Thrones, or Potentates = Ιδεαι η Αριθμοι.[1] Our Lord plainly interpreted the verse in the sense.[2]

41   pp 421–2, pencil | Elegy 1 *Ad Carolum Deodatum* lines 11–12

Jam nec arundiferum mihi cura revisere Camum,
Nec dudum vetiti me laris angit amor.

[Not now am I concerned to revisit the Reedy Cam, nor am I harrowed now by love of my Lares there, this long time denied me.]

---

[a] The note having been written on p 379, the PS begins on p 378 (opposite) and concludes on p 379

38[1] I.e. p 379: "O'er the works of thy hand thou mad'st him Lord,/ Thou hast put all under his lordly feet . . .".

39[1] Thomas Sternhold's metrical version of the Psalms (with some additions by John Hopkins in the 3rd ed of 1557) became the standard version for singing and was still widely used in C's time. C defends "Hopkins and Sternhold" in SOUTHEY *Wesley* **93**, though wishing for "a more dignified metrical version".

40[1] "Ideas or Numbers"—Platonic, not NT Greek. C habitually denied that there was any biblical authority for the story of the fall of the angels, e.g. LACUNZA **80**.

40[2] Christ alludes to Ps 82 in John 10.34, presumably the "interpretation" to which C refers.

[Warton's note:] *Nec dudum vetiti me Laris angit amor.* The words *vetiti Laris*, and afterwards *exilium*, will not suffer us to determine otherwise, than that Milton was sentenced to undergo a temporary removal or rustication from Cambridge.

I cannot agree with Warton. It seems to me far more probable that Deodati in a pedantic fit had called Milton's Vacation an Exile from the Muses—and that Milton ⟨tacitly or rather implicitè⟩ reproves his friend's Pedantry. But how Warton could have so utterly mistaken the sense of the 11 & 12 Lines is astonishing!

42   p 429 | Lines 69–70

> Nec Pompeianas Tarpëia Musa columnas
> Jactet, et Ausoniis plena theatra stolis.

[Let not now the Tarpeian Muse boast of Pompey's Columns, or of the theatres crowded with Ausonian stoles.]

Remarkable, that a man of so fine an ear as Milton, should have endured a short syllable before *st*—theatra *st*olis.

43   p 533, pencil | Sylvarum Liber *Ad Salsillum, Poetam Romanum aegrotantem* lines 6–7

> Adesdum, et haec s'is verba pauca Salsillo
> Refer . . .

[. . . stand by me, I pray, and bear, if you will, these few words to Salsilli . . .]

hœcce?[1]

43[1] A proposed emendation, substituting the emphatic suffix *-ce* for *s'is*: "bear *these*" rather than "bear, if you will, these".

HENRY MORE

1614–1687

Observations upon *Anthroposophia Theomagica*, and *Anima Magica Abscondita*. By Alazonomastix Philalethes. London 1650. 8°.

Bound as first with MORE *Second Lash*; see below. More's *Psychodia Platonica* or *Platonic Song of the Soul* (1642) was attacked by Thomas Vaughan under the pseudonym Eugenius Philalethes ("Gentleman Lover of Truth") in *Anima magica abscondita*, published with *Anthroposophia theomagica* in 1650; More defended himself in these *Observations*, writing under a pseudonym that means "Lash for braggarts"; and a controversy ensued, Vaughan's response *The Man-Mouse Taken in a Trap* (1650) being followed by More's *Second Lash* (1651) and finally Vaughan's *The Second Wash; or the Moore Scour'd Once More* (1651).

British Library C 43 a 20(1)

The title-page has traces of previous ownership, the name "Cha: Jackson" being written at the centre and "204" at the top together with symbols that may have to do with its purchase price—none of these in C's hand. On p $^-$2, in pencil, "J. H. Green's copy: lot 489 in his sale 28 July 1880." C's note **3** is written around a large pencilled date, "1593".

DATE. The content of C's notes, esp **4**, suggests a date in the 1820s—as would be appropriate for a book belonging to J. H. Green.

1 Title-page, pencil, overtraced in ink

I fear, that the same Remark[1] will apply ^{a}no less^b to the other Sex in Harams, Nunneries^c & English Girls-Boarding-Schools. Each Sex is necessary even ⟨to⟩ the *special* Virtues of the^c the other.[2] Man (whether male or female) was not made to live alone.   S. T. C.

$^{a-b}$ Not overtraced ^{c} Word not overtraced

1[1] I.e. **3** below, textus and note.

1[2] C's experience of and reflections upon relations between the sexes led him to speculate about the presence of masculine and feminine capacities in every individual, and to make the well-known observation that "a great mind must be androgynous" (*TT* 1 Sept 1832). A most interesting notebook entry of Dec 1829, analysing the character of Jacob in Gen 32, suggests that the presence of feminine characteristics in men may be more important and more admirable than that of masculine characteristics in women: ". . . why, it should be less accordant with truth to say, that in every good Woman there is the *Man* as an Under-song, than to say that in every true and manly Man there is a translucent Under-tint of the Woman—would furnish matter for a very interesting little Essay on Sexual Psychology" (*CN* v).

2   p 55, pencil

But this is to hold the *Anima*, the passive Spirit and celestiall water together. Our Theomagician here grows as imperious, as wrathfull *Xerxes*. Will you also fetter the Hellespont *Philalethes*? and binde the wind and waters in chains?

This is not quite fair, Master More!

3   p ⁻5 (p-d),ᵃ pencil, overtraced in ink, referring to p 56

[More quotes Vaughan, "Philalethes":] *But meethinks Nature complains of a prostitution, &c.* Did not I tell you so before, that *Philalethes* was a pander? and now hee is convinced in his own conscience and confesses the crime, and his ears ring with the clamours and complaints of Madam Nature, whom he has so lewdly prostituted. Sad Melancholist! thou art affrighted into the confession of crimes that thou art not only not guilty of, but canst not be guilty of if thou wouldst. . . . These are nothing but some unchast dreams of thy prurient and polluted phansie. . . . Thou hast not laid Madam Nature so naked as thou supposest, only thou hast, I am afraid, dream't uncleanly, and so hast polluted so many sheets of paper with thy Nocturnall Conundrums, which have neither life, sense, nor shape, head nor foot that I can find in them.

p. 56—and where not:
    This is an exquisite specimen of *university*ᵇ Wit and Manners in 1650—or rather of that style which is sure to prevail among Cœlibates & in works destined for the exclusive Reading of ⟨Cœlibates, whether⟩ young ~~and~~ᶜ or old Bachelors—! ᵈi.e. [? given/gross] even to emetica!ᶜ

4   p 63

[More quotes Vaughan:] *I am certain the world will wonder I should make use of Scripture to establish Philosophy, &c.* Here, *Philalethes*, you seem self-condemned even from your own speech, being conscious to your self, that all the world will bee against you in this superstitious abuse of the Scripture. For are you wiser than all the world beside in this matter, because you have pray'd away all your Logick in St. *Augustines* Letanie?

ᵃ C's note is written on a piece of paper (presumably one of the original end-papers) now pasted onto new end-paper
ᵇ Underlining (here italics) not overtraced
ᶜ "and" not overtraced, cancelled in ink; "or" may be overtracer's emendation
ᵈ⁻ᵉ Not overtraced

Q.ʸ Were such Men as Dʳ H. More in earnest in puncto identitatis SSSᵐ
et SS.ᵃˢ? ϱηματων ἐβϱᾶίϰων ϰαι λογων εϰ του Λογου;[1] N.b.—In this age
matured itself the abuse of "Philosophy" for "Science"—and (worse
still!) of "reason" for "understanding."[2]

---

[1] C's abbreviations are unusual: per-
haps *sanctissimum* ("most holy thing")
and *sanctissimus* ("most holy one"), and
so "in the point of identity of the most holy
thing [the Bible, Scriptures] and the most
holy one? of Hebrew *sayings* and *words*
from the WORD?" The goal of C's late so-
phisticated biblical criticism, especially in
CIS, is to clarify the relationship of the
Bible as a historical document to the eter-
nal Word.

[2] C's campaign for general recognition
of the importance of the distinction be-
tween reason and understanding is outlined
briefly in LEIGHTON COPY C 12 n 6.

Philosophical Poems, etc. Cambridge 1647. 8°.

Not located. Marginalia published from C. M. Ingleby's article (itself based on transcriptions) in *Transactions of the Royal Society of Literature* 2nd ser IX (1870) 430–3. Notes that Ingleby marked as dubious are omitted when they seem unlikely to be C's, but included with a textual note when reasonably characteristic.

CONTENTS. Prefaces; pp 1–298 *A Platonick Song of the Soul; treating, of the Life of the Soul, Her Immortalitie, The Sleep of the Soul, the Unitie of Souls, and Memorie after Death*; 299–334 An Addition of some few smaller Poems; 335–436 Notes to the *Song of the Soul*.

DATE. Perhaps as early as 1809–10, but more probably c 1822. C makes specific reference to More's *Song of the Soul* in *Omniana* § 97 (1812) I 197; RS's less sympathetic treatment of More appears in *Omniana* § 212 (1812) II 155–77. C returned to *The Song of the Soul* in Jul 1822, commenting on its anticipation of WW's "incomparable Ode" *Intimations of Immortality*, and quoting More extensively: *CN* IV 4910.

1   "front flyleaf"

Ah! what strength might *I* gather, what comfort might *we* derive, from the Proclo-plotinian Platonists' doctrine of the soul, if only they or their Spinosistic imitators, the nature-philosophers of present Germany, had told or could tell us what *they* meant by *I* and *we*, by pain and remorse! Poor *we* are nothing in *act*, but everything in suffering.[1]

2   "front flyleaf" | Textus a ms note in an earlier hand, possibly by Henry Bradshawe

Dr. More uses many words that are obsolete, many that are provincial, and many that are entirely his own coinage, which the novelty of his subject may in some degree have rendered necessary. His elisions appear to be more licentious than have either been adopted before or since.

Spenser, he acknowledges in his dedication, was a favourite author with him from childhood, and his partiality is sufficiently obvious from following his antiquated diction, and from writing in the same octave stanza, which Spenser borrowed from the Italian poets.

---

[1] C's note in KLUGE **33** clarifies the nature of his objection to the philosophical tradition that he sees as a descent from Plato through Proclus, Plotinus, and the Neoplatonists to Cambridge Platonists like More and so to the German Idealists of his own time (notably Schelling): if the soul is not identical with "I" or "we", "is there any *Subject*, of moral Amenability?"

Which is not an octave, but an ennead (*i.e.* a stanza of nine lines), and which Spenser did *not* borrow from the Italians, but, after many and various experiments, invented for himself, as a perfect* whole, as it is indeed, and it only.—[1]   S. T. Coleridge.

 * That, I mean, to which nothing can be added, and from which nothing can be removed.

3   p 67 (misprinted 76) | *Psychozoia* canto 3 st 55

> So bravely we went on withouten dread,
> Till at the last we came whereas a hill
> With steep ascent highly lift up his head . . .

Of very ancient usage for *to where*.

4   sig H [verso][a] | Preface to *Psychathanasia*

So I do verily think that the mind being taken up in some higher contemplation, if it should please God to keep it in that ecstasie, the body might be destroyed without any disturbance to the soul, for how can there be or sense or pain without animadversion.

Doubtless! but what is that in the body which enforceth the soul to attend? and where is the middle term between the *act* of attention and the *pass* of pain or pleasure?[1]

5   "back flyleaf", referring to p 108[b] | *Psychathanasia* bk 2 canto 1 st 7

> Those properties, who list it to recall
> Unto their minds; but now we'll let it fall
> As needlesse. Onely that vitality,
> That doth extend this great Universall,
> And move th' inert Materiality
> Of great and little worlds, that keep in memory.

[a] I.e. the pages of the Preface to the second part of *The Song of the Soul*, inserted between pp [72] and 73 of text

[b] Ingleby encloses this note in square brackets, indicating the possibility that it might not be by C

2[1] C is right: though the nine-line Spenserian stanza bears some resemblance to *ottava rima*, the incorporation of the ninth line, an alexandrine, made it Spenser's distinctive innovation. See his further remarks in ARIOSTO **1** and n 1.

4[1] Cf **1** above. C's most significant attempt to identify a "middle term" between the active and passive faculties of the mind is the analysis of imagination in *BL* (1817), but he was still working on the problem in 1828, when he wrote an essay "On the Passions" (BM MS Egerton 2801 ff 43–58 and Add MS 34225 f 164) coining the term "impetite" for something *between* passions and appetites.

p. 108.[a] As an instance of *humouring* a word into rhyme and metre, take ŭnīvĕrsăll.

6 p 128 | Bk 2 canto 3 sts 24–6

> Nor is she [the soul] chang'd by the susception
> Of any forms: For thus her self contraire
> Should be unto her self. But Union
> She then possesseth, when heat and cold are
> Together met: They meet withouten jarre
> Within our souls. Such forms they be not true
> You'll say. But of their truth lest you despair,
> Each form in purer minds more perfect hew
> Obtains, then those in matter we do dayly view.
>
> For there, they're mixt, soild and contaminate,
> But truth doth clear, unwcavc, and simplifie,
> Search, sever, pierce, open, and disgregate
> All ascititious cloggins; then doth eye
> The naked essence and its property.
> Or you must grant the soul cannot define
> Ought right in things; or you must not deny
> These forms be true that in her self do shine:
> These be her rule of truth, these her unerring line,
>
> Bodies have no such properties. . . .

What mere logomachy! All is first assumed in the definition of body, and then proved by applying of the definition to six or seven particular instances of this impossibility.[1] The Materialist need make no other answer than: Aye! but this is not what I mean by matter or body;[b] or, I deny[c] the truth of your definition.[2]

7 p 135 | Bk 3 canto 1 st 21

> But if't be so, how doth *Psyche* hear or see
> That hath nor eyes nor cares? She sees more clear

[a] Ingleby transcribes "103" but the word "universall" does not appear on that page
[b] Ashe reads "matter of body"   [c] Ashe reads "defy"

6[1] Thomas Ashe, printing this note in his ed of *Miscellanies, Aesthetic and Literary* (1892) 334–5, proposes an alternative textus—bk 1 canto 3 sts 23–6—that outlines six "degrees of life" and concludes "that the dark matter/ Is not that needful prop to hold up life" (st 26). This textus, however, does not contain the word "body", and it is found on pp 100–1, far away from C's note.

6[2] C's own tentative definitions of this important term appear in e.g. LEIGHTON COPY B 5 and n 6.

Then we that see but secondarily.
We see at distance by a *circular*
Diffusion of that spright of this great sphear
Of th' Universe: Her sight is tactuall.
The Sun and all the starres that do appear
She feels them in herself, can distance all,
For she is at each one purely presentiall.

Still, *we*: and in contra-distinction from our *soul*![1]

8   p 314[a] | *Resolution* lines 29–54

Then wilt thou say, *God rules the World*,
Though mountain over mountain hurl'd
Be pitch'd amid the foaming Maine
Which busie winds to wrath constrain.
His fall doth make the billowes start
And backward skip from every part.
Quite sunk, then over his senselesse side
The waves in triumph proudly ride.
Though inward tempests fiercely rock
The tottering Earth, that with the shock
High spires and heavie rocks fall down
With their own weight drove into ground;
Though pitchy blasts from Hell up-born
Stop the outgoings of the Morn,
And nature play her fiery games
In this forc'd Night, with fulgurant flames,
Baring by fits for more affright
The pale dead visages, ghastly sight
Of men astonish'd at the stoure
Of Heavens great rage, the rattling showers
Of hail, the hoarse bellowing of thunder
Their own loud shreekes made mad with wonder:
All this confusion cannot move
The purged mind freed from the love
Of commerce with her body dear
Cell of sad thoughts, sole spring of fear.

The outline of this paragraph seems to be taken from yᵉ 46th Psalm.[1]

---

[a] Ingleby prints this note twice, once as C's and once as possibly not C's

7[1] As in **1** above.   **8**[1] The ''yᵉ'' for the definite article, un-

9 p 353, cropped | Note on *Psychozoia* 1 stanza 59

Ahad, Aeon, Psyche, the Platonick Triad, is rather the τὸ θεῖον then θεὸς, the Divinity rather then the Deity. For God is but one indivisible unmovable self-born Unity, and his first born creature is Wisdome, Intellect, *Aeon, On*, or *Autocalon*, or in a word, the Intellectuall world, whose measure himself is, that is simple and perfect Goodnesse. το δε᾽ ἐστιν ἀνενδεὲς, ἱκανὸν ἑαυτῷ, μηδενος δεόμενον, μέτρον πάντων καὶ πέρας, δοὺς ἐξ αὐτοῦ νοῦν καὶ οὐσίαν καὶ ψυχην. that is. For he is without need, self-sufficient, wanting nothing, the measure and term of all things, yielding out of himself Intellect or *On*, and *Psyche*.

The three or four preceding pages convince me[1] that H. More was a poetical philosophist, who amused himself in calling Aristotelian abstractions by the names of Platonic ideas, but by no means a philosophic poet, formed in the life-light of a guiding Idea. The very phrase, a first *born creature*, which is a contradiction in terms, and the applying of creature to the Logos Sophia and ὁ ὦν are [. . . . .][a2]

10 "back flyleaf" (perhaps a PS to **4**)

It would be no trifling convenience in close reasoning on metaphysical subjects if we might dare coin the word *pass* or *pasch*, as the antithet or corresponding opposite of *act*.[1]

11 "back flyleaf"

The 5 main faults characteristic of our elder poets not of the first class, and of none more than of H. More, are—

1. that in the pursuit of truth and vigour they fall into, nay, eagerly rush upon, the hateful and loathsome, particularly the offensive to the sense of smell, aggravated by moral disgust and association of disease; "fed with stinking gore suck'd from corrupted corse". P. 74.[1]

---

[a] Ingleby: "the last words are cut off by the binder"

---

characteristic of C, may be the transcriber's habit, but the attribution of this note is at best doubtful. Ps 46: "God is our refuge and strength, a very present help in trouble. Therefore will not we fear, though the earth be removed, and though the mountains be carried into the midst of the sea" etc.

9[1] C's note is on p 353; the textus has been taken from pp 350–1.

9[2] One might guess that the missing word was "blasphemy" or its equivalent: Christ the Logos, "Word, Wisdom, and Being", being according to trinitarian doctrine not a creature or *product* of the Deity but one with it and "of the same substance".

10[1] Following upon the train of thought in **1** and **4** above, C proposes an antonym for "act", as "passive" (from the Latin *patior* and more remotely the Greek *paschein*, "to suffer") is an antonym for "active".

11[1] *Psychathanasia* bk 1 canto 1 st 5.

2. That from a predilection for the lively and exact in similitudes and descriptions, they recur to the mean, the ludicrous, and the odd.

3. That *generally* they are regardless of the influence of associations, not merely such as are the accidental growth of a particular age or fashion, but of those that are grounded on the nature of man and his circumstances.

4. That they sacrifice the grand *keeping*[2] and total impression to particular effects; and if only it be *bene* sonans *per se*,[3] care not though it should be dissonant in the concert.

5. That they construct their metre in correspondence to their own passionate, humouring, and often peculiar and *mannered* mode of reading or reciting their verses,—a mode always more influenced by what they intended the words to mean than by the necessary or obvious sense of the words themselves.—   S. T. Coleridge.

11[2] A term adopted from painting that C self-consciously introduces elsewhere, e.g. *BL* ch 14 (*CC*) ıı 15 and n, *Lects 1808–*   *1819* (*CC*) ıı 86 and n.

11[3] "*Well*-sounding *in itself*".

The Second Lash of Alazonomastix; conteining a solid and serious reply to a very uncivill answer to certain *Observations* upon *Anthroposophia Theomagica*, and *Anima Magica Abscondita*. Cambridge 1651. 8°.

Bound as second with MORE *Observations*, which see above.

British Library C 43 a 20(2)

DATE. Probably in the 1820s, as MORE *Observations*.

1 p +3, referring to p 44

He that is here, looks upon all things as one, and on himself, if he can then mind himself, as a part of the whole. And so hath no self-interest, no unjust malicious plot, no more then the hand hath against the foot, or the ear against the eye. This is to be godded with God, and Christed with Christ, if you be in love with such affected language.

P. 44.—This is one of the Peccata Originalia[1] of Platonism—at least, of Plotinism.[2]

2 pp +2–+3, referring to p 93

So that it was necessary for thee to have an idea of the *first Matter*, in thy mind when thou wentest about to find it out. Now tell me, what the idea of the *first Matter* can be, if not this? *A substance out of which all corporeall things are made, but it self out of nothing.*

Second Lash. p 9~~1~~3. The definition of the first matter, if we are to take it as an adequate definition, borders on absurdity. For f what is "made"? a term of faulty ambiguity, at best. *Created* it cannot stand for: since for B to be created out of A is a contradiction in terms. It must mean therefore either "*composed*" or "*formed*." But how ⟨can⟩ any thing be composed out of a simple incomposite and therefore indecomponible One? What can you *com*pose out of *one* element; more than ~~ought~~ out of space? By various remotions of the particles from each other?—But this

[1] "Original Sins".

[2] Cf C's objections to the doctrine of Plotinus about direct communion with God in *P Lects* Lect 7 (1949) 242: "But this is the difference between the works of Plotinus . . . and those of the ancient philosophers: in the works of Plato and Aristotle you see a painful and laborious attempt to follow thought after thought and to assist the evolution of the human mind from its simple state of information to the highest extent its faculties will reach; but in the works of Plotinus it is all beginning, no middle, no progress."

in propriety of language would be formation, or ~~the~~ a position of A so as to occasion a given Form in a relatively posited Percipient, B.—And if this form be called a Composition, it is because here are at least two Constituents, A and B. I say, at least—but when⟨ce⟩ comes the *Distances*? Whence got you the *Atoms* of this first *Matter*—How could A simply A dispart itself into an infinity of indistinguishable As?[1]—Will the Peripatetic *Privation* answer? Is the Idea, Space, really derived from any other? Above all, is it derived from Privation?[2] Does not the piece of Gold fill a Space, and is not Space as necessarily supposed in a Plenum as in a Vacuity?—No! were it convenient or expedient to assume a first matter at all, it must be defined $1 = 2, +, 2 = 1$: i.e. a one Substance, that of necessity manifests itself in (and as) two Opposites, that reciprocally suppose, each the other:/[3] or again προθετον τι, ὁ δηλουμενον γινετα[a] Θετον και Αντιθετο[b4]

3   pp 142–3

But all that thou dost or canst collect from what is in my Preface to the Canto *concerning the Sleep of the Soul*, is but this: that whether we see or imagine that both of these are but the very *Energie* of the Soul, and that the Soul doth not nor can perceive any thing immediately but her own *Energie*.⁎ But what of all this?

⁎ Esse = Percipi: the Sum and substance of Berklëianism.[1] But it is a mere Assertion in the first place: & 2ndly it is an absurd assertion, i.e. a contradiction in terms. For to see its own energy is to see one's seeing—and to see nothing but the invisible is = not to see.

[a] For γιγνεται   [b] For Αντιθετον

2[1] C repeatedly attacked atomism, e.g. in the outline history of atomism in *P Lects* Lect 12 (1949) 346, as no more than materialist hypothesising, "merely a supposition derived from another supposition, namely that of external matter".

2[2] C suggests that the followers of Aristotle, the Peripatetics, might attempt to account for the division of matter into atoms, and for the idea of space itself, by invoking the concept of privation that Aristotle introduced in *Physics* 1.7 (191ᵃ) as the contrary of that which underlies substance. C himself interprets it as a sort of anti-matter, in e.g. BÖHME **166** and n 1.

Space, which C describes in Kantian terms as "not an ens reale, but the universal Form . . . of sensuous Intuition" in JA-COBI *Ueber die Lehre* 4, he also describes in opposition to Kant as strictly indivisible: KANT *Metaphysische Anfangsgründe* 7, **8**.

2[3] This is the system of polarity expressed in the logical pentad of e.g. IRVING *Sermons* 2.

2[4] "A certain prothesis [something established beforehand] which, being made manifest, becomes Thesis and Antithesis". For "prothesis" as a logical term introduced by C see HEGEL **3** and n 1.

3[1] "To be is to be perceived", the formula associated with George Berkeley (1685–1753) *A Treatise Concerning the Principles of Human Knowledge* (1710): *Works* ed A. A. Luce and T. E. Jessop (9 vols 1948–57) II 42 ff. Cf C's allusions in *BL* ch 7 (*CC*) I 118 and n 1, *Logic* (*CC*) 66.

4 p 150–1

Is not the whole consistency of the body of Man, as a crudled cloud or coagulated vapour? and his Personality a walking Shadow and dark imposture?*

* More, I apprehend, means the Figure peculiar to & distinguishing each Individual—as in the phrase—He has a fine *Person*—Persona = the theatrical Mask, id per quod sonat Actor/[1]

5 pp 152–3, marked in the margin with an ink line

. . . heare this sober Aphorisme from me. If that those things which are confessedly true in Christianity were closely kept to by men, it would so fill and satisfie their souls with an inward glorious light and spirituall joy, that all those things that are with destroying zeal and unchristian bitternesse prosecuted by this and that Church, would, look all of them as contemptibly, as so many rush-candles in the light of the Sun.

⁎ This may be a sober but it is a somewhat silly. For the question is: whether this or that Church's rush-lights are not among the causes, that prevent the due sense & effectual Love of these Truths?

4[1] "That through which the Actor speaks": C indicates the then accepted etymology for the dramatic mask, as in DONNE *Sermons* COPY A **4**.

The Theological Works of the most pious and learned Henry More, D.D. sometime Fellow of Christ's College in Cambridge. . . . According to the author's improvements in his Latin edition. London 1708. F°.

British Library Ashley 5176

Bookplate of James Gillman on p ⁻4 (p-d). A few small pencilled crosses in margins by HNC, marking textus for *LR* III 156–67.

CONTENTS. Pp i–xiv Preface; 1–383 *An Explanation of the Grand Mystery of Godliness*; 387–716 *A Modest Enquiry into the Mystery of Iniquity*; 717–64 *A Prophetical Exposition of the Seven Epistles sent to the Seven Churches in Asia, from Him that is, and was, and is to come*; 765–70 *A Brief Discourse of the true Grounds of the Certainty of Faith in Points of Religion*; 773–823 *An Antidote against Idolatry*; 824–32 *Some Divine Hymns*; 833–56 Alphabetical Table.

DATE. Probably Dec 1823, when C made entries in a notebook about this work (*CN* IV 5066, 5068 and nn), but possibly also later, c 1827–8, given the extent of the similarity in content between these notes and notes to IRVING *Sermons* and LACUNZA.

1   pp ⁻3–⁻2, the first two words partly in pencil

⟨There are/—⟩ Three principal causes to which the imperfections and errors in the theological schemes and works of our elder Divines, the Glories of our Church, Men of almost unparallelled Learning, Genius, the rich and robust Intellects from the reign of Elizabeth to the death of Charles the Second, may, I think, be reasonably attributed. And striking, unusually striking instances of all three abound in this Volume—& in the works of no other Divine are they more worthy of being regretted. For hence has arisen a depreciation of Dʳ Henry More's theological Writings, which yet contain more original, enlarged and elevating views of the Christian Dispensation, than I have met with in any other single Volume. For More had both the philosophic and the poetic Genius, supported by immense erudition. But unfortunately, the two did not amalgamate. It was not his good fortune to discover, as in the preceding Generation William Shakspear ~~found~~ discovered, a mordaunt or common Base of both; and in which both, viz. the poetic and philosophic Power blended into one.—

These Causes are

1ˢᵗ and foremost, the want of that logical προπαιδεια docimastica,[1]

_____
1¹ "Examination preparatory to learning".

that Critique of the human intellect, which previous to the weighing and measuring of this or that begins by assaying the weights, measures, and scales themselves—that fulfilment of the heaven-descended, *Nosce teipsum*,[2] in respect to the intellective part of Man, which was commenced in a sort of tentative *broad-cast* way by Lord Bacon in his Novum Organum, and brought to a systematic Completion by Immanuel KANT in his Critik der rein[a] Vernunft, der Urtheilskraft, & die Metaphysiksche Anfangsgrunde der Naturwissenschafts.[3] From the want of this searching Logic there is a perpetual confusion of the Subjective with the Objective, in the Arguments of our Divines, together with a childish or anile over-rating of Human Testimony, and an ignorance in the art of sifting it, which necessarily engendered Credulity.

2. The ignorance of Natural Science, their Physiography scant in fact and stuffed out with fables, their Physiology embrangled with an inapplicable Logic and a misgrowth of Entia Rationalia,[4] i.e. substantiated Abstractions; and their Physiogony a Blank, or Dreams of Tradition & such "intentional Colors"[5] as occupy space but cannot fill it. Yet if Christianity is ⟨to be⟩ the Religion of the World, if Christ be that Logos or Word that was in the beginning, by whom all things *became*; if it was the same [Christ,][b] who said, Let there be *Light*;[6] who in and by the Creation commenced the great redemptive Process, the history of LIFE which begins in its detachment from Nature and is to end in its union with God[7]—if this be true, so true must it be, that the ~~Scheme~~ Book of Nature and the Book of Revelation with the whole history of Man as the intermediate Link must be the integral & coherent Parts of one great Work. And the conclusion is: that a Scheme of the Christian Faith which

---

[a] A slip for "reinen"

[b] Corner torn from the leaf; the text had been transcribed for *LR* before this damage occurred, and the word is supplied from *LR* III 158–60

[1][2] A variant of Juvenal 11.27, "It descended from heaven, *Know thyself*"—alluded to in e.g. *BL* ch 12 (*CC*) I 252 and n 1.

[1][3] C's view of Bacon as a precursor of Kant is consistent with his account of Bacon as a "British Plato" in the 1818 *Friend* (*CC*) I 488 ff and in *P Lects* Lect 11 (1949) 333, where "the true Baconic philosophy" is said to consist "in a profound meditation on those laws which the pure reason in man reveals to him, with the confident anticipation and faith that to this will be found to correspond certain laws in nature". In SCHELLING *Philosophische Schriften* 1, C

calls Bacon's *New Organon*, Kant's *Critique of Pure Reason*, and Spinoza's *Ethics* "the three greatest Works since the introduction of Christianity".

[1][4] "Entities of Reason", things that have only a rational or notional existence.

[1][5] Colours existing in and for the mind. In illustration of this scholastic use of "intentional", *OED* cites "intentional species" in More's own *Philosophical Poems*.

[1][6] Gen 1.3: "And God said, Let there be light: and there was light."

[1][7] This formula of C's appears also in LACUNZA 2.

does not arise out of and shoots its beams downward into, the Scheme of Nature, but stands aloof, as an insulated After-thought, must be false or distorted in all its particulars. In confirmation of this position, I may challenge any opponent to adduce a single instance in which the now exploded falsities of physical Science, thro' all its revolutions from the Second to the 17th Century of the Christian Æra did not produce some corresponding warps in the theological systems and dogmas of the several periods.

III.—The third and last cause, and especially operative in the writings of this Author, is the presence and *regnancy* of a̸ the false and fantastic Philosophy yet shot thro' with refracted Light from the not yet risen but rising Truth, a Scheme of Physics and Physiology compounded of Cartesian Mechanics, Empiricism (for it was the credulous Childhood of ~~the~~ Experimentalism) and a corrupt mystical theurgical Pseudo-platonism, which infected the rarest minds ~~of~~ under the Stewart Dynasty/ The only not universal Belief in Witchcraft and Apparitions, and the vindication of such Monster follies by such Men, as Sir M. Hales, Glanville, Baxter, Henry More, and a host of others, are melancholy proofs of my position.[8] Hence in the first Chapters of this Volume the most idle & fantastic Inventions of the Ancients are sought to be made credible by the most fantastic hypotheses and analogies. ⟨See PAGE 67., first half of.⟩[9]

To the man who has habitually contemplated Christianity as interesting all rational finite Beings, as the very "Spirit of Truth", the application of the Prophecies, as so many *Fortune-tellings*, and Soothsayings, to particular Events & Persons, must needs be felt as childish—faces seen in the Moon, or the sediments of a Tea-cup/ But reverse this—and a Pope, and a Bu⟨o⟩naparte can never be wanting—the Mole-hill becomes an Andes.—On the other hand, there are few [Writer]s,[a] whose

[a] Supplied from *LR*

[8] The prevalence of belief in witchcraft even among educated and eminent men in the late seventeenth century is a theme in e.g. C's lecture of 6 Mar 1818 on witches and magic: *Lects 1808–1819* (*CC*) II 196–211, esp 206–7, where Sir Matthew Hale (1609–76) and Richard Baxter (1615–91) are mentioned specifically. Joseph Glanville's *Saducismus triumphatus; or Full and Plain Evidence Concerning Witches and Apparitions* (1681) is the subject of notes made also in 1818 (*CN* III 4394, 4395 and nn), and C may have been familiar with the 1689 ed to which Henry More supplied a preface. Hale is mentioned in JON-SON **41** and n 1. More's belief in witches is exemplified in n 9 below.

[9] On p 67, arguing in favour of the probability of pagan heroes' having been the offspring of a god or goddess and a mortal, More reminds readers that in Virgil's *Georgics* mares are said to have conceived "of the wind", and that witches often claim to have had sexual intercourse with the Devil. He further observes, "For it is not the Matter of the Seed, but a grateful Contact or Motion fermenting or spiriting the place of conception, that make the Female fruitful."

works could be so easily defeated as More's. Mere Omission [would]*a*
suffice—& ~~surely~~ perhaps one *Half (an unusually large proportion)
would [come fo]rth*a* from the Furnace, pure Gold.   S. T. Coleridge.

* [If but a 4th, how] great [a G]ain!*b*

2   recto of leaf following title-page, pencil, overtraced

Dedicatio. Jesu Nazareno crucifixo Dei Filio . . . servorum Illius om-
nium indignissimus Henricus Morus . . .

[Dedication. To Jesus of Nazareth, crucified Son of God . . . Henry More, the
most unworthy of all His servants . . .]

Serv*us* indignissimus, or omnino indignus,[1] or any other *positive* Self-
abasement before God, I can understand; but how an express avowal of
unworthiness *comparatively* superlative can consist with the Job-like in-
tegrity and sincerity of Profession, especially required in a solemn Ad-
dress to Him, to whom all Hearts are open—this I do not understand.—
in the case of such men as Henry More, Jer. Taylor, R. Baxter, &c were,
and by *comparison* at least, with the multitude of evil doers, must have
believed themselves to be.*c*[2]

3   p 117, pencil, overtraced | Bk 5 ch 14 § 3

And therefore the *Martyrs* sharing so deeply in the Sufferings of Christ,
were permitted also in a measure to partake of that Glory and Honour
that is done to great Princes and Emperours after their Decease; to have
Images and Temples erected to their Name. This makes me not so much
wonder at that Passage of Providence which allowed so much Virtue to
the Bones of the Martyr *Babylas* once Bishop of *Antioch*, as to stop the
mouth of *Apollo Daphneus*, when *Julian* would have enticed him to
open it by many a fat Sacrifice: To say nothing of several other memo-
rable *Miracles* that were done by the Reliques of Saints and Martyrs in
those times.

Strange lingering of childish Credulity in the most learned & in many
respects *enlightened* Divines of the Prot. Episc. Church even to the time
of James II. The Popish Controversy at that time made a great clearance

---

a Supplied from *LR*
b The last two lines of ms are now partly effaced by handling
c "STC" inserted at the end, apparently—as at the end of **3**—by HNC

2[1] "A most unworthy servant" or "in
every way unworthy".
2[2] C compares More with two other sev-
enteenth-century divines whom he greatly

admired, and whose writings he copiously
annotated: the Dissenter Richard Baxter (**1**
n 8 above) and bp Jeremy Taylor (1613–
67).

tho' even at this day the *Oxford* men *hanker* after the four first Centuries & have not *heartily* forgiven Conyers Middleton.[a1]

4 p 119, pencil | § 10

I shall rather send him that doubts, to satisfy himself in the perusing of the Learned Writings of that incomparable Interpreter of Prophecies Mr. *Joseph Mede* . . . . Upon whose account I am not ashamed to profess, I think it clear both out of *Daniel* and the *Apocalypse* that the Scene of things in *Christendom* will be in due time very much changed, and that for the better.

At[b] one time Prof. Eichhorn had persuaded me that the Apocalypse was authentic—i.e. a Danielitic Dramatic Poem written *by* the Apostle & Evangelist John; and not merely under his name.[1] But the repeated Perusal of the Vision has sadly unsettled my Conclusions—The entire absence of all *spirituality* perplexes me, it forms so strong a contrast with the Gospel & I Epistle of John/ and then the too great appearance of an allusion to the fable of Nero's return to Life & Empire, to Simon Magus and Apollonius on the one hand—(i.e. the Eichhornian Hypothesis)[2] & the insurmountable Difficulties of Joseph Mede's—&c on to Bicheno and Faber, on the other[3]—in short, I feel just as both Luther & Calvin felt—i.e. not know what to make of it, so leave it alone.   S. T. C.

---

[a] "S. T. C." added in ink, apparently by HNC   [b] Word overtraced in ink

[3][1] C refers to Conyers Middleton's *Letter from Rome* (4th ed 1741) as early as in *Watchman* (*CC*) 52, where he says, "It was the policy of the early Christians to assimilate their religion to that of the Heathens in all possible respects. The ceremonies of the Romish church have been traced to this source by Middleton . . .". Oxford is mentioned not alluding to the Oxford Movement, which did not begin until 1833, but to the high-church traditions associated with Oxford, especially after William Laud (1573–1645) had been Chancellor of the University and reformed its statutes.

[4][1] Johann Gottfried Eichhorn *Commentarius in Apocalypsin Joannis* (2 vols Göttingen 1791), of which C annotated two copies c 1826 (*CM*—*CC*—ii 503–20), and which he was certainly familiar with much earlier. C's further debate with Eichhorn on the interpretation of Rev is recorded in

many of the 1827 notes to Lacunza, e.g. **70, 74, 87**.

[4][2] C alludes similarly to details of Eichhorn's interpretation of Rev as historical and prophetic elsewhere: to the identification of the dragon with the "Neronian Persecutions" in J. Smith 6, and to the coming of the "false Messiah" Apollonius of Tyana in Bible copy B **98**. Simon Magus, the sorcerer of Acts 8.9–24, is another example of the "false Messiah", a sect having been established under his name in the second century A.D.

[4][3] C also finds it impossible to accept any of the interpretations alternative to Eichhorn's. Joseph Mede (1586–1638), frequently and approvingly cited by More, was the author of *Clavis Apocalyptica* (1627) that described the visions of Rev as historical prophecies chronologically ordered, culminating in the millennium; closer to home, George Stanley Faber

It is much to be regretted that we[a] have no contemporary history of Apollonius, or of the Reports concerning him and the popular notions in his own time. For from the Romance of Philostratus we cannot be sure as to the *fact* of the Lies themselves/ It may be a Lie, that there ever was such or such a Lie in circulation/[4]

5   p 120, pencil | Ch 15 § 2

Fourthly, The *little Horn*, Dan. 7. that rules for *a Time and Times and half a Time*, it is evident that it is not *Antiochus Epiphanes*, because this *little Horn* is part of the Fourth Beast, namely the *Roman*; but *Antiochus* part of the *Greek* Empire.*

* Where is the Proof that the Macedonian was not the 4th Empire? 1. The Assyrian. 2. the Median. 3. the Persian. 4. the Macedonian.[1] And what a strange Prophecy that e confesso[2] having been fulfilled remains as obscure as before!

6   p 124, pencil | § 6

But the Signification is rather *Symbolical*, as the ten days are, *chap. 2. v.* 10. *And ye shall have the Tribulation of ten Days*, that is, the utmost Extent of Tribulation, beyond which there is nothing further, as there is no Number beyond *Ten*: By which therefore must be meant *Death*.

It means the very Contrary—Decem dierum is used even in Terence[1] for a very short time/ as we say, a 7 days' Wonder.

7   p 126, pencil | Ch 16 § 1

Where *Grotius* makes the Four Beasts, the *Lion, Calf, Man*, and *Eagle*, to be *Peter, James, Matthew*, and *Paul.* . . . Mr. *Mede*'s account seems

---

[a] The paragraph to this point overtraced in ink

(1773–1854), whose *Dissertation on the Mysteries of the Cabiri* C annotated (*CM—CC—*ii 573–85), published *A Dissertation on the Prophecies* (2 vols 1806), which C also read and may have marked: *CN* iii 3793; and James Bicheno (d 1831) published several works maintaining that contemporary events were the fulfilment of prophecies in Rev, e.g. *The Signs of the Times* (1793), on the French Revolution, and *The Destiny of the German Empire* (1801).

[4][4] C gives an account of Apollonius of Tyana and his biographer Philostratus

(c 170–c 245) in *P Lects* Lect 7 (1949) 240–1; Kathleen Coburn notes (425) that his source was Wilhelm Gottlieb Tennemann *Geschichte der Philosophie* (10 vols Leipzig 1798–1819) v 199–208.

[5][1] C gives a similar interpretation of the four kingdoms in Lacunza 4 (and n 1). For his view of Dan generally see Irving *Sermons* 20 n 3.

[5][2] "Avowedly".

[6][1] Terence *Heauton timorumenos* 909, *decem dierum vix mi est familia*, "My property will hardly hold out a fortnight" (tr John Sargeaunt LCL).

far more solid, as having . . . *the order of the Camp of Israel,* which
was distributed into four Parts, each Part being under a Standard or
Ensign . . .

Hard to say which of the two, Mede's or Gr., is the more improbable.
Beyond doubt, the Cherubim are meant as the Scenic Ornature borrowed
from the Temple[1]

8 p 126, pencil | § 2

* That this *Rider of the White-Horse* is Christ, they both [i.e. Mede and
Grotius] agree in . . .

* The White Horse is Victory, Triumph (i.e. of the Roman Power) fol-
lowed by Slaughter, Famine and Pestilence. All this is plain enough.
The difficulty commences after the Poet is deserted by his *historical
facts,* i.e. after the sacking of Jerusalem

9 p 131, pencil | § 5

. . . the *Seventh* and Last *Trumpet-Vision.* . . . *Grotius* interprets of the
Liberty the Christians had to profess their Religion at *Jerusalem,* when
the Jews were all banished thence. But . . . [i]t is very hard to interpret
κόσμος, and βασιλεῖα in the plural Number, of *Judaea* only.* . . . But
it is plain this *Seventh Trumpet* appertains to the Recovery of the Church
out of Apostacy . . .

* It would be no easy matter to decide, whether Mede + More[1] was at
a greater distance from the meaning, or Grotius from the poetry of this
Chapter—whether M. was more wild, or G. more tame, flat, and pro-
saic.

10 p 143, pencil | Ch 17 § 8

Let us therefore now consider what these *Two Witnesses* are. And truly,
according to the Richness of Prophetick Expression, I do not think they

---

[7][1] C is commenting on the views of the
two scholars as outlined in textus. "Cher-
ubim", however, are not mentioned in this
part of More's work. On p 399, in a discus-
sion of idolatry—specifically, the golden
calf—More explains that the Hebrew word
translated "calf" or "ox" (as here, of the
four beasts) also means "cherub", and is
used in OT of the cherubim "set on the
Mercy-seat for [God's] own worship"
(Exod 25.20, 22 etc).

[9][1] Throughout the chapter, More com-
pares Mede's interpretation of the pro-
phetic books with that of Grotius and aligns
himself with Mede. Earlier on this page,
for example, he cites admiringly Mede's
interpretation of the *"Serpentine Tails of
the Horses"* in Rev 9.19: "The Devil then,
that old Serpent, being ready to parly with
them [the Persians] and to seduce them to
Mahometanism."

are restrained to one single Signification, but type out at last these two things, *The Old and New Testament . . .*

Where is the probability of this, so long before the existence of the Collection, since called the N. T.—?

11   pp 146–7 | Bk 6 ch 1 § 2

For the Lord himself shall descend from Heaven with a Shout, with the Voice of the Archangel and with the Trump of God; and the Dead in Christ shall rise first. Then we which are alive and remain, shall be caught up together with them in the Clouds to meet the Lord in the air, and so shall we be ever with the Lord. *

* You may draw from this passage the strongest support of the Fact of the Ascension—or at least of S[t] Paul's (& of course of the first generations of Christians) belief of it. For had they not believed his Ascent, whence could they have derived the universal expectation of his Descent? his *bodily personal* Descent?—The only scruple is, that all these circumstances were parts of the Jewish Cabbala or Idea of the Messiah by the Spiritualists, before the Christian Æra, and therefore taken for granted with respect to Jesus as soon as he was admitted to be *the* Messiah.—[1]

12   p 147 | § 4

[More cites the prophecy of universal conflagration in 2 Pet 3.10.] The Explication of which Prophesie Mr. *Jos. Mede* has set down with a great deal of Caution and Judgment. To which I should wholly subscribe, did I not believe that this Execution of Fire were the very last visible Judgment God would do upon the Rebellious Generations of *Adam*, leaving them to tumble with the Devils in unsupportable Torment and Confusion.

O!

13   p 147, pencil | § 6

[Mede rejects the use of other texts in scripture to evade the threat of a final conflagration.] But light-minded Men whose Hearts are made dark with Infidelity, care not what Antick Distortions they make in interpret-

---

11[1] Following the historical analysis of such biblical scholars as Nathaniel Lardner (1684–1768), who devotes a chapter of his *Credibility of the Gospel History* (2nd ed rev 1730) 169–80 to the Jewish expecta- tions of a Messiah, C describes the "ruin- ous & fleshly fancies entertained by the Jews from the time of Alexander the Great of a Warrior Monarch & Conqueror" in Ir- ving *Sermons* **20**.

ing Scripture, so they bring it but to any shew of Compliance with their own Fancy and Incredulity.

Why so very *harsh* a censure? What moral, or spiritual, or even what physical Difference can be inferred from All men's dying, this of one thing, that of another, a third like the Marytyrs burnt alive—or *all* of the same/ In either case they *all* die and all pass to judgement—/.

14   p 180, pencil[a] | Ch 15 § 4

For as that excellent Interpreter *Hugo Grotius* has noted, the words are to be rendred, *yea tho' we might have known Christ after the Flesh*, that is to say, *Tho' I with others might have known Christ after the Flesh, and conversed with him here upon the Earth, nay have been something a-kin to him . . . yet henceforth . . . we should know him after this manner no more*, but as an Heavenly Prince . . .

With his semi-cartesian, semi-platonic, semi-christian notions Henry More makes a strange Jumble in his Assertion of chonochor-ʿ*istorical*[b] Xtnty.[1] One *decisive* reference to the Ascension of the visible & tangible ~~Jesus~~ Jesus from the surface of the Earth upward thro' the Clouds, pointed out by him in the Writings of Paul, or in the Gospel (or either of the three Facciamenti)[2] beginning as certainly did and as in the Copy according to Mark it now does with the baptism of John, or in the Writings of the Apostle John, would have been more effective in flooring old Nic of Amsterdam[3] and his Familiars, than Volumes of such "may be"s, perhapses, and "should be rendered", &c—

---

[a] The first three words are in ink
[b] For "chronochorhistorical", accidentally omitting the first "r" and using a Greek rough breathing for the third "h"

14[1] "Time-and-place-historical" Christianity, i.e. historically accurate in such details. The nonce-word is modelled on More's own bizarre coinages, present especially in the *Philosophical Poems* that C annotated. In *Omniana* (1812) § 97 C writes appreciatively of More's "picturesque words".

14[2] Matt, Mark, and Luke, which C like Eichhorn, Schleiermacher, and other contemporary biblical scholars considers as composite works (or "workings", *facimenti* being the Italian original of C's term). Cf "I, for whom the Gospel com-

mences with and from the Baptism of John" in IRVING *Sermons* 36 and n 2. "Rifacimento", which C usually spells "rifacciamento" (e.g. BÖHME 95 at n 7), had found its way into English, but not *facimento*.

14[3] C applies "Old Nick", a familiar name for the Devil, to the writer attacked by More throughout this section of his work, "H. Nicolas of Amsterdam" (p 171), i.e. Hendrik Niclaes (c 1502–c 1580), a mercer and founder of the Anabaptist sect of Familists: cf **15** and **17** below.

15   p 259, pencil | Bk 8 ch 2 § 6

I must confess our Saviour compiled no Books, it being a piece of Pedantry below so Noble and Divine a Person. . . . Nor did he wear any gay Clothes, but when by force the abusive Soldiers put a Scarlet Robe upon him in despight and mockery.

Alas! all this is *woefully* BENEATH the dignity of Henry More! and *shockingly* AGAINST the Majesty of the High & Holy so *very* unnecessarily compared with Hendrick Nikolas of Amsterdam, Mercer![1]

16   p 369, pencil, overtraced | Bk 10 ch 12 § 7

Mahometism could never have been set on foot but in a rude and illiterate Nation.

Q͞y—Cordova, Grenada, *continued* it could not be.[1]

17   pp 372–3, pencil[a] | Ch 13 § 5, 6

What Purchase therefore have you got by your *Allegorical* Mysteries? unless that you have been emboldned thereby to let go the *Historical Truth of the Gospel.* . . .
   If it be thus with you [Quakers], I dare appeal unto your own Consciences whether you keep so precisely to *the Light within you*, but that you have consulted with that blind Guide, *H. Nicolas*, and tasted of the treacherous sops of his abhorred Passover, whose fanatick Boldness has led the Dance to this mad Apostasy.

A new Sect naturally attracts to itself a portion of the madmen of the Time, and sets another portion into activity as Alarmists and Oppugnants—I can not therefore pretend to say what More might not have found in the writings or heard from the mouth, of some Lunatic who called himself a *Quaker*. But I do not recollect in any Work of an acknowleged "Friend" a *denial* of the Facts narrated by the Evangelists, as having really taken place—in the same sense, as any other Facts of History. If they were *Symbols* of *Spiritual* Acts and processes (as Fox and Penn contended,)[1] they must *have been*, or happened; else, how could they be Symbols?

a The first four words overtraced

15[1] See **14** n 3 above.

16[1] I.e. Cordoba and Granada, sophisticated cities in Spain where the religion of Islam had at least been established, though it did not constitute a serious challenge to the Christian Church.

17[1] C's sympathetic interest in Quakerism can be traced to his Cambridge days (*C Talker* 159) and was still strong in the days of the 1809–10 *Friend*, the title of which

It is too true, however, that the positive Creed of the Quakers is and ever has been extremely vague and misty. The Deification of the Conscience under the name of "The Spirit" seems the main Article of their Faith: and of the rest they form no opinion at all, considering it neither necessary or desirable. I speak of Quakers in general.[2]   S. T. C.

But what a lesson of experience does not this Chap. 13 of so great and good a man as H. More afford to *us*, who know what the Quakers really are!—Had the Followers of G. Fox, or any number of them collectively, acknowleged the mad notions of this H. Nicolas? If not[a]

18   p 621 | Bk 2 ch 2 § 8

[More attempts in this chapter to discredit Grotius's dating and interpretation of Rev. Grotius bases his dating of the composition of the work during the reign of Vespasian (A.D. 70–9) in part upon an interpretation of the seven heads of the beast in Rev 13 as referring to seven Roman emperors, starting with Claudius, who ruled A.D. 41–54. More suggests that Grotius's interpretation is at odds with some of the very authorities he cites, e.g. Epiphanius, who] tells us how St. *John* was impelled and constrained to write the Gospel . . . *when he was more than ninety Years old, after his return out of* Patmos, *which happened in* Claudius *his time.* . . . Now let us see what Service this *Magnus testis et Historiarum diligentissimus Inquisitor* [great witness and the most tireless Investigator among our Historians] (as *Grotius* calls him, as well as he doth *Petavius* who so plainly contradicts him in this very Point) can do this learned Interpreter in the present Case.

Q[y]—Has or has not Grotius been over-rated? If G. applied these words to Epiphanius *in* honest earnest and not ironically, he must have been greatly inferior in sound sense and critical tact both to Joseph Scaliger and ~~the~~ to Rhenferd.[1] Strange! that to H. More, a Poet & a man of fine

---

[a] C did not complete the note

---

was understood by some to refer to the Society of Friends. One of C's acquaintances, Thomas Clarkson, published *A Portraiture of Quakerism* (1806) and *Memoirs of the Private and Public Life of William Penn* (1813), with both of which C was probably familiar: *CN* III 3910n, 4169n; T. FULLER *Church-History* **4** n 1. But he certainly also read Penn himself; he quotes *Some Fruits of Solitude* in 1809 (*CN* III 3530), and in a letter to a Quaker acquaintance, Thomas Wilkinson, in Dec 1808 he writes, "Such

gratitude I owe and feel toward W. Penn. Take his Preface to G. Fox's Journal, and his Letter to his Son,—if they contain a faithful statement of genuine Christianity according to your faith, I am one with you" (*CL* III 156). His assertions about Fox and Penn here appear to be his own conclusions about the Quakers' attitude toward scripture rather than their actual words.

17[2] For other remarks about "Quakers in general" see AURELIUS **47** n 1.

18[1] Two eminent scholars who dis-

Imagination it should never have occurred, to ask himself whether this "Scene: Patmos", with which the Drama commences, was not a *part* of the Poem/ & like all other parts to be interpreted symbolically?²—That the poetic—& I see no reason for doubting, the real—date of the Apocalypse is under VESPASIAN, is so evidently implied in the 5 Heads preceding (for Vitellius, Otho, and Galba ~~never~~ were abortive Emperors) that it seems to me quite lawless to deny it.—³

That Λατεῖνος is the meaning of the 666, and the treasonable character of this, are both shewn by Irenæus's pretended rejection & his proposal of the perfectly senseless TITAN instead.⁴

---

counted the assertions of Epiphanius: Joseph Justus Scaliger (1540–1609), whose *De emendatione temporum* (1583) revolutionised the chronology of the ancient world; and Jacob Rhenferd (1654–1712), whose *Opera philologica* (Utrecht 1772) C annotated. In T. FULLER *Pisgah-Sight* 6, C refers to Rhenferd's "detection of the calumnious Lies and Blunders of Epiphanius, Irenæus & Co."

18² This is essentially the Eichhornian reading alluded to in **4** above: cf references to Rev as a symbolic poem or "Symbolic Drama" in LACUNZA **35, 47, 79**.

18³ C accepts Grotius's interpretation of the seven heads of the beast, as outlined by More p 617: "The Seven Heads of the Beast are seven *Roman* Emperors, *Claudius, Nero, Galba, Otho, Vitellius*; which five were fallen when St. *John* had this Vision, or at the least wrote it, as *Grotius* supposes. But *Vespasian* was then Reigning".

18⁴ C draws here upon his reading of Johann Christian Wolf *Curae philologicae et criticae* (Hamburg 1735) 547–52, which summarises the history of the interpretation of "the number of the beast" in Rev 13.18, beginning with Irenæus's discussion of three possible Greek equivalents, *Euanthas, Lateinos,* and *Teitan*. In his note on this passage, q *CN* III 3793n, C as here supports *Lateinos*: "it is at once the name of a man, and of the beast-like Latinus and the Latin Empire".

CESARE MUSSOLINI

fl 1794–1800

Italian Exercises, together with a collection of Italian and English dialogues, entirely new; containing a short history of the most distinguished personages in Great Britain, Ireland, and many other parts of Europe; also, a comparative view of the natives of various countries, and many other interesting subjects. The whole calculated to inform the minds of those who desire to improve themselves in the Italian language. . . . 2nd ed rev. London 1800. 12°.

Collection of Mrs Wallace Southam

DATE. 20 Apr 1813 (1).

1   p ⁻2

I have long meditated an Essay on the Taste, Judgement, Manners, and Morals of Dictionary & Grammar Writers. This Book, which I picked up this morning (20 April, 1813) is rich in materials.—I recommend it, as a morceau to Southey, for 10 minutes after dinner.—   S. T. C.—

Besides, the additional Merit of making an Exercise Book a Puffo universale[1]—In short, we quite grudge the Book—& should not send it, but that its folly & immorality are so laughably gross, that Sariola herself can suffer from no other cause than laughter—[2]

~~p. 55 excepted.~~—[3]

---

[1] "Universal Puff" or advertisement. ("Puffo" is not an Italian word, but C's playful construct.) The dialogues by means of which Mussolini teaches his language include the names and addresses of London shops and merchants.

[2] C was at this time living in London with the Morgans, at 71 Berners St. He plans to send this volume to Greta Hall for Mrs C (to whom this note is addressed) to use in her Italian lessons to SC. In a letter of 1812 he had reported that "Sara does honor to her Mother's anxieties, reads French tolerably and Italian fluently" (*CL* III 375).

[3] This is a scandalous dialogue in which the speaker complains of a corn on her foot but exonerates her shoemaker, who "makes always easy shoes for the ladies, notwithstanding Mrs. Willey preaches to her husband every night to make tight shoes for the ladies, with the intention to give some profit to the poor corn-doctors".

2 p iv | "To the Reader", at the end

The Dialogues are very curious, instructive, and entirely new . . .

N.B.—This I attest as truth. They are VERY curious,—but of the instructiveness the Deponent sayeth not ~~hi~~.—

NAPOLEON BONAPARTE
1769–1821

Codice di Napoleone il Grande pel Regno d'Italia. 2nd Florentine ed. Florence 1806. 4°.

British Library C 126 i 12

Inscribed "STC" on p ⁻2. "S. T. C." label on the title-page.

DATE. 1806? C was in Italy for the first six months of 1806 (the date of publication) and probably acquired and annotated this work during that period.

COEDITOR. David V. Erdman.

TEXTUS TRANSLATION. *The Code Napoleon . . . Translated from the Original and Official Edition, Published at Paris, in 1804. By a Barrister of the Inner Temple*. London 1824.

1   p ⁻2, pencil

P. 3	Ar. 25	P. 7. 8.[1]
Pag.	Art.	Par.
3.	25.	7.8.9.
7	64	— . . .
9	85	

1A   p 3, pencil | Bk 1 title 1 ch 2 sect 2 art 25

! Egli è incapace di contrarre un matrimonio che produca alcun effetto civile.

!!! Il matrimonio che avesse precedemente contratto, è disciolto per tutti i suoi effetti civili.

!!! Il conjuge ed i suoi eredi potranno rispettivamente far uso delle ragioni e delle azioni alle quali si farebbe luogo per la morte naturale.

[! He is incapable of contracting a marriage attended by any civil consequences.

!!! If he have previously contracted marriage, it is dissolved, as respects all civil effects.

1[1] This chart simply acts as a guide to   below. C's notes in the volume—**1A, 2, 2A**

932

!!! His wife and his heirs shall respectively exercise those rights and demands to which his natural death would have given rise.]

2   p ⁻2, referring to p 7, pencil | Title 2 ch 3 art 64

Una copi dell' atto di pubblicazione sarà e rimarrà affissa alla porta della casa del comune, duranti gli otto giorni d'intervallo dall' una all' altra pubblicazione. Il matrimonio non potrà celebrarsi prima del terzo giorno, da che sarà seguità la seconda pubblicazione, non compreso il giorno della medesima.!!

[An extract from the act of publication shall be affixed to the door of the town-hall, and remain so during the interval of eight days between the one and the other publication. The marriage shall not be celebrated until the third day exclusive after that of the second publication.!!]

If there lurk any Truth in Astrology, i.e. in Times and Seasons, something curious might result from a Nation of 40 Millions all wedding and bedding on Wednesdays—and only on Wednesdays.[1]

2A   p 9, pencil | Ch 4 art 85

!!! In qualunque caso di morte violenta occorsa nelle prigioni e case d'arresto, o per l'esecuzione delle sentenze di morte, non si farà nei registri veruna menzione di tali circonstanze, e gli atti di morte saranno semplicemente estesi nella forma prescritta dall' articolo 79.

[!!! In all cases of death, by violence, or in prisons and houses of seclusion, or by execution, no mention shall be made in the registers of these circumstances, but the acts of death shall be drawn up simply in the form prescribed by article 79.]

2[1] C's point is clarified by Art 63, which states that the two "publications"—notices of the names, families etc of the prospective bride and groom—must be posted on Sunday. After an "interval of eight days", i.e. a week from Sunday to Sunday inclusive, therefore, the earliest day on which the wedding could be held would be the following Wednesday.

NEMESIUS OF EMESA

fl 390

Nemesii philosophi clarissimi de natura hominis liber utilissimus. Georgio Valla Placentino interprete. Lyons 1538. 4°.

Harvard University (Houghton Library)

On a sheet of paper folded inside the book, slightly larger than the leaves: "Amico Suo Thomae Ryburn Buchanan Senatori Praeclaro Hocce Opus D. D. Ernestus Hartley 'S. T. Coleridge' Nepos. Jun. 17. MDCCCXCI.'' The signature "S. T. Coleridge'' in C's hand on p ⁻2.

DATE. 1816–18, possibly spring 1817. C's reference to his "Treatises on the Logos'' (**1** at n 4) suggests a general date of 1816–18, and Nemesius was especially on C's mind in the early months of 1817, when he suggested that HC translate Nemesius (*HCL* 14) and, in May, took an epigraph from this edition (*CL* IV 729).

TEXTUS TRANSLATION. W. Telfer ed *Cyril of Jerusalem and Nemesius of Emesa* (1955), adapted.

1　pp 32–3 | Ch 2

Cleantes igitur huiusmodi syllogismum texit: Non solùm, inquiens, corpore parentibus nostris similes gignimur, sed etiam animae perturbationibus, moribus, affectionibus. atqui corporis proprium est simile, ac dissimile, non autem rei incorporeae. ergo anima est corpus

[Cleanthes, then, made up this syllogism: "Not only do we resemble our parents in body,'' he said, "but also in soul, by our passions, manners and dispositions. Now 'like' and 'unlike' are applicable to bodies, but do not apply to the incorporeal. The soul therefore is corporeal.'']

⟨Modum nesciensmus, rem ipsam nego:[1] this may be cited, as⟩ A striking instance of the Sophism, A, the only known Means of B, not existing, B does not exist. This under the head of Elenchus ab Ignorantiâ.[2]—

---

[1] "We do not know how it happens, [therefore] I deny that it happens.'' C at first wrote "Not knowing how''. Cf "rem credimus, modum nescimus'' in DONNE *Sermons* COPY B **35**.

[2] Either C's variant of *ignoratio elenchi*, the traditional phrase in logic for proving a different conclusion from that which is desired in order to refute a proposition (thereby revealing that one does not know what the refutation requires); or a deliberate coinage, "Refutation from Ignorance'', for the specific fallacy exhibited here.

It is curious too, that Nemesius exposes this very same fallacy on the very next page: l. 18. "Hoc perinde est ac si quis &c".[3] Observe moreover, that this passage furnishes an instance in proof, that an exact and comprehensive *Logic* would or might have discovered, ⟨tho'⟩ not ~~only~~ the true theory (~~the~~ & even to this it might often lead), ~~but~~ yet the insufficiency of the grounds on which all false Theories have been built. This in my Λογος προπαιδευτικος, or Exposition of the Forms of Truth and Falsehood, with the application thereof to the purposes of active Life, in the Pulpit, the Bar, the Senate, and the Laboratory, I exemplify in the history of Chemy and Alchemy, Meteorology and Physiology.—See Treatises on the Logos anthropic and theanthropic, by S. T. Coleridge. Vol. I.[4]

2   p 33

Illud quoque aiunt, nihil incorporeum unà cum corpore pati, neque cum incorporeo corpus. patitur autem unà cum corpore anima aegrotante, & caeso, & corpus cum anima: pudore nanque suffusa anima, rubescit corpus: & metu perculsa, pallescit. corpus ergo anima est.

[Their next argument runs thus: "an incorporeal thing cannot be affected by what happens to a body, or *vice versa*, but one body is affected by what happens to another body. However, when the body is sick or hurt the soul suffers with it; and conversely, the body with the soul. For when the soul feels shame, the body blushes, and when the soul feels fear, the body blenches. Therefore the soul is corporeal."]

This is a weighty argument against the heterogenëity of the Body and Soul / but no argument at all in proof of the Soul's being a Body. For the body might as well be psychoid.—[1]

---

[3] The passage on p 33 to which C refers reads (tr), "It is as if someone said, 'No animal moves its upper jaw. A crocodile moves its upper jaw. Therefore, a crocodile is no animal.' The proposition is false." This is one of the arguments adduced against **2** textus. In commenting on Nemesius's text as "curious", C had perhaps overlooked, or been misled by the somewhat ambiguous sentence that precedes the textus, which indicates that Nemesius rejected Cleanthes' argument.

[4] C is evidently alluding not to the *Logic* as we have it, but to a portion of the projected "Logosophia, or [Treatises] on the Logos in man and Deity" (*CL* IV 736) frequently referred to in his correspondence after 1815, esp 1816–18: e.g. *CL* IV 589, 592, 687, 701, 736, 806–9. An account of it in Sept 1816 (*CL* IV 687) uses the phrase Λογος προπαιδευτικός ("propaedeutic Logic", or preliminary training in logic) as here; the application of logic to physical science is made in Jan 1818, *CL* IV 806–7.

[1] Not in *OED*: "soul-like", "in the form or likeness of the soul".

WILLIAM NICHOLSON

1753–1815

A Journal of Natural Philosophy, Chemistry, and the Arts. Vols XXII, XXVI, XXVII, XXVIII, XXX. London 1809, 1810, 1810, 1811, 1812. 8°.

The first series was in 5 vols 4°, 1797–1802; the second, "new series", in 36 vols 8°, 1802–13; after 1813 the *Journal* was incorporated in the *Philosophical Magazine*. C first became aware of *Nicholson's Journal* in May 1801 through Humphry Davy's contributions to it, and talked of subscribing at that time (*CL* II 735); he refers to it as late as 1825 in a marginal note in PEPYS *Memoirs*.

Not located; marginalia printed from MS TRANSCRIPT, upon which the text in *NTP* 237–46 was also based.

CONTENTS. Vol XXII (Jan–Apr 1809). JAN. Engravings: An Improved Goniometer; Views of the late Comet; Crystals of the Diopside; Life Boat. "An Account of a Goniometer invented by the Rev. E. J. Burrow" (1–2); William Herschel "Observations of a Comet" (3–14); "Remarks on the Diopside . . . By Mr. Tonnelier" (14–20); "Letter from Sir Thomas Clarges . . . [on] Lifeboats" (20–6); T. A. Knight "On the Origin and Office of the Alburnum of Trees" (27–33); P. Barlow "Letter on Polygonal Numbers" (33–5); William Brande "A Letter on the Differences in the Structure of Calculi . . . [in] the Urinary Passages" (35–51); Everard Home "Some Observations on Mr. Brande's Paper on Calculi" (51–4); Humphry Davy "Electro-Chemical Researches on the Decomposition of the Earths" (54–68); John Farey "On the supposed universal Distribution of Fossil Coal" (68–70); William Skrimshire, Jr. "Account of a British Vegetable Product, that may be substituted for Coffee" (70–3); "Account of some ferruginous Rocks . . . By Mr. Blavier" (74–5); J. C. Delametherie "On the Anthophyllite" (76); "Scientific News" (76–9); "Meteorological Table" (80). FEB. Engravings: Delphinus melas; Dr. W. Henry's Apparatus for the Analysis of . . . Gasses. T. S. Traill "Description of a new Species of Whale" (81–3); William Henry "Description of an Apparatus for the Analysis of the Compound Inflammable Gasses by slow Combustion" (83–100); William Herschel "Account of a new Irregularity . . . [in] the Planet Saturn" (100–3); Thomas Young "Hydraulic Investigations . . . on the Motion of the Blood" (104–24); Hericart de Thury "A Mineralogical Description of the Mountain and Silver Mine of Chalanches" (124–34); [Anon] "Effects of Gravity on the Balance of a Watch" (134–9); Richard Greene "An Account of . . . an artificial Cheltenham Water" (139–44); B. Cook "Second Letter on the Advantages of Coal Gas Lights" (145–8); James Scott "On the Superiority of Platina for making the Pendulum Spring of Watches" (148–9); [Anon] "On the Construction of Galvanic Batteries" (149–51); H. Lelivec "Account of an economical Method of evaporating the Water of Brine-springs" (151–3); John Goldingham "Eclipses of the Satellites of Jupiter" (153–6); "Scientific News"

Vol xxvi (May–Aug 1810). MAY. Engravings: Mr. Cavendish's Method; Prof. Copland's Insulating Handle; Mr. Robert Salmon's Man-trap; His Screw for fixing . . . in the Ground; His Method of building Pisé, or Earthen Walls. J. Bostock "Remarks upon Meteorology" (1–9); Mr. Cuthberton "On some Improvements in the Electrical Machine" (9–13); William Brande "Observations on Albumen" (13–22); John Saddington "Comparative Experiments on the Culture . . . of Kohl Rabi, . . . Cabbage, and Swedish Turnips" (23–5); Major Spencer Cochrane "On the Properties of Furze" (25–7); J. P. Hubbard "Account of several Varieties of British Marble" (27–30); Dr. Haldat "Inquiries concerning the Heat produced by Friction" (30–9); "Abstract of a Paper . . . by Messrs. Fourcroy and Vauquelin, on some Bones found in a Tomb" (39–43); Messrs. Fourcroy and Vauquelin "Experiments on the Tartarous Acid" (44–7); Henry Cavendish "On an Improvement in the Manner of dividing Astronomical Instruments" (47–54); Robert Salmon "Description of a Machine for securing Persons attempting Depredations" (55–8); Robert Salmon "Method of constructing commodious Houses with Earthen Walls" (58–68); [Anon] "Curious Property of the Toad" (68–9); J. A. de Luc "Communications on the Mode of Action of the Galvanic Pile" (69–72); Charles Sylvester "Observations on Galvanic Batteries" (72–5); J. D. Maycock "Remarks on . . . [the] doctrine of Radiant Heat" (75–8); "Scientific News" (78–9); "Meteorological Table". JUN. Engravings: Apparatus for analysing the Galvanic Pile; Continuous Galvanic Pile. Alexander von Humboldt "On the Volcanoes of Jorullo" (81–6); Mr. Klaproth "Chemical Inquiry into . . . ancient Bronze" (86–94); D. Viviani "On the Black Sand, or Menachanite" (94–8); Professor Tourte "Remarks on some Properties of Nickel" (99–102); "Abstract of a Paper on the Tenacity of ductile Metals . . . by Guyton-Morveau" (102–5); [Anon] "Improved Mode of preparing Phosphorus Bottles" (105–6); J. D. Maycock "Remarks on . . . [the] Doctrine of Radiant Heat" (106–11); Mr. Einhof "On the Acrid Principle of Horseradish" (111–13); J. A. de Luc "Analysis of the Galvanic Pile" (113–36); Everard Home "Hints on the Subject of Animal Secretions" (136–42); Mr. Trommsdorff "On the Saccholactic Acid" (142–7); "Letter from Mr. Hassenfratz . . . on the Oxidation of Iron" (147–52); E. Berard "On the Muriate of Tin" (152–7); Mr. Derosne "On the Formation of Acetic Ether in the Marc of Grapes" (157); [Anon] "Late sown Clover" (158); "Scientific News" (158–9); "Meteorological Table" (160). JUL. Engravings: An Escapement for a Clock; An Eye Bath; A Diagram . . . of the Rotary Motion of the Earth; A Method of securing the Beams of Ships; an Improvement in Linchpins. Theodore de Saussure "Observations on the Combustion of several Sorts of Charcoal" (161–76); George Prior, Jr. "Description of a Clock Escapement" (176–9); John Duckett Ross "An Eye Bath" (179–81); Richard Lovell Edgeworth "On Telegraphic Communications" (181–2); Professor Wood "New Theory of the Diurnal Motion of the Earth" (183–8); George Williams "Method of Securing the Beams of Ships" (188–9); J. Varty "Method to prevent the Accidents . . . from the Linchpins of Carriages breaking or coming out" (189–90); William Henry "An Analysis of several Varieties of British and Foreign Salt" (190–206); J. E. Berard "On the Proportions of the Elements of . . . the Alkaline Carbonates and Subcarbonates" (206–7); Marcel de Serres "On Chemical Printing" (208–12); Luke Howard "Observations on Dr. Bostock's Remarks upon Meteorology" (212–17); John Cuthbertson and G. J. Singer "Experiments on the comparative Powers of Cylinder and Plate electrical Machines'' (218–25); Richard Chevenix "Researches on Acetic Acid" (225–37); T. le Gay Brewerton "On the Precipitation of a solution of Sulphate of Lime by Sulphuric Acid" (237–8); "Scientific News" (238–9); "Meteorological Journal" (240). AUG. Engravings: An Iron Cylinder burst by Electricity; Arrangement of the Strata of the Hill at Durbuy; Mr. Mason's Trochar for the Relief of Hoven Cattle; Mr. Fisher's Churnstaff; Mr. Tansley's Shag Cutter. J. A. de Luc "Analysis of the Galvanic Pile" (241–72); Count Dunin Borkowski "On the Botryolite or Grapestone" (273); William Henry "An Analysis of several Varieties of British and Foreign Salt" (273–85); [Anon] "Action of the Electric Fluid" (285–8); J. C. Delametherie "Observations on the preceding Experiments" (288–90); J. J. Omalius de Halloy "Arrangement of the Strata of the Hill at Durbuy" (290–4); W. Wallis Mason "Method of stabbing Hoven Cattle" (294–6); Timothy Fisher "Description of a Swivelheaded Churn Staff" (296–8); Peter Tansley "Improvement in Cutting Silk Shag Edgings" (298–9); Theodore de Saussure "Observations on the Combustion of several Sorts of Charcoal" (300–9); J. Bostock "On Meteorological Nomenclature" (310–11); Count von Mellin "Method of increasing the Durability of Tiles" (312–14); "Extract of a Letter from Prof. Kries . . . on Radiant Heat" (314–16); [Anon] "Method of keeping Green Pease and French Beans" (316); [Anon] "On the Art of printing from Stone" (317); "Scientific News" (317–19); "Meteorological Journal" (320). SUPPLEMENT. Engravings: Mr. Davy's new Electrochemical Apparatus. Humphry Davy "The Bakerian Lecture for 1809. On some new Electro-chemical Researches" (321–39); Mr. Nose "On the Spinellane" (339–40); Richard Chevenix "Researches on Acetic Acid" (340–55); William Salisbury "On raising Grass Seeds" (355–60); William Lax "On a Method of examining the Divisions of astronomical Instruments" (360–71); Mr. von Humboldt "On a physical View of the Equatorial Regions" (371–8); Marcel de Serres "Observations on the Pleonast Spinel" (378–80); [Anon] "On the Nodules of Lava found in the Klingstein of the Rocks of Sanadoire" (381–2); Mr. Vauquelin "Chemical Examination of . . . Balsam of Mecca" (383–4); Count Dunin Borkowski "Of the Fettstein" (384); Index.

Vol XXVII (Sept–Dec 1810). SEPT. Engravings: Figures illustrating the Growth of Seeds. Agnes Ibbetson "On the Structure and Growth of Seeds" (1–17); Honoré Flaugergues "On the Ratio the spontaneous Evaporation of Water bears to Heat" (17–24); Charles Waistell "Method of ascertaining the Value of Growing Timber" (24–31); Mr. d'Arcet "Observations on Potash and Soda" (31–8); Humphry Davy "The Bakerian Lecture for 1809. On some new Electro-chemical Researches" (38–55); Thomas Forster "Times of Migration of some of the Swallow Tribe" (55–6); Thomas Young "The Croonian Lecture. On the Functions of the Heart and Arteries" (56–68); William Roxburgh "Natural Productions of the East Indies" (69–76); [Anon] "Cultivation of Poppies with Carrots" (76–7); [Anon] "Method of preserving and keeping in Vigour Fruit-trees" (77–8); "Scientific News" (78–9); "Meteorological Table" (80). OCT. Engravings: Mr. de Luc's Electric Column; Mr. Shute's Scarificator; Diagrams to illustrate . . . Capillary Attraction. J. A. de Luc "On the Electric Column" (81–99); Humphry Davy "The Bakerian Lecture for 1809. On some new Electro-chemical Researches" (99–111); Thomas Young "The Croonian Lecture. On the Functions of the Heart and Arteries" (112–23); Thomas Shute "Description of a Scarificator" (124–5); Thomas Knight "On the Theory of Capillary Attraction" (126–32); Dr. Baird "An Account of the Effects of Thirty Tons of Quicksilver escaping" (132–4); G. Cumberland "Scheme for preserving the Shipwrecked" (134–6); Charles Waistell "Method of ascertaining the Value of Growing Timber" (137–44); Mr. Laplace "Observations on Saturn's Ring" (144–6); Count De Vargas "On the Mines of Sardinia" (147–8); Mr. Klaproth "Analysis of various Minerals" (148–55); Richard Parkinson "Method of curing the Footrot in Sheep" (156); [Anon] "On . . . supporting the Vine and Hop" (156–7); Mr. Trommsdorff "Analysis of the Root of Valerian" (157–8); "Scientific News" (159); "Meteorological Table" (160). NOV. Engravings: Figures . . . [of] the Structure and Classification of Seeds; A Machine for raising large Stones. J. A. de Luc "On the Electric Column" (161–74); Agnes Ibbetson "On the Structure and Classification of Seeds" (174–84); Charles Waistell "Method of ascertaining the Value of Growing Timber" (185–93); P. Barlow "Demonstration of a curious Numerical Proposition" (193–205); Robert Richardson "Method of raising large Stones" (205–8); John Cuthbertson "An Account of a new Method of increasing the charging Capacity of coated Electrical Jars" (209–13); Marshall Hall "On the Combinations of Oxigen" (213–17); Thomas Forster "On the Migration of Swallows" (217–18); Everard Home "The Case of a Man, who died . . . of the Bite of a Rattlesnake" (219–25); Mr. Klaproth "Analyses of various Minerals" (225–31); L. Cordier "Description of the Dichroit" (231–6); Mr. John * "Analysis of the Naderlertz" (236–7); "Scientific News" (238–9); "Meteorological Table" (240). DEC. Engravings: Apparatus for Experiments on the Sonorous Properties of Gasses; Crystal of Apophyllite; A new Hygrometer; Mr. Congreve's Military Rockets. J. A. de Luc "On the Electric Column" (241–69); F. Kerby and Mr. Merrick, Jr. "Experiments on the Sonorous Properties of Gasses" (269–71); Mr. Haüy "Description of the Apophyllite" (272–5); W. Moore "On the Motion of Rockets" (276–85); Thomas Knight "Remarks on a new Principle . . . [in] Geometry" (285–7); Mr. Guyton-Morveau "Description of an Hygrometer for Gasses" (287–9); William Hyde Wollaston "The Croonian Lecture" (289–300); Charles Waistell "Method of ascertaining the Value of growing Timber" (300–9); [Anon] "Remarks on Professor Wood's new Theory" (309–11); Messrs. Bouillon-Lagrange and Vogel "An analytical Essay on the Scammonies of Aleppo and Smyrna" (311–16); "Scientific News" (317–19); "Meteorological Table" (320). SUPPLEMENT. Engravings: Cancer Fulgens; Medusa Pellucens. H. Davy "Researches on the Oximuriatic Acid" (321–37); J. Macartney "Observations upon Luminous Animals" (337–50); J. E. Berard "Note on the Water . . . in fused Soda" (351–3); Gillet Laumont "On a new Pitchlike Iron Ore" (354–5); Mr. Bucholz "Analysis of three Species of Pyrites" (356–7); Mr. Hersart "Description of a Phosphated Copper" (358–61); Henry Braconnot "Comparative Analysis of Gum-Resins" (361–70); Dr. Alexander Anderson "Communications concerning the Royal Botanical Garden at St. Vincent" (370–5); Thomas Thomson "On the Oxides of Iron" (375–84); Index.

Vol XXVIII (Jan–Apr 1811). JAN. Engravings: Electrical machine; Luminous animals. J. A. de Luc "Experiments concerning the Electric Machine" (1–13); A. Laugier "Comparative Examination of . . . Mucous Acid" (14–18); Thomas Thomson "Chemical Analysis of a Black Sand" (19–30); H. Davy "Researches on the Oximuriatic Acid" (31–6); C. Le Hardy "On the Culture of Parsneps"

(37–40); J. Macartney "Observations upon Luminous Animals" (41–55); G. Cumberland ". . . Printing from Autographs" (56–8); Marshall Hall "On the Classification of Chemical Agents" (59–62); Mr. Hume "Remarks on Military Rockets" (63–6); [Anon.] "Remarks on . . . Potassium and Sodium" (67–72); Honoré Flaugergues "Observations on . . . Thermometers" (73–4); A. Laugier "Analysis of the Amphibole of the Cape de Gattes" (75–6); "Scientific News" (77–9); "Meteorological Journal" (80). FEB. Engravings: Height of Meteors; Phaseolus Coccinea; Passion flower; Metallic Arborization. John Dalton "Inquiries concerning . . . the word Particle" (81–8); N. Bowditch "An Estimate of the Height . . . of the [Connecticut] Meteor" (89–97); Agnes Ibbetson "On the Method of Jussieu" (98–104); Robert Lyall "Remarks on the British Species of Drosera" (105–8); Robert Lyall "Remarks on the . . . Passion-Flower" (109–11); C. J. T. de Grotthuss "On . . . Metallic Arborizations" (112–24); W. T. Brande "Observations on the Effects of Magnesia" (125–31); J. Murray "Observations and Experiments on . . . Oximuriatic Acid" (132–52); [Anon] "Questions on the Nature of Water" (153–4); Thomas Knight "Remarks on . . . Capillary Action" (155–6); John Dalton "On Muriatic and Oximuriatic Acid" (157); Thomas Thomson "An Analysis of Fluor-Spar" (157–8); "Scientific News" (159); "Meteorological Journal" (160). MAR. Engravings: Motion of Rockets; Dissection of Petals; Corollas of Flowers. W. Moore "On the Motion of Rockets" (161–9); Agnes Ibbetson "The beautiful Tint of Flowers" (170–9); W. Gregor "An Analysis of a Soil" (180–3); J. H. Hassenfratz "Observations on the Oxides of Iron" (184–92); John Davy "Some Remarks [on] . . . Oximuriatic Acid" (193–205); N. Bowditch "An Estimate of the Height . . . of the [Connecticut] Meteor" (206–18); [Anon] "On Muriatic and Oximuriatic Acid" (219–21); W. H. Wollaston "On Cystic Oxide" (222–7); H. Braconnot "Comparative Analysis of Gum Resins" (228–37); "Scientific News" (238–9); "Meteorological Table" (240). APR. Engravings: Air Pump; Growth of the Bud. J. Murray "Observations . . . on the Alkaline Metalloids" (241–53); Agnes Ibbetson "On the Interior of Plants" (254–65); J. H. Hassenfratz "Observations on the Oxides of Iron" (266–74); T. A. Knight "On the Parts of Trees primarily impaired by Age" (275–9); John Bostock "Remarks on . . . the Manner in which Bodies combine with each other" (280–92); Thomas Forster "Effect of Changes in the State of the Atmosphere on Mr. De Luc's Electric Column" (293); J. Murray "On the Nature of Oximuriatic Acid" (294–309); [Anon] "Hypermuriate of Potash" (310–13); Robert Lyall "Observations respecting . . . the Barberry" (314–16); John Brinckley "The annual Parallax of a Lyrae" (317); "Scientific News" (317–19); "Meteorological Journal" (320). SUPPLEMENT. Engravings: Growth of the Bud; Machine for evaporating Liquids. Thomas Thomson "On the Gaseous Combinations of Hidrogen and Carbon" (321–35); F. R. Gowar "On a new Compound" (336–43); H. Braconnot "Comparative Analysis of Gum-Resins" (344–9); C. Duméril "On the Mechanism of Respiration in Fishes" (350–8); J. Murray "Further Experiments on . . . Potassium" (359–68); [Anon] "On the Affinity of Muriatic Acid for different Bodies" (369–72); Mr. Desormes and Mr. Clément "Description of an economical Process for Evaporation" (373–8); "Scientific News" (379).

Vol xxx (Sept–Dec 1811). SEPT. Engravings: Various Figures . . . representing the Hairs and minute Cryptogamiae on Plants. Agnes Ibbetson "On the

Hairs of Plants'' (1–9); [Anon] "Inquiry concerning . . . Ants" (10); Mr. Berthollet et al. "Report of a Committee . . . [on] a preservative Stucco" (10–16); George Pearson "Observations on Pus" (17–27); Grover Kemp "Method of preparing . . . White for Water Colours" (33–4); Luke Howard "The Natural History of Clouds" (35–62); Thomas Forster "An Account of the Thunderstorms on the 19th of August" (62–3); "Meteorological Journal" (64–5); Messrs. Gay-Lussac and Thenard "Abstract of a Memoir on the Analysis of Vegetable and Animal Substances" (66–74); Mr. Vauquelin "Chemical Examination of a white filamentous Substance" (74–5); Rev. John Simpson "An Account of the Burrknot Apple" (76); Sir Joseph Banks "A Short Account of a new Apple" (77); "Scientific News" (78–80). OCT. Engravings: Mr. Donkin's Tachometer; A Hippograph; Mr. Ross's Machine for separating Iron Filings; Mr. Marshall's Sash-frame. W. Moore "On the Destruction of an Enemy's Fleet at Sea by Artillery" (81–93); W. Moore "Correction . . . on the Motion of Rockets" (93–4); Mr. Malus "On a Property of reflected Light" (95–102); Mr. Biot "Experiments on the Transmission of Sound" (103–13); George Pearson "Observations . . . on Pus" (113–21); Bryan Donkin "Description of a Tachometer" (121–6); [Anon] "A Mode of conveying Intelligence" (126–7); J. D. Ross "Description of a Machine for separating Iron Filings" (127–8); G. Marshall "A New Method of constructing Sash Windows" (129–31); Thomas Forster "Observations on . . . Shooting Stars" (131–2); James Smithson "On the Composition of Zeolite" (133–7); J. Cloud "Extract . . . on the Discovery of Palladium" (137–40); Mr. d'Arcet "Analysis of the Cement of an antique Mosaic" (140–1); "Meteorological Journal" (142–3); Mr. Decandolle "Remarks on the Inclination of the Stems of Plants" (144–7); Sir Joseph Banks "On the Forcing-houses of the Romans" (147–54); Richard Cathery "Method of preparing Ox Gall" (154–5); "Letter from Mr. Vitalis . . . on the . . . Arbor Dianae" (156–7); "Scientific News" (157–60). NOV. Engravings: Peduncles of Leaves; Apparatus to explain the Decomposition of Water; Crystals of carbonated Lime. Mr. Malus "On a Property of the repulsive Forces, that act on Light" (161–8); Mr. Biot "Experiments on the Production of Sound" (169–73); Everard Home "Experiments to prove, that Fluids pass directly from the Stomach to the . . . Blood" (173–9); Agnes Ibbetson "Of the mechanical Powers in the Leaf Stalks" (179–83); Adam Anderson "On the Decomposition of Water" (183–9); Mr. Haüy "Description of . . . carbonated Lime" (189–92); Francis Delaroche "Extract . . . on Radiant Heat" (192–3); Marshall Hall "On Chemical Attraction" (193–202); Sir Joseph Banks "On the . . . Spanish Chestnut Tree" (202–4); Thomas Andrew Knight "On Potatoes" (204–8); [Anon] "A remarkable analytical Anomaly" (209–12); Dr. Traill "On the Migration of Swallows" (213–16); Professor Pictet "Account of . . . a Luminous Meteor" (216–18); Professor P. Prevost "Letter . . . on the Meteor of the 15th of May" (218–20); J. Hassell "Improvement in the Aquatinta Process" (220–6); J. Murray "On the Nature of the Oxymuriatic Acid Gas" (226–35); "Meteorological Journal" (236–7); Mr. Vauquelin "Experiments on . . . Potash" (238–9); "Scientific News" (239–40). DEC. Engravings: Plans and Sections of a Spire; Diagrams for the Demonstration of . . . the Lever. Richard Lovell Edgeworth "Description of a Spire of a new Construction" (241–8); Mr. Vauquelin "Experiments on . . . Gold" (248–56); Messrs. Fourcroy and Vauquelin "Experiments on Human Bones" (256–60); Mr. Berzelius "Letter . . . on the Analysis

MS TRANSCRIPT. VCL BT 37.7: transcript by SC. In the absence of the original, C's notes are printed from the transcript, which is also used (by its selection of textus) as a guide to the location of C's notes on the page; textus here, however, has been taken directly from a copy of the *Journal*.

DATE. Between Apr 1816 and Sept 1817? Although it is possible that the notes were written when the vols were first published, or that they were written at different times then or later, internal evidence suggests that most if not all of them were written during the brief period of C's comparatively uncritical acceptance of *Naturphilosophie*, c 1815–17. Since the vols from which the transcript was made were in Gillman's library at the time of C's death and may have been his rather than C's copies to begin with, the date of annotation can with some confidence be given as after Apr 1816, when C moved in with the Gillmans. **12** n 2 may be evidence of a later or further reading after Apr 1823.

1   XXII 162 | William Richardson "A Letter on the Alterations . . . in the Structure of Rocks . . . [in] the basaltic Country in the Counties of Derry and Antrim"

In a geological point of view, Nature* has been very kind to this district . . . [Footnote*:] By the word Nature, which frequently occurs in the course of this Memoir, I always mean, according to Ray's definition, the wisdom of God in the creation of the world.

Far better and more reverential, as well as more correspondent to the phænomena, would the following definition of Nature be, me saltem judice.[1] The Law, or constructive Powers,[2] excited in Matter by the influence of God's Spirit and Logos.

P.S. We have no other reason for continuing the inchoative acts of the Spirit and Word, after the Creative Week, than as all existence is grounded in the Abysmal Aseïty, the divine Nature as indivisibly distinguished from the divine Personeïty.[3]   S. T. C.

2   xxii 210 | "A Letter on Comets, addressed to Mr. Bode, Astronomer Royal at Berlin" 209–10

[The anonymous author speculates that the light from comets is phosphoric in nature, "some chemical decomposition" having produced "luciferous vapours".] Let us suppose, that a certain degree of proximity to the Sun is a circumstance determining either the production or the decomposition of these vapours; in other words, that the intensity of its rays is the chemical cause, that induces the luminous effects. I have been led to this idea by a phenomenon observed in our experiments, which displays some analogy with the supposition here made: certain bodies recently calcined, or calcined anew, such as oyster shells and the Bononian stone, after having been some time exposed to the *rays of the Sun*, are *luminous* in the dark. Euler imagined, that he could draw from this phenomenon an argument against Newton's theory of the *emission of light*, and in favour of his theory of vibrations: conceiving, that the effect of the rays of the Sun on these bodies was to produce in them *vibrations*, which continued for some time. On the contrary I deduce from it an argument militating directly against his theory: for he supposes, that the different *colours* of light are different kinds of *vibrations*; so that when these bodies are exposed to rays of certain *colours*, which can produce vibrations of their own kind only, the light afterwards emitted by these bodies in the dark must be of the same *colour*. Now from the experiments of Mr. Wilson, which I myself have seen, the light emitted by a calcined oyster shell is the same, whatever was the colour of the ray, to which it had been exposed. These oyster shells acquire dif-

[1] [1] "According to my judgment, at least".

[1] [2] The phrase "constructive Powers" is derived from the *Naturphilosophie* of Schelling and his followers, notably H. Steffens, whose major works C read carefully 1815–16, and reread later. Cf *TL* 50–9, e.g. 55: "If we pass to the construction of matter, we find it as the product, or *tertium aliud*, of antagonist powers of repulsion and attraction. Remove these pow-

ers, and the conception of matter vanishes into space . . .".

[1] [3] Aseity—underived or self-grounded existence, the quality by virtue of which a being exists in and from itself alone—is normally attributed only to God. Nature is derived from "the divine Nature", which is itself absolute. Cf *AR* (1825) 328, where C alludes to patristic and scholastic debate on "the obscure and *abysmal* subject of the Divine A-seity . . .".

ferent properties in this respect, according to the degree of calcination, or some other unknown circumstance. I have seen them emit red, green, and yellow light: but they never shine again, each with its own colour, except from the immediate action of the solar rays; and each single coloured ray causes them to emit the same colour, but more faintly, the ray of their *own colour* having no advantage over the rest. Hence, I infer, that the rays of the Sun produce a *decomposition* in these calcined substances, in consequence of which they give out the *light*, that entered into their composition.

In what way are we to conceive the matter of Light (= solar rays) to produce a decomposition or extrication of matter of Light (= rays chemically combined with matter not Light)? Not by homogeneous attraction, for the extrication continues after the removal of the solar rays, i.e. the attracting substances. By the motion then of the solar rays exciting correspondent motion in the calcined shells?—and what else is meant by vibrations? Mem. Experim. with various instruments (musical) of glass and steel on the Bononian stone, calcined Oyster shells, &c.[1]

3   xxii 212

[The anonymous author develops an analogy between the appearance of the comet and lightning, which is formed of the electrical fluid in the atmosphere interrupted in its otherwise straight course by "its strong tendency to unite with particles of the *air*", and consequently zigzags.] Suppose then, that a fluid in all other respects similar to the *electric* is formed on that side of a comet which is turned from the Sun; a fluid so rapid in its rectilinear motion, that it soon gets out of the sphere of gravity of that body, without being detained by its atmosphere, and which is rendered *luminous* by its decomposition on its course: thus we shall have the phenomenon of the *tail*, with a circumstance characteristic of these causes, namely, the *curvature* of these tails, the convexity of which is

---

2[1] As the textus indicates, calcined oyster shells (i.e. shells reduced to ashes) and Bononian or Bolognian (Bologna) Stone specially prepared were of interest to chemists for their phosphorescent properties: see e.g. W. T. Brande *A Manual of Chemistry* (1819) 72, a book which C studied. In trying to account for their gradual loss of phosphorescence—which cannot be attributed exclusively to the action of the sun on them, because it is observed to happen also in the dark—C disagrees with the author of the article and hopes by experiment with sound-waves to find support for the anti-Newtonian "theory of vibrations". The wave theory of light had been defended by Thomas Young (1773–1829) in contributions to *Phil Trans RS*, and it may have been Young's paper "Outlines of Experiments and Inquiries Respecting Sound and Light" ibid xc (1800) 106–50 that led C to think of experimenting with sound-waves: Levere 157.

turned toward the side to which they are moving; the cause of which appears to me to be as follows.

The particles of the fluid of the tail, as they are detached from the comet, possess the same *projectile* movement with it, and in the same direction. Accordingly they must continue to follow it. But if they extend very far, that is to say, if the tail become very long; the particles that proceed the farthest, continuing to move with the same velocity but in a larger orbit, must have a less *angular* movement. This must produce such a *curvature*, not to mention some degree of *resistance*, which these particles may experience in *space*, though with respect to large bodies it is imperceptible.

Bode in this very ingenious speculation assumes the absence of any perceptible action of gravity in this more refined and uncombining sort of electric fluid.[1] If so, how can the particles self-projected from the comet in the direction opposite to that in which the comet is moving, possess the *same* projectile movement? I ask *formâ pauperis*, not *ad confutandum*.[2] A stone thrown from a coach in full motion, I know, will follow the coach, or rather accompany it. But would a body projected from a pistol do so? i.e. supposing the earth's gravity removed. And the tail has been measured at 100 millions of miles!!—

What a prodigious idea—an outline of motion = A. extending 100,000,000 miles, and in the direction u, while all the area included, with exception of 500 or 1000 miles, is filled by particles moving in the opposite direction x.![3] Query. Would not the perpetual evolution of the phosphorescent vapour keeping up a continuum from the evaporating disk *sun fro*[a] to the end of the tail, like smoke issuing from the stern holes of a vessel sailing against the wind, supply a less startling hypothesis? The smoke of a steam-boat for instance. The expansive or more probably the self-projective power of the cometary vapour = p would be instead of the Wind = w[b] p : vapour :: w : m[4]

[a] Thus MS TRANSCRIPT; *NTP* prints *sunfro*. SC must have found the original illegible, and it is hard to guess what it might have been: "run thro' "?
[b] MS TRANSCRIPT leaves no space between "w" and "p"

3[1] C's opposition to theories that depend upon positing imponderable fluids is documented and explained in Levere 60–1, 146–7. The "ingenious speculation" belonged of course not to Bode but to the anonymous author.

3[2] "As a beggar", not "for the sake of confutation".

3[3] The nature of comets was a matter of keen scientific and popular interest in the early nineteenth century, and C maintained a consistently sceptical position with regard to theories about them that were based upon Newtonian assumptions. Two notes of c Jul 1818, responding to an article in *Blackwood's*, make a similar point about the disparity between the enormous tail of a comet and its comparatively small nucleus: *CL* IV 954–6, BM Egerton MS 2801 ff 71–2 (*SW & F—CC*).

3[4] I.e. "the projective power is to the vapour as wind to the motion of the boat".

4   xxɪɪ 316 | "An Essay on Electrical Attractions and Repulsions, by Mr. ***"

[The anonymous author is concerned with the conditions necessary to make glass conduct electricity.] We see above, that the author requires the ball of glass to be very thin: this is a necessary condition for producing the rotatory and revolving motion, for every thing made of glass in this state is moved by the slightest electric action; it kindles, as it were, like charcoal before the blowpipe; and being moved in one point, the neighbouring points tend by affinity to carry themselves in succession to the centre of activity.

This, the most important of all, is so expressed as to be utterly unintelligible. What does "it" mean?—and "tend by affinity to *carry* themselves?"—Does the Writer mean that what *each* point *would* do separately, but which neither (no one) *can* do, manifests itself in the motion of the *whole* as the representative of *all*? This would be something, could it be proved.

5   xxvɪ 31 | "Inquiries concerning the Heat produced by Friction. By Dr. Haldat, Secretary to the Academy of Nancy"

[Haldat introduces his own explanation of the properties of heat by presenting the theory of heat as a debate between the proponents of the fluid or caloric "hypothesis" on the one hand, and those who assert that heat is a product or manifestation of "a certain mode of being of the particles of bodies" (31) on the other. As he says, "each has adopted for their explanation that hypothesis, which appears to him the most natural, and their opinions are divided" (30).]

A striking and beautiful instance of the theory of Equation, arising in the attempt to objectivize Powers by substituting the sensuous products as their representatives. An hypothetic fluid, or an hypothetic motion, are really the same object in the mind—in the one, we borrow the [? void/word] by abstracting the act from the Image, in the other by abstracting the Image from the act.[1]   *S. T. C.*

6   xxvɪ 131 | "Analysis of the Galvanic Pile. By J. A. de Luc, Esq."[1]

. . . the different *modifications* which the *electric fluid* undergoes by pervading different *piles*, will become an important object in the course of the conclusions from the above experiments, to which I now come.

The steamboat was a recent introduction to British life; C records his own delight in travelling by it in 1825: *CL* v 497, 499.

5[1] SC's rather dubious transcription, "borrow the [? void/word]", does not obscure the general point, namely C's familiar objection to abstraction as a fiction of the human understanding inferior even to generalisation: cf *CN* ɪv 4538.

6[1] This paper and its successors ap-

The first of these conclusions will concern the fundamental *mode of action* of the *pile*, in its two different effects, *electric* and *chemical*. . . . for *electric effects*, the *efficient groups* consist simply of the *binary* associations of the two *metals*; each group being separated from the next by a *conducting substance non-metallic*.

For *chemical effects*, the *efficient groups* are *ternary*; they are composed of the two *metals*, having between them a *liquid* in contact with both, which here is in the *wet cloth*.

I dare not doubt the substantial merits of a Naturalist so highly admired, as De Luc is, by so competent a judge as Blumenbach.[2] But there is a complexity in all De Luc's experiments, with a multiplicity in his data, rendered more hopeless by the absence of ideas (or first principles) that for me amounts in the effect to positive entanglement. If he meant to prove that Chemismus or the power of composition and decomposition exercised by bodies on each other, is not the same as the Electrical, he is right; and Davy carried his anticipation too far.[3] But if De Luc meant, as he does, that the electrical power is the property of a peculiar Fluid, or rather but another word for the presence of that Fluid, and therefore as diverse from chemical agency, as from the ponderable bodies, the properties of which are denoted thereby; and that the chemical agency is as independent of the electrical, as the electrical of it; he is far astray, and deduces a falsity from a fiction. For his electrical fluid is a mere

---

peared in Nicholson's *Journal* after having been denied publication in *Phil Trans RS*. Jean André de Luc (1727–1817), Swiss geologist and meteorologist resident in England since 1773, set out to correct Davy's Bakerian Lecture of 1806 "On Some Chemical Agencies of Electricity" (*Phil Trans RS* xcvii—1807—1–56): his consequent distinction between the chemical and the electrical effects of the galvanic pile or battery led him to experiment with an exclusively "electric column" or "dry pile", which has since been considered the chief discovery of his distinguished career.

6[2] De Luc and Blumenbach were not only friends but allies in the attempt to use scientific evidence in support of the teachings of the Bible. The full title of one of de Luc's geological works is revealing: *Lettres sur l'histoire physique de la terre, adressées à M. le professeur Blumenbach, renfermant de nouvelles preuves géologiques et historiques de la mission divine*

de Moyse (Paris 1798). C wrote enthusiastically of Blumenbach's lectures and conversation in 1799 (*CL* I 494)—when, as it happens, de Luc was spending some time in Germany—and may have heard Blumenbach's opinion of him then; no special praise of de Luc has been traced in those published works of Blumenbach with which C was familiar.

6[3] C had himself described the conclusion reached in Davy's lecture (6 n 1 above) with great excitement (*CL* III 38): ". . . by the aid and application of his own great discovery, of the identity of electricity and chemical attractions, he has placed all the elements and all their intimate combinations in the power of man. . . . Davy supposes that there is only one power in the world of the senses; which in particles acts as chemical attractions, in specific masses as electricity, & on matter in general, as planetary Gravitation."

picture-word of the fancy, a short-hand hieroglyphic mark or memento of a class and series of phænomena, a generic name for a certain set of changes substituted and passed off for their common cause. Chemismus is the third and synthetic power, Magnetism being the *thetic* and the + and − Electricity the antithetic: while Galvanism is the transition of Electricity into Chemismus, or the co-adunation of Magnetism and Electricity.[4] As Depth to Length and Breadth, so Chemismus to Magnetism and Electricity. It is to Bodies what the corporific[5] power is to matter, the continuance of the same, as the reproductive and conserving power—analogous to the dogma of the Theologians, that the preservation of the Material World is but the continuance of the Creative Act.[6]

S. T. C.

7   xxvi 186 | "New Theory of the Diurnal Motion of the Earth round its Axis. In a letter from Professor Wood"

This principle I have employed to explain the tides, the trade winds, and the phenomena of falling stones. [Footnote:] Prof. Wood supposes the stones, that fall from the atmosphere, to be projected into it from volcanoes: and that, as the point from which they are thrown has its rotary velocity increased or diminished, while the stones retain that impressed on them at the time of their projection, they must consequently reach the Earth at a greater or less distance east or west of the volcano.

This hypothesis neither solves the heterogeneity of the *composition* of meteoric stones from any minerals, volcanic or otherwise, hitherto found in this Planet, nor their homogeneity with each other, which makes their volcanic origin from any Planet improbable, and suggests their being products of our atmosphere, analogous to hail, snow &c: whether by electrical re-aggregation of metallic particles that continually effluviate wherever exposed to the air and sun-light, or by contraction of the matter of fire, first magnetically and then electrically (or rather the union of both in the galvanic or constructive act) according to Heraclitus and the present *Natur-philosophen*, is to be decided.[1]

6[4] This sequence of constructive acts is basic to *Naturphilosophie*. Cf *TL* 91 and 1 n 2 above.

6[5] Not in *OED*: lit "body-making", that which causes something to assume a body or material form. The formation of discrete bodies precedes the dynamic chemical action by which they are preserved or adapted.

6[6] Cf 1 above for a similar reference to this version of the Neoplatonic emanation theory, and SPINOZA 12 for the concept of preservation as continuous creation. Spinoza himself introduces the concept with a Scholastic phrase, in *Ethics* pt 1 prop 24 cor: "From this it follows that God is not only the cause of things beginning to exist, but also of their persevering in existing, *or* (to use a Scholastic term) God is the cause of the being of things."

7[1] The first chemical analysis of meteorites was published in *Phil Trans RS* in

8 xxvi 243 | "Analysis of the Galvanic Pile. By J. A. de Luc, Esq. F.R.S. Part II."

Must we, *in the present state of our knowledge*, be satisfied with *electrical energies*, which might be considered as *essential properties of matter**? [Footnote*: "Mr. Davy's *Bakerian Lecture*, Ph. Trans. 1807, Part I, p. 39; or Journal, vol. xix, p. 50."] Or rather, in this very *state of our knowledge*, is it not already ascertained, that a particular *substance* exists, namely, the *electric fluid*, which, beside the effects here in view, produces greater and more general effects on our globe?

No! till De Luc tells what he means by a *substance*, and how a particular substance is to be *proved* except by weight and vision. De Luc quotes Bacon. Pity he had not learned from him, that the notion of cause and effect belongs to Logic—to the arrangement of *our* thoughts, and dare not be supposed in nature, or rather cannot without contradiction in terms.[1] And then a *particular* substance that exists *every where*! See p. 131.[2] It remains clear that the utmost which De Luc's experiments prove is that the electrical is not the same act or modification of power as the chemical, but different as Λ from Δ, or the power of 2 from that of 3. and this we grant on higher evidence than his experiments can afford.[3]

S. T. C.

9 xxvi 330 | Humphry Davy "The Bakerian Lecture for 1809. On some new Electrochemical Researches, on various Objects, particularly the metallic Bodies from the Alkalis, and Earths, and on some Combinations of Hidrogen"

Mr. Ritter's argument in favour of potassium and sodium being compounds of hidrogen is their extreme lightness. This argument I had in

1802; it led to much speculation about their composition and origin. W. T. Brande's *Manual of Chemistry* (1819), which C knew, summarises evidence and dismisses the theory of volcanic origin. C characteristically presents the German theorists— thinking perhaps of H. Steffens *Geognostische-geologische Aufsätze* (Hamburg 1810) 222–3—as revivers of an ancient theory, in this case Heraclitus's general principle of fire which is alternately kindled and extinguished.

8[1] De Luc was an avowed admirer of Bacon's and wrote two books about him, *Bacon tel qu'il est* (Berlin 1800) and *Précis de la philosophie de Bacon* (2 vols Paris 1803). It was in the earlier instalment of this article (*Journal* xxvi—1810—114) that he had actually quoted him. Although this anticipation of Hume is not usually attributed to Bacon, it finds some support in

Bacon's assigning the study of causes to the speculative branches of knowledge in *De augmentis* bk 3 ch 4 and in *New Organon* bk 2 aph 2 (*Works* ed Spedding et al IV 119–20, 343, 346; ed Mallet—1740—I 109–10, 313–14); and it is consistent with C's view of Bacon as a "British Plato" in *Friend* (*CC*) I 490.

8[2] The "electric fluid" here called a "particular substance" is affirmed on p 131 to exist universally. C objects to the contradiction in logic but also, at a deeper level, to what he considered to be a misuse of the term "substance" as equivalent to "matter" rather than to "divine essence".

8[3] Possibly, the a priori principles of *Naturphilosophie*; ultimately, the Book of Genesis. The Greek capital letters lambda and delta resemble one another but differ as two and three.

some measure anticipated, in my paper on the decomposition of the earths; no one is more easily answered. Sodium absorbs much more oxigen than potassium, and, on the hypothesis of hidrogenation, must contain much more hidrogen; yet, though soda is said to be lighter than potash in the proportion of 13 to 17 nearly, sodium is heavier than potassium in the proportion of 9 to 7 at least.

This is singular in Ritter, since his friend, Steffens, a year or more before Davy's experimental analysis of the Alkalis had deduced the metallicity of Soda and Potash, in very nearly the same proportions of metal to Oxygen found by Davy, from the polar theory—nay, had answered by anticipation this objection to their metallic nature from the levity of the asserted bases.[1]   *S. T. C.*

10 xxvi 330

On the theory which I have adopted, this circumstance is what ought to be expected. Potassium has a much stronger affinity for oxigen than sodium, and must condense it much more, and the resulting higher specific gravity of the combination is a necessary consequence.

Steffens would not have objected to Ritter, had he considered the two bases as metallic, no less than zinc or tin, yet as metals composed of Carbon and Hydrogen, the latter being the same as Nitrogen, only under the state of positive electricity as Nitrogen under that of + Magnetism $\times$ + pos. E = H $\times$ + pos. M = N.[1] But he would have contended that this must ever remain a *speculative* analysis, and the alkaline metals practically indecomponible equally with any other metal.

11 xxvii 38, continued on p +1 | H. Davy "The Bakerian Lecture for 1809 [cont] . . . iii. Experiments on Nitrogen, Ammonia, and the Amalgam from Ammonia"

One of the queries that I advanced, in attempting to reason upon the singular phenomena produced by the action of potassium upon ammonia

[9][1] There is no evidence that C knew the work of the eminent German scientist Johann Wilhelm Ritter (1776–1810) at first hand, but he had seen it respectfully cited by Davy and Steffens. Davy, who had succeeded in isolating sodium and potassium, from "caustic soda" (sodium hydroxide) and potash respectively, in 1807, exposes Ritter's error in believing them not to be metals; C in turn suggests that Davy's discovery had been anticipated not by practical experiment but by the systematic application of *Naturphilosophie*—specifically,

by the geologist Heinrich Steffens.

[10][1] On the "Compass of Nature" that C adapted from *Naturphilosophie* (e.g. *CN* iii 4420), hydrogen and positive electricity are found at the western pole and nitrogen and positive magnetism at the southern. A note of May 1819 that also prophesies that hydrogen and nitrogen would be found to be different modifications of the same "Stuff" reveals another aspect of the theory in its defence of "Mosaic Chemistry" and the biblical account of the Creation: *CN* iv 4536 and n.

was, that nitrogen might possibly consist of oxigen and hidrogen, or that it might be composed from water.

For important reasons I should rather say that Hydrogen is a modification of Nitrogen by $+$E.[1] But then it must not be forgotten that each of the four polar stuffs is composed of all and that this as their Ousia,[2] must be distinguished from their after-modifications.

A	B
B	D
C	C
D	A

S. T. C.

12 xxviii "blank leaf"[1]

De Luc's predilection for subtle fluids, with his abuse of occult properties and essential powers reminds me of Moore's anecdote—. The cruelty of the mode being objected to the scheme of sweeping Chimneys by dragging a goose down, the Proposer replied, "Why it is rather cruel; but two ducks will do as well."[2] Yet even this is not enough. To make it a full equivalent in absurdity, the Proposer must have substituted the *same* goose, but tied to and under the belly of a phœnix. For what but the never yet seen and exhibited phœnix is a fair parallel to these subtle fluids, with *specific properties*, i.e. each with the old goose under it?

S. T. C.

13 xxx 323 | "On the Place of a Sound, produced by a Musical String. In a Letter from Mr. John Gough"[1]

This discovery points out a distant analogy connecting the thundering noise of a drum and the smooth sounds of a harp or lute.

Smooth is not the appropriate term, I think. The first difference is that

11[1] As **10** n 1 above.

11[2] The Platonic term means "being, essence, true nature". In C's dynamic system, the two primary powers of light and gravitation generate the "four polar stuffs", but these in turn enter into new combinations in a complex process of ramification. C's columns are intended to show that each of the four includes all the others to some extent.

12[1] This is all the indication SC gives in ms transcript of the location of the note, which sums up C's reaction to the continuing series of de Luc's papers and returns specifically to the objection of **8** n 2. *NTP* 243–4 prints **8** and **12** as one note.

12[2] Presumably the Irish poet and well-known wit Thomas Moore (1779–1852). C does not appear to have met Moore before 1823, though he might have heard this story attributed to him before then. It is a topical joke, the conditions of climbing boys having been a focus for social reform since the 1780s, and various incentives having been offered for chimney-cleaning methods that did away with the need for child labour.

13[1] C might have been interested in this paper from his acquaintance with the author, the remarkable blind Quaker scientist John Gough of Kendal (1757–1825), to whom he had paid tribute in "The soul and its organs of sense" in *Omniana* (1812) § 174.

of *discrete* and *continuous*—but then comes another in the latter (the Drum)—viz—the want of all harmonic proportion between the last sound of the diminishing interval with the renewed sound given by the Drum-stick—this changes the continuous into confused, while the tone or specific quality from the cavity makes it rumbling.   *S. T. C.*

CHRISTOPH FRIEDRICH NICOLAI
1733–1811

Ueber meine gelehrte Bildung, über meine Kenntniss der kritischen Philosophie und meine Schriften dieselbe betreffend, und über die Herren Kant, J. B. Erhard, und Fichte. Ein Beylage zu den neun Gesprächen zwischen Christian Wolf und einem Kantianer. Berlin and Stettin 1799. 8°.

British Library C 126 g 2

"S. T. C." label on title-page verso. On p ⁻6, the "C" monogram of James Duke Coleridge. A short slanting line in the margin of p 118 may have been a slip of the pen: it does not mark a discrete passage.

MS TRANSCRIPT. VCL BT 22: unidentified hand.

DATE. ? 1813–16 or earlier.

COEDITORS. Lore Metzger, Raimonda Modiano.

1   p ⁻2, pencil

femur = outside of the Thigh
femen = inside D°
Talus = Ancle
Dorsi pars gracilis = Small of the Back
Lumbi   Loins
Coxæ   Hips
prolated, producted, protensed/
aquam reddere—[1]

2   p ⁻1

22	W		bl	le
7~~7~~6-77		W		lest
v 119			~~W W~~	
159			bl	
182			beauty	U
253[1]			beauty	

1[1] "To render water". C was evidently jotting down words and phrases from a medical book in Latin—unidentified.

2[1] These numbers all correspond to

954

3 p ⁻1

Nicolai's Arms.

In the center Ignorance, as a ~~Goose~~ander arching its neck in imitation of the Swans, (Lessing & Mend~~l~~eelsohn) who had swum on the same Lake with it, by accident[1]—The Supporters, Garrulous Egotism, as a Parrot; and darkling Hypo-criticism,[2] as a mousing Owl: the Crest, a coronet of Quills; the Motto— ~~ROGUE! FOOL!~~ "GABBLE! GABBLE! HOOT! HOOT! PRETTY POLL! PRETTY POLL!—"

If this wretched book-selling Book-maker has assured us once, that he does, that he must, understand Kant & all other philosophers, he has done ⟨it⟩ 20 times at least—how *should* it be, how *can* it be otherwise, because as why—and as how—&c, and yet ⟨in⟩ *every* remark on Kant he dolefully demonstrates himself old Nic.[3] the Berlin book-scribling Book-shopster & Book-monger.[4]   S. T. COLERIDGE

4 pp 20–1

[Footnote:] Man sollte sich zwar in unserer hochphilosophischen Zeit in Deutschland . . . eigentlich schämen, dass man noch so schwach ist, von der Weisheit, welche wir in allen Gegenständen sehen, auf einen allmächtigen und weisen Urheber durch eine *Induktion* zu kommen, da Herr Kant schon lange zu zeigen gesucht hat, dass sie nicht gelte. Hingegen versichert er freylich, wir wären verbunden einen lieben Gott *anzunehmen*, weil sonst sein neues moralisches System nicht vollständig seyn würde. . . . Wenn man, um Kants moralisches System vollständig

pages which C marked or annotated, perhaps on his first reading: **4A, 12A, 19, 25A, 25B, 27A,** below.

3[1] Nicolai recounts in this work the history of his friendship with G. E. Lessing and Moses Mendelssohn (whose works C also annotated) and his close intellectual association with the latter as a result of their membership in an exclusive society founded in Berlin in 1775. The 100 members of this society met twice a month to discuss the most challenging scientific and philosophical literature of the time. From Nicolai's report it appears that Kant's critical philosophy was a frequent topic of discussion in the society and that its members generally opposed Kant's ethical system (pp 44–5, 64–7 and passim). C may have had this society in mind when he invented a coat of arms for Nicolai.

3[2] "Hypo-criticism", not in *OED*, C's nonce-word for something passing itself off as criticism that is actually inferior to it, "beneath" criticism and also—by association with "hypocrite" and "hypocritical"—pretending to be better than it is.

3[3] "Old Nick", i.e. the Devil: cf MORE *Theological Works* 14 n 3.

3[4] C may be drawing on Kant's essay "Ueber die Buchmacherei, Zwei Briefe an Herrn Friedrich Nicolai", KANT *VS* III 377–88. In the second letter addressed to "Mr Friedrich Nicolai the Publisher", Kant accuses Nicolai of turning the book industry into a mercantile business keyed to the ephemeral taste of the public and to a work's market value rather than its intrinsic value (pp 385–8). Nicolai devotes a long section of his book (pp 105–95) to Kant's essay and to a rebuttal of Kant's charges. C's complaints about Nicolai as an editor of Lessing appear in e.g. LESSING *Sämmtliche Schriften* 1.

zu finden, *nothwendig* eine Idee *annehmen* muss, wovon uns Kant vorher behauptete, dass wir, weil sie übersinnlich ist, *von vorn nichts davon wissen . . . können*; so ist Kants moralisches *System in sich selbst mangelhaft und inkonsequent.*

[We should really be ashamed that in Germany in our highly philosophical age we are still so weak as to infer inductively an almighty and wise creator from the wisdom that we perceive in all things, since Mr Kant has long sought to demonstrate that this *induction* is invalid. On the other hand, he assures us, of course, that we are obliged to *assume* a God, because otherwise his new moral system would not be complete. . . . If, in order to find Kant's moral system complete, we must *necessarily assume* an idea about which Kant asserted before that *we cannot know anything a priori* because it is supersensible, then Kant's moral *system is in itself defective and inconsistent.*]

The whole of Kant's System of Theology proceeds on this plain Principle: *That*, the non-existence of which would involve the non-existence of ~~that~~ some other, which we *know* to exist, must itself have existence.[1] Thus we *know* the existence of the Law of Conscience, "Love thy neighbour as thyself", & the *generic* distinction between Regret & Remorse.[2] Now this would involve a contradiction, if Free Will did not exist—& by the same Process, from Free Will, a super-sensuous Nature is deduced; & again from this Immortality & a God.—But tho' Kant justly denies a positive *demonstrative* force to the arguments a posteriori, for the existence of God, does he not admit that they are inducements of such strength that a man would deserve to be deemed *mad*, who rejected them?

4A　p 22, marked with a horizontal line

"Wir begreifen zwar nicht die praktische unbedingte *Nothwendigkeit* desselben, wir *begreifen* aber doch seine *Unbegreiflichkeit.*" (*S. Metaphysik der Sitten* S. 128).

["We do not comprehend at all its unconditional practical *necessity*, but we do comprehend its *incomprehensibility.*" (See *Metaphysics of Morals*, p. 128.)]

5　p 48

Zwar fand ich beym Durchlesen dieses Werkes [*C d r V*] hin und wieder nicht wenig, was mir Herrn Kants Verheissungen zu widersprechen

---

[1] C's arguments are based on Kant's "Der einzig mögliche Beweisgrund zu einer Demonstration des Daseyns Gottes" (1763) and "The Ideal of Pure Reason" of the first *Critique*. Cf closely related passages in *P Lects* Lects 12 and 13 (1949) 364–5, 388–90.

[2] C used this distinction frequently, e.g. in a lecture of 1808 (*Lects 1808–1819—CC*—ɪ 63–4) and in *P Lects* Lect 12 (1949) 364.

schien, besonders fiel mir die *Arroganz* der meisten Anhänger Kants sehr auf.*

[In perusing this work [*C d r V*] from time to time, I certainly found not a few things that seemed to me to contradict Mr Kant's promises; I was especially struck by the *arrogance* of most of Kant's partisans.*]

* a precious "besonders"![1] and a satisfying proof of the fitness of Nicolai's Mind for the examination of a new Scheme of Philosophy! The Philosopher's Kitchen-maid's Second Cousin gave himself airs—and in the Study of the Philosopher's great Work *this* was what *especially* struck him. Exquisite Nicolai!

6   p 51

Moses [Mendelssohn] sah auch den Vorzug des *Kantischen* Idealismus vor dem *Berkeleyschen* sehr wohl ein. Aber er sah gewiss auch ein, dass diese Zurückführung *aller* Erkcnntniss auf ein angenommenes *rein* von-vorniges Wissen, abgezogen von allem was die Sinne gewähren, und mit Entsagung auf alle Induktionen daraus . . . dennoch entweder bloss in der Idee und Abstraktion bleiben muss, und nie auf die Sinnenwelt angewandt werden kann, oder bey der Anwendung die ärgsten Widersprüche herbeyführt . . .

[Moses [Mendelssohn], no doubt, also saw the superiority of the *Kantian* idealism over the *Berkeleian*. But he also saw, certainly, that the reduction of *all* cognition to a supposed *pure a priori* knowledge, abstracted from all that the senses impart, and with renunciation of all inductions therefrom, nevertheless either must remain merely in the realm of idea and abstraction and never be applied to the world of the senses or, if it is applied, must lead to the worst contradictions . . .]

Is it possible, that N. could really have read the K. d. r. V.? The very object of which is to prove, that without Inductions of the Senses all a priori Conceptions & Ideas "in blosser fruchtlosen Abstraction bleiben müssen"?[1]   *S. T. C.*

5[1] "Especially", in textus.

6[1] "Must remain in mere fruitless abstraction": C is adapting Nicolai's phrase to draw the opposite inference from Kant's premises. C refers to the "Transcendental Analytic" of the first *Critique* (B 146–9) where Kant emphasises the fact that *a priori* concepts of the understanding, though not derived from experience, "become knowledge for us only in so far as"

they are "related to objects of the senses" and "can be applied to empirical intuitions. . . . For as concepts of objects they are then empty, and do not even enable us to judge of their objects whether or not they are possible. They are mere forms of thought, without objective reality. . . . Only *our* sensible and empirical intuition can give them body and meaning" (tr Norman Kemp Smith).

7 p 56

. . . wahr ist's, dass ich die sogenannten *rein vonvornigen Voraussetz-ungen*, worauf ein grosser Theil der *Kritik der praktischen Vernunft* und mit ihr das kantische moralische System beruhet, für *ganz willkürliche Sätze* halte, wenn sie gleich der reinen Vernunft aufgebürdet und *Vernunftsbedürfnisse* betitelt werden . . .

[. . . it is true that I regard the so-called *pure a priori*[1] *principles*, on which a large part of the *Critique of Practical Reason* and with it the Kantian moral system is based, as *completely arbitrary hypotheses* even if they are attributed to pure reason and are labelled *needs of reason* . . .]

What? is the Law of Conscience a mere arbitrary assumption? Kant appeals to a Fact: those who find that Fact in their moral Reason cannot deny the deduction/—for those, who cannot find it, Kant has not written.[2] Such men must be made better, before they can become wiser, men.   *S. T. C.*

8 p 59

Wenn man dann mit grösster-Anstrengung und Unparteylichkeit, mit dem *deutlichsten Denken dieses moralischen Gesetzes*, Kants vermeinten kategorischen Imperativ in seinem Bewusstseyn nicht findet, wenn mehrere Menschen, deren moralisches Gefühl und deren moralische Thätigkeit nur ein Nichtswürdiger in Zweifel ziehen kann, in ihrem *Bewusstseyn* nicht finden können,* dass sie *nothwendig unbedingt* verpflichtet wären, Principe zur Gesetzgebung für alle vernünftige Wesen zu suchen; so darf man behaupten: ein solcher Satz könne kein *Imperativ* noch weniger *kategorisch* seyn . . .

[If, even with the greatest effort and impartiality, and with *the clearest conception of this moral law*, one cannot find in one's consciousness Kant's supposed categorical imperative, if several men whose moral sense and moral activity could be called in doubt only by someone contemptible cannot discover in their consciousness* that they might be *necessarily, unconditionally* obliged to seek principles of legislation for all rational beings, then one may maintain that such a maxim cannot be an *imperative*, still less *categorical*.]

* What vulgar Sophistry! When & where has Kant affirmed it to be a man's Duty to discover principles of Legislation for all intelligent Be-

7[1] For Nicolai's use of *von vorn* and *vonvornig* as equivalent to *a priori* see **17** and n 1.

7[2] Cf *P Lects* Lect 12 (1949) 364, where C, adapting Kant, writes: "We believe it [the existence of God] because it is not a mere idea but a fact, that our conscience bids us do unto others as we would be done by, and in all things to make that a maxim of our conduct, which we can conceive without a contradiction as being the law of all rational beings."

ings? He announces a simple Truth, that A = A. Let *me* act on the same principle, as in the same circumstances I should be obliged by my own reason to demand of another.

9   p 60

Jeder vernünftige Mensch darf also schliessen, man könne sehr moralisch handeln, *ohne* gerade diesen Satz *ausschliessend* zur Maxime seiner moralischen Handlungen zu machen. [Footnote:] Dies läugnen Kant und die Kantianer in dem Uebermasse der Strenge ihrer vonvornigen Moralität; und dies ist es eben wodurch ihr moralisches System *intolerant* wird, bis zur Ungereimtheit.

[Every rational human being may therefore infer that he could act very morally *without* adopting just this principle *exclusively* as the maxim of his moral actions. [Footnote:] This Kant and the Kantians deny, owing to the extreme severity of their *a priori* morality; and this is just how their moral system becomes *intolerant*, to the point of absurdity.]

No! It is absolutely impossible! His Actions may be right; but his Agency can not be moral, unless he does his Duty, because it is his Duty—or at least, strives after this—makes it his *maxim*.

10   p 62

. . . jetzt aber wird alles durch *Postulate* entschieden, welche *Eingebungen* einer *Philosophie* sind, die sich alles selbst *macht*, so wie sie es braucht.

[. . . but now everything is decided according to *postulates*, which are the *inspirations* of a *philosophy* that *creates* for itself everything it needs.]

But is it possible to ground any System except on Postulates? N. forgets the essential Difference of Mathematics & Metaphysics/[1] The latter always involves a certain quantum of *Will*.[2]

10[1] The distinction between mathematics and metaphysics or philosophy in general is frequently analysed by Kant. His pre-critical essay *Untersuchungen über die Deutlichkeit der Grundsätze der natürlichen Theologie und der Moral* (1763) deals specifically with the differences between the methods of achieving certainty in mathematical and philosophical knowledge. C annotated a copy of KANT VS II, which includes this essay.

10[2] Kant does not generally refer to the "quantum of *Will*" as an element of this distinction. C may possibly have in mind Kant's distinction between postulates of geometry and postulates of the moral law in *Critique of Practical Reason* tr T. K. Abbott bk 1 ch 1 § 7: "Pure geometry has postulates which are practical propositions, but contain nothing further than the assumption that we *can* do something if it is required that we *should* do it. . . . They are, then, practical rules under a problematical condition of the will; but here the rule says:—We absolutely must proceed in a certain manner. . . . The will is thought as

11 p 66

Da ich, nebst meinem eigenen Studium . . . mehrere Jahre lang Veranlassung hatte, alle Theile der kritischen Philosophie auf mancherley Art durch mündliche Vorträge und Erörterungen durchzudenken, so darf ich dann wohl glauben, ich verstehe was dazu gehört, und wisse was ihr rechter Gebrauch und ihr Missbrauch sey . . .

[Since, besides my own studies, I had for several years occasion to make a thorough study of all parts of the critical philosophy from various angles through oral discourses and debates, I may surely believe that I understand what pertains to it and know what its proper use or misuse might be . . . .]

This is the 20ᵗʰ or 30ᵗʰ time that Nicolai has anxiously assured us on his word & honor, that he really ~~can~~ does understand thoroughly the Kantéan Philosophy—for &c &c &c[1]—& yet he never makes a critical Remark which does not betray a Book-maker's Ignorance. A Book-making Book-seller! O LORD!   S. T. C.

12 p 67

Zu dem Zwecke dieser vortrefflichen vielleicht in ihrer Art einzigen Gesellschaft . . . war der oben gedachte, in der *deutschen Monatsschrift* gedruckte Aufsatz besonders geeignet. Die Sätze, die ich gegen das Ende . . . aufstelle, sonderlich die Maxime: "Lebe und handele stets *im Verhältnisse deiner Pflichten und Rechte,*" waren eigentlich der Gegenstand der damaligen mündlichen Diskussion.

[The essay referred to above, which was printed in the *Deutsche Monatsschrift*, was particularly adapted to the purposes of this admirable and unique society. The propositions which I advanced towards the end, particularly the maxim "Live and act always *in accordance with your duties and rights*", were really the subject of oral discussion in those days.]

In ~~ordin~~ other and plainer words, the grand maxim of Duty is, Do your Duty!—For what are Rights *morally* considered, but that which it is my Duty to claim—i.e. my Duty to myself.[1]

---

independent on empirical conditions, and, therefore, as pure will determined by *the mere form of the law* . . .".

11[1] Nicolai is indeed quite insistent in his self-praise as a competent reader of Kant. Just two pages before the passage annotated by C (p 64) he writes (tr), "I studied the critical philosophy for over *twelve years before I said any word about it publicly.* I examined and gave earnest and im

partial consideration to all of its parts. . . . One shouldn't therefore wonder that I am so well acquainted with it."

12[1] Like others of his generation subjected to the repetition of claims about the "rights of man"—and, indeed, like the authors of the French *Declaration of the Rights of Man and of the Citizen* (1789) itself—C habitually insisted on the reciprocity of rights and duties, e.g. in *Lects 1795*

12A pp 76–7, marked with ink line

[Footnote:] Im vorigen Jahre kam eine Schrift heraus: *Die Vernunft fordert die Säkularisirungen,* wo die Frage aus vonvornigen Gründen bejahet ward. Sogleich erschien eine Schrift: *Die Vernunft fordert die Säkularisirungen nicht,* worin sie aus eben so *allgemeingültigen vonvornigen* Gründen *verneint* wird. In dieser letztern Schrift wird die Kirche (man merke, dass von der *katholischen* Kirche die Rede ist) folgendergestalt definirt: Kirchen sind Gemeinen "denen sittlich religiöse Wahrheiten verkündigt werden;" ein Fürstbischof ist also, sagt der Verf. *ein Lehrer der Moral.* Da kann nun also die *Vernunft* nicht fordern, dass ein Fürst nicht die Moral lehren solle. *Q. E. D.*—Der Verfasser einer im J. 1797 herausgekommenen Schrift: *Versuch einer ausführlichen Erörterung der Frage:* In wie fern ist der *Successor singularis ex pacto et providentia maiorum, zur Anerkennung der Verträge und Handlungen des Vorfahrs verpflichtet?* behauptet, dass das Fürstliche Haus Taxis das *Postwesen* auch in den Reichs-Ländern jenseit des Rheins welche an die Franzosen abgetreten sind, (so wie der Burgundische Kreis), oder noch abgetreten werden möchten, nothwendig fortführen müsse. Im 11ten Theile verspricht der Verfasser "von dem kaiserlichen Reichspostregal zu handeln, und die Rechte des hochfürstlichen Hauses von Thurn und Taxis, in Bezug auf die Reichspostlehen vorzüglich *nach den Grundsätzen der kritischen Philosophie darzustellen.*" Man sieht aus der Recension dieses Buchs, in der *Salzburgischen Litteraturzeitung* (1798 No. LXIV. S. 1012) wo es gar sehr gelobt wird, dass der Verfasser auch im ersten Theile einen guten Anfang zu einer so originalen philosophischen Deduktion gemacht hat. Ich kenne das Buch nur aus der Recension, wünschte es aber zu besitzen. Ein *Reichspostlehen nach den Grundsätzen der kritischen Philosophie dargestellt,* ist etwas gar zu allerliebstes!—Ein Herr *Westphal,* ein pomposer politischer Quasikantianer, hat neue *Ideen zur Begränzung der einzelnen Gebiete des Naturrecht* (Rostock 1797[–]8.) zur Welt geboren, welche voll ähnlicher ernsthafter Possierlichkeiten sind. Sein *Naturrecht* behauptet: z.B. bey diesen bedrängten Zeiten solle nicht jedermann Pferde halten. "Aber," fährt er fort, "wie soll man denn des Vergnügens des *Spazierenreitens* geniessen, wie diese *Art der Kultur* der *reitenden* Menschen und der zu *reitenden Pferde* erwerben? Auch hier ist *die schönste Harmonie:* Mann mache es zu einem ausschliesslichem *Gegenstand des bürgerlichen* Er-

---

(*CC*) 43 and n 3. In *Watchman* (*CC*) 122* he expresses the relationship as here: "Those duties are called DUTIES which we exercise towards others; those duties are called RIGHTS which we exercise in favour of ourselves."

werbes, mit andern Worten; man bediene sich der *Miethpferde.*'' Nach diesem *Naturrechte* ist der *Haarpuder* ein Misbrauch gegen *die unveräusserlichen Rechte* der *Menschheit*; auch bringt er sonst noch gar feine vonvornige Anmerkungen über den *bürgerlichen Erwerb* und den *Luxus* vor. Daher wünscht auch Herr Westphal, recht treuherzig, seine Schrift möchte ins Französische übersetzt werden, (und ist nur besorgt wegen eines *guten Uebersetzers*), um sie vor den gesetzgebenden Ausschuss der *grossen Nation* zu bringen. Das kann ich nicht wünschen, denn die grosse Nation würde den Bürger Westphal durch eine Deputation aus Rostock abholen lassen, um ihn zu ihrem Finanzminister zu machen, und Deutschland würde ihn verlieren.

[A year ago there appeared a work (*Reason Demands Secularisations*) in which this question was answered in the affirmative on *a priori* grounds. At once there appeared a work (*Reason Does Not Demand Secularisations*) in which the question was answered *in the negative* on equally *universal a priori* grounds. In the latter publication the Church (notice that we are speaking of the *Catholic* Church) is defined in the following manner: churches are communities ''in which moral and religious truths are professed''; a Prince-Bishop, the author says, is, accordingly, *a teacher of morality*. Thus *reason* cannot predicate that a prince should not teach morality. *Q.E.D.*—The author of a work which appeared in 1797 (*An Attempt to Debate Fully the Question "To What Extent is the Successor singularis ex pacto et providentia maiorum* [as an individual [bound] by the prearranged agreement of ancestors] *Obligated to Honour the Agreements and Actions of an Ancestor?''*) contends that the royal house of Taxis has to maintain the *postal service* even in the imperial states on the other side of the Rhine which were surrendered to the French (as was the county of Burgundy) or which might be surrendered. In Part 11 the author promises ''to deal with the imperial postal prerogative and to present in particular the rights of the sovereign princely house of Thurn and Taxis regarding the imperial postal fief *according to the principles of critical philosophy''*. One can tell from the review of this book in the *Salzburgische Litteraturzeitung* (1798 no. 64 p 1012), where it was greatly praised, that in the first part of this work the author had already made a good start on such an original philosophical deduction. I know the book only from the review, though I should have liked to own it. An *imperial postal fief presented according to the principles of critical philosophy*—this is altogether charming! A certain Mr Westphal, a pompous political quasi-Kantian, has brought into the world new *Ideas Concerning the Boundaries of the Individual Provinces of Natural Law*, which is full of similar earnestly ludicrous ideas. His *natural law* states, for example, that in these hard times not everyone should be allowed to keep horses. ''But,'' he continues, ''how can one enjoy the amusement of *riding for pleasure*, and how does one attain the *civilised art* of the *horseman* and the *riding horse*? Here, too, there is *the most beautiful harmony*: one should make it into an exclusive *object of bourgeois* profit; in other words, one should make use of a *hired horse.*'' According to this *natural law*, *hair-powder* is a violation of the *inalienable rights* of *mankind*; he offers, moreover, quite fine *a priori* remarks concerning *bourgeois profit* and *luxury*. Hence

Mr Westphal desires quite candidly to have his work translated into French (and is only concerned about a *good translator*) in order to bring it before the executive committee of the *great Nation's* legislature. I cannot desire this, for the great Nation would send a delegation to fetch Citizen Westphal away from Rostock in order to make him their minister of finance, and Germany would lose him.]

13   pp 112–13

. . . Neigungen gehören eben so nothwendig zum Wesen des Menschen, als Verstand, Gedächtniss, Einbildungskraft u.s.w. . . . Sogar mit grosser Stärke der Neigungen und Leidenschaften kann man edel und vernünftig moralisch seyn, wenn man nur *sich selbst recht kennt*, und wenn die Kraft der Vernunft *stärker* ist als alle innere Triebe, um diese sicher zu regieren. . . . Es scheint . . . seine [Kants] Neigungen können seine Philosophie gar leicht *stören*, und was ihn *stört*, sey es Neigung oder Abneigung, möchte er sich gern kurzweg *vom Halse schaffen*, so wie z.B. mich.

[. . . Inclinations are just as indispensable to the being of man as understanding, memory, imagination, and so on. . . . Even when the inclinations and passions [become] more intense, one may nevertheless be noble and sensible if one *knows oneself well*, and if the power of reason is *greater* than all the inner impulses, so as to rule over them safely. . . . It appears . . . that his [Kant's] inclinations can very easily *disturb* his philosophy, and what *disturbs* him, be it inclination or disinclination, he would simply like to get rid of, like me, for example.]

What does Kant mean by Neigungen? Evidently, Hankerings, Proneness; from blind Feelings or Habits—& is there any moral man who does not with St Paul desire to be delivered *"from the Body of this Death?"*[1] But all ⟨old⟩ Nic's criticisms are of the same stamp—Ignorance with her two Supporters; the Parrot of garrulous Egotism, that for ever repeats "Pretty Poll!" and the mousing Owl of trifling ‡ Hypo-criticism.[2] Here he has confounded Neigung with Trieb.[3]

14   p 113

Ich hoffe, zur Ehre Herrn Kants, die Anekdote wenigstens der letzte Theil ist nicht auf diese Art wahr, und der Erzähler der recht aus dem Grunde loben will . . . hat nur nicht verstanden, wie man eigentlich einen berühmten Mann loben muss.

[I hope for Mr Kant's sake that the anecdote, at least the last part of it, is not

<hr>

13[1] Rom 7.24, q also in Luther *Colloquia* **47** at n 1.

13[2] Cf **3** above.

13[3] "Inclination" with "impulse".

true in this way, and that its author who wishes to praise profoundly . . . merely did not know how to praise a famous man properly.]

What if it had been?[1] Malice itself, one should think, would be puzzled to detect in it any thing worse than a Whim. As a young student, I should have been pleased to have so long fixed on me the eye & countenance of a Kant, even tho' the Want of a Button had been the cause. Any trifle is pleasing that brings one into connection with a truly great man. It makes a harmless anecdote for the family Fireside.   S. T. C.

15 p 114

. . . so darf ich ohne stolz oder eitel zu seyn, wohl wissen, dass ich nunmehr über das was Litteratur und Philosophie und ihren Gebrauch und Missbrauch betrift, wohl ein Wort mitsprechen und allenfalls mit Zuversicht die edelsten und einsichtsvollesten deutschen Gelehrten fragen kann: Ob es Herrn Kant nicht gebührt hätte, mit mir in dem anständigen Tone zu sprechen, den ich gegen ihn nie vergass . . .

[. . . without being proud or vain, I am surely entitled to voice an opinion on literature and philosophy and the use and abuse of them, and can at all events confidently ask the noblest and most judicious German scholars whether it had not been Mr Kant's duty to speak to me in that respectful tone which I never forget to use towards him . . .]

Hoot! Hoot! Pretty Poll! Pretty Poll![1]

16 p 115, partly pencil

. . . ich werde Gründe hinzuthun, woraus jeder Unparteyische sehen wird, dass Herr Kant verdient, dass ernsthaft und ohne Umschweife mit ihm gesprochen werde, damit er aus seinem vonvornigen Dünkel erwache. . . . Eben dieser Gründe wegen muss ich *weitläuftiger* werden als mir lieb ist.

[. . . I shall add reasons from which every impartial observer will see that Mr Kant deserves to be spoken to seriously and bluntly, so that he wakes up from his *a priori* arrogance. . . . Just for these reasons I shall have to go into *greater detail* than I should like.]

14[1] Nicolai reports an anecdote about Kant which appeared in an essay in *Jahrbücher der preussischen Monarchie* (Jan 1799). Apparently Kant, who was in the habit of staring at a student during his lectures, had for some time settled his gaze on a young man whose coat had a button missing. When the student finally replaced the button and appeared in class, Kant could not concentrate for the entire hour of his lecture and later called the student to his office in order to ask him to remove the button.

15[1] Cf **3, 11, 13** above.

Etwas gar zu allerliebstes!ᵃ "als ihm lieb ist!" [1] He is so Spartan in Brevity when he speaks of Himself!

17   p 116, pencil

[Footnote:] Irgend ein Recensent hat mich recht zutraulich ermahnet, mich doch zu schämen, dass ich *von vorn* anstatt *a priori* brauche; als ob es, an sich, etwa unrecht wäre philosophische Benennungen deutsch zu geben . . .

[Some reviewer has very frankly admonished me to feel ashamed because I use *von vorn* ["from before"] instead of *a priori*; as if it were improper in itself to give philosophical terms in German . . .

N. only confirms his ignorance by this Note; "Vonvornige" is not the translation, much less the meaning of *a priori*.[1]

18   p 118, pencil

Aber wahrlich, nicht erst die *Kritik der reinen Vernunft* durfte mich über den Unterschied der Erkenntnisse *a priori* und der Erfahrungserkenntnisse belehren. Leibnitz hat lange vor Herrn Kant gesagt, dass *Notwendigkeit* und *Allgemeinheit* Merkmale der Erkenntnisse *a priori* sind.

[But truly it was not the *C d r V* that first taught me the difference between judgments *a priori* and empirical judgments. Long before Mr Kant, Leibniz had said that *necessity* and *universality* are marks of knowledge *a priori*.]

True! Kant's Friend, Schmidt, in his Wörterbuch der K. Philos. had given Nic. this p scrap of philosophic History[1]

19   p 119, pencil

[Citing Leibniz *Essais*:] S. 33. "J'oppose les *verités nécessaires* ou de *raison*, aux *verités de fait*. Dans ce sens on doit dire que toute l'Arithmetique et toute la Géometrie sont innées et sont *en nous d'une manière virtuelle*, en sorte qu'on les y peut trouver en considerant attentivement et rangeant *ce qu'on a deja dans l'espirit*, sans se servir *d'aucune verité*

ᵃ Ink ends here, and pencil takes over

16[1] "How utterly charming! [more] 'than he likes!' " (the last words paraphrasing textus).

17[1] C's objection is justified. By "*a priori*" Kant means not antecedent to (*vonvornig*) but rather independent of experience.

18[1] In *Wörterbuch zum leichtern Gebrauch der Kantischen Schriften* (Jena 1788, 3rd ed 1795) 11–18, Carl Christian Erhard Schmid points out the resemblance between Kant's theory of knowledge *a priori* and Leibniz's doctrine of innate ideas. It is not known which edition of Schmid's dictionary C used.

apprise par l'experience.'' Hier findet man auch gerade das was Herr Kant von der Apriorität der mathematischen Kenntnisse behauptet.

[P. 33. "I oppose *necessary truths* or *truths of reason* to *truths of fact*. In this sense one may say that all arithmetic and all geometry are innate and are *in us virtually*, in such a way that one can find them by carefully considering and ordering *what already exists in the mind* without the assistance *of any truth learned by experience.''* Here one also finds precisely what Kant maintains about the apriority of mathematical judgments.]

But Leibnitz did not, and on his system could not explain the apodictic nature of Geometry: for he considered Space as confused Perception, of course, derived from experience.[1] Now Geometry consists in modifications of Space—ergo, dependent on experience—ergo, ought to be contingent. Kant's first great discovery was the a priority of the Forms of Space & T~~empus~~ime[2]—& thus was enabled, first of all philosophers, to explain the nature of Number, & the *synthetic* character both of Arithmetic & Geometry/ by which he has given the Death-blow to Hume's & Berkley's Scepticism./[3]

20   p 120, pencil

[Footnote:] Aber Leibnitz bemerkt auch sehr richtig S. 414: "Pour ce qui est des *verités éternelles* il faut observer, que dans le fonds elles sont toutes *conditionelles* et disent en effêt: *telle chose posée,* telle autre chose est. Par exemple disant: *toute figure qui aura trois cotés aura trois angles,* je ne dis autre chose que, *supposé* qu'il y ait une figure à trois cotés, *cette même figure* aura trois angles.'' Was Leibnitz hier und an andern Orten seines trefflichen Werks sagt, kann sehr zur Erläuterung dessen dienen, was Herr Kant von den *reinen synthetischen Begriffen a priori* behauptet. Es wird einem wieder ganz wohl zu Muthe, wenn man

19[1] Cf *Logic* (*CC*) 160, where C states that Leibniz "grievously erred in representing it [space] as nothing more than a confused perception arising out of the indistinctness of all particular figures . . .''. He echoes Kant's objections to Leibniz in the "Transcendental Dialectic'' of the first *Critique*.

19[2] Cf C's letter to Pryce of Apr 1818 on Kant's merit of explaining "the ground of the apodeixis in Mathematics: which neither Leibniz nor Plato had attained to—and this he did by proving that Space and Time were . . . the pure a priori forms of the intuitive faculty'': *CL* iv 852. In *De Mundi sensibilis atque intelligibilis forma*

et principiis (1770) §§ 15C and 15D, Kant argues that the principles of geometry are *a priori* and known with apodeictic certainty, and that Leibniz's theory of space had the effect of degrading geometry to a science based on empirical concepts.

19[3] I.e. to the two philosophical extremes (as C saw it) of materialism and idealism. Transcendental idealism integrates subject and object, perceiver and perceived, according to C's argument in *BL* ch 12 (*CC*) i 252–89. Kant discusses the concept of number and the synthetic character of mathematics in *C d r V* B 14–18, 205–6.

lange sich mit Kants dunkler und schwerfälliger Schreibart hat quälen müssen, Leibnitzens bestimmte Begriffe und deutliche Schreibart zu erblichen.*

[But Leibniz also observes very correctly on p 414: "As for the *eternal truths*, it must be observed that fundamentally they are all *conditional* and in effect mean: *if such a thing be posited*, such another thing exists. For example, when I say "Every figure that has three sides will have three angles", I am saying no more than "*Supposing* that there is a figure with three sides, *this same figure* will have three angles." What Leibniz says here and elsewhere in his excellent work is quite useful in elucidating what Mr Kant means by *pure synthetic concepts a priori*. After being forced to endure for a long time the agony of dealing with Kant's obscure and clumsy style of writing, one regains one's cheerfulness entirely when one comes across Leibniz's precise concepts and clear style of writing.*]

After all, this Division of innate or a priori, & a posteriori, is perhaps rather logico-psychological, than essential, or metaphysical: and originates in the limitation of our knowlege & intellectual Powers. We have ⟨no⟩ proof, that the Perception ⟨of a Tree⟩ is given in to, or mirrored in, the mind, by an exactly correspondent and distinct Arbor perceptus,[1] than of a pure Circle.—But Leibnitz in his "*conditionelles*"[2] confounds the auxiliary *Image* with the *Idea*,[3] and with the Truths evolved out of it—in our present state, by *occasion* of the Image.

* This quotation renders it suspicious, that L. had not a full & stedfast View of the essential Distinction between necessary ⟨truths⟩ & experimental *facts*[4]—This "*suppose*"[5] would imply that a mathematical Triangle was of the nature of a *Fact*. Besides, it is not true. We never think of an hypothesis—this *is* a Triangle &c—

21   p 121 pencil

Wenn ich—und wahrhaftig auch *Möser* und andere vernünftige Leute— Leibnitzens Schriften gelesen hatten, so bedurften wir wahrlich Herrn Kants Belehrung* über *a priori* nicht.

[After I—and indeed also Möser and other intelligent people—had read Leibniz's writings, we truly did not need Mr Kant to enlighten us* about *apriority*.]

20[1] "Tree perceived".

20[2] "*Conditional*" truths, from textus.

20[3] C consistently maintained the opposite characters of idea and image, as in *BL* chs 8, 12, 14 (*CC*) ɪ 135, 288–9, ɪɪ 17.

20[4] The definition of a "fact", as noted in KANT *C d r V* 5 n 3, was of considerable importance to C. In *Friend* (*CC*) ɪ 158 he works out the distinction between "*facts*, or things of *experience*" and "truths of *science* . . . which it is impossible to conceive otherwise"; on ɪ 358 he remarks, "how mean a thing a mere fact is, except as seen in the light of some comprehensive truth".

20[5] "Supposing", from textus.

* From Pythagoras & Plato down to Leibnitz without excepting Aristotle (rightly interpreted) on[a] any but the followers of Epicurus, all admitted the distinction between Truths & Facts.[1] Kant's merit is two fold/ 1. the full analysis & arrangement of the Reason as distinct from the Understanding. 2. the discovery of the *Forms* of Sense.[2]

22   p 122, pencil

[Footnote, on Kant's *Anthropologie*:] "*Man* sage ja nicht, dass wenigstens di *Mathematik* privilegirt sey, *aus eigener Machtvollkommenheit abzusprechen*; denn *wäre nicht die wahrgenommene durchgängige Uebereinstimmung der Urtheile des Messkünstlers mit dem Urtheile aller andern*, die sich diesem Fache mit Talent und Fleiss widmeten, *vorhergegangen*, so würde *sie selbst* der Besorgniss *irgendwo in Irrthum zu fallen, nicht entnommen seyn*." Man möchte fast seinen Augen nicht trauen, wenn man Hrn. Kants *beständige Behauptung* der *apodiktischen Kraft* der vonvornigen Begriffe kennt, und obiges Urtheil, sogar über die Mathematik, *in einer seiner Schriften* findet.

["*One* may not on any account say that at least *mathematics* should be privileged *to judge on its own authority*; for *even it itself* would *not be exempt from the* apprehension *of somewhere falling into error if it had not been preceded by the perceived universal correspondence of the geometrician's judgments with the judgments of all others* who devote themselves to this discipline with talent and diligence." One could hardly believe one's eyes, knowing Mr Kant's *constant assertion* of the *apodictic force* of *a priori* concepts and yet finding the above judgment concerning mathematics *in one of his writings*.]

This M[r] Nic. here confounds ⟨the⟩ *conception* of a Truth with the *feeling* of satisfaction & positiveness.[1] Kant is speaking of the Latter. Besides, Nic. did not notice or comprehend the force of the word "irgendwo"[2]— The Doubt would arise not from the component Truths, but in the Linking of them.

23   p 145, red crayon

Antwort: die *Kritik der praktischen Vernunft* lehret S. 64: "Was Pflicht ist, bietet sich jedermann von selbst dar—dem *kategorischen* Gebote der Sittlichkeit *Genüge zu leisten* ist *in jedes Gewalt zu aller Zeit*."—

[a] A slip for "or"?

21[1] See **20** n 4 above.

21[2] On Kant's "discovery of the *Forms* of Sense" see **19** above; the importance of the distinction between reason and understanding is outlined and glossed in Leighton copy c **12** esp nn 5, 6.

22[1] Cf Mendelssohn *Morgenstunden*

3, where C finds a similar confusion between "certainty" and "positiveness", and *Morgenstunden* 6, where C points out the "essential disparity" between certainty and positiveness in relation to the distinction between "sense" and "sensation".

22[2] "Somewhere", from textus.

Schön! da können wir ja unsere Pflicht *ganz* erfüllen, wenn wir gleich *ungern* daran gehen und die *Pflicht jederzeit* eine *Nöthigung* ist, obschon es zugleich auch *Pflichten* giebt, denen wir uns zu unterwerfen auch unmittelbare *Neigung* haben.

[Answer: the *Critique of Practical Reason* teaches on p 64: "What constitutes duty presents itself to everyone—*to do justice* to the *categorical* imperative of morality is *within everyone's power at all times*."—Fine! We can thus do our duty *completely* even if we undertake it *reluctantly*; and duty is *always* an *obligation*, although at the same time there are also *duties* to which we immediately feel *inclined* to submit.]

This Berlin*ᵃ* Bookseller of all blockhead Impertinents is the most impertinent Blockhead! His friend, Mendelssohn might have taught him that Nöthigung means a moral or hypothetical, not a physical, Necessity— the necessity, which every good mind acknowleges in "Thou *shouldst* do thy Duty—and *if* thou *wouldst then* thou *must* do so or so."

S. T. C.

24   p 146, red crayon

. . . und dennoch können wir, der *Sittenmetaphysik* S. 26 zufolge, in keinem *einzigen Falle* wissen, ob unsere *Maxime* . . . *lediglich* auf der *Vorstellung der Pflichte beruhe*, welche wir doch zu jeder Zeit in unserer Gewalt haben sollen? * Das läuft betrübt unphilosophisch unter einander!

[. . . and nevertheless, according to the *Metaphysic of Morals* p 26, can we know in any *single case* whether our *maxim* . . . is *based purely* on the *conception of duty* which we are supposed to have in our power at all times? * This jumbles everything in a sadly unphilosophical manner!]

* Yes! and so would a Picture of Raphael's to an Idiot with the gummy Tears of Dotage in his eyes.—He too would exclaim, like Nicolai "Das läuft betrübt unmahlerisch unter einander."[1]

25   pp 146–7, red crayon

Herr Kant hatte entweder S. 61 *vergessen, dass er S. 26 behauptet hatte, "es sey *schlechterdings unmöglich* in einem einzigen Falle zu wissen, ob die Maximen unserer Handlungen auf *moralischen* Gründen *lediglich* beruhten;" oder er muss der Meinung seyn, jeder Mensch könne *schlechterdings unmöglich* wissen, ob er sich *selbst verachten* und *innern Abscheu* gegen sich haben müsse . . .

ᵃ First two words in ink, overtraced in crayon

24[1] Adapting textus, "This jumbles everything in a sadly unpainterly manner."

[Either Mr Kant *forgot on p 61 that he had claimed on p 26 that "it is *absolutely impossible* to know in a single case whether the maxims of our actions are based *purely* on *moral* grounds", or he must be of the opinion that it is *absolutely impossible* for any man to know whether he ought to *despise himself* and feel an *inner loathing* towards himself . . .]

* Where lies the contradiction? I cannot, indeed, be empirically certain of the *absolute* purity of my motives in any one particular act; yet surely any, but a publishing Bookseller, would despise ⟨himself⟩ if he did not *aim* at doing his Duty *because* it is his Duty; if he did not make it his Maxim̶u̶m̶, i.e. principium maximum.[1]   S. T. Coleridge

25A   p 159, marked with a horizontal line

". . . schwarz gekleidet gingen, das Gebot des Stifters mit abdrucken liess: *Que les moins doivent être vêtus de* blanc."

[". . . they went dressed in black, the author's printed instruction read, 'That monks ought to be dressed in white'."]

25B   p 182, marked with a horizontal line

[Quoting Fénelon:] *Monseigneur, pourquoi me dites-vous des injures pour des raisons? auriez-vous pris mes raisons pour des injures?*

["Why, my lord, do you give me insults instead of reasons? Is it because you found my reasons insulting?"]

26   p 252, partly pencil

Selbst, wenn ein Philosoph sogar die Existenz Gottes läugnete, und er verwirrte nur nicht mit seinen grillenhaften Ideen die Gemüther der Jugend, welche noch nicht selbst denken kann, sondern Unterricht bedarf, dargestalt, dass sie zum bürgerlichen Leben untüchtiger würde, und es entstünde sonst keine Unruhe im Staate dadurch; so könnte man meines Erachtens solche leere Paradoxie sicher sich selbst überlassen . . .

[Even is a philosopher denied the existence of God, but if he did not with his eccentric ideas confuse the minds of young people who could not yet think for themselves and were in need of instruction to the extent that they became unfit for civic life, and if nevertheless no unrest in the state arose thereby, then one could, in my opinion, leave such empty paradoxes to their own fate . . .]

What a venemous Blind-worm this N! the malice in the "wenn er nur

25[1] C traces "maxim" to *principium maximum*, "greatest principle", in a variant of his usual etymology from *regula maxima*, "greatest rule", as in Leighton COPY C **30** at n 1.

nicht"[a1]—Don't injure Fichte! only drive him out of house and home, and shut up his Shop![2]

27 p 252, pencil

Fichtens Meinung über die *Realität der Existenz der Sinnenwelt* ist so beschaffen, dass man dieses beynahe glauben sollte. Er kann und wird niemand damit verwirren, als höchstens seine Zuhörer; denn man weiss, dass dergleichen junge Leute, sonderlich in spekulativen Dingen, alles glauben was ihr Professor sagt; wie könnte sonst jedes System der theoretischen Philosophie, sey es wie es sey, immer auf Universitäten so warme Anhänger finden!

[Fichte's view on the *real existence of the world of the senses* is so constituted that one ought almost to believe it. It cannot and will not confuse anyone except at most his listeners; for we know that such young people believe everything their professor says, especially in speculative matters; how else could every system of theoretical philosophy, no matter what it is like, always find such passionate followers in the universities!]

This low-born Wretch was, doubtless, entitled to judge of the minds & moods of Gentlemen at the University?—The impudence of his Ignorance, of this Chimney-sweep so proud of two or three patches of white left on his sooty Rags ~~by~~ after thrusting himself in among a Group of Meal-men & Millers!—   *S. T. C.*

27A p 253, marked with a line in the margin

Es gesellete sich zu den Widerspänstigen bald ein zahlreicher Pöbel, der schrie und lärmte, dass niemand sein Wort verstehen konnte. Der Civilobrigkeit ward bange, und sie schickte zum Kommandanten, um die unruhigen Köpfe durch militärische Gewalt auseinander zu treiben. Der General liess die Truppen anrücken, aber ehe sie sich hatten versammeln können, war der Pöbel zu tausend und mehr angewachsen, und erfüllte beynahe den ganzen Markt Kopf an Kopf. Von den andern Seite marschirte aus der Hauptstrasse das Militär in furchtbarer Ordnung auf, und dehnte sich über die ganze Breite des Marktes aus, mit einer Kanone auf jedem Flügel. Der General ritt vor, den unruhigen Haufen zu ermahnen

_____

[a] Quotation marks and remainder of note in pencil

26[1] Adapting textus, "if . . . [he] did not" or "so long as he did not".

26[2] C refers to Fichte's expulsion from Jena in 1798 after he published his friend F. K. Forberg's essay "Development of the Idea of Religion" with a prefatory essay of his own in the philosophical journal of which he was co-editor. He was accused of atheism, he was forced to resign his chair of philosophy at Jena, and his journal was confiscated. C refers to these events in *BL* ch 9 (*CC*) I 155 without identifying Fichte by name.

auseinander zu gehen, weil sonst seine Leute schiessen würden. Aber das Getümmel und das Drohen ward noch viel ärger. ''Nun!''—rief er— ''Ihr wollt es nicht anders haben! Schreibt euch nun selbst zu was geschehen wird!'' So ritt er zu seinen Leuten zurück.

[Soon a large mob joined the rebellious people, shouting and making a tumult so that no one could make out a word. The civil authorities were alarmed, and they sent for the commandant in order to disperse the troublemakers by military force. The general had the troops advance, but before they could assemble the mob had grown to over a thousand people and, tightly packed, filled nearly the entire market. On the other side the army marched from the main street in terrifying order, and spread over the entire width of the market with a cannon in each wing. The general was riding ahead in order to admonish the turbulent crowd to disperse, because otherwise his people would shoot. But the turmoil and the threats became much worse. ''All right!''—he shouted—''That's the way you want it! Blame yourselves for what happens!'' Thus he rode back to his people.]

28 p 255, pencil

[Nicolai is describing Voltaire's poem *Les systèmes*.] Es erschien zuerst der *Heil. Thomas von Aquino*. Er redete den lieben Gott an:

> *Vous êtes*, lui dit-il, *l'existence et l'essence,*
> *Simple avec attributs, acte pur, et substance,*
> *Dans les temps, hors des temps, fin, principe, et milieu,*
> *Toujours présent partout, sans être en aucun lieu.*

[First appeared St Thomas Aquinas. He addressed God: ''*You are*, he said to him, *existence and essence, singular with attributes; pure act, and substance, inside time, outside time; end, principle, and means, always omnipresent, yet nowhere.*'']

I can perceive the blasphemy in this poem (*if* RHYMES can make a poem, and those too FRENCH Rhymes) but for the Life of me, I cannot see the Wit. Even according to Voltaire's own account Thomas Aquinas uttered in those words (with exception of ''Dans les temps'',[1] which is V's own folly) more and more important truth, than Voltaire had Head to understand, or Heart to appreciate.

29 p 255

Darauf kam *Cartesius*:

> *Seigneur*, dit-il à Dieu, *ce bon homme Thomas*
> *Du rêveur Aristote a trop suivi les pas.*
>   Voici mon argument, que me semble invincible:
> *Pour être, c'est assez que vous soyez possible. . . .*

28[1] ''Within time'', from textus.

Nun kam *Spinoza*:

> Esprit subtil et creux, moins lu que célèbré,
> Caché sous le manteau de Descartes son maitre,
> Marchant à pas comptés, s'approcha du grand Etre.
> *Pardonnez-moi*, dit-il, en lui parlant tout bas;
> *Mais je pense, entre nous, que vous n'existez pas.*

[Thereupon came Descartes: *"Lord*, said he to God, *this fellow Thomas has followed that dreamer Aristotle too closely.* Here is my argument, which I think is invincible: *To be, it is enough that you should be possible."* . . . Now came Spinoza, "a subtle and hollow thinker, more widely known than read, hidden under the mantle of his master Descartes. With measured tread he approached the great Being. *Forgive me,* he said, speaking softly, *but between ourselves, I don't believe you exist."*]

I remember no Philosophers who have[a] so grossly misunderstood, as Des Cartes and Spinoza.[1]

30   p 259, pencil

Ich widerhole es: Ueber einen Mann, dem sein Einkommen oder seine bürgerliche Existenz genommen wird, kann kein Wohldenkender weder lachen noch auch einmal dessen Meinunge widerlegen.

[I repeat: No high-minded man can either laugh at or refute the opinions of a man who is deprived of his income and of his civil existence.]

nur wenn er nicht—Fichte ist![1]

31   p 259, pencil

Wir sind ja alle nichts als *Produkte* seines [Fichtes] übersinnlichen weltregierenden *Ich's.* Wir sind nichts als ein *Widerschein* seiner *Uebersinnlichkeit.* Er darf uns nur *nicht denken*, und siehe! wir sind *annihilirt.* Wir armen *Fichtischen Ideen!*

[Indeed, we are all nothing but *products* of his [Fichte's] supersensuous world-governing *"I"*. We are nothing but a *reflection* of his *supersensuousness.* He has only to *stop thinking* of us, and lo and behold! we are *annihilated.* We poor *Fichtean ideas!*]

What Gander's Gabble!—A green Eye-Glass might, at least ought to, have taught even old Nic better![1]

<hr>

[a] For "have been"?

29[1] C frequently complained that Spinoza and Descartes were misunderstood: e.g. JACOBI **3**, **4**, MENDELSSOHN *Morgenstunden* **11**, **12** (Spinoza); *Logic (CC)* 184* (Descartes).

30[1] Echoing **26**, "as long as he is not—Fichte!"

31[1] For "old Nic" see **3** and n 3.

JOSEPH NICOLSON

fl 1762

RICHARD BURN

1720–1785

Copy A

The History and Antiquities of the Counties of Westmorland and Cumberland. 2 vols. London 1777. 4°.

British Library C 126 k 3

Inscribed by C in pencil on I ⁻4: "S. T. Coleridge March 13ᵗʰ, 1804"; and again in pencil on II ⁻2: "S. T. Coleridge 7, Barnard's Inn Holborn at J. Tobin's Esqre March 13, 1804 bought at Mʳ Ryan's 353 Oxford Sᵗ." Inscribed by John Duke Coleridge on I ⁻4: "C" and "Coleridge Heath's Court 1892." "S. T. C." label on title-page of each volume and "S. T. C." inscribed on the title-page of I. Pencilled notes on I 53, 55 are not in C's hand, and passages associated with these notes by their use of small pencilled crosses on I 162 are also not recorded here. Notes **1, 4, 6, 7** in COPY A correspond to **1, 2, 3, 4** in COPY B.

DATE. C took these vols to Malta and Italy, and the annotation is of that period, Apr 1804 – Jul 1806: **9** is dated 29 Aug 1805, and cf *CN* II 2442, 2443.

1 I 1–2, pencil

Westmorland, *Westmoreland*, or as it is anciently written *Westmerland*, hath its name . . . from its being a *western moorish* country. . . . Nevertheless, there is not one ancient record that we have met with, wherein it is not expressly called *Westmerland*, and not *Westmorland*, or *Westmoreland* . . .

Why *not* the Westward *Mere* Land?/ It is ⟨so⟩ beyond all doubt/ Rydal*mere*, Thyrl*mere*, Gras*mere*, Winder*mere*, Kent*mere*, Coniston*mere*/ whereas in Cumberland the Lakes are, if I do not greatly mistake without any exception called *Waters*/ Derwent*water*, Wast*water*, Lows*water*, the water of Bassenthwaite ⟨or Broadwater,⟩ &c, and the only Lakes in Westmereland called Waters, (Ulswater, Broadwater, Hawswater) are on the very border of Cumberland/ I once started but immediately rejected, a new etymol. for Cumberland, to wit, Coomb-bruer-land, i.e. Hether dale land/ or Cum may be (thought I) = Cam, the Top or rather

974

ridge along the Top of the Mountain, as the Comb on the Cock's head—
exactly as Catcheda-*cam* on Helvellin/ *Comb*ruerland.

2 1 2, pencil

* If the county had bordered upon the *western sea*, it might have been
conjectured that it had received its name from thence; but as Cumberland
lies between this county and the sea on the west, it can scarcely admit
of that derivation.

* This Objection falls to the Ground, if you suppose that the People of
Durham & Northumberland gave the name.[1] Never the less it is not im-
probable, that it should be written *Wast*mereland, as *Wast*dale/. So the
waste Ward to the *North* of Calbeck is spoken and written Westward/
and often in the Cumberland Pronunciation I have heard Wast~~dale~~water
clipped into a sort of Wes (or Waes) water.

3 1 2, pencil

[The authors confess themselves unable to explain why it is that in West-
morland two miles by standard English measure are counted as three.
"It hath no reference to the Roman mile."] In some parts of Westmor-
land, the customary acre [4840 square yards] is measured to 7840 yards;
as if where the land is bad, they were willing to give so much the greater
measure. And there was good reason for this, inasmuch as they propor-
tioned the military duty according to the number of acres that a man
possessed. But this could be no rule as to the miles: there being no rea-
son, where the road was bad, that therefore they should make the miles
so much the longer.*

* May not the Reason be this: that in bad roads and mountain Countries
men are more home-tied, travel but a short way, yet have to travel it
daily or weekly/ & so by habit find it *short*. How wearisomely long a
new road seems, if we are rather anxious to be at the end of our journey,
than pleased with the road and its scenery/ and even then pleasure
equally with pain shall make it appear long by multiplying the con-
sciousnesses.

4 1 3, pencil

This county abounds with MOUNTAINS, which in the language of the
country are called *Fells*, this being the genuine Saxon appellation, and
the word is yet retained as an epithet in our language, to signify some-

2[1] Because Westmorland is west of those
counties.

thing that is wild and boisterous, as we say a *fell* tempest, a *fell* tyrant, or the like.*

* In this sense a playful Thought might not inaptly bemotto Cumber- & *Westmere*-land as "Fellest of the Fell". *Thomson's Seasons*.[1]

5 I 3, pencil

. . . in almost every little village there is water sufficient to carry a mill; which renders the precarious help of windmills superfluous: though, if need should be, there are few countries better situate for such like conveniences.

a somewhat droll way of saying, that it is an ill-weathered Climate.

6 I 8–9, pencil

* In modern military language, a *Maiden* fort signifies one that has never been taken, by reason of its extraordinary strength. But that could never be applicable to this small fortification upon Stanemore. It rather seems to be derived of the Anglo-Saxon *Mai* (*maigan, magan, magnum*) great, and *Dun* a hill.

* Is it not possible that *maden* may have been the participle of the old word, of which made is now both preterite and participle? = bid, bidden:[1] and that Maiden may be one of the many unconscious Puns in our language (Bird-cage Walk for Boccage)[2] when either the true word has become obsolete or the sense no longer *appropriate*. When the Roman Roads were the ⟨sole⟩ artificial roads, all others being only *Tracks*; when fortresses were chiefly natural strong-holds, or of stones without cement, á the *made* Road, the *made* Stronghold, would be a most appropriate and natural Phrase. Afterwards the appropriateness ceasing, the word altering, and another signification of the same Sounds (Maden) presenting no sense indeed, but a very pretty *Feeling* (and we do not seek for much more in names either of men, places or animals), the word became *Maiden*/ & was adopted in its new sense and appropriated in the modern Milit. Scien[ce.][a]

a Letters lost in cropping

4[1] From Thomson's *Seasons*, in the versions published 1728–38: "The spotted tyger, fellest of the fell" (*Spring* line 773). The passage was later rewritten and this line dropped. Cf COPY B **2** and n 1.

6[1] I.e. C speculates that by analogy with "bid" the simple past tense and past participle of "make" might once have been "made" and "maden". *OED* supports neither C's theory nor the one in textus.

6[2] Birdcage Walk in London, alongside St James's Park, was named for the aviary there that was extended, if not established, by Charles II. The source of C's incorrect etymology is not known; it may be his own.

7 I 21, pencil

. . . there was another tenure in Westmorland, which hath greatly puzzled antiquarians to explain or understand. It was called DRENGAGE. . . . Sir Henry Spelman . . . . conjectures upon the whole, that the *Drenges* were free tenants holding by military service.

I conjecture, that no particular Tenure is meant by Drengage, but that Dreng (Drenga) signifies *compulsory Service* in general, or its most complete, unmitigated state—that it ⟨is⟩ near akin to Thraldom, and might be translated, *oppressive* Service, and derived from dringen, to force forward or press upon as in a crowd—whence *gedränge*—the German prefixing the *ge* collective or cumulative, which we affix—so gehaüse = housa*ge*.[1]

8 I 24, pencil

And for this widow's estate is due to the lord an HERIOT . . . a recompence, in order to provide things necessary for the marching of the army; as the word *heriot* imports, being of Saxon original, derived of *here*, an army, and *yate* or *gate*, a march or expedition. And this *heriot* was anciently the best beast of the deceased.

Possibly the Lord's Due; was an den Herrn geht,[1] a *Herr yate/* what goes to the Lord/ Peace or War, the best of the quick or dead was the Lord's *Legacy*.

8A I 190, marked with a large pencilled cross

In the year 1723, John Kelsick of Ambleside gentleman devised to John Mackereth yeoman, George Cumpstone yeoman, and Tomas Knott clerk, all of Ambleside aforesaid, and to the survivors and survivor of them, their heirs and assigns for ever, all his lands at Ambleside, in trust, to sell part thereof for payment of debts and legacies, and to let the rest to farm, and with the profits and rents of the same to build a school-house as near the chapel in Ambleside as conveniently may be, and afterwards to pay the rents and profits to a schoolmaster to be chosen

---

7[1] C is speculating creatively, in the spirit of John Horne Tooke's *Diversions of Purley* (2 pts 1786—repr 1798—and 1805), politically and linguistically a radically reformist work that C may have read at Cambridge and had certainly read by Sept 1798: J. C. C. Mays "Coleridge's Borrowings from Jesus College Library, 1791–94" *Transactions of the Cambridge Bibliographical Society* VIII (1985) 557–81; and *CL* I 417. Current thinking, however, is that "drengage" comes from Old English *dreng*, "young man", whence "free tenant". Cf COPY B **4**.

8[1] German: "what goes to the Lord", as C says.

by them the said trustees. . . . The said lands produce to the schoolmaster at present about 40*l* a year.

9 ii ⁻1, pencil

As often when the Sun rises in sand- or brass-colored Vapor, we see him only by the greater Brightness of his *Shechinah*, not by any definite form—so in the Battle—there where the Fight was most vehement, there was the General—[1]   S. T. C.   29 Aug. 1805.—

or of suspecting from that greater blaze, & by little & little detecting/ = *bringing out* the melting outline of the Orb.

10 ii 115, pencil

The vicarage house is very small. . . . Mr. Murthwaite, one of the poor vicars, erected it, and put over the parlour chimney, *Fecit quod potuit* ["He made what he could"].

Piú vorrei, piú non posso.[1]

11 ii 293, pencil, lightly cropped[a]

In 1678, he [William Nicolson] was sent by Sir Joseph Williamson . . . to Leipsick, in order to get acquaintance with the *high Dutch and other septentrional languages.

* What does this mean? Is it a vulgar *pun-like* Translation of "Hoch-Teutch"[b] used in oppositio[n] to Platt-Teutch?[c1]—It is a strange Translation/ Dutch is a ridiculous Christening by the English/ All the Descendants of the supposed Teut are Teutche[d]/ distinguished from each ~~each~~ other by different names, Saxons, Schwabians, &c &c &c/ And the dialect of the united Provinces is Hollandic, ⟨and Niederlandish/⟩—In th[ose] cases therefore called the language of the 7 united Provinces *Dutch*/ the others divide into High—i.e. classical or book-German/ the others into N. or S. provincial German.

> [a] The whole note is written in an exceptionally untidy hand
> [b] "Hoch-Teutsch" intended
> [c] "Platt-Teutsch" intended
> [d] For "Teutsche"

9[1] If C is quoting, his source has not been traced. C's use of *Shekinah*, "the Glory of the Lord", is glossed in Eichhorn *Neue Testament* copy a **42** n 1.

10[1] "The more I wish to, the less I am able": an Italian saying, and a reminder of C's immediate circumstances.

11[1] "High German" (as in C's usage a few lines below) and "Low German".

12   II 316, pencil

Anciently, every bishop of Carlisle, at his death, was obliged to leave to his successor a certain number of books of divinity and canon law; and likewise 104 oxen, 16 heifers, and other quick goods in proportion.

An excellent Rule/ the Books, I mean/ the sorts not particularized. In every See, according to its Revenues, every Bishop should contribute annually from 20£ to 60£/ each striving to make some one class or department as perfect as possible. A. History. B. History. C. History. D. History. E. Voyages & Travels. F. Ditto. G. Ditto. H. Ditto. L. Poetry, ancient & modern, & of various nations. M. Ditto. N. Ditto. In this way I suppose two thirds of the revenue of the Library to be annually spent/ the remaining Third I supposed employed chiefly in keeping up the collection of Fathers, Schoolmen, Theologians, Pulpit Eloquence, &c &c &c, of which I take for granted that a large collection is the foundation of the Library.[1]

12[1] The subject of the textus is the cathedral library of Carlisle, whence C himself borrowed books in Apr 1801: *CN* I 937n, 937Fn.

Copy B

The History and Antiquities of the Counties of Westmorland and Cumberland. 2 vols. London 1777. 4°.

Wordsworth Library, Grasmere

WW's copy, with "Wm Wordsworth" (not holograph) on the title-page of I, "W Wordsworth, Rydal Mount" on the title-page of II. A bookplate on I ⁻3 (p-d) and II ⁻3 (p-d) indicates that the work was given to the Wordsworth Trust by Dorothy Dickson in 1967. A bibliographical note in pencil and an antiquarian note in ink, both written by Gordon Graham Wordsworth (d 1935) on slips of paper, are enclosed loose in Vol I, as is a pencilled note about family trees in Vol II. Prints of local views are pasted in at I 150/1, 160/1, 174/5, 406/7, 408/9; II 22/3, 68/9, 232/3, 242/3, 312/13, 334/5, 468/9, 478/9, 490/1, 494/5, 496/7. Notes in ink not in C's hand appear on I 148, 180 and II 317; a Crackanthorpe family tree is pasted in at I 370/1. Passages are marked in pencil, not by C, on I 194, II 40, and pencilled notes, most by G. G. Wordsworth, appear on I 164, 173, 368, 390, 397, 405, 428 and II 14.

DATE. Between Sept 1808 and Mar 1810, C's long period of domestication at Allan Bank. He evidently annotated WW's copy with some recollection of the notes made earlier in his own: see COPY A.

1   I 1, pencil

Westmorland, *Westmoreland*, or as it is anciently written *Westmerland*, hath its name . . . from its being a *western moorish* country. . . . Nevertheless, there is not one ancient record that we have met with, wherein it is not expressly called *Westmerland*, and not *Westmorland*, or *Westmoreland* . . .

No doubt,*Wast*mereland, i.e. of waste and meres.—Wast is in several instances written /West/—for in what sense & by [? ex] how few, at least, could it have^a emphatically called, *Western Lakes*—surely, the Lakes of Ennerdale, Wastdale, &c &c/ indeed, 2/3^rds of the Lakes of Cumberland have a superior claim to the Title. But it is observable, that in Cumberland *almost* all the Lakes are called *Waters*, Derwentwater, Broadwater, Crummock & Lowes' Water, &c &c, whereas all the Lakes of Westmoreland are called *meres*.¹   S. T. C.^b

2   I 3, pencil

This county abounds with MOUNTAINS, which in the language of the

___

^a For "have been"

^b A few words in pencil in another hand, following C's note and ending with a question mark, have been erased

1¹ Cf COPY A **1**.

country are called *Fells*, this being the genuine Saxon appellation, and the word is yet retained as an epithet in our language, to signify something that is wild and boisterous, as we say a *fell* tempest, a *fell* tyrant, or the like.

From the German, Fels, a rock/ Felsen, rocky mountains.—I doubt, that the adjective has any relationship/ I think it even more probable, that it is derived from the Latin "ferus", savage, by the substitut. of the softer for the harsher Liquid—unless it be from "felleus" bitter, full of Gall.[1]

3 ɪ 8

* In modern military language, a *Maiden* fort signifies one that has never been taken, by reason of its extraordinary strength. But that could never be applicable to this small fortification upon Stanemore. It rather seems to be derived of the Anglo-Saxon *Mai* (*maigan, magan, magnum*) great, and *Dun* a hill.

When artificial Roads were introduced by the Romans, "the *Made* way" would be an obvious and discriminative Name/ "Maiden" I hold therefore to be only a corruption of *Maden*; a corruption easily made from the pleasant & romantic ideas associated with "Maiden"—as well as the almost undistinguishable closeness of the Sound.[1]—In general, the Authors have*ᵃ* this Work have evinced little ingenuity and less Judgment in their Etymologies.   S. T. C.

4 ɪ 21

. . . there was another tenure in Westmorland, which hath greatly puzzled antiquarians to explain or understand. It was called Dᴿᴇɴɢᴀɢᴇ. . . . Sir Henry Spelman . . . . conjectures upon the whole, that the *Drenges* were free tenants holding by military service.

From Drang (in low German, Dreng) = Compulsion. "Why do you dregng me so?" = ["]why do you press so violently on me"—I have myself heard in the S.W. as well as N.S. Counties.[1]

5 ɪ 22

Pᴜᴛᴜʀᴇ, Sir Edward Coke explains as signifying *poture*, or drinking. It was a demand made by the officers of the forest, within the circuit of

---

ᵃ A slip for "of"?

2[1] For C's earlier and playful note on this passage see ᴄᴏᴘʏ ᴀ **4**. *OED* accepts the relationship between "fell" and the modern German *Fels*, but not C's Latin specu-

lations.

3[1] Cf C's similar note on this passage in ᴄᴏᴘʏ ᴀ **6**.

4[1] This note extends ᴄᴏᴘʏ ᴀ **7**.

their perambulation, of all kinds of victuals for themselves, their servants, horses, and dogs. Others, who call it *pulture*, explain the word as signifying a demand in general; and derive it from the monks, who before they were admitted, *pulsabant*, that is, knocked at the gates for several days together.

More probably from Puls, pultis—*Pulse*.[1]

5[1] *OED*, mentioning the possible derivation from *puls*, explains "puture" as meaning "food for man or beast", with the special significance in forest law of food or drink exacted by foresters from everyone within the forest boundaries.

SAMUEL NOBLE
1779–1853

An Appeal in behalf of the Views of the Eternal World and State, and the Doctrines of Faith and Life, held by the Body of Christians who believe that a New Church is signified (in the Revelation, Chap. XXI.) by the New Jerusalem: including answers to objections, particularly those of the Rev. G. Beaumont, in his work entitled "The Anti-Swedenborg." Addressed to the reflecting of all denominations. London 1826. 12º.

British Library Ashley 2885

Inscribed in pencil on p ⁻4: "Lucy Eleanor Gillman". Bookplate of T. J. Wise on p ⁻7 (p-d). Passages are marked in pencil with signs that do not resemble C's on pp 416, 429.

DATE. Apr 1827 (13).

1 p ⁻1, pencil, overtraced

How natural it is to mistake the weakness of an Adversary's Arguments for the strength of our own cause! This is especially applicable to Mʳ S. Noble's Appeal. Assuredly as far as Mʳ B.[1] &c &c are concerned, his Victory is complete.[a]

2 pp 48–9, pencil, marked with a line in the margin, and expanded in pencil by another hand[b]

Has not the change which has taken place during the last thirty or forty years, the seeds of which had been fermenting for twenty or thirty years previously, in the whole aspect of Europe, of Christendom, of the world, such as has filled with amazement every one who has witnessed it, every one who contemplates it? After every section of the great family of mankind has been seen struggling through convulsions which seemed to threaten the dissolution of all human society, does not order,—a new and improved order,—appear again to be emerging out of

---

[a] Written at the end in another hand (unidentified): "Pencil note by S. T. C."

[b] It appears that someone—possibly HNC, preparing text for *LR*—has added words at the end of the note, perhaps erasing others, in an attempt to make sense of it but in fact obscuring the meaning. The words that seem to have been added are here reported in textual notes

[1] The Rev Mr G. Beaumont, as on title-page and in **3A** below.

chaos? Are not extraordinary improvements, in every thing connected with the comforts of human life, and the advancement of the species in civilization, in knowledge, and, ultimately, in virtue, continually springing up? and are they not continually calling forth, from every quarter, exclamations of surprise, and expanding every bosom with the hope, that the opening of a new and happier day than the world has ever before seen is now dawning on mankind?

I grant that civilization has made most rapid strides—but what of this, compar[ing] this period to that of Luther, the reformation, the revolutions of our own and that of France*a* in*b* the Mind*c* *d*in a true*e* Philosophy

3   p 210

[Quoting from *The London Encyclopaedia*:] ". . . The intellectual spirit is moving upon the chaos of minds, which ignorance and necessity have thrown into collision and confusion; and the result will be, a new creation. * Nature (to use the nervous language of an old writer) 'will be melted down and recoined;' and all will be bright and beautiful."

* Alas! if this be possible, *now*—or at any time henceforward—whence came the *Dross*? If *Nature* be Bullion, that can be melted and thus purified by the conjoint action of Heat & Elective Attraction—I pray M*r* Noble to tell me, ~~by~~ to what Name or Genus he refers *the Dross*? Will he tell me, the Devil? Whence came the Devil? And how ~~does~~ was the pure Bullion so thoughtlessly made as to have an elective affinity for this Devil?

3A   p 226, marked with a pencil line

Mr. Beaumont, I am assured, frequently undertakes to inform his hearers, how the saints are endowed with the "spoils" of the fallen angels. When the latter, he tells them, were cast out of heaven, they left their thrones vacant behind them, with their crowns hung above them on pegs: every saint who dies enters on possession of one of the vacant thrones, and, taking the crown over it from its peg, places it on his head: and the occupying of the last throne and unloading of the last peg, will be the signal for the sounding of the last trumpet and the end of the world.

a Added in pencil: "& mark the influence"
b Changed to "on" in pencil
c Added in pencil: "of Man, it is running a parallel of [? Archiputum]". Some words of C's may have been erased here
d-e Overwritten in pencil: "with genuine"

4   p 227, marked with a pencilled cross in the margin

The common notions respecting angels and devils, are then, we find, sufficiently open to ridicule: Is it equally ridiculous to affirm, that angels and men are of the same family, and that heaven and hell are from the human race?*

* Augustine teaches the same doctrine as Swedenborg: there can be but three essentially different Genera of Being—Divine, Human, and Bestial. And Reason says the same/ The absolute rational, the finite Rational, and the Irrational—or 1. the Absolute. 2. the rational Finite. 3. the irrational Finite. God, Man, and Nature exhaust our conception.[1]

S. T. C.

5   pp 286–7

[Footnote:] . . . The next anecdote that I shall adduce is similar in its nature to the last. . . . The relater is Dr. Stilling, Counsellor at the court of the Duke of Baden, in a work intitled *"Die Theory der Geister-Kunde,"* printed at Nurcmberg in 1808. [Swedenborg was challenged to provide proof of his communication with the spirit world by telling the substance of a conversation that his challenger had had with a man since dead. The proof that Swedenborg gave consolidated the earlier incidents of "the Queen, the fire at Stockholm, and the mislaid receipt".]

Mr Noble is a man of too much English Good Sense ~~and~~ to have relied on Jung's (alias, Dr Stilling's) testimony, had he ever read the work in which this passage is found.[1] I happen to possess the work: and a more anile credulous solemn Fop never existed since the days of old Audley.[2]—It is strange that Mr Noble should not have heard, that the three anecdotes were first related by the celebrated Immanuel *Kant*, & still exist in his Miscell. Writings—/[3]

4[1] Like Noble, C defends Swedenborg, but by placing him in a central Christian tradition. C makes the same assertion about Augustine in HOOKER **21** and in *C&S* (*CC*) 169: the note to the latter passage identifies Augustinian texts that might have led C to this formulation, but no single explicit statement has been identified.

5[1] Johann Heinrich Jung or Jung-Stilling (1740–1817) *Theorie der Geister-Kunde* (Nürnberg 1808) 93–6, with the incidents of the Queen etc 91–3. C's annotated copy contains a note at p 92: see JUNG **14** and n 1.

5[2] Though the ms certainly reads "Audley", no one of that name seems a likely candidate for C's scorn, and the name appears nowhere else in C's writings. It is probably a mistake for "Aubrey"—i.e. John Aubrey (1626–97), whose *Miscellanies* (1721) C read and commented on in Mar 1818: *CN* III 4390, 4393. In the latter note C writes, "Poor John Aubrey's Miscellanies—the probable original of Congreve's Old omen-monger", i.e. Foresight in *Love for Love*, an "anile credulous solemn Fop".

5[3] Kant related these anecdotes more

6 pp 316–17

[Footnote (pp 301–28) giving evidence to show that Swedenborg was not mad; quoting "Gulielmus" in the *Colchester Gazette*:] ". . . Can he be a sane man who records the subsequent reverie as matter of fact? The Baron informs us, 'that on a certain night a man appeared to him in the midst of a strong shining light, and said, I am God the Lord, the Creator and Redeemer; I have chosen thee to explain to men the interior and spiritual sense of the sacred writings: I will dictate to thee what thou oughtest to write?' From this period, the Baron relates, he was so illumined, as to behold, in the clearest manner, what passed in the spiritual world, and that he could converse with angels and spirits as with men* . . ."

* I remember no such passage as this in Swedenborg's works. Indeed, it is virtually contradicted by their whole tenor. Sw. asserts himself to relate *visa et audita*[1]—His own experience, as a Traveller & Visitor, of the Spirit-world—not the words of another, as a mere Amanuensis. But altogether this Gulielmus must be *a silly Billy*.   S. T. C.

7 pp 321–2

[Still quoting Gulielmus:] ". . . The Apostolic canon in such cases is, 'Believe not *every* spirit, but *try the spirits whether they be of God*' (1 John iv. 1): and the touchstone to which they are to be brought is pointed out by the prophet: 'To the law and to the testimony: if they speak not according to this word, it is because there is no truth in them' (Isa. viii. 20). But instead of this canon, you offer another. . . . It is simply this: *Whoever professes to be the bearer of divine communications, is insane.** To bring Swedenborg within the operation of this rule, you quote, *as if from his own works*, a passage which is *nowhere to be found in them*, but which you seem to have taken from some Biographical Dictionary or Cyclopaedia, few or none of which give any thing like a fair account of the matter. . . ."

* Aye! My memory did not fail me, I find.[1]—As to insanity in the sense intended by Gulielmus, viz., as *Mania*, I should as little think of charging Sw^bg with it, as of ~~charging~~ calling a friend mad who laboured under an acyanoblepsia.[2]

---

than once, but C probably refers to the *Letter to a Noble Lady*: see JUNG **14** and n 1, KANT *VS* COPY C **16, 17**.

   6[1] "Things seen and heard", as in the title of one of the works by Swedenborg that C annotated, *De coelo et ejus mirabilis*

et inferno, ex auditas et visas.

   7[1] I.e. C's note **6** is supported by Gulielmus.

   7[2] A form of colour-blindness, the inability to distinguish blue tints.

8 pp 323–5 (the first misprinted 332)

[Continuation of footnote:] " . . . Did you never read of one who says, in words very like your version of the Baron's reverie, 'It came to pass, that, as I took my journey, and was come nigh unto Damascus, about noon, suddenly there shone from heaven a great light round about me: and I fell on the ground, and heard a voice saying unto me, Saul, Saul, why persecutest thou me? . . .' "

In the short space of four years the Newspapers contained three several cases, two of which I cut out and still have somewhere among my Ocean of Papers, as nearly parallel to Paul's as cases can well be—Struck with lightning—heard the thunder as an articulate voice—blind for a few days—& suddenly recovered their Sight. But then there was no Ananias, no confirming Revelation to another.[1] This it was, that justified St Paul as a wise man in regarding the incident as supernatural, or as more than a providential Omen. N.B. Not every revelation requires a sensible Miracle as the credential—but every Revelation of a *new* series of Credenda.[2] The Prophets appealed to records of acknowleged authority, and to their obvious sense literally interpreted. The Baptist needed no Miracle to attest his right of calling sinners to Repentance. See Exodus iv. v. 9–10.[3]

8A p 343, marked with a pencilled cross in the margin

Again then we see . . . there is no reason whatever for supposing that the Human Instrument appointed to announce the last, should accompany his announcement by the performance of natural miracles . . .

8B p 346, marked with a pencil line in the margin, partially erased

This sentiment,—that miracles are not the proper evidences of doctrinal truth, is, assuredly, the decision of the Truth itself; as is obvious from many passages of Scripture. We have seen that the design of the miracles of Moses, as external performances, was, not to instruct the Israelites in spiritual subjects, but to make them obedient subjects of a peculiar spe-

---

8[1] C alludes to the account of the conversion of Paul in Acts 9, where Paul's experience is corroborated by the vision to Ananias, Acts 9.10–16.

8[2] Of "Things to be believed".

8[3] In this chapter Moses doubts his ability to convince people, and God gives him miraculous signs of his calling. Exod 4.9–11: "And it shall come to pass, if they will not believe . . . , that thou shalt take of the water of the river, and pour it upon the dry land: and the water which thou takest out of the river shall become blood upon the dry land. And Moses said unto the Lord, O my Lord, I am not eloquent, neither heretofore, nor since thou hast spoken unto thy servant: but I am slow of speech, and of a slow tongue. And the Lord said unto him, Who hath made man's mouth? or who maketh the dumb, or deaf, or the seeing, or the blind? have not I the Lord?"

cies of political state. And though the miracles of Jesus Christ collaterally served as testimonies to his character, he repeatedly intimates that this was not their main design, and that they were only granted, in this respect, in accommodation to the hardness of Jewish hearts: and he condemns and laments the gross state of the people that could require them.

9   pp 347–8

At another time, more plainly still, he [Jesus] says, that it is "a wicked and adulterous generation (that) seeketh after a sign;"* on which occasion, according to Mark, "he sighed deeply in his spirit." How characteristic is that touch of the Apostle, "The Jews require a sign, and the Greeks seek after wisdom!" (where by wisdom he means the elegance and refinement of Grecian literature:) . . .

Agreeing in the main with ⟨the sentiments here expressed by⟩ this eloquent writer, as I do, I must notice that he has, hereow⟨ever⟩ mistaken the sense of the σημεῖον, which the Jews would have tempted our Saviour to shew[1]—viz. the signal for Revolt by openly declaring himself their King & leading them against the Romans—The foreknowlege that this superstition would shortly hurry them into utter ruin, caused the deep sigh—as on another occasion the bitter tears.[2] Again, by the σοφια[a] of the Greeks the⟨ir⟩ disputatious σοφιστικὴ[3] is meant. The Sophists pretended to teach *Wisdom* as an Art: and Sophistæ may be literally rendered—Wisdom-mongers, as we say, Iron-mongers.

10   pp 350–4

[Footnote, quoting from an earlier address of Noble's:] "Some, probably, will say, 'What argument can induce us to believe a man in a concern of this nature who gives no visible credentials to his authority? . . .' But let us ask in return, Is it worthy of a being wearing the figure of a man to require such proofs as these to determine his judgment? Are we not endowed with rationality? . . . The beasts act from the impulse of their bodily senses, but are utterly incapable of seeing from reason why they should so act: and it might easily be shewn, that while a man thinks and acts under the influence of a miracle, he is as much incapable

---

[a] A slip for σοφια

9[1] Noble takes *semeion*, "sign", as meaning "miracle" in the passage, Mark 8.12 (an issue discussed above in IRVING *For Missionaries* 8 and n 1); C proposed an alternative meaning, linking it to the messianic visions of the Jews (IRVING *Sermons*

20).

9[2] When, after betraying Christ, Peter "wept bitterly": Matt 26.75; Luke 22.62.

9[3] By "wisdom" (*sophia*) is meant "sophistry" (*sophistike*). C alludes to the verse cited in textus, 1 Cor 1.22.

of perceiving from any rational ground why he should thus think and act, as a beast is.

" 'What!' our opponents will perhaps reply . . . 'was it not by miracles that the prophets . . . testified their authority? Do you not believe these facts?'—Yes, my friends, I do most entirely believe them . . .''

There is so much of Truth in all this Reasoning on Miracles that I feel pain in the thought that the *result* is false—because it was not the *whole* truth. But this is the *grounding* & at the same time *pervading* error of the Swedenborgians—that they overlook the distinction between congruity with reason, truth of consistency, or internal possibility of this or that being *objectively* real, and the objective reality as fact. Miracles, quoad Miracles, can never supply the place of *subjective* evidence, i.e. of insight.[1] But neither can subjective Insight supply the place of Objective Sight. The certainty of the truth of a mathematical Arch can never prove the *fact* of its *existence*.[2]   S. T. C.

P.S. I anticipate the answers; but know that they likewise proceed from the want of distinguishing between *Ideas*, such as, God, Eternity, the responsible Will, the Good, &c, whose actuality is *absolutely* subjective, & includes both the relatively subjective$ & the relatively objective as á higher or transcendent Realities, which alone are the proper objects of FAITH, the great *Postulates* of Reason in order to its own admission of its own Being—the not distinguishing, I say, between these, and those positions which must be either matters of *fact* or fictions. For *such* positions it is that miracles are required in lieu of experience—i.e. A's testimony of Experience supplies the want of the same Experience for B. C. D &c. Ex. gr. how many thousands believe the existence of red snow on the testimony of Captn Parry.[3]—But who can expect more than *Hints* in a marginal note?—

10[1] It is this aspect of the argument against contemporary reliance on miracles that C usually emphasises: see LIGHTFOOT 2 n 1.

10[2] The arch was a favourite example of the discrepancy between ideal geometry and actual engineering: cf *Friend (CC)* I 176 (epigraph), 496–7.

10[3] C refers not to accounts of Arctic voyages by William Edward Parry (1790–1855) himself, but to an expedition in which Parry accompanied John Ross (1777–1856), who wrote about it in *A Voy-* *age of Discovery, Made under the Orders of the Admiralty, in His Majesty's Ships Isabella and Alexander, for the Purpose of Exploring Baffin's Bay, and Enquiring into the Probability of a North-West Passage* (2nd ed 2 vols 1819). Parry was commanding officer of the *Alexander*, but Ross led the expedition. There was lively controversy about the cause of the red snow that they reported (I 191–4), but the effect was eventually determined to have been produced by algae.

11 p 381, pencil

III. In the *general* views then which are presented in the writings of Swedenborg on the subject of heaven and Hell, as the abodes, respectively, of happiness and of misery, while there certainly is not any thing which is not in the highest degree agreeable both to Reason and Scripture, there also seems nothing which could be deemed inconsistent with the usual conceptions of the Christian world. I have therefore not thought it requisite to dwell upon the general subject further than was necessary to refute Mr. Beaumont's unjustifiable calumny . . .

What tends to render *thinking* readers a little sceptical is the want of a distinct Boundary between the Deductions from Reason, and the Articles thate truth of which is to rest on the Baron's personal testimony— his Visa et Audita.[1] Nor is the Baron himself (as it appears to me) quite consistent on this point.

12 pp 389–90, pencil, overtraced

[Quoting from a letter from Mrs M. Walker:] "The last time I had the pleasure of addressing her [Miss Bosanquet], my letter was conveyed to her hands by William Gilbert, Esq.,* a native of Antigua; in which I informed her that I had embraced the doctrine of the New Jerusalem Church, requesting her sentiments thereon. . . ."

* Bless us! I was *most* intimate with poor Gilbert, who was as mad as a March hare, & who has written letters to me referring to & prolixly repeating conversations of mine which not only never had, but never *could* have, taken place![1]   s. t. c.

13 p 434

[Footnote:] Witness, again, the poet Milton, who introduces active sports among the recreations which he deemed worthy of angels, and (strange indeed for a Puritan!) included even dancing among the number.*

* How *could* a man of Noble's Sense and Sensibility bring himself thus to profane the nam aweful name of Milton by associating it with Puritan?

14 pp +1–+3

I have often thought of writing a work, to be entitled, Vindiciæ Heterodoxæ, sive Celebrium Virorum παραδογματιζόντων ⟨Vindicatio—⟩ i.e.

11[1] See **6** n 1 above.
12[1] William Gilbert (c 1760–c 1825), author of *The Hurricane* (1796) and C's

friend in the Bristol period; "poor Gilbert" also in a letter of 1801 to DW: *CL* ii 673.

Vindication of great men unjustly branded—and at such times the ~~four~~ 4 names prominent to my mind's Eye have been Giordano Bruno, Jacob Behmen, Benedict Spinoza and Emanuel Swedenborg.[1] Of the last-mentioned especially nothing can be more unfair or more unthinking than the Language which our justly celebrated Poet, Historian and Critic, Robert Southey has permitted himself to use.[2]

Grant, that the ⟨Origin of the⟩ Swedenborgian Theology is a Problem. Yet on whichever of the three possible Hypotheses (possible, I mean, for Gentlemen, Scholars and Christians) it may be solved—namely, 1. Swedenborg's own Assertion and constant Belief in the hypothesis of a supernatural Illumination: or 2. That ~~thise~~ great and excellent Man was led into this belief by becoming the Subject of a very rare but not (it is said) altogether *unique*, conjunction of ~~thate~~ somniative faculty (~~on~~ by which the products of the Understanding, viz. Words, Conceptions, &c are rendered instantaneously into forms of Sense) with the voluntary and other powers of the waking state: or 3. the modest suggestion, that the first and second may not be so incompatible as they appear—still it ought never to be forgotten that the merit and value of Swedenborg's System ⟨do⟩ only in a very secondary degree depend$ on either of the three.   For even tho' the first were adopted, the Conviction and Conversion of such a Believer must, according to a fundamental principle of the "NEW Church", have been wrought by an Insight into the intrinsic Truth and Goodness of the Doctrines, severally and collectively, and their entire Consonance ⟨with⟩ the Light of the Eternal and of the Written Word—~~or~~ i.e. with the Scriptures and with the sciential and the practical Reason.—Or say, that the second hypothesis were preferred, and that by some hitherto unexplained affection of Swedenborg's Brain and nervous System he from the year 1743[3] thought and reasoned thro' the medium and instrumentally~~ity~~ of a series of appropriate and symbolic visual and auditual[4] Images spontaneously rising before him, and these so clear and so distinct as at length to ~~become~~ overpower perhaps his first

---

14[1] For the projected "Vindiciae Heterodoxae" (the title based presumably on C's rival Mackintosh's *Vindiciae Gallicae* of 1791 and RS's *Vindiciae Ecclesiae Anglicanae* of 1826) see JOHNSON **2** n 2.

14[2] Although C appears to be referring to a recent publication by RS, no trace of Swedenborg has been found in *Life of Wesley* (1820), *Book of the Church* (1824), or *Vindiciae Ecclesiae Anglicanae* (1826); and references in the *Quarterly Review* are not, in the 1820s, notably "unfair". An early review of D'Israeli's *Calamities of*

Authors, however, contains this intemperate remark: "Muggleton, Swedenborg, and Joanna Southcott, the craziest of the crazy, vulgarest of the vulgar, and the dullest of the dull, have found followers in England": *Quarterly Review* VIII (1812) 98.

14[3] The year of Swedenborg's conversion when, after a distinguished scientific career, he began to have direct contact with the spiritual world.

14[4] Cf the phrase used in **6** (n 1) and **11** above.

suspicions of their *subjective* nature and to become *objective* for him—i.e. in *his own* belief of their kind and origin—still the Thoughts, the Reasonings, the Grounds, the Deductions, the Facts illustrative or in proof, and the Conclusions, remain the same! and the Reader might derive the same benefit from them as from the sublime and impressive truths conveyed in the Vision of Mirza or the Tablet of Cebes.[5]—So much even from a very partial acquaintance with the works of Swedenborg I can venture to assert—that as a *moralist*, ~~and~~ Swedenborg is above all praise; and that as a Naturalist, Psychologist, and Theologian he has strong and varied claims on the gratitude and admiration of the professional and philosophical Faculties.—   S. T. Coleridge
                                                                      April 1827.
                                                           Grove, Highgate.

P.S. Notwithstanding all, that M[r] Noble says in justification of his arrangement, it is greatly to be regretted that the Contents of this work are so confusedly tossed together. It is, however, a work of great merit.

14[5] Two popular allegories of human life, Addison's *Spectator* 159 (referred to also in LUTHER *Colloquia* **72**) and *The Tablet of Cebes*, written c A.D. 100. C annotated the latter in Jeremy Collier's translation bound in with his AURELIUS (*CM* I 182–5) and uses it as an example of allegory in *Lects 1808–1819 (CC)* II 101 (and n 43).

4. Copy of Anthony van Dyck *Portrait of the Abbé Scaglia* (1634/5).
See NOTICE DES TABLEAUX **1, 2**
Koninklijk Museum voor Schone Kunsten, Antwerp; by permission

NOTICE DES TABLEAUX

Notice des tableaux exposés au Musée d'Anvers. [Antwerp] 1827. 8°.

Victoria College Library (Coleridge Collection)

EHC's description of the work as part of the "Green Bequest" is contained in a pocket attached to p ⁺3 (p-d), and his transcript of 2 inserted. Inscribed on p ⁻2: "A. H. B. Coleridge Nov 1945".

DATE. 2 Aug 1828 (2), in Antwerp.

1 p 26, pencil

ANTOINE VAN DYCK.

114. Portrait de *Caesar-Alexandre Scaglia*, un des négotiateurs pour L'Espagne au congrés de Munster: il est appuyé sur un piedestal, portant une inscription, qui faît connaître cette circonstance.

Ce Portrait ornait la ci-devant église des Recollets de cette ville.

[114. Portrait of *Caesar-Alexandre Scaglia*, one of the negotiators for Spain at the Congress of Munster. He is leaning on a pedestal bearing an inscription that makes known this fact. This portrait hung in the former Recollects' Church in this city.]

*adm*ᵃ¹

2 pp [2] (title-page verso) and [3], referring to p 26

2 August, 1828—

N.° 114 truly excellent—but on the whole, seldom have seldom seenᵇ a collection that has so disappointed me/

I am more and more sceptical concerning the validity of the almost universally received Opinion, that the Romish Church with its idolomaniacal polytheism and templar harlotry has exerted a beneficent influence on the Fine Arts, especially on Painting.—On Music, perhaps, it has/—But before the question can be wisely put, much more, an-

---

ᵃ For "admirable" perhaps; C has also marked the catalogue with a pencilled line in the margin
ᵇ For "seldom have I seen"?

1¹ The Abbé Scaglia died in 1641, and shortly thereafter the monastery of the Recollects sold his portrait, replacing it with the copy that C must have seen. The copy is now hung in the Museum voor Schone Kunsten in Antwerp, the original being in a private collection in England: Christopher Brown *Van Dyck* (Oxford 1982) 160. See Plate 4.

swered—it should be settled—1. at what age the ~~Christian~~ Latin Church ought to be called Romish—2. the Influences, it exerts as Religion independent of ~~wh~~ all by which it is contra-distinguished from the Protestant/ 3.—as public or corporate Wealth, generally/ Abstracting these, I should contend that its *peculiar* superstitions have been any thing but friendly to Painting—/ while the Gothic Cathedrals I would gladly assign to the religious Spirit, which it had not suffocated. But this, I suspect, is a little unfair on my part—.

HANS CHRISTIAN OERSTED
1777–1851

Ansicht der chemischen Naturgesetze, durch die neueren Entdeckungen gewonnen. Berlin 1812. 8°.

British Library C 43 a 17

DATE. c 1817, or later. The notes partly reflect C's study of Schelling.

COEDITORS. Lore Metzger, Raimonda Modiano.

1 p 24, slightly cropped

Vergleichen wir endlich die Metalle in Rücksicht ihrer Brennbarkeit, so finden wir noch ein neues Beispiel der mannichfaltigsten Abstufungen einer Eigenschaft in derselben Reihe. Man mache sich nur erst eine recht deutliche Vorstellung von der Brennbarkeit des Ammoniummetalls. Wir treffen in seinem Oxyde das Hydrogen an, das uns schon wegen seiner grossen Brennbarkeit bekannt war, aber in dem Metalle selbst muss etwas noch weit Brennbareres da seyn, als das Hydrogen; sonst könnte dessen Amalgam unmöglich eine so kräftige Wasserzersetzung bewirken. Was nun dieser brennbare Stoff weiter seyn mag, darüber haben wir nichts als Vermuthungen. Wollten wir mit mehreren vortrefflichen Chemikern es für ein desoxydirtes Hydrogen nehmen, so wäre das, was wir Hydrogen nennen, ein Oxyd, das sich durch zwei sehr auffallende Eigenschaften von andern Oxyden unterschiede; die eine, dass es sich mit Metallen verbindet, was kein Oxyd zu thun pflegt; die zweite, dass es mit keinem Oxyd, als solchem, in Verbindung tritt, welches ein durchaus entgegengesetzes Verhalten von allen übrigen Oxyden ist.

[Finally, if we compare the metals with regard to their combustibility we find yet another example of the manifold gradations of a property within the same series. But one must first form a very clear idea of the combustibility of ammonium metal. In its oxides we find hydrogen, which is already known to us for its great combustibility, but in the metal itself there must be something even more combustible than hydrogen; otherwise it would be impossible for its amalgam to cause such a powerful decomposition of water. Now, we have nothing but conjectures as to what this combustible matter might be. If, with many distinguished chemists, we wish to consider it a deoxidised hydrogen, then what we call hydrogen is an oxide that is distinguished from other oxides by two quite striking properties: first, that it combines with metals, which no oxide normally does; second, that it does not form compounds with any other oxide as such, which is entirely contrary to the behaviour of all other oxides.]

Q.^{y} Whether Dilative Power, or Dilatability, may not combine here with Contractive Power, or the capacity of contraction = combustibility? More and more, and by daily instances in proof, am I impressed with the practical no less than speculative importance of the distinction between Contraction and Attraction, Dilation and Repulsion, i.e. separative self-projection, or self-insulation.[1]

2   pp 28–32, pencil

. . . mit dem Kiesel, der Glucine, besonders aber mit der Thonerde, behaupten wir, dass das Hydrogenoxyd, das Wasser, grosse chemische Aehnlichkeit habe. Um dieses auf einmal recht klar zu sehen, denken wir uns unsere Erde versetzt in eine 200 Maass geringere Wärme, als die gegenwärtige. Das Wasser würde dann nicht bloss immer fest, sondern auch beinahe unschmelzbar erscheinen, in grossen Stücken als feste Krystalle, gepülvert wie eine weisse Erde. Man würde diese gleich auflöslich in Säuren und Alkalien finden, ungefähr wie wir den Thon; auch würde jenes Oxyd, wie dieses, keine grosse Abstumpfung, weder der Säuren noch der Alkalien, hervorbringen. . . . Wäre man nun aber ferner im Stande beide Oxyde durch Glühen mit Eisen oder dergleichen zu reduciren, so würde gewiss niemanden ein Zweifel darüber einfallen, ob nicht der brennbare Grundstoff im Eise eben sowohl wie der im Thone ein Metall sey. . . . Kehren wir nun aber in unsere Temperatur zurück, so ist das Eis flüssig, der Thon fest und für sich unschmelzbar, das Eismetall wird Luft seyn, das Thonmetall aber noch seine Festigkeit behalten, und nun würden wir die Verwandtheit dieser Stoffe nicht mehr anerkennen!—Was nun auch in diesem Gedankenexperiment unvollständig seyn mag, so wird doch so viel aus demselben hervorleuchten, dass der Unterschied des Hydrogen und seines Oxyds von den andern Metallen und Oxyden nur ein sehr relativer seyn kann. *

1[1] C often emphasised the importance of the distinction, which most of the German nature-philosophers neglected, between the substantive powers (attraction and repulsion, the polar powers of magnetism and gravitation represented by carbon at the North pole and nitrogen at the South pole of the ''compass of nature'') and the modifying powers (contraction and dilation, the polar powers of electricity and light represented by oxygen at the East pole and hydrogen at the West pole). Here, as in 4 below, he emphasises the importance of not confounding the powers that appear to be analogous in each pair. For expositions of the system of the compass of nature see *CN* III 4418 and n, 4420 and n; GOLDFUSS 1, 2 and nn; OKEN *Lehrbuch der Naturgeschichte* 1 n 9.

[We maintain that hydrogen oxide, water, has a great chemical resemblance to silica, glucina, and especially to clayey soil. In order to grasp this clearly and at once, let us imagine that the present temperature of our earth were reduced by a factor of 200. Water would then not always be purely solid, but would also appear almost unmeltable, in big pieces like solid crystals, pulverized like a white soil. One would find these pieces equally soluble in acids and alkalis, approximately as we now find clay; and the latter oxide, like the former, would produce no great neutralisation of either acids or alkalis. . . . Now, if one could further reduce both oxides by heating with iron or a similar substance, no one would entertain any doubts as to whether the combustible base in ice, like that in clay, is a metal. Returning to our own temperature, however, ice is fluid, clay is solid and in itself unmeltable; the ice-metal is air but the clay-metal retains its solidity, and thus we would no longer recognise the affinity between these substances! However imperfect this thought-experiment might be, this much it makes clear: that the difference between hydrogen and its oxide and the other metals and oxides can only be relative.*]

* In the Gedanken-Experiment of p. 27 from which this conclusion is drawn,[1] Oersted seems to me to assume, I. the fluidity of Hydrogen; and 2. the tautogenëity (= identity in *kind*) of fluidity with aerity.[2] As to first, there are both ideal grounds and inferences from facts in support and confirmation of the assumption—ideal grounds, because a dilative as well as its negative, a contractive power must be granted. Postulates in Material Dynamics, and the evident affinities and analogies between Hydrogen and positive Electricity, and of Oxygen and negative Elect. justify us in considering + E. as the fluxional or material, and Hydrogen as the Ponderable or corporeal, Symbol of the dilative, = fluidific, Force—inference from Facts, because the union indifferential of both (+ and − E, or Hyd. and Oxygen[)] constitutes the first visibility, water.[a3]

    [a] At the end of this paragraph C has drawn a line as though to mark the end of his note

2^1 "Thought-experiment": in textus.

2^2 C noted the same mistaken identity of fluidity with aerity in Steffens and Schelling and considered it to be the "most productive Error . . . common to all the Natur-philosophen", arising from the general confusion of substantive with modifying powers (see 1 n 1 above). In C's system hydrogen, as the symbol of fluidity or the force of dilation, corresponds to the positive pole (West) of the line of electricity, whereas nitrogen, the symbol of aerity or the force of repulsion, corresponds to the positive pole (South) of the opposite line of magnetism. As C explains in ZEITSCHRIFT 3, "Repulsion . . . which [is] the Principle of the Gaseous is opposite to Dilation or the Principle of the Fluid, as belonging to opposite Lines, and analogous only because they are both the positive Poles of the Lines to which they belong. Light and Darkness . . . are the two opposites, the primary Gegensätze of nature—the Gaseous is under the Pos. Pole of Darkness, the Fluid the Pos. Pole of Light—and here will be found the true solution of the difficulty."

2^3 This point is made also by the *Natur-philosophen*, e.g. STEFFENS *Grundzüge* p 48: "The indifference of the relative difference between oxygen and hydrogen is water itself." The theological significance of the primacy of water is brought out by C in

But Oersted's second Assumption—that Air, i.e. Azote, as far as it is Air, i.e. the symbol ponder. as + Magnetism is the symbol imponderable of the Repulsive Force, can by no means be so readily admitted. For it contradicts the ideal grounds, and ~~cannot~~ I know of no *fact* from which it can be legitimately ~~affirmed~~ inferred, that by mere Abstraction of Heat Azote could become a fixed coherent body: tho' there are facts numberless in proof, that it may be a component part of such bodies— as not improbably in Lime—/ but certainly, in the organs of living animals.[4] Here, however, its function is evidently that of resisting fixation, both positive solid & fluid. Oersted's arguments deduced from Carbon and Ammonia rest on the same confusion, common to all the schools, between Attraction and Contraction, Repulsion and Dilation.[5] Carbon and Ammonia are at different poles of the same Line, the positive pole of which is essentially aerific.[6]

3 p 31, pencil

Wenn es sich aber auch finden sollte, dass das Oxygen selbst vermittelst eines noch entfernteren Princips verbrennen könnte, so wird es doch immer gewiss seyn, dass nur der Körper, der dem Brennbaren als letzte äussere Bedingung aller Verbrennung gegenüber steht, das an sich Unverbrennliche ausmacht. Hieraus sieht man also deutlich, dass das Oxygen erfordert wird, um die Reihe der Metalle vollkommen zu schliessen, entweder als ein noch schwach verbrennlicher Stoff, oder als das Unverbrennliche selbst.

[Even if it should be found that oxygen itself could oxidate owing to a yet more remote principle, it is nevertheless certain that only the body that is to the combustible as a last exterior condition of all combustion constitutes that which is incombustible. From this we can clearly see that in order to close the series of metals completely, oxygen is required either as a weak combustible substance or as the incombustible itself.]

i.e. (according to the χολεριδγιαν[1] view) the contractive force can not

his commentaries on Genesis, e.g. *CN* III 4418.

2[4] Steffens, among others, argued that "vegetation produces silica, as animal life produces lime": *Beyträge* (Freiburg 1801) 45—a passage C annotated. In **10** below, C gives the example of the presence of nitrogen (azote) in the chyle of animals.

2[5] C refers to Oersted's discussion of the affinity between carbon and the metals,

pp 28–9 (tr): "Its [Carbon's] extremely close affinity with metals has been already recognised by many. . . . That its oxide is sufficiently volatile at a normal temperature to appear like air can no longer surprise us, as we are already acquainted with an aeriform oxide in ammonia."

2[6] I.e. the North-South line of magnetism.

3[1] "*Coleridgean*".

itself be contracted *ideally*, nor its symbol *practically*. But the same reason applies equally to the repulsive.

4   p 33, pencil

Man könnte diese der *Brennbarkeit* gegenüberstehende Eigenschaft die *feuernährende*, oder besser *zündungsfördernde* nennen.

[The property opposed to *combustibility* could be called *fire-nourishing*, or better, *ignition-stimulating.*]

Methinks the Combustible and the Combustive are sufficient.

5   pp 34–5, pencil

Bestände die Atmosphäre aus Hydrogengas, statt aus Oxygen, so würden die an Oxygen reichen Körper brennbare genannt worden seyn, und das Oxygengas selbst als ein brennbares angesehen werden.

[Should the atmosphere consist of hydrogen gas, instead of being composed of oxygen, bodies rich in oxygen would be called combustible, and oxygen gas itself would be looked upon as combustible.]

This again results from the same want of distinct dynamic Ideas. Let there be once an adequate conception of Fire generalized under the higher form of Contraction as the contra-action to that of Dilation, and Oersted's Hydrogen atmosphere would make no change. The Atmos: would be the Brennbar, the Combustible, and Oxygen the Comburent or Combustive, as in the present relations.—But a far deeper problem presents itself, on the supposition, that Hydrogen in a vessel excluding & free of atmospheric air is not inflammable by negative Electricity, and consequently that $-E$ must be combined with y in order to this effect. What is y?—The answer would probably contain the composition of Oxygen.

$$Q^y - E + -M = \text{Oxygen? or polarized Light} + \text{Carbon?}/[1]$$

5[1] C thought that the relationship between antithetical poles of one line necessitated intermediary elements from the opposite line. Thus in *CN* III 4420 f 18[v], referring to the interaction between carbon and azote, he speaks of "the necessity of an intermediate, which is either Oxygen or Hydrogen or both". His query as to whether oxygen is constituted by the negative poles of electricity and magnetism (oxygen + carbon), or by the entire line of electricity (polar light) and negative magnetism (carbon), is another instance of the close attention he paid to "the relations and complex antagonisms of the modifying to the substantial Powers": *CN* III 4420 f 17[v]. See **1** n 1 above. See also *CN* III 4435 and GOLDFUSS **1**, where C states that "Oxygen = Y in tendency of transition into X. or Light becoming [ponderable] Body is Oxygen".

6 p 36, pencil

So z.B. darf die Kohle, welche in höhern Temperaturen den grössten Theil der verbrannten Körper in den unverbrannten Zustand zurückführt, doch nicht als ein sehr brennbarer Körper betrachtet werden, denn in der gewöhnlichen Temperatur, in welcher wir alle Körper vergleichen müssen, weil wir sie in dieser am vollkommensten kennen, zeigt sie sich weit weniger oxydabel, als entweder Gold oder Platin, da sie nur sehr wenig von den Säuren angegriffen wird, welche jene oxydiren und auflösen. Auch finden wir die Kohle in den galvanischen Wirkungen mehr auf der negativen Seite, als irgend eins der edleren Metalle; welches, einer allgemeinen Erfahrung zufolge, anzeigt, dass sie weniger brennbar seyn muss.

[Thus coal, for example, which at higher temperatures converts most of its oxides to their unoxidised state, may not be considered very combustible. For at normal temperatures, at which all bodies must be compared because in that state we know them most completely, coal appears far less oxidisable than either gold or platinum, because it is affected only very slightly by those acids that oxidise and dissolve these metals. In voltaic batteries coal is found more on the negative side than any of the nobler metals; which shows, in accordance with common experience, that it must be less combustible.]

Oxydation allied to, but not the same as Combustion: it is moreover allied *with* the (lucific) Combustion, but not unigenous.

7 pp 37–8, pencil | **6** textus

Who but must suspect a substitution here of the Unigenous for the Analogous? That Coal may be less oxydable than even the noble Metals, yet more combustible? The relation of Hydrogen to Light, the convertibility of the Astrictive (= Carbon) to the Separative by the Dilative or rather ⟨thro'⟩ the Dilated & therefore Contractible Hydrogen these and other points must be brought into Question, in order to a plausible Theory of lucific Combustion. Something like this, Oersted indeed seems driving at; but from want of a distinct intuition of the original diversity of N.

and E, and of W and S in the w————e, he ends in empirical guessing.—

8 pp 42–3

Bekanntlich hat *Davy* in den neusten Zeiten behauptet, dass die sogenannte oxydirte Salzsäure ein einfacher Körper sey, dem der den Namen Chlorine giebt, und welcher mit dem Hydrogen die Salzsäure hervorbringt. . . . Was nun aber diesem entgegensteht, ist die grosse Analogie, welche die Chlorine mit der schwefelichten und saltpetrichten Säure hat. . . . Es ist also klar, dass man nicht, ohne sich in grosse Schwierigkeiten zu verwickeln, die oxydirte Salzsäure, oder Davysche Chlorine, für einen einfachen Stoff nehmen kann; ob aber diese Schwierigkeiten zu überwinden wären, müssen fortgesetzte experimentale Untersuchungen lehren.

[In recent times Davy, as is known, has asserted that the so-called oxidised hydrochloric acid is a simple body [i.e. an element] to which he gave the name chlorine, and which with hydrogen produces hydrochloric acid. . . . However, what contradicts this is the great analogy of chlorine to sulphuric and nitric acid. . . . It is therefore clear that one cannot, without getting entangled in serious difficulties, regard oxidised hydrochloric acid, or Davy's chlorine, as a simple substance; but continued experimental research must show whether these difficulties might be overcome.]

It is of highest importance in all departments of Knowlege to keep the Speculative distinct from the Empirical. As long as they run parallel, they are of the greatest service to each other: they never meet but to cut and cross. This is Oersted's fault—the rock of offence on which this Work strikes. Davy is necessarily right: for he follows the established Regula recta[1] of empirical Chemistry, viz. that all Bodies shall be considered as simple, till they shall have been *shewn* to be compound.[2] On this Rule Chlorine, and Iodine claim the title of simple Bodies (Stoffen) with the same right as Oxygen or the Metals: while the Speculative Chemist sees a priori, that all alike must be composite.[3]

9   p 49

Aber die Auflöslichkeit dieser Körper im Wasser nimmt in dieser Reihe, vom Ammoniak bis zum Kalke, so ausserordentlich ab, dass man mit keinem Schein von Recht behaupten könnte, dass nicht ein Alkali noch unauflöslicher seyn könne.

[But the solubility of these bodies in water decreases in this series, from ammonia to lime, so enormously that it cannot be maintained with any appearance of reason that no alkali could be more insoluble.]

Well! but wait till then.

8[1] "Right rule".

8[2] See Davy *Elements of Chemical Philosophy* (1812) 241: "Should oxygene ever be procured from it [chlorine], some other form of matter, possibly a new one, will at the same time, be discovered, as entering into its constitution, and till it is decompounded, it must be regarded, according to the just logic of chemistry, as an elementary substance." For Davy's view that chlorine and iodine are "simple Bodies"— i.e. elements—see OKEN *Lehrbuch der Naturgeschichte* 1 nn 6, 14.

8[3] I.e. because they are the unstable products of immaterial powers.

10   pp 70–1

* Der Stickstoff gehört, wie bekannt, vorzugsweise der thierischen Natur, ist aber durch seine Gegenwart in der Atmosphäre auch mit der anorganischen verbunden.

[*Nitrogen belongs, as is known, chiefly to organic nature, but through its presence in the atmosphere it is also tied to the inorganic.]

* One most pregnant fact—that ~~the~~ an equal quantity of Nitrogene in the chyle of graminivorous Animals as of carnivorous—& it has been proved that no nitrogene nor indeed Oxygene passes into the system thro' the Lungs.[1] This might suggest the thought that Nitrogen is Hydrogen in the state of positive Magnetism and Hydrogen = Nitrogen in the state of positive Electricity.

11   p 75

Und eben so wie es in der organischen Natur nur die entgegengesetzten Geschlechter sind, welche sich mit einander paaren, so sind es auch nur die entgegengesetzten chemischen Stoffe, welche ihre Vereinigungen mit Kraft und Lebhaftigkeit bilden. Die also, welche die chemischen Verbindungen unter die Bedingung einer Verwandtschaft stellten, hatten doch von einer gewissen Seite einen richtigen Blick; und die, welche das chemische Vereinigungsbestreben mit der Liebe in der organischen Natur verglichen, nicht weniger. Man halte diese Aehnlichkeit ja nicht für zufällig und oberflächlich. Es liegt in dem Wesen der Dinge, dass sich über die ganze Natur die entgegengesetzten Kräfte suchen müssen. Eine jede Kraft bedarf ihrer entgegengesetzten um ein Daseyn zu begründen . . .

[And just as in organic nature it is only opposite sexes that copulate with one another, likewise it is only opposite chemical substances that effect their fusions in a strong and vital way. Those, therefore, who have placed the chemical combinations under the condition of affinity have to a certain extent a correct view; and no less those who have compared the chemical striving after union with love in organic nature. One should not consider this resemblance accidental and superficial. It lies in the essence of things that in the whole of nature opposite powers must seek one another. Each power needs its opposite in order to achieve existence.]

10[1]   C refers to recent studies of "animal chemistry", and specifically (a) to the work of William Allen and William Heseldine Pepys on respiration, mentioned also in GOLDFUSS **5**, and (b) to the chemical analysis of chyle, blood, etc by William Thomas Brande. Brande first published his findings in *Phil Trans RS* CII (1812) 90–114 but added the information about graminivorous and carnivorous animals in his *Manual of Chemistry* (1819) III 463n, which was probably C's immediate source here as also in *CN* IV 4646.

Q? Is there not an equivocation here? An Alkali and an Acid are diverse as well as opposite; but the Woman is the *Counterpart* of the Man.[1] In the latter what, in an imitation of the French unworthy of a German, Oersted calls *Love*,[2] constitutes the Engtgegensetzung,[3] and is not the effect of it, and is a Babe a neutral Salt?—

12   p 77

Der brennbare Körper hat eine chemische Anziehung, ein Vereinigungsbestreben gegen das Oxygen, und dieses auch gegen jenen. Wenn der brennbare Körper bis auf einen gewissen Grad verbrannt ist, so hat er die Fähigkeit, unter den gegenwärtigen Umständen weiter zu brennen verloren, welches man so ausdrückt, der Körper ist mit Oxygen gesättiget. . . . Auf der andern Seite begegnet dem Oxygen dasselbe; auch es kann wie bekannt mit dem brennbaren Körper gesättiget werden, das ist: durch die Verbindung mit demselben an chemischer Anziehungskraft dafür eine Abnahme erleiden. . . . Da wir aber Kräfte, welche einander aufheben, *entgegengesetzte* zu nennen pflegen, so werden wir auch hier die chemischen Anziehungen der brennbaren Körper und des Oxygens gegen einander so benennen.

[The combustible body has a chemical attraction, a desire for union, towards oxygen, and so has oxygen towards the combustible body. When the combustible body is oxidised to a certain degree, it has lost the capacity for further combustion under the present circumstances, as is expressed in the phrase ''the body is saturated with oxygen''. . . . On the other hand, the same happens to oxygen; it too can, as is known, become saturated with the combustible body: that is, by combining with the combustible body it can suffer a loss of chemical attraction. . . . As we commonly call powers that annihilate one another *opposite*, here too we will thus designate the chemical attractions between combustible bodies and oxygen.]

The great Laws, by which the Powers at their maxima pass into their opposite poles, the dilative for instance (= Warmth) into the contractive (= Fire) contains an incomparably fuller solution than the arbitrary metaphors, attraction, Saturation, &c.

13   pp 86–9, cropped at the end

2. Vergleicht man unter einander die von den alkalisirbaren und säuer-

---

11[1] C often differentiated among the terms ''opposite'', ''contrary'', ''diverse'', and ''disparate'': cf OKEN *Lehrbuch der Naturgeschichte* **8** and n 1.

11[2] C makes a similar point in ENCYCLOPAEDIA LONDINENSIS **1**: ''This detest-able use of the word 'love' was introduced by the French; and is a good instance of the filthiness of mock-modesty.''

11[3] ''Opposition'', ''antithesis''—echoing on textus.

baren Körpern aufgenommenen Oxygenmengen, so findet man solche im Allgemeinen bei diesen weit grösser, als bei jenen. Die meisten ausgezeichneten Alkalien enthalten weniger als ein Viertheil ihres Gewichts an Oxygen, und kein einziges enthält davon die Hälfte. Bei den Säuren verhält sich dieses umgekehrt; in einigen derselben finden wir nahe an drei Viertheile von Oxygen, und in den allermeisten nicht weniger als die Hälfte.

[2. If we compare the quantities of oxygen absorbed by alkalisable bodies and by acidifying bodies, we find that in general the latter absorb far more oxygen than the former. Most of the important alkalis contain less than a fourth of their weight in oxygen, and none contains half its weight. In the case of the acids the situation is reversed; in some we find nearly three-fourths oxygen and in most acids no less than a half.]

2. This seems to me the essential distinction, the others only consequences of this—viz. in the Alkalis the Metallity (combustible quality) is uppermost, in Acids the Comburent, or anti-metallic. But when I meditate on the term, Metallity, and ~~of~~ that the ~~the axle-tree~~ metallic Series form the axle-tree on which all natural Bodies circumvolve, that Carbon and Azote are the − & +, the N. and S. Poles of the Line (or shall I risk a yet bolder Metaphor, and say, the solid Cylinder?) of Substantive Nature?/ I cannot suppress the suggestion that the qualitative Energies, the *inside*, of the metallic Bodies must be looked to, in order to discover the most proper Character of Metallity—and that one great purpose of the Noun Adject(ives) Oxygen + Chlorine + Iodine, and Hydrogen is to *express* their qualities—by destroying or exhausting their quantitative and outside power of Cohesion—or appropriative Attraction! That thus the *Con*tractive and the *Di*lative restore the conditions, under which the Qualities can be called from potence into act. The Twymetal, Iron, must be slightly oxydated in order to reveal its magnetic life. Even mechanic Divisions, as in filings, by overpowering the Cohesion enable the Metal to *communicate* its astringency: ~~t~~ its tonic Virtue is the force of Cohesion as changed into a transitive or causative Quality. But still more so in the state of Rust—or Rust endlessly divided by diluted Nitric Oxyd.—So the carbon is even so [. . . . .][a]

14   title-page verso, pencil, evidently referring to this section

[p 88:] . . . die verbrannten Körper, worin die Brennkraft noch einiges Uebergewicht hat, Alkalien sind; die aber, worin die Brennkraft so ganz überwältiget ist, dass die Zündkraft ein bedeutendes Uebergewicht darüber haben muss, sind Säuren. . . .

[a] Two words partly cropped, the second perhaps ''metallic''

[107–8:] Mit mehr Zuversicht wagen wir aber darauf aufmerksam zu machen, dass bei dem Neutralisationspunkt, wo ein ziemlich genaues Gleichgewicht der entgegengesetzten Kräfte Statt findet, auch der Wendepunkt der formenden Kräfte fällt. Es ist eben bei dem hiehergehörigen Mischungsverhältniss, wo fast alle Salze die Krystallisation annehmen.

[. . . the oxidised bodies in which the combustible power is to a certain extent dominant are alkalis; but those in which the combustible power is so subdued that the combustive power must have a significant dominance are acids. . . .

With more confidence we dare draw attention to the fact that the neutralising point at which a fairly even balance between the opposite powers takes place is also the turning point of the formative powers. It is just when this ratio is reached that almost all salts crystallise.]

All bodies divided chemically into Combustive, Combustible, and Neutral, or Acids, Alkalies, and Salts.[1] But I cannot with my present knowlege of Chemistry see the advantage of this division; and it strikes me as an objection to it, that it confounds the substantiative Forces with the modifying, by directing the whole attention to the Latter.[2] More simple in fact tho' far less so in sound and appearance, would be:

Hydrocarbonazotes. i.e. C $\mathcal{SL}$ with A. by H. under the
    predom. of C.[3]
Oxycarbonazotes
Hydrazotocarbons A [? in] C by H, C pred.
Oxazotocarbons.
Hydroxyds of Carbonazote
Oxhydrates of Carbonazote
Hydroxyds of Azotocarbons
Oxhydrates of Azotocarbons

Metals = indccomponible Carbonazotes with ~~indecomponible~~ inemancipable & latent Hydrogen, or Oxygen.
Water = decomponible Hydroxyd with latent Carbonazote, or Azotocarbon.

15 p 140, pencil

Es folgt also aus der Natur der Sache, und der Augenschein giebt es, dass *die Verbreitung der electrischen Kräfte nur in einer abwechselnden*

14[1] These are Oersted's categories, expounded in e.g. pp 39–43.

14[2] See **1** n 1 above.

14[3] C makes a counter-proposal for a chemical vocabulary to describe the relationships and proportions of elements in a compound. The symbol $\mathcal{SL}$ appears to mean "united with", so C's first category is "carbon united with azote [nitrogen] by hydrogen under the predominance of carbon".

Stöhrung und Wiederherstellung des innern Gleichgewichtes der Kräfte besteht. Hieraus ergiebt sich zugleich, dass *die electrischen Kräfte nur durch sich selbst (nämlich durch andre electrische Kräfte) geleitet werden.* Wer aber die Ueberzeugung mit uns theilt, dass es eben diese Kräfte sind, vermittelst welcher der Raum körperlich wird, muss diesen Ausdruck mit dem gewöhnlichen, dass *die Körper die Kräfte leiten,* doch gleichgeltend finden.[†]

[It is in the nature of things and it appears evident that *the propagation of the electric forces consists only in an alternating disturbance and restoration of their inner equilibrium.* From this it follows at once that *the electric forces are conducted only by themselves (that is, by other electric forces).* But those who share our conviction that it is just through those forces that space is materialised must find this expression equivalent to the usual one, that *the bodies conduct the forces.*[†]]

* Oersted is on a wrong scent. The + and − Forces of E. *qualify*, not substantiate. ⟨A. superficial⟩ as the union of + Subst. and Qual. is the Tetrad, Water ⊙ as A interior is = Gold.[1]

16   pp 140–2, pencil | **15** textus

[†] It would not be difficult to prove ⟨even⟩ the *logical* inadequacy of the electrical forces to the construction of a Body: as far as they are pure forces, or + 1 − 1 = 1: that is, $\frac{F}{2} = \frac{Power}{1}$.[1] The attempt and the failure are [a]an indirect proof therefore of the[b] truth of the other System: viz. that Electricity per se is neither Attractive nor Repulsive, but yet incapable of existing otherwise than either in the Attraction or in the Repulsion, as adjective to Substantive.

This which may be called the tetradic, or dynami-dynamic, System, alone reconciles the ancient elementary with the modern Gaseous Theories, Observation with experiment, Common Sense with Science, in

the constitution of Water. $\overset{\displaystyle N}{\underset{\displaystyle S}{|}}$ is substantia in Aquâ W •——• E = Aqua in

[a–b] Partly cropped at the foot of the page

15[1] The distinction between substantive and modifying powers is glossed in **1** n 1 above. In C's compass or sphere of nature, the substantive power of Attraction is manifest as a phenomenon at the *surface* level as water, and at the internal centre as gold (⊙ is the alchemical symbol for gold). C makes similar statements elsewhere, e.g. in a letter to Tulk in Sept 1817: ". . . Water as Hydrogen + Oxygen is in fact the first Cube of superficial Nature, under the predominance of Light . . . while Metal is the central Cube. In other words, Water is the Indifference or Balance of the four elements, each containing all the four elementary Powers but under the Dynasty of some one of the 4" (*CL* IV 772–3).

16[1] I.e. Force is to Power as 1 is to 2.

Substantiâ.[2]—Hence there are four Squares, Carbon, Azote, Oxygen, Hydrogen; and two Cubes, Water and Gold.

17 p 165

Sobald aber, durch erzwungene Leitung, eine grössere Kraftmenge den Körper durchdringt, als dieser selbstständig abzuleiten vermag, so wird auch das innerlich gestöhrte Gleichgewicht durch die eignen Kräfte der Körper nicht wiederhergestellt werden. . . . *Diese Zustand nun, wo das Gleichgewicht in jedem Punkte des Körpers gestöhrt ist, aber so dass es zu keiner sinnlich erkennbaren Trennung der Kräfte gekommen ist, giebt uns die Erscheinung der Wärme.*

[As soon as, through forced conduction, a greater force penetrates the body than it can conduct independently, the disturbed inner equilibrium will not be restored by the body's own forces. . . . *This state, then, in which the equilibrium is disturbed in every point of the body yet in such a way that no perceptible dissolution of the powers takes place, gives us the phenomenon of warmth.*]

I cannot think it philosophical, to use a name wholly subjective, such as Warmth in treating of an objective phænomenon.

18 p 165 | Continuing 17 textus

Diese Stöhrung des Gleichgewichts ist natürlicherweise mit einem Streben nach Wiederherstellung verbunden, das zwar nicht befriedigt wird, aber doch eine grosse innere lebendige Thätigkeit unterhält. Dieses veranlasst uns auch, *die Wärme als einen innern Wechselkampf der entgegengesetzten Kräfte anzusehen.*

[This disturbance of equilibrium is naturally linked with a striving for its restoration, which is not satisfied but maintains nonetheless a great and lively inner activity. This leads us *to regard warmth as an alternating inner struggle of opposite powers.*]

But this is not peculiar to Warmth. It is a universal condition of all action. Oersted appears to say a great deal, and says nothing. And then how empirical is the "erzwungene", the "gröss: Kraftm: als"!![1] These are but names for appearances, not solutions.

19 pp 178–9, pencil, slightly cropped

Die Härte, als eine Folge der besondern Thätigkeitsrichtungen in den Körpern, muss durch die Stöhrung des bestehenden innern Gleichgewichtes immer schwächer werden; denn erstlich müssen bei dem Zuwachs der allgemeinen innern Thätigkeit der Kräfte die Thätigkeiten in beson-

---

16[2] "Substance in Water . . . Water in Substance".

18[1] "Forced . . . greater force than": **17** textus.

dern Richtungen, wenn sie auch unverändert blieben, eine für das Ganze immer geringere Bedeutung erhalten; aber demnächst werden sie auch wirklich durch jenen inneren Wechselkampf gestöhrt, und in den meisten Körpern giebt es endlich einen Punkt, wo der Rest ihres gesammten Bestands plötzlich aufgehoben, und der Körper flüssig wird. . . . Das Verschwinden der bestimmten Form in dem Augenblick des Uebergangs von der Festigkeit zur Flüssigkeit, zeigt hinreichend, dass die Härte, wie überhaupt die Starrheit, von jener Bestimmtheit, und nicht unmittelbar von der Cohäsion herrührt. Was die gewöhnlichen Cohäsionsversuche mit festen Körpern zeigen, könnte man füglich die *Stärke* derselben nennen. Sie wird nicht bloss . . . durch die ursprüngliche Cohäsion und durch die Härte bestimmt, sondern auch durch die Dehnbarkeit . . .

[Hardness, as a result of the distinctive dynamic of bodies, must become increasingly weaker through the disturbance of the prevailing inner equilibrium. First, with the growth of the general inner activity of powers, the distinctive dynamic must have an ever smaller significance for the whole, even if they remain unchanged; next, they are really disturbed by the continuous alternating struggle, and in most bodies there finally comes a point at which all the stability it has left is suddenly destroyed and the body becomes fluid. . . . The disappearance of definite form at the moment of transition from a solid to a fluid state proves amply that hardness, like rigidity in general, is affected by that definiteness of form and not directly by cohesion. What the usual experiments on cohesion with solid bodies demonstrate cannot properly be called the *strength* of bodies. It is not determined only by primary cohesion and by hardness, but also by elasticity . . .]

Here again—fresh instances of the Maze of Cycles and Epicycles in

which the oversight of $\begin{array}{c} N \\ | \\ S \end{array}$ = W•——•E has bewildered the Author.

The latter, which is meant for a hemispheric Line, is always & exclusively modifying; but to modify is of itself in a certain degree to counteract, tho' by a still higher degree of counteraction, to A then to R,[1] or vice versâ, C. or D. may effectively *befriend* ⟨A or R.⟩ Let Z and X be direct antagonists: and Y to Z be $-\frac{1}{2}$, but to X -2, it is evident tha[t] Y is a poten[t] tho' indirect Auxiliary of Z.—Let Z represent the force of Attraction, X that of Repulsion, and Y that of Contraction, and the application is obvious.

What Oersted calls die Stärke, or Strength, is rather a complex force, in which A is assisted against R. by the power of Gravitation and the

---

19[1] Attraction and Repulsion, as below and in **1** and n 1 above.

Force of Dilation, with an intestine counteraction between the Allied
Powers themselves. N.B. Schelling has happily distinguished, tho' not
happily named, absolute and relative Hardness.[2]

20 p 228, pencil

Aus demselben Grunde, warum die schlechtesten Leiter am leichtesten
in den glühenden Zustand versetzt werden, wird auch das Licht am
leichtesten durch sie verbreiten, denn dieses ist nichts weiter, als dass
der Körper eine augenblickliche Glühung erleidet, welche aber . . .
nicht mit Wärme anfangt, sondern mit Licht, und daher auch nach lan-
gem Durchwirken des Lichts keine andre Wärme hinterlässt, als die,
welche durch die Hemmung des Lichts zuwege bracht wird. . . . In
derjenigen chemischen Wirkung, worin die grössten Gegensätze sich
aufheben, erscheint auch am häufigsten Licht, nemlich bei dem Ver-
brennen. Die in der Luft vorgehende Verbrennungen sind besonders
reich an Lichtentwicclung. . . . Nehmen wir dieses alles zusammen,
so begreifen wir, warum die langsame Verbrennung des Phosphors so
viel Licht und so wenig Wärme giebt. . . . Die ganze Atmosphäre also,
welche den Phosphor umgiebt, ist ein schlechter Leiter, von sehr gerin-
ger Masse in jedem Raumpunkte; sie wird also durch die Vereinigung
der Kräfte gar leicht zum Glühen gebracht, oder mit andern Worten, es
findet hier ein Glühen bei sehr geringer Wärme*menge* Statt. Diese Wär-
memenge zerstreuet sich nun leicht. . . . Ueberhaupt könnte man sagen,
dass Leuchten ohne bemerkbare Erwärmung erschiene bei dem Glühen
einer sehr geringen Masse, wenn Zerstreuung der Wärme damit verbun-
den ist.

[For the same reason that the worst conductors are the most easily brought to
incandescence, the propagation of light is easiest through these conductors; this
is but to say that the body undergoes an instantaneous incandescence which,
however, . . . begins not with warmth but with light and therefore, even after
having produced light for a long time, leaves behind no warmth except that
which is brought about through the blocking of light. . . . Light appears most
abundant in that chemical process in which the greatest oppositions are resolved,
that is, in combustion. Combustions that take place in air are particularly rich in
light formation. . . . If we take all this into account, we understand why the
slow combustion of phosphor gives off so much light and so little warmth. . . .
The whole atmosphere, then, which surrounds phosphor is a bad conductor, of
very small mass at every point in space; thus the union of powers brings it quite
easily to incandescence, or in other words, incandescence occurs with a small
amount of warmth. This amount of warmth disperses very easily. . . . Generally

19[2] E.g. in SCHELLING *Ideen zu einer*   344–7—a work which C annotated.
Philosophie der Natur (Landshut 1803)

one might say that glowing without noticeable warmth appears at the incandescence of a very small mass if the dispersion of warmth is connected with it.]

We often refer to the vis statum *conservandi*;[1] but if the chemical phænomena prove a more than the universal vis inertiæ[2] in sundry Stuffs, and consequently a τι ζωοειδες,[3] an analogon of *Life*—why not a vis statum *mutandi*?[4] an impatience of its present state? If the existing state be a statio coacta, eine Hemmung[5]—this must follow.

21 pp 247–50, pencil, lightly cropped

So kann man z.B. leicht durch eine genäherte geriebene Glasstange die Abstossung einer electrischen Säule ganz heben, und an ihrer Statt eine Anziehung oder entgegengesetzte Abstossung hervorbringen, und doch bleibt nicht bloss die chemische Wirkung ungestöhrt, sondern auch eine lange Wasserstrecke, wie ein in die Kette mit eingeschlossener feuchter Faden, leidet noch innerlich dieselbe chemische Veränderung wie sonst, ungeachtet sie durch eine Vertheilung von aussen einen ganz entgegengesetzten electroscopischen Zustand erhalten hat. Es scheint also, dass die Kräfte unter verschiedenen Wirkungsformen sich kreuzen oder entgegenkommen können, ohne einander zu stöhren. Die Wirkungsform in der Kette, oder die galvanische, steht zwischen der rein-electrischen und der magnetischen in der Mitte, indem die Kräfte in derselben weit mehr gebunden sind als in der ersten, und weit weniger als in der letzten.

[It is easy, for example, to neutralise the repulsive charge of an electric pile by bringing a rubbed glass rod near it, and to produce an attractive charge or an opposite repulsion in its place. And yet the *chemical* reaction is not merely unaltered, but even a long stretch of water, just like a moistened thread inside the chain [of a galvanic battery], experiences the same internal chemical transformation as usual, even when it has had an opposite electroscopic state visited upon it from without. It seems, then, that the powers can cross or meet each other under various forms of operation without disturbing each other. The chain form, or the galvanic, lies between the purely electric and the magnetic forms, as the powers are much more closely connected here than in the electric form, and much less than in the magnetic form.]

Here the action an[d] mode of action remain the same: and the change is confined to the relative direction. Thus a man in a crowded passage suffers the same pressure, which ever way the mass is moving to the

20[1] "Force for *preserving* a state".

20[2] "Force of inertia"—Newton's formulation in *Principia* bk 1 def 3.

20[3] "Something in the form of life".

20[4] "Force for *changing* a state".

20[5] A "forced state" (in the sense of one compelled from without), "a blocking". Oersted does not use the noun itself in this section of his work, but uses the adjective *gehemmt* p 220.

Inlet, for instance, of the Pit, or toward the Out-door of the Theatre. It is not clear, therefore, dass die Kräfte *thun* sich kreuzen.——. (a phrase by the bye that is genuine German, tho' unwisely dropt out of the modern Style.)[1] This indeed seems to be Oersted's own solution, in what follows. But a fuller solution is to be found in the position, that Galvanism is Electricity + Magnetism—that Elect. itself includes Magn. as Breadth includes Length (tho' I do not with Schelling make Breadth a simple production of Length, from the omni-productivity of the Point, the Space considered = 0, or the mere possibility of a productive Act.[2] On the contrary, I regard Space = principium continui[3]—the proper positive Figureless, and Breath[a] as the product of the infinitely repeated opposition of + Figure on the + Figure*less* or rather *Anti*-figure—and Galvanism as a re-action of the + Figure or Length on the Breadth, con*struct*ive, quasi con*strict*ive.

22   p 281, pencil

Die Gesetze der Verbrennung waren nicht genau genug bekannt, so lange man ein *materielles* Princip der Brennbarkeit annahm, indem daraus folgte, dass man die Verbrennung für eine Zerlegung hielt, da doch das deutlich materielle darin eine Verbindung ist. Unläugbar war es von der äussersten Wichtigkeit dieses zu erkennen. *Lavoisier* lehrte es uns, und brachte dadurch Licht in viele höchst verwickelte Erscheinungen.

[The laws of combustion were not accurately enough known so long as one assumed a *material* principle of combustibility, while it followed from this position that combustion had to be regarded as a [process of] decomposition, since the distinct material in it is a compound. It was undeniably of the greatest importance to recognise this. Lavoisier taught us this, and thereby threw light on many highly complex phenomena.]

Why Lav[r]? Mayhew more than a century before the Frenchman both taught and proved it. Nor was M. the first.[1]

***

[a] A slip for "Breadth"

21[1] "That the powers *do* cross one another": C modifies the phrasing of the textus by adding *thun*, "do" or "act".

21[2] Schelling's theory as expressed in *System des transcendentalen Idealismus* (Tübingen 1800) 176–85—a work which C annotated.

21[3] "Principle of continuum".

22[1] C characteristically offers an English alternative to the French hero of science Lavoisier (1734–94), namely John Mayow (1643–79), author of the *Tractatus quinque medico-physici* (1673), which includes an essay on the chemistry of combustion. Thomas Beddoes, whom C knew at Bristol, published a résumé of Mayow's work with commentary as *Chemical Experiments and Opinions. Extracted from a Work Published in the Last Century* (Oxford 1790).

23 Engraved plate verso, following p 298, pencil

Identity.
Thesis—Antithesis
    Synthesis
    Indifference.

Identity. I AM.
Thesis = Substantive
Antithesis   Verb
Synthesis = Participle
Indifference = Infinitive Mood/[1]

A   B   C   D[a]

---

[a] These letters written in a vertical column at the outer edge of the page

23[1] For a similar application of the pen-   *Sermons* **2**.
tad to elements of grammar see IRVING

LORENZ OKEN
1779–1851

Erste Ideen zur Theorie des Lichts, der Finsterniss, der Farben und der Wärme. IV. [*Half-title*:] Über Licht und Wärme als das nicht irdische, aber kosmische materiale Element. Jena 1808. 4°.

Bound as first with VALCKENAER *Diatribe* and with two other tracts not annotated by C, Heinrich S. Schwarzschild (1803–78) *De fungis capitis* (Heidelberg 1825) and Johann Martin Augustin Scholz (1794–1852) *Solemnia natalitia regis. . . . Commentatio de Golgotha . . .* (Bonn 1825).

British Library C 44 g 4(1)

A rough inscription is written diagonally around upper corner of the half-title: "M. Mrs Mrs Coat".

DATE. c 1820–5.

COEDITORS. Lore Metzger, Raimonda Modiano.

---

1   p 14

* Es ist nichts leichter, als *Newtons* Optik zu widerlegen; ohne allen Apparat, mit einigen Prismen von ganz gemeinem Glase, mit Linsen, gefärbtem Papier nebst einem finstern Zimmer ist alles abgethan; mehr aber wird erfodert, um die wahre Theorie des Lichtes durch Versuche zu beweisen, weil das Licht nicht in einem bloss mechanischen Brechen, Ablenken, Zerstreuen der Stralen besteht, sondern in einem chemischen Act, der bis ins Innerste der Materie wirkt und sie verändert, nicht etwa bloss durch Erwärmung, also Ausdehnung; sondern durch geistige Action, durch Polarisirungen, aus denen chemische Änderungen hervorgehen. Ich spreche hier stark und hart aber nicht ungerecht gegen *Newton*, nur um die Gelehrten mit Ernst auf die bisher gänge Theorie des Lichtes aufmerksam zu machen. In der Folge werde ich *Newtons* Lehre ganz ruhig widerlegen. †

[* Nothing is easier than to refute Newton's Optics; everything is disposed of without full equipment, with a few prisms made of quite ordinary glass, with lenses, coloured paper next to a dark room; more is required, however, in order to establish a truthful theory of light through experiments, for light consists not in a purely mechanical refraction, deflection, and dispersion of rays, but rather in a chemical act which affects the inmost aspect of matter and transforms it, not simply by causing heat, that is dilation, but by a spiritual action, by polar-

1013

isations that give rise to chemical changes. I am here speaking severely and harshly but not unjustly against Newton, only in order seriously to call to the attention of scholars the hitherto prevailing theory of light. From here on I shall quite calmly refute Newton's teaching.†]

*† Good Heaven! how much more good would Oken have done, how much more both with and wisdom would he have displayed, if instead of this rough Railing and d——n-your-eyes-you-lie Ipse-dixits, he had *begun* with this "*quite quiet* confutation of the Newtonian Doctrine," especially it being so very easy a task! Goëthe (not indeed "*ganz ruhig*"[1]) had attempted it in detail both by impeachment of Newton's Experiments, and by Counter-experiments of his own. And yet, G. himself confesses, that he had not succeeded in convincing or converting a single Mathematician, not even among his own friends and Intimates.——[2]

That a clear and sober Confutation of Newton's ~~Optics as far as~~ Theory of Colors, ~~are concern~~ is practicable, the exceeding unsatisfied state, in which Sir I. Newton's first Book of Optics leaves my mind—strongly persuades me. And it is Oken's Mountebank Boasting and Threatening that alone make me sceptical as to *his* ⟨own⟩ ability to perform the promise, here given by him ~~in his own person~~.   S. T. C.—

P.S. I readily admit, that the full exhibition of another Theory adequate to the Sum of the Phænomena, and grounded on more safe and solid principles, would be ⟨*virtually*⟩ the best confutation—but no one who knows[a]

2 pp 22–3

Nach unserer Theorie ist das Licht nur da, wo zwei Urpole sich gegen-

[a] The note remains unfinished

1[1] "Quite calmly": in textus. Cf C's "quite quiet".

1[2] C refers to Goethe's rejection of Newtonian optics, and specifically to the following passage from the Introduction to *Zur Farbenlehre* (2 vols Tübingen 1810) i xlvi, tr Charles Lock Eastlake (1840): "In looking a little further round us, we are not without fears that we may fail to satisfy another class of scientific men. By an extraordinary combination of circumstances the theory of colours has been drawn into the province and before the tribunal of the mathematician, a tribunal to which it cannot be said to be amenable. This was owing to its affinity with the other laws of vision which the mathematician was legitimately called upon to treat. It was owing, again, to another circumstance: a great mathematician had investigated the theory of colours, and having been mistaken in his observations as an experimentalist, he employed the whole force of his talent to give consistency to this mistake." C expressed his interest in Goethe's work and his own hostility to Newton's theory in a letter to Tieck in 1817 (*CL* IV 750); he also annotated a review of the *Farbenlehre*: see QUARTERLY REVIEW in *CM* (*CC*) IV.

über stehen, sonst nirgends und kann nirgends anders sein; also es ist in unserer Erdregion nur zwischen dem jedesmaligen Erdhorizonte, der der Sonne entgegengekehrt ist, und zwischen der Sonne durch den ganzen Raum hindurch: neben der Erde ist es daher stockfinster und hinter der Erde ebenfalls; wie es wohl die Nacht beweist. * So gehen Lichtsäulen von der Erde zu allen Sternen, und das ganze Universum ist durch*kreuzt* von Lichtsäulen; aber eine Lichtsphäre existirt nirgends, in der die Weltkörper schwömmen.

[According to our theory, light exists only where two primary poles confront each other; it exists and can exist nowhere else. On the earth it appears therefore only in the region between the existing horizons which are opposite to the sun, and throughout the whole space between them and it: near the earth it is pitchdark and behind the earth likewise, as the night clearly demonstrates. * Thus light shafts move from the earth to all the stars, and *crisscross* the whole universe; but nowhere does a luminous sphere exist in which the heavenly bodies float.]

* Are these (Sirius and our Earth, for instance) aboriginal Poles (*Urpole*) or not? If they are, ~~w~~how is it dark in spite of this Light-pillar, and of ten thousand other Pillars from the other fixt stars? In other words, what has Distance to do with a mere Act? The breath[a] of the Pillar is equal to the length of the Diameters of the Sun and the Earth, says Oken.[1] Of course, he means the *real* Diameters—. Is it so with the Earth & Sirius? Whence then the hair-like narrowness of the Shaft?—Is it otherwise? But how is this consistent with the assertion that the Light in all cases is ~~an~~ Centro-peripheric tension?[2]—Item: the Light of a Candle— of a Glow-worm—of rotten Wood?—Answer. The Power of Distance is

---

[a] A slip for "breadth"

[2][1] *Erste Ideen* 18: "Die Spannungssäule unserer Erde ist so breit, als die Durchmesser der Erde und der Sonne lang sind. [The tension pillar of our earth is as wide as the diameters of the earth and sun are long.]"

[2][2] C is taking up terms from *Erste Ideen* 15–20: "Durch diesen Gegensatz in der Schöpfung sondert sich die . . . Urmaterie in zwei Regionen; sie häuft sich im Centrum an und in der Peripherie, und der centroperipherische Gegensatz tritt nun zwischen der centralen und der peripherischen Masse hervor. . . . Die Spannung des Aethers gehört nicht zu seinem Wesen, sondern kömmt ihm nur zu, insofern in ihm ein Doppeltes, Centrum und Peripherie ist. Alle Polarisirung geht aber von Centrum aus, indem sie nichts anders ist, als ein Setzen des Centrums in der Peripherie. . . . *Die Spannung des Aethers . . . erscheint als Licht.* [Through this opposition in the universe the . . . primal matter divides itself into two regions; it accumulates in the centre and at the periphery, and thus the centro-peripheric opposition emerges between the central and the peripheral mass. . . . The tension of aether does not belong to its essence, but comes to it only in so far as there exists in aether a duality, centre and periphery. All polarisation starts from the centre, as it is nothing else than the placing of the centre in the periphery. . . . *The tension of aether . . . manifests itself as light.*]"

involved in the relation of the lesser to the larger Diameter—. Yet *still it puzzles* one, how that which applies equally to every two bodies in the universe, that of being peripheric to each other, should be the cause of a particular phænomenon.

3 p 23

Nach uns ist die Geschwindigkeit des Lichtes, vermöge der wir die Sonne in acht Minuten sehen, nicht ein schnelles Fortschleudern oder ein unbegreiflich gewaltsamer Stoss auf den Aether, sondern das augenblickliche Fortrücken des Spannungsprocesses.

[According to us, the velocity of light, which enables us to see the sun in eight minutes, is not a quick catapulting or an unbelievably violent thrust against the ether but the momentary forward pressure of the tension process.]

Nach Von Oken:[1] for Schelling or H. Stevens would have first shewn, if indeed shewn it can be, wherein a momentaneous Fortrücken[2] = Shoving forward a tergo[3] of a Tension, that yet required 8 minutes, differed from a Projection or a Propagation thro' the same Æther that took exactly the same time.[4] Von Oken (or Oken) did not see that not the velocity but the slowness of Light was the difficulty, he had to solve—instead of which Eight Minutes with him are the Synonyme of Instantaneous—

4 p 24

Der Aether ist Wärme und Licht zugleich, diese beiden aber sind Feuer. Feuer also ist das erste, was aus dem Nichts hervorgegangen . . .

[The ether is heat and light simultaneously, but both of these are fire. Fire is therefore the first element to have emerged from chaos . . .]

Far more convenient as well as more elegant is the Mosaic Formule— and a Nomenclature accordant.[1] The[a]

---

[a] The note remains unfinished

3[1] *"According to Von Oken"*—but C seems to have mistaken the "von" in "von Oken" ("by Oken") on the title-page for a prefix of nobility to which Oken had no claim.

3[2] "Forward pressure".

3[3] "From behind".

3[4] C probably refers to Heinrich Steffens's discussion of the tension between light and gravity in *Grundzüge der philosophischen Naturwissenschaft* (Berlin 1806), esp ch 2 pp 25–9; ch 3 pp 38–43, 53, 55, 62–3; ch 7 pp 143–5. For Schelling on light see *Erster Entwurf eines Systems der Naturphilosophie* (Jena and Leipzig 1799) pp 139–46, 236–40 and passim, and Schelling *Ideen zu einer Philosophie der Natur* (Landshut 1803) bk 1 ch 2 and ch 6.

4[1] Gen 1, upon which C wrote many commentaries, defending the biblical account of the creation from the point of view of contemporary science: e.g. *CL* IV 769– 71, 804–9, *CN* III 4418.

5   p 27

Nun ist der Sauerstoff das Determinirende, das primar Active, es ist der Sauerstoffpol der voltaischen Säule der primare, es ist die positive Electricität die beherrschende, es ist die Luft das spaltende, polarisirende, belebende Element, es muss also die Sonne dem Sauerstoffpol entsprechen; sie ist das Positive in der Weltspannung, der Planet ist das Negative, der Wasserstoffpol im Uebergewichte . . .

[Oxygen is now the determinant, the primary active element: the oxygenous pole of the voltaic pile is the primary one, positive electricity is the ruling element, and air is the dividing, polarising, vital element. The sun must therefore correspond to the oxygenous pole; it is the positive [force] in the tension of the universe, the planet being the negative, the hydrogenous pole being preponderant . . .]

Unluckily for Oken, the contrary is the Fact—the Hydrogenous being the Positive Pole.[1] But the discovery of Iodine and the elementary nature of Chlorine, render all remark superfluous[2]—unless indeed this—that the Natúr-philosophen ought never to have used such terms, as Ox. and Hydr.[3] But it was *Vanity*—impatience in Convert-making.

6   p 40

Gelb ist die Spannung des Rothen geneigt zum Weissen; *Blau* ist die Spannung des Rothen geneigt zum Schwarzen; oder Gelb ist ein weisses, Blau ist ein schwarzes Roth. Dieses sind die drei Farben und zwar die drei einzigen in der Natur; alle andern sind Uebergänge und Mischungen von ihnen.

[*Yellow* is the tension of red inclined towards white; *blue* is the tension of red inclined towards black; or yellow is a white [red], blue a black red. These are the three colours and indeed the only three colours in nature; all others are shades and mixtures of these.]

These, even these, are the passages that annoy me in the Natúr-philosophen! Yellow a white, and Blue a black, Red!! It is true, I know what

5[1] In C's schema of natural philosophy hydrogen represents the positive pole of the East–West line of electricity, or the force of dilation. See e.g. *CL* IV 772–3, 808; *TL* (1848) 57; *CN* III 4420; also OKEN *Lehrbuch der Naturgeschichte* 1 n 9.

5[2] These discoveries, announced and elaborated by Humphry Davy, suggest to C that Oken's version of the "Compass of Nature" is at least incomplete. There is a fuller account of the issue in OKEN *Lehr-*

buch der Naturgeschichte 1 nn 6, 14.

5[3] C complained repeatedly that the *Naturphilosophen* used such terms ambiguously to denote both powers (to which C thought they should be confined) and products: e.g. in his note to STEFFENS *Geognostisch-geologische Aufsätze* (Hamburg 1810) 250, where he says that Steffens forgot "the different sense in which he and the merely experimental Chemists use the words, Oxygen and Hydrogen".

Oken means *by* the words—but why Oken chose such words to convey such meanings, I do not know—tho' Vanity is so common a foible, and Quackery so ordinary a symptom & effect of that so common Foible, that I can pretty well guess. Goethe, & then Schelling & Steffens, had opposed to the Newtonian Optics the ancient doctrine of Light and Shadow on the grand principle of Polarity[1]—Yellow being the positive, Blue the negative, Pole, ~~and~~ Red the Culmination ⟨and Green the Indifference:⟩.[2] Oken follows them—but stop!—He waits, till they are out of sight.—Hangs out a new Banner (i.e. metaphor) and becomes a Leader himself.   S. T. C.

7   p 41

Das Lichte und das Dunkle vermischen sich so innig mit einander im Prisma, werden nur *eine* Substanz, dass der Schatten desselben als ein Zwitter zwischen Dunkelheit und Licht auf die Wand fällt, und daher nothwendig gefärbt ist—das Farbenbild ist ein gefärbter Schatten.

[Light and dark intermingle so closely in the prism, forming but *one* substance, that their shadow falls on the wall as a hybrid between darkness and light and therefore is necessarily coloured—the spectrum is a coloured shadow.]

—that its *shadow* is *not* a shadow?

8   p 43, pencil

Der Aether ist das *Durchleuchtige*. Das Durchleuchtige ist aber entweder in Action, Spannung oder in Ruhe; im ersten Falle ist das Durchleuchtige das *Lichte*, im zweiten das *Finstere*.

[The ether is the *illuminator*. The illuminator exists however either in action, tension, or at rest; in the first instance, the illuminator is the *light*, in the second, the *darkness*.]

Aristotle's το διαφανες εν ἐνεργεια = φως.[1]

6[1] For Goethe's opposition to Newton's *Optics* see **1** n 2 above. Steffens in "Ueber die Bedeutung der Farben in der Natur" *Schriften* (Breslau 1821) II 8–9 and Schelling in *Erster Entwurf* (1799) 32 reject Newton's theory of colours in favour of Goethe's dynamic system.

6[2] This schema of colours is essentially Goethe's: *Zur Farbenlehre* (1810) I 187–8 (§ 492), 289 (§ 764), 294 (§ 777), 300 (§ 801). In Steffens's system, however, red is the negative pole corresponding to the pole of oxygen or negative electricity, blue is the positive pole of hydrogen or positive electricity, and yellow is the indifference of the two. See "Ueber die Bedeutung der Farben in der Natur" *Schriften* II esp pp 13 and 22, and STEFFENS *Grundzüge* pp 53, 144. C's own polar system of colours appears in *CL* IV 773, *TT* 24 Apr 1832.

8[1] "Transparency in activity is light". C has significantly modified the definition of light in Aristotle *De anima* 419ᵃ 12, "the actuality [*entelecheia*] of transparency is light".

Lehrbuch der Naturgeschichte. 3 pts in 6 vols. Leipzig & Jena 1813–26. 8°.

Vols V, VI have a second title-page, *Lehrbuch der Zoologie.* By a binder's error the volume numbers of III and IV have been interchanged in this set, III being labelled IV and vice versa. The 4° volume of plates is not preserved with this set.

British Library C 126 g 6

Joseph Henry Green's copy with his autograph signature on VI ⁻4. The first note in Vol I is addressed to "My dear Green". "S. T. C." label on title-page verso of I, II, III, IV, and on the collective-title verso of V, VI. Several pages in II and III are unopened.

CONTENTS. I (1813) pt 1 Mineralogie; II (1825) pt 2 Botanik; III (1826) Botanik (cont); IV (1826) Botanik (cont), V (1815) pt 3 Zoologie; VI (1816) Zoologie (cont).

DATE. 1820–30: dated in ms 30 Sept 1820 (1), 6 Jul 1830 (25).

COEDITORS. Lore Metzger, Raimonda Modiano.

1   I ⁻2–⁻1, pencil, PS in ink

My dear Green[1]

  Oken is beyond doubt a man of genial Talents: tho', I fear, too bustling, snatching, and peremptory, to be hailed with a safe conscience a Man of Genius. I am too often tempted to class him as a Bastard or Blendling between the Hectors and Bobadils of the philosophic Realm.[2] The arbitrary introduction of the Elements and the exclusive attachment of Individuality to the Earth-element is an error in the first Concoction (see p. 2–4)[3] and involves his scheme in contradictions. For wherein (ex

1[1] This volume was owned by Joseph Henry Green (1791–1863), the London surgeon who became C's friend in 1817 and collaborated with him in the study of German philosophy and the development of an alternative philosophical system.

1[2] Bullies and braggarts—"Bobadil" being a generic name derived from the character so named in Ben Jonson's *Every Man in His Humour.*

1[3] Cf *Lehrbuch der Naturgeschichte* I 3: "Das Ird dagegen ist nicht Ird überhaupt und existirt gar nicht als ein Allgemeines, sondern immer und überall als ein Besonderes, Individuales. . . . Alle Individuen sind demnach bloss Individuen des Erdelements, *Irden*: denn Wasser, Licht, und Feuer zerfallen nicht in vielerlei Wasser, Lüfte, Feuer. Die Naturgeschichte ist daher eigentlich nur die Entwickelungsgeschichte der Erdelements, oder der *Irden* . . . [The earth-element, on the other hand, is not earth in general and does not exist as a universal, but always and everywhere as a particular, an individual. . . . All individuals are consequently mere individuals of the earth, *earths*: for water, light, and fire do not decompose into various waters, airs,

causâ)[4] lies the ground, that the unindividual, unindividualizable Air-element attracts & unites a small portion of the Brennstoff = Oxygen, and becomes a Protoxide = Nitrogen, while the same element put in contact, at least into the same portion of Space with ⟨the same⟩ Oxygen will yet attract none, & be pure Brinnstoff = Hydrogen.[5]—The same Error prevented him from anticipating (as I had done) Davy's, rather ~~of~~ from restoring Scheele's *diversity* of Chlorin from Oxygen[6]—& trecentum alia.[7] But I have but begun this first Volume and expect better things to come. I dare promise myself, that if he does not *teach*, he will *suggest*, much of much interest—Oaks from forgotten Acorns buried by a Magpie. But after all, Magpies are clever Birds—/eine *Spiel*art *der Wahrsagenden.*[8]

30 Sept[r] 1820.   S. T. Coleridge
Highgate

P.S. Compare Oken's confused *transmogrify* of H. Steffens's simple & in its simplicity elegant Scheme of the magnetic as modified by the electrical bipolar elements[9] with the original, notwithst. the advantages which Oken derived from the experiments of Davy & others from 1798–1800/ to 1813. And may I not say—*Contrast* it with our Scheme,[10] in

---

fires. Natural history therefore is strictly the history of the development of the earth-element, or of the *earths* . . .].''

1[4] "From what cause".

1[5] *Brennstoff* . . . *Brinnstoff*: "combustive . . . combustible substance". Cf **7, 9, 11** below.

1[6] Carl Wilhelm Scheele (1742–86) discovered chlorine in 1774 while studying the properties of manganese. In his own experiments, Davy confirmed Scheele's view that chlorine was an element, not—as the French chemists Lavoisier and Berthollet had believed—a compound of muriatic (hydrochloric) acid gas and oxygen. See H. Davy *Elements of Chemical Philosophy* (1812) 240–1 and the papers read before the Royal Society in 1810, 1811, 1818: *Collected Works* (1839–40) v 284–357, 524–7.

C claimed that the "compass of nature" had enabled him to predict the proof of the elementary nature of chlorine: e.g. in STEFFENS *Geognostisch-geologische Aufsätze* **9**, "Long before Sir H. Davy's attempts to establish the independent existence of the Oxymuriatic as Chlorine, I had

anticipated it a priori . . .''.

1[7] And "three hundred other things".

1[8] "A sort of soothsayers"—C's underlining drawing attention to the *Spiel* ("play") in the word for "sort" or "variety".

1[9] This is the system of the *Erdkugel* ("globe"), or what C calls the "Compass of Powers" (in **2** below) or "Compass of Nature" (*CN* III 4420 q n 14 below), the basis of which is the relationship between being and becoming, as expressed in e.g. Steffens *Grundzüge der philosophischen Naturwissenschaft* (Berlin 1806) 41 (tr): "The determinate line of a planet is the North–South line—its physical axis. The indeterminate, never being, always originating line of every planet is the East–West line. . . . The North–South polarity is represented by the magnetic antithesis, the East–West by the electric antithesis. . . . Not this quadruplicity, however, or the antithesis of antitheses, but much more the indifference of both . . . constitutes the real.''

1[10] The dynamic philosophy worked out over the years by C and Green, a system

which the *Substratum* modificabile[11] is subsumed in the creative Will, as a transcendent—while the powers *der Idee nach*[12] are named, each by the generic term, that best comprizes its Attributes, and the bodies, that best represent these powers, are named and treated of, *as* representing this or that power which in each is the Predominant, and not as *being* the powers.[13] Thus instead of Oxygen, we have the Contractive Power: & under it as the hitherto known primary, & in the *existing*[a] epoch of the Planet *immmutable*,[a] *Proportions* of this Power to those of the Attractive (= astrictive & appropriative) & ⟨to those⟩[b] of the Self-projective & Repulsive, we name Oxygen, Chlorine, and Iodine.[14] And in like manner the Dilative, with its *proportions* to the same bipolar line of Attraction & Repulsion.

2   1 2–4, pencil

Es kann nur das auf dem Planeten Gegenstand der Naturgeschichte werden, was wirklich ein Einzelnes ist, nicht aber das Allgemeine.* Die Elemente, woraus der Planet besteht, als das Ird (*Erdelement*), das Wasser, die Luft und zuletzt auch das Feuer oder der Aether, sind keine Einzelheiten, keine Körper, sondern Allgemeinheiten: nehmlich Arten der Materie überhaupt, des Aethers, nicht aber des Planeten.

---

[a] Underlined in pencil   [b] Insertion in pencil

---

that C sometimes playfully referred to as "Chloroesteesian" or "Gherano-Esteesian". "Esteesian" comes from "S. T. C."; *chloros* is Greek for "green"; "gherano" may be derived from the letters of "Green" or may be an allusion to the Greek *geranos*, "crane", for C was short and Green was 6'3". See RUNGE ii 46 (**20**).

1[11] "Modifiable *Base*".

1[12] "According to [this] conception"— a phrase used by Oken p 57 and repeated by C in **14** at n 3 below.

1[13] C frequently exposed the error, prevalent among *Naturphilosophen*, of regarding carbon, nitrogen, oxygen, and hydrogen as actual physical bodies rather than as mere symbols of the ideal powers of attraction, repulsion, contraction, and dilation. Thus, C points out in his commentary on STEFFENS *Beyträge* **14**, "it is an error . . . to speak of the Metals as composed of Carbon and Nitrogen—unless where these are taken as the names of the Power predominant in each. And even so, yet not as composed *of* them, but constituted *by*

them."

1[14] C believed that chlorine and iodine were also "*ideally* indecomponible" elements like carbon, nitrogen, oxygen, and hydrogen, and that they occupied an intermediary position between the South (nitrogen) and East (oxygen) poles of nature. Cf *CN* iii 4420 f 20: "But it must not be forgotten, that the Compass of Nature like the Mariner's Compass is not designated by the 4 great Points, N. S. E. and W. only, but by the intermediates—Of these we . . . know that we have discovered two, the position of which is probably between E. and South, or Oxygen, and Azote—namely, Chlorine and Iodine." C's inclusion of chlorine and iodine among the ideal elements of nature is based on Davy's claim that these substances were "simple bodies". The case of chlorine is outlined in n 6 above; on iodine cf Davy's papers read before the Royal Society in 1814, 1815, 1816: *Collected Works* v 437–77, 492–502, 510–16.

[Only those things on the planet which are truly particular can become the subject of natural history, not those which are universal.∗ The elements of which the planet consists, such as earth (*the earth-element*), water, air, and finally also fire or aether, are not particulars or bodies but universals; that is, forms of matter generally, of aether, but not of the planet.]

∗ But these very Elements are ⟨either⟩ mere Hypotheses—and very foolish ones to boot; or they are Personifications of the Powers and Forces manifested in Bodies, Numina (= νουμενα) rerum.[1] When a Philosopher shews me Carbon in its purest form of Diamond or Quarz, as the Body in which the ~~Attra~~ Power of Attraction or Astriction is best represented, & most predominant; and Nitrogen, as the Body in which the Power of Repulsion or Self-projection is paramountly represented—: and in like manner the power of Contraction in Oxygen, and of Dilation in Hydrogen, allotting to other Bodies, as Chlorine, Iodine, &c the intermediate points in this Compass of Powers:[2]—I know and understand what he means, and can give to the Ideal what subsists as Idea, and to the Real or ⟨Phænomenal,⟩ what exists as Phænomena. See the note in the Blank Leaf.[3]   S. T. Coleridge

3 ₁ 3, pencil

Das Wasser ist Wasser und nur eines. Es giebt nirgends zweierlei Wasser: die Mineralwasser haben ihre Verschiedenheit nicht innerlich, nicht von einer besondern Wasserheit; sondern von erdigen, salzigen Theilen, also nicht von sich selbst, sondern von einer fremden Individualität, und sind mithin als Wasser ohne Individualität.

[Water is water and exists only as one kind. Two kinds of water do not exist anywhere; the distinguishing properties of mineral waters do not reside within them, not in their particular essence of water, but in their earth and salt components; thus [mineral waters] do not have an individuality of their own but a foreign individuality, and therefore as water they have no individuality at all.]

Why is a Piece of Ice, i.e. Oxyd of Hydr. less individual than a piece of Quarz i.e. Oxyd of Silicon? What if all the Metallic Reguli[1] be Combinations of Carbon and Nitrogen in immutable Proportions?

4 ₁ 7–11, pencil

Die drei untern Elemente, Ird, Wasser und Luft sind zusammen dem

---

2[1] "The divinity of things": C makes his usual connection between the Latin word for the divine and the Greek for acts of mind, as in JOANNES 2 and n 6.

2[2] See the note on the Compass of Na-ture, **1** n 9 above.

2[3] I.e. **1** above.

3[1] A chemical term for the pure metals extracted from minerals.

Feuer untergeordnet, und nur soviel werth als es allein; daher sind zwei grosse Elementenabtheilungen zu unterscheiden, *planetarische* und *ätherische* oder solare.

Jene sind die unedlen, massigen Elemente, das Feuer das edle, geistige. . . . Die Pflanze ist daher eine Dreiheit der Elemente, aber eigentlich nur der planetaren. Die Pflanze ist ein Ebenbild des Planeten, ein Stein, der in sich alle planetaren Elemente in ihrer Vollkommenheit trägt—ein individualisirter Planet, oder *ein Planet auf dem Planet.*

Das Feuer, oder Wärme und Licht, wirken nicht mehr durch Masse, sondern nur durch polare, geistige Erregung. Durch sie werden die drei planetaren Elemente erst in ununterbrochener Thätigkeit erhalten. Eine Pflanze aber, welche auf geistige Weise sich bewegt, heisst *Thier.*

[The three lower elements, earth, water, and air, are subordinated to fire and together are worth only as much as fire alone; hence one can distinguish two broad divisions of elements, the *planetary* and the *ethereal* or solar elements.

The former are ignoble, massy elements; fire is the noble, spiritual one. . . . The plant is therefore a triplicity of elements, but only of the planetary ones exclusively. The plant is an image of the planet, a stone which carries within itself all the planetary elements in their perfection—an individualised planet, or *a planet on the planet.*

Fire, or warmth and light, no longer acts through mass, but only through polar, spiritual stimulation. By its means the three planetary elements are first obtained in uninterrupted activity. A plant that functions on a spiritual basis is called *animal.*]

It really tries, nay, *provokes*, one's patience to read these ¶s, which are either identical propositions, or A being A is A; or absurdities. Fire, Earth, Air and Water exist in a chrystal of Flint—Is it a Plant? No! because they do not maintain each the others in the specific proportions by specific intermutual Actions and Re-actions—But what places the Elements in these precise proportions, differing in each different plant, and in the same plant at each different period of its growth? What originates their specific reciprocal excitements?—What makes an Antecedent Whole of the same species necessary to the production of every Whole? We can dissolve Alum-Chrystals & reproduce them out of their component particles? *That* therefore, which cannot be produced out of the dissolved or comminuted Substance of the Plant, *is* the Plant—the Idea plantifica:[1] & not the Elements or phænomenal components, the co-existence, proportions, and renewals of which are themselves *Effects* of the Plant & presuppose it.—And then the intolerable Trash of the *geistig*[2] Element, Fire! If Oken means by Fire the sparks from Flint &

4[1] "Plant-making Idea". 4[2] "*Spiritual*"—in last para of textus.

Steel or any other igneous phænomenon, the ~~spiritual~~ phrase spiritual ⟨Fire⟩ is as absurd as a blue Sound/ if not, what is it but nicknaming a spiritual Agent or perhaps a tonic motion?

5   I $^{+}2-^{+}4$, probably referring to I 1–11, 24–5 | Cf **4** textus

6 July 1830.—I see no advantage, but on the contrary many inconveniences, in this Assumption of Elements and of Fire, as the Ground-element. Doubtless, Fire may be rightly regarded, as the symbol and manifestation of that ποθος δεινος,[1] that esurience and sitience of the non-absolute Will self-precipitated into mere potentiality, whose name is Chaos & Hades, dimly apprehensible by predicating of the same Subject innumerable Multeity by defect of Number and Unity of Indistinction by defect of ~~One~~ the Unific. This is, ⟨indeed,⟩ the GROUND of Matter, materia immateriata.[2] But so^a from being itself the Element of Fire, this latter supposes a series of contractions, & preceded by extröitions or extröitive tendencies, and the phænomenal Products of these, acting on which, combining with which, and finally bursting thro' which the primary Esurience manifests itself, as FIRE. But in no sense, that I am aware of, can ~~the~~ Fire be called an Element. In fact, the whole doctrine of Elements is worse than useless, assumed and interpreted as hath hitherto been the case, as *material* Entities. Only as Elementary *Forms*, have Earth, Air, Water and Fire any philosophic Significance—and to preclude the confusion it would be far better to say, the Aeriform, igniform, aquiform, &c. Theoretically and philosophically there are but two Elements, ⟨or primary Essences, viz.⟩ Light and Ether—(the Mosaic Darkness, which in the second Epoch became phænomenal) ~~as~~ but for which in consequence of the manifold modifications according to difference of relations, positions, and the Subjective Senses to which they correspond no ∅ two single Terms ⟨or names of Substances⟩ will be sufficiently general. If we named the first, Lumen or Luminëity, we must premise that it is ~~p~~ unum pro multis,[3] and includes Sound, Odor &c—Therefore it would be expedient to *enact* the terms, in the manner of the Old Alchemists—and the first might be called Αλλον, the other, ~~Met.~~ Μεταλλον,[4] or the Allëity and the Metallëity.—But even so, the word, Elements or Elementary Matters, is defective & partial—for in the necessary co-existence of both by virtue of the Oneness of the Power, of

---

^{a} Possibly a slip for "so far"

5[1] "Dreadful yearning".
5[2] "Matter unmattered".
5[3] "One thing [standing] for many".
5[4] Reduced to primitive meanings, C's

terms would mean "Other" and "In-quest-of-other", suggesting both the difference and the relationship between the two "primary Essences".

which these are the two polar forms or forces, the former will always sustain the *dynamic* Function, will appear as an Act, and the latter will be understood as the *Material* factor—i.e. the Metal⟨lon⟩ will be the Base, and the Allon the Act or Active Property. Thus, Sound is Light in Metal, Color Metal in Light—the first $= \frac{M}{L}$; the second $= \frac{L}{M}$.[5]

S. T. Coleridge

6   I 14–15, pencil

Wenn die obern Abtheilungen Klassen heissen, die zweiten Ordnungen, die dritten Sippschaften, die vierten Familien, die fünften Gattungen, die sechsten Arten; so sind die Klassen der Eintheilungsgrund der Ordnungen, diese der Sippschaften, diese der Familien, diese der Gattungen, diese der Arten.

[If the highest divisions are called classes, the second orders, the third tribes, the fourth families, the fifth species, the sixth varieties; then the classes provide the principle of classification for the orders, the orders for the tribes, the tribes for the families, the families for the species, the species for the varieties.]

I should propose the following terms of Classification. Class: Animal. Order: Mammalia. Kind: Man. Race: European. Tribe: Gothic. Family: Teutonic. House or Household: English—or where the number of permanent Distinctions required an additional Division, Branch might be interposed between Family and House

7   I ⁺3, referring to I 25

Dass es nur zwei Urstoffe gibt, liegt im Wesen des ersten Elements, des Feuers. Dieses hat ein Substrat, welches passiv verbrennt (ver*brinnt*) und ein Attribut, von dem jenes verbrannt wird (welches ver*brennt* oder zündet) daher nenne ich jenes *Brinnstoff*, dieses *Brennstoff* oder *Zündstoff*. . . . Der Brinnstoff heisst Brinnstoffgas oder *Stickgas*, der Brennstoff Brennstoffgas oder *Sauerstoffgas*, Lebensluft.

[The fact that there are only two primary substances is determined by the properties of the first element, fire. It contains a substratum that is passively burned up and an attribute by which the former is burned (i.e. which burns or ignites); hence I call the former the *combustible*, the latter the *combustive* or *igniting*

5⁵ Cf the similar schema of the relationship between sound and light in *CL* IV 773: "Color is Gravitation under the power of Light . . . while Sound on the other hand is Light under the power . . . of Gravitation." C substitutes here "Gravitation" for "Metal", metal representing for C, as for Steffens, the North–South line of nature which is the line of gravitation, as the East–West line is the line of light. On the relationship between light and gravitation cf Steffens *Grundzüge* ch 2 pp 16–35, ch 3 pp 36–43.

substance. . . . The combustible substance is called combustible gas or *nitrogen*, the combustive substance combustive gas or *oxygen*, vital air.]

P. 25.

This representation of the Brinnstoff, i.e. the combustible, and the Brennstoff, i.e. the combustive, by Azote and Oxygen is singularly injudicious—it being notorious that the Azote performs its functions mainly by its incombustibility.

8   1 ⁺ 3, referring to 1 26

[Stickgas] Macht den andern Bestandtheil der Luft aus und bleibt nach Verbrennungen oder Athmungen zurück. Ist in allem das Gegentheil vom Sauerstoffgas.

[Nitrogen constitutes the other component of air and remains behind after combustion or respiration. In all respects it is the opposite of oxygen.]

P. 26. "Gegentheil" used confusedly by Oken, now as Opposite, now as Contrary. In this instance, the Nitrogen is characterized as the Contrary of Oxygen—Oxygen & Hydrogen are Opposites—and Carbon and Nitrogen.—This is the advantage of my Signs,

)(disparate	✳ opposite,	✳ contrary.
Green)(Grey	Sweet ✳ Sour	Sweet ✳ Bitter.[1]

9   1 ⁺4, referring to 1 28

Dieser Brinnstoff scheint aber ganz rein von Sauerstoff zu sein, daher er sehr leicht mit Flamme brinnt, und dabei wieder zu Wasser wird.

[This combustible substance seems however to be completely free of oxygen; thus it is very easily made to burn and thereby converted again into water.]

p. 28. Daher er sehr leicht mit Flamme brinnt—what is the *Logic* of this "Daher."[1] But the whole hypothesis of Oxygen and Nitrogen being the two only Elements or primary Stuffs is so baseless, so mere a hypopoiesis (i.e. a *Suffiction* rather than a Sup*position*)[2] that it is worth picking holes in.

8[1] These symbols marking the distinctions among the terms "disparate", "opposite", and "contrary" appear often in C's notes, e.g. *CN* III 4241 and n, GOLDFUSS 2.

9[1] I.e. of the "thus" or "therefore" in "thus it is very easily made to burn", in textus.

9[2] C's earliest definition of the term as distinct from "hypothesis" appears in *CN* III 3587: "Hypothesis: the placing of one known fact under others as their *ground* or foundation. Not the fact itself but only its position in a . . . certain relation is imagined. Where both the position and the fact are imagined, it is Hypopœesis, subfiction not supposition."

According to Oken's own scale of the proportion in which Oxygen combines with Nitrogen in the AIR, (in which, by the bye, it is yet proved that is[a] chemically combined at all!) in Nitrous Oxyd, Nitrous Gas, Nitrous Vapor, and Nitric Gas,[3] the portion of Oxygen combined with the supposed Base of Nitrogen, this *Brinnstoff*,[4] must be extremely small—less than is known to exist in many combustible Bodies which yet burn readily & with Flame. It would be far more plausible to suppose Nitrogen & Carbon the same Stuff, in the opposite states of Astriction, and Repulsion. Q.y Does the Diamond or pure Carbon, burn with Flame?—If it does, would it not rather suggest that the Diamond is not pure Carbon but contains a portion of Hydrogen?[5]—Q.y—the refractive power of Nitrogen—does this favor the supposition of its being an oxidated Hydrogen?—[6]

10 ɪ 29, pencil

Die Natur und die voltaische Säule haben das Vermögen, durch eine schnelle Wasserzersetzung, statt des Sauerstoffgas einen ihm entsprechenden aber viel kräftigern Zündstoff aus dem Wasser zu entwickeln.* Mit Wasserstoff bildet er *Salzsäure*, und ihn selbst nannte man *oxydirte Salzsäure*, jetzt *Halogen*.

[Nature and the voltaic pile have the power, through quick decomposition of water, to develop an igniting substance from water corresponding to but much stronger than oxygen.* With hydrogen it forms *muriatic acid*, and it is itself called *oxidised muriatic acid*, now *halogen*.]

* I thought, that Davy had detected the error and explained the results

---

[a] For "it is yet to be proved that it is"?

9[3] Cf *Lehrbuch der Naturgeschichte* ɪ 27 (tr): "Nitrogen is capable of various degrees of oxidation. It is remarkable how it absorbs only a specific quantity of oxygen. 20 O + 80 N form air; 50 O + 100 N nitrous gas; 50 O + 50 N nitrous oxide; 25 O + 150 N nitrous vapour; finally, 200 O + 100 N nitric acid . . .".

9[4] "Combustible substance"—from textus.

9[5] Cf Humphry Davy's paper "Some Experiments on the Combustion of Diamond and other Carbonaceous Substances" read before the Royal Society in 1814, *Collected Works* v 478: "MM. Biot and Arago, from the high refractive power of the diamond, have supposed that it may

contain hydrogen; I ventured to suggest in my third Bakerian Lecture . . . that a minute portion of oxygen may exist in it . . .". Oken (*Lehrbuch der Naturgeschichte* ɪ 33) and Steffens (*Beyträge* p 264) shared the view that the diamond contains oxygen.

9[6] This supposition is discussed by Humphry Davy in his "Bakerian Lecture for 1809" *Collected Works* v 246: "One of the queries that I advanced, in attempting to reason upon the singular phenomena produced by the action of potassium upon ammonia was, that nitrogen might possibly consist of oxygen and hydrogen, or that it might be composed from water. . . . My results have been for the most part negative . . .".

of this imagined production of Muriatic Acid and Chlorin from water, before the year 1813.—[1]

11 I 31

Das allgemeine Trennungsmittel in der Natur ist das Licht. Es wirkt aber nicht allein sondern bald durch die Luft, bald durch das Wasser auf die Erden. Wenn diese daher in ihre zwei Urstoffe zersetzt werden, so empfangen die letztern bald vom Wasser, bald von der Luft, bald vom Licht Eigenschaften, und es wird daher einen Wasser- einen Luft- und einen Licht-Erdstoff geben.

[The universal decomposing agent in nature is light. It does not however act by itself on the earths but acts sometimes through air, sometimes through water. Thus when these substances are decomposed into their two primal elements, the latter two receive their characteristics sometimes from water, sometimes from air, sometimes from light, and therefore a water-earth, an air-earth, and a light-earth substance will result.]

Incomparable.[a] First, the Brinn- and Brenn-stoffe[1] are *all*—and here when the product is decomposed into these two, they are diversely potenziated by Light, by Air, and by Water! i.e. by themselves!!

12 I ⁻4, referring to I 31–2

Der Wasser-Erdstoff hat sich mithin durch einen kalten, langsamen, verborgenen Process in der Erdmasse selbst entwickelt, gleich dem Faulungsprocess der Wurzel der Pflanze; er wird sich als *Kohlenstoff* zeigen. Der Licht-Erdstoff ist durch einen heissen, schnellen, offenen Process entstanden ausserhalb der Erdmasse . . . gleich dem Blühten- oder Begattungsprocess der Pflanze, der nur ein augenblicklicher ist; er wird sich als *Metall* zeigen. Der Luft-Erdstoff ist durch einen Process entstanden, der das Mittel zwischen beiden hält, weder kalt noch warm, feucht noch trocken, sondern beides, electrisch ist, wie der Laubprocess der Pflanze; er wird sich als *Schwefel* zeigen. . . . Wenn die Erden nicht durch einen schnellen Begeistungsprocess angegriffen, sondern nur durch eine Art von Verwitterung zersetzt werden; so treten Zünd- und Brinnstoff verändert hervor.

[a] Two full stops in ms

10[1] In *Elements of Chemical Philosophy* (1812) 250, Davy wrote, "Those persons who suppose chlorine to be a compound of an unknown body, and oxygene, conceive muriatic acid gas to be a compound of its weight of water, and the same hypothetical substance; but as no oxygene has yet been shewn to exist in chlorine, so no such moisture has been proved to exist in muriatic acid gas."

11[1] "Combustible and combustive substances", as in **1** above at n 5.

[The water-earth substance has therefore developed itself through a cold, slow, concealed process in the earth, similar to the process of putrefaction of plant roots; it will manifest itself as *carbon*. The light-earth substance has originated in a hot, fast, overt process below the earth . . . similar to the process of flowering or pollination in plants, which is instantaneous; it will manifest itself as *metal*. The air-earth substance has originated in an electrical process like the formation of leaves in plants, a process which is the mean between the two, neither cold nor warm, neither wet nor dry; it will manifest itself as *sulphur*. . . . When the earths are not seized by a spiritualising process, but only disintegrate through some sort of decomposition, then the igniting and combustible substances appear in a changed form.]

P. 31, 32. What a strange illogical Hyberno-fumiflammant Head Oken must have![1]—His Brinn- and Brenn-stoffe[2] are the two elementary Bases of all Matter—then they assume different forms, accordingly as they are potenziated by Light, Air and Water—i.e. by themselves—and this won't do—No! Metaphors must be called in—and these stuffs are again differenced and become Carbon, Metal, Sulphur, by putrefaction, by *Verwitterung*,[3] and by half in half—they are Carbon is rotten Roots, the Metals Blossoms, the Sulphur Leaves/ &c &c—

13 ɪ 41, pencil

* Das Queck ist das <u>Radical</u> der Metalle.

[* Quicksilver is the <u>radical</u> of metals.]

* Alchemistische Nonsens,[1] unworthy of Oken who ought to have known that the Radical of the Metals must be a *Dynamis*,[2] not a *Thing*.

12[1] Considering Oken's theories to be self-contradictory, C coins a compound epithet. "Hyberno-" with a capital letter suggests the Irish, whom C and his contemporaries associated with Irish bulls (as in *BL* ch 4—*CC*—ɪ 72 and n); but it might also—or alternatively—be intended for "hiberno-", i.e. wintry, referring to the cold process outlined in the textus, and in contrast with "fumiflammant", i.e. "smoky-fiery".

12[2] See 11 n 1.

12[3] "Decomposition"—in textus.

13[1] "Alchemical nonsense". Oken shows partiality to the alchemists, arguing that their discoveries were unjustly discredited by contemporary scientists. He points out that the alchemists were well acquainted with the composition of earths and their transformation into metals (p 37), and in his classification of metals he restores the system of signs which the alchemists had used to denominate each metal and planet (pp 51–6). These signs are reproduced in BOERHAAVE 3.

13[2] "Force" or "power". For C, the metals are constituted by the interaction between the opposite poles of the magnetic line represented by carbon (North), the pole of negative magnetism or absolute coherence, and nitrogen (South), the pole of positive magnetism or absolute fluidity. Cf *CN* ɪɪɪ 4420: the metals perhaps "are different proportions of Carbon and Azote indifferenced by the minimum of Hydrogen or Oxygen".

14 I 57–9, pencil

1. Das schwache Ird-End, welches den Schwefel zur Basis hat, muss auf der sauren Seite liegen, und da es im Wasser auflöslich ist, selbst *Säure* sein. Die Säurenbasis wäre demnach Schwefel, ein Resultat, das mir ungeheuer wichtig vorkommt. Die Basis der Hauptsäure wäre mithin der Idee nach Schwefel. . . .

2. Das schwache Ird-End, welches die Kohle zur Basis hat, muss auf der laugen Seite liegen, und da es im Wasser auflöslich ist, selbst *Lauge* sein. Die Laugenbasis wäre demnach Kohle, ein Resultat, das mir nicht weniger ungeheuer wichtig vorkommt. . . . Die Basis der Hauptlauge wäre mithin der Idee nach Kohle. . . .

3. Das neutrale Ird, welches das Metall zur Basis hat, muss im gewöhnlichen, natürlichen Zustand im Wasser unauflöslich sein, eben so in der Luft und im Feuer. Was unschmelzbar, unverbrennlich . . . unauflöslich ist, ist *Erde*. Die Erdbasis wäre demnach Metall . . .

[1. The weak pole of the earth, which has sulphur as its base, must be on the acid side and, since it is soluble in water, must itself be an *acid*. The acid base would consequently be sulphur, a result that seems to me enormously significant. . . . The base of the main acid would therefore be, according to [this] conception, sulphur. . . .

2. The weak pole of the earth, which has carbon as its base, must be on the alkaline side and, since it is soluble in water, must itself be an *alkali*. The alkali base would consequently be carbon, a result which seems to me no less enormously significant. . . . The base of the main alkali would therefore be, according to [this] conception, carbon. . . .

3. The neutral earth, which contains metal as its base, must be in its normal, natural state insoluble in water, and likewise in air and fire. That which is unmeltable, incombustible . . . insoluble is *earth*. The base of earth would consequently be metal . . .]

In the name of wonder what can these monstrous Importants, diese ungeheure Wichtigkeiten,[1] mean? Oken has just before stated the Metals below 5 sp. gr. as the bases of Earths and Alkalies.[2] If he mean that

14[1] I.e. "these enormous significances"—based on textus.

14[2] *Lehrbuch der Naturphilosophie* I 36: "Wenn man irgend eine Erde oder Lauge . . . einer starken galvanischen Batterie aussetzt; so entwickelt sich Sauerstoff und es bleibt ein Metallkorn übrig. . . . Am leichtesten sind die Laugen und laugigen Erden zu zersetzen. Man hat bereits folgende in Metalle verwandelt. Diese Metalle nennt man Metalloide. . . . Die Metalloide zeigen, das Gewicht ausgenommen, alle Eigenschaften der Metalle. [When any particular earth or alkali . . . is placed in a strong galvanic battery, oxygen develops and a metallic kernel remains behind. . . . The alkalis and alkaline earths are the easiest to decompose. The following have already been converted into metals. These metals are called metalloids. . . . Metalloids show, with the exception of specific gravity, all the properties of metals.]" Oken does not mention the figure of 5 s.g. as a determining factor in his

these metallic Bases are themselves composed (*der Idee* nach),[3] those of the Earths, of Carbon and Sulphur with a great predominance of the latter, and those of the Alkalines of Sulphur & Carbon, with a great predominance of Carbon—what is this but a mere echo of H. Steffens's Theory, published 14 or 15 years before him[4]—only changing the name of the old Phlogiston from Azote (= Hydrogen in + Magn: instead of H + Elect., or Hydr. so called) to Sulphur? But then wherein do the *Metals*, considered as Bases, differ from the Metalloids as Bases?[5]

15   I 58, pencil

Alle Säuren ohne Unterschied sind im Wasser auflöslich, und ein Stoff, der es nicht ist, kann nicht Säure genannt werden; die meisten sind selbst immer flüssig. Ihre Natur ist so wasserig, dass keine einzige ohne Wasser bestehen kann, nicht einmal die Metallsäuren.

[All acids are without exception soluble in water, and a substance that is not water-soluble cannot be called an acid; most acids are themselves always fluid. They are so watery by nature that none can exist without water, not even the metallic acids.]

The Uric Acid I expect?[1]

16   I 58, pencil

. . . die Wurzel aller Säuren, die Salzsäure, ist weiter nichts als ein über-oxydirtes Wasser, oder Wasser verbunden mit dem Halogen.

[. . . the basis of all acids, muriatic acid, is nothing more than hyper-oxidised water, or water combined with halogen.]

false[1]

---

classification; it appears to be C's inference from Oken's examples. He may have had a table of specific gravities at hand: cf **21** below.

  14[3] "According to [this] conception", as in **1** at n 12.

  14[4] C may have in mind ch 6 of Steffens *Grundzüge* (1806) 88–133, which deals with the metals and the earths. In Steffens's system the earths are distributed along the magnetic axis, like the metals, with the silex series corresponding to the North pole and the lime series corresponding to the South pole. Steffens points out (p 90) that because of the disappearance of the

magnetic opposition in earths, the two series relate to one another like acids to alkalis, not like coherent to non-coherent metals. Hence the silex series represents the acids (at the North pole) and the lime series the alkalis (at the South pole, i.e. nitrogen). Steffens also discusses the relationship among metals, earths, and alkalis in *Geognostisch-geologische Aufsätze*, e.g. pp 225–54.

  14[5] On metalloids cf n 2 above.

  15[1] C offers uric acid as an exception, since it can be crystallised and therefore is not "always fluid".

  16[1] See **17**.

17   I 59, pencil

The French Chemists have lately produced a true hydatic Acid, by simple hyperoxygenation of Water.[1] Q[y] Has it been attempted to combine Halogen (= Chlorine) with Hydrogen in the proportion of Oxygen in Water, by the Electrical Spark?[2]

18   I 59, pencil

a. *Elementensäuren*:
1. Luftsäure = Salpetersäure   . .   1
2. Wassersäure = Salzsäure   . .   2
3. Irdsäure = Flussspathsäure   . .   3

[a. Elementary Acids:
1. Air-acid = nitric acid   . .   1
2. Water-acid = muriatic acid   . .   2
3. Earth-acid = fluoric acid   . .   3]

Discerptive Gas. Q[y] Nitrog. + Oxyg.? or $\frac{N}{C}$, as a metallic Base = Phthorium—[1]

19   I 60, pencil

[Oken classifies the vegetable acids into a main type (acetic acid) and two secondary classes (mucic acid and excreted acids), each subdivided into several varieties (malic, tartaric, saccharic, tanic, quinine, benzoic etc). The animal acids are similarly divided into a main type (phosphoric acid) and three varieties (uric, lactic, formic).]

Is not this a Classification grounded on mere Assertions, & sic mihi placets?[1]

20   I 62

* *Kohlensäure, Acidum carbonicum*, scheint Irdsaurstoff mit Wasser verbunden zu sein wie die Salzsäure, gasig, schwerer als Luft, besteht aus 62,3 Sauerstoff, 23,3 Kohlenstoff, 14,4 Wasser . . .

17[1] C refers to Thenard's discovery in 1819 of hydrogen peroxide, which he called *eau oxygené* ("oxygenated water"). It was reported promptly in British periodicals, e.g. *Philosophical Magazine* LIV (Jul 1819) 70–1.

17[2] Davy describes the process of combining hydrogen and chlorine in the proportion of one volume of hydrogen to one of chlorine by applying an electrical charge, but he does not mention experiments in the proportion of two to one: *Elements of Chemical Philosophy* (1812) 249.

18[1] C uses the French chemists' name for an element that had yet to be isolated, and that Davy named "fluorine" because it was known to be present in fluorspar.

19[1] *Sic mihi placet*, "as it pleases me"; so "whims".

[* *Carbonic acid* (*Acidum carbonicum*) seems to be lime oxide combined with water like muriatic acid; it is gaseous and heavier than air, and is composed of 62.3 [per cent] oxygen, 23.3 carbon, 14.4 water . . .]

* Pure Oxygen + diamond = Carb. Acid. Is then 14 Water here? Did not Tennant decompose it?[1]

21 I 67, pencil

In einer starken galvanischen Säule werden die beiden festen Laugen in Metall verwandelt. . . . Als Metall können sie demnach in der Natur nicht bestehen und dürfen mithin auch nicht zu den Metallen gerechnet werden.* Kein Metall bleibt für sich im Wasser aufgelöst.

[The two solid alkali are converted into metal in a strong galvanic pile. . . . They can therefore not exist as metals in nature and may thus also not be counted as metals.* No metal remains itself when dissolved in water.]

* i.e. They *are* Metals; but must not be called Metals, because they are the Metals, that they are, & not other metals?? The difference in sp. gr. between Potassium & Cerium is far less than Cerium & Platinum[1]

22 I 169, pencil

Man benennt die Farben meist nach den Körpern, an denen sie vorkommen. Diese Methode, welche die Mineralogen befolgen, sollte in allen Wissenschaften nachgeahmt werden, weil nie ein Streit über eine Farbe entstehen kann, da man den Stein oder andere Körper, nach denen die Farbe benannt ist, beliebig anschn kann.*

[Colours are named mostly after the bodies on which they appear. This method, which mineralogists adhere to, should be imitated in all the sciences, because no quarrel can ever arise over a colour since one can always look at the stone or the other substances after which the colour is named.*]

* Yes! if the color in bodies of the same name were always the same—

20[1] According to Davy "M. Lavoisier first determined that carbonic acid was formed from diamond; and Messrs. Tennant, Allen, and Pepys, have demonstrated by some refined experiments that it produces about the same quantity as an equal weight of charcoal": *Elements of Chemical Philosophy* (1812) 312. Davy refers to Smithson Tennant's paper "On the Nature of the Diamond" William Nicholson ed *A Journal of Natural Philosophy, Chemistry, and the Arts* I (1797) 177–9, e.g. 179: "The quantity of fixed air which was thus produced by the diamond does not differ much from that which, according to M. Lavoisier, might be obtained from an equal weight of charcoal."

21[1] C objects to Oken's classification of potassium as an alkali rather than as a metal like cerium and platinum. Davy, who discovered it, refers to it as a metal, e.g. in *Elements of Chemical Philosophy* (1812) 321, as does W. T. Brande, in a work C is known to have used, *A Manual of Chemistry* (1819) 183. The specific gravity of potassium is 0.862, of cerium 6.77, of platinum 21.45.

if every Sapphire had the same shade of Blue. Ex. gr. *rose*-colored—
which Rose? in what stage of growth?

23 I 243, pencil | **24** and **25** textus

It is such pages as this and the next, and alas! of too frequent occurrence!
that create an excusable prejudice against the Author and his works at
large.

24 I 243, pencil

Das vollkommenste Individuum, der Mensch ist ein Ganzes nur durch
verschiedenartige Theile. Die Theile sind wieder zweierlei, entweder
einfache, wie Nerven, Gefässe, Knochen, Muskeln, welche man *ana-
tomische Systeme* zu nenne pflegt, oder aus diesen zusammengesetzte,
als Lunge, Arm, Aug, Ohr, welche *Organe* heissen; diese machen durch
ihre Aneinandersetzung und stattliche Verbindung den *Leib* aus. Die or-
ganischen Systeme sind aus Urformen zusammengesetzt, wie die Druse,
welche bald *Zellen* (Zellgeweb), bald *Kugeln* (Knochen), bald *Fasern*
(Fleisch), bald *Puncte* (Nerv) sind.

[The most perfect individual, man, is a whole only through [the union of] dif-
ferent parts. The parts are again of two kinds, either simple, such as the nerves,
blood vessels, bones, muscles, which one used to call *anatomical systems*, or a
combination of these parts, such as the lung, arm, eye, ear, which are called
organs; these compose the *body* through their close connection and their mar-
vellous unity. Organic systems are composed of primal forms, such as the
druses, which are now *cells* (tissue), now *globules* (bone), now *fibres* (flesh),
now *points* (nerve).]

* Q̲ᵧ What is the difference between a *large Punct* (Point) and a very
minute Ball (Kugel)?

25 I 244–5, pencil

Den thierischen Organen müssen irdige Organe entsprechen, also Zu-
sammensetzungen aus den Irden, welches Berge, Gebirgsarten, *Felsen*
sind. 4. Der thierische *Leib* ist endlich aus diesen Organen zusammen-
gesetzt, so muss die Zusammensetzung der Gebirgsarten einen irdigen
Leib hervorbringen, welches *Planet* ist.∗

[Earthly organs must correspond to animal organs, that is, combinations of the
earths, which are mountains, rocky terrain, *cliffs*. 4. Just as the animal *body* is
finally composed of these organs, so the composition of rocky terrain must pro-
duce a terrestrial body, which is the *planet*.∗]

* But why stop here? Where are the Sexes? Is it a Monandria Poly-

gynia,[1] the Planets the Sun's Wives? And where are the little Master & Miss Planets? Or is the Analogy to be taken from the Rabbit Woman?[2]

26   v 2–3, pencil

Der Mensch ist Mass und Messer der Schöpfung; sein Leib mithin Mass und Messer der Thierleiber; er gibt den Thieren Stellung und Namen.

Der Leib theilt sich ein in *Kopf* und *Stamm*;

Der Stamm in *Rumpf* und *Glieder*;

Der Rumpf in *Brust, Bauch* und *Becken*. . . . Brust, Bauch und Becken bestimmen die vordere Rumpfhöhle, der Rückmarkskanal die hintere; jene wird vom Blutsystem bestimmt, diese vom Rückenmark. . . .

Der Kopf zerfällt auch in Rumpf und Glieder. . . .

Das Gesicht besteht aus Brust- und Bauchhöhle, jene *Nase*, diese *Mund*.

[Man is measure and measurer of creation; his body therefore is measure and measurer of the animal body; he gives to animals a place and a name. The body is divided into *head* and *trunk*; the trunk into *torso* and *limbs*; the torso into *chest*, *abdomen*, and *pelvis*. . . . The chest, abdomen, and pelvis determine the anterior body cavity, the spinal canal the posterior cavity; the former is determined by the circulatory system, the latter by the spinal marrow. . . . The head is also divided into trunk and limbs. . . . The face consists of chest and abdomen cavity, the latter [consisting] of the *nose*, the former of the *mouth*.]

* Even this is an instance of the Hurry in which Oken writes. P. 1. the Stamm is distinguished into Rumpf und Glieder; the R. in Br. Bauch & Becken, & here all at once we find a prior division of Rumpf in vordere and hintere![1] Observe too the confusion so idly occasioned by making fanciful analogies the ground of *names* in the nomenclature of the first & by right therefore the simplest Classification. Why in the name of the Goat-imp, CAPRICCIO,[2] should the Nose be called Belly-hole, more than

25[1] In the Linnaean botanical system, the name for a class of plants with flowers that have a single stamen and more than 12 styles; it signifies literally "one male many females".

25[2] A notorious fraud: Mary Toft or Tofts (? 1701–63) was reported as having given birth to a litter of rabbits after being frightened by a rabbit in a field. The achievement was repeated and aroused medical and popular interest, but after being caught trying to procure rabbits she confessed the imposture.

26[1] "Trunk . . . torso and limbs . . . torso into chest, abdomen and pelvis . . . torso into anterior and posterior": all in textus.

26[2] C complains again of Oken's whimsicality (as in **19**), taking "capriccio" in the sense of "caprice" to be a "little goat" or "offspring of a goat" (from the Latin *caper*).

the Belly Nose-hole?—Man is Mass und Messer der Schöpfung[3]—& yet his Limbs &c are to have Fishes for their Godfathers—Kiefer, Kiemen![4]

27 v 8–11, pencil

* Die Lunge bildet sich aus zum Lungensinn, *Nase*; Fleisch u. Knochen bilden sich aus z. Knochensinn, *Ohr*; Nerv bildet sich aus zum Nerven-sinn, *Aug*.

[* The lung develops into the sense of the lung, the *nose*; flesh and bones develop into the sense of bones, the *ear*; the nerves develop into the sense of nerves, the *eye*.]

[1]* Are then the Nerves of less necessity to the sense of Smelling and Hearing than to that of seeing? Are they not in all alike the primary and sole *proper* Agents: & to who̶m̶ich the other parts are but the stands, joints, bolts, channels, tubes, &c. & sometimes little more than the protecting *Cases*? Is it not a presumption against Oken's Scheme, that the eye appears in almost the lowest & most Nerveless Animals? And why? Because (if we do not confound mere *Feeling* or *sensation* of Stimulus with the *Sense* of *Touch*)[2] the Eye is of all the Senses the least *reflective*, the most superficial. Hence, the number of Eyes in Insects, whose Life is the life of Irritability, i.e. the electrical or *surface* Power, the *objective* selfless Sensibility ✶ the *subjective* or proper Sensibility.[3] But further. Insects have neither Lungs nor Gills; yet their Smell is almost miraculous. Mͬ R. Southey dipped some Beetles in oil. They remained to all appearance dead. He put aside 2 or 3 in another Room. To the rest he brought a female Beetle: in a few seconds the Males evinced signs of returning animation, & within a minute or two were pursuing the female briskly. The former, that were put aside, remained dead—died.

26[3] "Measure and measurer of creation": in textus.

26[4] "Jawbones, gills": the words appear in the paragraph following **26** textus, where Oken describes the arms and legs as the upper and lower jawbones of the body, and the blood vessels in the placenta as the gills of the foetus.

27[1] This note and **29** and **36** below appear in a slightly expanded form in N29 f 53 in an entry entitled "Notes on Oken's Natur-geschichte" with specific references to II 8, 12.

27[2] On the distinction between feeling and touch cf *CL* IV 773–4, where C defines feeling as the state of "Indifference" or union of all the senses, and touch as one of the five senses which emerge through the differentiation of feeling.

27[3] In *TL* (1848) 75, adopting an aspect of the system of Heinrich Steffens, C identifies the insect world with the "surface" power of electricity and the vital response of irritability. He frequently expressed the conviction that sight was commonly misrepresented as the highest of the senses, especially in his objections to "the despotism of the eye", e.g. *BL* ch 6 (*CC*) I 107, JOANNES 5, KLUGE 2.

28   v 9, pencil, and ⁺2, ink

Es giebt Thiere, in denen noch kein Nerv entwickelt ist; Eingeweid-
würmer, gallerige Quallen, Korallen, Polypen, Infusorien. Die ganze
Masse ist Nerv.

[There are animals in which no nerve has yet developed; tapeworms, gelatinous
jellyfish, corals, polyps, infusoria. The whole mass consists in nerve.]

Capital!
      P. 9. ''There are animals in which no nerve exists—Intestinal worms,
gelatinous Molluscæ, Corals, Polypes, Infusoria. *The whole Mass is
Nerve.*'' Now this I call *cutting* a Knot.

29   v 12–13, pencil

? 1. *Elemententhiere* werfen sich sehr leicht heraus; wie ursprünglich
die Elemente in Atome aufgelöst sind, so werden diese Thiere nur die
Atome des Thierreichs vorstellen, nur Puncte, Linien, Flächen oder ein-
förmige Kugeln sein, nur aus der ersten organischen Materie, *Schleim*
bestehen, *Schleimpuncte* sein.* Sie sind nothwendig die untersten, und
verhalten sich zu den andern Thieren wie die Elemente zu andern Ma-
terien, d.h. sie sind der Urstoff aller Thiere.

[? 1. *Elemental animals* are easily brought forth; just as originally the elements
are dissolved into atoms, so these animals represent only the atoms of the animal
kingdom; they will be only points, lines, planes, or uniform balls; they will
consist only of the primal organic matter, *slime*; they will be *points of slime.**
They are necessarily the lowest, and stand in the same relation to the other ani-
mals as the elements to other substances: that is, they are the primary substance
of all animals.]

* Strange to meet with one of Buffon's adopted Brats, but to which he
could not bequeath a mite of his reputation, in a Natur-philosoph of
1815!¹ Organische Atome—i.e. organisch ut mons (alias movens) a non

29¹ C may refer to Buffon's theory that
''all animals . . . and every species of ve-
getable, are composed of living organic
particles'' which are beings ''less orga-
nized than animals'' but enjoy ''a species
of life and motion''. These particles ''are
more abundant in the seminal fluids of both
sexes, and in the seeds of plants. . . .
When this organic matter, which may be
considered as an universal semen, is as-
sembled in great quantities, as in the sem-
inal fluids, and in the mucilaginous part of
the infusions of plants, its first effect is to
vegetate, or rather to produce vegetating
beings. These zoophytes swell, extend,
ramify, and then produce globular, oval,
and other bodies of different figures, all of
which enjoy a species of animal life'': Buf-
fon *Natural History* ed William Smellie
(3rd ed 1791) II ch 8 pp 214–19, 252–3. It
is not known which edition of Buffon's
Natural History C used.

movendo!²—They are "*wahre* Atome"³ too! the right genuine *Atoms*,
the indivisible primary ⟨*All-*⟩*Component Minima, composed of! Coal!
Water: Air and Light!* Okeno Trismegisto, inter Atheos alter Athanasius,
Laus et Gloria!⁴ Amen.

30 v 28, pencil

[Oken mentions a controversy over whether primitive wormlike forms
when present together can justly be regarded as one animal with one
will, or as many:] Zu einer Zeit, wo man die Aeusserungen des Willens
von den Kräften des Körpers unabhängig wähnte . . . ist solcher Streit
begreiflich. Jedes Thier hat allerdings seinen eigenen Willen; wenn es
sich aber mit andern verbindet, so geschieht es, weil sich die organ-
ischen Kräfte anziehen* . . .

[At a time when the manifestations of the will were considered to be independent
of the body's powers . . . such a controversy is understandable. Every animal
has indeed a will of its own; if nevertheless it connects itself with others, it
happens because the organic powers attract each other* . . .]

* Might not the same be said of every Mob? Besides, "unverbunden"
is surely a safer subject of Blume than unabhängig.¹ No thinking man
will assert the former; but many, I trust, the latter.

31 v 28–9, pencil

Wenn eine mesmerirte Person mit der mesmerirenden verbunden ist, so
ist auch nur *ein* Wille da, und jene gehorcht nicht nur dieser, sondern
sie will, was diese will, weil beider organische Kräfte sich gleichförmig
vertheilt haben, und in einander geflossen sind.

[When a mesmerised person is connected with the mesmeriser, only *one* will
exists, and the former not only obeys the latter but wills what the latter wills,
because the organic powers of both have evenly distributed themselves and are
intermingled.]

Mercy! What a fact to found *such* a principle on!! Etna on a lamp post

29² "Organic atoms—i.e. organic as a
mountain (moving others) by not being
moved!" C alludes to a favourite etymo-
logical joke that appears also in e.g. *CN* III
4134 and n.
29³ "*True* atoms", Oken's phrase later
on this page.
29⁴ "To Oken Trismegistus, amid the
Atheists another Athanasius, Praise and
Glory!" On Oken's atheism cf **35** below,

OKEN *Lehrbuch der Naturphilosophie* 2
and n 5.
30¹ I.e. "unconnected" a safer subject
of "flower" than "independent". Oken is
discussing the lowest forms of animal life,
which often appear closely akin to plant
life. *Unabhängig* appears in textus, and
C's "unverbunden" echoes the textus *ver-
bindet*.

were nothing to it! Nay! the pretended fact itself is at variance with other facts resting on the same Authority, proving a contrariety of Will in the Somnambulist intense even to the danger of life, when the Magnetizer has exercised an impure Will.[1]

32 v 29, pencil

[Characteristics of globular animalcules:] Bei den Milen ist aber alles eingeschachtelt, und alles durch Zusammensetzung entstanden; es ist völlig gleich, welche Hypothese man durch sie beweisen will, nur beweisen sie keine Einschachtelung in mehre Generationen hinaus, denn ihre Vervielfältigung ist nur eine Trennung der Puncte. Die sich trennenden Puncte sind aber nicht etwa eingeschachtelt, sondern die Mile fressen, und was sie auch immer fressen mögen, ist wieder organische Puncte.

[In infusoria, however, everything is enclosed and everything originates by means of combination; it does not matter which hypothesis one wishes to prove by them; only they do not prove that they have been enclosed for several generations, since their reproduction consists only in the division of points. The self-dividing points are, however, not enclosed by chance; rather, the infusoria eat, and whatever they eat constitutes in turn organic points.]

Fressende Puncte!!![1]

33 v 33, pencil

[Characteristics of spermatic animalcules, p 32] Sippschaft. . . . *Kreisel.*

  1 Gattung. *Schweifel*; kolbig, geschwänzt.
  2 Gattung. *Halsel*; kolbig, m. schwanzähnlichem Hals. . . .
  [p. 33] 4 Art. *Grünes Schweifel, C[ercaria] viridis*; walzig, hinten zweispitzig, grün, mehrgestaltig. . . . Es ist in unzählbarer Menge.

[Family. . . . *Spherical Infusoria.*
  First species. *Cercaria*; shaped like a club, with tail.
  Second species. *Trachelius*; shaped like a club, with tail-like neck. . . .
  Fourth variety. *Green Cercaria, C[ercaria] viridis*; cylindrical, double-pointed posterior, green, variously shaped. . . . It exists in numberless multitudes.]

If Prof. Oken could demonstrate that these physical points that concur in this moment to form the Green Schweifel, for instance, do in the next

31[1] C read of several such cases in his study of mesmerism, e.g. in the annotated KLUGE, pp 190–1, 198–203, 315–19. An example is Wienholt's case (p 199) of a patient made to kiss her magnetiser; she was subsequently afflicted with cramps and died of epilepsy six months later.

32[1] ''Points that eat!''

motion & interchange form a Halsel, or Kreisel[1] & so on—then I might
believe him to be in his right wits.

34　v 42, pencil

[Characteristics of Rotifera:] 2. Gattung. *Wirrel, Rotifer*; Räderthier
. . . dieses Thier ist ein wahrer Proteus, durch Einziehen der Räder,
Verkürzen des Schwanzes nimmt es die wunderlichsten Gestalten an.
ɪ. Art. *Gemeines Wirrel; Rotifer vulgaris*. . . . Durchs Suchglas
sichtbar, man will zwei Augen an ihm bemerkt haben, wenn die Räder
eingezogen sind. Streckt zwischen den Rädern eine Art Schnauze her-
aus, die es auch einziehen kann, schwimmt hurtig mittels der Räder,
kriecht schlecht und dann spannenmessend mit Schnauze wie Blutegel,
setzt sich mit dem Schwanz fest, wirbelt dann mit den Rädern, zieht die
Nahrung, kleine Mile durch diese Röhren ein bis zum Magen, der sich
beständig bewegt. Schwanz hat Einschiebsel wie Fernrohre, unten drei,
oben zwei Sporen. . . . Ausser den vielen wunderlichen Stellungen und
Figuren, die es annimmt, kann es sich auch zu einer Kugel zusammen-
ziehen, dass Schwanz, Sporne, Räder, Schwänze, Zapfen, Magen, alles
weg ist, bleibt so lange liegen; lässt sich zwar in feuchtem Sand lang
erstarrt aufbewahren, einmal vertrocknet bleibt es aber todt. Sein Aufer-
stehen ist ein Mährchen.

[Second species. *Rotifer*; Wheel-animal . . . this animal is a true Proteus; by
drawing in the wheels and shortening the tail it takes the most wonderful shapes.
First variety. *Common Rotifer, Rotifer vulgaris*. . . . It is visible through a
magnifying glass; two eyes have been noticed on it when the wheels are drawn
in. Between the wheels there protrudes a kind of snout which it can also draw
in; it swims swiftly by means of the wheels, crawls badly and then, advancing
with its snout like a leech, it fastens itself with the tail, then whirls around with
the wheels, draws its nourishment (infusoria) in through these tubes into the
stomach, which moves constantly. The tail has an inserted piece like a telescope
with three spores below, two above. . . . Among the many wonderful positions
and figures that it assumes, it can also gather itself into a sphere so that tail,
spores, wheels, tails, uvula, stomach all disappear, and it remains lying for a
long time; it preserves itself stiff for a long time in wet sand, but once it dries
up it remains dead. Its resurrection is a fairy tale.]

Then Blumenbach & I were cheated by our own eyes.[1] But what strikes

33[1] C refers to the literal meanings of
the German names: "little tail . . . little
neck . . . little circle". C objects again (as
in **29**) to the concept of elementary build-
ing-blocks of living matter, and to the no-
tion that in varying combinations they
could produce all the variety of living
forms.

34[1] C attended lectures on natural his-
tory given by J. F. Blumenbach at Göttin-
gen in 1799, and thought of translating
Blumenbach's textbook: *CL* ɪ 518, 590–1.
(He was also on friendly terms with Blu-
menbach's son, but it is surely to the fa-
mous father that he refers here.) He implies
that he and Blumenbach actually witnessed

me is the oddity of 2 or 300 or 000 or million of the *phys.* points have all at once such co-incident and yet diverse *Wills.* Here a set agreeing to form an *eye*; another set a wheel; a third a Tail &c!—[2]

35   v 51, 54–6, pencil

[Characteristics of hydrozoan polyps:] Anfangs erscheint nur ein Knötchen, das sich in einen Zapfen verlängert, dann zeigen sich die Arme als Knötchen. . . . Wird das Thier zerschnitten, so schliesst sich das Armstück hinten, das Hinterstück treibt vorn Knöpfchen und Arme, und es sind zwei Doldel. So kann jedes wieder zerschnitten werden, auch in mehre Stücke; jedes Stück wird wieder ein ganzes Thier. . . . Man kann sie umstülpen, indem man sie mit einer Borste hinten kitzelt; nun ist die äussere Wand die innere und verdaut. Das Verdaute speien sie wieder aus, weil der After fehlt. Die Reproductionskraft dieser Thiere hat seit *Trembley* viel Lärm gemacht. Das Wunder ist aber eben nicht gross.* Der ganze Leib ist eine gleichförmige, körnige oder aus Mulbeln bestehende Masse, die in jedem Theil lebt wie im Ganzen. Was auch weggeschnitten werden mag, ist dennoch kein Verlust, so wenig als eine Quecksilberkugel etwas an ihrer Kugelgestalt verliert, wenn sie zerschnitten wird.

[At the beginning there appears only a little knot that lengthens into a tail; then the arms appear [in the shape of] little knots. . . . If the animal is cut, the part of the arm closes behind, the posterior part puts forth armlets and arms, and there appear two polyps. Thus, each can be cut again into several parts; each part becomes again the whole animal. . . . One can turn them upside down by tickling them with a bristle; now the external wall is the internal one, and it digests [food]. They vomit the digested [food] because they have no anus. Since Trembley much fuss has been made about the reproductive power of these animals. The miracle, however, is not all that great. * The whole body is a uniform granicular mass or consists of monads, every part of which is alive like the whole. Whatever may be cut off nevertheless occasions no loss, any more than a quicksilver ball loses its globular shape when it is cut up.]

The Deuce it isn't! What causes these Life-Atoms always to make arms at the same places? Why a mouth only? and not an anus? Why a mouth at all? The Quicksilver forms endless globules—but does it arrange these Globules?[a] Besides, what mouth or for whom do these Life-points

---

[a] At this point C ran out of space on v 51 and accidentally turned over two leaves to continue on v 54; realising his mistake, he then wrote on v 51 "*" and marked the continuation on v 54 with "*"

---

the resurrection of the wheel-animal that Blumenbach describes in *Handbuch der Naturgeschichte* (Göttingen 1799) 471–2.

34[2] This note takes up the questions

about the independence of will in individual animals and about elementary animals as building-blocks that were raised in **30**, **31**, and **33**.

form? Does it admit the same *Mulbels*[1] only as the ones already congregated? What then is there to digest and spit out? And why receive these Accretions from *within*?—But *who* eats? Not the atoms: *they* form the Channel only of the Food? WHO digests? If each point has the same Life as the Whole, the Whole must have no other life or instinct than that in each—Therefore if one formed a Knot, *all* must form a Knot—no subordination could exist? But the joke is, that this Polyp is but one of very many kinds, each diverse yet always the same—& yet all composed of the same Mulbels, or Life-atoms!—Atheism has driven Oken mad: unless Oken was mad. And Atheism found *him*.

36 v 56, pencil

Das Thierreich fängt also an mit schleimigen Punkten, die so klein sind, dass sie nur durch dreihundertmalige Vergrösserung wahrgenommen werden können. . . . Diese Punkte verbinden sich, und werden Bläschen, die sich zu Röhren verlängern. Das umgebende Element wirkt auf ihre Aussenfläche, diese verhärtet zu Gallerte und wird äussere Röhre, in der das Thier steckt wie ein Darm. Die Gallerte wird endlich hautartig, dann papierartig, fest, zuletzt setzt sich selbst hornige und steinige Masse darinn ab, und diese einfachen Thiere gehen in Irdenthiere über.

[The realm of animals begins therefore with mucous points which are so small that they can be perceived only when they are magnified three hundred times. . . . These points combine and become little bubbles that stretch out into tubes. The surrounding element acts on their outer surface; this hardens into a gelatine and becomes an outer tube in which the animal sticks like an intestine. The gelatine finally becomes as firm as skin, then as firm as paper, [and] at last a horn-like stony mass settles within it, and these simple animals turn into terrestrial animals.]

Worthless as these *Okenisms* are in themselves, they are fit objects for serious reflection: for to these or their like, must all Pantheism come, as soon as it is applied to Physiology and the World that exists for us. What should we think of a man who seriously set about to explain the origin of York Cathedral by a pretended Discovery of the ultimate Chrystals, or of the original *Shape* of the Atoms of the Stones, with which the Walls had been built?

37 v +1–+2, pencil

I give Oken due credit for the *ingenuity* shewn by him in the Nomencla-

35[1] "Monads": in textus.

ture of the microscopic Animals, which would have done honor to a
Swift, had he given us a Natural History of Lilliput. But the want of
Common Sense is marvellous. For whom are these names invented? For
Germans only? And for those Germans, who are ignorant of the Latin,
and have no means of acquiring even so much as is requisite for pro-
nouncing a Latin *name*? And of these how many are like to study the
*Atom*ology of Animal Life, and thro' Oken's Volumes?—But for all the
rest of the World Oken's names have *no* meaning. f And even for *Ger-
mans*, it is notoriously more difficult to carry in mind a set of strange
new-minted words formed fancifully out of old words, & these for the
greater part obsolete or provincial, and as unknown to the common us-
age as Sanscrit—than to learn a new term for a new Object.—Had it
been Oken only, this would not merit noticing. But is[a] a common, a
fashionable Affectation with German Naturalists, Chemists, &c. What
if the English, French, Italians, &c did the same? Each must be confined
to the works in their own Language, or learn half a dozen Proper Names
for each Stone, Plant & Animal, instead of the one conventional Term
constructed from á one and the same fixed Language, the knowlege of
which may be presumed in every man of Letters & Science.—

In many of the German works of comparative Anatomy this silly Prac-
tice is downright provoking—for in addition to its *especial* Silliness, it
is a serious Inconvenience to a learned Foreigner who very probably
would not recognize the vulgar name of a Bone or Viscus even in his
own Mother-tongue, supposing any such word to exist in it.

38 VI 8, pencil

Die in der Tiefe lebenden Fische kommen nie an die Oberfläche und
können auch nicht, um Luft zu schlucken; sie müssen daher aus dem
verschluckten Wasser Saurstoffgas absondern, da man in ihrer Blase fast
reines Saurstoffgas findet.

[Fish that live in the depths do not and cannot ever come to the surface in order
to swallow air; they must therefore extract the oxygen gas from swallowed wa-
ter, since almost pure oxygen gas is found in their bladder.]

? But some Sorts of Fish have not Air-bladders; and from individuals
they have been cut out and the Fish recovered and lived without it.

39 VI 143, pencil

Tetradon mola. . . . Leuchtet bei Nacht, wahrscheinlich durch den
Schleim, von dem er überzogen ist, daher Mondfisch. Fleisch weiss wie

[a] For "it is"

Schnee, löst sich am Feuer in einer Art Gallert auf, schmeckt aber nach Oel.*

[*Tetradon mola*. . . . Shines at night, probably owing to the mucus with which it is covered; hence [it is called] moonfish. Flesh white as snow, dissolves over heat into a kind of gelatine but tastes of oil.*]

* The Fish stinks like putrid Carrion: we could not bear it on the open Deck beyond a minute or two.[1]

40   vi 256–7, completed in pencil

Die Natur des Giftes weder chemisch, noch pathologisch bekannt. Physiologisch kann es nichts anders als der höchste Ausdruck des Speichels sein, durch welche Ansicht aller Speichel in die Bedeutung des Giftes tritt. * Man will behaupten, dass giftige Thiere sich nicht wechselseitig tödten können, was physiologischen Lehren nicht gemäss ist.

[The nature of the poison is neither chemically nor pathologically known. Physiologically it can be nothing but the highest form of saliva, in which case all saliva enters the realm of poison. * It has been maintained that poisonous animals cannot kill each other, but this does not accord with physiological theory.]

* I could not deduce this, in my present knowlege of the circulating Fluids in snakes; but so far from deeming it incongruous with physiologic principles, I should have so far conjectured it as to ask, whether it was so or no? [a]Whether it might not be! At all events, the Assertion or traditional Belief (Man will behaupten, dass[1]—) suggests a series of highly interesting experiments, in which the effects of the viper-poison on the different Classes, instead of, as hitherto on different *sizes*, in the same class, should be tried.

41   vi 360, pencil

Die *Anlage* zum Jungen wird in Pflanzen und Thieren von der Mutter gemacht, ohne dass aber die Keime eingeschachtelt wären. Der männliche Samen verhält sich zur Keimanlage wie die Sonne zu den Planeten.

[The process of producing offspring is begun by the mother in plants and animals, but in such a way that the germ cells are not encased. The male sperm is to procreation what the sun is to the planets.]

* More, far more than this, must the Seed be, to account for Mules.[1]

[a] The note is written in pencil from here to the end

39[1] C must be referring to personal experience—presumably the voyage to (1804) or from (1806) the Mediterranean.
40[1] "It has been maintained that": in textus.

41[1] As the offspring of a he-ass and a mare, a mule is distinctly different from both its parents and consequently is an exception to Oken's general rule.

42 VI 440, pencil

[Characteristics of the robin:] . . . Rothbrüstchen; 6″ l[ang], schmutzig olivengrün, Kehle und Brust gelbroth. * Europa überall, Zugvogel, in Gärten, Hecken, Wäldern, lockt *Sifi! sifi sri!*, singt angenehm, munter auf Zweigen und Erde, zänkisch. Nistet 2mal auf die Erde, in Steinritzen, Baumlöcher, Nest zugebaut, hat nur einen Eingang.

[Redbreast: 6″ long, dirty olive green, throat and breast yellow-red. * Throughout Europe, vagrant bird, in gardens, hedges, woods, calls *Sifi! sifi sri!*, sings pleasantly, active on branches and on the ground, quarrelsome. Nests twice [a year] on the ground, in stone crevices, tree holes, enclosed nest with only one entrance.]

* If the Redbreast has the same habits in Germany as with us, it is odd that Oken says no more of our pretty winter warbler, the pious Bird that seeks the Cotter's Hearth.

43 VI 466, pencil

4. Gattung. *Corvus*, Rabe; Schn[abel] stark, grad, oben gewölbt . . . Kieferänder messerf[örmig], Naslöcher rundlich . . . Zunge knorpelig, kurz, gespalten, Füsse stark, erstes Zehenglied verwachsen, Flügel lang, Federn im Flug ausgesperrt, fressen Gewürm und Gesäme, schreiten und hüpfen, ätzen ausm Schlund, wenns nur Gewürm ist, ausm Schnabel, wenns Mäuse, Vögel sind. Stehlen gern, und verstecken es, besonders Futter und Metall, leben gesellig, schreien viel und unangenehm.

[Fourth species. *Corvus*, Crow; bill strong, straight, curved on top . . . edges of jaw shaped like a knife, nostrils round . . . tongue cartilaginous, short, forked, legs strong, first toe overgrown, wings long, feathers spread out in flight; [they] eat worms and seeds, walk and hop, take in food with the throat when there are only worms and with the bill when there are mice [or] birds. Like to steal and hide what they have stolen, especially food and metal; gregarious, screech much and unpleasantly.]

A very meagre & imperfect account of the Corvus—Rabe—Raven, Carrion Crow, Rook. ~~The latter not in Germany, but Oken might have found it described in Blumenbach~~ ⟨a mistake of mine⟩[a][1]

44 VI 652, pencil

Das Eijunge erhält seinen Oxydations- also Lebensprocess nicht von der

[a] Written above the note

43[1] Blumenbach describes the rook, *Corvus frugilegus*, in *Handbuch der Naturgeschichte* (Göttingen 1799) 202, describing it as a useful bird found throughout Europe; C's error was believing it not to appear in Germany. For C's early use of Blumenbach's work cf *CN* I 1738–53nn.

Mutter, sondern von der äussern Luft, welche ins Ei dringt: bei den Sucken aber tritt das Sauerstoffgas an das Blut der Mutter, und von diesem an den Mutterkuchen des Kindes, der also *Kieme und nicht Ernährungsorgan ist.*

[The embryo receives its oxidation—i.e. its life process—not from its mother but from the external air which penetrates the ovum; but in mammals the oxygen gas enters the mother's blood and through it enters the placenta of the child, which therefore is an *organ for breathing and not for nourishment.*]

What then *is*? the Amnion?[1]

45 vi 657, pencil

Die Hüllen des Jungen sind Chorion (Aderhaut), Amnion (Schafhaut), Harnhaut (*Allantois*), Darmblase (*Tunica erythroides = Vesicula umbilicalis*). Weiter gibt es keine. Sie sind nicht da, um wie ein todtes Gefäss nur das Junge einzuschliessen, sondern sie sind wesentliche Organe des Jungen selbst, die aber nur schnell ihren Lebenslauf vollenden und absterben.* Aus dem Chorion entsteht das Gefässsystem, Leber, Lunge, Hirn, Fleisch, Knochen, das Junge athmet damit; aus dem Amnion ernährt sich das Junge . . .

[The embryo's membranes are the chorion, the amnion, the allantois, the umbilical vesicle (*Tunica erythroides = Vesicula umbilicalis*). There are no others. They do not serve merely to envelop the embryo like a dead vessel but are, rather, the essential organs of the embryo itself, which however quickly complete their life cycle and die.* From the chorion the circulatory system develops, the liver, lungs, brain, flesh, bones; the embryo breathes through it; from the amnion the embryo draws its nourishment . . .]

* Then it should seem, that these Envelopes rather *are*, than can be said to inclose, the Fœtus. Or yet more truly, that the Chorion is *the* Child, which compleats itself out of the Allantois & the Vesic. Umb.?

46 vi 658, pencil

Wenig Thiere werden so alt als der Mensch, vielleicht nur der Elephant wird älter. Die wenigsten erreichen 30 Jahre, die meisten kaum ein Dutzend, wohin besonders die Kleinen gehören. Es ist zu bemerken, dass die Grösse lediglich hierauf Einfluss hat, nicht die Verschiedenheit der Geschlechter,* wohl aber die der Geschlechter, indem das Männchen meist grösser, stärker, hurtiger als das W[eibchen] ist.

[Few animals grow as old as man; possibly only the elephant grows older. Very

44[1] The amnion is described as one of the four membranes of the foetus in **45** below.

few animals reach the age of thirty; most [live] barely twelve years—this applies especially to the small ones. It is worth noting that only size influences this: not the difference between genera* but rather that between sexes, since the male is usually larger, stronger, nimbler than the female.]

* The same word for Genera & Sexes?[1] Is it meant for Wit, an *intentional* Conundrum?

47 vi 663, pencil

Es ist doch sonderbar, dass Wale bald sterben, wenn sie aufs Trockene kommen, wo ihnen doch der Athemprocess nicht verändert wird. * Man kennt ein Beispiel, dass eine Menge gestrandeter in wenig Tagen verreckte, und nur ein altes Männchen 5 Tage lebte.

[It is indeed strange that whales die when they are stranded although their breathing process does not change. * An instance is known of a number who were stranded and died while only an old male lived for five days.]

* ~~Hea~~ Hectic *fever*, from accumulation of Heat in the absence of the abstracting Fluid? Hence the *old* one lived the longest?

48 vi 806

Einige meinen, sie [versteinerte Elephanten] seien durch Ueberschwemmung aus Indien hergebracht worden, andere sie wären nur, aber plötzlich ertränkt, oder durch schnelle Klimaveränderung getödtet worden. Allein es ist wahrscheinlich, dass sie ruhig an Ort und Stelle starben, so wie unser Vieh. . . . * dass sich einige mit Meerproducten finden, beweist nicht, dass sie in einer Ueberschwemmung umgekommen sind. . . . Von Elephantenknochen wimmelt es in Siberien, vorzüglich gegen das Eismeer, und hier sogar am meisten auf dem Inseln. . . . Man findet sie längs der ungeheuren Flüsse Wolga, Don . . . kurz an allen Flüssen vom Don bis Kamtschatka, meist in trocknen Ebenen, nicht an den Hochgebirgen und nicht in Sümpfen, aber oft unter Schichten von Meerthieren.

[Some think that they [fossil elephants] were brought from India by floods, others that they just drowned suddenly or were killed by a quick change of climate. It is more probable, however, that they died quietly on the spot, like our cattle. . . . * The fact that a few have been found along with sea creatures does not prove that they perished in a flood. . . . Bones of elephants abound in Siberia, especially near the polar sea and there mostly on the islands. One finds them along the large rivers Volga and Don . . . in short, along all rivers from the Don to Kamchatka, mostly on dry plains, not in high mountains, nor in swamps, but often underneath strata of marine animals.]

46[1] I.e. *das Geschlecht*, in textus.

* What then does it prove? How came the Strata of marine animals (p. 807) over them?

49 VI 1042–3, pencil

[Characteristics of different breeds of dogs.]

Oken prefaces his work by describing it as unusually full & particular respecting the Habits, Manners & Instincts of animals. Surely he has forgotten his promise just where it might have been expected that he would performed[a] it most at large & with most delight.

50 VI +6, pencil

Heron, Hern/[1]

---

[a] A slip for "perform" or "have performed"

50[1] C records "Hern" as an archaic English form for "heron": the connection (if there is any) with Oken is obscure, though Oken does include the heron (*Reiher*) in the catalogue of animals in this volume: VI 570–1.

Lehrbuch der Naturphilosophie. 2 pts in 1 vol. Jena 1809. 8°.

The volume is imperfectly bound, with a second copy of pp 225–8 bound at pp vi/vii.

British Library C 126 g 1

"S. T. C." label at head of title-page. At pp 56/7 a leaf is tipped in with three notes referring to Wolfart: see WOLFART.

DATE. Aug–Sept 1818, coinciding with a series of notebook entries: *CN* III 4427–9.

COEDITORS. Lore Metzger, Raimonda Modiano.

TEXTUS TRANSLATION. Alfred Tulk tr *Elements of Physiophilosophy* Ray Society Publications no 10 (1847); since Tulk worked from a later edition than C's, his translations have been modified where necessary.

1   half-title, pencil, badly rubbed | Dedication

One Pound—
  [? Lathmete]
    Coach   1.6
  [? Ba . . .] 3.6   remain—9.

———

$15 \times 3 = 45$
$45 + 11 = 56$ for steward 57.

    $3 + 9$ 12—[? Therefore . . .] $12 - 2$
    the offer at present, 1.0.7
    after one answerable for all [. . .]

    To Mr Murray,   13. 6.
    To Mrs Coleridge   4. 6.
    Dinner, &c
  during the while
      Same—
    Paid for Tea   2
    Coach to the Stage   4[1]

———

[1] These memoranda and calculations of expenses obscurely suggest a recent journey (perhaps C's trip to Essex in Jun 1818: *CL* IV 867–9) and a small debt, perhaps for books, to the publisher John Murray.

2 p [2], pencil, lightly cropped | § 1

* 1. Die höchste mathematische Idee, oder das Grundprincip aller Mathematik ist das Zero = 0.

[* The highest mathematical idea, or the fundamental principle of all mathematics, is the zero = 0.]

* How completely does the very first ¶ betray the Γοητην καὶ Θαυματουργον,[1] the quacking Paradox-monger! The highest mathematical Idea, and its grounding Principle is = 0! Now as the Mathemata are distinguished from Philosophemata (of course Mathesis from Philosophy) by ~~its~~ the compulsive evidence of its Axioms, this position ought to force assent the moment it is enunciated. An Axiom, that requires a commentary, is a contradiction in terms.[2] And truly Oken has given none—. But whether it is not requisite, let those determine who like me read the assertion, that all numbers then first acquire significance and reality when they are capable of being stated equal to 0, with a Stare and an inward—What, the deuce! can the Man mean?

From the History of my own reasoning I perceive, that this absurd position is a necessary Consequence of the pantheistic or rather atheistic Absolute, as the mera nuda [? mysteria][3] in which all = 0 & 0 = all.[4]

3 pp 4–6, pencil, lightly cropped, rubbed | §§ 3–4

3. Wenn daher die Mathematik eine <u>reale</u> Wissenschaft sein will, so ist es nicht genug, dass sie nur das höchste Princip habe, sondern sie muss in eine Menge von Einzelnheiten zerfallen, nehmlich zunächst in Zahlen und endlich in Sätze. Alle Realität kann sich nur in der Vielheit offenbaren; wo diese nicht ist, ist die Wirklichkeit verschwunden, sie ist Zero geworden. Es ist folglich der erste Act des Realwerdens, des Etwaswerdens ein Entstehen von Vielem, also von etwas Bestimmtem, oder überhaupt von etwas Begränztem, Endlichem. Es frägt sich, wie es zugeht, dass die Mathematik eine Vielheit, oder was dasselbe ist, dass sie eine Realität, ein Etwas wird.

4. Wenn das Zero das höchste Princip ist, auf das sich alles Einzelne, alles Endliche, alle Zahl der Mathematik reduciren lässt, und von dem

2[1] ''Wizard and Wonder-worker'': the following phrase is a more cynical translation.

2[2] C echoes Kant's analysis of the difference between mathematical and philosophical knowledge and his conclusion that axioms belong to mathematics alone; he mentions the distinction also in NICOLAI

10.

2[3] ''Pure, bare [? mystery]''.

2[4] The foundation of C's objections to post-Kantian *Naturphilosophie* in general was its tendency to atheism: cf *CN* III 4429, and *CL* IV 873–6, a letter of 30 Sept 1818 to J. H. Green, mentioning Oken.

alles begründet ist; so kann alle Zahl, und alles, was in die Mathematik gehört, keine andere Quelle haben, als das Zero.

[3. In order, therefore, that mathematics may become a real science, it is not enough that it have only the highest principle; rather, it must subdivide into a number of details, namely, first of all into numbers and finally into propositions. All reality can manifest itself only in multiplicity; without this, reality disappears, it becomes zero. The first act of becoming real or of becoming something is, accordingly, a coming into existence of many, that is of something definite, or generally something limited, finite. The question arises how it happens that mathematics becomes a multiplicity or, what is the same thing, a reality, a something.

4. If zero constitutes the highest principle to which every particular, every finite [thing], every number of mathematics can be reduced and in which all are grounded, then every number and everything belonging to mathematics has no other source than zero.]

What does Oken mean by a *real* Science? Is there then an *unreal* Science, in any sense of the word that leaves Geometry *real*? But if it mean a Science adequately realizable in the World of the Senses, i.e. extra mentem[1]—Mathematics are not a *real* Science. Oken's ¶. 3. demands that we should read *Verstehen*schaft instead of Wissenschaft.[2] But in fact all these ¶s are rank lazy Truisms, that borrow all their semblance of Depth from tautology—they all amount to the indistinguishable cannot [. . . . .]*a*

The 4th ¶ is false logic. The Zero even of Oken's own doctrine is not the *Fountain*—for a Fountain means more than the passive water of the Fountain—viz. ~~with~~ an ebullient or projective power + the Wat[er] which therefore neither is; has been; or can be = 0. In short the parent and prolific error (το πρωτον ψευδος)[3] of *all* the *Schellingia[ns]* consists in the ANTEDATING of *Potentiality*: of *Polarity*, the latter being a vicious ⟨equivoque.⟩ Deus nempe = ens realissimum, sive Realitas actuosissima, sine ullâ potentialitate.[4] S. T. C. But in the line A——B,

---

a One line of ms cropped

3[1] "Outside the mind".

3[2] "Understanding" instead of "science": C coins the term *Verstehenschaft* from the verb *verstehen*, "to understand", by analogy with *Wissenschaft* ("science"), formed from the verb *wissen*, "to know".

3[3] "The fundamental error": an often-used phrase that C renders as "Mother-lie" in **4** below.

3[4] "God indeed = the most real being, or most fully active Reality without potentiality." C invoked this scholastic definition of God many times, e.g. in *BL* ch 9 (*CC*) I 143. His dissent from the system of *Naturphilosophie* expounded by Schelling and his followers rests in his belief in an absolute unity antecedent to the polar pattern of thesis and antithesis and the varying relations between them: cf **11** below, and *CL* IV 873–6.

when B repels A—the attractive force is [? natural/notional] in B. actual. Ergo, ubi nulla potentialitas, nulla polaritas—at in Deo nulla pot., ergo, nulla pol:⁵—Q: E. D.

4 p 8, pencil | § 11

Beim Realwerden der Monas muss durchgehends das Gegentheil auftreten. Da geht die Einheit, Klarheit, Gleichartigkeit, Ununterscheidbarkeit verloren, und verwandelt sich in Vielheit, Getrübtheit, Verschiedenheit: Das Ewige zeitlich gesetzt, ist ein Fortlaufendes ohne Ende, die Einheit vielfach gesetzt, ist ein Ausgedehntes ohne Ende, aber immer dasselbe bleibend. Das Realwerden ist ein Extendiren des Absoluten seiner selbst.

[With the realisation of the [mathematical] monad the opposite must appear throughout. Thereby unity, clarity, homogeneity, indistinguishability are lost, and are converted into multiplicity, obscurity, diversity. The eternal posited temporally is limitless continuum, unity posited manifoldly is limitless expansion, which however always remains the same. The realisation is an extension of the absolute itself.]

¶. 11. is utterly false: and the πρωτον ψευδος,¹ the Mother-Lie of the whole Brood of Okenisms.

5 p 8, pencil | § 12, following **4** textus

Die erste Form dieses Extendirens der Monas ist die Zweiheit, und diese ist das + −. Alles Manchfaltige der Mathematik löst sich zuletzt, ehe es in das Zero übergeht, in + − auf. Die ganze Arithmetik beruht auf zwei Zahlenreihen, auf der positiven und negativen; eine Zahlenreihe ist aber nur eine Wiederholung eines + 1 oder eines − 1, folglich reducirt sich die ganze Arithmetik auf + 1 − 1.

[The first form of this expansion of the monas is duality, and this is the + −. Every manifold of mathematics, before passing into zero, is finally reduced to + −. The whole of arithmetic depends on two numerical series, the positive and the negative; a numerical series is, however, only a repetition of a + 1 or a − 1; consequently, the whole of arithmetic reduces itself to + 1 − 1.]

¶. 12. No! not 01 = 1: 0 = 1 = 111. Die erste Form ist die Dreiheit.¹

6 p 8, pencil | § 13

Was ist aber ein + 1 oder ein − 1? Offenbar nichts anders, als ein ein-

3⁵ "Therefore where there is no potentiality there is no polarity—as there is in God no potentiality, therefore no polarity."

4¹ "Fundamental error" as in **3** above at n 3.

5¹ "The first form is the triad."

faches + oder −. Die Ziffer ist ganz überflüssig, und man kann statt
+ 1 setzen +, statt − 1 aber − schlechtin. Ueberhaupt ist die ganze
Zahlenreihe nichts anders als eine Wiederholung von + oder − ins
Unendliche; die Reihe + 1 + 1 + 1 ist gleichbedeutend der + + +,
oder statt 3 kann man setzen + + +, und so für jede beliebige Zahl.

[What, however, is a + 1, or a − 1? Obviously nothing other than a single + or
−. The figure is quite superfluous, and instead of + 1 we can posit +, instead
of − 1 simply −. The whole numerical series is generally nothing other than a
repetition of + or − ad infinitum; the series + 1 + 1 + 1 is synonymous with
+ + +, or instead of 3 we may posit + + +, and so on for any number ad
libitum.]

¶. 13. *Shallow* as well as false—5 is not the same as + + + + + but
5 = 1 = 11111. 7 is as like a unit as 1, where ever 1 and 7 are ejusdem
essentiae[1]—i.e. where it is a *unit* and not = 0

7   p 14 | § 31

Durch das Negiren wird das Endliche mit dem Absoluten verbunden.
Alles Verschwinden des Endlichen ist ein Zurückgehen ins Absolute,
oder ein Endliches kann nicht vergehen, ohne wieder ins Absolute zu-
rückzugehen, denn woher es gekommen, dahin muss es wieder ge-
langen. Es ist aus dem Nichts entstanden, ist selbst das seiende Nichts,
daher muss es auch wieder in das Nichts zurückgehen.

[Through negation the finite becomes united with the absolute. Every disappear-
ance of the finite is a retrogression into the absolute, or nothing finite can perish
without again returning to the absolute; for it must return to whence it came. It
has arisen out of nothing, is itself the existing nothing; it must therefore return
again into the nothing.]

This affect[?ivish]ation of Buddhaism is truly characteristic Oken.

Oken   = 7½.
Genius = 2½
Talent = 4½
Sense = 0½
─────────
         7½

8   p 15, pencil | §§ 33, 34

Gott ist das selbstbewusste Nichts, oder das seiende (selbstbewusste)
Nichts ist Gott. . . . Was in unserem Bewusstsein die Vorstellungen
sind, das sind die einzelnen Erscheinungen der Welt im Bewusstsein

6[1]   "Of the same essence".

Gottes. Die weltlichen Dinge haben für Gott nicht mehr Realität, als unsre Gedanken für unser Bewusstsein. Wir tragen eine Welt in uns, und schöpfen in jedem Momente eine, indem wir denken, oder uns poniren; ebenso hat Gott erschaffen in dem Momente, in dem er zum Selbstbewusstsein kam, und er erschafft ewig, weil er ewig zum Selbstbewusstsein kömmt, weil er das ewige Selbstbewusstsein, und nichts anders ist.

[God is self-conscious nothingness, or the existing (self-conscious) nothingness is God. . . . What ideas are in our consciousness, the individual appearances of the world are in God's consciousness. Worldly things have no more reality for God than our thoughts have for our consciousness. We carry a world within us and create one each moment that we think or posit our existence; just so God created the moment he became self-conscious, and he creates eternally because he becomes self-conscious eternally, because he is the eternal self-consciousness itself and nothing else.]

N.B. all this is sad Common-place, the only approach to Novelty consisting in the strangeness of calling the Eternal I Am *Nothing*—and even this is but a poor plagiarism from the Burmese, and the dreaming Faquirs of Budda—/[1] not to add, that it is either a stupid Contradiction in terms—if we are to understand it as—An Eternal Mind = Nothing i.e. = A and not = A—/ or it is a silly Equivoque—God is no *Thing*.

9   p 19, pencil | §§ 39–48

Nennt man diese drei Formen Ideen, so kann man sagen, das Absolute zerfalle ursprünglich in drei Ideen, aus welches alle Manchfaltigkeit hervorgeht. . . . Die erste Idee ist die ursprüngliche, also durchaus unabhängige, aus sich selbst entstandene, kurz die ewige = 0 = aoristos Monas. . . . Die beiden andern Ideen sind . . . nur ausgegangen aus der ersten Idee, obschon ihr gleich, ja sie selbst, aber ausgegangen aus sich selbst, sich erscheinend = *Monas determinata* oder *Dyas aoristos* und *Trias aoristos*. Die erste Idee als ein Ewiges ist von Ewigkeit her bemüht oder vielmehr erfreut, sich in die zwei anderen Ideen zu verwandeln. Das Thun Gottes oder das Leben Gottes besteht darinn, sich ewig selbst zu erscheinen, ewig sich selbst anzuschauen in der Einheit und Zweiheit, ewig sich zu entzweien und doch eins zu bleiben.

[If one calls these three forms ideas, then one may say that the absolute divides itself originally into three ideas, from which all multiplicity arises. . . . The first idea is the original, therefore that which is thoroughly independent, which has originated from itself, in short, the eternal = 0 = *aoristos Monas* [infinite Monad]. . . . The two other ideas have . . . merely emerged from the first idea, though resembling it; yea, they have themselves issued out of themselves [and

8[1]   An elaboration of the charge of "affectation of Buddhaism" in **7**.

are] self-manifesting = *Monas determinata* [fixed Monad] or *Dyas aoristos* [infinite Dyad] and *Trias aoristos* [infinite Triad]. The first idea, as something eternal, labours or, rather, rejoices from all eternity to transform itself into the two other ideas. The action of God or the life of God consists in eternally manifesting itself, eternally contemplating itself in unity and duality, eternally dividing itself and still remaining one.]

This Chapter is a far better (and indeed very near to the Orthodox) statement of the Trinity in Unity, than could have been expected from the preceding Jargon.

10   p 20 | §§ 49–51

Gott ist in seiner Uridee die absolute Identität, das 0, die *Monas aoristos.* . . . Das *Ousia* ist das nicht Darstellbare, das nie Erscheinende, das überall Seiende, aber sich immer Entziehende . . . kurz das Geistige, welches sich in alles verwandelt, aber doch dasselbe bleibt.

[In the primary idea, God is absolute identity, 0, the *Monas aoristos* [infinite Monad]. . . . This *Ousia* [Being] is the non-representable, the never-apparent, the omnipresent yet always withdrawing . . . in short, the spiritual which transforms itself into everything yet remains the same.]

For a pantheistic System, this is as near to the Truth as was perhaps possible. But the exquisite absurdity of calling the same X Nichts (Nothing) and Ousia (Being) is Oken all over!

11   pp 22–3, pencil | §§ 59–60

Alle Activität der Dinge, alle Kräfte sind Entelechien, entspringen aus der Urentelechie, aus dem Selbsterscheinungsacte Gottes. Es gibt daher keine einfache Kraft in der Welt, jede ist eine Selbsterscheinung, eine Position von + − , oder eine *Polarität.*

[All activity of things, all their forces, are entelechies that originate from the primal entelechy, from God's act of self-manifestation. There is, therefore, no single force, but each is self-manifesting, a placing of + and − , or a *polarity.*]

* Here lies the fundamental Falsity of the *Natur-philosophie.*—It places Polarity in the Eternal, in God. All its other Errors are consequences of this.[1]

12   p 41, pencil | § 123

Da nun die Sphäre aus dem Nichts entstanden ist, so ist auch die Schwere aus demselben entstanden. Die Form ist ein geformtes Nichts, die Form ist aber keine Form ohne innere formende Kräfte, wozu die

---

11[1] See **3** n 4 above.

Schwere gehört. Geformtsein und Schwersein ist eins. Die Schwere ist ein gewichtiges Nichts, ein schweres, central strebendes Wesen, *Ousia*, Realwerdung der ersten göttlichen Idee.

[Now, as the sphere has originated out of nothing, so also has gravity originated out of the same. The form is a formed nothing; the form is however no form without internal forming forces, among which gravity is one. The being of form and the being of gravity are one. Gravity is a weighty nothing, a heavy essence, *Ousia* [Being], striving towards the centre, the becoming real of the first divine idea.]

Other Philosophers have given, as a solution of the problem, a part of the problem to be solved; ~~to~~ but D̠ʳ Oken boldly turns the whole problem into the Solution. Every thing is nothing, differenced therefrom by being 0 + 0; and Nothing is *every thing*, differenced from *Something* by being 0 = 0!!

13   p 41, pencil | §§ 125–6

Von der Materie gilt alles, was von der Schwere gesagt worden; denn Materie ist nur ein anderes Wort für Schwere. Ein schweres Ding ist ein materiales Ding.

126. Zur Totalität eines Dinges gehört nicht blos seine Figur, nicht blos seine Spannung oder Bewegung, sondern auch seine Schwere; diese ist aber die *Ousia*, die Materie ist mithin totale Position Gottes, ist Dreiheit der Ideen. Gott als vollendetes Object ist Materie; Materie ist der schwere Gott. Die materiale *Ousia* nenne ich Substanz.

[Everything which has been said of gravity holds good with respect to matter; for matter is only another term for gravity. A heavy thing is a material thing. 126. To the totality of a thing belongs not merely its figure, not merely its tension or motion, but also its gravity; this is, however, the *Ousia* [Being], [and] matter is consequently a total placing of God, a trinity of ideas. God as perfected object is matter; matter is the weighty God. The material *Ousia* I call substance.]

The cavalier manner, in which Oken—*not* unfolds, but enfolds all the phænomena of the Universe in his God Nothing, and instead of explaining Matter, Gravity, &c coolly assures his Readers, that they are all mere Synonymes of + and − Nichts, is very amusing.

14   p 45, pencil | § 143

* Das sich aus dem Aether Individualisirende kann nichts anders als wieder eine Sphäre sein. Der Aether zerfällt in unendlich viele untergeordnete rotirende Aethersphären, und er muss darein zerfallen, weil die Welt kein Ganzes ohne Theile, sondern nur ein Ganzes in den Theilen, nur eine Wiederholung von Positionen ist.

[* Whatever is individuated from aether can be nothing other than a sphere again. The aether subdivides into infinitely many subordinate rotating spheres, and so it must be, because the universe is not a whole devoid of parts, but only a whole in the parts, only a repetition of positions.]

Exquisite. It must be so for if it were not *so*, it would be *so*—but A being A − B cannot be B − A!—

15 p 83, pencil | § 268

Der Sauerstoff ist das überall Thätige, alles Aufregende, Belebende, Bewegende, das Licht im Irdischen. Der Stickstoff das Träge, Todte, Indifferente, heisst bezeichnend *Azot* . . .

[Oxygen is that which is everywhere active, everything that excites, animates, moves; it is the light of the terrestrial. Nitrogen is [that which is everywhere] inert, dead, indifferent; significantly, it is called *azote* . . .]

May Common Sense dare ask H. v. Oken how it happens that Oxygen Gas is heavier than the Azotic; Oxyds than the Metals?[1]

16 p 89, pencil | § 292

Das Wasser ist sphärisch in seinen kleinsten Theilen, denn es ist der aus sich getretene Punct; die Erde aber ist überall nichts als Punct, * daher concret, jeder Theil für sich bestehend, während das Wasser nur durch die Allheit aller Wassertheilchen besteht . . .

[Water is spherical in its smallest parts, for it is the point that goes out from itself; but earth is everywhere nothing but a point, * [and is] thus concrete, each part existing independently, while water exists only through the totality of all water particles . . .]

* It would be *almost*, perhaps, worth the while to analyse this curious position. A Point having no length or breadth; whence is Earth extended?

17 p 93, pencil | §§ 296–302

296. Die nächste Verdunkelung des Lichts, oder sein unmittelbarer Uebergang in Materie ist der polare Urstoff, der *Sauerstoff*. Sauerstoff ist das leibliche Licht. . . .

298. Die Sonne ist der Sauerstoffkörper, das Wassern im Weltraume, der Planet aber ist der Strickstoffkörper, die Erde im Weltraume, der Aether ist zwischen allen als die Himmelsluft verbreitet. . . .

15[1] Oken does not assert that nitrogen (azote) is heavier than oxygen, but C takes this conclusion as implied in Oken's definition of nitrogen as the body of gravity and of oxygen as the body of light. The name "azote" signifies "unable to support life"—though the *OED* points out that it was based on a false etymology.

301. Durch das Licht wird in der Materie der negative, sein Gegenpol hervorgerufen. Die Sonne setzt sich entgegen den Planeten als *Stickstof-figes*.*

302. Das Licht tendirt von der Sonne zur Erde, nicht blos weil es Radialität ist, sondern weil die Erde der Stickstoffpol der Sonne ist . . .

[296. The next obscuration of light, or its immediate transition into matter, is the polar primary matter, *oxygen*. Oxygen is embodied light. . . . 298. The sun is the body of oxygen, the water in the world-space; the planet, however, is the body of nitrogen, the earth in the world-space. The aether is diffused between the two as the air of heaven. . . . 301. Through light the negative, its opposite pole, has been evoked in matter. The sun opposes itself to the planets as *azotic*.* 302. The light tends from the sun to the earth, not merely because light is radiality, but because the earth is the azotic pole of the sun . . .]

—gen? Dative Plural agreeing with Planeten?[1] If not, it seems a direct contradiction to ¶ 298.

This Stickstoffpol[2] is Stuff that will not stick in my pole & how comes it to be the −pol?

* In addition to his extravagance, Oken seems to aim at Obscurity and to perplex: 296 Light embodied [? but] becomes Oxygen. 301. The Sun opposes itself to the Planets, as azotic—i.e. the Sun is azote in relation to the Planets.—298: The direct contrary.

18　p 95, pencil | § 312

Alle durchsichtige Körper müssen das Licht brechen. Die Körper sind aber dichter als der Aether, daher muss das Licht, welches aus einem dünneren Mittel in ein dichteres geht, gegen das Centrum (Einfallsloth) gebrochen werden, und im umgekehrten Falle umgekehrt.

[All transparent bodies must refract light. The bodies are, however, denser than the aether; therefore light which passes from a rarer into a denser medium must be refracted towards the center (plummet of incidence), and in the reverse case the other way round.]

It is so, we know: but why? Oken has forgot to explain.

19　p 96, pencil | § 317

Die Durchsichtigkeit kömmt nur denjenigen Körpern zu, welche noch eine Duplicität in sich haben. Es wird sich zeigen, dass die Metalle absolut identische Materien sind, und daher ihre Undurchsichtigkeit. Die Metalle sind die einzigen undurchsichtigen Körper.

17[1] C's suggestion that Oken's term should be *Stickstoffigen* would make the planets, rather than the sun, nitrogenous bodies.

17[2] "Azotic pole"—at end of textus.

[Transparency belongs only to those bodies which have in themselves a twofold character. It will be shown that the metals are absolutely uniform substances, whence comes their opacity. Metals are the only opaque bodies.]

Gold Leaf?[a]

Can it be supposed, that the Hammering produces a slight Oxydation and that this is the cause of the Green Light seen thro' the Gold Leaf?

20   pp 98–9, pencil | §§ 324–5

Das Substrat des Lichts, der Aether, hat daher zwei extreme Zustände, und nur zwei, den gespannten und den ungespannten; jener ist der *lichte*, dieser der *finstere*. . . . Die mittlere Aetherspannung, das Licht mit Finsterniss gemischt, heisst *Farbe*.

[The substratum of light, the aether, therefore has two extreme conditions, and only two, the tensed and the untensed; the one is *light*, the other *dark*. . . . The mean tension of aether, light mingled with darkness, is called *Colour*.

Licht = gespanntes Æther. Ergo: Licht − Spannung = ungespanntes Æther.—

But Licht material ponirt = L − Sp: ergo = ungespanntes Æther.

So Licht = ungesp. Æther = Weiss; yet ungesp. Æther = Licht = Schwarz![1] This is swearing Black White with a vengeance.

21   p 99, pencil | §§ 325–7, continuing **20** textus

Farbe ist ein endliches, ein fixirtes Licht, der leibhafte Uebergang des Lichts in Materie. Eine immateriale Farbe ist ein Unding.

326. Keine Materie kann ungefärbt sein. Eine ungefärbte Materie ist auch ein Unding. . . .

327. Das klare Licht material ponirt ist *Weiss*.*

Der ungespannte Aether material gesetzt ist *Schwarz*.

[Colour is a finite, fixed light, the embodied transition of light into matter. An immaterial colour is a non-thing. 326. No matter can be colourless. A colourless matter, too, is a non-thing. . . . 327. Pure light materially posited is *White*.* The untensed aether materially posited is *Black*.]

* The clear unturbid Light is tense (gespanntes)Æther. By losing its tension, it becomes material (material ponirt)[1]—And the clear Light *material ponirt*—i.e. becoming darkness is *white*. Is not this nonsense?

[a] C has written "*" here and has continued the note in the foot-margin starting with another "*"

20[1] "Light = tensed aether. Therefore: light minus tension = untensed aether.— But light materially posited = light minus tension: therefore = untensed aether. Thus light = untensed aether = white; yet untensed aether = light = black!"

21[1] C's terms come from **20** and **21** textus.

22 p 99, pencil | § 331

Es ist nichts sichtbar als die Farbe, nichts als die gefärbte Materie. <u>Kein Körper ist sichtbar.</u>
    Die Finsterniss ist der Grund aller Sichtbarkeit. Gäbe es keine Finsterniss, so gäbe es keine Welt für das Auge.

[There is nothing visible but colour, but coloured matter. <u>No body is visible.</u> Darkness is the cause of all visibility. Were there no darkness, there would be no world for the eye.]

O wonder of wonders! Nought could we see: for nothing would be there to be seen!

23 p 113 | §§ 384–5

Der Electrismus existirt unter zwei Formen, als Lichtstoff- und als Schwerestoffelectrismus. Man nennt diese zwei Zustände + E. und − E, vielleicht mit Unrecht.
    385. Das + E ist das energischere, in sich selbst active, polare; es ist der Lichtelectrismus dargestellt im Sauerstoffe. Das − E ist das indifferente, trage, usiale, oder schwere.

[Electricity exists under two forms, as the electricity of the substance or body of fire [light], and as the electricity of the planet [gravity]. These two conditions are called, perhaps incorrectly, + E and − E. 385. The + E is the more energetic, active in itself, polar; it is the electricity of fire represented in oxygen. The − E is the indifferent, inert, basic, or heavy.]

The German Philosophers either use the terms, + and − in the reverse sense that we do: or they mistake the fact. The Oxygen or Contractive Power is the Negative Pole. The Hydrogen or Dilative is the positive. So the Attractive or North Pole is Negative Magnetism; Nitrogen, the Repulsive, is the + Magnetism.[1]

24 p 113 | § 386

Diese elektrischen Zustände müssen in der Luft immer wechseln, je nachdem von aussen die geringste Einwirkung geschieht. In diesem Wechsel der elektrischen Pole besteht die Luft. Wechselten sie nicht, so wäre die Luft ein festes Element. Die Erde ist eine Luft mit *fixer* Elektricität.

[23][1] The four-pole scheme, with carbon and nitrogen as the attractive and repulsive poles of the line of magnetism and oxygen and hydrogen as the contractive and dilative poles of the line of electricity, is basic to C's system of natural philosophy: see OKEN *Lehrbuch der Naturgeschichte* **1** n 8 and the letter of 30 Sept 1818 cited in **2** n 4 above. By "we" in this note C probably means himself and J. H. Green, his fellow investigator.

[These electrical conditions must always be changing in the air, according as the slightest influence is brought to bear upon them from without. The air consists in this change of electrical poles. Were the poles not to change, the air would be a solid element. The earth is an air with *fixed* electricity.]

Oken sees only half the truth. The Atmosphere is not $+E + -E$ but $+$ Magn. $+ -E$.

25   p 128, pencil | §§ 426–34 "Werth der Krystallographie"

An interesting Chapter, even in spite of the swaggering bull-frog assertional *"You be damned!"* and *"blast my eyes,*[a] *if it an't"* style, so (in degree at least if not in kind) exclusively characteristic of this Writer as to be well implied in the term, OKENISM.—It would not be below Heinrich Steffens to answer it.[1]

26   p 134, pencil | §§ 435–9

[Die Erdmasse] ist das Kind der Finsterniss, der Trockenheit, der höchsten Cohäsion.

Sie ist mithin das Azotische der Erde rein dargestellt ohne den Sauerstoff, ist elementarischer Kohlenstoff, ist das Verbrennliche auf dem Planeten vorzugsweise.

437. Dieser Kohlenstoff, oder die Identität der Erde rein und abgesondert von dem feindlichen, spaltenden Lichtprincip ist das *Erz.*

438. Was fest und oxydabel ist, ist Erz.

439. Das Erz ist das allein Verbrennliche in der Materie . . .

[The earth-mass is the child of darkness, dryness, of the utmost cohesion. It is therefore the azotic of the earth itself, in its pure form devoid of oxygen; it is elementary carbon; it is above all the combustible on the planet. 437. This carbon, or the identity of the earth in a pure state and separated from the inimical dividing principle of light, is *ore*. 438. Whatever is solid and oxydisable constitutes ore. 439. Ore is the only combustible element of matter . . .]

Oken has not merely an *itch*, he has a positive *letch*, for Paradoxy. Das Erz ist das allein verbrennliche[1]—therefore Inflammable Air or Hydrogen Gas must of course be *Erz*, i.e. metallic Ore. But the Erz = Carbon, is the product (Kind) of the maximum of Cohesion, das am meisten feste.[2] Therefore Hydrogen is Carbon in its greatest positive &c.

[a] Both "You be damned" and "blast my eyes" have a line above instead of under them, but the intent appears to have been the same as underlining for emphasis

25[1] The chapter is concerned with the formation of the earth, a subject treated extensively by Steffens, especially in *Geognostisch-geologische Aufsätze* (Hamburg 1810), which C annotated and on the whole admired.

26[1] "Ore is the only combustible element"—in textus.

26[2] "The most solid".

27 p. 147, pencil | §§ 482–3

Erde ist ein wasser- und feuerbeständiger Körper. . . . . Das Erz ist im Wasser nicht auflösbar, dagegen im Feuer entweder verbrennbar oder reducirbar.

[*Earth is a water- and fire-proof body.* . . . . Ore is not soluble in water; on the contrary, it is either oxydisable or reducible in fire.]

What can this man mean? That Lime under one set of agents does not exhibit the same phænomena as Lime under another?

28 pp 194–5, pencil | §§ 669–73

Das Eisen konnte nirgends anders entstehen als um die Pole, das Silber nur unter dem Aequator. Der Magnetismus ist daher ganz unabhängig von der Erdachse, aber er fällt doch nothwendig mit ihr zusammen. . . .

671. Es kömmt auf die Lage der Metallmassen unter dem Aequator und unter den Polen an, welche Richtung die Magnetnadel nimmt.

672. Die Magnetnadel muss daher an jeder Stelle auf der Erde eine andere Richtung annehmen. . . .

673. Im Ganzen muss aber die Richtung doch nach den Polen gehen. Dieses sind die Phänomene der *Abweichung* der Nadel.

[Iron could not originate anywhere except near the poles, silver only below the equator. Magnetism is thus entirely independent of the earth's axis, but it necessarily coincides with it. . . . 671. The direction which the magnetic needle takes depends on the position of the metallic masses below the equator and below the poles. 672. The magnetic needle must therefore assume a different direction on every part of the earth. . . . 673. Upon the whole, however, the direction must tend towards the poles. Such are the phenomena of *declination* of the magnetic needle.]

Was Oken drunk when he wrote this? Surely, he could not be ignorant of silver mines far on this side of the tropics—in Hungary & even in Norway.

The fault, however, lies more in the Author's broad bankless Gush and Boast of Assertion than in the Conception itself. Had Oken applied to the three Metals the same qualification that he attributes to the Compass-needle, ¶s 671, 672, 673, so that the Silver im ganzen[1] is a Tropical Product—all would have been plausible at least. Accidents or subordinate Laws might have exposed certain Tracks lying between Masses of Iron and Lead to a greater intensity of Light-action than belonged to their geographical position.   S. T. C.

28[1] "Upon the whole"—in textus.

29   p 198 | § 687

Als Wassermetall ist die Entelechie der Metallität (Magnetismus) im Arsenik aufgehoben, und es hat sich dagegen die Wasserentelechie in ihm fixirt.

[The entelechy of metallity (magnetism) is neutralised in arsenic as metallic water, and the entelechy of water becomes fixed in it instead.]

Most unsatisfactory! If either, it is Air = azote, not Water that Arsenik metallizes, i.e. repeats metallically. But Oken throughout is blind to the

———— and its four Poles.[1]

29[1] To the "compass of nature": see **23** n 1.

OMNIANA

Omniana, or horae otiosiores. 2 vols. London 1812. 12°.

British Library C 45 a 3–4

Heraldic bookplate of James Gillman on p ⁻5 (p-d) of each vol. On ɪ ⁻3, in pencil in an unidentified hand, a 4-line jingle in a mixture of Italian, Latin, and English. Although the volumes were cropped after C wrote his notes, most of the notes were saved by the pages having been folded in before cropping.

The first of RS's "omniana" appeared in a series of anonymous articles in the correspondence section of John Aikin's new miscellany, *The Athenaeum*, in 1807–8. In 1812 RS made a selection from the original series and added substantially to it for the two-volume *Omniana*. Although the title-page does not indicate his authorship, RS's name appears to have been printed on the original paper wrappers (*SW & F—CC*), and it has always been known as his. C may have contributed one entry to the original series; then in the collection of 1812, he assisted RS by writing 45 entries which are marked with asterisks in the Table of Contents of each volume and identified in a footnote as being "by a different writer". In the annotations he claims two others (**2A, 10**) and part of a third (**1A**). The "Omniana 1809–16" included in *LR* ɪ 338–95 are extracts from C's notebooks assembled by the editors; they were not so designated by C himself. The full text of C's contribution to *Omniana* appears in *SW & F (CC)*.

MS TRANSCRIPTS. (*a*) VCL BT 37: SC transcript, made after the original had been cropped. (*b*) Humanities Research Center, University of Texas: a transcript of C's notes made by Sir George Grove in another copy of the work. Neither transcript is complete.

DATE. Late 1819: **24** is dated 27 Dec 1819. C appears to have annotated this copy specifically for James Gillman.

1 ɪ [iii] | Contents

The articles with the asterisks prefixed were furnished by S. T. Coleridge all the others by R. Southey.

1A ɪ 28 | 17 "Hell"

* Bellarmin makes sweating and crowding one of the chief torments of Hell, which Lessius (no doubt after an actual and careful survey,) affirms to be exactly a Dutch mile, (about a league and a half English,) in diameter. But Ribera, grounding his map on deductions from the Apocalypse, makes it 200 Italian miles. Lessius, it may be presumed, was a protestant, for whom, of course, a smaller Hell would suffice.

S. T. C.

2 ɪ 58, cropped | 37 [RS] "Anthony Purver"

I am he who am, is better than *I am that I am*.

No! The sense of *that* is = because, or in that—[I a]m, in [tha]t I am![a] [meani]ng I [affir]m myself [and], affir[min]g myself to be, I am. Causa Sua.[1] My own [ac]t is the Ground of my own existence.[2]

2A ɪ 77–9 | 45

* Thomas O'Brien Mac Mahon[b]

3 ɪ 103–5 | 60 [RS] "Small Wit"

[C's note at the end of the article is a comment on the whole, to which the first lines provide a suitable introduction:] "Many there are (says an old writer) that will lose their friend rather than their jest, or their quibble, pun, *punnet* or *pundigrion*, fifteen of which will not make up one single jest."

The Pun may be traced from its Minimum, in which it exists only in the violent intention and desire of the Punster to make one. ⟨This is⟩ the fluxion or pre-nascent Quantity, the Infinitesimal first Moment, or Differential, of a Pun—as that of the Man who hearing Lincoln mentioned, grumbling most gutturally, shaking his head, and writhing his nose, muttered,—*Lincoln*s, indeed! Lɪɴccoln! Lɪɴccoln! You may well call it *Link*coln!—(a pause)—I was never so bit with Bugs in a place, in my whole Life before!—" Here the reason (i.e. vindictive anger striving to ease itself by Contempt—the most frequent origin of Puns, next to that of scornful Triumph exulting and insulting (see Parad. Lost, VI.)[1] or cause of the impulse or itch to let a pun was substituted for the Pun itself, which the man's wit could not light on. This, therefore, is the Minim. At the other extreme lies the Pun polysyllabic—of which accept the following as a specimen:

Two Nobles in *Madrid* were straddling side by side,
Both shamefully diseased: espying which, I cried—
What *figures* these men make! the Wight, that Euclid cons,
Sees plainly that they are—Parallel o'*pippy*-Dons!—[2]

S. T. C.

[a] This "am" is written large, but not in capitals
[b] Signed "*S. T. C.*" at the end of the article

2[1] "Self-cause".
2[2] RS's entry comments on the work of a Quaker translator of the Bible. C is defending the AV translation of Exod 3.14, a crucial text for him, as in e.g. *BL* ch 13

(*CC*) ɪ 275*.
3[1] *Paradise Lost* vɪ 607–27, Satan and Belial exulting over the success of their artillery in the war in heaven.
3[2] Like several other close friends of

4 ɪ 132–3, cropped | 68 [RS] "Cupid and Psyche"

[RS summarises Calderón's allegorical version of the myth of Cupid and Psyche in three and a half pages, then concludes:] Calderon has another *Auto* upon the same subject; the characters differently named, but with little variation of story. He says in his preface to these Autos (72 in number) that they have all but one subject and one set of characters; the greater, therefore, must his merit be, if he resembles nature, who makes so many faces with nothing but eyes, nose, and mouth, and yet no two alike.*

I do not find fault with this [o]utline of the Fable and Plot of Calderon's [C]upid and Psyche;[1] but with R.S. for [g]iving this only. Half a dozen passages [s]elected from the 72 Autos Sacramentales, and translated as Southey would have translated them—and the sketch of the Plot we should have thanked him ~~as~~ for, as an agreeable though unnecessary Over-weight.   S. T. C.

5 ɪ 135 | 70 [RS] "Lions of Romance"

There is a distinction made in Palmerin de Oliva between *Leones Coronados*, and *Leones Pardos*. The former, who may be called Lions Royal, are those who know blood-royal instinctively, and respect it, I suppose, as a family sort of tie. The others have no such instinct.

There is a much better reason for this distinction: & I wonder that our zoo-logists have not noticed the evident diversity (the *variety*, at least) of the Leones Pardos, or Leopard Lions, with low round foreheads, and the Eyes almost at the top of the face, as contrasted with the magnificent Leone Coronado with high *square* forehead &c.—[1]

C's, Gillman was fond of a pun, and C's letters often indulged him: e.g. *CL* v 185. The joke here involves a somewhat unusual use of "pippy" as "covered with spots" or perhaps (from "the pip") just generally "diseased", besides the pun on "parallel-epipedon"—an older form of "parallelepiped", in geometry the term for the "figure" (as C says) of a prism having a parallelogram as its base (*OED*).

4[1] Calderón's elaborate allegory, in which Psyche is "Faith", the youngest daughter of Old World, courted by Cupid and Apostasy, is similar in approach to, though different in detail from, C's later in-terpretation of the "parable" in *AR* (1825) 278.

5[1] C's observation may be based on en-graved pictures such as the plates illustrat-ing the genus *Felis* in Rees's *Cyclopaedia*, in which the first shows the square-headed lion and second the leopard and other big cats, all with rounded heads. (The *Cyclopaedia* was published in parts 1802–20; the vols of plates all appeared in 1820, proba-bly after these notes were written by C.) An earlier and widely circulated set of wood-cuts that would prove C's point is Thomas Bewick *A General History of Quadrupeds* (1790) 164 ff: see Plate 5.

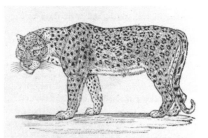

T H E   L I O N,

T H E   L E O P A R D.

T H E   T I G E R

T H E   P A N T H E R

5. "The Lion", "The Leopard", "The Tiger", "The Panther": from Thomas Bewick *A General History of Quadrupeds* (1790). See OMNIANA **5**

6 I 146 | 76 [RS] "The Gossamer"

Spenser calls the gossamer

> The fine nets, which oft we woven see
> Of scorched dew.

Henry More alludes to this opinion, which seems to have been then commonly held.

From a Glossary of Hard Words printed in the reign of James I. I find the true derivation of Gossamere—Coma virginis, Coma Matris Dei—God's Dame's Hair—. So Gossip is God's SIB, or Cousin—the still nearer baptismal Relations being God-father, God-mother.[1] S. T. C.

7 I 191 | 93 [RS] "Tractors"

The *Tractors* are no new mode of quackery,—witness this extract from one *of the rogues of the days of old: "How famous is that martial ring, which carried in some fit place, or *rubbed on some such part*, will allay and cure the pains of the teeth and head, the cramp, quartain ague, falling sickness, vertigo, apoplexy, plague, and other diseases! . . ."

* Southey should have recollected that the very same Philosophers & the same Medical Board, who denounced Animal Magnetism in Paris, confirmed after a series of experiments the positive ćeffect of Iron applied externally to the body, in rheumatism &c.—Perkins' Tractors have considerable, but not any peculiar, powers.[1]

6[1] C repeats in slightly different form the assertion he had made in Jul 1810 in WHITE *Works* 5 without reference to a glossary. The etymology he proposes has never been given in its English form, but he would have found precedents in Latin and German than in Stephen Skinner *Etymologicon Linguae Anglicanae* (1671), which gives "Unser Frawen haar (i.e.) Capilli B. M. Virg."

7[1] Elisha Perkins's "metallic tractors", in vogue in England 1798–1800, were a pair of metal rods—normally in fact not iron but brass and steel—the stroking of which was supposed to cure a range of diseases from burns to rheumatism and toothache. In the "Essay on Scrofula" of Sept–Oct 1816 C had dismissed the tractors as a fraud along with mesmerism and "touching for the Evil" (*SW & F—CC*), but in 1817 he was led to take mesmerism or animal magnetism more seriously, and other unconventional modes of healing with it. The allusion to philosophers and the "Medical Board" is puzzling, since neither the 1784 official reports of the "philosophers" under Franklin and Bailly and of the "Medical Board" of Mauduyt, Andry, and Caille, nor the minority medical report of A. L. de Jussieu, nor any subsequent official report by the same commissioners supports C's claim. He may have been misled by some hitherto untraced publication in favour of animal magnetism, however, for his reading in that subject was extensive.

8 ɪ 195, pencil | 96 [RS] "Tostatus"

The works of this voluminous commentator had a luckier resurrection from the deep than even Frith's Treatises. Cardinal Ximenes . . . sent the manuscript to Venice to be printed; the ship in which they were embarked, encountered a violent storm . . . all the lading was thrown overboard to lighten her, and the bishop's works among the rest. The passengers with great difficulty got to shore; and the next day they saw the chest which contained these papers come floating safely to the beach. . . . It is not to be wondered at, that the Catholics were disposed to believe this circumstance miraculous, considering the specific gravity of the contents of the chest.

N.b. By putting sp. gr. for heaviness Southey has spoilt this own joke.

9 ɪ 212 | 107 [RS] "Hereticks of the Early Ages"

* A large class consists of those who resisted the various corruptions of Christianity step by step, from Cerinthus down to Berengar.

* Hush! hush!—dear Southey! do not write on what you do not know.— The subjects are so few, with which you are *not* acquainted, that this abstinence would be but a trifling sacrifice & the occasions of rare occurrence. You might as well have placed Luther and Tom Payne together, as Berengar & Cerinthus![1]   S. T. C.

10 ɪ 216 | 110 [C] "Egotism"[a]

. . . the passion of Contempt, which is the concentrated Vinegar of Egotism.

Contempt is Egotism in ill-humour.

Appetite without moral ᴏʀ Affection, social sympathy, and even without passion and imagination—(in plain English, mere lust)⟨—⟩is the basest Form of Egotism, and being infra-human, or below Humanity should be pronounced with the harsh Breathing (or Asperate) as Hegoatism.

10A ɪ 220 | 113 [C] "Bulls"

. . . a confusion of (what the Schoolmen would have called) *Objectivéity* with *Subjectivéity* . . .

[a] C has signed this entry at the end "S. T. C.", thereby claiming it as his own composition

9[1] C's objection is to the yoking of a subtle theologian, Berengar of Tours (c 999–1088), whose work contributed to the refinement of the doctrine of transubstantiation, with the Gnostic heretic Cerinthus (fl c 100). C has a late poem on Berengar: *PW* (EHC) ɪ 460–1.

10B ɪ 220 | 114 [C] "Wise Ignorance"

Ne curiosƗus quaere causas omnium
Quaecunque libris vis prophetarum indidit,
Afflata caelo, plena veraci Deo:
Nec operta sacri supparo silentii
Irrumphere aƗude; sed prudenter praeteri!
Nescire velle quae magister optimus
Docere non vult, erudita inscitia est.[1]

[Do not in your curiosity seek the causes of all things whatever the power of prophets, inspired by heaven and filled with God's truth, has imparted to books; and do not have the audacity to break in on what is concealed by the veil of sacred silence. But pass by in silence! To be willing not to know what the best of teachers is not willing to teach—that is an educated ignorance.]

11 ɪ 226–7 | 116 [RS] "Gift of Tongues"

There is a curious question concerning the gift of tongues, in what mode the miracle was effected: many theologians . . . opining that the miracle took place in the atmosphere, and not in the ears of the hearers . . .

¶ 116. ℵ In no instance is the Love of the Marvellous more strikingly exhibited than in the ordinary interpretations of this plain and simple narration of Sᵗ Luke's.[1]—On the inrush of the Spirit the new converts ⟨to Jesus,⟩ from all parts of the Roman Empire, then met at Jerusalem/[a] rushed out of the house, and addressed the crowd, each his own countrymen, and to the scandal of some & surprize of all, in the vernacular ⟨dialects⟩ instead of the sacred (Syro-chaldaic) Language—just as if a man should pray aloud in a Catholic Church in any other than Latin Prayers.—The Apostles sate still the while. At length, observing the workings in the minds of the Auditors, the 12 rose at once: and Peter as the Foreman, made the address recorded, & expressly tells them, that the *miracle*, they had witnessed, was a fulfilment of Joel's Prophecy—viz. that Laymen should preach in the Spirit in the Common Tongue.[2]

12 ɪ 254–5 | 135 [RS] "Early English Metre"

A remarkable rhyme occurs in the metrical Romance of Octouian Imperator.

---

[a] The oblique stroke looks at first glance like a closing parenthesis or a greatly elongated comma

10B[1] The lines are by Joseph Scaliger, as RS's note indicates. C corrects two typographical errors.
11[1] In Acts 2. Publishing this note in

NTP 139–40, SC defended C's views upon the "gift of tongues" in an appendix, 409–15.
11[2] Acts 2.16–18.

Whan they were seght alle yn same,
And Florence herde Florentyne's name,
Sche swore her oth be Seynt Jame
    Al so prest,
So hyght my sone that was take *fra me*
    In that forest.

Mr. Weber observes . . . that "this singular rhyme strongly supports
the opinion of Wallis and of Tyrwhitt . . . that the final *e* which is at
present mute, was anciently pronounced obscurely like the *e* feminine
of the French." [But against this view RS quotes from Gower:]

For love is ever fast *byme*
Which taketh none hede of due tyme.

[And, after a second example from Gower, "the first stanza of Troilus
and Creseide" as "another instance of contraction":]

The double sorow of Troilus to tellen
That was King Priamus sonne of Troy.
In loving how his aventuris fellen
From wo to wele, and after out of joy,
My purpose is, er that I part *froy*.

The last couplet with the "froy" from Chaucer is very strong and I think
decisive: but the first line of the first couplet seems too catalectic and
unmetrical even for Gower, on the supposition of "byme" being a
monosyllable

$$\cup - \mid \cup - \mid \cup - \mid - :$$

unless it can be shewn from other passages that Gower meant it to be
read,

For Lovè is evèr fast byme

$$\cup \quad - \cup - \cup - \quad - \quad -$$

or that we ought to read "evermore" for "ever."

13   ɪ 296–7 | 153 [RS] "Aqua Vitae"

One Theoricus . . . wrote a proper treatise of Aqua Vitae, says Stani-
hurst, wherein he praiseth it unto the ninth degree. "He distinguisheth
three sorts thereof, *Simplex, Composita*, and *Perfectissima*. He declar-
eth the simples and ingredience thereto belonging. He wisheth it to be
taken as well before meat as after. It drieth up the breaking out of hands,

and killeth the flesh worms, if you wash your hands therewith. It scoureth all scurf and scalds from the head, being therewith daily washt before meals. Being moderately taken, saith he, it sloweth age, it strengtheneth youth, it helpeth digestion, it cutteth phlegm, it abandoneth melancholy . . ."

Even this is not so hearty, so heart-felt an eulogy on Aqua vitæ, the Brannte (= Brandy) wein, as I met with painted on a Board in a Public House on the skirts of the Harz in N. Germany.[1]

> Des Morgens ist das Brannt-wein gut,
> Desgleichen zum Mittage;
> Und wer am Abend ein Schlückgen thut,
> Der ist frei von aller Plage:
> Auch kann es gar kein Schade seyn
> Zum Mitternacht, *das* BRANNTE WEIN!

i.e. Of a morning is the Brandy-wine good, and the like at noon day; and he who takes a Sip at evening tide is free from all care. Likewise it can sure be no harm At midnight, the BRANDY-WINE!

13A I 308 | 158 [C] "Sense and Common Sense"

> "If it is not me, I be not I, he'll bark and he'll rail;
> "But if I be I, he'll wag his little tail."[1]

13B I 312 | 159 [C] "Toleration"

It is its [the state's] duty to prevent a present evil, as much at least as to punish the perpetrators of it. Besides, preaching and publishing are overt acts. Nor has it yet been proved, though often asserted, that a Christian sovereign has nothing to do with the external happiness or misery of the fellow creatures entrusted to his charge.

14 II title-page, cropped

Epitaph
On an *insignificant*.
Tis CYPHER lies beneath this crust,
Whom Death *created* into Dust.[1]
S. T. [C.]

13[1] C made this walking tour in mid-May 1799 with a group mainly of English friends (*CL* I 497–516, *CN* I 410–20), one of whom jovially recorded the same discovery: Clement Carlyon *Early Years and*

Late Reflections (1836) I 38.
13A[1] The line makes fun of illogical arguments on the philosophical problem of personal identity: cf *CN* I 1235.
14[1] *PW* (EHC) II 954 var; cf *CN* I 625.

15　II [iii], pencil, cropped | Contents of the Second Volume

Those with * supplied by S. T. Coleri[dge.]

16　II 35 | 182 [RS] "Instinct"

A drake, which had been hatched with a brood of chicken, was <u>killed</u> because it could not be kept from treading the hens.

Why? What harm did *that* do?

17　II 38 | 184 [RS] "Beer and Ale"

[RS quotes two verses on beer: one in English from the time of Henry VIII; the other in Latin by] the Norman poet, Henry of Araunches, in which the said Henry speaks with notable indecorum of this nectar of Valhalla.

> * *Nescio quod Stygiae monstrum conforme paludi*
> *Cervisiam plerique vocant; nil spissius illa*
> *Dum bibitur, nil clarius est dum mingitur, unde*
> *Constat quod multas faeces in ventre relinquit.*

[There's a sort of monstrosity not unlike a Stygian bog which many people call *beer*. Nothing is muddier when you drink it, or clearer when you piss it—from which it follows that it leaves a lot of sediment in your belly.]

* I remember a similar German Epigram on the Goslar Ale, ~~of~~ which may be englished thus—

> This Goslar Ale is stout and staunch;
> But sure 'tis brew'd by Witches!
> Scarce do you feel it warm in paunch,
> Odsblood! tis in your Breeches![1]
> 　　　　　　　　S. T. C.—

18　II 54–7, cropped | 191 [RS] "Beards"

There is a female Saint, whom the Jesuit Sautel, in his Annus Sacer Poeticus, has celebrated for her beard, . .[a] a mark of divine favour bestowed upon her for her prayers.

Pereant qui ante nos nostra dixere![1] What, can nothing be one's own? This is the more vexatious, for at the age of 18 I lost a L[egacy] of 50£

---

[a] Two points of ellipsis thus in original

17[1] The German original was recorded in 1799: *CN* I 429.

18[1] "A curse on those who say what we do before us!'": attributed to Aelius Donatus by St Jerome. Cf *CN* I 1284, *CL* v 454.

for the following Epigram on my Godmother's beard, w[hich] she had
the *barbarity* to revenge by striki[ng] me out of her will—

> So great the charms of Mrs Munday,
> That men grew rude a Kiss to gain:
> This so provok'd the Dame that one [day]
> T[o Pallas chaste] did she complai[n.]

> Nor vainly she address'd her prayer,
> Nor vainly to that Power applied:
> The Goddess bade a length of Hair
> In deep recess her muzzle hide.

> Still persever! to Love be callous!
> For I have your petition heard:
> To snatch a Kiss were vain (cried Pall[as)]
> Unless you first should shave your be[ard.][2]
> S. T. C.

19   II 64 | 195 [RS] ''Amphibious Fish''

[RS quotes a long passage from Captain James Cook's *First Voyage*
describing a singular kind of small amphibious fish that hopped away
''by the help of the breast fins, as nimbly as a frog''.]

Q^y The Tadpole of the Rana paradoxa?—[1]

20   II 66, cropped

Yet I have been assured that small fish have been found in India, after a
shower, upon the roof of a house. The thing was affirmed so positively
that it could not be disbelieved without rejecting the direct testimony of
one whose veracity there was every reason for believing . . .

* The fact is, I believe, out of doubt. The Showers may possibly have
originated in Land or Lake Water-spouts by electrical Sussorption[1]—
and the Fish or the already pregnated Sperm have [. . . . .]

18[2] *PW* (EHC) II 976. Being cut out of
wills for tactlessness was a standard joke
(though in fact C's godmothers were
named ''Mundy''—*CL* I 311): cf C's con-
tinuation of ''Maxilian'' in BM Add MS
34225 ff 81–3.

19[1] The Paradoxical Frog is so called
because it shrinks from a ten-inch tadpole
to a two-inch frog. The source of C's infor-

mation was perhaps Erasmus Darwin *The
Temple of Nature* (1803) canto 1 line 343n:
''Of the rana paradoxa the larva or tadpole
is as large as the frog, and dwells in Suri-
nam, whence the mistakes of Merian and
of Seba, who call it a frog fish.''

20[1] Apparently C's coinage on the
model of ''absorption'', and meaning
''suck in underneath''.

21   II   111–12 | 200 [RS] "Gigantic Bird"

[RS combines the discovery in Russia of bird-claws a yard long, the account of a bird at Nootka big enough to carry off a whale in its talons, and Cook's description of an enormous nest in New Holland:] *"it was built with sticks upon the ground, and was no less than six and twenty feet in circumference, and two feet eight inches high."*

More probably a Syngenesia Species, like that Bush Bird in Caffraria.[1]

22   II   131, cropped | 207 [RS] "French-English"

It is curious to observe how the English Catholicks of the 17th century wrote English like men who habitually spoke French. Corps is sometimes used for the living body, . .[a] and when they attempt to versify, their rhymes are *only rhymes according to a French pronunciation.

> This path most fair I walking winde
> By shadow of my pilgrimage,
> Wherein at every step I find
> An heavenly draught and image
> Of my frail mortality,
> Tending to eternity.
>
> *   *   *
>
> The tree that bringeth nothing else
> But leaves and breathing verdure
> Is fit for fire, and not for fruit
> And doth great wrong to Nature.

* I doubt [it]. It seems mor[e] likely that "b[y] shădŏw ŏf[" is] isochronous [? with] an Amphibr[ach] ◡ — ◡, two [of] the Breves, being equ[al] to one Lon[g,] and that [the] remainde[r of] the Line is a Ditrochæus, — ◡ — ◡, grī[măge] rhyming to Image—and Vērdŭre an asson[ant] to Nātŭre

23   II   147 | 211 [RS] "Valentine Gretrakes"

[RS quotes from Henry More:] "This I can speak by experience of myself, especially when I was young, that every night, when going to bed

[a] Two points of ellipsis thus in original

21[1] "Syngenesia", a botanical term loosely meaning "bunched", applied to animals occasionally by C (e.g. *CN* IV 4814) probably in imitation of Oken; "Caffraria", a province in South Africa, and by extension South Africa as a whole. C alludes to an account of the community or "clumps of nests" of a South African bird in John Barrow *An Account of Travels into the Interior of Southern Africa* (2 vols 1801–4) I 393–4.

I unbuttoned my doublet, my breast would omit a sweet aromatick smell, and every year about the end of winter, or approaching the spring, I had unusually sweet herbous scents in my nostrils, no external object appearing from whence they came. Nay, my urine would smell like violets . . .''

Q̇ Had not the philosophic Divine been eating Asparagus?

24   II   157 | 212 [RS] ''Henry More's Song of the Soul''

There is perhaps no other poem in existence, which has so little that is *good in it, if it has any thing good. Henry More possessed the feelings of a poet; but the subject which he chose is of all others least fitted for poetry, and in fact there is no species of poetry so absurd as the didactic.

* 27 Decr 1819. M^r (J. H.) Frere, of all men eminently φιλοκαλος, of the most exquisite Taste,[1] observed this very day to me—how very very grossly Southey had wronged this Poem.[2] I cannot understand in what mood S. could have been: it is so unlike him.

25   II   162

Old Mnemon remarks upon this story,

> A lecture strange he seem'd to read to me,
> And though I did not rightly understand
> His meaning, yet I deemed it to be
>   Some goodly thing.

Henry More's readers seem to have agreed with old Mnemon, in thinking it *strange and in not understanding it. Yet this is the best part of the whole allegory, and of the whole poem.

* false, cruelly false! Again and again I puzzle myself to guess in what most unsoutheyian mood Southey could have been when he thought & wrote the above.   S. T. C.—

24[1] John Hookham Frere (1769–1846), diplomat, poet, translator of Aristophanes, an encouraging and useful friend to C from about 1816. In 1818 C wrote to a correspondent, ''I know no man now alive, whose Taste, Judgment, Manners and Principles I love and admire so unmixedly'' (*CL* IV 881): cf *C&S* (*CC*) 6 and n. He regularly applied this Greek epithet to him,

e.g. *CL* VI 542, 559n, 713, 735.

24[2] C's own early views of More's poetry had been critical, and he mildly makes fun of More's vocabulary in one of his contributions to *Omniana* (§ 97, *SW & F—CC*); MORE *Theological Works* 1, a note written at Highgate, asserts however that ''More had both the philosophic and poetic Genius, supported by immense erudition''.

26 II 162–3 | Continuing **25** textus

He soon begins to imitate John Bunyan in his nomenclature, . .^a but oh! what an imitation of that old King of the Tinkers!

And the phrase, old King of the Tinkers! applied to the Author of the inimitable Pilgrim's Progress, that model of beautiful, pure, and harmonious *English*, no less than of still higher merits, outrages my moral Taste.[1]

27 II 167–74, pencil, overtraced

The following extract [from More's *Song of the Soul*] is the best specimen that can be given of the strain of feeling, which Henry More could express in no better language than an inharmonious imitation of Spenser's, barbarized by the extremes of carelessness the most licentious, and erudition the most pedantic.

> In silent night when mortalls be at rest,
> And bathe their molten limbs in slothful sleep,
> My troubled ghost strange cares did straight molest,
> And plunged my heavie soul in sorrow deep:
> Large floods of tears my moistned cheeks did steep,
> My heart was wounded with compassionate love
> Of all the creatures: sadly out I creep
> From men's close mansions, the more to improve
> My mournfull plight; so softly on I forward move.

[RS quotes nineteen more stanzas.]

After so very sharp a censure, of the justice of which the following extract is to be the proof, who would have expected a series of Stanzas for the greater part at least so chaste in language, and easy in versification? Southey must have wearied himself out with the Poem, till the Mist from its swamps and stagnants had spread over its green and flowery Plots and Bowers.

28 II 190 | 219 [RS] "The Stigmata"

In intolerant and barbarous bigotry indeed the writer [of "the Telemacomanie"] is only surpassed by the Eclectic reviewer, who affirms that "thousands of unhappy spirits and thousands yet to increase their num-

---

^a Two points of ellipsis thus in original

26[1] C objects to the condescension implied in RS's phrase as, in 1810, he had objected to sneers about the "tinker" Bunyan in Sedgwick *Hints* iii 28–9.

ber, will everlastingly look back with unutterable anguish on the nights
and days in which Shakespeare ministered to their guilty delights.''*

> * —Churlish Priest!
> A blessed Angel shall my sweet Shakspear be,
> When thou lyest howling!—
>
> *Hamlet*[1]

29   II 272 | 242 [RS] "Glow-Beast"

[In the Valley of Calchaquina, on the borders of Peru and Chile, it] ''is
reported that in the night there is a sort of creature seen here which casts
a mighty light from its head, and many are of opinion that light is caused
by a carbuncle; but as yet this creature could never be taken or killed,
because it suddenly baffles all the designs of men, leaving them in the
dark, by clouding that light.'' . . . The author of the verse-Argentina,
D. Martin del Barco, says he had seen this beast, and often hunted it in
vain, and that happy man would he be who should catch one. Ruy Diaz
Melgarejo, he adds, had been thus fortunate. He had caught a carbuncle-
beast, and taken out the stone, . . [a] but the canoe in which he embarked
with it upset, and the jewel was lost. I, says D. Martin, saw him la-
menting his evil fortune, and heard him say, that if he had not lost the
carbuncle, he would have presented it to King Philip.*

* Q.y A large Lanthorn-fly that had settled by accident on the Forehead
of a wild ox?

[a] Two points of ellipsis thus in original

28[1] *Hamlet* v i 262–4 var, used also in a
lecture in 1808: *Lects 1808–1819 (CC)* I 133.

SAMUEL O'SULLIVAN
1790–1851

The Agency of Divine Providence Manifested in the Principal Transactions Religious and Political, Connected with the History of Great Britain from the Reformation to the Revolution in 1688. Dublin 1816. 8°.

British Library C 126 h 13

Inscribed on the title-page, "To S. T. Coleridge Esqʳ by the Author." "S. T. C." label on the title-page, and John Duke Coleridge's monogram on p ⁻2. The book is unopened from 173 to the end (as of 1987).

DATE. Presumably c 1816–17, at or shortly after the presentation of the volume.

1   p 37, pencil

He [Henry VIII] spent much time in the study of the fathers, of whom Thomas Aquinas was his favourite; and thereby contracted a dislike to every project of Reformation.

*the Schoolmen.*¹

2   pp 48–9, pencil

The most objectionable and offensive parts of Popery, were, for a considerable time, retained, in their full extent; and the doctrines of that church, the most unreasonable and extravagant, authoritatively asserted. To deny the doctrine of purgatory, or of the real presence,* subjected the incredulous to the most rigorous penalties.

* Mʳ O Sullivan is sadly inaccurate in his statements. The fiercest Papist could not assert the doctrine of the real presence with more or bitterer Zeal than did the Lutheran Divines—or have wished it to have been affirmed in more unqualified terms than our own Cathecism¹ has done. Not the fact but the *mode* of the real presence was the point in dispute—²

1¹ The term "Fathers of the Church" is properly applied only to ecclesiastical authorities of the first few centuries A.D. such as Augustine and Jerome; Aquinas belongs among the "schoolmen", teachers of philosophy and theology at the medieval universities.

2¹ This is presumably a slip for "Catechism" rather than for "Catholicism". C refers, as in LACUNZA **30**, to continuing controversy about the real presence, i.e. the actual and not simply symbolic presence of the body and blood of Christ in the Eucharist. On this issue the BCP catechism defines the bread and wine as "the outward part or sign" and the body and blood of Christ as "the inward part, or thing signified".

2² C's concern with "the *mode* of the real presence" is outlined in *CCD* 175–6.

3 pp 62–3, pencil

This reformer [Cranmer] seems to have considered the grossness of su-
perstition not more hostile to the interests of true religion, than the ge-
nius of a !!*purely spiritual and fanatical form of worship, repugnant to
the spirit of Gospel truth, and averse from the restraints of civil govern-
ment.

* A purely *spiritual form* of worship repugnant to the *Spirit* of the
Gospel which commands us to worship God in spirit and in truth, indif-
ferent alike to Jerusalem and to the Mountain!!¹ And this too *fanatical*—
this contempt of Fanes fanatical!! Enthusiastic it might be—but fanat-
ical?—²

4 p 157

His [Charles II's] disposition naturally humane, tempered the rigorous
severity with which the church party, now reinstated in the possession
of power, were disposed to animadvert upon their adversaries.

!! Just as much as one who had set a Toad and a huge Spider by the
ears—and occasionally held them asunder in order to prolong the Sport
and secure, if possible, the destruction of both. Charles would not let
the Toad crush the Spider, till the Spider-fang had emptied its venom-
bag in the body of the Toad—Such, I mean, was the wish and purpose
dictated by the playful and humane disposition of this engaging Ti-
berius.—¹

3¹ John 4.21–4.

3² C objects to O'Sullivan's violation of
etymology: "fanatic" and "fane" are both
derived from the Latin *fanum*, "temple".
Cf a statement in *BL* ch 2 (*CC*) I 31: "The
sanity of the mind is between superstition
with fanaticism on the one hand; and en-
thusiasm with indifference and a diseased

slowness to action on the other."

4¹ With calculated irony C likens
Charles II—"profligate tyrant" in LA-
CUNZA 5—to the Roman emperor Tiberius
(42 B.C.–A.D. 37), whom C used as a
touchstone of depravity in e.g. *Lects 1795*
(*CC*) 159, *EOT* (*CC*) I 414.

WILLIAM FITZWILLIAM OWEN
1774–1857

Narrative of Voyages to Explore the Shores of Africa, Arabia, and Madagascar; performed in H. M. Ships Leven and Barracouta, under the direction of Captain W. F. W. Owen, R.N. by command of the Lords Commissioners of the Admiralty. 2 vols. London 1833. 8°.

Not located; marginalia published from MS TRANSCRIPT.

MS TRANSCRIPT. VCL BT 37, transcript by SC. The initials "S. T. C." written at the end of **1, 2, 5,** and **7** are here omitted as being probably the transcriber's convention for identifying the marginal note.

DATE. Between Jun 1833, the month of publication, and C's death in Jul 1834.

1 ɪ "front flyleaf"

All instruments made by man seem to have been provided by Lord Melville &c for this Expedition,[1] only not the instrument made by God—that is, Men fitted for the adventure and countries—Not even a good *shot*, or experienced sportsman among them.—No astronomer—and the Naturalists were very sentimental, shooting *at* Hippopotami with pewter bullets![2] A double charge of sparrow shot would have shewn better sense!—

2 ɪ 5 | Ch 1

Ask the young and thoughtless midshipman, whose tender frame and boyish cheek seem little suited for the adventurous sailor's life, why he leaves his parent's arms to seek a distant, friendless shore? His sanguine imagination will answer—honour, promotion, wealth, and all that fancied something so often seen in the glittering sunshine of romance, but which sad reality so soon blackens into shadow and disappointment.

Nonsense!—If the boy answered at all but by an uneasy stare, he would have said, "Because I wanted to be *somewhere else*: and I had a *fancy* for this."

1[1] Henry Dundas, Viscount Melville (1742–1811), First Lord of the Admiralty when the expedition was formed "by command of the Lords Commissioners of the Admiralty" as the title-page indicates.

1[2] Cf **4** textus, where they do not shoot at all.

3 ɪ 91 | Ch 4

[A surveying boat's crew, their boat having been shattered by the attack of a hippopotamus, came ashore for repairs.] The sky was clear and brilliantly starlight; not a sound was heard but[a] the crackling of our immense fires, the snorting of the hippopotami, and an occasional splash, as they rushed in and out of the water whilst pursuing their rough pastime . . .

—but—what?—Why, half a dozen sounds! Better to have said—The sense of the silentness was enhanced, rather than interrupted by the crackling &c.

4 ɪ 92

On arrival at the side of a creek they unexpectedly came upon an hippopotamus of the largest size sleeping on the mud. As they had only small shot they could not hope to gain a victory over him, and therefore hurried back to the encampment . . .

It seems strange that on such an expedition Rifles with steel bullets were not part of the Traveller's equipment. But I forgot.—They were sentimental Travellers.

5 ɪ 258–9 | Ch 13

On the 2nd, a party of Zoolos were seen about a mile from the fort. The Commandant immediately sent three soldiers to chase them away. Of these one was killed on the spot, and the other two were badly wounded. One actually returned with his entrails in his arms; but death soon relieved him from his sufferings. We afterwards learnt that this man was one of four soldiers, who, at Mozambique, had murdered a young Englishman named Dowling. Upon this matter there was much correspondence between the Governments of Calcutta, Goa, Mozambique, London, and Lisbon, his father being in the service of the East India Company at Bengal. But atrocious as the act was, there did not appear any just reason for the interference of British authority, as, at the time, Mr. Dowling was actually serving as master of a Portuguese merchant vessel.

But an atrocious murder of an Englishman, tho' for the time in the service of a Portuguese vessel, might well justify the interference of the English Government. If Mr Dowling had been taken fighting against Eng-

---

[a] "but" is underlined in the transcription of textus (not in the printed version), perhaps indicating that it was underlined by C

land, the King of England would have *hung* him—and when he retains his power of *hanging*, he is bound to protect or avenge.

6 I 396 | Ch 20

This monster [the elephant], unless by the agency of reason, never could have been brought beneath the power of man, but, conquered by its strength alone, he falls at his feet his most humble and willing slave. The young savage who here destroys him has not half so much intelligence as the brute that he subdues; but one possesses only instinct, while the other, gifted with reason, is enabled to obtain by sure and simple means that which the other never could succeed in.

Deserves to be quoted, as confirming and illustrating the *diversity*, the more than difference, of reason and understanding, as first taught explicitly in Coleridge's Aids to Reflection.[1]

7 II 218 | Ch 18

In every succeeding visit since our first arrival at Delagoa, we had observed that the natives were becoming still more unhappy; many, it appeared, had voluntarily sold themselves to slavery in order to avoid the miseries of starvation: for so great had been the ravages of the Hollontontes that even onions, which were once so plentiful and highly prized by the inhabitants, had become exceedingly scarce.

After reading such accounts, as these, of the state of the Negroes in their own country, surely it is pardonable to think, that if the power and wisdom of Law, enforced by powerful and wise Governments, had regulated the Middle Passage, and secured the right treatment, gradual Christianizing, and final emancipation of the Slave after his arrival in the Colonies, the transportation would have been a blessed Providence for the poor Africans!—[1]

6[1] *AR* (1825) 207–28: see also LEIGH-TON COPY C **12**.

7[1] This is of course not a reversal of C's abolitionist position (as stated in e.g. *Lects 1795—CC*—232–51) but an acknowledgment of the preferability of controlled emigration to starvation at home.

JOHN OXLEE
1779–1854

The Christian Doctrines of the Trinity and Incarnation Considered and Maintained on the Principles of Judaism. 2 vols. London 1815, York 1820. 8°.

British Library C 126 f 2

Inscribed on p ⁻2 of both volumes: "From the Author". John Duke Coleridge's monogram on I ⁻4; "S. T. C." label on the title-page verso of both vols. A note by EHC is guarded in before I 1: "These notes are pub. . . . Oxlee linguist born 1779. died 1854 knew 120 languages as he survived S. T. C so far I wonder how he liked the publicⁿ of the notes" (i.e. in *LR* and *NED*). Following I 137, with the exception of II 301–4, the pages are unopened, i.e. the leaves are joined in pairs at the top; 17 shows, however, that C might still have read a page at random.

DATE. 1827 (1), probably the latter part of the year (2 n 1).

COEDITOR. J. Robert Barth, S.J.

1   I ⁻2

Strange yet from the date of the Book of the Celestial Hierarchies of the pretended Dyonisius the Areopagite to the Translator, Joannes Scotus Erigena,[1] the Contemporary of Alfred, and from Scotus to the Revᵈ J. O. 1815, not unfrequent Delusion of mistaking Pantheism disguised in a fancy-dress of pious phrases for a more spiritual and philosophic Form of Christian Faith!—Nay, stranger still—to imagine with Scotus, and Mʳ O., that ₰ in a Scheme, which ~~even~~ ⟨even⟩ more directly than the grosser species of Atheism, precludes all moral responsibility and subverts all essential difference of Right and Wrong, ₰ they have found the means of proving and explaining "the Christian doctrines of the Trinity and Incarnation"[2]—i.e. the great and only sufficient ~~Bulwarks~~ Antidotes of the right faith against this insidious poison. For Pantheism, ~~is~~ trick it up as you will, is but a painted Atheism—A Mask of

---

[1]¹ Joannes Scotus Erigena (c 810–60), whose *De divisione naturae* C annotated, translated, and commented on the writings of the mystical theologian Dionysius (fl c 500), also known as the Pseudo-Dionysius. C's spelling of the name follows that of Joannes, as in a passage about Dionysius copied from *De divisione naturae* in 1803: *CN* I 1369. The *Celestial Hierarchy* "explains how the nine orders of angels mediate God to man" (*ODCC*).

[2]² C quotes Oxlee's title.

perverted Scriptures may hide its ugly face, but cannot change a single Feature!—[3]

S. T. Coleridge 1827

2 1 4–5

In the infancy of the Christian Church, and immediately after the general dispersion, which necessarily followed the sacking of Jerusalem and Bither; the Greek and Latin Fathers had the fairest opportunity of disputing with the Jews, and of evincing the truth of the Gospel dispensation; but unfortunately for the success of so noble a design, they were totally ignorant of the Hebrew Scriptures; and so wanted, in every argument, that stamp of authority, which was equally necessary to sanction the principles of Christianity, and to command the respect of their Jewish antagonists. For the confirmation of this remark, I may appeal to the Fathers themselves, but especially to Barnabas, Justin, and Irenaeus; who in their several attempts at Hebrew learning betray such portentous signs of ignorance and stupidity, that we are covered with shame at the sight of their criticisms.

M[r] Oxlee would be delighted in reading Jacob Rhenferd's Disquisition on the Ebionites & other supposed Heretics among the Jewish Christians.[1] And I cannot help thinking that Rhenferd who has so ably anticipated M[r] Oxlee on this point, and in Jortin's best manner[2] displayed the gross ignorance of the Gentile Fathers in all matters relating to Hebrew Learning and the ludicrous yet mischievous results thereof, has formed a juster tho' very much lower opinion of these Fathers, with a few exceptions, than M[r] Oxlee. I confess that till the Light of the two-foldness of the Christian Church dawned on my mind,[3] the study of the history and literature of the Church during the three or four first Centuries in-

---

1[3] This note repeats C's comment in JOANNES **3**.

2[1] C annotated a copy of the *Opera philologica* (Utrecht 1722) of the "truly excellent and enlightened Theologian" Jacob Rhenferd (1654–1712) in Jul 1827, so it was fresh in his mind when he turned to Oxlee. He is referring here to two essays on "supposed Heretics", *De fictis Judaeorum haeresibus* and *De fictis Judaeorum & judaizantium haeresibus*, both of which he annotated with admiration for the biblical scholarship—especially in Hebrew—that allowed Rhenferd to expose the ignorance of the early Christian writers, e.g. RHENFERD **14**, "a capital specimen of the malignant credulity of the Fathers respecting those, whom they considered as Heretics".

2[2] John Jortin (1698–1770), ecclesiastical historian and philologist, whose work C quotes appreciatively in a letter of Feb 1793 (*CL* 1 50, source identified *Friend— CC*—1 61 n 1). What C liked in Jortin was his "wit and humor & classical taste" (RHENFERD **2**).

2[3] C means presumably the two aspects of the Church as on the one hand spiritual and timeless and on the other hand worldly and historical—the "ecclesia" and "enclesia" of *C&S* (*CC*) 45.

fected me with a spirit of doubt and disgust which required a frequent recurrence to the Writings of John and Paul to preserve me *whole* in the faith.[4]   S. T. C.

3 ɪ 17

The truth of the doctrine ["that God is an immaterial and spiritual being"] is vehemently insisted on, in a variety of places, by the great R. Moses ben Maimon; who founds upon it the unity of the Godhead, and ranks it among the fundamental articles of the Jewish religion. [Oxlee then quotes from a celebrated letter of Maimonides, in Hebrew with English version, to the Jews of Marseilles.]

But what is obtained by quotations from Maimonides, more than from Alexander of Hales, or any other Schoolman of the same Age?[1] The metaphysics of the learned Jew are derived from the same source—viz. Aristotle: and his object the same as that of the Christian Schoolmen— viz. to systematize the religion, he professed, on the form and in the principles of the Aristotelian Philosophy.

4 ɪ 19

[Oxlee cites four other passages in Hebrew (and English) from various authors.]

It is a serious defect in Mʳ Oxlee's work that he does not give the age of the Writers, from whom he cites. He cannot have expected all his Readers to be as learned as himself.

5 ɪ 26

Seeing, however, that we assert the Godhead to be not only immaterial, but spiritual; whereby is meant, that it has the property of putting matter in motion; it may not be amiss to annex a few testimonies to shew, that this also is the opinion of the Jewish church.

Mʳ Oxlee seems too much inclined to identify the Rabbinical Interpretations of Scripture Texts with their sense: when in reality the Rabbis themselves not seldom used them as a convenient & popular mode of

---

2[4] C makes a similar remark about these touchstones of his faith in *BL* ch 10 (*CC*) ɪ 201: "For a very long time indeed I could not reconcile personality with infinity; and my head was with Spinoza, though my whole heart remained with Paul and John."

3[1] C's point is that although one was Jewish and the other Christian, both Moses Maimonides (1135–1204) and his contemporary Alexander of Hales (c 1170–1245) started from the same philosophical premises.

conveying their own philosophic opinions. Neither have I ever been able to admire the Logic so general among the Divines of both Churches, according to which if one, two, or perhaps three Sentences in any one of the Canonical Books assert a tenet the same as we now hold, one assertion of a different character must have ⟨been⟩ meant metaphorically.

6 ı 26–31

The prophet Isaiah, too, clearly inculcates the spirituality of the Godhead in the following declaration . . . "But Egypt is man, and not . . . God; and their horses flesh, and not spirit." . . . In the former member, the Prophet declares, that Egypt was man, and not God; and then in terms of strict apposition enforces the sentiment by adding, that their cavalry was flesh, and not spirit; which is just as if he had said . . . "But Egypt, which has horses . . . in war, is only man, that is, flesh, and not God, who is spirit."

* Assuredly this is a false interpretation—& utterly unpoetic. It is even doubtful whether Ruach in this place means *Spirit* in contradistinction from *Matter* at all; and not rather Air or Wind.[1] At all events, the poetic decorum, the proportion, and the antithetic parallelism demand a somewhat as much below God, as the Horse is below Man.—The opposition of Flesh & Spirit in the Gospel of John who *thought* in Hebrew tho' he *wrote* in Greek, favors our Version—flesh and not Spirit;[2] but the place in which it stands, namely, in one of the first Forty chapters of Isaiah, and therefore written long before the Captivity,[3] together with the majestic simplicity characteristic of Isaiah's Muse, gives perhaps a greater probability to the other—Egypt is Man and not God; and her Horses Flesh and ⟨not⟩ *Wind*. If Mr Oxlee renders the verse in the Psalms (Ps. 104.) He maketh Spirits his Messengers (for our version, He maketh his Angels Spirits, is senseless),[4] this is a case in point, for the use of the word, Spirits, in the sense ⟨of⟩ incorporeal Beings—& (Mr Oxlee will hardly attribute the opinion of some later Rabbis that God alone & exclusively is a Spirit, to the Sacred Penmen/ easy as it would be to quote

---

6[1] Oxlee follows AV in rendering the Hebrew word *ruach* in Isa 31.3 as "spirit"; C, aware of its complex significance as "breath", "wind", "life" etc, objects to making so sharp a distinction.

6[2] E.g. John 6.63: "It is the spirit that quickeneth; the flesh profiteth nothing".

6[3] A point made (and glossed) also in JAHN *History* 9 and n 3.

6[4] C tests Oxlee's translation of *ruach* against his own in another text, Ps 104.4 (AV), "Who maketh his angels spirits; his ministers a flaming fire". (The BCP text is virtually identical.) "Angels" may be construed as "messengers"—as in JUNG 8 and HACKET *Sermons* 16—because NT uses the same Greek word, *angelos*, for both.

a score of texts in proof of the contrary.)—I however cannot doubt that the true rendering of the 4th v. of the 104 Ps. is—He maketh the Winds his Angels, or Messengers, and the Lightnings his ministrant Servants.—N.B. *Abstract* for pure Intelligences,[a] and even pure Intelligences for incorporeal, I deem a lax use of terms.—But as to the point in question, the truth seems to be this—The ancient Hebrews certainly distinguished the principle or ground of Life, Understanding, & Will, from ponderable visible Matter—the former they considered & called Spirit, & believed it to be an emission from the Almighty Father of Spirits—the latter they called Body: and in this sense they doubtless believed in the existence of in*corporeal* Beings.—But that they had any notion of im*material* Beings in the sense of Des Cartes, is contrary to all, we know of them & of every other people in the same degree of cultivation.[5]—Air, Fire, Light express the degrees of ascending refinement— In the infancy of Thought the Life, Soul, Mind, are supposed to be air— anima, animus i.e. ανεμος, Spiritus, πνευμα[6]—in the Childhood they are Fire—Mens ignea, ignicula[7]—& God himself πῦρ νοερον, πῦρ αειζων.[8] Lastly, in the youth of Thought, they are refined into Light; & ⟨that Light is⟩ capable of existing in a latent state, the experience of the stricken flint, of lightning from the clouds, &c seemed to prove: it at least, supplied a popular answer to the objection—If the Soul be Light, why is it not visible?/ That the purest Light is invisible to our gross sense; and that visible Light is a compound of Light and Shadow; were answers of a ~~more~~ later & more refined period.—Observe, however, that the Hebrew Legislator precluded all unfit applications of the materializing Fancy ~~to God~~ by forbidding the People to *imagine* at all concerning God. For the Ear alone, to the exclusion of all other bodily sense was he to be designated/—viz. by the Name[9]—All else was for the Mind—by Power, Truth, Wisdom, Holiness, Mercy &c—   S. T. C.

7 I 36

Now the vision of Micaiah [2 Chron 18.18] is a manifest proof, that

[a] Written "Intelligences for pure" and marked for transposition

6[5] The distinction invoked by C here is the distinction between body and matter forcibly expressed in IRVING *Sermons* 29 and n 12, where the failure of the Cartesian system is also concerned.

6[6] C lists words in Latin and Greek that originate as words for "air" or "breeze" or "breath" but come to mean "spirit" or "life" or "consciousness". The Latin *ani-mus* is itself based, as he observes, on the Greek word for "wind", *anemos*.

6[7] "Mind [is] fiery, a spark".

6[8] "Intellectual fire, everlasting fire".

6[9] C alludes to the Ten Commandments in Exod 20, esp 20.4 ("Thou shalt not make unto thee any graven image") and 20.7 ("Thou shalt not take the name of the Lord thy God in vain").

angels are spirits, and, that they subsist many in number. . . . In this extraordinary vision, the prophet represents the divinity as attended on both sides with a numerous train of angels; and, that the reader may not doubt of their being all individual spirits, the subsisting spirit of pseudo-prophecy, it is declared, stood forth in the council, and devised the means of decoying the king of Israel.

I fear I must ~~give up~~ surrender my hope that Mr Oxlee ~~i~~was an exception to the Rule, that the Study of Rabbinical Literature either finds a man *whimmy*[1] or makes him so.—If neither the demands of poetic Taste nor the peculiar character of oracles were of avail, yet morality & piety ought to have convinced Mr O. that this Vision was the poetic form, the Veil of the Prophet's Meaning. And a most sublime Meaning it was. ~~Does~~ Is Mr O. ignorant, that the forms & personages of *Visions* are all symbolical?

8   ɪ 40–1

It will not avail us much, however, to have established their incorporeity or spirituality, if what R. Moses affirms be true; That, by reason of their incorporeity, they cannot, without being embodied, or standing in the correlation of cause and effect, be subject to number; or in other words, that the sameness of their substance neither does nor can exist in a diversity of persons.

To what purpose then are the crude metaphysics of these later Rabbis (differing in no other respect from the theological dicta of ~~the~~ our School Divines but that they are written in a sort of Hebrew) brought forward?—I am far from denying that an Interpreter of the Scriptures may derive important aids from the Jewish Commentators—Aben Ezra especially was a truly great man.[1] But of this I am certain, that he only will be benefited who can *look down* upon the Works, he is studying— i.e. He must thorughly[a] understand their weaknesses, superstitions, rabid Appetite for the marvellous & monstrous—and then read them as an enlightened Chemist of the present day would read the Writings of the Alchemists, or a Linneus the works of Pliny & Aldrovandus.[2] If he can do this, well—if not, he will line his skull with Cobwebs.

[a] A slip for "thoroughly"

7[1] I.e. prone to whims; not in *OED*.
8[1] Ibn Ezra, i.e. Abraham ben Meir Ibn Ezra (c 1092–1167), great Jewish scholar born in Spain but widely travelled, author of Hebrew grammars and of commentaries on the Pentateuch; praised by Spinoza,

whose opinion may be the basis of C's.
8[2] An application of the golden rule (based on a remark by Socrates about Heraclitus) expressed in *BL* ch 12 (*CC*) ɪ 232, *"until you understand a writer's ignorance, presume yourself ignorant of his un-*

9 I 41–2

But how, I would ask, is this position to be defended? Surely, not by contradicting almost every part of the inspired volumes, in which such frequent mention occurs of different and distinct angels appearing to the patriarchs and prophets, sometimes in groups, and sometimes in limited numbers; nor by denying, what the Talmudists have ever regarded as a most important truth, that the deity has a particular messenger for every particular errand; much less by arguing, that Michael, Gabriel, and Raphael, are but one and the same angel.

I am so far from agreeing with Mr O. on these points, that I not only doubt whether before the Captivity any fair proof of the existence of Angels in the present sense can be adduced from the inspired Writings; but think a strong proof of the divinity of Christ, and for his presence under the Patriarchs & the Law rests on the contrary—viz. that the Seraphim were no less symbolic Images than the Cherubim—[1]

10 I 43

That there is a number, indeed, of angelic spirits, is the constant and uniform language of the Jewish Church; and it is certainly matter of astonishment, that either Maimonides, or Kimchi, should deviate so far from the principle of their religion, as to inculcate a doctrine, which is in diametrical opposition to the authority of the fathers.

O surely it is not ~~exp too much~~ expecting too much of a clergyman of the Church of England to expect that he would measure the importance of a theological tenet by its bearings on our moral and spiritual duties, by its practical tendencies!—What is it to us whether Angels are the Spirits of just men made perfect, or a distinct class of moral & rational Creatures?[1] Augustine has well & wisely observed, that Reason recognizes only three *essential* Kinds—God, Man, Beast.[2] Try as long as you will—you can never make an Angel anything but a Man with wings on his Shoulders.[3]

---

derstanding''. C cites an eminent eighteenth-century scientist, the Swedish botanist Linnaeus, and his earlier counterparts Pliny the Elder (c 23–79) and Ulissi Aldrovandi (1522–1605).

9[1] A fuller version of this note appears in HACKET *Sermons* **16**, where C suggests that the notion of angels, for which—and especially for the fall of which—he finds no authority in OT (cf LACUNZA **27** n 2, *C Talker* 219), was "probably . . . a pro-

verbial expression, derived from the Cherubim in the Temple: as the country-folks used to say to Children—Take care! the Fairies will hear you''. The cherubim were Temple ornaments: cf MORE *Theological Works* **7** and n 1.

10[1] The former suggestion C noted in LEIGHTON COPY B **14**.

10[2] See NOBLE **4**.

10[3] This note recalls both HACKET *Sermons* **16** (as **9** above) and HOOKER **21**.

11 I 58

But this deficiency in the Mosaic account of the creation is amply supplied by early tradition,*!! which inculcates, not only that the angels were created; but that they were created, either on the second day, according to R. Juchanan; or on the fifth, according to R. Chanina.

Inspired Scripture amply supplied by ~~the~~ Talmudic and Rabbinical *Traditions*—this from a Clergyman of the Protestant Church of England!

12 I 59, pencil

To begin, then, with what the Cabbalists call the seven inferior numerations of the Godhead, the highest intelligences to which the term angel has ever been given; is it not unanimously maintained, that they all emanated essentially from the Deity, and do not differ from him in any other manner, than as the flames of a burning coal may differ in substance from the coal itself?

I am, I confess, greatly disappointed. I had expected, I scarce know why, to have had some light thrown on the existence of the Cabbala in its purest form, from Ezekiel to Paul and John.[1] But M[r] Oxlee takes it as he finds it—gravely ascribes this patch-work of corrupt Platonism or Plotinism, with Chaldean, Persian, and Judaic Fables and Fancies to the Jewish Doctors, as an original, profound, and pious Philosophy in its Fountain-head!!—

13 I 60–5

Similar to this is the declaration of R. Moses ben Maimon. . . . "For that influx, which flows from the Deity to the actual production of abstract intelligences, flows also from the intelligences to their production from each other in succession; until that active intelligence, which is the soul of matter, be caused to exist: and with that terminates the production or creation of abstract intelligences."

The indispensable Requisite not only to a profitable but even to a safe study of the Cabbala is a familiar knowlege of the Docimastic Philosophy[1]—i.e. that which has for its object the Trial and *Testing* of the Weights and Measures themselves/ the first principles, definitions,

---

12[1] As Brerewood **1** n 4—a comprehensive note on C's interest in the subject—indicates, C rejected the view that the Cabbala was a medieval compilation and believed it to belong to a much earlier period.

13[1] C characteristically takes a term over from science to philosophy, but the point is the familiar one of the need for a Kantian "propaedeutic logic", as in Nemesius **1** and n 4.

postulates, axioms of Logic & Metaphysic. But this is in no other way possible but by ⟨an enumeration of the mental Faculties and⟩ an investigation of the Constitution, Functions, Limits, and applicability ad quas res,[2] of each. Of the application of the Rules & Forms of the Understanding, or discursive Logic, or even of the intuitions of the Reason itself, if *Reason* be assumed as the *First & Highest*, has Pantheism for its necessary Result. But this the Cabbalists did: and consequently the Cabbalistic Theosophy is pantheistic: and Pantheism, in whatever drapery of pious phrases disguised, is (where it forms the whole of a System) Atheism, & precludes moral responsibility, and the essential difference of Right and Wrong[3]—One of the two contra-distinctions of the Hebrew Revelation is the doctrine of the positive Creation. ~~in~~ This, if not the only is the ~~def~~ easiest and surest Criterion between the idea of God and the notion of a Mens agitans molem.[4] But this the Cabbalists evaded by their double-meaning of the term, *Nothing*—viz. Nought, = 0, and no *thing*—~~&~~ by their use of the term, as designating God. Thus in *words* ~~the~~ and to the *ear* they taught, that the World was made out of *Nothing*; but in fact they meant & inculcated, that the World was God himself *expanded*.[5] It is not therefore half a dozen passages respecting the three first Proprietates in the Sephiroth,[6] that will lead a ⟨wise⟩ man to expect the true doctrine of the Trinity in the Cabbalistic Scheme; ~~who~~ for he knows that the ~~one thoroughly~~ *scholastic* Value, the *theological* necessity of this doctrine consists in its ~~being~~ exhibiting an idea of God, which *rescues* our faith from both extremes, Cabbalah = Pantheism/, & Anthropomorphism. It is, I say, to prevent the necessity of the Cabbalistic inferences that the ⟨full and distinct developement of the⟩ doctrine of the Trinity becomes necessary ~~as an article of faith~~ in every Scheme of Dogmatic Theology. If the three first *Proprietates* are God, so are the Seven: ⟨and so are all Ten.⟩ God according to the Cabbalists is all in each and one in all.

N.B. I do not say, there is not a great deal of truth in this; but I say, that it is not, as the Cabbalists represent it, the *whole* truth. Spinoza himself describes his own philosophy as in substance the same with that of the ancient Hebrew Doctors, the Cabbalists—~~but~~ only unswathed from the biblical dress.[7]   S. T. C.

13[2] "To what things".

13[3] Cf 1 above.

13[4] "Mind setting mass in motion".

13[5] On the issue of creation "from nothing" see JOANNES 5 and n 1.

13[6] Oxlee claims that the Cabbala distinguishes the first three of ten sephiroth—

the attributes or emanations of God—as "eternal subsistences of the godhead" (I 344) and uses this fact as an example of the kinship between the Hebrew tradition and orthodox Christianity.

13[7] In a letter (LXXIII) to Henry Oldenburg written in Nov or Dec 1675: "Like

14 I 61, pencil | **12** textus

How much trouble would Mr O. have saved himself, had he in sober earnest asked his own mind, what he meant by emanation? and whether he could attach any intelligible meaning to the term at all? as applied to Spirit?[1]

14A I 63, pencil

!! The latter part of this pasuk is <u>beautifully</u> illustrated by Onkelos, the paraphrast . . .

15 I 65, pencil, partly overtraced by C

Thus having, by variety of proofs, demonstrated the fecundity of the godhead, in that all spiritualities, of whatever gradation, have originated essentially and substantially from it, like streams from their fountain; I avail myself of this as another sound argument, that in the sameness of the divine essence subsists a plurality of persons.

~~How~~ A plurality with a vengeance! Why, this is the very *Scoff* of a late Unitarian Writer—only that he ^{a}inverts the^b order: Mr Oxlee proves ten trillions of Trillions in the Deity in order to deduce a fortiori the rationality of^c Three: the Unitarian from the Three pretends to^c deduce the^c equal rationality of as many Thousands.—[1]

16 I 66

So, if without detriment to piety great things may be compared with small, I would contend, that every intelligency, descending by way of emanation or impertition from the godhead, must needs be a personality of that godhead, from which it has descended; only so vastly unequal to it in personal perfection, that it can form no part of its proper existency. *

$^{a-b}$ Overtraced. Overtracing resumed at ''rationality'', except for the few words marked *c*
^{c} Word in pencil, not overtraced

Paul, and perhaps also like all ancient philosophers, though in another way, I assert that all things live and move in God; and I would dare to say that I agree also with all the ancient Hebrews as far as it is possible to surmise from their traditions, even if those have become corrupt in many ways'': *The Correspondence of Spinoza* tr and ed A. Wolf (1928) 343; in C's copy of Spinoza *Opera quae supersunt omnia* ed H. E. G. Paulus (Jena 1802–3) I 509.

14[1] C may have been prompted to this remark not so much by Oxlee's own words in **12** textus as by his quotation from a cabbalistic work on I 60: ''The fourth way is called the receptecular intelligency; and is so termed, because from it emanate all spiritual powers by a subtilty of emanation, whereby they emanate one from another by virtue of the primordial emanator, the supreme being, blessed is he.''

15[1] C may have a more recent case in mind, but this is an extension of the argument of Joseph Priestley, e.g. in *A History of the Corruptions of Christianity* (2nd ed 2 vols 1793) I 100.

* Is not this to all intents & purposes ascribing partibility to God?/ What is indeed the necessary consequence of the emanation Scheme?—Unequal!—Aye, *vicious wicked* personalities of the Godhead!! How does this rhyme?—Even as a metaphor, Emanation is an ill-chosen term: for it applies only to Fluids, ~~un~~ Ramenta, unravellings, threads, would be more germane.—[1]

17   ɪ 173

[Quoting Rabbi Shabtai, first in Hebrew and then in English:] "Let the doctrine be illustrated under the figure of a tree. First, there is its root; from the root issues the stem, and from the stem issue the branches; which are three degrees or orders of existence, namely, the root, the stem, and the branches; and yet they are all but one tree . . ."

Vide Par. Lost. B. V. L. 470–490.[1]

16[1] For C's views on the problems of the concept of emanation see **14** above and LUTHER *Colloquia* 62 and n 2.

17[1] *Paradise Lost* v 469–90, the archangel Raphael's account to Adam of the scale of being. C cites this—to him immensely important—passage in *BL* ch 10 (*CC*) ɪ 173–4 and comments on it in ANDERSON COPY B **27** as an *almost* perfect "enunciation of the only true System of Physics".